Introduction to Psychology

Exploration and Application

Introduction to Psychology
Exploration and Application

Fourth Edition

Dennis Coon
Department of Psychology
Santa Barbara City College, California

West Publishing Company
St. Paul   New York   Los Angeles   San Francisco

A study guide has been developed to assist you in mastering the concepts presented in this text. The study guide clarifies concepts by presenting them in concise, condensed form. It reinforces your understanding of terms, concepts, and individuals and also provides a programmed review and self-test questions. The study guide is available from your local bookstore under the title, *Study Guide to Accompany Introduction to Psychology: Exploration and Application*, prepared by Faren Akins.

A *Mastery Study Guide* written by Tom Bond also is available to accompany this book. The *Mastery Study Guide* is specially designed for self-paced, or PSI, courses. It is also highly appropriate for any course in which true mastery of concepts is the goal.

If you cannot locate either of these books in the bookstore, ask your bookstore manager to order them for you.

Library of Congress Cataloging-in-Publication Data

Coon, Dennis.
 Introduction to psychology.

 Bibliography: p.
 Includes index.
 1. Psychology. I. Title.
BF121.C625 1986   150   85-31500
ISBN 0-314-93167-8
1st Reprint—1986

Cover: *Lovers* by Yankel Ginzburg reproduced by permission of the artist and S&Y Art, Ltd.

Text illustrations: Barbara Barnett
Anatomical illustrations: Marsha Dohrmann
Photo research: Stuart Kenter
Design: Janet Bollow
Production Coordination: Janet Bollow Associates
Composition: The Clarinda Company

Acknowledgments   The author is indebted to the following for permission to reproduce copyrighted materials.

Fig. 1—1 (*upper right*) © Art Sweezy, Stock Boston; (*upper left*) © Bruce Rosenblum, The Picture Cube; (*lower right*) Story Litchfield, Stock Boston; © Susan Van Etten, The Picture Cube.
Fig. 1—3 © Susan Kuklin, Photor Researchers.
Fig. 1—4 Brown Brothers.
Fig. 1—5 Brown Brothers.
Fig. 1—6 Brown Brothers.
Fig. 1—7 United Press International

Fig. 1—8 The Bettmann Archive
Fig. 1—9 © Ted Polumbaum
Fig. 1—11 The Bettmann Archive.
p. 23 Ulrich, R. E., Stachnik, T. J., and Stainton, N. R. Student acceptance of generalized personality interpretations. PSYCHOLOGICAL REPORTS, 1963, 13, 831–834.
p. 28 van Lawick-Goodall, Jane. *In The Shadow of Man*. Houghton Mifflin Co., 1971. World Rights: William Collins Sons & Co. Ltd., London.
Fig. 2—1 © Richard Wood, The Picture Cube.
Fig. 2—2 National Geographic Society Magazine. Photo by Baron Hugo van Lawick.
p. 33 Courtesy of Peter Mueller.
Fig. 2—7 © Jean-Claude Lejeune, Stock Boston.
p. 57 Gazzaniga, M. S. *The Bisected Brain*. Plenum Publishing Co., 1970.
p. 58 Ornstein, R. E. *The Psychology of Consciousness*. W. H. Freeman & Co., 1972.
Fig. 3—16 © Michael Serino, The Picture Cube.
Fig. 4—10 (*left*) © Harvey Eisner, Taurus; (*right*) © David M. Campione, Taurus.
Fig. 4—12 © Jeffry W. Myers, Stock Boston.
Fig. 4—15 © Jon L. Barken, The Picture Cube.
Fig. 4—25 The Bettmann Archive.
Fig. 4—26 NASA.
Fig. 5—1 Photo by Kevin McMahon.
Fig. 5—4 © E. R. Degginger, Animals, Animals.
Fig. 5—8 © Enrico Ferorelli/DOT.
Fig. 5—10 B. Julesz. *Foundations of Cyclopean Perception*. Copyright © 1971, University of Chicago Press.
Fig. 5—16 M. C. Escher "Still Life and Street" © BEELDRECHT, Amsterdam/VAGA, New York Collection Haags Gemeentemuseum—The Hague.
Fig. 5—17 From "Pictorial Perception and Culture" by J. B. Deregowski. Copyright © 1972 by *Scientific American*, Inc. All rights reserved.
Fig. 5—18 The Bettmann Archive.
Fig. 5—20 Baron Wolman
Fig. 5—21 © Dan Francis, Mardan Photography.
Fig. 5—26 Erdelyi, M. H. and A. G. Appelbaum, "Cognitive Masking: The Disruptive Effect of an Emotional Stimulus Upon the Perception of Contiguous Neutral Items." *Bulletin of the Psychonomic Society*. 1973, 1, 59–61.
p. 128 Kapleau, Philip. *The Three Pillars of Zen*, Harper & Row, 1966.
Fig. 6—1 Dan Francis, Mardan Photography.
Fig. 6—2 Dan Francis, Mardan Photography.
Table 6—1 Stanford Hypnotic Scale, adapted from Weitzenhofler and Hilgard. Stanford University Press, 1959.
Fig. 6—4 Spectrum and Continuum of Drugs, Dr. Robert W. Earle, University of California, Irvine.
p. 145 Cartoon courtesy of Chronicle Features.
Fig. 6—5 D. Coon.
Fig. 6—6 Blood Alcohol Content Chart, courtesy of Jozef Cohen.
Table 6—2 Facts About Drugs from *The Resource Book for Drug Abuse Education*. National Education Association, 1969.
Fig. 6—7 "Beware Marijuana" Poster courtesy of Dr. Lester Grinspoon, Harvard Medical School.

(continued following Index)

Contents in Brief

Part Seven

Self and Others 565

Contents

Part Two

Foundations of Human Consciousness   47

Chapter 3
The Biology of Behavior   48

Chapter 4
The Sensory World and Reality   76

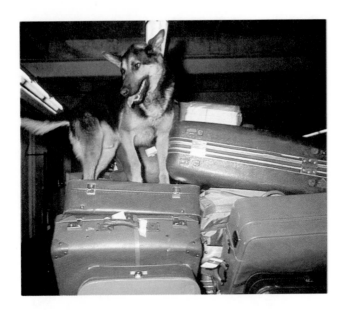

Chapter 9

Conditioning and Learning II   211

Chapter 10

Memory   233

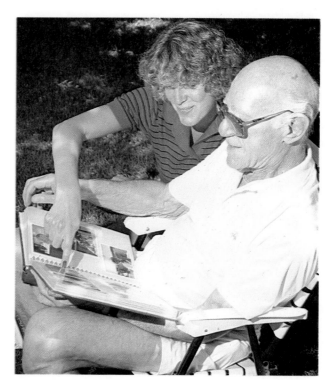

Chapter 11
Thinking, Problem Solving, and Creativity 258

Part Four

─────────────────────────────

Actions and Reactions 283

Chapter 12
Motivation 284

Chapter 16

Challenges of Development: The Cycle of Life   385

Chapter Preview: Life with Billy   385

Resources

Part Six

Abnormal Behavior and Psychotherapy   481

Chapter 20

Deviance and Disorder:
The Unhealthy Personality   482

Chapter 21

Psychosis   504

Preface to the Fourth Edition

To the Student

Psychology is a large and rapidly growing field. It is at once familiar, exotic, commonplace, surprising, and challenging. Most of all, psychology is changing. Indeed, this book can be no more than a "snapshot" of a colorful passing scene. And yet, it is this rapid change that makes psychology especially fascinating: What, really, could be more intriguing than our evolving understanding of human behavior?

In a very real sense, psychology is about each of us. Psychology asks, "How can we step outside of ourselves for a more objective look at how we live, think, and act?" Psychologists believe the answer is "through careful thought, observation, and inquiry." As simple as this may seem, it is the guiding light for everything that follows in this book.

I sincerely hope that you will find psychology as fascinating as I have. In this text, I have done all that I could imagine to make your first encounter with psychology enjoyable and worthwhile. To help you get off to a good start, Chapter 1 includes a discussion of how to study effectively. The ideas covered there will help you get the most out of this text, class lectures, and your psychology course as a whole. In the remaining chapters, I hope that the delight I have found in my own students' curiosity, insights, imagination, and interests will be apparent. Please view this book as a long letter from me to you. It is, in a very real sense, written about you, for you, and to you.

To the Instructor

This book differs from traditional texts in a number of important ways. If you are already familiar with its format, a description of Fourth Edition changes follows shortly. If the text is unfamiliar, a brief account of its design and underlying philosophy is in order.

A Book for Students As an instructor I have learned that selection of a textbook is half the battle in teaching a course. A good text does much of the work of imparting information to students. This leaves class time free for discussion, and it leaves students asking for more. When a book overwhelms students or cools their interest, teaching becomes an uphill battle. For this reason, I have worked hard to make this a clear, readable, and interesting text.

This book is a concise introduction to psychology. I believe an important question to ask of the introductory course is, "What will students remember next year, or in 10 years?" Consequently, I have tried to give students a clear grasp of major concepts, rather than bury them in details. At the same time, I have tried to show the value of a variety of theoretical perspectives. I think students will find this book full of intellectual challenge, and teachers will find traditional topics covered to their satisfaction. In addition, I have made a special effort to relate psychology to common experiences and to practical problems of daily life.

A major feature of the book is the Applications section in each chapter. These sections explicitly bridge the gap between psychological theory and practical application. I believe students have every right to ask, "Does this mean anything to me? Can I use it? Why should I learn it if I can't use it?" No matter how interesting or intellectually stimulating, a text that fails to show the practical value of new ideas is irrelevant in a very basic sense. The Applications sections therefore spell out how students can use the principles of psychology. By doing so, they breathe life into its concepts.

At the end of each chapter you will find a separate Exploration section. These sections cover current issues, topics from psychology's frontiers, or subjects likely to promote thought and discussion. In essence, they serve as "mini-articles" to provide a taste of changing issues and ideas in psychology. Because Explorations conclude each chapter, they are easy to assign or delete at your discretion.

A Format for Learning Before this book first appeared, psychology texts made surprisingly little use of learning principles to teach psychology. The extensive use of learning aids herein is based on my belief that students can be guided into more effective study and reading habits while learning course content. Basically, each chapter is built around the well-known SQ3R study-reading formula. Thus, in addition to helping students learn psychology, the chapter format encourages the development of valuable study skills. Student response to this feature of the text has been very positive, with many students reporting that they transfer the SQ3R technique to their other texts as well.

Each chapter is divided into five major parts: a *Preview, Resources, Applications, Chapter Summary, and an Exploration.* Chapter Previews are used to arouse reader interest, to give an overview of the chapter, and to focus attention on the task at hand. Each Preview concludes with a series of *Survey Questions* to further orient the reader and aid the survey step of the SQ3R method. The Resources section that follows presents major concepts of the chapter. Next comes an Applications section that shows how concepts can be applied. After that a Chapter Summary offers a point-by-point review of key ideas. Finally, an Exploration section rounds out the chapter, expands student horizons, and provides a basis for thought and discussion. Explorations end with a list of *Questions for Discussion* that many teachers find useful in class.

Throughout each chapter, *guide questions* are used to maintain reader attention and to make reading an active learning experience. Despite its appearance, this is not just a question-and-answer format. Rather, it takes the form of a dialogue in which student questions and reactions are anticipated. Guide questions cue students to look for important points in the paragraphs that follow, thus fulfilling the *question* part of SQ3R. And, significantly, they also allow clarification of difficult points through a lively give-and-take between questions and responses.

If you glance through the text, you will immediately notice the *Learning Checks* that appear throughout. These are short, noncomprehensive quizzes that allow readers to gauge recall and understanding of preceding material. Students who cannot answer Learning Check questions are directed to review the previous section before reading more. Completing Learning Checks also serves as a form of recitation to enhance learning (the fourth step in SQ34). The last SQ3R step (review) is aided by the detailed Chapter Summary.

To supplement its SQ3R format, *Introduction to Psychology* employs a full array of traditional learning aids. These include: part outlines, boldface type and phonetic pronunciations for important terms, bullet summaries, a detailed glossary (also with pronunciations), summary tables, a detailed index, and a robust new illustration program.

Chapters throughout the text have been kept short so each can be read in a single session. This brevity provides excellent flexibility regarding the order in which chapters are assigned. It also gives students a sense of closure or completion at the end of each assignment. Finally, and perhaps most importantly, the readability of each chapter has been carefully controlled for maximum student involvement and comprehension.

Fourth Edition Changes

The last 3 years has been a fertile and productive period for psychology. Perhaps as never before, researchers are revising long-standing ideas and pioneering new topics of study. Reporting these developments has been stimulating and rewarding: With this revision, *Introduction to Psychology* has become more than ever the text I always dreamed it could be.

Illustrations The most visible change in this edition is the use of color in every chapter. Added color has made it possible to improve almost all drawings, graphs, tables, and photographs so that they present information more clearly and effectively. Beyond this, the text's enhanced visual appeal should have a positive effect on student interest and motivation.

Chapter Format The format for this edition has evolved in several ways. A prominent example is the addition of an entirely new feature called *Highlights* to each chapter. These brief discussions of high-interest topics are set off from the main body of the text. Although I have long resisted using "boxes" within chapters, I believe that the new Highlights will not be unduly distracting to readers. They are very short and they are placed where they will least interrupt the general flow of ideas. Most Highlights focus on current research, interesting controversies, or novel viewpoints. I think students will like them very much.

Another notable change is that Applications now *precede* each Chapter Summary. This switch was made to more closely tie Applications to core chapter content. The Exploration sections, on the other hand, still follow chapter summaries. As mentioned before, this placement makes it easy to treat Explorations as separate reading assignments if desired. All Explorations now include Learning Checks to aid comprehension.

Content Changes   This Fourth Edition reflects an extensive updating, and it introduces a long-awaited (and often requested) new chapter on applied psychology. Virtually every chapter has been rewritten, reorganized, or improved, with much new information evident at every turn of a page. I have drawn on hundreds of new references (many as recent as 1985) to revise existing chapters and to create the new Applied Psychology chapter (Chapter 27).

The chapters that follow contain over 50 new Highlights, a new Preview, several revised Applications, an entirely new Application, and 11 new Explorations. Combined with line-by-line updates, the content changes in this edition are far too numerous to describe here. The following is just a sampling of the new or revised topics. These include: study skills (Chapter 1); relationships in psychology (Chapter 2); brain transplants, hypopituitary dwarfism (Chapter 3); the brain and vision, artificial hearing, motion sickness (Chapter 4); innate understanding of drawings, ESP research (Chapter 5); hypnosis, sensory deprivation, drug effects, meditation (Chapter 6); circadian rhythms, jet lag, behavioral remedies for insomnia (Chapter 7); higher order conditioning, stimulus control, behavioral self-management (Chapter 8); CAI, skill learning, TV as a model (Chapter 9); state dependent learning, hypnosis and memory, exceptional memory, types of memory (Chapter 10); mental imagery, insight, animal intelligence, intuition (Chapter 11); obesity, high achievement, anorexia and bulimia (Chapter 12); emotional expression, lie detectors, love as an emotion (Chapter 13); burnout, stress and hassles, test anxiety, stress management (Chapter 14); social referencing, birth and bonding, enrichment, genetics and reproduction (Chapter 15); parenting styles, "hurried adolescents," biological aging, child abuse (Chapter 16); multiple intelligences, teaching intelligence (Chapter 17); traits and situations, androgyny, identical twins and personality (Chapter 18); self-reinforcement, characteristics of self-actualizers, the morality of caring (Chapter 19); sexual deviance, posttraumatic stress disorder, postpartum depression (Chapter 20); Alzheimer's disease, biological research on depression and psychosis, the Genain quadruplets (Chapter 21); family therapy, large group awareness training, media psy-

chologists (Chapter 22); rapid smoking, cognitive behavior therapy, covert reinforcement (Chapter 23); sexual scripts, the double standard (Chapter 24); attribution theory, selecting a mate, resisting compliance pressures, social traps (Chapter 25); anger control, aggression and pornography, sociobiology (Chapter 26).

The new Applied Psychology chapter concludes the text with a discussion of industrial/organizational psychology, environmental psychology, consumer behavior, educational psychology, health and sports psychology, vocational choice, and the psychology of living in space. It is worth noting again that this and the preceding list are really just a sample of the new information to be found in this edition.

Careers in Psychology   Appendix A, Careers in Psychology, is another prominent addition to this edition. Appendix A is designed to help students decide whether an undergraduate major in psychology would be appropriate for them. Employment opportunities at each degree level are described, along with projections of future job availability. Special emphasis is placed on the broad applicability of an undergraduate psychology degree to various careers and occupations. At the same time, the advantages of more advanced training are clearly stated. Appendix A answers many preliminary questions about careers in psychology and provides a general overview of the field. Psychology majors and nonmajors alike should find it worth reading.

Study Guides   Two excellent study guides will again be available to accompany the text. To structure learning, each chapter of Faren Akins' *Study Guide* provides a list of key terms and concepts, a programmed review, and a practice test. Tom Bond's *Mastery Study Guide* is designed for use in PSI courses. It offers a very thorough review and a chance to practice concepts presented in the text. It also includes a list of important terms and individuals, learning objectives (with space for student responses), two tests ("Do You Know the Information?", "Can You Apply the Information?"), and a fill-in-the-blanks Chapter Review.

WESTUDY   A new mircocomputer study program called WESTUDY is available to accompany this edition of the text. WESTUDY poses questions to students in three easy-to-run formats: a multiple-choice review, a race, and a college bowl contest. When used by one or more students, WESTUDY is a motivating and enjoyable study aid.

IM and Test Bank   Carol Woodward has done a super job of enlarging and updating the *Instructor's Manual*. The IM includes extensively updated film annotations and resource materials, as well as new demonstrations and class exercises created by Carol Woodward and Bill Titus. Carol, George W. Johnson, and Steven Pollock combined their talents to revise the *Test Bank*, which now contains over 2500 questions. A special effort was made to ensure that these questions include general conceptual items as well as items that test recall of the text. The *Test Bank* is again available on computer tape or disks.

Transparencies   I am very pleased to report that Bill Dwyer, who has previously enhanced this text in other ways, has created a set of transparencies to enliven classroom presentations. Bill's transparencies are on acetate, in color, and they look so good I am anxious to use them myself. Contact your West representative for more information.

Psychware   Another exciting development is the debut of *Psychware*, a CAI package to enrich the introductory course. Robert S. Slotnick and the New York Institute of Technology have developed a stimulating collection of tutorials, simulations, and experiments for use on microcomputers. Each exercise is highly interactive and features engaging graphics. By using *Psychware* students can apply the principles of operant conditioning, they can test their short-term memory, they can explore social behavior or gain insight into Piaget's stages of cognitive development, and much more.

Summary   I sincerely hope that teachers and students will consider this book and its supporting materials a refreshing change from the ordinary. Writing and revising it has been quite an adventure. In the pages that follow, I think the reader will find an attractive blend of the theoretical and the practical, plus many of the most exciting ideas in psychology.

Acknowledgments   The enterprise of psychology is a cooperative effort requiring the talents and energies of a large community of scholars, teachers, researchers, and students. As with earlier versions of this text, this edition has combined the efforts of a large number of people. I would like to thank first the many students who sent comments, suggestions, and letters of encouragement. To the professional users/reviewers who gave their time and expertise, I extend my sincere thanks. I deeply appreciate the contributions of all those who have, over the years, contributed to this text's evolution. I especially wish to thank those who helped make this edition a reality:

Brian R. Bate
Cuyahoga Community College

Michael Bardo
University of Kentucky

Tom Bond
Thomas Nelson College

Anne Bright
Jackson State Community College

Lorry Cology
Owens College

William F. Ford
Bucks County Community College

David Gershaw
Arizona Western College

Carolyn A. Gingrich
South Dakota State University

David A. Griesé
State University Agricultural and Technical College, New York

Edward McCrary
El Camino College

James P. B. O'Brien
Tidewater Community College

Frances O'Keefe
Tidewater Community College

Mark W. Vernoy
Palomar College

Sharon Whelan
University of Kentucky

Michael Zeller
Mankato State University

I would also like to thank the individuals whose work has so obviously enhanced this text and its supporting materials: Faren Akins, Tom Bond, Bill Dwyer, George Johnson, Steven Pollock, Bob Slotnick, William Titus, and Carol Woodward. It has been a pleasure working with such talented and inspired psychologists.

Getting a text into print seems almost miraculous at times. With this fact in mind, I would like to thank Jane Fischer and Carole Grumney for ongoing editorial support, and Bill Stryker for talents that have again made possible the seemingly impossible. Thanks also to Stuart Kenter for exceptional photographic research, to Elizabeth Hannan for getting the word out, to Dan and Marietta Francis for photographic excellence, to Marsha Dohrmann for wonderful anatomical art, and to Barbara Barnett for the colorful figures that appear throughout this text. These individuals, and many others at West Publishing Company, share greatly in the credit for this book's final form.

Finally, I would like to express my continuing gratitude to Clyde H. Perlee, Jr., everyone's favorite Editor in

Chief, for his patience, inspiration, and friendship. This is his book as well as mine. I am equally indebted to Janet Bollow for passing up retirement at C.S.L. in order to grapple with the design problems of this text. A glance at my manuscript, and then at Janet's pages, should be enough to convince anyone that miracles do happen.

Last of all, I would like to thank my wife Sevren, whose emotional support and countless hours of help made this book possible.

Dennis Coon

Part One

An Introduction to Psychology and Psychologists

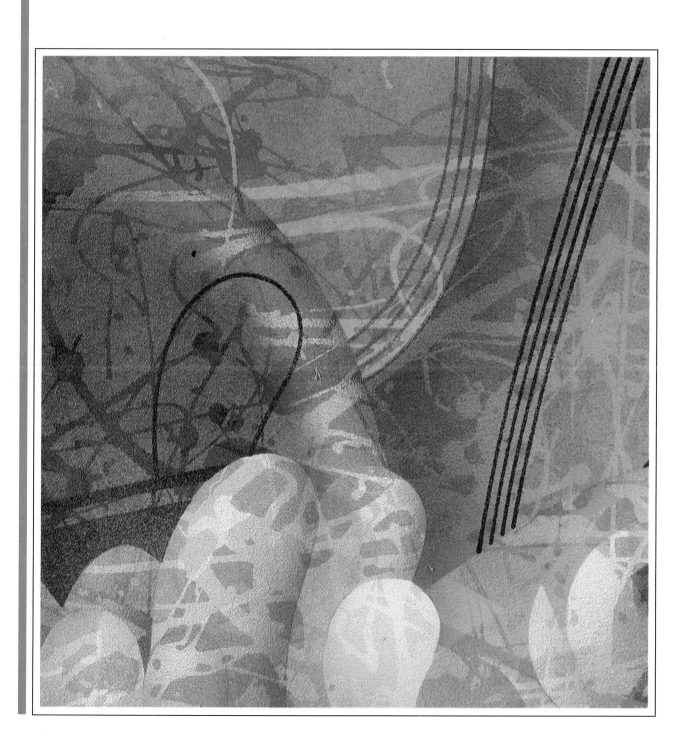

Chapter 1

An Introduction to Psychology and Psychologists

Chapter Preview
Why Study Psychology?

You are a universe, a collection of worlds within worlds. Your brain is possibly the most complicated and amazing device in existence. Through its action you are capable of art, music, science, philosophy, and war. Your capacities for love, compassion, and dedication coexist with your potential for aggression, hatred, and . . . murder? You are the most frustrating riddle ever written, a mystery at times even to yourself. You are at one and the same time a unique event in human history and like everyone who has ever lived. Your thoughts, emotions, and actions, your behavior and conscious experience are the subject of this book.

Look around you. Newspapers, magazines, radio, and television abound with psychological information. Psychology is discussed in homes, schools, businesses, and bars. Psychology is an explosive, exciting, and ever-changing panorama of people and ideas. You can hardly consider yourself "educated" without knowing something about it.

There is another reason for studying psychology. Socrates said, "Know thyself," and although we must envy those who have set foot on the moon, looked into an atom, or cruised the dreamlike landscapes of the ocean's depths, the ultimate frontier still lies close to home. Psychologist D. O. Hebb put it this way: "What is psychology all about? Psychology is about the mind: the central issue, the great mystery, the toughest problem of all" (Hebb, 1974).

Psychology is a journey into inner space. This book is a travel guide. Psychologists can't claim to have "the answers" to all of your questions, but they can show you the contours of the landscape already explored. More importantly, you may find skills in psychology that will aid you in your own search for answers. Ultimately, the answers must be your own, but studying psychology is a rich starting point. In this chapter you will find a definition of psychology, a description of various kinds of psychologists and what they do, a brief history of ideas in psychology, and some tips on studying.

Resources

"The elephant," said the blind man as he felt the elephant's leg, "is very much like a tree."

"Why how foolish!" said a second blind man (who had hold of the elephant's tail). "The elephant is like a rope."

The third blind man, having encountered the beast's trunk, said, "You're both wrong, the elephant is like a snake."

Psychology: Psyche = Mind; Logos = Knowledge or Study

Question: What is psychology?

Psychology is: memory, stress, psychotherapy, love, persuasion, hypnosis, perception, death, conformity, creativity, conditioning, personality, aging, intelligence, sexuality, emotion, and so many more topics that for a time you may be in a position similar to that of the blind men. Psychology has become such an enormous and colorful beast that no short description can do it justice.

It is important, then, to be open-minded as you begin this course. Consider your introduction to psychology an adventure, and judge after you have seen what it has to offer. By the time you have read this entire book, you will begin to have an overall picture of what psychology is, and what psychologists do. For now, let's just say that **psychology** *is the scientific study of human and animal behavior.* Its goals are to **describe, understand, predict,** and **control** behavior. Beyond this, psychology's ultimate goal, like that of other sciences, is to gather knowledge for the benefit of humanity.

Question: What does "behavior" refer to in the definition of psychology?

Behavior   Anything you do—eating, sleeping, talking, thinking, or sneezing—is a "behavior." So is dreaming, gambling, taking drugs, watching TV, learning Spanish, basket weaving, or reading this book. Notice that the word *behavior*, as used here, includes *covert* (private, internal) processes, such as thinking, as well as *overt* (visible) actions. To a psychologist, even hidden activities, such as thinking or perceiving, are "behaviors" because they are things that you do.

Much of our overt behavior can be studied by direct observation. But how do we study problem solving, daydreaming, or memory? In such cases we must *infer* what is happening "internally" from what we can observe directly. For example, try answering these questions: "Is a horse bigger than a mouse?"; "Is a collie bigger than a German shepherd?" If you are like most people you answered the first question faster than the second. Why? Most people report forming mental images of the animals to compare their size. A difference in the time it takes to answer, therefore, suggests that comparing images close in size is more difficult (Moyer & Bayer, 1976). Although we couldn't directly observe thinking, we were able to learn something interesting about it just the same.

Question: It seems from this example that psychologists try to be objective in their observations. Is that correct?

Yes. Psychologists have a special respect for **empirical evidence**—that is, information gained by direct observation and measurement, rather than through opinion, argument, or reliance on authority. Would you say it's true, for instance, that "you can't teach an old dog new tricks"? Why argue about it? A psychologist would get 10 "new" dogs, 10 "used" dogs, and 10 "old" dogs and then try to teach them all new tricks to find out!

Empiricism   Whenever possible, psychologists settle differences by direct investigation. This allows them to compare what they have observed and draw accurate conclusions. As self-evident as the empirical approach may seem in fields like biology or physics, in psychology we are still often tempted to accept what seems plausible or sensible rather than what *is*. For example, see if you can tell, on the basis of personal experience or common sense, which of the following statements are true. Then we will compare your answers to those found empirically.

True or False?

1. If you happened to step on a nail, you would feel it instantly. (Chapter 3)
2. A one-eyed man could not land an airplane. (Chapter 5)
3. When the moon is low in the sky, its image is greatly magnified by the atmosphere. (Chapter 5)
4. When hypnotized, witnesses to crimes can be made to have perfect memory for what they saw. (Chapter 6)
5. Brain activity almost ceases at various times during sleep. (Chapter 7)
6. Punishment is the most effective way to reinforce the learning of new habits. (Chapter 9)
7. All memories are permanent, if only there were some way to retrieve them. (Chapter 10)
8. People with high IQs are also highly creative, in most instances. (Chapter 11)

Fig. 1–1 *The variety and complexity of human behavior make psychological investigation challenging.*

9. A person facing major surgery would be better off if he or she worried about it as little as possible. (Chapter 13)
10. Stress is almost always bad for you. (Chapter 14)
11. Intelligence is completely inherited from one's parents. (Chapter 17)
12. Those who threaten suicide rarely actually commit suicide. (Chapter 20)
13. Schizophrenics have two or more distinct personalities. (Chapter 21)

14. If your car breaks down, you are more likely to get help from a passerby on a busy highway than on a lightly traveled country road. (Chapter 26)

Scoring this quiz is easy because all of the statements are *false*. (To find out why, you may want to look ahead at the chapters shown in parentheses.) If you missed some questions, don't despair. The point is simply this: Psychology became a science when psychologists began to perform experiments, make observations, and seek evidence, and you will become a better observer of human behavior to the extent that you do the same.

Question: I've heard that psychology isn't scientific. You have said that it is. Is it?

Science Psychology has been described by some as an "almost science" because scientific study of some of its topics is not yet possible. But the same is true of almost all sciences. Like other scientists, psychologists are sometimes unable to answer questions because of moral or practical concerns. What would happen if a child were placed in a soundproof, lightproof box for the first 5 years of life? This question will probably never be directly answered. (Many times, however, an indirect answer can be obtained by studying animals.) In other cases, research must await a receptive social climate. Very little was known about human sexual response, for instance, until William Masters, a gynecologist, and Virginia Johnson, a psychologist, directly recorded physical responses that occurred during sexual intercourse. Such research would have been impossible to carry out and publish 30 years ago. Likewise, much of what we know about the psychology of death was learned in the last 10 years, as this once-taboo subject has come under study.

More often, psychological questions remain unanswered for lack of a suitable *method.* For years the reports of people who said they never dream had to be considered accurate. But with an advance in technology, the EEG (electroencephalograph or brain wave machine) was developed. It then became possible to tell objectively when a person is dreaming. People who "never dream," it turns out, dream frequently and remember their dreams vividly when awakened during one. Through use of the EEG, the study of dreaming is becoming quite scientific. Many people think of scientific research as dull and painstaking. But as you can see, it often takes a great deal of creativity to find new methods for answering long-standing questions in psychology. Moreover, what we *do* know adds up to a large and highly useful body of knowledge.

Animals Notice from our definition that psychology includes the study of animals, as well as people. As a group psychologists are interested in natural laws governing the behavior of *any* living creature—from flatworms to humans. Indeed, specialists known as **comparative** psychologists may spend their entire careers studying rats, cats, dogs, turtles, chimpanzees, or other animals (Fig. 1–3). Comparative psychologists *compare* the behavior of different animals to learn what principles apply to all species, and which are unique to a particular creature. As they do,

they must be very careful to avoid the **anthropomorphic fallacy** (AN-thro-po-MORE-fik: attributing human thoughts, feelings, or motives to animals).

The temptation to assume that an animal is "angry," "jealous," "bored," or "guilty" can be strong, but it often leads to false conclusions. As an example, let's say I observe gorillas in the wild (where food is plentiful) and conclude that by nature gorillas are not "greedy." On the other hand, you place two hungry gorillas in a cage with a banana, stand back to watch the action, and conclude that gorillas are in fact *very* "greedy." Actually, all we have observed is that competition for food is related to the availability of food. Allowing the human concept of greed into the picture just clouds our understanding of gorilla behavior.

Question: Are comparative psychologists the only ones who study animals?

No. Many psychologists use animal research to discover principles that prove useful for solving human problems. Studies of topics as diverse as obesity, memory, stress, psychosis, therapy, and aging have used animals as subjects. More importantly, in some instances, animals serve as **models,** to provide the *only* information available on a particular subject. For example, the majority of what is known about the human brain is based on animal research. You just can't go around destroying parts of hu-

Fig. 1–2 *The scientific study of dreaming has been made possible by use of the EEG, a device that records the tiny electrical potentials generated by the brain of a sleeping subject. The EEG converts these electrical potentials to a written record of brain activity.*

Fig. 1–3 *Some of the most interesting research with animals has focused on attempts to teach primates to communicate. (See Chapter 10 for more information.)*

man brains to find out how they work. (The author, at any rate, has had a hard time finding volunteers.)

Animals, in return, have benefited from psychology. For example, behavioral research has provided ways to avoid the killing of animals, such as coyotes, crows, or deer, that destroy crops or livestock. The successful breeding and raising of endangered species in zoos also relies on behavioral research, as does the training of guide dogs for the blind (Miller, 1985). For these and other reasons, animals are very much a part of psychology.

Goals   To conclude this discussion, let's return for a moment to the goals of psychology. What do they mean in practice? Assume that we would like to answer these questions: What happens when a person has an injury on the right side of the brain? Is there more than one type of memory? How does creative problem solving differ from routine thought? Do autistic children react differently to their parents than to other adults? The answer to each question would require a careful **description** of behavior, the first goal of psychology.

Question: But a description doesn't explain anything, does it?

Right. Useful knowledge in psychology begins with accurate description, but description fails to answer the important "why" questions. *Why* do more women attempt suicide, and why do more men complete it? *Why* does

frustration encourage aggression? *Why* are bystanders often unwilling to help in an emergency?

Psychology's second goal, **understanding** behavior, is satisfied when we can explain why a phenomenon occurs or exists. Take the last question as an example. Research on "bystander apathy" has shown that people often fail to help when *other* potential helpers are present. This causes a "diffusion of responsibility" so no single bystander feels obligated to help. Generally, the greater number of potential helpers present, the less likely it is that help will be given (Darley & Latane, 1968) (see Chapter 26 for more information).

Psychology's third goal is **prediction**. Notice that the explanation for bystander apathy makes a prediction about the chances of getting help. Anyone who has been stranded by car trouble on a busy freeway will recognize the accuracy of this prediction. Of course, prediction in psychology is rarely as precise as it is in "hard sciences" like physics or chemistry. Just the same, psychological predictions are often quite useful. For example, psychological theory predicted that students high in test-taking anxiety would show improved performance if given reassurance and advice during testing—a prediction that proved true when tried (Sarason, 1975).

Question: Description, explanation, and prediction seem reasonable, but is control a valid goal for psychology?

Control is a frequently questioned and misunderstood goal of psychology, probably because it sounds like a threat to personal freedom. It should be realized, however, that to most psychologists "control" simply means altering conditions that influence behavior in predictable ways. For example, if a psychologist suggests changes in classroom procedures so that children learn more effectively, the psychologist has exercised control. If the psychologist uses conditioning principles to help a person overcome a crippling fear of heights, control is involved. Control is also present if psychological research is used to design an instrument panel that reduces airline pilot errors. Clearly, psychology can provide the means for changing behavior, but it does not say what changes should be made. As is the case with knowledge in other areas, psychological principles must be used wisely and humanely.

In summary, psychology's goals are a natural outgrowth of our desire to understand behavior. For various topics in psychology, the goals boil down to asking:

What is the nature of this behavior? (description)
Why does it occur? (explanation)
Can we predict when it will occur? (prediction)
What conditions affect it? (control)

Learning Check

To improve your memory of this chapter, see if you can answer these questions. If you miss any, skim over the preceding material before continuing, to make sure you understand what you just read.

1. Psychology is the ___Scientific___ study of the ___behavior___ of organisms.

2. Information gained through direct observation and measurement is called ___empirical___ evidence.

3. The ___anthropomorphic___ fallacy involves attributing human feelings and motives to animals.

4. Which of the following questions relates most directly to the goal of *understanding* behavior?
   a. Do men and women differ in intellectual abilities?
   b. Why does a blow to the head cause memory loss?
   c. Will productivity in a business office increase if room temperature is raised or lowered?
   d. How can test anxiety be prevented?

Answers: 1. scientific, behavior 2. empirical 3. anthropomorphic 4. b

A Brief History of Psychology's Brief History

Psychology has a long past but a short history. Psychology's past is centuries old because it includes **philosophy,** the study of knowledge, reality, and human nature. In contrast, psychology's history began only about 100 years ago. As sciences go, psychology is a new kid on the block: Easily 9 out of 10 persons to ever work in the field are alive today. Of course, to some students this history is still "not short enough"! Yet, the ideas in psychology's past are intimately tied to the present. To understand where psychology is now, let's take a brief look at its short history.

Into the Lab Psychology's history began in 1879 at Leipzig, Germany. There, the "father" of psychology, **Wilhelm Wundt** (VILL-helm Voont), created the first psychological laboratory to study *conscious experience.* How, he wondered, are sensations, images, and feelings formed? To find out, Wundt observed and carefully measured **stimuli*** of various kinds (lights, sounds, weights). He then used **introspection,** or "looking inward," to examine his reactions to them. Wundt called this approach **experimental self-observation** (Blumenthal, 1979). Over the years he used it to study vision, hearing, taste, touch, reaction time, memory, feelings, time perception, and a host of other topics. Along the way Wundt wrote some 60,000 printed pages. It may be a good thing that word processors didn't exist then: When a student gave Wundt a typewriter, a rival psychologist grumbled that this "evil" gift would only allow him to write more!

*Stimulus: singular; stimuli (STIM-you-lie): plural.

Experimental self-observation became a highly developed skill, much like that needed to be a professional wine taster. Wundt's subjects had to make at least 10,000 practice observations before they were allowed to describe their sensations in a real experiment (Lieberman, 1979). With such emphasis on careful observation and measurement, psychology was off to a good start.

Structuralism Wundt's ideas were carried to the United States by one of his students, a psychologist named E. B. Titchener (TICH-in-er). There, Titchener and others launched a school of thought called **structuralism.** The structuralists hoped to develop a sort of "mental chemistry" by *analyzing* experience into basic "elements" or "building blocks."

Question: How could they do that? You can't analyze experience like you can a chemical compound, can you?

Perhaps not, but the structuralists tried, mostly by using introspection. In this approach an introspectionist might heft an apple and then decide that he or she had experienced the elements "hue" (color), "roundness," and "weight." Another example of the kind of question that might have interested a structuralist is, "What elemental tastes mix together to create complex flavors as different as liver, lime, bacon, or burnt-almond fudge?"

It soon became evident that introspection was a poor way to answer many kinds of questions. The most troublesome problem was that introspectionists frequently *disagreed.* And when they did, introspection provided no method for settling differences. If two structuralists came up with different lists of elementary taste sensations, who was to say which was right? Despite such limitations, "looking inward" is still a part of modern psychology. The study of hypnosis, meditation, drug effects, problem solving, and many other topics would be incomplete without reports of subjective experiences.

Functionalism   William James, an American psychologist, agreed with Wundt and the structuralists that psychologists should study the mind. However, he broadened the scope of psychology to include animal behavior, religious experience, abnormal behavior, and a number of other interesting topics.

Question: Did James use introspection?

James and other **functionalists** were willing to use introspection, experimentation, and even a dash of armchair philosophizing to study mental life. The term *functionalism* comes from James' interest in how the mind *functions* to adapt us to our environment. To James, consciousness was an ever-changing *stream* or *flow* of images and sensations—not a collection of lifeless building blocks as the structuralists claimed.

The functionalists were strongly influenced by Charles Darwin. According to Darwin, organisms evolve, through **natural selection,** in directions that favor their survival. This means that features that help adapt animals to their environment are retained in evolution. Similarly, the functionalists wanted to learn how thought, perception,

habits, and emotions aid human adaptation. In short, they wanted to study the mind *in use.*

Question: What effect did functionalism have on modern psychology?

Functionalism brought the study of animals into psychology by linking human and animal adaptation. It also encouraged the development of **educational psychology.** Functionalists emphasized that learning improves personal adaptability, and they urged psychologists to help improve education. Today, modern educational psychologists develop tests and conduct research on classroom dynamics, teaching styles, and learning. Functionalism also spurred the development of **industrial psychology,** a speciality involving the study of people at work (see Chapter 27).

Behaviorism: Stimulus-Response   Psychology
Functionalism was soon challenged by a new school of thought called **behaviorism.** Behaviorist John B. Watson objected to defining psychology as the study of the "mind" or "conscious experience," and he considered introspection unscientific. Watson quickly learned that he could study animals quite effectively even though he couldn't ask them questions or know what they were thinking. He simply observed the relationship between **stimuli** (events in the environment) and an animal's **responses** to them. Why not, he argued, apply the same objectivity to the study of humans?

Fig. 1–4 *Wilhelm Wundt, 1832–1920.*   **Fig. 1–5** *William James, 1842–1910.*   **Fig. 1–6** *John B. Watson, 1878–1958.*

Watson soon adopted Russian physiologist Ivan Pavlov's (ee-VAHN PAV-lahv) **conditioned response** concept as a way of explaining most behavior. (A conditioned response is a learned reaction to a particular stimulus.) Watson's enthusiasm for conditioning had obviously reached extremes when he proclaimed:

Give me a dozen healthy infants, well-formed, and my own special world to bring them up in and I'll guarantee to take any one at random and train him to become any type of specialist I might select—doctor, lawyer, artist, merchant-chief, and yes, beggarman and thief. (Watson, 1913.)

Question: Would most psychologists agree with Watson's claim?

Today, most would probably consider it an overstatement. Just the same, behaviorism has had a profound effect on modern psychological thought. The best known and most influential modern behaviorists, B. F. Skinner, has said,

The environment is the key causal matrix. . . . In order to understand human behavior we must take into account what the environment does to an organism before and after it responds. Behavior is shaped and maintained by its consequences. (Skinner, 1971.)

Skinner, too, has been criticized. Skinner's emphasis on stimulus-response relationships, and his tendency to ignore thought and subjective experience, have led some observers to charge that Skinnerian psychology has "lost consciousness." Despite such criticisms, a majority of psychologists would probably agree that most human behavior is influenced in one way or another by learning.

The behavioristic approach is responsible for much of what we know today about learning, memory, conditioning, and the effective use of reward and punishment. A direct descendant of behavioristic thought is a type of therapy known as **behavior modification.** In behavior modification, conditioning principles are used to treat problems such as overeating, phobias, and childhood misbehavior. (See Chapter 23 for more information.)

Gestalt Psychology   Imagine for a moment that you have just heard a familiar tune such as "Yankee Doodle" played on a tuba. Next it is played on a high-pitched violin. Even though none of the original sounds are used, the melody will still be recognizable—*if the relationship* between notes is the same. Now, what if the original notes were played in the correct order, but at a rate of one per hour? What would we have? Nothing. The separated notes would no longer be a melody. The melody is somehow more than the sum of its parts. It was observations such as

this that launched the **Gestalt** school of thought in psychology.

The German word *Gestalt* (geh-SHTALT) means form, pattern, or whole. The Gestalt viewpoint, first advanced by the German psychologist Max Wertheimer (VERT-himer), held that it is a mistake to analyze psychological events into pieces or "elements" as the structuralists did. Instead, the Gestaltists tried to study experiences as *wholes.* Their slogan was, "The whole exceeds the sum of its parts."

Question: What did they mean by that?

A perceptual illusion called the **phi phenomenon** provides a good example. The illusion is created by placing two light bulbs a few inches apart in a darkened room. The left bulb is turned on, then off, and a split second later the right bulb is turned on. When this is done, a single bulb appears to move from left to right. No real movement occurs, so the whole experience is more than the sum of its parts. The same effect causes the apparent movement of stationary lights on computerized billboards and theater signs.

Like a melody or the phi phenomenon, many other experiences resist analysis into "parts" or "pieces." For this reason, the Gestalt viewpoint remains influential in the study of perception and personality.

Psychoanalytic Psychology   As the mainstream of psychology grew more objective, scientific, and experimental, an Austrian physician named Sigmund Freud was developing his own theory of behavior. Freud's point of departure was his belief that mental life is like an iceberg: Only part is exposed to view. According to Freud, vast areas of **unconscious** thoughts, impulses, and desires, which cannot be known directly, influence our behavior. This idea added a new dimension, not only to psychology, but to art, literature, and history as well.

Freud theorized that many unconscious thoughts are of a threatening, sexual, or aggressive nature. Hence, they are *repressed* (actively held out of consciousness). But sometimes, he said, they are revealed by dreams, emotions, or slips of the tongue. ("Freudian slips" are often humorous, as when a student who is tardy for class says, "I'm sorry I couldn't get here any later.") Also notable was Freud's insistence that all thoughts, emotions, and actions are *determined* (nothing is an accident); his emphasis on the importance of childhood in later personality development ("the child is father to the man"); and his development of a method of psychotherapy called **psychoanalysis.**

Freud had not held sway for very long before some of

his students, such as Carl Jung, began to break away from him. (See Table 1–1.) These psychologists developed their own theories and became known as **neo-Freudians** (*neo* means new or recent). Today, Freud's ideas have been enlarged, altered, revised, and adapted to the point that few strictly psychoanalytic psychologists are left. However, Freud's legacy is still evident in various **psychodynamic** approaches to psychology, which emphasize the interplay of internal forces in the personality.

Table 1–1   The Early Development of Psychology

Approximate Origin	Date	Notable Events
Experimental psychology	1875	■ First experimental psychology course offered by William James
	1878	■ First American Ph.D. in psychology awarded
	1879	■ Wilhelm Wundt establishes first psychology laboratory in Germany
	1883	■ First American psychology lab founded at Johns Hopkins University
	1886	■ First American psychology textbook published by John Dewey
Structuralism	1898	■ Edward Titchener advances psychology based on introspection
Functionalism	1890	■ James publishes *Principles of Psychology*
	1892	■ American Psychological Association founded
Psychoanalytic psychology	1895	■ Sigmund Freud publishes first studies
	1900	■ Freud publishes *The Interpretation of Dreams*
Behaviorism	1906	■ Ivan Pavlov reports his research on conditioning
	1913	■ John Watson presents behavioristic view
Gestalt psychology	1912	■ Max Wertheimer and others advance Gestalt viewpoint
Neo-Freudianism	1914	■ Carl Jung breaks with Freud

Humanistic Psychology   A fairly recent development in psychology is a point of view known as **humanism.** Humanism is sometimes called the "third force" in psychology. (Psychodynamic psychology and behaviorism are the other two.)

Question: How is the humanistic approach different?

Psychologists Carl Rogers, Abraham Maslow, and others developed the humanistic viewpoint to counter the negativity they saw in psychoanalysis and early versions of behaviorism. Humanists reject the Freudian idea that personality is ruled by unconscious forces and the behavioristic idea that we are controlled by the environment. Although humanists admit that one's past affects personality, they emphasize the importance of **free will,** the human ability to make choices.

The humanists also brought a new emphasis to psychological needs for love, self-esteem, belonging, self-expression, and creativity. According to the humanists, such needs are as important as biological needs for food and water. For example, newborn infants who are deprived of human love and warmth may die just as surely as they would if deprived of food.

Question: How scientific is the humanistic approach?

Humanists collect data and seek evidence to support their ideas, but for the most part they tend to be less interested in attempts to treat psychology as a science. Since they are basically interested in solving human problems, humanists show less interest in research with animals or laboratory studies of behavior. Instead, they stress the importance of such *subjective* factors as one's **self-image, self-evaluation,** and **frame of reference.** It is possible, however, to apply scientific methods to humanistic goals, and some humanists do so.

One of the most distinctive contributions of the humanistic approach is Maslow's description of **self-actualization.** Self-actualization is the need to develop one's potential fully, to lead a rich and meaningful life, and to become the best person one can become. According to the humanists, everyone has this potential. The humanists seek ways to allow it to emerge.

Psychology Today   At one time schools of thought functioned almost like political parties in the profession of psychology. Loyalty to a particular viewpoint was often fierce, and clashes between schools were common. Today, several of the traditional schools of thought have given way to a blending of ideas and perspectives. Although loyalties and specialties still exist, many psychologists can be described as **eclectic** (ek-LEK-tik: drawing

Fig. 1–7 *Max Wertheimer, 1880–1941.*

Fig. 1–8 *Sigmund Freud, 1856–1939.*

Fig. 1–9 *Abraham Maslow, 1908–1970.*

from many sources) in their approach. Even so, five major perspectives are evident in modern psychology. These are the **behavioristic, humanistic,** and **psychodynamic** views, plus the increasingly important **biological** and **cognitive** perspectives.

The value of biological approaches for understanding behavior has risen dramatically in recent years. This is largely due to an explosive growth in knowledge about how the brain works and its relation to thought, feelings, perception, abnormal behavior, and other important topics. A similar trend has occurred for cognitive psychology. Cognition means thinking or knowing, so cognitive psychologists study thoughts, expectations, language, perception, problem solving, consciousness, creativity, and other mental processes. Some of these topics were neglected for so many years that it may be fair to say that psychology has recently "regained consciousness."

Whatever their theoretical leanings, most modern psychologists share a preference for facts and principles that have survived rigorous scientific testing.

In the next section we will further explore what contemporary psychologists do, as well as take a look at some of their specialties. But first, see if you can correctly match the items in the following Learning Check.

Learning Check

Match:

1. ____ Philosophy
2. ____ Wundt
3. ____ Structuralism
4. ____ Functionalism
5. ____ Behaviorism
6. ____ Gestalt
7. ____ Psychoanalytic
8. ____ Humanistic
9. ____ Cognitive

A. Against analysis; studied whole experiences

B. "Mental chemistry" and introspection

C. Emphasizes self-actualization and personal growth

D. Interested in unconscious causes of behavior

E. Gave rise to educational and industrial psychology

F. Studied stimuli and responses, conditioning

G. Part of psychology's "long past"

H. Concerned with thinking, language, problem solving

I. Used "experimental self-observation"

J. Also known as engineering psychology

Answers: 1. C 2. I 3. B 4. E 5. F 6. A 7. D 8. C 9. H

Psychologists— Guaranteed Not to Shrink

Question: What is the difference between a psychologist and a psychiatrist?
Answer: About $20 an hour. (And going up.)

Confusion often exists about the differences among **psychologists, psychiatrists, psychoanalysts, counselors,** and other mental health professionals. It is quite inaccurate to think of them all as "shrinks." Each title reflects distinct differences in training and emphasis.

A psychologist usually has a master's degree or a doctorate in psychology; that is, from 3 to 8 years of specialized postgraduate training in psychological theory and research methods. Depending on their interests, psychologists may teach, do research, administer psychological tests, or serve as consultants to business, industry, government, or the military. (This statement applies to psychiatrists and psychoanalysts too.) Psychologists interested in human emotional problems and their treatment specialize either in **clinical psychology** or **counseling psychology** (see Table 1–2).

To enter the profession of psychology today, you would probably find it necessary to have the doctorate (Ph.D., Psy.D., or Ed.D) in order to be licensed or to qualify or compete for positions. (For more information, see Appendix A, Careers in Psychology, at the end of the text.) Most clinical psychologists now have a Ph.D. or a Psy.D. (Doctor of Psychology) degree. The Psy.D. is a newly created degree that places emphasis on practical clinical skills rather than on research (McNett, 1982).

Like clinical psychologists, psychiatrists are also interested in human problems, but they are trained differently. A psychiatrist is a medical doctor (M.D.). After training in general medicine, psychiatrists specialize in abnormal behavior and psychotherapy. Psychiatrists often become "talking doctors" who spend much of their time doing psychotherapy. In practice, then, the major difference between clinical psychologists and psychiatrists is that psychiatrists are trained to treat the physical causes of psychological problems. In the vast majority of cases, they do so by prescribing drugs, which is something a psychologist cannot do.

To be a psychoanalyst, you must have a moustache and goatee, spectacles, a German accent, and a well-padded couch—or so the TV and movie stereotype goes. Actually, to become an analyst, you must have an M.D. or Ph.D. degree and then receive specialized training in the theory and practice of Freudian psychoanalysis. In other words, either a psychologist or a psychiatrist may become

an analyst by completing additional training. Analysts typically undergo psychoanalysis themselves before applying the method to others.

Question: Is psychoanalysis widely used?

The fact that traditional Freudian analysis is expensive and time consuming is gradually making psychoanalysts something of a rare breed. Nowadays, few psychologists or psychiatrists become analysts, and fewer clients seek analysis. In practice many psychotherapists find that a flexible and eclectic approach is most effective.

In many states counselors (such as marriage and family counselors, child counselors, or school counselors) also do mental health work. To be a licensed counselor typically requires a master's degree plus 1 or 2 years of full-time supervised counseling experience. Almost all of a counselor's postgraduate education is directly related to practical counseling skills, with little emphasis on research. The practice of counseling is usually limited to adjustment problems not involving serious mental disorders.

Question: Do psychologists have to have a license?

Before the American Psychological Association (APA) began a push for licensing and certification, it was possible in many states for virtually anyone to purchase an inexpensive license and "hang out a shingle" as a "psychologist."

Today, to be legally called a psychologist, a person must meet a rigorous set of educational requirements. To work as a clinical or counseling psychologist, he or she must have a license issued by a state examining board. However, the law does not prohibit you from calling yourself anything else you choose—Gestalt therapist, primal feeling facilitator, cosmic aura balancer, or Rolfer—or from selling your "services" to anyone willing to pay. Beware of people advertising under such self-proclaimed titles. Even if their intentions are honorable, their training often is limited or nonexistent. A fully trained, certified psychologist who chooses to use a particular type of therapy is not the same as someone "trained" only in that technique.

Unfortunately, psychology, like medicine, has attracted a fringe of opportunists, quacks, and charlatans who seek to profit by taking advantage of human needs, fears, and suffering. When the escapades of these "not-really psychologists" make the news, or when a friend or relative has a bad experience with one, psychologists often pay the price in negative public attitudes toward psychology in general. This is indeed unfortunate since psychologists adhere to a professional code established by the APA which stresses: (1) accurate representation of one's professional qualifications; (2) confidentiality in handling of personal information in teaching, practice, or research; and above all, (3) protection of the client's welfare. The APA also encourages psychologists to make their services available to anyone who seeks them, regardless of his or her ability to pay.

How to Be a Psychologist— Let Us Count the Ways

Question: Do all psychologists do therapy and treat abnormal behavior?

Even when combined, clinical and counseling psychology account for only about 40 percent of psychologists. The rest are found in a large number of other specialties. At present, there are 42 divisions of the APA, each reflecting a special skill area or interest. Some of the major specialties are listed in Table 1–2. (Also see Fig. 1–10.) Over 50 percent of psychologists are employed full time by schools. In this setting they teach and may also do research, consultation, or therapy. Those engaged in research may do **basic research,** seeking knowledge for the sake of knowledge, or **applied research,** in which immediate uses are planned for the information gained.

Question: What kinds of things would a typical psychologist at a university do research on?

Here is a sampling of representative research topics.

Comparative   "I have always been interested in basic questions about animal behavior, but my current research is applied. I am investigating ways of preventing abnormalities that result when an animal is kept in social isolation for extended periods of time. My goal is to help the space program. If I can provide a way to keep animals 'mentally' healthy while in space, the effects of prolonged weightlessness can be studied."

Developmental   "I am interested in development from conception until death. I am trying to learn how people grow and change over time. My interests stretch over the whole lifespan, but I am especially interested in early childhood. My colleagues and I seek the principles whereby a child develops the ability to think, speak, perceive, and act. Broadly speaking, I am interested in how adult personality and skills emerge from childhood, but my current research is more limited. I am studying the effects of stimulating childhood environments on the development of intelligence."

Learning   "I'm also interested in how people get to be the way they are, but in a much more abstract sense. I believe that most human behavior is learned. At any given moment I would describe your behavior as the result of your personal learning history. By studying various kinds of learning, conditioning, and memory in humans and animals, I am helping construct theories about how learning occurs and what factors affect it. My doctoral dissertation was on avoidance learning. I had rats learn to press a bar to avoid receiving an electric shock that followed the onset of a signal light. Right now I'm studying the effects of patterns of reinforcement on learning in pigeons."

Personality   "In many ways my area is both the most rewarding and the most frustrating. Personality theorists draw on the findings of all other research areas as well as

Fig. 1–10   (a) *Specialties in psychology. Percentages are approximate (from* A Career in Psychology, *APA, 1970);* (b) *Where psychologists work. (From Boneau & Cuca, 1974.)*

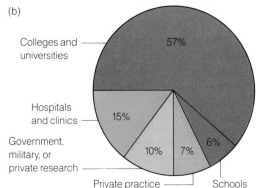

Table 1-2   Kinds of Psychologists and What They Do

Specialty		Typical Activities
Clinical and counseling psychologists	A*	Does psychotherapy and personal counseling, helps with emotional and behavioral problems, researches clinical problems, is involved in community mental health.
Industrial psychologist	A	Selects job applicants, does skills analysis, evaluates on-job training, improves work environments and human relations in work setting.
Educational psychologist	A	Conducts research on classroom dynamics, teaching styles, and learning variables; develops educational tests, evaluates educational programs, acts as consultant for schools.
Consumer psychologist	A	Researches and tests packaging, advertising, and marketing methods; determines characteristics of product users, conducts public opinion polling.
School psychologist	A	Does psychological testing, emotional and vocational counseling of students; detects and treats learning disabilities; improves learning and motivation in the classroom.
Developmental psychologist	A, B	Carries out basic and applied research on child development, adult developmental trends, and aging; does clinical work with disturbed children; acts as consultant to preschools, programs for the aged, and so forth.
Engineering psychologist	A	Does applied research on design of machinery, controls, airplanes, automobiles, and so on for business, industry, and the military.
Medical psychologist	A	Studies the relationship between stress, personality, and disease (heart attacks, high blood pressure, ulcers); manages emotional problems associated with illness or disability.
Environmental psychologist	A, B	Studies the effects of urban noise pollution, crowding, attitudes toward environment, and human use of space; acts as consultant for design of industrial environments, schools, housing for elderly, and urban architecture.
Forensic psychologist	A	Studies problems of crime and crime prevention, rehabilitation programs in prisons, courtroom dynamics, psychology and law; selects candidates for police work.
Experimental psychologist	B	Applies scientific research methods to study of human and animal behavior; may conduct research in the areas of comparative animal behavior, learning, sensation/perception, personality, physiology, motivation/emotion, social behavior, or cognition.

*Research is typically: applied (A); basic (B); or both.

their own in an effort to create as total a picture and understanding of human personality as possible. I concern myself with the structure and dynamics of personality, motivation, and individual differences. I am studying the personality profiles of college students who score high on tests of creativity."

Sensation and Perception   "How do we come to know the world? How does information 'get into' our ner-

vous systems? How is it processed and given pattern and meaning? These are my concerns. I am using an information-processing theory called signal detection to study the visual perception of random shapes."

Physiological Psychology   "The brain and nervous system are my meat . . . so to speak. It is my belief that ultimately all other areas in psychology—learning, perception, even personality and abnormal behavior—will be explained by the action of nerve cells and brain chemicals. I have been doing some exciting research on the role of the hypothalamus in hunger. I find that if I remove part of the hypothalamus in a rat's brain, the rat will eat and gain weight until it looks like a furry water balloon. If I remove an area just a few millimeters away, the rat will starve to death if not force-fed."

Social Psychology "I study people in a group setting or under any circumstance in which social factors play a part. Social psychologists in general are interested in attitudes, social influence, riots, conformity, leadership, racism, friendship, and a growing list of other topics. My personal interest is interpersonal attraction. I place two strangers together in a room for a short time and investigate factors that affect their degree of attraction toward each other."

This small sample should give you some idea of the diversity of psychological research. It also gives a hint of some of the kinds of information covered later in this book.

Giving Psychology Away— An Introduction to Applications

Question: What can I learn from psychology that will benefit me personally?

More than you might think. A special quality of psychology is that its concepts are available to everyone. As former APA president George Miller has said:

> The secrets of our trade need not be reserved for highly trained specialists. Psychological facts should be passed out freely to all who need and can use them. (Miller, 1969.)

To this day, Miller (1980) remains convinced that psychologists should "give psychology away," and that's exactly what this book is meant to do.

To help you get the most out of psychology, each chapter includes a specific Applications section like the one that follows. There, information and ideas of immediate usefulness are discussed. In our first Applications, we will investigate how psychology can help you study more effectively.

Learning Check

See if you can answer these questions before continuing.

1. Which of the following can prescribe drugs?
   psychologist   psychiatrist   psychoanalyst   counselor

2. Two kinds of psychologists specialize in treating human emotional difficulties. One specialty is called _____ psychology. The other is _____ psychology.

3. Roughly 40 percent of psychologists specialize in counseling psychology.   T or F?

4. Seeking knowledge for the sake of knowledge is called _____ research.

Match the following research areas with the topic they cover.

5. ____ Developmental
6. ____ Learning
7. ____ Personality
8. ____ Sensation and perception
9. ____ Physiological psychology
10. ____ Social psychology
11. ____ Comparative

A. Attitudes, groups, leadership
B. Conditioning, memory
C. The psychology of law
D. Brain and nervous system
E. Child psychology
F. Individual differences, motivation
G. Animal behavior
H. Information processing

12. Who among the following would most likely be involved in the detection and treatment of learning disabilities?
   a. consumer psychologist   *b.* forensic psychologist   *c.* experimental psychologist   *d.* school psychologist

Answers: 1. psychiatrist 2. clinical, counseling 3. F 4. basic 5. E 6. B 7. F 8. H 9. D 10. A 11. C 12. *d*

Applications

The Psychology of Studying

Do you find learning challenging and rewarding? Or painful and intimidating? The second reaction is common even among bright students, if they lack basic "tools of the trade." Even if you're not one of those students, you may be able to improve your study skills. Would you like to learn more in less time? There is a good chance you can, if you apply the methods described here.

The SQ3R Method—How to Tame a Textbook

Have you ever completed a reading assignment, only to discover afterward that you remembered little of what you read? This problem has plagued students for decades. Fortunately, an excellent solution exists. Over 40 years ago, educator Francis Robinson developed a superb reading technique called the **SQ3R method.**

Robinson's method is simply a way of combining studying with reading. The symbols S-Q-R-R-R stand for *survey, question, read, recite,* and *review.* Following these five steps can help you understand ideas quickly, remember more, and review effectively for tests (Robinson, 1941):

S = *Survey.*   Look ahead through a chapter before you begin reading. As you do, read only topic headings, captions for illustrations, and any chapter summary or review. This step should give you an overall picture of what lies ahead.

Q = *Question.*   To focus your attention as you read, turn each topic heading into one or more questions. For example, the heading "Stages of Sleep" could raise questions such as: "Is there more than one stage of sleep?" "What are the stages of sleep?" "How do they differ?" "How is each identified?" And so forth. Asking questions will increase your interest, and it will help relate new ideas to what you already know, for better comprehension.

R1 = *Read.*   The first *R* in SQ3R refers to *read.* As you read, try to answer the questions you asked.

Read in short "bites" from one *topic heading* to the next, then stop. (If the material is very difficult, you may want to read only a paragraph or two at a time.)

R2 = *Recite.*   The second *R* stands for *recite.* After you have read from one topic heading to the next, you should stop and recite. That is, try to silently answer your questions or to summarize what you've read by writing brief notes. If you can't summarize main ideas in your own words, scan back over the section until you can. Until you can remember what you just read, there's little point to reading more.

After you have completed one section in this way, turn the next topic heading into questions. Then read to the following heading. Again, you should look for answers as you read, and you should recite before moving on. Repeat the question-read-recite cycle until you've read the entire chapter.

R3 = *Review.*   When you've finished reading, skim back over the chapter, or read your notes. Then check your memory by reciting and quizzing yourself again. Or better yet, get someone to ask you questions about each topic to see if you can answer in your own words.

Question: Does this method really work?

Experiments show that using the SQ3R method improves both reading comprehension and grades (Boker, 1974; Driskell & Kelly, 1980). Simply reading straight through a chapter often leads to a case of intellectual "indigestion." That's why it's important that you stop often to think, question, recite, review, and "digest" information.

How to Use this Text   With practice, you can apply the SQ3R method to any book. However, as you have probably guessed by now, its steps are built into this text to help you use them.

Each chapter opens with a short Preview, followed by

Applications: The Psychology of Studying

Survey Questions to help you get oriented. After you have read these two sections, take a minute or two to make your own survey of the chapter. As you read, questions woven into the text will help clarify ideas and focus your attention. Research shows that this arrangement leads to improved learning and memory (Boker, 1974; Melton, 1978).

Every few pages, Learning Checks allow you to "recite" by testing your memory of important points. (Again, you should also take notes or recite on your own.) Near the end of each chapter is a Chapter Summary you can use for review. Then, to extend your knowledge, a short Exploration on an interesting topic completes each chapter.

As you read, new terms will be defined where they first appear in the text. Key terms are printed in **boldface type** and are often followed by pronunciations. (Capital letters show which syllables are accented.) As a further study aid, a **glossary,** or mini-dictionary, of terms also appears near the end of this book. Perhaps you should take a moment to find it now.

Together, these features should make learning psychology enjoyable and effective, but there is still more you can do on your own.

Effective Note Taking—Good Students, Take Note!

Question: The SQ3R method may be good for reading, but what about taking notes in class when it's difficult to know what's important?

Effective note taking requires active listening. **Active listeners** know how to control their attention to avoid classroom daydreaming. Here's a listening/note-taking plan that works for many students. The important steps are summarized by the letters in the word **LISAN,** pronounced "listen" (Carman & Adams, 1985).

L = *Lead. Don't follow.*   Try to anticipate what the instructor is going to say. As in SQ3R, use questions as guides. Questions can come from the instructor's study guides or the reading assignments.

I = *Ideas.*   Every lecture is based on a core of important ideas. Usually an idea is introduced and

examples or explanations are given. Ask yourself often, "What is the main idea now? What ideas support it?"

S = *Signal words.*   Listen for words that tell you the direction the instructor is taking. For instance, here are some groups of signal words:

There are three reasons why . . .	Here come ideas
Most important is . . .	Main idea
On the contrary . . .	Opposite idea
As an example . . .	Support for main idea
Therefore . . .	Conclusion

A = *Actively listen.* Sit where you can hear and where you can be seen if you need to ask a question. Look at the instructor while he or she talks. Bring questions you want answered from the last lecture or from your reading. Raise your hand at the beginning of class or approach your instructor before the lecture begins. Do anything that helps you to be active.

N = *Note taking.* As you listen, write down only key points. Listen to everything, but be selective and don't try to write down everything. If you are too busy writing, you may not grasp what is said. Any gaps in your notes can be filled in immediately after class.

Here is something more you should know: A recent study (Palkovitz & Lore, 1980) found that most students do make reasonably good notes—and then don't use them! Most students wait until just before exams to review their notes—which have, by then, lost much of their meaning. If you don't want your notes to seem like hieroglyphics or "chicken scratches," it pays to review them *on a regular basis.* And remember, whenever it is important to listen effectively, the letters LISAN are a good guide.

Study Habits—Avoiding the Last-Minute Blues

It is important to realize that virtually every topic is interesting to someone, somewhere. Although I may not

Applications: The Psychology of Studying

be interested in the sex life of the South American tree frog, a biologist might be fascinated. If you wait for your teachers to "make" their courses interesting, you are missing the point. Interest is a matter of *your attitude*. No teacher can "make" a course interesting without your participation. If you bring an inquiring mind and a positive attitude to your studies, you will find learning challenging and interesting. If you wait to be entertained, learning will be a chore. Students and teachers *together* make a class interesting.

   With these thoughts in mind, let's consider a few things you can do to make your study habits more productive.

Study in a Specific Place   It goes almost without saying that you should study in a quiet, well-lighted area that is free of distractions. If possible, you should also have at least one place where you *only study*. Do nothing else at that spot: Keep magazines, radios, friends, pets, posters, games, puzzles, food, lovers, sports cars, elephants, pianos, televisions, hang gliders, kazoos, and other distractions out of the area. In this way, studying will become strongly linked with one specific place (Beneke & Harris, 1972). This association makes it easier to get work done. Rather than trying to force yourself to study by "willpower," all you have to do is go to your study area. Once there, you'll find it relatively easy to get started.

Use Spaced Study Sessions   It is quite reasonable to review intensely before an exam. However, if you are actually learning information for the first time (cramming), you are asking for trouble. Psychological research suggests that **spaced practice** is a more efficient way to study. Spaced practice consists of a large number of relatively short study sessions, rather than one or two long ones (called *massed practice*). (It might be worth remembering that if you "massed up" your studying you probably messed it up too.) Cramming places a tremendous burden on memory. It is far better to learn small amounts on a daily basis and to review frequently.

Try Mnemonics   Students sometimes complain about having to memorize for classes. But learning has to start somewhere, and memorizing is often the first step.

Psychologists now know a great deal about how to improve memory. Since many of the most important points are summarized in Chapter 10, let's consider just one technique here.

   A **mnemonic** (nee-MON-ik) is a memory aid. Most mnemonics link new information to ideas or images that are easy to remember. For example, to remember the early schools of psychology (structuralism, functionalism, behaviorism, Gestalt, psychoanalytic, and humanistic), it might be helpful to make up a sentence like this: *Strut*ting is *fun behavior, guessed* the *psycho-human*. As silly as this may seem, it could provide the extra cues you need when you are under pressure on a test. As another example, imagine you want to remember that the Spanish word for duck is *pato* (pronounced POT-oh). To use a mnemonic, you could picture a duck in a pot or a duck wearing a pot for a hat (Pressley et al., 1980). Obviously, the possibilities for creating mnemonics are numerous. If you would like to learn more, look ahead to Chapter 10.

Test Yourself   Many students overlook one of the best ways to improve test scores: When studying, you can arrange to take several practice tests before the real one in class. In other words, studying should include **self-testing** by use of flash cards, Learning Checks, a study guide, or questions you ask yourself. As you study, ask as many questions as you can and be sure you can answer them. Studying without testing yourself is like practicing for a basketball game without shooting any baskets.

Overlearn   When you study, there is something else to keep in mind: Many students *underprepare* for exams, and most *overestimate* how well they will do on exams (Murray, 1980). A solution to both problems is **overlearning**. To overlearn, you should continue studying beyond bare mastery of a topic. This means that you need to give yourself time for extra study and review *after* you think you are prepared for a test. Another reason for overlearning is provided by the following experiment:

The Perils of Multiple Choice

College students were given 15 minutes to study a passage on human rights. Students were told to expect either an

Applications: The Psychology of Studying

essay, multiple-choice, "memory," or unspecified type of test. In fact, all students took the same test, which included multiple-choice and short-answer questions. Students expecting multiple-choice questions scored *lowest,* even on the multiple-choice questions (Foos & Clark, 1984).

Before tests, students always ask, "Will it be essay or multiple-choice?" But as the experiment shows, it is probably best to approach all tests as if they were essays. By doing so, you will learn information more completely, so that you will really "know your stuff" when you take the test.

Question: All of these study techniques are fine. But what can I do about procrastination?

Procrastination

A tendency to procrastinate is almost universal among college students. (When campus workshops on procrastination are offered, many students never get around to signing up!) Even when procrastination doesn't lead to failure, it can cause much suffering. Procrastinators put off work until the last possible moment, work only under pressure, skip classes, give false reasons for late work, and feel ashamed of their last-minute efforts (Burka & Yuen, 1983).

Question: Why do so many students procrastinate?

It is fairly natural to put off long-range assignments, at school and elsewhere. However, there are additional reasons for student procrastination. Psychologists Jane Burka and Lenora Yuen observe that many students seem to equate performance in school with their *personal worth.* By procrastinating, students can blame poor work on a late start, rather than a lack of ability—after all, it wasn't their best effort, was it?

Perfectionism is a related problem. If you have high expectations for yourself, you may find it hard to start an assignment. Students with high standards expect the impossible from themselves and end up with all-or-nothing work habits (Burka & Yuen, 1983).

Time Management   Burka and Yuen supervise a program for procrastinators at the University of California, Berkeley. Eventually, they say, most procrastinators must face the self-worth conflict, but progress can be made by learning better study skills

and more effective time management. Since we have already discussed study skills, let's consider time management.

A **formal time schedule** can do much to prevent procrastination and maintain motivation in school. To prepare your schedule, make a chart showing all of the hours in each day of the week. Then fill in times that are already committed: sleep, meals, classes, work, team practices, lessons, appointments, and so forth. Next, fill in times when you will study for various classes, and label them. Finally, label the remaining hours as open or free times.

The beauty of keeping a schedule is that you *know* you are making an honest effort to do well in your classes. In addition to getting more done, you will avoid the trap of yearning to play while you work and feeling guilty about not working when you play. The key to time management is to treat your study times as serious commitments, like class meetings or a job, and to respect your free times as well.

Taking Tests—Are You "Test Wise"?

Question: If I have read and studied effectively, is there anything else I can do to improve my grades?

Learning is only a first step. You must then be able to show what you know on a test. Here are some guidelines for improving your test-taking skills.

Objective Tests   Objective tests (multiple-choice and true-false items) test your ability to recognize a correct statement among wrong answers or a true statement against a false one. If you are taking an objective test, try this:

1. Read the directions carefully; they may give you good advice or clues. If the directions are not clear, ask the instructor to clarify them.
2. Read *all* of the choices for each question before you make a decision. If you immediately think "a" is correct, for instance, and stop reading, you might miss seeing a last choice like "both a and d" that is a better answer.
3. Read rapidly and skip items you are uncertain about. Later questions may give you "free" information that will help you answer difficult items. Return to skipped items if time allows.

Applications: The Psychology of Studying

4. Eliminate certain alternatives. With a four-choice-per-item, multiple-choice test, the odds are 1 in 4 in that you could guess right. If you can eliminate two alternatives, your guessing odds improve to 50–50. Unless there is a penalty for guessing, be sure to answer every question.

5. There is a bit of folk wisdom that says, "Don't change your answers on a multiple-choice test. Your first choice is usually right." Careful study of this idea has shown it is *false*. Students who switch answers are more likely to change from wrong to right than the reverse (Davis, 1975; Edwards & Marshall, 1977). This is especially true if you feel *very* uncertain of your first answer. ("When in doubt, scratch it out!") When you have strong doubts, your second answer is more likely to be correct (Johnson, 1975).

Essay Tests   Essay questions are a weak spot for many students simply because of poor organization, poor support of main ideas, or not writing directly to the question. When you take essay exams, try the following:

1. Read the question carefully. Make sure that you note key words, such as *compare, contrast, discuss, evaluate, analyze,* or *describe*. These words all demand a certain emphasis in your answer.

2. Think about your answer before putting words on paper. It's a good idea to make a brief list of the points you want to make. Just list them in any order as they come to mind. Then rearrange your ideas in the order you want to write them.

3. Don't beat around the bush or pad your answer. Be direct. Make a point and support it. Get your list of ideas into words.

4. Look over your essay for spelling errors, sentence errors, and grammatical errors. Save this step for last. Your *ideas* are of first importance. You can work on spelling and grammar separately if they affect your grades.

A Final Word   There is a distinction made in Zen between "live words" and "dead words." Live words come from personal experience; dead words are "about" a subject. This book can only be a collection of dead words without your personal involvement. It is designed to help you learn psychology, but it cannot learn for you. You will find many helpful, useful, and exciting ideas in the pages that follow. To make them yours, you must set out to *actively* learn as much as you can. The ideas presented here should get you off to a good start. Good luck!

For more information, consult any of the following books:

Annis, L. F. *Study Techniques:* Brown, 1983.

Burka, J. B., & L. M. Yuen. *Procrastination: Why You Do It; What to Do about It.* Addison-Wesley, 1983.

Carman, R. A., & W. R. Adams. *Study Skills: A Student's Guide for Survival.* Wiley, 1985.

Deese, J., & E. K. Deese. *How to Study.* McGraw-Hill, 1979.

Ellis, A., & W. J. Knaus. *Overcoming Procrastination.* Rational Living, 1977.

Learning Check

1. The three *R*s in SQ3R stand for read, recite, and review.   T or F?
2. When using the LISAN method, students try to write down as much of a lecture as possible so that their notes are complete.   T or F?
3. Spaced study sessions are usually superior to massed practice.   T or F?
4. According to recent research, you should almost always stick with your first answer on multiple-choice tests.   T or F?
5. To use the technique known as overlearning, you should continue to study after you feel you have begun to master a topic.   T or F?
6. Procrastination is related to seeking perfection and equating self-worth with grades.   T or F?

Answers: 1. T 2. F 3. T 4. F 5. T 6. T

Chapter Summary

- Psychology is the scientific study of human and animal behavior. Its goals are to *describe, understand, predict,* and *control* behavior.

- Whenever possible, psychologists seek *empirical* (objective and observable) *evidence.*

- Not all psychological questions are answerable, usually because of moral, practical, technological, or methodological limitations.

- Psychologists study animals as well as people, either out of interest in animals themselves or to use animals as models for human behavior. One danger in studying animals is the *anthropomorphic fallacy,* the tendency to treat animals as if they had human characteristics.

- Accurate description is one goal of psychology, but psychologists also seek understanding and the ability to predict and control behavior. Psychologists engage in control when they alter conditions that affect behavior in predictable ways.

- The history of psychology begins with *philosophy,* an armchair approach to understanding human behavior.

- The first psychological laboratory was established in Germany by *Wilhelm Wundt,* who tried to apply scientific methods to the study of conscious experience.

- The first school of thought in American psychology was *structuralism,* a kind of "mental chemistry" based on *introspection.*

- Structuralism was followed by *functionalism, behaviorism,* and *Gestalt* psychology. The *psychoanalytic* approach, which emphasizes unconscious determinants of behavior, developed separately. A more recent development is *humanistic* psychology.

- Three mainstreams of thought that can still be seen in modern psychology are *behaviorism, humanism,* and the *psychodynamic* approach, but there is a strong trend toward blending the best features of many viewpoints. A fourth perspective that has grown in importance recently is the *cognitive* viewpoint, which emphasizes thinking, knowing, perceiving, and other internal events. *Biological* approaches comprise a fifth major perspective for understanding behavior.

- *Psychologists, psychiatrists, psychoanalysts,* and *counselors* work in the field of mental health, although their training and methods differ considerably.

- *Clinical* and *counseling* psychologists, who do psychotherapy, represent only one of dozens of specialties in psychology. Other representative areas of specialization are: *industrial, educational, consumer, school, developmental, engineering, medical, environmental, forensic, psychometric,* and *experimental.*

- Psychological research may be *basic* or *applied.* Some common research specialties are: comparative, learning, sensation, perception, personality, physiology, motivation and emotion, social, cognitive, and developmental.

- The elements of *effective study skills* include: the SQ3R method, active listening and note taking, a positive attitude toward learning, use of a specific study area, spaced practice, mnemonics, self-testing, overlearning, time management, and test-taking skills.

▶▶▶ **Exploration**

Pseudo-Psychologies—Palms, Planets, and Personality

Pseudo-psychologies (SUE-doe-psychologies) are dubious and unfounded systems superficially resembling psychology. Many pseudo-psychologies offer highly developed systems that give the appearance of science but are actually false. *(Pseudo* means false.) Let's begin by considering some of the less convincing pseudo-psychologies.

Palmistry   Palmistry claims that lines in the hand are indicators of personality and a person's future. Lines that are longer or shorter, more or less bent, clear or distinct supposedly predict destiny, fortune, length of life, occupation, health, and so on. The fact that palmistry assumes that the hands tell the story of the whole body is hard enough to swallow, but ignoring the effects of dishwater, manual labor, or hand lotion is inexcusable. Even so, palmists can still be found in many cities cheerfully separating the gullible from their money.

Phrenology   During the 19th century, a German anatomy teacher, Franz Gall, popularized the theory that personality is revealed by the shape of the skull. Phrenologists assumed that parts of the brain responsible for various "mental faculties" caused bumps on the head. By feeling these bumps, the phrenologist claimed to read a person's abilities.

Fig. 1–11 *Phrenology was an attempt to assess characteristics of various areas of the skull. Phrenologists used charts such as the one shown here as guides.*

Phrenology faded rapidly when greater understanding of the brain showed that this is impossible. For instance, the area of the brain that controls hearing was listed on phrenologists' charts as the center for combativeness and destructiveness!

Graphology   Graphologists believe that personality is revealed by handwriting. Graphology is only moderately popular in the United States, although at least 500 companies in this country use handwriting analysis to evaluate job applicants. In European countries, graphology is widely

used for job placement and advancement. These uses are somewhat distressing to psychologists because studies show that graphologists score close to zero in tests of accuracy in rating personality (Guilford, 1959). In fact, in a recent study, professional graphologists did no better than untrained college students in rating personality and sales success, based on the handwriting of a group of salespersons (Rafaeli & Klimoski, 1983). (The failure of graphology as a means of personality evaluation should be distinguished from its proven value for the detection of forgeries.)

Question: If the pseudo-psychologies have no scientific basis, how do they survive and why are they popular?

There are several reasons, all of which can be demonstrated by a brief discussion of astrology.

Astrology   Astrology—probably the most popular pseudo-psychology—is based on the assumption that the position of the stars and planets at the time of a person's birth determines personality characteristics and affects behavior. Like other pseudo-psychologies, astrology has repeatedly been shown to have no scientific validity (Jerome, 1975). The objections to astrology are numerous and devastating, as shown by the following:

Exploration: Pseudo-Psychologies—Palms, Planets, and Personality

Problems in the Stars*

1. The zodiac has shifted by one full constellation since astrology was first set up. However, few astrologers take this shift into account. In other words, if astrology calls you a Scorpio, you are really a Libra, and so forth.

2. There is no connection between the "compatibility" of the astrological signs of couples and their marriage and divorce rates.

3. Studies have found no connection between astrological signs and leadership, physical characteristics, career choice, or personality characteristics.

4. The force of gravity exerted by a physician, standing near the mother at birth, is greater than that exerted by the stars. Also, astrologers have failed to explain why the moment of birth should be more important than the moment of conception.

5. A study of over 3000 predictions made by famous astrologers found that only a small percentage were fulfilled. These "successful" predictions tended to be vague ("There will be a tragedy somewhere in the eastern United States in the spring") or easily guessed from current events.

In short, astrology doesn't work.

Question: Then why does it so often seem to work?

Uncritical Acceptance   If you have ever had your astrological chart done, you may have been impressed with its seeming

*Sources: "Astrology and Astronomy," 1983; Culver & Ianna, 1979; Pasachoff, 1981; Randi, 1980.

accuracy. Careful reading shows many such charts to be made up of a preponderance of flattering traits. Naturally, when your personality is described in *desirable* terms, it is hard to deny that the description has the "ring of truth." How much acceptance would astrology receive if the characteristics of a birth sign read like this:

Virgo: You are the logical type and hate disorder. Your nitpicking is unbearable to your friends. You are cold, unemotional, and usually fall asleep while making love. Virgos make good doorstops.

Positive Instances   Even when an astrological description of personality contains a mixture of desirable and undesirable traits, it may seem accurate. To find out why, read the following personality description.

You have a strong need for other people to like you and for them to admire you. You have a tendency to be critical of yourself. You have a great deal of unused energy which you have not turned to your advantage. While you have some personality weaknesses, you are generally able to compensate for them. Your sexual adjustment has presented some problems for you. Disciplined and controlled on the outside, you tend to be worrisome and insecure inside. At times you have serious doubts as to whether you have made the right decision or done the right thing. You prefer a certain amount of change and variety and become dissatisfied when hemmed in by restrictions and limitations. You pride yourself on being an independent thinker and do

not accept other opinions without satisfactory proof. You have found it unwise to be too frank in revealing yourself to others. At times you are extroverted, affable, sociable, while at other times you are introverted, wary, and reserved. Some of your aspirations tend to be pretty unrealistic.†

Does this describe your personality? A psychologist read this summary individually to 79 college students who had taken a personality test. Of these students, 29 said it was an "excellent" description of their personality; 30 said it was "good"; 15 said it was "average"; and 5 said it was "poor." Thus, only 5 students out of 79 felt that the description failed to adequately capture their personality.

Reread this description and you will see that it contains both sides of several personality dimensions ("At times you are extroverted . . . while at other times you are introverted"). Its apparent accuracy is an illusion based on the **fallacy of positive instances** in which a person remembers or notices things that confirm his or her expectations and forgets the rest. The pseudo-psychologies thrive on this effect. For example, you can always find "Leo characteristics" in a Leo. If you looked, however, you could also find "Gemini characteristics," "Scorpio characteristics," or whatever.

†Reprinted with permission of author and publisher from: R. E. Ulrich, T. J. Stachnik, and N. R. Stainton, "Student acceptance of generalized personality interpretations," *Psychological Reports,* 1963, **13,** 831–834.

Exploration: Pseudo-Psychologies—Palms, Planets, and Personality

The Barnum Effect   P. T. Barnum, the famed circus showman, had a formula for success: Always have a little something for everybody. Like the astrological personality description, palm readings, fortunes, horoscopes, and other products of pseudo-psychology are stated in such *general* terms that they can hardly miss. There is always "a little something for everybody." If you doubt this, read *all 12* of the daily horoscopes found in newspapers for several days. You will find that predictions for other astrological signs fit events in your life as well as those for your own sign do.

Question: Couldn't that be because commercial horoscopes don't take into account a person's specific time of birth?

If they did, they would probably not be any more accurate, just more convincing. In a recent experiment people were given standardized horoscopes. Some had provided only their sign, others the year, month, and day of their birth. All received the same personality description, but those who had provided more detailed information considered their horoscope more accurate (Snyder & Schenkel, 1975). Thus, the more "hocus pocus" a fortune teller, palmist, or astrologer goes through, the more believable are the results.

A Final Note   Astrology's continuing popularity shows the difficulty many people have in separating valid psychology from systems that seem valid but are

not. The goal of this discussion, then, has been to make you a more critical observer of human behavior and to clarify what is, and is not, psychology. In Chapter 2, you will get a chance to further sharpen your critical skills as we investigate the research methods used in psychology. In the meantime, here is what the "stars" say about your future.

Emphasis now on education and personal improvement. Learning experience of lasting value awaits you. Take care of scholastic responsibilities before recreation. Research new possibility. The number 2 figures prominently in your efforts.

Learning Check

1. _____ is the outdated theory that personality is revealed by the shape of the skull. It was popularized by Franz _____.
2. The fallacy of positive instances refers to graphology's proven value for the detection of forgeries.   T or F?
3. Personality descriptions provided by pseudo-psychologies are stated in general terms, which provide "a little something for everybody." This fact is the basis of the
   a. palmist's fallacy   *b.* uncritical acceptance pattern   *c.* fallacy of positive instances   *d.* Barnum effect
4. The more accurate the information given an astrologer concerning a person's time and place of birth, the more accurate the astrological descriptions of personality become.   T or F?

Answers: 1. Phrenology; Gall   2. F   3. d   4. F

Questions for Discussion

1. The goals of psychology are a refinement of things we do everyday. Can you relate instances in which you have sought to describe, predict, understand, and control behavior? Do you consider control of behavior an acceptable goal for psychology? Why or why not?

2. Should psychologists study animals? Most people anthropomorphize pets. How could this be a problem in the objective study of animals? In your opinion can we learn anything about humans by studying animals?

3. In what ways is your behavior controlled by the environment? Do you believe that you have free will? Is there any way to tell if a "free choice" is really determined by your past?

4. How did you picture psychology and psychologists before reading the first chapter? Has your image changed? How accurate are television and movie portrayals of psychologists? What psychological specialty do you consider the most interesting at this point?

5. Can you name additional systems of thought that you suspect are pseudo-psychologies? What are their claims? Can you use the points made in the Exploration section to explain their attraction for believers?

6. Return to the quiz at the beginning of this chapter. Why are all the statements false? Explain those that you can.

7. Discuss the limitations of the following widely used "psychological" terms and "insights" (dubbed "psycho-babble" by one critic): I "flashed on" what he meant and really felt like we were "getting into each other's heads." She's really "together," you know, really "laid back." "I hear you." He gives me "good vibes," he's really "high energy," and you can always tell where he's "coming from." You gotta "go with your feelings" and "let it happen" if you don't want to be "uptight." We give each other the "space" to be our "true selves."

Chapter 2

Research Methods in Psychology

Chapter Preview

From Common Sense to Controlled Observation

Comment overheard on campus: "I don't know why he bothers taking psychology classes. Psychology is just common sense." Is psychology common sense? Is common sense a good source of information?

Consider some "commonsense" statements: Let's say that your grandfather has gone back to college. What do people say? "Ahh . . . never too old to learn." And what do they say when he loses interest and quits? "Well, you can't teach an old dog new tricks." Let's examine another commonsense statement. It is frequently said that "absence makes the heart grow fonder." Those of us separated from friends and lovers can take comfort in this knowledge—until we remember that it's also "out of sight, out of mind"! Much of what passes for common sense is equally vague and inconsistent. Notice also that these B.S. statements work best after the fact. (B.S., of course, stands for Before Science.)

Common sense can be a set of blinders that prevents us from seeking better information or seeing the truth. Einstein reportedly said, "Common sense is the layer of prejudice laid down in our minds before we are 18." In the early stages of the scientific revolution, people laughed at the idea that the world is round. Anyone with eyes could see that it wasn't. They laughed at Pasteur when he proposed that microorganisms cause disease. How could creatures too small to be seen kill a healthy human? Certainly, ideas such as these contradicted the common sense of their time. Now few people argue with the findings of established sciences such as chemistry, physics, or biology. But many still write off psychology as "just common sense."

Jab a hat pin into your finger. The sensation of pain seems instantaneous. We can go no further with personal observation. However, by using electrical recorders to measure the speed of nerve impulses, psychologists have found the top speed to be 120 meters per second. This is one-third the speed of sound. That's fast but certainly not instantaneous. Pain from the finger takes at least a hundredth of a second to reach the brain.

As you can see, research psychologists use careful measurement and a number of specialized approaches to improve observation and to avoid the pitfalls of "common sense." Their techniques are the topic of this chapter.

Survey Questions   How do psychologists collect information? What are the advantages and disadvantages of each approach? How is an experiment performed? How dependable is psychological information found in the popular press? What ethical questions does psychological research raise?

Resources

Scientific Method— Can a Horse Add?

In the United States today it is still possible to find people who believe that the earth is flat. To the "flat-earther" the earth is disk shaped, with the North Pole at the center and the South Pole ringing the outer edge.

Question: How could anyone believe such a thing after seeing the astronauts' photographs of the earth?

Flat-earthers point out that the opposite side of large lakes can be seen through binoculars; therefore, the earth must be a flat surface. Also, a person who jumps up in the air for one second does not come down 190 miles away. Surely, they say, this fact proves that the earth cannot be a rotating globe (McCain & Segal, 1969).

Obviously the flat-earthers have made the wrong observations, in the wrong way, and for the wrong reasons—*if* they are interested in the truth. In many ways psychologists in search of accurate information must avoid the same trap of faulty observation. To do so they use the **scientific method,** which is based on the collection of solid observable evidence, accurate description and measurement, precise definition, controlled observation, and consistent confirmation of results. In its ideal form the scientific method has five steps:

1. Observation
2. Defining a problem
3. Proposing a hypothesis
4. Experimentation
5. Theory formulation

Question: What is a hypothesis?

A **hypothesis** (hi-POTH-eh-sis) is a tentative explanation of an event or observation. In common terms a hypothesis is a clearly stated and *testable* "hunch" or "educated guess" about the causes of behavior. For example, on the basis of your own observations you might form the hypothesis that "aggression is encouraged by frustration." How would you test this hypothesis? First, you would have to

decide how you were going to frustrate people. (This part might be fun.) Then you would have to devise a way of measuring whether they became more aggressive. (Not so fun.) The procedures you chose would provide **operational definitions** of frustration and aggression. Operational definitions state the exact procedures used to represent a concept.

Forming a hypothesis and other steps in the scientific method can be illustrated with the story of Clever Hans, a "wonder horse" owned by a mathematics instructor (Rosenthal, 1965). Clever Hans seemed to be able to solve math problems, which he answered by tapping his foot. If you asked Hans, "What is 12 times 2, minus 18," Hans would tap his foot 6 times. Hans was so astonishing that he eventually attracted the attention of an inquiring scientist who discovered how Hans was able to perform. Assume that you are the scientist and that you are just itching to find out how Hans *really* does his trick.

Your investigation of Hans' mathematical abilities would probably begin with careful **observation** of both horse and owner while Hans was performing. If these observations fail to reveal any obvious deception, the *problem* becomes more clearly **defined:** What signals Hans to start and stop tapping his foot? Your first **hypothesis** might be that the owner is giving Hans a signal. Your proposed test (an **experiment** of sorts) would be to make the owner leave the room. Then someone else could ask Hans questions. Your proposed test would either confirm or deny this possibility and thereby support or eliminate the hypothesis. By changing the conditions under which you observe Hans, you have **controlled** the situation to gain more information from your observations.

Incidentally, Hans could still answer when his owner was out of the room. But a brilliant series of controlled observations revealed Hans' secret. If Hans couldn't see the questioner, he couldn't answer. It seems that questioners always *lowered their heads* (to look at Hans' foot) after asking a question. This was Hans' cue to start tapping. When Hans had tapped the correct number, the questioner would always *look up* to see if Hans was going to stop. This was Hans' cue to stop tapping!

Question: What about theory formulation?

Since Clever Hans' ability to do math was an isolated problem, no theorizing was involved. However, in actual psychological research, theory formulation is often important. A **theory** allows the results of a large number of observations to be summarized in a way that accounts for existing data, predicts new observations, and guides further research. Theories of forgetting, personality, mental illness, and the like are valuable products of psychological research. Without them psychologists would drown in a sea of seemingly disconnected facts.

Fig. 2–1 *Applying the scientific method to the study of behavior requires careful observation. Here, a student programs a computer to record a rat's responses in a learning experiment.*

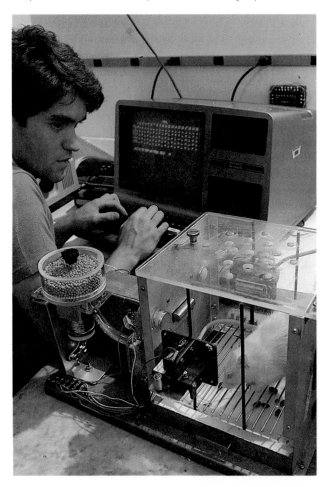

In their search for accurate information and useful theories, psychologists investigate behavior in many ways: They observe behavior as it unfolds in natural settings (**naturalistic observation**); they make measurements to discover relationships between events (**correlational method**); they use the powerful technique of controlled experimentation (**experimental method**); they study unique problems and therapeutic solutions in the psychological clinic (**clinical method**); and they use questionnaires and surveys to poll large groups of people (**survey method**). Let's see how each of these is used to advance psychological knowledge.

Naturalistic Observation— Psychology Steps Out!

Instead of waiting to encounter haphazardly whatever they are interested in, psychologists may set out to **actively observe** subjects in a **natural setting**. A good example of this style of research is the work of Jane Goodall. She and her staff have been observing chimpanzees in Tanzania since 1960. A quote from her book *In the Shadow of Man* captures the excitement of a scientific discovery:

> Quickly focusing my binoculars, I saw that it was a single chimpanzee, and just then he turned my direction. . . . Cautiously I moved around so that I could see what he was doing. He was squatting beside the red earth mound of a termite nest, and as I watched I saw him carefully push a long grass stem into a hole in the mound. After a moment he withdrew it and picked something from the end with his mouth. I was too far away to make out what he was eating, but it was obvious that he was actually using a grass stem as a tool. (van Lawick-Goodall, 1971.)

Notice that naturalistic observation only provides *descriptions* of behavior. To explain what we observe often requires more information from other research methods. Just the same, Goodall's discovery forced many scientists to change their definition of humans. Previously, humans had been regarded as the only toolmaking animals.

Question: Chimpanzees in zoos use objects as tools. Doesn't that demonstrate the same thing?

Not necessarily. One of the advantages of naturalistic observation is that the behavior being studied has not been tampered with by outside influences. Only by observing chimps in their natural environment can we tell if they use tools without human interference.

Question: But doesn't the presence of human observers in an animal colony affect their behavior?

Effects of the Observer   Yes. The presence of an observer may change the behavior of the observed. Naturalists studying animal colonies must be careful to keep their distance and to avoid the temptation to "make friends" with the animals. Likewise, if you are interested in student-teacher interactions in an elementary school classroom, it would hardly do for you to walk in and begin taking notes. A stranger in the room would undoubtedly affect both the students and the teacher. When possible, this problem is minimized by **concealing the observer.** For example, Arnold Gesell and his associates (1940) were able to determine at what age children develop the ability to sit up, walk, talk, and so forth by observing preschoolers through one-way vision screens.

Observer bias is a closely related problem, in which observers see what they *expect* to see, or record only selected details. Teachers in one study were told to watch elementary school children who had been labeled as either learning disabled, mentally retarded, emotionally disturbed, or normal. The ratings teachers gave the children differed markedly, depending on the label applied to the child (Foster & Ysseldyke, 1976).

Question: Then should naturalistic observation be used at all?

Psychologists doing naturalistic studies make a special effort to know their biases and to keep **careful records** of observations to minimize such errors. In the final analysis naturalistic observation can be very valuable (Sommer, 1977). It provides a large amount of information in a relatively short time, raises interesting questions, defines new problems for study, and suggests initial hypotheses. In any scientific investigation it is an excellent starting point.

Correlational Studies— In Search of the Perfect Relationship

Let's say that a psychologist notes a correspondence between the IQs of children and their parents, between physical attractiveness and social popularity, between anxiety and test performance, or even between riots and weather conditions. In each instance two observations or events are **co-related** (linked together in some orderly fashion). A **correlational study** is one that determines the degree of correlation, or relationship, between two existing traits, behaviors, or events (Myers, 1980). Unlike naturalistic observation, correlational studies can be done either in the lab or in the natural environment. Two factors of interest are measured, and then a statistical technique is used to determine their degree of correlation. (See Appendix B for more information.) For example, we could find the correlation between the average number of hours slept each night and daytime anxiety levels. If the correlation is large, knowing the number of hours slept would allow us to predict anxiety level. Likewise, knowing anxiety level would allow prediction of sleep needs.

Question: How is the degree of correlation expressed?

Correlations can be expressed as a **coefficient of correlation,** which is simply a number falling somewhere between + 1.00 and − 1.00. (See Appendix B.) If the num-

Fig. 2–2   *A special moment in Jane Goodall's naturalistic study of chimpanzees—a chimp uses a grass stem to extract a meal from a termite nest. (Photo by Baron Hugo van Lawick, © National Geographic Society.)*

Highlight 2–1
Relationships in Psychology

Do students who study more get better grades? To answer this question we could record the number of hours different students study each week. Then we could match hours studied with grades earned. Suppose we find that low study times correspond with low grades and high amounts of studying are linked with high grades. If this were the case, there would be a **positive relationship** between studying and grades. Similarly, we might discover that students who watch many hours of television tend to get lower grades than those who watch few hours. (This is the well-known TV zombie effect.) This time, a **negative relationship** would exist. That is, low viewing times go with high grades, and high viewing times go with low grades. Obviously, these examples are only hypothetical. However, when real relationships of this sort can be identified, they have great value. Relationships summarize large amounts of data and allow prediction as well.

Drawing graphs of relationships often helps clarify their nature. For example, Figure 2–3 shows the results of an experiment on memory. Before being tested, subjects learned from 1 to 20 word lists. The question was, how well would they remember the last list? The graph shows that when the subjects memorized no other lists, they remembered 80 percent of the test list. When they memorized 3 other lists, their scores on the last list dropped to 43 percent (blue arrows). When they

memorized 10 other lists, recall fell even farther, to 22 percent (red arrows). Overall, there was a negative relationship between the number of lists memorized and recall of the last list. (The meaning of this finding is discussed in Chapter 10. For now, let's just say that you shouldn't memorize the telephone book before studying for a test.)

Some graphs reveal a **linear** (or straight-line) **relationship**. Others are **curvilinear** (kur-vih-LIN-ee-er: consisting of a curved line) like Figure 2–3. In either case relationships need not be perfect to be useful. Suppose, for instance, that we randomly select 10 people. We then compare the number of years of college completed for each to his or her income at age 25. If we were to obtain results like those shown in Figure 2–4, it would be clear that there is a strong positive relationship between education and earnings. A pattern like this might be of great interest to a high school student thinking about whether to attend college.

The shaded area and the colored line in Figure 2–4 show that the relationship is approximately linear but not perfect. (If it were perfect, all of the dots would lie on the colored line.) The correlation coefficient *(r)* also shows that the relationship is strong, and positive, but not perfect. (How often do you find a perfect relationship?) If the relationship *were* perfect, the coefficient would be 1.00. For comparison, Figure 2–5 plots further hypothetical

---

ber is zero or close to zero, it indicates a weak or nonexistent relationship. For example, the correlation between shoe size and intelligence is zero. (Sorry, size 12 readers.) If the correlation is +1.00, a **perfect positive relationship** exists; if it is −1.00, a **perfect negative relationship** has been discovered.

Correlations in psychology are rarely perfect. Most fall somewhere between zero and plus or minus one. The closer the correlation coefficient is to +1.00 or −1.00, the stronger the relationship. For example, identical twins are likely to have almost identical IQs, whereas parents and their children have IQs that are only generally similar.

The correlation between IQs of parents and children is .35; that between identical twins is .86.

Question: What do the terms "positive" and "negative" correlation mean?

In a positive correlation increases in one measure are matched by increases in the other (or decreases are accompanied by decreases). For example, there is a positive relationship between high school grades and college grades; students who do better in high school tend to do better in college (and the reverse). In a negative correlation *increases* in the first measure are associated with *decreases* in

Highlight 2–1

Relationships in Psychology, continued

Fig. 2–3 *Effects of interference on memory. A graph of the approximate relationship between percentage recalled and number of different word lists memorized. (Adapted from Underwood, 1957.)*

Fig. 2–4 *The relationship between years of college completed and personal income. (Hypothetical data.)*

Fig. 2–5 *The relationship between air temperature and amount of coffee consumed. (Hypothetical data.)*

data. Assume that the manager of a college cafeteria has recorded the amount of coffee sold on 10 different days and the air temperature each day. Notice again that the relationship appears to be linear. However, this time it is negative. Also, note how the shaded area and the correlation coefficient both indicate a weaker relationship. Even so, the relationship between temperature and

coffee consumed would be helpful to anyone planning how much "mud" to brew each morning. On a higher plane, psychologists seek to identify relationships concerning memory, perception, stress, aging, therapy, and a host of similar topics. Much of this book is a summary of such relationships.

the second. We might observe, for instance, that the higher the air temperature, the lower the activity level of animals in a zoo. (Also, see Highlight 2–1.)

Question: Would that show that air temperature causes changes in activity level?

It might seem so, but we cannot be sure without performing an experiment. Correlational studies help us discover relationships and make useful predictions. However, correlation *does not demonstrate causation.* (There is an exception, but it involves an advanced technique beyond the scope of this book.) The animals' activity might be affected

by seasonal changes in weight, by hormone levels, or even by the zoo's feeding schedule.

Consider another example of mistaking correlation for causation: What if a psychologist detected a certain chemical in the blood of schizophrenic patients that was not found in the blood of people functioning normally? Would this demonstrate that the chemical *causes* schizophrenia? It may seem so, but schizophrenia could cause the chemical to form. Or, both schizophrenia and the chemical might be caused by some unknown third factor. Just because one thing *appears* to cause another does not *confirm* that it does. This fact can be seen clearly in the case of obviously noncausal relationships. For example, there is a correlation between the number of churches in American cities and the number of bars; the more churches, the more bars. Does this mean that drinking makes you religious? Does it mean that religion makes you thirsty? No one, of course, would leap to the conclusion that any one of these events *caused* the other, but in more realistic situations to do so is a temptation.

Exactly 9 months after a major power failure in New York State, doctors and nurses in New York hospitals no-ticed a sharp rise in the birthrate. News reports of this event assumed that when the lights and TVs went off, people had nothing better to do, and the result was a "baby boom" 9 months later. A closer look at the birthrate would show that it fluctuates up and down all year. The "baby boom" was but one of dozens of small peaks, and therefore not necessarily linked to the power failure at all. The best way to be confident that a cause-effect relation-ship exists is to perform a controlled experiment. You'll learn how in the next section.

Learning Check

Before reading on, answer the following questions about what you just read.

1. Most of psychology can rightfully be called common sense because psychologists prefer naturalistic observation to controlled observation.   T or F?

2. A hypothesis is any careful observation made in a controlled experiment.   T or F?

3. Two problems in naturalistic observation are:
   a. getting subjects to cooperate and identifying correlations
   b. defining a problem and proposing a hypothesis
   c. effects of the observer and observer bias
   d. running the experiment and making careful records

4. Correlation typically does not demonstrate causation.   T or F?

5. Which correlation coefficient represents the strongest relationship?
   a. −0.86   b. +0.66   c. +0.10   d. +0.09

6. A relationship that does not form a straight line when it is graphed is described as _____.

Answers: 1. F 2. F 3. c 4. T 5. a 6. curvilinear

The Psychology Experiment— Where Cause Meets Effect

One of the most powerful research tools available is the **experiment.** Research psychologists carefully control con-ditions in an experiment to gain reliable information and to identify cause-effect relationships. An experiment con-tains three essential elements:

1. **Independent variables,** which are conditions altered, applied, or varied in known ways by the experimenter. Independent variables are the suspected *causes* in an experiment.
2. **Dependent variables,** which measure the outcome of the experiment. Dependent variables reveal the *effects* of independent variables.

3. **Extraneous variables,** which are conditions the re-searcher wishes to prevent from affecting the experi-ment.

The simplest psychological experiment is based on two groups of **subjects** (animals or people). One group is called the **experimental group;** the other becomes the **control group.**

Question: How do these groups differ?

The control group and the experimental group are treated exactly alike except for one condition, the **independent variable.** (For the moment just think of a variable as any condition that can change or vary and that might affect the outcome of the experiment.) Suppose you notice that you study better with background music on. This suggests

CONTROL GROUP   OUT OF CONTROL GROUP

the hypothesis that music improves learning. We could test this idea experimentally by forming two groups of people. One group studies with music. The other studies without music. Then we could compare their scores on a test. The group exposed to music is the experimental group because the independent variable (music) is present. The group not exposed to music is the control group.

Question: Is a control group really needed? Can't people just study with music on to see if they do better?

Without a control group it would be impossible to tell if music had any effect on learning. The control group provides a *point of reference* to which scores of the experimental group can be compared. If the average test score of the experimental group is higher than that of the control group, it can be concluded that music improves learning efficiency. If the average is lower than the control group, we will know that music hampers learning. If there is no difference, we know that the independent variable had no effect on learning. In this experiment the "amount learned" (indicated by scores on the test) is the **dependent variable.** In an experiment we are asking the question, "Does the independent variable *affect* or influence the dependent variable?" (Does music affect or influence learning?) Another way to think of this is that results of an experiment are measured by the dependent variable, which *depends* on the independent variable. (The amount learned depends on whether music accompanied study.)

Question: How do we know that people in one group aren't more intelligent than those in the other group?

It's true that differences in personal characteristics of subjects might influence the outcome of an experiment. However, these can be eliminated by *randomly* assigning

subjects to the two groups. **Random assignment** means that a subject has an equal chance of being a member of either the experimental group or the control group. Even in fairly small groups, this selection method results in few differences in the number of people in each group who are geniuses or dunces, hungry, hung over, Democrat, Republican, tall, music lovers, or whatever.

Other **extraneous,** or outside variables—such as the amount of study time, the sex of subjects, the temperature of the room, the time of day, the amount of light, and so forth—must also be prevented from affecting the outcome of an experiment. But how? Usually by making all conditions except the independent variable *exactly the same* for both groups. If every possible condition is the same for subjects in both groups, *except* the presence or absence of music, and if there is a difference in the average amount learned, then that difference *must* be caused by the music (Fig. 2–6).

Now let's summarize more formally. In a psychological experiment two or more groups of subjects are treated differently with respect to the independent variable. In all other ways they are treated the same. That is, extraneous variables are identical for all groups in the experiment. This prevents conditions we are not interested in from affecting the results of the experiment. The effect of the independent variable (or variables) on some behavior (the dependent variable) is then measured. In a carefully controlled experiment, differences in the independent variable can be the only possible **cause** for any **effect** noted in the dependent variable. This allows clear cause-and-effect connections to be identified. (Also see Highlight 2–2.)

Question: Experiments seem to set up artificial situations. Do experimental findings have anything to do with the real world?

Fig. 2—6 *Elements of a simple psychological experiment to assess the effects of music during study on test scores.*

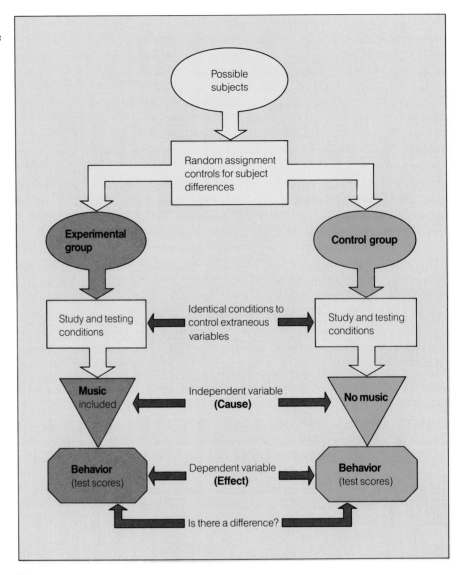

Field Experiments There are many advantages to being able to "custom design" conditions in a laboratory experiment. But there is also a degree of artificiality. An alternative is the **field experiment,** which uses the "real world" as a laboratory. Here is an illustration:

One Good Flat Deserves Another

James Bryan and Mary Test (1971) were interested in whether people are more likely to help a person in distress when they have recently seen someone else being helped. To find out, they parked a car with a flat tire on a busy street. An inflated tire leaned against the car, and a young woman stood nearby. Of 2000 cars that passed, only 35 stopped in this control condition. In the experimental condition a second car was parked one-quarter mile back from the test car. The second automobile was raised on a jack, and a woman stood watching a man change a tire. Of 2000 vehicles that passed this staged helping scene, 58 stopped to help the woman in the test car.

Such "real life" experiments are becoming increasingly popular among psychologists as a way to bridge the gap between laboratory studies and everyday life. You may have even taken part in an experiment without knowing it!

Question: Is the difference between 35 helpers and 58 helpers really enough to draw a conclusion?

Significance The problem of deciding whether an independent variable made a difference is handled statistically. Articles in psychology journals almost always include the statement, "Results were statistically significant." What this means is that a difference like that observed between the experimental and control groups would occur very rarely *by chance alone*. For a difference to be considered significant, it usually must be sufficiently large so that it would occur by chance in less than 5 experiments out of 100. (See Appendix B for more information.)

Placebo Effects— Sugar Pills and Salt Water

Assume that we want to perform an experiment to see if Dexedrine (a powerful central nervous system stimulant) affects learning. An accurate test of the drug would *not* occur if, before studying, members of the experimental group were given a Dexedrine pill and the control group got nothing.

Question: Why not? The experimental group gets the drug and the control group doesn't. If there is a difference in learning scores, it must be due to the action of the drug. Right?

No, because an error has been made: The experimental group and the control group have been treated differently with respect to more than just the presence or absence of the drug. Members of the experimental group swallowed a pill, and control subjects did not. Without using a **placebo** (plah-SEE-bo), it is impossible to tell if the drug has affected learning. It might be that those who swallowed a pill *expected* to do better. This alone might affect their performance.

Question: What is a placebo?

A placebo is a fake pill or injection. A placebo's beneficial effects come from what it suggests rather than from what it contains. Sugar pills and saline (saltwater) injections are common placebos.

Although they have little or no direct chemical effect, placebos can have a tremendous *psychological* impact. As an example of how powerful the **placebo effect** can be, one study showed that an injection of saline solution was 70 percent as effective as morphine in reducing pain for hospital patients (Beecher, 1959). This fact is well known to physicians, who for years have prescribed placebos for complaints they believe have no physical basis (Jospe, 1978). Exactly how placebos relieve pain is not fully un-

**Highlight 2–2
Could You Repeat That, Please?**

A key element in the scientific pursuit of truth is the ability to **replicate** (repeat) observations or experiments. In contrast, a failure to replicate observations is a major failing of **parascience** (that which resembles science but is not truly scientific). A good example is the idea that plants have feelings. This claim, which received wide media coverage, was largely based on "experiments" performed by Cleve Backster, a polygraph expert. (The polygraph is commonly referred to as a lie detector. See Chapter 13.) Backster claimed that plants wired to a lie detector responded to music, threats (such as lighting a match nearby), and other stimuli. However, when scientists tried to repeat the experiments, using either identical or improved methods, the results were completely negative (Galston & Slayman, 1983). A long list of other purported phenomena—from pyramid power to dowsing to moon madness—likewise have disappeared in the light of careful scrutiny.

Psychology, too, has admittedly had its share of unrepeatable results. But what separates psychology and other sciences from parascience is that they are self-correcting. When scientists cannot repeat a finding, they discard it. Maintaining such high standards can be frustrating at times. Among other things, it requires a willingness to change one's beliefs as new or better evidence becomes available. Yet, the end result is highly satisfying. High standards of evidence and a demand for repeatability ensure that science moves slowly, but surely, toward the truth.

derstood, but recent experiments suggest that expecting to feel better may trigger the release of brain chemicals called **endorphins** (Cohen, 1977; Levine et al., 1979). Endorphins are similar to pain-killing opiate drugs such as morphine.

To control for placebo effects, a psychologist doing drug research could use a **single-blind** arrangement. In this approach *all* subjects get a pill or injection. The experimental group gets the real drug and the control group gets a

Fig. 2–7 *The placebo effect is a major factor in medical treatments.*

placebo. Thus, subjects are *blind* as to whether they received the drug. But this is not enough. Experimenters must also be blind as to whether they are giving drugs or placebos to subjects. In a **double-blind** experiment both subjects and experimenters are kept in the dark concerning drugs and placebos. Typically, this is done by having someone else prepare the pills or injections so that experimenters don't know until after the experiment is over who

got what. The double-blind arrangement prevents researchers from unconsciously influencing their subjects.

Question: How could the researcher influence the subject?

The Experimenter Effect Psychological researchers face an interesting problem not shared by physicists and chemists. Human subjects are very sensitive to hints from an experimenter about what is expected of them. The **experimenter effect**, as this is called, can have a powerful influence on a subject's behavior (Rosenthal, 1976).

The experimenter effect even holds outside the laboratory, where expectations have been shown to influence people in interesting ways. Psychologist Robert Rosenthal (1973) reports a typical example: At the U.S. Air Force Academy Preparatory School 100 airmen were randomly assigned to one of five math classes. Their teachers were unaware of this random assignment. Instead, the teachers were told that their students were selected for high or low levels of ability. Students in the supposed "high-ability" classes improved substantially more in math scores than those in "low-ability" classes. Yet, initially, the classes were all of equal ability. Apparently, the teachers subtly communicated their expectations to students. This, in turn, created a **self-fulfilling prophecy** that affected students' performance. That is, the students tended to perform as they expected to perform. In short, people sometimes become what we prophesy for them. It is wise to remember that others tend to live *up* or *down* to our expectations for them.

Learning Check

1. To understand cause and effect, psychologists perform experiments using two groups: the _____ group and the _____ group.

2. Anything that can change (vary) and that might affect the behavior of subjects is called a _____.

3. There are three types of variables to consider in an experiment: an _____ variable; a _____ variable; and _____ variables.

4. A researcher performs an experiment to learn if room temperature affects the amount of aggression displayed by college students under crowded conditions in a simulated prison environment. In this experiment the independent variable is (circle):

room temperature   the amount of aggression   crowding   the simulated prison environment

5. A procedure used in drug experiments to control both the placebo effect and the experimenter effect is the:
a. correlation method   *b.* extraneous prophecy   *c.* double-blind technique   *d.* random assignment of subjects

Answers: 1. experimental, control   2. variable   3. independent, dependent, extraneous   4. room temperature   5. c

The Clinical Method— Data by the Case

Many experiments that might be informative or revealing are impractical, immoral, or impossible to perform. In instances such as these, information may be gained from **case studies.** A case study is an in-depth focus on all aspects of a single subject. Case studies are used heavily by clinical psychologists.

Case studies may sometimes be thought of as **natural experiments.** Gunshot wounds, brain tumors, accidental poisonings, and similar disasters have provided much information on the functioning of the human brain. One remarkable case from the history of psychology was reported by Dr. J. M. Harlow (1868). Phineas Gage, a young foreman on a work crew, had a 13-pound steel rod blown through the front of his brain by an excavating charge. Amazingly, he survived the accident, but not without undergoing a profound personality change. Dr. Harlow carefully recorded all the details of what was perhaps the first well-done case study of an accidental *frontal lobotomy* (the destruction of front brain matter).

Over 120 years later, a Los Angeles carpenter named Michael Melnick was the victim of a similar freakish accident. Melnick fell from the second story of a house and impaled his head on a steel reinforcing rod. Incredibly, he recovered completely, with no sign of lasting ill effects (*Los Angeles Times*, 1981). Melnick's very different reaction to a similar injury shows why psychologists prefer controlled experiments and often use lab animals for studies of the brain. But when a purely psychological problem is under study, the clinical method may be the *only* source of information.

A classic psychological case study is *The Three Faces of Eve* (Thigpen & Cleckley, 1957). Eve White was a mild, restrained, suburban housewife who in the course of psychiatric treatment revealed the existence of a second, separate personality. This second personality, Eve Black, was the antithesis of Eve White. Eve Black was childish, mischievous, and erotically flirtatious. Eve Black knew about Eve White and openly talked about the times she had disobeyed her parents or gotten drunk and then "went into" Eve White. After Eve Black's escapades, Eve White faced her punishment or bore her hangover with bewilderment because she did not know of Eve Black's existence. Eventually, this duality was resolved when a third personality— who called herself Jane—emerged. Jane ultimately separated from Eve White's husband and began a relatively stable new life marked by the slow development of a progression of other personalities.

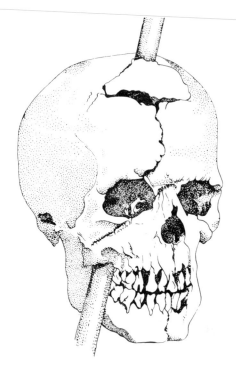

Fig. 2–8 *Some of the earliest information on the effects of damage to frontal areas in the brain came from a case study of the accidental injury of Phineas Gage.*

Now in her 50s, the former Eve White has manifested 21 different personalities over the years. The careful recording of all pertinent facts in cases such as this one is essential to psychology. *Multiple personality* is a rare event, and there are no experimental means for producing it. (Multiple personality is discussed further in Chapter 20.)

Survey Method— Here, Have a Sample

Sometimes psychologists would like to ask everyone in the world a few well-chosen questions: "Have you ever smoked marijuana?" "Have you engaged in premarital sexual intercourse?" "What is your marital status now, and were your parents ever separated or divorced?" "Do you favor abortion?" The answers to questions such as these can reveal much about significant psychological events in the lives of large groups of people. But since it is impractical to question everyone, psychologists use the **survey method.** In a survey, people in a **representative sample** are asked a carefully worded series of questions. A representative sample includes the same proportion of men, women, white-collar workers, Republicans, Democrats, blacks, and so on as found in the population as a whole.

A careful survey can provide an accurate picture of how large segments of the general population feel about current issues, even though only a small percentage of people are polled. However, some psychologists have questioned—tongue in cheek—psychology's claim that its conclusions apply to people in general. The distinguished psychologist Edward Tolman once noted that much of American psychology is based on two sets of subjects: rats and college sophomores. Tolman urged his colleagues to remember that rats certainly are not people and that college sophomores may not be!

Question: How accurate is the survey method?

Modern surveys like the Gallup and Harris polls are quite accurate. The Gallup poll has erred in its election predictions by only 1.5 percent since 1954. This level of accuracy has not always been the case. During the 1936 presidential election, a well-known magazine, the *Literary Digest*, predicted that Alfred Landon would defeat Franklin Roosevelt by a large margin. In actuality, Roosevelt defeated Landon by a landslide!

Question: How could the poll have been so wrong?

The answer lies in the way the sample was taken. Most people in the poll were contacted by *telephone*. In 1936, during the Depression, people who had phones were much more wealthy than average, and the wealthy favored Landon. Thus, the sample was biased rather than representative.

Even when questions are carefully stated and the sample is representative, a survey may be limited by another prob-

lem. If a psychologist asked you detailed questions about your sexual history and current sexual activities, how accurate would your replies be? Would you be self-conscious and perhaps not completely frank? Or might you have a tendency to exaggerate? Replies to survey questions are not always *accurate or truthful*. Many people show a distinct **courtesy bias,** or tendency to give answers that are agreeable and socially acceptable. For example, pollsters working on a 1979 election found that black persons talking to white interviewers were less likely to admit support for a black candidate. Similarly, white persons talking to black interviewers were more likely to claim support for the black candidate (McKean, 1984).

Despite such limitations, surveys frequently produce useful information. For instance, in recent years working women have complained of sexual harassment at their jobs. How widespread is this problem? A recent survey of working men and women conducted by psychologist Barbara Gutek provides an answer. Gutek (1981) found that 53 percent of women but only 37 percent of men had experienced some form of sexual harassment at work. Although such information does not solve the problem of sexual harassment, it is a first step toward understanding it and remedying it.

A Look Ahead   To complete our discussion, this chapter's Applications offers a critical look at psychological information reported in the popular press. Following that is an Exploration section on the ethics of psychological research. You should find these topics an interesting way to conclude our look at research in psychology.

Learning Check

1. Case studies can often be thought of as natural experiments and are used frequently by clinical psychologists.   T or F?

2. For the survey method to be valid, a representative sample of people must be polled.   T or F?

3. The phenomenon of multiple personality would most likely be investigated by use of:
   a. a representative sample   *b.* field experiments   *c.* the double-blind procedure   *d.* case studies

4. A problem with the survey method is that answers to questions may not always be _____

   or _____.

Answers: 1. T 2. T 3. d 4. accurate, truthful

Applications

Psychology in the News— Notes on Reading the Popular Press

Question: Is so much emphasis on "research" really necessary in psychology?

In a word, yes. As we have seen, "science" is a powerful way of asking questions about the world, a way of getting trustworthy answers. More importantly, we might ask, "What is the alternative to using the scientific method?" In most areas of knowledge, including psychology, wiping out scientific advances would mean a return to the Dark Ages. Awareness of this fact, along with your understanding of psychological research methods, should do much to make you a more critical observer of human behavior. Below are some additional pointers to sharpen your skills.

Notes on Reading the Popular Press

The tremendous popularity of psychology has spurred extensive coverage of psychological research and theories in popular magazines and daily newspapers. Unfortunately, much of what is covered is based on wishful thinking rather than science. Here are some suggestions for telling the difference.

Suggestion 1   Be skeptical.   Psychological reports in the popular press tend to be made uncritically and with a definite bias toward the reporting of sensational findings. Remember, saying "That's incredible" means "That's not believable"—which is quite often true.

Example: A few years ago stories appeared in the press reporting research in the Soviet Union and the United States on "dermo-optical perception." According to these stories, people had been found who could identify colors and read print (even under glass) while blindfolded. These feats were supposedly performed using the fingertips and were given as an indication of the existence of a "sixth sense," or "X-ray eyes." Martin Gardner, a scientist whose hobby is magic, suggests that such "abilities" are based on what professional performers call a "nose peek." Gardner says that it is impossible to prepare a blindfold

(without doing damage to the eyes) that does not leave a tiny space on each side of the nose through which a person can peek. In accordance with Gardner's criticism, the phenomenal ability of individuals who performed in the first dermo-optical perception experiments disappeared each time the opportunity to peek was controlled (Gardner, 1966).

Here is another indication of the need to be skeptical. Psychologist Philip Zimbardo tells with amusement about his mentioning to a reporter that in the back wards of two mental hospitals in which he had worked, women patients seemed to use a greater number of obscenities than male patients. Zimbardo emphasizes that this was nothing more than a casual statement and that it was not based on data of any kind. When it was reported in *The New York Times,* however, it became an "observation" that he had "noted" over a long period of time. When *Newsweek* reported the *Times* article to its readers, the relationship that was "noted" became one that had been "found." Ultimately, *Playboy's* version stated that "a number of psychologists, *The New York Times* reports, have found that women of every social level have become increasingly uninhibited in their use of obscene language" (*Playboy,* 1969). Zimbardo notes that the only authority mentioned to confirm this "fact" was himself (Ruch & Zimbardo, 1971)!

Suggestion 2   Consider the source of information.
It should come as no surprise that information given by an individual or a company intent on selling a product often reflects a desire for profit rather than the objective truth. Here is a typical advertising claim: "Government tests prove that no pain reliever is stronger or more effective than Brand X aspirin." A statement like this usually means that there was *no difference* between the product and others tested. No other pain reliever was stronger or more effective, but none was weaker either.

Keep the source in mind when reading the claims of makers of home biofeedback machines, sleep-learning devices, and the like. Remember also that psychological services may be merchandised as well.

Applications: Psychology in the News—Notes on Reading the Popular Press

Expensive courses that promise instant mental health and happiness, increased efficiency, memory, ESP or psychic ability, control of the unconscious mind, an end to the smoking habit, and so on are usually supported by a few testimonials and many unsupported claims.

"Psychic" phenomena should be viewed with special caution. Stage mentalists make their living by deceiving the public. Understandably, they are highly interested in promoting belief in their nonexistent powers. Psychic phenomena when (and if) they do occur are quite unpredictable. It would be impossible for a mentalist to do three shows a night, six nights a week without consistently using deception.

Question: I've seen some amazing things on TV. Could you give an example of how I may have been fooled?

Here is a typical stage mentalist's routine. The mentalist picks a member of the audience "at random" and begins telling him personal things that "he could not possibly know." How does he do it? Easy! One of his many assistants stood in line outside the theater and eavesdropped on the person's conversations before the show. The assistant then made careful note of where the person was seated and passed on the location and information to the mentalist. The mentalist then announces, "You have an aunt . . . Aunt Bessie . . . she has been very ill . . . you were thinking about her earlier this evening . . . you had a flat tire on the way here this evening."

Suggestion 3 Ask yourself, "Was there a control group?" The essential importance of a control group in any experiment is frequently overlooked by the unsophisticated—an error to which you are no longer susceptible! The popular press is full of reports of "experiments" performed without control groups: "Talking to Plants Speeds Growth"; "Special Diet Controls Hyperactivity in Children"; "Food Shows Less Spoilage in Pyramid Chamber"; "Theater Reports Increased Beverage Sales during Showing of *Lawrence of Arabia*."

Consider the last example for a moment. Almost every year it seems a theater somewhere will claim that a movie has had an unusual effect on viewers. If the showing of *Lawrence of Arabia* were accompanied by increased beverage sales, would this indicate that

viewers had been influenced by the desert scenery? Actually, they may have been influenced, but since there is no control group (people who watch another movie under identical conditions), it is impossible to tell if the temperature in the theater, the time of year, the kind of crowd attracted, or the movie itself affected beverage consumption.

Suggestion 4 Look for errors in distinguishing between correlation and causation. An earlier discussion should make it clear that it is dangerous to presume that one thing has *caused* another just because there is a correlation between the two. In spite of this, you will encounter numerous claims based on questionable correlations. Recently, a nutritionist was quoted in the news as saying that excessive consumption of milk may cause juvenile deliquency. (This must have been a real hit with the National Dairy Association.) On what did he base this conclusion? Adolescent males who are often in trouble, he said, drink greater than average amounts of milk. Certainly, this correlation is interesting. But in no way does it demonstrate that milk causes delinquency. The situation could easily be, for instance, that young males who mature early are more likely to be aggressive or get into trouble. Maturing early involves rapid growth. And rapid growth promotes hunger. It is entirely possible that this is the only link between milk and delinquency. Or, perhaps some other unknown factor is involved.

Here's another example of mistaking correlation for causation. Jeanne Dixon, a popular astrologer, once answered a group of prominent scientists—who had declared that there is no scientific foundation for astrology—by saying: "They would do well to check the records at their local police stations, where they will learn that the rate of violent crime rises and falls with lunar cycles" (Dixon, 1975). Dixon, of course, is implying that the moon affects human behavior.

Question: If it is true that violent crime is more frequent at certain times of the month, doesn't this prove her point?

Far from it; increased crime could be due to darker nights, the fact that bills fall due at the first of the month, or any number of similar factors.

Applications: Psychology in the News—Notes on Reading the Popular Press

Suggestion 5   Be sure to distinguish between observation and inference. If you see a person *crying,* is it correct to assume that he or she is *sad*? Although making this assumption seems reasonable, it is actually quite risky. We can observe objectively that the person is crying, but to *infer* sadness may be in error. It could be that the individual has just peeled 5 pounds of onions or just won a million-dollar lottery or is trying contact lenses for the first time. Psychologists, politicians, physicians, scientists, and other experts often go far beyond the available facts in their claims. This does not mean that their inferences, opinions, and interpretations have no value; the opinion of an expert on the causes of mental illness, criminal behavior, learning problems, or whatever can be very revealing. But be careful to distinguish between fact and opinion. Here is an example that illustrates why this is important.

A 54-year-old schizophrenic patient was rewarded for holding a broom that was given to her by a ward attendant. If she held the broom after it was handed to her, she was given a cigarette by another attendant. The purpose of this experiment was to determine if rewards should be used to alter the patient's rather listless behavior (she had been hospitalized for 23 years and refused to do anything on the ward). Soon the patient spent much of her time holding the broom. At this point two psychiatrists were invited to observe the patient through a one-way mirror. One psychiatrist's interpretation of the "broom-holding behavior" was that it was a symbolic expression of deep-seated unfulfilled desires. According to him, the broom could be a symbol for:

1. "a child that gives her love and she gives him in return her devotion,
2. a phallic symbol,
3. the sceptre of an omnipotent queen" (Ayllon et al., 1965).

The psychiatrist *observed* that the patient spent much of her time holding a broom. He *inferred* that this behavior had deep psychological meaning. In fact she held the broom for one reason: She received cigarettes for doing so!

Suggestion 6   Beware of over-simplifications, especially those motivated by monetary gain. Courses or programs that offer a "new personality in three sessions," "six steps to love and fulfillment in marriage," or newly discovered "secrets of unlocking the powers of the mind" should be immediately suspect. An excellent example of oversimplification is provided by a brochure entitled, "Dr. Joyce Brothers Asks: How Do You Rate as a 'Superwoman'?" Dr. Brothers, a media psychologist who has no private practice and is not known for research, wrote the brochure as a consultant for the Aerosol Packaging Council of the Chemical Specialties Manufacturers Association. A typical suggestion in this brochure tells how to enhance marriage: "Sweep him off to a weekend hideaway. Tip: When he's not looking, spray a touch of your favorite *aerosol* cologne mist on the bedsheets and pillows" (italics added). Sure, Joyce. . . .

Suggestion 7   Remember, "for example" is no proof. After reading this chapter, you should be sensitive to the danger of selecting single examples. If you read, "Law student passes state bar exam using sleep-learning device," don't rush out to buy one. Systematic research has shown that these devices are of little or no value (Koukkou & Lehmann, 1968). A corollary to this suggestion is to ask, "Are the reported observations important or widely applicable?"

Summary   Journalist Alvin Toffler and others have suggested that we are in the midst of an "information explosion." Indeed, we are all bombarded daily with such a mass of new information that it is difficult to adequately absorb it. The available knowledge, even in a limited area like psychology, biology, medicine, or contemporary rock music, is so vast that no single person can completely know and comprehend it. With this situation in mind, it becomes increasingly important that you become a critical, selective, and informed consumer of information. And if you think the value of scientific thought is restricted to the laboratory, remember the words of Oliver Wendell Holmes: "All life is an experiment."

Applications: Psychology in the News—Notes on Reading the Popular Press

Learning Check

1. Newspaper accounts of dermo-optical perception have generally reported only the results of carefully designed psychological experiments.   T or F?
2. Stage mentalists and psychics often use deception in their acts.   T or F?
3. Blaming variations in the rate of violent crime on changes in the lunar cycle is an example of mistaking correlation for causation.   T or F?
4. Psychiatric interpretations of a patient's "broom-holding behavior" (described previously) show the importance of using a control group in experiments.   T or F?

Answers: 1. F   2. T   3. T   4. F

Chapter Summary

Many of the important ideas in this chapter are summarized in the accompanying comparison chart. A few additional points to remember follow it.

	Advantages	Disadvantages
Naturalistic observation	Behavior is observed in a natural setting; much information is obtained and hypotheses and questions for additional research are formed.	Little or no control is possible; observed behavior may be altered by the presence of the observer; observations may be biased; causes cannot be conclusively identified.
Correlational method	Demonstrates the existence of relationships; allows prediction; can be used in lab, clinic, or natural settings.	Little or no control is possible; relationships may be coincidental; cause-effect relationships cannot be confirmed.
Experimental method	Clear cause-effect relationships can be identified; powerful controlled observations can be staged; no need to wait for natural event.	May be somewhat artificial; some natural behavior not easily studied in laboratory (field experiments may avoid these objections).
Clinical method	Takes advantage of "natural experiments" and allows investigation of rare or unusual problems or events.	Little control is possible; subjective interpretation is often necessary; a single case may be misleading or unrepresentative.
Survey method	Allows information about large numbers of people to be gathered; can address questions not answered by other approaches.	Obtaining a representative sample is critical and can be difficult to do; answers may be inaccurate; people may not do what they say or say what they do.

■ The *scientific method* is used to improve on common sense and avoid the pitfalls of casual observation. Important steps in scientific investigation usually include: *observing, defining a problem, proposing a hypothesis, experimenting,* and *forming a theory.*

■ *Naturalistic observation* is a starting place in many investigations. Three problems with this approach are: the effects of the observer on the observed, observer bias, and an inability to explain observed behavior.

■ In the *correlational method,* relationships between two

traits, responses, or events are measured. Then a *correlation coefficient* is calculated to gage the strength of the relationship. Correlations allow prediction, but they are usually insufficient to demonstrate cause-and-effect connections.

■ Relationships in psychology may be *positive* or *negative*, *linear* or *curvilinear*. Relationships are often clarified by graphing.

■ Cause-effect relationships are best identified by *controlled experiments*. In an experiment, two or more groups of *subjects* are formed. These groups differ only with regard to the *independent variable* (condition of interest as a cause in the experiment). *Effects* on the *dependent variable* are then measured. All other conditions (*extraneous variables*) are held constant. It must be possible to *replicate* (repeat) observations or experiments for them to be meaningful.

■ In experiments testing drugs, a *placebo* (a fake pill or injection) must be used to control psychological expectations associated with taking a drug. Drug research also frequently employs a *double-blind* procedure so that neither subjects nor experimenters know who is receiving the drug.

■ A related problem is the *experimenter effect*. This is the tendency for experimenters to subtly and unconsciously influence the outcome of an experiment. Expectations can create a *self-fulfilling prophecy*, in which a person changes in the direction of the expectation.

■ The *clinical method* employs *case studies*, which are in-depth records of a single subject. Case studies provide important information on topics that would not be studied any other way.

■ In the *survey method*, people in a *representative sample* are asked a carefully worded series of questions. Responses to these questions provide information on the attitudes and psychological functioning of large groups of people.

■ Information in the popular media varies greatly in quality and accuracy. It is wise to approach such information with skepticism and caution. This is especially true with regard to the *source* of information, *uncontrolled observation*, *correlation* and *causation*, *inferences*, *oversimplification*, and *single examples*.

Smile, You're on Candid Camera!—
The Ethics of Psychological Research

Several years ago, social psychologist Philip Zimbardo and his associates set up a simulated prison at Stanford University. Their goal was to probe the effects of imprisonment on otherwise healthy individuals. Students were recruited to play the roles of prisoners and guards. Much to everyone's surprise, the experiment had to be called off soon after it began. The "guards" had become so sadistic that 4 of the 10 "prisoners" suffered severe emotional reactions, including crying, depression, anxiety, and rage (Zimbardo, Haney, & Banks, 1973). (This experiment is discussed further in Chapter 26.)

The Stanford prison experiment is only one of several that have raised serious ethical questions. Were the participants permanently harmed? Did the information gained justify the emotional costs? Are such experiments dehumanizing? Questions like these have drawn attention to three issues to which researchers must be particularly sensitive. These are: use of *deception, invasion of privacy,* and *lasting harm.* Each issue is illustrated by the following three experiments. See if you think they are ethical.

Deception   In many experiments the true interests of a researcher are hidden by deception. This approach is often considered necessary to obtain genuine reactions. For example, a researcher interested in guilt once led subjects to believe that they

had broken an expensive piece of machinery. During the experiment, the machine suddenly popped loudly, released a plume of smoke, and sputtered to a stop. As embarrassed subjects were about to leave, the experimenter asked them to sign a petition he was supposedly circulating. The petition called for a doubling of tuition fees at the school. Almost all control subjects had refused to sign the same petition. However, because of their guilt, more than 50 percent of the experimental subjects signed (reported by Rubin, 1970). Was deception really necessary to investigate guilt?

Invasion of Privacy   A second area of debate concerns the extent to which invasions of privacy should be allowed in psychological research. One study that has been both criticized and defended involved secret observation of men in a restroom. Psychologist Eric Knowles was interested in the stress caused by "personal space" invasions. An observer concealed himself in a toilet stall in a public restroom and used a hidden periscope to monitor activity at the urinals. As predicted, urination took longer to begin when an assistant occupied a urinal next to the unsuspecting subject (Middlemist, Knowles, & Matter, 1976; Koocher, 1977). This finding is interesting, but does it justify the invasion of privacy used to obtain it?

Lasting Harm   Do psychological experiments ever do lasting harm

to participants? This is perhaps the most serious ethical question of all. A classic experiment on obedience to authority illustrates the problem. In the study, subjects thought they were inflicting painful and dangerous electrical shocks on another person (Milgram, 1974). (No shocks were actually given— see Chapter 25.) Belief that they were hurting someone proved extremely stressful for most subjects. Many left the experiment shaken and upset. Some presumably suffered guilt and distress for some time afterward.

This experiment may sound clearly unethical, but the researcher, Stanley Milgram, did follow-up studies on participants afterwards. Most felt positive about their experience and claimed they were glad they had taken part. Many added that they had learned something of value about themselves. But what about the few who felt otherwise?

As in medical research, no easy answers exist to the ethical questions raised by psychology. Most students find the studies just described interesting and informative. How can the search for knowledge be properly balanced with human rights? As a reply to this question, the American Psychological Association has adopted guidelines that state in part: "Psychologists must carry out investigations with respect for the people who participate and with concern for their dignity and welfare." To ensure this, most

Exploration: Smile, You're on Candid Camera!—The Ethics of Psychological Research

college psychology departments have ethics committees that oversee proposed research. Nevertheless, no easy answers exist for the ethical questions raised by some research. How do *you* think a psychologist should decide if his or her research is ethical?

Becoming a Subject   The ethics of research often turn out to be highly pertinent for many students.

As mentioned earlier, college students are frequently asked to serve as subjects in psychology experiments. If you become a subject, what should you expect? First of all, count on having an interesting and educational experience. There is no better way to learn how research is done than to observe it firsthand. Beyond that, you have a right to expect that your reactions will remain confidential; that you will be

debriefed about the purpose of the research; that you will receive an interpretation of your responses or test results; and finally, that the results of the research project will be made available to you.

Psychological research can be truly fascinating. If you do participate as a subject, you may end up wanting to try experiments or answer questions of your own. Many careers in psychology were launched in just this way.

Learning Check

1. Deception is regarded as a necessary part of almost all psychology experiments.   T or F?
2. Most of the subjects who participated in Milgram's obedience experiment felt that they had not been harmed.   T or F?
3. The major ethical question raised by the Stanford prison experiment concerned an invasion of privacy.   T or F?
4. In the United States the American Psychological Association must rule on whether an experiment is ethical before it is performed.   T or F?

Answers: 1. F   2. T   3. F   4. F

Questions for Discussion

1. Let's say you are interested in investigating the unspoken rules that govern the spacing of people in public places. What research techniques would you use? Can you propose some field experiments that might be performed?
2. What type of correlation would you expect to find between noise levels and productivity in an office? Between income and education? Between physical attractiveness and frequency of dating? Between class attendance and grades? Between use of alcohol by parents and by their children? How would you demonstrate a causal link in any of these cases?
3. Regarding self-fulfilling prophecies, how have the expectations of teachers, parents, or friends affected your expectations for yourself?
4. In your opinion is it dishonest or unethical for a physician to administer placebos to patients? Why or why not?

5. Have you ever taken part in a survey? On the basis of your participation, how accurate do you think surveys are? What are the flaws of typical "person on the street" surveys often done by local newspapers?
6. Compared with things done regularly by the government, the military, business, and educational institutions, most psychology experiments are pretty tame. With this point in mind, what is your position on the ethical questions raised in the Exploration section?
7. Do you consider the experiments described in the Exploration section ethical? Why or why not? What changes would you make if you were repeating the experiments?
8. There is a loophole in the statement, "I've been taking vitamin C tablets, and I haven't had a cold all year." What is it?

Part Two

Foundations of Human Consciousness

Chapter 3 | The Biology of Behavior

Chapter Preview
Worlds within Worlds within Worlds

Imagine yourself smaller than the period at the end of this sentence. Then join me as we enter a bizarre microscopic world. Surrounding us is a tangle of spidery branches, delicate fibers, and transparent globes. As we watch, pulsing waves of electrical energy flash through the fibers, arriving and scattering in thousands of directions. Meanwhile, all is bathed in a swirling sea of exotic chemicals. We are indeed in a strange realm. Yet there is beauty here, and mind-bending complexity—for we have just stepped into that most amazing of all computers, the human brain.

Crack open the fragile shell of the skull and you find, in the truest sense, "worlds within worlds within worlds." The human brain is a mass of spongy tissue about the size of a large grapefruit. Weighing a little over 3 pounds, it consists of some 100 billion individual nerve cells called **neurons** *(NEW-rons). All human behavior can ultimately be traced to the activity of these tiny cells. Each neuron in the brain's "enchanted loom" is connected to as many as 10,000 others. This network provides an exceedingly large capacity for combining and storing information. Scientists estimate that the number of possible pathways between neurons in a single human brain exceeds the number of atoms in the entire universe!*

Psychologists have long known that the brain is the organ of consciousness and action. But only in recent years has it become possible to demonstrate this directly. To prove the point, researcher José Delgado once entered a bullring with a cape and a radio transmitter. The bull charged. Delgado retreated. At the last possible instant the speeding bull stopped short. Why? Because Delgado's radio activated electrodes implanted deep within the bull's brain. These, in turn, stimulated "control centers" that brought the bull to a halt.

Physiological psychology *is the study of how the brain and nervous system relate to behavior, including the effects of damage to these delicate systems. The physiological psychologist occupies an exotic midground between mind and brain, biology and psychology. Let us enter this fascinating realm for a closer look at our biological heritage and human potential.*

Survey Questions How do nerve cells operate and communicate? What are the functions of major parts of the nervous system? What happens when the brain is injured? How does the glandular system relate to the nervous system? How do right- and left-handed individuals differ? Can the brain be controlled artificially?

Resources

Neurons— Building a "Biocomputer"

As physiological psychologist Paul MacLean once remarked, the towering question before the world concerns whether humans can master their brains and behavior before they have blown themselves to smithereens through their mastery of physics and chemistry. One of the most powerful keys to understanding the brain is the study of individual nerve cells. Unlike other cells in the body, neurons are specially designed to carry information. They are the basic units of the human "biocomputer."

Question: How do neurons carry information?

Parts of a Neuron   If we think of the nervous system as long "chains" of communicating cells, then neurons are the links. No two neurons are exactly alike in size or shape, but most have four basic parts (Fig. 3–1). Notice first the **dendrites** (DEN-drytes), which look like the roots of a tree. The dendrites specialize in receiving information from other neurons. The cell body, or **soma** (SOH-mah), also gathers incoming information, which it collects and combines. Periodically, the soma sends nerve impulses down a long thin fiber called an **axon** (AK-sahn).

Some axons are only about 0.1 millimeter long. (That's about the width of a pencil line.) Other axons stretch up to a meter through the nervous system of an adult. Axons act like miniature cables carrying messages from the sensory organs to the brain, from the brain to muscles or glands, or simply from one nerve cell to the next. Most axons branch at their ends to form an array of **axon terminals.** These branches connect the neuron to the dendrites and somas of other nerve cells.

The Nerve Impulse   Each neuron can be thought of as a tiny biological battery ready to be discharged. Nerve cells are filled with, and surrounded by, electrically charged molecules called **ions** (EYE-ons), especially sodium and potassium ions (Fig. 3–2). Differing amounts of these ions are found inside and outside the cell. As a result, a tiny difference in electrical charge exists across the cell membrane (or "skin"). In humans this electrical charge, called a **resting potential,** is about minus 70 millivolts (a millivolt is one-thousandth of a volt).

Messages arriving from other neurons alter the resting potential until it reaches a **threshold,** or trigger point, for firing. The threshold for human neurons averages about minus 50 millivolts. (See Fig. 3–2.) When a neuron reaches this point, a nerve impulse, or **action potential,** sweeps down the axon. The threshold for firing makes the action potential an **all-or-nothing** event; an impulse occurs completely or not at all. Thus, you might find it helpful to picture the axon as a fuse. This "fuse" is normally lit at the soma and burns rapidly to the axon terminals.

After each nerve impulse occurs, the cell briefly drops below its resting level. This drop, called a **negative afterpotential,** occurs while the neuron is recharging. It takes about one-thousandth of a second for a neuron to fire an impulse and return to the resting level. For this reason about 1000 nerve impulses per second are possible. However, firing rates of one to several hundred per second are more typical (Steven, 1979).

Question: How fast do nerve impulses travel along the axon?

Impulses travel at about 2.5 meters (roughly, 8 feet) per second in small, thin axons and up to 100 meters per second (about 225 miles per hour) in large axons. The speed of nerve impulses is also higher when **myelin** (MY-eh-lin) is present. Myelin forms a layer of fatty insulation around some axons. Where the layer is broken by small gaps, nerve impulses move faster by jumping from gap to gap. As you can see, nerve impulses are far from instantaneous. If someone steps on your toes, it takes one-fiftieth of a second for your brain to get the message!

Question: How is information carried from one neuron to another?

Neurotransmitters   We have seen that the nerve impulse is primarily an electrical event. This is why behavior is affected when the brain is stimulated electrically. (A good example is José Delgado's "electronic bullfighting" described in the Chapter Preview.) In contrast, communication between neurons is *chemical.* A nerve impulse that reaches the tips of the axon terminals causes **neurotransmitters** (NEW-row-TRANS-mit-ers) to be released. These potent chemicals cross the tiny gap, or **synapse** (SIN-aps), between neurons. Transmitter molecules then attach to special **receptor sites** on the dendrites and soma of the next neuron (Fig. 3–3). (This is also how neurotransmitters activate muscles and glands.)

Synapse (see Fig. 3–3 for an enlarged view)

Other neuron

Axon terminals

Nerve impulse

Myelin

Neurilemma

Soma (cell body)

Axon

Axon collateral (branch)

Nerve fiber

Myelin sheath

Axon

Dendrites

Fig. 3-1   *An example of a neuron, or nerve cell, showing several of its important features. The right foreground shows a nerve fiber in cross section, and the upper left inset gives a more realistic picture of the shape of neurons. The nerve impulse usually travels from the dendrites and soma to the branching ends of the axon. The neuron shown here is a motor neuron. Motor neurons originate in the brain or spinal cord and send their axons to the muscles or glands of the body.*

Question: Does the arrival of a neurotransmitter trigger an action potential in the next neuron?

Not always. Neurotransmitters may *excite* the next neuron (move it closer to firing) or *inhibit* it (make an impulse less likely). At any instant each neuron receives messages from hundreds or thousands of others. If several "exciting" messages arrive close in time, and they are not canceled by "inhibiting" messages, the neuron reaches its threshold for firing. This means that chemical messages are *combined* before a neuron "decides" to send on its all-or-nothing message. Multiply these events by 100 billion neurons and 100 trillion synapses and you have a computer of astounding capacity—all fit into a space one-half the size of a shoe box.

There are now some 30 known or suspected neurotransmitters in the brain. Among the more important "chemical messengers" are acetylcholine, adrenaline, noradren-

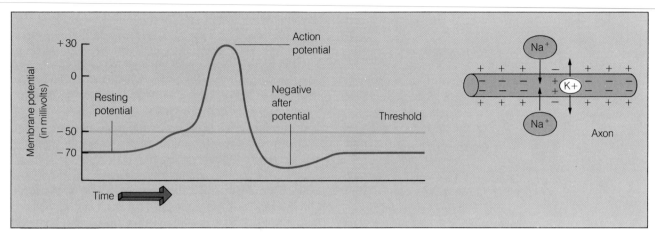

Fig. 3-2 *Electrochemical changes in a nerve cell generate an action potential. When positively charged sodium (Na+) ions rush into the cell, its potential briefly becomes positive. This is the action potential. After the action potential, an outward flow of positive potassium (K+) ions restores the negative charge of the resting potential. (See text for further explanation.)*

aline, serotonin, dopamine, histamine, and various amino acids (Krieger, 1983). The large variety of transmitter chemicals is one reason why there are literally thousands of drugs that affect the brain. Many drugs operate by imitating, duplicating, or canceling the actions of neurotransmitters. For example, one of the best known transmitters is **acetylcholine** (AS-ih-til-KOH-leen), which normally activates muscles. The drug **curare** (cue-RAH-ree), however, prevents nerve cells from activating muscle cells (Evarts, 1979). As a result, a person or animal given curare will be paralyzed—a fact known to South American Indians of the Amazon River Basin, who use curare as an arrow poison. The mind-altering drug mescaline, which is similar to noradrenaline, is an example of a drug that imitates a brain transmitter; the drugs LSD and psilocybin ("magic mushrooms") do the same (Iversen, 1979).

Neural Regulators A stunning series of recent discoveries has revealed a new class of brain transmitters called **neuropeptides** (NEW-row-PEP-tides), or, simply, brain peptides. Rather than carrying messages directly, these chemicals seem to *regulate* the activity of other neurons. In doing so, they affect memory, pain, emotion, pleasure, mood, hunger, sexual behavior, and other basic processes (Krieger, 1983). An example of a brain peptide in action is shown in Figure 3–4. As you can see in the drawing, some neurons have specific receptor sites for opiate drugs, such as morphine.

Fig. 3-3 *A highly magnified view of the synapse shown in Fig. 3-1. Transmitter chemicals cross the synaptic gap to affect the next neuron. The size of the gap is exaggerated here; it is actually only about one-millionth of an inch. Transmitter chemicals vary in their effect: Some excite the next neuron and some inhibit its activity.*

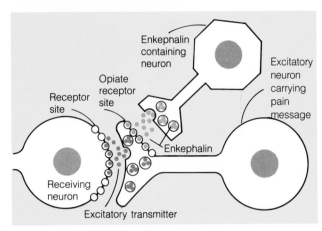

Fig. 3-4 *This simplified diagram shows how natural opiates may operate in the brain to relieve pain. Neurons carrying pain messages appear to have receptor sites for opiatelike transmitters called* enkephalins. *Release of enkephalins by "regulator" neurons suppresses activity in pain-carrying neurons. This suppression blocks or reduces the flow of pain messages. (Adapted from Iversen, 1979.)*

Question: Why would the brain have opiate receptors? After all, the human body isn't born with opium in it.

This is exactly the question that started a search for natural opiatelike peptides in the brain. Scientists found that the body produces natural opiates called **enkephalins** (en-KEF-ah-lins) to relieve pain and stress (Iversen, 1979). It now appears that phenomena as diverse as "runner's high," the placebo effect, and acupuncture may be explained by the action of enkephalins. (See Chapter 4 for more information.) Ultimately, an understanding of brain peptides may help explain depression, schizophrenia, drug addiction, and other puzzling problems.

General Neuroanatomy— Wired for Action

Picture two people playing catch with a Frisbee. To an outside observer this activity appears to be interesting but certainly not amazing. Yet, consider what is going on inside the body. In order to launch or catch the Frisbee, an incredible amount of information must be sensed, interpreted, and directed to countless muscle fibers. The neural circuits of the body are ablaze with activity. Let us consider in more detail the "wiring diagram" that makes this possible.

Neurons and Nerves

Question: Are neurons the same as nerves?

No. Nerves can be seen with the unaided eye. Rather than being single cells, nerves are bundles of axons and dendrites. Many nerves have a whitish color because they are made up mainly of axons coated by myelin. Most nerve fibers outside of the brain and spinal cord also have a thin layer of cells called the **neurilemma** (NEW-rih-LEM-ah) wrapped around them (see Fig. 3–1).

The neurilemma is important because it provides a "tunnel" through which damaged nerve fibers can grow when repairing themselves. If you were to accidentally sever a finger, and if it were sewn back on, there is a good chance the nerves would regenerate. In fact, you could expect feeling to creep back at a rate of about 1 millimeter per day. Neurons in the *brain* and *spinal cord* cannot be replaced by the body, so they must last a lifetime. If the spinal cord is torn, cut, or crushed, a person may permanently lose use of the body below the point of injury. Also, if the cell body of a neuron is destroyed *anywhere* in the nervous system, the cell will die. This is the cause of polio, a crippling disease in which the cell bodies of neurons controlling muscles are destroyed. (For a fascinating exception to the preceding statements, see Highlight 3–1.)

The Nervous System

Taken as a whole, the nervous system is a single unified structure. Dividing it into smaller parts, however, makes it easier to understand. As seen in Figures 3–5 and 3–7, a distinction can be made between the **central** and the **peripheral nervous systems**. The central nervous system (CNS) consists of the brain and spinal cord.

Question: How are the CNS and the peripheral nervous system related?

The Peripheral Nervous System   The peripheral system consists of nerves that carry information to and from the CNS. The peripheral system has two subparts: (1) the **somatic** system, which carries messages to and from the sense organs and the skeletal muscles; and (2) the **autonomic** system, which serves the internal organs and glands of the body. The autonomic nervous system (ANS) can be further divided into the **sympathetic** and **parasympathetic** branches. Both branches are important in the control of emotional response (Fig. 3–6).

The ANS, along with the somatic system, coordinates the inner and outer worlds of the body. If a large and angry-looking dog lunges at you unexpectedly, the somatic

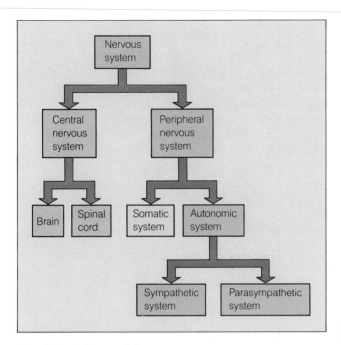

Fig. 3-5 *Subparts of the nervous system.*

Fig. 3-6 *Sympathetic and parasympathetic branches of the autonomic nervous system. Both branches control involuntary functions. The sympathetic system generally activates the body whereas the parasympathetic system generally quiets it. The sympathetic branch relays through a chain of ganglia (clusters of cell bodies) outside the spinal cord.*

Highlight 3–1
Brain Transplants

Transplanting brain tissue may sound more like science fiction than fact. Nevertheless, it seems likely that brain grafts will someday be used to correct a variety of brain diseases and injuries.

As you know, damaged brain cells are lost forever. The natural question then becomes, "Can they be replaced artificially?" There is growing evidence that in some cases the answer is yes. Damage can sometimes be repaired with grafts of healthy brain cells. In one experiment, for example, the brains of rats were damaged in an area that affects learning. Some of the rats then received implants of healthy brain tissue in the damaged region. Others remained untreated. Next, a maze-learning test was conducted, with encouraging results: Rats that received transplants did significantly better than those left untreated (Labbe et al., 1983). In addition, the grafts appeared to have "taken," or actually linked up with existing brain tissue.

Implants may also provide a cure for some brain-centered diseases. For instance, the crippling effects of Parkinson's disease are caused by a loss of brain cells that release dopamine. (Recall that dopamine is a transmitter substance.) In Sweden two human patients with severe Parkinson's disease recently had dopamine-producing tissue from their own adrenal glands grafted into their brains. In each case the patients improved noticeably (Kolata, 1983).

Obviously, it's a little early to think about seeking a brain graft to get you through final exams. Transplants are highly experimental at present, and it is not known if foreign tissue can be transplanted in humans, as it has been in animals. Just the same, brain grafting has profound implications. By doing transplants, it may become possible to repair some brain and spinal injuries that are now irreversible. Imagine what that could mean to a person confined to a wheelchair or someone suffering the aftereffects of a stroke. Although it is unwise to raise false hopes, the basic elements of a solution to such problems are beginning to fall into place.

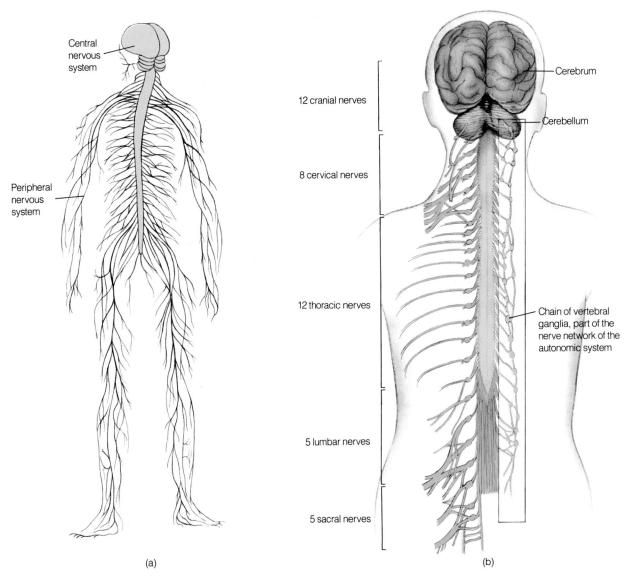

Central nervous system

Peripheral nervous system

12 cranial nerves

8 cervical nerves

12 thoracic nerves

5 lumbar nerves

5 sacral nerves

Cerebrum

Cerebellum

Chain of vertebral ganglia, part of the nerve network of the autonomic system

(a)

(b)

Fig. 3-7   (a) *Central and peripheral nervous systems.* (b) *Spinal nerves, cranial nerves, and the autonomic nervous system.*

system will help control the muscles for running, while the autonomic system raises blood pressure, quickens the heart, and so forth.

Question: How do the branches of the autonomic system differ?

The sympathetic branch prepares the body for "fight or flight" during times of emergency or emotion. In essence it mobilizes the body's resources for action. The parasympathetic branch, on the other hand, is most active im-

mediately *after* a stressful or emotional event. Its role is to quiet the body and return it to a lower level of arousal. It also helps maintain vital functions such as heart rate, breathing, and digestion at moderate levels. (See Chapter 13 for more information on the autonomic system.)

The Spinal Cord   The spinal cord is especially important because it acts like a cable connecting the brain to other parts of the body. If you were to cut through the spinal cord, you would see columns of **white matter**—

nerve tissue made up of axons that leave the spinal cord at various points to form peripheral nerves. As you can see in Figure 3–7b, there are 30 pairs of **spinal nerves** leaving the spinal cord and 1 pair leaving the bottom tip. The 31 pairs, together with an additional 12 nerves that leave the brain directly (the **cranial nerves**), place the entire body in sensory and motor communication with the brain.

Question: How is the spinal cord related to behavior?

Within the spinal cord itself the simplest behavior pattern (a **reflex arc**) can be carried out without any direct participation from the brain (see Fig. 3–8). Imagine that one of our Frisbee players steps on a thorn. This is detected in the foot by a **sensory neuron,** and a message (in the form of an action potential) is fired off to the spinal cord.

The sensory neuron synapses with a **connector neuron** (or **interneuron**) inside the spinal cord. The connector neuron in turn activates another connector cell (in this case a **motor neuron**) that leads back to muscle fibers. The muscle fibers are made up of **effector cells,** which contract and cause the foot to withdraw. Note that brain activity was not required for a reflex arc. The body can react to protect itself without any help from the brain.

In reality, more complex activity usually accompanies even a simple reflex. For example, muscles of the limb on the opposite side of the body must contract to support the shift in weight. Even this can be carried out by the spinal cord, but it involves many more cells and several levels of the spinal nerves. Perhaps you have already realized how adaptive it is to have a spinal cord capable of responding on its own. Such automatic responses leave the brain of our Frisbee ace free to deal with more important information—such as the whereabouts of trees, lampposts, and attractive onlookers—as he or she makes a grandstand catch.

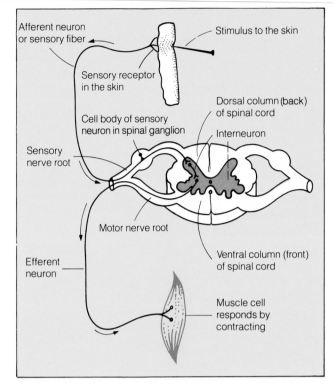

Fig. 3–8   *A simple sensory-motor (reflex) arc. A simple reflex is set in motion by a stimulus to the skin (or other part of the body). The nerve impulse travels to the spinal cord and then back out to a muscle, which contracts. Reflexes provide an "automatic" protective device for the body.*

Learning Check

Before reading further, see if you can answer these questions.

1. The _____ and _____ are receiving areas where information from other neurons is accepted.

2. Nerve impulses are carried down the _____.

3. The point of interchange between two neurons is called a myelin.   T or F?

4. The _____ potential becomes an _____ potential when a neuron passes the threshold for firing.

5. Neuropeptides are a newly discovered class of transmitter substances that include naturally occurring opiatelike chemicals called enkephalins.   T or F?

6. The somatic and autonomic systems are part of the _____ nervous system.

7. Sodium and potassium ions cross the synapse to trigger a nerve impulse in the receiving neuron.   T or F?

8. The simplest behavior sequence is a _____.

9. The parasympathetic nervous system is most active during times of high emotion.   T or F?

Answers: 1. dendrites, soma   2. axon   3. F   4. resting, action   5. T   6. peripheral   7. F   8. reflex arc   9. F

The Cerebral Cortex— My, What a Big Brain You Have!

In many respects humans are pretty unimpressive creatures. Fragile, weak, born naked and helpless, humans are excelled by other animals in almost every category of strength, speed, and sensory sensitivity. The one area in which humans excel is intelligence.

Question: Do humans have the largest brain?

Surprisingly, no. Elephant brains weigh 13 pounds and whale brains, 19 pounds. At 3 pounds the human brain seems puny—until we figure the proportion of brain weight to body weight. We then find that an elephant's brain is 1/1,000 of its weight; the ratio for sperm whales is 1 to 10,000. The ratio for humans is 1 to 60 (Cohen, 1974). If someone says you have a "whale of a brain," be sure to find out if they mean size or ratio!

Question: What about dolphins?

The only other creatures that compare well with humans in both brain size and brain-body ratio are dolphins and porpoises. It is possible, although not established, that these animals may be as intelligent (or more so) as humans. Researchers have already shown that dolphins communicate with a system of sounds as complex as our own (Wursig, 1979). On the other hand, whales and elephants use large portions of their brains to coordinate their massive bodies. It may be that dolphins and porpoises likewise use much of their brains for "lower" sensory and motor functions.

So, relatively speaking, humans have very highly developed brains. More importantly, as we move from lower to higher animals, there is an ever-increasing proportion of brain tissue devoted to the **cerebral cortex** (SER-eh-brel or seh-REE-brel) (see Fig. 3–9). In humans the cerebral cortex accounts for no less than 70 percent of the neurons in the central nervous system.

Corticalization   The cortex covers most of the visible portions of the brain with a mantle of **gray matter** (spongy tissue made up mostly of cell bodies and unmyelinated axons). In humans the cerebral cortex looks a little like a giant, wrinkled walnut. The cortex in lower animals is small and smooth; in humans it is the largest brain structure. Human intellectual superiority appears to be related to this **corticalization** (KORE-tih-kal-ih-ZAY-shun), or increase in the size and wrinkling of the cortex.

Cerebral Hemispheres   The cortex is composed of two halves, or **hemispheres.** At first glance the hemispheres appear to be mirror images of each other, but they actually differ slightly in shape and wrinkling (Corballis, 1980). The two hemispheres are connected by a thick band of fibers called the **corpus callosum** (KORE-pus kah-LOH-sum). Surprisingly, the two halves control opposite sides of the body. The left side of the brain mainly controls the right side of the body, and the right half of the brain mainly controls left body areas.

Hemispheric Specialization

We turn now to some remarkable findings. In 1981 Roger Sperry of the California Institute of Technology won a Nobel Prize for his work on the special abilities of the cerebral hemispheres. Sperry and other psychologists have shown that the right and left sides of the brain perform differently on tests of language, perception, music, and other capabilities.

Question: How is it possible to test only one side of the brain?

One way is to work with people who have had a type of surgery for severe epilepsy that literally *disconnects* the hemispheres. The result of these "split-brain" operations is essentially a person with two brains in one body (Sperry,

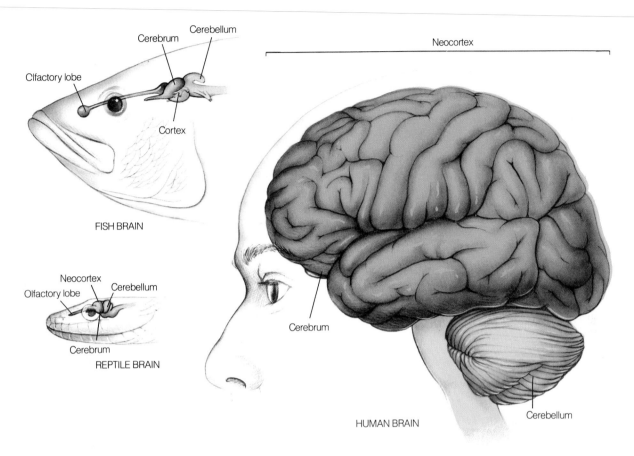

Fig. 3-9   *An illustration showing the increased size of the human cerebral cortex, a significant factor in human adaptability and intelligence.*

1968). After the surgery it is a simple matter to route information to one hemisphere or the other (see Fig. 3–10).

"Split Brains"   In both animals and humans, separation of the hemispheres consistently results in a doubling of consciousness. As Sperry (1968) says:

In other words, each hemisphere seems to have its own separate and private sensations; its own perceptions; its own concepts; and its own impulses to act.

Question: How does a split-brain person function after the operation?

On occasion having two "brains" in one body creates quite a dilemma. Another researcher, Michael Gazzaniga, recounts that one of his split-brain patients would:

. . . sometimes find himself pulling his pants down with one hand and pulling them up with the other. Once, he grabbed his wife with his left hand and shook her violently, while with

the right trying to come to his wife's aid in bringing the belligerent left hand under control. (Gazzaniga, 1970, p. 107.)

It is far more typical, however, for split-brain individuals to act normally in most situations. The reason is that both halves of the brain experience approximately the same thing at the same time. Also, if any conflict arises, one hemisphere tends to override the other (To find out which of your brain hemispheres is dominant, see the Applications section of this chapter.)

Split-brain effects become most apparent in specialized testing. For example, a dollar sign can be flashed to the right brain and a question mark to the left brain. (Figures 3–10 and 3–11 show how this is possible.) If the person is asked to draw (out of sight) with the left hand what he or she saw, the dollar sign will be drawn. If then asked to point with the right hand to a picture of what the left hand drew, the subject will point to a question mark (Sperry, 1968). In short, for the split-brain person, one hemisphere does not know what is happening in the other. This

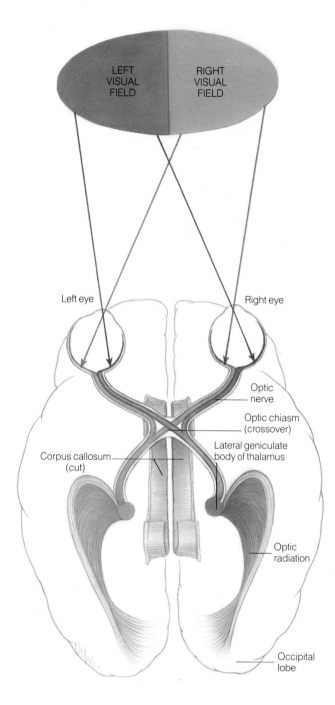

has to be the ultimate case of the right hand not knowing what the left hand is doing!

Question: Earlier it was stated that the hemispheres differ in abilities. In what ways do they differ?

Right Brain/Left Brain   The brain divides up its work in interesting ways. For example, language is a specialty of the left hemisphere. Roughly 95 percent of all adults use the left side of the brain for speaking, writing, and comprehending language. In addition, the left hemisphere is superior at math, judging time and rhythm, and at ordering or coordinating complex movements (especially those needed for speech) (Corballis, 1980). In contrast, the right hemisphere responds to only the simplest elements of language and numbers. Working with the right hemisphere is a little like talking to a child who only understands a dozen words or so. To express itself, the right hemisphere must point to objects or make other nonverbal responses (see Fig. 3–11).

At one time the right brain was regarded as the "minor" hemisphere. But we now know that it has talents of its own. The right hemisphere is superior at perceptual skills such as recognizing patterns, faces, and melodies, and it is involved in detecting and expressing emotion (Geschwind, 1979). The right brain is also better at tasks requiring visualization, and manipulo-spatial skills, such as arranging blocks to match a sample pattern, putting together a puzzle, or drawing a picture (Gazzaniga & Le Doux, 1978).

The superiority of the right hemisphere at spatial tasks leads to another intriguing split-brain observation. A common test of spatial ability involves solving a geometric puzzle. On this test the split-brain patient's left hand typically can perform quite well, but the right cannot. Robert Ornstein (1972) reports that:

> Professor Sperry often shows an interesting film clip of the right hand attempting to solve the problem and failing, whereupon the patient's left hand cannot restrain itself and "corrects" the right—as when you know the answer to a problem and watch me making mistakes, and cannot refrain from telling me the answer.

Question: Do people normally solve puzzles with just their right hemisphere? Do they do other things with just the left?

If you were to solve a puzzle like the one mentioned, your spatially oriented right hemisphere would indeed be more active than the left. But at the same time, your left hemisphere would be more active than it was before you started the puzzle. Thus, while activity may focus on one hemisphere, the skills of both sides of the brain are *combined*

Fig. 3–10 *Basic nerve pathways of vision. Notice that the left portion of each eye connects only to the left half of the brain; likewise, the right portion of each eye connects to the right brain. When the corpus callosum is cut, a "split brain" results, and visual information can be directed to one hemisphere or the other.*

LEFT BRAIN
- Language
- Speech
- Writing
- Calculation
- Time Sense
- Rhythm
- Ordering of complex movements

RIGHT BRAIN
- Nonverbal
- Perceptual skills
- Visualization
- Recognition of patterns, faces, melodies
- Recognition and expression of emotion
- Spatial skills
- Simple language comprehension

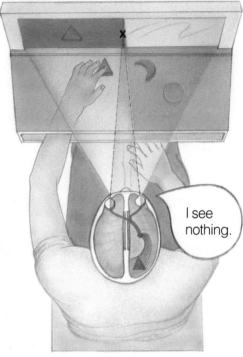

LEFT HEMISPHERE

RIGHT HEMISPHERE

Fig. 3-11 *If a circle is flashed to the left brain and the person is asked to say what he or she saw, the circle is easily named. The person can also pick out the circle by touching shapes with the right hand, out of sight under a tabletop (shown semi-transparent in drawing). However, the left hand will be unable to identify the shape. If a triangle is flashed to the right brain, the person cannot say what was seen (speech is controlled by the left hemisphere). The person will also be unable to identify the correct shape by touch with the right hand. Now, however, the left hand will have no difficulty picking out the hidden triangle. Separate testing of each hemisphere reveals distinct specializations, as listed above. (Figure adapted from an illustration by Edward Kasper in McKean, 1985.)*

in most activities. Perhaps this is why lawyers, artists, and psychologists showed no differences in a test of right and left hemisphere activity (Arndt & Berger, 1978; Ornstein & Galin, 1976). (Also see Fig. 3–12.) Such findings also suggest that books purporting to teach you to use the "right brain" to be more creative, and the like, ignore the fact that the entire brain is used at all times.

Cerebral Maps of Reality

In addition to the hemispheres, the cerebral cortex can be divided into several smaller areas, or **lobes** (see Fig. 3–13).

Question: What is known about the function of the lobes?

The functions of various areas in each of the lobes have been "mapped" by clinical and experimental studies. Experimentally, the surface of the cortex can be activated by touching it with a small electrified needle or wire called an **electrode**. When this is done to a patient undergoing brain surgery—using only local painkillers— the patient can report what effect the stimulation had. The functions of the cortex have also been identified by clinical studies of changes in personality, behavior, or the senses caused by brain diseases or injuries. Let us consider the outcome of such studies.

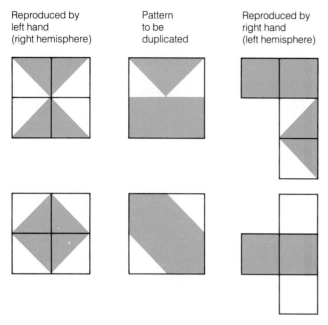

| Reproduced by left hand (right hemisphere) | Pattern to be duplicated | Reproduced by right hand (left hemisphere) |

Fig. 3-12 *Results from tests of pattern reproduction in a "split-brain" human. Examples of errors made by each hand-hemisphere combination are shown. Notice that both hemispheres made errors and that the types of errors differ. Apparently, both hemispheres contribute to successful completion of most tasks, even those that are primarily "nonverbal." (Adapted from Geschwind, 1979, p. 181.)*

The Occipital Lobes   The occipital lobes (ok-SIP-ih-tal), which are located at the back of the brain, are the primary **visual area** of the cortex. Patients with *tumors* (cell growths that interfere with brain activity) in the occipital lobes develop blind spots in areas of the visual field.

Question: Do the visual areas of the cortex correspond directly to what is seen?

Visual images are mapped onto the surface of the cortex but not in a one-to-one fashion. The map is greatly distorted; it is as if you printed a picture on a sheet of rubber and stretched it in various directions (Carlson, 1981). Therefore, it is important to avoid thinking of the visual area as being like a little TV screen in the brain. Visual information creates complex patterns of activity in nerve cells; it does *not* make a TV-like image. Even if we were tempted to visualize this activity as a "picture," we would still have to ask, "Who's watching the TV?" It is a classic error to think of the brain in terms of some **homunculus** (ho-MUN-cue-lus: "little man") that makes decisions or observes incoming information. (See the Highlight in Chapter 4 on how the brain sees the world.)

The Parietal Lobes   The parietal lobes (puh-RYE-ih-tal) are located just above the occipital lobes. Touch, temperature, pressure, and other somatic, or bodily sensations are channeled to the **somatosensory area** (SO-mat-oh-SEN-so-ree) on the parietal lobes. The correspondence between areas of the parietal lobes and parts of the body is not a perfect one. The distorted body in Figure 3–13 shows that, as a map of bodily sensations, the cortex represents the sensitivity of body areas, not their size. For example, the lips are large in the drawing because of their great sensitivity, while the back and trunk, which are less sensitive, are much smaller. Notice also that representation of the body is "upside down" on the cortex: Sensations from the foot register at the top, followed downward by the leg, hip, trunk, shoulder, neck, arm, hand, fingers, face, lips, and tongue.

The Temporal Lobes   The temporal lobes are located on each side of the brain and extend below to the underside of the cortex. Auditory information projects directly to the temporal lobes, making them the site where hearing registers. If we were to stimulate the **primary auditory area** of a temporal lobe, our subject would "hear" a series of sounds. These sounds would increase in pitch as we moved from the top to the bottom; stimulating in another direction, we would find that sound sensations would undergo an orderly change in loudness (Carlson, 1981). This indicates that sound qualities are precisely mapped out on the surface of the cortex.

For most people the left temporal lobe also contains a language "center." (For some this area is on the right temporal lobe.) Damage to this center can severely limit ability to use language meaningfully. More on this later.

The Frontal Lobes   The frontal lobes perform a mixture of functions. For one thing, **olfactory** (smell) information registers on the underside of the frontal lobes. Another important area is the **motor cortex,** an arch of tissue running roughly ear-to-ear over the top of the brain. This area directs the body's muscles. If the motor cortex is stimulated with a brief electrical current, muscular twitches will be observed in various parts of the body. Like the somatosensory area, the motor cortex corresponds to the importance of bodily areas, not to their size. The hands, for example, get more area than the feet (see Fig. 3–13).

Also related to the frontal lobes are behaviors of a more complex nature. When areas of the frontal lobes other than motor cortex are removed, animals lose the ability to judge the passage of time, to hold the solution to a problem in mind, or to respond to emotionally unpleasant sit-

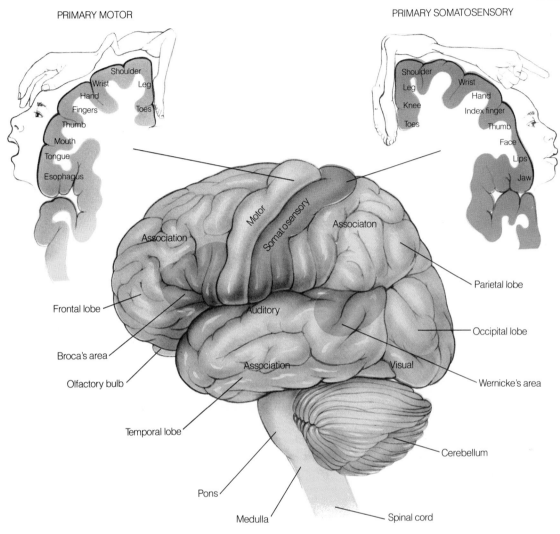

PRIMARY MOTOR

PRIMARY SOMATOSENSORY

Fig. 3-13 *The drawing shows the lobes of the cerebral cortex and the primary sensory, motor, and association areas on each. The top diagrams show (in cross section) the relative amounts of cortex "assigned" to the sensory and motor control of various parts of the body.*

uations. Damage to the frontal lobes in humans tends to decrease emotionality and ability to perform tasks requiring thinking, reasoning, or planning (Thompson, 1967).

Question: The sensory and motor areas leave a lot of the cortex unaccounted for. What do the remaining areas do?

Associative Areas In the human brain areas that are specifically sensory or motor in function make up only a small part of the cerebral cortex. All other areas (including parts of all the lobes previously described) have been collectively called the **association cortex.** The association cortex seems to process and combine information from the various senses. When stimulated, it yields reponses more complex than simple sensations or movements. The loss of thinking skills after damage to the frontal lobes is an excellent example. Additional clues to the workings of the association cortex come from studies of humans with brain injuries.

Brain Injuries

As you might imagine, damage to the right brain often leaves the left side of the body paralyzed, and vice versa for damage to the left brain. More importantly, the special abilities of the left and right hemispheres may also be affected. A person with a stroke or other damage in the left brain may lose the ability to speak, read, write, or spell. Yet, the same person may remain able to draw or hum with skill. Persons with right brain damage may be unable to dress themselves properly or may get lost while driving, but they can speak and read as before (Gardner, 1975). To make another comparison, a person with left brain damage may not understand what you say, but he or she will pick up your emotional tone. With right hemisphere damage the person can understand what is said but fails to recognize if it is spoken in an angry or humorous way (Geschwind, 1975).

Question: Is it fair to say that damage to the left hemisphere is usually more serious?

Generally it is, because speech and language are so essential. However, if you are an artist, the right brain may be the "major" hemisphere from your point of view. It has been observed, for instance, that painters can still create art after left brain damage. But an artist with right brain damage may neglect the left side of the canvas, or distort outlines, or portray bizarre and repulsive subject matter (Gardner, 1975).

Aphasia   Two areas of the cortex are particularly related to language. One, called **Broca's area** (BRO-cahs), lies on the left frontal lobe. The second, known as **Wernicke's area** (VER-nick-ees), is found on the left temporal lobe (see Fig. 3–12). Injury to either area can cause **aphasia** (ah-FAZE-yah), meaning an impaired ability to use language.

Question: What kinds of impairment take place?

Persons with damage in Broca's area can read and can understand the speech of others, but they have great difficulty speaking or writing themselves. Typically, their grammar and pronunciation is poor and their speech is slow and labored. For example, the person may say "bife" for bike, "seep" for sleep, or "zokaid" for zodiac. Generally the person knows what he or she wants to say but can't seem to get it into words (Geschwind, 1979).

In Wernicke's aphasia the person has problems with the *meaning* of words, not grammar or pronunciation. Whereas someone with Broca's aphasia might say "tssair" when shown a picture of a chair, a Wernicke's patient might say "stool." People with injuries to Wernicke's area often speak in incredibly roundabout ways to avoid using certain nouns. While discussing her son's career, one patient said: "Well he was two years away, away down for nothing. He didn't do it and got out and said I want to go over there and . . . how to do things, what he's doing now" (Goodglass, 1980). It is obvious that both Broca's area and Wernicke's area are crucial for normal language use. It is not surprising, then, to find that they are interconnected in the brain.

"Mindblindness"   One of the most fascinating results of brain injury is **agnosia** (ag-KNOW-zyah). This condition is sometimes referred to as "mindblindness" because it involves an inability to identify seen objects. If shown a candle, for instance, someone with an agnosia might describe it as a long narrow object tapering at the top, or may draw it accurately and yet fail to name it. However, if the person is permitted to feel the candle, he or she will name it immediately (Benton, 1980).

Question: Are agnosias limited to objects?

No. A particularly interesting form of mind-blindness is facial agnosia, the inability to identify familiar persons. For instance, one patient with facial agnosia was unable to recognize her husband or mother when they visited her in the hospital, and she could not identify pictures of her children. However, as soon as visitors spoke, she knew them immediately from their voices (Benton, 1980). Study of facial agnosias shows that a brain area devoted to recognizing others is located on the underside of the occipital lobes. These areas appear to have no other function. Why would part of the brain be set aside solely for recognizing faces? From an evolutionary standpoint this is not really so surprising. After all, we are social animals, for whom facial recognition is very important (Geschwind, 1979). This specialization is an additional example of what a marvelous organ of consciousness we possess.

Learning Check

See if you can successfully match the following.

1. _____ Corpus callosum   **A.** Visual area

2. _____ Occipital lobes   **B.** Language, speech, writing

3. ____ Parietal lobes

4. ____ Temporal lobes

5. ____ Frontal lobes

6. ____ Association cortex

7. ____ Aphasias

8. ____ Corticalization

9. ____ Left hemisphere

10. ____ Right hemisphere

11. ____ "Split brain"

12. ____ Agnosia

C. Motor cortex and abstract thinking

D. Spatial skills, visualization, pattern recognition

E. Speech disturbances

F. Causes sleep

G. Increased ratio of cortex in brain

H. Bodily sensations

I. Treatment for severe epilepsy

J. Inability to identify seen objects

K. Fibers connecting the cerebral hemispheres

L. Cortex that is not sensory or motor in function

M. Hearing

Answers: 1. K   2. A   3. H   4. M   5. C   6. L   7. E   8. C   9. G   10. D   11. I   12. J

The Subcortex— At the Core of the (Brain) Matter

Question: What do brain areas below the cortex do?

A person can lose large portions of the cerebrum and still survive. As a matter of fact, if damage is limited to the less crucial areas of the cortex, little visible change may take place. Not so with the brain areas below the cortex. Most of these are so basic to normal functioning that damage may endanger a person's life.

Question: Why are the lower brain areas so important?

Below the cerebral cortex and completely covered by it are structures that are collectively termed the **subcortex**. The subcortex can be divided into three general areas called the **brainstem** or **hindbrain**, the **midbrain**, and the **forebrain**. (The forebrain also includes the cerebral cortex, which was discussed earlier because of its size and importance.) For the purpose of this discussion the midbrain can be viewed primarily as a link between the brain structures above and below it. Therefore, let us focus on the hindbrain and the forebrain to more fully appreciate their importance (see Fig. 3–14).

The Hindbrain

As the spinal cord enters the skull to join the brain, it widens into the brainstem, consisting principally of the **medulla** (meh-DUL-ah) and the **cerebellum** (ser-ah-BEL-um). The *medulla* contains centers important for the reflex control of vital life functions, including heart rate, breathing, swallowing, and the like. For example, the medulla receives information about the carbon dioxide content of the blood and the tension of the muscles that expand the chest for breathing. Combining this information, the medulla *excites* the muscles so that you will inhale, then *inhibits* this excitement to cause exhalation. You can, of course, override this reflex by voluntarily holding your breath; but if you hold your breath long enough to pass out, the higher brain centers relinquish control, and once again you will begin reflex breathing. Various drugs, diseases, or injuries can interrupt the vital functions of the medulla enough to end or endanger life. That's why a karate chop to the back of the neck, like those depicted in movies, can be extremely dangerous.

The *cerebellum*, which looks like a miniature cerebral cortex, lies at the base of the brain. The cerebellum is closely connected to many areas in the brain and spinal cord and functions primarily to regulate posture, muscle tone, and muscular coordination.

Question: What happens if the cerebellum is injured?

Without the cerebellum, seemingly simple tasks like walking, running, or playing catch would be impossible. The importance of the cerebellum is indicated by the effects of a crippling disease called *spinocerebellar degeneration*. The first symptoms of this disease include tremor, dizziness, and muscular weakness. Soon, affected persons find that they underreach or overreach for objects and have difficulty standing, walking, or even feeding themselves.

Reticular Formation   In a space within the medulla and brainstem is a *network* of fibers and cell bodies called the **reticular** (reh-TICK-yuh-ler) **formation** (RF).

Question: What does the reticular formation do?

The RF is important for several reasons. First, it acts as a kind of central clearinghouse for most of the information coming to and from the brain. Second, the reticular formation gives priority to some incoming messages, while excluding others. This is basically what we mean by *attention*. Without the RF we would be overwhelmed with useless information from the environment. Third, and perhaps most important, the reticular formation is responsible for alertness and wakefulness.

Incoming impulses from the sense organs branch into the reticular formation, where they form a **reticular activating system** (RAS). The RAS bombards the cortex with

stimulation, keeping it active and vigilant (Malmo, 1975). Researchers have found that destroying the RAS causes animals to enter a permanent coma resembling sleep. In contrast, electrical stimulation of the same area instantly awakens sleeping animals (Moruzzi & Magoun, 1949; Lindsley, Bowden, & Magoun, 1949). The sleepy driver who snaps to attention when an animal appears in the middle of the road can thank the RAS for arousing the rest of the brain.

The Forebrain

Like gemstones of nerve tissue, two of the most important parts of the body lie buried deep within the center of the

Fig. 3-14   *This simplified drawing shows the main structures of the human brain and describes some of their most important functions.*

CEREBRUM
(Surface: cerebral cortex) Voluntary movements; sensations, learning, remembering, thinking, emotion; consciousness

HYPOTHALAMUS
Control of hunger, thirst, temperature, and other visceral and bodily functions

PITUITARY GLAND
The "master gland" of the endocrine system

MEDULLA
Centers for control over breathing, swallowing, digestion, heartbeat

CORPUS CALLOSUM
Band of fibers connecting the two hemispheres

THALAMUS
Relay station to cortex for sensory information

MIDBRAIN
Conduction and switching center

CEREBELLUM
Muscle tone; body balance; coordination of skilled movement

RETICULAR FORMATION
Arousal system

SPINAL CORD
Conduction paths for motor and sensory impulses; local reflexes (reflex arc)

Forebrain
Midbrain
Hindbrain

brain. The **thalamus** (THAL-ah-mus), and an area just below it called the **hypothalamus** (HI-po-THAL-ah-mus), are part of the forebrain (see Fig. 3–14).

Question: How could these be any more important than other areas already described?

The thalamus is a football-shaped structure that acts as a final "switching station" for sensory information on its way to the cortex. Not only does information from vision, hearing, taste, and touch relay through the thalamus, it undergoes preliminary processing and analysis there as well. Injury to even small areas of the thalamus could cause deafness, blindness, or loss of any other sense, except smell.

The hypothalamus in the human is about the size of a thumbnail. Yet small as it may be, the hypothalamus is related to the control of behaviors as diverse as sex, rage, temperature control, hormone release, eating and drinking, sleep, waking, and emotion. The hypothalamus is a sort of crossroads that connects with many other areas of the cortex and subcortex. As such, it acts as a final path for many kinds of behavior leaving the brain. You might think of the hypothalamus as the last area in the brain where many behaviors are organized or "decided on." (See Chapter 12 for a discussion of the role of the hypothalamus in hunger and thirst.)

The Limbic System   The hypothalamus, parts of the thalamus, and several structures buried within the cortex have been collectively labeled the **limbic system.** Although the specific function of some parts of the limbic system is unclear, as a group they share an unmistakable role in the production of *emotion* and motivated behavior. Rage, fear, sexual response, and other instances of intense arousal have all been obtained from various points in the limbic system. For example, cats made aggressive by electrical stimulation of the limbic system will crouch, hiss, expose their claws, lean forward, and tense their muscles—all characteristic of defense or attack. (See this chapter's Exploration.)

One part of the limbic system appears to be important for the formation of long-term memories. This is the **hippocampus** (HIP-oh-CAMP-us), found at the core of the temporal lobes. A link between the hippocampus and memory may explain why stimulating the temporal lobes can produce memorylike or dreamlike experiences. (See Chapter 10 for more information on this point.)

One of the most exciting discoveries in psychology was the finding that animals will learn to press a lever in order to deliver electrical stimulation to the limbic system as a reward (Olds & Milner, 1954). Since the original discovery, many additional areas of the limbic system have been shown to act as reward or "pleasure" pathways in the brain. Many are found in the hypothalamus, where they overlap with areas associated with drives such as thirst, sex, and hunger (Olds, 1977) (see Chapter 8). In addition, punishment, or "aversive" areas have also been found. When these areas are stimulated, animals show discomfort and will work to turn off the stimulation. Since a great deal of human and animal behavior is directed by the pursuit of pleasure and the avoidance of pain, these discoveries continue to fascinate psychologists.

The Brain in Perspective— Beyond the Biocomputer

We have seen that the human brain is an impressive living assembly of billions of sensitive cells and nerve fibers. The brain controls vital bodily functions, keeps track of the external world, issues commands to the muscles and glands, generates complex responses to current needs, creates the magic of consciousness, and regulates its own behavior—*all* at the same time. Each of these basic needs is met by the action of cne or more of the three main brain divisions: Control of vital bodily functions is carried out by the hindbrain (with some assistance from the hypothalamus in the forebrain); gathering sensory information and issuing motor commands takes place at all three levels of the brain; response selection, learning, memory, and higher thought processes are controlled by the forebrain, particularly the cortex and association areas.

Redundancy   A final note of caution is now in order. For the sake of simplicity we have assigned functions to each "part" of the brain as if it were a computer. This is only a half-truth. In reality the brain always functions as a unit. Incoming information scatters to structures all over the brain and converges again as it goes out to muscles and glands. The overall system acts in ways that go far beyond any view that considers only "parts" or "brain centers" (Nauta & Fiertag, 1979). To say the least, the brain is much, much more complicated than implied here.

One reason for the brain's great complexity is the fact that it shows tremendous **redundancy,** or duplication throughout. The brain may use dozens of areas to carry out a function that any one area could manage alone. Because of such redundancy, the brain has an impressive ability to reorganize itself after injury.

Question: Does it make any difference at what age a person experiences a brain injury?

Plasticity   Yes. In response to brain damage, children usually show greater **plasticity** (or flexibility) of brain reorganization than adults. Like adults, children cannot replace destroyed brain cells. But even when there is severe damage to the left hemisphere, children under the age of 7 can usually shift language processing to the right brain. In fact, people have been located who were born without corpus callosums, having, in effect, "natural" split brains. As adults these people can answer questions from both hemispheres, write with both hands, draw with both hands, and solve block-design puzzles with both hands (Sperry, 1974). After age 10, such plasticity becomes rare.

Much of the plasticity of early childhood derives from the rapid growth and development of the brain during this period. For the same reason the brain is more subject to damage of another type at this time. Animal research (Lewin, 1975) indicates that **malnutrition** can reduce the number of brain cells in the cerebellum (causing clumsiness). It can also diminish the size of axons and lower the number of synapses in the cortex by 40 percent. This fact is well worth remembering, since malnourished children show a variety of physical and intellectual losses that researchers have had little success in reversing.

Potential   In the final analysis the brain is both highly vulnerable and amazingly resilient. In one astounding case a child had the entire left hemisphere of his brain removed at age 5. As an adult he was paralyzed on the right side and blind in his right visual field. But he was able to speak, read, write, and comprehend so well that he maintained a double major in college and has an above-average IQ (Smith & Sugar, 1975).

Cases such as the one just described bring realization that full use of the brain's potential may still lie ahead. At the same time that such injuries help us understand the brain's limitations, they raise questions about how the undamaged brain might be used more fully. Perhaps the future will see significant breakthroughs in the enhancement of memory or intelligence or in recovery from brain damage. For now it is exciting to think that the human brain hasn't yet yielded all its secrets.

The Glandular System— Slow but Sure Messenger Service

The nervous system is not the only communication network in the body. The **endocrine system** (EN-duh-krin) is made up of a number of glands that release chemicals directly into the bloodstream (see Fig. 3–15). These chemicals, called **hormones**, are transported throughout the body, where they affect bodily functioning and behavior.

Question: How do hormones affect behavior?

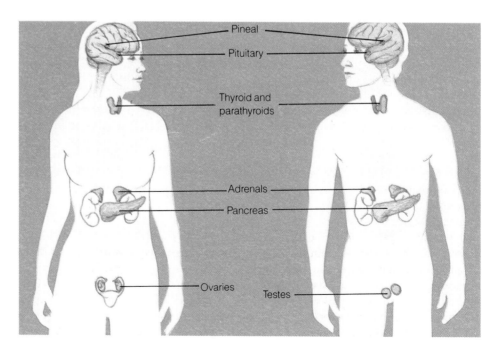

Fig. 3-15   *Locations of the endocrine glands in the male and female.*

Pineal

Pituitary

Thyroid and parathyroids

Adrenals

Pancreas

Ovaries

Testes

Although we are seldom aware of them, hormones affect us in a multitude of ways. Here is a brief sample: Hormone output from the adrenal glands rises during stressful situations; androgens ("male" hormones) are related to the sex drive in both males and females; hormones secreted during times of high emotion intensify memory formation; at least some of the emotional turmoil of adolescence is due to elevated hormone levels; different hormones predominate when a person is angry than when he or she is fearful (Hoyenga & Hoyenga, 1984). Since this is just a sample, let's consider some additional effects hormones have on the body and behavior.

The **pituitary** is a small grape-sized structure hanging from the base of the brain (return to Fig. 3–14). One of the pituitary's more important roles is regulation of growth. During childhood the pituitary secretes a hormone that speeds bodily development. If too little **growth hormone** is released, a person may remain far smaller than average (see Highlight 3–2). Too much growth hormone produces **giantism** (see Fig. 3–16). Secretion of too much growth hormone late in the growth period causes the arms, hands, feet, and facial bones to become enlarged. This condition, called **acromegaly** (AK-row-MEG-uh-lee), distorts appearance in a way that some people have turned into successful careers as sideshow entertainers, wrestlers, and the like.

The pituitary also regulates the functioning of other glands (especially the thyroid, adrenal glands, and ovaries or testes). These glands in turn regulate such bodily processes as reproduction, metabolism, and responses to stress. In women the pituitary also controls the production of milk during pregnancy. Because of its many effects, the pituitary is often called the "master gland." But the master has a master: The hypothalamus, which lies directly above the pituitary in the brain, directs the activity of the pituitary and hence affects glands throughout the body. This then is the major link between the brain and the glandular system (Schally et al., 1977).

The **thyroid gland** consists of tissue found in the neck on each side of the windpipe. The thyroid regulates **metabolism**—the rate at which energy is produced and expended in the body. As a consequence it can have a sizable effect on personality. A person with an overactive thyroid (termed **hyperthyroidism**) tends to be thin, tense, excitable, and nervous. An underactive thyroid (**hypothyroidism**) in an adult can cause inactivity, sleepiness, slowness, and overweight. In infancy hypothyroidism limits development of the nervous system and can bring about severe mental retardation (see Chapter 17).

When you are frightened or angry, a number of important actions take place in your body to prepare it for action:

Highlight 3–2
A Short Topic

Children who lag far behind in growth may suffer lasting emotional scars from rejection by peers or adults. One of the more common causes of limited growth is insufficient production of growth hormone. If this condition is not treated, a child may fall 6 to 12 inches behind age-mates in height. As adults some will be **hypopituitary dwarfs** (HI-po-pih-TU-ih-ter-ee). Such individuals are perfectly proportioned but tiny.

For many years dwarfism could be treated only with injections of human growth hormone. Supplies were extracted from the pituitary glands of human cadavers—a painstaking and expensive process. Now, a relatively cheap synthetic growth hormone has become available. Regular injections of this hormone can raise a hypopituitary child's height by several inches, usually to the short side of average.

Unfortunately, synthetic growth hormone may bring problems as well as good. If not carefully administered, it can cause giantism, acromegaly, diabetes, or other medical problems. There are also ethical concerns. Already, some parents and children have been bitterly disappointed and further upset when the child failed to grow as much as expected after taking the growth hormone. In addition, some children have found it difficult to adjust to becoming more "ordinary." Many go from playing with younger children to being ignored by age-mates. There may even be a risk that some competitive parents will pressure physicians to increase growth of "normal short" children. With all this in mind, perhaps it is fair to say that the success of growth hormone therapy should be measured by increased emotional well-being—not merely by an increase in stature. (Abstracted from Franklin, 1984.)

Your heartbeat and blood pressure are raised; stored sugar is released into the bloodstream for quick energy; the muscles tense and receive more blood; and the blood is prepared to clot more quickly in the event of injury. These changes are brought about by the hormones **adrenaline** and **noradrenaline**, which are produced by the **adrenal**

Fig. 3-16 *Underactivity of the pituitary gland may produce a dwarf; overactivity, a giant.*

glands. (As mentioned earlier, the same substances also act as neurotransmitters.)

The adrenal glands are located just under the back of the rib cage, atop the kidneys. The **adrenal medulla,** or inner core of the adrenal glands, is the source of adrenaline and noradrenaline. The **adrenal cortex,** or outer "bark" of the adrenal glands, produces a second set of important hormones called **corticoids** (KOR-tih-coids). One of their jobs is to regulate salt balance in the body. A deficiency of certain corticoids can evoke a powerful craving for the taste of salt in humans (Beach, 1975). The corticoids also help the body adjust to stress, and they are a secondary source of sex hormones. (For a full discussion of the role of sex glands in development, see Chapter 24.)

Perhaps you have heard about the use of anabolic steroids by athletes who want to "bulk up" or promote muscle growth. These drugs are a synthetic version of one of the male corticoids. Like all of the corticoids, they are quite powerful and therefore dangerous. There is no evidence that they improve performance, and they may cause voice deepening or baldness in women and testicle shrinkage or breast enlargement in men (*Sexual Medicine,* 1980).

An oversecretion of the auxiliary sex hormones can cause **virilism,** in which a woman grows a beard or a man's voice becomes so low it is difficult to understand. Oversecretion in children may cause **premature puberty,** resulting in full sexual development. One of the most remarkable cases on record is that of a 5-year-old Peruvian girl who gave birth to a son (Strange, 1965).

In this brief discussion of the endocrine system, we have considered only a few of the more important glands. Nevertheless, this should give you an appreciation of how completely your behavior and personality are tied to the ebb and flow of hormones in the body. In the upcoming Applications section we return to the brain to see how hand preference relates to brain dominance. In the Exploration that concludes the chapter, we will examine the fascinating effects of stimulating the brain electrically.

Learning Check

Here is a chance to check your memory of the preceding discussions.

1. Three major divisions of the brain are the brainstem or _____, the _____, and the _____.

2. Reflex centers for heartbeat and respiration are found in the (circle):

cerebellum   thalamus   medulla   RF

3. A portion of the reticular formation, known as the RAS, serves as an _____ system in the brain.
a. activating   *b.* adrenal   *c.* adjustment   *d.* aversive

4. The _____ is a final relay or "switching station" for sensory information on its way to the cortex.

5. "Reward" and "punishment" areas are found throughout the _____ system, which is also related to emotion.

6. Redundancy and early plasticity underlie the brain's surprising capacity for recovery from some types of brain injuries in early childhood.   T or F?

7. Undersecretion from the thyroid can cause (circle):

dwarfism   giantism   overweight   mental retardation

8. The body's ability to resist stress is related to the action of the adrenal _____.

Answers: 1. hindbrain, midbrain, forebrain 2. medulla 3. *a* 4. thalamus 5. limbic 6. T 7. overweight, mental retardation (in infancy) 8. cortex

Applications

Handedness—If Your Brain Is Right, What's Left?

In the English language, "what's right is right," but what's left may be wrong. We have left-handed compliments, leftovers, people with "two left feet," those who are left behind, left out, and . . . left-handed. On the other hand (so to speak), we have the right way, the right whale, the right angle, the right-hand man (or woman), righteousness, and . . . the right-handed.

The Sinister Hand   Left-handedness has a long and undeserved bad reputation. Southpaws have been accused of being clumsy, stubborn (for refusing to use their right hand), and maladjusted. One 1930s psychologist described the left-handed as: "Awkward in the house, and clumsy in their games, they are fumblers and bunglers at whatever they do." But as any lefty will tell you, and modern psychology has confirmed, none of this is true. The supposed clumsiness of lefties is merely a consequence of living in a right-handed world: If it can be gripped, turned, folded, held, or pulled, it's probably designed for the right hand. Even toilet handles are on the right side.

What causes handedness? Why are there more right-handed than left-handed people? How do left-handed and right-handed people differ? Does being left-handed really create problems? Are there any benefits to being left-handed? The answers to most of these

questions lead us back to the brain, where handedness begins. Let's see what recent research has revealed about handedness, the brain, and you.

Hand Dominance   To begin with, you might find it interesting to compare your hands by copying the accompanying design on a piece of paper, once with your right hand and once with your left. You should notice a definite superiority in the copy done by your dominant hand. The interesting thing about this exercise is that there's no real difference in the strength or dexterity of the hands themselves. The agility of the dominant hand is an outward expression of superior motor control on one side of the brain (Herron, 1980).

Question: If a person is left-handed, does that mean the right hemisphere is dominant?

Not necessarily. It's true that the right hemisphere controls the left hand, but a left-handed person's language-producing, dominant hemisphere may be on the opposite side of the brain.

Brain Dominance   About 97 percent of right-handers process speech in the left hemisphere and are left-

Applications: Handedness—If Your Brain Is Right, What's Left?

brain dominant. A good 60 percent of left-handers produce speech from the left hemisphere, just as right-handed people do. About a quarter of all lefties, and 3 percent of righties use their right brain for language. And approximately 15 percent of left-handers use *both* sides of the brain for language processing (Corballis, 1980; Herron, 1980).

Question: Is there any way for a person to tell which of his or her hemispheres is dominant?

For a time some psychologists believed that hemispheric dominance could be revealed by eye movements. But recent experiments offer little support for this idea (Erlichman & Weinberger, 1978). A better approach is based on the way you write. Right-handed individuals who write with a straight hand, and lefties who write with a hooked hand, are left-brain dominant for language. Left-handed people who write with their hand below the line, and righties who use a hooked position, are right-brain dominant (Levy & Redd, 1976; Pines, 1980). Are your friends right-brained or left-brained? (See Fig. 3–17.)

Question: How common is left-handedness, and what causes it?

Handedness   Animals, such as monkeys, show definite hand preferences. However, in most animal groups there is a 50-50 split of right and left "handedness." Among humans the split is about 90-10, with right-handedness being most common. The prevalence of right-handedness in humans probably reflects the left brain's specialization for language production (Corballis, 1980). Evidence exists that the majority of humans have been right-handed for at least 50 centuries (Coren & Porac, 1977).

It was long believed that children don't express clear-cut handedness until they are 4 or 5. But a recent study shows that hand preference for many children is stabilized by 18 months of age or earlier (Gottfried & Bathurst, 1983). Such early preferences underscore the fact that handedness cannot be dictated. Parents should never try to force a left-handed child to use the right hand. To do so may invite speech or reading problems because handedness is hereditary (Herron, 1980).

Fig. 3-17   *Recent research suggests that the hand position used in writing indicates which brain hemisphere is used for language. (Redrawn from an illustration by M.E. Challinor.)*

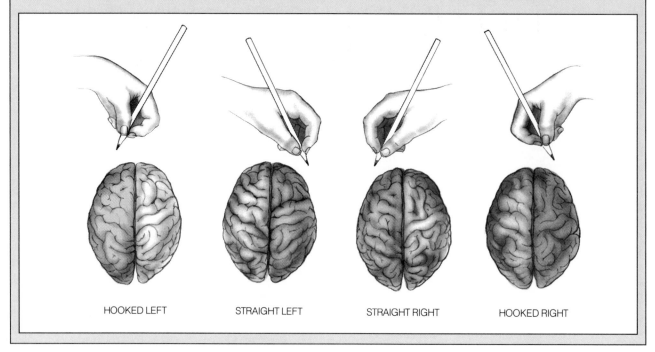

HOOKED LEFT   STRAIGHT LEFT   STRAIGHT RIGHT   HOOKED RIGHT

Applications: Handedness—If Your Brain Is Right, What's Left?

Question: Are there any drawbacks to being left-handed?

Other than the fact that lefties must live in a right-handed world, there seem to be none. A recent large-scale study of high school students in California found no differences in school achievement between left- and right-handers and no physical or mental defects associated with left-handedness (Hardyck et al., 1976). In fact, there may actually be some advantages to being left-handed.

Advantage Left Throughout history a notable number of artists have been lefties—from Leonardo da Vinci and Michelangelo, to Pablo Picasso and M. C. Escher. Conceivably, since the right hemisphere is superior at imagery and visual abilities, there is some advantage to using the left hand for drawing or painting (Pines, 1980). Whether this is true or not, the left-handed do seem better at putting together verbal and pictorial symbols or ideas—which may be why there are more left-handed architects than would be expected (Herron, 1980).

One striking feature of lefties is that they are generally less **lateralized** than right-handed persons are. This means that there is less distinct specialization in the two sides of their brains. In fact, even the physical size and shape of the cerebral hemispheres are more identical in left-handed persons. If you are a lefty, you can take pride in fact that your brain is less lopsided than the brains of your right-handed friends (Corballis, 1980)! In general left-handers are more symmetrical on almost everything, including eye dominance, fingerprints—even foot size (Corballis, 1980).

In some situations less lateralization may be a real advantage. For instance, individuals who are moderately left-handed or ambidextrous seem to have better than average pitch memory, which is a basic musical skill (Deutsch, 1978). Correspondingly, more musicians are ambidextrous than would normally be expected. It's not clear, however, if those who are musically gifted were initially less lateralized or if playing music develops both hands, or possibly both sides of the brain (Pines, 1980). The clearest advantage of being left-handed shows up when there is a brain injury. Because of their milder lateralization, left-handed individuals typically experience less language loss after damage to either brain hemisphere, and they recover more easily (Geschwind, 1979). Maybe having "two left feet" isn't so bad after all.

Learning Check

1. About 97 percent of left-handed people process language on the left side of the brain, the same as right-handed people do.   T or F?
2. Left-handed individuals who write with their hand below the line are right-brain dominant.   T or F?
3. Most animals, like most humans, show a preference for the right limb.   T or F?
4. In general left-handed individuals show less lateralization in the brain and in fact throughout the body.   T or F?
5. A recent study of high school students demonstrated that left-handed individuals are superior in school achievement.   T or F?

Answers: 1. F 2. T 3. F 4. T 5. F

Chapter Summary

- The brain and nervous system are made up of linked nerve cells called *neurons*. Neurons are arranged in long chains and dense networks. They pass information from one to another through *synapses*.
- The basic conducting structures of neurons are *axons*, but *dendrites* (a receiving area), the *soma* (the cell body and also a receiving area), and the *axon terminals* (the branching ends of an axon) are also involved in communication.
- The firing of an *action potential* (nerve impulse) is basically electrical, whereas communication between neurons is chemical. Neurons release chemicals called *neurotransmitters* at the synapse. These cross to *receptor sites* on the receiving cell, causing it to be excited or inhibited. Transmitters called *neuropeptides* appear to regulate activity in the brain.
- Nerves are made of axons and associated tissues. Neurons and nerves in the peripheral nervous system can often *regenerate*; damage in the central nervous system is *permanent*, unless repair is attempted by *implantation* of healthy tissue.
- The nervous system can be divided into the *central nervous system* (the brain and spinal cord) and the *peripheral nervous system*, which includes the *somatic* (bodily) and *autonomic* (involuntary) nervous systems. The autonomic system has two divisions: the *sympathetic* (activating) and the *parasympathetic* (conserving).
- The human brain is marked by advanced *corticalization*, or enlargement of the *cerebral cortex*. The *left cerebral hemisphere* contains speech or language "centers" in most people. It also specializes in writing, calculation, judging time and rhythm, and ordering complex movements. The *right hemisphere* is largely nonverbal. It excels at spatial and perceptual skills, visualization, and recognition of patterns, faces, or melodies.
- "*Split brains*" have been created experimentally in animals, and for medical reasons in humans, by cutting the *corpus callosum*. The split-brain individual shows a remarkable degree of independence between the right and left hemispheres. Under some circumstances the hemispheres function as separate brain units.
- The most basic functions of the *lobes* of the cerebral cortex are: *occipital* lobes—vision; *parietal* lobes—bodily sensation; *temporal* lobes—hearing and language; *frontal* lobes—olfaction, motor control, speech, and abstract thought.
- There are a number of *association* areas on the cortex that are neither sensory nor motor in function. These are related to more complex skills such as language, memory, recognition, and problem solving. Damage to either *Broca's area* or *Wernicke's area* causes speech and language problems known as *aphasias*. Damage in other areas may cause *agnosia*, the inability to identify objects by sight.
- The brain as a whole can be subdivided into three general areas: the *forebrain*, *midbrain*, and *hindbrain*.
- The *subcortex* includes several crucial brain structures. The *medulla* contains centers essential for reflex control of heart rate, breathing, and other "vegetative" functions. The *cerebellum* maintains coordination, posture, and muscle tone. The *reticular formation* directs sensory and motor messages, and part of it, known as the RAS, acts as an activating system for the brain. The *thalamus* carries sensory information to the cortex. The *hypothalamus* exerts powerful control over eating, drinking, sleep cycles, body temperature, and other basic motives and behaviors. The *limbic system*, which is made up of several structures, serves as an emotional system in the brain. It also contains distinct reward and punishment areas and an area known as the *hippocampus* that is important for forming memories.
- The *endocrine system* provides *chemical* communication in the body through the release of *hormones* into the bloodstream. Many of the endocrine glands are influenced by the *pituitary* (the "master gland") which in turn is influenced by the hypothalamus. The endocrine glands influence behavior, body configuration, and even personality.

►►► Exploration

ESB—The Promise and Peril of Brain Control

Question: What is ESB and how is it done?

ESB refers to **electrical stimulation** of the **brain,** a technique that has made direct control over the machinery of the brain a reality. In some instances ESB is capable of calling forth animal and human behavior with almost robotlike precision. ESB begins with **electrode implantation:** the placing of electrical stimulating devices in strategic areas of the brain. Usually, these are fine steel or platinum wires or needles, inserted through the skull, run under the scalp, and collected at a single external socket. By this means as many as two dozen or more separate brain sites can be electrically stimulated on command.

Advances in electronics have made it possible for such electrodes to be activated at a distance by use of radio transmitters and receivers. Further developments promise increasingly smaller receivers and stimulating devices, eventually the size of a postage stamp or smaller. In addition to removing any outward signs of ESB implants, miniaturization may eventually allow placement of a microcomputer in the brain, perhaps as a means of controlling epileptic seizures or of artificially increasing intelligence.

Question: How is ESB used now?

ESB is used extensively in animal research as a means of exploring brain-behavior connections. An important advantage of ESB is that it allows an animal (or person) to function normally, with the brain intact, while the experimenter turns various brain areas on and off. An early ESB experiment by W. R. Hess demonstrated that full-blown rage could be elicited from cats. Since then, ESB has proved capable of putting animals and humans through the paces of most basic behaviors. Stimulation applied to the proper brain area can instantly bring about terror, anxiety, rage, sexual desire, aggression, alertness, escape, eating, drinking, sleeping, movement of limbs, euphoria, memories, speech, tears, and more.

Question: How do humans respond to ESB?

ESB experiments with humans have understandably been limited to situations involving extraordinary medical need. For example, ESB may be used to identify brain areas that are triggering violent outbursts so that such areas may be removed surgically. When tested by ESB, one patient reacted with a sudden outburst of anger on stimulation of the amygdala (ah-MIG-dah-lah, a part of the limbic system), saying, "I feel like I want to get up from this chair! Please don't let me do it! Don't do this to

me. I don't want to be mean!" When asked by the interviewer if she would like to hit him, she said, "Yeah I want to hit something. I want to get something and just tear it up!" The patient was then given a stack of paper, which she tore to shreds (King, 1961). Later, she explained that she had not really been angry at the interviewer but just had an overwhelming desire to hit or destroy anything and everything.

Electrodes at other locations produce decidedly different reactions. Upon stimulation of electrodes in the temporal lobe, one patient giggled and made funny comments, saying she enjoyed the stimulation very much. Repetition of the stimulation made the patient flirtatious and forward, and she ended by openly expressing her desire to marry the therapist. When stimulation ceased, she again became quiet, reserved, and proper, without familiarity or excessive friendliness.

Question: Could ESB be used to control a person against his or her will?

José Delgado of Yale University, who has done some of the most advanced work with ESB, believes it could not. As evidence he cites research on stimulated aggression in animal colonies. Monkeys receiving ESB become aggressive in direct proportion to their rank in the pecking order of the colony.

Exploration: ESB—The Promise and Peril of Brain Control

When they are at the bottom of the pecking order, stimulation causes few attacks on other monkeys. When they are near the top, aggressive outbursts and attacks are easily triggered. Thus, to the question, "Could a ruthless dictator stand at a master radio transmitter and stimulate the brains of a mass of hopelessly enslaved people?" Delgado replies, "Fortunately it is beyond the theoretical and practical limits of ESB."

So at this point in its development, ESB cannot really cause a person to behave like a robot. It is true, as we have seen, that a person's emotional reactivity can be influenced, making the person more aggressive or amorous, for instance. But in most cases the behavioral details of these feelings are modified by the individual's personality and by the situation. If someone were intent on controlling or disrupting the behavior of another person, it would be far easier to do it with drugs. Even minute traces of some drugs, such as LSD, can alter activity throughout the brain. A threat by terrorists to put LSD in a city water supply would be a far more realistic danger than ESB could ever be.

What, then, does the future hold for ESB? Will it provide a way to overcome epileptic seizures, end uncontrollable violence, reverse some forms of mental retardation, or link the brain to a computer? What are the ethical implications of present ESB research? Will more precise brain control become possible? What impact does ESB research have on your conceptions of personality, mind, and free will? (Sources: Delgado, 1969, 1970; London, 1971.)

Learning Check

1. ESB is done primarily by electrically stimulating the spinal cord.   T or F?
2. Stimulation of the amygdala causes a person to become hostile and aggressive.   T or F?
3. Behaviors induced by ESB are, for the most part, unaffected by external circumstances.   T or F?
4. The chance of ESB being used to control the behavior of a large number of people against their will is very low.   T or F?

Answers: 1. F   2. T   3. F   4. T

Questions for Discussion

1. If you could change the brain or nervous system in any way to improve them, how would you do it and why?

2. What effect would you expect a drug to have if it raised the firing threshold for neurons? If it blocked passage of neurotransmitters across the synapse? If it mimicked the effect of a neurotransmitter? If it stimulated the RF? If it suppressed activity in the medulla?

3. Have you known someone who had a stroke or other brain injury? What were the effects? How did the person cope with the injury?

4. A member of your family has been having outbursts of hostile and aggressive behavior. In the past year this person has become virtually uncontrollable. ESB has been recommended as the only remaining possible treatment. Would you condone its use? What limitations (if any) do you think should be imposed on ESB procedures?

5. Do you think a sharp distinction between right- and left-hemisphere function is valid? For example, are there verbal skills involved in music, dance, or art?

6. Robert Ornstein has urged us to recognize that full use of human potential should take advantage of the specialized skills of both cerebral hemispheres. Roger Sperry has charged that "our educational system . . . tends to neglect the nonverbal form of intellect. What it comes down to is that modern society discriminates against the right hemisphere." Do you agree? If you do, what changes would you make in educational systems?

7. What would be some of the possible advantages and disadvantages to having a "split brain"?

8. If a person were kept alive with only the spinal cord intact, what kinds of responses would be possible? What if both the spinal cord and medulla were functioning? The spinal cord, medulla, and cerebellum? The spinal cord, medulla, cerebellum, and subcortex? All brain areas except the association cortex?

9. If your brain were removed, replaced by another, and moved to a new body, which would you consider to be yourself, your old body with the new brain or your new body with the old brain?

10. Can the brain ever expect to understand itself completely? Or is the brain studying the brain like trying to lift yourself by your bootstraps?

11. If the parents of a normal-sized child wanted to give the child growth hormone to make him or her taller, would you consider this ethical? Why or why not?

Chapter 4

The Sensory World and Reality

Chapter Preview
Sensation and Reality

At this very moment you are bathed in a swirling kaleidoscope of light, heat, pressure, vibrations, molecules, radiation, mechanical forces, and other physical energies. Without your senses, all of this would seem like a void of darkness and silence. The next time you drink in the beauty of a sunset, a flower, or a friend, remember this: **Sensation** *makes it all possible.*

It is apparent that the world as we know it is created from sensory impressions. Less obvious is that what passes for "reality" is shaped by the senses. Our sensory organs can detect only a limited range of physical energies. Thus, events go unrecorded when the senses are not attuned to them. We have, for instance, no receptors for atomic radiation, X rays, or microwaves. For this reason it is possible to be injured by each of these energies without being aware of it.

Yellow Is Amazing but Red Is Best *What would the world be like if new senses could be added—if we could "see" gamma rays, "hear" changes in barometric pressure, or "taste" light? We can only guess. It is far easier to imagine losing or regaining a sensory system. Consider the words of Bob Edens, who had his sight restored at age 51 after being blind since birth:*

> I never would have dreamed that yellow is so . . . so yellow. I don't have the words, I'm amazed by yellow. But red is my favorite color. I just can't believe red. I can't wait to get up each day to see what I can see. And at night I look at the stars in the sky and the flashing lights. You could never know how wonderful everything is. I saw some bees the other day, and they were magnificient. I saw a truck drive by in the rain and throw a spray in the air. It was marvelous. And did I mention, I saw a falling leaf just drifting through the air?

If you are ever tempted to take everyday sensory impressions for granted, remember Bob Edens. As his words show, sensation is our window on the world. All our meaningful behavior, our awareness of physical reality, and our ideas about the universe ultimately spring from the senses. It may be no exaggeration then, to claim that our topic for this chapter is quite . . . sensational.

Survey Questions   In general, how do sensory systems function? What are the limits of our sensory sensitivity? How do each of the major senses work, and what causes common sensory problems, such as deafness or color blindness? Why are we more aware of some sensations than others? How can pain be reduced or controlled in everyday situations? What causes motion sickness and what can be done about it?

Resources

Sensory Receptors— What You See Is What You Get

We begin with a paradox. On one hand we have the magnificent power of the senses. In one instant you can view a star light-years away, and in the next you can peer into the microscopic universe of a dewdrop. Yet vision, like the other senses, is also carefully limited in sensitivity, so that it acts as a **data reduction system.** That is, our senses routinely "boil down" floods of information into a select stream of useful data. Such selection can be seen in the fact that "light" is only a small slice of a broader range of energies. In addition to visible light, the **electromagnetic spectrum** includes infrared and ultraviolet light, radio frequencies, television broadcasts, gamma rays, and other energies (see Fig. 4-2). If the eyes were not limited to "light" sensitivity, "seeing" would be like getting hundreds of different "channels" at once. The confusion would be overwhelming. Obviously, *selection* of information is important.

Question: How are selection and data reduction accomplished?

Some selection occurs simply because sensory receptors act as biological *transducers.* A **transducer** is a device that converts one kind of energy into another. For example, a phonograph needle converts *vibrations* into electrical signals. Scrape the needle with your finger and the speakers will blast out sound. However, if you shine a light on the needle, or put it in cold water, the system will remain silent. (The owner of the stereo, however, may get quite loud at this point!) Similarly, each sensory organ is most sensitive to a select range of energy, which it most easily translates into nerve impulses.

As they transduce information, many sensory systems **analyze** the environment into important *features* before sending messages to the brain. For example, frog eyes are especially sensitive to small, dark, moving spots. Researcher Jerome Lettvin (1961) calls sensitivity to this fea-

ture a "bug detector." It seems that the frog's eyes are "wired" to detect bugs flying nearby. But, the insect (spot) must be moving. A frog may starve to death surrounded by dead flies.

In addition to selection and analysis, then, sensory systems **code** important features of the world into messages understood by the brain (Hubel & Wiesel, 1979). To see coding at work, try this simple demonstration:

> Close your eyes for a moment. Then take your fingertips and press firmly on your eyelids. Apply enough pressure to "squash" your eyes slightly. Do this for about 30 seconds and observe what happens. (Persons with eye problems should not try this.)

If you followed the instructions, you probably saw stars, checkerboards, and flashes of color called **phosphenes** (FOSS-feens). The reason for this is that the receptor cells in the eye, which normally respond to light, are also somewhat sensitive to pressure. Notice, though, that the eye is only prepared to code stimulation—including pressure—into *visual* features. As a result you experience *light sensations*, not pressure. Also important in producing this effect is **localization of function** in the brain.

Question: What does localization of function mean?

It means that specific brain areas receive messages from each of the senses. Thus, the sensation you experience depends ultimately on which area of the brain is activated.

One practical implication of such localization is that it may be possible to artificially stimulate specific brain areas to restore sight, hearing, or other senses. For example, researchers have already tested a system that uses a miniature television camera to create electrical signals that are applied to the visual cortex of the brain (Dobelle et al., 1974) (see Fig. 4–1). Unfortunately, artificial vision of this type still faces major hurdles. However, artificial hearing is proving more workable—as we will see later.

It is fascinating to realize that experiences such as

TV camera   Computer   Electrodes

Fig. 4–1 *Artist's concept of an artificial visual system. Images received by an artificial eye would be transmitted to electrodes placed in the visual area of the brain (shown in cutaway view). The artificial eye, which operates like a television camera, might be placed in the eye socket as shown in the drawing. A major barrier to such systems is the brain's tendency to reject implanted electrodes.*

"seeing" and "hearing" ultimately take place in the brain, not in the eye or ear. Each sense organ is only the first link in a long chain that ends in the vast cell and fiber forest of the brain. Much as we may be tempted to think so, our sensory systems simply do not operate like cameras or tape recorders, sending back "pictures" of the world. Rather, they collect, transduce, analyze, code, and transmit a never-ending flow of data to an active, information-hungry brain. This incoming flow of information is what we refer to as **sensation.** (When the brain organizes sensations into meaningful patterns, we speak of *percep-*

Table 4–1 Absolute Thresholds	
Sensory Modality	**Absolute Threshold**
Vision	Candle flame seen at 30 miles on a clear dark night.
Hearing	Tick of a watch under quiet conditions at 20 feet.
Taste	A teaspoon of sugar in 2 gallons of water.
Smell	A drop of perfume diffused into a three-room apartment.
Touch	A bee's wing falling on your cheek from 1 centimeter above.

(From Galanter, 1962.)

tion, which is the topic of Chapter 5.) In a moment we will see how each of the senses operates. But first, let's explore the question of how sensitive we are to our "sensational" world.

Psychophysics— Taking It to the Limit

Question: What is the quietest sound that can be heard? The weakest light that can be seen? The lightest touch that can be felt?

The sense organs are our link to reality. What are their limits? An approach called **psychophysics** provides some answers. In psychophysics, changes in *physical* stimuli are measured and related to *psychological* sensations, such as loudness, brightness, or taste. A basic question psychophysics asks is, "What is the absolute minimum amount of stimulation necessary for a sensation to occur?" The answer defines the **absolute threshold** for a sensory system. For example, if the eardrum moves as little as one-billionth of a centimeter (one-tenth the diameter of a hydrogen atom), a sound can be heard (Bekesy, 1957a). This threshold is so low that your ears would be less sensitive if they were more sensitive! That is, if your ears could detect quieter sounds, you would hear random movements of air molecules. This would cause a constant roaring noise that would make it very difficult to hear anything else.

The absolute threshold for vision is equally spectacular. A **photon** (FOE-tahn) is the smallest possible particle or "package" of light energy, yet it takes only *three* photons of light striking the back of the eye to produce a sensation. This is the equivalent of seeing a candle flame 30 miles away! Table 4–1 gives the approximate absolute thresholds for the five major senses.

It is interesting to note that some sensory systems have upper limits as well as lower ones. For example, when the ears are tested for pitch (higher and lower tones), we find that humans can hear sounds down to 20 **hertz** (vibrations per second) and up to about 20,000 hertz. This is an impressive range, from the lowest rumble of a pipe organ to the highest squeak of a stereo tweeter. Again the lower threshold is as low as practical. If the ears could respond to tones below 20 hertz, you would hear the movements of your own muscles (Oster, 1984). Imagine how disturbing it would be to hear your body creak and groan like an old ship each time you moved.

The 20,000-hertz upper threshold for human hearing, on the other hand, could easily be higher. Dogs, bats, cats, and other animals can hear sounds well above this limit. That's why a "silent" dog whistle (which may make sounds as high as 40 or 50 thousand hertz) can be heard by dogs but not by humans. For dogs the sound exists. For humans it is beyond awareness. It's easy to see how thresholds define the limits of the sensory world in which we live. (If you want to buy a stereo for your dog, you will have a hard time finding one that reproduces sounds above 20,000 hertz!)

Perceptual Defense and Subliminal Perception

Question: Wouldn't the absolute threshold be different for different people?

Not only do absolute thresholds vary from person to person, they also vary from time to time for a single person. The type of stimulus, the state of one's nervous system, and the costs of false "detections" all make a difference. Emotional factors are also important. Unpleasant stimuli, for example, may *raise* the threshold for recognition. This effect is called **perceptual defense.** It was first demonstrated in experiments on the recognition of "dirty" and "clean" words (McGinnies, 1949). So-called dirty words such as *whore, rape, bitch,* and *penis* were briefly flashed on a screen. These words consistently took longer to recognize than did "clean" words such as *wharf, rope, batch,* and *pencil.*

Question: Couldn't it be that people wanted to be really sure they had seen a word like penis *before saying it?*

Yes. For many years psychologists worried about this and other flaws in the original experiment. But later research that avoided these problems suggests that perceptual defense does occur (Erdelyi, 1974). Apparently, it is possible to process information on more than one level and to resist information that causes anxiety, discomfort, or embarrassment (Dember & Warm, 1979).

Question: Is this "subliminal" perception?

Basically, yes. Anytime information is processed below the normal **limen** (LIE-men: threshold or limit) for awareness, it is **subliminal.** Subliminal perception was recently demonstrated by an experiment in which people saw a series of shapes flashed on a screen for $\frac{1}{1000}$ second each. Later, they were allowed to see these shapes, and other "new" shapes, for as long as they wanted. At that time they rated how much they liked each shape. Even though they could not tell "old" shapes from "new," they gave "old" shapes higher ratings (Kunst-Wilson & Zajonc, 1980). Apparently, the "old" shapes had become familiar and thus more "likable"—but at a level below normal awareness.

Question: Could this finding be applied to advertising?

The urge to manipulate shoppers must be strong, since many businesses have tried subliminal advertising over the years. But do subliminal sales pitches actually work? Let's see.

In one early attempt at subliminal advertising, a New Jersey theater flashed the words *Eat popcorn* and *Drink Coca-Cola* on the screen for $\frac{1}{3000}$ second every 5 seconds during movies. Since the words were presented so briefly, they were below the normal threshold for awareness. During the 6 weeks the messages ran, the firm claimed an increase of 57.5 percent in popcorn sales and 18.1 percent in Coca-Cola sales.

In the uproar that followed this "experiment," some states rushed to pass laws against the "invisible sell." However, they really had nothing to fear. Subliminal advertising has proved largely ineffective (McBurney & Collings, 1984). Such early "experiments" appeared to succeed only because they didn't take into account weather conditions, time of year, films shown, type of audience, snack bar displays, and so forth.

To summarize, there is evidence that subliminal perception occurs. However, well-controlled laboratory experiments have shown that subliminal stimuli are basically weak stimuli. An advertiser would be better off using the loudest, clearest, most attention-demanding stimulus available—as most do. Despite the evidence, some advertisers still use subliminal messages. Maybe *they* haven't gotten the message.

Difference Thresholds

Another kind of threshold studied in psychophysics is the **difference threshold.** Here we are asking, "How much must a stimulus change (increase or decrease) before it becomes *just noticeably different?*" The study of just noticeable differences (**JNDs**) led to one of psychology's first natural "laws." Called *Weber's Law* (VAY-bears), it can be roughly stated as: The amount of change needed to produce a JND is a constant *proportion* of the original stimulus intensity.

Question: What does this mean in practice?

Let's take an example. Pretend that you are sitting in a room in which there are 10 candles burning—that is, the original stimulus intensity is 10 candles. Let's say that we begin lighting candles until the room becomes just noticeably brighter. If this takes 3 more candles, how many additional candles would be needed to cause a just noticeable increase in brightness in a room in which 20 candles were burning? Your first guess may be 3, but remember, the

JND is a *proportion*. We will have to light 6 additional candles if we start with 20, 9 if we start with 30, and 12 if we start with 40. Here are Weber's proportions for some common judgments:

Pitch	1/333 (1/3 of 1 percent)
Weight	1/50
Loudness	1/10
Taste	1/5

Notice the big difference in auditory sensitivity (pitch and loudness) compared to taste. Very small changes in hearing are easy to detect. A voice or a musical instrument that is off pitch one-third of 1 percent will be noticeable. For taste we find that a 20 percent change is necessary to produce a JND. If a cup of coffee has 5 teaspoons of sugar in it, 1 more (⅕ of 5) will have to be added before there is a noticeable increase in sweetness. It takes a lot of cooks to spoil the broth.

Weber's Law is really just an approximation because it applies mainly to stimuli in the midrange. For other than pure sensory judgments, it is even more approximate. In spite of this, there is a lesson to be learned from it. Consider judgments of money, for instance. If you discovered that you had been overcharged $5 on the purchase of a shirt, would you return to demand your money? If you discovered that you had been overcharged $5 on the purchase of an automobile, would you return to demand your money? If your answer to the first question is yes, then rationally your answer to the second should be too. It may not be, however, because the larger base price of a car makes $5 seem a very small difference.

It's now time to examine each of the senses in more detail. In the next section we will begin with vision, which is perhaps the most magnificent sensory system of all.

Learning Check

Before you read more, it might be a good idea to stop for a quick check on some of the ideas we have covered.

1. Sensory receptors are biological _____, or devices for converting one type of energy to another.

2. Lettvin found that the frog's eyes are especially sensitive to phosphenes.   T or F?

3. Important features of the environment are transmitted to the brain through a process known as:
   a. phosphenation   *b.* coding   *c.* detection   *d.* programming

4. The minimum amount of stimulation necessary for a sensation to occur defines the _____ _____.

5. A stimulus that causes discomfort or embarrassment may have to be viewed longer before it is perceived because of _____ _____.

6. Subliminal stimuli have been shown to have a powerful effect on the behavior of viewers, especially when embedded in movies.   T or F?

Answers: 1. transducers 2. F 3. b 4. absolute threshold 5. perceptual defense 6. F

Vision— Catching Some Rays

Question: Which of the senses is most essential?

There really isn't an answer to this question. Nevertheless, for most people loss of vision is the single most devastating sensory disability. Because of its tremendous importance, we will explore vision in more detail than the other senses. Let's begin with the basic dimensions of light and vision.

Dimensions of Vision   Recall that the room in which you are sitting is filled with **electromagnetic radiation,** in-

cluding light and other energies. The **visible spectrum** is made up of light of various wavelengths. The spectrum starts at wavelengths of 400 nanometers (nan-OM-et-ers). A nanometer (nm) is one-billionth of a meter. Wavelengths at this end of the spectrum produce sensations of purple or violet. Longer wavelengths of light produce sensations of blue, green, yellow, and orange, until red, with a wavelength of 700 nm, is reached (Fig. 4–2).

This physical property of light, its *wavelength*, corresponds to the psychological experience of **hue,** or the specific color of a stimulus. White light is made up of a mixture of frequencies from the entire spectrum. Colors

WHITE LIGHT

When a white light is directed through a prism, the visible light spectrum results.

PRISM

INVISIBLE LONG WAVES VISIBLE LIGHT SPECTRUM INVISIBLE SHORT WAVES

Infrared rays (beyond red)

Ultraviolet rays (beyond violet)

1500 1000 700 600 500 400 300

Radio TV Microwaves Infra-red U-V X-rays Gamma rays Cosmic rays

Fig. 4–2 *The visible spectrum.*

produced by a very *narrow band* of wavelengths are said to be very **saturated,** or "pure." A third dimension of vision, **brightness,** corresponds roughly to the *amplitude* (or "height") of light waves; light of greater amplitude carries more energy and appears brighter.

Structure of the Eye

Question: Is it true that the eye is like a camera?

If we were willing to push the issue a bit, the eye could be used as a camera. When the light-sensitive back surface of the eye is bathed in alum solution, the last image to strike it will appear like a tiny photograph. This fact might make for a great murder mystery, but it's obviously not much of a way to take a photograph. In any case, several basic elements of eyes and cameras are similar. Both have a **lens** that focuses images on a light-sensitive layer at the back of a closed space. In a camera this layer is the film; in the eye it is a layer of **photoreceptors** (light-sensitive cells) about the size and thickness of a postage stamp, called the **retina** (see Fig. 4–3).

Question: How does the eye focus?

Focusing The front of the eye has a clear covering called the **cornea.** The curvature of this transparent "window" bends light rays inward. Next, the lens, which is elastic, is stretched or thickened by a series of muscles, so that more or less additional bending of light occurs. This bending, fattening, and stretching of the lens is called **accommodation.** In cameras focusing is done more simply—by changing the distance between the lens and the film.

Visual Problems The overall shape of the eye also affects focusing. If the eye is too short, nearby objects cannot be focused, but distant objects are clear. This is *farsightedness,* or **hyperopia** (HI-per-OH-pea-ah). If the eye is too long, the image falls short of the retina, and distant objects cannot be focused. This condition results in *nearsightedness,* or **myopia** (my-OH-pea-ah). When the cornea or the lens is *misshapen,* some of the visual field will be focused and some will be fuzzy, a problem called **astigmatism** (ah-STIG-mah-tiz-em). All three visual problems can be corrected by placing eyeglasses or contact lenses in front of the eye. These added lenses change the path of incoming light to restore crisp focusing (see Fig. 4–4).

Sometimes, with age, the lens grows less flexible and less able to accommodate. Since the lens must do its greatest bending to focus nearby objects, the result is **presbyopia** (prez-bee-OH-pea-ah, "old vision," or farsightedness due to aging). Perhaps you have seen a grandparent or older friend reading a newspaper at arm's length because

Fig. 4–3 *The human eye, a simplified view.*

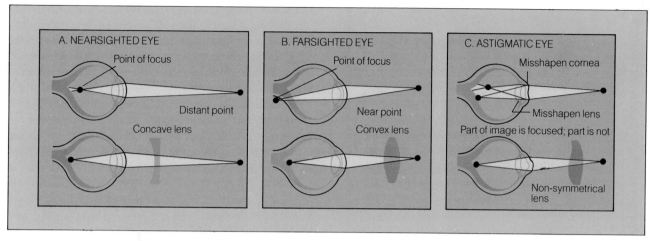

Fig. 4—4 *Visual defects and corrective lenses: (a) A myopic (longer than usual) eye. The concave lens spreads light rays just enough to increase the eye's focal length. (b) A hyperopic (shorter than usual) eye. The convex lens increases refraction (bending), returning the point of focus to the retina. (c) Astigmatic (lens or cornea not symmetrical) eye. In astigmatism parts of vision are sharp and parts are unfocused. Lenses to correct astigmatism are non-symmetrical.*

of presbyopia. Also, if you now wear glasses for nearsightedness, you may need bifocals as you age. Bifocal lenses correct near vision *and* distance vision.

Light Control   There is one more major similarity between the eye and a camera. In front of the lens in both is a mechanism to control the amount of light entering. This mechanism in a camera is the diaphragm; in the eye it is the **iris** (see Fig. 4–5). The iris is a colored circular muscle that expands and contracts to control the size of the **pupil,** or opening at the center of the eye.

The iris is extremely important for normal vision. The retina can adapt to changing light conditions but only very slowly. By making rapid adjustments, the iris allows us to move quickly from darkness to bright sunlight or the reverse. In dim light the pupils **dilate** (enlarge) and in bright light they **constrict** (narrow). At the largest opening of the iris, the pupil is 17 times larger than at the smallest. Were it not for this, you would be blinded for quite some time on walking into a darkened room.

Rods and Cones   At this point our eye-camera comparison breaks down. From the retina on, vision becomes a complex system for analyzing patterns of light (see Highlight 4–1). Besides, the eye would make a very strange camera. First of all, the eye has two types of "film," consisting of receptor cells called **rods** and **cones.** The cones, numbering about 6.5 million in each eye, work best in bright light. They also produce *color* sensations and pick

up fine details. In contrast, the rods, numbering about 100 million, are unable to detect colors. Pure rod vision is black and white. However, the rods are much more sensitive to light than the cones. The rods therefore allow us to see in very dim light.

Compared with the film in a camera, the visual receptors are backward. The rods and cones point toward the *back* of the eye, away from incoming light (see Fig. 4–7). In addition, the "film" has a hole in it. Each eye has a **blind spot** because there are no receptors where the optic nerve leaves the eye (see Fig. 4–8). And last, the eye is constantly in motion. This would be disastrous for a camera, but as we shall see later, motion is essential for normal vision.

Question: Are there other differences between the rods and cones?

Visual Acuity   The cones lie mainly at the center of the eye. In fact there is a small cup-shaped area in the middle

Fig. 4—5 *The diaphragm and iris.*

Highlight 4–1
How the Brain Sees the World

Early ideas of vision often assumed an almost movielike projection of "pictures" to the brain. But, as mentioned in Chapter 3, this mistaken notion immediately raises the question, "Who's watching the movie?" Thanks to the Nobel Prize–winning work of psychobiologists David Hubel and Torsten Wiesel, we now know that vision acts more like a computer than like a television or movie camera.

Hubel and Wiesel directly recorded the activities of single cells in the visual cortex of the brain. As they did, they noted the area of the retina to which each cell responded. Then they shone lights of various sizes and shapes on the retina and recorded how often the corresponding brain cell fired nerve impulses (see illustrations). The results were fascinating. Many brain cells responded only to lines of a certain width or orientation. These same cells didn't get the least bit "excited" over a dot of light or overall illumination. Other cells responded only to lines at certain angles, or lines of certain lengths, or lines moving in a particular direction (Hubel, 1979; Hubel & Wiesel, 1979).

The upshot of such findings is that cells in the brain, like the frog's retina described earlier, act as feature detectors. The brain seems first to analyze incoming information into lines, angles, shading, movement, and other basic features. Then, other brain areas combine these features into meaningful visual experiences. Reading the letters on this page is a direct result of such feature analysis. Given the size of the task, it's little wonder that as much as 30 percent of the human brain may be involved in vision.

Fig. 4–6 *The top drawing (a) shows how much of the total field of vision a "typical" brain cell responds to. The bar graph below (b) illustrates how a brain cell may act as a feature detector. Notice how the cell primarily responds to just one type of stimulus. (Adapted from Hubel, 1979.)*

of the retina called the **fovea** (FOE-vee-ah) that contains *only* cones—about 50,000 of them. If you look at your thumbnail at arm's length, its image just about covers the fovea. Like a newspaper photograph made of many small dots, the tightly packed cones of the fovea produce the greatest visual **acuity,** or sharpness. In other words, vision is sharpest when an image falls on the fovea. It then steadily decreases as images are moved to the edge of the retina.

Figure 4–9 describes a widely used rating system for acuity. If vision can be corrected to no better than 20/200 acuity, a person is considered legally blind. With 20/200 vision the world is nothing but a blur.

Question: What is the purpose of the rest of the retina?

Peripheral Vision Areas outside the fovea also get light, creating a large region of **peripheral** (side) **vision.**

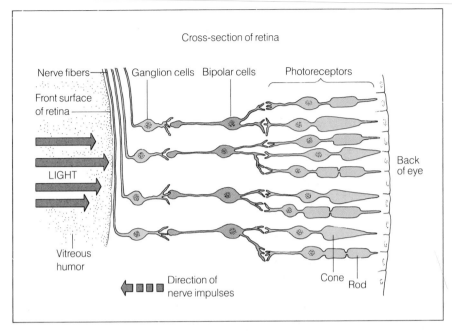

Fig. 4—7 *Anatomy of the retina, light-sensitive element of the eye. Note that light does not fall directly on the rods and cones. It must first pass through the outer layers of the retina. Only about one-half of the light falling on the front of the eye reaches the rods and cones—testimony to the eye's amazing light sensitivity.*

The rods are most numerous about 20 degrees from the center of the retina; hence, much peripheral vision is rod vision. Fortunately, the rods are quite sensitive to *movement*. Thus, while the eye gives its best acuity to the center of vision, it maintains a radarlike scan for movement in side vision. Seeing "out of the corner of the eye" is important for sports, driving, and walking down dark alleys. Those who have lost peripheral vision suffer from **tunnel vision,** a condition much like wearing blinders.

Sailors, pilots, astronomers, and military spotters have long made use of another interesting fact about peripheral vision. Although the rods give poor acuity, they are many

Fig. 4—8 *Experiencing the blind spot. (a) With the right eye closed, stare at the upper right cross. Hold the book about 1 foot from your eye and slowly move it back and forth. You should be able to locate a position that causes the black spot to disappear. When it does, it has fallen on the blind spot. (b) Repeat the procedure described but stare at the lower cross. When the white space falls on the blind spot, the black line will appear to be continuous. This may help you understand why you do not usually experience a blind spot in your visual field.*

Fig. 4–9 *Tests of visual acuity. Above are some common tests of visual acuity. In (a) sharpness is indicated by the smallest grating still seen as individual lines. Part (b) requires that you read rows of letters of diminishing size until you can no longer distinguish them. The Landolt rings (c) require no familiarity with letters. All that is required is a report of which side has a break in it. Normal acuity is designated as 20/20 vision: At 20 feet in distance you can distinguish what the average person can see at 20 feet. If your vision is 20/40, you can see only at 20 feet what the average person can see at 40 feet. If your vision is 20/200, you need glasses! Vision that is 20/12 would mean that you can see at 20 feet what the average person must be 8 feet nearer to see, indicating better than average acuity. American astronaut Gordon Cooper, who claimed to see railroad lines in northern India from 100 miles above, had 20/12 acuity.*

times more responsive to light than are the cones. Since most rods are 20 degrees to each side of the fovea, the best night vision is obtained by looking *next to* an object you wish to see. Test this yourself some night by looking at, and next to, a very dim star.

Color Vision— There's More to It Than Meets the Eye

What would you say is the brightest color? Red? Yellow? Blue? Actually, there are two answers to this question, one for the rods and one for the cones. The differing *maximal color sensitivity* of the rods and cones has practical importance. The cones are most sensitive to the *yellowish green* region of the spectrum. In other words, if all colors are tested in daylight (with each reflecting the same total amount of light), then yellowish green appears *brightest*. The increased use of yellow fire trucks, and of Day-Glo yellow vests worn by roadside work crews, reflects this fact (Fig. 4–10).

Question: To what color are the rods most sensitive?

Remember first that the rods do not produce color. If very dim, colored lights are used, no color will be seen, but one light will appear brighter than the others. When tested this way, the rods are most sensitive to *blue-green* lights. Thus, at night or in dim light, when rod vision prevails, the brightest-colored light will be one that is blue or blue-green. For this reason, police and highway patrol cars in many states now have blue emergency lights for night work. Also, you may have wondered why the taxiway lights at airports are blue. This may seem like a poor choice, but blue is actually highly visible to pilots.

Color Theories

Question: How do the cones record color sensations?

No short answer can do justice to the complexities of color vision, but, briefly, here is the best current explanation. The **trichromatic** (or three-color) **theory** of color vision holds that there are three types of cones, each most sensitive to a specific color: red, green, or blue. Other colors are assumed to result from combinations of these three areas of the spectrum, whereas black and white sensations are produced by the rods.

A basic problem with the trichromatic theory is that four colors seem psychologically primary: red, green, blue, and yellow. A second view, known as the **opponent-process theory,** was developed to explain why you can't have a reddish green or a yellowish blue. According to this theory, the visual system analyzes information into either-or color messages. It is assumed that the visual system can produce messages for either red or green, yellow or blue, black or white. Coding one color in a pair (red, for instance) seems to block the opposite message (green), so a reddish green is impossible, but a yellowish red (orange) can occur. According to the theory, fatigue caused by making one response causes an **afterimage** of the opposite color as the system recovers. To experience an afterimage of this type, see Fig. 4–11 and follow the instructions given there.

Question: Which color theory is correct?

Both! The three-color theory seems to apply to the retina, where three types of visual pigments with sensitivity peaks in approximately the red, green, and blue regions have been found. The opponent-process theory seems to explain events recorded in the optic pathways after information leaves the eye. So both appear to be correct at a particular level in the visual system.

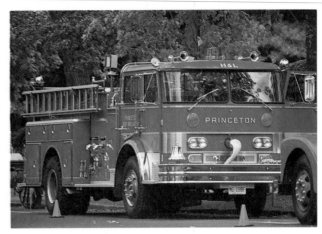

Fig. 4–10 *Yellow-green fire trucks are far more visible in daylight because their color matches the cones' sensitivity peak. However, many cities continue to prefer red trucks because of tradition.*

Color Blindness and Color Weakness

Do you know anyone who regularly draw hoots of laughter by wearing clothes of wildly clashing colors? Or someone who sheepishly tries to avoid saying what color an object is? If so, you probably know someone who is color blind.

Question: What is it like to be color blind? What causes color blindness?

A person who is completely **color blind** sees the world as if it were a black and white movie. How do we know? In a few rare cases people have been color blind in only one eye and can compare (Hsia & Graham, 1965). Two colors of equal brightness look exactly alike to the color-blind individual. The color-blind person either lacks cones or has cones that do not function normally (Rushton, 1975).

Total color blindness is rare. **Color weakness,** or partial

Fig. 4–11 *Negative afterimages. Stare at the dot near the middle of the flag for at least 30 seconds. Then look immediately at a plain sheet of white paper or a white wall. You will see the American flag in its normal colors. Reduced sensitivity in yellow, green, and black receptors in the eye, caused by prolonged staring, results in the appearance of complementary colors. Project the afterimage of the flag on other colored surfaces to get additional effects.*

(a)   (b)   (c)

Fig. 4–12 *Color blindness and color weakness. Photograph on left* (a) *illustrates normal color vision. Middle photograph* (b) *is printed in blue and yellow and gives an impression of what a red-green colorblind person sees. Right image* (c) *simulates total color blindness.*

color blindness, is more common. Approximately 8 percent of the male population (but less than 1 percent of women) are red-green color blind. (Another form of color weakness, involving yellow and blue, is extremely rare.) Red-green color blindness is a recessive, sex-linked trait. This means that it is carried on the X, or female chromosome. Women have two X chromosomes, so if they receive only one defective color gene, they still have normal vision. Color-blind men, however, only have one X chromosome, so they can inherit the defect from their mothers (who are usually not color blind themselves). The red-green color-blind individual perceives both reds and greens as the same color, usually a yellowish brown (Rushton, 1975). (See Fig. 4–12.)

Question: Then how can color-blind individuals drive? Don't they have trouble with traffic lights?

Red-green color-blind individuals have normal vision for yellow and blue, so their main problem is to tell red lights from green. In practice this is not difficult. In the United States the red light is always on top, and the green light is brighter than the red. Also, to help remedy this situation, most modern traffic signals have a "red" light that has a background of yellow light mixed with it, and a "green" light that is really blue-green.

Question: How can a person tell if he or she is color blind?

A common test for color blindness and weakness is the **Ishihara** test. In the test, numbers and other designs made up of dots are superimposed on a background also made

of dots. The background and the numbers are of different colors (red and green, for example). A person who is color blind sees only a collection of dots. The person with normal color vision can detect the presence of the numbers or designs. Figure 4–13 is a replica of the Ishihara test. You should not consider Fig. 4–13 a true test of color vision, but it may give you some idea of whether or not you are color blind.

Dark Adaptation— Let There Be Light!

Question: What happens to the eyes when they adapt to a dark room?

Dark adaptation is the dramatic increase in light sensitivity that occurs after you enter the dark. Consider walking into a theater. If you enter from a brightly lighted lobby, you practically need to be led to your seat. After a short time, however, you can see the entire room in detail (including the couple kissing over in the corner). Studies of dark adaptation show that it takes about 30 to 35 minutes of complete darkness before your eyes reach maximum sensitivity (Fig. 4–14). When dark adaptation is complete, the eye can detect lights 10,000 times weaker than those to which it was originally sensitive.

Question: What causes dark adaptation?

Both the rods and cones contain light-sensitive chemicals known as **visual pigments**. When struck by light, these

ARE YOU COLOR BLIND?

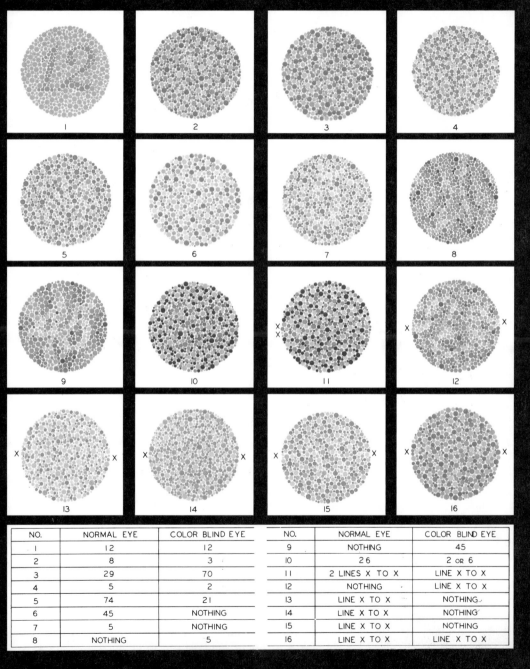

NO.	NORMAL EYE	COLOR BLIND EYE
1	12	12
2	8	3
3	29	70
4	5	2
5	74	21
6	45	NOTHING
7	5	NOTHING
8	NOTHING	5

NO.	NORMAL EYE	COLOR BLIND EYE
9	NOTHING	45
10	26	2 OR 6
11	2 LINES X TO X	LINE X TO X
12	NOTHING	LINE X TO X
13	LINE X TO X	NOTHING
14	LINE X TO X	NOTHING
15	LINE X TO X	NOTHING
16	LINE X TO X	LINE X TO X

Fig. 4-13 *Replica of a test for color blindness.*

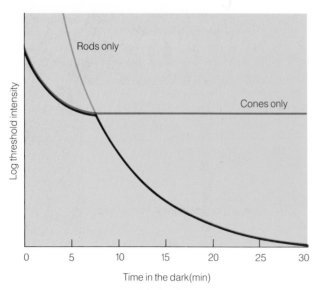

Fig. 4–14 *Time course of dark adaptation. Lowering of the threshold for vision after varying amounts of time in the dark is plotted by the black line. (A lower threshold means that less light is needed for vision.) Colored lines show that the cones adapt first but reach maximum sensitivity quickly. Rods adapt slowly but continue adding to night vision after the cones have adapted.*

Fig. 4–15 *Red light allows dark adaptation to occur because it provides little or no stimulation to the rods.*

pigments bleach, or break down chemically. (The after-images caused by flashbulbs are a direct result of this bleaching.) To restore light sensitivity, the visual pigments must recombine, which takes time. Night vision is due mainly to an increase of the rod pigment, **rhodopsin** (row-DOP-sin). When completely dark-adapted, the human eye is almost as sensitive to light as the eye of an owl.

Before artificial illumination, gradual adaptation at sunset posed few problems. Now we are often caught in temporary semiblindness. Usually this isn't dangerous, but it can be. Even though dark adaptation takes a long time, it can be wiped out by just a few seconds of viewing bright light. Try this demonstration:

Spend 15 or 20 minutes in a darkened room. At the end of this time, you should be able to see clearly. Now, close your left eye and cover it tightly with your hand. Turn on a bright light for 1 or 2 seconds and look at it with your right eye. With the light off again, compare the vision in your two eyes, first opening one and then the other. You will be completely blinded in your right eye.

This experience should convince you of the wisdom of the oft-repeated warning to avoid looking at the headlights of approaching cars during night driving. Under normal conditions glare recovery takes about 20 seconds, plenty of time for an accident. After a few drinks, it may take 30 to 50 percent longer, because alcohol dilates the pupils, allowing more light to enter.

Question: Is there any way to speed up dark adaptation?

The rods are *insensitive* to extremely red light. To take advantage of this lack of sensitivity, submarines and airplane cockpits are illuminated with red light. So are the ready rooms for fighter pilots and ground crews (Fig. 4–15). In each case this allows people to move quickly into the dark without adapting. Since the red light doesn't stimulate the rods, it is as if they had already spent time in the dark.

Question: Can eating carrots really improve vision?

One of the "ingredients" of rhodopsin is **retinal,** which the body makes from vitamin A. When too little vitamin A is available, less rhodopsin is produced. Thus, a person suffering from vitamin A deficiency may develop **night blindness.** In night blindness the person sees normally in bright light while using the cones but becomes totally blind at night when the rods must function. Since carrots are an excellent source of vitamin A, they could improve night vision for someone suffering a deficiency, but not the vision of anyone with an adequate diet (Carlson, 1981).

Learning Check

After such an extended discussion of vision, you may find it helpful to review the following questions.

1. The _____ _____ is made up of electromagnetic radiation with wavelengths between 400 nm and 700 nm.

2. Match:

    ____ Myopia   **A.** Farsightedness

    ____ Hyperopia   **B.** Elongated eye

    ____ Presbyopia   **C.** Farsightedness due to aging

    ____ Astigmatism   **D.** Lack of cones in fovea

                           E. Misshapen cornea or lens

3. In dim light, vision depends mainly on the _____; color and fine detail are produced by the _____.

4. The fovea has the greatest visual acuity due to the large concentration of rods found there.   T or F?

5. Hubel and Wiesel found that cells in the visual cortex of the brain function as _____ _____.

6. The term 20/20 vision means that a person can see at 20 feet what can normally be seen from 20 feet.   T or F?

7. When using the cones, the most visible color is (circle):

    reddish orange   blue-green   yellow-orange   yellowish green

8. The eyes become more sensitive to light at night due to a process known as _____ _____.

Answers:

1. visible spectrum 2. B, A, C, E 3. rods, cones 4. F 5. feature detectors 6. T 7. yellowish green 8. dark adaptation

---

Hearing— Good Vibrations

Rock, classical, jazz, country, pop—whatever your musical taste, you have probably been moved or soothed by the riches of sound. Hearing also provides the brain with a wealth of information not available through the other senses, such as the approach of an unseen car or the information imparted by spoken language.

Question: What is the stimulus for hearing?

If you throw a stone into a quiet pond, a circle of waves will spread from it in all directions. In much the same way sound travels as a series of invisible waves of **compression** (peaks) and **rarefaction** (RARE-eh-fak-shun: valleys) in the air. Any object set in motion—a tuning fork, the string of a musical instrument, or the vocal cords—will produce **sound waves** as it vibrates. The **frequency** of sound waves (the number of waves per second) corresponds to the **pitch** of a sound. The **amplitude**, or "height" of a sound wave

tells how much energy it contains, so amplitude corresponds to **loudness** (see Fig. 4–16).

Question: How are sounds converted to nerve impulses?

What we call the ear is only the **pinna** (PIN-ah), or visible, external part of the ear. In addition to being a good place to wear earrings or balance pencils, the pinna acts like a funnel to concentrate sounds. After they are guided into the ear, sound waves collide with the **eardrum,** which is like a tight drumhead within the ear canal. The sound waves set the eardrum in motion, which in turn causes three small bones called the **auditory ossicles** (OSS-ih-kulz) to vibrate (see Fig. 4–17). The third ossicle is attached to a second membrane, or drumhead, called the **oval window.** As the oval window moves back and forth, it makes waves in a fluid within the **cochlea** (KOCK-lee-ah). The cochlea is really the organ of hearing, since it is here that waves in the fluid are detected by tiny **hair cells,** which generate nerve impulses to be sent to the brain.

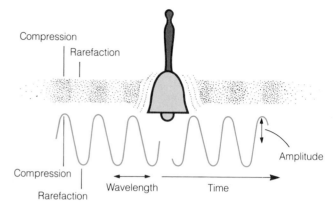

Fig. 4—16 *Waves of compression in the air, or, vibrations are the stimulus for hearing. The frequency of sound waves determines their pitch. The amplitude determines loudness.*

Fig. 4—17 *Anatomy of the ear. The entire ear is a mechanism for changing waves of air pressure into nerve impulses. Inset in foreground shows that as the stapes move the oval window, the round window bulges outward, allowing waves to ripple through fluid in the cochlea. The waves move membranes near the hair cells, causing the cells to bend. The hair cells then generate nerve impulses carried to the brain. (See enlarged cross sections of cochlea.)*

Highlight 4—2
Artificial Hearing

The late Helen Keller, who was blind and deaf from early infancy, once commented: "Silence sits immense upon my soul." If Keller were alive today, there is a chance her hearing could be partially restored. Researchers have recently found that in many cases of "nerve" deafness, the nerve is actually intact. This finding has spurred development of **cochlear implants** that bypass hair cells and stimulate the auditory nerves directly (see Fig. 4–18). As you can see, wires from a microphone carry electrical signals to an external coil. A matching coil under the skin picks up the signals and carries them to one or more areas of the cochlea. Early implants allowed recipients to hear only low-frequency sounds, such as a dog's bark or the horn of a speeding car. Newer multichannel models make use of place theory to separate higher and lower tones. This has allowed some formerly deaf persons to hear human voices and other higher frequency sounds (Franklin, 1984).

   At present, artificial hearing remains crude. Most implant recipients describe the sound as "like a radio that isn't quite tuned in." In fact 30 percent of adults who have tried implants have given up on them (Dreyfuss, 1985). But the implants are sure to improve. And even now it is hard to argue with

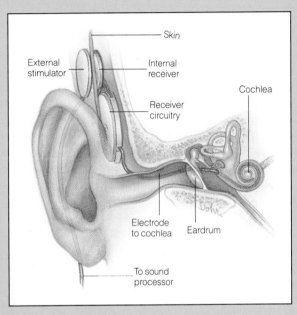

Fig. 4—18 *A cochlear implant, or "artificial ear."*

enthusiasts like 22-year-old Kristen Cloud. Shortly after Ms. Cloud received an implant, she was able to hear a siren and avoid being struck by a speeding car (Williams, 1984). She says simply, "The implant saved my life."

Question: How are higher and lower sounds detected?

The **frequency theory** of hearing states that as pitch rises, nerve impulses of the same frequency are fed into the auditory nerve. This explains how sounds up to about 4000 hertz reach the brain. But higher tones require a different explanation. The **place theory** of hearing states that high tones register most strongly at the base of the cochlea (near the oval window). Lower tones, on the other hand, mostly move hair cells near the outer tip of the cochlea. Pitch is therefore signaled by the area of the cochlea most strongly activated. Place theory also explains why hunters sometimes lose hearing in a narrow pitch range. Hunter's notch, as this is called, occurs when hair cells are damaged in the area activated by the pitch of gunfire.

Question: What causes other types of deafness?

Deafness   There are three principal types of deafness. **Conduction deafness** occurs when the eardrums or ossicles are damaged or immobilized by disease or injury. Such damage reduces the transfer of sounds to the inner ear. In many cases conduction deafness can be overcome by a hearing aid, which makes sounds louder and clearer. **Nerve deafness** is a hearing loss resulting from damage to the hair cells or auditory nerve. Hearing aids are of no help in this case, because auditory messages are completely blocked from reaching the brain. However, a new artificial hearing system is making it possible for some victims of nerve deafness to break through the wall of silence. (See Highlight 4–2.)

A third problem, called **stimulation deafness,** is of special interest, because many jobs, hobbies, and pastimes can cause it. Stimulation deafness occurs when very loud sounds damage hair cells in the cochlea (as in hunter's notch). If you work in a noisy environment, or if you enjoy loud music, motorcycling, snowmobiling, hunting, or similar pursuits, you may be risking stimulation deafness. The hair cells, which are about as thick as a cobweb, are extremely fragile and easily damaged.

Question: How loud must a sound be to be hazardous?

The danger of hearing loss depends on both the loudness of sound and the length of exposure. Daily exposure to 85 decibels or more may cause permanent hearing loss. Short periods of exposure to 120 decibels (a rock concert) may cause a **temporary threshold shift,** or temporary loss of hearing. Even brief exposure to 150 decibels (jet airplane nearby) can cause permanent deafness (Apfel, 1977; Lipscomb, 1974).

You might find it interesting to check the decibel ratings of some of your activities in Fig. 4–19 as a way of estimating hearing risk. Notice that music, as well as noise, can do damage. People who sit directly in front of the speaker columns at highly amplified musical concerts run considerable risk of hearing loss. "Walkman" style stereo headphones also present a danger. If the sound from the headset you are wearing can be heard by someone standing next to you, the volume is probably damaging your ears.

If a ringing sensation known as **tinnitus** (tin-NYE-tus) follows exposure to loud sounds, chances are that hair cells have been damaged (McFadden & Wightman, 1983; Dunkle, 1982). Almost everyone experiences tinnitus at times. But after repeated sounds that produce this warning, you can expect to become permanently hard-of-hearing (Apfel, 1977). The next time you are exposed to an excessively loud sound, remember Figure 4–19 and take precautions against damage. (Remember, too, that for temporary ear protection fingers are always handy.)

Fig. 4–19 *The loudness of sound is measured in decibels. Zero decibels is the faintest sound most people can hear. Sound in the range of 110 decibels is uncomfortably loud. Prolonged exposure to sounds above 85 decibels may damage the inner ear. Rock music, which may rate 120 decibels, is known to have caused hearing loss in musicians and may affect audiences as well. Sounds of 130 decibels pose an immediate danger to hearing.*

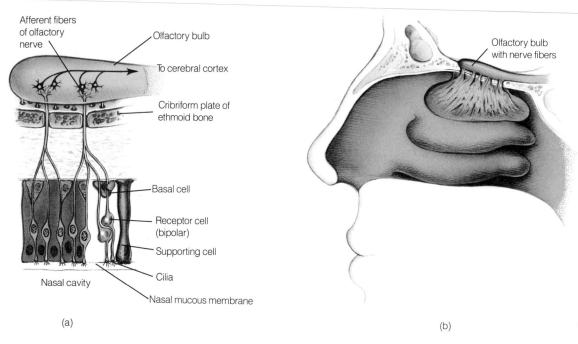

Fig. 4–20   *Receptors for the sense of smell (olfaction). Olfactory nerve fibers respond to gaseous molecules. Receptor cells are shown in cross section at left of part (a).*

Smell and Taste—The Nose Knows When the Tongue Can't Tell

Unless you are a wine taster, a perfume blender, chef, or gourmet, you may think of **olfaction** (smell) and **gustation** (taste) as least important among the senses. Certainly, a person could survive without these two **chemical senses.** Just the same, the chemical senses occasionally prevent poisonings and daily add pleasure to our lives. Let's see how they operate.

The Sense of Smell   The receptors for smell respond primarily to gaseous molecules carried in the air. As air enters the nose, it passes over millions of nerve fibers embedded in the lining of the upper nasal passages. Airborne molecules passing over the exposed fibers trigger nerve signals that are sent to the brain (see Fig. 4–20).

Question: How are different odors produced?

This is still something of a mystery. One hint comes from the fact that it is possible to develop a sort of "smell blindness" for a single odor. This loss, called an **anosmia** (an-NOSE-me-ah) suggests that there are specific receptors for different odors. Indeed, scientists have noticed that molecules having a particular odor are quite similar in shape.

Specific shapes have been identified for the following odors: *floral* (flowerlike), *camphoric* (camphorlike), *musky* (Have you ever smelled a sweaty musk ox?), *minty* (mintlike), and *etherish* (like ether or cleaning fluid). Scientists currently believe that there are different shaped "holes," or depressions, on the odor receptors. Like a piece fit in a puzzle, a molecule produces an odor when it matches up with a hole of the same shape. This is called the **lock and key theory.** Although there are some exceptions, the theory seems to explain many odors.

Taste   There are at least four basic taste sensations: sweet, salt, sour, and bitter. We are most sensitive to bitter, next to sour, less sensitive to salt, and least sensitive to sweet. This order may have helped prevent poisonings during earlier times when humans foraged for food, because bitter and sour foods are more likely to be inedible.

Question: If there are only four tastes, how can there be so many foods with different flavors?

Flavors seem more varied than suggested by the four taste qualities because we tend to include sensations of texture, temperature, smell, and even pain ("hot" chili peppers) along with taste. Smell is particularly important in determining flavor. Small bits of apple, potato, and onion

Fig. 4–21 *Receptors for taste: (a) Position of receptors (taste buds) especially sensitive to four taste qualities; (b) Detail of a taste bud within the tongue. The buds also occur in other parts of the digestive system.*

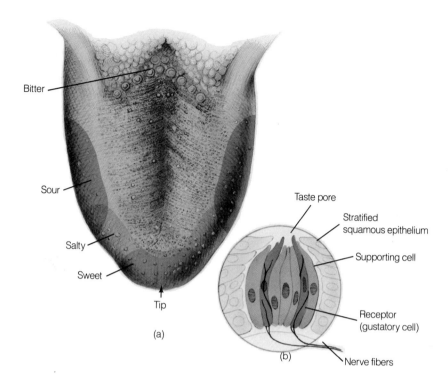

Bitter

Sour

Salty

Sweet

Tip

(a)

Taste pore

Stratified squamous epithelium

Supporting cell

Receptor (gustatory cell)

Nerve fibers

(b)

"taste" almost exactly alike when the nose is plugged. It is probably no exaggeration to say that subjective flavor is one-half smell. This is why food loses its "taste" when you have a cold.

The four primary tastes are detected by **taste buds** located mainly on the top of the tongue but also at other points inside the mouth (see Fig. 4–21). As food is chewed, it dissolves and enters the taste buds, where it sets off nerve impulses to the brain. As you can see in Fig. 4-21, taste receptors are not equally distributed: Some areas of the tongue are more sensitive to each of the tastes than others.

Question: People seem to have very different tastes. Why is that?

Some differences are genetic. The chemical phenylthiocarbamine (FEN-ul-thi-oh-CAR-bah-meen), or PTC, tastes bitter to about 70 percent of those tested and has no taste for the other 30 percent. The sense of taste also varies with age. Taste cells have a life of only several days. With aging, cell replacement slows down, so the sense of taste diminishes (Beidler, 1963). This is why many foods you disliked in childhood have become acceptable to you as an adult. Children who will not eat vegetables, spinach, liver, and so on may be having a very different taste ex-

perience than the adult urging the child to eat. Aside from this fact, however, most taste preferences are acquired. Would you eat the coagulated secretion of the modified skin glands of a cow after it had undergone bacterial decomposition? If you would, you are a *cheese* fancier (Matthews & Knight, 1963)!

The Somesthetic Senses— Flying by the Seat of Your Pants

A gymnast "flying" through a routine on the uneven bars may rely as much on the **somesthetic senses** as on vision. Even the most routine activities, such as walking, running, or passing a sobriety test, would be impossible without somesthetic information from the body.

Question: What are the somesthetic senses?

The somesthetic senses (*soma:* body; *esthetic:* feel) include the **skin senses** (touch), the **kinesthetic senses** (receptors in the muscles and joints that detect body position and movement), and the **vestibular senses** (receptors in the inner ear that signal balance—and cause motion sickness). Because of their importance, let us focus on the skin senses.

Skin receptors produce at least five different sensations: *light touch*, *pressure*, *pain*, *cold*, and *warmth*. Receptors with particular shapes appear to specialize somewhat in various sensations (see Fig. 4–22). However, the surface of the eye, which only has free nerve endings, produces all five sensations, so receptor shape is not critical (Carlson, 1981). Altogether, the skin has about 200,000 nerve endings for temperature, 500,000 for touch and pressure, and 3 million for pain.

Question: Does the number of receptors in an area of skin relate to its sensitivity?

Yes. Your skin could be "mapped" by applying heat, cold, touch, pressure, or pain to points all over your body. This procedure would show that the skin receptors are found in varying numbers and that sensitivity corresponds roughly to the number of receptors in a given area. As a rough-and-ready illustration, try this two-point touch test:

> The density of touch receptors on various body areas can be checked by having a friend apply two pencil points to your skin a number of times, varying the distance between the points each time. Without looking, you should respond "one" or "two" each time. Record the distance between the pencils whenever you experience the touch as two points rather than one.

You should find that two points are recognizable when they are ⅒ inch apart on the fingertips, ¼ inch on the nose, and 3 inches at the middle of the back. Generally

Fig. 4–22 *The skin senses include touch, pressure, pain, cold, and warmth. This drawing shows different forms the skin receptors can take. Other shapes were once recognized, but most turned out to be variations of the shapes shown. The only clearly specialized receptor is the Pacinian corpuscle, which is highly sensitive to pressure. Free nerve endings are receptors for pain and any of the other sensations. For reasons that are not clear, cold is sensed near the surface of the skin, and warmth is sensed deeper. (Carlson, 1981.)*

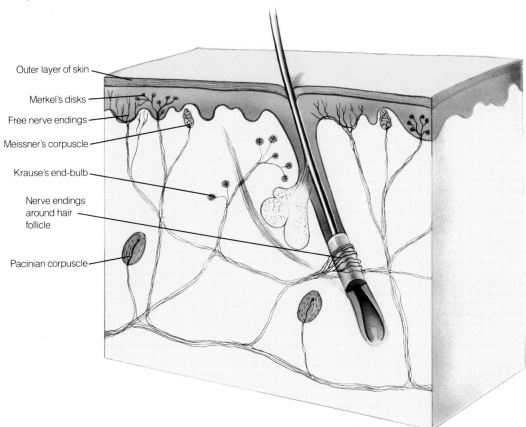

Outer layer of skin

Merkel's disks

Free nerve endings

Meissner's corpuscle

Krause's end-bulb

Nerve endings around hair follicle

Pacinian corpuscle

speaking, important areas such as the lips, tongue, face, hands, and genitals have higher concentrations of receptors.

Question: There are many more pain receptors than other kinds. Why is pain so heavily represented, and does the concentration of pain receptors also vary?

Like the other skin senses, pain receptors vary in their distribution. There is an average of about 232 pain points per square centimeter behind the knee, 184 per centimeter on the buttocks (an area preferred by many parents for spankings), 60 on the pad of the thumb, and 44 on the tip of the nose (Geldard, 1972). (Is it better, then, to be pinched on the nose than behind the knee? It depends on what you like!)

Actually, there are two kinds of pain. Pain carried by *large* nerve fibers is sharp, bright, fast, and associated with specific body areas. This is the body's **warning system.** Give yourself a small jab with a pin and you will feel this type of pain. As you do this, notice that warning pain quickly disappears. Much as we may dislike warning pain, it is usually a signal that the body has been, or is about to be, damaged. Without warning pain we would be unable to detect or prevent injury (Melzack & Dennis, 1978).

A second type of pain is carried by *small* nerve fibers. This type is slower, nagging, aching, widespread, and very unpleasant. It gets worse if the pain stimulus is repeated. This is the body's **reminding system** (Melzack & Dennis, 1978). A sad thing about the reminding system is that it often produces agony even when the reminder is useless, as in terminal cancer or when pain continues after an injury has healed. Later in the chapter we will return to pain to learn how it can be controlled. If you got carried away with the pin demonstration, maybe you should read ahead now. . . .

Adaptation, Attention, and Gating— Tuning In and Tuning Out

Even though each of the senses we have described is continuously active, many sensory events never reach awareness. One reason for this is *sensory adaptation*, a second is *selective attention*, and a third is *sensory gating*. Let's see how information gets filtered by these processes.

Sensory Adaptation Think about walking into a house where fried fish, sauerkraut, and head cheese were prepared for dinner. (Some dinner!) You would probably pass out at the door, yet people who have been in the house for some time will be unaware of the food odors

because of **sensory adaptation.** Sensory adaptation refers to a decrease in sensory response that accompanies a constant or unchanging stimulus.

Fortunately, the olfactory (smell) receptors are among the most quickly adapting. When exposed to a constant odor, they send fewer and fewer nerve impulses to the brain until the odor is no longer noticed. Adaptation to sensations of pressure from a wristwatch, waistband, ring, or glasses is based on the same principle. Sensory receptors generally respond best to *changes* in stimulation. As David Hubel says, "We need above all to know about changes; no one wants or needs to be reminded 16 hours a day that his shoes are on" (Hubel, 1979).

Question: If change is necessary to prevent sensory adaptation, why doesn't vision undergo adaptation like the sense of smell does? If you stare at something, it certainly doesn't go away.

The rods and cones, like other receptor cells, would respond less to a constant stimulus were it not for the fact that the eye normally makes thousands of tiny movements every minute. These movements are caused by tremors in the eye muscles known as **physiological nystagmus** (nih-STAG-mus). Although they are too small to be seen, these movements shift visual images from one receptor cell to another. Constant shifting ensures that images always fall on fresh, unfatigued receptors. Evidence for this comes from experiments in which subjects are fitted with a special contact lens that has a miniature slide projector attached to it (see Fig. 4–23a). Since the projector follows the exact movements of the eye, an image can be stabilized on the retina. When this is done, projected geometric designs fade from view within a few seconds (Pritchard, 1961). You can get the same effect by staring at Figure 4–23b. Since the lighter circle does not form a distinct edge, the retina adapts to the brightness difference, and the circle gradually disappears.

Selective Attention Also dependent on the functioning of sensory systems is the "seat-of-your-pants phenomenon." As you sit reading this chapter, receptors for touch and pressure in the seat of your pants are sending nerve impulses to your brain. Even though these sensations have been present all along, you were probably not aware of them until just now. The seat-of-your-pants phenomenon is an example of **selective attention.** Through selective attention, we are able to tune in on any of the many sensory messages bombarding us while excluding others. Another familiar example of this is the "cocktail party effect." When you are in a group of people, surrounded by voices, you can still select out and attend to the voice of the person with whom you are conversing. Or if that person gets dull, you can eavesdrop on conversations all over the room. (Be sure to smile and nod your head occasionally!)

Question: What makes this possible?

Selective attention appears to be based on the ability of various brain structures to select and divert incoming sensory messages (see Chapter 3). But what about messages on their way to the brain? Is it possible that some are blocked while others are allowed to pass? Recent evidence suggests there are **sensory gates** that control the flow of incoming nerve impulses in just this way.

Sensory Gating   A fascinating example of sensory gating is provided by the work of Ronald Melzack and Patrick Wall, who are studying "pain gates" in the spinal cord (Melzack & Dennis, 1978; Wall, 1976). Melzack and Wall noticed, as you may have, that one type of pain will sometimes cancel another. This suggests that pain messages from different nerve fibers pass through the same neural "gate" in the spinal cord. If the gate is "closed" by one pain message, other messages may not be able to pass through.

Question: How is the gate closed?

Messages carried by large, fast nerve fibers seem to close the spinal pain gate directly. Doing so can prevent slower, "reminding system" pain from reaching the brain. Pain clinics use this effect by applying a mild electrical current to the skin. Such stimulation, felt only as a mild tingling, can greatly reduce more agonizing pain (Melzack & Dennis, 1978).

Messages from small, slow fibers seem to take a different route. After going through the pain gate, they pass on to a "central biasing system" in the brain. Under some circumstances the brain then sends a message back down the spinal cord, closing the pain gates (Melzack & Dennis, 1978) (see Fig. 4–24). Melzack and Wall believe this type of gating explains the pain-killing effects of **acupuncture.** As the acupuncturist's needles are twirled, heated, or electrified, they activate small pain fibers. These relay through the biasing system to close the gates to intense or chronic pain.

Acupuncture has an interesting side effect not predicted by sensory gating. People undergoing acupuncture often report feelings of light-headedness, relaxation, or euphoria. How are these feelings explained? The answer seems to lie in the body's newly discovered ability to produce opiatelike chemicals. To combat pain the brain releases a chemical called **beta-endorphin** (BAY-tah–en-

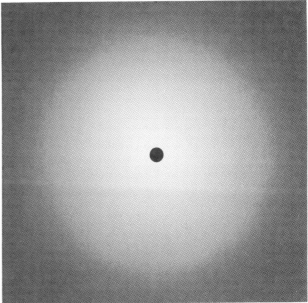

Fig. 4–23   *Stabilized images. (a) Miniature slide projector attached to a contact lens moves each time the eye moves. As a result the projected image disappears in a few seconds because it does not move on the retina. (b) A similar effect occurs when changes in brightness do not define a distinct edge. In this case eye movements cannot prevent adaptation: Therefore, if you stare at the dot, the lighter area will disappear. (After Cornsweet, 1970.)*

DOR-fin), which is similar to morphine (Snyder & Childers, 1979). (Endorphins belong to a class of brain chemicals known as enkephalins discussed in Chapter 3.) Both acupuncture and electrical stimulation cause a buildup of endorphins in the brain. In other words, the nervous sys-

Fig. 4—24 *Diagram of a sensory gate for pain. A series of pain impulses going through the gate may prevent other pain messages from passing through. Or, pain messages may relay through a "central biasing mechanism" that exerts control over the gate, closing it to other impulses.*

Fig. 4—25 *An acupuncturist's chart. Modern research has begun to explain the pain-killing effects of acupuncture. (See text.)*

tem makes its own "drugs" to block pain. Actually, this ties in nicely with the idea of pain gates. The central biasing system, which closes pain gates in the spinal cord, is highly sensitive to morphine and other opiate painkillers (Melzack & Dennis, 1978).

The discovery of endorphins and their pain-killing effect has caused quite a stir in psychology. At long last it appears possible to explain a number of puzzling phenomena, including runner's "high," masochism, acupuncture, and the euphoria sometimes associated with childbirth and painful initiation rites in primitive cultures. In each instance there is reason to believe that pain and

stress cause the brain to release endorphins (Kruger & Liebskind, 1984). These in turn induce feelings of pleasure or euphoria similar to morphine intoxication (Cannon et al., 1978). The "high" often felt by long-distance runners serves as a good example of this effect. In one experiment subjects were tested for pain tolerance. After running 1 mile, each was tested again. In the second test all could withstand pain about 70 percent longer than before. The runners were then given naloxone, a drug that blocks the effects of endorphins. Following another mile run the subjects were tested again. This time they had lost their earlier protection from pain (Haier et al., 1981). People who say they are "addicted" to running may be closer to the truth than they realize. And more importantly, we may at last have an explanation for those hardy souls who take hot saunas followed by cold showers!

Since you may not want to try acupuncture or electrical stimulation to control everyday pain, the Applications section that follows describes some practical ways of reducing pain. Before we turn to this useful topic, here's a Learning Check.

Learning Check

1. Which of the following is *not* important for the transduction of sound?   (circle)

   pinna   ossicles   phosphenes   oval window   hair cells

2. Daily exposure to sounds with a loudness of _____ decibles may cause permanent hearing loss.

3. Cochlear implants have been used primarily to overcome
    a. conduction deafness   *b.* stimulation deafness   *c.* nerve deafness   *d.* tinnitus

4. Olfaction appears to be at least partially explained by the _____ theory of molecule shapes and receptor sites.

5. From the standpoint of survival, we are fortunate that bitter tastes register primarily on the tip of the tongue.   T or F?

6. Which of the following is a somesthetic sense?   (circle)

    gustation   olfaction   rarefaction   kinesthesis

7. Warning pain is carried by _____ nerve fibers.

8. Sensory adaptation refers to an increase in sensory response that accompanies a constant or unchanging stimulus.   T or F?

9. The brain-centered ability to influence what sensations we will receive is called   (circle):

    sensory gating   central adaptation   selective attention   sensory biasing

10. The pain-killing effects of acupuncture appear to result from _____ _____.

Answers:
1. phosphenes 2. 85 3. c 4. lock and key 5. F 6. kinesthesis 7. large 8. F 9. selective attention 10. sensory gating

---

Applications

Controlling Pain—This Won't Hurt a Bit

Earlier sections of this chapter have dealt with useful information about each of the senses. Because so many applications have already been discussed, this will be a short discussion. Let's see how several ideas from this chapter can help you cope better with pain.

There are many indications that pain may be controlled psychologically. In India, fakirs pierce their cheeks with needles or sit on beds of spikes. In other cultures people endure tatooing, stretching, cutting, burning, and the like, with little apparent pain. How is such insensitivity achieved? There is no evidence that these people lack normal pain responses. Very likely the answer lies in four factors that can be used by anyone to alter the amount of pain felt in a particular situation. These are: (1) **anxiety**, (2) **control**, (3) **attention**, and (4) **interpretation**.

Anxiety   The basic sensory message of pain can be separated from emotional reactions to it (Melzack, 1978). Studies have consistently shown that fear or high levels of anxiety increase pain (Barber, 1959). A dramatic reversal of this effect is the surprising *lack* of pain displayed by soldiers wounded in battle. Being excused from further combat apparently produces such relief that it leaves many soldiers insensitive to wounds that would agonize a civilian (Melzack, 1974).

Control   A moment's reflection should convince you that pain over which you have no control is particularly upsetting. Loss of control seems to increase pain by increasing anxiety and emotional distress. People who are allowed to regulate, avoid, or control a painful stimulus suffer less (Craig, 1978). In general, the more control one *feels* over a painful stimulus, the less pain experienced (Kruger & Liebskind, 1984).

Attention   Distraction can also radically reduce pain. Pain, even though it is highly persistent, can be selectively tuned out (at least partially) just like any other sensation. Subjects in one experiment who were exposed to intense pain experienced the greatest relief when they were distracted by the task of viewing color

Applications: Controlling Pain—This Won't Hurt a Bit

slides and describing them aloud (Kanfer & Goldfoot, 1968). In another experiment pain was lessened when subjects concentrated on trying to name all their high school courses and teachers (Ahles et al., 1983). For the same reason you may have temporarily forgotten about a toothache or similar pain while absorbed in a movie or book.

Interpretation   The meaning or interpretation given a painful stimulus also affects pain (Keefe, 1982). For example, if you give a child a swat on the behind while playing, you'll probably get a burst of laughter. Yet the same swat given as punishment may bring tears. Childbirth provides a similar example. In some cultures birth is considered a relatively painless natural event, which it usually is for women reared in the culture. In our culture childbirth tends to be associated with fear and stress (Bresler & Trubo, 1979). It's not surprising, then, that painkillers are often required by women giving birth in the United States. The effects of interpretation have also been demonstrated in the lab. In one experiment it was found that thinking of pain as pleasurable (denying the pain) greatly increased pain tolerance (Neufeld, 1970).

Coping with Pain

Question: How can these facts be applied?

In a sense they have already been applied to childbirth. **Prepared childbirth training,** which emphasizes birth without drugs or painkillers, utilizes all four factors. To prepare for natural childbirth, the prospective mother learns in great detail what to expect at each stage of labor. This greatly relieves her fears and anxieties. During labor she pays attention to important sensations indicating the progress of labor and adjusts her breathing accordingly. Her attention is directed to sensations other than pain, and her positive attitude is maintained by use of the term *contractions* rather than *labor pains.* Finally, because of her months of preparation, and because of her active participation, she feels *in control* of the situation.

Reduced anxiety, redirected attention, and added control can be applied to other painful circumstances. In any situation where pain can be anticipated (a trip to the doctor, dentist, and so on), lowered anxiety may be achieved by making sure that you are *fully informed.* Be sure that everything that will happen or could happen to you is explained, and fully discuss any fears you have. If you are physically tense, the use of relaxation exercises can help lower your level of arousal. (Relaxation techniques are described in detail in the Chapter 23 Applications section. The desensitization procedure described there may also help reduce anxiety.)

Distraction and Reinterpretation   Some dentists are now equipped to help you shift attention away from pain. Patients are actively distracted with video games and with headphones carrying music. Some dentists even put a clothespin on the patient's ear as a pain aid. In other situations you can shift attention away from pain by focusing on some external object. Pick a tree outside a window, a design on the wall, or some other stimulus and examine it in great detail. Prior practice in meditation can be a tremendous aid to such attention shifts. (Meditation techniques are described in Chapter 6.) Recent research suggests that distraction of this type works best for mild or brief pain. For chronic or strong pain, reinterpretation is more effective (McCaul & Malott, 1984).

Question: Is there any way to increase control over a painful stimulus?

Counterirritation   Practically speaking, the possibilities may be limited. You may be able to arrange a signal with a doctor or dentist that will give you control over whether a painful procedure will continue. A second possibility is more unusual. Ronald Melzack's gate-control theory of pain suggests that sending *mild* pain messages to the spinal cord and brain may effectively close the neurological gates to more severe or unpredictable pain. Medical texts have long recognized this effect. Physicians have found that intense surface stimulation of the skin can control pain from other parts of the body, and that a brief, mildly painful stimulus can relieve more severe pain. Such procedures, known as **counterirritation,** are evident in some of the oldest techniques used to control pain: applying ice packs, hot-water bottles, or mustard packs to other parts of the body (Melzack, 1974).

This suggests a way to minimize pain that is based

Applications: Controlling Pain—This Won't Hurt a Bit

on increased control, counterirritation, and production of endorphins. If you pinch yourself, you can easily *create and endure* pain equal to that produced by many medical procedures (receiving an injection, having a tooth drilled, and so on). The pain doesn't seem too bad because you have control over it, and it is predictable. This fact might be used to *mask* one pain with a second painful stimulus that is under your control. For instance, if you are having a tooth filled, try pinching

yourself or digging a fingernail into a knuckle while the dentist is working. Focus your attention on the pain you are creating, and increase its intensity any time the dentist's work becomes more painful. This suggestion may not work for you, but casual observation suggests that it can be a useful technique for controlling pain in some circumstances. Generations of children have used it to take the edge off of a spanking.

Learning Check

1. Like heightened anxiety, increased control tends to increase subjective pain.   T or F?
2. In one experiment, subjects given the task of viewing color slides and describing them aloud experienced relief from pain.   T or F?
3. Imagining a pleasant experience can be an effective way of reducing pain in some situations.   T or F?
4. The concept of counterirritation holds that relaxation and desensitization are key elements of pain control.   T or F?

Answers   1. F   2. T   3. T   4. F

Chapter Summary

- Sensory organs *transduce* physical energies into nerve impulses. Due to limited responsiveness, selectivity, *feature detection*, and *coding* patterns, the senses act as *data reduction systems*. Sensory response can be partially understood in terms of *localization of function* in the brain.

- The minimum amount of physical energy necessary to produce a sensation defines the *absolute threshold*. The amount of change necessary to produce a *just noticeable difference* in a stimulus defines a *difference threshold*. The study of thresholds and related topics is called *psychophysics*.

- Threatening or anxiety-provoking stimuli may raise the threshold for recognition, an effect called *perceptual defense*. Any stimulus below the level of conscious awareness is said to be *subliminal*. There is some evidence that *subliminal perception* occurs, but subliminal advertising is largely ineffective.

- The *visible spectrum* consists of electromagnetic radiation in a narrow range. The eye is in some ways like a camera, but ultimately it is a visual system, not a photographic one. Individual cells in the visual cortex of

the brain act as feature detectors to analyze visual information.

- Four common visual defects, correctable with glasses, are *myopia* (nearsightedness), *hyperopia* (farsightedness), *presbyopia* (loss of accommodation), and *astigmatism*.

- The *rods* and *cones* are *photoreceptors* making up the *retina* of the eye. The rods specialize in night vision, black and white reception, and motion detection. The cones, found exclusively in the *fovea* and otherwise toward the middle of the eye, specialize in color vision, *acuity* or perception of fine detail, and daylight vision. Much *peripheral vision* is supplied by the rods.

- The rods and cones differ in color sensitivity. Yellowish green is brightest for cones, blue-green for the rods (although they will see it as colorless). Color vision is explained by the *trichromatic theory* in the retina and the *opponent-process theory* in the visual system beyond the eyes.

- Total color blindness is rare, but 8 percent of males and 1 percent of females are red-green color blind or color weak. Color blindness is a sex-linked trait carried on the X chromosome. Color blindness is revealed by the *Ishihara test*.

■ *Dark adaptation*, an increase in sensitivity to light, is caused by increased concentration of visual pigments in both the rods and the cones, but mainly by recombination of *rhodopsin* in the rods. Vitamin A deficiencies may cause *night blindness*.

■ *Sound waves* are the stimulus for hearing. They are transduced by the *eardrum, auditory ossicles, oval window, cochlea*, and ultimately, the *hair cells*. The *frequency* and *place theories* of hearing together explain how various pitches are sensed. Three basic types of deafness are: *nerve deafness, conduction deafness*, and *stimulation deafness*.

■ *Olfaction* (smell) and *gustation* (taste) are *chemical* senses responsive to airborne or liquified molecules. The *lock and key* theory partially explains smell. Specific areas on the tongue are more responsive to sweet, salty, sour, and bitter tastes.

■ The *somesthetic* senses include the *skin senses, vestibular senses*, and *kinesthetic senses*. The skin senses include touch, pressure, pain, cold, and warmth. Sensitivity to each is related to the number of receptors present.

■ Incoming sensations are affected by *sensory adaptation* (a reduction in the number of nerve impulses sent), by *selective attention* (selection and diversion of messages in the brain), and by *sensory gating* (blocking or alteration of messages flowing toward the brain). Selective gating of pain messages apparently takes place in the spinal cord.

■ Pain is greatly affected by *anxiety, attention, control* over the stimulus, the *interpretation* placed on an experience, and by *counterirritation*. Pain can therefore be reduced by controlling these factors.

Exploration

Sensation in Space—Adapting to an Alien Environment

On television, astronauts are often shown playfully enjoying the acrobatics made possible by weightlessness (Fig. 4–26). But adapting to life in space is not as easy or pleasant as such images imply (Johnson, 1984). Indeed, if you were to ride in the space shuttle, chances are about 50-50 that your first experience in orbit would be throwing up (Joyce, 1984). At least one-half of all astronauts have suffered from **space adaptation syndrome,** or "space sickness."

Question: Is that like sea sickness?

Space Sickness   Space sickness is a type of motion sickness. Like sea sickness, car sickness, and air sickness, its initial signs are dizziness and mild disorientation. However, space sickness usually does not produce the pallor, "cold sweating," and nausea so common on earth. In most types of motion sickness, these signs warn that vomiting is about to occur. But in space, vomiting is usually sudden and unexpected. Seeing another astronaut drift by upside down or viewing the earth at an odd angle is often all it takes to trigger repeated vomiting. (Connors, Harrison & Atkins, 1985).

The Vestibular System

Question: What causes motion sickness?

Motion sickness is directly related to the vestibular system (Fig. 4–27). Fluid-filled sacs called **otolith**

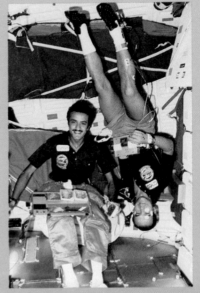

Fig. 4–26   *Weightlessness presents astronauts with a real challenge in sensory adaptation.*

organs (OH-toe-lith) contain tiny crystals in a soft, gelatinlike mass. The tug of gravity or rapid head movements can cause the mass to shift. This, in turn, stimulates hairlike receptor cells, allowing us to sense gravity and movement.

Three fluid-filled tubes called the **semicircular canals** are also part of the vestibular system. If you could climb inside these tubes, you would find that head movements cause the fluid to swirl about. As the fluid moves, it bends a small "flap" or "float" within a wider part of the canal, called an **ampulla** (am-PULL-ah). This bending again stimulates hair cells that signal head rotation.

Motion Sickness   The most widely accepted explanation of motion sickness is the **sensory conflict theory.** According to the theory, dizziness and nausea occur when sensory information from the vestibular system fails to match information received from the eyes and body. You can create an example of sensory conflict by turning around repeatedly until you become dizzy. Doing so sets the fluid spinning in the semicircular canals. When you stop, the fluid continues to swirl about, so the brain thinks your head is still moving. This causes the eyes to move involuntarily and makes the world seem like it is spinning.

On earth information from the vestibular system, vision, and kinesthesis usually matches. However, in a heaving, pitching boat, car, or airplane, a serious mismatch can occur—causing disorientation, and finally, heaving of another kind.

Question: Why would sensory conflict cause nausea?

The most popular theory is that evolution is to blame (or thank). Many poisons disturb the coordination of messages from the vestibular system, vision, and the body. Therefore, we may have evolved so that we react to sensory conflict by vomiting to expel poison. (The value of this reaction, however, may be of little comfort to anyone who has ever been "green" and miserable with motion sickness.)

Exploration: Sensation in Space—Adapting to an Alien Environment

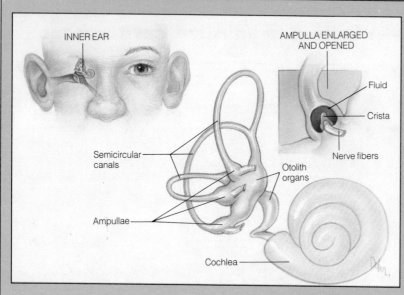

INNER EAR

AMPULLA ENLARGED
AND OPENED

Fluid

Crista

Nerve fibers

Semicircular
canals

Otolith
organs

Ampullae

Cochlea

Fig. 4—27 *The vestibular system.*

In space, sensory conflict can be especially intense. During weightlessness merely pulling on one's shoes can result in a backward somersault. Under such conditions the otolith organs send unexpected signals to the brain, and head movements are no longer confirmed by the semicircular canals. Few of the messages the brain receives from the vestibular system and kinesthetic receptors agree with a lifetime of past experience (Engle & Lott, 1980).

Question: How long does it take to adapt to weightlessness?

Space sickness usually disappears in 2 or 3 days. Recent research suggests that this adaptation occurs because astronauts shift to using visual cues instead of vestibular information. Later, this same shift can cause "earth sickness." Immediately after returning to earth (especially after very long missions), some astronauts have experienced dizziness and nausea. All had considerable difficulty in standing with their eyes closed for the first day or two (von Baumgarten et al., 1984).

How to Minimize Motion Sickness

Researchers trying to prevent space sickness have learned a great deal about what helps and what doesn't. The following points may be of some aid to you here on Earth.

■ Medical treatment for space sickness has concentrated on drugs. The most successful so far is scopolamine, which is available by prescription. Nonprescription sea sickness pills also offer some protection. Alcohol and other intoxicating drugs, however, usually make motion sickness worse.

■ Soviet cosmonauts have had some success with a system that limits head movements for the first 2 days in space. In a boat, car, or airplane it helps to move your head as little as possible. You may even want to place a towel around your neck to restrict head movement. (If it doesn't help, you may soon find another use for it!)

■ To minimize sensory conflict, stay out of the cabin on boats. In cars and airplanes try closing your eyes. Or, as an alternative, fixate your eyes on an unmoving point (such as the horizon) or look above the horizon at the unmoving sky.

■ If possible you should lie down. The otoliths are less sensitive to vertical movements when you are horizontal, and your head will move less.

■ Anxiety seems to intensify motion sickness. Some of the astronauts have had success at learning to focus their attention on pleasant, distracting thoughts. If you do the same, be sure to also breathe slowly and deeply. (Breathing can, in fact, be a good focus for attention [Nicogossian & Parker, 1982].)

■ Space sickness is only one of the behavioral challenges of space travel. In fact, the long-term effects of space flight are still largely unknown. Although space missions now seem routine, astronauts remain true pioneers in a strange and alien sensory environment.

Exploration: Sensation in Space—Adapting to an Alien Environment

Learning Check

1. At least 50 out of every 200 astronauts have suffered from space sickness.   T or F?
2. Head movements are detected primarily in the semicircular canals, gravity by the otolith organs.   T or F?
3. Sensory conflict theory appears to explain space sickness, but it does not seem to apply to other types of motion sickness.   T or F?
4. The drug amphetamine has been used successfully to prevent motion sickness.   T or F?

Answers   1. F 2. T 3. F 4. F

Questions for Discussion

1. Is your brain sitting on a laboratory table somewhere? It is theoretically possible that your brain was donated to science some time ago. Let's say that it was preserved and recently reactivated and that a sophisticated computer is artificially generating patterns of nerve activity in the cortex by mimicking normal sensory messages in the nerves. These messages duplicate the sights, sounds, odors, and sensations of sitting in a college classroom. If this were happening—right now—could you tell? Would you be able to discover that you had no body? Defend your answer.

2. William James once said, "If a master surgeon were to cross the auditory and optic nerves, then we would hear lightning and see thunder." Can you explain what James meant?

3. Let's say that you would like to design a system that uses touch to convey "images" to a blind person. How would you proceed? What would be the advantages and disadvantages of using various body areas (hands, back, forehead, and so on)?

4. What changes would be likely to take place if the absolute thresholds for vision and hearing were changed so that we could see infrared and ultraviolet light and hear sounds up to 50,000 cycles per second? (Consider lighting systems, the design of stereo equipment, and so forth.)

5. In Zen Buddhism there is a familiar *koan*, or riddle, that says, "Last night I dreamt I was a butterfly. How do I know today that I am not a butterfly dreaming I am a man?" Can you relate this to the idea that we construct a version of reality out of the more basic world of physical energies surrounding us?

6. Why do you think your voice sounds so different when you hear a tape recording of yourself speaking? (Hint: How else might vibrations from the voice reach the cochlea?)

Chapter 5 | Perception

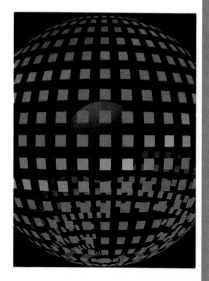

Chapter Preview
Murder!

The following is a true account. Only the degree of exaggeration has been changed for educational purposes.

I was in a supermarket when a girl suddenly came running around a corner. She looked back and screamed, "Stop! Stop! You're killing him! You're killing my father!" Naturally I was interested! As I hurriedly retraced her path, I was greeted by a grisly scene. There was a man stretched out on the floor with another on top of him. The guy on top was huge; at 6 feet 6 inches tall and 300 pounds, he looked only half human. He had his victim by the throat and was beating his head against the floor. There was blood everywhere. I decided to do the right thing. I ran. . . .

By the time the store manager and I returned to the "scene of the crime," the police were just arriving. It took quite a while to straighten things out, but here are the facts that emerged: The "guy on the bottom," had passed out and hit his head. This caused the cut (actually quite minor) that accounted for the "blood everywhere." The "guy on top" had seen the first man fall and was trying to prevent him from further injuring himself while unconscious. He was also loosening the man's collar.

If I had never returned, I would have sworn in court that I had seen a murder. The girl's description completely determined my own perceptions. This perhaps is understandable. But what I will never forget is the shock I felt when I met the "murderer"—the man I had seen a few moments before, in broad daylight, as a huge, vicious, horrible-looking creature. The man was not a stranger. He was a neighbor of mine. I had seen him dozens of times before. I know him by name. He is a rather small man.

The last chapter discussed sensation, the process of bringing information into the nervous system. This chapter is about **perception,** or how we assemble sensations into a usable "picture" of the world. As we perceive events, the brain actively selects, organizes, and integrates sensory information. These mental processes are done so automatically that we are rarely aware of them. It may, in fact, take misperceptions as drastic as the one just described to call attention to this marvelous process. Perception creates faces, melodies, works of art, illusions, and on occasion, "murders" out of the raw material of sensation. Let us see how this is accomplished.

Survey Questions   What are perceptual constancies and what is their role in perception? What basic principles do we use to group sensations into meaningful patterns? How is it possible to see depth and to judge distance? What effect does learning have on perception? How is perception altered by motives, values, and expectations? How reliable are eyewitness reports? Is extrasensory perception possible?

Resources

Perceptual Constancies— Taming an Unruly World

What would it be like to have your vision restored after a lifetime of blindness? In reality a first look at the world can be disappointing. A newly sighted person must *learn* to identify objects, read clocks, numbers, and letters, and to judge sizes and distances (Senden, 1960). Indeed, learning to "see" can be quite frustrating. Richard Gregory (1977) has described the experiences of Mr. S. B., a 52-year-old cataract patient who had been blind since birth.

After an operation restored his sight, Mr. S. B. struggled to use his vision. At first, for instance, he could only judge distance in situations already familiar to him. One day, he was found crawling out of his hospital room window to get a closer look at the automobile traffic on the street. His curiosity is understandable, but he had to be restrained. His room was on the fourth floor!

Question: How could Mr. S. B. try to crawl out of a fourth-story window? Couldn't he at least tell distance from the size of the cars?

No, because using size to judge distance requires familiarity with the appearance of objects. Try holding your left hand a few inches in front of your eyes and your right hand at arm's length. The image of your right hand should be about half the size of your left hand. Still, because of the countless times you have viewed your hands from different distances, you know your right hand has not shrunk. This is called **size constancy**: The perceived size of an object remains the same even though the size of its retinal image changes.

In order to perceive your hand accurately, you had to draw on past experience. Some perceptions—like seeing a line on a piece of paper—are so basic they seem to be **native** (inborn). But much perception is **empirical,** or based on prior experience (Julesz, 1975). For example, Turnbull (1961) tells of the time he brought a Pygmy from the dense rain forests of Africa to the vast African plains. The Pygmy had no past experience with seeing objects at great distance. Hence, the first time he saw a herd of buffalo in the distance, he thought they were a swarm of insects. Imagine his confusion when he was then driven toward the animals. He concluded that witchcraft was being used to fool him because the "insects" seemed to grow into buffalo before his eyes.

Perhaps you have also experienced the failure of size constancy in unfamiliar situations. When viewed from an airplane, cars, houses, and people no longer seem normal in size; instead, they begin to look like toys.

A second important constancy is **shape constancy.** Shape constancy can be demonstrated by looking at this page from directly overhead and then from an angle. Obviously, the page is rectangular, but most of the time the image that reaches your eye is distorted. In spite of this, there is no tendency for you to assume the book changes shape when the image does. (For additional examples see Fig. 5–1.)

Let's say that you are outside in bright sunlight with a friend who is wearing a white blouse. Suddenly a cloud shades the sun. It might seem that the blouse would grow dimmer, but it still appears bright white. This happens because the blouse continues to reflect a larger *proportion* of light than surrounding objects. The principle of **brightness constancy** states that the apparent brightness of an object stays the same under changing lighting conditions. It's interesting to note, though, that brightness constancy applies only when objects receive the same amount of light. If a gray piece of paper is placed in bright light and a white piece of paper is next to it, in deep shadow, the gray will look white and the white will look gray.

To summarize, the energy patterns reaching our senses are constantly changing, even when they come from the same object. Size, shape, and brightness constancy rescue us from a potentially confusing world in which objects would seem to shrink and grow, change shape as if made of rubber, and light up or fade like neon lamps. Establishing these constancies was only one of the hurdles Mr. S. B. faced in learning to "see." In the next section we will consider some others.

Fig. 5–2 *A reversible figure-ground design. Do you see two faces in profile or a wineglass?*

Perceptual Grouping— Getting It All Together

William James said that "to the infant the world is just a big, booming, buzzing confusion." Like an infant, Mr. S. B. had to find meaning in his visual sensations. He was soon able to tell time from a large wall clock and to recognize block letters he had previously known only from touch. At a zoo he recognized an elephant from descriptions he had heard. However, handwriting meant nothing to him for more than a year after he regained his sight, and many objects remained meaningless to him until he touched them. Thus, while Mr. S. B. had visual *sensations*, his ability to *perceive* remained limited.

Question: How are sensations organized into meaningful perceptions?

The simplest organization is to group some sensations into an object, or "figure," that stands out on a plainer background. **Figure-ground** organization is probably inborn, since it is the first perceptual ability to appear when a cataract patient regains sight (Hebb, 1949). In normal figure-ground perception only one figure is seen. However, in **reversible figures** figure and ground can be switched. In Fig. 5–2 it is equally possible to see either a wineglass figure on a dark background or two face profiles on a white background. As you shift from one possibility to the other, you should get a clear sense of what figure-ground organization means.

Fig. 5–1 *Shape constancy. (a) When a door is open, its image actually forms a trapezoid. Shape constancy is indicated by the fact that it is still perceived as a rectangle. (b) With great effort you may be able to see this design as a collection of flat shapes. However, if you maintain shape constancy, the distorted squares strongly suggest the surface of a sphere. (From "Spherescapes 1," by Scott Walter & Kevin McMahon, 1983.)*

Question: What causes the formation of a "figure"?

The Gestalt psychologists studied this question in detail. Even if you were seeing for the first time, they concluded, the following factors would bring some order to your perceptions (refer to Fig. 5–3).

1. **Nearness.** Stimuli that are near each other tend to be grouped together (see Fig. 5–3*a*).
2. **Similarity.** "Birds of a feather flock together"—stimuli that are similar in size, shape, color, or form tend to be grouped together (see Fig. 5–3*b*).
3. **Continuation, or continuity.** Perceptions tend toward simplicity and continuity. In Fig. 5–3*c* it is easier to visualize a wavy line on a squared-off line than it is to see a complex row of shapes.
4. **Closure.** Closure refers to the tendency to *complete* a figure, so that it has a consistent overall form. Each of the drawings in Fig. 5–3*d* has one or more "gaps," yet each is perceived as a recognizable figure. The

Fig. 5–3 *Perceptual grouping illustrations.*

Fig. 5—4 *An example of perceptual organization. Once the camouflaged insect (known as a Giant Walkingstick) becomes visible, it is almost impossible to view the picture again without seeing it.*

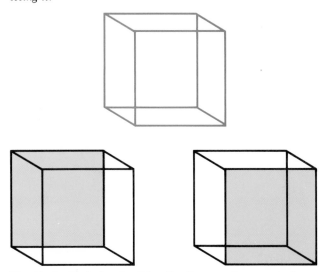

Fig. 5—5 *Necker's cube. Visualize the top cube as a wire box. If you stare at the cube, its organization will change. Sometimes it will seem to project upward, like the lower left cube; other times it will project downward. The difference lies in how the brain interprets the same information.*

Fig. 5—6 *An impossible figure—the "three-pronged widget."*

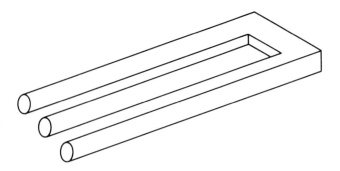

white "shapes" that appear in the middle of the right two drawings in Fig. 5–3*d* are called **illusory figures** (Parks, 1984). Even young children see these implied shapes, despite knowing that they are "not really there." Illusory figures reveal that our tendency to form shapes—even with minimal cues—is powerful.

In addition to these principles, learning and past experience greatly affect perceptual organization. Contrast Mr. S. B.'s immediate recognition of letters to his inability to read handwriting. Also, take a moment and look for the camouflaged insect in Fig. 5–4. **Camouflage** patterns are those that break up figure-ground organization. If you had never seen an insect before, could you have located the one pictured? Mr. S. B. would have been at a total loss to find meaning in such a picture.

In a way we are all detectives, seeking patterns in what we see. In this sense a meaningful pattern represents a **perceptual hypothesis,** or "guess" held until the evidence contradicts it. Have you ever seen a "friend" in the distance, only to have the friend turn into a stranger as you drew closer? Pre-existing ideas and expectations *actively* guide our interpretation of sensations (McBurney & Collings, 1984).

The active nature of perceptual organization is perhaps most apparent in the case of **ambiguous stimuli** (patterns allowing more than one interpretation). If you look at a cloud, you may discover dozens of ways to organize its contours into fanciful shapes and scenes. Even clearly defined stimuli may permit more than one interpretation. Stare at the design in Fig. 5–5 if you doubt the active and fluctuating nature of perception. In some instances a stimulus may present such a conflict that perceptual organization becomes impossible. For example, the tendency to make a three-dimensional object out of a drawing is frustrated by the "three-pronged widget" (Fig. 5–6), an **impossible figure.** Impossible figures are patterns that cannot be organized into stable or consistent images of three dimensional objects.

Question: Is the ability to understand drawings learned?

The best evidence so far on this question comes from studies of prehistoric cave paintings, drawings made by the blind, and the reactions of adults unfamiliar with drawing. Such studies suggest that some types of information in drawings are universally recognized. Humans almost always appear to understand lines that represent the *edges of surfaces.* We also have no problem with a single line used to depict the *parallel edges* of a narrow object, such as a rope. One thing that we *do not* easily recognize is lines that show color boundaries on the surface of an object (Kennedy, 1983).

To illustrate the last point, let's pay a brief visit to the Songe, a small tribe in Papua New Guinea. Before they were tested, the Songe had never made nor seen line drawings—not even doodles scratched on the ground. As a test, the Songe were shown drawings like those in Fig. 5–7. When this was done, they easily recognized the hand and the parrot from simple outlines. But lines showing color boundaries confused them. The half-moons on the fingernails, for example, made them think that the nails had been damaged and new ones were growing in. Similarly, they thought the parrot must have been cut repeatedly. This was true even though the lines in the drawing match color markings of parrots found in Songe territory (Kennedy, 1983).

One of the most amazing feats of perceptual organization deserves a separate discussion. Our capacity to create three-dimensional space from flat retinal images and from two-dimensional drawings is explored in the next section.

Fig. 5–7 *Stimuli similar to those used by Kennedy (1983) to study the kinds of information universally recognized in drawings. (See text for explanation.)*

Learning Check

Try these questions before reading more.

1. Which of the following are subject to basic perceptual constancy? (circle)

   figure-ground   size   ambiguity   brightness   continuity   closure   shape   nearness

2. The first and most basic perceptual organization to emerge when sight is restored to a blind person is:
   a. continuity *b.* nearness constancy *c.* recognition of numbers and letters *d.* figure-ground

3. At times, meaningful perceptual organization represents a _____, or "guess," held until the evidence contradicts it.

4. Ambiguous figures have more than one meaningful organization.   T or F?

5. The design known as Necker's cube is a good example of an impossible figure.   T or F?

6. There is evidence that humans universally recognize line drawings depicting the edges of _____ and narrow parallel lines.

   Answers: 1. size, brightness, shape 2. *d* 3. hypothesis 4. T 5. F 6. surfaces.

Depth Perception— What If the World Were Flat?

Depth perception is the ability to see three-dimensional space and to accurately judge distances. Without depth perception you would be unable to successfully drive a car or ride a bicycle, play catch, shoot baskets, thread a needle, or simply navigate around a room. The world would look like a flat surface.

Question: Mr. S. B. had trouble with depth perception after his sight was restored. Does this mean that depth perception is learned?

Some psychologists (nativists) hold that depth perception is inborn. Others (the empiricists) view it as learned. Most likely, depth perception is partly learned and partly innate. Evidence of innate depth perception comes from work with the **visual cliff** (see Fig. 5–8). The visual cliff is basi-

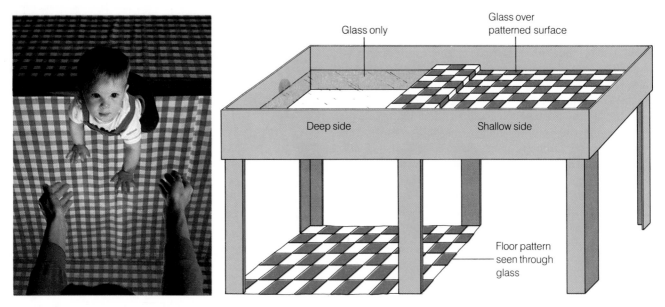

Fig. 5—8 *Human infants and newborn animals refuse to go over the edge of the visual cliff.*

cally a table covered with glass. On one side there is a checkered surface directly beneath the glass. On the other side, the checkered surface is 4 feet below. This makes the glass look like a tabletop on one side and a cliff or drop-off on the other.

In a test for depth perception, 6- to 14-month-old infants were placed in the middle of the visual cliff. This gave them the choice of crawling to the "shallow" side or the "deep" side. (The glass prevented them from doing any "skydiving" if they chose the deep side.) The majority of infants chose the shallow side. In fact most refused the deep side even when their mothers tried to call them toward it (Gibson & Walk, 1960). Psychologist Jane Gwiazada has recently tested babies in another interesting way. Gwiazada fits infants with goggles that make some designs stand out three-dimensionally, while others remain flat. By monitoring the babies' head movements, Gwiazada can tell when the infants first become aware of the 3-D designs. For most infants this occurs at age 4 months, give or take about 2 weeks. Together with evidence from the visual cliff, this work suggests that a basic level of depth perception is innate.

Question: Then why do some babies crawl off of tables or beds?

As soon as infants become active crawlers, they refuse to cross the deep side of the visual cliff (Campos et al., 1978). But even babies who perceive depth may not be able to catch themselves if they slip. A lack of coordina-tion—not an inability to see depth—probably explains most "crash landings" after about 4 months of age.

Question: How do adults perceive depth?

A number of **depth cues** combine to produce our experience of three-dimensional space. Depth cues are features of the environment, or messages from the body, that supply information about distance and space. Some cues will work with just one eye (**monocular cues**), while others require two eyes (**binocular cues**).

Muscular Cues   As their name implies, muscular cues come from within the body. One is **accommodation,** a monocular cue for depth perception. You may recall from Chapter 4 that the lens in each eye must bend or bulge to focus nearby objects. Sensations coming from the muscles that support the lens are channeled back to the brain. Differences in these sensations help us judge distances that fall within about 4 feet of the eyes. Beyond 4 feet accommodation contributes little to depth perception. Obviously, accommodation is more important to a watchmaker or a person trying to thread a needle than it would be to a basketball player or an airline pilot.

A second bodily source of depth is **convergence,** a binocular cue. When you look at a distant object, the lines of vision from your eyes are parallel. However, when you look at something 50 feet or less in distance, your eyes must converge (turn in) to focus the object (see Fig. 5–9).

You are probably not aware of it, but whenever you

estimate a distance under 50 feet (as when you approach a stop sign, play catch, or zap flies with your personal laser), you are using convergence. How? Again there is a relationship between muscle sensations and distance. Convergence is controlled by a group of muscles attached to the eyeball. These feed information on eye position to the brain to aid it in judging distance. You can feel convergence by exaggerating it: Focus on your fingertip and bring it toward your eyes until they almost cross. At this point you can feel sensations from the muscles that control eye movement.

Stereoscopic Vision   The most important source of depth perception is **retinal disparity,** also a binocular cue. Retinal disparity is based on the simple fact that the eyes are about 2½ inches apart. Because of this, each eye receives a slightly different view of the world. When the resulting two images are *fused* into one overall image, **stereoscopic vision** occurs. This produces a powerful sensation of depth (see Fig. 5–9). Retinal disparity can be used to produce 3-D movies by filming with two cameras separated by several inches. Later, both images are simultaneously projected on a screen. The audience then wears glasses that filter out one of the images to each eye. Since each eye gets a separate image, normal stereoscopic vision is duplicated. Try this demonstration of retinal disparity and fusion:

Roll a piece of paper into a tube. Close your left eye. Hold the tube to your right eye like a telescope. Look through the tube at some object in the distance. Place your left hand against the tube halfway down its length and in front of your left eye. Now open your left eye. You should see a "hole" in your hand. You couldn't expect a professional photographer to do a better job of blending the two images than your visual system does automatically.

Question: How does retinal disparity produce depth?

Perceiving depth is more than a blending of two images. In Fig. 5–10c you will find two squares of random dots. Notice that they contain no lines, edges, or distinct patterns. Just the same, when these **random dot stereograms** are properly viewed (one to each eye), a center area seems to float above the background. Researcher Bela Julesz believes the designs show that the brain is very sensitive to any **mismatch** of information from the eyes. In this example, depth comes from shifting dots in one square so the center areas do not quite match (Julesz, 1971; Ross, 1976). To a large extent, three-dimensional space is woven from countless tiny differences between what the right and left eyes see.

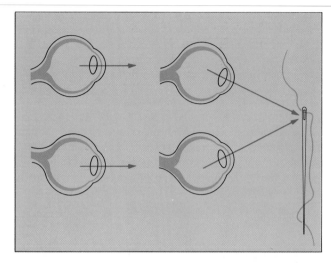

Fig. 5—9   *The eyes must converge or turn in toward the nose to focus close objects.*

Question: If disparity is so important, can a person with one eye perceive depth?

A one-eyed person lacks convergence and retinal disparity, and accommodation is only helpful for judging small distances. This means that a person with only one eye will have restricted depth perception. Try driving a car or riding a bicycle for some time with one eye closed. You will find yourself braking too soon or too late, and you will have difficulty estimating your speed. ("But officer, my psychology text said to. . . .") In spite of this, you will be able to drive, although with greater difficulty than usual. A person with one eye can even successfully land an airplane—a task strongly dependent on depth perception.

Pictorial Cues for Depth— A Deep Topic

A good movie, painting, or photograph can give a convincing sensation of depth where none exists, and as noted, a one-eyed person can learn to accurately gauge depth.

Question: How is the illusion of depth created on a two-dimensional surface, and how is it possible to judge depth with one eye?

The answers lie in the **pictorial depth cues,** all of which are monocular (they will work with just one eye). These

Fig. 5—10   (a) *Stereoscopic vision.* (b) *The photographs show what the right and left eye would see when viewing a vase. Hold a file card or small piece of paper (4 or 5 inches tall) vertically between the two photos. Place the bridge of your nose on the card so that each eye sees only one photo. Relax your eyes until the vase fuses into one image. The third dimension appears like magic.* (c) *Now do the same with the random dot stereogram, but with your eyes 8 or 10 inches from the page. With luck you will see a diamond shape hovering over the background. (See text for explanation.) Most readers will not be able to get the effect without using a prism to perfectly fuse the right and left dot squares. (Julesz, 1971; reprinted by permission of the University of Chicago Press.)*

(a)

(b)

(c)

cues contain much of the information present when a person looks at a real three-dimensional scene (Haber, 1980). To understand how the pictorial cues work, imagine that you are looking outdoors through a window. If you traced everything you saw onto the glass, you would have an excellent drawing, with convincing depth. If we then analyzed what was on the glass, we would find the following features.

Pictorial Depth Cues

1. **Linear perspective.** This refers to the apparent convergence of parallel lines in the environment. If you stand between two railroad tracks, they appear to come together near the horizon. Since you know they are parallel, this seeming convergence implies great distance (see Fig. 5–11).

2. **Relative size.** If an artist wishes to depict two objects of the same size at different distances, the artist makes the more distant object smaller (see Fig. 5–12). The films *Star Wars* and *Return of the Jedi* cre-

ated sensational illusions of depth through rapid changes in the image size of planets, space stations, and starships.

3. **Light and shadow.** Most objects in the environment are lighted in such a way as to create definite patterns of light and shadow. Appropriate distribution of light and shadow can give a two-dimensional design a three-dimensional feeling (see Fig. 5–13).

4. **Overlap.** Overlap (also known as *interposition*) describes a depth cue caused by one object partially blocking the view of another. Hold your hands up and have a friend try to tell from across the room which is nearer. Relative size will give the answer if the difference between the two hands is large. But if one hand is only slightly closer than the other, your friend may have difficulty—until you slide one hand in front of the other. Overlap then removes any doubt (see Fig. 5–14).

5. **Texture gradients.** Changes in texture also contribute to depth perception. If you are standing in the middle of a cobblestone street, the street looks coarse near

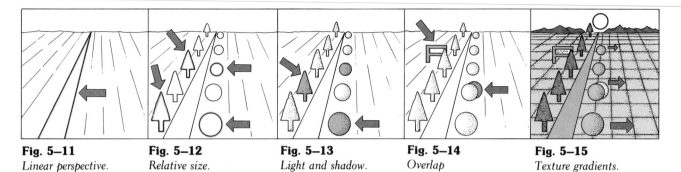

Fig. 5—11
Linear perspective.

Fig. 5—12
Relative size.

Fig. 5—13
Light and shadow.

Fig. 5—14
Overlap

Fig. 5—15
Texture gradients.

your feet, but the texture of the stones gets smaller and finer as you look off into the distance (see Fig. 5–15).

6. **Aerial perspective.** Smog, fog, dust, and haze add to the apparent distance of an object. Objects seen at great distance tend to be hazy, a washed-out color, and lacking in detail due to aerial perspective. This is true even in clear air but is increasingly the case in our industrial society. As a matter of fact, aerial haze is often most noticeable when it is missing. If you have traveled the wide open spaces of states such as Colorado or Wyoming, you may have seen mountain ranges that looked only a few miles away, and then were shocked to find that you were actually viewing them through 50 miles of crystal-clear air.

7. **Relative motion.** Relative motion, also known as *motion parallax* (PAIR-ah-lax), can be seen by looking out a window and moving your head from side to side. You will notice that objects near you appear to move a sizable distance as your head moves. Trees, houses, and telephone poles at a greater distance appear to move slightly in relation to the background, and distant objects like hills, mountains, or clouds don't seem to move at all.

When combined, pictorial cues can create a powerful illusion of depth (see Fig. 5–16).

Question: Is motion parallax really a "pictorial" cue?

Strictly speaking, it is not, except in movies, television, or animated cartoons. However, when it is present, depth almost always prevails. Much of the apparent depth of a good movie comes from relative motion captured by the camera. People who can only see with one eye depend heavily on motion parallax. Many of them make frequent head movements to exaggerate parallax and improve depth perception.

Question: Are pictorial depth cues universal, like the understanding of basic drawings noted earlier?

Not entirely. Some cultures use only selected pictorial cues to represent depth. People in these cultures may not easily recognize other cues (Deregowski, 1972). For example, researcher William Hudson has tested members of remote tribes who do not use relative size to show depth. These people see simplified drawings as two-dimensional designs (see Fig. 5–17).

Question: How do the depth perception cues relate to daily experience?

The Moon Illusion   Like the bodily depth cues, you constantly use the pictorial cues to gauge depth and judge distances. This can be seen through an intriguing illusion.

Fig. 5—16   *Pictorial depth. Look closely! The artist has used many of the pictorial depth cues to fool the eye. (M. C. Escher, Still Life and Street.© M. C. Escher Heirs c/o Cordon Art, Baarn, Holland. Collection Haags, Gemeentemuseum—The Hague. Reproduced by permission.)*

Fig. 5–17 *A Hudson test picture. Two-dimensional perceivers assume the hunter is trying to spear the distant elephant rather than the nearby antelope. Some acquaintance with conventions for representing depth in pictures and photographs seems necessary. (From "Pictorial Perception and Culture" by J. B. Deregowski.© 1972 by Scientific American, Inc. All rights reserved.)*

When the moon is on the horizon, it tends to look as large as a silver dollar. When it is directly overhead, it looks like a dime, very much smaller than it did earlier the same evening. Contrary to what some people believe, the moon's image is not magnified. If you take a photograph of the moon and measure its image, you will find that it is not larger on the horizon. But the moon *looks* larger when it's low in the sky. This is because the **appar-**ent distance of the moon is greater when it is on the horizon than when it is overhead.

Question: But if it seems farther away, shouldn't it appear smaller?

No. When the moon is overhead, there is an absence of depth cues. In contrast, when the moon is on the horizon, it is seen behind houses, trees, telephone poles, and mountains. These objects add numerous depth cues, which cause the horizon to seem more distant than the sky overhead (Dember & Warm, 1980).

To better understand the moon illusion, picture two balloons, one 10 feet away and the other 20 feet away. Suppose the more distant balloon is inflated until its image matches that of the nearer balloon. We know the more distant balloon is larger because its image is the same size as a balloon that is closer. Similarly, the moon makes the same size image on the horizon as it does overhead. However, the horizon seems more distant because of the depth cues present. As a result, the horizon moon must be perceived as larger (Rock, 1962).

This explanation is known as the **apparent distance hypothesis.** You can test it by removing the normal depth cues present when you look at a full moon. Try looking at the moon through a rolled-up paper tube, or make your hands into a "telescope" and look at the next large moon you see. It will immediately "shrink" when viewed without depth cues.

Learning Check

If you have difficulty with any of these questions, skim back over the previous material.

1. The visual cliff uses retinal disparity to test for depth perception.   T or F?

2. Write an "M" or a "B" after each of the following to indicate if it is a monocular or binocular depth cue.

   accommodation _____   retinal disparity _____   motion parallax _____

   convergence _____   linear perspective _____

3. List one muscular cue for depth perception: _____

4. Interpretation of pictorial depth cues requires no prior experience.   T or F?

5. The moon's image is greatly magnified by the atmosphere near the horizon.   T or F?

Answers: 1. F 2. accommodation (M), convergence (B), retinal disparity (B), linear perspective (B), motion parallax (M)   3. accommodation or convergence 4. F 5. F.

Perceptual Learning—
What If the World Were Upside Down?

There is a story, perhaps fictional, about a visit to the London symphony made by a diplomat from India. According to the story, the diplomat, to his great embarrassment, began clapping loudly after the orchestra finished tuning up. The point of this anecdote is that learning has a powerful impact on perception, something we have already seen in several ways.

Question: How does learning affect perception?

Perceptual Habits   One way that learning affects perception is through established patterns of organization and attention, referred to as **perceptual habits.** Stop for a moment and look at Fig. 5–18. The left face looks somewhat unusual, to be sure. But the distortion appears mild—until the page is turned upside down. Viewed normally, the face looks quite grotesque. Why is there a difference? Apparently, most people have little experience with upside down faces. Perceptual learning, therefore, has less impact on our perceptions of an upside-down face. With a face in normal position you know what to expect and where to look.

Before we continue, read aloud the short phrase in Fig. 5–19. Did you read "Paris in the spring"? If so, look again. The word *the* appears twice in the phrase. Because of past experience with the English language, the repeated word is frequently overlooked. Again, the effects of perceptual learning are apparent.

Magicians make use of perceptual habits when they use sleight of hand to distract observers while performing their tricks. Another kind of "magic" is related to consistency in the environment. It is usually safe to assume that the overall shape of a room is approximately that of a simple box. This need not be true, however. A decidedly lopsided room can be made to appear square by carefully distorting the proportions of the walls, floor, ceiling, and windows. One such room, called an **Ames room,** after the man who designed it, presents a unique problem for the perceptual habits and organization of an observer.

Since the left corner of the Ames room is farther from a viewer than the right, a person standing in that corner looks very small, whereas one standing in the right corner looks very large (see Fig. 5–20). If a person walks from the left corner of the room to the right, an observer is faced with maintaining shape constancy by perceiving the room as square, or maintaining size constancy by refusing to see the person "grow." Most people choose shape constancy and see people "shrink" and "grow" before their eyes.

As mentioned in the previous chapter, the brain is especially sensitive to important **features** of the environment. At least some of this sensitivity appears to be learned. Colin Blakemore and Graham Cooper of Cambridge University raised kittens in rooms with only vertical stripes or horizontal stripes on the walls. When returned to normal

Fig. 5–18   *The effects of prior experience on perception. The doctored face looks far worse when viewed right-side up, because it can be related to past experience.*

Fig. 5–19

Paris
in the
the spring

environments, the "horizontal" cats could easily jump onto a chair, but when walking on the floor they bumped into chair legs. "Vertical" cats, on the other hand, had no difficulty avoiding chair legs, but they missed when trying to jump to horizontal surfaces. The cats reared with vertical stripes were "blind" to horizontal lines, and the "horizontal" cats acted as if vertical lines were invisible (Lewin, 1974). Other experiments show that there is an

actual decrease in brain cells tuned to the missing features (Grobstein & Chow, 1975).

Question: Would it be possible, then, for an adult to adapt to a completely new perceptual world?

Inverted Vision An answer is offered by experiments in which people have worn lenses that invert visual images. In one such experiment a subject wore goggles that turned the world upside down and reversed objects from right to left. At first even the simplest tasks—walking, eating, and so forth—became extremely difficult. Imagine trying to reach for a door handle and watching your hand shoot off in the wrong direction.

Subjects also reported that head movements made the world swing violently through space, causing severe headaches and nausea. Yet, incredible as it may seem, after several days they began adapting to inverted vision. Their success was not complete, but it was impressive. Such a

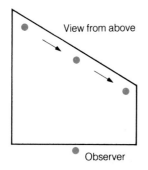

Fig. 5–20 *The Ames room. From the front the room looks normal; actually, the right-hand corner is very short, and the left-hand corner is very tall. In addition, the left side of the room slants away from viewers. The diagram shows the shape of the room and reveals why people appear to get bigger as they cross the room toward the nearer, shorter right corner.*

high degree of adaptation apparently is related to superior human learning abilities. If the eyes of goldfish are surgically turned upside down, the fish swim in circles and rarely adapt (Sperry, 1956).

Question: Did everything turn upright again for the humans?

No. While they wore the goggles, their visual images remained inverted. But, subjects regained ability to perform most routine activities, and their upside-down world began to seem relatively normal. In more recent experiments subjects wearing inverting lenses have successfully driven cars, and one subject even flew an airplane after a few weeks of adaptation (Kohler, 1962). These feats are the equivalent of driving or flying upside down and backwards. Some ride!

Active movement in a new visual world seems to be the key to rapid adaptation. In one experiment people wore glasses that grossly distorted vision. Those who walked on their own adapted more quickly than subjects pushed around in a wheeled cart (Held, 1971). Why does movement help? Probably because commands sent to the muscles can be related to sensory feedback (McBurney & Collings, 1984). Remaining immobile would be like watching a weird movie, over which you have no control. There would be little basis for any perceptual learning to occur.

Adaptation Level An important factor affecting perception is the external **context** in which a stimulus is judged. For example, a man 6 feet in height will look "tall" when surrounded by others of average height and "short" among a group of professional basketball players. In Fig. 5–22 the center circle is the same size in both designs. But, like the man in different company, the circle takes on a different apparent size depending on context. The importance of context is also shown by Fig. 5–23. What do you see in the middle? If you read across, context causes it to be organized as a 13. Reading down makes it a B.

In addition to external contexts we all have *internal* **frames of reference,** or standards by which stimuli are judged. If you were asked to lift a 10-pound weight, would you label it "light," "medium," or "heavy"? The answer to this question depends on your **adaptation level** (Helson, 1964). This is your own personal "medium point," or frame of reference. Each person's adaptation level is constantly modified by experience. If most of the weights you lift in day-to-day life *average* around 10 pounds, you will call a 10-pound weight "medium." If you are a watchmaker and spend your days lifting tiny watch parts, you

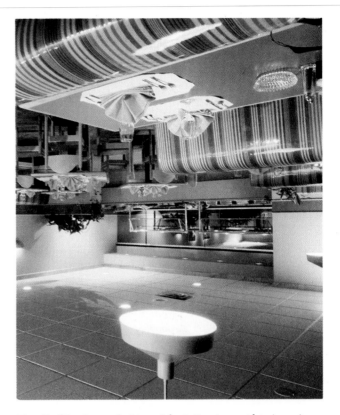

Fig. 5–21 *Inverted vision. Adaptation to complete inversion of the visual world is possible but challenging.*

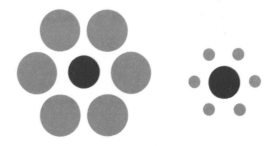

Fig. 5–22 *Are the center dots in both figures the same?*

Fig. 5–23 *Context alters the meaning of the middle figure.*

will probably call a 10-pound weight "heavy." If you work as a furniture mover, your adaptation level will exceed 10 pounds, and you will call a 10-pound weight "light." If you are an aging rock star, you will no doubt call everything "heavy," man.

Illusions   Perceptual learning is responsible for a number of **illusions.** In an illusion, length, position, motion, curvature, or direction is consistently misjudged (Gillam, 1980). Illusions differ from **hallucinations** in that illusions distort stimuli that actually exist. People who are hallucinating perceive objects or events that have no external reality (for example, they hear "voices" that are not there). If you think you see a 3-foot tall butterfly, you can confirm you are hallucinating by trying to touch its wings. To detect an illusion, it is often necessary to measure a drawing or apply a straight-edge to it.

Illusions are a fascinating challenge to our understanding of perception. On occasion they also have practical uses. An illusion called **stroboscopic movement** (strobe-oh-SKOP-ik) is responsible for putting the "motion" in motion pictures. The strobe lights sometimes used on dance floors reverse this illusion. Each time the strobe flashes, it "freezes" dancers in particular positions. However, if the flashes are speeded up sufficiently, normal motion is seen. In a similar way movies project a rapid series of "snapshots" on the screen, so the gaps in motion are imperceptible.

Question: Can other illusions be explained?

Not in all cases, or to everyone's satisfaction. Generally speaking, size and shape constancy, habitual eye movements, continuity, and perceptual habits combine in various ways to produce the illusions in Fig. 5–24. Rather than attempt to explain all of the pictured illusions, let's focus on one "simple" example.

Consider drawing *a,* the familiar **Müller-Lyer illusion** (MUE-ler–LIE-er). In this illusion the horizontal line with arrowheads appears shorter than the line with V's on each end. A quick measurement will show that they are the same length. How can we explain this illusion? Evidence suggests it is based on a lifetime of experience with

Fig. 5–24   *Some interesting perceptual illusions.*

(a) Which of the horizontal lines is longer

(b) Is the diagonal line straight? Check it with a ruler.

(c) Is this a drawing of a staircase descending from upper left to lower right . . . or is it the view of the underneath of a staircase from lower right to upper left?

(d) Are these lines parallel? Cover some of the slash marks to see.

(e) Which line is longer, horizontal or vertical?

(f) Notice how the background distorts the square.

(g) Which quadrilateral is larger?

(h) Which column is shortest? Which is longest.

the edges and corners of rooms and buildings. Richard Gregory (1977) believes you see the horizontal line with the V's as if it were the corner of a room viewed from inside (see illustration). The line with arrowheads, on the other hand, suggests the corner of a room or building seen from outside (see Fig. 5–25).

Earlier, to explain the moon illusion, we said that if two objects make the same size image but one is more distant, the more distant object must be larger. This is known formally as **size-distance invariance**. Gregory believes the same concept explains the Müller-Lyer illusion. Thus, if the V-tipped line looks farther away than the arrowhead-tipped line, you must compensate by seeing the V-tipped line as larger. This explanation of the Müller-Lyer illusion presumes that you have had years of experience with straight lines, sharp edges, and corners—a pretty safe assumption in our culture.

Question: Is there any way to show that past experience causes this illusion?

If we could test someone who as a child had seen only curves and wavy lines, we would know if experience with a "square" culture is important. Fortunately, in South Africa there is a tribe of people, the Zulus, who live in a "round" culture. In their daily lives Zulus rarely encounter a straight line: Huts are shaped like rounded mounds and are arranged in a circle; tools and toys are curved; and there are no straight roads or square buildings.

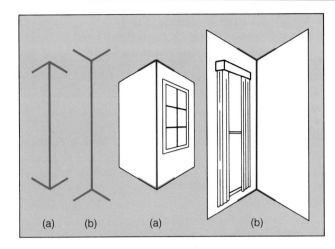

Fig. 5–25 *Why does line (b) in the Müller-Lyer illusion look longer than line (a)? Probably because it looks more like a distant corner than a nearer one. Since the vertical lines form images of the same length, the more "distant" line must be perceived as larger.*

Question: What happens if a Zulu looks at the Müller-Lyer design?

The typical Zulu does not experience the illusion. At most he or she sees the V-shaped line as *slightly* longer than the other (Gregory, 1977). This seems to confirm the importance of past experience and perceptual habits in determining our view of the world.

Learning Check

1. Perceptual habits may become so ingrained that they lead us to misperceive a stimulus.   T or F?
2. Perceptual learning seems to program the brain for sensitivity to important _____ of the environment.
3. The Ames room is used to test for adaptation to inverted vision.   T or F?
4. An important factor in adaptation to inverted vision is:
   a. learning new categories
   b. active movement
   c. overcoming illusions
   d. the stroboscopic movement effect
5. Size-distance relationships appear to underlie which two illusions? _____ and _____.
6. An adaptation level represents a personal "medium point" or internal _____

Answers: 1. T 2. features 3. F 4. b 5. moon illusion and Müller-Lyer illusion 6. frame of reference

Motives and Perception— May I have Your . . . Attention!

You are surrounded by sights, sounds, odors, tastes, and tactile sensations. Which are you aware of? The first stage of perception is *attention*—selection of incoming messages.

Attention Very *intense* stimuli are attention getting. Stimuli that are brighter, louder, or larger tend to capture attention: A gunshot in a library would be hard to ignore. Big, bright cars probably get more tickets than small, dull ones. Loud, irritating comedian Don Rickles has made a career out of the first principle of attention.

Repetitious stimuli, repetitious stimuli, repetitious stimuli, repetitious stimuli, repetitious stimuli, repetitious stimuli are also attention getting. A dripping faucet at night makes little noise by normal standards, but because of repetition it may become as attention getting as a single sound many times louder. This effect is used repeatedly, so to speak, in television and radio commercials. ATTENTION IS ALSO FREQUENTLY RELATED TO *contrast* OR *change* IN STIMULATION. Change is perhaps the most basic source of attention. We quickly **habituate** (respond less) to an unchanging stimulus.

Question: How does habituation differ from sensory adaptation?

Habituation As described in Chapter 4, *adaptation* decreases the actual number of sensory messages sent to the brain. When messages do reach the brain, the body makes a sort of "What is it?" reaction known as the **orientation response** (OR). An OR is characterized by enlarged pupils, brain wave changes, a short pause in breathing, increased blood flow to the head, and turning toward the stimulus (Dember & Warm, 1979). If you have ever seen someone do a double take, you have observed an orientation response.

Now, think about what happens when you buy a new record album. At first the album holds your attention all the way through. But when the album becomes "old," a whole side may play without your really attending to it. When a stimulus is repeated *without change*, the OR habituates, or decreases.

Motives Motives also play a role in attention. If you are riding in a car and are hungry, you will notice restaurants and billboards picturing food. If you are running low on gas, your attention will shift to gas stations. Advertisers, of course, know that their pitch will be more effective if it gets your attention. Ads are therefore loud, repetitious, and intentionally irritating. They are also designed to take advantage of two motives that are widespread in our society: *anxiety* and *sex*.

Everything from mouthwash to automobile tires is merchandised using sex as a source of attention. For instance, a recent ad for Triple Sec liqueur ran in national magazines under the heading "Sec's Appeal." Another liquor ad shows a woman in a seductive velvet dress as she says, "Feel the velvet." And what could be more obvious than ads for designer jeans that feature a shapely posterior pointed at the camera? Other ads combine sex with anxiety. Mouthwash, deodorant, soap, toothpaste, and countless other articles are pushed in ads that play on desires to be attractive or have sex appeal, and to avoid embarrassment.

In addition to directing attention, motives may alter what is perceived:

> As part of a supposed study of "the dating practices of college students," male volunteers were shown a picture of a female student and asked to give a first impression of how attractive she was. Before making these ratings, each subject read one of two short written passages: one was sexually arousing and the other was not. The important finding was that subjects who read the more arousing passage rated the female as more attractive (Stephan, Bersheid, & Walster, 1971).

This result may come as no surprise to you if you have ever been infatuated with someone and then "fallen out of love." A person who once seemed highly attractive may look quite different when your feelings change.

Another interesting experiment demonstrates that an emotional stimulus can shift attention away from other information. In this experiment members of a Jewish organization watched as pictures like Fig. 5–26 were flashed on a screen for a split second. Their recognition for symbols at the edge of the figure was impaired when the central item was an emotional symbol like the pictured swastika (Erdelyi & Appelbaum, 1973). This effect probably explains why fans of opposing sports teams often act as if they have seen two completely different games.

Perceptual Expectancies— On Your Mark, Get Set

Question: What is a perceptual expectancy?

A runner in the starting blocks at a track meet is **set** to respond in a certain way. In perception, past experience, motives, context, or suggestion may create a **perceptual expectancy** that sets you to perceive in a certain way. If a car backfires, runners at a track meet may jump the gun.

As a matter of fact, we all frequently jump the gun when perceiving. To relate this idea to an earlier one: An expectancy is a perceptual hypothesis we are *very likely* to apply to a stimulus—even if it is inappropriate.

We respond according to perceptual set by seeing what we expect to see. For example, let's say you are driving across the desert. You are very low on gas. Finally you see a distant sign. On it are the words FUEL AHEAD. You relax, knowing you will not be stranded. But as you draw nearer, the words on the sign become FOOD AHEAD. Most people have had similar experiences in which expectations altered their perceptions. To observe perceptual expectancies firsthand, perform the experiment described in Fig. 5–27.

Many perceptual expectancies are created by *suggestion*. This is especially true when one is perceiving other people. For example, a psychology professor once arranged an experiment in which a guest lecturer taught his class. Half the students in the class were given a page of notes that described the lecturer as a "rather *cold* person, industrious, critical, practical, and determined." The other students received notes describing him as a "rather *warm* person, industrious, critical, practical, and determined" (Kelley, 1950; italics added). Students who received the "cold" description perceived the lecturer as unhappy and irritable and didn't volunteer in class discussion. Those who got the "warm" description saw the lecturer as happy

Fig. 5–26 *Emotionally significant stimuli influence attention. (Erdelyi & Appelbaum, 1973, p. 50. Reprinted by permission.)*

and good-natured, and they actively took part in discussion with him.

Expectancies may even explain why celebrities and persons of high status can seem "larger than life." In one experiment an individual was introduced to students as either a student, an assistant, a lecturer, or a professor at a prestigious university. When asked to estimate his height, students judged him to be progressively taller as his status

Fig. 5–27 *"Young woman/old woman" illustrations. As an interesting demonstration of perceptual expectancy, show some of your friends View I and some View II (cover all other views). Next show your friends View III and ask them what they see. Those who saw View I should see the old woman in View III; those who saw View II should see the young woman in View III. Can you see both? (After Leeper, 1935.)*

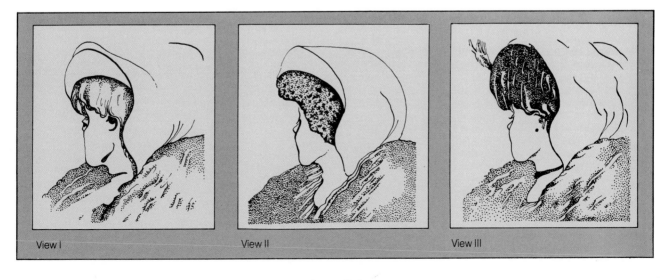

View I   View II   View III

increased (Wilson, 1968). Short people take note! Forget the high heels and get an education!

Categories Have you ever seen playing cards with a *red* ace of spades or a *black* four of hearts? Psychologist Jerome Bruner used a *tachistoscope* (tah-KIS-toh-scope: a device for projecting pictures for very short periods) to flash pictures of cards on a screen. He found that subjects misperceived cards that did not fit their expectations. For instance, a *red* six of spades would be misperceived as a normal six of hearts (Bruner & Postman, 1949). Bruner believes that perceptual learning builds up a set of mental **categories**. Experiences are then "sorted" into categories somewhat as if the categories were slots or pigeonholes. Since subjects had no category for a red six of spades, they saw it as a six of hearts. Categories such as *punk, mental patient, queer, honky, bitch,* and so on are particularly likely to distort perception.

Question: Those are extremes. Does it really make that much difference what you call someone, or something?

Perceptual categories, especially those defined by labels, do make a difference. This is particularly true when we are perceiving people. Even trained psychologists may be influenced by labels and categories. For example, in one study psychotherapists were shown a 15-minute videotaped interview. Half of the therapists were told the man being interviewed was applying for a job. The rest were told that the man was a mental patient. Therapists who thought the man was a job applicant perceived him as "realistic," "sincere," and "pleasant." Those who thought he was a mental patient perceived him as "defensive," "dependent," and "impulsive" (Langer & Abelson, 1974).

In this chapter we have moved from basic perceptions of form to the complexities of perceiving people and events. In the Applications section we will continue this progression with a look at "objectivity" and eyewitness testimony. Before we continue, here's a Learning Check.

Learning Check

1. Attention is elicited by all but one of the following. Which does not fit?
   a. habituation   *b.* repetition   *c.* change   *d.* intensity

2. The presence of an orientation response shows that habituation is complete.   T or F?

3. Changes in brain waves and increased blood flow to the head are part of an OR.   T or F?

4. Research shows that heightened sexual arousal can cause a person to perceive someone of the opposite sex as more physically attractive.   T or F?

5. When a person is prepared to perceive events in a particular way, it is said that a perceptual expectancy

   or _____ has been created.

6. Perceptual expectancies are greatly influenced by the existence of mental categories and labels.   T or F?

Answers: 1. *a*   2. F   3. T   4. T   5. set   6. T

Applications

Perception and Objectivity—Believing Is Seeing

Have you ever seen the sun set? An odd question perhaps, since we see the sun "go down" every day. Yet, in reality we know that the sun does not "set." Instead, our viewing angle changes as the earth turns, until finally the sun is blocked by the horizon. Want to try the alternative? Tonight stand facing the west. With practice you can learn to feel yourself being swept backward on the rotating surface of the earth—as you watch an unmoving sun recede in the distance (Fuller, 1969).

This radical shift in perspective illustrates the limitations of "objective" observation. As with most other perceptions, seeing a "sunset" is an active and creative **reconstruction** of events. As we have seen, perception reflects the needs, expectations, attitudes, values, and beliefs of the perceiver. In this light the phrase "Seeing is believing" must be modified. Clearly, we see what we believe as well as believe what we see.

In some cases the highly subjective quality of perception contributes to the uniquely personal vision valued in art, music, poetry, and the creative parts of scientific research. Too often, though, it is a real liability.

Eyewitness   In the courtroom eyewitness testimony can be a key element in establishing guilt or innocence. The claim, "I saw it with my own eyes," carries a lot of weight with a jury. But, to put it bluntly, eyewitness testimony is frequently wrong. In fact, recent experiments show that a person's confidence in his or her testimony has almost no bearing on its accuracy (Wells & Murray, 1983)!

Psychologists interested in perception are gradually convincing lawyers, judges, and police officers of the fallibility of eyewitness testimony (Loftus & Monahan, 1980). In one court case a police officer testified that he saw the defendant, a black man, shoot the victim as both stood in a doorway 120 feet away. Measurements made by a psychologist showed that, at that distance, light from the dimly lit doorway was extremely weak—less than a fifth of that from a candle. To further show that identification was improbable, a black juror stood in the doorway under identical lighting conditions. None of the other jurors could identify him. The defendant was acquitted (Buckhout, 1974).

Unfortunately, perception rarely provides an instant replay of events. Even in broad daylight eyewitness testimony is untrustworthy. After a disastrous DC-10 airliner crash in Chicago in 1979, 84 pilots who saw the accident were interviewed. Forty-two said the DC-10's landing gear was up, and 42 said it was down! As one investigator commented, the best witness may be a "kid under 12 years old who doesn't have his parents around" (McKean, 1982). Adults, it seems, are easily swayed by their expectations.

Perceptions formed when a person is surprised, threatened, or under stress are especially prone to distortion. This is why witnesses to crimes so often disagree. As a dramatic demonstration of this problem, an assault was staged on a college campus in which a professor was attacked by an actor. Immediately after the event, 141 witnesses were questioned in detail. Their descriptions were then compared with a videotape made of the staged "crime." The total accuracy score for the group (on features such as appearance, age, weight, and height of the assailant) was only *25 percent* of the maximum possible (Buckhout, 1974).

Question: Wouldn't the victim of a crime remember more than a mere witness?

A recent experiment found that eyewitness accuracy was virtually the same for witnessing a crime (seeing a pocket calculator stolen) as it was for being a victim (seeing one's own watch stolen) (Hosch & Cooper, 1982). Jurors who place more weight on the testimony of victims may be making a serious mistake. Also, it is worth repeating that witnesses who are confident in their testimony are no more likely to be accurate than those who have doubts.

In many crimes victims also fall prey to the phenomenon of **weapon focus.** Understandably, victims often fix their entire attention on the knife, gun, or other weapon used by an attacker. In doing so, they fail to perceive details of appearance, dress, or other clues to identity (Loftus, 1979).

Applications: Perception and Objectivity—Believing Is Seeing

Implications   How often are our everyday perceptions as inaccurate or distorted as those of an emotionally distraught eyewitness? The answer we have been moving toward is, "very frequently." Bearing this in mind may help you develop tolerance for the views of others and be more cautious about the "objectivity" of your own perceptions. It may also encourage more frequent **reality testing** on your part.

Question: What do you mean by reality testing?

Reality Testing   In any situation having an element of doubt or uncertainty, reality testing involves obtaining additional information as a check on perceptions. Even simple designs like those in Fig. 5–28 are easily misperceived. One of the designs in the drawing is a continuous line; the other is not. Most people cannot perceive this difference spontaneously. Instead, they must carefully trace and compare the two designs as a check on pure perception (Julesz, 1975).

Psychologist Sidney Jourard provided a more pertinent example of reality testing. One of Jourard's students believed her roommate was stealing from her. The student gradually became convinced of her roommate's guilt but said nothing. As her distrust and anger grew, their relationship turned cold and distant. Finally, at Jourard's urging, she confronted her roommate. The roommate cleared herself immediately and expressed relief when the puzzling change in their relationship was explained (Jourard, 1974). With their friendship reestablished, the true culprit was soon caught. (The cleaning woman did it!)

Fig. 5–28   *Limits of pure perception. (Adapted from patterns devised by Marvin L. Minsky and Seymour A. Papert.)*

If you have ever concluded that someone was angry, upset, or unfriendly without checking the accuracy of your perceptions, you have fallen into a subtle trap. Personal objectivity is an elusive quality, requiring frequent reality testing to maintain. At the very least it pays to ask a person what he or she is feeling when you are in doubt. Undoubtedly, most of us could learn to be better "eyewitnesses" to daily events.

Question: Do some people perceive things more accurately than others?

Perceptual Awareness   Humanistic psychologist Abraham Maslow (1969) felt that some people are unusually accurate in perceptions of themselves and of others. Maslow characterized these people as especially alive, open, aware, and mentally healthy. He found their perceptual styles were marked by: immersion in the present; a lack of self-consciousness; freedom from selecting, criticizing, or evaluating; and a general "surrender" to experience. The kind of perception Maslow described is like that of a mother with her newborn infant, a child at Christmas, or two people in love.

Other researchers have tested Zen masters for habituation to repeated stimuli. The results indicate that Zen masters fail to show the expected habituation (Kasamatsu & Hirai, 1966). This finding lends some credibility to claims that Zen masters perceive a tree as vividly after seeing it 500 times as they did the first time.

Attention   Whereas the average person has not reached perceptual restriction of the "if you've seen one tree, you've seen them all" variety, the fact remains that most of us tend to look at a tree and classify it into the perceptual category of "trees in general" without really appreciating the miracle standing before us. How then can we bring about a **dishabituation** of perception (without going through years of meditative discipline as a Zen master does)? The deceptively simple answer is: *Pay attention.*

The following quote summarizes the importance of attention:

Applications: Perception and Objectivity—Believing Is Seeing

One day a man of the people said to Zen Master Ikkyu: "Master, will you please write for me some maxims of the highest wisdom?"

Ikkyu immediately took his brush and wrote the word "Attention."

"Is that all?" asked the man. "Will you not add something more?"

Ikkyu then wrote twice running: "Attention. Attention."

"Well," remarked the man rather irritably, "I really don't see much depth or subtlety in what you have just written."

Then Ikkyu wrote the same word three times running: "Attention. Attention. Attention."

Half angered, the man demanded, "What does that word 'Attention' mean anyway?"

And Ikkyu answered gently: "Attention means attention." (Kapleau, 1966)

To this we can add only one thought, provided by the words of poet William Blake: "If the doors of perception were cleansed, man would see everything as it is, infinite."

Learning Check

1. Most perceptions can be described as active reconstructions of external reality.   T or F?
2. Inaccuracies in eyewitness perceptions obviously occur in real life, but they cannot be reproduced in psychology experiments.   T or F?
3. Accuracy scores for facts provided by witnesses to staged crimes may be as low as 25 percent correct.   T or F?
4. Victims of crimes are more accurate eyewitnesses than are impartial observers.   T or F?
5. *Reality testing* is another term for dishabituation.   T or F?

Answers: 1. T   2. F   3. T   4. F   5. F

Chapter Summary

- *Perception* is the process of assembling sensations into a usable mental representation of the world.
- In vision the image projected on the retina is constantly changing, but the external world appears stable and undistorted because of *size, shape,* and *brightness constancy.*
- The most basic organization of sensations is a division into *figure* and *ground* (object and background). A number of factors contribute to the organization of sensations. These include: *nearness, similarity, continuity, closure,* and *combinations* of the preceding. Basic elements of line drawings appear to be universally recognized.
- A perceptual organization may be thought of as a *hypothesis* held until evidence contradicts it. Perceptual organization shifts for *ambiguous stimuli. Impossible figures* resist stable organization altogether.
- *Depth perception* (the ability to perceive three-dimensional space and judge distances) is present in rudimentary form soon after birth, as shown by testing on the *visual cliff.*
- Depth perception depends on the *muscular cues* of *accommodation* (bending of the lens) and *convergence* (inward movement of the eyes). *Stereoscopic vision* is created mainly by *retinal disparity* and the resulting overlap and *mismatch* of visual images.
- A number of *pictorial cues* also contribute to depth perception. These are: *linear perspective, relative size, light and shadow, overlap, texture gradients, aerial haze,* and *relative motion* (motion parallax). All are monocular depth cues (only one eye is needed to make use of them).
- The *moon illusion* is at least partially explained by the *apparent distance hypothesis,* which emphasizes the

greater number of depth cues present when the moon is on the horizon. Another way of saying this is that a *size-distance invariance* underlies the moon illusion.

■ The organization and interpretation of sensations are greatly influenced by the development of *perceptual habits*. Studies of *inverted vision* show that even the most basic organization is subject to a degree of change. *Active movement* speeds adaptation to a new perceptual environment.

■ Perceptual judgments are not made in a vacuum. They are almost always related to *context*, or to an internal frame of reference called the *adaptation level*.

■ One of the most familiar of all perceptual illusions, the *Müller-Lyer illusion*, seems to be related to perceptual learning, linear perspective, and size-distance invariance relationships.

■ Attention is closely related to *stimulus intensity*, *repetition*, *contrast*, and *change*. Attention is accompa-

nied by an *orientation response*. When a stimulus is repeated without change, the orientation response undergoes *habituation*.

■ Personal *motives* and *values* often alter perceptions by changing the evaluation of what is seen or by altering attention to specific details.

■ Attention, prior experience, suggestion, and motives combine in various ways to create perceptual *sets*, or *expectancies*. These prepare a person to perceive, or misperceive, in a particular way. Expectancies are often related to preexisting mental *categories* and *labels*.

■ Perception is an active *reconstruction* of events. This is one reason why *eyewitness testimony* is surprisingly unreliable and unrelated to the *confidence* of the witness. Eyewitness accuracy is further damaged by *weapon focus*. Perceptual accuracy is enhanced by *reality testing*, *dishabituation*, and conscious efforts to pay *attention*.

Exploration

Extrasensory Perception—Do You Believe in Magic?

In a quiet laboratory Uri Geller, a self-proclaimed "psychic," has agreed to demonstrate his claimed abilities. In the course of testing Geller was supposedly able to: select from a row of 10 film canisters the one that contained an object, correctly guess 8 out of 8 times the number that would come up on a die shaken in a closed box, and reproduce drawings sealed in opaque envelopes.

Question: Was Geller cheating, or was he using some ability beyond normal perception?

There is now little doubt that Geller was cheating (Randi, 1980). But how? The answer lies in a discussion of **extrasensory perception (ESP)**—the purported ability to perceive events in ways that cannot be explained by accepted perceptual principles.

Parapsychology

Parapsychology is the study of ESP and other **psi** (sie) phenomena—events that seem to defy accepted scientific laws. Parapsychologists seek answers to the questions raised by three basic forms that ESP could take. These are:

1. Clairvoyance: the ability to perceive events or gain information in ways that appear unaffected by distance or normal physical barriers.
2. Telepathy: extrasensory perception of another person's thoughts, or, more simply, an ability to read someone else's mind.
3. Precognition: the ability to perceive or accurately predict future events. Precognition may take the form of *prophetic dreams* that foretell the future.

While we are at it, we might as well toss in another purported psi ability:

4. Psychokinesis: the ability to exert influence over inanimate objects by will power ("mind over matter"). (Psychokinesis cannot be classed as a type of perception, extrasensory or otherwise, but it is frequently studied by parapsychologists.)

Question: Have parapsychologists confirmed the existence of ESP and other psi abilities?

American psychologists as a group remain skeptical about psi abilities. If you doubt ESP, then you should know that some experiments seem to support its existence. If you are among those who believe in ESP, then you should know why the scientific community doubts many of these experiments!

Coincidence   Anyone who has ever had an apparent clairvoyant or telepathic experience may find it hard to question the existence of ESP. Yet, the difficulty of excluding *coincidence* makes natural ESP occurrences less conclusive than they might seem. For example, consider this typical psychic experience: During the middle of the night, a woman away for a weekend visit suddenly had a strong impulse to return home. When she arrived, she found the house on fire, with her husband asleep inside (Rhine, 1953). An experience like this is striking, but it does not confirm the existence of ESP. If, by coincidence, a "hunch" turns out to be correct, it may be *reinterpreted* as a premonition or case of clairvoyance (Marks & Kammann, 1979). If it is not confirmed, it will simply be forgotten. Most people don't realize it, but such coincidences occur so often that we should *expect* them, not consider them strange or unexplainable (Alcock, 1981).

The formal study of psi events owes much to J. B. Rhine. Rhine established the first parapsychological laboratory at Duke University and spent the rest of his life trying to document ESP. To avoid problems of coincidence and after-the-fact interpretation of "natural" ESP events, Rhine tried to study ESP objectively. Many of his experiments made use of the **Zener cards** (see Fig. 5–29). In a typical clairvoyance test subjects tried to guess the symbols on the cards as they were turned up from a shuffled deck. Pure guessing in this test will produce an average score of 5 "hits" out of 25 cards.

Unfortunately, some of Rhine's most dramatic early experiments used badly printed Zener cards that allowed the symbols to show

Exploration: Extrasensory Perception—Do You Believe in Magic?

Fig. 5–29 *ESP cards used by J. B. Rhine, an early experimenter in parapsychology.*

through faintly on the back. Note also that it is very easy to cheat by marking cards with a fingernail or by noting marks on the cards caused by normal use. Even if this were not the case, there is evidence that early experimenters sometimes unconsciously gave subjects cues about the cards with their eyes, facial gestures, or lip movements. In short, none of the early studies in parapsychology were done in a way that eliminated the possibility of fraud (Alcock, 1981).

Modern parapsychologists are now well aware of the need for double-blind experiments, maximum security and accuracy in record keeping, meticulous experimental control, and repeatability of experiments (Rhine, 1974a). In the

last 10 years hundreds of experiments have been reported in parapsychology journals, many of them supporting the existence of psi abilities (Hyman, 1979).

Question: Then why do most psychologists remain skeptical about psi abilities?

For one thing, fraud continues to plague the field. Walter J. Levy, former director of Rhine's laboratory, was caught faking records, as have some others who got positive results. Even honest scientists have been fooled by various frauds and cheats, so there is reason to remain skeptical and on guard.

Statistics and Chance   A major criticism of psi research has to do with inconsistency. For every study with positive results, there are others that fail (Hansel, 1980). It is rare—in fact, almost unheard of—for a subject to maintain psi ability over any sustained period of time (Jahn, 1982; Schmeidler, 1977). ESP researchers consider this "decline effect" an indication that parapsychological skills are fragile and unpredictable (Rhine, 1977). But critics argue that subjects who only temporarily score above chance have just received credit for a **run of luck**. When the run is over, it is not fair to assume that ESP is temporarily gone, these critics say. We must count *all* attempts.

To understand the run-of-luck criticism, consider an example. Say that you flip a coin 100 times and record the results. You then flip another coin 100 times, again

recording the results. The two lists are compared. For any 10 pairs of flips we would expect heads or tails to match 5 times. Let's say that you go through the list and find a set of 10 pairs where 9 out of 10 matched. This is far above chance expectation. But does it mean that the first coin "knew" what was going to come up on the second coin? The idea is obviously silly.

Now, what if a person makes a guess each time a coin is flipped. Out of 100 tosses we might find a set of 10 guesses that matches the results of flipping the coin. Does this mean that the person, for a time, had precognition—then lost it? Parapsychologists tend to believe the answer is yes. Skeptics assume that nothing more than random matching has occurred, like in the two-coin example.

Research Methods
Unfortunately, many of the most spectacular findings in parapsychology simply cannot be **replicated** (repeated) (Gardner, 1977; Hyman, 1977). More importantly, improvements in research methods usually result in fewer positive results. Proponents of parapsychology feel that they can point to experiments that meet all possible criticisms. But in virtually every case, the results cannot be repeated by doubters. Believers in ESP, such as ex-astronaut Edgar Mitchell, assume that other factors explain such negative results: "The scientist has to recognize that his own mental processes may influence the phenomenon he's observing. If he's really a total skep-

Exploration: Extrasensory Perception—Do You Believe in Magic?

tic, the scientist may well turn off the psychic subject." This may sound convincing, but skeptics consider it unfair. With Mitchell's argument in effect, anyone attempting an objective experiment can only get two results: He or she may find evidence of ESP or be accused of having suppressed it. This makes it impossible to disprove ESP to believers, even if it truly does not exist.

Reinterpretation is also a problem in psi experiments. For example, Mitchell claimed he conducted a successful telepathy experiment from space. Yet news accounts never mentioned that on some trials Mitchell's "receivers" scored above chance, while on others they scored *below* chance. The second outcome, Mitchell decided, was also a "success" because it represented intentional "psi missing." But, as skeptics have noted,

if both high scores and low scores count as "successes," how can you lose?

Stage ESP   Skeptics and serious researchers in ESP both agree on one point. If psychic phenomena do occur, they cannot be controlled well enough to be used by entertainers. Stage ESP (like stage magic) is based on a combination of sleight of hand, deception, and patented gadgets (see Fig. 5–30). A case in point is Uri Geller, a former nightclub magician who "astounded" audiences—and some scientists—from coast to coast with apparent telepathy, psychokinesis, and precognition.

Geller's performance on tests was described earlier. Not mentioned is what University of Oregon professor Ray Hyman calls the "incredible sloppiness" of these tests. One example is Geller's reproduc-

tions of sealed drawings. These, it turns out, were done in a room next to the one where the drawings were made. Original reports of Geller's alleged "ability" failed to mention that there was a hole in the wall between the two rooms, through which Geller could easily hear discussions of the pictures being drawn. Also unreported was the fact that Geller's friend Shipi Stang was present at every test. Geller's manager has since testified that Stang frequently acted as Geller's accomplice in trickery (Alcock, 1981). Is it a coincidence that when a picture of a rocket ship was drawn, Stang hummed the theme music from the motion picture *2001: A Space Odyssey*? A similar lack of control pervaded every other test. In the "die in the box" tests, for instance, Geller was allowed to hold the box, shake it, and have the honor of opening it

Fig. 5–30 *Fake psychokinesis.* (left) *The performer shows an observer several straight keys. While doing so, he bends one of the keys by placing its tip in the slot of another key. Normally, this is done out of sight, behind the "psychic's" hand. It is clearly shown here so you can see how the deception occurs.* (middle) *Next, the "psychic" places the two keys in the observer's hand and closes it. By skillful manipulation, the observer has been kept from seeing the bent key. The performer then "concentrates" on the keys to "bend them with psychic energy."* (right) *The bent key is revealed to the observer. "Miracle" accomplished!* (Adapted from Randi, 1983.)

Exploration: Extrasensory Perception—Do You Believe in Magic?

(Randi, 1980; Wilhelm, 1976). Why weren't such pertinent details reported?

Sensational and uncritical reporting of apparent paranormal events is widespread. Hundreds of books, articles, and television programs are produced each year by people who have become wealthy promoting unsupported claims. If a person did have psychic powers, he or she would not have to make a living by entertaining, giving demonstrations, or making personal appearances. A quick trip to the gaming tables of Las Vegas would allow the person to retire for life.

Conclusion   After close to 100 years of investigation, it is still im-possible to say conclusively that psi events occur, or that they don't. As we have seen, a close look at psi experiments often reveals serious problems of evidence, procedure, and scientific rigor (Alcock, 1981; Hansel, 1980; Marks & Kammann, 1979; Randi, 1980). Yet, being a skeptic does not mean a person is against something. It means that he or she is unconvinced. The purpose of this discussion, then, has been to balance the *uncritical* acceptance of psi events that is rampant in the media.

Question: What would it take to scientifically demonstrate the existence of ESP?

Quite simply, a set of instructions that would allow any competent, unbiased observer to produce a psi event under standardized conditions (Moss & Butler, 1978). Undoubtedly, some intrepid researchers will continue their attempts to supply just that. Others remain skeptics, and some consider 100 years of inconclusive efforts reason enough to abandon the concept of ESP. At the least it seems essential to be carefully skeptical of evidence reported in the popular press or by researchers who are uncritical "true believers." But then, you already knew I was going to say that, didn't you!

Learning Check

1. Four purported psi events investigated by parapsychologists are clairvoyance, telepathy, precognition, and _____.
2. The _____ cards were used by J. B. Rhine in early tests of ESP.
3. Natural or "real life" occurrences are regarded as the best evidence for the existence of ESP.   T or F?
4. Skeptics attribute positive results in psi experiments to statistical runs of luck.   T or F?
5. Replication rates are high for ESP experiments.   T or F?

Answers: 1. psychokinesis 2. Zener 3. F 4. T 5. F

Questions for Discussion

1. Return for a moment to the incident described in the Chapter Preview. What perceptual factors were involved in the first version of the "murder"? How did the girl affect what was seen?

2. Do you think your perceptions of an argument or fight with a friend, parent, spouse, or lover are accurate? What perceptual factors might affect your viewpoint?

3. Motorcyclists often complain that automobile drivers act as if cyclists are invisible. What perceptual factors might cause drivers to "look right at" motorcyclists without seeing them.

4. A professional basketball player is at the free-throw line for the last shot in a tied championship game. What depth cues are available to him? A professional golfer is making the last putt for a $10,000 prize; what depth cues is she using? A pilot is landing at an unfamiliar airport; what cues are available to her or him? You are looking through a microscope with one eye; what depth cues can you use?

5. Describe a situation you have misperceived. What influenced your perceptions?

6. What role might habituation play in industrial accidents (especially on production lines) and in driving on arrow-straight superhighways? What changes would you make in work procedures or highway design to combat habituation?

7. In view of the Chapter Preview and Applications, how dependable do you think eyewitness testimony is in a courtroom? What factors other than accuracy of original perceptions might contribute to inaccuracies in testimony?

8. If you believe ESP occurs, what would it take to convince you that it does not? If you do not believe that ESP occurs, what would it take to convince you that it does?

Chapter 6

Altered States of Consciousness

Chapter Preview
Young Dervishes

Were you a "spinner" as a child? Sooner or later, most children discover the joys of whirling around and around, until they collapse in a giggling heap. What attraction does spinning hold for children? Here is what some 10-year-olds had to say about it: "It gets you dizzy and makes you feel good." "It's like flying." "I like the floating feeling" (Weil, 1977).

Like spinning children, people throughout history have sought ways to alter their conscious experience. A more dramatic example is the sweat lodge ritual of the Sioux Indians. During the ritual, several men sit in total darkness inside a small chamber heated by a bed of coals. Cedar smoke and the aroma of sage fill the air. Sudden explosions of steam boil into the lodge, as water is poured on the coals. The men chant rhythmically. The heat builds. At last they can stand no more. The door is thrown open. Cooling night breezes rush in. And then? The heating cycle begins again—often to be repeated four or five times more. Among the Sioux this ritual is viewed as a cleansing of mind and body. When it is especially intense, it brings altered awareness and personal revelation.

*What do the experiences of the spinning children and the Sioux Indians have in common? Though they are worlds apart, both involve **altered states of consciousness**, the topic of this chapter.*

Some altered states are sought primarily for pleasure, as is often true of drug intoxication. Yet, changes in consciousness cannot be dismissed as mere pleasure seeking. All people experience altered states, such as sleep, dreaming, and daydreaming. Also, almost every known religion has accepted at least some altered states of awareness as pathways to mystical experience. Accepted avenues have ranged from fasting, meditation, prayer, isolation, sleep loss, whirling, and chanting, to self-inflicted pain and psychedelic drugs. In everyday life significant changes in consciousness may accompany long-distance running, listening to music, or making love. This chapter examines the nature of several states of consciousness, as well as their uses and abuses.

Survey Questions What are the characteristics of altered consciousness? What is hypnosis like, and what are its limitations? How does sensory deprivation affect consciousness? What are the effects of the more commonly used psychoactive drugs? How is meditation done? What are its benefits? Why is drug abuse so widespread in our culture?

136

Resources

States of Consciousness— Beyond Normal Awareness?

William James described consciousness as a stream, or everchanging flow of awareness. Ordinary **waking consciousness** includes a mixture of sensations from the outside world, sensations from your body, memories of the past, thoughts and images, and expectations about the future. Waking consciousness is organized, meaningful, clear, perceived as real, and associated with a familiar sense of time and place (Marsh, 1977). But as James also noted:

> Our normal waking consciousness . . . is but one special type of consciousness, whilst all about it, parted from it by the filmiest of screens, there lie potential forms of consciousness entirely different. (James, 1958.)

States of consciousness related to fatigue, delirium, hypnosis, meditation, drugs, and ecstasy differ significantly from what might be considered "normal" awareness. As mentioned earlier, everyone experiences at least a few altered states, such as sleep, dreaming, and daydreaming. Depending on personal experience and cultural training, a person may add drunkenness, drug highs, meditation, and the like to his or her personal list of states of consciousness.

Question: It's clear that there are many altered states of consciousness. How do they differ from normal awareness?

An **altered state of consciousness** (ASC) represents a distinct change in the *quality* and *pattern* of mental functioning. ASCs differ from normal waking consciousness with regard to: sense impressions, body image, emotions, memory (gaps, loss, or enhancement), time sense, feelings of personal identity, self-control, suggestibility, and the meaning given to events (Tart, 1975). Definitions aside, most people have little difficulty recognizing that they have experienced an ASC.

Question: Other than drugs, what causes ASCs?

The list of causes is practically endless. In addition to sources already mentioned, we could add: sensory overload (for example, a light show, Mardi Gras crowd, or disco), monotonous or restricted stimulation ("highway hypnotism" on long drives is a good example), religious and mystical experiences (revivals and religious conversions), unusual physical conditions (high fever, hyperventilation, dehydration, sleep loss), and too many other possibilities to mention.

Because nearly one-third of your life is spent asleep, sleep and dreaming will be covered in a separate chapter. Here, we will focus on examples of four major ways in which consciousness is changed. These are: hypnosis (suggestion), stimulus deprivation (unusual sensory conditions), drugs (psychoactive chemicals), and meditation (mental exercises).

To get right to the questions raised by altered states of consciousness, let's begin with hypnosis.

Hypnosis— Look into My Eyes

"Your body is becoming heavy. Your eyes are so tired you can barely keep them open. You feel warm and relaxed and very heavy. You are so tired you can't move. Relax. Sleep, sleep, sleep." These are the last words a book should ever say to you and the first a professional hypnotist might say.

Hypnosis has always had a certain aura of mystery surrounding it. Yet hypnosis has been accepted by most psychologists as a valid phenomenon. Most would agree that **hypnosis** is a *trancelike, altered state of consciousness, characterized by narrowed attention and an increased openness to suggestion.*

Interest in hypnosis began in the 1700s with Franz Mesmer (whose name is the basis for the term **mesmerize**). Mesmer, an Austrian physician, believed that he could cure diseases by passing magnets over the body. For a time, mesmerism enjoyed quite a following. In the end, however, Mesmer's theories of "animal magnetism" were rejected by the medical profession, and he was branded a quack and a fraud. The term *hypnosis* was coined later by a respected English surgeon named James Braid. The Greek word *hypnos* means "sleep," and Braid used it to describe the hypnotic trance. Today we recognize that hypnosis is *not* sleep, since EEG (brain wave) recordings made during hypnosis are similar to those obtained when a person is awake. Confusion about this point remains because some hypnotists give the suggestion, "Sleep, sleep." However, hypnosis shown in movies and on television bears little resemblance to the real thing.

Question: Can anyone be hypnotized?

Approximately 8 people out of 10 can be hypnotized, but only 4 out of 10 will be good hypnotic subjects. If you are

Table 6–1 Stanford Hypnotic Susceptibility Scale	
Suggested Behavior	**Criterion of Passing (yielding score of +)**
1. Postural sway	Falls without forcing.
2. Eye closure	Closes eyes without forcing.
3. Hand lowering (left)	Lowers at least 6 in. by end of 10 sec.
4. Immobilization (right arm)	Arm rises less than 1 in. in 10 sec.
5. Finger lock	Incomplete separation of fingers at end of 10 sec.
6. Arm rigidity (left arm)	Less than 2 in. of arm bending in 10 sec.
7. Hands moving together	Hands at least as close as 6 in. after 10 sec.
8. Verbal inhibition (name)	Name unspoken in 10 sec.
9. Hallucination (fly)	Any movement, grimacing, acknowledgment of effect.
10. Eye catalepsy	Eyes remain closed at end of 10 sec.
11. Posthypnotic (changes chairs)	Any partial movement response.
12. Amnesia test	Three or fewer items recalled.

(Adapted from Weitzenhoffer & Hilgard, 1959.)

willing to be hypnotized, chances are good that you could be. Hypnotic susceptibility can be measured by making a series of suggestions to a person and recording the number of suggestions to which he or she responds. A typical hypnotic test is the **Stanford Hypnotic Susceptibility Scale** shown in Table 6–1 (also see Fig. 6–1).

Question: How is hypnosis done? Could anyone be hypnotized against his or her will?

There are as many different hypnotic routines as there are hypnotists. The actual method of hypnotic induction doesn't seem to be too important. Common factors in all techniques are that they encourage a person: (1) to focus attention on what is being said, (2) to relax and feel tired, (3) to "let go" and accept suggestions easily, and (4) to use vivid imagination (Tart, 1975).

In deeper stages of hypnosis, "reality testing" may be relaxed so that a partial suspension of normal "will power" is achieved. But at first one must cooperate willingly in order to become hypnotized. Many theorists believe that all hypnosis is really **self-hypnosis** and that the hypnotist simply serves as a guide to help the subject achieve an altered state of awareness that could be achieved alone.

Question: What does it feel like to be hypnotized?

You might be surprised at some of the actions you performed during hypnosis, and you might experience mild feelings of floating, sinking, anesthesia, or separation from your body. Personal experiences vary widely. However, in all but the deepest stages of hypnosis, people remain aware of what is going on.

A key element in hypnosis is the **basic suggestion effect.** Hypnotized persons feel that suggested actions or experiences are involuntary—they seem to just "happen" without effort (Kihlstrom, 1985). Here is one subject's description of his hypnotic session:

I felt lethargic, my eyes going out of focus and wanting to close. My hands felt real light. . . . I felt I was sinking deeper into the chair. . . . I felt like I wanted to relax more and more. . . . My responses were more automatic. I didn't have to *wish* to do things so much or *want* to do them. . . . I just did them. . . . I felt floating. . . . very close to sleep. (Hilgard, 1968.)

Hypnosis often causes a *dissociation* or "split" in awareness. To illustrate, researcher Ernest Hilgard asks hypnotized subjects to plunge their hand into a painful bath of ice water. Subjects told to feel no pain say they feel none. The same subjects are then asked if there is any part of their mind that does feel pain. Many write, "It hurts," or "Stop it, you're hurting me," but continue to act as if they are completely comfortable (Hilgard 1977, 1978). One part of the hypnotized person says there is no pain and acts as if there is none. Another part, which Hilgard calls the **hidden observer,** is aware of the pain but remains in the background.

Question: Could someone be made to perform an immoral act while hypnotized?

Generally speaking, a person will not do something when hypnotized that he or she would not normally do. However, a person who would not undress in public *might* undress if given the suggestion that he or she is at home alone and that it is bedtime (Eysenck, 1957). Also, hypnosis may *disinhibit* a person by providing an excuse to engage in forbidden behavior. If you were hypnotized and told to throw a cream pie in your teacher's face, you would probably comply because you couldn't be held responsible. After all, you were hypnotized, weren't you?

Question: What can be achieved with hypnosis?

A vast array of abilities has been tested for responsiveness to hypnotic suggestion. In some cases the evidence is incomplete or contradictory, but the following conclusions seem reasonably justified (Kihlstrom, 1985):

1. **Superhuman acts of strength.** Hypnosis has no more effect on physical strength than instructions that encourage a subject to make his or her best effort (Barber, 1970).

2. **Memory.** There is some evidence that hypnosis can enhance memory. However, it also frequently increases the number of false memories as well (Dywan & Bowers, 1983). For this reason many states now bar persons who have been hypnotized from testifying in court cases. (See Chapter 10 for more information.)

3. **Amnesia.** Hypnotic subjects can be instructed to forget what occurred during the trance. It is not yet certain if they do forget or just won't say what they remember. However, the pattern of memory errors made by hypnotized subjects suggests that some amnesia may actually occur (Kihlstrom, 1985).

4. **Pain relief.** Hypnosis can relieve pain (Hilgard & Hilgard, 1983). Therefore, it can be especially useful in situations where chemical painkillers cannot be used or are ineffective. One such situation is control of *phantom limb pain.* (Phantom limb pains are recurring pains that amputees sometimes feel coming from the missing limb.)

5. **Age regression.** Through hypnosis subjects have been "regressed" to childhood. Some theorists believe that regressed subjects are only acting childlike. Doubt is also cast by the fact that age-regressed persons continue to use knowledge they could only have learned as adults. The validity of age regression, therefore, remains doubtful (Kihlstrom, 1985).

6. **Sensory changes.** Hypnotic suggestions concerning sensations seem to be among the most effective. Given the proper instructions, a person can be made to smell a small bottle of ammonia and respond as if it were a wonderful perfume. It is also possible to alter color vision, hearing sensitivity, time sense, perception of illusions, and many other sensory responses (Kihlstrom, 1985).

Fig. 6–1 *In one test of hypnotizability, subjects attempt to pull their hands apart after hearing suggestions that their fingers are "locked" together.*

Generally, hypnosis seems to have greatest value as a tool for inducing relaxation, as a means of controlling pain (in dentistry and childbirth, for example), as an aid to maintaining motivation (to study, diet, quit smoking, and so forth), and as an adjunct to other forms of psychological therapy and counseling. The effects that can be obtained with hypnosis are useful but seldom amazing (Hilgard, 1974; Rieger, 1976; Williams, 1974).

Stage Hypnotism

On stage the hypnotist intones, "When I count to three, you will imagine that you are on a train to Disneyland and growing younger and younger as the train approaches. . . ." Responding to these suggestions, grown men and women begin to giggle and squirm like children on their way to a circus.

Question: How do entertainers use hypnosis on stage to get people to do strange things?

They don't. Little or no hypnosis is necessary to do a good stage hypnosis act. T. X. Barber, an authority on hypnosis, says that stage hypnotists make use of several characteristics of the stage setting to perform their act (Barber, 1970).

1. **Waking suggestibility.** We are all more or less open to suggestion, but on stage people are usually cooperative because they don't want to ruin the act. As a result they will readily follow almost any instruction given by the entertainer.

2. **Selection of responsive subjects.** Participants in stage hypnotism (all *volunteers*) are first "hypnotized" as a group. Thus, anyone who doesn't succumb (respond to instructions) is eliminated.

3. **The hypnosis label disinhibits.** As we noted before, once a person has been labeled "hypnotized," he or she can sing, dance, act silly, or whatever, without fear of embarrassment. Being "hypnotized" takes away all personal responsibility for one's actions.

4. **The hypnotist as a director.** After participants loosen up and respond to a few suggestions, they find that they are suddenly the star of the show. Audience response to the antics on stage brings out the "ham" in many participants so that all the "hypnotist" need do is direct the action.

5. **The stage hypnotist uses tricks.** Stage hypnosis is about 50 percent taking advantage of the situation and 50 percent deception. Here is a common deception:

One of the more impressive stage tricks is to suspend a person horizontally between two chairs and then to stand on the person's chest. This is astounding only because the audience does not question it. Anyone can do it, as is dem-

onstrated in the photographs and instructions in Fig. 6–2. Try it!

Question: If entertainers don't hypnotize people, why do those who have been on stage say they were hypnotized?

Some may have been hypnotized, but since most people don't know what it feels like to be hypnotized, the combination of bright lights, nervousness, and the things they did convince them they were. A prime example occurred when the "Amazing Kreskin," a stage mentalist, told talk show host Johnny Carson he could be hypnotized without knowing it. Kreskin suspended Carson between two chairs and asked singer Bette Midler to sit on Carson's stomach. And what was Carson's response to this? "You've proved your point," he said. "I'm wide awake, but I must be hypnotized because I feel as comfortable as a duck in a pond" (Weisinger, 1977).

To summarize, hypnosis is real and is capable of causing a significant change in conscious experience. It is a useful tool that has been effectively applied in a variety of settings. The TV or nightclub stage, however, is not one of these settings. Stage "hypnotists" entertain; they rarely hypnotize.

Sensory Deprivation— Life on a Sensory Diet

Throughout history **sensory deprivation** (SD) has been one of the most frequently used means of altering consciousness. Sensory deprivation refers to any major reduction in external stimulation.

Fig. 6–2 *Arrange three chairs as shown. Have someone recline as shown. Ask him to lift slightly while you remove the middle chair. Accept the applause gracefully!*

Question: What happens when stimulation is greatly reduced?

A hint comes from reports by prisoners in solitary confinement, arctic explorers, high-altitude pilots, long-distance truck drivers, and radar operators. Under conditions of reduced or monotonous stimulation, these people have at times had dangerous lapses in awareness, bizarre sensations, and wildly distorted perceptions. To find out why, D. O. Hebb and his associates paid volunteers to undergo sensory deprivation under controlled conditions.

Subjects spent several days lying on their backs in a small cubicle. To prevent vision, they wore darkened goggles. Gloves and cardboard cuffs restricted touch. In the background a constant hissing noise masked all other sounds. Do these conditions sound interesting? If you were placed in similar circumstances, you might be in for a surprise. Few subjects could take more than two or three days of sensory deprivation without "pushing the panic button." Most lost track of time, had difficulty concentrating, and underwent a variety of perceptual changes (Heron, 1957).

Disruptive Effects

Question: What sort of changes does sensory deprivation cause?

The most consistent disturbances after sensory deprivation are a distortion of colors, heightened visual illusions, slower reactions, and a brief warping of visual lines and spaces. Some participants in early experiments also reported disturbing hallucinations. One subject screamed in panic, "There is an animal having a long slender body with many legs. It's on the screen, crawling in back of me!" (Heron, 1957). Spurred by such reports, researchers soon created an ingenious array of sensory deprivation environments, and volunteers flocked to experiments seeking a drugless "high." Most were disappointed, however. We now know that true hallucinations are rare during sensory deprivation (Zubek, 1969b).

Question: But what about John Lilly's experiments?

The Womb Tank John Lilly, M.D., who is better known for his work on communication with dolphins, pioneered the use of an unusual sensory deprivation environment. Subjects in Lilly's experiments wore a face mask with darkened goggles and floated naked in a tank of body-temperature water (Lilly, 1972). As they floated weightlessly in this womblike, "hypodynamic" environment, subjects were effectively cut off from smell, touch, vision,

hearing, and taste sensations. Under these conditions—with almost no sensations coming in—subjects often had vivid mental images. However, other research has shown that these are basically **hypnogogic images** (hip-no-GAH-jik), not hallucinations (Zubek, 1969b). Many people associate hallucinations with Lilly's experiments because he sometimes took LSD before entering the tank.

Hypnogogic images are similar to those experienced just before falling asleep. They are dreamlike, very vivid, and often surprising. However, they are rarely mistaken for real objects in the environment. Their occurrence is linked to an increase in the amount of **theta waves** produced by the brain. These brain waves normally occur during the brief time between sleep and waking, but sensory deprivation also increases their occurrence (Taylor, 1983).

Benefits of Sensory Restriction

Early studies of sensory deprivation focused mainly on its negative or disruptive effects. More recently, psychologists have begun to explore some possible benefits. Much of this work has involved mild sensory restriction in small isolation tanks like the one pictured in Fig. 6–3.

Question: How could sensory deprivation be beneficial?

Sensory Enhancement One of the most consistent after-effects of sensory deprivation is increased sensory acuity. That is, vision, hearing, touch, and taste temporarily become more sensitive (Suedfeld, 1975; Zubek, 1969b). Some people report using this after-effect to aid creative thinking or constructive work (Hutchison, 1984). At the

Fig. 6–3 *Sensory isolation chamber. Small flotation tanks like the one pictured have been used by psychologists to study the effects of mild sensory deprivation. Subjects float in darkness and silence. The shallow body-temperature water contains hundreds of pounds of Epsom salts, so that subjects float near the surface.*

very least it seems that wearing earplugs for a day might be an interesting prelude to attending a musical concert!

Relaxation   As we noted, most people find prolonged sensory deprivation stressful and aversive. Yet, paradoxically, brief periods of restricted sensation are very relaxing (Suedfeld, 1980). An hour or two spent in a flotation tank, for instance, causes a large drop in blood pressure, muscle tension, and other signs of stress. Of course, it could be argued that a warm bath has the same effect. But to date evidence suggests that a brief exposure to sensory deprivation is one of the surest ways to induce deep relaxation.

Changing Habits   Psychologist Peter Suedfeld, at the University of British Columbia, has found that sensory deprivation can help people quit smoking or lose weight. In one of his first experiments of this type, Suedfeld compared the effects of standard antismoking messages to the same messages combined with sensory deprivation. He found that roughly equal numbers of people succeeded in stopping smoking with either treatment. But 3 months later, members of the sensory deprivation group were smoking 40 percent less than the others (Suedfeld, 1980). Another study found similar prolonged benefits for people

in a weight-loss program based on sensory deprivation (Borrie & Suedfeld, 1980).

Question: How does sensory deprivation help?

Tape-recorded suggestions to eat less or to stop smoking are played for clients while they are isolated in a flotation tank. Suedfeld speculates that deep relaxation makes a person less likely to argue against, or otherwise resist suggestions. Also, some mental confusion usually accompanies sensory deprivation. This, he believes, helps unfreeze or "loosen" belief systems. Unfreezing, in other words, may make it easier to bring about lasting changes in beliefs that maintain bad habits.

Prospect   After years of being viewed only as a disruptive state, sensory deprivation may yet prove to have other benefits. Research is presently under way on using sensory deprivation as an aid to treating phobias (irrational fears). Preliminary evidence also suggests that sensory deprivation sessions can help people cut down on alcohol and drug abuse. In addition, continued study of sensory deprivation should add to our understanding of brainwashing attempts, isolation at remote weather outposts, the aftereffects of eye surgery, and the problems of extended space flight. Clearly, there is much yet to be learned from studying "nothingness."

Learning Check

Here are a few questions to test your memory of our discussion so far.

1. Altered states of consciousness are defined mainly by changes in alertness.   T or F?

2. The term *hypnotism* was coined by a British surgeon named:
   a. Franz Mesmer   *b.* James Stanford   *c.* T. A. Kreskin   *d.* James Braid

3. Only 4 out of 10 people can be hypnotized.   T or F?

4. Which of the following can most definitely be achieved with hypnosis?
   a. superhuman acts of strength   *b.* pain relief   *c.* memory loss   *d.* sleeplike brain waves

5. Could someone be made to perform an immoral act while hypnotized?   Yes or No?

6. Which of the following is not a disruptive effect observed during or immediately after sensory deprivation?
   a. impaired time sense   *b.* difficulty concentrating   *c.* elevated blood pressure   *d.* heightened visual illusions

7. Vivid images during sensory deprivation usually can be best described as:
   a. daydreams   *b.* hypnogogic   *c.* hallucinations   *d.* hypodynamic

8. Prolonged periods of sensory deprivation induce deep relaxation.   T or F?

Answers:

1. F 2. d 3. F 4. b 5. Generally no; however, hypnosis may provide an excuse to engage in prohibited behavior. 6. c 7. c 8. F

Drug-Altered Consciousness— The High and Low of It

Alcohol, heroin, amphetamines, barbiturates, marijuana, cocaine, LSD, caffeine, nicotine . . . The list of consciousness-altering drugs—legal and illegal—is extensive. The surest way to alter human consciousness is to administer a **psychoactive drug.** A psychoactive drug is a substance capable of altering attention, memory, judgment, time sense, self-control, emotion, or perception (Ludwig, 1966).

Facts about Drugs   Most psychoactive drugs can be placed on a scale ranging from **stimulation** to **depression.** Figure 6–4 shows the approximate relationships among various drugs and their effects on the central nervous system. A more complete summary of the most frequently abused psychoactive drugs is given in Table 6–2 (pp. 144–145).

Drug dependence falls into two broad categories. When a person compulsively uses a drug to maintain bodily comfort, a **physical dependence** exists. Physical dependence, commonly referred to as **addiction,** occurs most often with drugs that cause **withdrawal symptoms** (painful or even agonizing reactions that take place when the drug is withheld). Addiction is often accompanied by a **drug tolerance,** in which the user must take larger and larger doses to achieve the desired effect. When a person develops a **psychological dependence,** he or she feels a drug is necessary to maintain emotional or psychological well-being. No withdrawal symptoms or physical cravings are involved, and yet psychological dependence may affect a drug user as powerfully as physical dependence does.

Note in Table 6–2 that the drugs most clearly associated with physical dependence are: heroin, morphine, codeine, methadone, barbiturates, alcohol, amphetamines, and tobacco. *All* of the drugs listed can lead to psychological dependence.

Some drugs, of course, have a higher potential for abuse than others. However, this is only one side of the picture. Often, it is as useful to classify drug-taking *behavior* as it is to classify drugs. For example, some people remain social drinkers for a lifetime, whereas others become alcoholics within weeks of taking their first drink. In this sense drug use can be classified as **experimental** (short-term use motivated by curiosity), **social-recreational** (occasional social use considered pleasurable by participants), **situational** (use to cope with a specific problem such as boredom or staying awake for night work), **intensive** (daily use having elements of dependence), or **compulsive** (intense use and extreme dependence) (National Commission on Marijuana and Drug Abuse, 1973). The last three categories of drug taking tend to be damaging no matter what drug is used. The discussion that follows will focus on the drugs most frequently abused by college students.

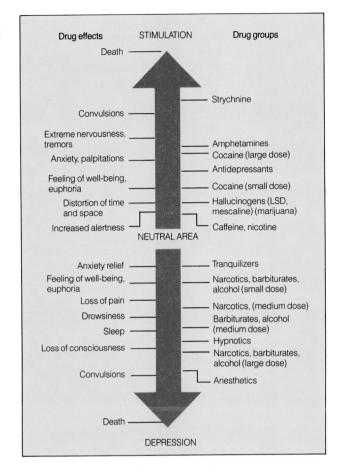

Fig. 6–4   *Spectrum and continuum of drug action. Drugs can be placed on a continuum of stimulation-depression according to their effect on the central nervous system.*

Uppers— Amphetamines, Cocaine, Caffeine, Nicotine

Amphetamines form a large group of synthetic stimulants. Drugs commonly available in this group are *Dexedrine*, *Methedrine*, and *Benzedrine*. Amphetamines were once widely prescribed by doctors to aid weight loss or to combat mild depression. Both practices are now discouraged because patients frequently become dependent on their "legal" amphetamines. The only fully legitimate medical

Table 6–2   Comparison of Psychoactive Drugs

Name	Classification	Medical Use	Usual Dose	Duration of Effect
Heroin	Narcotic	Pain relief	Varies	4 hr.
Morphine	Narcotic	Pain relief	15 milligrams	6 hr.
Codeine	Narcotic	Ease pain and coughing	30 milligrams	4 hr.
Methadone	Narcotic	Pain relief	10 milligrams	4–6 hr.
Cocaine	Stimulant, local anesthesia	Local anesthesia	Varies	Varied, brief periods
Marijuana (THC)	Relaxant, euphoriant; in high doses, hallucinogen	Treatment of glaucoma	1–2 cigarettes	4 hr.
Barbiturates	Sedative-hypnotic	Sedation, relief of high blood pressure, hyperthyroidism	50–100 milligrams	4 hr.
Amphetamines	Stimulant	Relief of mild depression, control of appetite and narcolepsy	2.5–5 milligrams	4 hr.
LSD	Hallucinogen	Experimental study of mental function, alcoholism	100–500 micrograms	10 hr.
Mescaline	Hallucinogen	None	350 micrograms	12 hr.
Psilocybin	Hallucinogen	None	25 milligrams	6–8 hr.
Alcohol	Sedative-hypnotic	Solvent, antiseptic	Varies	1–4 hr.
Tobacco (Nicotine)	Stimulant	Emetic (nicotine)	Varies	Varies
Caffeine	Stimulant	Counteract depressant drugs, treatment of migraine headaches	Varies	Varies

(Question marks indicate conflict of opinion. It should be noted that illicit drugs are frequently adulterated and thus pose unknown hazards to the user.)

*Persons who inject drugs under nonsterile conditions run a high risk of contracting hepatitis, abscesses, or circulatory disorders.

Table 6–2   Comparison of Psychoactive Drugs (Continued)

Effects Sought	Long-Term Symptoms	Physical Dependence Potential	Psychological Dependence Potential	Organic Damage Potential
Euphoria, prevent withdrawal discomfort	Addiction, constipation, loss of appetite	Yes	Yes	No*
Euphoria, prevent withdrawal discomfort	Addiction, constipation, loss of appetite	Yes	Yes	No*
Euphoria, prevent withdrawal discomfort	Addiction, constipation, loss of appetite	Yes	Yes	No
Prevent withdrawal discomfort	Addiction, constipation, loss of appetite	Yes	Yes	No
Excitation, talkativeness	Depression, convulsions	Debated	Yes	Yes
Relaxation; increased euphoria, perceptions, sociability	Possible lung cancer, other health risks	No	Yes	Yes
Anxiety reduction, euphoria	Addiction with severe withdrawal symptoms, possible convulsions, toxic psychosis, addiction	Yes	Yes	No
Alertness, activeness	Loss of appetite, delusions, hallucinations, toxic psychosis	Yes	Yes	Yes
Insightful experiences, exhilaration, distortion of senses	May intensify existing psychosis, panic reactions	No	No?	No?
Insightful experiences, exhilaration, distortion of senses	May intensify existing psychosis, panic reactions	No	No?	No?
Insightful experiences, exhilaration, distortion of senses	May intensify existing psychosis, panic reactions	No	No?	No?
Sense alteration, anxiety reduction, sociability	Cirrhosis, toxic psychosis, neurologic damage, addiction	Yes	Yes	Yes
Alertness, calmness, sociability	Emphysema, lung cancer, mouth and throat cancer, cardiovascular damage, loss of appetite	Yes	Yes	Yes
Wakefulness, alertness	Insomnia, heart arrhythmias, high blood pressure	No	Yes	Yes

Adapted and updated from: *Resource Book for Drug Abuse Education*. NEA, 1969.

uses of amphetamines are to treat narcolepsy (sleep attacks) and to counteract overdoses of depressant drugs. Illicit use of amphetamines is widespread among individuals seeking an easy way to stay awake or who think drugs can improve mental or physical performance. Truck drivers, athletes, factory workers, and students cramming for exams frequently abuse amphetamines for these purposes.

Amphetamines rapidly produce a drug tolerance. Most abusers begin with one or two pills a day and soon progress to dozens a day to get the same effect. At this point the habitual user may take amphetamines in large doses or may switch to injecting Methedrine ("speed") directly into the bloodstream to produce euphoria, alertness, and a heightened sense of mental and physical energy and well-being. The true speed freak typically goes on binges lasting several days, after which he or she "crashes" from lack of sleep and food.

Question: How dangerous are amphetamines?

The dangers of amphetamine usage are multiple. To stay "high," the speed freak must take more and more of the drug as the body's tolerance increases. Higher doses can cause nausea, vomiting, high blood pressure, life-threatening heart arrhythmias, and crippling strokes. Also, it is important to realize that amphetamines speed the expenditure of bodily resources; they do not magically supply energy (AMA, 1968). Hence, the after-effects of an amphetamine high can be quite dangerous and uncomfortable. Possible effects include fatigue, depression, terrifying nightmares, confusion, and uncontrolled irritability and aggression. Repeatedly overextending one's body by speeding may lead to:

> considerable weight loss, sores and nonhealing ulcers, brittle fingernails, tooth grinding, chronic chest infections, liver disease, a variety of hypertensive disorders, and in some cases cerebral hemorrhage. (Canadian Government's Commission of Inquiry, 1971.)

Question: What is the meaning of the phrase "speed kills"?

It should be obvious that amphetamines are physically dangerous drugs. Further danger lies in the fact that amphetamines can cause a loss of contact with reality known as **amphetamine psychosis**. Amphetamine psychosis is similar to extreme paranoia. Affected individuals feel threatened and suffer from delusions that someone is out to get them. Acting on these delusions, the speed freak may become violent, resulting in self-injury or injury to others. At least one drug authority (Snyder, 1972) believes that it is in this sense that the slogan "speed kills," is most accurate: More persons may die from amphetamine-caused violence than from overdoses of the drug itself.

Cocaine   Cocaine is a powerful central nervous system stimulant derived from the leaves of the coca plant. Its subjective effects are sensations of alertness, euphoria, well-being, power, boundless energy, or exhilaration. There is often an increase in talkativeness, restlessness, and excitement, but there is no loss of thinking abilities or motor coordination. Hence a cocaine high is not easily detected by others (Spotts & Shontz, 1980).

Cocaine has a long history of use and misuse in the United States. At the turn of the century, dozens of non-prescription potions and cure-alls containing cocaine were sold. It was during this time that Coca-Cola was indeed the "real thing." From 1886, when it was first concocted, until 1906, when the Pure Food and Drug Act was passed, Coca-Cola contained cocaine (which has since been replaced with caffeine) (Grinspoon & Bakalar, 1977). Today, cocaine is becoming one of the most widely abused drugs. An estimated 4 to 5 million Americans use it at least once a month (Hammer & Hazleton, 1984).

Question: How does cocaine differ from amphetamines?

The two are very much alike in their effect on the central nervous system, so much so that when experienced users are given both they can't tell the difference (Resnick et al., 1977). At high dosages the main difference is that amphetamine effects may last several hours; cocaine is quickly metabolized, so its effects last only about 15 to 30 minutes.

Question: How dangerous is cocaine?

Scientists are currently reevaluating earlier ideas about cocaine's dangers. Some are beginning to think it is physically addicting, especially as more dependent abusers have begun to show up. However, at present there is little evidence that withdrawal symptoms occur when a person stops taking cocaine. On the other hand a temporary tolerance does develop during "runs" of cocaine use. That is, the abuser can take a dose at the end of a binge that might have been deadly at the beginning. However, such tolerance does not carry over from one drug-taking episode to the next. Therefore, it may still be most accurate to say that cocaine is not physically addicting in the classic sense.

Even if cocaine proves not to be physically addicting, there is little doubt about its tremendous potential for abuse. Cocaine is one of the most rewarding of all known chemicals. When rats and monkeys are given free access to cocaine, they find it irresistible. Many, in fact, end up dying of convulsions from self-administered overdoses of the drug (Hammer & Hazelton, 1984). Cocaine increases activity in brain pathways sensitive to the chemical messengers dopamine (DOPE-ah-meen) and noradrenaline (nor-ah-DREN-ah-lin). Noradrenaline arouses the brain, and increased dopamine produces an orgasmic rush of pleasure. This combination is so powerfully rewarding that compulsive cocaine use is highly likely. In short, the potential for psychological dependence is immense.

Cocaine's rewarding effects are followed by a period of emotional and physical depression (similar to an amphetamine letdown). To combat depression, the user often takes another dose, which is followed by another letdown and another dose. After repeating this cycle regularly, heavy users often suffer chronic nervousness, irritability, depression, and paranoia. Since cocaine is usually inhaled, or snorted, nasal damage is also possible (*Science News*, 1977).

Cocaine's potential for abuse would probably be even higher were it not for its absurdly high price. Currently, about 1 user in 10 becomes a compulsive abuser. If cocaine were cheaper, some authorities estimate that the figure would be 9 out of 10. The following is a list of increasingly serious signs of cocaine abuse (Pursch, 1983).

Compulsive use. If cocaine is available, say at a party, you will undoubtedly use it. You can't say no to it.

Loss of control. Once you have had some cocaine, you will keep using it until you are exhausted or the cocaine is gone.

Disregarding consequences. You don't care if the rent gets paid, your job is endangered, your lover disapproves, or your health is affected, you'll use cocaine anyway.

Cocaine has quite a reputation as a glamour drug. It is becoming increasingly clear, however, that its capacity for abuse and social damage rivals that of the decidedly unglamourous drug, heroin. Anyone who thinks he or she may be developing a cocaine problem should seek advice at a drug clinic or a Cocaine Anonymous meeting.

Caffeine Caffeine is the most frequently used psychoactive drug in the United States. Caffeine stimulates the brain by blocking chemicals that normally inhibit or slow nerve activity (Julien, 1985). Its effects become apparent with doses as small as 100 to 200 milligrams (the amount found in about two cups of brewed coffee).

Caffeine has various effects on the body: It speeds the heart, promotes the release of stomach acid, and increases urine production; also, it dilates some blood vessels while narrowing others. In large amounts caffeine may cause convulsions, but this is highly unlikely. It takes about 10 grams of caffeine, the equivalent of 100 cups of coffee, to run a serious risk of death (Julien, 1985). Psychologically, caffeine suppresses fatigue or drowsiness and increases feel-

ings of alertness; some people have a hard time starting a day without it.

How much caffeine did you consume today? It is common to think of coffee as the major source of caffeine, but there are many others. Caffeine is found in tea, many soft drinks (especially colas), chocolate, and cocoa. Over 2000 nonprescription drugs also contain caffeine, including stay-awake pills, cold remedies, and many name-brand aspirin products. Table 6–3 gives the approximate caffeine content of several foods.

Question: Are there any serious drawbacks to using caffeine?

Serious abuse of caffeine may result in an unhealthy dependence known as **caffeinism** (Levitt, 1977). People with caffeinism suffer from insomnia, irritability, loss of appetite, chills, racing heart, and elevated body temperature (Fig. 6–5). It is not uncommon to find that such individuals are consuming 15 or 20 cups of coffee a day. Even in the absence of caffeinism there are some caffeine-related health risks. Caffeine encourages the development of breast cysts in women, and it may contribute to insomnia, stomach problems, heart problems, and high blood pressure. Also, many drug experts recommend that women restrict their caffeine intake during the first 3 months of pregnancy. It is customary in our culture to think of caffeine as a nondrug. But as this discussion shows, it is wise to remember that it *is* a drug and to use it in moderation.

Nicotine Nicotine is a naturally occurring stimulant found mainly in tobacco. Next to caffeine, it is the most widely used psychoactive drug (Julien, 1985).

Question: How does nicotine compare with other stimulants?

Table 6–3 Average Caffeine Content of Various Foods
Instant coffee (5 oz.), 64 mg.
Percolated coffee (5 oz.), 108 mg.
Drip coffee (5 oz.), 145 mg.
Decaffeinated coffee (5 oz.), 3 mg.
Black tea (5 oz.), 42 mg.
Canned ice tea (17 oz.), 30 mg.
Cocoa drink (6 oz.), 8 mg.
Chocolate drink (8 oz.), 14 mg.
Sweet chocolate (1 oz.), 20 mg.
Colas (12 oz.), 50 mg.
Soft drinks (12 oz.) 0–52 mg.

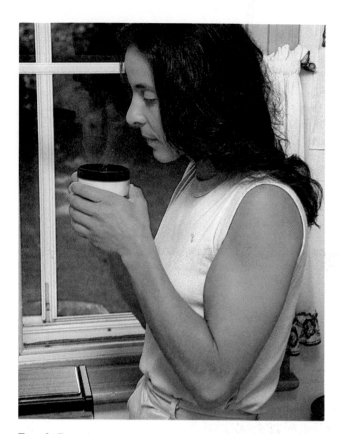

Fig. 6—5 *Like other drugs, caffeine is subject to abuse by some users.*

Nicotine is a potent drug. It is so toxic that it is sometimes used as an insecticide! In large doses it causes stomach pain, vomiting and diarrhea, cold sweats, dizziness, confusion, and tremors. In very large doses nicotine may cause convulsions, respiratory failure, and death (Levitt, 1977). For a nonsmoker, 50 to 75 milligrams of nicotine could be lethal (smoking about 17 to 25 cigarettes will produce this dosage). Most beginning smokers get sick on 1 or 2 cigarettes. In contrast, a heavy smoker may consume 40 cigarettes a day without feeling ill. This difference indicates that regular smokers build a tolerance for nicotine (Levitt, 1977).

Question: Is it true that nicotine can be addicting?

There is growing evidence that for some smokers nicotine is addicting. For many, withdrawal from nicotine causes headache, sweating, cramps, insomnia, digestive upset, irritability, and a sharp craving for cigarettes (Shiffman, 1980).

Question: How serious are the health risks of smoking?

A burning cigarette releases more than 6800 different chemicals. Many of these are potent *carcinogens* (car-SIN-oh-jins: cancer-causing substances). In addition, nicotine itself may be cancer causing (Bock, 1980). Lung cancer and other cancers caused by smoking are now considered the single most preventable cause of death in the United States. Among men, 97 percent of lung cancer deaths are caused by smoking. For women, 74 percent of all lung cancers are due to smoking, a rate that has risen sharply in recent years. Altogether, smoking is responsible for about one-third of all cancer deaths in the United States (Reif, 1981).

If you think smoking is harmless, or the link between smoking and cancer is unproven, you're kidding yourself. As one expert says, "The scientific link between tobacco smoking and cancer is now as firmly established as any link between cause and effect in a human disease is likely to be" (Reif, 1981). As if this weren't enough, smoking is also linked to heart disease, emphysema, and birth defects (Schwartz et al., 1980). An estimated 340,000 Americans die yearly of smoking-related diseases.

Smokers, unless they have a death wish, must be getting something out of smoking. Most claim that smoking helps them concentrate, feel sociable, or calm down. But psychologist Stanley Schachter asserts, "The heavy smoker gets nothing out of smoking. He smokes only to prevent withdrawal" (Schachter, 1978). Schachter has shown that smoking does not improve the mood or the performance of heavy smokers compared with nonsmokers. On the other hand, heavy smokers who are *deprived* of nicotine feel worse and perform worse than nonsmokers. Schachter has done experiments showing that heavy smokers adjust their smoking to keep bodily levels of nicotine constant. Thus, when smokers are given lighter cigarettes, they smoke more. Also, if they are under stress (which speeds the removal of nicotine from the body), they smoke more (Schachter, 1978). The link between stress and nicotine probably explains why students smoke more during stressful periods such as final exams, or at parties, which are also stressful.

Question: Is it better for a person to quit smoking abruptly or to taper down gradually?

Many authorities recommend cutting down gradually or at least switching to a low-tar cigarette. But Schachter and others believe it is better to quit "cold turkey" rather than to merely cut down or smoke lighter cigarettes. Schachter's work shows that smokers who cut down are in a constant state of withdrawal. This causes irritability and discomfort without really ending smoking. Smokers who switch to lighter cigarettes often end up smoking more to get the same total nicotine input. In doing so, they may expose themselves to more cancer-causing substances than before (Schachter, 1978; Shiffman, 1980). Whichever approach is taken, quitting smoking is not easy. Yet tens of millions of people have quit.

Downers— Barbiturates and Alcohol

Question: How do downers differ from the stimulant drugs?

The most widely used downers, or depressant drugs, are alcohol, barbiturates, and tranquilizers. These drugs are very much alike in their effects. Let's examine their properties.

Barbiturates

Barbiturates are **sedative** drugs that depress activity in the brain. Medically, they are used to calm patients or to induce sleep. In mild doses barbiturates have an effect similar to alcohol intoxication, but an overdose can cause coma or death. Barbiturates combined with alcohol are particularly dangerous, as the combined effects of the two drugs are multiplied by a **drug interaction** (one drug enhances the effect of another). Barbiturates are often taken in excessive amounts, because a first dose may be followed by a second or third as the user becomes uninhibited or forgetful. Marilyn Monroe, Judy Garland, and other well-known personalities have died of barbiturate overdoses. An overdose of barbiturates first causes unconsciousness and then so severely depresses activity in brain centers controlling heartbeat and respiration that death results.

Abuse   The most frequently abused downers are newer short-acting barbiturates such as *Seconal* and *Tuinal*. Closely related to these (and to alcohol) is the nonbarbiturate drug *methaqualone (Quaalude, Sopor,* and *Parest* are its trade names). These drugs seem to be preferred because they take effect quickly, and the rush of intoxication only lasts from 2 to 4 hours. Like the other depressants, repeated use can cause a physical dependence and emotional depression. Freddie Prinze, a popular television comedian, was on Quaaludes before he committed suicide.

All too often, the short-acting depressants are gulped down with alcohol or added in uncounted quantities to a "spiked" punch bowl. This is the combination that left a young woman named Karen Ann Quinlan in a coma that lasted 10 years, ending with her death in 1985. It is no exaggeration to restate that mixing barbiturates with alcohol can be fatal.

Alcohol

Contrary to popular belief, alcohol is not a stimulant. The apparent gaiety at drinking parties is due to alcohol's effect as a central nervous system **depressant**. As Fig. 6–6 shows, small amounts of alcohol reduce inhibition and produce feelings of relaxation and euphoria. Greater amounts of alcohol cause progressively more dangerous impairment of brain function until the drinker loses consciousness. Alcohol is also not an aphrodisiac. It usually impairs sexual performance, particularly in males. As William Shakespeare observed long ago, drink "provokes the desire, but it takes away the performance."

Abuse   Alcohol, America's favorite depressant, generates this country's biggest drug problem. Over 100 million Americans use alcohol, and an estimated 10 to 13 million of these have a serious drinking problem. A particularly alarming trend is a recent dramatic increase in alcohol abuse among adolescents and young adults. It is estimated that 20 percent of youths between the ages of 14 and 17 are problem drinkers (Chafetz, 1979). A recent national

THE FAR SIDE   By GARY LARSON

The real reason dinosaurs became extinct

Fig. 6–6 *The behavioral effects of alcohol are related to blood alcohol content and the resulting suppression of higher mental function. (From Jozef Cohen, Eyewitness Series in Psychology, p. 44. Copyright © by Rand McNally and Company. Reprinted by permission.)*

ALCOHOL CONSUMED	NEURAL REPRESENTATION	BEHAVIORAL EFFECT
2 oz. 90 proof whiskey .05% blood alcohol		Affects higher nervous centers. Drinker loses inhibitions, foregoes conventions and courtesies. Relaxes.
6 oz. 90 proof whiskey .15% blood alcohol		Affects deeper motor areas. Drinker staggers, has slurred speech, is overconfident, acts on impulse.
10 oz. 90 proof whiskey .25% blood alcohol		Affects emotional centers of midbrain. Drinker has impaired motor reactions and unsteady gait. Sensations are distorted. Tends to see double, to fall asleep.
16 oz. 90 proof whiskey .4% blood alcohol		Affects sensory area of cerebellum. Senses are dulled. Drinker is in stupor.
24 oz. 90 proof whiskey .6% blood alcohol		Affects perceptual areas. Drinker loses consciousness. Only functions of breathing and heartbeat remain.
32 oz. 90 proof whiskey .8% blood alcohol		Affects entire brain. Heartbeat and respiration stop. **Death.**

survey of college students found that 17 percent (more than 1 out of 6) are heavy drinkers. For college males the figure was 25 percent, or 1 out of 4 (Olmstead, 1983).

The costs of alcohol abuse are high. Of all drivers involved in traffic accidents resulting in death or bodily injury, 73 percent have blood alcohol levels of 0.2 percent or more (Cohen, 1970). It is probably no exaggeration to say of alcohol that:

Its abuse has killed more people, sent more victims to hospitals, generated more police arrests, broken up more marriages and homes, and cost industry more money than has the abuse of heroin, amphetamines, barbiturates, and marijuana combined. (Bengelsdorf, 1970.)

Question: What are the signs of alcohol abuse?

Recognizing Problem Drinking Because alcohol abuse is such a common problem, it is important to recognize the danger signals of alcoholism. Progression from a social drinker to a problem drinker to an alcoholic is often subtle. Jellinek (1960) has detailed the steps in the development of a drinking problem:

1. Initial phase. Initially, the social drinker begins to turn more frequently to alcohol to relieve tension or to feel good. Four danger signals in this period that signal excessive dependence on alcohol are:

More **Increasing consumption.** The individual drinks more and more and may begin to worry about his drinking.

Morning drinking. Morning drinking is a dangerous sign, particularly when it is used to combat a hangover or to "get through the day."

Mourning **Regretted behavior.** While drunk the individual engages in extreme behavior that leaves him feeling guilty or embarrassed. *Mourning*

Memory Loss **Blackouts.** Excessive drinking may be accompanied by an inability to remember what happened during intoxication.

2. Crucial phase. A crucial turning point comes as the person begins to lose control over drinking. At this stage there is usually control over when and where a first drink is taken, but one drink starts a chain reaction leading to a second and a third and so on.

3. Chronic phase. At this point alcoholics drink compulsively and continuously. They eat infrequently, become intoxicated from far less alcohol than before, and feel a powerful need for alcohol when deprived of it. Work, family ties, and social life all deteriorate. Their self-drugging is usually so compulsive that when given the choice, the bottle comes before friends, relatives, employment, and self-esteem. The alcoholic is an addict.

To add to this summary, Highlight 6–1 may help you form a clearer picture of how alcoholism begins.

One of the major stumbling blocks to early detection of an alcohol problem is our society's dual attitude toward drinking. Drinking is promoted, approved, and encouraged as an escape from problems, a means of relaxing, and as a source of entertainment at social gatherings. But this approval suddenly turns to rejection when the drinker has had too much or drinks too often. "Too much," however, is a hazy and undefined standard (Chafetz, 1979).

Many social-recreational drinkers could do a far better job of managing their alcohol consumption. Almost everyone has been to a party or social gathering spoiled by someone who drank too much too fast. Those who avoid overdrinking have a better time, and so do their friends. But how do you avoid drinking too much when "the conscience dissolves in alcohol"? The work of psychologists Roger Vogler and Wayne Bartz (1982) provides a partial answer.

Vogler and Bartz observe that drinking remains pleasant as long as blood alcohol stays below a level of about 0.05.

Highlight 6–1
The Devleopment of a Drinking Problem

Early Warnings
You are beginning to feel guilty about your drinking.

You drink more than you used to and tend to gulp your drinks.

You try to have a few extra drinks before or after drinking with others.

You have begun to drink at certain times or to get through certain situations.

You drink to relieve feelings of boredom, depression, anxiety, or inadequacy.

You are sensitive when others mention your drinking.

You have had memory blackouts or have passed out while drinking.

Signals Not to Be Ignored
There are times when you need a drink.

You drink in the morning to overcome a hangover from previous drinking.

You promise to drink less and are lying about your drinking.

You often regret what you have said or done while drinking.

You have begun to drink alone.

You have weekend drinking bouts and Monday hangovers.

You have lost time at work or school because of drinking.

You are noticeably drunk on important occasions.

Your relationship to family and friends has changed because of your drinking.

In this range people feel relaxed, euphoric, and sociable. At higher levels they go from moderately intoxicated to thoroughly drunk. Later, as blood alcohol begins to fall, those who overdrink become sick and miserable. Table 6–4 shows the approximate amount per hour that can be consumed without exceeding the 0.05 blood alcohol level. (Even at this level driving may be affected.) By pacing themselves, those who choose to drink can remain comfortable, pleasant, and coherent throughout a long party or other event. In short, if you drink, it might be wise to learn your "magic" number from Table 6–4.

Treatment   Treatment for alcoholism begins by sobering the person up and cutting off the supply. This procedure is referred to as **detoxification.** It frequently produces all the symptoms of drug withdrawal and can be excruciatingly unpleasant for the alcoholic. The next step is to try to restore the alcoholic's health. Continued heavy use of alcohol usually causes severe damage to the body and nervous system. Food, vitamins, and medical care cannot fully reverse this damage, but a reasonable state of health can be obtained. When they have "dried out" and health has been restored, alcoholics may be treated with tranquilizers, antidepressants, or psychotherapy. Unfortunately, the success of these procedures has been limited.

One lay group approach that has been fairly successful is Alcoholics Anonymous (AA), which functions on the premise that it takes a former alcoholic to understand and help a current alcoholic. Of those who remain in AA over one year, 81 percent get through the following year without a drink (Sexias, 1981). AA's success rate may simply reflect the fact that members participate voluntarily, meaning they have admitted to themselves that they have a serious problem. Sadly, it seems that problem drinkers often will not admit their problems until they have really

"hit bottom," but if they are willing, AA presents a practical approach to the problem.

Marijuana—
What's in the Pot?

If you pick any 20 college students at random, approximately 8 or 10 will have tried marijuana. A government survey recently estimated that 40 to 50 million Americans have tried marijuana, and approximately 15 million people regard themselves as regular users. Marijuana can no longer be considered a counterculture drug; it is used by professionals, elected officials, business people, and suburbanites (Carr & Meyers, 1980).

Marijuana and **hashish** are derived from the hemp plant **Cannabis sativa.** The main active chemical in cannabis is tetrahydrocannabinol, or **THC** for short. THC is a mild **hallucinogen** (hal-LU-sin-oh-jin)—a substance that alters sensory impressions. The range between a psychoactive dose and a toxic dose of THC is enormous. There have been no overdose deaths from marijuana use reported in the United States (Carr & Meyers, 1980). However, enough is now known about the effects of marijuana to make it clear that it cannot be considered harmless. Particularly worrisome is the fact that THC accumulates in the body's fatty tissues, especially in the brain and reproductive organs. Even if a person smokes marijuana just once a week, the body is never entirely free of THC (Nahas, 1979a).

Question: Does marijuana produce physical dependence?

Some signs of withdrawal symptoms have been observed in volunteers given large doses of THC in a clinical setting. However, studies of long-term heavy users of marijuana in Jamaica, Greece, and Costa Rica failed to find any physical dependence (Carter, 1980; Rubin & Comitas, 1975; Stefanis et al., 1977). Marijuana's potential for abuse lies primarily in the realm of psychological dependence, not addiction.

Immediate Effects of Marijuana   Marijuana's typical psychological effects are: a sense of euphoria or well-being, relaxation, altered time sense, and perceptual distortions (Carr & Meyers, 1980). Being "stoned" on marijuana impairs short-term memory and slows learning. Lists of words and numbers learned when a person is intoxicated are forgotten when he or she is sober again (Nahas, 1979b). Marijuana's interference with learning can become a serious problem for frequent users.

All considered, marijuana intoxication is relatively subtle by comparison to a drug such as alcohol (Carter,

Table 6–4	Moderated Drinking
Your Weight	Approximate number of drinks per hour to stay below 0.05 blood alcohol.*
100	.75
120	1.00
140	1.25
160	1.30
180	1.50
200	1.60
220	1.80
One drink	= 12 oz. beer
	= 4 oz. wine
	= 2.5 oz. brandy
	= 1.25 oz. 80 proof liquor

*Table entries are approximate, due to individual differences in metabolism, recency of meals, and other factors. Estimates are derived from tables prepared by Vogler and Bartz (1982).

Fig. 6–7 *An outdated antimarijuana poster demonstrates the kind of misinformation that has long been attached to this drug. Research is beginning to sort out what risks are associated with continued use of marijuana.*

1980). It may even be necessary for marijuana users to learn to experience an alteration of consciousness. At low dosages inexperienced users often report that they feel no effect at all (Carr & Meyers, 1980). Very large dosages can cause hallucinations, and some first-time users of larger amounts have feelings of losing control or panic. However, most marijuana smokers gauge their intake so that the high attained remains controlled. Despite this it is now well established that driving a car or operating machinery while high on marijuana can be extremely hazardous (Carr & Meyers, 1980). As a matter of fact, driving under the influence of any intoxicating drug is dangerous.

Question: There have been very alarming reports in the press about the dangers of marijuana. Are they accurate?

Dangers of Marijuana Use   As one pharmacologist put it, "Those reading only *Good Housekeeping* would have to believe that marijuana is considerably more dangerous than the black plague." Unfortunately, an evaluation of marijuana's risks has been clouded by emotional debate. Let's see if we can make a realistic appraisal.

In the early 1970s it was widely reported that marijuana causes brain damage, genetic damage, loss of motivation, and a reduction in the body's natural immunity to diseases. These are serious charges, but each has been criticized for being based on poorly done or inconclusive research (Brecher, 1975a; Julien, 1985; NIDA, 1976, Zinberg, 1976). In addition, recent studies in Jamaica,

Greece, and Costa Rica failed to find any serious health problems or mental impairment in long-term marijuana smokers (Carter, 1980; Rubin & Comitas, 1975; Stefanis et al., 1977). Does this mean that marijuana gets a clean bill of health? Not really. As is true of alcohol, some adults become highly dependent on marijuana. Frequent use of *any* psychoactive drug can seriously impair mental, physical, and emotional development—especially in children and adolescents (Nahas, 1979b; Zinberg, 1976).

Another legitimate concern is the possible adulteration of street drugs. For example, Mexican-grown marijuana has in recent years frequently been laced with the dangerous herbicide paraquat. On occasion street marijuana has been found to have PCP ("angel dust") or strychnine in it; both are *very* dangerous substances.

One more point to consider is that the possession and use of marijuana is illegal. True, some states have undertaken a **decriminalization** of marijuana laws. In these states possession brings a citation and a fine comparable to a traffic ticket. In most states, however, possession of any amount of marijuana is a misdemeanor, and in all states a person caught with larger amounts may be charged with a felony. Unless the laws change, marijuana usage can be costly in terms of a career or future employability.

Health Risks   After many years of conflicting and inadequate information, some of marijuana's potential health hazards have been clarified. After an extensive review of research, the National Academy of Sciences concluded in 1982 that marijuana's long-term effects include several health risks.

1. Marijuana smoke is quite irritating to the lungs. In regular users it causes chronic bronchitis and precancerous changes in lung cells. At present no direct link between marijuana and lung cancer has been established, but it is suspected. A recent study by Swiss researchers found that marijuana smoke contains 50 percent more cancer-causing hydrocarbons than does tobacco smoke. Some doctors estimate that smoking several joints a week is the equivalent of smoking a dozen cigarettes a day (Nahas, 1979a).

2. Marijuana temporarily lowers sperm production in males, and some studies show an increased number of abnormal sperm in men who use it. This could be a problem for a man who is marginally fertile and wants to have a family.

3. In experiments with female monkeys, THC causes abnormal menstrual cycles and disrupts ovulation. It is not known if the same applies to human females. Other animal studies show that THC causes a higher rate of miscarriages and that it can reach the developing fetus (Nahas, 1979a). As is true for so many other drugs, it appears that marijuana should be avoided during pregnancy.

When the preceding findings are compared with the studies of veteran marijuana users in other countries, it is clear that no one can say with complete certainty that marijuana is extremely harmful or completely safe. At present it appears to be in a class with tobacco and alcohol, but much is still unknown (Carter, 1980). Only future research will tell for sure "what's in the pot."

Learning Check

1. Circle the letters of all the drugs listed below that are known to cause a physical dependence:
   a. heroin   c. codeine   e. barbiturates   g. caffeine
   b. morphine   d. methadone   f. alcohol   h. amphetamines

2. Amphetamine psychosis is similar to extreme _____ in which the individual feels threatened and suffers from delusions.

3. Cocaine is very similar to _____ in its effects on the central nervous system.
   a. Quaaludes   b. codeine   c. cannabis   d. amphetamines

4. The combination of _____ and alcohol can be fatal.

5. One drink starts a chain reaction leading to a second and a third in the crucial phase of problem drinking.   T or F?

6. This country's biggest drug problem centers on abuse of:
   a. marijuana   b. alcohol   c. tobacco   d. cocaine

7. Most experts now acknowledge that marijuana is physically addicting.   T or F?

Answers: 1. All but g 2. paranoia 3. d 4. barbiturates 5. T 6. b 7. F

Applications

Meditation—The 20-Minute Vacation

A final form of consciousness alteration has been reserved for this Applications section because of its potential usefulness. Many psychologists now regard **meditation** as a practical way to lower stress and enhance well-being. Meditation refers to any mental exercise designed to produce relaxation and heighten awareness.

Question: How is meditation done?

Concentrative meditation, which is the simplest of several related techniques, is easily learned. In one experiment (Maupin, 1965), college students were instructed to concentrate on breathing:

> While you are sitting let your breath become relaxed and natural. Let it set its own pace and depth if you can. Then focus your attention on your own breathing: the movements of your belly, not your nose and throat. Do not allow extraneous thoughts or stimuli to pull your attention away from your breathing. This may be hard to do at first, but keep directing your attention back to it. Turn everything else aside if it comes up. (Maupin, 1965.)

Not all subjects responded to this exercise, but at the end of a two-week period those who did reported satisfying changes in consciousness. Their experiences included deep concentration, pleasant bodily sensations, and extreme detachment from outside worries and distractions.

An alternative approach you may want to try involves the use of a **mantra.** Mantras are smooth, flowing words that are easily repeated. Instead of focusing on breathing, you can silently chant a mantra. Two widely used mantras are "Om" and "Om mani padme hum." Like breathing, a mantra is basically used as a focus for attention. If other thoughts arise during meditation, one should return attention to the mantra as often as necessary to maintain meditation.

The Relaxation Response A principal claim of commercial meditation courses is that they offer a mantra tailored to the needs of each individual. But medical researcher Herbert Benson of Harvard Medical

School has demonstrated that the physical benefits of meditation are the same no matter what word is used. These include lowered heart rate, blood pressure, muscle tension, and other signs of lowered stress.

Benson believes that the core of meditation is the **relaxation response.** By this he means an innate physiological pattern that opposes activation of the body's fight-or flight mechanisms. Benson feels, quite simply, that most of us have forgotten how to deeply relax. Subjects in his experiments have had considerable success in producing the relaxation response by following these instructions:

> Sit quietly in a comfortable position. Close your eyes. Deeply relax all your muscles, beginning at your feet and progressing up to your face. Keep them deeply relaxed.
>
> Breathe through your nose. Become aware of your breathing. As you breathe out, say the word "one" silently to yourself.
>
> Do not worry about whether you are successful in achieving a deep level of relaxation. Maintain a passive attitude and permit relaxation to occur at its own pace. Expect distracting thoughts. When these distracting thoughts occur, ignore them and continue repeating "one" (adapted from Benson, 1977).

Question: What effects does meditation have, other than producing relaxation?

Effects of Meditation Many extravagant claims have been made about meditation. For example, members of the Transcendental Meditation (TM) movement have stated that 20 minutes of meditation is as restful as a night's sleep. This, however, is simply not true. One recent study, for instance, found that merely resting for 20 minutes produces the same bodily effects as meditation (Holmes et al., 1983). Long-term meditators have also claimed improvements in memory, alertness, creativity, and intuition. Again, such claims must be judged cautiously. Most are based on personal testimonials or poorly controlled studies. Contrary to such claims, a recent study by Warrenburg and Pagano (1983) found no

Applications: Meditation—The 20-Minute Vacation

improvements in verbal, musical, or spatial skills that could be linked to TM.

Before you dismiss meditation, however, let's explore a little further. A thorough review of studies on meditation leads to a number of interesting conclusions (Pagano & Warrenburg, 1983).

As already stated, meditation does reliably elicit the relaxation response. The fact that other activities will do the same does not cancel the value of meditation as a way to control relaxation. Meditation may be the best choice for people who find it difficult to "turn off" upsetting thoughts when they need to relax.

Early reports that meditators produce more alpha waves (a brain wave pattern associated with lowered stress) have proved false. Meditation most often produces a *decrease* in alpha waves. Instead, meditators fall into hypnogogic drowsiness like that associated with sensory deprivation. In other words, they tend to remain in a twilight state between sleep and wakefulness (Pagano & Warrenburg, 1983; Schuman, 1980).

Regular meditators consistently report lower levels of day-to-day stress and a greater sense of well-being. This effect appears to be genuine. It is interesting to note, however, that similar stress reduction occurs when people set aside time daily to engage in other restful activities. Muscle relaxation, positive daydreaming, and even leisure reading can bring similar benefits.

There is some evidence that those who meditate regularly react more strongly to stressful stimuli during laboratory testing. However, they recover faster than nonmeditators and say they felt less stressed.

As you can see, the effects of meditation are positive and beneficial, but far from magical. In fact, it must be concluded that many activities will elicit the relaxation response. Benson (1975) believes that the key elements for producing the relaxation response are:

1. a quiet environment
2. decreased muscle tension
3. a mental device (such as a repeated word) that helps shift thoughts away from ordinary, rational concerns
4. a passive attitude toward whether you are "succeeding" at becoming relaxed

Summary   To summarize, recent research suggests that meditation is only one of several ways to elicit the relaxation response. For many people sitting quietly and resting can be as effective. However, if you are the type of person who finds it difficult to ignore upsetting thoughts, then concentrative meditation might be a better way to promote relaxation. More important than the method you choose, however, is a willingness to set aside time each day to intentionally relax. Meditation and similar techniques provide a valuable, stress-lowering time-out from the normal clamour of thoughts and worries—something almost everyone could use in our fast-paced society.

Learning Check

1. During meditation there is an increase in hypnogogic drowsiness.   T or F?
2. Mantras are words said silently to oneself to end a session of meditation.   T or F?
3. Research conducted by Herbert Benson indicates that careful selection of a mantra is necessary to obtain the physical benefits of meditation.   T or F?
4. The most immediate benefit of meditation appears to be its capacity for producing the relaxation response.   T or F?

Answers: 1. T   2. F   3. F   4. T

Chapter Summary

- States of awareness that differ significantly from normal, alert, waking consciousness are called *altered states of consciousness* (ASCs). Altered states are particularly associated with hypnosis, sensory deprivation, psychoactive drugs, and meditation.

- *Hypnosis* is an altered state characterized by narrowed attention, increased suggestibility, and a dissociation or split in awareness. Many effects of hypnosis are in doubt, but it seems definitely capable of producing relaxation, controlling pain, maintaining motivation, and altering perceptions. *Stage hypnotism* makes use of deception and several characteristics of the stage setting to simulate hypnosis.

- Extreme or unusual stimulus conditions often induce altered states of consciousness. A prime example is *sensory deprivation*. Prolonged sensory deprivation is stressful and linked to a variety of perceptual and cognitive disruptions. Brief exposure to sensory deprivation, however, can produce sensory enhancement and relaxation. Sensory deprivation also appears to aid the breaking of long-standing habits.

- A *psychoactive* drug is a substance capable of altering functioning of the brain and nervous system in ways that alter consciousness. Most psychoactive drugs can be placed on a scale ranging from *stimulation* to *depression*.

- Drugs may cause a *physical dependence* (addiction) or a *psychological dependence*, or both. The physically addicting drugs are: heroin, morphine, codeine, methadone, barbiturates, alcohol, amphetamines, tobacco, and possibly cocaine. All psychoactive drugs can lead to psychological dependence.

- Drug use can be classified as *experimental, recreational, situational, intensive,* and *compulsive*. Drug abuse is most often associated with the last three.

- *Amphetamines* are powerful stimulants. They are subject to drug tolerance and can be very destructive to physical health. Heavy use is associated with paranoid delusions (*amphetamine psychosis*) and outbursts of violence.

- *Cocaine* is a stimulant almost identical to amphetamine. It differs from amphetamine in that no lasting tolerance develops and its effects last a shorter time. Cocaine has a high dependence potential owing to its powerful rewarding effects and after-use depression.

- *Caffeine* is a relatively mild CNS stimulant found in many foods and drug preparations. Caffeine's abuse potential is relatively low, but *caffeinism* sometimes occurs. Excessive caffeine consumption is unhealthy.

- *Nicotine* is a powerful stimulant. There is evidence that heavy smokers develop a tolerance to nicotine and undergo withdrawal if they stop smoking. Heavy users smoke mainly to regulate internal nicotine levels. Smoking causes lung cancer and other health problems.

- *Barbiturates* are depressant drugs whose action is similar to alcohol intoxication. The overdose level for barbiturates is quite close to the intoxication dosage, making them dangerous drugs. Mixing barbiturates and alcohol may be fatal.

- *Alcohol* is, in terms of potency and sheer numbers of people affected, the most damaging and heavily abused drug in common use today. The development of a drinking problem is usually marked by an *initial phase* of increasing consumption, a *crucial phase*, in which a single drink can set off a chain reaction, and a *chronic phase*, in which a person lives to drink and drinks to live.

- The immediate effects of *marijuana* include relaxation, sensory distortions, and euphoria. Marijuana is subject to an abuse pattern similar to alcoholism, although large numbers of people use it recreationally without evidence of serious problems. Studies of long-term users have failed to find any drastic health changes due to marijuana. However, animal studies and laboratory studies have implicated marijuana as a possible source of lung cancer and other health risks.

- *Concentrative meditation* is a mental exercise used to alter consciousness and elicit relaxation. Many of the benefits of meditation can be achieved in other ways, but the technique remains a viable means of lowering stress and enhancing perceived well-being.

▶▶▶▶ **Exploration**

Perspectives on Drug Abuse

Drug Abuse— Many Questions, Few Answers

Question: Why do people use drugs?

People seek drug experiences for a variety of reasons, ranging from curiosity and a desire to belong to a group to a search for meaning or an escape from feelings of inadequacy (Lipinski & Lipinski, 1970). Some observers believe that drug use is so deeply ingrained in modern society that "we are addicted to addiction. This is to say that, with few exceptions we subscribe to the premise . . . that life cannot be lived without drugs." We are so used to having our own way that we have come to believe "that we should be able to will ourselves to be calm, cheerful, thin, industrious, creative—and moreover, to have a good night's sleep" (Farber, 1966). Farber believes that the medical profession, well meaning but misguided, has accepted these premises wholeheartedly, and unnecessarily encourages drug use. Indeed, one psychologist observed:

Depression, social inadequacy, anxiety, apathy, marital discord, children's misbehavior, and other psychological and social problems of living are now being redefined as medical problems, to be solved by physicians with prescription pads. (Rogers, 1971.)

Perhaps physicians and laymen alike can be partially excused for placing undue faith in the value of drugs because each group is the target of multimillion-dollar advertising campaigns aimed at encouraging drug use. Even the lowly aspirin is now pushed as a means of relieving "nervous tension." Advertisements directed at physicians encourage overuse of drugs even more blatantly. An ad pictures a distraught mother with a child and asks, "Her kind of pressures last all day . . . shouldn't her tranquilizer?" Another reads:

School, the dark, separation, dental visits, monsters. The everyday anxiety of children sometimes gets out of hand.

A child can usually deal with his anxieties. But sometimes the anxieties overpower the child. Then he needs your help. Your help may include Vistaril. (Rogers, 1971.)

Drugs, of course, have legitimate uses and have alleviated much suffering. The problem is that drugs strong enough to ease pain, induce sleep, end depression, or otherwise alter consciousness have a high potential for abuse.

Drug abuse in the United States has reached epidemic proportions in recent years. Problems once restricted to drug-related subcultures and the urban disadvantaged are now seen regularly among high school and college students and among the vast middle classes (McGlothlin, 1975). One study of *junior high* students found that almost one-quarter claimed to have used illicit drugs (Anhalt & Klein,

1976). A few years ago, country western singer Charlie Pride was proclaiming in song that, "We don't smoke marijuana in Muskogee." But information indicates that rural areas and smaller towns have been absorbed into the national drug culture. Only extremely small towns of less than 2500 population still report relatively low rates of drug use (Bowker, 1976). Also giving cause for concern is a strong trend toward multidrug use, often involving use of drugs in combination (Gould, 1977).

Question: What, if anything, should be done about drug abuse?

Prevention   Traditional approaches have emphasized strict law enforcement, legal penalties, and limiting drug supplies. Limiting supplies has been relatively successful in the case of some drugs. But drug abuse and the legality of a drug are two relatively independent issues. This distinction becomes clear when it is recognized that one of the most potent, destructive, and potentially dangerous drugs available is alcohol. Another indication of the overuse of legally manufactured drugs can be found in the 12 billion amphetamine tablets produced each year by American drug companies. This volume is enough to supply every American with 35 to 50 tablets (Grinspoon & Hedblom, 1972).

Facts such as these have led some observers to conclude that anyone who seeks drug-induced

Exploration: Perspectives on Drug Abuse

consciousness alteration will find a drug, legal or illegal, to achieve it. Psychiatrist Thomas Szasz (1972) believes that it is therefore futile for the government to attempt to "legislate morality" by regulating what drugs a person chooses to take. Szasz suggests that current drug regulations have an effect similar to that produced by the prohibition of alcohol; that is, they encourage a black market, organized crime, disrespect for the law, and occasional poisonings from adulterated drugs.

After an extensive review of research on drugs, drug abuse, and drug laws, *Consumer Reports* magazine drew the same conclusion and added these recommendations (Brecher, 1972):

Stop publicizing the horrors of the "drug menace." Scare publicity has functioned not as warnings, but to popularize drugs and as a lure to recreational drug use.

Stop misclassifying drugs. Our current legal classification system treats alcohol and nicotine—two of the most harmful drugs—essentially as nondrugs, while marijuana is equated with heroin—a shocking and harmful bit of foolishness. Cocaine is still listed as a narcotic when it is clearly a stimulant. A scientifically based legal system must replace the current politically based one.

Whereas it is true that drug *use* is essentially a victimless crime, the fact remains that *abuse* of drugs—legal or illegal—represents a serious loss in terms of the productivity and mental health of self-drugged citizens. The point of view expressed by Szasz—that government regulation of drugs is futile— is obviously controversial. Many, in fact, believe that the answer to drug problems is to be found in stricter penalties and law enforcement. And yet, a sober look at drug abuse makes it clear that

some psychoactive drugs are almost always available. In general, Americans tend to overlook the frequency of abuse of legal drugs such as tranquilizers or alcohol and overestimate the misuse of illegal drugs (Drug Abuse Council, 1980). Although millions of dollars have been spent on drug enforcement since 1970, there has been an increase in the overall level of drug use by young adults in the United States (*The National Household Survey on Drug Abuse,* 1982). Given this fact, some experts believe prevention through education and early intervention is the answer to drug problems. What do you think?

Learning Check

1. Advertising campaigns directed at physicians tend to overstate the need for treating behavioral problems with drugs.   T or F?
2. There has been an increasing trend toward multidrug use in the United States in recent years.   T or F?
3. Thomas Szasz believes that it is time for the government to take a lead in "legislating morality" with regard to drug use.   T or F?
4. Current laws in the United States have been accused of misclassifying some drugs.   T or F?

Answers: 1. T 2. T 3. F 4. T

Questions for Discussion

1. Do you agree or disagree with the idea that prohibition of drug use leads to adulteration, black markets, organized crime, unwillingness of abusers to seek help, and greater injury through imprisonment than is caused by the drugs themselves? What arguments can you give to support your position?

2. Why do you think there is such a contrast in the laws regulating marijuana in contrast to alcohol and tobacco?

3. In the novel *Brave New World* Aldous Huxley describes an imaginary drug called *soma* that makes people feel continuously happy and cooperative. If such a drug existed, what controls would you impose on its use? Why? If a drug that could enhance creativity were discovered, what use would you allow for it? What about a drug to improve memory?

4. If you have ever seen a stage hypnotist or participated in a hypnosis demonstration, how did your experience compare with Barber's analysis of stage hypnosis?

5. Have you ever been in a situation that produced sensory deprivation (such as a commercial flotation center or a radar room)? How did you react? Why do you think brief sensory deprivation is restful and longer periods are stressful?

6. Do you think that seeking altered states of consciousness is "natural." What altered states does our culture accept? About which states is it ambivalent? What altered states does it clearly reject? How do you think such differences developed?

7. What rationale can you provide for alcohol's becoming the drug of choice for so many adolescents and young adults?

8. If you had a totally free hand, how would you handle this country's drug abuse problem?

Sleep, Dreaming, and Arousal

Chapter 7

Chapter Preview

A Living Nightmare and Life beyond Time

January 1959, New York's Times Square: To raise money for charity, disc jockey Peter Tripp has agreed to go without sleep for 200 hours. But all too soon his vigil turns brutal. After 100 hours Tripp begins to have visual hallucinations. He sees cobwebs in his shoes, and he watches in terror as a tweed coat becomes a suit of furry worms. When Tripp crosses the street to a hotel to change clothes, a dresser drawer seems to burst into flames.

After 170 hours Tripp's agony becomes almost unbearable. He struggles with the simplest thought, reasoning, and memory problems. His brain wave patterns look like those of sleep, and he is no longer sure who he is. By the end of 200 hours, Tripp is unable to distinguish between his waking nightmares, hallucination, and reality (Luce, 1965). He has been ravaged by his need for sleep.

Life beyond Time   In a scene far removed from Peter Tripp's ordeal, French scientist Michel Siffre entered Midnight Cave near Del Rio, Texas, on February 14, 1972 (Siffre, 1975). A small nylon tent deep inside the cave became Siffre's home for the next 6 months.

Living alone within the depths of the cave, Siffre was completely isolated from clocks, calendars, the sun, the moon, and other reminders of time's passing. Siffre's strange quest was undertaken to learn what effect such isolation would have on the natural rhythms of human life. In the cave he lived by sleep-waking "cycles," rather than by days. After each period of sleep, he signaled the above-ground support crew to switch on the lights in his living area to begin a cycle. When he felt that a "day" had passed, the lights were turned off.

In addition to the scientific interest of Siffre's experience, there are practical concerns. For example, if two days could be perceived as one, the emotional strain of space flight, or the lengthy isolation on nuclear submarines, or life at lonely radar outposts could be eased. In partial support of such possibilities, Siffre's "days" averaged 28 hours. But at several points they lasted 30, 40, or even 50 hours—and seemed completely normal to him.

Both Siffre and Tripp are voyagers into a realm that is both familiar to us all and a source of great mystery. This chapter is a further investigation into sleep, dreaming, and points beyond.

Survey Questions   How much sleep do we need? What are the effects of sleep loss or changes in sleep patterns? Are there different stages of sleep? How does dream sleep differ from dreamless sleep? What are the causes of sleep disorders and unusual sleep events? Do dreams have meaning? Can dreams be used to promote self-understanding?

Resources

Sleep— A Nice Place to Visit

Each of us will spend some 25 years of life in a strange state of semi-consciousness called sleep. Contrary to common belief, we are not totally unresponsive during sleep. Experiments show that you are more likely to awaken if your own name is spoken instead of another (Webb, 1978). Likewise, a sleeping mother may ignore a jet rumbling overhead but wake at the slightest whimper of her child. Some people can even do simple tasks while asleep. In one experiment subjects learned to avoid an electric shock by touching a switch each time a tone sounded— eventually they could do it without waking. (Turning off an alarm clock without waking up is a similar response.) Of course sleep does impose limitations. There is no evidence, for instance, that a person can learn math, a foreign language, or other complex skills while asleep—especially when the snooze takes place in class (Aarons, 1976).

Because of its many contradictions, sleep has always aroused curiosity. What do we know about this daily retreat from the world?

The Need for Sleep

Question: How strong is the need for sleep?

Sleep expert Wilse Webb (1975) describes sleep as a "gentle tyrant." Webb considers sleep an innate biological rhythm that can never be entirely sidestepped. But, if flexibility is needed, sleep will give way temporarily, especially at times of great danger. As comedian Woody Allen put it, "The lion and the lamb shall lie down together, but the lamb will not be very sleepy." You could choose, then, to stay awake for an extended period. But there *are* limits. Animals with brain operations that prevent sleep fall into a coma and die after several days (Kleitman, 1963).

Early in his career Webb tried, in every way he could imagine, to teach animals to do without sleep. In one experiment rats were placed on a moving treadmill over a pool of water to prevent sleep. Even so, sleep won out. The animals soon began to engage in repeated microsleeps (Goleman, 1982). A **microsleep** is a brief shift in brain activity to patterns normally found in sleep. Microsleeps also occur in humans. Have you ever realized, while driving late at night, that you were dangerously unaware of your surroundings for a few seconds? Many automobile accidents occur during such microsleeps.

Question: How long could a person go without sleep?

Sleep Deprivation   With few exceptions 4 days or more without sleep becomes hell for anyone, but longer sleepless periods are possible. The world record for continuous wakefulness is held by Randy Gardner—who at age 17 went 268 hours (11 days) without sleep. Surprisingly, Randy needed only 14 hours of sleep to recover (Dement, 1972). It is usually not necessary to completely replace lost sleep. In fact, most symptoms of sleep deprivation are removed by a single night's rest.

What are the costs of sleep loss? Age and personality make a big difference. Randy Gardner remained coherent to the end of his vigil, whereas Peter Tripp's behavior became quite bizarre. In general most persons show no impairment on complex mental tasks after 2 days without sleep. But most grow irritable, and their ability to pay attention, remain vigilant, and follow simple routines declines (Webb, 1978). If you were mildly deprived of sleep, you would probably find that you could rouse yourself for more complex, engaging, or challenging tasks. What usually suffers most is low-level, boring, self-motivated tasks. As Wilse Webb says, "It's not your thinking or memory that goes, it's your will to continue; you would prefer to be asleep" (Goleman, 1982).

Greater sleep loss can occasionally produce a temporary **sleep-deprivation psychosis** like that suffered by Peter Tripp. Common elements of this reaction are confusion and disorientation, delusions (false or distorted beliefs), and hallucinations. Hallucinations may be visual, like Tripp's "coat of furry worms," or tactile, such as feeling cobwebs on the face. Fortunately, such "crazy" behavior is less common than once thought. Hallucinations and delusions, if they occur at all, are never evident before 60 hours without sleep. The most common reactions to extended sleep loss are inattention, staring, trembling hands, drooping eyelids, and an increased sensitivity to pain (Webb, 1978).

Biological Rhythms

Question: Sleep was described as an innate biological rhythm. What does that mean?

Scientists have long known that the body operates like a finely tuned instrument, guided by internal biological clocks. Every 24 hours the body undergoes a complex cycle of changes called **circadian** (sur-KAY-dee-un) **rhythms** (*circa*: about; *diem*: a day).

Throughout the day large changes take place in body temperature, blood pressure, urine volume, amino acid level, and in activity of the liver, kidneys, and endocrine glands. These bodily activities, and many others, peak sometime each day (Moore-Ede et al., 1982). Especially important is the output of the hormone adrenaline, which causes general arousal. Adrenaline is often three to five times greater during the day than at night (Luce, 1971).

Most people are more energetic and alert during the high point of their circadian rhythm (Horne et al., 1980).

Such differences are so basic that when a "day person" rooms with a "night person," both are more likely to give their relationship a negative rating (Watts, 1982). This is readily understandable: What could be worse than having someone bounding around cheerily when you're half asleep, or the reverse?

Sleep is closely linked to circadian rhythms. It is easiest to get to sleep, for instance, when body temperature begins to drop. Rhythms of sleep and waking are so steady that they continue for many days even when clocks and light-dark cycles are eliminated. However, under such conditions humans eventually shift to a rhythm that averages 25 hours, not 24 (Sulzman, 1983) (see Fig. 7–1). This finding suggests that external time markers, especially light and dark, help tie our body rhythms to a normal 24-hour day. Otherwise, some people would eventually drift into their own unusual sleep patterns—as Michel Siffre did in his cave experiment.

In a moment we will discuss some practical aspects of circadian rhythms. But first, let's examine normal sleep patterns in more depth.

Question: What is the normal range of sleep?

Sleep Patterns According to medical records there is a man in England who gets by on only 15 minutes to 1 hour of sleep each night—and feels perfectly fine. However, this is quite a rarity. Only 8 percent of the popula-

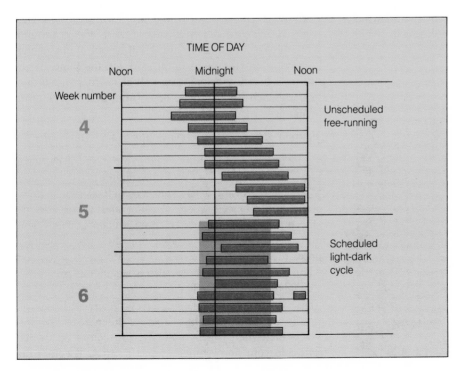

Fig. 7–1 *Circadian rhythms. Bars show periods of sleep during the fourth, fifth, and sixth weeks of an experiment with a human subject. During unscheduled periods the subject was allowed to select times of sleep and lighting. The result was a circadian rhythm of about 25 hours. Notice how this free-running rhythm began to advance around the clock. When periods of darkness were scheduled (colored area), the rhythm quickly resynchronized with 24-hour days. (Adapted from Czeisler, 1981.)*

tion averages 5 hours of sleep or less per night. The majority sleep on a familiar 7- to 8-hour-per-night schedule. It is quite normal, however, to sleep as little as 5 hours per night, or as much as 11. Urging everyone to sleep 8 hours would be like advising everyone to wear medium-size shoes. There is one difference worth noting, however: In general **long sleepers** tend to be daytime worriers. **Short sleepers,** in contrast, are typically nonworriers (Hartmann, 1981). (If you sleep a lot, try not to worry about it!) This difference may reflect the restorative function of sleep. That is, people who worry may need more rest each night.

Question: Do elderly people need more sleep?

They may need it, but they seldom get it. Increasing age usually brings a *reduction* in sleep time. People over the age of 50 average only 6 hours of sleep a night. In contrast, infants spend up to 20 hours a day sleeping, usually in 2- or 4-hour cycles. With increasing age most children go through a nap stage and eventually settle into a steady cycle of sleeping once a day (see Fig. 7–2). Some people, of course, maintain the afternoon siesta as an adult pattern.

There is a great temptation to try to reduce sleep time. The late Buckminster Fuller, inventor of the geodesic dome, claimed he often slept only 2 hours a day by napping whenever he felt like it. Before you try the same thing, you should know that such schedules are usually less efficient than sleeping once a day. Why should this be true? As long as a person gets 8 hours of sleep a day, what

Fig. 7–2 *Development of sleep patterns. Short cycles of sleep and waking gradually become the night-day cycle of an adult. (After Williams, 1964.)*

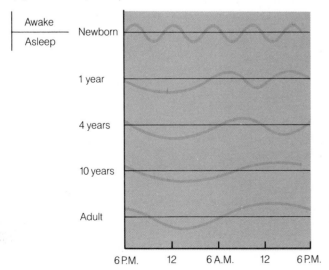

difference would it make? The problem is that people on *shortened* cycles—for example, 3 hours of sleep to 6 hours awake—often can't get to sleep when the cycle calls for it (Webb, 1978). The underlying circadian rhythm simply won't cooperate. This is why astronauts continue to sleep on their normal earth schedule once in space (Goleman, 1982).

A more promising possibility is to adapt to *longer* than normal days. Such days can be tailored to match natural **sleep patterns,** which show a ratio of *two to one* between time awake and time asleep. One such schedule was tested in an experiment in which 28-hour days were set up. It was found that younger subjects adapted more easily to longer days of this sort—presumably because their circadian rhythms were less firmly established (Kleitman & Kleitman, 1953). However, on very long, 36-hour cycles (24 awake and 12 asleep), all subjects did poorly. Most couldn't use the entire 12-hour sleep period, so they lost sleep over several cycles (Webb, 1978). As with sleep needs, we see again that sleep is a gentle tyrant. Sleep patterns and circadian rhythms may be bent and stretched, but they rarely yield entirely to human whims.

Shift Work and Jet Lag   The effects of sleep-waking cycles become especially noticeable whenever there is a major shift in time schedules. It is well documented, for example, that businesspersons, diplomats, athletes, and other time-zone travelers often make errors or perform poorly when their body rhythms are disturbed by jet lag. If you travel great distances east or west, the peaks and valleys of your circadian rhythms will be out of phase with the physical environment. Shift work has the same effect, causing a loss of efficiency, as well as fatigue, irritability, upset stomach, nervousness, depression, and a decline in mental agility (Akerstedt, Torsvall, & Gillberg, 1982).

Question: How fast do people adapt to such time shifts?

For major time-zone shifts (5 hours or more) it can take from several days to 2 weeks to resynchronize. Adaptation to jet lag is slowest when you stay indoors—in a hotel room, for instance—where sleeping and eating can be done on the old schedule. Getting outdoors, where you must sleep, eat, and socialize on the new schedule, speeds the process (Moore-Ede et al., 1982).

The *direction* of travel also affects adaptation. If you fly west, adapting is relatively easy, taking an average of 4 to 5 days. If you fly east, adapting takes 50 percent longer or more (see Fig. 7–3). Why is there a difference? The answer is that when you fly east, the sun comes up earlier relative to your home time. As you fly west, it comes up later. Recall that the circadian rhythm naturally runs longer than 24 hours. For this reason it is easier to advance (stay up later and sleep in) than it is to shift backwards. When you travel east, you must go to sleep during your former afternoon and get up when your body thinks it is the middle of the night. Likewise, work shifts that rotate backward (night, evening, day) are more disruptive than those that advance (day, evening, night). Best of all are work shifts that do not change: Even continuous night work is less disruptive than changing shifts.

Question: What does all of this have to do with those of us who are not shift workers or world travelers?

There are few college students who have not at one time or another burned the midnight oil, especially for final exams. During this or any other strenuous period, it is wise to remember the effects of disturbed bodily rhythms. Any major deviation from your regular schedule is likely to cost more than it's worth. Often, you can accomplish as much during 1 hour in the morning as you could have in 3 hours of work after midnight. The 2 hours difference in efficiency might as well be spent sleeping. If you feel you must depart from your normal schedule, do it gradually over a period of days.

In general if you can anticipate an upcoming body rhythm change (when traveling, before finals week, or when doing shift work), it is best to *preadapt* yourself to your new schedule beforehand. Before traveling, for instance, you should go to sleep 1 hour later, or earlier, each day until your sleep cycle matches the time at your destination.

Stages of Sleep—
The Nightly Roller Coaster Ride

Question: What causes sleep?

Early sleep experts thought that some substance related to fatigue must accumulate in the bloodstream and cause sleep. But studies of Siamese twins (individuals whose bodies are joined at birth) show this is false. One twin frequently can be observed sleeping while the second is awake (see Fig. 7–4). During extended wakefulness a sleep-promoting chemical collects in the brain and spinal cord, *not* in the blood. If this substance is extracted from one animal and injected into another, the second animal will fall asleep (Pappenheimer, 1976). Notice, however, that this experiment does not fully explain sleep. For example, how do we account for the well-rested student who must fight to stay awake during a boring lecture?

All that can be said with certainty is that sleep is *actively* generated by several structures in the brain: the hypothal-

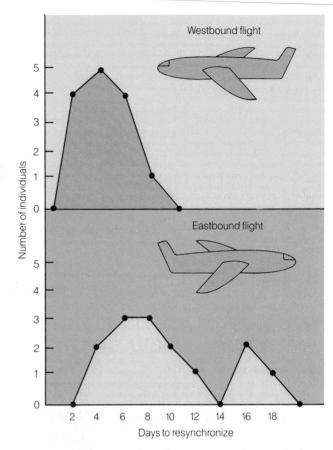

Fig. 7–3 *Time required to adjust to air travel across six time zones. The average time to resynchronize was faster for westbound travel than for eastbound flights. (Data from Beljan et al., 1972; cited by Moore-Ede et al., 1982.)*

Fig. 7–4 *These Siamese twins share the same blood supply, yet one sleeps while the other is awake. (Photo by Yale Joel,* Life *magazine. ©1954 Time, Inc.)*

amus, the reticular formation, and a "sleep center" in the brainstem. Rather than shutting down during sleep, the brain changes the *pattern* of its activity, not the amount.

Question: Why should the brain be programmed so that we regularly become unconscious?

No one really knows, but there are some hints. Sleep may simply lower activity, body temperature, and metabolism to conserve energy and lengthen life. For example, shrews have a high metabolic rate and rarely sleep. By contrast bats sleep up to 20 hours a day. The life span of the shrew is about 2 years, whereas bats of the same size live up to 18 years. Thus the bat's ability to "turn itself off" may result in a ninefold increase in life span (Allison & Van Twyver, 1970). During the course of evolution, natural selection may also have favored sleep. Those animals who did not retire to burrow, tree, cave, or hollow had a higher chance of going out at night and getting into trouble or of being killed (Greenberg, 1978). (No doubt they had more fun, though.)

Question: What happens when you fall asleep?

The Stages of Sleep　The changes that come with sleep can be measured with an **EEG (electroencephalograph,** or brain wave machine). The brain gives off tiny electrical signals that can be amplified and recorded. When a person is awake and alert, the EEG shows a pattern of small fast waves called **beta waves** (see Fig. 7–5). Immediately before sleep the EEG shifts to a different pattern of larger and slower waves called **alpha waves.** (Alpha waves also occur at other times when one is relaxed and thoughts are allowed to drift.) As the eyes close, breathing becomes slow and regular, the pulse rate slows, and body temperature drops.

Stage 1　As the person loses consciousness and enters **light sleep,** the heart rate slows even more. Breathing becomes more irregular; the muscles of the body relax. This sometimes triggers a reflex muscle contraction called **myoclonus** (MY-oh-KLOE-nus), which is quite normal. In Stage 1 sleep the EEG is made up mainly of small, irregular waves with some alpha. Persons awakened at this time may or may not say they were asleep.

Stage 2　As sleep deepens, the EEG begins to show short bursts of activity called **sleep spindles,** and body temperature drops even more noticeably (see Fig. 7–5). Sleep spindles seem to mark the true boundary of sleep. Within 4 minutes after they appear, the majority of subjects who are awakened report that they were asleep (Bonnet & Moore, 1982).

Stage 3　In Stage 3 a new brain wave called **delta** begins to appear. Delta waves are very large and slow. Delta waves signal deeper sleep and a further loss of consciousness.

Stage 4　About an hour after sleep begins, **deep sleep** is reached. In Stage 4 the brain wave pattern becomes almost pure delta waves, and the sleeper is in a state of

Fig. 7–5　(a) *Photograph of an EEG tracing.* (b) *Changes in brain wave patterns associated with various stages of sleep. Actually, most wave types are present at all times, but they occur more or less frequently in various sleep stages.*

(a)

Awake — Beta waves

Eyes closed, relaxed — Alpha waves

Stage 1 — Small irregular waves

Stage 2 — Sleep spindles

Stage 3 — Delta waves appear

Stage 4 — Mostly delta

(b)

Fig. 7–6 *Typical changes in stages of sleep during the night. (After Van de Castle, 1971.)*

nearly complete oblivion. If a loud noise is sounded during Stage 4, the sleeper will awaken in confusion and may not remember the noise.

After spending some time in Stage 4, the sleeper returns (through Stages 3 and 2) to Stage 1. Further shifts between deeper and lighter sleep occur throughout the night (see Fig. 7–6).

Two States of Sleep   Along with the discovery of sleep stages, it was noticed that at various times the eyes of a sleeper make rapid movements. These rapid eye movements (or **REM**s) are strongly associated with dreaming. Roughly 85 percent of awakenings made during ongoing REMs produce reports of dreams (Cartwright, 1978). REMs usually occur in Stage 1 sleep. An exception is the very first Stage 1 period, which is usually free of REMs and dreams. **REM sleep** is easy to observe in pets, such as dogs and cats. Watch for movement of the eyes under the eyelids and for facial movements and irregular breathing. In addition to twitching their ears, whiskers, and paws, cats and dogs may also move their legs in synchrony, as if they were trying to run.

The two most basic states of sleep now appear to be REM sleep, with its associated dreaming, and **non-REM (NREM) sleep,** which occurs during Stages 2, 3, and 4 (Cartwright, 1978). NREM sleep is dream free about 90 percent of the time. While it's true that people awakened during NREM sleep occasionally say they were dreaming, dreams reported during REM sleep are usually longer, clearer, more detailed, and more vivid or dreamlike (Foulkes & Schmidt, 1983).

NREM sleep seems to help us recover from fatigue built up during the day. It increases with exercise or physical exertion (Horne & Staff, 1983). In comparison REM sleep increases when a person is subjected to added daytime stress. Although REM sleep totals only about 1½ hours per night (about the same as a feature movie), its connection with dreaming makes it as important as NREM sleep. REM sleep may become pronounced when there is a death in the family, a major occupational change, marital conflict, or other emotionally charged event (Hartmann, 1973).

Learning Check

See if you can answer these questions before reading on.

1. A momentary shift in brain activity to a pattern characteristic of sleep is referred to as:
   a. delta sleep   *b.* light sleep   *c.* microsleep   *d.* deprivation sleep

2. Delusions and hallucinations may continue for several days after a sleep-deprived individual returns to normal sleep.   T or F?

3. When external indications of time's passing are removed, the human circadian rhythm eventually averages about _____ hours.

4. It is usually easier to adapt sleep-waking cycles to eastward time-zone shifts than to westward travel.   T or F?

5. Older adults, and particularly the elderly, sleep more than children because they are more easily fatigued.   T or F?

6. Most studies of sleep patterns show a consistent ratio of two to one between time awake and time asleep.   T or F?

7. Rapid eye movements (REMs) indicate a person is in deep sleep.   T or F?

8. Match the following:

____ Awake, re-laxed	**A.**	Sleep spindles
	B.	Dreaming
____ Stage 2	**C.**	Myoclonus
____ Stage 4	**D.**	Delta waves
____ Stage 1, REM	**E.**	Alpha waves

Answers: 1. c 2. F 3. 25 4. F 5. F 6. T 7. F 8. E, A, D, B

REM Sleep— In the Theater of Dreams

When researchers Nathaniel Kleitman and Eugene Aserinsky discovered REM sleep in 1952, they ushered in a golden era of dream inquiry that has allowed us to answer some age-old questions. Let us consider some of the most interesting.

Question: Does everyone dream? Do dreams occur in an instant?

Most people dream four or five times a night, but not all people remember their dreams. "Nondreamers" are often shocked by the vividness of their dreams when first awakened during REM sleep. Dreams are usually spaced about 90 minutes apart, with each succeeding dream lasting a little longer. The first dream lasts only about 10 minutes; the last averages 30 minutes and may run as long as 50. Dreams, therefore, occur in real time, not as a "flash" (Cartwright, 1978; Dement, 1960).

Question: What happens to the body when a person dreams?

REM Sleep As discussed before, the brain returns to light sleep and rapid eye movements begin (see Fig. 7–7). Some eye movements correspond to dream activity. For instance, if you dream that you are watching a tennis match, you will probably move your eyes from side to side (Dement & Kleitman, 1957).

Because there is a return to Stage 1, dreaming has been called **paradoxical sleep.** It looks like the sleeper is about to awaken, but he or she is actually harder to arouse. This may be partially explained by the fact that noises and other stimuli are often incorporated into dreams (Dement & Wolpert, 1958). (Have you ever made your alarm clock into a "telephone call" in a dream?)

REM sleep is a time of high emotion. The heart beats irregularly, and blood pressure and breathing waver. Both males and females appear to be sexually aroused: Males usually have an erection, and genital blood flow increases in women. This occurs for all REM sleep, so it is not strictly related to erotic dreams. When an erotic dream does occur, evidence of sexual arousal becomes more pronounced (Cartwright, 1978). Despite all this emotional activity, the body becomes quite still during REM sleep. It is as if the person is paralyzed. If we imagine the results of acting out dreams, it seems that REM-sleep paralysis prevents some hilarious nighttime escapades. Fortunately, changing positions takes place *between* REM periods. This occurs about every 15 minutes, or 20 to 40 times a night. Interestingly, poor sleepers tend to move less and spend more time on their backs (De Koninck, Gagnon, & Lallier, 1983).

Question: How important are dreams? Are they essential for normal functioning?

Dreams To answer these questions, dream researcher William Dement awakened subjects each time they entered REM sleep. People who were thus prevented from dreaming for several nights in a row showed an increased tendency to dream. By the fifth night, 20 or 30 awakenings often were necessary to prevent dreaming. When continuous sleep was finally allowed, subjects dreamed extra amounts. This effect, called the **REM rebound,** explains why alcoholics often have horrible nightmares after they quit drinking (Dement, 1960). Alcohol suppresses REM sleep and sets up a powerful rebound effect when it is withdrawn. It's worth remembering that while alcohol may help a person get to sleep, it often greatly reduces sleep quality.

While they were deprived of dream sleep, Dement's subjects complained of memory lapses, difficulty in concentrating, and feelings of anxiety during the day. For a time this result led to widespread belief that a person would go crazy if kept from dreaming. But sleep researchers now refer to this as the "REM myth." Recent experiments indicate that missing out on *any* particular sleep stage can cause a rebound for that stage. More importantly, daytime disturbances are generally related to the total *amount* of sleep lost, not the type of sleep lost (Cartwright, 1978; Johnson et al., 1972).

What, then, is the purpose of REM sleep? There are several interesting possibilities. Early in life, dream sleep may provide stimulation for the developing brain. Newborn babies spend about 50 percent of their sleeping time in REM sleep. This amounts to a hearty 8 or 9 hours a day of dream time. Premature babies get even more REM sleep (up to 75 percent). By age 5, when the nervous system is more mature, REM time drops to 20 percent, about the same as for an adult (Allison & Van Twyer, 1970; Feinberg & Carlson, 1967).

In adulthood REM sleep may serve other purposes. For one thing REM sleep increases after learning, so it may help restore brain chemicals needed for learning and memory (Hartmann, 1981; Stern, 1981). There is further evidence that dreams help integrate information learned during the day, prevent sensory deprivation during sleep, and aid the processing of emotional events. Although we have much to learn, it seems clear that REM sleep and dreaming are valuable for keeping the brain in good working order.

Sleep Disturbances—
Showing Nightly: Sleep Wars!

In the last 10 years a new kind of treatment center has appeared in hospitals. Sleep clinics, as they are called, now treat thousands of people who suffer from sleep disorders or complaints. Let's see what has been learned about a few of the most common problems.

Sleepwalking and Sleeptalking   Like many sleep disturbances, sleepwalking is an eerie and fascinating phenomenon. **Somnambulists** (som-NAM-bue-lists) negotiate obstacles, descend stairways, climb trees, and on rare occasions may step out of windows or in front of automobiles. The sleepwalker's eyes are usually open, and he or she is able to respond to commands or questions. Sleepwalkers move as if they can see, but a blank face, lack of recognition, and shuffling feet show they are still asleep. Children of sleeptalkers and sleepwalkers are likely to have the same problems, which suggests that these sleep disturbances are at least partially hereditary (Abe et al., 1984).

Question: Does sleepwalking occur during dreaming?

It was long supposed that sleepwalkers were acting out dream events, but EEG studies have shown that somnam-

Fig. 7–7   *John Herman of the University of Texas may look like he just stepped out of the movie* Star Wars, *but he is actually involved in dream research. Herman is wearing goggles that electronically monitor eye movements during sleep. Use of such devices has greatly extended our understanding of dreaming.*

bulism occurs during Stages 3 and 4. **Sleeptalking** also occurs in NREM stages of sleep and appears to be an outlet for NREM "thinking." The association of sleepwalking and sleeptalking with the deeper stages of sleep seems to explain why sleeptalking makes little sense and why a sleepwalker who is awakened is confused and remembers little (Jacobson et al., 1965; Luce, 1974). Remember, too, that a person is paralyzed during REM sleep, so vigorous actions do not normally occur.

Nightmares and Night Terrors   Stage 4 sleep is also the realm of **night terrors,** severely frightening experiences that can be distinguished from the normal nightmare (see Table 7–1). A **nightmare** is simply a bad dream that takes place during REM sleep. Nightmares are usually brief.

Table 7–1   Was It a Nightmare or a Night Terror?

	Nightmare	Night Terror
Stage of sleep	☐ REM	☐ NREM
Activity	☐ Slight or no movement	☐ Violent body movement, sits up, cries out, may run
Emotion	☐ Fear or anxiety	☐ Terror and disorganizing panic
Mental state when awakened	☐ Coherent, can be calmed	☐ Incoherent, disoriented, cannot be calmed, may be hallucinating
Physiological changes	☐ No perspiration	☐ Perspires heavily
Recall	☐ Dream activity usually remembered	☐ Amnesia for episode

(Adapted from Woods & Greenhouse, 1974.)

The person awakens and remembers the dream in complete detail. During Stage 4 night terrors, a person experiences blind panic and may hallucinate frightening dream images into the room itself. The attack may last 15 or 20 minutes. When it is over, the person awakens drenched in perspiration but has only a vague memory of the terror itself. Since night terrors occur during NREM sleep when the body is not immobilized, the victim may sit up, get out of bed, or run around the room. Night terrors are most common in childhood, but continue to plague some adults throughout their lives (Kales & Kales, 1973; Kanner, 1957).

Narcolepsy   One of the most dramatic sleep problems is **narcolepsy** (NAR-koe-lep-see). Narcoleptics suffer from sudden, repeated, and irresistible sleep attacks. These last anywhere from a few minutes to a half hour. The attacks are so overpowering that victims fall asleep while standing, talking, or even driving. Most victims also suffer from **cataplexy** (CAT-ah-plex-see), a sudden temporary paralysis of the muscles, leading to complete body collapse.

Question: What causes such drastic reactions?

When monitored on an EEG, narcoleptics tend to fall directly into REM sleep. (Recall that the first REM period normally occurs about 90 minutes after sleep begins.) The narcoleptic's sleep attacks and muscle paralysis apparently result from an intrusion of REM into the waking state. Fortunately, narcolepsy is quite rare. It tends to run in families, which suggests that it too is hereditary. This has been confirmed by breeding several generations of narcoleptic dogs (Guilleminault et al., 1976). (These dogs, by the way, are simply outstanding at learning the trick, "Roll over and play dead.") For humans, there is no known cure for narcolepsy, but stimulant drugs may cut down the frequency of attacks.

Insomnia   While some people sleep when they don't want to, a far greater number have trouble getting enough sleep. An estimated 40 million Americans suffer from chronic insomnia (Kripke & Simons, 1976). **Insomnia** includes difficulty in going to sleep, frequent nighttime awakenings, waking too early, or any combination of these. Almost everyone has had an occasional bout of insomnia.

Americans spend more than one-half billion dollars each year on drugs to help them sleep. There is real irony in this expenditure. Nonprescription sleeping pills such as Sominex, Nytol, and Sleep-eze have little or no sleep-inducing effect (Kales & Kales, 1973). Even worse are most prescription *sedatives*. These drugs (usually barbiturates) decrease both Stage 4 and REM sleep and thereby drastically reduce sleep quality. In addition a drug tolerance rapidly builds so that the initial dosage becomes ineffective. Many users become "sleeping-pill junkies" as an ever greater number of pills is required to produce sleep. The resulting **drug-dependency insomnia** is a serious problem. Victims must be painstakingly withdrawn from their sleeping pills. Otherwise, terrible nightmares and sleep disturbances drive them back to drug use.

Question: If sleeping pills are a poor way to treat insomnia, what can be done?

Actually, there is a new drug called triazolam (try-AS-o-lam) that appears to be effective for some cases of insomnia. All traces of this drug are out of the body within 4 hours, so it doesn't cause grogginess the next day. In comparison, other sedatives remain in the body for 20 to 40 hours (Seidel et al., 1984). Even when drugs are effective, it is inadvisable to use them repeatedly. Often, it is far better to learn behavioral techniques to treat insomnia.

Temporary insomnia caused by worry, stress, or excitement usually sets up a cycle in which heightened physical arousal interferes with sleep. Then, frustration and anger resulting from inability to sleep causes more arousal. This further interferes with sleep, which causes more frustration, and so on. This cycle suggests that one of the best ways to beat temporary insomnia is to avoid fighting it. Usually it is best to get up and do something useful or satisfying when you have difficulty sleeping (reading a textbook might not be a bad choice of useful activities).

Some insomniacs have been found to have a drop in blood sugar during the night. The restlessness and hunger this causes can be avoided by having a small snack before sleeping. Also, it has been discovered that the amino acid **tryptophan** (TRIP-tuh-fan) can help people sleep—especially those who sleep poorly, rather than those who are just slow in getting to sleep (Lindsley, Hartmann, & Mitchell, 1983). Interestingly, tryptophan can be found in a glass of milk. So grandma was right after all! But she apparently didn't know that an egg-tuna-cottage cheese-soybean-cashew-chicken-turkey sandwich would be even better for inducing sleep. All of the listed foods are also high in tryptophan (Hartmann, 1978).

Question: What about more serious cases of insomnia?

Treatment for **chronic insomnia** usually begins with training in relaxation techniques to lower arousal before sleep. (See the Chapter 23 Applications section for more about relaxation.) Stimulus control procedures are also helpful. For example, patients are told to strictly avoid doing any activities other than sleeping when they go to bed. They are not to study, eat, watch TV, read, or even think in bed. In this way only sleeping becomes associated with retiring (Bootzin, 1973). One of the most helpful techniques for combating insomnia is also the simplest. Many insomniacs have scattered sleep habits. For these people adopting a regular schedule (getting up and going to sleep at exactly the same time each day) helps establish a firm body rhythm and greatly improves sleep. These and other ways of combating insomnia are summarized in Highlight 7-1.

Sleep Apnea   Some sage once said, "Laugh and the whole world laughs with you; snore and you sleep alone." If your family tree is like most, it probably includes at least one outrageous snorer. Nightly "wood sawing" is often harmless, but it can signal a serious problem. A person

---

Highlight 7-1
Behavioral Remedies for Insomnia

All of the approaches listed here have been shown effective for treating insomnia (Borkovec, 1982). With a little experimenting you should be able to find a combination that works for you.

Stimulants   Avoid stimulants such as coffee or cigarettes. Remember too that alcohol, while not a stimulant, impairs sleep quality.

Relaxation   Learn a physical or mental strategy for relaxing, such as progressive muscle relaxation (Chapter 23), meditation (Chapter 6), or blotting out worries with calming images. Strenuous exercise during the day promotes sleep, but it is usually too stimulating in the evening. Very light evening exercise may be helpful, however.

Stimulus control   Link only sleep with your bedroom so that it does not trigger worrying: (1) Go to bed only when you are feeling sleepy. (2) Avoid naps. (3) Awaken at the same time each morning. (4) Avoid nonsleep activities in bed. (5) Always leave the bedroom if sleep has not occurred within 10 minutes. (6) Do something else when you are upset about not being able to sleep.

Paradoxical intention   To remove the pressures of trying to get to sleep, try instead to keep your eyes open (in the dark) and stay awake as long as possible. This allows sleep to overtake you unexpectedly and lowers performance anxiety.

---

who snores loudly, with short silences and loud gasps or snorts, may suffer from **sleep apnea** (ap-NEE-ah). In sleep apnea breathing stops for periods of 20 seconds to 2 minutes. As the need for oxygen becomes intense, the person wakes a little and gulps in air. He or she then settles back to sleep, but soon breathing stops again. This cycle is repeated hundreds of times a night (Guilleminault, 1979). Understandably, apnea victims complain of insomnia, morning headaches, or daytime sleepiness.

Question: What causes sleep apnea?

Some apnea occurs because the brain stops sending signals to the diaphragm to maintain breathing. Another cause is blockage of the upper air passages. In either case the person can breathe normally during the day, so he or she may be unaware of the problem. Drinking alcohol aggravates apnea, and the problem becomes more common after age 60 (Scrima et al., 1982). Apnea should be suspected any time very loud snoring is present. In addition to causing much misery, apnea seriously endangers health. Persons who suspect they are apneic should seek treatment at a sleep clinic (Hales, 1980).

Sleep apnea is especially dangerous in infancy, when it is suspected as one cause of **sudden infant death syndrome** (SIDS), or "crib death." SIDS is the most frequent cause of death for infants under 1 year of age. Each year it claims 10,000 victims in the United States alone (Naeye, 1980). In the typical crib death, a slightly premature or small baby with some signs of a cold or cough is put to bed. A short time later, when parents return to the crib, the child is dead.

Some doctors think that SIDS is caused by apnea due to immaturity of breathing centers in the brainstem (Hales, 1980). Others suspect direct blockage of the nose

is responsible. Most infants will cry, flail, and kick if the nose is blocked for a few seconds—responses that can save them if they roll face down. But some babies remain passive when breathing is blocked. These infants run a much higher risk of crib death (Lipsett, 1980). Such babies must be carefully watched for the first 6 or 7 months of life. To aid parents in this task, a special monitor may be used that sounds an alarm when breathing becomes weak (Naeye, 1980). Before we stop for a learning check, here is a list of danger signals to be aware of:

Some Warning Signs for SIDS

The mother is a teenager or smoker.

The baby is premature.

The baby has an unusual, high-pitched cry.

The baby engages in "snoring" breath holding, or frequent awakening at night.

The baby breathes mainly through an open mouth.

The baby remains passive when its face rolls into a pillow or blanket.

Learning Check

Match the following:

A. REM sleep
B. NREM sleep

1. ____ Paradoxical sleep

2. ____ Nightmares

3. ____ Night terrors

4. ____ Sleepwalking

5. ____ Sleeptalking

6. ____ Emotion and sexual arousal

7. ____ Relaxed muscles, little movement

8. ____ Narcolepsy

9. Adults generally spend more time in REM sleep than do children.   T or F?

10. Somnambulists usually also suffer from cataplexy.   T or F?

11. Sleep apnea is suspected as a major cause of SIDS.   T or F?

Answers: 1. A 2. A 3. B 4. B 5. B 6. A 7. A 8. A 9. F 10. F 11. T

Dreams and Beyond—
A Separate Reality

Question: What do people usually dream about?

Calvin Hall, a noted authority on dreams, has collected and analyzed over 10,000 dreams. Hall (1966; Hall et al., 1982) found that most dreams are extensions of everyday experiences. The favorite dream setting is familiar rooms in a house. Action usually takes place between the dreamer and two or three other people with whom the dreamer is emotionally involved—friends, enemies, parents, or employers. Actions in dreams are also predominantly familiar: running, jumping, riding, sitting, talking, and watching. About half of the recorded dreams had sexual elements. Dreams of flying, floating, and falling occur less frequently. Hall also found that if you're dreaming more now, you may be enjoying it less. Unpleasant emotions such as fear, anger, and sadness are more frequent in dreams than pleasant emotions are.

Question: Do the dreams of men and women differ?

The dreams of men and women (in our culture) seem to reflect traditional sex roles. Compared with men, women's dreams are more emotional, less aggressive, less focused on sexual themes, more often indoors, and more often about home and family. Male characters appear more often than female characters in the dreams of both men and women; but in men's dreams they are more likely to be rivals or antagonists. In describing dreams men use more action words such as run, hit, or drive; women use more words of feeling or emotion. Women are more often pursued or endangered in their dreams than men are (Winget & Kramer, 1979).

Question: How meaningful are dreams?

Interpreting Dreams

Most theorists agree that dreams reflect our waking personalities. For one thing, dreams are similar in many ways to daytime fantasies and thoughts (Winget & Kramer, 1979). Also, a large body of research shows that dream content reflects waking emotional concerns and styles (Cartwright, 1978). (See Highlight 7–2.) Thus, a better question might be, "How deep should we dig in interpreting dreams?" Some theorists believe that dreams have deeply hidden meanings. Others see dreams as a fairly simple extension of waking thought. Let's examine both views.

Highlight 7–2
A Lesson from the Dream People?

Dreams play a minor role in our culture. Are we missing out on something? If you posed the question to a member of the Senoi tribe in Malaysia, the answer would be a resounding yes.

The Senoi daily practice a type of dream therapy in which adults analyze the dreams of children or discuss their own dreams. Like many Western theorists the Senoi believe dreams reveal facets of the dreamer's personality. In addition, the Senoi believe that every person should learn to control his or her dream world. Thus, if a child reports a frightening falling dream, he or she is encouraged to redream the episode as a pleasant flying dream. Similarly, adults are encouraged to continue their dreams to a satisfactory ending, or even to finish them when awake. For example, a dreamer who has an argument with an acquaintance in a dream must apologize to her or him in real life (Stewart, 1969).

Is this emphasis on dreams what allows the Senoi to function without need of a police force, jails, or psychiatric hospitals? Probably not. It is likely that *any* reason to air feelings and resolve conflicts would be equally beneficial. Still, the Senoi offer a hint that discussing and understanding dreams may have considerable emotional value.

Psychodynamic Dream Theory Sigmund Freud's book *The Interpretation of Dreams* (1900) opened a whole new world of psychological investigation. Upon analyzing his own dreams, Freud felt that many represented **wish fulfillment.** Thus, a student who is angry at a teacher may dream of successfully embarrassing the teacher in class; a lonely person may dream of romance; or a hungry child may dream of food. Although Freud's view of dreaming is attractive, there is evidence against it. For example, volunteers in a study of the effects of prolonged starvation showed no particular increase in dreams about food and eating (Keys, 1950).

Freud's response to this fact probably would have been that not all wish fulfillment is so direct. He believed that dreams often express *unconscious* desires and conflicts.

Highlight 7–3

Common Freudian Dream Interpretations and Their Symbols

1. Parents—emperors, empresses, kings, queens
2. Children (brothers and sisters)—small animals
3. Birth—water
4. Death—journey
5. Nakedness—clothes, uniforms
6. Male genitals—sticks, umbrellas, poles, trees, anything elongated, pointed weapons of all sorts
7. Erection—balloons, airplanes, zeppelins, dreamer himself flying
8. Male sexual symbols—reptiles, fishes, serpents, hands or feet
9. Female genitalia—pits, hollow caves, jars, bottles, doors, ships, chests
10. Breasts—apples, peaches, other fruit
11. Intercourse—mounting a ladder or stairs, entering a room, walking down a hall or into a tunnel, horseback riding, and so forth

Many such desires are so threatening that they must be represented in disguised form so as not to directly arouse the person's conscience. A woman sexually attracted to her best friend's husband might dream of stealing her friend's wedding ring and placing it on her own hand, an indirect symbol of her true desires. (For a discussion of dream analysis in psychotherapy, see Chapter 22.)

To unlock dreams, Freud identified four **dream processes** that he believed disguise the hidden meanings of dreams. The first is called **condensation.** Through condensation a single character in a dream may represent several people at once. A character in a dream who looks like a teacher, acts like your father, talks like your mother, and is dressed like your employer might be a condensation of prominent authority figures in your life. A second means of diguising dream content is **displacement.** Through displacement the most important emotions of a dream may be redirected toward "safe" or seemingly unimportant images. A student angry at his parents might dream of accidentally wrecking their car instead of directly attacking them.

A third dream process is **symbolization.** This is one of the most controversial of Freud's ideas. Freud believed that dreams are usually expressed in images that are sym-

bolic rather than literal in their meaning. The list in Highlight 7–3 summarizes some of these symbols. Notice that the interpretations strongly emphasize sexual motives and tend to be highly imaginative. Many psychologists reject such interpretations as misleading.

A process called **secondary elaboration** is the fourth method by which the meaning of dreams is disguised. Secondary elaboration is the tendency to make a dream more logical and to add details when remembering it.

Question: Do all dreams have hidden meanings?

Probably not. Even Freud realized that some dreams are trivial or unimportant "day residues," or carryovers from ordinary waking events. Also, you may be relieved to learn that Freud's is not the only approach to dream interpretation. For example, Carl Jung, a rebellious student of Freud's, came to believe that dreams have no fixed symbolic meanings. Jung considered it important to learn a person's own symbolic language by studying a *series* of dreams. At the same time, he emphasized the presence of universal images, or **archetypes** (AR-keh-types) in dreams. Let us say, for instance, that a man dreams of dancing with his sister. To Freud this would probably be a sign of hidden incestuous feelings. For Jung the sister might represent an unexpressed feminine side of the man's personality, or the cosmic dance that intertwines "maleness" and "femaleness" in all lives.

The Activation-Synthesis Hypothesis   A radically different view of dreaming is offered by scientists Allan Hobson and Robert McCarley (1977). After studying REM sleep in cats, Hobson and McCarley believe that dreams are made in this way: During REM sleep, certain brain cells are activated that normally control eye movements, balance, and actions. However, messages from the cells are blocked from actually reaching the body, so no movement occurs. But the cells continue to tell higher brain areas of their activities. Struggling to interpret this information, the brain searches through stored memories and manufactures a dream. Hobson and McCarley call this explanation of dreaming the **activation-synthesis hypothesis.**

Question: How does this help explain dream content?

Let's use the classic chase dream as an example. In such dreams we feel we are running but not going anywhere as a pursuer bears down on us. Hobson and McCarley suggest that in such dreams the brain is being told that the body is running, but it gets no confirming feedback from the motionless body. As it tries to make sense of this information, the brain creates a chase drama.

A Look Ahead   The activation-synthesis hypothesis certainly seems to explain some dream experiences. Most psychologists, however, continue to believe that dreams have deeper meaning (Cartwright, 1978; Winget & Kramer, 1979). Moreover, there seems little doubt that dreams can make a difference in our lives: Veteran sleep researcher William Dement once dreamed that he had lung cancer. In the dream a doctor told Dement he would die soon. At the time, Dement was smoking two packs of cigarettes a day. He says, "I will never forget the surprise, joy, and exquisite relief of waking up. I felt reborn." Dement quit smoking the following day (Hales, 1980).

In recent years the idea that dreams can only be interpreted by a professional has given way to an appreciation of the personal nature of dream meanings. As a result many psychologists now urge people to collect and interpret their own dreams. The Applications section that follows offers some practical suggestions for doing just that.

Learning Check

1. The favored setting for dreams is: *a.* work   *b.* school   *c.* outdoors or unfamiliar places   *d.* familiar rooms

2. Unpleasant emotions such as fear, anger, and sadness are more frequent in dreams than pleasant emotions are.   T or F?

3. Dream content typically reflects one's waking personality and roles.   T or F?

4. In secondary elaboration a single dream character stands for several others.   T or F?

5. List four dream processes identified by Freud.

_____   _____

_____   _____

6. According to the activation-synthesis model of dreaming, dreams are constructed from _____ to explain messages received from nerve cells controlling eye movement, balance, and bodily activity.

Answers: 1. d   2. T   3. T   4. F   5. condensation, displacement, symbolization, secondary elaboration   6. memories

Applications

Exploring Your Dreams

An uninterpreted dream is like an unopened letter.

The Talmud

As we have seen, Freud considered the meaning of dreams to be deeply hidden. But there are other points of view. Dream theorist Calvin Hall (1966, 1974) prefers to think of dreams as plays and the dreamer as a playwright. Hall does admit that the images and ideas in dreams tend to be more *primitive* than those experienced when one is awake. Nevertheless, much can be learned simply by considering the **setting, cast of characters, plot,** and **emotions** portrayed in a dream.

Another dream researcher, Rosalind Cartwright (1969, 1978) suggests that dreams be considered primarily as feeling statements. The overall **emotional tone** of a dream is a major clue to its meaning. Is the dream comical, threatening, joyous, or depressing? Were you lonely, jealous, frightened, in love, or angry? Cartwright encourages use of everyday dream life as a source of varied experience and personal enrichment and considers dream explorations as an avenue for personal growth.

Dream theorist Ann Faraday (1972) also believes in the value of studying one's own dreams. Faraday considers dreams a message *from* yourself *to* yourself. Thus, the way to understand dreams is to remember them, write them down, look for the message they contain, and become deeply acquainted with *your* own symbol system. Here's how:

How to Catch a Dream

1. Before retiring, plan to remember your dreams. Keep a pen and paper or a tape recorder beside your bed.
2. If possible arrange to awaken gradually without an alarm. Natural awakening is almost always from a REM period.
3. If you rarely remember your dreams, you may want to set an alarm clock to go off an hour before you usually awaken. Although less desirable than awakening naturally, this method may let you catch a dream.
4. On awakening lie still and review the dream images with your eyes closed. Try to recall as many details as possible.
5. If you can, make your first dream record (whether by writ-

ing or by tape) with your eyes closed. Opening your eyes will disrupt dream recall.
6. Review the dream again and record as many additional details as you can remember. Dream memories disappear quickly. Be sure to describe feelings as well as the plot, characters, and actions of the dream.
7. Put your dreams into a permanent dream diary. Keep dreams in chronological order and review them periodically. This procedure will reveal recurring themes, conflicts, and emotions. It almost always produces valuable insights.
8. Remember, a number of drugs suppress dreaming (see Table 7–2).

Since each dream has several possible meanings or levels of meaning, there is no fixed way to work with it. Telling the dream to others and discussing its meaning can be a good start. Describing it may help you relive some of the feelings in the dream, and family or friends may be able to offer interpretations you would be blind to yourself. Watch for verbal or visual puns and other playful elements in dreams. If, for example, you dream that you are in a wrestling match and your arm is pinned behind your back, it may mean that you feel someone is "twisting your arm" in real life.

The meaning of most dreams will yield to careful scrutiny and a little detective work. If you still have trouble seeing the meaning of a dream, you may find it helpful to use a technique developed by Fritz Perls. Perls, the originator of Gestalt therapy, considered most dreams a special message about what's missing in our lives, what we avoid doing, or feelings that need to be

Table 7–2   Effects of Selected Drugs on Dreaming

Drug	Effect on REM Sleep
Alcohol	Decrease
Amphetamines	Decrease
Barbiturates	Decrease
Caffeine	None
Cocaine	Unknown
LSD	Slight increase
Marijuana	Slight decrease or no effect

Applications: Exploring Your Dreams

"reowned." Perls believed that dreams are a way of filling in gaps in personal experience (Perls, 1969).

An approach that Perls found quite helpful in understanding a dream is to "take the part of" or "speak for" each of the characters and objects in the dream. In other words if you dream about a strange man standing behind a doorway, you would speak aloud to the man, then answer for him. To use Perls' method, you would even speak for the door, perhaps saying something like, "I am a barrier. I keep you safe, but I also keep you locked inside. The stranger has something to tell you. You must risk opening me to learn it."

A particularly interesting dream exercise is to continue a dream as waking fantasy so that it may be concluded or carried on to a more meaningful ending. It is also revealing to set up dialogues between people or objects in the dream, especially those that stand in opposition to one another. Speak for them both and you will perhaps discover conflicting aspects of yourself. As the world of dreams and your personal dream language become more familiar, you will doubtless find many answers, paradoxes, intuitions, and insights into your own behavior.

Using Your Dreams

History is full of cases where dreams have been a pathway to creativity and discovery. A striking example of a dream breakthrough is provided by Otto Loewi, a pharmacologist and Nobel Prize winner. Loewi had spent years on research relating to the chemical transmission of nerve impulses. A tremendous breakthrough came when, for three nights in a row, he dreamed of an experiment. The first two nights he woke up and scribbled the experiment on a pad, but the next morning he was unable to tell what the notes meant. On the third night he got up after having the dream and instead of making notes went straight to his laboratory and performed the crucial experiment. Loewi later commented that if the experiment had occurred to him while he was awake he would have rejected it.

Loewi's experience gives some insight into the potential value of dreams for producing creative solutions. The dream state is one of reduced inhibition and may be especially useful in solving problems that require a fresh point of view.

The likelihood of being able to take advantage of dreams for problem solving is improved if you "set" yourself before retiring by thinking intently about a problem you wish to solve. Try to steep yourself in the problem by stating it clearly and reviewing all relevant information. Then use the suggestions listed in the previous section to catch your dreams. While this approach cannot be guaranteed to produce a novel problem solution or a new insight, it is certain to be an adventure.

Lucid Dreaming   If you would like to press further into the territory of dreams, you may want to learn lucid dreaming. During a **lucid dream** the dreamer "wakes" within an ordinary dream and feels capable of normal thought and action. Lucid dreamers know they are dreaming, but they feel fully conscious within the dream world (La Berge, 1981a).

Stephen La Berge and his colleagues at the Stanford University Sleep Research Center have used a unique approach to show that lucid dreams are real and that they occur during REM sleep. In the sleep lab, lucid dreamers agree to make prearranged signals when they become aware that they are dreaming. One such signal is to look up abruptly in a dream, causing a distinct upward eye movement. Another signal is to clench the right and left fists (in the dream) in a prearranged pattern. Corresponding muscle changes in the wrists can then be recorded electrically. Such signals show very clearly that lucid dreaming and voluntary action in dreams is possible (La Berge et al., 1981a; La Berge, 1981b).

Question: How would a person go about learning to have lucid dreams?

La Berge (1980) found he could greatly increase lucid dreaming by following this simple routine: When you awaken spontaneously from a dream, take a few minutes to try to memorize it. Next, engage in 10 to 15 minutes of reading or any other activity requiring full wakefulness. Then, while lying in bed and returning to sleep, say to yourself, "Next time I'm dreaming, I want to remember that I'm dreaming." Finally, visualize yourself lying in bed asleep, while in the dream just rehearsed. At the same time, picture yourself realizing that you are dreaming. Follow this routine each time

Applications: Exploring Your Dreams

you awaken (substitute a dream memory from another occasion if you don't awaken from a dream).

Question: Why would anyone want to have lucid dreams?

Researchers are interested in lucid dreams because they provide a new tool for understanding dreaming. Using subjects who can signal while they are dreaming may make it possible to explore dreams with firsthand data from the dreamer's world itself (La Berge, 1981b).

On a more personal level, lucid dreaming can convert dreams into a nightly workshop for emotional growth, as practiced by the Senoi. Consider, for example, a recently divorced woman who kept dreaming that she was being swallowed by a giant wave. Rosalind Cartwright (1978) asked the woman to try swimming the next time the wave engulfed her. She did, with great determination, and the nightmare lost its terror. More importantly, her new dream gave her a sense that she could cope with life again.

Learning Check

1. Calvin Hall's approach to dream interpretation emphasizes the setting, cast, plot, and emotions portrayed in a dream.   T or F?
2. Rosalind Cartwright stresses that dreaming is a relatively mechanical process having little personal meaning.   T or F?
3. Both alcohol and LSD cause a slight increase in dreaming.   T or F?
4. Taking the part of or speaking for dream elements is a dream interpretation technique originated by Fritz Perls.   T or F?
5. Recent research shows that lucid dreaming occurs primarily during NREM sleep or microawakenings.   T or F?

Answers: 1. T   2. F   3. F   4. T   5. F

Chapter Summary

■ Sleep is an innate *biological rhythm* essential for survival. Higher animals and people deprived of sleep experience involuntary *microsleeps.*

■ Moderate sleep loss mainly affects vigilance and performance on routine or boring tasks. Extended sleep loss can (somewhat rarely) produce a temporary *sleep deprivation psychosis.* It is not necessary to make up for most lost sleep.

■ *Circadian rhythms* of bodily activity are closely tied to sleep cycles. Time zone travel or shift work can seriously disrupt sleep and bodily rhythms. Traveling east intensifies jet lag; backward work shift rotations are also more stressful. *Preadapting* to new time schedules can minimize these effects.

■ *Sleep patterns* show some flexibility, but 7 to 8 hours remains the average under most conditions. The amount of daily sleep decreases steadily from birth to old age. Once-a-day sleep schedules, with a two-to-one ratio of hours awake to hours asleep, are most efficient for most people.

■ During sleep the *pattern* of brain activity changes rather than the amount. Sleep is actively generated by brain structures and is not directly caused by fatigue. A sleep-inducing chemical has been found in the brain and spinal cord.

■ Sleep occurs in four *stages.* Stage 1 is *light sleep,* and Stage 4 is *deep sleep.* The sleeper alternates between Stages 1 and 4 (passing through 2 and 3) several times each night.

■ There are two basic sleep states, *rapid eye movement* (REM) sleep and *non-REM* (NREM) sleep. REM sleep is much more strongly associated with dreaming than is non-REM sleep.

■ Dreaming and REMs occur mainly during Stage 1. Everyone dreams, usually four to five dreams per night. Dreaming is accompanied by emotional arousal but relaxation of the skeletal muscles. REM sleep is often referred to as *paradoxical* sleep.

■ People deprived of dream sleep show a *REM rebound* when allowed to sleep without interruption. Consistent loss of any sleep stage can be disruptive, but total sleep loss seems to be the most important factor.

■ *Somnambulism* (sleepwalking) and *sleeptalking* occur during NREM sleep. Except in rare instances, neither is dangerous or particularly significant. The tendency to sleepwalk or sleeptalk appears to be at least partially hereditary.

■ *Nightmares* are brief and upsetting REM dreams. *Night terrors* occur in NREM sleep and produce a panic-like terror.

■ *Narcolepsy* (sleep attacks) is caused by the sudden occurrence of Stage 1 REM patterns during normal waking hours. Narcolepsy is frequently accompanied by *cataplexy* (paralysis). Studies of animals indicate a genetic or hereditary basis for narcolepsy.

■ *Insomnia* may be temporary or chronic. When it is treated through use of drugs, sleep quality is often lowered and *drug-dependency insomnia* may develop. *Behavioral approaches* to managing insomnia have been shown to be effective.

■ One source of insomnia, or daytime exhaustion, is *sleep apnea*. Individuals suffering from apnea repeatedly stop breathing while asleep, and they snore loudly. Apnea is suspected as a major cause of *sudden infant death syndrome* (SIDS).

■ Most dreams are about familiar settings, people, and actions. Dreams appear to reflect waking personality and roles. Negative emotions are more common in dreams than positive emotions are.

■ The Freudian, or *psychodynamic*, view is that dreams express unconscious wishes, impulses, or emotions. Freud held that the meaning of dreams is hidden by *condensation*, *displacement*, *symbolization*, and *secondary elaboration*. Many theorists have questioned Freud's view of dreams. For example, the *activation-synthesis model* portrays dreaming as a physiological process.

■ Dreams may be used to promote self-understanding. Hall's emphasis on the *setting*, *cast*, *plot*, and *emotions* of a dream can be helpful in this regard. Cartwright's view of dreams as *feeling statements* and Perls' technique of speaking for dream elements are also helpful. Dreams may be used for creative problem solving, especially when dream control is achieved through *lucid dreaming*.

Exploration

Biorhythms—Fact or Fallacy?

Because of its recent popularity, you have probably heard of *biorhythm theory*. Perhaps you have been curious about it. What does biorhythm theory claim? What evidence is there to support it? Is there any value to having your biorhythms charted?

Biorhythm Theory

Biorhythm theory states that we are all subject to three separate cycles: a physical cycle lasting 23 days, an emotional or sensitivity cycle of 28 days, and a 33-day intellectual cycle. The first half of each cycle is supposedly positive (made up of good days) and the second half negative. According to the theory, all three cycles begin at birth and flow in and out of synchronization throughout one's life. The day on which a cycle changes from positive to negative is termed a "critical" day. When the critical days for all three cycles occur simultaneously, the chances for disaster or accident are supposedly quite high.

Although you can easily chart your own biorhythms, an incredible number of commercial charting services would like to do it for you. Other firms sell hand calculators or computer programs for determining biorhythms. Most of these businesses promote themselves by describing case histories of celebrities who made serious errors, had accidents, or performed exceptionally well when biorhythms were working "for" or "against" them. What these companies usu-

ally overlook, however, are all the cases that don't fit. For example, Reggie Jackson, while still an outfielder for the New York Yankees, went on an incredible hitting streak to lead his team to victory in the 1977 World Series. And what, we might ask, were Jackson's biorhythms doing at that time? They were all at rock bottom (Louis, 1978).

Question: But what about companies that have cut accident rates by charting employees' biorhythms? Doesn't that support the theory?

It might seem so, but there is a catch. Consider an example: When they arrive for work, bus drivers for the Ohmi Railway Company in Japan receive a card that warns them if they are about to have a critical day, as predicted by their biorhythms. Drivers who receive cards are urged to be extra careful for that day. Since this program began, there has been a dramatic reduction in accidents. Does this confirm the theory? Not at all. What if the drivers were selected at *random* and warned to be extra careful? If they heeded the warnings, we would expect an overall drop in accident rates, even if the warnings had no connection to biorhythms.

Save Your Money   The surface similarity between circadian rhythms and biorhythm theory has led many people to assume that biorhythm theory is based on fact. However, some of the logical prob-

lems with biorhythm theory may already have occurred to you. Why should the three cycles begin at birth? After all, the fetus is alive before birth. Are we to believe, as well, that a Caesarean birth can change a person's entire life? Or that being born a few days earlier or later can make a lifelong difference? And why should the cycles last exactly 23, 28, and 33 days for everyone on earth?

The strongest evidence against biorhythm theory comes from accident studies and other attempts to match cycles with outcomes. For instance, one researcher compared 100 no-hit baseball games pitched in the major leagues to biorhythm charts for the pitchers. He found no connection between cycles and these performances (Louis, 1978). In Canada the Workmen's Compensation Board of British Columbia studied over 13,000 occupational accidents. The outcome? Accidents are no more likely to occur on "critical" days than at any other time (Nelson, 1976). Other studies have found absolutely no correlation between aviation accidents and pilots' biorhythms, or between biorhythms and recovery from surgery, time of death, or the scores of golf pros (Holmes et al., 1980; Wolcott et al., 1977).

In summary, the evidence is strongly against biorhythm theory. If you fail a test, have an accident, lose a game, insult your boss, or dissolve your marriage, don't look to a biorhythm chart for the explanation.

Questions for Discussion

1. How would your life change if you had to sleep 15 hours per day? How would it change if you only needed 2 hours a day?

2. Would you give up sleep if you could?

3. Have you ever gone without sleep for an extended period, or have you had to adapt to an unusual sleep schedule, shift work, or jet lag? If so, what were your reactions? Your greatest difficulties?

4. Describe a recent dream you have had. How does it relate to your daytime experiences and feelings? What additional meanings can you find in it?

5. How important are your dreams to you? What value do they have? Do you think recording your dreams would be a worthwhile practice?

6. Have you ever solved a problem in your dreams? How much control do you have over what you dream?

7. You have a friend who claims never to dream. How could you realistically prove to your friend that he or she does dream?

8. Respond to the statement: "The REM state is not sleep at all; during REM we are paralyzed and hallucinating." Do you agree?

9. If you were dreaming right now, how could you prove it?

10. Why do you think that false and overly simplified systems such as biorhythm theory appeal to so many people?

Part Three

Learning, Memory, and Thinking

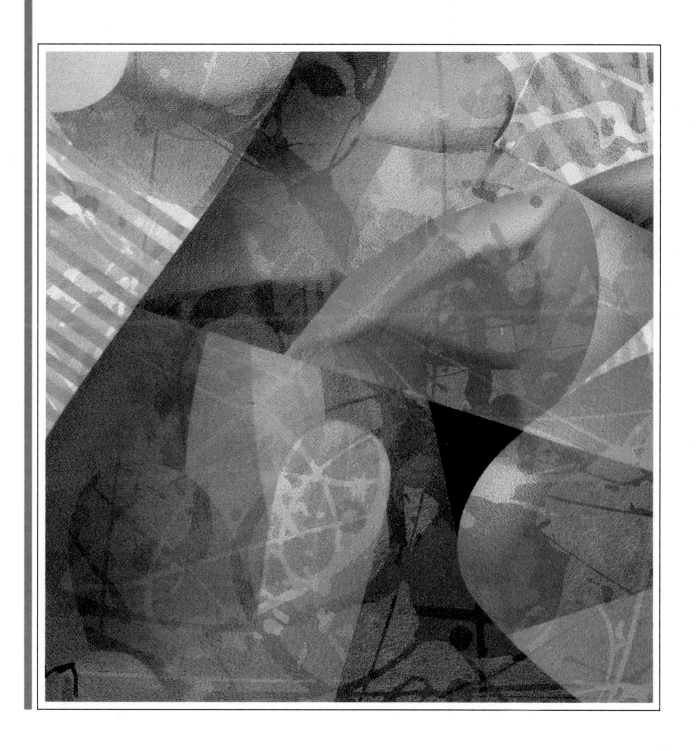

Chapter 8 | Conditioning and Learning I

Chapter Preview
What Did You Learn in School Today?

When your author was in college, students discovered an interesting "game" that could be played with the plumbing in the dorms. If a toilet was flushed while someone was taking a shower, the water became scalding hot. Naturally, the shower victim screamed in terror as his reflexes caused him to leap back in pain. Soon it was further discovered that if several students flushed all the toilets at once, the effects were multiplied many times over!

A flushing toilet has to be one of the world's most uninspiring stimuli. But for a time a whole flock of college students twitched involuntarily whenever they heard a toilet flush. Their reactions were the result of a form of learning called classical conditioning. Details of how and why classical conditioning occurs are explored in this chapter.

Consider another learning situation. Let's say that you are at school and that you are "starving to death." Locating a vending machine, you deposit your last quarter to buy a candy bar. You press the button, and . . . nothing happens. Being civilized and in complete control, you press the other buttons, try the coin return, and look for an attendant. Still nothing. Your stomach growls. Being no longer either civilized or self-controlled, you give the machine a little kick (just to let it know how you feel). Then, as you turn away, the machine begins to whirr and out pops a candy bar plus 15 cents change. Once this happens, chances are you will repeat the "kicking response" in the future. If it pays off several times more, kicking vending machines may become a regular feature of your behavior. In this case learning is based on operant conditioning (also called instrumental learning).

Classical and operant conditioning underlie much human behavior. In fact conditioning reaches into every corner of our lives. You should certainly find it useful to learn more about it. Are you ready to learn more about learning? If so, read on!

Survey Questions How is learning defined? What is classical conditioning, and what is its role in human learning? What is operant conditioning? How does conditioning alter behavior? How are conditioning principles applied to practical problems?

Resources

What Is Learning— Does Practice Make Perfect?

The weaverbird is a curious little creature that ties a special knot with grass to hold its nest together. How does it learn to make the knot? It doesn't! Weaverbirds raised in total isolation for several generations still tie the knot at their first opportunity to build a nest.

Knot tying in the weaverbird is a **fixed action pattern** (FAP), or instinctual chain of movements found in all members of a species. Like other **innate** (inborn) **behaviors** fixed action patterns help animals meet major needs in their lives. A simpler innate behavior is a **reflex,** such as blinking when your eyelashes are touched. More complicated behaviors, like the maternal instinct in lower animals, combine both fixed action patterns and reflexes.

Question: Do humans have instincts?

Humans have reflexes but not instincts. To be instinctual a behavior must be both complex and species specific. **Species specific behaviors** are those that occur uniformly in all members of a species. Actually, it is fortunate that we are not as rigidly programmed as animals. Such programming, though usually helpful, can also be very limiting. If a spider begins a cocoon and its silk glands are removed, it will continue to make all 6400 spinning movements to complete the job. Then it will lay eggs in the nonexistent cocoon (Eibl-Eibesfeldt, 1970)!

Learning versus Instinct What humans lack in instinctual "programming" is more than made up for in learning capacity. Our ability to learn is so advanced that the majority of our daily activities are learned or affected by learning. Imagine what you would be like if you suddenly lost everything you had ever learned. What could you do? You would be unable to read, write, or speak. You couldn't walk, feed yourself, find your way home, drive a car, or party. Needless to say, you would be totally incapacitated. Dull too!

Question: Learning is obviously important. What's a formal definition of learning?

Learning is a *relatively permanent change in behavior due to experience.* Notice that this definition excludes temporary changes caused by motivation, fatigue, maturation, disease, injury, or drugs. Each of these can alter behavior, but none qualifies as learning.

Question: Isn't learning the result of practice?

It depends on what you mean by practice. Repeating a response will not necessarily produce learning—*unless* some type of *reinforcement* is present. **Reinforcement** refers to any event that increases the chances that a response will occur again. If I want to teach a dog a trick, I could reinforce correct responses by giving the dog food each time it sits up. Similarly, a child who consistently gets praise or a hug for picking up toys will learn to be neat. These, of course, are only examples. As we will see later, there are many ways in which learning can be reinforced.

Antecedents and Consequences Unlocking the secrets of learning begins with noting what happens just before, and just after, a response. Events before a response are called **antecedents.** Those that follow a response are called **consequences.** Paying careful attention to the "before and after" of learning is a key to understanding it.

In classical conditioning all the "action" occurs before a response. We begin with a stimulus that already triggers a response. For example, a puff of air to the eye (the stimulus) will make you blink (the response). This occurs without any prior learning. Now, assume that we sound a horn (another stimulus) just before each puff of air hits your eye. If the horn and the air puff occur together many times, what happens? Soon, the horn alone will make you blink. Since you didn't respond to the horn before, learning has occurred. Similarly, if your mouth waters each time you eat a sweet roll, you may learn to salivate when you merely *see* a sweet roll.

Classical conditioning, then, involves learning to *associate* antecedent events with one another. A stimulus that does not produce a response is associated with one that does. Learning is evident when the new stimulus also begins to elicit (bring forth) the response.

Operant conditioning involves learning affected by *consequences.* Each time a response is made, it may be followed by reinforcement, punishment, or nothing. These results determine whether a response is likely to be made again. For example, if you wear a particular shirt or blouse and get lots of compliments (reinforcement), you are likely to wear it more often. If people snicker, insult you, call the police, or scream (punishment), you will probably wear it less often.

Now that you have an idea of what happens in the two basic kinds of learning, let's look at classical conditioning in more detail.

Classical Conditioning— Does the Name Pavlov Ring a Bell?

Question: How was classical conditioning discovered?

At the beginning of the twentieth century, something happened in the lab of the Russian physiologist **Ivan Pavlov** that brought him international recognition. The event was so unastounding that a lesser man might have ignored it: Pavlov's experimental subjects drooled at him.

Actually, Pavlov was studying digestion. In order to observe salivation, he placed meat powder or some tidbit on a dog's tongue. After a time, Pavlov noticed that his animals were salivating *before* the food was placed in their mouths. Later, the dogs even began to salivate at the mere sight of Pavlov entering the room. Pavlov recognized this as something more than misplaced affection. Salivation is normally a reflex (automatic, nonlearned) response. Some form of learning had to be taking place in order for the animals to salivate at the sight of food. Pavlov called this form of learning **conditioning**. Because of its importance in psychology's history, it is now called **classical conditioning** (also known as **respondent conditioning**).

Question: How did Pavlov study conditioning?

Pavlov's Experiment   After Pavlov observed that meat powder caused reflex salivation, he began his classic experiments. To begin, he rang a bell. Then immediately afterward, he placed meat powder on the dog's tongue. Each time Pavlov rang the bell, he followed it with meat powder, which always caused salivation. This sequence was repeated many times: bell/meat powder/salivation, bell/meat powder/salivation. Eventually (as conditioning

took place), the bell alone would cause salivation (see Fig. 8–2). By association the bell began to have the same effect as food. This was shown by sometimes ringing the bell and observing that the dog salivated.

Psychologists use several special terms to describe these events. The bell in Pavlov's experiment is a **conditioned** (learned) **stimulus (CS)**. The meat powder is an **unconditioned stimulus (US)** (because the dog does not have to learn to respond to it). Unconditioned stimuli typically produce reflex responses. Since a reflex is "built in," it is called an **unconditioned** (nonlearned) **response (UR)**. In Pavlov's experiment salivation was the UR. When the bell alone causes salivation, the response can no longer be called a simple reflex. Instead, it is a **conditioned** (learned) **response (CR)** (Fig. 8–2).

Question: Are all these terms and code letters really necessary?

In a word, yes, because they help us recognize similarities in various instances of classical conditioning. As an example see if you can apply the terms to explain the effects of the shower and flushing toilet described in the chapter Preview.

1. What is the unconditioned (nonlearned) response?

   _____

2. What is the unconditioned stimulus that causes the response?

   _____

3. What is the conditioned stimulus?

   _____

Fig. 8–1 *Pavlov's conditioning apparatus. In Pavlov's early experiments a tube carried saliva from the dog's mouth to a lever that activated a recording device (far left). The placing of a dish of food in front of the dog was paired with various other stimuli for conditioning.*

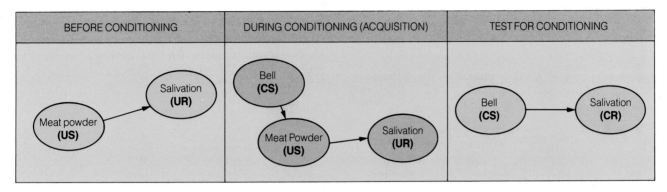

| BEFORE CONDITIONING | DURING CONDITIONING (ACQUISITION) | TEST FOR CONDITIONING |

Fig. 8–2 *The conditioning procedure.*

Now let's see if you understand the terms. The unconditioned, or nonlearned, response was a reflex jump from the hot water. The unconditioned stimulus was the hot water. The conditioned stimulus was the sound of a flushing toilet. That is, the flushing sound was at first neutral. But, due to conditioning it began to elicit a reflex.

Elements of Classical Conditioning—Teach Your Little Brother to Salivate

A number of interesting events occur during classical conditioning. To observe them, you could ring a bell, squirt lemon juice into a child's mouth, and condition salivation to the bell. The child's reactions might then be used to demonstrate additional features of conditioning.

Acquisition During **acquisition,** or training, a conditioned response must be **reinforced,** or strengthened (see Fig. 8–3). In classical conditioning, reinforcement occurs whenever the CS is followed by, or paired with, an unconditioned stimulus (US). For our child, the bell is the CS; salivating is the UR; and the US is the sour lemon juice. To reinforce salivation to the bell, we must pair the bell with lemon juice. Conditioning will be most rapid if the US follows *immediately* after the CS. For most reflexes the optimal delay between CS and US is from ½ second to about 5 seconds (Schwartz, 1984).

Higher Order Conditioning Once a response is learned, it can form the basis for **higher order conditioning.** In higher order conditioning a well-learned CS is used to reinforce further learning. Let's illustrate again with our salivating child. Because of prior learning, the bell now elicits salivation, without the lemon juice. To go a step further, you could clap your hands and then ring the bell. (No lemon juice would be used.) As before the child will soon learn to salivate when you clap your hands. (This little trick should be a real hit with friends and neighbors.)

Through higher order conditioning learning can be extended one or more steps beyond the original conditioned stimulus. Many advertisers try to use this effect by pairing images associated with good feelings (such as people smiling and having fun) with pictures of their products. Obviously, they hope that you will learn to feel good when you see their products.

Fig. 8–3 *Acquisition and extinction of a conditioned response. (After Pavlov, 1927)*

Question: After conditioning has occurred, what would happen if the US no longer followed the CS?

Extinction and Spontaneous Recovery   If the US never again follows the CS, conditioning will **extinguish**. If the bell (in our example) is rung repeatedly and not followed by lemon juice, the child's tendency to salivate

Fig. 8–4   (a) *Stimulus generalization. Stimuli similar to the CS also elicit a response.* (b) *This cat has learned to salivate when it sees a catfood box. Because of stimulus generalization, it also salivates when shown a similar-looking detergent box.*

(a)

(b)

to the ringing of the bell will be *inhibited* (or suppressed). Thus, we see that classical conditioning can be reversed by consistently omitting reinforcement (Fig. 8–3). This process is called **extinction**.

Question: If conditioning takes a while to build up, shouldn't it take time to reverse?

Yes. After one session in which the bell is rung until the child quits responding, we might assume that extinction is complete. However, the next day, if the bell is rung, it would initially elicit a response. This reaction is called **spontaneous recovery**. Because of it, several extinction sessions may be necessary to completely reverse conditioning. Spontaneous recovery explains why a person who has been in a terrifying car accident may need many slow, calm rides before his or her fear is completely extinguished.

Generalization   Once a person or an animal has learned to respond to a conditioned stimulus, other stimuli *similar* to the CS may also trigger a response. For example, we might expect the child in our conditioning experiment to salivate to sounds like the ringing of a telephone or doorbell. **Stimulus generalization,** as it is called, has been demonstrated many times in experiments involving humans and animals (Kimble, 1961).

It is easy to see the importance of stimulus generalization. Consider, for instance, the child who accidentally burns a finger while playing with matches. Conditioning principles predict that the sight of a lighted match will become a conditioned stimulus for fear. But will the child's fear be limited only to matches? Because of stimulus generalization, the child should also show a healthy fear of flames produced by cigarette lighters, fireplaces, stoves, and so forth. Fortunately, generalization tends to extend learning to new situations and similar circumstances. Were it not for this, we would all be far less adaptable.

An important point to keep in mind about stimulus generalization is that it does have limits. Experiments show that there is a gradual decrease in generalization as test stimuli become less like the original CS (Siegel et al., 1968). In other words if you condition a person to blink each time you play a particular note on a piano, blinking will decline as you play higher or lower notes. If the notes are *much* higher or lower, the person will not respond at all (Fig. 8–4).

Discrimination   Let's consider one more possibility with our salivating child (who by now must be ready to hide in the closet). Suppose that the child is again conditioned with a bell as the CS. As an experiment we occasionally sound a buzzer instead of the bell but never follow it with the US (lemon juice). At first the buzzer would produce salivation (due to generalization). But after the buzzer is presented several times more, the child ceases to respond to it. The child has now learned to *discriminate*, or respond differently to, the bell and the buzzer. In essence the child's generalized response to the buzzer has extinguished.

Stimulus discrimination is an important element of learning. As an example you might remember the feelings of anxiety or fear you experienced as a child when your mother's or father's voice changed to its your-about-to-get-swatted tone. Most children quickly learn to discriminate voice qualities associated with pain from voice qualities associated with praise or affection.

Classical Conditioning in Humans— An Emotional Topic

Question: How much human learning is based on classical conditioning?

In its simplest form classical conditioning depends on reflex responses. To expand a little on what we have said, a *reflex* is a dependable, inborn stimulus-response connection. For example, pain causes reflex withdrawal of various parts of the body. The pupil of the eye reflexively narrows to bright lights. Various foods cause salivation. It is entirely possible for humans to associate any of these— or other—reflex responses with a new stimulus. At the very least you have probably noticed how your mouth waters when you see or smell a bakery. You may even have salivated to pictures of food (a picture of a lemon is great for this).

Of greater importance, perhaps, are more subtle ways in which conditioning affects human behavior. In addition to simple reflexes, more complex *emotional* or "gut" responses may be conditioned to new stimuli. For instance, if your face reddened as part of your emotional reaction to being punished as a child, you may blush now as an adult when you are embarrassed or ashamed. Or, think of the times you have experienced pain at a dentist's office. On your next visit did your heart pound and your palms sweat *before* the dentist began? Many *involuntary*, autonomic nervous system responses are linked to new stimuli and situations by classical conditioning.

Another common example of such conditioning is a **phobia** (FOE-bee-ah). Phobias are fears that persist even when no realistic danger exists. People who fear animals, water, heights, thunder, automobiles, or bugs can often trace their fear to a few unfortunate experiences in which they were frightened, injured, upset emotionally, or subjected to pain in the presence of the feared object or stimulus. Reactions of this type, called **conditioned emotional responses (CERs)**, are often broadened into phobias by stimulus generalization (see Fig. 8–5). In fact a therapy

Fig. 8–5 *Hypothetical example of a CER becoming a phobia. Child approaches dog (a) and is frightened by it (b). Fear generalizes to other household pets (c) and later to virtually all furry animals (d).*

technique called **desensitization** is now widely used to extinguish or countercondition fears, anxieties, and phobias. (Desensitization is described in detail in Chapter 23.)

Vicarious, or Secondhand, Conditioning   The importance of conditioned emotional responses is extended by the fact that they can be learned indirectly. One experiment, for example, showed that people could be conditioned to give an emotional response to a light, merely by watching another person get an electric shock each time the light came on. Even though subjects never directly received a shock, they developed a conditioned emotional response to seeing the light come on (Bandura & Rosenthal, 1966). Children who learn to fear thunder by watching their parents have undergone similar conditioning.

Vicarious classical conditioning, as it is called, probably affects emotional reactions in many situations. For example, the film *Jaws* made ocean swimming a conditioned fear stimulus for many viewers. If movies can affect us, we might expect the emotional reactions of parents, friends, and relatives to have even more impact. How, for instance, does a city child learn to fear snakes and to respond emotionally to mere pictures of them? Perhaps the child has been told that "snakes are dangerous," but the child's *emotional* response has probably been learned by observing the negative reactions of others.

The emotional attitudes we develop toward certain foods, political parties, minority groups, escalators—whatever—are probably not only conditioned by direct experience but vicariously as well. Parents may do well to look in a mirror if they wonder how or where a child has "picked up" a particular fear or emotional attitude.

Learning Check

Make certain you can answer these questions before continuing.

1. Complex responses known as _____ help many animals adapt to their environment.
   a. generalizations   b. unconditioned discriminations   c. fixed action patterns   d. releasers

2. Classical conditioning, studied by the Russian physiologist _____, is also referred to as _____ conditioning.

3. Classical conditioning is strengthened or reinforced when the _____ follows the _____.
   a. CS, US   *b.* US, CS   *c.* UR, CR   *d.* CS, CR

4. Training that inhibits, or causes the loss of a conditioned response is called _____.

5. When a conditioned stimulus is used to reinforce the learning of another conditioned stimulus, higher order conditioning has occurred.   T or F?

6. Many phobias very likely begin with a CER that generalizes to similar situations.   T or F?

7. Conditioning brought about by observing pain, joy, or fear of others is called _____ conditioning.

8. A dependable, inborn stimulus-response connection is called a/an:
   a. unconditioned stimulus   *b.* CER   *c.* reflex   *d.* reinforcer

Answers: 1. c   2. Ivan Pavlov, respondent   3. b   4. extinction   5. T   6. T   7. vicarious   8. c

Operant Conditioning— Can Pigeons Play Ping-Pong?

As stated earlier, **operant conditioning** concerns how we learn to associate responses with their consequences. The basic principle of operant conditioning is quite simple: Acts followed by reinforcement tend to be repeated. Think of the earlier example of the vending machine. Because kicking the machine was followed by reward, the odds of repeating the "kicking response" were increased.

As we have seen, classical conditioning is passive and involuntary. It simply "happens to" the learner when a CS and US are associated. In operant conditioning, the learner actively "operates on" the environment. Thus, operant conditioning refers mainly to learning *voluntary* re-

Table 8–1 Comparison of Classical Conditioning and Operant Conditioning

	Classical Conditioning	Operant Conditioning
Nature of response	Involuntary, reflex	Spontaneous, voluntary
Reinforcement	Occurs *before* response (Conditioned stimulus paired with reinforcing stimulus)	Occurs *after* response (Response is followed by reinforcing stimulus or event)
Role of subject	Passive (Response is *elicited*)	Active (Response is *emitted*)
Nature of learning	Association between antecedent stimuli	Probability of response altered by consequences

sponses. For example, waving your hand in class to get a teacher's attention is a learned operant response. (See Table 8–1 for a further comparison of classical and operant conditioning.)

The idea that reward affects learning is certainly nothing new to parents (and other trainers of small animals). However, parents, as well as teachers, politicians, businesspeople, supervisors, and even you, may use reward in ways that are haphazard, inexact, or misguided. A case in point is the very term *reward*. To be correct, it is better to say *reinforcer*. Why? Because rewards do not always increase responding. If you try to give licorice candy to a child as a reward for good behavior, the reward will work only if the child likes licorice. As a practical rule of thumb, psychologists therefore define an **operant reinforcer** as any event that follows a response and increases its probability.

Acquisition of an Operant Response Most laboratory research on operant learning takes place in some form of **conditioning chamber** (also called a "Skinner box," after B. F. Skinner, who invented for experiments in operant conditioning) (see Fig. 8–6). A look into a typical Skinner box will clarify the process of operant conditioning.

The Adventures of Mickey Rat

A hungry rat is placed in a small cagelike chamber. The walls are bare except for a metal lever and a tray from which food pellets may be dispensed (see Fig. 8–6).

Frankly, there's not much to do in a Skinner box. This situation increases the chances that our subject will make the response that we want to reinforce, which is pressing the bar. Hunger also ensures that the animal will actively *emit*, or freely give off, a variety of responses.

Fig. 8–6 *The Skinner box. This simple device, invented by B. F. Skinner, allows careful study of operant conditioning. When the rat presses the bar, a pellet of food or a drop of water is automatically released.*

Light Screen

Water Lever

Food tray

Now let's take another look at our subject.

Further Adventures of Mickey Rat

For a while our subject walks around, grooms, sniffs at the corners, or stands on his hind legs—all typical rat behaviors. Then it happens. He places his paw on the lever to get a better view of the top of the cage. *Click!* The lever depresses, and a food pellet drops into the tray. The rat walks to the tray, eats the pellet, and then grooms himself. Up and exploring the cage again, he leans on the lever. *Click!* After a trip to the food tray, he returns to the bar and sniffs it, then puts his foot on it. *Click!* Soon the rat's behavior settles into a smooth pattern of frequent bar pressing.

Notice that the rat did not acquire a new skill in this situation. He already had the responses necessary to depress the bar. Reward only alters how *frequently* he presses the bar. In operant conditioning reinforcement is used to alter the frequency of responses or to assemble them into new patterns.

A good example of using operant reinforcement to change behavior patterns is shown in Fig. 8–7. The results are from an effort to reduce the number of deviant behaviors performed by children in a special classroom. (Deviant behavior was defined as fighting, crying, and temper tantrums.) As you can see, chaos reigned during the initial, baseline period. However, when good behavior (such as paying attention or remaining seated) was reinforced, disruptive actions declined rapidly (O'Leary & Becker, 1967).

To be effective, operant reinforcement like that used in the special classroom must be **response contingent.** That is, reinforcement is given only when a desired response is made. Contingent reinforcement also affects the *performance* of responses already learned. This is evident in situations ranging from childrearing to job performance and pay (see Fig. 8–8).

Shaping   Even in a Skinner box, it might be a long time before a rat accidentally pressed the bar and received a food pellet. We might wait forever for more complicated responses to occur. For example, you would have to wait a long time for a duck to accidentally walk out of its cage, turn on a light, play a toy piano, turn off the light, and walk back to its cage. If this is what you wanted to reward, you would never get the chance.

Question: Then how are the animals on TV and at amusement parks taught to perform complicated tricks?

The answer lies in **shaping.** Let's look again at our subject, Mickey Rat.

Mickey Rat Shapes Up

Assume that the rat has not yet learned to press the bar. He also shows no signs of interest in the bar. Instead of waiting for the first accidental bar press, we can shape his behavior patterns. At first, we settle for just getting him to face the bar. Any time he turns toward the bar, he is reinforced with a bit of food. Soon Mickey spends much of his time facing the bar. Next, we reinforce him every time he takes a step toward the bar. When he turns toward the bar, then walks away, nothing happens. But when he faces the bar and takes a step forward, *click!* His responses are being shaped.

By changing the rules regarding what makes a successful response, the rat can gradually be trained to approach the bar and to press it. We can reward responses that come closer and closer to the final desired pattern until it occurs. The basic principle of shaping, then, is that *successive approximations* to the desired response are reinforced.

Fig. 8–7 *Reinforcement and human behavior. The amount of deviant behavior engaged in each day by children in a classroom setting is shown. Before reinforcement of good behavior began, disruptive actions were the rule. The effectiveness of reinforcement is indicated by the rapid drop in crying, fighting, and tantrums that occurred. (Adapted from O'Leary & Becker, 1967.)*

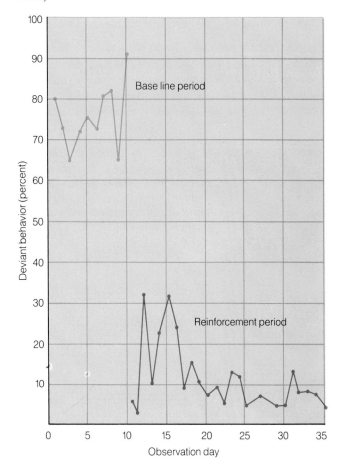

B. F. Skinner once taught two pigeons to play Ping-Pong in this way. (See Fig. 8–9 and Highlight 8–1.)

Shaping applies to humans, too. Let's say, for example, that you want to study more, clean the house more often, or exercise more. Success in each case would be aided if you set a series of gradual, daily goals and rewarded yourself for each small step in the right direction (Watson & Tharp, 1981).

Extinction   You might expect that a rat's bar pressing would immediately stop if food delivery ceased. Actually, the rat would stop pressing the bar but not immediately. Just as acquiring an operant response takes time, so does extinction. If a learned response is not reinforced, it gradually drops out of an organism's behavior. Extinction, therefore, refers to the same general phenomenon it did in classical conditioning.

Even after extinction seems complete, there may be a return of the previously rewarded response. If a rat is removed from a Skinner box after extinction and given a short rest, the rat will begin pressing the bar when returned to the Skinner box.

Question: Does extinction take as long the second time?

If reinforcement is still withheld, bar pressing will extinguish again, usually more quickly. The brief return of an operant response after extinction is another example of *spontaneous recovery* (mentioned earlier regarding classical conditioning). Spontaneous recovery seems to be very adaptive. The rat responds again in a situation that produced food in the past: "Just checking to see if the rules have changed!"

Operant Reinforcement— What's Your Pleasure?

As we have seen, reinforcement is a key element in learning. Reinforcers clearly have a large impact on our daily lives. Let's examine the reinforcement of operant behavior in more detail.

When dealing with humans, an effective reinforcer may be anything from an M&M candy to a pat on the back. In categorizing reinforcers, useful distinctions can be made among *primary reinforcers*, *secondary reinforcers*, *generalized reinforcers*, and *prepotent responses*.

Primary Reinforcement

Primary reinforcers are natural, or unlearned. Hence, they apply almost universally to a species. They are usually biological in nature and produce comfort, end discomfort, or fill an immediate physical need. Food, water, and

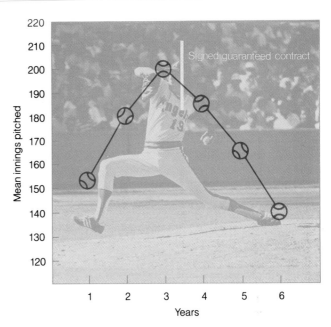

Fig. 8–8   *Mean number of innings pitched by major league baseball players before and after signing long-term guaranteed contracts. The performance of 38 pitchers who signed multiyear contracts for over $100,000 per season is shown. When salary was no longer contingent on good performance, there was a rapid decline in innings pitched and in the number of wins. During the same six-year period, the performance of pitchers on one-year contracts remained fairly steady. (Data from O'Brian et al., 1981.)*

sex are obvious primary reinforcers. Every time you open the refrigerator, walk to a drinking fountain, turn up the heat, or make a trip to an ice cream parlor, your actions reflect the effect of primary reinforcement.

In addition to the most obvious examples, there are other less natural primary reinforcers. One of the most un-

Fig. 8–9   *Operant conditioning principles were used to train these pigeons to play Ping-Pong.*

Highlight 8–1
Biological Constraints—
The Reluctant Raccoon

B. F. Skinner's success in shaping pigeons to play Ping-Pong was based on the fact that pigeons naturally peck objects. At one time psychologists assumed that almost any voluntary response could be taught by operant conditioning. In recent years, however, it has become clear that responses are not created equal. Animals, especially, will learn some responses much more easily than others. This observation suggests that there are a number of **biological constraints**, or limits, to learning. For example, two noted psychologists, Keller and Marion Breland, went into business training animals for television shows, zoo displays, and amusement parks. Along with their many successes came some revealing failures.

In one instance the Brelands tried to condition a raccoon to place coins in a piggy bank for an advertisement. Instead, the raccoon repeatedly rubbed the coins together in a miserly looking fashion (Breland & Breland, 1961). No amount of reinforcement would change this behavior. The Brelands ran into similar difficulties with other animals. In each case an innate behavior pattern intruded on learned responses. The Brelands called this problem **instinctive drift**: Learned responses tend to "drift" toward innate ones. The "miserly" behavior of the raccoon was simply an innate food-washing response. In view of such observations, it is wise to remember that the laws of learning operate within a framework of biological limits and possibilities (Adams, 1980).

they revive, they begin pressing again. If the reward circuit is not turned off, an animal will ignore food, water, and sex in favor of bar pressing.

One shudders to think what might happen if brain implants were easy and practical to do. (They are not.) Every company from *Playboy* to General Motors would have a device on the market, and we would have to keep a closer watch on politicians than usual!

Secondary Reinforcement

In some primitive societies learning is still strongly tied to primary reinforcement. Most of us, however, respond to a much broader range of rewards and reinforcers. Money, praise, attention, approval, success, affection, and grades all serve as *learned*, or **secondary reinforcers**.

Question: How does a secondary reinforcer gain its ability to reward responding?

A secondary reinforcer may simply be associated with a primary reinforcer. This can be demonstrated experimentally in this way:

The Button-Down Rat

A rat caged in a Skinner box has learned through operant conditioning to press the bar for food pellets. Each rewarded bar press is also followed by a brief auditory tone. After a period of training in which bar-pressing, food, and the tone are associated, the rat is moved to a new cage. This cage has no bar, but it does have a button mounted on the wall. If the rat pushes the button, the tone sounds, but no food is delivered. Even though no primary reinforcement (food) is given, the rat learns to press the button to turn on the tone. Because of its prior association with food, the tone has become a secondary reinforcer.

Tokens   Secondary reinforcers may also gain their value more directly when they can be *exchanged* for primary reinforcers. Printed money obviously has little or no value on its own. You can't eat it, drink it, or sleep with it. However, it can be exchanged for water, lodging, and other . . . necessities.

In a series of classic experiments, chimpanzees were taught to work for **tokens**.

Chimps were first trained to put poker chips into a "Chimp-O-Mat" vending machine that dispensed a few grapes or raisins for each chip. Once the animals had learned to exchange tokens for food, they would learn new tasks to earn the chips. They also learned to lift a heavy weight to obtain them. Value of the tokens was maintained by occasionally allowing the chimps to use the "Chimp-O-Mat" to exchange chips for food (Cowles, 1937; Wolfe, 1936) (see Fig. 8–11).

usual (and powerful) is **intra-cranial stimulation** (ICS). ICS involves direct stimulation of "pleasure centers" in the brain (Olds & Fobes, 1981) (see Fig. 8–10).

Wiring a Rat for Pleasure

Use of brain stimulation for reward requires the permanent implantation of tiny electrodes in specific areas of the brain. A rat "wired for pleasure" can be trained to press the bar in a Skinner box to deliver electrical stimulation to its own brain. Some rats will press the bar thousands of times per hour to obtain brain stimulation. After 15 or 20 hours of constant pressing, animals sometimes collapse from exhaustion. When

Fig. 8–10 *In the apparatus shown in (a), the rat can press a bar to deliver mild electric stimulation to a "pleasure center" in the brain. Humans also have been "wired" for brain stimulation, as shown in (b).*

One problem with primary reinforcers is that people and animals receiving them may *satiate* quickly. (To be satiated means to be fully satisfied or to have reduced desire.) If, for example, you wanted to use candy to reinforce a retarded child for correctly naming things, the child might only show interest while still hungry. A major advantage of tokens is that they do not lose their reinforcing value as quickly as primary reinforcers do. This is why tokens (plastic chips, gold stars, and the like) have been quite useful in work with troubled children, adolescents, adults in special programs, and in education of the mentally retarded (see Fig. 8–12). Tokens are even used at times in ordinary elementary school classrooms. In each case the goal is to provide an immediate, tangible reward as an incentive for learning. Typically, tokens may be exchanged for food, desired goods, special privileges, or trips to movies, amusement parks, and so forth. (See Chapter 23 for more information on the use of tokens in therapy.)

Question: People sometimes hoard money even when all their needs are taken care of. Why is that?

Generalized Reinforcers Interestingly, the chimps working for tokens also tended to hoard them, even when hungry. This and similar observations suggest that money may become a **generalized reinforcer**—that is, a secondary reinforcer that has become largely independent of its link to primary reinforcers. Not only can money be exchanged for primary rewards, it may also lead to other secondary reinforcers, such as prestige, attention, approval, status, or power. This property makes its value so

general in our society that people sometimes pursue and hoard money just for the sake of having it.

Prepotent Responses Discovering what will serve as a reinforcer can sometimes be tricky. Praise, candy, or a

Fig. 8–11 *Poker chips normally have little or no value for chimpanzees, but this chimp will work hard to earn them once he learns that the "Chimp-O-Mat" will dispense food in exchange for them.*

Fig. 8–12 *Reinforcement in a token economy. This graph shows the effects of using tokens to reward socially desirable behavior on a mental hospital ward. Desirable behavior was defined as cleaning the ward, bed making, attending therapy sessions, and so forth. Tokens earned by constructive behavior could be exchanged for basic amenities such as meals, snacks, coffee, game-room privileges, or weekend passes. (Adapted from Ayllon & Azrin, 1965.)*

pat on the back may be reinforcing for one person but not another. One way out of this dilemma is to apply the **Premack principle**. The idea, advanced by David Premack (1965), is that any high-frequency (or prepotent) response can be used to reinforce a low-frequency response. Let's say you love to listen to music and do so frequently. In contrast, you hate to take out the trash and rarely do it. If this were the case, by requiring yourself to take out the trash before turning on the stereo, you would increase the low-frequency response. As another example, access to video games has proved to be a very effective reinforcer for managing the behavior of many children (Buckalew & Buckalew, 1983).

If you are interested in applying reinforcement to change your own behavior (your study habits, for instance), remember that anything you do frequently (watching television, talking with friends, listening to music) can serve as a reinforcer.

Delay of Reinforcement

Reinforcement has its greatest effect on operant learning when there is a short time lapse between a response and its consequences. This point can be demonstrated in a simple experiment.

Mickey Rat and Friends Get Delayed

Several groups of rats are trained to press the bar in a Skinner box for a food reward. For some of the animals, a bar press is followed immediately by a food pellet. Other animals are trained with ever greater amounts of delay between a bar press and a reward. When the delay reaches about 50 seconds, very little learning occurs. If delivery of the food pellet follows a bar press by more than about 1½ minutes, no learning occurs (Perin, 1943) (see Fig. 8–13).

If you wish to reward either an animal or a person for a correct response, reward will be most effective if it is given *immediately* after the response.

Question: Let's say I work hard all semester in a class to get an A. Wouldn't the delay in reinforcement keep me from learning anything?

No, for several reasons. First, as a human you can anticipate future reward. Second, you get reinforced throughout the semester by quiz and test grades. Third, a single reinforcer can often maintain a long *chain* of responses. A simple example of **response chaining** is provided by Barnabus, a rat trained by psychologists at Brown University.

The Great Barnabus

By carefully working backward from the last response to the first, Barnabus was trained to make an ever longer chain of responses to obtain a single food pellet. When in top form, Barnabus was able to: climb a spiral staircase, cross a narrow bridge, climb a ladder, pull a toy car with a chain, get into the car, pedal it to a second staircase, climb the staircase, wriggle through a tube, climb onto an elevator and descend to a platform, press a lever to receive a food pellet, and . . . . start over (Pierrel & Sherman, 1963)!

Many of the things we do every day involve similar response chains. The long sequence of events necessary to prepare a meal, for instance, is rewarded by the final eating. A violin maker may spend three months carrying out thousands of operations for the final reward of hearing the first note from an instrument. Tying a shoelace is a short but familiar response chain.

Superstitious Behavior   Reinforcement affects not only the last response that precedes it but also other responses occurring shortly beforehand. This helps account for the learning of many human superstitions. If a golfer

Fig. 8–13 *The effect of delay of reinforcement. Notice how rapidly the learning score drops when reward is delayed. Animals learning to press a bar in a Skinner box showed no signs of learning if food reward followed a bar press by more than 100 seconds. (Perin, 1943.)*

Fig. 8–14 *Many gamblers rely on charms for good luck. Such superstitious behavior occurs because the charm is occasionally associated with reinforcement (winning).*

taps her club on the ground three times and then hits an unusually fine shot, the success of the shot rewards not only the correct swing but also the three taps. During operant training animals often develop similar unnecessary responses. If a rat scratches its ear just before its first bar press, it may continue to scratch its ear before each subsequent bar press. Pressing the bar is all the animal actually has to do to receive food, but it may continue "superstitiously" scratching its ear each time, as if this were necessary.

Question: But if the superstitious behavior is unnecessary, why does it continue?

Superstitious acts probably *appear* to pay off to the person or animal. For example:

Why Pigeons Shouldn't Gamble

A pigeon has been placed in a Skinner box, where it is allowed to peck at the key three times to obtain food. Then the key is turned off. At random intervals food falls into the tray as the pigeon continues pecking. *There is no connection between pecking and food*, but there *appears* to be. During 20 testing periods, 20 minutes in length, the pigeon made an average of 2700 "superstitious" pecks (Neuringer, 1970).

Many human superstitions seem to be based on the same phenomenon. If you get the large half of a wishbone and have good fortune soon thereafter, you may credit the wishbone for your luck (see Fig. 8–14). If you walk under a ladder and then break a leg, you may avoid ladders in the future. Each time you avoid a ladder and nothing unusually bad occurs, your superstitious response is reinforced. Belief in magic can also be interpreted along these lines. Primitive rituals to produce rain, ward off illness, or produce abundant crops very likely earned the faith of participants by occasionally appearing to succeed. Besides, better safe than sorry!

Learning Check

1. Responses in operant conditioning are _____, whereas those in classical conditioning are passive, _____ responses.

2. Changing the rules so that an animal (or person) is gradually trained to respond as desired is called _____.

3. Extinction in operant conditioning is also subject to _____ of a response.
   a. successive approximations   *b.* shaping   *c.* automation   *d.* spontaneous recovery

4. Reinforcement in operant conditioning depends on the consequences of a response, or what happens after it is made.   T or F?

5. Primary reinforcers are those learned through classical conditioning.   T or F?

6. Tokens basically are _____ reinforcers.

7. Superstitious responses are those that are:
   a. shaped by secondary reinforcement   b. extinguished   c. prepotent   d. unnecessary to obtain reinforcement

Answers: 7. d   6. secondary   5. F   4. T   3. d   2. shaping   1. voluntary, emitted, involuntary or elicited

Partial Reinforcement— Las Vegas, a Human Skinner Box?

SERENDIPITY (*n*): to discover one thing while looking for another

B. F. Skinner, so the story goes, was studying operant conditioning when he ran short of food pellets. In order to continue, he arranged for a pellet to reward every other response. Thus began the formal study of **schedules of reinforcement.** Until now we have treated reward in operant conditioning as if it were continuous. **Continuous reinforcement** means that reward follows every response. This is fine for the laboratory but has little to do with the real world, where successful responses are more inconsistently and unpredictably rewarded. **Partial reinforcement,** which does not follow every response, may be given in a number of patterns. Each has an effect on the rate at which a response is performed. In addition to these specific effects (to be explored in a moment), there is a general effect: *Responses acquired under conditions of partial reinforcement are highly resistant to extinction.* For some obscure reason, forever lost in the lore of psychology, this is called the **partial reinforcement effect.** It applies to both classical and operant conditioning.

Question: How does getting reinforced part of the time make a habit stronger?

If you have ever visited Las Vegas or a similar gambling mecca, you have probably been amused by the sight of row after row of people pulling slot machine handles. To get the flavor of what's happening here and to gain insight into partial reinforcement effects, imagine that you are making your first visit to Las Vegas. You put a nickel in a slot machine and pull the handle. Twenty-five cents in nickles spills into the tray. Taking one of your newly won nickels, you pull the handle again. Again there is a small payoff. Let's say this continues for 15 minutes. Every pull is followed by a payoff. Then, without your knowing it

someone turns off the payoff mechanism. Suddenly each pull is followed by nothing. Obviously, you would respond several times more before giving up. However, when continuous reinforcement is followed by extinction, the message soon becomes clear: No more payoffs.

Contrast this with partial reinforcement. You begin by placing five nickels in the machine, without a payoff. You are just about to quit, but decide to play one more. Bingo! The machine returns $2 in change. After this, payoffs continue on a partial schedule; some are large and some are small. All are unpredictable. Sometimes you hit two in a row, and sometimes 20 or 30 pulls go unrewarded. Now let's say the payoff mechanism is turned off again. How many times do you think you would respond this time before your handle-pulling response extinguished? Since you have developed the expectation that any play may be "the one," it will be hard to resist just one more play . . . and one more . . . and one more. Also, since acquisition on a schedule of partial reward includes long periods of nonreward, it will be harder to discriminate between conditions of reinforcement and extinction. It is no exaggeration to say that the partial reinforcement effect has left many people penniless. Even psychologists visiting Las Vegas often get cleaned out—and they should know better!

Schedules of Partial Reinforcement

The patterns in which partial reinforcement could be given are limitless. We will consider only the four most basic possibilities.

Fixed Ratio (FR)   During continuous reinforcement every response is followed by a reinforcer. A simple variation would be to follow every other response with reinforcement. Likewise, we could follow every third, fourth, fifth, or *n*th response with reinforcement. Each of these possibilities is a **fixed ratio (FR) schedule.** The ratio of reinforcers to responses is fixed: FR-2 means every other response is rewarded; FR-3 means every third response is reinforced; and so forth.

Question: What effect does an FR schedule have?

The most prominent characteristics of fixed ratio schedules is that they produce *very high rates of response* (Fig. 8–16). A hungry rat on an FR-10 schedule will quickly run off 10 responses, pause to eat, and will then run off 10 more. A similar situation occurs when factory or farm workers are paid on a piecework basis. When a fixed number of items must be produced for a set amount of pay, work output is high.

Variable Ratio (VR)   A **variable ratio (VR) schedule** is a slight variation on fixed ratio. Instead of reinforcing, for example, every fourth response (FR-4), a person or animal on a VR-4 schedule gets rewarded *on the average* every fourth response. Sometimes a response must be made two times to obtain a reinforcer, sometimes five times, sometimes four, and so on. The actual number of responses required varies, but it averages out to four (in this example).

Variable ratio schedules also produce high response rates, although not quite as high as FR. Since reinforcement is less predictable, VR schedules tend to produce slightly greater resistance to extinction than fixed ratio schedules. Playing a slot machine is an example of behavior maintained by a variable ratio schedule of reward. Another would be a child asking for a treat at the supermarket. The number of times the child must ask varies, so the child becomes quite persistent. Golf, tennis, and many other sports are also reinforced on a variable ratio basis: An average of 1 good shot in 5 or 10 may be all that's needed to make a person into a sports fanatic.

Fixed Interval (FI)   Another pattern involves reinforcing only the first response that occurs after a fixed amount of time has passed. In other words a rat on a FI-30-second schedule must wait 30 seconds after the last reinforced response before a bar press will pay off again. The rat can press the bar as often as it wants during the interval, but it will not be rewarded. **FI schedules** produce *moderate response rates*. These are punctuated by spurts of activity mixed with periods of inactivity. Animals working on an FI schedule seem to develop a keen sense of the passage of time. For example:

Mickey Rat Gets Put on Hold

Mickey Rat, trained on a FI 60-second schedule, has just been reinforced for a bar press. What does he do? He saunters around the cage, grooms himself, hums, whistles, reads

Fig. 8–15   *The one-armed bandit (slot machine) is a dispenser of partial reinforcement.*

Fig. 8–16   *Typical response patterns for reinforcement schedules. Results such as these are obtained when a cumulative recorder is connected to a Skinner box. The device consists of a moving strip of paper and a mechanical pen that jumps upward each time a response is made. Rapid responding causes the pen to draw a steep line; a horizontal line indicates no response. Small tick marks on the lines show when a reinforcer was given.*

Highlight 8–2
Stimulus Control

The role of discriminative stimuli may be clarified by an interesting feat achieved by Jack, a psychologist friend of the author's. Jack decided to teach his cat to say its name. Here is how he proceeded. First he gave the cat a pat on the back. If the cat meowed in a way that sounded anything like its name, Jack immediately gave the cat a small amount of food. If the cat made this unusual meow at other times, it received nothing. This process was repeated many times each day. By gradual shaping the cat's meow was made to sound very much like its name. Also, this peculiar meow came under stimulus control: When it received a pat on the back the cat said its name; without the pat it remained silent or meowed normally. Psychologists symbolize a stimulus that precedes reinforced responses as an **S+**. Discriminative stimuli that precede unrewarded responses are symbolized as **S−** (Schwartz, 1984). Thus, the accompanying diagram summarizes the cat's training.

I should add at this point that I was unaware that Jack had a new cat or that he had trained it. I went to visit him one night and met the cat on the front steps. I gave the cat a pat on the back and said, "Hi, kitty, what's your name?" Imagine my surprise when the cat clearly replied, "Ralph"!

ANTECEDENT	RESPONSE	CONSEQUENCE
S+ ⟶	"Ralph" ⟶	Food
S− ⟶	"Ralph" ⟶	Nothing
S+ ⟶	"Meow" ⟶	Nothing

Question: Are there human examples of FI schedules?

Pure examples of fixed interval schedules are somewhat rare, but some situations come close. A parallel would be having a paper due in a class every 2 weeks. Immediately after turning in a paper, your work would probably drop to zero for a week or more, until the next due date draws near. Another example is checking a Thanksgiving turkey in the oven. Usually, the frequency of checking increases as the time for the turkey to be done draws near (Schwartz, 1984).

Variable Interval (VI) VI schedules are a logical variation on fixed intervals. Here, reinforcement is given for the first response made after a varied amount of time has passed. A VI 30-second schedule means that reinforcement follows an interval that *averages* 30 seconds duration. VI schedules produce *slow, steady rates* of response and tremendous resistance to extinction. When you dial a phone number and get a busy signal, reward (getting through) is on a VI schedule. You may have to wait 30 seconds or 30 minutes. If you are like most people you will doggedly dial over and over again until you get a connection. Success in fishing is also on a VI schedule—which may explain the bull dog tenacity of many anglers (Schwartz, 1984).

Stimulus Control—
Putting Habits on a Leash

Thus far, we have focused on the consequences of making a response. The time has come to consider behavior in combination with the situation in which it occurs. Antecedent stimuli, or events that come before a response, also affect operant conditioning. If a response is reinforced in a particular situation, it tends to come under the control of stimuli present in that situation. This is called **stimulus control**. Notice how this works with our friend Mickey Rat.

Lights Out for Mickey Rat

While learning the bar-pressing response, Mickey has been in a Skinner box illuminated by a bright light. During several training sessions the light is alternately turned on and off. When the light is on, a bar press will produce food. When the light is off, bar pressing goes unrewarded. We soon observe that the rat presses vigorously when the light is on and ignores the bar when the light is off.

In this example the light signals what consequences will follow if a response is made. A similar situation would be a child learning to ask for candy when her mother is in a

magazines, and polishes his nails. After 50 seconds, he walks to the bar and gives it a press—just testing. After 55 seconds have passed, he gives it two or three presses. Fifty-eight seconds, and he settles down to rapid pressing, 59 seconds, 60 seconds, and he hits the reinforced press. After one or two more presses (unrewarded), he wanders off again for the next interval.

good mood but not asking at other times. In operant conditioning stimuli that precede a rewarded response tend to influence *when* and *where* the response will occur. Evidence for stimulus control could be shown in the example above by turning the food delivery *on* when the light is *off*. A well-trained rat would never discover that the rules had changed.

Generalization   Two important aspects of stimulus control are **generalization** and **discrimination.** Let's return to the example of the vending machine (from the chapter Preview) to illustrate these concepts. First, generalization.

Question: Is generalization the same in operant conditioning as it is in classical conditioning?

Basically, yes. Responses followed by reinforcement tend to be made again when similar antecedents are present. Assume, for instance, that you have been consistently rewarded for kicking one particular vending machine. Your kicking response tends to occur in the presence of that machine. It has come under stimulus control. Now let's say that there are three other machines on campus identical to the one that pays off. Because they are similar, your kicking response will very likely transfer to them. If each of these machines also pays off in response to a kick, your kicking response may *generalize* to other machines bearing only mild similarity to the original.

A good example of generalization is the way children use new words. One child studied by psychologist Melissa

Bowerman (1977) first used the word *snow* while handling snow outdoors. For a while, however, the child also called each of the following *snow*: the white tail of a toy horse, a white toy boat, a white flannel blanket, and spilled milk on the floor. Similar generalization explains why children may temporarily call all men *daddy*—much to the embarrassment of their parents.

Discrimination   Meanwhile, back at the vending machine . . . . As stated earlier, to **discriminate** means to respond differently to different stimuli. Because one vending machine reinforced your kicking response, you began kicking other identical machines (generalization). Because these also paid off, you began kicking similar machines (more generalization). If kicking these new machines has no effect, the kicking response that generalized to them will extinguish due to nonreinforcement. Thus, your response to machines of a particular size and color is consistently rewarded, whereas the same response to different machines is extinguished. You have learned to discriminate between antecedent stimuli that signal reward and nonreward. As a result your response pattern will shift appropriately in the presence of these **discriminative stimuli.** (See Fig. 8–17 and Highlight 8–2.)

Stimulus discrimination is aptly illustrated by the "sniffer" dogs used at airports and border stations to locate drugs and explosives. Operant discrimination training is used to teach these dogs to recognize contraband. During training the dogs are reinforced only for approaching con-

Fig. 8–17 *Stimulus control. Operant shaping was used to teach Flo, the pictured Walrus, first to cover her face (left) and then to douse her trainer. A fish is her reward. Notice the trainer's hand signal, which serves as a discriminative stimulus to control Flo's performance. (Photographs ©1984, Los Angeles Times.)*

Fig. 8–18 *Operant discrimination training is used to sharpen the skills of "detective" dogs.*

tainers baited with drugs or explosives (Fig. 8–18). Stimulus discrimination also has a tremendous impact on human behavior. Learning to recognize different automobile brands, birds, animals, wines, types of music, or even the answers on psychology tests all depend, in part, on operant discrimination learning.

Coming Attractions Some of the examples in this chapter are simplified and perhaps a little unrealistic. They were selected to clearly express the basic principles of conditioning. To complete our discussion, the upcoming Applications section covers more realistic examples of human and animal learning. After that, an Exploration proposes a personal experiment in applying operant conditioning to your own behavior. Don't miss these coming attractions!

Learning Check

1. Two aspects of stimulus control are _____ and _____.

2. Responding tends to occur in the presence of discriminative stimuli associated with reinforcement and tends not to occur in the presence of discriminative stimuli associated with nonreinforcement.   T or F?

3. When stimuli similar to those that preceded reward also bring forth a response, this is called stimulus generalization.   T or F?

4. When a reward follows every response, it is called:
   a. continuous reinforcement   b. fixed reinforcement   c. ratio reinforcement   d. controlled reinforcement

5. Partial reinforcement tends to produce slower responding and reduced resistance to extinction.   T or F?

6. The schedule of reward associated with playing slot machines and other types of gambling is:
   a. fixed ratio   *b.* variable ratio   *c.* fixed interval   *d.* variable interval

Answers: 1. generalization, discrimination 2. T 3. T 4. *a* 5. F 6. *b*

Applications

Conditioning in Everyday Situations

A technology of behavior is emerging. A later chapter of this book (Chapter 23) is largely devoted to applying conditioning principles to human problems. Conditioning principles have found their way into business, education, industry, and the home. If you understand these principles, you will find frequent uses for them. It is impossible to detail all the possibilities, but a number of examples should extend your understanding.

Conditioning Pets

One of the most common mistakes people make with pets (especially dogs) is hitting them if they do not come immediately when called. Calling the animal then becomes a conditioned stimulus for fear and withdrawal. No wonder it disobeys when summoned on future occasions.

Question: How can conditioning be used to correct this?

Obviously the situation needs to be reversed. A "stop" command can be used to control an animal when it is running away, and return on command can be rewarded. A stop command can be used in conditioning a dog by attaching a 20-foot-long rope to the dog's collar. During training, if the dog walks or bolts beyond a radius of about 5 or 10 feet, take a firm grip on the rope, give the stop command, and begin walking away from the dog. When the dog hits the end of the rope, the dog is jolted (this will not hurt the dog and is not cruel). Very soon, the stop command will bring the dog up short. The rope then becomes unnecessary.

An excellent way to train an animal to come when you call it is to give a distinctive call or whistle daily during feeding. This makes the signal a discriminative stimulus for reward (food). Effectiveness of the signal is greatly enhanced if it is also used at other times and in other settings and is followed first always, then frequently, then occasionally with a little food. Ultimately, very few "bribes" will be necessary to maintain the effectiveness of the signal if it is conditioned on a partial schedule of reward. Later, petting and praise can be substituted for food.

Question: What can be done about an animal that begs at the table?

Pets beg at the table for only one reason: They have been rewarded occasionally for doing so. The problem is usually that the owner finds begging bothersome most of the time and seeks to discourage it by not rewarding it with food. But there is always that time when Fido is just too cute to resist. If the owner gives in then, begging has been reinforced on a partial schedule, which makes it very resistant to extinction. Also, persistence has been reinforced. If you don't want your pets to beg, never give in and reward them. If you want them to beg quietly, reward them after a period of silence, not after a particularly sorrowful plea. Then, gradually extend the length of the silent period.

Conditioning in Business

Most business and industrial applications of reinforcement principles focus on the effects of various bonuses, payment schedules, incentives, commissions, and profit-sharing plans on overall productivity. Before this trend most people worked for either a straight salary or for an hourly wage. A straight salary can be thought of as a fixed interval schedule of reward. There is little relationship between the amount of effort expended from one paycheck to the next and the amount of pay. This is also partially true of an hourly wage. While it is true that more hours worked means a larger paycheck, an employee gets paid the same amount for an hour of productive work as he or she does for an hour of goofing off. It can be very demoralizing to see others do less work and receive the same pay.

With these facts in mind, industrial psychologists have sought to make pay relate more directly to work output. The simplest alternative to hourly wages or salary is payment on a piecework (fixed ratio) basis. If an individual is paid a small amount for each item handled, pound picked, shirt sewed, or whatever, work

Applications: Conditioning in Everyday Situations

output tends to be high because more items mean more pay. Piecework pay has something of a bad reputation because some employers pay so little on a per-item basis that tremendous amounts of work are necessary to earn a reasonable wage. But this need not be the case. For example, employees of a small leather factory in Los Angeles are paid for making a pre-arranged number of items per week (billfold backs, handbag handles, and so on). Employees are allowed to work as many or as few hours per day as they choose, and they can work at any rate. This allows great flexibility for the workers, and the company pays only for the work it gets.

The most widely used business adaptation of schedules of reinforcement is a combination of hourly wages and incentives for extra effort. Fixed interval rewards (hourly wage or salary) guarantee a good overall level of productivity and give workers a secure base pay, whereas fixed ratio reinforcement (incentives, bonuses, commissions, or profit sharing) ties extra effort to increased pay or other rewards. For example, in one recent study clerks in a department store were given a chance to earn paid time off by meeting minimum standards for selling and stockwork. This strategy brought about a significant improvement in their performance. In comparison, a control group's behavior remained the same (Luthans, Paul, & Baker, 1981).

Conditioning and Children

Children seem to have an almost endless craving for attention. This makes attention and approval from a parent a very powerful reinforcer.

Question: How does this affect a child?

Parents often unknowingly reinforce *negative attention seeking* in children. Generally, children are *ignored* when they are quiet or are playing constructively. They get attention as they get louder and louder, when they yell "Hey Mom!" at the top of their lungs, when they throw a tantrum or show off, or when they break something. Granted, the attention they get is often a scolding, but it is still attention, and it still reinforces negative attention seeking. To avoid this, parents could ignore children when they seek attention this way. However, if attention seeking declines because it is not reinforced,

some other behavior must be rewarded to take its place. Parents report dramatic changes in their children's behavior when they make a special effort to actively praise, attend to, or spend time with their children when the children are quiet or playing constructively.

Question: What can be done about a child who throws tantrums in a store if he or she isn't allowed to buy candy?

Children are realists. If you say, "No you may not buy candy" and stick to it, the child will get the message. Children can discriminate between what is said in a situation and the *actual* possibility of a reward. Children learn to throw tantrums with one parent but not the other; they learn to discriminate between parents' and grandparents' susceptibility to their requests; and they discriminate between a casual no and an angry no. The problem is that no occasionally becomes, "OK, but shut up!" If so, whining or crying has been rewarded on a partial schedule, and it will occur even more frequently in the future. Consistency is the key. If tantrums *never* pay off, they will be abandoned.

Question: But what if the tantrum is really embarrassing? Sometimes parents are willing to do anything to quiet a child.

Beginning a program of nonreward for tantrums may require considerable courage, but it does work. If you don't mind the idea of buying a treat, but dislike the tantrum, try requiring the child to "help" you in some (quiet) way as a condition for receiving the treat. If necessary, walk away from the child and return only when the child has quieted down, or leave the store with the child when a tantrum starts and allow a return to the store only when the child has quieted down.

Conditioning Other Adults

Students seldom realize how much power they have over their teachers. Even tough-skinned veteran teachers are (believe it or not) still human and therefore sensitive to whether they are succeeding in class and being accepted by students. This fact can be used in a demonstration of the effects of reward on human behavior.

Applications: Conditioning in Everyday Situations

Shaping a Teacher

For this demonstration, approximately one-half (or more) of the students in a classroom must participate. First, a target behavior should be selected. This should be something like "lecturing from the right side of the room." (Keep it simple; teachers aren't too clever.) Begin training in this way: Each time the instructor turns toward the right side of the room or takes a step in that direction, participating students should look *really* interested. Also, smile, ask questions, lean forward, and make eye contact. If the teacher turns to the left or takes a step in that direction, participating students should lean back, yawn, check out their split ends, close their eyes, or generally look bored. Soon, without being aware of why, the instructor should be spending most of his or her time each class period lecturing from the right side of the classroom.

This trick has been a favorite of psychology graduate students for decades. For a time one of my professors delivered all of his lectures from the right side of the room while toying with the venetian blind cords. (We added the cords the second week!)

As was pointed out in the discussion of reinforcement with children, attention and approval are powerful rewards for human behavior. This is something to keep in mind when interacting with others.

Question: But how can this be applied?

An excellent example is provided by the work of two educators, Paul S. Graubard and Harry Rosenberg, who taught "incorrigible," "deviant," and "socially outcast" students to use reinforcement on classmates. They cite the example of Peggy, an attractive, intelligent student who was unable to make friends. Peggy encountered so much hostility that she was miserable and unhappy and because of this did poorly in school.

When asked to name three other students she would like to have as friends, Peggy named three students who frequently insulted her. Here is how Peggy began to put into effect the reinforcement principles she had learned: She began by ignoring Doris if Doris said anything bad to her. When Doris said anything nice, Peggy complimented her or sat down and asked Doris to join her. Doris soon began to say nice things about Peggy, to sit by her in class, and for the first time ever, they were able to ride on the bus together without fighting.

Peggy dealt with another student's hostility in the same way. Whenever Elwyn said something bad to her, she turned her back on him. But the first time he walked past her without saying something bad, she gave him a big smile and said, "Hi, Elwyn, how are you today?" The authors add that after Elwyn recovered from his initial shock, he grew to be Peggy's best friend (Graubard & Rosenberg, 1974).

Experimental Living   In 1948, B. F. Skinner published *Walden Two*, a utopian novel about a model community based on behavioral engineering. Would such a community work? On a small scale the answer appears to be yes. One such operant community organized at the University of Kansas has been quite successful. College students took part in an Experimental Living Project in which 30 men and women shared a large house (Miller, 1976). In this "community" work, leadership, and self-government were tied directly to behavioral principles.

Worksharing provides a good example of the Project's operant approach. Basic jobs such as preparing food and cleaning are divided into approximately 100 tasks. Each task is described in terms of its expected end result. Residents perform all of these tasks themselves, and one community member checks daily to see that each job has been completed. (This role is rotated periodically.) To maintain job performance, credits are assigned for each of the tasks. At the end of the month residents who have collected 400 credits get a sizable rent reduction.

This system has been very effective in maintaining day-to-day work habits. As anyone who has shared living quarters knows, good intentions are no guarantee that the chores will get done. More importantly, residents rated the Project as superior to dormitory living and similar alternatives. Most were highly satisfied with the system (Miller, 1976). The Experimental Living Project is a good example of the possibilities of applying conditioning principles to human behavior.

The examples cited here should give you an idea of the value of understanding conditioning and of applying conditioning principles to everyday problems. Their successful use requires practice, but your efforts are sure to foster a deeper appreciation for their application. Give them a try!

Applications: Conditioning in Everyday Situations

Learning Check

1. Pets who beg for food are often very persistent because they have been rewarded on a schedule of partial reinforcement.   T or F?
2. A straight salary can be thought of as fixed interval reinforcement, whereas piecework pay is a fixed ratio schedule.   T or F?
3. Negative attention seeking refers to the idea that parents tend to reward negative attention from their children.   T or F?
4. Compliments, attention, and approval can serve as powerful reinforcers of human behavior.   T or F?

Answers: 1. T   2. T   3. F   4. T

Chapter Summary

■ *Classical* or *respondent* conditioning and *instrumental* or *operant* conditioning are two basic types of learning. In classical conditioning a previously neutral stimulus begins to elicit a response through *association* with another stimulus. In operant conditioning the frequency and pattern of voluntary responses are altered by their *consequences*.

■ Many animals are born with *innate* behavior patterns far more complex than *reflexes*. These are organized into *fixed action patterns* (FAPs), whch are stereotyped, *species-specific* behaviors.

■ *Learning* is a relatively permanent change in behavior due to experience. Learning due to basic conditioning processes depends on *reinforcement*. Reinforcement increases the probability that a particular response will occur.

■ Classical conditioning, studied by Pavlov, occurs when a *conditioned stimulus* (CS) is associated with an *unconditioned stimulus* (US). The US causes a reflex called the *unconditioned response* (UR). If the CS is consistently paired with the US, then the CS begins to produce a response by itself. This is called a *conditioned* (learned) *response* (CR).

■ When the conditioned stimulus is followed by the unconditioned stimulus, conditioning is *reinforced* (strengthened). A well-learned CS can also be used to reinforce further learning in a process known as *higher order conditioning*. When the CS is repeatedly pre-

sented alone, conditioning is *extinguished* (weakened or inhibited). Temporary reappearance of a conditioned response after extinction seems to be complete is called *spontaneous recovery*.

■ Through *stimulus generalization* stimuli similar to the conditioned stimulus will also produce a response. Generalization gives way to *stimulus discrimination* when an organism learns to respond to one stimulus but not to similar stimuli.

■ Conditioning applies to visceral or emotional responses as well as to simple reflexes. As a result *conditioned emotional responses* (CERs) also occur. Irrational fears called *phobias* may be learned CERs. Conditioning of emotional responses can occur *vicariously* (secondhand) as well as directly.

■ Operant conditioning occurs when a voluntary action is followed by a *reinforcer*. Reinforcement in operant conditioning increases the frequency or probability of a response.

■ Complicated operant responses can be taught by reinforcing *successive approximations* to a final desired response. This is called *shaping*. It is particularly useful in training animals. However, learning in animals is limited at times by various *biological constraints*, such as *instinctive drift*.

■ If an operant response is not reinforced, it may *extinguish* (disappear). But after extinction seems complete, it may temporarily reappear (*spontaneous recover*).

■ *Primary reinforcers* are natural, physiologically based rewards. *Intra-cranial stimulation* of "pleasure centers" in the brain can also serve as a primary reinforcer.

■ *Secondary reinforcers* are learned. They typically gain their reinforcing value by direct association with primary reinforcers or by being subject to exchange for primary reinforcers. *Tokens* and money gain their reinforcing value in this way. Money may be exchanged for so many other reinforcers that it sometimes becomes a *generalized reinforcer. Prepotent*, or high-probability, responses can be used to reinforce low-frequency responses.

■ *Delay* of reinforcement greatly reduces its effectiveness, but long *chains* of responses may be built up in which a single reinforcer rewards many responses. *Superstitious behaviors* often become part of response chains because they *appear* to be associated with reinforcement.

■ Reward or reinforcement may be given *continuously* (after every response) or on a *schedule of partial reinforcement*. Partial reinforcement produces greater resistance to extinction. Four of the most basic schedules of reinforcement are: *fixed ratio, variable ratio, fixed interval*, and *variable interval*.

■ Stimuli that precede a reinforced response tend to control the response on future occasions *(stimulus control)*. Two aspects of stimulus control are *generalization* and *discrimination*. In generalization, an operant response tends to occur when stimuli similar to those preceding reinforcement are present. In discrimination, responses are given in the presence of *discriminative stimuli* associated with reinforcement (S +) and withheld to stimuli (S −) associated with nonreinforcement.

▶▶▶▶ **Exploration**

Behavioral Self-Management

This discussion could be the start of one of the most personal "explorations" in this book. There is now little doubt that self-administered reward affects behavior (Watson & Tharp, 1981). Many people have learned to successfully use self-administered reinforcement to alter or manage their own behavior. At the very least trying self-management can make you more aware of your behavior and what controls it. This Exploration, then, is an invitation to carry out a self-management project of your own. Would you like to increase the number of hours you spend studying each week? Would you like to exercise more, attend more classes, concentrate longer, or read more books? All these activities and many others can be improved by following the rules described here.

1. Choose a target behavior. Identify the activity you want to change.
2. Record a baseline. Record how much time you currently spend performing the target activity or count the number of desired or undesired responses you make each day.
3. Establish goals. Remember the principle of shaping and set realistic goals for gradual improvement on each successive week. Also, set daily goals that add up to the weekly goal.
4. Choose reinforcers. If you meet your daily goal, what reward will you allow yourself? Daily rewards might be watching television, eat-

ing a candy bar, socializing with friends, playing a musical instrument, or whatever you enjoy. Also establish a weekly reward. If you reach your weekly goal, what reward will you allow yourself? A movie? A dinner out? A weekend hike?
5. Record your progress. Keep accurate records of the amount of time spent each day on the desired activity.
6. Reward successes. If you meet your daily goal, collect your reward. If you fall short, be honest with yourself and skip the reward. Do the same for your weekly goal.
7. Adjust your plan as you learn more about your behavior. Overall progress will reinforce your attempts at self-management.

If you have trouble finding rewards or if you don't want to use the entire system, remember that anything *done often* can serve as reinforcement (the Premack principle). For example, if you watch television every night and want to study more, make it a rule not to turn on the set until you have studied for an hour (or whatever length of time you choose). Then lengthen the requirement each week.

   Here is a sample of one student's plan:

1. *Target behavior:* number of hours spent studying for school
2. *Recorded baseline:* an average of 15 minutes per day for a weekly total of 1¼ hours
3. *Goal for first week:* an increase in study time to 20 minutes per day;

weekly goal of 2 hours total study time. Goal for second week: 25 minutes per day and 2½ hours per week. Goal for third week: 30 minutes per day and 3 hours per week. Ultimate goal: to reach and maintain 8 hours per week study time.
4. *Daily reward for reaching goal:* 1 hour of guitar playing in the evening; no playing if the goal is not met. Weekly reward for reaching goal: go to a movie or buy a record album.

Self-Recording   Even if you find it difficult to give and withhold the rewards in your program, you are likely to succeed. Simply knowing that you are reaching a desired goal can be reward enough. The key to any self-management program therefore becomes accurate record keeping. This concept is demonstrated by a study in which some students in an introductory psychology course recorded study time and graphed daily and weekly study behavior. Even though no extra rewards were offered, students who recorded their study time earned better grades than those who did not (Johnson & White, 1971).

Contracting   If you try the techniques discussed and have difficulty sticking with them, you may want to try **behavioral contracting**. In a behavioral contract you state a *specific* problem behavior you want to control or a goal you want to achieve. Also state the rewards you will receive, privileges you will forfeit, or punishments you must

Exploration: Behavioral Self-Management

accept. The contract should be typed and signed by you and a person you are close to.

A behavioral contract can be quite motivating, especially when mild punishment is part of the agreement. Here's an example reported by Nurnberger and Zimmerman (1970): A student working on his Ph.D. had completed all requirements but his dissertation, yet for 2 years he had not written a single page. A contract was drawn up for him in which he agreed to meet weekly deadlines on the number of pages he would com-

plete. To make sure he would meet the deadlines, he wrote postdated checks. These were to be forfeited if he failed to reach his goal for the week. The checks were made out to organizations he despised (the Ku Klux Klan and American Nazi Party). From the time he signed the contract until he finished his degree, the student's work ouput was greatly improved.

Getting Help   Attempting to manage or alter your own behavior may be more difficult than it sounds. If you feel you need more

information, consult either of the books listed below. You will also find helpful advice in the Applications for Chapters 9 and 23. If you do try a self-modification project but find it impossible to reach your goal, be aware that professional advice is available.

For more information, consult:

Watson, D. L., & Tharp, R. G. *Self-Directed Behavior.* Brooks/Cole, 1981.

Williams, R. L., & Long, J. D. *Toward a Self-Managed Life Style.* Houghton Mifflin, 1979.

Learning Check

1. After a target behavior has been selected for reinforcement, it's a good idea to record a baseline so you can set realistic goals for change.   T or F?
2. Self-recording, even without the use of extra rewards, can bring about desired changes in target behaviors.   T or F?
3. The Premack principle states that behavioral contracting can be used to reinforce changes in behavior.   T or F?
4. A self-management plan should make use of the principle of shaping by setting a graduated series of goals.   T or F?

Answers: 1. T   2. T   3. F   4. T

Questions for Discussion

1. Lately you have been getting a shock of static electricity every time you touch a door handle. You begin to notice a hesitation in your door-opening movements. Can you analyze this situation in terms of classical conditioning?

2. Over the years, balloons have occasionally popped in your face when you were blowing them up. Now you squint and feel tense whenever you blow up a balloon. What kind of conditioning is this? What schedule of reinforcement has contributed to the conditioning? How could you extinguish the response?

3. You are in charge of a group of fifth-grade children that meets regularly for recreation. Other members of the group have excluded a younger girl and a very shy boy from activities. How could you use reinforcement principles to improve this situation? Include techniques aimed at both the excluded children and the group.

4. What role has reinforcement played in your selection of a major? Friends? A job? The clothes you wore to school today?

5. From your point of view, what would be the ideal way to be paid at a job? Should pay be weekly, hourly, daily? Should it be tied to work output? Should rewards other than money be offered? If you owned a business, what would you consider the ideal way to pay your employees?

6. How many situations can you list in which rewards are haphazardly or inefficiently applied (for example, tax breaks for people who have children instead of those who don't; better seats for those who take "cuts" in line, etc.)? How would you feel about applying a behavioral engineering approach to such problems?

7. How might operant conditioning principles be used to encourage people to pick up litter (what rewards could be offered, and how might the cost of rewards be kept low)?

8. In what ways would instinctive drift be adaptive for an animal? In what ways would it be maladaptive? Do you think human learning shows signs of any biological constraints?

Conditioning and Learning II

Chapter 9

Chapter Preview

Human history becomes more and more a race between education and catastrophe.

H. G. Wells

Any subject can be taught effectively in some intellectually honest form to any child at any stage of development.

Jerome Bruner

Dr. Moore's "Learning Machine"

Teaching two- to five-year-olds to read, write, type, and compose stories may sound impossible. However, under the proper conditions it can become a reality. In the early 1960s Omar Khayyam Moore of Yale University designed a "responsive learning environment" to take full advantage of children's intellectual curiosity. In Moore's lab children were allowed to "play" with a "talking typewriter." When a child pressed a key, the corresponding letter appeared on the paper and a voice named it through a loudspeaker. Surprised by this response, the children tried other keys. Soon the connection between keys and letters began to form.

After several sessions in which typing was fairly random, a new game began. Whenever a child's attention wandered, a letter appeared on a screen and was named aloud. Children who returned to random key pressing suddenly found that the keys no longer worked—until they pressed the key matching the letter on the screen. Then, the correct letter printed and the voice named it. Soon, a new letter appeared on the screen. Later, words began to appear. If a child pressed the key for the first letter, a pointer moved to the second letter. When the child had correctly typed all the letters of a word such as dog, *the machine pronounced the word. Then a new word appeared. By working with the talking typewriter, children rapidly went from random typing to reading and writing. Then they composed their own sentences and stories—all before age five (Pines, 1963)!*

Today, pocket-size electronic games duplicate many of the educational feats of Moore's bulky apparatus. And, by comparison to popular video games like "Space Invaders" or "Pac Man," Moore's talking typewriter looks pretty tame. Just the same, children in Moore's lab became lost in the joy of discovery, simply because. the environment was responsive to their actions. As these children show, an ability to learn is every human's birthright. This chapter extends the discussion begun in Chapter 8. An important theme to watch for as you read is that learning is based on information.

Survey Questions   What do classical conditioning and operant conditioning have in common? What is feedback and how does it affect learning? What impact does punishment have on learning? What is cognitive learning? Does learning occur by imitation? How are motor skills best learned? What can be done to break a bad habit? How serious are the effects of television violence?

Resources

Conditioning in Perspective— Great Expectations

An ice cream truck approaches with its bell ringing. A boy runs to the truck, buys an ice cream, and eats it, salivating as he does. What kind of learning is this? If it seems to you that both classical and operant conditioning are present in this example, you are right.

Two-Factor Learning

In the real world classical and operant conditioning are often intertwined. As you can see in Figure 9–1, the boy's behavior reflects both kinds of learning. Due to classical conditioning, the boy will salivate each time he hears the truck's bell. Also, the bell is a discriminative stimulus (S+) signaling that reward is available if certain responses are made. When he hears the bell, the boy will run to the truck, buy, and eat an ice cream (operant conditioning).

The boy's involuntary responses are altered by classical conditioning while his voluntary behavior is shaped by operant conditioning.

Question: Other than the fact that they often occur together, do operant and classical conditioning have anything in common?

Information   Psychologists used to picture conditioning as a mechanical "stamping in" of responses. Now, many think of learning in terms of *information processing*. According to this **informational view,** learning creates mental **expectancies** (or expectations) about events. Once acquired, these expectancies alter behavior. For example, researcher Robert Rescorla (1980) explains classical conditioning this way: Because the conditioned stimulus reliably precedes the unconditioned stimulus, the CS *predicts* the US. When the CS is present, the brain *expects* the US to follow. Therefore, the brain prepares the body to respond to the US. In our example whenever the boy

Fig. 9–1 *Two-factor learning.*

hears the bell or sees the truck, his mouth waters to prepare for eating ice cream. Similarly, when you are about to get a shot with a hypodermic needle, your muscles tighten and there is a catch in your breathing as your body prepares for discomfort.

If you think about it, operant reinforcers also supply information. In operant conditioning we learn to *expect* that a certain response will have a certain effect at certain times (Bolles, 1979). From this point of view, reward tells a person or an animal that a response was "right" and worth repeating. Likewise, stimuli or events preceding actions tell what response to make to get a reinforcer. Thus, when the boy hears the bell, he *expects* that running to the truck and paying for an ice cream will lead to eating it. If his expectation changes, his behavior will too. Picture what would happen if the ice cream truck changed its route, and the boy repeatedly ran out to find, instead, a garbage truck with its safety bell ringing. Rapid extinction would follow as the boy's expectancy changed from "bell means ice cream" to "bell means garbage."

The adaptive value of information helps explain why much human learning occurs without obvious reinforcement by food, water, and the like. Humans readily learn responses that merely have a desired effect or that bring them closer to a goal. Let's explore this idea further.

Feedback

Imagine that you are asked to throw darts at a target. Each dart must pass over a screen, which prevents you from telling if you hit the target. If you threw 1000 darts this way, we would expect little improvement in your performance, because no **feedback** is provided. Feedback (information about what effect a response had) is particularly important in human learning. Recall, for instance, that O. K. Moore's "learning machine" did not explicitly reward children for correct responses. Yet, because it provided feedback, rapid learning took place.

The value of feedback (also called **knowledge of results, or KR**) is one of the most useful lessons to be gained from studies of learning. Increased feedback almost always improves learning and performance.

Question: How can feedback be applied?

There are numerous possibilities, many already widely used. If you want to learn to play a musical instrument, to sing, to speak a second language, or to deliver a speech, tape-recorded feedback can be very helpful. In sports videotapes are used to improve everything from ten-

nis serves to pick-off moves in baseball. If you would like to make similar use of feedback, it's worth knowing that taped replays are most helpful when a skilled coach directs attention to key details (Salmoni, Schmidt, & Walter, 1984).

Learning Aids Feedback is valuable in education too. In recent years operant learning and feedback have been combined in two interesting ways. These are *programmed instruction* and *computer-assisted instruction.*

Question: How do such techniques make use of feedback?

For feedback to be most effective, it should be *frequent*, *immediate*, and *detailed*. **Programmed instruction** teaches students in a format that requires precise answers about information as it is presented. This arrangement supplies frequent feedback to keep learners from practicing errors. It also has the advantage of letting students work at their own pace. (The Learning Check that follows this discussion is done in a programmed format so that you can see what one looks like.)

In **computer-assisted instruction (CAI)** students work at individual computer terminals. The computer displays lessons on a screen, and students respond by typing answers. In addition to giving immediate feedback, the computer can *analyze each answer*. This allows use of a **branching program** that supplies extra information and questions when errors are made.

Elementary school children seem to do especially well with a "computer tutor" due to the rapid feedback and individualized pacing. Adults, too, benefit from computer-assisted instruction. For example, CAI has been found to speed electronics training in the military, and it accelerates learning for various college subjects (Dossett & Hulvershorn, 1983: Kulic et al., 1980). Although the final level of skill or knowledge is no higher than that gained with conventional methods, CAI can save much time and effort (Wexley, 1984).

The simplest computerized instruction consists of self-paced **drill and practice**. In this format students answer questions similar to those found in printed workbooks. Some critics believe this makes the computer nothing more than an electronic page-turner. However, even at this level CAI offers advantages. In addition to immediate feedback, the computer can give extra KR not normally available. If you were to use such a program, for example, you might be told how fast you worked, your percentage of correct responses, or how your work compared with previous scores (Lepper, 1985).

Fig. 9–2 *Computer-assisted instruction. Screen on the left shows a typical drill-and-practice math problem, in which students must find the hypotenuse of a triangle. Center screen presents the same problem as an instructional game to increase interest and motivation. In the game a child is asked to set the proper distance on a ray gun in the hovering space ship to "vaporize" an attacker. The right screen depicts an educational simulation. Here, students place a "probe" at various spots in a human brain. They then "stimulate," "destroy," or "restore" areas. As each area is altered, it is named on the screen, and the effects on behavior are described. This allows students to explore basic brain function on their own.*

Higher level CAI programs include **instructional games** and **educational simulations.** Instructional games use stories, competition with a partner, sound effects, and gamelike graphics to increase interest and motivation (see Fig. 9–2). In educational simulations students face problems in an imaginary situation or "microworld." By observing the effects of their choices, students discover basic principles of physics, biology, psychology, or other subjects (Lepper, 1985).

Psychologists are only now beginning to fully explore the value and limits of computer-assisted instruction. Nevertheless, it seems likely that their efforts will improve not only education but our understanding of human learning as well.

Learning Check

To give you an idea of what programmed instruction is like, this Learning Check is presented in a programmed format. To use it, cover the words on the left, and then uncover each answer after you have filled in a blank.

classical two- classical expectancies knowledge results feedback drill	In many learning situations both _____ and operant conditioning occur simultaneously. This circumstance is referred to as _____ factor learning. Often, a reinforcer that strengthens an operant response also serves as an unconditioned stimulus for _____ conditioning. The informational view of learning states that both classical and operant conditioning create mental _____ that alter behavior. Much human learning is based on informational feedback about the effects a response has had. Feedback is also known as KR or _____ of _____. Programmed instruction is self-paced and gives immediate _____ to the learner. The simplest form of computer assisted instruction is _____ and practice.

Punishment—
Putting the Brakes on Behavior

For better or worse punishment is one of the most popular ways to control behavior in our society. Spankings, reprimands, loss of privileges, fines, jail sentences, firings, failing grades, and the like all reflect a widespread reliance on punishment (Fig. 9–3). Clearly, no account of learning can be complete without discussing punishment. Before we begin, however, let's return briefly to reinforcement.

Negative Reinforcement versus Punishment   Until now we have concentrated on **positive reinforcement,** which occurs when pleasant or desirable consequences follow a response. The time has come to also consider the "dark side" of conditioning: **Negative reinforcement,** as it is called, occurs when a response causes the *removal* of an *unpleasant* event. Like positive reinforcement, negative reinforcement also increases responding. However, it does so by *ending discomfort*. For example, if you have a headache and take an aspirin, your aspirin taking will be reinforced if the headache stops. Likewise, a rat could be taught to press a bar to get a food pellet (positive reinforcement); or, the rat could be shocked mildly until it pressed a bar that turned off the shock (negative reinforcement). Either way, bar pressing would increase. Often, positive and negative reinforcement combine. If you are uncomfortably hungry, eating a meal is reinforced by the good-tasting food (positive reinforcement) and by an end to nagging hunger (negative reinforcement).

Many people mistake negative reinforcement for punishment. However, **punishment** is "any event that follows a response and *decreases* its likelihood of occurring again" (Adams, 1980). As noted, negative reinforcement *increases* responding. The difference can be seen in a hypothetical example. Let's say you live in an apartment and your neighbor's stereo is blasting so loudly that your ears hurt. If you pound on the wall and the volume drops (negative reinforcement), future wall pounding will be more likely. If you pound on the wall and the volume increases (punishment), or the neighbor comes over and pounds on you (more punishment), pounding on the wall becomes less likely. For a more realistic example consider the case of a drug addict undergoing withdrawal. Taking the drug ends painful withdrawal symptoms temporarily. Drug taking, therefore, is negatively reinforced. If the drug intensified pain (punishment), the addict would quickly stop taking it.

Question: Isn't it also punishing to have privileges, money, or other positive things taken away?

Yes. Punishment is either the addition of an aversive (painful or disliked) event or the removal of a positive event. Parents who "ground" their teenage children for misbehavior are using the second kind of punishment. For your convenience Figure 9–4 summarizes what we have covered so far.

Variables Affecting Punishment

Question: Reinforcement strengthens a response. Does punishment weaken a response?

Many people assume that punishment abolishes undesired behavior. Is this always true? Psychologists have learned that the effectiveness of punishment depends greatly on its *timing, consistency,* and *intensity.* Punishment suppresses behavior best when it occurs while a response is being made, or *immediately* afterward (timing), and when it is given *each time* a response occurs (consistency). Thus, a dog that has developed a habit of constantly barking can be effectively (and humanely) punished by spraying water on its nose each time it barks. Ten to fifteen such treatments are usually enough to greatly reduce barking. This would not be the case if punishment were applied occasionally or much later. If you discover that your dog dug up and ate a tree while you were gone, it will do little

Fig. 9–3 *Punishment has long been used to suppress undesirable behavior.*

> ### Edict of Louis XI, King of France
> ### A.D. 1481
>
> "Anyone who sells butter containing stones or other things (to add to the weight) will be put into our pillory, then said butter will be placed on his head until entirely melted by the sun. Dogs may lick him and people offend him with whatever defamatory epithets they please without offense to God or King. If the sun is not warm enough, the accused will be exposed in the great hall of the gaol in front of a roaring fire, where everyone will see him."

TYPE OF EVENT

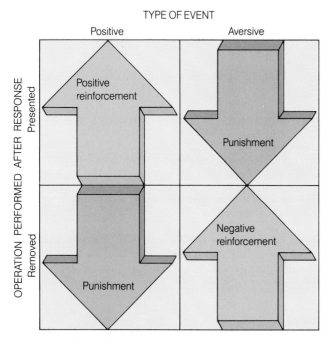

Fig. 9–4 *Types of reinforcement and punishment. The impact of an event depends on whether it is presented or removed after a response is made. Each square defines one possibility: Arrows pointing upward indicate that responding is increased; downward-pointing arrows indicate that responding is decreased. (Adapted from Kazdin, 1975.)*

good to punish him hours later. Likewise, the commonly heard childhood threat of, "Wait 'til your father comes home, then you'll be sorry," does more to make father an ogre than it does to effectively punish an undesirable response.

Severe punishment can be extremely effective in stopping behavior. If a child sticks a finger in a light socket and gets shocked, that may be the last time the child *ever* tries it. More often, however, punishment only temporarily *suppresses* a response. If the response is still reinforced, punishment may be particularly ineffective. Responses suppressed by **mild punishment** usually reappear later. If a child sneaks a snack from the refrigerator before dinner and is punished for it, the child may pass up snacks for a short time. But since snack sneaking was also rewarded by the sneaked snack, the child will probably try sneaky snacking again, sometime later.

This fact was demonstrated experimentally by arranging for rats to be slapped on the paw when bar pressing in a Skinner box. Two groups of well-trained rats were placed on extinction. One group was punished with a slap for each bar press, while the other was not. It might be ex-

pected that the slap would cause bar pressing to extinguish more quickly. Yet this was not the case, as can be seen in Fig. 9–5. Punishment temporarily slowed responding, but it did not cause more rapid extinction. Slapping the paws of rats or children has little permanent effect on a reinforced response. It is worth stating again, however, that intense punishment may permanently suppress a response. Experiments show that actions even as basic as eating can be suppressed. Animals severely punished while eating may never eat again (Bertsch, 1976).

Question: Then should punishment be used in the learning process?

Using Punishment Wisely   Parents, educators, animal trainers, and the like have three basic tools available to control simple learning: (1) *reinforcement* (or reward) strengthens a response; (2) *nonreinforcement* causes a response to extinguish; (3) *punishment* suppresses a response. These tools work best in combination. When punishment is mild, as it should be, its effect may be limited if reinforcers are still available in the situation. If you choose to use punishment, it is best to also reward an alternate, desirable response. Used alone, punishment tells a person or animal that a response was "wrong," but it *does not teach new behaviors*. If reinforcement is missing from the formula, punishment becomes less effective.

In a situation that poses immediate danger, such as when a child reaches for the top of a stove or a dog runs into the street, mild punishment may prevent disaster. Punishment in such cases is most effective when it produces responses *incompatible* with the undesired response. Let's say a child reaches toward a stove burner. Would a swat on the bottom serve as effective punishment? Probably so. It would be better, however, to slap the child's outstretched hand so it will be withdrawn in the presence of the stove.

Question: Are there drawbacks to the use of punishment?

Yes, several. Let's consider the case against punishment.

Side Effects of Punishment

The basic problem with punishment is that it is usually *aversive* (painful or uncomfortable). As a result people and situations associated with punishment tend, through classical conditioning, to also become aversive (feared, resented, or disliked). This association, perhaps, is why children so often choose school windows to break when others are available. The aversive qualities of punishment make it especially inappropriate to use when teaching children to eat politely, or for toilet training.

Escape and Avoidance   A second major problem is that aversive stimuli usually encourage **escape learning** and **avoidance learning**. Escape learning simply reflects the operation of negative reinforcement:

> A dog is placed in a two-compartment cage called a shuttle box. If it is shocked in one of the compartments, it will quickly learn to jump to the second compartment to *escape* the shock. If a buzzer is sounded 10 seconds before the shock is turned on, the dog will soon learn to associate the buzzer with shock. It will then *avoid* pain by jumping *before* the shock begins (Solomon & Wynne, 1953).

Psychologists have theorized that avoidance involves two-factor learning, described earlier. An animal first learns, through classical conditioning, to feel fear in the presence of the buzzer. Then leaping from the compartment is rewarded by negative reinforcement in the form of a reduction in fear (this is operant learning).

Once avoidance is learned, it is very persistent. The shock can be turned off and the dog will continue to leap from the compartment each time the buzzer sounds. This fact is rather puzzling: If the buzzer is never followed by shock, why doesn't fear of the buzzer extinguish? In informational terms the dog has learned to expect that the buzzer is followed by shock. If the dog leaves before the shock would normally occur, it gets no new information to change the expectancy (Schwartz, 1984).

Question: How do escape and avoidance learning relate to punishment?

Escape and avoidance learning are a regular part of daily experience. For instance, if you work with a loud and obnoxious person, you may at first escape from conversations with him; later you may learn to avoid him altogether. Each time you sidestep him, your avoidance is reinforced by a sense of relief. In many situations involving frequent punishment, similar desires to escape and avoid are activated. For example, children who run away from punishing parents (escape) may soon learn to lie about their behavior (avoidance) or to spend as much time away from home as possible (also an avoidance response).

Aggression   A third problem with punishment is that it can greatly increase *aggression*. Researchers have shown that animals consistently react to pain by attacking whomever or whatever is around (Azrin et al., 1965). A common example of this effect is the faithful dog that nips its owner while undergoing a painful procedure at a veterinarian's office.

We also know that one of the most common responses to frustration is aggression (Fig. 9–6). Generally speaking, punishment is painful, frustrating, or both. Punishment therefore sets up a powerful learning environment for the promotion of aggression. When a child is spanked, the child may feel angry, frustrated, and hostile. What if the child then goes outside and hits a brother, sister, or a neighbor? The danger is that the child may feel good because anger and frustration have been released. If so, aggression has been rewarded and will tend to occur again in other frustrating situations. One study found that overly aggressive adolescent boys had been severely punished for aggression at home. Since aggression was suppressed at home, parents were frequently surprised to learn that their "good boys" were in trouble at school for fighting and other forms of aggression (Bandura & Walters, 1959).

Fig. 9–5 *The effect of punishment on extinction. Immediately after punishment, the rate of bar pressing is suppressed, but by the end of the second day, the effects of punishment had disappeared. (After B. F. Skinner, The Behavior of Organisms. © 1938. D. Appleton-Century Co., Inc. Reprinted by permission of Prentice-Hall, Inc.)*

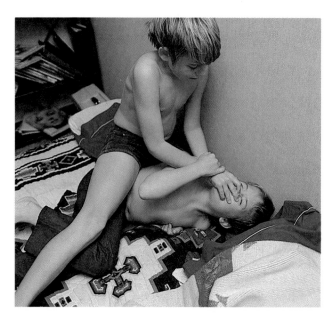

Fig. 9–6 *Frustration and aggression are frequent side effects of punishment.*

To summarize, the most common error in the use of punishment is to rely on it exclusively as a means of training or discipline. The overall emotional adjustment of a child or pet disciplined mainly by reward is usually superior to one disciplined mainly by punishment. Frequent punishment makes a person or an animal unhappy, confused, anxious, aggressive, and fearful of the source of punishment. Children who receive a lot of punishment from parents or teachers learn not only to dislike parents and teachers but also to dislike and avoid the activities associated with punishment (schoolwork or household chores, for instance) (Munn, 1969). It is not entirely unreasonable with three- to five-year-old children to occasionally use mild physical punishment (see the Chapter 16 Applications section). Otherwise, it would seem that the adage "Spare the rod and spoil the child" should at least be changed to "Use the rod sparingly or spoil the child" and perhaps simply to "Spare the rod."

Cognitive Learning— Beyond Conditioning

Question: Is all learning just a connection between stimuli and responses?

Some learning can be thought of this way. But, as we have seen, even basic conditioning has "mental" elements. As a further example of this fact, assume that you have been conditioned—by the pairing of a light with shock—to feel fear each time the light comes on. If the shock is then turned off and the light is presented many times, your fear will gradually extinguish. Now, what would happen if you were simply *told* that shock would not follow the light again? The surprising finding is that your fear would disappear almost immediately (Grings & Lockhart, 1963; Wickens et al., 1963). As a human, you can anticipate future reward or punishment and react accordingly, even to the point of overriding a conditioned response. (You may wonder why this doesn't seem to work when a doctor or dentist says, "This won't hurt a bit." Here's why: They lie!)

There is no doubt that human learning includes a large *cognitive*, or mental, dimension. As humans, we are greatly affected by information, expectations, perceptions, mental images, and the like. Loosely speaking, **cognitive learning** refers to understanding, knowing, anticipating, or otherwise making use of higher mental processes. Cognitive learning extends beyond basic conditioning into the realms of memory, thinking, problem solving, and language. Since these topics are covered in later chapters, our discussion here is limited to an initial look at learning beyond conditioning.

Cognitive Maps   How do you navigate around the town you live in? Is it fair to assume that you have simply learned to make a series of right and left turns to get from one point to another? It is far more likely that you have developed an overall mental picture of how the town is laid out. This **cognitive map** (internal representation of relationships) acts as a guide even when you must detour or take a new route.

Question: Are animals capable of cognitive learning?

A little psychological "monkey business" shows that they are. In one experiment chimpanzees watched as a psychologist hid pieces of fruit in a field at various places. Later, the chimps were released into the field. Chimps who watched the hiding found about 12 pieces of fruit each. Control group chimps averaged only 1 find each—mostly by following the informed monkeys and sharing the "fruits of their labors" (Menzel, 1978). Actually, it's not surprising that higher animals are capable of cognitive learning. Even the lowly rat—not exactly a mental giant—learns *where* food is found in a maze, not just which turns to make to reach the food (Tolman, 1946).

Latent Learning   Cognitive learning is also revealed by **latent** (or hidden) **learning**. That is, learning sometimes occurs without obvious reinforcement and remains hidden until reinforcement is provided:

Mickey Rat II Learns Where the Action Is

Two groups of rats are allowed to explore a maze. Rats in one group find food at the far end of the maze and soon learn to make their way rapidly through the maze when released. Rats in the second group are unrewarded and show no signs of learning. But later, when the same rats are given food, they run the maze as well as the rewarded group (Tolman & Honzik, 1930).

Although there was no outward sign of it, the unrewarded rats had learned their way around the maze. Their learning, therefore, remained latent at first (see Fig. 9–7).

Question: How did they learn if there was no reinforcement?

Apparently, satisfying curiosity can be enough to reward learning (Harlow & Harlow, 1962). In humans, latent learning is probably related to higher level abilities, such as anticipation of future reward. For example, if you give an attractive classmate a ride home, you may make mental notes about how to get to his or her house, even if a date only seems to be a remote future possibility.

Learning to Learn   *Learning to learn* is another interesting cognitive effect. It too can be demonstrated by an animal experiment. A monkey is given the problem of picking which of two objects has a raisin under it. On the first trial a raisin is placed under a cup; to the right of it is a box with nothing underneath. The monkey chooses the cup and gets the raisin. On the next trial the position of the objects is reversed, but the cup still has the raisin. This time the monkey chooses the box, apparently selecting by position, not by object. After a large number of trials, the monkey learns that the treat is always under the cup, regardless of position. Then a new problem is presented, this time using a dish and a toy car. Again, the

monkey's learning is gradual. However, after several hundred trials and many new problems, the monkey will develop a **learning set,** or preparedness for further learning. Given a new problem, it gets it right on the first or second trial (Harlow, 1949). Humans given similar problems catch on immediately. Perhaps it could be said that persistence is the monkey's forte, and learning to learn, the human's.

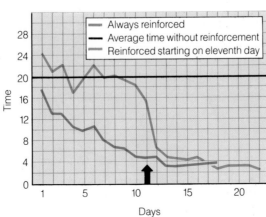

Fig. 9–7 *Latent learning. The maze used by Tolman and Honzik to demonstrate latent learning by rats (left). Results of the experiment are on the right. Notice the rapid improvement in performance that occurred when food was made available to the previously unreinforced animals. (Adapted from Tolman & Honzik, 1930.)*

Discovery Learning   Much of what is meant by cognitive learning is summarized by the word *understanding*. Each of us has, at times, learned ideas by *rote* (repetition and memorization). Although rote learning is efficient, many psychologists believe that learning is more lasting when people *discover* facts and principles on their own (Lepper, 1985). In **discovery learning**, skills are gained by insight and understanding instead of by rote (Bruner, 1968).

Question: As long as learning occurs, what difference does it make?

Figure 9–8 illustrates the difference. Two groups of students were taught to calculate the area of a parallelogram. Some were encouraged to see that a "piece" of a parallelogram could be "moved" to create a rectangle. Later, they were better able to solve unusual problems than were students who simply memorized a rule (Wertheimer, 1959). As this suggests, discovery learning tends to produce better understanding of new problems and situations (Lepper, 1985). In sum it seems worthwhile to take extra steps to foster insight and deeper understanding, even if learning by discovery takes longer.

Modeling— Do as I Do, Not as I Say

The class watches intently as a skilled potter pulls a spinning ball of clay into the form of a vase. There is little doubt that many skills are learned by what Albert Bandura (1971) calls **observational learning, modeling**, or, simply, imitation. The value of learning by observation is obvious: A seemingly simple skill, such as throwing a small pot, would take pages and pages to describe in words. Even then, a beginner still might not know how to begin. Many responses simply cannot be effectively learned by verbal instruction. Imagine trying to *tell* someone how to tie a shoelace, do a dance step, crochet, or play a guitar.

Question: It seems obvious that we learn by observation, but how does it occur?

By observing a **model** (someone who serves as an example), a person may: (1) learn new responses, (2) learn to carry out or avoid previously learned responses (depending on what happens to the model for doing the same thing), or (3) learn a general rule that can be applied to various situations (Rosenthal & Zimmerman, 1978).

Fig. 9–8 *Learning by understanding and by rote. For some types of learning, understanding may be superior, although both types of learning are useful. (After Wertheimer, 1959.)*

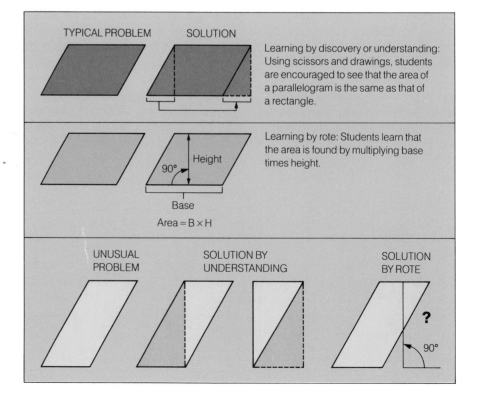

For observational learning to occur, several things must take place. First, the learner must pay *attention* to the model and *remember* what was done. (A beginning auto mechanic might be interested enough to watch an entire tune-up but unable to remember all the steps.) Next, the learner must be able to *reproduce* the modeled behavior. (Sometimes this is a matter of practice, but it may be that the learner will never be able to perform the behavior. I may admire the feats of world-class gymnasts, but with no amount of practice could I ever reproduce them.) If a model is *successful* or *rewarded*, the learner is more likely to imitate the behavior. This is also the case for models who are attractive, admired, or high in status (Bandura & Walters, 1963). Finally, once a new response it tried, normal *reinforcement determines if it will be repeated thereafter.*

Modeling has a powerful effect on behavior. In a classic experiment children watched an adult attack a large blowup Bo-Bo doll. Some children saw an adult sit on the doll, punch it, hit it with a hammer, and kick it around the room (Fig. 9–9). Others saw a color movie of these actions. A third group saw a cartoon version of the aggression. Later, the children were frustrated (by having some attractive toys taken away from them) and then allowed to play with the Bo-Bo doll. Most imitated the attack they had seen the adult perform. Some even added new aggressive acts of their own! Interestingly, the cartoon was only slightly less effective in encouraging aggression than the live adult model and the filmed model (Bandura, Ross, & Ross, 1963).

Question: Then do children blindly imitate adults?

No. Remember that observational learning equips a person to duplicate a response, but whether it is actually imitated depends on whether the model was rewarded or punished for what was done. Nevertheless, research shows that when parents tell a child to do one thing, but model a completely different response, children tend to imitate what the parents *do*, and *not* what they *say* (Bryan & Walbek, 1970). Thus, through modeling children learn not only attitudes, gestures, emotions, and personality traits, but fears, anxieties, and bad habits as well.

Consider a typical situation. Little Shawn-Erin-Ringo-Jeremy Jones has just been interrupted at play by his little brother. Angry and frustrated, he hits his little brother. This behavior interrupts his father's TV program. Father promptly spanks little Shawn-Erin-Ringo-Jeremy, saying, "This will teach you to hit your little brother." And it will. Because of modeling effects, it is unrealistic to expect a child to "Do as I say, not as I do." The message the father has given the child is clear: "You have frustrated me; therefore, I will hit you." Is it any wonder that the child does the same when he is frustrated?

Question: Can television serve as a model for observational learning?

There is reason to believe that it can. As a convicted criminal once told *TV Guide* magazine, "TV taught me how to steal cars, how to break into establishments, how to go about robbing people, even how to roll a drunk. Once after having watched *Hawaii Five-O*, I robbed a gas station. The show showed me how to do it." The rash of "repeat performances" that followed TV coverage of the first successful airline hijackings gives similar evidence of TV's power as a model.

In addition to teaching new antisocial actions, television may **disinhibit** dangerous impulses that viewers already have. For example, many TV programs give the message that violence is normal acceptable behavior (see Highlight 9–1). For some people this message can lower inhibitions against acting out hostile feelings (Berkowitz, 1984). Disinhibition may even extend to self-destructive

Fig. 9—9 *A nursery school child imitates the aggressive behavior of an adult model he has just seen in a movie. (Photos courtesy of Albert Bandura.)*

Highlight 9–1

Television: An Unflattering Portrait

Did you know that the world is populated primarily by males, professionals, whites, and members of the middle class? Did you know that women make up only 28 percent of the population; that one-half of all women are teenagers or in their early twenties; that more than one-third are unemployed or have no identifiable purpose beyond offering emotional support to men or serving as objects of sexual desire? That minorities are generally service workers, criminals, victims, or students? That over one-half of all villains have accents (usually German or Russian)? If you watch much TV, these are the impressions you get daily on the tube (U.S. Commission on Civil Rights, 1977).

Televised violence is even more disturbing. Some 80 percent of all TV dramas, and 95 percent of televised cartoons, contain violence. Foreigners and nonwhites are more likely to die on TV than are whites. TV lawmen more often than not contribute to violence, rather than prevent it (Oskamp, 1984; U.S. National Commission on the Causes and Prevention of Violence, 1970).

Are the distortions and stereotypes of "TV land" cause for concern? It would seem so. In over 99 percent of all United States households, TV is practically a member of the family. By 1984 average daily TV viewing in America had exceeded 7 hours. If forced to choose between having indoor plumbing or television, many families would find it difficult to decide! Clearly, television is a major influence in the lives of most children and many adults (Oskamp, 1984).

impulses. There is evidence that after a television soap opera character commits suicide, real suicides increase among viewers (Phillips, 1982).

Many psychologists are especially concerned about the effects of televised violence on children. Given the influence of television in our culture, TV's impact as a model deserves further examination—something we will undertake in this chapter's Exploration.

Learning Check

1. Negative reinforcement increases responding; punishment suppresses responding.   T or F?

2. Three factors that greatly influence the effects of punishment are timing, consistency, and _____.

3. Mild punishment tends to only temporarily _____ a response that is also reinforced.   (circle)

   enhance   aggravate   replace   suppress

4. Three undesired side effects of punishment are: (1) conditioning of fear and resentment, (2) encouragement of aggression, and (3) the learning of escape or _____ responses.

5. In humans extinction of a conditioned response can be influenced by expectation.   T or F?

6. An internal representation of relationships is referred to as a _____ _____.

7. Learning that suddenly appears when a reward or incentive for performance is given is called:
   a. discovery learning *b.* latent learning *c.* rote learning *d.* reminiscence

8. Albert Bandura uses the term _____ to describe observational learning.

9. If a model is successful, rewarded, attractive, or high in status, his or her behavior is:
   a. difficult to reproduce *b.* less likely to be attended to *c.* more likely to be imitated *d.* subject to positive transfer

10. Children who observed a live adult behaving aggressively became more aggressive; those who observed movie and cartoon aggression did not.   T or F?

Answers: 1. T 2. intensity 3. suppress 4. avoidance 5. T 6. cognitive map 7. b 8. modeling 9. c 10. F

Learning Principles in Action— Biofeedback

Psychologists have recently discovered that humans can learn to control bodily activities formerly believed to be involuntary. For years Yoga and Zen masters have demonstrated extraordinary control over "involuntary" functions like heart rate, blood pressure, oxygen consumption, and temperature of parts of the body. Now, Western technology is showing that under the proper conditions anyone can learn to duplicate these "impossible" effects.

Question: How is this possible?

Electronic Yoga?   By applying the general principle of feedback to the control of bodily responses, we arrive at **biofeedback.** If I were to say to you, "Raise the temperature of your right hand," you probably couldn't because you wouldn't know when you were succeeding. However, your task could be made easier by attaching a sensitive thermometer to your hand. With the thermometer wired so that an increase in temperature would activate a signal light, all you would have to do is try to keep the light on as much as possible. With practice you could then learn to raise your hand temperature at will.

Question: If you succeed at raising hand temperatures, what are you actually doing?

If asked to describe what you did, you might say, "I thought warm thoughts," or, "I just had a feeling when the light was on and I kept trying to recapture that feeling." The point is that when you are given feedback, you can repeat successful responses, even if they are subtle mental states. In this sense biofeedback involves cognitive learning: Bodily processes are monitored (usually electronically) and converted into a clear signal that provides *information* about bodily activity.

Neal Miller and his research associates have found that almost any bodily function can be voluntarily controlled if feedback or reward follows a change in the function. In a typical experiment Miller taught rats to change the speed of their heart rate. Their reward was electrical stimulation of "pleasure centers" in the brain (Miller & DiCara, 1967). Miller initially thought the animals were directly speeding and slowing their hearts. But later experiments suggest the animals altered heart rate by moving their voluntary muscles (Miller & Dworkin, 1974). In any case Miller and others have shown that rats can also learn to change their blood pressure, the blood flow to their stomach or kidneys, and the frequency of stomach contractions. They can even increase blood flow in one ear without affecting the other (Miller, 1969). Can you blush in your left ear?

Question: Of what value is this?

Applications of Biofeedback

Biofeedback holds considerable promise as a means of treating psychosomatic problems (illnesses caused mainly by stress or psychological factors) (see Fig. 9–10). For example, Elmer and Alyce Green have successfully trained people to prevent migraine headaches. With sensors taped to their hands and foreheads, patients are taught to redirect blood flow away from the head to their extremities. Since migraine headaches are caused by excessive blood flow to the head, biofeedback training equips patients to short-circuit headaches before they develop (Luce & Peper, 1971).

"He said his first words today—'Bang you're dead.'"

Fig. 9–10 *Biofeedback training involving muscle tension and blood flow has been used to relieve headaches and to promote relaxation. Here, a biofeedback signal is routed back to the patient through headphones, allowing him to alter bodily activities.*

Early successes led many to predict that biofeedback would offer a cure for psychosomatic illnesses, anxiety, phobias, drug abuse, and a long list of other problems. In reality biofeedback has proved helpful but not an instant cure. Biofeedback definitely can relieve muscle-tension headaches and migraine headaches (Adler & Adler, 1976; Budzynski, 1977). It shows promise for lowering blood pressure and alleviating irregular heart rhythms (Kristt & Engel, 1975). Some control of the digestive system seems possible through biofeedback, which may be helpful for ulcer patients. Biofeedback has even been used with some success to control epileptic seizures (Sterman, 1977). But questions about the value of biofeedback remain. Many of the benefits reported may simply reflect *general relaxation* (Blanchard & Epstein, 1978).

Question: Does biofeedback apply to brain waves?

Alpha Control   Alpha waves are one of several distinctive patterns of brain activity that can be recorded with the EEG (electroencephalograph, or brain wave machine). Several years ago psychologist Joseph Kamiya developed a technique whereby subjects are signaled by a tone or light whenever they produce alpha waves (Kamiya, 1968). Subjects in early alpha-control experiments reported that high levels of alpha were linked with sensations of pleasure, relaxation, passive alertness, or peaceful images. Some people saw these findings as a potential avenue to "instant bliss." But more recently, serious questions have been raised about the use of alpha training to promote deep relaxation. Research has shown that for some people in-

creased alpha output is the product of relaxation, but for others it occurs at times of *heightened* arousal (Orne & Wilson, 1978). For the moment it seems that the age of electronic yoga is not yet quite with us.

Learning Principles in Action—Learning Skills Skillfully

A motor skill is a series of actions molded into a smooth and efficient performance. Typing, walking, pole vaulting, shooting baskets, playing golf, driving a car, writing, and skiing are examples of motor skills.

Question: How are motor skills learned?

Many begin as simple response chains. However, as skills improve, we typically develop **motor programs** for them (Blumenthal, 1976). Motor programs are mental plans or models of what a skilled movement should be like. A good example of this kind of learning is provided by a guitarist friend of the author's. The guitarist once cut the first finger of his right hand before a performance. Normally he did his finger-picking with his thumb and first two fingers. How could he perform with an injured finger? No problem! He used the second and third fingers instead. His musical skills were in his head (as a motor program), not in his fingers.

Question: How do motor programs guide movement?

To perform an action, such as walking, we use feedback from the body and senses to compare our actions to an internal ideal (or program). Such monitoring, plus rapid corrections, is what allows us to walk on ice, sand, rocks, and stairs with no loss of skill. Motor programs also underlie many sports skills. A basketball player, for instance, may never make exactly the same shot twice in a game. This makes it almost impossible to practice every shot that might occur. Instead, the skilled athlete learns a variety of general programs, not a collection of set responses (Klausmeir, 1975).

New skills usually require conscious guidance. Think of when you learned to drive a car. Initially, almost all of your attention was focused on steering, signaling, accelerating, and braking; holding a conversation or tuning the radio was probably out of the question. However, as motor programs develop, we can pay less attention to specific movements. Eventually, skills become *automated*, or nearly automatic. This frees higher brain centers to make decisions and attend to other information (Singer, 1978). Thus, a skilled skier can enjoy the scenery on a downhill run, a knitter can watch television, or a driver can think about things other than driving.

Question: Are motor skills easily lost?

A concert pianist or a ballet dancer may require constant practice to maintain performance. On the other hand you have probably observed that you were able to type, roller-skate, swim, ride a bicycle, and so forth after years without practice. Perhaps it is not surprising that such everyday skills resist loss. Most are greatly **overlearned** (practiced far beyond basic mastery of the skill). But what about skills somewhere between typing and ballet? How well are they retained? For instance, can we expect astronauts to retain landing skills at the end of long space flights? Or might they become dangerously rusty without practice? Figure 9–12 suggests an answer.

Figure 9–12 shows how much learning is retained after varying amounts of time. People who learned a new motor pattern (keeping a pointer on a rotating target) showed little loss of skill after 10 weeks without practice. Those who learned a list of nonsense syllables (meaningless three-letter words) remembered very few at the end of the same period. This and a large number of similar studies show that *well-practiced motor skills are very resistant to loss* (Annett, 1979). The astronauts we left hanging in space a moment ago should have no trouble landing.

Question: Does Figure 9–12 also show that motor skills are retained better than words?

It is almost impossible to answer this question because there is no way to equate motor tasks and verbal tasks. It is true that verbal learning is often rapidly lost (think about how much you remember from classes taken last semester). Still, some verbal learning—a song or a poem, for example—may be retained for life. One reason for the rapid forgetting of words is that new learning often conflicts with old (see the discussion of interference in Chapter 10). In contrast, motor skills seem relatively free of such conflicts. Ultimately, all that can be said with certainty is that motor skills are quite lasting. It's a good thing they are, too. Imagine leaving your car at a garage and returning in 2 weeks—only to find your driving skills so shot that you are a menace to society on the way home!

Becoming Skilled

Question: Why is there a jump in the motor skill curve after practice has stopped?

Improved performance of a motor skill *after* practice is called **reminiscence**. Reminiscence is explained in this way: Learning increases during practice, but so does fatigue, boredom, and loss of motivation. These negative

Fig. 9–11   *Strobe-light photograph of a motor skill. Multiple exposures reveal the complexity of skilled movement. Motor skills are guided by mental plans or programs.*

Fig. 9–12   *The curves of forgetting for a simple motor skill and simple verbal learning. Notice that there is less rapid forgetting of the motor skill and that there is actually an improvement shortly after practice has ended. (After Leavitt & Scholsberg, 1944.)*

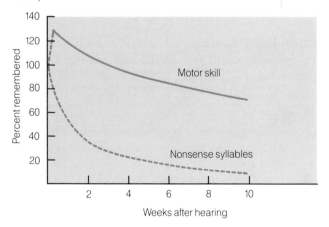

Fig. 9–13 *Performance curves for massed and spaced practice. Subjects learned to keep a pointer on a moving target. During the first learning session the spaced-practice group performed better. After a rest period performance was similar for both groups, but further trials again lowered performance in the massed-practice group. (From Jones & Ellis, 1962.)*

factors lower *performance* toward the end of a practice session even though *learning* continues. Later, when a rest period removes fatigue, performance rises sharply (Drowatzky, 1975).

Figure 9–13 gives another example of reminiscence and shows a related effect. Improvement in the performance of a motor skill is most rapid when short practice sessions are alternated with rest periods. This pattern, called **spaced practice,** helps keep fatigue and boredom to a minimum. It can also prevent the learner from practicing errors while tired. (Perfect practice makes perfect.) The opposite of spaced practice is **massed practice,** in which little or no rest is given between learning sessions. Notice in Figure 9–13 that massed practice lowers performance.

After a short rest it can be seen that massed and spaced practice produce similar amounts of learning. However, in the long run skills learned with spaced practice are retained better than those learned by massed practice (Drowatzky, 1975). This suggests that you should keep practice sessions short and well spaced if you are learning to type, play a musical instrument, juggle, or master some other motor skill.

Skillful Skill Learning   You should also keep in mind the following points for optimal skill learning (sources: Drowatzky, 1975; Gagne & Fleishman, 1959; Klausmeir, 1975; Meichenbaum, 1977; Singer, 1978):

1. Begin by observing and imitating a *skilled model.* Modeling provides a good mental picture of the skill. At this point try simply to grasp a visual image of the skilled movement.
2. Learn *verbal rules* to back up motor learning. Such rules are usually most helpful in the early phases of skill learning. When first learning cross-country skiing, for example, it is helpful to say "left arm,

right foot, right arm, left foot." Later, as a skill becomes more automated, internal speech may actually get in the way.
3. Practice should be as *lifelike* as possible so that artificial cues and responses do not become a part of the skill. A competitive diver should practice on the board, not on a trampoline. If you want to learn to ski, try to practice on snow, not straw.
4. Get *feedback* from a mirror, videotape, coach, or observer. Whenever possible, get someone experienced in the skill to direct attention to *correct responses* when they occur.
5. When possible, it is better to practice *natural units* rather than break the task into artificial parts. When learning to type, it is better to start with real words rather than exercises or nonsense syllables.
6. Learn to *evaluate* and *analyze* your own performance. Remember you are trying to learn a motor program, not just train your muscles. Motor skills are actually very mental.

The last point leads to one more suggestion. Research has shown that merely thinking about or imagining a skilled performance can aid learning (Annett, 1979). This technique, called **mental practice,** seems to help by refining motor programs (see inset box). The more familiar you are with a skill, the more mental rehearsal helps (Drowatzky, 1975; Meichenbaum, 1977). When you begin to get really good at a skill you are interested in, give mental practice a try. You may be surprised at how effective it can be.

Transfer of Training   Most skiing enthusiasts are familiar with the graduated length method. In this approach the beginning skier learns on short, easily managed skis and moves to progressively longer skis as skill develops.

This technique is an intuitive application of the principle of **positive transfer.** Positive transfer is said to have taken place when mastery of one task aids mastery of a second task. Another example would be learning to balance and turn on a bicycle before learning to ride a motorcycle or moped.

Question: Is there such a thing as negative transfer?

There is indeed. In **negative transfer,** skills developed in one situation conflict with those required for mastery of a new task. Learning to back a car with a trailer attached is a good example. Normally, when you are backing a car, the steering wheel is turned in the direction you want to go, the same as when moving forward. However, with a trailer attached, the steering wheel must be turned *opposite* from the direction you want the trailer to go. This situation results in negative transfer and regularly creates comical scenes at campgrounds and boat launching ramps. On a more serious note similar problems eventually led to standardization of airplane cockpits after many tragic crashes caused by negative transfer. Fortunately, negative transfer is usually brief and it occurs less often than positive transfer (Drowatzky, 1975). Negative transfer is most likely to occur when a new response must be made to an old stimulus. If you have ever encountered a pull type handle on a door that must be pushed open, you will appreciate this final point.

 Mental Gymnastics

In the following paragraph a member of the United States Olympic team describes a gymnastics routine he performs on the high bar. Notice how his mental review of the routine includes a series of reminders about important details of good form. Such self-coaching during mental practice helps perfect underlying motor programs.

OK, high-start mount, stay away from the bar, inside Stalder, get your feet in fast, push out fast, good easy giant swing, Gienger, throw the bar away, good hard toes, look for the bar, grab it, straddle cut catch, open up your body, stretch through the bottom, kick your toes hard again, Gienger, re-catch, Stalder up, nice and easy, reverse, Stalder, California hop, giant swing, good pressure on the jam, push it out, inverted swing, open at the top, inverted hop pirouette, push away from the bar, nice fast easy giants, good relax at the bottom, good relax, kick hard, twist, look for the ground, firm landing. ("High Bar," 1984.)

(Have you got that, future Olympians?)

Learning Check

1. Biofeedback is a type of meditation in which the body is made very quiet so that bodily functioning can be detected.   T or F?

2. Rats given electrical brain stimulation as a reward can be made to alter such bodily functions as heart rate, blood pressure, and stomach contractions.   T or F?

3. Biofeedback can definitely relieve:
   a. depression   *b.* diabetes   *c.* stomach ulcers   *d.* muscle-tension headaches

4. Joseph Kamiya developed a technique whereby subjects can gain control over the brain's production of _____ _____.

5. An important step in the mastery of many motor skills is achieved when the skill becomes
   a. reversible   *b.* automated   *c.* graduated   *d.* fixed

6. Mental models, called _____ _____, appear to underlie well-learned motor skills.

7. In motor skill learning, massed practice generally produces performance that is superior to spaced practice.   T or F?

8. Learning verbal rules to back up motor learning is usually most helpful in the early stages of acquiring a skill.   T or F?

Answers: 1. F   2. T   3. d   4. alpha waves   5. b   6. motor programs   7. F   8. T

Applications

Good Ways to Break Bad Habits

Question: How can I use learning principles to break a bad habit?

The following techniques offer some helpful possibilities. They combine ideas drawn both from this chapter and the last.

1. Try to discover what is reinforcing a habit and *remove, avoid,* or *delay* the *reinforcement.*

Example: A student who developed a habit of taking longer and longer breaks when studying realized that the breaks usually were lengthened by TV watching. A chance to watch TV was also reinforcing more frequent break taking.

Comment: To improve study habits, the student should either resolve to stay out of the room where the TV is located until work is done, or else require 2 hours of study for ½ hour of TV watching.

Example: Pam has a slightly different problem. When she reads in the evening, her periods of concentration last only about 15 minutes. They are usually followed by a trip to the kitchen for a snack. In addition to falling behind in her reading, she is gaining weight.

Comment: Snacking is rewarding her impulse to avoid reading. She should do her reading at school or at a library, so that there is a delay between the impulse to eat and the reward of snacking. At home she should keep only staples on hand or foods that require preparation, so that a separate trip to a store is required for "goodies." Requiring a walk around the block before eating a snack would also help (Ferster et al., 1962).

2. Try to get the same *reinforcement with new responses.*

Example: A young mother realized she was yelling at her children more often than she would like. This habit seemed to be reinforced by the periods of relative quiet that followed when she raised her voice.

Comment: To avoid this habit (which is negatively reinforced), she should (as much as possible) ignore her children when they are noisy and should make a special effort to praise them, show approval, and pay attention to them when they are playing quietly and constructively.

Example: Frank has been drinking increasing amounts of beer after getting home from work in the evening. He usually feels more relaxed but often drinks too much and gets into arguments with other family members.

Comment: Frank's need to unwind and dissipate the frustrations of the workday might be better achieved by participation in an athletic activity, such as jogging, swimming, bowling, handball, and so forth. An organized team sport might ensure that he will actually stick with his substitute activity.

3. *Avoid* or *narrow down cues* that elicit the bad habit.

Example: A student has begun to notice how much impulse buying he does at the grocery store. As a first step in avoiding this habit, he has begun to shop after he has had a meal because he has observed that hunger is a cue for his food buying.

Comment: He should also make a shopping list and stick to it so that he only looks at items he intends to buy.

Example: A father has noticed that he nags and criticizes his 4-year-old son almost nightly because the boy pours ketchup all over his dinner. He is upset about this and other daily instances of criticizing the boy.

Comment: The father has identified one cue for his excessive criticizing. It could be avoided by giving the boy a small bowl of ketchup to prevent the regular dinner battle. Other cues for nagging can be avoided in similar ways as they are identified (Schmidt, 1976).

Example: Raul is not ready to give up smoking, but would like to cut down. He has taken many smoking cues out of his daily routine by removing ashtrays, matches, and extra cigarettes from his house, car, and office. He also has been making an effort to avoid situations in which most of his smoking occurs by staying away from other smokers, taking a walk after meals (leaving his cigarettes at home), and putting a piece of gum in his mouth when he feels nervous.

Comment: To improve his control of smoking, Raul should try narrowing cues. He could begin by smoking only inside buildings, never outside or in his car. He could then limit his smoking to home. Then to only one room at home. Then to one chair at home. If he succeeds in getting this far, he may want to limit his smoking to only one uninteresting place: a bathroom, basement, or garage, for example (Goldiamond, 1971).

Applications: Good Ways to Break Bad Habits

4. Make an *incompatible response* in the presence of stimuli that usually precede the bad habit.

Example: A sprinter has developed a habit of jumping the gun at track meets and is frequently disqualified.

Comment: The sprinter should prepare for meets by remaining in the blocks while his coach fires the starter's pistol several times.

Example: A child has developed the habit of throwing her coat on the floor after coming in the front door. After being scolded, she would hang it up.

Comment: The parents should recognize that scolding has become the cue for hanging the coat up. The girl should not just be scolded, but should put her coat on again, go outside, come in the door, and hang her coat up. Soon, coming in the door will become the cue for hanging the coat up.

Example: June bites her nails so much they are painful and unsightly. She has identified several situations in which she is most likely to bite her nails and would like to break the connection between these and her habit.

Comment: June should make a list of incompatible behaviors she can engage in when she has the urge to bite her nails. These might include: putting her hands in her pockets, taking notes in class, sketching pictures, crossing her arms, leaning against something with her hands, chewing gum, playing a musical instrument, or combing her hair (Perkins & Perkins, 1976).

5. Use *negative practice* to associate a bad habit with discomfort.

Example: Rick has a facial tic that appears when he is nervous or tired. The tic looks like a wink made with his right eye.

Comment: In negative practice a response is repeated until it becomes boring, painful, or produces fatigue. This increases awareness of the habit and tends to discourage its recurrence. Rick should stand in front of a mirror and repeat the tic until the muscles used become quite uncomfortable. Similarly,

if you have a habit of saying "you know" or "uh" too often when speaking, set aside 15 minutes a day and repeat the error over and over while thinking, "I hate the way this sounds when someone else says it."

6. Utilizing *feedback* is one of the most direct of all approaches to changing bad habits.

Example: Four college students who are renting a house together are concerned about their high utility bills. Also, they would like to make an effort to conserve energy. To date, however, their good intentions have not lowered their electric bill.

Comment: The roommates should keep a daily record of their energy consumption by writing down and posting the numbers shown on their electric meter. A study of families given this kind of daily feedback showed that their energy use was greatly reduced (Palmer et al., 1977).

The last technique described is worth emphasizing. As noted in the Exploration for Chapter 8, almost any habit will benefit simply from keeping score. Keep track of the number of times daily that you arrive late to class, smoke a cigarette, watch an hour of TV, drink a cup of coffee, bite your fingernails, swear, or whatever other response you are interested in changing. A simple tally on a piece of paper will do, or you can get a small mechanical counter like those used to keep golf scores or count calories.

Throughout this chapter and the last, we have tried to emphasize the practical applications of learning theories to everyday problems. Many simple difficulties can be handled effectively without special training. If you have a really troublesome habit, such as overeating or excessive use of alcohol, cigarettes, or marijuana, you may find it most expedient to consult a professional counselor. Additional learning techniques for overcoming mild difficulties can be found in Chapter 23, Chapter 12, and Chapter 8.

Learning Check

1. Removing or avoiding reinforcement of a bad habit can help eliminate it, but delaying reinforcement has no effect.   T or F?
2. A mother who praises her children when they are quiet instead of yelling at them when they are noisy has received the same reinforcement for an alternate response.   T or F?
3. Restricting smoking to only one room in a house is an example of using feedback to alter a bad habit.   T or F?

Applications: Good Ways to Break Bad Habits

4. To break the link between an undesired response and various situations in which it occurs, it can be helpful to practice making an incompatible response in the same situations.   T or F?

5. In negative practice we learn to avoid or narrow down cues that elicit a bad habit.   T or F?

Answers: 1. F   2. T   3. F   4. T   5. F

Chapter Summary

■ Many real world situations involve *two-factor learning*—a combination of classical conditioning and operant conditioning.

■ From an *informational viewpoint* conditioning creates *expectancies*, which alter response patterns. In classical conditioning the CS creates an expectancy that the US will follow. In operant conditioning learning is based on the expectation that a response will have a specific effect.

■ *Feedback* or *knowledge of results* aids learning and improves performance. It is most effective when it is *immediate, detailed,* and *frequent.*

■ *Programmed instruction* breaks learning into a series of small steps and provides immediate feedback. *Computer-assisted instruction* (CAI) does the same but has the added advantage of being able to provide alternate exercises and information when needed. Three variations of CAI are *drill and practice, instructional games,* and *educational simulations.*

■ In *positive reinforcement* a reward or a pleasant event follows a response. In *negative reinforcement* a response ends discomfort and is therefore repeated. Punishment decreases responding. *Punishment* is either the presentation of an aversive event or the removal of a positive event after a response is made.

■ *Punishment* is most effective when it is *immediate, consistent,* and *intense.* Mild punishment tends only to temporarily suppress responses that are reinforced or were acquired by reinforcement.

■ The undesirable side effects of punishment include: conditioning of *fear* to punishing agents and situations associated with punishment, the learning of *escape* and *avoidance* responses, and the encouragement of *aggression.*

■ *Cognitive learning* involves higher mental processes, such as understanding, knowing, or anticipating. Even in relatively simple learning situations, animals and people seem to form *cognitive maps* (internal representations of relationships). In *latent learning,* learning remains hidden or unseen until a reward or incentive for performance is offered. *Learning to learn* is revealed by progressive improvements in the ability to solve similar problems. *Discovery learning* emphasizes insight and understanding, in contrast to *rote learning.*

■ Much human learning is achieved through observation or *modeling.* Modeling (or *observational learning*) is influenced by many factors, especially the personal characteristics of the model and the success or failure of the model's behavior. Studies have shown that aggression is readily learned and released by modeling.

■ During *biofeedback,* bodily processes are monitored and converted to a signal that indicates what the body is doing. With practice biofeedback allows alteration of many bodily activities. It shows promise for the alleviation of some stress-related illnesses. Its long-term effectiveness is still being evaluated. The usefulness of *alpha control* (voluntary control of brain waves) is debatable.

■ *Motor skills* are nonverbal response chains assembled into a smooth performance. Motor skills are guided by internal mental models called *motor programs.* Motor skills are resistant to forgetting and often show improvement *after* practice *(reminiscence).* Motor skill learning is usually best when practice is *spaced,* rather than *massed.* Depending on the relationship between prior learning and a new task, motor skills may show *positive* or *negative transfer* (carryover to a new situation).

Modeling and Television—The Tube as Teacher

An indication of the potential impact of TV can be found in these figures: By the time the average person has graduated from high school, he or she will have viewed some 15,000 hours of TV, compared with only 11,000 hours spent in the classroom. In that time, such viewers will have seen some 18,000 murders and countless acts of robbery, arson, bombing, torture, and beatings. Prime-time TV dramas average 8 acts of violence per hour and children's cartoons average 22 an hour (Oskamp, 1984).

Question: Earlier, the effects of observational learning were described. Do they apply to TV violence?

Television and Aggression
Where the effects of TV violence on children are concerned, the answer appears to be yes. At this point, hundreds of studies, involving well over 10,000 children from every conceivable background, have been completed. The vast majority point to the same conclusion: "If large groups of children watch a great deal of televised violence, they will be more prone to behave aggressively" (Comstock et al., 1978; Liebert et al., 1973; National Institute of Mental Health, 1982; Rubinstein, 1978).

Question: How does TV violence affect children?

As Albert Bandura showed in his Bo-Bo doll study, children may learn new aggressive actions by watching violent or aggressive behavior, or they may learn that violence is "OK." Either way, they are more likely to act aggressively. Also, remember that the children in Bandura's study imitated a cartoon almost as much as they did live human models. The claim that cartoons are "harmless," or "all in fun" becomes questionable in this light. Some TV stations now refuse to carry "Tom and Jerry," "Bugs Bunny," and "Roadrunner" cartoons because their violence levels are so high.

In addition to encouraging imitation of aggression, TV violence tends to lower sensitivity to violent acts. As anyone who has seen a street fight or a mugging can tell you, TV violence is sanitized and unrealistic. The real thing is gross, ugly, and gut wrenching. Even when it is graphic, TV violence is viewed in the relaxed and familiar setting of the home. For at least some viewers this combination diminishes emotional reactions to violent scenes. When Victor Cline and his associates showed a bloody fight film to a group of boys, they found that heavy TV viewers (averaging 42 hours a week) showed much less emotion than those who watched little or no TV (Cline et al., 1972). Television, in other words, can cause a *desensitization* to violence (see Chapter 23 for more on desensitization).

Question: Is it fair to say, then, that televised violence causes aggression in children?

No. That would be an exaggeration. Televised violence can make aggression more likely, but it does not cause it to occur (Freedman, 1984). Many other factors affect the chances that hostile thoughts will be translated into actions (Berkowitz, 1984). Among children one such factor is the extent to which a child *identifies* with aggressive characters (Huesmann et al., 1983). That's why it is so sad to find TV *heroes* behaving aggressively, as well as villains.

Question: Couldn't TV's impact also be used constructively?

TV as a Positive Model   There is no denying TV's tremendous power to inform and entertain. When these features are combined, as they have been in specials such as "Roots" or "Holocaust," the effect can be quite constructive. Perhaps the best examples of TV as a positive social force are the educational programs "Sesame Street," "The Electric Company," and "Mr. Rogers' Neighborhood." Over 150 research reports have dealt with the impact of these programs. An overwhelming majority of these evaluations are positive. Clearly, television can teach children while holding their voluntary interest and attention (Rubinstein, 1978).

As a model for prosocial attitudes and responses, TV could be used to promote helping, cooperation, charity, and brotherhood in the same way that it has tended to stereotype and encourage aggres-

---

Exploration: Modeling and Television—The Tube as Teacher

sion. To illustrate, children in one experiment watched a TV program that emphasized helping (a "Lassie" episode). Later these children were more willing than others to help a puppy in distress even when it meant skipping a chance to win prizes (Rubinstein et al., 1974).

Almost since the first TVs blinked to life in living rooms across the country, television has been damned and defended, praised and put down. In view of our discussion, you might want to think about these questions: Why is so much violence shown on TV? Do you think your views or behav-

ior have been influenced by TV? Given what you know about modeling, what changes would you make in TV programming? Would others watch the programs you propose? Would you?

Learning Check

1. The highest number of violent acts per hour is found in prime-time commercial television dramas.   T or F?
2. Heavy exposure to television appears to result in lowered emotional sensitivity to violence.   T or F?
3. Psychological research indicates that televised violence causes aggressive behavior in children.   T or F?
4. Research indicates that positive actions portrayed on television have little or no effect on viewers.   T or F?

Answers: 1. F   2. T   3. F   4. F

Questions for Discussion

1. Can you think of anything you do that is not affected in some way by learning?
2. How could you include more feedback (or more immediate feedback) in your study habits?
3. If you could change procedures in an elementary school classroom to enhance learning, what would you do? What changes would you make in a high school classroom?
4. Corporal punishment has been banned in many schools. In your opinion, what would be the pros and cons of banning corporal punishment in homes?
5. Draw a map of your school's campus as you picture it now. Draw a map of the campus as you pictured it after your first visit. How have the maps changed? How has reinforcement affected the changes?
6. How would your life change if motor skills were highly subject to loss?

7. Choose a bad habit you would like to break. How could you apply the principles discussed in this chapter to breaking this habit?
8. What incompatible responses can you think of that could be performed in public to prevent the following behaviors: smoking, knuckle cracking, swearing, fingernail biting, hand wringing, eyelash plucking?
9. How would you explain the many distortions of commercial television? Do you think that people watch television because of such distortions or in spite of them?
10. In your opinion should TV programs come with a violence rating scale, like the ratings of tar and nicotine on cigarette packages, or a rating system, such as that used for movies? What, if anything, would you suggest be done about the quality of TV programming and the amount of TV violence?

Memory

Chapter 10

Chapter Preview
"What the Hell's Going On Here?"

February, 1978: Steven Kubacki is cross-country skiing on the ice of Lake Michigan. He stops for a moment, pausing to enjoy the winter solitude. It's cold, colder in fact than he had realized. Steven decides to turn back. In a few minutes comes a new realization: He is lost. Wandering on the ice, he grows numb and very, very tired.

Put yourself in Steven Kubacki's shoes, and you will appreciate the shock of what happened next. Steven clearly recalls wandering lost and alone on the ice. Immediately after that, he remembers waking up in a field. But as he looked around, Steven knew something was wrong. It was spring! The backpack beside him contained running shoes, swimming goggles, and a pair of glasses—all unfamiliar. As he looked at his clothing—also unfamiliar—Steven thought to himself, "What the hell's going on here?" Fourteen months had passed since he left to go skiing (Loftus, 1980). How did he get to the field? Where did the strange gear come from? Steven couldn't say. He had lost over a year of his life to total amnesia.

As Steven Kubacki's amnesia vividly shows, life without memory would be meaningless. Imagine the terror and confusion of having all of your memories wiped out, from birth to the present. You would have no identity, no knowledge, no life history, no recognition of friends or family. Your past would be a total blank. In a very real sense we are our memories.

This chapter discusses memory and forgetting. As an inquiring person you should find the information interesting. Also included is a large section on improving memory skills. As a student you should find this discussion particularly helpful. Almost anyone (including you) can learn to use memory more effectively.

Survey Questions   How do we store information in memory? Is there more than one type of memory? How is memory measured? What are "photographic" memories? What causes forgetting? How accurate are everyday memories? How can memory be improved?

Resources

Stages of Memory—Do You Have a Mind Like a Steel Trap? Or a Sieve?

"A dusty storehouse of facts." That's how many people think of memory. In reality, **memory** is an *active system* that receives, stores, organizes, alters, and recovers information. In some ways memory acts like a computer (Fig. 10–1). Information to be recorded is first **encoded,** or changed into a usable form. This step is like punching data onto cards before feeding it into a computer. Next, information is **stored,** or held in the system. (As we will see in a moment, human memory actually has three separate storage systems.) Finally, memories must be **retrieved,** or taken out of storage, to be useful. In order to "remember" something, encoding, storage, and retrieval all must take place.

Question: What are the three separate memory systems just mentioned?

Psychologists have identified three stages of memory. To be stored for a long time, information must pass through all three (please refer to Fig. 10–2).

Fig. 10–1 *In some ways a computer acts like a mechanical memory system. Both systems process information, and both allow encoding, storage, and retrieval of data.*

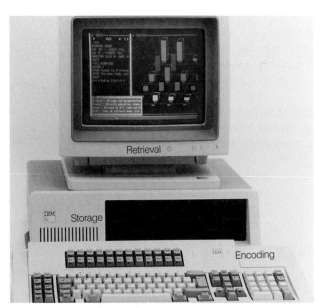

Sensory Memory   Let's say a friend asks you to pick up several things at a market. How do you remember them? Incoming information first enters **sensory memory.** Sensory memory holds an exact copy of what is seen or heard for a few seconds or less. For instance, if you see an object, an **icon** (EYE-kon) (image) persists for about one-half second afterward (Klatzky, 1980). To witness an icon, hold your hand in front of your face. Then, close your eyes and blink them rapidly open and closed again. You will continue to see a fleeting image of your hand for a split second after closing your eyes. Similarly, information you hear is held as a brief **echo** in sensory memory for up to 2 seconds (Klatzky, 1980). In general, sensory memory holds information just long enough to transfer it to the second memory system.

Short-Term Memory   Not everything seen or heard is kept in memory. Let's say a radio is playing in the background as your friend reads you her shopping list. Do you remember what the announcer says too? Probably not, because *selective attention* (discussed in Chapter 4) determines what information moves on to **short-term memory (STM).** Short-term memories are also brief, but longer than sensory memories. Attending to your friend's words will place the shopping list in short-term memory (while allowing you to ignore the voice on the radio saying, "Buy Burpo Butter").

Question: How are short-term memories encoded?

Short-term memories can be stored as images. But more often they are stored by *sound,* especially in recalling words and letters (Klatzky, 1980). Thus, if you are introduced to Tim at a party and you forget his name, you are more likely to call him by a name that *sounds like* Tim (Jim, for instance) than a name that sounds different (such as Bob or Tod). Your friend with the shopping list will be lucky if you don't bring home peas instead of cheese and soap instead of soup!

Short-term memory acts as a *temporary* storehouse for *small amounts* of information. Unless the information is important, it is quickly "dumped" from STM and forever lost. Short-term memory prevents our minds from collecting useless names, dates, telephone numbers, and other trivia (Miller, 1964). At the same time, it provides a **working memory** where we do much of our thinking. Dialing a phone number, doing mental arithmetic, remem-

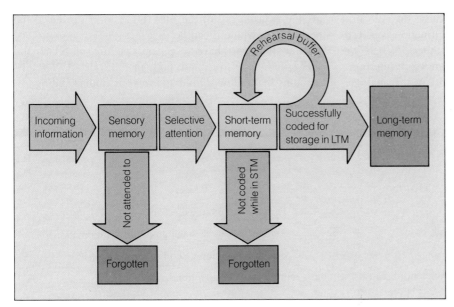

Fig. 10—2 *Memory is thought to involve at least three steps. Incoming information is first held for a second or two by sensory memory. Information selected by attention is then transferred to temporary storage in short-term memory. If new information is not rapidly encoded, or rehearsed, it is forgotten. If it is transferred to long-term memory, it becomes relatively permanent, although retrieving it may be a problem. The preceding is a useful model of memory; it may not be literally true of what happens in the brain.*

bering a shopping list, and the like all rely on STM (Atkinson & Shiffrin, 1971).

As you may have noticed when dialing a telephone, STM is very sensitive to *interruption* or *interference* (Adams, 1967). You've probably had the following experience with STM. You look up a number and walk to the phone, repeating it to yourself. You dial the number and get a busy signal. Returning a few minutes later, you find that you must look up the number again. This time as you are about to dial, someone asks you a question. You answer, turn to the phone, and find that you have forgotten the number.

Question: If short-term memory is brief, easily interrupted, and limited in "size," how do we remember for greater lengths of time?

Long-Term Memory   Information that is important or *meaningful* is transferred to the third memory system, called long-term memory. In contrast to STM, **long-term memory (LTM)** acts as a permanent storehouse for information. LTM contains everything you know about the world—from aardvark to zucchini, math to Monopoly, facts to fantasy. And yet, there appears to be no danger of running out of room in LTM. LTM has a nearly limitless storage capacity (Klatzky, 1980).

Question: Are long-term memories also encoded as sounds?

No. Information in LTM is stored on the basis of *meaning* and importance, not by sound. If you make an error in recall from LTM, it will probably be related to meaning.

For example, if you are trying to recall the word BARN from a memorized list, you are more likely to mistakenly say SHED or FARM than BORN.

When new information enters STM, it is related to knowledge stored in LTM. This gives the new information meaning and makes it easier to store it in LTM. As an example, try to memorize this story:

> With hocked gems financing him, our hero bravely defied all scornful laughter. "Your eyes deceive," he had said, "An egg, not a table, correctly typifies this unexplored planet." Now three sturdy sisters sought proof. Forging along, days became weeks as many doubters spread fearful rumors about the edge. At last from nowhere welcome winged creatures appeared, signifying momentous success. (Adapted from Dooling & Lachman, 1971.)

This story emphasizes the impact of meaning on forming lasting memories. People given the title of the story were able to remember it far better than those not given a title. See if the title helps you as much as it did them. The title is "Columbus Discovers America."

Dual Memory   Most of our daily memory chores are handled by STM and LTM. To summarize their connection, picture short-term memory as a small desk at the front of an immense warehouse full of filing cabinets (LTM). As information is brought into the warehouse, it is first placed on the desk. Since the desk is small, it must be quickly cleared off to make room for new information.

Some items are simply tossed away because they are unimportant. Meaningful or important information is placed in the permanent files (long-term memory). When we want to use knowledge from LTM to answer a question, the information is returned to STM. Or, in the analogy, a copy is taken out of the files (LTM) and moved to the desk (STM) where it can be used.

Now that you have a general picture of STM and LTM, it is time to explore both in more detail. The discussions that follow should add to your understanding.

Learning Check

Match:

A. Sensory memory   **B.** STM   **C.** LTM

1. _____ Working memory

2. _____ Holds information for a few seconds or less

3. _____ Stores an icon or echo

4. _____ Permanent, unlimited capacity

5. _____ Temporarily holds small amounts of information

6. _____ Selective attention determines its contents

7. STM is improved by interruption or interference because attention is more focused at such times.   T or F?

Answers: 1. B   2. A   3. A   4. C   5. B   6. B   7. F

Short-Term Memory— Do You Know the Magic Number?

Question: How much information can be held in short-term memory?

For an answer read the following numbers once. Then close the book and write as many as you can in the correct order.

| 8 | 5 | 1 | 7 | 4 | 9 | 3 |

This is called a **digit-span test.** If you were able to correctly repeat this series of 7 digits, you have an average short-term memory. Now try to memorize the following list of digits, reading them only once.

| 7 | 1 | 8 | 3 | 5 | 4 | 2 | 9 | 1 | 6 | 3 |

This series was probably beyond your short-term memory capacity. Psychologist George Miller has shown that short-term memory is limited to what he calls the magic number **seven** (plus or minus two) **bits** of information (Miller, 1956). It is as if short-term memory has 7 "slots" or "bins" into which separate items can be placed.

When all of the "slots" in STM are filled, there is no room for new information (Klatzky, 1980). Picture how this works at a party: Let's say your hostess begins introducing everyone who is there, "Ted, Barbara, Donna, Roseanna, Wayne, Shawn, Linda. . . ." "Stop," you think to yourself. But the hostess continues, "Eddie, Jay, Gordon, Frank, Marietta, Dan, Patty, Glen, Ricky." The hostess leaves, satisfied that you have met everyone. And you spend the evening talking with Ted, Barbara, and Ricky, the only people whose names you remember!

Recoding   Before we continue, try your short-term memory again, this time on letters. Read the following letters once, then close the book and try to write them in the proper order.

| TVF | BIJF | KY | MCA |

Notice that there are 12 letters, or "bits" of information. This should be beyond the 7-item limit of STM. However, since the letters are presented as 4 groups, or **chunks** of information, many students are able to memorize them.

Question: How does chunking help?

Chunking **recodes** information into larger units. Most often it does so by taking advantage of units already in LTM. For example, in the letter list above, you may have noticed that KY is the abbreviation for Kentucky. If so, the 2 bits "K" and "Y" become one chunk. In a memory experiment involving the list you have just memorized, subjects remembered best when the letters were read as: TV . . . FBI . . . JFK . . . YMCA (Bower & Springston, 1970). If you recoded the letters this way, you undoubtedly remembered the entire list.

Chunking suggests that STM holds about 7 of whatever units we are using, be they numbers, letters, words, phrases, or familiar sentences (Klatzky, 1980). Picture STM as a small desk again. Through chunking we combine several individual items into one "stack" of information. This allows us to place 7 stacks on the desk where before there was only room for 7 separate items.

Question: How long do short-term memories last?

Rehearsal   Short-term memories appear to weaken and disappear very rapidly. However, a short-term memory can be prolonged quite easily by silently repeating it until it is needed. Remembering a telephone number you intend to use only once is often done this way.

Keeping a short-term memory alive by silently repeating it is called **rehearsal**. The longer a short-term memory is rehearsed, the greater its chances of being stored in LTM. What if rehearsal is prevented, so a memory cannot be recycled or moved to LTM? Without rehearsal STM is incredibly short.

In one experiment subjects heard meaningless syllables like XAR followed by a number like 67. As soon as subjects heard the number, they began counting backwards by threes (to prevent them from repeating the syllable). After only 18 seconds of delay, memory scores fell to zero (Peterson & Peterson, 1959).

After *18 seconds* without rehearsal, the short-term memories were gone forever! Keep this in mind when you get only one chance to hear information you want to remember. For example, if you are introduced to someone, and his or her name slips out of STM, there is no way to retrieve it. To escape this awkward situation, you might try saying something like, "I'm curious, how do you spell your name?" But unfortunately, the response is often an icy reply like, "B-O-B S-M-I-T-H, it's really not too difficult." To avoid embarrassment, pay careful attention to the name, repeat it to yourself several times, and try to use it in the next sentence or two—before you lose it.

Long-Term Memory— Where the Past Lives

An electrode was placed at location number 11 on the patient's brain. She immediately said, "Yes, sir, I think I heard a mother calling her little boy somewhere. It seemed to be something happening years ago. . . . It was some-body in the neighborhood where I live." A short time later the electrode was applied to the same spot. Again the patient said, "Yes, I hear the same familiar sounds, it seems to be a woman calling, the same lady" (Penfield, 1958). These statements were made by a woman undergoing brain surgery for epilepsy. Only local anesthetics were used (there are no pain receptors in the brain), so the patient was awake as her brain was electrically stimulated (Fig. 10–3). When activated, some brain areas seemed to produce vivid memories of long-forgotten events.

Question: Does this mean that every experience a person has ever had is recorded in memory?

Permanence   Results like those described led neurosurgeon Wilder Penfield to claim that the brain records the past like a "continuous strip of movie film, complete with sound track" (Penfield, 1957). But as you now know, this is an exaggeration. Many events never get past short-term memory. More importantly, there is reason to doubt Penfield's conclusion. In only about 3 percent of cases does brain stimulation produce memorylike experiences. Most reports resemble dreams more than memories, and many

Fig. 10–3   *Exposed cerebral cortex of a patient undergoing brain surgery. Numbers represent points that reportedly produced "memories" when electrically stimulated. A critical evaluation of such reports suggests that they are more like dreams than memories. This fact raises questions about claims that long-term memories are permanent. (From Wilder Penfield,* The Excitable Cortex in Conscious Man, *1958. Courtesy of the author and Charles C Thomas, Publisher, Springfield, Illinois.)*

Highlight 10–1
Hypnosis, Imagination, and Memory

In 1976 near Chowchilla, California, 26 children were abducted from a school bus and held captive for a ransom. Under hypnosis the bus driver recalled the license plate number of the kidnappers' van. This memory helped break the case and led to the children's rescue. Such successes seem to imply that hypnosis can improve memory. But does it? Read on and judge for yourself.

Recent research has shown that a hypnotized person is more likely than normal to use imagination to fill in gaps in memory. Also, when hypnotized subjects are given false information, they tend to weave it into their memories (Sheehan, Grigg, & McCann, 1984). It has been shown that "leading" questions asked during hypnosis can alter memories (Sanders & Simmons, 1983). And, even when a memory is completely false, the hypnotized person's confidence in it can be unshakable (Laurence & Perry, 1983). Most telling of all is the fact that hypnosis increases false memories more than it does true ones. Subjects in one experiment, for instance, were able to slightly improve their memory scores under hypnosis. But they did so at great cost: Eighty percent of their new memories were *incorrect* (Dywan & Bowers, 1983).

Overall, it can be concluded that hypnosis does not greatly improve memory (Kihlstrom, 1985). Even when hypnosis uncovers more information, there is no way to tell which memories are true and which are false. Clearly, hypnosis is not the magic bullet against forgetting that some police investigators hoped it would be.

Constructing Memories   There is another reason to doubt Penfield's claim. As new long-term memories are formed, older memories are often updated, changed, lost, or *revised* (Cofer, 1975). Consider this illustration: Loftus and Palmer (1974) showed subjects a filmed automobile accident. Afterward, some subjects were asked to estimate how fast the cars were going when they "smashed" into each other. For others the words "bumped," "contacted," or "hit" replaced "smashed." One week later subjects were asked, "Did you see any broken glass?" Those asked earlier about the cars that "smashed" into each other were more likely to say yes. (No broken glass was shown in the film.) The new information ("smashed") was included in subjects' memories and altered them.

Updating memories is called **constructive processing.** Recent research shows that gaps in memory, which are common, may be filled in by logic, guesses, or new information (Loftus, 1977, 1980). Indeed, it is possible to have "memories" for things that never happened (such as remembering broken glass at an accident when there was none). People in Elizabeth Loftus' experiments who had these **pseudo-memories** (false memories) were often quite upset to learn they had given false "testimony" (Loftus, 1980).

The updating of long-term memory is a common problem in police work. For example, a witness may select a photo of a suspect from police files or see a photo in the news. Later, the witness identifies the suspect in person (in a lineup or in court). Did the witness really remember the criminal? Or the more recently seen photograph? Even if the suspect is innocent, he or she may be "remembered" as the criminal. It is quite possible for a photo to update or *blend* with the original memory. Many tragic cases of mistaken identity have occurred in this way.

Question: Couldn't hypnosis be used to avoid such problems?

News stories often give the impression that it can. Is this true? For an answer see Highlight 10–1.

Organization   Long-term memory may record 1 quadrillion separate bits of information in a lifetime (Asimov, 1967). How is it possible, then, to quickly find specific memories? The answer is that each person's "memory index" is highly organized.

Question: Do you mean that information is arranged alphabetically, as in a dictionary?

Not a chance! If I ask you to name a black and white animal that lives on ice, is related to a chicken, and can-

are clearly fictional. Memory experts Elizabeth and Geoffrey Loftus have carefully examined Penfield's work and other research on "truth serums" and hypnosis. They conclude there is little evidence that long-term memories are absolutely permanent (Loftus & Loftus, 1980). It is probably most accurate to say that long-term memories are *relatively* permanent, or long lasting.

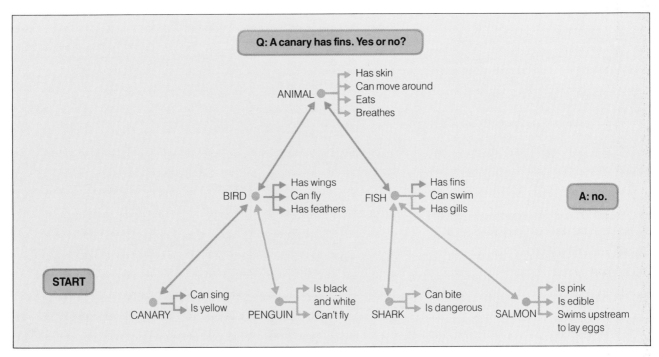

Fig. 10—4   *Hypothetical network of facts about animals shows what is meant by the structure of memory. Small networks of ideas such as this are probably organized into larger and larger units and higher levels of meaning. (Adapted from Collins & Quillian, 1969.)*

not fly, you don't have to go from aardvark to zebra to find the answer. Probably you will only think of black and white birds living in the Arctic. Which of these cannot fly? Voilà, the answer is penguin.

The arrangement of information in LTM may be based on rules, images, categories, symbols, similarity, formal meaning, or personal meaning (Atkinson & Shiffrin, 1971). In the last 10 years psychologists have begun to develop a picture of the **structure,** or arrangement, of memories. One example will serve to illustrate this research.

You are given the following two statements, to which you must answer yes or no: *A canary is an animal. A canary is a bird.* Which do you answer more quickly? Collins and Quillian (1969) found that *A canary is a bird* produced a faster yes than *A canary is an animal.* Why should this be so? Collins and Quillian believe a **network**

model of memory explains why. According to them, LTM is organized as a network of linked ideas (see Fig. 10—4). When ideas are "farther" apart, it takes a longer chain of associations to connect them. The more two items are separated, the longer it takes to answer. In other words *canary* is probably close to *bird* in your "mental dictionary." *Animal* and *canary* are farther apart. Remember, though, this has nothing to do with alphabetical order. We are talking about organization based on meaning.

Psychologists still have much to learn about the nature of long-term memory. For now, one thing stands out clearly: People who have good memories excel at organizing information and making it meaningful (Mandler, 1968). With this in mind, the Applications for this chapter tells how you can use organization and meaning to improve your memory.

Learning Check

1. The digit-span test is commonly used to measure LTM.   T or F?

2. There is evidence that STM lasts about 18 seconds, without rehearsal.   T or F?

3. Information can be held indefinitely in STM by   (circle):

chunking   recoding   networking   rehearsal

4. Constructive processing is often responsible for creating pseudo-memories.   T or F?

5. Electrical stimulation of the brain has shown conclusively that all memories are stored permanently, but not all memories can be retrieved.   T or F?

6. Memories elicited under hypnosis are more vivid, complete, and reliable than normal.   T or F?

7. _____ of related information are an example of the structure or organization found in LTM.

Answers: 1. F 2. T 3. rehearsal 4. T 5. T 6. F 7. Networks

Measuring Memory— The Answer Is on the Tip of My Tongue

Initially, it might seem that you either remember something or you don't. But a moment of thought should convince you that this is not always true. For instance, have you ever recognized someone you only saw once before and thought you had completely forgotten? If so you have used a form of partial memory called *recognition*. Partial memory is also demonstrated by the **tip-of-the-tongue phenomenon**. This is the experience of having an answer or a memory just out of reach—on the "tip of your tongue."

In one study of the tip-of-the-tongue effect, university students read the definitions of words such as *sextant*, *sampan*, and *ambergris*. Students who "drew a blank" and couldn't name a defined word were asked to give whatever other information they could about it. Often, they could accurately guess the first and last letter and even the number of syllables of the word they were seeking. They were also able to give words that sounded like or meant the same as the defined word (Brown & McNeill, 1966).

Because memory is not an all-or-nothing event, there are several ways of measuring it. Three commonly used **memory tasks** are *recall*, *recognition*, and *relearning*. Let's see how they differ.

Recall   What is the name of the first song on your favorite record album? Who won the World Series last year? Who wrote the *Gettysburg Address*? If you can answer these questions, you have demonstrated recall. To **recall** means to supply or reproduce facts or information. Tests of recall often require *verbatim* (word-for-word) memory. If you study a poem or a speech until you can recite it without looking, you will have recalled it. Recall is also used when you take an *essay* exam and provide facts and ideas without prompting. Essay tests tend to be difficult because they offer few cues to aid memory.

The order in which information is memorized has an interesting effect on recall. To experience it, try to memorize the following list, reading it only once:

BREAD, APPLES, SODA, HAM, COOKIES, RICE, LETTUCE, BEETS, MUSTARD, CHEESE, ORANGES, ICE CREAM, CRACKERS, FLOUR, EGGS.

If you are like most people, you will have the greatest difficulty recalling items from the middle of the list. Figure 10–5 shows the results of a similar test. Notice that the greatest number of errors is found for middle items. This is called the **serial position effect**. The last items on a list appear to be remembered best because they are still in STM. The first items are also remembered because they entered an "empty" short-term memory where they could be rehearsed (Tarpy & Mayer, 1978). The middle items are neither held in STM nor moved to LTM, so they are often lost.

Recognition   If you tried to write down all the facts you could remember from a class taken last year, you might conclude that you had learned very little. However, a more sensitive testing procedure based on **recognition** could be used. For instance, you could be given a *multiple-choice* test covering the facts and ideas from the course. Since multiple-choice tests only require you to recognize the correct answer, you would probably find evidence of considerable learning.

Recognition memory can be amazingly accurate for pictures, photographs, or other visual input. One investigator showed subjects 2560 photographs at a rate of one every 10 seconds. Subjects were then shown 280 pairs of photographs. One in each pair was from the first set of photos and the other was similar but new. Subjects could tell with 85 to 95 percent accuracy which photograph they had seen before (Haber, 1970). This finding may explain why people so often say, "I may forget a name, but I never forget a face."

Recognition is usually superior to recall. This is why police departments use photographs or a lineup to identify criminal suspects (Fig. 10–6). Witnesses who disagree in their recall of a suspect's height, weight, age, or eye color often agree completely when recognition is all that is required.

Question: Is recognition always superior?

It depends greatly on the kind of **distractors** used. These are false items included along with an item to be recognized. If the distractors are very similar to the correct item, memory may be poor. A reverse problem sometimes occurs when only one choice looks like it could be correct. This can produce a **false positive**, or false sense of recognition. For example, there have been instances in which witnesses described a criminal as black, tall, or young. Then a lineup was held in which a suspect was the only black among whites, the only tall suspect, or the only young person (Loftus, 1980). Under such circumstances a false identification is very likely.

Relearning   In a classic experiment on memory, a psychologist read a short passage in Greek to his son. This was done daily when the boy was between 15 months and 3 years of age. At age 8 the boy was asked if he remembered the Greek passage. He showed no evidence of recall. He was then given selections from the passage he had heard and selections from other Greek passages. Could he recognize the one he had heard as an infant? "It's all Greek to me!" he said, indicating no recognition (and drawing a frown from everyone in the room).

Had the psychologist stopped, he might have concluded that no memory of the Greek remained. However, the child was then asked to memorize the original quotation and others of equal difficulty. This time his earlier learning became evident. The boy memorized the passage he had heard in childhood 25 percent faster than the others (Burtt, 1941). As this experiment suggests, relearning is typically the most sensitive measure of memory.

When a person is tested by **relearning,** how do we know a memory still exists? As with the boy described, relearning is measured by a **savings score.** Let's say it takes you 1 hour to memorize all the names in a telephone book. (It's a small town.) Two years later you relearn them in 45 minutes. Because you "saved" 15 minutes, your savings score would be 25 percent (15 divided by 60 times 100). Savings of this type are a good reason for studying a wide range of subjects. It may seem that time spent learning

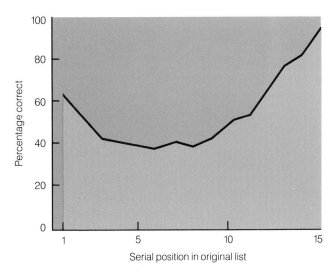

Fig. 10–5   *The serial position effect. Graph shows the percentage of subjects correctly recalling each item in a 15-item list. Recall is best for the first and last items. (Data from Craik, 1970.)*

algebra, history, or a foreign language is wasted because little is remembered a year or two later. But if you ever need such information, you will find you can relearn it in far less time.

Fig. 10–6   *Police lineups make use of the sensitivity of recognition memory.*

Ψ   Highlight 10–2
Can Exceptional Memory Be Learned?

In the beginning SF could remember 7 digits—a typical score for a college student. Could he improve with practice? For 20 months psychologist William Chase guided SF as he practiced memorizing ever longer lists of digits. Ultimately, SF was able to memorize around 80 digits, like this sample:

92842048050842268953990190252912807999706606574717310601080585269726026357332135

How did SF reach such lofty heights of memory? He worked by chunking digits into meaningful groups containing 3 or 4 digits each. SF's avid interest in long-distance running helped greatly. For instance, to him the first 3 digits from the preceding sample represent 9 minutes and 28 seconds, a good time for a 2-mile run. When running times wouldn't work, SF used other associations, such as ages or dates, to chunk digits (Ericsson & Chase, 1982).

Chase and psychologist Anders Ericsson believe SF's performance shows that exceptional memory—even like that displayed by Mr. S—is merely a learned extension of normal memory. As further evidence they note that SF's short-term memory did not improve during his months of practice. For example, he could still memorize only 7 consonants. SF's phenomenal memory for numbers grew as he figured out ways to encode digits so he could rapidly store them in LTM.

The idea that Mr. S had a normal memory is, perhaps, open to debate. Mr. S could memorize, with equal ease, strings of digits, meaningless consonants, mathematical formulas, and poems in foreign languages. His memory was so powerful that he had to devise ways to forget—such as writing information on a piece of paper and then burning it.

In sum there is evidence that exceptional memory can be learned. It's an open question, however, about whether some exceptional memories, like Mr. S's, are based on unusually vivid images or other rare abilities.

Redintegration   There is a fourth way in which memories may be revealed. Imagine finding a picture taken on your sixth birthday or tenth Christmas. As you look at the photo, one memory leads to another, which leads to another, and another. (Picture this as following some of the "branches" of your memory network.) Soon you have unleashed a flood of seemingly forgotten details. This process is called **redintegration** (ruh-DIN-tuh-GRAY-shun). Many people find that such memories are also touched off by distinctive odors out of the past, from a farm visited in childhood, Grandma's kitchen, the seashore, a doctor's office, the perfume or after-shave of a former lover, and so on. The key idea in redintegration is that one memory serves as a cue to trigger another. As a result an entire past experience may be reconstructed from one small recollection. Such memories usually involve personal experience rather than formal learning.

Eidetic Imagery— Picture This!

Question: What is a photographic memory? How is it different from the types of memory already described?

Eidetic (eye-DET-ik) **imagery,** known informally as photographic memory, occurs when a person has visual images clear enough to be "scanned" or retained for at least 30 seconds. Eidetic imagery occurs most often in childhood, with about 8 children out of 100 having eidetic images (Haber, 1969).

In one series of tests children were shown a picture from *Alice in Wonderland* (Fig. 10–7). To test your eidetic imagery, look at the picture and read the instructions there. Now, let's see how much you remember. Can you say (without looking again) which of Alice's apron strings is longer? Are the cat's front paws crossed? How many stripes are on the cat's tail? After the picture was removed from view, one 10-year-old boy was asked what he saw. He replied, "I see the tree, gray tree with three limbs. I see the cat with stripes around its tail." Asked to count the stripes, the boy replied, "There are about 16" (a correct count!). The boy then went on to describe the remainder of the picture in striking detail (Haber, 1969).

Don't be disappointed if you didn't do too well when you tried your eidetic skills. Most eidetic imagery disappears during adolescence and becomes quite rare by adulthood (Haber, 1974). Actually, this change may not be too much of a loss. The majority of eidetic memorizers have no better long-term memory than average.

Internal Images   Eidetic images are "projected" out in front of a person. Many psychologists believe that a second type of imagery is also used in memory. Can you remember how many doors there are in your house or apartment? To answer a question like this, many people form **internal images** of each room and count the doorways they "see."

Kosslyn, Ball, and Reisler (1978) found an interesting way to show that memories do exist as images. Subjects first memorized a sort of treasure map similar to the one shown in Figure 10–8a. They were then asked to picture a black dot moving from one object, such as the tree, to another, such as the hut at the top of the island. Did subjects really form an image to do this task? It seems they did. As shown in Figure 10–8b, the time it took to "move" the dot was directly related to actual distances on the map.

Some people may have internal images so vivid that they too have "photographic" memory. A notable example was reported by A. R. Luria (1968) in his book, *The Mind of a Mnemonist*. Luria studied a man (Mr. S) who had practically unlimited memory for visual images. Mr. S could remember almost everything that ever happened to him with incredible accuracy. When Luria tried to test Mr. S's memory by using longer and longer lists of words or numbers, he discovered that no matter how long the list Mr. S was able to reproduce it without error. Psychologists used to think that such exceptional memory was a biological gift and could not be learned. However, recent research has raised questions about this conclusion (see Highlight 10–2).

As fantastic as it might sound to a struggling student, Mr. S's memory caused great difficulty. He remembered

Fig. 10–7   *Test picture used to identify children with eidetic imagery. To test your eidetic imagery, look at the picture for 30 seconds. Then look at a blank surface and try to "project" the picture on it. If you have good eidetic imagery, you will be able to see the picture in detail. Return now to the text and try to answer the questions there. (Redrawn from an illustration in Lewis Carroll's* Alice in Wonderland.)

Fig. 10–8   *"Treasure map" similar to the one used by Kosslyn, Ball, and Reisler (1978) to study images in memory. (See text for explanation.)*

(a)

(b)

so much that he could not separate important facts from trivia. For instance, if he were tested on the contents of this chapter after reading it, he might remember not only every word, but all the images each word made him think of and all the sights, sounds, and feelings that occurred as he was reading. Finding the answer for a specific question, writing a logical essay or even understanding a single sentence therefore became very difficult for him.

Learning Check

Unless you have a memory like Mr. S's, it might be a good idea to see if you can answer these questions before reading on.

1. Four common techniques for measuring or demonstrating memory are: _____, _____, _____, and _____.

2. Multiple-choice tests primarily require _____ memory.

3. Essay tests require _____ of facts or ideas.

4. As a measure of memory, a "savings" score is associated with: (circle)

   recognition   eidetic images   relearning   reconstruction

5. Children with eidetic imagery typically have no better than average long-term memory.   T or F?

Answers: 1. recall, recognition, redintegration, relearning 2. recognition 3. recall 4. relearning 5. T

Why We, Uh, Let's See; Why, We, Uh . . . Forget!

Question: Why are some memories lost so quickly? For example, why is it hard to remember information a week or two after taking a test in class?

Generally speaking, most forgetting occurs immediately after memorization. In a famous set of experiments, **Herman Ebbinghaus** (1885) tested his own memory at various times after learning. Ebbinghaus wanted to be sure he would not be swayed by prior learning, so he memorized **nonsense syllables.** These are meaningless three-letter words such as GEX, CEF, or WOL. The importance of using meaningless words is shown by the fact that VEL, FAB, and DUZ are no longer used on memory tests. Subjects who recognize these words as detergent names find them very easy to remember.

By waiting various lengths of time before testing himself, Ebbinghaus constructed a **curve of forgetting** (see Fig. 10–9). Owing to the great care Ebbinghaus took in his work, these findings remain valid today. Notice that forgetting is rapid at first and is then followed by a slow decline. As a student you should see that forgetting is minimized when there is little delay between review and taking a test. However, don't misinterpret this as a reason for cramming. The error most students make is to cram *only.*

If you cram, you don't have to remember for very long, but you may not learn enough in the first place. If you use short, daily study sessions, and, in addition, review intensively before a test, you will get the benefit of good preparation and a minimum time lapse.

"I'll never forget old, old . . . oh, what's his name?" Forgetting is both frustrating and embarrassing. Why *do* we forget? The Ebbinghaus curve gives a general picture of forgetting, but it doesn't explain it. For explanations we must search further.

Encoding Failure

Whose head is on a United States penny? Which way is it facing? What is written on the top side of a penny? Can you accurately draw and label a penny? In a recent experiment Nickerson and Adams (1979) asked a large group of students to draw a penny. Few could. Well, then, could the students at least recognize a drawing of a real penny among fakes? (See Figure 10–10.) Again, few could.

The most obvious reason for forgetting is also the most commonly overlooked. In many cases we "forget" because a memory was never formed in the first place. Obviously, few of us ever encode the details of a penny. If you are bothered by frequent forgetting, it is wise to ask yourself, "Have I been storing the information in the first place?"

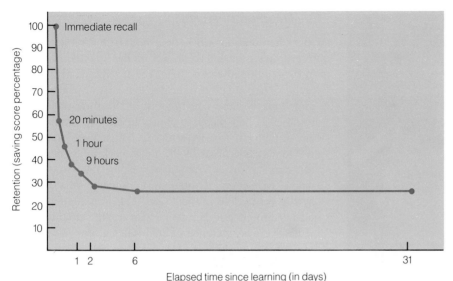

Fig. 10–9 *The curve of forgetting. This graph shows the amount remembered (measured by relearning) after varying lengths of time. Notice how rapidly forgetting occurs. Material learned was nonsense syllables. Meaningful information is not forgotten so quickly. (After Ebbinghaus, 1885.)*

Decay

One view of forgetting says that **memory traces** (changes in nerve cells or brain activity) fade, or **decay,** over time. Decay appears definitely to be a factor in the loss of sensory memories. Such fading also applies to short-term memory. Information stored in STM seems to initiate a brief flurry of activity in the brain that quickly dies out (Shiffrin & Cook, 1978). Short-term memory therefore operates like a "leaky bucket": New information constantly pours in, but it rapidly fades away and is replaced by still newer information (Miller, 1956).

Disuse   Is it possible that the decay of memory traces also explains long-term forgetting? That is, could long-

term memory traces fade from **disuse** and eventually become so weak they cannot be retrieved? As tempting as this possibility may seem, there are reasons to doubt it. One already mentioned is the recovery of seemingly forgotten memories through redintegration. Another is that disuse fails to explain why some unused memories fade, while others are carried for life. A third contradiction will be recognized by anyone who has spent time with the elderly. People growing older may become so forgetful that they can't remember what happened a week ago. Yet at the same time your Uncle Oscar's recent memories are fading, he may have vivid memories of trivial and long-forgotten events from the past. "Why I remember it as clearly

Fig. 10–10 *Some of the distractor items used in a study of recognition memory and encoding failure. Penny A is correct but was seldom recognized. Pennies G and J were popular wrong answers. (Adapted from Nickerson & Adams, 1979.)*

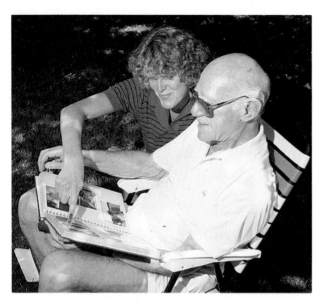

Fig. 10–11 *Because of the many cues they provide, photographs often bring back numerous memories.*

as if it were yesterday," he will say, forgetting that the story he is about to tell is one he told earlier the same day. In short, disuse alone does not adequately explain long-term forgetting.

Question: If decay and disuse don't fully explain forgetting, what does?

There are several additional possibilities. Let's briefly consider each.

Fig. 10–12 *The effect of mood on memory. Subjects best remembered a list of words when their mood during testing was the same as their mood when they learned the list. (Adapted from Bower, 1981.)*

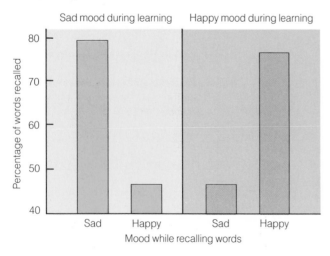

Cue-Dependent Forgetting

Often memories appear to be *available* but not accessible. An example is having an answer on the tip of your tongue. You know the answer is there, but it remains just "out of reach." This situation indicates that many memories are "forgotten" because **cues** present at the time of learning are absent when the time comes to retrieve information. For example, if you were asked, "What were you doing on Monday afternoon of the third week in September 2 years ago?" your reply might be, "Come on. How should I know?" However, if you were reminded, "That was the day the courthouse burned," or "That was the day Mary had her automobile accident," you might remember immediately. The presence of such cues almost always enhances memory (Fig. 10–11)

State-Dependent Learning   Nearly everyone has heard the story about the drunk who misplaced his wallet and had to get drunk again to find it. Although this tale is often told as a joke, it is not too farfetched. The *bodily state* that exists during learning can be a strong cue for later memory (Overton, 1985). For this reason information learned under the influence of a drug is best remembered when the drugged state occurs again—an effect known as **state-dependent learning.**

A similar effect applies to emotional states. For instance, Gordon Bower (1981) found that people who learned a list of words while in a happy mood recalled them better when they were again happy. People who learned a list while they felt sad remembered best when they were sad (see Fig. 10–12). The link between emotional cues and memory may explain why couples who quarrel often end up remembering—and rehashing—old arguments.

Interference

Further understanding of forgetting comes from an experiment in which college students learned lists of nonsense syllables. After studying, students in one group slept for 8 hours and were then tested for memory of the lists. A second group remained awake for 8 hours and went about business as usual. When members of the second group were tested, they remembered *less* than the group that slept (see Fig. 10–13). This difference is based on the fact that new learning can **interfere** with previous learning (Shiffrin, 1970). Such interference seems to apply to both short-term and long-term memories (Klatzky, 1980).

It is not completely clear if new memories alter existing memory traces or if they make it harder to "locate" (retrieve) earlier memories. In either case there is no doubt that interference is a major cause of forgetting. College students who memorized 20 lists of words (1 list each day) were only able to recall 15 percent of the last list. Students who learned only 1 list remembered 80 percent (Underwood, 1957) (see Fig. 10–14).

Inhibition The sleeping college students remembered more because **retroactive** (RET-ro-AK-tiv) **inhibition** was held to a minimum. Retroactive inhibition refers to the tendency for new learning to interfere with the retrieval of old learning. Avoiding new learning prevents retroactive inhibition from occurring. This fact doesn't exactly mean you should hide in your closet after you study for an exam. However, you should avoid studying other subjects until the exam. Sleeping after study can improve your memory, whereas reading, writing, or even watching TV may cause interference.

Retroactive inhibition is easily demonstrated in the laboratory by this arrangement:

Experimental group:	Learn A	Learn B	Test A
Control group:	Learn A	Rest	Test A

Imagine yourself as a member of the experimental group. In Task A you learn a list of telephone numbers. In Task B you learn a list of Social Security numbers. How do you do on a test of Task A (the telephone numbers)? If you do not remember as much as the control group that *only* learns Task A, retroactive inhibition has occurred. The second thing learned interfered with memory of the first thing learned; the interference went "backward," or was "retroactive" (see Fig. 10–15).

A second basic type of interference is **proactive** (pro-AK-tiv) **inhibition.** Proactive inhibition occurs when prior learning interferes with later learning. A test for proactive inhibition would take this form:

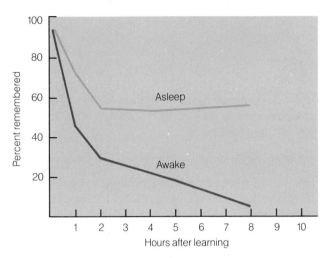

Fig. 10–13 *The amount of forgetting after sleep or waking activity. Notice that sleep causes less memory loss than waking. (After Jenkins & Dallenbach, 1924.)*

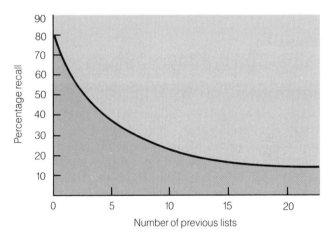

Fig. 10–14 *Effects of interference on memory. A graph of the approximate relationship between percentage recalled and number of different word lists memorized. (Adapted from Underwood, 1957.)*

Fig. 10–15 *Retroactive and proactive inhibition. The order of learning and testing shows whether interference is retroactive (backward) or proactive (forward).*

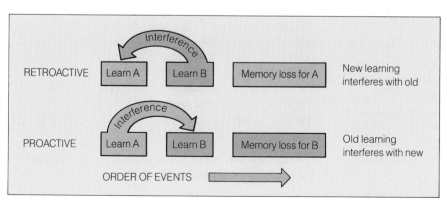

Experimental group:	Learn A	Learn B	Test B
Control group:	Rest	Learn B	Test B

If the experimental group remembers less than the control group on a test of Task B, then learning Task A interfered with memory of Task B.

Question: Then proactive interference goes "forward"?

Yes. For instance, if you cram for a psychology exam and then later the same night cram for a history exam, your memory for the second subject studied (history) will be less accurate than if you had studied only history. (Due to retroactive inhibition, your memory for psychology would probably also suffer.) The greater the similarity in the two subjects studied, the more interference takes place. The moral, of course, is don't procrastinate in preparing for exams.

Repression

Take a moment from reading and scan over the events of the last few years of your life. What kinds of things most easily come to mind? This is a question that interested psychologist Marigold Linton. Linton (1979) kept a careful record of everything that happened to her over a 6-year period and compared her memories to her record. Linton found that she tended to remember happy, positive events better than disappointments and irritations. A clinical psychologist would call this tendency **repression,** or motivated forgetting.

Through repression, painful, threatening, or embarrassing memories are held out of consciousness by forces within one's personality. The forgetting of past failures, upsetting childhood events, the names of persons you dislike, or appointments you don't want to keep may indicate repression.

Question: If I try to forget a test I have failed, am I repressing it?

No. Repression can be distinguished from **suppression,** an active attempt to put something out of mind. By not thinking about the test, you have merely suppressed a memory. If you choose to, you can remember the test. Clinicians consider true repression an *unconscious* event. When a memory is repressed, we are unaware that forgetting has even occurred. (See Chapter 14 for more information on repression.)

An interesting, unanswered question is why some traumatic events are vividly remembered, whereas others are repressed. Psychologists Roger Brown and James Kulik (1977) use the term **flashbulb memories** to describe lasting images that are frozen in memory at times of personal tragedy, accident, or loss. One reason such memories can be so vivid is that the hormones adrenaline and ACTH are secreted at times of stress. Both substances have been shown to enhance memory formation, possibly by altering brain chemistry (McGaugh, 1983).

Memory Formation— Some "Shocking" Findings

One possibility overlooked in our discussion of forgetting is that memories may be lost as they are being formed. For example, a head injury may cause a "gap" in memories preceding the accident. **Retrograde amnesia,** as it is called, can be understood by assuming that transferring memories from short-term storage to long-term memory takes a certain amount of time. The forming of a long-term memory is called **consolidation** (John, 1967). You can think of consolidation as being somewhat like writing your name in wet concrete. Once the concrete is set, the information (your name) is fairly lasting, but while it is setting it can be wiped out (amnesia) or scribbled over (interference).

Consider a classic experiment on consolidation, in which a rat is placed on a small platform. The rat steps down to the floor and receives a painful electric shock. After one shock, the rat can be returned to the platform repeatedly, but it will not step down. Obviously, the rat remembers the shock. Would it remember if consolidation were disrupted?

Interestingly, one way to prevent consolidation is to give a different kind of shock called **electroconvulsive shock (ECS)** (Jarvik, 1964). ECS is an electric shock to the brain. It does not harm the animal, but it does destroy any memory that is being formed. If each painful shock (the one the animal remembers) is followed by ECS (which wipes out memories during consolidation), the rat will step down over and over. Each time, ECS will erase the memory of the painful shock. (ECS has been employed as a psychiatric treatment for severe depression in humans. Used in this way, electroshock therapy also causes memory loss. See Chapter 21 for details.)

Question: What would happen if ECS were given several hours after the learning?

If enough time is allowed to pass between learning and ECS, the memory is unaffected, apparently because consolidation is already complete. This is why people with head injuries usually only lose memories from immediately before the accident, while older memories remain intact (Baddeley, 1976). Likewise, you would forget more if you studied, stayed awake 8 hours, and then slept 8 hours than you would if you studied, slept 8 hours, and were then awake for 8 hours. Both cases involve the passage of 16 hours. However, in the second instance forgetting is reduced, because more consolidation takes place before interference begins.

Question: Can memory be improved with drugs?

Drugs and Consolidation   The possibility of chemically improving memory has long intrigued psychologists. We have known for some time that various stimulating drugs speed up consolidation if given just after learning. Note, however, that this only reduces the time during which interference can take place; it does not magically improve memory. Also, the drugs involved (metrazol, strychnine, nicotine, caffeine, and amphetamine) must be given in carefully controlled dosages. If the dosage is too high by even a small amount, memory will be *disrupted* (McGaugh, 1970).

Question: What effect does alcohol have on memory?

Memory losses are common when a person overindulges in alcohol. This may be due, in part, to state-dependent learning. At higher levels of intoxication, alcohol seems to directly impair encoding and consolidation of memories. A person suffering an alcohol blackout may lose anywhere from a few minutes to several hours of memory. Research makes it clear that studying while drunk is an excellent way to *lower* test scores (Birnbaum et al., 1978). In general alcohol blackouts are most likely when a person (1) gulps a large amount of alcohol very quickly, (2) is very tired, or (3) has also taken a tranquilizer or sedative (Loftus, 1980).

Question: What part of the brain causes consolidation?

From STM to LTM   Actually, many areas of the brain are responsible for memory, but the **hippocampus** is of particular importance. This structure, buried deep within the brain, seems to act as a sort of "switching station" between short-term and long-term memory.

Humans who have had the hippocampus damaged show a striking inability to store new memories. HM, a patient described by Brenda Milner, is typical. Two years after an operation that affected the hippocampus, HM continued to give his age as 27 (it was actually 29) and reported that it seemed that the operation had just taken place (Milner, 1965). His memory of events before the operation remained clear, but HM found forming new long-term memories almost impossible. When his parents moved to a new house a few blocks away on the same street, HM could not remember the new address, and he was observed to read the same magazines over and over again without finding their contents familiar. If you were to meet HM, he would seem fairly normal since he still has short-term memory. But if you were to leave the room and return 15 minutes later, HM would act as if he had never seen you before (Milner, 1965). Years ago HM's favorite uncle died, but HM suffers the same grief anew each time he is told of the death. Lacking the ability to form lasting memories, HM lives eternally in the present.

The Brain and Memory— Will We Eat College Professors?

Somewhere within the 3-pound mass of the human brain lies all we know: zip codes, faces of loved ones, history, favorite melodies, the taste of an apple, and much, much more. Where is this information? Karl Lashley, a pioneering brain researcher set out in the 1920s to find an **engram,** or memory trace. Lashley taught animals to run mazes and then removed parts of their brains to see how memory of the maze changed. After 30 years he had to concede defeat: Engrams are not located in any one area of the brain. It mattered little which part of the brain's cortex he removed. Only the *amount* removed correlated to memory loss.

By the 1960s researchers began to suspect that memory might be stored in "macro-molecules" such as **RNA** (ribonucleic acid). RNA is similar to DNA, the master molecule of heredity, in its ability to code information. An interesting early test of the RNA hypothesis involved teaching a simple response to planaria (plan-NAIR-ee-ah: flatworms). The "trained" planaria were ground up and fed to "untrained" planaria. When this experiment was first performed, the "cannibal worms" supposedly showed evidence of learning (McConnell, 1962). For a time this led to jokes about not wasting the brains of old college professors (you can guess the rest). However, other researchers were unable to repeat the experiment, and enthusiasm for RNA as the basis for memory waned.

Question: Then how are memories recorded in the brain?

Fig. 10–16 *An Aplysia. The relatively simple nervous system of this sea animal allows scientists to study memory as it occurs in single nerve cells.*

Scientists studying simple animals are beginning to identify the exact mechanisms by which individual nerve cells record information. There is now extensive evidence that learning alters the electrical activity, structure, and chemistry of the brain (McGaugh, 1983). For example, Eric Kandel and his colleagues have studied learning in the marine snail *Aplysia*. Kandel has found that learning in *Aplysia* occurs when certain nerve cells in a circuit alter the amount of transmitter chemicals they release (Kandel, 1976) (see Fig. 10–16). Such changes essentially determine which circuits get strengthened and which become weaker. Other researchers have shown that an increase in receptor cites for transmitter chemicals occurs during learning (Lynch & Baudry, 1984).

On the basis of such breakthroughs, scientists are now studying a bewildering array of chemicals and brain processes that affect memory (McGaugh, 1983). Should this research succeed, it may be possible to help the millions of persons who suffer from memory impairment. Will researchers ever produce a "memory pill" for those with normal memory? Some neuroscientists are confident that memory can be and will be artificially enhanced. At present, however, the possibility of something like a "physics pill" or a "math pill" seems especially remote.

Learning Check

1. According to the Ebbinghaus curve of forgetting, we forget slowly at first and then a rapid decline occurs.   T or F?

2. Which explanation seems to account for loss of short-term memories?   (circle)

    decay   disuse   repression   interference

3. When memories are available but not accessible, forgetting may be cue dependent.   T or F?

4. When learning one thing makes it more difficult to recall another, forgetting may be caused

    by _____.

5. You are asked to memorize long lists of telephone numbers. You learn a new list each day for 10 days. When tested on list 3, you remember less than a person who only learned the first three lists. Your larger memory loss is probably due to: (circle)

    disuse   retroactive inhibition   regression   proactive inhibition

6. Repression is thought of as a type of motivated forgetting.   T or F?

7. Retrograde amnesia results when consolidation is speeded up.   T or F?

8. Researchers have clearly established that engrams are stored in RNA molecules.   T or F?

Answers: 1. F   2. both decay and interference   3. T   4. interference or inhibition   5. retroactive inhibition   6. T   7. F   8. F

How to Improve Your Memory—Keys to the Memory Bank

While you're waiting around for the development of a memory pill, let's focus on some ways of improving your memory right now.

Knowledge of Results   Learning proceeds most effectively when feedback or knowledge of results allows you to check to see if you are learning. Feedback also helps you identify material that needs extra practice, and it can be rewarding to know that you have remembered or answered correctly. A prime means of providing feedback for yourself when studying is *recitation.*

Recitation   Recitation means repeating to yourself what you have learned. If you are going to remember something, eventually you will have to retrieve it. Recitation forces you to practice retrieving information as you are learning. When you are reading a text, you should stop frequently and try to remember what you have just read by summarizing it aloud. In one experiment the best memory score of all was earned by a group of students who spent 80 percent of their time reciting and only 20 percent reading (Gates, 1958). Maybe students who talk to themselves aren't crazy after all.

Overlearning   Numerous studies have shown that memory is greatly improved when study is continued beyond bare mastery. In other words after you have learned material well enough to remember it once without error, you should continue to study the material. Overlearning is your best insurance against going blank on a test because of nervousness or anxiety.

Selection   The Dutch scholar Erasmus said that a good memory should be like a fisherman's net: It should keep all the big fish and let the little ones escape. If you boil down the paragraphs in most textbooks to one or two important terms or ideas, you will find your memorization chores more manageable and you will probably remember more than you would if you tried to retain everything. Practice careful and selective marking in your texts and use marginal notes to further summarize ideas. Most students mark their texts too much instead of too little. If everything is underlined, you haven't been selective.

Spaced Practice   Spaced practice generally is superior to massed practice. By improving concentration, and consolidation, three 20-minute study sessions can produce more learning than 1 hour of continuous study. Perhaps the best way to make use of this principle is to *schedule* your time. If most students were to keep a totally honest record of their weekly activities, they would probably find that very few hours were spent really studying. To make an effective schedule, designate times during the week before, after, and between classes when you will study particular subjects. Then treat these times just as if they were classes you had to attend.

Organize   Assume that you must memorize the following list of words: *north, man, red, spring, woman, east, autumn, yellow, summer, boy, blue, west, winter, girl, green, south.* This rather difficult list could be reorganized into *chunks* as follows: *north-east-south-west, spring-summer-autumn-winter, red-yellow-green-blue, man-woman-boy-girl.* This simple reordering made the second list much easier to learn when college students were tested on both lists (Deese & Hulse, 1967). In another experiment students who made up stories using long lists of words to be memorized learned the lists better than those who didn't (Bower & Clark, 1969). Organizing class notes and outlining chapters can be helpful when studying. It may even be helpful to outline your outlines, so that the overall organization of ideas becomes clearer and simpler.

Whole versus Part Learning   If you had to memorize a speech, would it be better to try to learn it from beginning to end or in smaller parts like paragraphs? Generally it is better to practice whole packages of information rather than smaller parts. This is especially true for fairly short, organized information. An exception is that learning parts may be better for extremely long, complicated information. Try to study the largest *meaningful* amount of information possible at one time.

For very long or complex material, try the *progressive part method.* In this approach you break a learning task into short sections. At first, you study part A until it is mastered. Next, you study parts A and B; then A, B, and C; and so forth. This is a good way to learn the lines of a play, a long piece of music, or a poem. After the material is learned, you should also practice it by starting at points other than A (at C, D, or B, for example). This helps prevent getting "lost," or going blank in the middle of a performance.

Serial Position   Whenever you must learn something in *order,* be aware of the *serial position effect.* As you will recall, this is the tendency to make the most errors in remembering the middle of a list. If you are introduced to a long line of people, the names you are likely to forget will be those in the middle, so you should make an extra effort to attend to them. The middle of a list, poem, or speech should also be given special attention and extra practice.

Sleep   Remember that sleeping after study produces the least interference. Since you obviously can't sleep after every study session, or can't study everything just before you sleep, your study schedule (see the "Spaced Practice" section) should include ample breaks between subjects. Using your breaks and free time in a schedule is as important as living up to your study periods.

Review   If you have spaced your practice and have overlearned, review will be like icing on your study cake. Re-

viewing shortly before an exam cuts down the time during which you must remember details that may be important for the test but not otherwise meaningful to you. When reviewing, hold the amount of new information you try to memorize to a minimum. It may be realistic to take what you have actually learned and add a little more to it at the last minute by cramming, but remember that more than a little new learning will confuse you and interfere with what you already know.

If you consistently use the principles reviewed here, you should get grades at least one step higher without increasing your study time, or you should get the same grades after spending less time. Give this an honest try—the results are almost guaranteed. Besides, if you haven't adopted the SQ3R and LISAN techniques described in the first chapter, it might be time to give them a try.

Learning Check

1. To improve memory, it is reasonable to spend as much or more time reciting as reading.   T or F?
2. Organizing information while studying has little effect on memory because memory is already highly organized.   T or F?
3. The progressive part method of study is best suited for long and complex learning tasks.   T or F?
4. Sleeping immediately after studying is highly disruptive to the consolidation of memories.   T or F?

Answers: 1. T 2. F 3. T 4. F

Applications

Mnemonics—Memory Magic

Question: Some stage performers use memory as part of their acts. Do they have eidetic imagery?

Various "memory experts" entertain by giving demonstrations in which they memorize the names of everyone at a banquet, the order of all the cards in a deck, long lists of disconnected words, or other seemingly impossible amounts of information. Such feats may seem like magic, but if they are, you can have a magic memory too. These tricks are performed through the use of **mnemonics** (nee-MON-iks). A mnemonic is any kind of memory system or aid.

Some mnemonic systems have become so common

that almost everyone knows them. If you are trying to remember how many days there are in a month, you may find the answer by reciting, "Thirty days hath September. . . ." Physics teachers often help their students remember the colors of the spectrum by giving them the mnemonic "Roy G. Biv": *red, orange, yellow, green, blue, indigo, violet.* The budding sailor who has trouble telling port from starboard may remember that port and left both have four letters or may remind himself, "I *left* port." And what beginning musician hasn't remembered the notes represented by the lines and spaces of the musical staff by learning "face" and "*every good boy does fine.*"

Applications: Mnemonics—Memory Magic

Mnemonic techniques are ways of avoiding *rote learning* (learning by simple repetition). The superiority of mnemonic learning as opposed to rote learning has been demonstrated many times. For example, Bower (1973) asked college students to study five different lists of 20 unrelated words. At the end of a short study session, subjects were asked to recall all 100 items. Subjects using mnemonics remembered an average of 72 items, whereas a control group using simple, or rote, learning remembered an average of 28.

Stage performers rarely have a naturally superior memory. Instead, they make extensive use of memory systems to perform their feats. Few of these systems are of practical value to the student, but the principles underlying mnemonics are. By practicing mnemonics you should be able to greatly improve your memory with little effort.

The basic principles of mnemonics are:

1. Use mental pictures. There are at least two kinds of memory, *visual* and *verbal*. Visual pictures or images are generally easier to remember than words. Turning information into mental pictures is therefore very helpful (Paivio, 1969).

2. Make things meaningful. Transfer of information from short-term to long-term memory is aided by making the information meaningful. If you encounter technical terms that have little or no immediate meaning for you, *give* them meaning, even if you have to stretch the term to do so. (This point is clarified by the examples following this list.)

3. Make information familiar. Connect it to what you already know. Another way to get information into long-term memory is to connect it to information already stored there. If some facts or ideas in a chapter seem to stay in your memory easily, associate other more difficult facts with them.

4. Form bizarre, unusual, or exaggerated mental associations. When associating two ideas, terms, or mental images, you will find that the more outrageous and exaggerated the association, the more likely you are to remember it later.

A sampling of typical applications of mnemonics should make these four points clear to you.

Example 1   Let's say you have 30 new vocabulary words to memorize in Spanish. You can proceed by rote memorization (repeat them over and over until you begin to get them) or you can learn them with little effort by using the **key word method** (Pressley et al., 1980). To remember that the word *pajaro* (pronounced PA-ha-ro) means bird, you can link it to a "key" word in English: *Pajaro* (to me) sounds like "parked car-o." Therefore, to remember that *pajaro* means bird, I will visualize a parked car jam packed full of birds. I will try to make this image as vivid and exaggerated as possible, with birds flapping and chirping and feathers flying everywhere. Similarly, for the word *carta* (which means letter), I will imagine a shopping *cart* filled with postal letters. If you link similar key words and images for the rest of the list, you may not remember them all, but you will get most without any further practice. As a matter of fact, if you have formed the *pajaro* and *carta* images just now, it is going to be almost impossible for you to ever see these words again without remembering what they mean.

Question: What if I think pajaro means "parked car" when I take my Spanish test?

This is why you should form one or two extra images so that the important feature (bird, in this case) is repeated.

Example 2   Let's say you have to learn the names of all the bones and muscles in the human body for biology. You are trying to remember that the jawbone is the *mandible*. This one is easy because you can associate it with a *man nibbling,* or maybe you can picture a *man dribbling* a basketball with his jaw (make this image as ridiculous as possible). If the muscle name *latissimus dorsi* gives you trouble, familiarize it by turning it into *"the ladder misses the door, sigh."* Then picture a ladder glued to your back where the muscle is found. Picture the ladder leading up to a small door at your shoulder. Picture the ladder missing the door. Picture the ladder sighing like an animated character in a cartoon.

Question: This seems like more to remember, not less; and it seems like it would cause you to misspell things.

Mnemonics are not a complete substitute for normal memory; they are an aid to normal memory. Mnemonics are not likely to be helpful unless you make extensive use of *images.* Your mental pictures will come back to you easily. As for misspellings, mnemonics can be thought of as a built-in hint in your memory. Often, when taking a test, you will find that the slightest hint is all you need in order to remember correctly. A mnemonic image is like having someone leaning over your shoulder who says, "Psst, the name of that muscle sounds like 'ladder misses the door, sigh.'" If misspelling continues to be a problem, try to create memory aids for spelling, too.

Applications: Mnemonics—Memory Magic

Here are two more examples to help you appreciate the flexibility of a mnemonic approach to studying.

Example 3   Your art history teacher expects you to be able to name the artist when you are shown slides as part of an exam. Many of the slides you have only seen once before in class. How will you remember them? As the slides are shown in class, make each artist's name into an object or image. Then picture the object *in* paintings done by the artist. For example, you can picture van Gogh as a *van* (automobile) *going* through the middle of each van Gogh painting. Picture the van running over things and knocking them down. Or, if you remember that van Gogh cut off his ear, picture a giant bloody ear in each of his paintings.

Example 4   If you have trouble remembering history, try to avoid thinking of it as something from the dim past. Picture each historical personality as a person you know right now (a friend, teacher, parent, and so on). Then picture these people doing whatever the historical figures did. Also try visualizing battles or other events as if they were happening in your town or make parks and schools in your town into foreign countries. Use your imagination.

Question: How can mnemonics be used to remember things in order?

Here are three techniques that are helpful.

1. Form a chain. To remember lists of ideas, objects, or words in order, try forming an exaggerated association (mental image) connecting the first item to the second, then the second to the third, and so on. To remember the following short list in order: *elephant, doorknob, string, watch, rifle, oranges,* picture a full-sized *elephant* balanced on a *doorknob* playing with a *string* tied to him. Picture a *watch* tied to the string, and a *rifle* shooting oranges at the watch. This technique can be used quite successfully for lists of 20 or more items. Try it next time you go shopping and leave your list at home.

2. Take a mental walk. Mnemonics were well known to ancient Greek orators, who would take a mental walk along a familiar path to associate ideas they wanted to cover in a speech to the images of statues found along the walk. You can do the same thing by "placing" objects or ideas along the way as you mentally take a familiar walk.

3. Use a system. Many times the first letter or syllables of words or ideas can be formed into another word that will serve as a reminder of order. "Roy G. Biv," just cited, is an example. As an alternative, learn the following: 1 is a bun, 2 is a shoe, 3 is a tree, 4 is a door, 5 is a hive, 6 is sticks, 7 is heaven, 8 is a gate, 9 is a line, 10 is a hen. To remember in order, form an image associating bun with the first item on your list. For example, if the first item is "frog," picture a "frog-burger" on a bun to remember it. Then, associate shoe with the second item, and so on.

If you have never used mnemonics, you may still be skeptical, but give this approach a fair trial. Most people find they can greatly extend their memory through the use of mnemonics. But remember, mnemonics only supplement the memory tips given earlier; they do not replace them. Like most things worthwhile, remembering takes effort.

Learning Check

1. Memory systems and aids are referred to as _____.
2. Which of the following is least likely to improve memory?
   a. using exaggerated mental images
   b. forming a chain of associations
   c. turning visual information into verbal information
   d. associating new information with information that is already known or familiar
3. Picturing your knee moaning as it tries to remember something could serve as a mnemonic for the term mnemonic.   T or F?
4. Bower's 1973 study showed that, in general, mnemonics only improve memory for related words or ideas.   T or F?

Answers: 1. mnemonics 2. c 3. T 4. F

Chapter Summary

■ *Memory* is an active, computerlike system that *encodes*, *stores*, and *retrieves* information.

■ Humans appear to have three interrelated memory systems: *sensory memory*, *short-term memory* (also called *working memory*), and *long-term memory*.

■ Sensory memory is *exact* but very brief. Through *selective attention* some information is transferred to STM.

■ STM has a capacity of about *seven bits* of information, but this can be extended by *chunking* or *recoding*. Short-term memories are brief and very sensitive to *interruption* or *interference*; however, they can be prolonged by *rehearsal*.

■ LTM functions as a general storehouse of information, especially *meaningful* information. Long-term memories are *relatively* permanent, or lasting. LTM seems to have an almost unlimited storage capacity.

■ LTM is subject to *constructive processing*, or ongoing revision and updating. LTM is highly *organized* to allow retrieval of needed information. The pattern, or *structure*, of memory *networks* is the subject of current memory research.

■ *Hypnosis* may improve memory to a small degree, but it also increases the number of *false memories* reported.

■ The *tip-of-the-tongue phenomenon* shows memory is not an all-or-nothing event. So, memories may be revealed by *recall*, *recognition*, *relearning*, or *redintegration*.

■ In recall, memory proceeds *without explicit cues*, as in an *essay exam*. Recall of listed information often reveals a *serial position effect* (middle items on the list are most subject to errors). A common test of recognition is the *multiple-choice* question, which requires selection of a correct answer. In relearning, "forgotten" material is learned again and memory is indicated by a *savings score*. In redintegration, memories are *reconstructed* as each memory serves as a cue for the next memory.

■ *Eidetic imagery* (photographic memory) occurs when a person is able to project an image onto a blank surface. Such images allow brief, nearly complete recall in some children. Eidetic imagery is rarely found in adults. However, many adults have *internal memory images*, which can be very vivid.

■ *Exceptional* memory can be learned by finding ways to directly store information in LTM. Learning has no effect on the limits of STM. Some people may have exceptional memories that exceed what can be achieved through learning.

■ Forgetting and memory were extensively studied by *Herman Ebbinghaus*, whose *curve of forgetting* shows

that forgetting is most rapid immediately after learning. This is one reason why *periodic review* can be helpful in studying.

■ *Failure to encode* information is a common cause of "forgetting." Forgetting in sensory memory and STM probably reflects *decay* of *memory traces* in the nervous system. Decay or *disuse* of memories may also account for some LTM loss, but much forgetting cannot be explained in this way.

■ Often forgetting is *cue dependent*. That is, information is stored and *available* but is not *accessible*, because the cues necessary to retrieve it are missing. The power of cues to trigger memories is revealed by *state-dependent learning* and the link between moods and memory.

■ Much forgetting in both STM and LTM can be attributed to *interference* of memories with one another. When recent learning interferes with retrieval of prior learning, *retroactive inhibition* has occurred. If old learning interferes with new learning, *proactive inhibition* has occurred.

■ *Repression* is the forgetting of painful, embarrassing, or traumatic memories. Repression is thought to be unconscious, in contrast to *suppression*, in which one consciously tries to avoid thinking about something.

■ *Retrograde amnesia* and the effects of electroconvulsive shock (ECS) may be explained by the concept of *consolidation*. Consolidation theory holds that *engrams* (permanent memory traces) are formed during a critical period after learning. Until they are consolidated, long-term memories are easily destroyed. The *hippocampus* is a brain area that has been connected to consolidation of memories.

■ The search within the brain for engrams, once focused on RNA, has now settled on changes in individual nerve cells. The best documented changes are alterations in the amounts of *transmitter chemicals* the cells release and the number of *receptor cites* on them.

■ Memory can be improved by using *feedback* and *recitation*, by *overlearning*, by *selecting* and *organizing* information, and by using *spaced practice* and the *progressive part method*. Effects of *serial position*, *sleep*, and *review* should also be kept in mind when studying or memorizing.

■ *Mnemonic systems* use mental images and unusual associations to link new information with familiar memories already stored in LTM. Such strategies organize information and give it personal meaning to make recall easier.

▶▶▶ **Exploration**

How Many Types of Memory Are There?

As we have seen, "memory" is an umbrella term that includes both short- and long-term memory. Beyond this it is becoming clear that more than one type of long-term memory exists. Let's probe a little further into the mysteries of memory.

Skill Memory and Fact Memory   A curious thing happens to many people who develop amnesia. A patient like HM, described earlier, may be unable to learn a telephone number, an address, or a person's name. And yet HM, like many such patients, could learn the frustrating task of drawing while watching his hands reversed in a mirror. Likewise, amnesiac patients may learn to complete complex puzzles in the same amount of time as normal subjects (McKean, 1983) (see Fig. 10–17). Observations like these and others have led many psychologists to conclude that long-term memories fall into at least two categories. One of these might be called **procedural memory** (or skill memory). The other is sometimes called **fact memory**.

Procedural memory includes basic conditioned responses and response chains like those involved in typing, solving a puzzle, or swinging a golf club. Memories such as these can be fully expressed only as actions. It is likely that skill memories register in "lower" brain areas and that they appeared early in the evolution of

the brain (Tulving, 1985). They appear to represent the more basic "automatic" elements of conditioning, learning, and memory.

Fact memory is the ability to learn specific information, such as names, faces, words, dates, or ideas. This is the memory that a person with amnesia lacks, and that most of us take for granted. Some psychologists believe that fact memory can be further divided into two other types, called semantic and episodic memory (Tulving, 1985).

Semantic Memory   Most of our basic *factual knowledge* about the world is almost totally immune to forgetting. The names of objects, the days of the week or months of the year, simple math skills, the seasons, words and language, and other general facts are all quite

lasting. Such facts make up a part of LTM called **semantic memory.** Semantic memory serves as a mental dictionary or encyclopedia of basic knowledge.

Episodic Memory   Semantic memory has no connection to times or places. It would be rare, for instance, to remember when and where you first learned the names of the seasons. In contrast **episodic memory** (ep-ih-SOD-ik) is "autobiographical." It records life events (or episodes) day after day, year after year: Can you remember your seventh birthday, your first date, an accident you witnessed, the first day of college, ideas you have read in this text, what you had for breakfast three days ago? All are episodic memories.

Question: Are episodic memories as lasting as semantic memories?

Fig. 10–17   *The Tower Puzzle. In this puzzle all of the colored disks must be moved to another post, without ever placing a larger disk on a smaller one. Despite his amnesia HM learned to solve the puzzle in 31 moves, the minimum possible. Even so, each time he began he protested that he did not remember ever solving the puzzle before and that he did not know how to begin. Evidence like this suggests that skill memory is distinct from fact memory.*

Exploration: How Many Types of Memory Are There?

In general, episodic memories are more easily forgotten than semantic memories. This is because new information constantly pours into episodic memory. Stop for a moment and remember what you did last summer. That was an episodic memory. Notice that you now remember that you just remembered something. You have a new episodic memory in which you remember that you remembered while reading this text! It's easy to see how much we ask of our memory system.

How Many Memories? In answer to the question posed by the title of this Exploration, it is very likely that three kinds of long-term memories exist (procedural, semantic, and episodic). Although other types may be discovered in the future (Tulving, 1985), it appears that some pieces of the puzzle called memory are falling into place.

Questions for Discussion

1. What type of classroom testing do you prefer? Why? What would you consider an ideal way to be tested? ("Never" does not count as an answer!)

2. Would you like to have a memory like the man studied by A. R. Luria? What would be the advantages and disadvantages of such a memory? If, as an adult, you retained eidetic memory, how would you use it?

3. If you were forced to give up either STM or LTM, which would you choose? Think carefully about your answer.

4. We have seen that there are several reasons for forgetting. Which does the use of mnemonics most directly combat? How would you minimize the other major causes of forgetting?

5. You must study French, Spanish, psychology, and biology in one evening, and you have little time for breaks. What do you think would be the best ordering of subjects to minimize interference? Why?

6. If scientists perfect a drug that improves memory, do you think it should be widely available? Would you want to try it? If a drug were perfected that could cause selective forgetting of memories, would you support its use for victims of rape, assault, disaster, or a horrifying accident?

7. What mnemonic strategies have you used in studying? Which have been most helpful? How could a person with poor mental imagery use mnemonics?

8. What have you done to cope with remembering longer zip codes?

9. Describe a case of mistaken identity you have seen in the news. What aspect of memory contributed to the mistake?

10. In view of the text's discussion, do you think memories that occur during hypnosis should be allowed as evidence in court? One expert has suggested videotaping sessions during which witnesses or victims are questioned under hypnosis. If such tapes were available to juries, do you think testimony based on hypnosis would be more trustworthy? Why or why not?

Chapter 11

Thinking, Problem Solving, and Creativity

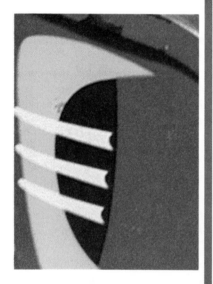

Chapter Preview
Chess Anyone?

David Levy was in trouble. It was the fourth game of a six-game chess match and Levy was trying a new strategy. If he lost the match, Levy would forfeit $2500 of his own money. Game one was a tie. Levy won games two and three. Now in game four, he was locked in a sharp tactical battle, and he was losing. What was wrong? In the earlier games Levy relied on the kind of wide open maneuvering that had made him an International Master. In contrast his opponent's strength was a powerful short-term, or tactical, style of play. Maybe "powerful" isn't the right word. Unbeatable is closer to the truth, as Levy soon learned. For the moment David Levy had met his match. He watched silently as the robot arm of Chess 4.7 made its final move, winning game four.

Chess 4.7 is a computer program. In 1977 it won the Minnesota Open Chess Tournament—against humans. However, David Levy, the reigning Scottish champion, proved to be a tougher opponent. After losing game four, Levy quickly returned to his original style of play—and won the match (Ehara, 1980). For all their raw power computers are only able to plan five or six chess moves in advance (by considering over one billion possibilities). They don't make mistakes in the short run, but they can be beaten by strategy and foresight.

David Levy's victory symbolizes one of the most unique of all human capacities: the ability to think intelligently and creatively. We know how computers "think" because we created them. But how do we explain David Levy's creativity and problem-solving ability? Or yours? Thinking, problem solving, and creativity are the challenging topics of this chapter.

Survey Questions What is the nature of thought? What basic units are used in thinking, and how do they differ? How do concepts and language influence thought? Can animals think? Can they be taught to use language? What do we know about effective problem solving and creativity? Can creativity be learned? How accurate is intuition?

Resources

What Is Thinking?— It's All in Your Head!

Thinking refers to many things: daydreaming, fantasy, problem solving, and reasoning—to name but a few. Stated more formally, **thinking,** or **cognition,** refers to the mental manipulation and combination of images, concepts, words, rules, symbols, and precepts. Although an ability to think is not limited to humans, imagine trying to teach an animal to match the feats of Hans Eberstark, a "lightning calculator." Eberstark can multiply two 12-digit numbers in his head, supplying the correct answer in about 2 minutes!

Question: To what extent are animals capable of thought?

Most pet owners can readily supply stories about apparent thinking in animals. A friend might say, "Wow, you should have seen Studebaker figure out how to get into the closet where I hid the dog food." Are animals actually thinking in such situations? In a rudimentary sense they are. At its most basic, thinking is the **internal representation** of a problem or situation. (Picture a chess player who mentally tries out several possible moves before actually touching a chesspiece.)

Animals demonstrate internal representation in **delayed response problems.** For example, a hungry animal could be allowed to watch as food is hidden under one of three goal boxes. After a delay the animal is released. Can it select the correct box? If the delay is brief, the answer is yes (Hunter, 1913). Animals also show apparent problem-solving ability far exceeding that just described. In fact German psychologist Wolfgang Köhler felt that higher animals such as chimpanzees are capable of insight.

Insight is a sudden reorganization of the elements of a problem whereby the solution becomes evident. To test for insight, Köhler challenged Sultan, his brightest chimp, with a **multiple-stick problem.** In this problem several sticks of increasing length were arranged between the cage and a banana (see Fig. 11–1). To reach the banana, Sultan had to use the first stick to retrieve the second stick (which was longer than the first). The second stick could then be used to retrieve an even longer stick, which could then be used to reach the banana (Köhler, 1925).

When confronted with this problem, Sultan looked at the banana, then at the sticks . . . then at the banana. Picking up the first stick, Sultan smoothly and without further hesitation solved the problem and raked in the banana.

Psychologists have long debated whether Köhler's chimps actually displayed insight. More recently, however, David Premack (1983) has provided additional evidence of insightful problem solving by a chimp. In one fascinating experiment Premack showed a chimpanzee a videotape of an actor jumping up and down below a bunch of bananas. The chimp was then shown several still photographs of the actor in various positions. From these, the chimp chose a photograph of the actor stepping up onto a chair. Note that this choice makes sense only if the chimp understood that the actor was trying to reach the bananas.

In recent years evidence for animal intelligence and thinking ability has continued to grow—but not without controversy (see Highlight 11–1).

Basic Units of Thought In the Chapter Preview we used chess playing as an example of human thought. Let's briefly consider another chess example. Chess Grand Mas-

Fig. 11–1 *Psychologist Wolfgang Köhler believed that solution of a multiple-stick problem revealed a capacity for insight.*

Highlight 11–1
How Intelligent Are Animals?

Evidence for the idea that animals are capable of intelligent thought is varied and, to many researchers, convincing:

- Monkeys can learn to select, from among three objects, the one that differs from the other two.
- When a container of sugar water is moved a set distance farther from a beehive each day, the bees begin to go to the new location *before* the water is moved.
- Pigeons can learn to select photographs of humans from a group of photos that includes various objects.
- A chimpanzee is allowed to see itself in a mirror. It is then anesthetized and a red spot is placed on its forehead. When it awakens and looks in the mirror, it tries to rub away the colored spot.

Do such examples really demonstrate thinking by animals? Some psychologists say yes; some say no. What would it take, then, to verify animal thinking? Psychologist Donald Griffin suggests that we must observe behavior that is versatile and appropriate to changing circumstances. He also believes that thinking is implied by actions that appear to be planned with an awareness of likely results. As one example of animal cognition, Griffin describes an incident in which a pair of ravens dropped rocks on humans who climbed too close to their nest. In similar fashion sea otters select suitably sized rocks and use them to hammer shellfish loose for eating. They then use the rock to open the shell (Fig. 11–2).

As convincing as such examples may seem, they have not gone unchallenged. For example,

Fig. 11–2 *Does the seemingly intelligent behavior of sea otters and other animals reflect thinking ability, instinct, or conditioning? The evidence remains inconclusive, so psychologists disagree.*

Epstein, Lanza, and Skinner have conditioned pigeons to duplicate seemingly insightful behavior like that claimed for higher animals. David Premack, however, replies that the pigeons only achieved the *appearance* of thinking, because their behavior was strongly guided by reinforcement.

As stated before, it seems reasonable to assume that animals do think. However, debate is sure to continue about the limits of their intelligence and about whether specific examples demonstrate thinking, instinct, or conditioning. (Sources: Epstein et al., 1981; Griffin, 1984; Herrnstein, 1979; Premack, 1983; Rose, 1984.)

---

ter Miguel Najdorf once simultaneously played 45 chess games while *blindfolded*. It is estimated that over 3600 different positions arose during the evening of the exhibition (Hearst, 1969).

How did Najdorf perform his feat? Like most people he used several types of internal representation. The *basic units of thought* include (1) **images,** (2) **muscular responses,** (3) **concepts,** and (4) **language,** or **symbols.** All four units are usually combined in situations requiring complex thought and internal representation. Indeed, in some situations people need all the help they can get. To accomplish their mental feats, blindfolded chess players report that they use a combination of visual images, muscular sensations involving "lines of force," concepts ("Game 2 is an English opening"), and the special notational system or "language" used by chess players (Hearst,

1969). Because of their obvious importance, each of the units of thought is discussed in greater detail in the following pages.

Mental Imagery— Does a Frog Have Lips?

A survey of 500 people found that 97 percent have visual images and 92 percent have auditory images. Over 50 percent had imagery that included movement, touch, taste, smell, and pain (McKellar, 1965). When we speak of images, we usually think of mental "pictures." But as you can see, "images" may involve the other senses as well. For example, your image of a bakery may include its delicious odor, as well as its appearance. Some people even have a rare form of imagery called **synesthesia** (sin-es-THEE-zyah). For these individuals, images cross normal sensory barriers (Marks, 1978). To the synesthetic individual, for instance, hearing music may include a burst of colors or tastes as well as sound sensations. Despite such variations it is generally accepted that most people use images to think and solve problems.

In recent years Stephen Kosslyn of Harvard University and other researchers have added greatly to our understanding of mental imagery. For instance, Kosslyn (1983) discovered that mental images are not flat, like photographs.

Question: How could he determine that?

To sample Kosslyn's work, think about the following question: Does a frog have lips and a stubby tail? Unless you often kiss frogs, you will probably tackle this question by using mental images. To answer, most people report that they picture a frog, "look" at its mouth, and then mentally *rotate* the frog to check its tail (Kosslyn, 1983). Mental images, then, are not necessarily flat, and they can be moved about as needed (also see Fig. 11–3).

Question: How are images used to solve problems?

Stored images can be used to bring prior experience to bear on problem solving. If you were given the question, "How many uses can you think of for an old automobile tire?" you might begin by picturing all the uses you have already seen. To generate more original solutions, you might use **created images**. Recent research indicates that people who have good imaging ability tend to score higher on tests of creativity (Shaw & Belmore, 1983). Thus, an artist may completely picture a proposed sculpture before beginning work.

Does the "size" of a mental image make any difference in thinking? To find out, first picture a cat sitting beside a housefly. Now try to "zoom in" on the cat's ears so you see them clearly. Next, picture a rabbit sitting beside an elephant. How quickly can you "see" the rabbit's front feet? Did it take longer than picturing the cat's ears?

When a rabbit is pictured with an elephant, the rabbit's image must be small because the elephant is large. Using such tasks, Kosslyn (1975) found that the smaller an image is, the harder it is to "see" its details. To put this finding to use, try forming oversized images of things you want to think about. For example, to understand electricity, picture the wires as large pipes with electrons the size of golf balls moving through them; to understand the human ear, explore it (in your mind's eye) like a large cave; and so forth.

Muscular Imagery

Question: How do muscular responses relate to thinking?

It is somewhat surprising to recognize that we think with our bodies as well as our heads. Jerome Bruner (1966) believes that we often represent things in a kind of **muscular imagery** created by actions or *implicit* actions. For example, people who "talk" with their hands are using gestures to help themselves think as well as to communicate. A

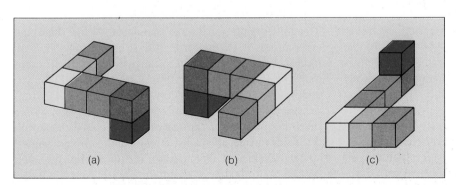

Fig. 11–3 *Imagery in thinking. Subjects were shown a drawing similar to* (a) *and drawings of how* (a) *would look in other positions, such as* (b) *and* (c). *Subjects could recognize* (a) *after it had been "rotated" from its original position. However, the more* (a) *was rotated in space, the longer it took to recognize it. This result suggests that subjects actually formed a three-dimensional image of* (a) *and rotated the image to see if it matched. (Shepard, 1975.)*

(a)   (b)   (c)

great deal of information is contained in *kinesthetic sensations* (feelings from the muscles and joints). As one talks, these sensations help structure the flow of ideas (Horowitz, 1970). If you try to tell a friend how to knead bread dough, you may find it impossible to resist moving your hands as you describe the proper motion.

Most thinking is accompanied by an undercurrent of muscular tension and **micromovements** throughout the

body. In one classic study a subject was asked to imagine that he was hitting a nail with a hammer. As he did, there was a clearly recorded burst of activity in the muscles of his unmoving arm (Jacobson, 1932). If you would like to demonstrate the link between muscular activity and thinking, ask a friend who was in a sporting event to describe what occurred. Along with a description, you will probably get an "instant replay" of the high points!

Learning Check

1. A _____ _____ problem can be used to show that animals are capable of simple representative thought.

2. There is evidence that chimpanzees are capable of insightful solutions to problems, but some psychologists remain unconvinced that true thinking is involved.   T or F?

3. List four basic units of thought:

   _____ , _____

   _____ , _____.

4. Synesthesia is the use of kinesthetic sensations as a vehicle for thought.   T or F?

5. Our reliance on imagery in thinking means that problem solving is impaired by micromovements.   T or F?

6. Humans appear capable of forming three-dimensional images that can be moved or rotated in space.   T or F?

Answers: 1. delayed response 2. T 3. images, muscular responses, concepts, and language or symbols 4. F 5. F 6. T

Concepts— I'm Positive, It's a Whatchamacallit

A **concept** is a word or idea that represents a class of objects or events. Concepts provide a powerful tool for thought because they allow us to think more *abstractly*, free from distracting details. Imagine, for instance, that you have shown a 5-year-old child two big toy frogs and four little frogs. You then ask the child, "Are there more frogs or more baby frogs?" When Markman and Seibert (1976) asked kindergarten children the same question, most children erred and said, "More baby frogs." The researchers then introduced the concept of *family* to the problem ("This is a family of frogs. Are there more frogs or more baby frogs?"). Adding the concept dramatically reduced the children's thinking errors.

Question: How are concepts learned?

Concept formation is the process of classifying information into meaningful categories. In early childhood much concept formation simply involves experience with **positive** and **negative instances** of the concept. This is not as

simple as it might seem: Imagine a child learning the concept of *dog*.

Dog Daze

A child and her father go for a walk. At a neighbor's house, they see a medium-sized dog. The father says, "See the dog." As they pass the next yard, the child sees a cat and says, "Dog!" Her father corrects her, "No, that's a *cat*." The child now thinks, "Aha, dogs are large and cats are small." In the next yard she sees a Pekingese and says, "Cat!" "No, that's a dog," replies her father.

The child's confusion is understandable. At first she might even mistake a Pekingese for a dust mop. However, with more positive and negative instances the child will eventually recognize everything from Great Danes to Chihuahuas as examples of the same category—dogs. As adults we more often acquire concepts by learning or forming **rules**. For example, a *triangle* must be a closed shape with three sides made of straight lines. Rule learning is generally more efficient than examples, but examples remain important (Rosenthal & Zimmerman, 1978). It is unlikely that memorizing a series of rules would allow an uninitiated listener to accurately categorize *punk*, *new wave*, *fusion*, *salsa*, and *techno-pop music*.

Question: Are there different kinds of concepts?

Several general types of concepts have been identified. A **conjunctive concept** refers to a class of objects having one or more features in common. Conjunctive concepts are sometimes referred to as *and concepts:* To belong to the concept class, an item must have "this feature, *and* this feature, *and* this feature." For example, a *motorcycle* must have two wheels, *and* an engine, *and* a seat, *and* handlebars. **Relational concepts** classify objects on the basis of their relationship to something else, or by the relationship between features of an object. *Large, above, left, north*, and *upside down* are all relational concepts. **Disjunctive concepts** refer to objects that have at least one of several possible features. These are *either-or concepts*. To belong, an item must have "this feature, *or* that feature, *or* another feature." For example, in the game of baseball, a *strike* is *either* a swing, *or* a miss, *or* a pitch down the middle, *or* a foul ball. The either-or quality of disjunctive concepts makes them difficult to learn.

When you think of the concept *bird*, do you make a mental list of features that birds have? Probably not. In addition to rules and features, most people also use **prototypes**, or ideal models to identify concepts (Rosch, 1977). A robin, for instance, is a model bird, whereas an ostrich is not. What this tells us is that not all examples of a concept are equally representative. For example, which of the drawings in Figure 11–4 best represents a cup? At some point a cup that is made taller or wider becomes a vase or a bowl. How do we know when the line is crossed? Probably by comparing objects to an "ideal" cup, like number 5. The upshot of this discussion is that identifying concepts is difficult when we cannot come up with a prototype relevant to what we see. What, for example, are the objects shown in Fig. 11–5?

Generally speaking, concepts have two types of meaning. The **denotative meaning** of a word or concept is its explicit definition. The **connotative meaning** is its emotional or personal meaning. For example, the denotative meaning of the word *naked* (having no clothes) is the same for a nudist as it is for a movie censor, but we could expect their connotations to differ.

Question: Can you give a clearer statement of what a connotative meaning is?

Researcher Charles Osgood (1952) used a method called the **semantic differential** to measure connotative meaning (see Fig. 11–6). Osgood found that when words or concepts are rated on a series of scales, most of their conno-

Fig. 11–4 *When does a cup become a bowl or a vase? Deciding if an object belongs to a conceptual class is aided by relating it to a prototype or ideal example. Subjects in one experiment chose number 5 as the "best" cup. (After Labov, 1973.)*

tative meaning boils down to the dimensions: *good–bad*, *strong–weak*, and *active–passive*. (Sounds like a good movie title, doesn't it: *The Good the Bad, the Strong the Weak, the Active and the Passive*.) Because concepts vary on these dimensions, words or phrases having roughly the same denotative meaning may have very different connotations. For example, I am *conscientious*; you are *careful*; he is *nit-picking!*

Fig. 11–5 *Use of prototypes in concept identification. Even though its shape is unusual, item (a) can be related to a model (an ordinary set of pliers) and thus recognized. But what are items (b) and (c)? If you don't recognize them, look ahead to Fig. 11–7. (After Bransford & McCarrell, 1977.)*

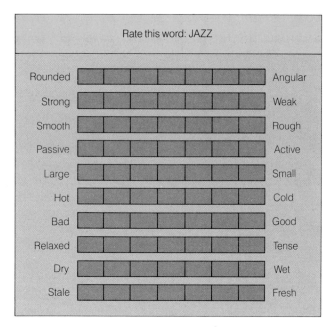

Rate this word: JAZZ

Rounded							Angular
Strong							Weak
Smooth							Rough
Passive							Active
Large							Small
Hot							Cold
Bad							Good
Relaxed							Tense
Dry							Wet
Stale							Fresh

Fig. 11—6 *This is an example of Osgood's semantic differential. Connotative meaning of the word* jazz *can be established by rating it on the scales. Mark your own rating by placing dots or X's in the spaces. Connect the marks with a line; then have a friend rate the word and compare your responses. It might be interesting to do the same for* rock and roll, disco, *and* classical. *You also might want to try the word* psychology. *(From C. E. Osgood. Copyright © 1952 American Psychological Association. Reprinted by permission.)*

Language— Give Us a Sign, Washoe

As we have seen, thinking sometimes takes place without language. Everyone has had the experience of searching for a word to express an idea that exists as a vague image or feeling. Nevertheless, most thought leans heavily on

Fig. 11—7 *Context can substitute for a lack of appropriate prototypes in concept identification.*

language, because it allows the world to be **encoded** into symbols that are easy to manipulate.

Study of the meaning of words and language is called **semantics**. It is here that the connection between language and thought becomes most evident. Suppose, on an intelligence test, you were asked to circle the word that does not belong in this series:

SKYSCRAPER   CATHEDRAL   TEMPLE   PRAYER

If you circled PRAYER, you answered as most people do. Now try another problem, again circling the odd item:

CATHEDRAL   PRAYER   TEMPLE   SKYSCRAPER

Had you seen only this question, you probably would have circled SKYSCRAPER. There is a subtle change in meaning caused by re-ordering the words (Judson & Cofer, 1956; cited by Mayer, 1977).

Semantic problems often arise when a word has dual, or unclear, meaning: Does the sentence, "Tom was seated by the waiter," mean the waiter gave Tom a seat or that Tom was seated beside the waiter? Choice of words may directly influence thinking about important events by shifting meaning: Has one country's army "invaded" another? Or "effected a protective incursion"? Is the city reservoir "half full" or "half empty"? Would you rather eat "prime beef" or "dead cow"?! (See Fig. 11—8.)

Question: What does it take to make a language?

The Structure of Language

First of all, a language must provide *symbols* that can stand for objects and ideas. The symbols we call words are built out of **phonemes** (FOE-neems: basic speech sounds) and **morphemes** (MORE-feems: speech sounds collected into meaningful units). The units of speech can be arranged into countless combinations. Consider the possibilities in just four morphemes: *reach, to, able, un*. From these we can make: *able to, unable to, reach to, to reach, able to reach, unable to reach, reachable, unreachable, reachable to, unreachable to, unto, unto Able.*

The second requirement of language is that it have a **grammar,** or set of rules for combining sounds into words and words into sentences. One part of grammar is known as **syntax,** or rules for word order in sentences. Syntax is very important because rearranging words almost always changes the meaning of a sentence: "Dog bites man" versus "Man bites dog."

Traditional grammar has been concerned with "surface" language—the actual sentences spoken. More recently, American linguist Noam Chomsky has drawn attention to the rules used to change core ideas into various sentences.

Fig. 11–8 *The Stroop interference task. Test yourself by naming the colors in the top two rows as quickly as you can. Then name the colors of the ink used to print the words in the bottom two rows (do not read the words themselves). The greater difficulty of naming colors in the bottom rows shows how intimately thought is linked to language. The meaning of words has a powerful impact on our response to them. (After Tzeng & Wang, 1983.)*

Chomsky (1968) argues that we do not learn all the sentences we might ever say. Rather, we actively *create* them by applying **transformation rules.** For example, the core sentence "Dog bites man" can be transformed to the following patterns (and others as well):

Past: The dog bit the man.
Passive: The man was bitten by the dog.
Negative: The dog did not bite the man.
Question: Did the dog bite the man?

Children show evidence of using transformation rules when they form sentences such as "I runned home." The child has applied the past tense rule to the irregular verb *to run.*

The third, and perhaps most essential, characteristic of language is that it is **productive.** The great strength of any true language is that it can produce new thoughts or ideas. Because words do not resemble the things they represent, they can be rearranged to produce an infinite variety of meaningful sentences (Bruner, 1966). Some are silly: "Please don't feed me to the goldfish." Some are profound: "We hold these truths to be self-evident, that all men are created equal." In either case it is the productive quality of language that makes it such a powerful tool for thought.

Question: Do animals use language?

Animals do communicate. The cries, gestures, and mating calls of animals have broad meanings immediately understood by other animals of the same species (Premack, 1983). For example, vervet monkeys make several distinct distress calls, including a leopard alarm, an eagle alarm, and a snake alarm. In one study monkeys in the wild responded to a tape-recorded leopard signal by climbing into the nearest tree. The eagle alarm, in contrast, sent them diving into thick vegetation. When the taped python alarm was played, the monkeys stood on their hind legs while looking all around for the nonexistent snake (Seyfarth, Cheney, & Marler, 1980). (Unfortunately, there is no vervet cry for "Sorry guys, just kidding.")

For the most part natural animal communication is quite limited. Even apes and monkeys make only a few dozen distinct cries, which carry messages such as "attack," "flee," or "food here." More importantly, animal communication seems to lack the productive quality of human language. For example, when a monkey gives an eagle distress call, it means something like, "I see an eagle." The monkey has no way of saying "I don't see an eagle," or "Thank heavens that wasn't an eagle," or "That sucker I saw yesterday was some huge eagle" (Glass, Holyoak, & Santa, 1979).

Question: Could an animal be taught to use language?

Psychologists have made several intriguing attempts to teach animals to use language. Let's consider some of their successes and failures.

Talking Chimps   Early attempts to teach chimps to talk were a dismal failure. The world record for talking was held by Viki, a chimp who could say only four words (*mama, papa, cup,* and *up*) after 6 years of intensive training (Fleming, 1974; Hayes, 1951). (Actually, all four words sounded something like a belch.) Then there was a breakthrough. Beatrice Gardner and Allen Gardner of the University of Reno, Nevada, used a combination of operant conditioning and imitation to teach a female chimp named Washoe to use **American Sign Language**

(ASL). ASL is a set of hand gestures used by the deaf (each gesture stands for a word).

Washoe's communication skills blossomed rapidly as her "vocabulary" grew. Soon she began to put together primitive sentence strings like: "Come-gimme sweet," "Out please," "Gimme tickle," and "Open food drink." She now has a vocabulary of about 240 signs and can construct six-word sentences. She even communicates with other chimpanzees using sign language, and she is "teaching" her adopted son Loulis to use signs (Gardner & Gardner, 1969; Rose, 1984).

Some critics are skeptical about Washoe's achievements, since her arrangement of "words" is somewhat haphazard. Children quickly learn the difference between word orders like "Give me candy" and "Me give candy." An answer to this criticism has come from the work of David Premack (1970), who taught a female chimp named Sarah to use 130 "words" consisting of plastic chips arranged on a magnetized board (see Fig. 11–9).

From the beginning of her training, Sarah was required to use proper word order. She has learned to answer questions, to label things "same" or "different," to classify objects by color, shape, and size, and to construct com-

Fig. 11–9 *After reading the message, "Sarah insert apple pail banana dish" on the magnetic board, Sarah performed the actions as directed. (From "Teaching Language to an Ape" by Ann J. Premack and David Premack. Copyright © 1972 by Scientific American, Inc. All rights reserved.)*

pound sentences (Premack & Premack, 1983). One of her most outstanding achievements is use of sentences involving **conditional relationships**: "If Sarah take apple, then Mary give Sarah chocolate"; "If Sarah take banana, then Mary no give Sarah chocolate."

Questions: Can it be said with certainty that the chimps understand such interchanges?

Most researchers working with chimps believe that they have indeed communicated with them. Especially convincing are the chimp's spontaneous responses. Washoe once "wet" on psychologist Roger Fouts' back while riding on his shoulders. When Fouts asked, with some annoyance, why she had done it, Washoe signed, "It's funny!"

Some of the most convincing evidence on language comprehension by an animal has come from recent work by Penny Patterson. Patterson has trained a young gorilla named Koko to use over 300 signs. Patterson considers conversations held about *past events* and *feelings* a strong indication of Koko's comprehension. For example, 3 days after Koko bit Patterson, the following conversation took place:

Me: "What did you do to Penny?"
Koko: "Bite."
Me: "You admit it?"
Koko: "Sorry bite scratch. Wrong bite."
Me: "Why bite?"
Koko: "Because mad."
Me: "Why mad?"
Koko: "Don't know."
(Adapted from Patterson, 1978, p. 459.)

Such interchanges are impressive. But communication and actual language use are two different things. Several psychologists have recently expressed doubt that apes can really use language. For one thing the chimps rarely "speak" without prompting. Many of their seemingly original sentences turn out to be responses to questions or imitations of signs made by the teacher. Also, it appears that the apes may be simply performing chains of *operant responses* to get food or other goodies (Savage-Rumbaugh et al., 1979). By using such responses, the apes then manipulate their trainers to get what they want.

You might say that the critics believe the apes have made monkeys out of their trainers. However, psychologists Roger and Debbi Fouts have recently countered such criticism. An analysis they performed of some 6000 conversations between chimps showed that only 5 percent had anything to do with food. The Fouts have also videotaped conversations between chimps that took place when no humans were present to cue them. So, maybe the chimps will make monkeys out of the critics. Although the issue is far from resolved, such research promises to unravel some of the mysteries of language learning. In fact it has already proved helpful for teaching language to aphasic children (children with serious language impairment) (Huges, 1974).

Learning Check

Before you read more, it might be a good idea to see if you can answer these questions.

1. A *mup* is defined as anything that is small, blue, and hairy. *Mup* is a _____ concept.

2. The connotative meaning of the word *naked* is "having no clothes." T or F?

3. True languages are _____ because they can be used to generate new possibilities.

4. The basic speech sounds are called _____; the smallest meaningful units of speech are

called _____.

5. One of the chimpanzee Sarah's most outstanding achievements has been the construction of sentences involving: (circle)

negation adult grammar unprompted questions conditional relationships

6. Critics consider "sentences" constructed by apes to be simple _____ responses having little meaning to the animal.

Answers: 1. conjunctive 2. F 3. productive 4. phonemes, morphemes 5. conditional relationships 6. operant

Problem Solving— Getting an Answer in Sight

A good way to start off a discussion of problem solving is to solve a problem. Give this one a try.

> A famous ocean liner (the *Queen Ralph*) is steaming toward port at 20 miles per hour. It is 50 miles from shore when a seagull takes off from its deck and flies toward port. At the same instant, a speedboat leaves port at 30 miles per hour. The bird flies back and forth between the speedboat and the *Queen Ralph* at a speed of 40 miles per hour. How far will the bird have flown when the two boats pass?

If you don't immediately see the answer to this problem, read it again. (The answer is revealed in the "Solution by Insight" section that follows.)

We all do a tremendous amount of problem solving every day. Problem solving can be as commonplace as figuring out how to make a nonpoisonous meal out of the leftovers in the refrigerator or as significant as developing a cure for cancer. In either case we begin with an awareness that an answer probably exists and that by proper manipulation of the elements of thought a solution can be found. A number of different approaches to problem solving can be identified.

Mechanical Solutions Mechanical solutions may be achieved by *trial and error* or by *rote*. If I have forgotten the combination to my bike lock, I may be able to discover it by trial and error. In an era of high-speed computers, many trial and error solutions are best left to machines. A computer could generate all possible combinations of the five numbers on my lock in a split second.

When a solution is achieved by rote, we mean that thinking advanced according to a learned set of rules. If you have a good background in mathematics, you may have solved the problem of the bird and the boats by rote. (I hope you didn't. There is an easier solution.)

Solutions by Understanding Many problems are unsolvable by mechanical means or by the use of habitual modes of thought. In this case a higher level of thinking based on *understanding* is necessary. A classic series of studies on this type of thinking has been performed by German psychologist Karl Duncker (1945). Duncker gave college students this problem:

> Given an inoperable stomach tumor and rays which at high intensity will destroy tissue (both healthy and diseased), how can the tumor be destroyed without damaging surrounding tissue? (Students were also shown the sketch in Fig. 11–10).

Fig. 11–10 *A schematic representation of Duncker's tumor problem. The dark spot represents a tumor surrounded by healthy tissue. How can the tumor be destroyed without injuring surrounding tissue? (After Duncker, 1945.)*

Question: What did this problem show about problem solving?

Duncker asked the students to think aloud as they worked. By "eavesdropping" on their thoughts, he found that there were two phases to successful problem solving. First, students had to discover the **general properties** of a correct solution. Once they realized that the intensity of the rays had to be lowered on their way to the tumor, a number of **functional** (workable) **solutions** could be proposed. This marked the second stage of problem solving, during which a specific solution was selected. (The correct solution is to focus weak rays from several sources on the tumor, or to rotate the person's body so that the exposure of healthy tissue is minimized.)

Solution by Insight   Recall that Köhler's apes sometimes seemed to show *insight* in their problem solving.

Fig. 11–11 *Solution to the hat-rack problem.*

With humans we say that insight has occurred when an answer suddenly appears after a period of unsuccessful thought. An insight is usually so rapid and clear that we often wonder how such an "obvious" solution could have been missed.

Perhaps you experienced insight when trying to solve the problem of the boats and the bird. Because the boats will cover the 50-mile distance in exactly 1 hour, and the bird flies 40 miles per hour, the bird will have flown 40 miles when the boats meet. No math is necessary if you have insight into this problem.

Question: What, really, does it mean to have an insight?

Psychologists Robert Sternberg and Janet Davidson (1982) have studied people as they solve problems that require insight or "leaps of logic" for solution. According to their work, insight involves three abilities. The first is **selective encoding,** which refers to the ability to select information that is relevant to a problem, while ignoring that which is not. For example, consider the following problem:

> If you have white socks and black socks in your drawer, mixed in the ratio of 4 to 5, how many socks will you have to take out to make sure you have a pair of the same color?

A person who fails to recognize that, "mixed in a ratio of 4 to 5" is irrelevant information will be less likely to come up with the correct answer of three socks.

According to Sternberg and Davidson, a second source of insights is **selective combination.** Selective combination brings together seemingly unrelated bits of useful information. Try this sample problem:

> With a 7-minute hourglass and an 11-minute hourglass, what is the simplest way to time the boiling of an egg for 15 minutes?

Answering this problem requires using both hourglasses in combination. First, the 7-minute and the 11-minute hourglasses are started running. When the 7-minute hourglass runs out, it's time to begin boiling the egg. At this point 4 minutes remain on the 11-minute hourglass. Thus, when it runs out, it is simply turned over. When it runs out again, 15 minutes will have passed.

A third source of insight is **selective comparison,** which is the ability to compare new problems to old information or to problems already solved. A good example is the hat-rack problem. This problem calls on subjects to build a structure in the middle of a room that will support an overcoat. Subjects are given only two long sticks and a C-clamp to work with. The solution, shown in Fig. 11–11, is to clamp the two sticks together, so they are wedged between floor and ceiling. If you were given this problem, you would be more likely to solve it if you first thought of the way pole lamps are wedged between floor and ceiling.

Fixations   The ease with which problems are solved is related to a variety of factors. One of the most important barriers to problem solving is called **fixation.** Fixation is the tendency to get "hung up" on wrong solutions or to become blind to other alternatives. A prime example of fixation is **functional fixedness.** Functional fixedness is the inability to see new uses (functions) for familiar objects or for objects that have been used in a particular way. If you have ever used a dime as a screwdriver, you've overcome functional fixedness.

Question: How does functional fixedness affect problem solving?

Karl Duncker, who originated the concept of functional fixedness, performed a clever study to demonstrate its operation. Duncker challenged students to mount a candle on a vertical board so that it could burn in the normal way. Duncker gave each student three candles, some matches, some cardboard boxes, some thumbtacks, and other items. Half of Duncker's subjects received these items *inside* the cardboard boxes. The others received all the items, including the boxes, laid out on a tabletop. Duncker found that when the items were in the boxes, solution of the problem was very difficult. This is because the boxes were seen as *containers*, not as items that might be part of the solution. (If you haven't guessed the solution, check Fig. 11–12.)

Functional fixedness is just one example of the mental blocks that prevent insight. Here's another: How would you remove a $5 bill placed below a stack of precariously balanced objects (without touching or moving the objects)? A good answer is to split the bill at the edge and tear it in half, gently pulling from opposite ends. Many people fail to see this solution because they have learned not to destroy things of value. In a book entitled *Conceptual Blockbusting,* James Adams (1980) lists other sources of fixations (see box).

Creative Thinking— Fluency, Flexibility, and Originality

Question: What distinguishes creative thinking from more routine problem solving?

As we have noted, problem solving may be the result of thinking that is mechanical, insightful, or based on understanding. To this we can add that thought may be **inductive** (going from specific facts or observations to general

principles) or **deductive** (going from general principles to specific situations). Thinking may also be **logical** (proceeding from given information to new conclusions on the basis of explicit rules) or **illogical** (intuitive, associative, or personal—see this chapter's Exploration).

Creative thinking involves all these styles of thought (in varying combinations) *plus* fluency, flexibility, and originality (Guilford, 1950). The meaning of these terms can be illustrated by returning to an earlier example. Let's say that you would like to find a creative use (or uses) for the millions of automobile tires discarded each year. The crea-

Fig. 11–12   *Materials for solving the candle problem were given to subjects in boxes* (a) *or separately* (b). *Functional fixedness caused by condition* (a) *interfered with solving the problem. The solution to the problem is shown in* (c).

(a)   (b)   (c)

Highlight 11–2
Daydreams, Fantasy, and Creativity

Has your reading of this chapter been interrupted by a daydream? Clinical psychologist Jerome Singer (1974) found that most people daydream sometime each day. What do we know about this unique form of thought?

Content   Two of the most common daydream "plots" are the **conquering hero** and the **suffering martyr** themes. In a conquering hero fantasy the daydreamer gets the starring role as a famous, rich, or powerful person: a celebrity, athlete, musician, famous surgeon, brilliant lawyer, or magnificent lover. Themes such as these seem to reflect needs for mastery and escape from the frustrations of everyday life. Suffering martyr daydreams center on feelings of being neglected, hurt, rejected, or unappreciated by others. In such fantasies others end up regretting their past actions and realizing what a *wonderful person* the daydreamer was all along.

Benefits   Daydreams often fill a need for stimulation when a person must perform a routine or monotonous task. They also improve the ability to delay immediate pleasures so that future goals can be achieved. And, in everyday terms, fantasy can be an outlet for frustrated impulses. If you have a momentary urge to kill the fool in front of you on the highway, substituting fantasy for action can avert disaster (Biblow, 1973).

Perhaps the greatest value of fantasy is its contribution to creativity. In the imaginative realm of fantasy, nothing is impossible—a quality allowing for tremendous fluency and flexibility of thought. For most people fantasy and daydreaming are associated with positive emotional adjustment, lower levels of aggression, and greater mental flexibility or creativity (Singer, 1974). Perhaps this is why Albert Einstein, one of the world's most celebrated thinkers, was, in his own words, "disorderly and a dreamer."

tivity of your suggestions could be rated in this way: **Fluency** is defined as the total number of suggestions you are able to make. **Flexibility** is defined as the number of times you shift from one class of possible uses to another. **Originality** refers to how novel or unusual your suggestions are. By totaling the number of times you showed fluency, flexibility, and originality, we could rate the creativity of your thinking on this problem. Speaking more generally, we would be rating your capacity for **divergent thinking**. (See Highlight 11–2.)

Divergent thinking is the most widely used measure of creative problem solving. In routine problem solving or thinking, there is one correct answer, and the problem is to find it. This leads to **convergent thought** (lines of thought that converge in the correct answer). Divergent thinking is the reverse, in which many possibilites are developed from one starting place.

There are several tests of divergent thinking. In the **Unusual Uses Test** a person is asked to think of as many uses for an object (such as the tires just mentioned) as possible. In the **Consequences Test** the object is to answer a question such as, "What would be the results if everyone suddenly lost the sense of balance and were unable to stay in an upright position?" Subjects are to list as many reactions as possible. In the **Anagrams Test** subjects are given a word such as *creativity* and asked to make as many new words as possible by rearranging the letters. Each of these tests can be scored for fluency, flexibility, and originality. (For an example of other tests of divergent thought, see Fig. 11–13.)

Question: Isn't creativity more than divergent thought? What if a person comes up with a large number of useless answers to a problem?

A good question. Divergent thought is definitely an important part of creative thinking, but there is more to it. To be creative, the solution to a problem must be more than novel, unusual, or original. It must also be potentially useful or meaningful, and it must meet the demands of the problem (MacKinnon, 1962). This is the dividing line between a "harebrained scheme" and a "stroke of genius." (See Fig. 11–14 and Fig. 11–15.)

Question: Is there any pattern to creative thinking?

Stages of Creative Thought   A good summary of the sequence of events in creative thinking proposes five stages that usually occur:

1. **Orientation.** As a first step, the problem must be defined and important dimensions identified.

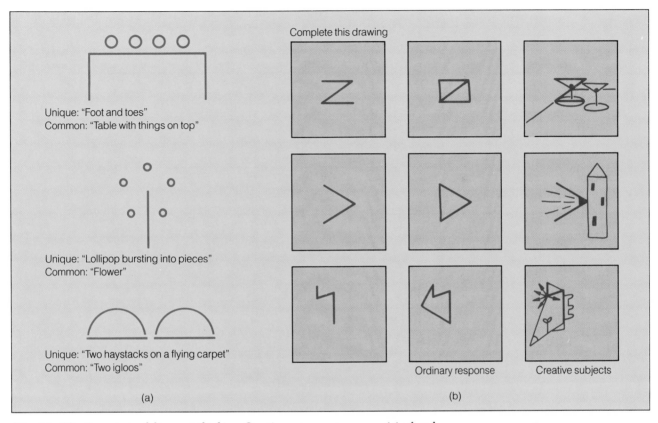

Fig. 11–13 *Some tests of divergent thinking. Creative responses are more original and more complex.* [(a) *After Wallach & Kogan, 1965;* (b) *after Barron, 1958.*]

2. Preparation. In the second stage, creative thinkers saturate themselves with as much information pertaining to the problem as possible.

3. Incubation. Most major problems produce a period during which all attempted solutions will have proved futile. At this point problem solving may proceed on a subconscious level: While the problem seems to have been set aside, it is still "cooking" in the background.

4. Illumination. The stage of incubation is often ended by a rapid insight or series of insights. These produce the "Aha!" experience, often depicted in cartoons as a light bulb appearing over the thinker's head.

5. Verification. The final step is to test and critically evaluate the solution obtained during the stage of illumination. If the solution proves faulty, the thinker reverts to the stage of incubation.

Of course, creative thought is not always so neat. Nevertheless, the stages listed are a good summary of the most typical sequence of events.

You may find it helpful to attach the stages to the following more or less true story. Legend has it that the king of Syracuse (a city in ancient Greece) once suspected that his goldsmith had substituted cheaper metals for some of

Fig. 11–14 *Creative ideas combine originality with feasibility. (Adapted from McMullan & Stocking, 1978.)*

Creativity Profile

The following qualities have repeatedly been found to characterize creative individuals:

1. An unusual awareness of people, events, and problems.

2. A high degree of verbal fluency.

3. Flexibility with numbers, concepts, media; flexibility in social situations.

4. Originality of ideas and expressions, a sense of humor.

5. An ability to abstract, organize, and synthesize.

6. A high energy/activity level.

7. Persistence at tasks of interest.

8. Impatience with routine or repetitive tasks.

9. A willingness to take risks.

10. A vivid and spontaneous imagination; in childhood this may take the form of "fibbing" or imaginary companions.

(Source: Meeker, 1978.)

Fig. 11–15 *Hat-tipping device. According to the patent, it is for "automatically effecting polite salutations by the elevation and rotation of the hat on the head of the saluting party when said person bows to the person or persons saluted." In addition to being original or novel, a creative solution must fit the demands of the problem. Is this a creative solution to the "problem" of hat tipping?*

the gold in a crown and had pocketed the difference. Archimedes, a famous mathematician and thinker, was presented with the problem of discovering whether the king had been cheated.

Archimedes began by defining the problem (orientation): "How can I determine what metals have been used in the crown without damaging it?" He then investigated all known methods of analyzing metals (preparation). All involved cutting or melting the crown, so he was forced to temporarily set the problem aside (incubation). Then one day as he stepped into his bath, Archimedes suddenly knew he had the solution (illumination). He was so excited he is said to have run naked through the streets shouting, "Eureka, eureka!" (I have found it, I have found it!)

On observing his own body floating in the bath, Archimedes realized that different metals would displace different amounts of water. All that remained was to test the solution (verification). Archimedes placed an amount of gold (equal to that given the goldsmith) in a tub of water. He marked the water level and removed the gold. He then placed the crown in the water. Was the crown pure gold? If it was, it would raise the water to exactly the same level. Unfortunately, the purity of the crown and the fate of the goldsmith are to this day unknown!

Question: What makes a person creative?

The Creative Personality   According to the popular stereotype, highly creative people are eccentric, introverted, neurotic, socially inept, unbalanced in their interests, and, frequently, on the edge of madness. Although some well-known artists and musicians cultivate a public image to fit the stereotype, there is little truth in it. Studies by psychologist Donald MacKinnon paint a very different picture of the creative person. After extensive interviews and testing of creative writers, architects, mathematicians, and scientists, MacKinnon (1968) and others have drawn these conclusions:

1. At any given level of IQ, some people are creative and some are not. There is little correlation between creativity and IQ (Nelson & Crutchfield, 1970; Taylor, 1978).

2. Creative people usually have a greater than average range of knowledge and interests, and they are more fluent in combining ideas from various sources.

3. Creative people have an openness to experience. They accept irrational thought and are uninhibited about their feelings and fantasies.

4. MacKinnon's subjects enjoyed symbolic thought, ideas, concepts, and possibilities. They tended to be interested in truth, form, and beauty, rather than in recognition or success. Their creative work was an end in itself.

5. Highly creative people value independence and have a preference for complexity. However, they are unconventional and nonconforming primarily in their work; otherwise, they do not have particularly unusual, outlandish, or bizarre personalities. Indeed, most creative personalities resemble the profile in the accompanying box.

Question: Can creativity be learned?

Most of what we know about creativity remains preliminary. Nevertheless, it is beginning to look as if some of the thinking skills that contribute to creative problem solving can be taught. In the Applications section of this chapter you will find a brief discussion of some helpful strategies.

Learning Check

1. Insight refers to rote, or deductive, problem solving.   T or F?

2. The first phase in problem solving by understanding is to discover the general properties of a correct solution.   T or F?

3. The term *fixation* refers to the point at which a helpful insight becomes fixed in one's thinking.   T or F?

4. Functional fixedness is usually an aid to problem solving.   T or F?

5. Fluency, flexibility, and originality are characteristics of:
   a. convergent thought   *b.* deductive thinking   *c.* creative thought   *d.* trial and error solutions

6. List the stages of creative thinking in the correct order:

   _____, _____,

   _____, _____,

   _____.

7. An ability to organize, abstract, and synthesize ideas blocks creativity; these are noncreative qualities.   T or F?

8. To be creative, an original idea must also be practical or feasible.   T or F?

9. According to Sternberg and Davidson, insights are the result of selective encoding, selective combination, and selective _____ of information.

Answers:

1. F 2. T 3. F 4. F 5. c 6. orientation, preparation, incubation, illumination, verification 7. F 8. T 9. comparison

Applications

Steps to Better Thinking and Problem Solving

We all at one time or another experience difficulties in thinking and problem solving. The following should alert you to some of the more common problems.

Rigid Mental Set   Try the problems pictured in Fig.11–16. If you have difficulty, try asking yourself what *assumptions* you are making. The problems are designed to demonstrate the limiting effects of a mental set. (The answers to these problems, along with an explanation of the mental sets that prevent their solution, are found on p. 276.) In addition to the assumptions and mental sets we bring to a problem, problems themselves may produce a disruptive set. A simple example is the following: The name *Polk* is pronounced "poke," the word *folk* is pronounced "foke," and the white of an egg is pronounced _____? Here is another example. See if you can unscramble each set of letters to make a word that uses all the letters:

MEST_____

LFAE_____

DUB_____

STKAL_____

OTOR_____

LTEPA_____

Fig. 11–16   (a) *Nine dots are arranged in a square. Can you connect them by drawing four continuous straight lines (without lifting your pencil from the paper)? (b) Six matches must be arranged to make four triangles. The triangles must be the same size, with each side equal to the length of one match. (The solutions to these problems appear on page 276.)*

(a)   (b)

Now try a new list:

FINEK_____

OPONS_____

KROF_____

PUC_____

SDIH_____

LTEPA_____

Did you notice that the last set of letters was the same in each list? Many people don't and end up solving the problem twice. To complete the first list *(stem, leaf, bud, stalk, root)*, the item LTEPA is usually unscrambled as PETAL. In the second list *(knife, spoon, fork, cup, dish)* LTEPA becomes PLATE for many people.

Now that you have been forewarned about the danger of faulty assumptions, see if you can correctly answer the following questions.

1. Argentineans do not have a fourth of July.   T or F?
2. How many birthdays does the average person have?
3. A farmer had 19 sheep. All but 9 died. How many sheep did he have left?
4. It is not unlawful for a man living in Winston-Salem, North Carolina, to be buried west of the Mississippi River.   T or F?
5. Some months have 30 days, some have 31. How many months have 28 days?
6. I have two coins that together total 55 cents. One of the coins is not a nickel. What are the two coins?
7. It would be far better to have an elephant eat you than a gorilla.   T or F?

These questions are designed to cause thinking errors. Here are the answers:

1. F. Of course they have a fourth of July. What would they do, go from the third to the fifth?   **2.** One, celebrated each year.   **3.** 19—9 alive and 10 dead.   **4.** F. It is against the law to bury a living man anywhere.   **5.** All of them.   **6.** A half-dollar and a nickel. One of the coins is not a nickel, but the other one is!   **7.** F. It would be better to have the elephant eat the gorilla. (Read it again.)

If you got caught on any of the questions, consider it an additional reminder of the value of actively challenging the assumptions you are making in any instance of problem solving.

Applications: Steps to Better Thinking and Problem Solving

Problems with Logic   A major thinking difficulty centers on the process of *logical reasoning*. Simple sequences of logical thought can be arranged as a set of *premises* (assumptions) and a *conclusion*. This format is called a **syllogism**. A syllogism can be evaluated for the *validity* of its *reasoning* and for the *truth* of its *conclusion*. It is entirely possible to draw true conclusions using faulty logic, or to draw false conclusions using valid logic. The examples below show how this is possible.

Syllogism I

>   All humans are mortal. (Major premise)
>   All women are human. (Minor premise)
>   Therefore, all women are mortal. (Conclusion)

Comment: As you can see from the diagram in Fig. 11–17, the logic of the syllogism is valid. Since our premises are true, this means the conclusion is true. The diagram shows all women included within the boundaries of mortals.

Syllogism II

>   All women are humans.
>   All humans are mortal.
>   Therefore, all mortals are women.

Comment: In this example the conclusion drawn is false because the reasoning is invalid. The diagram for Syllogism I shows that all mortals are not women. Notice how little the syllogism has to be changed to produce a false conclusion. Now consider Syllogism III.

Syllogism III

>   All psychologists are weird.
>   Mary is a psychologist.
>   Therefore, Mary is weird.

Fig. 11–17

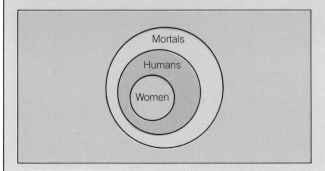

Comment: In this case the reasoning is valid, but the conclusion is false, because the first premise is false. All psychologists are *not* weird. (Honest!) Now, let's consider one more syllogism.

Syllogism IV

>   All ducks have wings.
>   All birds have wings.
>   Therefore, all ducks are birds.

Comment: This syllogism shows the importance of paying close attention to logic. The reasoning appears to be valid since the conclusion is true, but substitute *bats* or *airplanes* for *ducks* and see how the conclusion reads. It is a good idea to get in the habit of questioning the logic used by politicians and advertisers—psychologists, too, for that matter.

Oversimplification   It may be an oversimplification to say so, but oversimplification is another basic source of thinking errors. There are two types of oversimplification that are particularly troublesome. The first is **all-or-nothing thinking.** Classifying things as absolutely right or wrong, good or bad, acceptable or unacceptable, or honest or dishonest prevents appreciation of the complexity of most life problems. The second problem is thinking in terms of **stereotypes.** Stereotypes are particularly troublesome when human relationships are involved. An overly simplified, inaccurate, or rigid picture of men, blacks, women, Republicans, liberals, police officers, or any other group of people leads to muddled thinking about individual members of the group. Look for this and the other errors in your own thinking habits.

Enhancing Creativity—Brainstorms

Thomas Edison once explained his creativity by saying, "Genius is 1 percent inspiration and 99 percent perspiration." Many studies of creativity show that "genius" owes as much to persistence and dedication as it does to inspiration (Hunt, 1982). Once it is recognized that creativity can be hard work, then something can be done to enhance it. Here are some suggestions on how to begin (from Hayes, 1978, and indicated sources).

1. Define the problem broadly. Whenever possible enlarge the definition of a problem. For instance, assume your problem is, "Design a better doorway." This is likely to lead to ordinary solutions. Why not change the problem to, "Design a better way to get through a

Applications: Steps to Better Thinking and Problem Solving

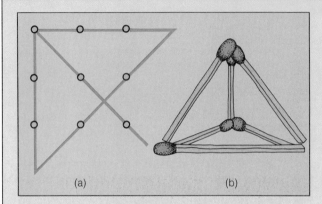

(a)   (b)

Fig. 11–18 *Problem solutions. (a) The dot problem can be solved by extending the lines beyond the square formed by the dots. Most people assume incorrectly that they may not do this. (b) The match problem can be solved by building a three-dimensional pyramid. Most people assume that the matches must be arranged on a flat surface.*

wall"? Now your solutions will be more original. Best of all might be to state the problem as, "Find a better way to define separate areas for living and working." This could lead to truly creative solutions (Adams, 1980).

Let's say that you are the leader of a group interested in designing a new can opener. Wisely, you ask the group to think about *opening* in general, rather than about can openers. This was just the approach used in developing the pop-top can. As the design group discussed the concept of opening, one member suggested that nature has its own openers, like the soft seam on a pea pod. Instead of a new can-opening tool, the group invented the self-opening can (Fig. 11–19) (Stein, 1974).

Fig. 11–19

2. Create the right atmosphere. A variety of experiments show that people make more original, spontaneous, and imaginative responses when exposed to others (models) doing the same (Amabile, 1983). If you want to become more creative, spend time around creative people. This is the premise underlying much education in art, theater, dance, and music.

3. Allow time for incubation. Trying to hurry, or to force a problem's solution, may simply encourage fixation on a dead end. In one experiment subjects were asked to list as many consequences as possible that would follow if people no longer needed to eat. Most subjects rapidly produced several ideas and then ran dry. After working for a time, some subjects were interrupted and required to do another task for 20 minutes. Then they returned to the original question. The interruption improved their scores, even though they worked no longer than the control group (Fulgosi & Guilford, 1968).

4. Seek varied input. Remember, creativity requires divergent thinking. Rather than digging deeper with logic, you are attempting to shift your mental "prospecting" to new areas. As an example of this strategy, Edward de Bono (1970) recommends that you randomly look up words in the dictionary and relate each to the problem. Often this activity will trigger a fresh perspective or open a new avenue. For instance, let's say you are asked to come up with new ways to clean oil off a beach, and you draw a blank. Following de Bono's suggestion, you would read the following randomly selected words, relate each to the problem, and see what thoughts are triggered: *weed, rust, poor, magnify, foam, gold, frame, hole, diagonal, vacuum, tribe, puppet, nose, link, drift, portrait, cheese, coal.*

5. Look for analogies. As the principle of selective comparison (described earlier) suggests, many "new" problems are really old problems in new clothing. Representing a problem in a variety of ways is often the key to solution. Most problems become easier to solve when they are effectively represented. For example, consider this problem:

Two backpackers start up a steep trail at 6 a.m. They hike all day, resting occasionally, and arrive at the top at 6 p.m. The next day they start back down the trail at 6 a.m. On the way down they stop several times and vary their pace. They arrive back at 6 p.m. On the way down one of the hikers, who is a mathematician, tells the other that she has realized that they will pass a point on the trail at exactly the same time as they did the day before. Her nonmathematical friend

Applications: Steps to Better Thinking and Problem Solving

finds this hard to believe, since on both days they have stopped and started many times and have changed their pace. The problem: Is the mathematician right?

Perhaps you will see the answer to this problem immediately. If not, think of it this way: What if there were *two* pairs of backpackers, one going up the trail, the second coming down, and both hiking on the *same day*? It becomes obvious that the two pairs of hikers will pass each other at some point on the trail. Therefore, they will be at the same place at the same time. The mathematician was right (adapted from Hayes, 1978).

6. Delay evaluation. Various studies suggest that people are most likely to be creative when they are given the freedom to play with ideas and solutions without having to worry about being evaluated. In the first stages of creative thinking, it is important to avoid criticizing your efforts. Worrying about the correctness of solutions tends to inhibit creativity (Amabile, 1983). This idea is expanded in the discussion that follows.

An alternative approach to enhancing creativity is called *brainstorming*. Although brainstorming is a group technique, it can be applied to individual problem solving as well.

Brainstorming The essence of brainstorming is that *production* and *criticism* of ideas are kept separate. To encourage divergent thinking in group problem solving, participants are encouraged to produce as many ideas as possible without fear of criticism or evaluation. Only *after* a brainstorming session is complete are ideas reconsidered and evaluated (Haefele, 1962). As ideas are freely generated, an interesting **cross-stimulation effect** takes place in which one participant's ideas trigger ideas for others. The four basic rules for successful brainstorming are:

1. Criticism of an idea is absolutely barred. All evaluation is deferred until after the session.
2. Modification or combination with other ideas is encouraged. Don't worry about giving credit for ideas or keeping them neat. Mix them up!
3. Quantity of ideas is sought. In the early stages of brainstorming, quantity is more important than quality. Try to generate lots of ideas.

4. Unusual, remote, or wild ideas are sought. Let your imagination run amok!

Question: How is brainstorming applied to individual problem solving?

The essential point to remember is to *suspend judgment*. Ideas should first be produced without regard for logic, organization, accuracy, practicality, or any other evaluation. In writing an essay, for instance, you would begin by writing ideas in any order, the more the better, just as they occur to you. Later you would go back and reorganize, rewrite, and criticize your efforts.

As an aid to achieving steps 2, 3, and 4 of the brainstorming method, you might find the following checklist helpful for encouraging original thought. It can be used to see if you have overlooked a possible solution (adapted from Parnes, 1967).

Creativity Checklist

1. Redefine. Consider other uses for all elements of the problem. (This is designed to alert you to fixations that may be blocking creativity.)
2. Adapt. How could other objects, ideas, procedures, or solutions be adapted to this particular problem?
3. Modify. Imagine changing anything and everything that could be changed.
4. Magnify. Exaggerate everything you can think of. Think on a grand scale.
5. Minify. What if everything were scaled down? What if there were no differences between elements of the problem? "Shrink" the problem down to size.
6. Substitute. How could one object, idea, or procedure be substituted for another?
7. Rearrange. Break the problem into pieces and shuffle them.
8. Reverse. Consider reverse orders, opposites, and turn things inside out.
9. Combine. This one speaks for itself.

By making a habit of subjecting a problem to each of these procedures, you should be able to greatly reduce the chances that you will overlook a useful, original, or "creative" solution.

Learning Check

1. In evaluating a syllogism, it is possible to draw a true conclusion with faulty logic, or a false conclusion with valid logic.   T or F?

Applications: Steps to Better Thinking and Problem Solving

2. Stereotyping is an example of oversimplification in thinking.   T or F?
3. Exposure to creative models has been shown to enhance creativity.   T or F?
4. In brainstorming, each idea is critically evaluated as it is generated.   T or F?
5. Defining a problem broadly produces a cross-stimulation effect that can inhibit creative thinking.   T or F?

Answers: 1. T 2. T 3. T 4. F 5. F

Chapter Summary

■ Thinking is the manipulation and combination of *internal representations* of external stimuli or situations.

■ Animals reveal a capacity for thought when they solve *delayed response problems* and, in some cases, problems that appear to require understanding or *insight*. Some psychologists remain unconvinced about such abilities, however.

■ Four basic units of thought are *images, concepts, muscular responses,* and *language*.

■ Most people have internal images of one kind or another. Images may be *stored* or *created*. Sometimes they cross normal sense boundaries in a type of imagery called *synesthesia*. Images used in problem solving may be three-dimensional, and their size may change.

■ Muscular images are created by memory of actions or by *implicit actions. Kinesthetic sensations* and *micromovements* seem to help structure the flow of thought for many people.

■ A *concept* is a generalized idea of a class of objects or events. *Concept formation* is often based on *positive* and *negative instances* and on *rule learning*. In practice concept identification frequently makes use of *prototypes*, or general models of the concept class. Concepts may be classified as *conjunctive* (*and* concepts), *disjunctive* (*either-or* concepts), or *relational*.

■ The *denotative* meaning of a word or concept is its dictionary definition. *Connotative* meaning is personal or emotional. Connotative meaning can be measured with the *semantic differential*.

■ Language allows events to be *encoded* into *symbols* for easy mental manipulation. Thinking in language is influenced by meaning. The study of meaning is called *semantics*.

■ Language carries meaning by combining a set of symbols according to a set of rules (*grammar*), which includes rules about word order (*syntax*). A true language is *productive* and can be used to generate new ideas or possibilities.

■ Animal communication is relatively limited because it lacks *symbols* that can be rearranged easily. Attempts to teach chimpanzees systems such as American Sign Language suggest to some that primates are capable of language use. Others question this conclusion.

■ The solution to a problem may be arrived at *mechanically* (by trial and error or by rote application of rules), but mechanical solutions are frequently inefficient or ineffective except where aided by computer.

■ Solutions by *understanding* usually begin with discovery of the *general properties* of an answer. Next comes proposal of a number of *functional solutions*.

■ When understanding leads to a rapid reorganization of a problem whereby the solution becomes obvious, it is said that *insight* has occurred. Three elements of insight are *selective encoding, selective combination,* and *selective comparison*.

■ Insight and other problem solving can be blocked by *fixation. Functional fixedness* is a common fixation, but *emotional blocks, cultural values, learned conventions,* and *perceptual habits* are also problems.

■ Creative thinking requires *divergent* thought, characterized by *fluency, flexibility,* and *originality*. To be creative, a solution must be useful or meaningful as well as original. *Fantasy* is a source of much divergent thinking.

■ Five stages often seen in creative problem solving are *orientation, preparation, incubation, illumination,* and *verification*. Not all creative thinking fits this pattern.

■ Studies suggest the *creative personality* has a number of identifiable characteristics, most of which contradict popular stereotypes. There appears to be little or no correlation between IQ and creativity.

■ *Rigid mental set, faulty logic,* and *oversimplification* are major sources of thinking errors. Various strategies, including *brainstorming,* tend to enhance creative problem solving.

Exploration

Intuition—Mental Shortcut? Or Dangerous Detour?

Decision 1: An epidemic breaks out and 600 people are about to die. Doctors have two choices. If they give drug A, 200 lives will be saved. If they give drug B, there is a one-third chance that 600 people will be saved and a two-thirds chance that none will be saved. Which drug should they choose?

Decision 2: Again, 600 people are about to die, and doctors must make a choice. If they give drug A, 400 people will die. If they give drug B, there is a one-third chance that no one will die and a two-thirds chance that 600 will die. Which drug should they choose?

Most people choose drug A for the first problem and drug B for the second. This is fascinating because the two problems are identical. The only difference is that the first is stated in terms of lives saved, the second in lives lost. Yet, even people who realize their answers are contradictory find it difficult to change them (Kahneman & Tversky, 1972, 1973).

Intuition   As the example shows, we often make decisions on the basis of intuition, rather than by logic. Doing so may provide quick answers, but it can also be misleading and sometimes disastrous. Two noted psychologists, Daniel Kahneman and Amos Tversky, have spent nearly 20 years studying how people make decisions and predictions in situations involving a large element of uncertainty. They have found, to put it bluntly, that human judgment is often seri-

ously flawed (Kahneman et al., 1982). Understanding the thinking errors they have identified may help you avoid them. Let's explore some common errors.

Representativeness   One very common pitfall in judgment is illustrated by the following question.

Which is more probable?
a. Bjorn Borg will lose the first set of a tennis match but win the match.
b. Bjorn Borg will lose the first set.

Tversky and Kahneman (1982) found that most people regard A as more probable than B. However, this intuitive answer overlooks an important fact: The likelihood of two events occurring together is lower than the probability of either alone. (For example, the probability of getting one head when flipping a coin is one-half, or .5. The probability of getting two heads when flipping two coins is .25, or one-fourth.) Therefore, A is less likely to be true than B.

Tversky and Kahneman believe that such faulty conclusions are based on an intuitive error called **representativeness.** That is, a choice that seems to be representative of what we already know is given greater weight. Tversky and Kahneman believe that the information given in the question about Borg is compared with a mental model of what a tennis pro's behavior should be like. The first choice seems to better represent

this model and therefore seems more likely, even though it isn't.

Underlying Odds   A second common error in judgment involves ignoring the **base rate,** or underlying probability of an event. In one experiment, for instance, subjects were told that they would be given descriptions of 100 people—70 lawyers and 30 engineers. Subjects were then asked to guess, without knowing anything about a person, whether he or she was an engineer or a lawyer. All correctly stated the probabilities as 70 percent for lawyer and 30 percent for engineer. Subjects were then given this description:

> Dick is a 30-year-old man. He is married with no children. A man of high ability and high motivation, he promises to be quite successful in his field. He is well liked by his colleagues.

Notice that the description gives no new information about Dick. He could still be either an engineer or a lawyer. Therefore, the odds should again be estimated as 70–30. However, most people changed the odds to 50–50. Intuitively, it seems that Dick has a 50 percent chance of being either an engineer or a lawyer. But this guess completely ignores the underlying odds.

Perhaps it is fortunate that we do at times ignore underlying odds. Were this not the case, how many people would get married in the face of a 50 percent divorce rate?

Exploration: Intuition—Mental Shortcut? Or Dangerous Detour?

Or how many would start high-risk businesses? On the other hand people who smoke, drink and then drive, or skip wearing auto seat belts ignore rather high odds of injury or illness. In many high-risk situations ignoring base rates is the same as thinking you are an exception to the rule.

Framing   Perhaps the most general conclusion from Kahneman and Tversky's work is that the way a problem is stated, or **framed**, affects decisions (Tversky & Kahneman, 1981). As the first example in this discussion revealed, people often give different answers to the same problem posed in slightly different ways. Here's another example of framing:

   When you arrive at a musical concert, you realize that you have lost your $20 ticket. The management cannot issue you a replacement. Would you buy another ticket?

   You arrive at a musical concert to pay for a $20 ticket you previously reserved. As you are about to pay,

you discover that you've lost $20 from your pocket. Would you still buy the ticket? (Assume that you have enough cash left to do so.)

Again, the way a problem is stated affects the choice made. Both problems involve a loss of $20. Yet, most people will buy a ticket after losing $20 in cash but not after losing the ticket. Why? According to Kahneman and Tversky, most people set up a mental account for going to a concert in the first problem and charge it $20. Thus, if you buy another ticket, your concert account will be down $40—which may be more than you are willing to spend. In the second problem, you can charge the lost $20 to some other account such as lunch money or next month's gasoline bill (Mckean, 1985; Tversky & Kahneman, 1981).

   Usually, the broadest way of framing or stating a problem produces the most rational decisions. However, people often state problems in increasingly narrow terms until a single, seemingly "obvious"

answer emerges. For example, to select a career, it would be wise to consider pay, working conditions, job satisfaction, needed skills, future employment outlook, and many other factors. Instead, such decisions are often narrowed to thoughts such as, "I like to write, so I'll be a journalist," "I want to make good money and law pays well," or "I can be creative in photography." Framing decisions so narrowly greatly increases the risk of making a poor choice.

Conclusion   We have discussed only some of the intuitive errors made in the face of uncertainty. The study of intuitive decision making is rapidly finding application to medical diagnosis, business decisions, military strategy, investing and finance, international relations, and more. In each area people are learning to think twice before they decide. With practice you too can learn to spot errors like those described: Remember, shortcuts to answers often short-circuit clear thinking.

Learning Check

1.   Kate is single, outspoken, and very bright. As a college student she was deeply concerned with discrimination and other social issues and participated in several protests. Which statement is more likely:

   a. Kate is a bank teller.
   b. Kate is a bank teller and a feminist.

2.   The probability of two events occurring together is lower than the probability of either one occurring alone.   T or F?

3.   Almost everyone agrees that there are many bad drivers on the road. Almost no one believes that he or she is a bad driver. The second belief ignores the underlying _____ _____ for bad drivers.

4.   Usually, the broadest way of _____ a problem yields the most rational decisions.

Answers: 1. a 2. T 3. base rate 4. framing

Questions for Discussion

1. If you suddenly lost your ability to internally represent problems, what changes would you have to make?
2. In your opinion are chimps that have been trained to use hand signs really using language? Why or why not?
3. Describe a time when you have used imagery to solve a problem. What are the advantages and disadvantages of imagery compared with other units of thought?
4. How do differences in connotative meaning contribute to arguments and misunderstandings? Do you think connotative meaning could or should be standardized?
5. The text implies that animals communicate but do not use language in the human sense. Do you agree? Can you give an example of animal communication that qualifies as language?
6. Think of the most creative person you know. What is that person like? How does he or she differ from your less creative acquaintances?
7. In your opinion should measures of divergent or creative thinking be used to select students for college admission? Why or why not?
8. What effects would you expect the following to have on fantasy: Television? Highly realistic toys? Free or unstructured time? High levels of stress or anxiety? Skits, role taking, or acting? Sensory deprivation? Sensory overload?
9. Can you provide a real-life example of each of Kahneman and Tversky's concepts (representativeness, base rates, and framing)?

Part Four

Actions and Reactions

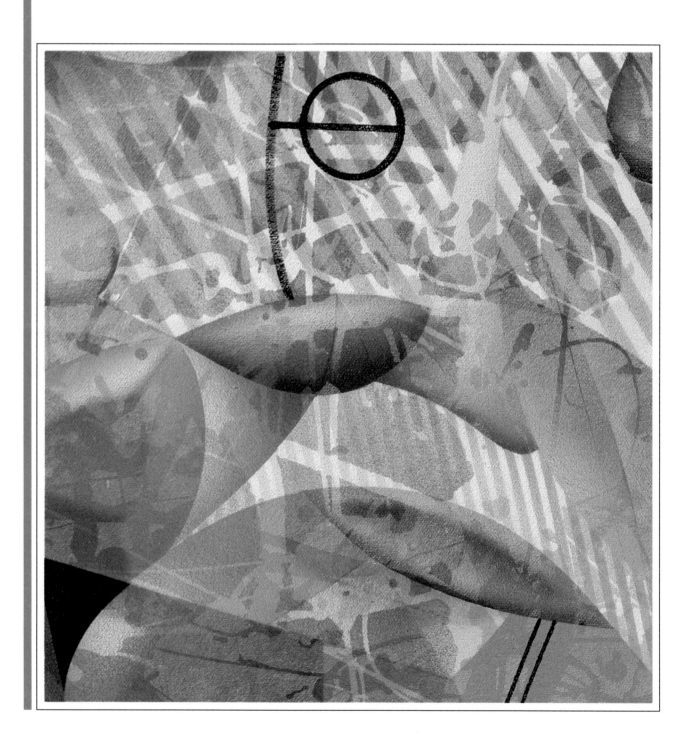

Chapter 12 | Motivation

Chapter Preview

Flight of the *Gossamer Albatross*

What would it feel like to pedal an airplane over the English Channel? In 1979 cyclist Bryan Allen found out the hard way by serving as pilot and "engine" for the first human-powered flight from England to France. Allen pedaled a delicate aircraft, the Gossamer Albatross, *in a grueling 3-hour flight. The flight took Allen to the limits of endurance, as he fought head winds, thirst, leg cramps, and exhaustion. The following excerpts are from Allen's (1979) account:*

> 6:59 A.M. At last, word comes over the radio . . . "We have France in sight—four miles to go . . ."
>
> Four miles or four hundred. I'm fading now and know it. Gradually the head winds have been building up . . . I talk to myself . . . Don't give up now, you *can* do it! As I waver between hope and despair, the radio crackles again:
>
> "Altitude six inches, six inches; get it up, you've got to get it up!"
>
> 7:29 A.M. One mile. Less distance than I had flown *Gossamer Condor* two years before for the original Kremer prize. Then, however, there were no head winds or turbulence, no thirst, no cramps. . . . Despite the cramps, I struggle back up to five feet. "Against all hope," I repeat to myself, "against all hope."
>
> 7:36 A.M. Four hundred yards to shore. . . . One hundred yards now. I am running on reserves I never knew I had. . . .

Motivation   *This chapter is about goals, needs, and the dynamics of behavior. Bryan Allen's final burst of effort ("I am running on reserves I never knew I had") is but one example of highly motivated behavior—behavior ranging from eating and drinking to feats like Allen's historic flight. How do we explain such diversity? The answer is by considering a broad sweep of ideas—from "feeding systems" in the brain to Abraham Maslow's concept of self-actualization. The pages that follow are an introduction to some of the most interesting and useful of these ideas.*

Survey Questions   Are there different types of motives? What causes hunger? Thirst? Overeating? In what ways are pain avoidance and the sex drive unusual? How does arousal relate to motivation? How are motives learned? Are some motives more basic than others? What is intrinsic motivation? Can psychology be applied to dieting? What causes eating disorders?

Resources

Motivation— Forces That Push and Pull

We move. We seek different goals, some more vigorously than others. The same goal may be pursued for different reasons, or different goals may be pursued for the same reasons. We use the concept of motivation to explain each of these basic aspects of behavior. To be more specific, **motivation** refers to "the dynamics of behavior, the process of initiating, sustaining, and directing activities of the organism" (Goldenson, 1970).

Question: Can you clarify that?

Yes. Let's relate the concept of motivation to a simple sequence of activity:

Liz is studying (psychology, of course) in the library. She begins to feel hungry and has difficulty concentrating. Her stomach growls. She grows restless and decides to buy an apple from a vending machine. The machine is empty, so she goes to the cafeteria. Closed. She returns to the library, packs up her books, and drives home, where she prepares a meal and eats. At last her hunger is satisfied, and she again resumes studying.

Liz's food seeking was *initiated* by her bodily need for food; it was *sustained* because her need was not immediately met; and her activities were *directed* by possible sources of food. Notice too that her food seeking was *terminated* by achieving her goal.

A Model of Motivation   Many motivated activities can be thought of as beginning with a **need**. The need that initiated Liz's search was a depletion of necessary substances within the cells of her body. Needs cause a psychological state or feeling called a **drive** to develop. (In Liz's case the drive was hunger.) Drives activate a **response** (or a series of actions) designed to attain a **goal** that will satisfy the need. Meeting the need temporarily ends the motivational sequence. Thus, a simple model of motivation can be shown in this way:

Question: Why use the terms "need" and "drive"? Aren't they the same thing?

Both terms are necessary because the strength of needs and drives can differ. If you were to begin fasting, your bodily need for food would increase daily, but you would probably be less "hungry" on the seventh day than you were on the first. Your need steadily increases, but the hunger drive comes and goes.

Before we assume that we have a complete model of motivation, let us observe Liz's eating behavior on another occasion:

For dinner, Liz has just eaten soup, salad, a large steak, a large baked potato, one-half of a loaf of bread, two pieces of cheesecake, and four cups of coffee. After the meal she remarks about her discomfort from overeating. Soon after, Liz's roommate arrives with a strawberry pie. Liz exclaims that strawberry pie is her favorite dessert and proceeds to eat three good-sized pieces and has a cup of coffee to wash them down.

Is this hunger? Certainly we can believe that Liz's extra large meal was enough to satisfy her biological needs for food.

Question: How does that change the model of motivation?

The story illustrates that motivated behavior can be energized by the "pull" of external stimuli as well as by the "push" of internal needs. The pull exerted by a goal is called its **incentive value.** Some goals are so desirable (strawberry pie, for example) that they motivate behavior in the absence of internal need. Other goals are so low in incentive value that they will be rejected even though they might meet the internal need. Fresh, live grubworms, for instance, are considered a delicacy in some parts of the world, but it is doubtful that the average American could eat one no matter how hungry he or she might be.

In most instances it is helpful to recognize that actions are energized by a combination of internal needs *and* external incentives, and that a strong state of need may make a less attractive incentive into a desirable goal. You may never have eaten a grubworm, but chances are good that you have eaten some pretty horrible "leftovers" when the refrigerator was bare. Incentives also help account for motives that do not seem to have any identifiable internal need, such as drives for success, status, or approval (see Fig. 12–1).

Types of Motives   For the purpose of study, motives can be divided into three major categories:

Fig. 12–1 *Needs and incentives interact to determine drive strength (top). (a) Moderate need, combined with a high-incentive goal, produces a strong drive. (b) Even when a strong need exists, drive strength may be moderate if a goal's incentive value is low. It is important to remember, however, that incentive value lies "in the eye of the beholder" (photo). No matter how hungry, few people would be able to eat the pictured grub worms.*

1. **Primary motives** are based on biological needs that must be met for survival. The most important primary motives are hunger, thirst, pain avoidance, and needs for air, sleep, elimination of wastes, and regulation of body temperature. Primary motives are innate.
2. **Stimulus motives** also appear to be innate, but they are not necessary for mere survival of the organism.

Their purpose seems to be to provide the nervous system with useful information and stimulation. The stimulus motives include activity, curiosity, exploration, manipulation, and physical contact.

3. **Learned, or secondary, motives** account for the great diversity of human activities suggested by the Chapter Preview. Behavior like Bryan Allen's flight over the English Channel is probably best understood in terms of learned motives or goals. Many secondary motives are related to acquired needs for power, affiliation (the need to be with others), approval, status, security, and achievement. The important motives of fear and aggression also appear to be subject to learning.

Primary Motives and Homeostasis— Keeping the Home Fires Burning

How important is food in your life? Water? Sleep? Air? Temperature regulation? For most of us, satisfying these biological needs is so habitual we tend to overlook how much of our behavior they actually direct. But exaggerate any of these needs through famine, shipwreck, poverty, near-drowning, or exposure, and their powerful grip on behavior becomes evident. We are, after all, still animals in many ways.

Biological drives are essential because they maintain **homeostasis** (HOE-me-oh-STAY-sis), or bodily equilibrium (Cannon, 1932).

Question: What is homeostasis?

The term *homeostasis* means standing steady, or steady state. Within the body there are "ideal" levels for body temperature, for concentration of various chemicals in the blood, for blood pressure, and so forth. When the body deviates from these ideal levels, automatic reactions restore equilibrium. You might find it helpful to think of the homeostatic mechanisms as being similar in operation to a *thermostat* set at a particular temperature.

A (Very) Short Course on Thermostats

If room temperature falls below the level set on a thermostat, the heat is automatically turned on to warm the room. When the heat equals or slightly exceeds the ideal temperature, it is automatically turned off. In this way room temperature is maintained in a state of equilibrium hovering around the ideal level.

In the human body the first reactions to disequilibrium are also automatic. For example, if you become too hot, blood flow to body surfaces is increased and perspiring begins, thus lowering body temperature. We become aware of the need to maintain homeostasis only when driven by continued disequilibrium to seek shade, warmth, food, or water.

Since hunger is one of the most interesting and better understood of the primary drives, we will examine it in detail before we discuss biological drives in general. Before reading more you may find it helpful to complete the Learning Check that follows.

Learning Check

1. Motives _____, sustain, and _____ activities.
2. Needs provide the _____ of motivation, whereas incentives provide the _____.

Classify the following needs or motives by placing the correct letter in the blank.

A. Primary motive   **B.** Stimulus motive   **C.** Secondary motive

3. ____ curiosity   6. ____ thirst
4. ____ status   7. ____ achievement
5. ____ sleep   8. ____ physical contact
9. The maintenance of bodily equilibrium is called thermostasis.   T or F?
10. A goal high in incentive value may create a drive in the absence of any internal need.   T or F?

Answers: 1. initiate, direct   2. push, pull   3. B   4. C   5. A   6. A   7. C   8. B   9. F   10. T

Hunger— Pardon Me, That's Just My Hypothalamus Growling

Question: What causes hunger?

When you feel hungry, you probably associate a desire for food with sensations from your stomach. This, sensibly enough, is where the search for hunger began. In an early study Cannon and Washburn (1912) decided to see if the contractions of an empty stomach cause hunger. To do this, Washburn trained himself to swallow a balloon. Once it was in his stomach, the balloon was inflated through an attached tube so that stomach contractions could be recorded (see Fig. 12–2). Cannon and Washburn observed that when Washburn's stomach contracted, he felt "hunger pangs." They concluded that hunger is nothing more than stomach contractions.

Later research contradicted this conclusion. Perhaps you already guessed that something more than the stomach is involved in hunger. Many people experience hunger as an overall feeling of weakness or shakiness that does not seem to be associated with the stomach. And, while eating *is* limited when the stomach is distended (full), it can be

shown that the stomach is not essential for experiencing hunger.

Question: How has that been demonstrated?

For one thing, cutting the sensory nerves from the stomach (so that the stomach sensations can no longer be felt) does not abolish hunger. Even more convincing is the fact that many people have had their stomachs removed surgically. These people continue to feel hungry and to eat regularly. It would seem that some *central* factor must be the cause of hunger. One important element now appears to be the level of sugar in the blood. If insulin is injected in a human, it produces **hypoglycemia** (HI-po-gli-SEE-me-ah: low blood sugar) and stimulates feelings of hunger and stomach contractions (Hoyenga & Hoyenga, 1984). Strange as it may seem, the liver may also affect hunger.

Question: The liver?

Yes, the liver. Recent evidence suggests that the liver responds to a lack of bodily "fuel" by sending nerve impulses to the brain, thus triggering the desire to eat (Friedman & Stricker, 1976).

Question: What part of the brain controls hunger?

Fig. 12–2 *In Cannon's early study of hunger, a simple apparatus was used to simultaneously record hunger pangs and stomach contractions. (After Cannon, 1934.)*

When you are hungry, many brain areas are affected, so no single "hunger center" exists. However, one of the most important areas for the control of hunger is the **hypothalamus** (HI-po-THAL-ah-mus), a small structure near the base of the brain (see Fig. 12–3).

Cells in the hypothalamus are sensitive to levels of sugar (and perhaps other substances) in the blood. The hypothalamus also receives messages from the liver and the stomach (Hoyenga & Hoyenga, 1984). These messages combine to produce hunger. One area of the hypothalamus acts somewhat like a **feeding system**. If the *lateral hypothalamus* is activated electrically, even a well-fed animal will immediately begin eating. (The term *lateral* simply means the sides of the hypothalamus.) If the same area

Fig. 12–3 *Location of the hypothalamus in the human brain.*

Hypothalamus

is destroyed, the animal will refuse to eat and will die if not force-fed (Anand & Brobeck, 1951).

A second area within the hypothalamus seems to serve as a **satiety system** (or "stop system") for eating. If the *ventromedial hypothalamus* is destroyed, dramatic overeating results. (*Ventromedial* refers to the bottom middle of the hypothalamus.) Rats with such damage overeat to the point of total obesity. Some balloon up to weights of 1,000 grams or more and get so large that they can barely move (see Fig. 12–4). A normal rat weighs about 180 grams. To picture this weight change in human terms, envision someone you know who weighs 180 pounds growing to a weight of 1,000 pounds!

It should come as no surprise that there is more to hunger than simple "start" and "stop" systems in the brain. Recent evidence suggests that fat stored in the body also influences hunger. The body acts as if there is a **set point** for the *proportion* of body fat that is maintained (Le Magnen, 1980). That is, the set point acts like a "thermostat" for body fat. Your personal set point is the weight you maintain when you are making no effort to gain or lose weight. When your body goes below its set point, you are likely to feel hungry most of the time (Friedman & Stricker, 1976).

Question: Do people have different set points?

Yes. The set point appears to be partly inherited and partly determined by early feeding patterns. Persons with overweight parents are much more likely to be overweight themselves. Also, the set point may be lastingly altered when a child is overfed. If a weight problem begins in childhood, the person will, as an adult, have *more* fat cells and *larger* fat cells in the body. If the person does not become overweight until adulthood, his or her fat cells will be larger, but their number usually does not increase. Thus, when a weight problem begins in childhood, it is much more difficult to control.

Question: Why do people overeat?

Obesity   Set points are only one piece in a complex puzzle that scientists are still trying to solve. Their search is fueled by the fact that obesity is a major health risk and, for many, a source of social stigma and low self-esteem (Brownell, 1982).

Perhaps if eating were controlled only by internal needs, fewer people would overeat. As noted earlier, however, the sight or aroma of food often makes people want to eat, even when they do not feel hungry. It seems that many people are sensitive to **external eating cues** (signs and signals linked with food) (Rodin, 1978). If you are sensitive to external cues, you are most likely to eat when food is attractive, highly visible, and easy to obtain (Schachter & Rodin, 1974).

Even the time of day can influence eating. In one intriguing experiment subjects were allowed to nibble on some crackers while waiting in a room. On the wall was a clock that could be adjusted to run fast or slow. When obese subjects were led to believe it was closer to mealtime than it actually was (fast clock), they ate more crackers than when they thought dinnertime was farther away than it actually was (slow clock). Subjects of normal weight *decreased* their eating when they thought it was closer to mealtime (Schachter & Gross, 1968). When the clock read 5 minutes after 6, the reaction of fat subjects seems to have been, "Hmm, dinnertime, I must be hungry!"

Question: Does that mean that people who are overweight are more sensitive to external eating cues?

Until recently, the obese were thought to be "externally cued eaters." Lean people, in contrast, were assumed to be better attuned to internal hunger signals. Unfortunately, this idea is now recognized as too simple. People of all weights can be found who are unusually sensitive to external eating cues, so this is not strictly a problem of the obese (Rodin, 1981). Just the same, eating cues do appear to be a factor in some overeating. For example, psychologist Judith Rodin found that externally responsive girls were most likely to gain weight at a 2-month summer camp (Rodin, 1978).

It is highly likely that **diet** also contributes to overeating. Placing animals on a "supermarket" diet, for instance, can lead to gross obesity. In one experiment, rats were

Fig. 12–4   *Damage to the hunger-satiety system in the hypothalamus can produce a very fat rat, a condition called hypothalamic hyperphagia (overeating). This rat weighs 1080 grams. (The pointer has gone completely around the dial and beyond.) (Photo courtesy of Neal Miller.)*

given meals of chocolate chip cookies, salami, cheese, bananas, marshmallows, milk chocolate, peanut butter, and fat. Rats on this diet gained almost three times as much weight as controls who ate only standard laboratory rat chow (Sclafani & Springer, 1976). (Rat chow is a dry mixture of several bland foods. If you were a rat, you'd probably eat more cookies than rat chow too!) We humans also appear to be sensitive to dietary content. In general *sweetness*, high *fat content*, and *variety* tend to encourage overeating (Ball & Grinker, 1981). It seems that our culture may provide the worst possible kinds of foods for those with a tendency toward obesity.

It is tempting to assume that fatness comes from constant overeating, but this is a myth. Studies by Albert Stunkard (1980) and Judith Rodin (1978) show that overeating occurs mainly when a person is gaining weight. Once excess weight is gained, it can be maintained with a normal diet. Theoretically, it takes only 100 extra calories a day to gain 10 pounds in a year. This amounts to one extra muffin, one pear, one cup of soup, or one small piece of cheese per day (Bennet & Gurin, 1982). An

Ψ Highlight 12–1
The Dieter's Dilemma

If dieting works, why are hundreds of "new" diets published each year? The answer is that while dieters do lose weight, most regain it soon after the diet ends. Indeed, many people experience a rebound that can push weight higher than before the diet began. Why should this be so? Many theorists now believe that dieting (starving) alters the physiology of the body. In effect, dieting causes the body to become highly efficient at *conserving* calories and storing them as fat (Bennet & Gurin, 1982; Hoyenga & Hoyenga, 1984).

Apparently, evolution has prepared us to save energy when food is scarce and to stock up on fat when food is plentiful. Briefly starving yourself, therefore, may have little lasting effect on weight. To avoid ineffectively bouncing between feast and famine requires a change in basic eating habits—a topic covered in this chapter's Applications.

added problem is that as people gain weight, many reduce their activity level and burn fewer calories. As a result some overweight persons may continue to gain weight while consuming fewer calories than their slimmer neighbors (Ball & Grinker, 1981).

Question: Is it true that people also overeat when they are emotionally upset?

Yes. People with weight problems are just as likely to eat when they are anxious, angry, bored, or distressed as when hungry (Bruch, 1973; Hoyenga & Hoyenga, 1984). Furthermore, unhappiness often accompanies obesity in our fat-conscious culture (Rodin, 1978). The result is a pattern of overeating that leads to emotional distress and still more overeating, making weight control extremely difficult.

To summarize, overeating is the result of a complex interplay of internal and external influences, diet, emotions, genetics, exercise, and many other factors (Rodin, 1978). To answer the question we began with, people become obese in different ways and for different reasons. Clearly, scientists are still a long way from winning the "battle of the bulge." (For another perspective on overeating, see Highlight 12–1.)

Other Factors in Hunger

As research on overeating suggests, "hunger" is affected by more than bodily needs for food. Let us consider some additional factors of interest.

Cultural Factors Learning to think of some foods as desirable and others as revolting obviously has much to do with eating habits. In America we would never consider eating the eyes out of the steamed head of a monkey, but in some parts of the world this dish is considered a real delicacy. By the same token our willingness to consume large quantities of meat, to eat cows, and to cook fish would be considered barbaric in many cultures. Thus, **cultural values** greatly affect the incentive value of various foods.

Taste Even tastes for "normal" foods may vary considerably. One experiment demonstrated that the hungrier a person is, the more pleasant a sweet food tastes (Cabanac & Duclaux, 1970). It is also interesting to note that a **taste aversion** can be easily learned if a food causes sickness, or if it is eaten just before nausea is caused by something else (Nachman, 1970). Not only will such foods be avoided, they too can become nauseating. A friend of the author's, who once became ill after eating a cheese Danish (well, actually, *several*), has never again been able to come face to face with this delightful pastry.

Question: If getting sick occurs long after eating, how does it become associated with the food eaten?

A good question. Taste aversions are a type of classical conditioning. And, as stated in Chapter 8, a long time delay usually prevents conditioning. For this reason psychologists theorize that there is a biological tendency to associate an upset stomach with food eaten earlier. Such learning usually helps protect both animals and people (Garcia et al., 1974). Yet, sadly, many human cancer patients suffer taste aversions long after the nausea of their drug treatment has passed (Bernstein, 1978).

If you like animals, you will be interested in an imaginative approach to an age-old problem. In many parts of the country, predators are poisoned, trapped, or shot on sight by livestock owners. These practices have virtually extinguished the timber wolf, and in some areas the coyote faces a similar end. How might the coyote be saved, without an unacceptable loss of livestock?

In a now classic experiment, coyotes were given lamb tainted with lithium chloride. Coyotes who took the bait rapidly became nauseated and vomited. After one or two such treatments, they developed **bait shyness**—a lasting distaste for the tainted food (Gustavson & Garcia, 1974). If applied consistently, taste aversion conditioning might solve many predator-livestock problems at less expense than traditional methods (Fig. 12–5). Perhaps this technique could even be used to protect roadrunners from the Wiley Coyote!

Specific Hungers Evidence exists that animals and people are able to develop **specific hungers** for nutritional substances lacking in their diet. For example, if animals are made ill by being deprived of vitamin B, they develop a marked preference for foods containing this essential vitamin (Scott & Verrey, 1947).

Question: Then do humans have specific hungers?

There is some direct evidence of specific hungers occurring in humans, particularly in children. In one classic experiment on **self-selection feeding,** human infants were given a daily "cafeteria" choice of foods. Over a period of several months they selected a balanced diet, and their health and growth were normal (Davis, 1928). In fact one child who began the study suffering from rickets voluntarily drank large amounts of foul-tasting cod-liver oil and apparently cured himself of his nutritional disease.

It should be noted, however, that the "wisdom of the body" is actually fairly limited. In the experiment described, the babies could only select from nutritious foods. If candy had been a choice, they might not have done so well. Even by early childhood, learned food preferences tend to override specific hungers, so that poor diets of sweets and junk food are not uncommon in our society.

Primary Motives Revisited— The Strange Case of Sex and Pain

The pattern we have observed in the control of hunger is similar to that found for most of the other primary motives. For example, thirst is only partially related to dryness of the mouth and throat. When drugs are used to keep the mouth constantly wet or dry, thirst and water intake remain normal. Like hunger, thirst appears to be controlled through the hypothalamus, where separate *thirst* and *thirst-satiety* systems are found. Also like hunger, thirst is strongly affected by individual learning and by cultural values.

Question: Is there such a thing as a "specific thirst"?

In a sense there is. Before the body can retain water, minerals lost through perspiration (mainly salt) must be re-

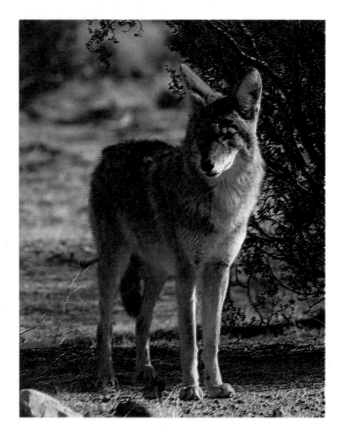

Fig. 12–5 *Like humans and other animals, coyotes develop taste aversions when food is associated with nausea.*

placed. Therefore, animals develop a marked preference for salt water when their salt levels are lowered experimentally (Carlson, 1981).

You may not have noticed, but there are actually two kinds of thirst. **Extracellular thirst** occurs when there is a loss of water from the fluids surrounding the cells of your body. Bleeding, vomiting, diarrhea, sweating, and drinking alcohol cause this type of thirst (Houston, 1985). When a person loses both water and minerals in any of these ways—especially by perspiring—a slightly salty liquid may be more satisfying than plain water. Among some nomadic peoples of the Sahara Desert, blood is a highly prized beverage, perhaps because of its saltiness. (Maybe they should try Gatorade?)

A second type of thirst occurs when you eat a salty meal. In this instance your body does not lose fluid. Instead, an increase in salt causes fluid to be drawn out of cells. As the cells "shrink," **intracellular thirst** is triggered. Thirst of this type is best quenched by plain water.

The drives for food, water, air, sleep, and elimination are all fairly similar in that they are generated by a combination of activities in the body and the brain, are modified by learning and culture, and are influenced by external factors. Two of the primary drives are unlike the others. These are the sex drive and the drive to avoid pain. Each differs from the other primary drives in some interesting ways.

Question: How is the drive to avoid pain different?

Pain   Drives such as hunger, thirst, and sleepiness come and go in a fairly regular cycle each day. Pain, by contrast, is an **episodic drive** (ep-ih-SOD-ik). That is, it occurs in distinct episodes, since it is aroused only when damage to the tissues of the body takes place. Most of the primary drives cause a person to actively seek a desired goal (food, drink, sleep, and so forth). The pain drive has as its goal the avoidance or elimination of pain.

The desire to end pain seems so basic that it may come as a surprise that avoiding pain appears to be partially learned. This fact was demonstrated by a study in which dogs were totally isolated (in special cages) from the normal bumps, bites, and other pains of puppyhood. As adults the dogs reacted strangely to pain. For example, when a lighted match was held near their noses, many pushed toward it as if they felt no pain (Melzack & Scott, 1957). Apparently, the dogs had not learned the meaning of pain or how to avoid it.

Human pain avoidance is also affected by learning. Some people, for instance, feel they must be "tough" and not show any discomfort; others complain loudly at the smallest ache or pain. As you might expect, the first attitude raises pain tolerance, and the second lowers it (Klienke, 1978). Such attitudes explain why members of some societies endure cutting, burning, whipping, tatooing, and piercing of the skin that would agonize the typical American.

The Sex Drive   Sexual motivation is quite unusual compared with other biological motives. In fact many psychologists do not think of sex as a primary motive because sex (contrary to anything your personal experience might suggest) is not necessary for *individual* survival. It is necessary, of course, for *group* survival among humans and other creatures.

In lower animals the sex drive is directly related to the action of bodily hormones. Females of the lower species are only interested in mating when their fertility cycle is in the stage of **estrus,** or "heat" (caused by secretion of the hormone **estrogen** into the bloodstream). Hormones are important in the male animal as well. In most lower animals castration will abolish the sex drive. But in contrast to the female, the normal male animal is always ready to mate. His sex drive is primarily aroused by the behavior of a receptive female. In animals, mating is therefore closely tied to the fertility cycle of the female.

Question: How much do hormones affect the sex drive in humans?

The link between hormones and the sex drive grows weaker as we ascend the biological scale. Hormones do affect the human sex drive but only to a limited degree. For example, one careful study found no connection between female sexual activity and the monthly menstrual cycle (Udry & Morris, 1977). In humans, mental, cultural, and emotional factors determine sexual expression. However, our liberation from hormones is not total. Human males show a loss of sex drive after castration, and some women lose sexual desire when using birth control pills (McCauley & Ehrhardt, 1976).

Human sexual behavior and attitudes are discussed in detail in Chapter 24. For now it is enough to note that the sex drive is largely **nonhomeostatic.** In humans the sex drive can be aroused at virtually any time by almost anything. It therefore shows no clear relationship to deprivation (the amount of time since the drive was last satisfied). True, an increase in desire may occur as time passes. But on the other hand recent sexual activity does not prevent sexual desire from occurring again. The sex drive is also unusual in that its arousal is as actively sought as its reduction.

The nonhomeostatic quality of the sex drive can be shown in this way: An animal is allowed to copulate until it seems to have no further interest in sexual behavior. Then a new sexual partner is provided. Immediately the animal resumes sexual activity. This pattern is called the *Coolidge effect* after former United States President Calvin Coolidge. What, you might ask, does Calvin Coolidge have to do with the sex drive? The answer is found in the following story. While touring an experimental farm, Coolidge's wife reportedly asked if a rooster mated just once a day. "No, ma'am," she was told, "he mates dozens of times each day." "Tell that to the president," she said, with a faraway look in her eyes. When President Coolidge reached the same part of the tour, his wife's message was given to him. His reaction was to ask if the dozens of matings were with the same hen. No, he was told, different hens were involved. "Tell *that* to Mrs. Coolidge," the president is said to have replied.

Learning Check

1. Systems for the control of hunger and thirst are found in the _____ of the brain.

2. The satiety system in the hypothalamus signals the body to start eating when it receives signals from the liver or detects changes in blood sugar.   T or F?

3. Varied diets containing high levels of sweets and fats tend to encourage overeating only for people who tend to eat when they are anxious.   T or F?

4. Bait shyness occurs when:
   - *a.* a specific hunger develops
   - *b.* the set point for body fat is altered
   - *c.* the hypothalamus is activated electrically
   - *d.* a taste aversion is formed

5. If an animal is deprived of a necessary food substance, the animal may develop a/an: (circle)

   taste aversion   estrus drive   specific hunger

6. Thirst may be either intracellular or _____.

7. Pain avoidance is an _____ drive.

8. Sexual behavior in animals is largely controlled by estrogen levels in the female and the occurrence of estrus in the male.   T or F?

Answers: 1. hypothalamus   2. F   3. F   4. d   5. specific hunger   6. extracellular   7. episodic   8. F

Stimulus Needs—Skydiving, Horror Movies, and the Fun Zone

"Curiosity killed the cat," is sometimes said, but nothing could be further from the truth. Drives for **exploration**, **manipulation**, or simply for **curiosity** seem to exist in most animals. As mentioned earlier, such drives might be explained by the life-and-death necessity of keeping track of sources of food, danger, and other important details of the environment. However, the curiosity drives seem to go beyond such needs.

Monkey Business

In an experiment, monkeys confined to a dimly lit box learned to perform a simple task to open a window that allowed them to view the outside world (Butler & Harlow, 1954). In a similar experiment, monkeys quickly learned to solve a mechanical puzzle made up of interlocking metal pins, hooks, and hasps (Butler, 1954) (see Fig. 12–6). In both situations no external reward was offered for exploration or manipulation.

The monkeys described seemed to work for the sheer fun of it. An interest in video games, chess, puzzles, Rubick's cube, and the like offers a human parallel. Curiosity, the drive to *know*, also seems to be powerful in humans. Scientific investigation, intellectual curiosity, and other advanced activities may be an extension of this basic drive.

Closely related to curiosity is the need for sensory stimulation. It is now well established that humans and animals demand and actively seek stimulation (Reykowski, 1982). As discussed in Chapter 6, people who have undergone prolonged or severe **sensory deprivation**—for ex-

Fig. 12–6 *Monkeys happily open locks that are placed in their cage. Since no reward is given for this activity, it provides evidence of the existence of stimulus needs. (Photo courtesy of Harry F. Harlow.)*

ample, prisoners, arctic explorers, radar operators, and truck drivers—often report sensory distortions and disturbed thinking. The nervous system seems to require varied, patterned stimulation in order to respond normally (Suedfeld, 1975).

The drive for stimulation can even be observed in infants. When babies are shown patterns of varying complexity (Fig. 12–7), they spend more time looking at complex patterns than at simpler ones (Berlyne, 1966). Indeed, human infants seem to have an almost limitless appetite for stimulation. By the time a child can walk, there are few things in the home that have not been tasted, touched, viewed, handled, or, in the case of toys, destroyed!

Question: Are stimulus needs homeostatic?

Arousal Theory

Some psychologists would argue that they are not. However, by relating drives for stimulation to the concept of homeostasis, we get a useful model for understanding many human activities. This position, called the **arousal theory** of motivation, assumes that there is an ideal level of arousal for various activities and that individuals behave in ways that keep arousal near this ideal level (Hebb, 1966).

Fig. 12–7 *Berlyne studied curiosity in infants by showing them these designs. Babies looked first at the more complex patterns on the right. (From Science 153:25–33. Copyright © 1966 by the American Association for the Advancement of Science.)*

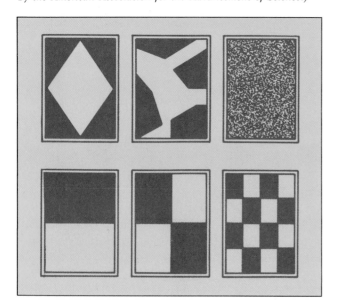

Question: What do you mean by "arousal"?

Arousal refers to variations in activation of the body and the nervous system. Arousal is zero at death; it is low during sleep; it is moderate during daily activities; and it is high at times of excitement, emotion, or panic. Arousal theory assumes that an individual becomes uncomfortable when arousal is too low (as when a person is bored) or when it is too high (as might be the case during intense fear, anxiety, or panic). Curiosity and the drive to seek stimulation can be interpreted as an attempt to raise the level of arousal when it is too low. Most adults seem to vary their activities to maintain a comfortable level of activation. Music, parties, athletics, conversation, sleep, and many other activities may be mixed to keep arousal at moderate levels, thus preventing both boredom and overstimulation.

Question: Do people vary in their needs for stimulation?

Sensation Seekers   The city dweller who visits the country complains that it is "too quiet," and seeks some "action." The country dweller finds the city "hectic," "overwhelming," or "too much," and seeks peace and quiet. The arousal theory of motivation also assumes that the ideal level of arousal varies from one person to the next and that individuals learn to seek a particular arousal level.

Marvin Zuckerman has devised a test to measure such differences. The *Sensation-Seeking Scale* (SSS), as he calls it, includes statements like the samples shown here (from Zuckerman et al., 1978).

Thrill and Adventure Seeking

I would like to try parachute jumping.
I think I would enjoy the sensations of skiing very fast down a high mountain slope.

Experience Seeking

I like to explore a strange city or section of town myself, even if it means getting lost.
I like to try new foods that I have never tasted before.

Disinhibition

I like wild, "uninhibited" parties.
I often like to get high (drinking liquor or smoking marijuana).

Boredom Susceptibility

I can't stand watching a movie that I've seen before.
I like people who are sharp and witty, even if they do sometimes insult others.

People who score high on the full-length version of this test tend to be extroverted, independent individuals who value change and stimulation (Fig. 12–8). In addition high scorers are more likely to smoke and to prefer spicy, sour, and crunchy foods over blander foods. Low sensation seekers are orderly, nurturant, giving, and enjoy the company of others (Zuckerman, 1978). Which are you? (Most people fall somewhere in between.)

Question: Is there an ideal level of arousal?

Levels of Arousal   Discounting individual differences, performance of a task is usually best when arousal is moderate. Let's say that you have to take an essay exam in one of your classes. If you are sleepy or feeling lazy (arousal level too low), your performance will suffer. If you are in a state of anxiety or panic about the test (arousal level too high), you will also perform below par. This relationship between arousal and efficiency of behavior can be expressed as an **inverted U function** (see Fig. 12–9). At very low levels of arousal, the body is not sufficiently energized to perform effectively. With increased arousal, performance continues to improve up to the middle regions of the curve; then it begins to drop off as an individual becomes emotional, frenzied, or disorganized. Such disorganization might occur if you were trying to start a car stalled on a railroad track, with a speeding train bearing down on you.

Question: Is performance always best at moderate levels of arousal?

No, the optimal level of arousal depends on the complexity of the task to be performed. For simple tasks, greater activation runs little risk of disorganizing performance. If a task is relatively *simple*, the optimal level of arousal will be *high*. When a task is more *complex*, the best performance occurs at *low* levels of arousal. This relationship is

Fig. 12–8   *Thrill seeking is an element of the sensation-seeking personality.*

called the **Yerkes-Dodson law** (see Fig. 12–9). It applies to a wide variety of tasks and to measures of motivation other than arousal.

Some examples of the Yerkes-Dodson law in operation might be helpful. At a track meet it is almost impossible for a sprinter to get too aroused for a race. The task is direct and uncomplicated: Run as fast as you can for a short distance. On the other hand a golfer making the last putt in an important tournament faces a more sensitive and complex task, as does a basketball player making a game-deciding free throw. Excessive arousal is almost certain to hurt such performances. In school most students have had experience with "test anxiety" as a familiar example of the effects of excessive arousal on performance.

Fig. 12–9   (a) *The general relationship between arousal and efficiency can be described by an inverted U curve. The optimal level of arousal or motivation is higher for a simple task* (b) *than for a complex task* (c).

(a) Inverted U function

(b) Simple task

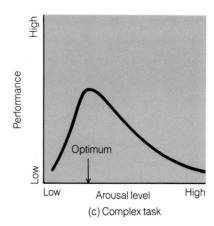

(c) Complex task

Question: Then is it true that by learning to calm down, a person would do better on tests?

Usually, but not always. Studies of anxious students show that they typically are most anxious when they don't know the material. If this is the case, calming down simply means you will remain calm while failing. One of the best ways to overcome test anxiety is to be overprepared (Spielberger et al., 1976). (For more information on test anxiety, see the Exploration in Chapter 14.)

Learned Motives— Cheap Thrills and the Pursuit of Excellence

Many motives are acquired directly. It is easy enough to see that praise, money, success, pleasure, and similar reinforcers affect our goals and desires. But how do people learn to enjoy activities that are at first painful or frightening? Why do people climb rocks, jump out of air-

Fig. 12–10 *A sport parachutist takes the plunge. The typical emotional sequence for a first jump is: anxiety before, terror during, and relief after the jump. After many jumps the emotional sequence becomes: eagerness before, a thrill during, and exhilaration after a jump. The new sequence strongly reinforces skydiving.*

planes, run marathons, take sauna baths, or swim in frozen lakes? For an answer let's examine a related situation.

When a person first tries a drug such as heroin, he or she feels a "rush" of pleasure. However, as the drug wears off, a period of discomfort or craving occurs. The easiest way to end the discomfort is to take another dose of the drug—as most drug users quickly learn. But in time habituation takes place; the drug stops producing pleasure, although it will end discomfort. At the same time, the after-effects of the drug grow more painful. At this point the drug user has acquired a powerful new motive. In a vicious cycle, heroin relieves discomfort, but it guarantees that the withdrawal will occur again in a few hours.

Psychologist Richard Solomon (1980) offers an intriguing explanation for drug addiction and other learned motives. According to his **opponent-process theory,** if a stimulus causes strong emotion, such as fear or pleasure, an opposite emotion tends to occur when the stimulus ends. For example, if you are in pain, and the pain ends, you will feel a pleasant sense of relief. If you feel pleasure, as in drug use, and the pleasure ends, it will be followed by craving or discomfort. If you are in love and feel good when you are with your lover, you will be uncomfortable when he or she is absent.

Question: What happens if the stimulus is repeated?

Solomon assumes that when a stimulus is repeated, our response to it habituates, or gets weaker. First-time skydivers, for instance, are almost always terrified. But with repeated jumps, fear lessens, until finally the skydiver feels a thrill instead of terror. In contrast, emotional after-effects get stronger with repetition. After a first jump, beginning parachutists experience a brief but exhilarating sense of relief. After many such experiences, seasoned skydivers can get a "rush" of euphoria that lasts for hours after a jump (see Fig. 12–10). With repetition, the pleasurable after-effect gets stronger and the initial "cost" (pain or fear) gets weaker. The opponent-process theory thus explains how skydiving, rock climbing, ski jumping, and other hazardous pursuits become reinforcing. If you are a fan of horror movies or of carnival rides, your motives may be based on the same effect.

Social Motives

Competition and achievement are highly valued in American culture. In less industrialized nations the desire to achieve may be minimal. Some of your friends are more interested than others in success, money, possessions, status, love, approval, grades, dominance, power, or belonging to groups. In each case we are referring to differences in **social motives** or goals. Social motives are acquired in complex ways through socialization and cultural conditioning. The behavior of outstanding artists, scientists, athletes, educators, and leaders is best understood in terms of such learned needs, particularly the need for achievement.

The **need for achievement (nAch)** is certainly not the only social motive of importance, but it is a prominent motive in American culture. To many people, being "motivated" means being interested in achievement. In other chapters we will investigate the motives behind aggression, love, affiliation, and seeking approval. For now, let us focus on the need for achievement.

The need for achievement can be defined as a desire to meet some *internalized standard of excellence* (McClelland, 1961). The person with high needs for achievement strives to do well in any situation in which evaluation takes place.

Question: Is that like the aggressive businessperson who strives for success?

Not necessarily. Needs for achievement may lead to material wealth and prestige, but a person who is a high achiever in art, music, science, or amateur athletics may be striving for excellence without concern for material reward. The need for achievement differs from a **need for power,** which is a desire to have *impact* or control over others (McClelland, 1975). People with strong needs for power want their importance to be visible: They buy expensive possessions, read flashy magazines, and try to exploit relationships.

David McClelland (1958, 1961) and a number of other psychologists have been interested in the effects of high or low needs for achievement. Using a simple measure of nAch, McClelland found that he could predict the behavior of high and low achievers in many situations. In one study, for example, the occupations of college graduates were compared with scores on a need for achievement test given in their sophomore year. Fourteen years after graduation, those who scored high in nAch were found more often in careers involving an element of risk and responsibility than were those with low nAch scores (McClelland, 1965). Interestingly, scores for achievement motivation have declined for students in recent years (Lueptow, 1980). Some psychologists believe this may help account for the dramatic decline in *Scholastic Aptitude Test* scores observed in the last decade (Hoyenga & Hoyenga, 1984).

Characteristics of Achievers In front of you are five targets placed at various distances from where you are

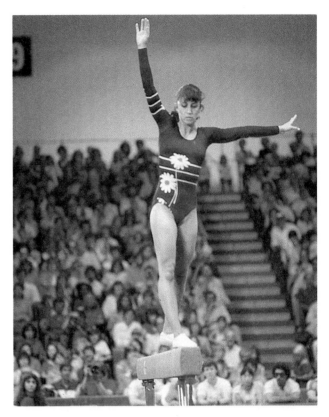

Fig. 12–11 *The person with high needs for achievement strives to do well in any situation in which evaluation takes place.*

standing. You are given a beanbag to toss at the target of your choice. Target A, anyone can hit; target B, most people can hit; target C, some people can hit; target D, very few people can hit; target E is rarely if ever hit. If you hit A, you will receive $2; B, $4; C, $8; D, $16; and E, $32. You get only one toss. Which one would you choose? McClelland's research suggests that if you have a high need for achievement, you will select C or perhaps D.

Those high in nAch are *moderate* risk takers. When faced with a problem or challenge, persons high in nAch avoid goals that are too easy because such goals offer no sense of satisfaction. They also avoid long shots because there is no hope of success or because if success occurs, it will be due to luck rather than skill. Persons low in nAch select either sure things or impossible goals. Either way, there is no risk of personal responsibility for failure.

Desires for achievement and calculated risk taking are converted into successful performances of tasks in many situations. People high in nAch do better on various tasks in the laboratory. They are more likely to complete diffi-

Highlight 12–2
Who's Afraid of a Little Success?

Which of the following statements do you agree with?

1. I am happy only when I am doing better than others.
2. Achievement commands respect.
3. It is extremely important for me to do well in all things that I undertake.
4. Often the cost of success is greater than the reward.
5. I believe that successful people are often sad and lonely.
6. I think "success" has been emphasized too much in our culture.

(Source: Zuckerman & Allison, 1976.)

Agreement with the first three statements shows a positive attitude toward success. People who agree with the last three statements tend to avoid success. It might seem that avoiding success is always undesirable. In reality an overemphasis on achievement can be as big a handicap as avoidance of success. Our society is notorious for its successful but unhappy workaholics. In the final analysis a truly successful life strikes a balance between achievement and other needs.

cult tasks. They earn better grades in high school and college, and they tend to excel in their chosen occupations. College students high in nAch tend to attribute success to their own ability and failure to insufficient effort (Kleinke, 1978). Thus, high nAch students are more likely to renew their efforts when faced with a poor performance. When the going gets tough, high achievers get going.

Fear of Success   Have you ever hidden your talents in favor of blending into a group? Have you ever backed off from "winning" in sports or school? Have you ever "played dumb" with friends? Everyone has probably done so at times. Each of these actions involves an avoidance, or fear, of success (see Highlight 12–2). Obviously, fearing success can stifle efforts to achieve.

Why would anyone avoid success? Most often because:

(1) Success can require a stressful shift in self-concept; (2) many people fear rejection when they stand out in a group; and (3) some people fear the extra demands of being a "successful person" (Tresemer, 1977). All three reasons are illustrated by a secretary who quit when she was offered a job as a supervisor. When asked why she quit, she said it was because she didn't want to be a "career woman," because she feared her former friends in the office would reject her, and because she disliked telling others what to do.

Question: Do fears of success occur more in women or men?

Both men and women appear to be equally subject to success fears (Kearney, 1984). But in our culture there is often an extra conflict for women. By adulthood many men and women have learned to consider it "unfeminine" for a woman to excel (de Charms & Muir, 1978). Understandably, then, successful women are most often those who define achievement as an acceptable feminine quality (Kleinke, 1978). Perhaps the women's movement and changing attitudes will help remove this unnecessary stumbling block for future generations of talented and aspiring women.

The Key to Success?   What does it take to achieve extraordinary success? Educational psychologist Benjamin Bloom recently completed a study of America's top performers in six fields: concert pianists, Olympic swimmers, sculptors, tennis players, mathematicians, and research neurologists. Bloom (1985) found that drive and determination, not great natural talent, led to success in the lives of the high achievers studied.

The development of Bloom's subjects began when parents exposed the child to music, swimming, scientific ideas, and so forth, "just for fun." Many of the children were initially quite ordinary in their skills. One Olympic swimmer, for instance, remembers repeatedly losing races as a 10-year-old. At some point, however, the children began to get recognition for their abilities and pursued them more actively. Before long, parents became aware of the child's rapid progress and sought out a more expert instructor or coach. After more successes and encouragement, the youngsters began "living" for their talent. Most spent many hours each day practicing their skills. This continued for many years before they reached truly extraordinary heights of achievement.

The upshot of Bloom's work is that talent is nurtured through dedication and hard work. It appears that this is most likely to happen when parents give their wholehearted support to a child's special interest, and when they place emphasis on doing one's best at all times. The old belief that "talent will out" of its own accord is largely a myth.

Motives in Perspective— A View from the Pyramid

As you may recall from Chapter 1, humanistic psychologist Abraham Maslow defined self-actualization as the full development of personal potential. As a sidelight to his work on self-actualization, Maslow proposed that there is a **hierarchy** (or ordering) of human needs. By this he meant that some needs are more basic or powerful than others. Think for a moment about the needs that influence your behavior. Which seems strongest? Which do you spend the most time and energy satisfying? Now look at Maslow's hierarchy (Fig. 12–12).

Note that physiological needs are at the bottom. Since these are necessary for survival, they tend to be *prepotent*, or dominant over the higher needs. It could be said, for example, that "to a starving person, food is god."

Maslow believed that higher needs are expressed only when the prepotent physiological needs are satisfied. This is also true of needs for safety and security. Until there is a basic amount of order and stability in meeting the lower needs, a person may have little interest in higher pursuits. For this reason Maslow described the first two levels of the hierarchy as **basic needs.** Higher, or **growth needs,** include love and belonging (family, friendship, caring), needs for esteem and self-esteem (recognition and self-respect), and self-actualization needs (Fig. 12–13). Although Maslow believed that a desire for self-actualization is universal, he placed it at the top of the hierarchy. This placement indicates that he viewed it as fragile and easily interrupted by lower needs.

Question: How are needs for self-actualization expressed?

Maslow called the less powerful but humanly important actualization motives **meta-needs** (Maslow, 1970). These are listed in Table 12–1. According to Maslow, there is a tendency to move up the hierarchy to the meta-needs. A person whose survival needs are met, but whose meta-needs are unfulfilled, falls into a "syndrome of decay" and experiences despair, apathy, and alienation.

Maslow's hierarchy is not well documented by research, and questions can be raised about it. How, for instance, do we explain the use of fasting as a means of social protest? How has the meta-need for justice overcome the more basic need for food? (Perhaps the answer is that fast-

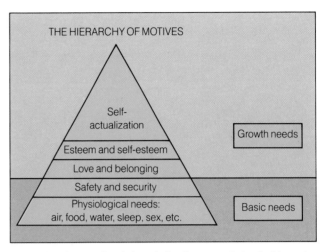

Fig. 12–12 *Maslow believed that lower needs in the hierarchy are dominant. Basic needs must be satisfied before growth motives are fully expressed. Desires for self-actualization are reflected in various meta-needs (see text).*

ing is temporary.) Despite such objections Maslow's views have been widely influential as a way of understanding and appreciating the rich interplay of human motives.

Question: Did Maslow believe that many people are motivated by meta-needs?

Maslow estimated that only about 1 person in 10 is primarily motivated by self-actualization needs. Most are

Fig. 12–13 *Wheelchair athletes engage in vigorous competition. Maslow considered such behavior an expression of needs for self-actualization.*

Table 12–1 Maslow's List of Meta-Needs	
Meta-needs are seen as an expression of tendencies for self-actualization, the full development of personal potential.	
1. Wholeness (unity)	**8.** Beauty (rightness of form)
2. Perfection (balance and harmony)	**9.** Goodness (benevolence)
3. Completion (ending)	**10.** Uniqueness (individuality)
4. Justice (fairness)	**11.** Playfulness (ease)
5. Richness (complexity)	**12.** Truth (reality)
6. Simplicity (essence)	**13.** Autonomy (self-sufficiency)
7. Aliveness (spontaneity)	**14.** Meaningfulness (values)

more concerned with esteem, love, or security. Perhaps this is because incentives and rewards in our society are slanted to encourage conformity, uniformity, and security in schools, jobs, and relationships. When was the last time you met a meta-need?

Intrinsic and Extrinsic Motivation

Some people cook for a living and consider it hard work. Others cook for pleasure and dream of opening a restaurant. For some people carpentry, gardening, writing, photography, or jewelry making is fun. For others the same activities are drudgery they must be paid to do. How can the same activity be "work" for one person and "play" for another?

When you undertake an activity for enjoyment, to demonstrate competence, or to gain skill, your motivation is usually *intrinsic*. **Intrinsic motivation** occurs when there is no obvious external reward or ulterior purpose behind your actions. The activity is an end in itself. Intrinsic motivation is closely related to the higher levels of Maslow's hierarchy.

In contrast, **extrinsic motivation** stems from obvious external factors, such as pay, grades, rewards, obligations,

or approval. Most of the activities we think of as "work" are extrinsically rewarded.

Turning Play into Work   It might seem that increasing extrinsic incentives would strengthen motivation, but this is not always the case. Research with children shows that excessive rewards can undermine spontaneous interest (Ross et al., 1976). For instance, children lavishly rewarded for drawing with Magic-Markers (felt-tip pens) later showed little interest in playing with them (Greene & Lepper, 1974). Apparently, "play" can be turned into "work" by *requiring* a person to do something he or she would otherwise enjoy. A similar effect occurred when adult college students were rewarded for working on puzzles (Daniel & Esser, 1980).

Question: How can the concept of intrinsic motivation be applied?

Motivation can't always be intrinsic. Nor should it be. Not every worthwhile activity is intrinsically satisfying. In addition extrinsic motivation is often needed if we are to develop enough skill or knowledge for an activity to become intrinsically rewarding. This effect can be observed in learning to read, to play a musical instrument, or to enjoy a sport. At first, external encouragement or incentives may be needed to get a person to the level of ability needed for intrinsic motivation to occur.

So, both extrinsic and intrinsic motivation are necessary. But extrinsic motivation should not be overused. Greene and Lepper (1974) summarize: (1) If there is no intrinsic interest in an activity to begin with, there is nothing to lose by using extrinsic rewards; (2) if needed skills are lacking, extrinsic rewards may be necessary to begin; (3) extrinsic rewards may focus attention on an activity so that real interest can develop—this is especially true for motivating learning in children; (4) if extrinsic rewards or incentives are to be used, they should be as small as possible, used only when absolutely necessary, and faded out as soon as possible. By following these rules, you can avoid taking spontaneous interest and satisfaction out of motivation for others, especially children.

Learning Check

1. Drives for exploration, manipulation, and curiosity provide evidence for the existence of _____ needs.

2. People who score high on the SSS tend to be extroverted, independent, and to value change.   T or F?

3. When a task is complex, the ideal level of arousal is _____; when a task is simple, the optimal level of arousal is _____.

4. The overall relationship between arousal and efficiency can be described as:
a. nonhomeostatic   *b.* a negative correlation   *c.* an inverted U function   *d.* an SSS score

5. The need for achievement can be described as a desire to meet an internalized _____ of _____.

6. People with high nAch are attracted to "long shots" and "sure things."   T or F?

7. Fears of success are common in men but occur less often for women.   T or F?

8. According to Maslow, meta-needs are the most basic and prepotent sources of human motivation.   T or F?

9. Intrinsic motivation is often undermined in situations in which obvious external rewards are applied to a naturally enjoyable activity.   T or F?

Answers: 1. stimulus   2. T   3. low, high   4. c   5. standard, excellence   6. F   7. F   8. F   9. T

Applications

Behavioral Dieting—Kicking the Food Habit

The goal of the previous discussion was to help you better understand a number of basic motives. In this section we will consider an application of motivational research by looking at psychological techniques for weight control.

Most people today are aware that obesity may be hazardous to health, yet all around us are people who suffer from being overweight. The overweight run a high risk of developing heart and kidney diseases, of encountering dangerous complications in surgery, and of simply living fewer years than slimmer people (Lappe, 1971).

Question: What can be done to control weight?

For years the basic approach has been to "diet"; that is, to restrict food intake drastically for a brief period. This, of course, is perfectly sensible in theory: You must eat less to lose weight. As noted earlier, however, most people who lose weight by dieting regain it rapidly. And, as the Exploration that follows points out, there may be other risks in dieting as well.

What is really needed if one wishes to lose weight is to overhaul *eating habits* and to control *cues* for eating. The person who succeeds in changing eating habits can expect a permanent weight reduction. This approach, called **behavioral dieting,** is greatly superior to simple dieting for weight control. The following list sum-marizes several behavioral techniques that have proved helpful (compiled from Kiell, 1973; Lake, 1973; Mayer, 1968; Trotter, 1974).

1. Begin any weight control program with a physical checkup. About 5 percent of all weight problems are physical.

2. Learn your eating habits by observing yourself and keeping a diet diary. Begin by making a complete record of your eating habits for 2 weeks. Record when and where you eat, what you eat, and the feelings and events that occur just before and after eating. How do others around you respond to your eating? Is someone encouraging you to overeat?

3. Count calories, but don't starve yourself. To lose, you must eat less, and calories allow you to keep an accurate record of your food intake.

4. Develop techniques to control the act of eating. Begin by taking smaller portions. Carry only what you plan to eat to the table. Put all other food away before leaving the kitchen. Eat slowly, finish one mouthful before taking another, count your mouthfuls, leave food on your plate, avoid eating alone (you're less likely to overeat in front of others).

5. Learn to weaken your personal eating cues. When you have learned when and where you do most of your eating, avoid these situations. Try to restrict your eating

---

Applications: Behavioral Dieting—Kicking the Food Habit

to one room, and do not read, watch TV, study, or talk on the phone while eating. Require yourself to interrupt what you are doing in order to eat. Be especially aware of the "night-eating syndrome." Most calories are consumed late in the day or at night. Keep food out of sight and find things to do to keep yourself busy during this dangerous period.

6. Avoid snacks. Buy low-calorie foods that require preparation, and fix only a single portion at a time. If you have an impulse to snack, set a timer for 20 minutes and see if you are still hungry then. Delay the impulse to snack several times if possible. Dull your appetite by filling up on raw carrots, bouillon, water, coffee, or tea.

7. Exercise. Physical activity burns calories. Stop saving steps and riding elevators. Add activity to your routine in every way you can think of. Contrary to popular opinion, regular exercise does not increase appetite. For reasons that are not well understood, exercise lowers the body's set point for fat storage (Bennett & Gurin, 1982).

8. Get yourself committed to weight loss. Involve as many people in your program as you can.

9. Make a list of rewards you will receive if you change your eating habits and punishments that will occur if you don't. You may find it helpful to set up specific rewards (see Chapter 23 for more details). Don't reward yourself with food!

10. Chart your progress daily. Record your weight, the number of calories eaten, whether you met your daily goal. (Set realistic goals by cutting down calories gradually. About a pound per week weight loss is realistic, but remember, you are changing habits, not just losing weight.) Take pride in your successes. Post your chart in a prominent place. This feedback on your progress is possibly the most important of all the techniques.

Be patient with this program. It takes years to develop eating habits. You can expect it to take at least several months to change them. If you are unsuccessful at losing weight with these techniques, you might find it helpful to seek the aid of a psychologist familiar with behavioral weight-loss techniques.

Learning Check

1. According to behavioral dieting specialists, about 45 percent of all weight problems are physical.   T or F?
2. In addition to burning calories, physical exercise can lower the body's set point.   T or F?
3. For behavioral dieting you should maintain a diet diary and chart your progress, but you should avoid the trap of counting calories.   T or F?

Answers: 1. F 2. T 3. F

Chapter Summary

- Motives *initiate, sustain,* and *direct* activities. Motivation typically involves the sequence: *need, drive, goal,* and *goal attainment* (need reduction).
- Behavior can be activated either by *needs* (push) or by *goals* (pull). The attractiveness of a goal and its ability to initiate action are related to its *incentive value*.
- Three principal types of motives are: *primary motives* (based on biological survival needs), *stimulus motives* (which serve needs for activity, exploration, manipulation, and so forth), and *secondary motives* (activated by learned needs and valued goals). Most primary motives operate to maintain *homeostasis*.

- Hunger is influenced by a complex interplay of factors. These include fullness of the stomach, blood sugar levels, metabolism in the liver, and fat stores in the body. The most direct control of eating is effected by the *hypothalamus*, which has areas that act like *feeding* and *satiety* systems.
- Other factors influencing hunger are: the body's *set point, external eating cues,* the attractiveness and variety of *diet, emotions,* learned *taste preferences* or *taste aversions,* and *cultural values.*
- Lack of nutritional substances in the diet can sometimes produce *specific hungers,* as demonstrated by *self-*

selection feeding experiments with animals and infants.

■ Like hunger, thirst and other basic motives are affected by a number of bodily factors but are primarily under the central control of the hypothalamus. Thirst may be either *intracellular* or *extracellular*.

■ Pain avoidance is an unusual primary drive because it is *episodic* as opposed to *cyclic*. Pain avoidance and pain tolerance are partially learned. The sex drive is also unusual in that it is *nonhomeostatic* (both increases and decreases in drive level are actively sought).

■ The stimulus motives include needs for *exploration, manipulation, change,* and *sensory stimulation*. Stimulus motives appear to be innate because they operate independent of other rewards.

■ Drives for stimulation are partially explained by the *arousal theory*, which states that an ideal level of bodily arousal will be maintained if possible. The desired level of arousal or stimulation varies from person to person. Stimulus needs have been measured with the *Sensation Seeking Scale (SSS)*.

■ Optimal performance on a task usually occurs at moderate levels of arousal. This relationship is described by an *inverted U function*. An added qualification, known as the *Yerkes-Dodson law*, states that for simple tasks the ideal arousal level is higher, and for complex tasks it is lower.

■ *Social motives* are learned through socialization and cultural conditioning. Such motives account for much of the diversity of human motivation.

■ One of the most prominent and intensely studied social motives is the *need for achievement (nAch)*. Achievement striving differs from the *need for power*. High nAch is correlated with success in many situations, with occupational choice, and with moderate risk taking. There is evidence that at times both men and women experience a *fear of success*.

■ Maslow's *hierarchy of motives* categorizes needs as *basic* and *growth oriented*. Lower needs in the hierarchy are assumed to be *prepotent* (dominant) over higher needs. Self-actualization, the highest and most fragile need, is reflected in *meta-needs*.

■ Higher needs in Maslow's hierarchy are closely related to the concept of *intrinsic motivation*. In many situations *extrinsic motivation* (that which is induced by obvious external rewards) can reduce intrinsic motivation.

■ Because of the limitations of traditional dieting, changing basic eating patterns and habits is usually more effective. *Behavioral dieting* brings about such changes by use of self-control techniques.

Anorexia and Bulimia—Hungering for Control

Under the sheets of her hospital bed Krystal looks like a starved skeleton. To counter a life-threatening weight loss, Krystal's doctors are feeding her intravenously. Yet, her desire to lose weight is so intense that when the nurse leaves, Krystal turns off the IV. If her self-destructive course cannot be changed, Krystal may die of malnutrition.

How could things go so desperately wrong with a motive as basic as hunger? Recent attempts to understand problems like Krystal's provide a fascinating look at motivation gone awry.

Eating Disorders

Serious cases of undereating like Krystal's are called **anorexia nervosa** (AN-uh-REK-see-yah ner-VOH-sah). Victims of anorexia, who are mostly adolescent females (5 to 10 percent are male), suffer devastating weight loss from self-inflicted starvation.

Question: Do anorexics lose their appetite?

Anorexia nervosa is not a simple loss of desire for food. Many anorexics continue to feel hunger, and yet they struggle to starve themselves. The problem can best be described as a *relentless pursuit of excessive thinness*. Persons who suffer from anorexia nervosa have an obsessive fear of gaining weight. Often, the problem starts with normal dieting that gradually begins to dominate the person's life. In time, anorexics suffer physical weakness, absence of men-

strual cycles, and a dangerous risk of infection. Five to eight percent (that's more than 1 in 20) die of malnutrition or related health problems. The death of popular singer Karen Carpenter is a case in point. Some victims of anorexia nervosa realize the harmfulness of their excessive dieting, but they feel powerless to stop.

Bulimia (bue-LIHM-ee-yah), also known as the binge-purge syndrome, is a second major eating disorder. Bulimics gorge on food, then induce vomiting or take laxatives to avoid gaining weight. The prevalence of bulimia is currently unknown, but its incidence is probably very high among women in their early 20s. One psychologist, who was mentioned in a newspaper as an expert on binge eating, received over 1500 letters asking for help. Like anorexia, bulimia is far more prevalent in women than in men.

In a culture that values slimness, bulimia may seem relatively harmless. However, like anorexia nervosa, bingeing and purging can cause serious health problems. Typical risks include sore throat, hair loss, muscle spasms, kidney damage, dehydration, erosion of tooth enamel, swelling of the salivary glands, menstrual irregularity, loss of sex drive, and even heart attack.

Recognizing Trouble

Question: Could a person be both anorexic and bulimic?

Yes. Close to 50 percent of anorexics are also bulimic. It is not unu-

sual, for instance, for the parents of anorexics to plead with them to eat more. However, if the anorexic gives in to such coaxing, she may just disappear into the bathroom to secretly vomit.

Although they are related, anorexia and bulimia are separate problems. Anorexic individuals suffer a weight loss of at least 25 percent of their original body weight. Some anorexics lose weight by fasting and dieting. Those who are also bulimic alternate between bingeing and purging. Either way, weight loss is severe for anorexics. In contrast, persons who are only bulimic may be from any weight group, from thin to heavy. Most, in fact, are only slightly below average weight.

Of the two disorders, bulimia is harder to detect because weight often remains nearly normal, and bingeing and purging can be hidden. However, bulimia is indicated if any *three* of the following conditions are present: binge eating; hiding the amount eaten during a binge; gorging on food, followed by self-induced vomiting or abdominal pain; repeated attempts to lose weight by severe dieting; use of vomiting, laxatives, or diuretics to lose weight; frequent weight changes of more than 3 pounds; awareness that one's eating is abnormal, coupled with an inability to change; anxiety or depression following binges.

Question: What causes anorexia and bulimia?

Causes Both anorexics and bulimics have exaggerated fears of

Exploration: Anorexia and Bulimia—Hungering for Control

becoming fat and unrealistic views of what constitutes normal size. Anorexics, especially, have distorted body images. Most overestimate their body size by 25 percent or more and continue to see themselves as "fat" when in fact they are wasting away.

Anorexics are usually described as "perfect" daughters—helpful, considerate, conforming, and obedient. Many are would-be high achievers who frantically try to excel in many areas. However, because of their inexperience in making decisions and dealing with normal adolescent stresses, many feel overwhelmed. At this point they decide to be "perfect" in one area—to have complete control over their weight and to be perfectly slim. Losing weight thus gives anorexics a sense of pride, self-worth, and effectiveness. The thought of gaining weight, in contrast, fills them with terror—they literally feel that they are losing control.

Bulimics also seem to be concerned with control. For them, however, maintaining control is an ongoing struggle. Bulimics are obsessed with thoughts of weight, food, eating, and ridding themselves of food. As a result most feel guilt, shame, self-contempt, and anxiety after a binge. For many vomiting reduces the anxiety triggered by a binge. This makes purging highly reinforcing.

Dieting   Recent research suggests that dieting may actually encourage bingeing. Most bulimics, for instance, go through a period of "normal" dieting before they begin to purge too.

Question: How does dieting contribute to bingeing?

Psychologists Janet Polivy and Peter Herman have found that dieters eat *more* after first eating a large meal than they do if they ate nothing beforehand. It is as if dieters are barely able to keep the brakes on eating. When they feel that they have "broken" their diet, the suppressed urge to eat is released and a binge follows. This effect can occur even when dieters merely are *told* they ate a high-calorie meal (that was actually low in calories). Thus, as long as dieters *believe* they are "in control," and their diet is intact, they eat with restraint. But when they believe their diet has been violated, they can no longer control eating and tend to gorge themselves. In short, societal pressures to diet, and the link between dieting and bingeing, may be contributing to an increase in bulimia.

Treatment   In almost all cases, a person with anorexia or bulimia will need professional help to restore normal eating. Treatment for anorexia usually begins with admitting the person to a hospital. There, a carefully controlled diet is used to restore weight and health. As a second step the client enters counseling to work on the personal conflicts and family issues that led to weight loss. For bulimia, psychologists have had some success with behavioral counseling that includes careful self-monitoring of food intake and work on extinguishing the urge to vomit after eating.

Although much progress is being made in treating eating disorders, most anorexics do not seek help, and many actively resist it. Bulimics will sometimes seek treatment but usually not until their eating habits become intolerable. In either case it may take strong urging by family or friends to get victims into treatment. With this in mind, it is worth emphasizing again that anorexia nervosa and bulimia are serious, health-threatening problems that rarely disappear on their own. (Sources: DSM III, 1980; Moore, 1981; Polivy & Herman, 1985; Rosen & Leitenburg, 1982; Schlessier-Stroop, 1984.)

Learning Check

1.   Anorexia nervosa is also known as the binge-purge syndrome.   T or F?
2.   A person can suffer from both anorexia nervosa and bulimia at the same time.   T or F?
3.   Anorexics underestimate their body size by 25 percent or more.   T or F?
4.   A dieter who eats a large meal will typically eat more soon afterward than will a dieter who did not eat before.   T or F?

Answers: 1. F   2. T   3. F   4. T

Questions for Discussion

1. Which of the primary drives do you consider the strongest? Why? Which occupies the greatest amount of your time and energies? How could the strength of the primary drives be established for animals?

2. Discuss some of the factors that contribute to overeating at Thanksgiving or a similar feast.

3. The sex drive is not essential for individual survival, and it can be easily interrupted by any of the other primary drives. Why do you think so much energy is directed toward sexuality in our culture?

4. In what ways have you observed the stimulus motives at work in human behavior? Does learning contribute to curiosity or needs for stimulation?

5. Does the American emphasis on competition (in your opinion) encourage achievement or discourage it? (Consider the effects, for example, when only one person can be considered the "winner" in many situations.)

6. How could you apply the concept of incentives to improve your motivation to study?

7. In *Lady Windermere's Fan*, playwright Oscar Wilde said, "In this world there are only two tragedies. One is not getting what one wants, and the other is getting it. The last is the real tragedy." What do you think Wilde meant? Where does your motivation come from?

8. If you had a guaranteed income, would you "work"? What do you think you would spend your time doing? For how long? What, if anything, does this reveal about sources of intrinsic motivation?

9. How has our culture contributed to eating problems such as obesity, anorexia nervosa, and bulimia? In some cultures a degree of fatness is considered desirable as a hedge against starvation. Do we apply the definition "fat" to people who are perfectly healthy?

Emotion

Chapter 13

Chapter Preview
Voodoo Death

Few events are more bizarre than sudden death caused by voodoo or "magic." Yet, many explorers and anthropologists have witnessed this strange phenomenon. Here is an account of what happens in one tribe when a man discovers that he has been cursed by an enemy:

> He stands aghast, with his eyes staring at the treacherous pointers, with his hands lifted as though to ward off the lethal medium. . . . His cheeks blanch and his eyes become glassy and the expression of his face becomes horribly distorted. . . . His body begins to tremble and the muscles twist involuntarily. He sways backwards and falls to the ground. . . . From this time onwards he sickens and frets, refusing to eat and keeping aloof from the daily affairs of the tribe. Unless help is forthcoming in the shape of a counter-charm, death is only a matter of a comparatively short time. (Basedow, 1925; cited in Cannon, 1942.)

At first glance voodoo deaths seem to require belief in the power of magic. Actually, all they require is belief in the power of emotion. Walter Cannon (1942), a well-known physiologist, studied a large number of voodoo deaths and concluded that they really do occur.

Question: How could a voodoo curse cause death?

Cannon believed that these deaths are explained by changes in the body that accompany strong emotion. Specifically, he believed that cursed victims experience fear so intense and lasting that it causes a heart attack or other bodily disaster.

More recent research suggests that Cannon's explanation was only partly correct. It now appears that such deaths are caused not by fear itself but by the body's reaction to fear. After a period of strong emotion, the parasympathetic nervous system normally restores balance by reversing the bodily changes caused by emotion. For example, during intense fear, heart rate is dramatically increased; to counteract this increase, the parasympathetic system later slows the heart. It is now believed that the cursed person's emotional response is so intense that the parasympathetic nervous system overreacts and slows the heart to a stop (Seligman, 1974).

There is more to this story, as we will see in a later section of this chapter. For now it is enough to say that emotions are not only the "spice of life," for some they may be the spice of death as well.

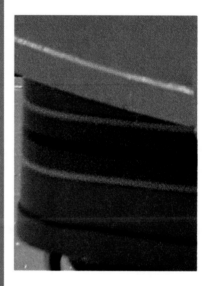

Survey Questions   What causes emotion? How do psychologists explain emotions? What happens to the body during emotion? Can "lie detectors" really detect lies? How do emotions develop? How accurately are they expressed by "body language" and the face? What do we know about coping with threatening situations, helplessness, death, and depression? Is love an emotion?

Resources

Dissecting an Emotion— How Do You Feel?

Have you ever waited until someone was in a good mood to ask for a favor? If so, you are aware that emotions have a powerful influence on everyday behavior. On the plus side, for example, it is easier to make decisions when you are in a good mood (Isen & Means, 1983). Likewise, people who are feeling happy are more likely to help others in need (O'Malley & Andrews, 1983). And who would deny the importance of love, optimism, acceptance, and joy in human relationships? It is apparent, however, that emotions also have negative effects. Hate, anger, contempt, disgust, and fear all disrupt our behavior and relationships. Even brief encounters may be colored by emotion. In one recent study, researchers found that just 5 minutes with a person trained to act depressed induced feelings of depression in college students (Marks & Hammen, 1982). (To get the full flavor of this finding, imagine being stuck in an elevator with the most anxious, depressed, or angry person you know.) Clearly, emotion is an important dimension in our lives.

Fig. 13-1 *How accurately do facial expressions reveal emotion? After you have guessed what emotion these people are feeling, turn to page 318.*

The root of the word **emotion** means "to move," and emotions do, indeed, move us. First, the body is physically aroused during emotion. Such bodily stirrings are what cause people to say they were "moved" by a play, a funeral, or an act of kindness. Second, we are often motivated, or moved to take action, by emotions such as fear, anger, or joy. Underlying all this, perhaps, is the fact that emotions are linked to such basic **adaptive behaviors** as attack, retreat, seeking comfort, helping others, reproduction, and the like (Plutchik, 1980). Again, we must realize that human emotions can be disruptive—as in having stage fright or "blowing" an athletic performance. But more often, emotions aid survival. This seems to be why emotional reactions were retained in evolution.

Most people closely identify a pounding heart, sweating palms, and "butterflies" in the stomach with emotion. This observation is valid since **physiological changes** within the body are a major element of fear, anger, joy, and other emotions. These changes include alterations in heart rate, blood pressure, perspiration, and other bodily stirrings. (More on this later.) Most such reactions are caused by release of **adrenaline** into the bloodstream. Adrenaline is a hormone that stimulates the sympathetic nervous system, which in turn activates the body.

Emotional expressions, or outward signs of what a person is feeling, are a second major element of emotion. For example, when you are intensely afraid, your hands tremble, your face contorts, and your posture becomes tense and defensive. Emotion is also revealed by marked shifts in voice tone or modulation. Other signs of emotion range from nonstop verbal abuse during rage to the surprisingly subdued last words found on flight recorders after air disasters (a common last word is "Damn," spoken calmly). Such emotional expressions are particularly important because they communicate emotion from one person to another (Fig. 13–1).

Question: Are some emotions more basic than others?

Based on his research, Robert Plutchik (1980) believes there are eight **primary emotions: fear, surprise, sadness, disgust, anger, anticipation, joy,** and **acceptance** (receptivity). If the list seems too short, it's because each listed emotion can vary in *intensity*. Anger, for instance, may vary from rage to simple annoyance.

One of Plutchik's most interesting ideas concerns the mixing of primary emotions. As shown in Fig. 13–2, adjacent emotions can be mixed to yield a third, more complex emotion. Other mixtures are also possible. For example, a child about to eat a stolen cookie may feel both joy and fear. The result? Guilt—as you may recall from your own childhood. Likewise, jealousy could be considered a mixture of love, anger, and fear.

Theories of Emotion—
Four Ways to Fear a Bear

Question: What is the typical sequence of events in experiencing an emotion?

There are many theories about what takes place during emotion. Let's take a brief look at four of the most popular views.

The Commonsense Theory of Emotion Common sense tells us that when we see a bear, we feel fear, become aroused, and run (and sweat and yell). For various reasons psychologists have questioned this ordering of events. The theories of emotion that follow tell why. (Refer to Figure 13–3.)

The James-Lange Theory (1884—1885) In the 1880s American psychologist William James (the functionalist) and Danish psychologist Carl Lange proposed a different relationship between emotional feelings and the body. James and Lange suggested that, "We are afraid of a bear because we run, or are angry because we strike." In doing so, they turned the tables on our usual view of emotion. According to James and Lange, bodily arousal (such as increased heart rate) does not follow a feeling such as fear. Instead, they argued, *emotional feelings follow bodily arousal.* Thus, we see a bear, run, are aroused, and *then* feel fear as we become aware of our bodily reactions.

To support this line of thought, James pointed out that we often do not experience an emotion until after reacting. For example, imagine that you are driving and that a car suddenly pulls out in front of you. You swerve and skid to an abrupt halt at the side of the road. Only after you have come to a stop do you notice your pounding heart, rapid breathing, and tense muscles—and recognize your fear.

The Cannon-Bard Theory (1927) American physiologist Walter Cannon and his student Phillip Bard found a number of reasons to question the James-Lange theory. While agreeing that the body becomes stirred up during emotion, Cannon and Bard noted that the physical changes accompanying various emotions are almost identical. This fact casts doubt on the idea that emotional feelings come primarily from the body.

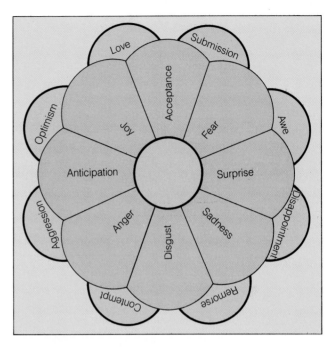

Fig. 13-2 *Primary and mixed emotions. In Robert Plutchik's model there are eight primary emotions, as listed in the inner areas. Adjacent emotions may combine to give the emotions listed around the perimeter. Mixtures involving more widely separated emotions are also possible. (Adapted from Plutchik, 1980.)*

Fig. 13-3 *Theories of emotion.*

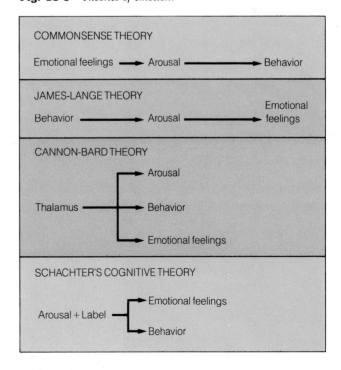

Question: What does account for the variety of emotions, the body or the brain?

For the reason just stated, and a number of others, Walter Cannon (1932) proposed that emotional feelings and bodily arousal are both organized in the brain. In this version seeing a bear activates the thalamus, which in turn alerts both the cortex and the hypothalamus for action. The cortex is responsible for emotional feelings and emotional behavior. The hypothalamus is responsible for arousing the body. Thus, if the bear is seen as dangerous, bodily arousal, running, and feelings of fear will all be generated at the same time by brain activity.

Schachter's Cognitive Theory of Emotion (1971)

The previous theories are mostly concerned with emotion as a physical response. In Stanley Schachter's view, cognitive (mental) factors also enter into emotion. According to Schachter, emotion occurs when a particular *label* is applied to general physical *arousal*. Schachter assumes that when we are aroused, we have a need to interpret our feelings. Assume, for instance, that someone sneaks up behind you on a dark street and says, "Boo!" No matter who the person is, your body will be aroused (pounding heart, sweating palms, and so on). If the person is a total stranger, you may interpret this arousal as fear; if the person is a close friend, the arousal may be labeled as surprise or delight. The label (such as anger, fear, or happiness)

applied to bodily arousal is influenced by past experience, the situation, and the reactions of others.

Support for the cognitive theory of emotion comes from an experiment in which subjects watched a slapstick movie (Schachter & Wheeler, 1962). Before viewing the movie, one-third of the subjects received an injection of adrenaline, one-third got a placebo injection, and the remaining subjects were given a tranquilizer. Subjects who received the adrenaline rated the movie funniest and showed the most amusement while watching it. In contrast those given the tranquilizer were least amused, and the placebo group fell in between.

According to the cognitive theory of emotion, subjects who received adrenaline had a stirred-up body but no explanation for the way they were feeling. Consequently, subjects became happy when the movie implied that their arousal was due to amusement. This and similar experiments make it clear that emotion is much more than just an agitated body. Perception, experience, attitudes, judgment, and many other more clearly "mental" factors also affect emotion. Schachter would predict, then, that if you met a bear, you would be aroused. If the bear seemed unfriendly, you would interpret your arousal as fear; and if the bear offered to shake your paw, you would be happy, amazed, and relieved!

Attribution   We now move from slapstick movies and fear of bear bodies to appreciation of bare bodies. Stuart Valins (1967) has added an interesting refinement to Schachter's theory of emotion. According to Valins, arousal can be attributed to various sources—a process that alters perceptions of emotion. To demonstrate such **attribution**, Valins (1966) showed undergraduate male students a series of slides of nude females. While watching the slides, subjects heard an amplified heartbeat that they believed was their own. In reality they were listening to a recorded heartbeat carefully designed to beat *louder* and *stronger* when some, but not all, of the slides were shown.

After viewing the slides, subjects were asked to say which they found most attractive. Students exposed to the false heartbeat consistently rated slides paired with a "pounding heart" as the most attractive. In other words when a subject saw a slide and heard his heartbeat become more pronounced, he attributed his "emotion" to the slide. His interpretation then seems to have been, "Now that one I like!" His next reaction, perhaps, was "But why?" Recent research suggests that subjects persuade themselves that the slide really is more attractive in order to explain their apparent arousal (Truax, 1983).

Question: That seems somewhat artificial. Does it really make any difference what arousal is attributed to?

Fig. 13-4 *Which theory of emotion best describes the reaction of these people? Given the complexity of emotion, each theory appears to possess an element of truth.*

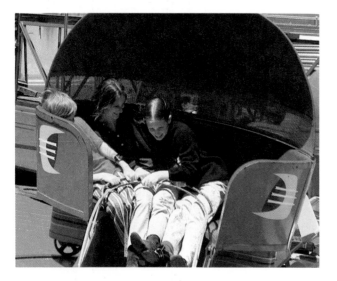

Yes. To illustrate how attribution works in the real world, consider what happens when parents interfere with the budding romance of a son or daughter. Often, trying to break up a young couple's relationship *intensifies* their feelings for one another. Parental interference adds frustration, anger, and fear or excitement (as in seeing each other on the sly) to the couple's feelings. Since they already care for one another, they are likely to attribute all this added emotion to "true love" (Walster, 1971).

Attribution theory predicts that you are most likely to "love" someone who gets you stirred up emotionally, even when fear, anger, frustration, or rejection is part of the formula. Thus, if you want to successfully propose marriage, take your intended to the middle of a narrow, windswept suspension bridge over a deep chasm and look deeply into his or her eyes. As your beloved's heart pounds wildly (from being on the bridge, not from your irresistible charms), say "I love you." Attribution theory predicts your companion will conclude, "Oh wow, I must love you too."

The preceding is not as farfetched as it may seem. In an ingenious study a female experimenter interviewed men in a park, some on a swaying suspension bridge 230 feet above a river and others on a solid wooden bridge just 10 feet above the ground. After the interview each subject was given the experimenter's telephone number, so he could "find out about the results" of the study if he wanted. Men interviewed on the suspension bridge were much more likely to give the "lady from the park" a call (Dutton & Aron, 1974). Apparently, these men experienced heightened arousal, which they interpreted as attraction to the experimenter—a clear case of love at first fright! (Love is discussed further in this chapter's Exploration.)

Learning Check

Check your comprehension by answering these questions.

1. Many of the physiological changes associated with emotions are caused by secretion of the hormone
   a. atropine   *b.* adrenaline   *c.* attributine   *d.* amoduline

2. Emotional _____ often serves to communicate one's emotional state to others.

3. Awe, remorse, and disappointment are among the primary emotions listed by Robert Plutchik.   T or F?

4. According to the James-Lange theory of emotion, we see a bear, are frightened, and run.   T or F?

5. The Cannon-Bard theory of emotion says that bodily arousal and emotional experience occur _____.

6. According to Schachter's cognitive theory, bodily arousal must be labeled or interpreted for an emotional experience to occur.   T or F?

7. Subjects in Valin's false heart-rate study attributed increases in their heart rate to the action of a placebo.   T or F?

Answers: 1. b   2. expression   3. F   4. F   5. simultaneously   6. T   7. F

Physiology and Emotion— Arousal, Sudden Death, and Lying

To a large degree, the physical aspects of emotion are innate, or built into the body. The physical reactions of an African Bushman frightened by a wild animal and an urbane city dweller frightened by a prowler are quite similar. Unpleasant emotions produce especially consistent reactions. Among the most frequent are: pounding heart, muscular tenseness, irritability, dryness of the throat and mouth, sweating, butterflies in the stomach, frequent urination, trembling, restlessness, sensitivity to loud noises, and a large number of internal reactions (Shaffer, 1947). The consistency of these reactions is tied to the fact that they are caused by the **autonomic nervous system (ANS)**. As you may recall from the discussion in Chapter 3, the reactions of the ANS are *automatic* and not normally under voluntary control. There are two divisions of the ANS, one called the **sympathetic branch** and the other the **parasympathetic branch**.

Question: What do these do during emotion?

Fight or Flight   The sympathetic branch prepares the body for emergency action—"fight or flight"—by arousing a number of bodily systems and inhibiting others. (Sympathetic nervous system effects are listed in Table 13–1.) These changes have a purpose. Sugar is released into the bloodstream for quick energy, the heart beats faster to distribute blood to the muscles, the unnecessary process of digestion is temporarily inhibited, blood flow in the skin is restricted to reduce bleeding, and so forth. Most of the

sympathetic reactions increase the chances that a person or an animal will survive an emergency. (To learn about an interesting sidelight of sympathetic arousal, see Highlight 13–1.)

The actions of the parasympathetic branch generally reverse emotional arousal and calm and relax the body. After a period of high emotion, the heart is slowed, the pupils return to normal size, blood flow shifts away from the muscles and back to the internal organs, and so forth. In addition to restoring balance, the parasympathetic system helps build up and conserve bodily energy.

The parasympathetic system responds much more slowly than the sympathetic. This is why increased heart rate, muscular tension, and similar signs of arousal do not subside for 20 or 30 minutes after you experience an intense emotion, such as fear.

Sudden Death   As we noted in the Chapter Preview, the parasympathetic system may overreact during intense fear, sometimes causing death. Voodoo curses are not the only cause of such deaths. There is evidence that in times of war the pressures of combat can be so intense that some soldiers literally die of fear (Moritz & Zamchech, 1946). Even in civilian life such deaths apparently are possible. In one case a terrified woman was admitted to a hospital because she felt she was going to die. A backwoods midwife had predicted that the woman's two sisters would die before their sixteenth and twenty-first birthdays. Both died as predicted. The midwife also predicted that this woman would die before her twenty-third birthday. She was found dead in her hospital bed the day after she was admitted. It was 2 days before her twenty-third birthday (Zimbardo, 1975). The woman was an apparent victim of her own terror.

Question: Is the parasympathetic nervous system always responsible for such deaths?

Probably not. In the case of older individuals or people with heart problems, the direct effects of sympathetic activation may be enough to bring about heart attack and collapse. For example, at a memorial concert honoring the late Louis Armstrong, his widow was stricken with a heart attack as she played the final chord of "St. Louis Blues." Psychiatrist George Engel (1977) has studied hundreds of similar occurrences and concludes that many lead to death. He found that almost half of all sudden deaths are associated with the extremely traumatic disruption of a close relationship or the anniversary of the loss of a loved one. Clearly, relationships are one of the most potent sources of human emotional response.

Table 13–1 Autonomic Nervous System Effects		
Organ	Parasympathetic System	Sympathetic System
Pupil of eyes	Constricts to diminish light	Dilates to increase light
Tear glands Mucous membrane of nose and throat Salivary glands	Stimulate secretion	Inhibit secretion, cause dryness
Heart	Slowing, constriction of blood vessels	Acceleration, dilation of blood vessels to increase blood flow
Lungs, windpipe	Constrict bronchi of lungs to relax breathing	Dilate bronchi to increase breathing
Esophagus Stomach Abdominal blood vessels	Stimulate secretion and movement	Inhibit secretion and movement, divert blood flow
Liver	Liberates bile	Retains bile
Pancreas	———	Releases blood sugar
Intestines	Stimulate secretion	Inhibit secretion
Rectum Kidney Bladder	Excitation, expulsion of feces and urine	Inhibition, retention of feces and urine
Skin blood vessels	Dilate, increase blood flow	Constrict; skin becomes cold and clammy
Sweat glands	Inhibited	Stimulated to increase perspiration
Hair follicles	Relaxed	Tensed to make hair stand on end

Highlight 13-1
Emotion—The Eyes Have It

Question: Is there any truth to the idea that the eyes can reveal emotion?

The eyes have long been considered "windows on the soul" and indicators of emotion. For instance, if you doubt someone's word, you may ask them to "look you in the eye." Many seasoned poker players claim to have detected a bluff by watching the eyes of their opponents. Psychologist Eckhard Hess (1975) believes that in such instances we are mainly interested in the size of a person's *pupils.* As shown in Table 13–1, emotion affects the pupils. Specifically, *arousal, interest,* or *attention* can activate the sympathetic nervous system and cause the pupils to dilate (enlarge).

Dilation of the pupils can occur during both pleasant and unpleasant emotions (Woodmansee, 1970). Despite this fact most people tend to interpret *large* pupils as a sign of pleasant feelings and *small* pupils as a sign of negative feelings. To illustrate, Hess (1975) showed two photos of an attractive young woman to a group of men. In one photograph the woman's pupils had been retouched to make them larger. In the other they were retouched to make them smaller. The men consistently described the woman with large pupils as "soft," "feminine," or "pretty." The same woman, with small pupils, was described as "hard," "selfish," and "cold" (Fig. 13–5).

The reactions of the men in Hess's experiment

Fig. 13-5 *Select the face you think looks more attractive, warm, or friendly. Research by Eckhard Hess (1975) suggests you will choose the face on the left because the pupils of the eyes are larger.*

may explain why the drug belladonna was once popular among women. When put into the eyes, belladonna (which means "pretty lady") causes the pupils to dilate. Until it was restricted, many women used belladonna to make themselves more "beautiful." This effect, of course, does not apply only to women. In another experiment subjects were introduced to two individuals of the opposite sex and asked to choose one as a partner for the experiment. One person in each pair had been given eye drops to dilate his or her pupils, and the other had not. Subjects of both sexes tended to select the person with the larger pupils as a partner. Perhaps at long last we know why the bad guys in movies always have beady eyes!

Lie Detectors   Because bodily changes caused by the autonomic nervous system are good indicators of emotion, several ways of measuring them have been developed. One use of such measures is the "lie detector." If you have not yet done so, chances are good that sooner or later you will take a lie detector test. Of course this doesn't mean you are likely to become a criminal. It simply reflects the fact that a growing number of businesses use lie detectors to screen job applicants and to check the honesty of current employees. These practices must be questioned for two reasons: First, the lie detector's accuracy is doubtful; and second, such testing is often a serious invasion of privacy (Lykken, 1981).

Question: What is a lie detector? Do lie detectors really detect lies?

The lie detector is more accurately referred to as a **polygraph** (Fig. 13–6). A polygraph (the word means "many writings") is a portable device capable of drawing a record of changes in **heart rate, blood pressure, breathing rate, and the galvanic skin response (GSR).** (The GSR is recorded from the surface of the hand by electrodes that measure skin conductance, or, more simply, sweating.) The polygraph has become popularly known as a lie detector because of its frequent use in criminology and job interviewing. In reality the polygraph is not a lie detector at

Fig. 13-6   *A typical polygraph* (left) *includes devices for measuring heart rate, blood pressure, respiration, and galvanic skin response. Pens mounted on the top of the machine make a record of bodily responses on a moving strip of paper. Changes in the area* (right) *marked by the arrow indicate emotional arousal. If such responses appear when a person answers a question, he or she may be lying, but other causes of arousal are also possible.*

all. As critic David Lykken (1981) points out, there is no unique "lie response" that everyone gives when not telling the truth. The machine only records *general emotional arousal*—it can't tell the difference between fear, anxiety, lying, or excitement.

When attempting to detect a lie, the polygraph operator begins by asking a number of **irrelevant** (nonemotional) **questions.** ("What is your name?" "What did you have for lunch?" and so forth). This procedure establishes a "baseline," or normal emotional responsiveness. Then **relevant questions** can be asked: "Did you murder Hensley?" A person who lies presumably will become anxious or emotional when answering relevant questions.

Question: Wouldn't a person be nervous just from being questioned?

Yes, and to minimize this problem, a skilled polygraph examiner asks a *series* of questions with critical items mixed among them. An innocent person may respond emotionally to the whole procedure, but supposedly only a guilty person will show increased response to key questions. For example, a suspected bank robber might be shown a picture and asked, "Was the teller who was robbed this person? Was it this person?" (Lykken, 1974). As an alternative, subjects may be asked **control questions**

for comparison to critical questions (Saxe, Dougherty, & Cross, 1985). Control questions are designed to make almost anyone anxious: "Have you ever stolen anything from a place you worked?" Typically, control questions are extremely difficult to answer truthfully with an unqualified "No." In theory they allow the examiner to see how a person reacts to doubt or misgivings. The person's reaction to critical questions can then be compared with his or her response to control questions.

Even when questioning is done properly, "lie detection" may be inaccurate. For example, in August 1978, Floyd Fay was convicted of murdering his friend Fred Ery. To prove his innocence, Fay volunteered to take a lie detector test, which he failed. Fay spent 2 years in prison before the real killer confessed to the crime. Psychologist David Lykken (1981) has documented three such cases in which innocent people spent from 1 to 5 years behind bars after being convicted on the basis of polygraph evidence.

Question: If Floyd Fay was innocent, why did he fail the test?

Put yourself in his place, and it's easy to see why. Imagine the examiner asking, "Did you kill Fred?" Since you knew Fred, and you are a suspect, it's no secret that this is a critical question. What would happen to *your* heart rate, blood pressure, breathing, and perspiration under such circumstances?

Proponents of lie detection claim 90 to 95 percent accuracy. But in one laboratory experiment accuracy was lowered to 25 percent by subjects who intentionally thought exciting or upsetting thoughts during questioning (Smith, 1971). Similarly, the polygraph may be thrown off by self-inflicted pain or by people who can lie without anxiety. One recent experiment showed that tranquilizing drugs interfere with the detection of lies (Waid & Orne, 1982). Worst of all, the test's most common error is to label an innocent person guilty, rather than a guilty person innocent (Lykken, 1981). In field studies involving real crimes and criminal suspects, an average of approximately 1 innocent person in 5 was rated as guilty by the "lie detector" (Saxe, Dougherty, & Cross, 1985). In some instances these false positives reached 75 percent, or 3 persons out of 4.

Each year hundreds of thousands of ordinary workers are forced to take polygraph exams. In some cases unsatisfactory results or failure to submit to an exam may lead to demotion, transfer, or outright firing. In view of what we have said here, it is ironic that only a few states have passed laws requiring operators of lie detection devices to be licensed. True, some states have adopted laws forbidding employers to require job applicants to take polygraph tests. The fact remains, however, that there is a good chance you will at some time be given a "lie detector" test. Should this occur, the best advice is to remain calm; then actively challenge the outcome if your honesty is wrongly questioned.

Learning Check

See if you can correctly answer these questions.

1. Emotional arousal is closely related to activity of the _____ nervous system.

2. The sympathetic system prepares the body for "fight or flight."   T or F?

3. The parasympathetic system inhibits digestion and raises blood pressure and heart rate.   T or F?

4. What bodily changes are measured by a polygraph? _____
   _____

5. The polygraph is really an _____
   detector.

6. The pupils of the eyes dilate during pleasant emotions and constrict during unpleasant emotions.   T or F?

Answers:

1. autonomic 2. T 3. F 4. heart rate, blood pressure, breathing rate, galvanic skin response 5. arousal or emotion 6. F

Development and Expression of Emotions—Feeling Babies and Talking Bodies

Question: How soon do emotions develop?

Even the basic reactions of **anger**, **fear**, and **joy**—which appear to be unlearned—take time to develop. General **excitement** is the only emotional response newborn infants clearly express. However, as any parent can tell you, the emotional life of a baby blossoms rapidly. One researcher (Bridges, 1932) observed a large number of babies and found that all the basic human emotions appear before age 2. Bridges found that there is a consistent order in which emotions appear and that the first basic split is between pleasant and unpleasant emotions (see Fig. 13–7).

More recent research suggests that even by the end of the first year, babies can express happiness, surprise, fear, anger, sadness, disgust, and interest (Saarni, 1982). This is an important development because it contributes to a fascinating interplay of emotions between infants and adults. For example, when new parents see and hear a crying baby, they feel annoyed, irritated, disturbed, or unhappy. In addition, their blood pressure and perspiration increase (Frodi et al., 1978). Such reactions encourage

Fig. 13-7 *In the human infant, emotions are rapidly differentiated from an initial capacity for excitement. (After K. M. B. Bridges, 1932. Reprinted by permission of The Society for Research in Child Development, Inc.)*

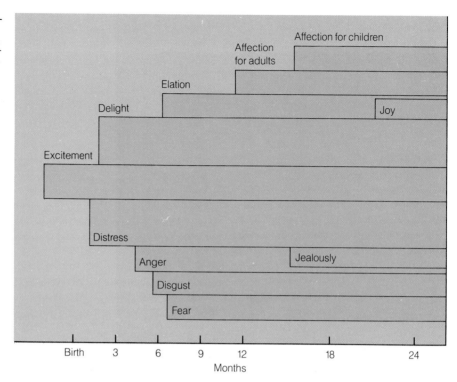

Fig. 13-8 *The "yawn" of this baboon is actually a threat. Emotional expressions allow dominance relationships among animals to be maintained with little actual fighting.*

parents to tend to a baby's needs, thus increasing its chances for survival.

Question: Does the ordering Bridges observed apply to children of all cultures?

Development of the ability to express emotion is probably related to maturation of the brain, since children of all cultures show a similar pattern (Greenberg, 1977). Babies the world over, it seems, rapidly become capable of letting others know what they like and dislike. (Prove this to yourself sometime by driving a baby buggy.)

Emotional Expression

Are human emotional expressions a carryover from more primitive and animal-like stages of human evolution? Charles Darwin thought so. Darwin (1872) observed that tigers, monkeys, dogs, and human beings all bare their teeth in the same way during rage. Darwin believed that emotional expressions were retained during the course of human evolution because communicating feelings to others is an aid to survival (Fig. 13–8). (For more information on the link between facial expressions and emotion, see Highlight 13–2.)

Question: Are emotional expressions the same for all people?

Highlight 13–2
Emotional Expression—Making Faces

It may seem like a case of the tail wagging the dog, but scientists have recently found that "making faces" alters activity in the rest of the body. Paul Ekman and his colleagues carefully guided subjects as they arranged their faces, muscle by muscle, into expressions of surprise, disgust, sadness, anger, fear, and happiness (Fig. 13–9). At the same time, subjects' bodily reactions were monitored. Contrary to what might be expected, making faces brought about changes in the autonomic nervous system, as reflected by heart rate and skin temperature. In addition, each facial expression produced a different pattern of activity. An angry face, for instance, raised heart rate and skin temperature, whereas disgust lowered heart rate and skin temperature (Ekman, Levenson, & Friesen, 1983).

It appears, then, that not only do emotions determine expressions, but expressions may determine emotions (Laird, 1984). Such findings also emphasize the central role played by the face in emotion—as first suggested by Charles Darwin. They may also help explain an interesting effect you have probably observed. When you are feeling "down" or sad, forcing yourself to smile will sometimes be followed by an actual improvement in your mood (Laird, 1974).

Fig. 13-9

The most basic expressions appear to be fairly universal. Children who are born deaf and blind and who therefore have little opportunity to learn emotional expressions from others use the same facial gestures as others to display joy, sadness, disgust, and so on (Knapp, 1978). In fact the gestures of such children may be one of the few examples of "pure" emotional expression. By adulthood most people have learned to carefully control facial expression so that many gestures become unique to various cultures. Among the Chinese, for example, sticking out the tongue is a gesture of surprise, not of disrespect or teasing. Despite such differences, facial expressions of *fear, surprise, sadness, disgust, anger,* and *happiness* are recognized by people of all cultures (Ekman, 1980). Notice that this covers most of the primary emotions listed earlier in the chapter. It's also nice to note that a smile is the most universal and easily recognized facial expression of emotion.

Body Language   If a friend approached you and said, "Hey, ugly, what are you doing?" would you be offended? Probably not, because such expressions are usually accompanied by a big grin. The facial and bodily gestures of emotion speak a language all their own and add an additional message to what is said verbally. The study of communication through body movement, posture, gestures, and facial expressions is called **kinesics** (ki-NEE-ziks) and is informally referred to as body language.

Question: What kinds of messages are sent with body language?

Most of the popular books on body language (for example, Fast, 1970) tend to list particular meanings for gestures. For instance, a woman who stands rigidly, crosses her arms over her chest, or sits with her legs tightly crossed supposedly is sending a "hands off" message. But researchers in the field of kinesics emphasize that gestures are rarely this fixed in meaning (Swensen, 1973). The message might simply be, "This room is cold." Being more realistic, we would say that an overall **emotional tone** is usually communicated by body language.

The most expressive and frequently noticed part of the body is the face. Physiologists estimate that the face is capable of producing some 20,000 different expressions. Most of these are **facial blends,** involving a mixture of two

Fig. 13-10 *Facial and bodily gestures do not always allow an observer to accurately "read" emotion. The agonized expression on the face of Frank De Vito is deceptive. Mr. De Vito and his wife have just learned that he has won $1 million in the New Jersey state lottery.*

or more basic expressions. Imagine, for example, that you just received an F on an unfair test. Quite likely, your eyes, eyebrows, and forehead would show anger, while your mouth would express sadness (Knapp, 1978).

Most of us believe we can fairly accurately tell what others are feeling by observing facial expressions. If thousands of facial blends occur, how do we make such judgments? The answer seems to lie in the fact that facial expressions can be boiled down to basic dimensions of **pleasantness-unpleasantness, attention-rejection,** and **activation** (or arousal) (Schlosberg, 1954). By smiling when giving a friend a hard time, you add the emotional message of pleasantness and acceptance to the verbal insult and change its meaning. As they say in movie Westerns, it makes a big difference to "smile when you say that, pardner."

Other emotional feelings are telegraphed by the body. The most general seem to be **relaxation** or **tension,** and **liking** or **disliking.** Relaxation is expressed by casual positioning of the arms and legs, leaning back (if sitting), and spreading the arms and legs. Liking is expressed mainly by leaning toward a person or object (Mehrabian, 1969) (Fig. 13–11). Thus, body positioning can reveal feelings that would normally be concealed. Who do you "lean toward"?

Imagine that you are standing 30 yards from a classroom in which test grades are being announced. As students file out, do you think you could tell—without the aid of facial expressions—who got A's and who got F's? Actually, your task might not be too difficult. Recent research suggests that overall *posture* can also indicate one's emotional state. Specifically, when a person is successful, his or her posture is likely to be more erect (Weisfeld & Beresford, 1982) (see Fig. 13–12). It remains debatable whether this tendency is a product of evolution or is simply learned. In any case standing tall with pride and slumping with dejection do seem to be consistent patterns.

Question: Does body positioning or movement ever reveal lying or deception?

If you know a person well, you may be able to detect deception from expressive changes (Ekman & Friesen, 1975). But don't count on it. Most people learn to maintain careful control over their facial expressions. A good example is smiling to avoid hurting someone's feelings when you have received a disappointing gift. Often because of such control, deception is best revealed by the lower body. Tense leg positions and restless or repetitive foot and leg movements are associated with fibbing in most people (Ekman & Friesen, 1975). Even a good con artist may be too busy attending to his or her voice and face to control bodily cues.

Coping with Emotion— "Am I Okay or in Trouble?"

Situation: You have been selected to give a speech to 300 people. Or, a physician has informed you that you must undergo a dangerous and painful operation. Or, the one true love of your life walks out the door. What would your emotional response to these events be? How do you cope with an emotional threat? According to Richard Lazarus (1975, 1981), there are two important steps in the process of coping with a threatening situation. The first is **primary appraisal,** in which you decide if a situation is relevant or irrelevant, positive or threatening. In essence this appraisal answers the question, "Am I okay or in trouble?" (Lazarus & Folkman, 1984). Then you make a **secondary appraisal,** during which you choose a means of meeting the threat or challenge. ("What can I do about this situation?")

The emotional effects of appraising a threatening situation were demonstrated in a fascinating experiment by Joseph Spiesman and his associates (1964). These researchers used a graphic film called *Subincision* to stimulate emotional responses in volunteer subjects. Subincision is a ritual used to initiate adolescent boys into manhood in a primitive Australian tribe. The filmed procedure begins with three or four adults holding a boy down to prevent escape. Then a crude and obviously painful operation is performed in which the adolescent's penis is slit on the underside for its entire length. To add insult to injury, the operation is performed with a sharpened flintstone. Needless to say, American viewers respond emotionally to the gory details of this film.

The film was shown in four different versions to test the emotional effects of different appraisals. The first had no sound track. The second emphasized the painful and traumatic aspects of the operation. The third treated the operation in an intellectual and distant way. The fourth glossed over the threatening aspects of the operation and denied that it was painful.

Question: Did the sound tracks affect emotional reactions?

Recordings of heart rate and GSR showed quite clearly that appraisal of a situation affects emotional response. The film emphasizing traumatic aspects of the operation produced an increase in emotion over that caused by the silent film. On the other hand the intellectual and denial sound tracks reduced emotion. The way a situation is "sized up" therefore becomes very important to coping with it. Public speaking, for instance, can be appraised as an intense threat or as a challenge and a chance to perform. Emphasizing the threat by imagining failure, rejection, or embarrassment obviously invites disaster.

Fig. 13-11 *Emotions are often unconsciously revealed by gestures and body positioning.*

Coping with Threat   After a person makes a secondary appraisal, his or her coping attempts can be either problem-focused or emotion-focused (Lazarus & Folkman, 1984). **Problem-focused coping** is aimed at managing or altering the distressing situation itself. In **emotion-focused coping** the person tries instead to control his or her emotional reaction.

Fig. 13-12 *Posture and success. These drawings show the endpoints of a five-point rating scale used to measure erectness of posture. Success by human subjects in various situations was found to be reflected by erect posture. (Adapted from Weisfeld & Beresford, 1982.)*

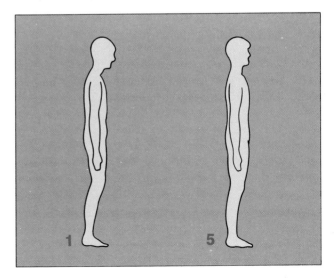

Question: Couldn't both types of coping occur together?

Yes. Sometimes problem- and emotion-focused coping aid one another. Say, for example, that a woman experiences anxiety as she steps to the podium to give a speech. If she does some deep breathing to reduce her anxiety (emotion-focused coping), she will be better able to glance over her notes to improve her delivery (problem-focused coping). It is also possible, however, for the two types of coping to clash or impede one another. If you have to make a difficult decision, for instance, you may suffer unbearable emotional distress. In such circumstances there is a temptation to make a premature and ill-advised choice, just to end the emotional suffering. Doing so may allow you to cope with your emotions, but it shortchanges problem-focused coping (Lazarus & Folkman, 1984).

Coping effectively with emotional reactions is a major topic in its own right. In the following chapter we will further discuss reactions to stressful, threatening, and emotional situations. To conclude our discussion here, let's see what happens when coping attempts fail.

Learned Helplessness— Is There Hope?

Question: What would happen if a person appraised a threatening situation as hopeless?

Bruno Bettelheim (1960), who survived imprisonment in Nazi concentration camps, has described a reaction he calls "give-up-itis." Many of the prisoners felt so helpless that they developed a "zombie-like" detachment that made them into "walking corpses." Martin Seligman (1974) has described a similar reaction in Vietnam prisoner of war camps. Seligman reports the case of a young marine who had adapted unusually well to the stresses of being a POW. His health was apparently related to a promise made by his captors that if he would cooperate he would be released on a certain date. As the date approached, his spirits soared. Then came a devastating blow. He had been deceived. His captors had never intended to release him. Immediately, he lapsed into a deep depression, refused to eat or drink, and died shortly thereafter.

Examples such as these are extreme, but they demonstrate once again the power of emotions. Recent attempts to understand such events have focused on the concept of **learned helplessness.**

Learned helplessness has been demonstrated in the laboratory with animals tested in a shuttle box (Fig. 13–13). If placed in one side of a divided box, dogs will quickly learn to leap to the other side to escape an electric shock. If they are given a warning before the shock occurs (for example, a light dims), most dogs will learn to avoid the shock by leaping the barrier before the shock arrives. This is true of most dogs but not those who have learned to feel helpless.

Question: How is a dog made to feel helpless?

Before being tested in the shuttle box, some dogs were placed in a harness (from which they could not escape)

Fig. 13-13 *In the normal course of escape and avoidance learning, a light dims shortly before the floor is electrified (a). Since the light does not yet have meaning for the dog, the dog receives a shock (noninjurious, by the way) and leaps the barrier (b). Dogs soon learn to watch for the dimming of the light (c) and to jump before receiving a shock (d). Dogs made to feel "helpless" rarely even learn to escape shock, much less to avoid it.*

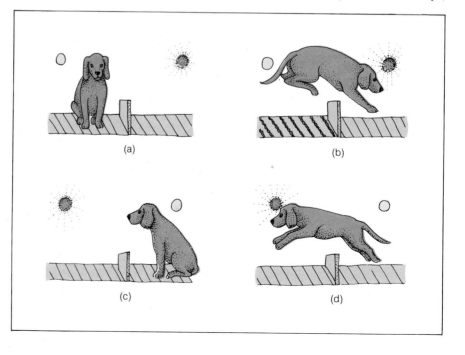

and were given several painful shocks. The animals were helpless to prevent these shocks (Overmier & Seligman, 1967). When placed in the shuttle box, these dogs reacted to the first shock by crouching, howling, and whining. None tried to escape. They helplessly resigned themselves to their fate—after all, they had already learned that there was nothing they could do about shock.

Similar effects occur when humans are made to fail or receive punishment they cannot predict or prevent (Fox & Oakes, 1984). However, where humans are concerned, attributions (remember attribution?) have a large effect on helplessness. Persons who are made to feel helpless in one situation are more likely to act helpless in other situations if they blame their failure on *lasting, general* factors. An example would be concluding "I lack intelligence" after failing to solve a series of puzzles. In contrast, attributing failure to specific factors in the original situation ("I'm not too good at puzzles") tends to prevent learned helplessness from spreading (Alloy, Peterson, Abramson, & Seligman, 1984; Anderson, Anderson, Fleming, & Kinghorn, 1984).

Question: What does learned helplessness have to do with emotion?

Depression Seligman and his associates have drawn attention to the similarities between learned helplessness and depression. Symptoms that occur in both depression and learned helplessness include: feelings of powerlessness and hopelessness, decreased activity, lowered aggression, loss of sexual drive and appetite, and, in humans, a tendency to see oneself as failing, even when this is not the case (Miller, Rossellini, & Seligman, 1977).

Depression is one of the most widespread emotional problems, and it undoubtedly has many causes. However, Seligman has made a good case for learned helplessness as a major factor in many cases of depression and hopelessness. For example, Seligman (1972) describes the fate of Archie, a 15-year-old boy. For Archie school is an unending series of shocks and failures. Other students treat him as if he's stupid; in class he rarely answers questions be-

cause he doesn't know some of the words. He feels knocked down every direction he turns. These may not be electric shocks, but they are certainly psychological "shocks," and Archie has learned to feel helpless to prevent them. When he leaves school, his chances of success will be poor. He has learned to passively endure whatever shocks life has in store for him.

Question: Does Seligman's research give any clues about how to "unlearn" helplessness?

Hope With dogs one effective technique has been to forcibly drag them away from the shock into the "safe" compartment. After this is done several times, the animals regain "hope" and feelings of control over the environment. Just how this can be accomplished with humans is a question for further research. It seems obvious, however, that someone like Archie would benefit from an educational program that would allow him to "succeed" repeatedly. This prediction is backed up by other animal experiments. When animals are given **mastery training**, they become more resistant to learned helplessness (Volpicelli, Ulm, Altenor, & Seligman, 1983). For example, animals that first learned to successfully escape shock were more persistent later in trying to escape inescapable shock. In effect they wouldn't give up, even when the situation was hopeless.

Such findings suggest that we might even be able to "immunize" people against helplessness and depression by giving them experience at mastering seemingly impossible challenges. The Outward Bound schools, in which people pit themselves against the rigors of mountaineering, whitewater canoeing, and wilderness survival, might serve as a model for such a program.

As a final note, the value of hope should not be overlooked. As fragile as this emotion seems to be, it is a powerful antidote to depression and helplessness. As an individual, you may find hope in religion, nature, human companionship, or even technology. Wherever you find it, remember its value: Hope is among the most important of all human emotions.

Learning Check

1. The first recognizable emotional response in a newborn baby is fear. T or F?

2. The pattern of emotional development in human infants varies greatly from one culture to another. T or F?

3. Charles Darwin held that emotional expressions aid survival for animals. T or F?

4. A formal term for "body language" is _____.

5. Circle the three dimensions of emotion communicated by facial expressions:

pleasantness-unpleasantness   complexity   attention-rejection   anger   curiosity-disinterest   activation

6. According to Richard Lazarus, coping with threatening situations can be both problem-focused and _____ focused.

7. Depression in humans is similar to _____ _____ observed in animal experiments.

Answers:

helplessness
1. F 2. F 3. T 4. kinesics 5. pleasantness-unpleasantness, attention-rejection, activation 6. emotion- 7. learned

Applications

Coping with Death and Depression—Problems for Everyone

DEAR ABBY: Do you think about dying much?

CURIOUS

DEAR CURIOUS: No, it's the last thing I want to do.

There are a number of situations in each person's life that are heavily charged with emotion. The second most difficult to handle is probably the death of a close friend or relative; the first is one's own impending death.

Death is a topic of importance to us all. The statistics on death are very convincing: One out of one dies. In spite of this, there tends to be a conspiracy of silence surrounding the topic of death. Perhaps this is because most of us would rather not be reminded of our ultimate demise. Modern medical practice and the funeral industry have also served to insulate most people from

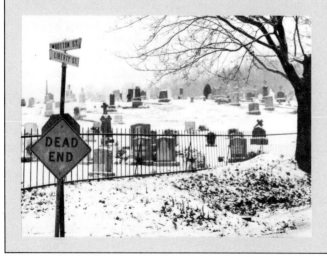

contact with death. As a result most of us are poorly informed about a process that is as basic as birth.

We have seen in this chapter that it is valuable to understand one's own emotions and those of others. With this in mind, this section begins with an investigation of emotional responses before, during, and after death.

Fears of Death

Fears of death are not so extensive as might be supposed. In a public opinion poll of 1500 adults, only about 4 percent showed evidence of directly fearing their own death (Kastenbaum & Aisenberg, 1972). It might seem that as people grow older they would become more fearful of death. However, a recent study of individuals ranging in age from 30 to 82 found no overall differences in death anxiety associated with age (Conte, Weiner, & Plutchik, 1982). However, those fears that do exist apparently change with age. Hall (1922) found that younger individuals fear the *occurrence* of death, whereas older people fear the *circumstances* of death.

These findings seem to indicate a general lack of fear about death, but there is another possible interpretation. It may be more accurate to say that they reflect a deeply ingrained tendency to deny death. The mere fact that death has been something of a taboo subject suggests that underlying fears do exist. When *Psychology Today* surveyed its readers on the subject of death, it found that less than one-third of those who replied grew up in families in which death was openly discussed (Schneidman, 1971). The average person's

Applications: Coping with Death and Depression—Problems for Everyone

exposure to death unfortunately consists of the artificial and unrealistic portrayals of death on TV. It has been estimated that by the time a person is 14 years old, he or she will have witnessed 18,000 TV deaths. With few exceptions these will have been *homicides,* not deaths due to illness or aging (Tobin, 1972).

The Stages of Death

A more direct indication of emotional responses to death comes from the work of Elisabeth Kübler-Ross (1975). Kübler-Ross, a **thanatologist** (THAN-ah-TOL-oh-jist: one who studies death), has spent hundreds of hours at the bedsides of the terminally ill. She has found that dying persons tend to go through a series of emotional stages in order to prepare for death. The five basic stages are:

1. Denial and isolation. The initial reaction to impending death is an attempt to deny its reality and to isolate oneself from all information confirming that death is really going to occur. Initially, the person may be convinced that "It's all a mistake," that lab reports or X-rays have been mixed up, or that a physician is in error. Such denial may proceed to attempts to ignore or avoid any reminder of the situation.

2. Anger. In this stage the dying say, "Why me?" As they face the ultimate frustration of having everything ever valued stripped away, their anger spills over into rage or envy toward those who will continue living. Even good friends may temporarily become enemies because their health is envied.

3. Bargaining. During this period the dying bargain with themselves or with God. The dying person says, "Just let me live a little longer and I'll do anything to earn it." Individuals may bargain for time by trying to be "good" ("I'll never smoke again"), by righting past wrongs, or by praying that if they are granted more time they will dedicate themselves to their religion.

4. Depression. As death draws nearer and the person begins to recognize that it cannot be prevented, feelings of futility, exhaustion, and deep depression set in. The person recognizes that he or she will be separated from friends, loved ones, and the familiar routines of life, and this causes a profound sadness.

5. Acceptance. Assuming that death is not sudden, many people eventually reach a stage during which they calmly accept death. The dying are neither happy nor sad but are at peace. This is usually a quiet time

when the struggle with death has been resolved. The need to talk about death is ended, and silent companionship from others is frequently all that is desired.

Not all terminally ill individuals experience all these stages, and the stages may not always occur in this order. Individual styles of dying vary greatly, according to emotional maturity, religious belief, age, education, the attitudes of relatives, and so forth. Some psychologists believe that Kübler-Ross' description of dying has been taken too literally by the public. It is probably best not to think of the stages as a fixed series that one goes through, with later stages being "more advanced." Rather, the stages describe typical and appropriate reactions to impending death. In this sense Kübler-Ross' work is a good summary of emotional reactions to the difficult process of dying. It is also interesting to note that many of the same reactions accompany any major loss, be it divorce, loss of a home due to fire, death of a pet, or loss of a job.

Question: How can I make use of this information?

This information can be put to use in a number of ways. First of all, it can help both the dying individual and survivors recognize and cope with periods of depression, anger, denial, and bargaining. Secondly, it is helpful to realize that close friends or relatives of the dying person may go through many of the same emotional stages before or after the person's death because they, too, are facing a loss.

Perhaps the most important thing to recognize is that the dying person may have a need to share feelings with others and to discuss death openly. Too often, the dying person feels isolated and separated from others by the wall of silence erected by doctors, nurses, and family members. Adults tend to "freeze up" with a dying person, saying things such as, "I don't know how to deal with this."

Understanding what the dying person is going through may make it easier for you to offer support at this important time. A simple willingness to be with the person and to honestly share his or her feelings can help bring dignity, acceptance, and meaning to death.

Bereavement   After a friend or relative has died, a period of grief typically follows. Grief is a natural and normal reaction to loss, and most psychologists regard it as an essential part of adjusting to death. In our culture funeral services frequently serve as useful outlets for

Applications: Coping with Death and Depression—Problems for Everyone

grief by encouraging the release of emotions.

Grief usually follows a predictable pattern (Parkes, 1979; Schulz, 1978). Grief normally begins with a period of **shock** or numbness. For a brief time the bereaved remain in a dazed state in which they may show little emotion. Most find it extremely difficult to accept the reality of their loss. This phase usually ends by the time of the funeral, which unleashes tears and bottled-up feelings of despair.

Initial shock is followed by sharp **pangs of grief.** These are episodes of painful yearning for the dead person and, sometimes, anguished outbursts of anger. During this period the wish to have the dead person back is intense. Often, mourners continue to think of the dead person as alive; they may hear his or her voice or may encounter the deceased in vivid dreams. During this period agitated distress alternates with silent despair, and suffering is acute.

The first powerful reactions of grief gradually give way to weeks or months of **apathy, dejection,** and **depression.** The person faces a new emotional landscape with a large gap that cannot be filled. Life seems to lose much of its meaning, and a sense of futility dominates the person's outlook. The mourner is usually able to resume work or other activities after 2 or 3 weeks, but insomnia, loss of energy and appetite, and similar signs of depression may continue.

Little by little the bereaved person accepts that which cannot be changed and makes a new beginning. Pangs of grief may still occur, but they are less severe and less frequent. Memories of the dead person, though still painful, now include positive images and nostalgic pleasure. At this stage the bereaved person can be said to be moving toward **resolution.** As was true of approaching death, individual reactions to grief vary considerably. In general, however, a month or two typically passes before the more intense stages of grief have run their course.

As you can see, grief allows survivors to discharge their anguish and to prepare to go on living. A person who avoids this "grief work" by suppressing feelings may later experience a much more severe and lasting depression. Therefore, it is important for people who suffer a loss to accept the need to grieve and for those around them to encourage this necessary expression of emotion (Schulz, 1978). Some additional suggestions for coping with grief are given in Table 13–2.

Table 13–2   Coping with Grief

- Face the loss directly and do not isolate yourself.
- Discuss your feelings with relatives and friends.
- Do not block out your feelings with drugs or alcohol.
- Allow grief to progress naturally; neither hurry nor suppress it.

(From Coni, Davison, & Webster, 1984.)

Coping with Depression

Recent studies show that during the school year up to 78 percent of students at American colleges suffer some of the symptoms of depression. At any given time roughly one-quarter of the student population is involved (Beck & Young, 1978). Why should so many students be "blue"? A variety of problems typically contribute to such depressive feelings. Among the most common are:

1. Stresses from the increased difficulty of college work and pressures to make a career choice often leave students feeling that they are missing out on fun or that all their hard work is meaningless.

2. Isolation and loneliness are common when a student leaves his or her support group behind. Formerly, family, a circle of high school friends, and often an intimate boyfriend or girlfriend could be counted on for support or encouragement.

3. Problems with studying and grades frequently trigger depression. Many students enter college with high aspirations and little former experience with failure. At the same time, many lack basic skills necessary for academic success.

4. Another common cause of college depression is the breakup of an intimate relationship, either with a former boyfriend or girlfriend or with a newly formed college romance (Beck & Young, 1978).

Recognizing Depression   Most people know, obviously enough, when they are "down." Aaron Beck, a nationally recognized authority on depression, suggests you should assume that more than a minor fluctuation in mood is involved when five conditions exist:

1. You have a consistently negative opinion of yourself.
2. You engage in frequent self-criticism and self-blame.

Applications: Coping with Death and Depression—Problems for Everyone

3. You place negative interpretations on events that usually wouldn't bother you.

4. The future looks bleak and negative.

5. You feel that your responsibilities are overwhelming.

Question: What can be done to combat depression?

Combating Depression   Beck and Greenberg (1974) suggest that you begin by making a *daily schedule* for yourself. Try to schedule activities to fill up every hour during the day. It is best to start with easy activities and progress to more difficult tasks. Check off each activity as it is completed. In this way you will begin to break the self-defeating cycle of feeling helpless and falling further behind (depressed students spend much of their time sleeping). A series of small accomplishments, successes, or pleasures may be all you need to get going again. However, if you are lacking skills needed for success in college, ask for help in getting them. Don't remain "helpless."

Beck and Greenberg also believe that feelings of worthlessness and hopelessness are supported by thoughts such as those listed in the five preceding conditions. They recommend writing down self-critical or negative thoughts as they occur, especially those that immediately precede feelings of sadness. After you have collected these thoughts, write a rational answer to each. For example, the thought, "No one loves me," should be answered with a list of people who do care. (See Chapter 23 for more information on this point.)

Attacks of the "college blues" are common and should be distinguished from more serious cases of depression. Severe depression is a serious problem that can lead to suicide or a major impairment of emotional functioning.

Question: How can mild depression be distinguished from more serious problems?

This is a rather difficult judgment to make because it is related to many psychological dimensions. Practically

speaking, a useful answer can be found in a list of 10 danger signals compiled by the National Association for Mental Health to help people distinguish normal depression from reactions that require professional help. Here is the list:

1. A general and lasting feeling of hopelessness and despair.

2. Inability to concentrate, making reading, writing, and conversation difficult. Thinking and activity are slowed because the mind is absorbed by inner anguish.

3. Changes in physical activities such as eating, sleeping, and sex. Frequent physical complaints with no evidence of physical illness.

4. Loss of self-esteem, which brings on continual questioning of personal worth.

5. Withdrawal from others due to immense fear of rejection.

6. Threats or attempts to commit suicide, viewed as a way out of a hostile environment and a belief that life is worthless.

7. Hypersensitivity to words and actions of others and general irritability.

8. Misdirected anger and difficulty in handling most feelings. Self-directed anger because of perceived worthlessness may produce general anger directed at others.

9. Feelings of guilt in many situations. A depressed person assumes he or she is wrong or responsible for the unhappiness of others.

10. Extreme dependency on others. Feelings of helplessness and then anger at the helplessness.

No single item (except number 6) necessarily indicates dangerous depression, but if several are observed, it should be assumed that seeking professional help would be wise.

Learning Check

1. The majority of deaths portrayed on TV involve elderly people who die of some fatal disease.   T or F?

2. In the stage that Küber-Ross describes as bargaining, the dying individual asks, "Why me?"   T or F?

3. A dazed state of shock or numbness is typical of the first phase of grief.   T or F?

4. Many authorities stress that suppression of grief often leads to later problems, such as severe depression.   T or F?

Chapter Summary

■ There is evidence that voodoo deaths actually occur. They are probably caused by intense and prolonged emotion. Despite this, emotions were probably retained in evolution because they are linked to many basic *adaptive behaviors*.

■ Two major parts of an emotion are *physiological changes* in the body and *emotional expressions* (outward signs of emotion).

■ The following are considered to be *primary emotions: fear, surprise, sadness, disgust, anger, anticipation, joy,* and *acceptance*. Other emotions seem to represent mixtures of the primaries.

■ The *James-Lange theory* of emotion says that emotional *experience* follows the bodily reactions of emotion. In contrast the *Cannon-Bard theory* says that bodily reactions and emotional experience occur at the same time and that emotions are organized in the brain.

■ Schachter's *cognitive theory* of emotion emphasizes the importance of labels or interpretations applied to feelings of bodily arousal. Also important is the process of *attribution*. Attribution refers to the effects of associating bodily arousal with a particular person, object, or situation.

■ Physical changes associated with emotion are caused by the action of *adrenaline*, a hormone released into the bloodstream, and by activity in the *autonomic nervous system* (ANS).

■ The *sympathetic branch* of the ANS is primarily responsible for arousing the body, the *parasympathetic branch* for quieting it. Sudden death due to prolonged and intense emotion is probably a parasympathetic effect. Heart attacks caused by sudden intense emotion are more likely due to sympathetic arousal.

■ The *polygraph*, or "lie detector," measures emotional arousal by monitoring *heart rate, blood pressure,* *breathing rate,* and the *galvanic skin response* (GSR). The accuracy of the lie detector has been challenged by many researchers.

■ Emotions develop from the *generalized excitement* observed in newborn babies. Three of the basic emotions—*fear, rage,* and *joy*—may be unlearned. Basic emotional expressions, such as smiling, frowning, or baring one's teeth when angry, also appear to be unlearned. *Facial expressions* appear to be central to emotion. As a result some psychologists consider them a carryover from earlier stages of evolution.

■ Body gestures and movements (body language) also express feelings, mainly by communicating *emotional tone* rather than specific messages. Three dimensions of facial expressions are *pleasantness-unpleasantness, attention-rejection,* and *activation*. The formal study of body language is known as *kinesics*.

■ The *primary appraisal* of a situation greatly affects emotional response to it. Fear reactions in particular are related to the appraisal of threat. During a *secondary appraisal* some means of coping with a situation is selected. Coping may be either *problem-focused* or *emotion-focused*.

■ The concept of *learned helplessness* has been used to explain failure to cope with threatening situations, and as a model for understanding *depression*. *Mastery training* acts as one major antidote to helplessness.

■ Typical emotional reactions to impending death are *denial, anger, bargaining, depression,* and *acceptance*. Bereavement also brings forth a typical series of reactions ranging from shock to final acceptance.

■ *Depression* is a major, and surprisingly common, emotional problem. Actions and thoughts that counter feelings of helplessness tend to reduce depression.

Love—Stalking an Elusive Emotion

When the topic is love, everyone is a philosopher. And why not? Love is one of the most intense of all emotions. Moreover, love figures prominently in many major life decisions. At one time or other, most people must ask themselves, "Is this love or lust?" "Is it real or infatuation?" "What am I really feeling?" All of which raise the question: What is love?

To quote one author, love is: "a preoccupation with another person. A deeply felt desire to be with the loved one. A feeling of incompleteness without him or her" (Pope, 1980). While this captures some of the essence of *romantic* love, it obviously falls short as a general definition. Think, for instance, about differences in the love you feel for parents, siblings, friends, or a spouse or lover. Clearly, love can take many forms. At the very least love can be: erotic, playful, friendly, affectionate, dependent, obsessive, jealous, altruistic (given without expectation of gain), or practical.

Question: How different are different kinds of love? Do they have anything in common?

These questions were recently addressed by psychologists Robert Sternberg and Susan Grajeck at Yale University. In an interesting study, subjects' love for their mothers, fathers, siblings, best friends, and lovers was measured with a questionnaire and written tests. By combining this data with a personal "love history" for each sub-

ject, Sternberg and Grajeck (1984) were able to probe and analyze patterns of love.

As you might expect, the *intensity* of love differed in various relationships. Opposite-sex lovers, for example, were the target of the most intense feelings of love. In contrast, love for siblings was weakest. Sternberg and Grajeck also found that the happiest families were the most loving (or, loving families were the happiest). However, the intensity of love within a family was unrelated to the amount of love felt for persons (including lovers) outside the family. Another interesting finding was that, for most people, love felt for a best friend was least like that felt in other close relationships. Such findings, however, were only a sidelight to a more interesting discovery.

The Core of Love?

The key finding of Sternberg and Grajeck's study is that the relationships studied all had something in common. No matter how else they differed, each loving relationship had a "common core," consisting of a high level of *interpersonal communication, sharing, and support.* Sternberg and Grajeck believe that various types of love occur when other emotions and motives are added to this common core. Possible extra "ingredients" you may experience in some of your relationships are: jealousy, physical attraction, irrational feelings, sexual desire, security, com-

petition for affection, a sense of personal growth, and so forth. Undoubtedly many other factors could be listed. Nevertheless, Sternberg and Grajeck believe that the various loves one experiences are not, at core, different.

Question: Then why does romantic love seem so different?

Passionate Love   The chief feature that sets romantic love apart from other types is probably *heightened arousal.* **Passionate love** is a wildly emotional state—a mixture of tenderness and sexuality, elation and pain, anxiety and relief, altruism and jealousy (Walster & Walster, 1978). Passionate love is often associated with restlessness (in the absence of one's lover), appetite loss, agitation, emotional activation, and other signs of arousal. Also, passionate love frequently occurs against a backdrop of danger, adversity, stress, or frustration—especially in soap operas and romance novels!

As discussed earlier in this chapter, some psychologists believe that heightened arousal, no matter what its cause, may be interpreted as passionate love in a romantic relationship (Bersheid & Walster, 1974b). Other psychologists argue that lovers not only increase arousal for one another but also reduce it—which may explain why being together is so powerfully reinforcing for lovers (Kenrick & Cialdini, 1977). In any case a variety of experiments support the idea that passionate love is associ-

Exploration: Love—Stalking an Elusive Emotion

ated with heightened emotional arousal.

Companionate Love   Do you believe that to be truly in love is to be in love forever? Do you believe that as long as two people love each other, they can overcome any obstacle? Do you believe that a person should marry whomever he or she loves, regardless of circumstances? If you agree with such statements, you probably believe strongly in the importance of passionate love. If so, you are not alone. Our culture tends to place great emphasis on passion as the basis for "falling" in love. This tendency, however, overlooks a second major kind of love. **Companionate love** refers to affection and deep attachment that is built on respect, shared interests, and firm friendship. Companionate love is lower key emotionally than passionate love. However, it is steady, long term, and tends to grow with time (Walster & Walster, 1978).

Question: Are you suggesting that one type of love is better than the other?

A Delicate Balance?   Passionate love is certainly responsible for launching many relationships. However, the passionate, breathless stage of love typically lasts only about 6 to 30 months (Walster & Walster, 1978). What happens when this period ends? Quite often, people separate. There is a degree of danger, then, in expecting to live forever on a romantic cloud. People who are primarily caught up in passionate love may neglect to build a more lasting relationship. In this sense companionate love—the "kind of affection we feel for those with whom our lives are deeply intertwined"—is as important as passionate love (Walster & Walster, 1978).

Rather than downplaying companionate love, it is helpful to realize that lovers must also be friends. It could even be said that

passionate love merely brings people together long enough so that they can become friends as well as lovers. Companionate love, by the way, is not necessarily a prescription for a boring relationship. Although passionate love tends to decline even in lasting marriages, companionate love tends to grow and can still include emotional highs (Cimbalo, Faling, & Mousaw, 1976). All considered, the best relationships probably involve a mixture of both types of love.

In this brief discussion we have singled out only two of the many types of love that may occur. Whatever form your own love relationships may take, you might find it valuable to remember Sternberg and Grajeck's findings: The core of love is communication, sharing, and mutual support.

Learning Check

1.   Essentially, all types of love can be described as a preoccupation with another person.   T or F?
2.   Sternberg and Grajeck found that love for parents is typically more intense than love for siblings.   T or F?
3.   According to Sternberg and Grajeck's work, the core of various types of love is security, sharing, and dependency.   T or F?
4.   In most instances a key element in romantic love is the presence of irrational thoughts.   T or F?
5.   _____ love is the kind of affection we feel for those with whom our lives are deeply intertwined.

Answers: 1. F   2. T   3. F   4. F   5. Companionate

Questions for Discussion

1. Do you consider yourself more or less emotional than average? What role has learning played in the development of your emotional life? (Consider the influence of family, friends, and culture.)

2. In what ways have emotions contributed to your enjoyment of life? In what ways have they caused problems for you?

3. There is an element of truth to each of the theories of emotion. Which seems to apply best to your own emotional experience?

4. What would be the advantages and disadvantages of being emotionless? (You might use Mr. Spock from "Star Trek" as a model for answering this question.)

5. In your opinion what limits, if any, should be placed on the use of lie detection devices by businesses? By the military? By government?

6. How general are the emotional stages of death described by Kübler-Ross? Do they describe the reactions of people you know who have died?

7. Why do you think dying individuals so often feel isolated? How could the emotional needs of dying persons be better served than they are now in hospitals and nursing homes?

8. Did you learn "body language" from your parents? How similar are your facial and hand gestures to theirs?

9. In what ways do schools, parents, and the government encourage feelings of helplessness? In what ways do they (or could they) add to feelings of confidence, competence, or hope?

Chapter 14

Frustration, Conflict, Stress, and Defense

Chapter Preview
How to Build a Human Time Bomb

When he was arrested, John was sitting atop a 3-ton bulldozer staring into space. Behind him lay a mile-long path of destruction, for John had cut a broad, straight path through yards, roads, and fields. The path led back to his house where the dozer was usually kept. Why did he do it? John explained that his father had denied him use of the family car that morning. Hours later, his anger reached the exploding point.

Question: What would cause someone to react so drastically to a family disagreement?

In John's case, the answer is that he was frustrated—*very frustrated! Perhaps you have been as frustrated as John must have been when he climbed into the driver's seat. For example, picture yourself looking for a parking place in a crowded lot. Imagine that you are late for a test and have already been delayed by an irritating traffic jam. After 15 minutes of frantic searching, you finally spy an empty space, but as you start toward it, a Volkswagen darts around the corner and into the space. A car behind you begins to honk impatiently. Your car's radiator boils over. In such a situation you might be seized by an overwhelming desire to run over anything in sight—cars, pedestrians, lampposts, trees, and flower beds. Few people actually carry out such impulses, but the feeling is common. Aggressive urges frequently accompany frustration.*

Question: Is frustration the same as anger?

No. **Frustration** *can be defined as a negative emotional state that occurs when one is prevented from reaching a goal. John's desire to use the family car was blocked by his father. Similarly, in the imaginary parking lot the goal of finding a parking space was blocked by the presence of other cars.*

This chapter will discuss frustration and some of the ways people deal with it. We will also discuss some common forms of **conflict**. *Conflicts develop when a person has two or more competing or contradictory motives or goals. Choosing between college and work, marriage and single life, or study and failure are conflicts many students face.*

Frustration and conflicts are major causes of stress. **Stress** *occurs when demands are placed on an organism to adjust or adapt. Stress is a normal part of life, but when it is severe or prolonged, it can do much damage. Therefore, the Applications section of this chapter focuses on ways for you to cope with frustration, conflict, and stress.*

Survey Questions What causes frustration and what are typical reactions to it? When and why do people use psychological defense mechanisms? Are there different types of conflict? How is stress related to health and disease? What can be done to manage stress? How does stress interfere with taking tests?

Resources

Sources of Frustration—
Blind Alleys and Lead Balloons

Question: What causes frustration?

Obstacles of many kinds cause frustration. A useful distinction can be made between *external* and *personal* sources of frustration. **External frustration** is based on conditions outside the individual that impede progress toward a goal. All of the following are external frustrations: getting stuck with a flat tire, having a marriage proposal rejected, finding the cupboard bare when you go to get your poor dog a bone, finding the refrigerator bare when you go to get your poor tummy a T-bone, finding the refrigerator gone when you return home, being chased out of the house by your starving dog. In other words external frustrations are based on *delay*, *failure*, *rejection*, *loss*, and other direct blocking of motives.

Notice that external obstacles can be either *social* (slow drivers, tall people in theaters, people who cut into lines) or *nonsocial* (stuck doors, a dead battery, rain on the day of the game). If you ask 10 of your friends what has frustrated them recently, most will probably mention someone's behavior ("My sister wore one of my dresses when I wanted to wear it"; "My supervisor is unfair"; "My history teacher grades too hard"). As social animals we humans are highly sensitive to social sources of frustration.

Frustration usually increases as the **strength, urgency,** or **importance** of a blocked motive increases. An escape artist submerged in a tank of water and bound with 200 pounds of chain could be expected to become *quite* frustrated by the jamming of a trick lock. Remember too that motivation becomes stronger as we near a goal. As a result frustration is more intense when a person encounters an obstacle very close to a goal. If you've ever missed an A grade by two points, you were probably very frustrated. If you've missed an A by *one* point—well, frustration builds character, right?

A final factor affecting frustration is summarized by the old phrase "the straw that broke the camel's back." *Repeated* frustrations can accumulate in their effect until a small irritation unleashes an unexpectedly violent response. The boy who bulldozed the countryside probably had been frustrated many times before by his father.

Personal frustrations are based on an individual's personal characteristics. If you are 4 feet tall and aspire to be a professional basketball player, you very likely will be frustrated. If you want to go to medical school but can only earn D grades at best, you will likewise be frustrated. In both examples, frustration is ultimately based on personal limitations, although the resulting failures may be *experienced* as externally caused. We will return to this point in the Applications section of this chapter. In the meantime let's look at some typical reactions to frustration.

Reactions to Frustration—
Irresistible Force
Meets Immovable Object

Question: Does frustration always cause aggression? Aren't there other reactions?

Although the connection is strong, frustration does not always provoke aggression. Later, in Chapter 26, we will explore factors that influence when and where aggression is likely to occur. For now it is enough to note that **aggression** is one of the most persistent and frequent responses to frustration (Miller, 1941). The frustration-aggression link is so common, in fact, that experiments are hardly necessary to show it. A glance at almost any newspaper will provide examples such as the one that follows.

Justifiable Autocide

Burien, Washington (AP)—Barbara Smith committed the assault, but police aren't likely to press charges. Her victim was a 1964 Oldsmobile which failed once too often to start.

When Officer Jim Fuda arrived at the scene, he found one beat-up car, a broken baseball bat, and a satisfied 23-year-old Seattle woman.

"I feel good," Ms. Smith reportedly told the officer. "That car's been giving me misery for years and I killed it."

Aggression is not usually the first reaction to frustration. More often, frustration is met with **persistence** characterized by more **vigorous efforts** and more **variable responses.** For example, if you put your last quarter in a vending machine and find that pressing the button has no effect, you will probably press harder and faster (vigorous effort), and then you will press all the other buttons (varied response). Persistence may help you get *around* a barrier and achieve your goal. However, if the machine *still* refuses to deliver or to return your quarter, you may then become aggressive and kick the machine (or at least tell it what you think of it). (See Fig. 14-1 for a summary of common reactions to frustration.)

Persistence can be very adaptive. Overcoming a barrier ends the frustration and satisfies the need or motive directed toward the goal. The same is true of aggression that removes or destroys a barrier. Picture a small band of primitive humans, parched with thirst but separated from a water hole by a menacing animal. It is easy to see that attacking the animal may ensure their survival. In modern society such direct aggression is seldom acceptable. If you encounter a long line at the drinking fountain, aggression is hardly an appropriate response. Since direct aggression is disruptive and generally discouraged, it is frequently *displaced.*

Question: How is aggression displaced? Does displaced aggression occur often?

Directing aggression toward a source of frustration may be impossible or it may be too dangerous. If you are frustrated by your boss at work or by a teacher at school, the cost of

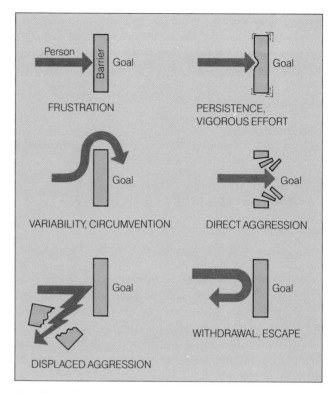

Fig. 14-1   *Frustration, and reactions to it.*

direct aggression may be too high (loss of a job or failure of a needed class). Instead, the aggression may be displaced or *redirected* toward whomever or whatever is available (see cartoon).

Targets of **displaced aggression** tend to be "safer," or less likely to retaliate, than the original source of frustration. Attacking the helpless countryside when the real source of frustration is one's father is a clear case of displaced aggression. Sometimes long *chains* of displacement can be observed, in which one person displaces aggression to the next. For instance, a businessman who is frustrated by high taxes reprimands an employee, who swallows his anger until he reaches home and then yells at his wife, who in turn yells at the children, who then tease the dog; the dog chases the cat, who later knocks over the canary cage.

Psychologists attribute much hostility and destructiveness in our society to displaced aggression. A disturbing example is the finding that when unemployment increases, so does child abuse (Steinberg et al., 1981). Particularly damaging is a pattern known as **scapegoating.** A scapegoat is a person who has become a habitual target of

"Bills, bills, bills! I'll remember this when it comes time for your Christmas tip."

displaced aggression. A tragic example of scapegoating on a large scale is the fact that in the United States between 1880 and 1930 there was a strong correlation between the price of cotton and the number of lynchings of blacks in the South. As the price of cotton went down (and frustration increased), the number of lynchings increased (Dollard et al., 1939). Despite recent progress many minority groups continue to suffer from hostility based on scapegoating.

Question: I have a friend who dropped out of school to hitchhike around the country. He seemed very frustrated before he quit. What type of response to frustration is this?

Another major reaction to frustration is **escape,** or **withdrawal.** Being frustrated is unpleasant. If other reactions do not reduce feelings of frustration, a person may try to escape. Escape may mean actually leaving a source of frustration (dropping out of school, quitting a job, leaving an unhappy marriage), or it may mean *psychologically* escaping. Two common forms of psychological escape are *apathy* (pretending not to care) and the *use of drugs* such as alcohol, marijuana, or narcotics.

Thus far we have examined only the most obvious responses to frustration. A whole class of *defensive* reactions also exists. Let's see how they operate.

Learning Check

Be sure you can answer these questions before continuing.

1. When progress toward a goal is blocked, the resulting psychological state is called _____.

2. Delays, rejections, and losses may be thought of as what kind of frustration? _____

3. Which of the following is *not* considered a common reaction to frustration?
   a. ambivalence   *c.* displaced aggression
   b. aggression   *d.* persistence

4. Scapegoating can be thought of as a type of displaced aggression.   T or F?

5. Sampson Goliath is 7 feet tall and weighs 300 pounds. He has failed miserably in his aspirations to become a jockey. The source of his frustration is mainly _____.

6. As a reaction to frustration, apathy may be viewed as a form of _____.

7. Being very close to a goal when a barrier is encountered typically increases the intensity of frustration.   T or F?

Answers: 1. frustration 2. external 3. *d* 4. T 5. personal 6. escape or withdrawal 7. T

Psychological Defense— Mental Karate?

Situations causing frustration, conflict, or stress are often accompanied by an unpleasant emotion known as **anxiety.** A person who is anxious becomes tense, uneasy, apprehensive, worried, and feels vaguely threatened. Since anxiety is unpleasant and uncomfortable, we are usually motivated to avoid it. Anxiety caused by stressful situations, or by our own shortcomings and limitations, frequently leads to use of **psychological defense mechanisms.**

Question: What are psychological defense mechanisms and how do they lessen anxiety?

A defense mechanism is any technique used to avoid, deny, or distort sources of anxiety. Defense mechanisms are also used to maintain an idealized self-image, so that we can comfortably live with ourselves. Many of the defenses were first identified by Sigmund Freud, who assumed they operated *unconsciously.* Often, unconscious defensiveness creates large blind spots in awareness, as when an extremely stingy person fails to recognize that he or she is a tightwad. Everyone has at one time or another used such defenses. Let's consider a few of the most common. (A more complete listing is given in Table 14–1.)

Table 14–1   Psychological Defense Mechanisms

Compensation	Counteracting a real or imagined weakness by emphasizing desirable traits or by seeking to excel in other areas.
Denial	Protecting oneself from an unpleasant reality by refusing to perceive it.
Fantasy	Fulfilling frustrated desires in imaginary achievements or activities.
Intellectualization	Separating emotion from a hurtful, threatening, or anxiety-provoking situation by talking and thinking about it in formal or intellectual terms.
Isolation	Separating contradictory thoughts or feelings into "logic-tight compartments" so that no conflict is created.
Projection	Attributing one's own feelings, shortcomings, or unacceptable impulses to others.
Rationalization	Justifying one's own behavior by giving reasonable and rational but false reasons for it.
Reaction formation	Preventing dangerous impulses from being expressed by exaggerating opposite behavior.
Regression	Retreating to an earlier level of development or to earlier, less demanding habits or situations.
Repression	Preventing painful or dangerous thoughts from entering consciousness.
Sublimation	Working off frustrated desires, or unacceptable impulses, in activities that are constructive.

Denial   One of the most basic defense mechanisms is **denial**. Denial means to protect oneself from an unpleasant reality by refusing to accept it or believe it. Denial is closely linked with experiences such as death, illness, and similar painful and threatening situations. For instance, if you were told that you had only 3 months to live, how would you react? Your first thoughts might be: "Aw, come on, someone must have mixed up the X-rays," or "The doctor must be mistaken," or, simply, "It can't be true!" Similar denial and disbelief are common reactions to the unexpected death of a friend or relative: "It's just not real. I don't believe it. I just don't believe it!"

Repression   Freud noticed that his patients had tremendous difficulty recalling shocking or traumatic events from childhood. It seemed that powerful forces were holding these painful memories from awareness. Freud called this **repression**. Apparently, we protect ourselves by repressing thoughts or impulses that are painful or threatening. Feelings of hostility toward a loved one, the names of disliked people, and past failures and embarrassments are common targets of repression.

Repression may seem similar to denial, but there is a difference. Let's say you are often criticized by others for being selfish. If you are aware of the criticism, but refuse to believe that it is meant seriously, you are using denial as a defense. On the other hand if you repress (forget) the times your selfishness is mentioned, you will remain totally unaware of your fault.

Reaction Formation   Reaction formation is a defense in which impulses are not only repressed, they are also held in check by exaggerated opposite behavior. For example, a mother who unconsciously resents her children may, through reaction formation, become absurdly overprotective and overindulgent. Her real thoughts of "I hate them" and "I wish they were gone" are replaced by "I love them" and "I don't know what I would do without them." The mother's hostile impulses are traded for "smother" love, so that she will not have to admit her dislike of her children. The basic idea in reaction formation is that the individual acts out an opposite behavior in order to block threatening impulses or feelings.

Regression   In its broadest meaning **regression** refers to any return to earlier, less demanding situations or habits. Most parents who have a second child have to put up with at least some regression by the older child. Frustrated by a new rival for attention, an older child may regress to childish speech, bed-wetting, or infantile play after the new baby arrives. However, regression is usually less severe. The child at summer camp who gets homesick and longs for the security of familiar surroundings is undergoing mild regression. An adult who throws a temper tantrum or a married adult who "goes home to mother" is also regressing.

Projection   Projection is an unconscious process that protects us from the anxiety that would occur from recognizing our own faults or unacceptable traits.

Question: How does projection work?

A person who is **projecting** tends to see his or her own shortcomings or unacceptable impulses in others. By exaggerating the unacceptable traits of *others*, the individual lessens his or her own failings.

The author once worked for a greedy shop owner who cheated many of his customers. This same man considered himself a pillar of the community and a good Christian. How did he justify to himself his greed and dishonesty? He believed that everyone who entered his store was bent on *cheating him* any way they could. In reality few, if any, of his customers shared his motives, but he projected his own greed and dishonesty onto them.

Rationalization Every teacher is familiar with a strange phenomenon that occurs whenever a test is scheduled. On the day of the exam, an incredible wave of disasters sweeps through the city. An amazing number of mothers, fathers, sisters, brothers, aunts, uncles, grandparents, friends, relatives, and pets become ill or die. Motors suddenly fall out of automobiles. Books are lost or stolen. Alarm clocks go belly-up and ring out no more.

The making of excuses comes from a natural tendency to explain one's behavior. When the explanation offered is reasonable, rational, and convincing—but not the real reason—we say a person is *rationalizing*. **Rationalization** unconsciously provides us with reasons for behavior we ourselves find somewhat questionable. Here is a typical example of rationalization. A student who fails to turn in an assignment he has known about since the beginning of the semester explains:

> My car broke down 2 days ago and I couldn't get to the library until yesterday. Then I couldn't get all the books I needed because some were checked out, but I wrote what I could. Then last night, as the last straw, the ribbon in my typewriter broke, and since all the stores were closed I couldn't finish the paper on time.

If asked why he left the assignment until the last minute (the real reason for its being late), the student would probably launch into another set of rationalizations. If these are questioned, the student will probably become emotional as he is forced to see himself without the protection of his rationalizations.

Sour grapes and **sweet lemons** reactions are two variations of rationalization. Sour grapes refers to making an unobtainable goal seem less appealing. For example, if you apply for a job and fail to get it, you may review its "sour" points to soften your disappointment. In contrast sweet lemons rationalization involves convincing yourself that a bad situation is really positive. Imagine, for example, that you just bought a car stereo. A week later, you hear another stereo that sounds better than yours and that cost less than you paid. Under such circumstances you would probably make a mental list of the advantages (other than price and sound!) of owning the stereo you selected.

Question: All of the defense mechanisms described seem pretty undesirable. Do they have a positive side?

People who overuse defense mechanisms become less adaptable, because they consume greater amounts of emotional energy to control anxiety and to maintain an unrealistic self-image. Defense mechanisms do have value, however. Often, they help keep us from being overwhelmed by immediate threats. This can provide time for learning to cope with continuing threats and frustrations. If you recognize some of your own behavior in the descriptions here, it is hardly a sign that you are hopelessly defensive. As noted earlier, most people make occasional use of defense mechanisms.

Two defense mechanisms that have a decidedly more positive quality are *compensation* and *sublimation*.

Compensation Compensation is a form of behavior in which a person tries to make up for some personal defect or fault. **Compensatory reactions** are defenses against feelings of inferiority. A person who has a deficiency or weakness (real or imagined) may go to unusual lengths to overcome the weakness or to compensate for it by excelling in other areas.

Two of the better known muscle men in America are Jack LaLanne and Charles Atlas. Both made successful careers out of body building, in spite of the fact that as young men they were thin and sickly. Perhaps it would be more accurate to say *because* they were thin and sickly. There are dozens of examples of compensation at work. A childhood stutterer may excel in debate at college. Franklin D. Roosevelt's outstanding achievements in politics came after he was stricken with polio. Although she was unable to see or hear, Helen Keller became an outstanding thinker and writer. Doc Watson, Ray Charles, Stevie Wonder, Ronnie Milsap, and a number of other well-known musicians are blind.

Sublimation Sublimation (sub-lih-MAY-shun) is defined as working off frustrated desires (especially sexual desires) in substitute activities that are constructive and accepted by society (Fig. 14-2). Freud believed that art, music, dance, poetry, scientific investigation, and most other creative activities can serve to rechannel sexual energies into productive and acceptable behavior. Freud also believed that almost any strong desire can be sublimated. For example, a very aggressive person might find social acceptance as a professional soldier, boxer, or football

Fig. 14-2 *For some players—and fans—football probably allows sublimation of aggressive urges.*

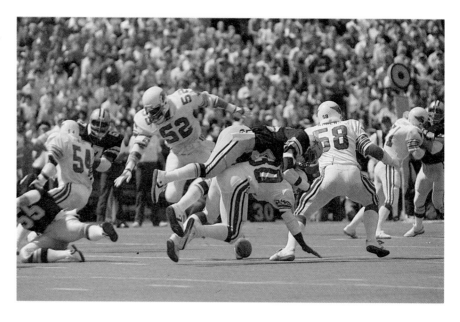

player. Greed may be refined into a successful business career. Lying may be sublimated into storytelling, creative writing, or politics.

Sexual motives appear to be the most easily and widely sublimated. Freud would have had a field day with such modern pastimes as surfing, motorcycle riding, drag racing, and dancing to or playing rock music, to name but a few. People enjoy each of these activities for a multitude of reasons, but it is hard to overlook the rich, sexual symbolism possible in each.

Conflict— Yes-No-Yes-No-Yes-No-Yes-No-Yes-No . . . Well, Maybe

Conflict creates a special kind of frustration. When an individual must make a decision between *incompatible* or *contradictory* needs, desires, motives, wishes, or external demands, he or she experiences conflict. There are four basic forms of conflict, each with its own characteristics (Lewin, 1935) (see Fig. 14-3 and Fig. 14-4).

Approach-Approach Conflicts The simplest conflict comes from having to choose between two *positive*, or desirable, alternatives. Choosing between tutti-frutti-coconut-mocha-champagne-ice and orange-marmalade-peanut-butter-coffee-swirl at the ice cream parlor may throw you into a temporary conflict, but if you really like both choices, your decision will be quickly made. Even when

more important decisions are involved, **approach-approach conflicts** tend to be the easiest kind of conflict to resolve. The old fable about the mule who died of thirst and starvation while standing between a bucket of water and a bucket of oats is clearly unrealistic. When both alternatives are positive, the scales of decision are easily tipped one direction or the other.

Avoidance-Avoidance Conflicts Avoidance conflicts are based on being forced to choose between two *negative*, or undesirable, alternatives. A person in an avoidance conflict is "caught between the devil and the deep blue sea" or "caught between the frying pan and the fire." In real life avoidance conflicts involve choosing between things like studying and failure, unwanted pregnancy and abortion, the dentist and tooth decay, a monotonous job and poverty.

Question: Suppose I don't object to abortion. Or suppose that I consider any pregnancy sacred and not to be tampered with?

Notice that these examples can only be defined as conflicts on the basis of an individual's own needs and values. If a woman wants to terminate a pregnancy and has no personal objection to abortion, she experiences no conflict. Or, if she would not consider abortion under any circumstances, there is no conflict.

Avoidance conflicts often have a "damned if you do, damned if you don't" quality. In other words both choices are negative, but *not choosing* is impossible or equally un-

Fig. 14-3 *Three basic forms of conflict.*

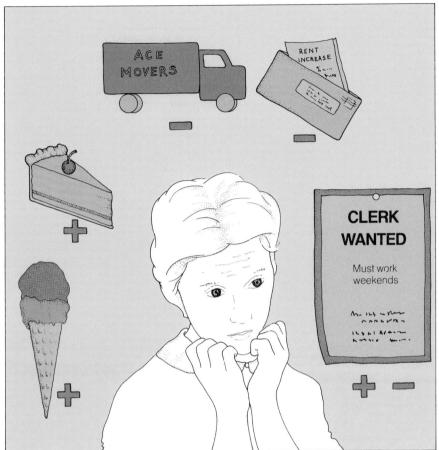

Fig. 14-4 *Conflict diagrams. As shown by the colored areas in the graphs (below), desires to approach, and to avoid, increase near a goal. The effects of these tendencies are depicted below each graph. The "behavior" of the ball in each example illustrates the nature of the conflict above it. An approach conflict (left) is easily decided. Moving toward one goal will increase its attraction (graph) and will lead to a rapid resolution. (If the ball moves in either direction, it will go all the way to one of the goals.) In an avoidance conflict (center), tendencies to avoid are deadlocked, resulting in inaction. In an approach-avoidance conflict (right), approach proceeds to the point where desires to approach and avoid cancel each other. Again, these tendencies are depicted (below) by the action of the ball. (Graphs after Miller, 1944.)*

desirable. To illustrate, imagine the plight of a person trapped in a hotel fire 20 stories from the ground. Should the person jump from the window and almost surely die on the pavement? Or should he or she try to dash through the flames and almost surely die of smoke inhalation and burns? When people are faced with choices such as these, it is easy to see why they often *freeze*, finding it impossible to decide or to take action. A trapped individual may first think about the window, approach it, and then back away after looking down 20 stories. Next the person may try the door and again back away as heat and smoke billow in. In actual disasters of this sort, people are often found dead in their rooms, victims of an inability to take action.

Indecision, inaction, and freezing are not the only reactions to avoidance conflicts. Since avoidance conflicts are stressful and rarely solved, people sometimes pull out of avoidance situations entirely. This reaction, called *leaving the field*, is a form of escape. It may explain the behavior of a student the author knows who could not afford to attend school unless he worked. However, if he worked, he could not earn passing grades. His solution after much conflict and indecision? He joined the navy.

Approach-Avoidance Conflicts Approach-avoidance conflicts are also difficult to resolve. Since people seldom escape them, such conflicts are in some ways more troublesome than avoidance conflicts. A person in an **approach-avoidance conflict** is "caught"—being simultaneously attracted to, and repelled by, the same goal or activity. Attraction keeps the person in the situation, but its negative aspects cause turmoil and distress. For example, a high school student arrives to pick up his date for the first time. He is met at the door by her father, who is a professional wrestler—7 feet tall, 300 pounds, and entirely covered with hair. The father gives the boy a crushing handshake and growls that he will break him in half if the girl is not home on time. The student considers the girl attractive and has a good time. But does he ask her out again? It depends on the relative strength of his attraction and his fear. Almost certainly he will feel *ambivalent* about asking her out again, knowing that another encounter with her father is involved.

Ambivalence (mixed positive and negative feelings) is a central characteristic of approach-avoidance conflicts. Am-

bivalence is usually translated into *partial approach* (Miller, 1944). Since our student is still attracted to the girl, he may spend time with her at school and elsewhere but may not actually date her again. Some more realistic examples of approach-avoidance conflicts are: planning marriage to someone your parents strongly disapprove of, wanting to be an actor but suffering stage fright, wanting to buy a car but not wanting to be tied to monthly payments, wanting to eat when overweight, and wanting to go to school but hating to study. Many of life's important decisions have approach-avoidance dimensions.

Question: Aren't real-life conflicts more complex than the ones described here?

In reality, conflicts are rarely as clear-cut as those described. People in conflict are usually faced with several dilemmas at once, so several types of conflict are intermingled. The fourth type of conflict moves us closer to this realistic state of affairs.

Double Approach-Avoidance Conflicts You are offered two jobs, one with good pay but poor hours and dull work, the second with interesting work and excellent hours, but low pay. Which do you select? This situation is more typical of the choices we must usually make. It offers neither completely positive, nor completely negative, alternatives. It is, in other words, a **double approach-avoidance conflict,** since each alternative has both positive and negative qualities.

When faced with double approach-avoidance conflicts, people tend to **vacillate,** or waver, between the alternatives. Just as you are about to choose one alternative, its undesirable aspects tend to loom large, so you swing back toward the other. If you have ever been romantically attracted to two people at once, each having qualities you like and dislike, then you have probably experienced vacillation.

On a day-to-day basis, most double approach-avoidance conflicts are little more than an annoyance. When they involve major life decisions, such as choice of a career, school, mate, job, whether to have children, and so forth, they add significantly to the amount of stress experienced.

Learning Check

1. The psychological defense known as denial refers to the natural tendency to explain or justify one's actions.   T or F?

2. Fulfilling frustrated desires in imaginary achievements or activities defines the defense mechanism of:
   a. compensation   *b.* isolation   *c.* fantasy   *d.* sublimation

3. In compensation, one's own undesirable characteristics or motives are attributed to others.   T or F?

4. Of the defense mechanisms two that are considered relatively constructive are: (circle)

    compensation denial isolation projection regression rationalization sublimation

5. Conflict is related to the presence of contradictory _____ or an attempt to reach contra-

    dictory _____.

6. The easiest type of conflict to resolve is typically an _____ conflict.

7. Inaction and freezing are most characteristic of avoidance conflicts.   T or F?

8. Approach-avoidance conflicts produce mixed feelings called _____.

Answers: 1. F 2. c 3. F 4. compensation and sublimation 5. motives, goals 6. approach-approach 7. T 8. ambivalence

Stress— Invisible Killer on the Loose

It is common to assume that stress is always bad or that a complete lack of stress is ideal. However, as stress researcher Hans Selye (1976) observes, "To be totally without stress is to be dead." Stress occurs anytime we must adjust or adapt to the environment. Naturally, unpleasant situations such as work pressures, marital problems, or financial troubles produce stress. But so do travel, sports, a new job, ski jumping, dating, and other pleasant activities. Even if you aren't a thrill seeker, a healthy lifestyle may include a fair amount of stress.

Question: Why is stress sometimes damaging and sometimes not?

Psychologists are learning that stress reactions in humans are more complex than once thought. Let's examine some of the chief factors that determine whether stress is harmful.

When Is Stress a Strain?   It goes almost without saying that some situations are inherently more stressful than others. Police officers, for instance, suffer from an unusually high rate of stress-related diseases. The threat of injury or death, coupled with periodic confrontations with drunk or belligerent citizens, takes a toll. A major factor here is the *unpredictable* nature of police work. An officer who stops to issue a traffic ticket never knows if he or she will encounter a cooperative citizen or an armed fugitive.

The effect of unpredictability in creating stress is shown by an interesting experiment involving three groups of rats. In the experiment one group was given shocks preceded by a warning tone; a second group got shocks without warning; the third group received no shocks but heard the tone. Later, autopsies were performed on the rats. It was found that animals that received no shocks had no stomach ulcers; those receiving unpredictable shocks had severe ulcers; and those given predictable shocks showed little or no ulceration (Weiss, 1972).

Pressure is another element in stress, especially job stress. **Pressure** occurs when activities must be speeded up, when deadlines must be met, when extra work is added unexpectedly, or when a person must work at, or near, maximum capacity for long periods. Most students who have survived final exams are familiar with the effects of pressure.

Question: What if I set deadlines for myself? Does it make a difference where the pressure comes from?

Yes. People generally experience more stress in situations over which they have little **control.** For example, DeGood (1975) subjected male college students to an unpleasant shock-avoidance task. Some subjects were allowed to select their own rest periods, while others rested at times selected by the experimenter. Subjects allowed to control their own rest periods showed lower stress levels (as measured by blood pressure) than those given no choice (Fig. 14–5). Notice that being unable to control stressors is similar to conditions that cause learned helplessness, as described in Chapter 13.

Another experiment shows that lack of control even carries over to the after-effects of stress. Subjects jolted by uncontrollable blasts of noise did more poorly later on tests of concentration than people given control over the noise (Glass & Singer, 1972). If you have ever worked in a noisy office, factory, child-care center, restaurant, or similar setting, you will recognize this effect.

The evidence we have reviewed indicates that when emotional "shocks" are *intense* or *repeated, unpredictable, uncontrollable,* and linked to *pressure,* stress will be mag-

Fig. 14-5 *Assembly line work can be quite stressful, due to the lack of control employees have over the pace of work.*

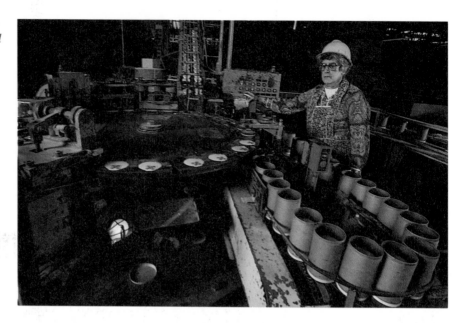

nified and damage is likely to result. At work, such damage sometimes takes the form of **burnout,** a pattern of emotional exhaustion described in Highlight 14–1.

As important as *external* conditions may be, they are not the whole story where stress is concerned. You have probably noted, for instance, that some people are stressed by events that others view as a thrill or a stimulating challenge. Ultimately, stress depends on how a situation is perceived. As you may recall from Chapter 13, whenever a stressor is appraised as a *threat*, a powerful stress reaction follows (Lazarus et al., 1985; Roskies & Lazarus, 1980). Further, stress is increased when a person believes he or she lacks *competence* to meet a particular demand (Bandura, 1977; Woolfolk & Richardson, 1978). Thus, the intensity of the body's stress response often depends on what we think and tell ourselves about stressors.

Psychosomatic Disorders

Chronic or repeated stress can damage physical health, as well as upset emotional well-being (Selye, 1976). Prolonged stress reactions are related to a large number of psychosomatic (SI-koh-so-MAT-ik) illnesses. Most people recognize that stomach ulcers are stress related, but so are many other illnesses. In **psychosomatic disorders** (*psyche:* mind; *soma:* body) psychological and emotional factors are associated with actual damage to tissues of the body. Psychosomatic problems, therefore, are *not* the same as *hypochondria.* **Hypochondriacs** (HI-po-KON-dree-aks) suffer

from imaginary diseases. There is nothing imaginary about a bleeding ulcer. A severe case could be fatal. The person who says, "Oh, it's *just* psychosomatic," misunderstands the seriousness of stress-related diseases.

Question: What diseases are psychosomatic? Who gets them?

The most common problems are gastrointestinal and respiratory (ulcers and asthma, for example), but there are many others. Included are problems such as eczema (skin rash), hives, migraine headaches, rheumatoid arthritis, hypertension (high blood pressure), colitis (ulceration of the colon), and heart disease. Actually, these represent only the major problems. Lesser health complaints are also frequently stress related. Typical examples include muscle tension, headaches, neckaches, backaches, indigestion, constipation, fatigue, insomnia, and sexual dysfunction (Brown, 1980; Hurst, Jenkins, & Rose, 1979). It is estimated that one-half or more of all patients who see a doctor have a psychosomatic disorder or have an illness complicated by psychosomatic symptoms.

It would be a mistake to assume that stress is the sole cause of psychosomatic diseases. Usually several factors combine to produce damage. These include hereditary differences, specific organ weaknesses, and learned reactions to stress. Personality also enters the picture. To a degree there are "ulcer personalities," "asthma personalities," and so on. The best documented of such patterns is the "cardiac personality"—an individual prone to heart disease.

Highlight 14–1
Burnout—The High Cost of Caring

■ A young nurse realizes with dismay that she has changed from a caring person at work to a cynic who has "lost all patience with her patients" and wishes they would "go somewhere else to be sick."

■ A teacher thinks of his students as "little monsters"; he no longer cares if they learn anything, and he desperately longs to change careers.

Reactions like these are clear signs of job burnout, a condition in which an employee is physically, mentally, and emotionally drained (Farber, 1983). What does it mean to be "burned out"? Psychologist Christina Maslach (1982) has identified three aspects of the problem.

First of all, burnout involves *emotional exhaustion.* Affected persons are fatigued, tense, apathetic, and suffer various physical complaints. They feel "used up" and have an "I don't give a damn anymore" attitude toward work. A second aspect of burnout is *depersonalization,* or detachment from others. Burned out workers coldly treat clients as if they were objects and find it difficult to care about them. The third aspect of burnout is a feeling of *reduced personal accomplishment.* Workers who have burned out do poor work and feel helpless, hopeless, or angry. Their self-esteem suffers and they yearn to change jobs or careers.

Burnout may occur in any job, but it is a marked problem in emotionally demanding helping professions, such as nursing, teaching, social work, counseling, or police work. The risk of burnout is especially high for workers who face many demands or complaints while getting little positive feedback or appreciation (Farber, 1983).

The irony of burnout is that the same work that tends to produce it can also be highly rewarding. If our society wishes to keep caring, committed people in the helping professions, several changes may be needed. A good start might include redesigning jobs, work loads, and responsibilities to create a better balance between demands and satisfactions. Building stronger social support systems at work could also be helpful. A good example is the increased use of support groups by nurses and other caregivers. Such groups allow workers to give and receive emotional support as they talk about feelings, problems, and stresses (Scully, 1983). Ultimately, however, the best solution may be for each of us to show greater understanding of the stresses felt by those whose work requires caring about the needs of others.

Type A   Two noted cardiologists, Meyer Friedman and Ray Rosenman, offer a glimpse at how some people create unnecessary stress. On the basis of a long-term study of heart problems, Friedman and Rosenman (1974) classified people into two categories: **Type A personalities** (those who run a high risk of heart attack) and **Type B personalities** (those who are unlikely to have a heart attack). Friedman and Rosenman then did an 8-year follow-up, finding more than twice the rate of heart disease in Type A's than in Type B's (Rosenman et al., 1975).

Question: What is the Type A personality like?

Type A people are hard driving, ambitious, highly competitive, achievement oriented, and striving (Fig. 14–6).

Type A people believe that with enough effort they can overcome any obstacle, and they "push" themselves accordingly. In tests of physical capacity (on a treadmill), Type A's work close to their actual limits of endurance but say they are less fatigued than do Type B people (Glass, 1977). Type A's don't know when to quit!

Perhaps the most telltale of all Type A characteristics are *time urgency* and chronic *anger* or *hostility.* Type A's seem unsatisfied with the normal pace of events. They hurry from one activity to another, racing the clock in self-imposed urgency. As they do, they feel a constant sense of frustration, anger, and hostility. Feelings of anger and hostility, in particular, are strongly related to increased risk of heart attack (Lenfant & Schweizer, 1985).

Fig. 14-6 *Individuals with Type A personalities feel a continuous sense of time pressure.*

Question: Some recent news reports have stated that Type A behavior is not a factor in heart attacks. Why is that?

It's true that some studies have failed to show a link between Type A behavior and heart attacks (Case et al., 1985). However, many researchers believe it is possible that these studies did not accurately classify people as Type A's and Type B's in the first place. Beyond that, hundreds of studies *have* supported the validity of the Type A concept. At this point it still seems that Type A's would be wise to take their increased health risks seriously.

Question: How are Type A people identified?

Many of the destructive habits of Type A people are summarized in the short self-identification test presented in Table 14–2. If all or most of the list applies to you, you may be a Type A. Your future plans may also provide a clue. When asked what they would do after college, 60 percent of Type A's said "go to graduate or professional school." In contrast 70 percent of Type B's said, "go to work, get a job" (Glass, 1977).

Since our society places a premium on achievement, competition, and mastery, it is not surprising that many

---

Table 14—2 Characteristics of the Type A Person*

Check the items that apply to you.

Do you:

_____ Have a habit of explosively accentuating various key words in ordinary speech even when there is no need for such accentuation?

_____ Finish other persons' sentences for them?

_____ *Always* move, walk, and eat rapidly?

_____ Quickly skim reading material and prefer summaries or condensations of books?

_____ Become easily angered by slow moving lines or traffic?

_____ Feel an impatience with the rate at which most events take place?

_____ Tend to be unaware of the details or beauty of your surroundings?

_____ Frequently strive to think of or do two or more things simultaneously?

_____ Almost always feel vaguely guilty when you relax, vacation, or do absolutely nothing for several days?

_____ Tend to evaluate your worth in quantitative terms (number of A's earned, amount of income, number of games won, and so forth)?

_____ Have nervous gestures or muscle twitches such as grinding your teeth, clenching your fists, or drumming your fingers?

_____ Attempt to schedule more and more activities into less time and in so doing make fewer allowances for unforeseen problems?

_____ Frequently think about other things while talking to someone?

_____ Repeatedly take on more responsibilities than you can comfortably handle?

*Shortened and adapted from Meyer Friedman and Ray H. Rosenman, *Type A Behavior and Your Heart.* New York: Alfred A. Knopf, 1974.

people develop Type A personalities. The best way to avoid the destructive stress this produces is to adopt behavior that is the opposite to that listed in Table 14–2 (Suinn, 1982). It is entirely possible to succeed without sacrificing your health in the process. (For additional suggestions on combating Type A behavior, consult Friedman and Rosenman, *Type A Behavior and Your Heart.*)

A very basic question remains unanswered in our discussion of stress. How does stress, and our response to it, translate into bodily damage? The answer seems to lie in the body's defenses against stress, a pattern of reactions known as the **general adaptation syndrome.**

The General Adaptation Syndrome Study of the general adaptation syndrome (G.A.S.) began when Canadian physiologist Hans Selye (1976) noticed that the initial symptoms of almost any disease or trauma (poisoning, infection, injury, or stress) are almost identical. After more research Selye concluded that the body responds in the same way to any stress, be it infection, failure, embarrassment, adjustment to a new job, school difficulties, or a stormy romance.

Question: What pattern does the body's response to stress take?

The G.A.S. consists of three stages: an *alarm reaction*, a *stage of resistance*, and a *stage of exhaustion* (Selye, 1976).

In the **alarm reaction** the body mobilizes its resources to cope with added stress. The pituitary gland secretes a hormone that causes the adrenal glands to step up their output of adrenaline and noradrenaline. As these hormones are added to the bloodstream, some bodily processes are speeded and others are slowed, to concentrate bodily resources where they are needed.

In the first phase of the alarm reaction, people have such symptoms as headache, fever, fatigue, sore muscles, shortness of breath, diarrhea, upset stomach, loss of appetite, and lack of energy. Notice that these are also the symptoms of being sick, of stressful travel, of high-altitude sickness, final exams week, and (possibly) of falling in love!

Soon the body's defenses are stabilized, and symptoms of the alarm reaction disappear. Physically the body has made adjustments to resist stress. However, the outward appearance of normality is maintained at a high cost. During the **stage of resistance,** the body is better able to cope with the original source of stress (see Fig. 14–7), but resistance to other stresses is lowered. For example, animals placed in an extremely cold environment become more

resistant to the cold, but more susceptible to infection. It is during the stage of resistance that the first signs of psychosomatic disorders begin to appear.

If stress continues, the **stage of exhaustion** may be reached. In this stage the body's resources are exhausted and the stress hormones are depleted. Unless a way of alleviating stress is found, the result will be a psychosomatic disease, organ failure, serious loss of health, or complete collapse.

The stages of the G.A.S. may sound melodramatic if you are young and healthy or if you have never had a personal encounter with prolonged stress. However, stress is not to be taken lightly. When Selye examined animals in the later stages of the G.A.S., he found enlargement and discoloration of their adrenal glands; intense shrinkage of the thymus, spleen, and lymph nodes; and deep bleeding stomach ulcers (Cox, 1978). In addition to such direct effects, there is growing evidence that stress can disrupt the body's immune system, making people more susceptible to illness (Jemmott & Locke, 1984). There is even evidence that severe life stresses, such as the death of a spouse, frequently precede the appearance of some forms of cancer (Eysenck, 1983).

Question: How do I know if I am subjecting myself to too much stress?

Although much has been learned about stress, this question remains difficult to answer. We can get some help, however, from research that links stressful events to changes in health, as described in the next section.

Fig. 14-7 *The General Adaptation Syndrome. During the initial alarm reaction to stress, resistance falls below normal. It rises again as bodily resources are mobilized, and it remains high during the stage of resistance. Eventually, resistance falls again as the stage of exhaustion is reached. (From* The Stress of Life *by Hans Selye. Copyright© 1956, 1976 by Hans Selye. Used by permission of McGraw-Hill Book Company.)*

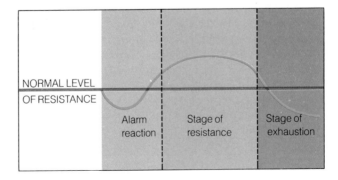

Stress and Health— The Hazards of Hassles

At the University of Washington, Dr. Thomas Holmes and his associates have confirmed something long suspected: Stressful events reduce the body's natural defenses against disease and increase the likelihood of illness (Holmes & Masuda, 1972). Holmes found that disaster and sorrow often precede illness. More surprising is the finding that almost any major *change* in one's life requires adjustment and increases susceptibility to accident and illness.

Life Change Units   Holmes and his associates have developed a rating scale to estimate the potential health hazards faced when stresses accumulate. Their **Social Readjustment Rating Scale (SRRS)** is reprinted in Table 14–3. Notice that the effect of life events is expressed in **life change units (LCU's).**

As you read the scale, notice too that a positive life event may be as costly as a disaster. Marriage rates 50 life change units, even though it is usually considered a happy event. Notice also that many items read "Change in . . . " This means that an improvement in life conditions is as costly as a decline.

To use the scale, add up the LCU's for all life events you have experienced during the last year and compare the total with these standards:

0 to 150—No significant problems

150 to 199—Mild life crisis (33 percent chance of illness)

200 to 299—Moderate life crisis (50 percent chance of illness)

300 or over—Major life crisis (80 percent chance of illness)

When the LCU total exceeds 300 points, there is an 80 percent chance of illness or accident in the near future.

A more conservative rating of stress can be obtained by totaling LCU points for events occurring only during the previous 6 months. Studies of U. S. Navy personnel produced these figures for 6-month totals (Rahe, 1972):

Table 14–3   Social Readjustment Rating Scale (SRRS). The SRRS lists significant life events and offers a rating of their contribution to susceptibility to illness.

Rank	Life Event	Life Crisis Units	Rank	Life Event	Life Crisis Units
1	Death of spouse	100	23	Son or daughter leaving home	29
2	Divorce	73	24	Trouble with in-laws	29
3	Marital separation	65	25	Outstanding personal achievement	28
4	Jail term	63	26	Wife begins or stops work	26
5	Death of a close family member	63	27	Begin or end school	26
6	Personal injury or illness	53	28	Change in living conditions	25
7	Marriage	50	29	Revision of personal habits	24
8	Fired at work	47	30	Trouble with boss	23
9	Marital reconciliation	45	31	Change in work hours or conditions	20
10	Retirement	45	32	Change in residence	20
11	Change in health of family member	44	33	Change in school	20
12	Pregnancy	40	34	Change in recreation	19
13	Sex difficulties	39	35	Change in church activities	19
14	Gain of new family member	39	36	Change in social activities	18
15	Business readjustment	39	37	Take out loan less than $20,000	17
16	Change in financial state	38	38	Change in sleeping habits	16
17	Death of close friend	37	39	Change in number of family get-togethers	15
18	Change to different line of work	36	40	Change in eating habits	15
19	Change in number of arguments with spouse	35	41	Vacation	13
20	Take out mortgage or loan for major purchase	31	42	Christmas	12
21	Foreclosure of mortgage or loan	30	43	Minor violations of the law	11
22	Change in responsibilities at work	29			

Adapted with permission from "Social Readjustment Rating Scale," by T. H. Holmes and R. H. Rahe, *Journal of Psychosomatic Research,* 1967. Reprinted with permission from Pergamon Press, Ltd.

LCU's	Average number of illnesses reported for 6-month period
0 to 100	1.4
300 to 400	1.9
500 to 600	2.1

Question: Many of the listed life changes don't seem relevant to young adults or college students. Does the SRRS apply to these people?

The SRRS tends to be more appropriate for older, more established adults. However, recent research has shown that the health of college students is also affected by stressful events, such as entering college, changing majors, or the breakup of a steady relationship (Martin et al., 1975).

The SRRS is not a foolproof way to rate stress, and some studies have failed to confirm the LCU-illness link (Schless, 1977). Nevertheless, a high LCU score should be taken seriously. It would be a good idea to total your LCU's once or twice a year as a rough index of stress levels. If your score goes much over 300, an adjustment in your activities or lifestyle may be called for. Remember, "to be forewarned is to be forearmed."

Question: There must be more to stress than major life changes. Isn't there a link between ongoing stresses and health?

Hassles In addition to their immediate impact, major life changes often create a kind of ripple effect—that is, countless daily frustrations and irritations spring from the original event. In addition many of us face ongoing stresses at work or at home that do not involve major life changes. In recognition of these facts, psychologist Richard Lazarus and his associates recently studied the impact of minor, but frequent stresses. Lazarus (1981) aptly refers to such stresses as **hassles**, which he defines as distressing daily annoyances. Hassles range from traffic jams to losing classroom notes; from an argument with a roommate to an employer's unrealistic demands.

In a year-long study Lazarus had 100 men and women keep track of the frequency and severity of the hassles they encountered. Subjects in the study also filled out questionnaires concerning their physical and mental health. As Lazarus and his associates had suspected, frequent and severe hassles turned out to be better predictors of day-to-day psychological and physical health than were major life events. However, major life events did predict changes in health a year or two after the events took place. So, it appears that daily hassles are closely linked to immediate health, whereas major life changes have more of a long-term impact.

In follow-up work, Lazarus and others have found that the personal importance of hassles affects the amount of stress they produce (Lazarus et al., 1985). Hassles that are viewed as central to one's self-worth are most likely to cause trouble. For many people central hassles are linked to work, family, and relationships. But as psychologist Rand Gruen notes, "Taking care of paperwork or being organized can be central for some people" (Fisher, 1984). This observation again emphasizes that stress occurs in people, not in the environment. Stress is always related to personality, values, perceptions, and personal resources.

Question: What can be done about a high LCU score or feeling excessively hassled?

A good response is to use **stress management** skills. For serious problems stress management should be learned directly from a therapist or at a stress clinic. When ordinary stresses are involved, there is much you can do on your own. This chapter's Applications section will give you a start. In the meantime, take it easy!

Learning Check

1. Ulcers developed by persons in high-stress occupations and by animals in stress experiments are an example of a _____ disorder.

2. Greater control over a source of stress is usually associated with a reduction in the amount of stress experienced.   T or F?

3. People suffering from hypochondria have serious tissue damage caused by stress or prolonged emotion.   T or F?

4. Which of the following is *not* classified as a psychosomatic disorder?
   a. hypertension *b.* colitis *c.* eczema *d.* thymus

5. The first stage of the G.A.S. is called the _____ reaction.

6. Most outward symptoms of stress disappear during the stage of _____.

7. According to Friedman and Rosenman, Type A persons tend to be angry or hostile but they rarely suffer from a sense of time urgency.   T or F?

8. Holmes's SRRS appears to predict long-range changes in health, whereas the frequency and severity of daily hassles is closely related to immediate ratings of health.   T or F?

Answers: 1. psychosomatic 2. T 3. F 4. d 5. d 6. resistance 7. F 8. T

Applications

Stress Management

The simplest way of coping with stress is to modify or remove its source—by leaving a stressful job, for example. Obviously this is often impossible, which is why learning to manage stress is so important.

As shown in Figure 14–8, stress triggers *bodily effects, upsetting thoughts,* and *ineffective behavior.* Also shown is the fact that each element worsens the others in a vicious cycle. Indeed, the basic idea of the "Stress Game" is that once it begins, *you lose*—unless you take action to break the cycle. The information that follows tells how. (Stress management techniques are derived from Davis, McKay, & Eshelman, 1980; Meichenbaum, 1977; Woolfolk & Richardson, 1978, and other sources as indicated.)

Bodily Reactions

Much of the immediate discomfort of stress is caused by the body's fight/flight emotional response. The body is ready to act, with tight muscles and a pounding heart. When action is prevented, we merely remain "uptight." A sensible remedy is to learn a reliable, drug-free way of relaxing.

Exercise   Because stress prepares the body for action, its effects can be dissipated by using the body. Any full-body exercise can be effective. Swimming, dancing, jumping rope, yoga, most sports, and especially walking are valuable outlets. Be sure to choose activities that are vigorous enough to relieve tension, yet enjoyable enough to be done repeatedly. Exercising for stress management is most effective when it is done daily.

Meditation   Many stress counselors recommend meditation for quieting the body and promoting relaxation. The meditation technique described in Chapter 6

is a good starting place. Remember that meditation is easy to learn—taking an expensive commercial course is unnecessary. Remember too that listening to or playing music, taking nature walks, doing hobbies, and the like can be meditations of sorts.

Progressive Relaxation   Progressive relaxation refers to a method in which people learn to relax systematically, completely, and by choice. To learn the full technique, consult Chapter 23 of this book. The basic idea is to tighten all the muscles in a given area of the body (the arms, for instance) and then voluntarily relax them. By tensing and relaxing each area of the body, it is possible, with practice, to greatly reduce tension.

Ineffective Behavior

Stress is often made worse by our response to it. The following suggestions may help you deal with stress more effectively.

Slow Down   Remember that stress can be self-generated. Try to deliberately do things at a slower pace—especially if your pace has speeded up over the years. Tell yourself, "What counts most is not if I get there first, but if I get there at all." Or, "My goal is distance, not speed."

Organize   Disorganization creates stress. Try to take a fresh look at your situation and get organized. Setting priorities can be a real stress fighter. Ask yourself what's really important and concentrate on the things that count. Learn to let go of trivial but upsetting irritations. And above all, when you are feeling stressed, remember to K.I.S.: *Keep It Simple.*

Strike a Balance   Work, school, family, friends, interests, hobbies, recreation, community, church—there

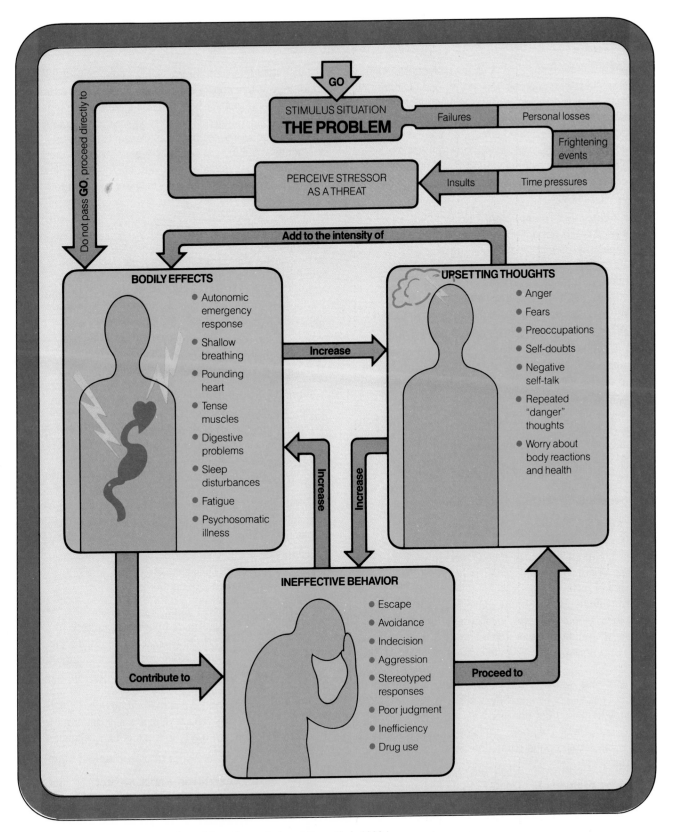

Fig. 14-8   *The stress game. (adapted from Rosenthal and Rosenthal, 1980.)*

Applications: Stress Management

are many important elements in a satisfying life. Damaging stress often comes from letting one element get blown out of proportion, especially work or school. Your goal should be *quality* in life, not quantity. Try to strike a balance between "good stress" and relaxation. Remember, when you are "doing nothing," you are actually doing something very important: Set aside time for "me acts" such as loafing, browsing, puttering, playing, napping.

Recognize and Accept Your Limits   Many of us set unrealistic and perfectionistic goals. Given that no one can ever be perfect, this attitude leaves many people feeling inadequate, no matter how well they have performed. Set gradual, achievable goals for yourself. Also, set realistic limits on what you try to do on any given day. Learn to say no to added demands or responsibilities.

Seek Social Support   Studies have shown that close, positive relationships with others facilitate good health and morale (Cobb, 1976). One reason for this is that support from family and friends serves as a buffer to cushion the impact of stressful events (Pardine et al., 1981). Talking out problems and expressing tensions can be incredibly helpful. If things really get bad, seek help from a therapist, counselor, or clergyman (please note that bartender is not on the list).

Upsetting Thoughts

Assume you are taking a test. Suddenly you realize you are running short of time. If you say to yourself, "Oh no, this is terrible, I've blown it now," your body's response will probably be sweating, tenseness, and a knot in your stomach. On the other hand, if you say, "I should have watched the time, but getting upset won't help now, so I'll just take one question at a time," your stress level will be much lower. (More information on test taking and anxiety appears in this chapter's Exploration section.)

   As stated earlier, stress is greatly affected by the views we take of events. Physical symptoms and a tendency to make poor decisions are increased by negative thoughts or "self-talk." In many cases what you say to yourself can be the difference between coping and collapsing.

Coping Statements   Donald Meichenbaum of the University of Waterloo, Canada, has recently popularized a technique called **stress inoculation**. In it, clients

learn to fight fear and anxiety with an internal monologue of positive **coping statements**. First, clients learn to identify and monitor **negative self-statements**. Negative, self-critical thoughts are a problem because they tend to directly elevate physical arousal (Schuele & Wiesenfeld, 1983). To counter this effect, clients learn to replace negative statements with coping statements from a supplied list. Eventually, they are encouraged to make their own lists.

Question: How are coping statements applied?

Coping statements are used to block out, or counteract, negative self-talk in stressful situations. In giving a short speech, for instance, you would replace "I'm scared," "I can't do this," "My mind will go blank and I'll panic," or "I'll sound stupid and boring" with "I'll give my speech on something I like," or "I'll breathe deeply before I start my speech," or "My pounding heart just means I'm psyched up to do my best." Additional examples of coping statements follow.

   Preparing for a Stressful Situation

   I'll just take things one step at a time.
   If I get nervous, I'll just pause a moment.
   Tomorrow I'll be through it.
   I've managed to do this before.
   What exactly do I have to do?

   Confronting the Stressful Situation

   Relax now, this can't really hurt me.
   Stay organized, focus on the task.
   There's no hurry, take it step-by-step.
   Nobody's perfect, I'll just do my best.
   It will be over soon, just be calm.

Meichenbaum cautions that saying the "right" things to yourself may not be sufficient to bring about real improvement in stress tolerance. You must practice this approach in actual stress situations. Also, it is important to develop your own personal list of coping statements by finding what works for you. Ultimately, the value of learning this, and other stress management skills, ties back into the idea that much stress is self-generated. Knowing that you *can* manage a demanding situation is, in itself, a major antidote for stress.

Coping with Frustration and Conflict

A psychologist studying frustration placed rats on a small platform at the top of a tall pole. Then he forced

Applications: Stress Management

them to jump off the platform toward two elevated doors, one locked and the other unlocked. If the rat chose the correct door, it swung open and he landed safely on another platform. If he chose the locked door, he bounced off it and fell into a net far below.

The problem of choosing the open door was made unsolvable and very frustrating by randomly alternating which door was locked. After a time most rats adopted a **stereotyped response.** That is, they chose the same door every time. This door was then *permanently* locked. All the rat had to do was to jump to the other door to avoid a fall, but time after time the rat bounced off the locked door (Maier, 1949).

Question: Isn't this an example of persistence?

No. Persistence that is not *flexible* can become "stupid," stereotyped behavior like that of a rat on a jumping stand. When dealing with frustration, it is important to know when to quit and establish a new direction. Here are some suggestions to help you avoid needless frustration.

1. Try to identify the source of your frustration. Is it internal, external, or personal?
2. Is the source of frustration something that can be changed? How hard would you have to work to change it? Is it under your control at all?
3. If the source of your frustration can be changed or removed, are the necessary efforts worth it?

The answers to these questions help determine if persistence will be futile. There is value in learning to accept gracefully those things that cannot be changed.

It is also important to distinguish between *real* barriers and *imagined* barriers. All too often we create our own imaginary barriers. For example:

Anita wants a part-time job to earn extra money. At the first place she applied, she was told that she didn't have enough "experience." Now she complains of being frustrated because she wants to work but cannot. She needs "experience" to work but can't get experience without working. She has quit looking for a job.

Is Anita's need for experience a real barrier? Unless she applies for *many* jobs, it is impossible to tell if she has overestimated its importance. For her the barrier is real enough to prevent further efforts, but with persistent looking she might locate an "unlocked door." If a reasonable amount of persistence does show that "experience" is essential, it might be obtained in other ways—through temporary volunteer work, for instance.

Question: How can I handle conflicts more effectively?

Most of the suggestions just made also apply to conflict. However, here are some additional things to remember when you are in conflict or must make a difficult decision.

1. Don't be hasty when making important decisions. Take time to collect information and to weigh pros and cons. Hasty decisions are often regretted. Even if you do make a faulty decision, it will trouble you less if you know that you did everything possible to avoid a mistake.
2. Try out important decisions *partially* when possible. If you are thinking about moving to a new town, try to spend a few days there first. If you are choosing between colleges, do the same. If classes are in progress, sit in on some. If you want to learn to skin-dive, rent equipment for a reasonable length of time before buying.
3. Look for workable compromises. Again, it is important to get all available information. If you think that you only have one or two alternatives and they are undesirable or unbearable, seek the aid of a teacher, counselor, minister, or social service agency. You may be overlooking possible alternatives these people will know about.
4. When all else fails, make a decision and live with it. Indecision and conflict exact a high cost. Sometimes it is best to select a course of action and stick with it unless it is *very obviously* wrong *after* you have taken it.

Learning Check

1. Exercise, meditation, and progressive relaxation are considered effective ways of countering negative self-statements. T or F?
2. Research shows that social support from family and friends has little effect on the health consequences of stress. T or F?

Applications: Stress Management

3. One element of stress inoculation is training in the use of positive coping statements.   T or F?

4. Stereotyped responding can be particularly troublesome in coping with frustration.   T or F?

Answers: 1. F   2. F   3. T   4. T

Chapter Summary

■ *Frustration* is the negative emotional state that occurs when progress toward a goal is blocked. Sources of frustration may be usefully classified as *external* or *personal*.

■ External frustrations are based on *delay, failure, rejection, loss,* and other direct blocking of motives. Personal frustration is related to *personal characteristics* over which one has little control. Frustrations of all types become more intense as the *strength, urgency,* or *importance* of the blocked motive increases.

■ Major behavioral reactions to frustration include *persistence, more vigorous responding, circumvention, direct aggression, displaced aggression* (including *scapegoating*), and *escape* or *withdrawal*.

■ Frustration and attendant feelings of anxiety or inadequacy frequently lead to use of *psychological defense mechanisms*. A large number of defense mechanisms have been identified, including *compensation, denial, fantasy, intellectualization, isolation, projection, rationalization, reaction formation, regression, repression,* and *sublimation*. Each helps people to deny, avoid, or distort sources of anxiety.

■ Conflict occurs when one must choose between contradictory alternatives. Four major types of conflict are: *approach-approach* (choice between two desirable alternatives); *avoidance-avoidance* (both alternatives are negative); *approach-avoidance* (a goal or activity has both positive and negative aspects); and *double approach-avoidance* (both alternatives have advantages and disadvantages).

■ Approach-approach conflicts are usually the easiest to resolve. Avoidance conflicts are difficult to resolve and are characterized by *inaction, indecision, freezing,* and a *desire to escape* (called *leaving the field*). People usually remain in approach-avoidance conflicts but fail to fully resolve them. Approach-avoidance conflicts are associated with *ambivalence* and *partial approach*. *Vacillation* (a wavering between alternatives) is probably the

most common reaction to double approach-avoidance conflicts.

■ *Stress* occurs when demands are placed on an organism to adjust or adapt. When stress is intense or prolonged (especially when associated with negative emotional response), it may cause damage in the form of ulcers and other *psychosomatic* problems. Psychosomatic (mind-body) disorders have no connection to *hypochondria,* the tendency to imagine that one has a disease.

■ Stress is more damaging in situations involving *pressure,* a lack of *control, unpredictability* of the stressor, and *intense* or *repeated* emotional shocks. Stress is intensified when a situation is perceived as a *threat* and when a person does not feel *competent* to cope with it. In work settings prolonged stress, especially when associated with caregiving, can lead to *burnout*.

■ People with *Type A personalities* are competitive, striving, frequently angry or hostile, and they have a chronic sense of time urgency. These characteristics combine to double the chances of heart attack.

■ The body reacts to stress in a series of stages called the *general adaptation syndrome* (G.A.S.). The stages of the G.A.S. are *alarm, resistance,* and *exhaustion*. The pattern of bodily reactions and changes in resistance observed in the G.A.S. follow closely the pattern observed in the development of psychosomatic disorders. In addition stress may lower the body's immunity to disease.

■ Work with the *Social Readjustment Rating Scale* indicates that an accumulation of life changes can increase susceptibility to accident or illness. However, immediate psychological and mental health is more closely related to the intensity and severity of daily annoyances, or *hassles*.

■ A sizable number of coping skills can be applied to manage stress. Most of these focus on one of three areas: *bodily effects, ineffective behavior,* and *upsetting thoughts*.

▶▶▶ **Exploration**

Test Anxiety—Stress in the Classroom

When taking tests, I often

a. feel extremely tense and anxious
b. spend much of my time worrying about whether I will pass
c. "go blank," even when I should know the answer
d. feel hurried, inadequate, or panicked

When you take tests, does your mind race out of control, filled with thoughts of disaster? Or do you cruise on a cushion of cool confidence? It's no secret that some people are more anxious than others during exams. If most of the answers to the question above apply to you, you probably have a high level of **test anxiety**. If you do, you may have learned the hard way that anxiety can bring test scores crashing downward.

Inside Test Anxiety

Question: How does test anxiety lower performance?

There is now much evidence that test anxiety involves excessive *worry* (thoughts and fears of failure, embarrassment, and frustration) during test taking. As anyone who has ever "freaked out" during a test can tell you, heightened *physiological arousal* (uneasiness, tension, sweating, pounding heart, nervousness) is also a major part of test anxiety. This combination—worry plus arousal—tends to distract students with a rush of upset-

ting thoughts and feelings (Mueller & Thompson, 1984).

Question: Which is worse, worrying or being too aroused?

Both worry and arousal are related to lower test scores. But worry is the greater culprit. Almost everyone gets nervous when taking tests, so heightened arousal is not limited to those with high test anxiety. In fact, during actual tests, people with high test anxiety show no more arousal on physical measures than do those with low test anxiety. (However, test-anxious students may pay more attention to distracting physical sensations.)

Worries, Worries "I'm not sure about any of these answers. I must be stupid. I can't do this. I'll never pass. Look how much time is gone already. What if I flunk? Suppose I blow this test so bad that I can't even pass the course. I might have to drop out of school. What will my friends think? What will my parents say?" Worries like these are the real heart of test anxiety because they directly interfere with thinking about the test (Eysenck, 1984; Salame, 1984). Some test-anxious students actually spend as much time worrying as they do working on the test. To make matters worse, worries tend to "fill up" working memory, further limiting ability to solve problems or answer questions (Eysenck, 1984). Interference of this type probably explains why anxious students so often complain of going blank or forgetting known facts. With a storm of doubts, fears, and worries raging inside, who could think clearly?

Treating Test Anxiety

Psychologists have become relatively successful in treating test anxiety. Let's see what can be learned from their efforts.

Preparation The most direct antidote for test anxiety is *hard work*. Many test-anxious students simply study too little and too late for exams (Becker, 1982). And, paradoxically, the more a student expects to fail, the less he or she is likely to study. Thus, one solution for test anxiety is to *overprepare* by studying well in advance of the "big day." Students who are well prepared score higher, worry less, and are less likely to become overly aroused (Lazarus & Folkman, 1984).

Relaxation (Again) As in other stressful situations, learning to relax can help lower test anxiety (Ricketts & Galloway, 1984). As mentioned earlier, students interested in learning self-relaxation skills should look ahead to Chapter 23, where a relaxation technique is described. Test anxiety is also lowered by support from others (Sarason, 1981). If you tend to be overly anxious during tests, you may find it helpful to discuss the problem

Exploration: Test Anxiety—Stress in the Classroom

with your professor. Preparing for the test with a supportive friend or classmate can also help.

If none of these strategies works, there is still something else you can try. Nervousness during tests can often be lessened by carefully *rehearsing* in your imagination how you will cope with upsetting events. Imagine yourself going blank, running out of time, or feeling panicked. Then calmly plan how you will handle each situation—by keeping your attention on the task, by focusing on one question at a time, and so forth (Watson & Tharp, 1981). As you rehearse, remember that feeling some anxiety during tests is normal. Your goal should be to manage anxiety, not to prevent it completely.

Restructuring Thoughts   Because worries are such a major part of test anxiety, changing self-defeating thinking patterns can be the best solution of all (Wise & Haynes, 1983).

Test-anxious students often benefit from listing the kinds of distracting and self-defeating thoughts they have during exams. They then work on learning to counter their worries with calming, rational replies (or *coping statements*, to use Meichenbaum's term).

Let's say, for example, that a student thinks, "I'm going to fail this test, and all my friends will think I'm stupid." To counter this upsetting thought, he or she might say, "If I prepare well and control my worries, I will probably pass

the test. Even if I don't, it won't be the end of the world. My friends will still like me, and I can try to improve on the next test." If you would like to work on countering test worries, watch especially for irrational beliefs that lead to distracting thoughts. For instance, it is irrational to believe that you should know absolutely everything, or that you should be 100 percent at ease, or that you must be perfect (Topman & Jansen, 1984).

Students who cope well with testing typically take a practical attitude and try to do the best they can, even under trying circumstances. With practice most students can learn to do the same, so they will be less testy at test time.

Learning Check

1. Preoccupation with thoughts of failure, embarrassment, and self-doubt is a major element of test anxiety.   T or F?
2. For most people who suffer from test anxiety, excess arousal is a greater problem than worry is.   T or F?
3. The more students expect to fail a test the more they tend to study for it.   T or F?
4. Mentally rehearsing ways to calmly deal with anticipated test-taking problems can help lower test anxiety.   T or F?

Answers: 1. T   2. F   3. F   4. T

Questions for Discussion

1. How could you reduce conflict or avoid an unfortunate decision in the following situations: choosing a school to attend, choosing a major, deciding about marriage, choosing a job, buying a car?

2. Calculate your life change score. If your score is elevated, what could you do to reduce the chances of illness? If it is low, what could you do to put more excitement in your life?! Can you see any relationship between previous periods of illness and the number of life changes or hassles that preceded them?

3. What do you consider the most prominent sources of stress in our society? What do you think should or could be done to combat these stresses?

4. Over a decade ago, journalist Alvin Toffler predicted that large numbers of people would become victims of "future shock." According to Toffler, future shock is a condition of shattering stress and disorientation brought on by overly rapid social change. In your view is there any truth to the idea that we are "future shocked" or that we may be in the near future?

5. The defense mechanisms listed in this chapter were described in psychodynamic terms; that is, in terms of the balance of forces within the personality. Can you advance a learning-theory explanation for any of the defenses? (Hint: Think in terms of avoidance learning and the rewards connected with defensive responses.)

6. What are the advantages and disadvantages of using defense mechanisms? Do you think it would be possible for a person to be completely free of defense mechanisms?

7. Defend or deny the following statement (attributed to Professor P. T. Barnumandbailey Circuits): "Television is the opiate of the people. If all the TV tubes in the United States suddenly went blank, the mental health of the nation would crumble because people could no longer escape their problems by watching television."

8. How could you best deal with the following sources of frustration: delays, losses, lack of resources, failure, rejection?

9. An atmosphere of competition and evaluation pervades many schools. How might this contribute to test anxiety? Do you think that the amount of testing done in schools should be increased or decreased? If testing were decreased, what alternatives would you propose?

Part Five

Human Development and Personality

Chapter 15 | Human Development

Chapter Preview
Alien Minds

You may not have noticed. Not everyone has. There are alien creatures among us. More arrive daily. They look a lot like you and me, but they're smaller, and they think differently. Their speech is strange. They ask many questions. It's obvious they are trying to understand how we live. Their goal is to inhabit the planet Earth in our place. Who are these creatures? Where are they from? You need not be alarmed; they come not from outer space, but from inner space. They are the product of a biological union—of life perpetuating life. They are children.

Studying children helps answer the question, "How did I become the person I am today?" To understand ourselves as adults, we must get to know the child in our past. This fact makes the study of children rewarding, but there is another reason for interest: A child's understanding of the world is qualitatively different from yours and mine. Entry into a child's circle of awareness has much of the intrigue of meeting a person from another culture. It might even be compared to an encounter with an alien mind. In short, children are extremely interesting creatures, and a tremendous amount of psychological research has focused on them.

Question: What branch of psychology studies children?

*The study of children is the heart of **developmental psychology**. However, you should recognize that developmental psychologists are interested in every stage of life from "the womb to the tomb." Developmental psychology can therefore be described as the* study of progressive changes in behavior and abilities from conception to death. *With a definition like this, it's clear that developmental psychology includes many topics—so many, in fact, that some appear in other chapters.*

In this chapter you will find a number of general principles of development, including an account of the far-reaching events in the first years of life. Perhaps learning about development will contribute to your own development. Find out by reading more!

Survey Questions What can newborn babies do? How aware are infants of their surroundings? How do heredity and environment affect prenatal development, self-awareness, motor skills, and learning? How important are parenting styles? Of what significance is a child's emotional attachment to parents? How do children acquire language and thinking abilities? What are the effects of a poor early environment? What can be done to enhance early development? How have sex selection, genetic counseling, and the like affected parents and children?

Resources

The Newborn Baby—The Basic Model Comes with Options

At birth the human **neonate** (NEE-oh-NATE, *neo:* new; *nate:* born) is completely helpless and will die if not cared for. Newborn babies cannot lift their heads, turn over, or feed themselves. Does this mean they are inert and unfeeling? Definitely not! Neonates can see, hear, smell, taste, and respond to pain and touch. Although their senses are less acute at birth, babies are immediately responsive to their surroundings. Babies will, in fact, follow a moving object with their eyes and will turn in the direction of sounds.

A number of adaptive *reflexes* can also be observed in the newborn. An object pressed into the neonate's palm will be grasped with surprising strength. The **grasping reflex** is so strong that many infants can hang from a raised bar, like little trapeze artists. Very likely, the grasping reflex improves an infant's chances of survival by helping to prevent falling. Another adaptive reflex can be demonstrated by touching a baby's cheek. Immediately the baby will turn toward your finger, as if searching for something.

Question: How is such turning adaptive?

The **rooting reflex,** as this is called, helps the infant to find a bottle or breast. Then, when a nipple touches the infant's mouth, the **sucking reflex** helps the baby obtain needed food. At the same time, food rewards nursing, which rapidly increases in vigor during the first days after birth. Thus, we see that learning begins immediately in the newborn.

Also of interest is the **Moro reflex.** If a baby's head is allowed to drop, or if the baby is startled by a loud noise, the infant will make movements similar to an embrace. These movements have been compared with those used by baby monkeys to cling to their mothers. (It is left to the reader's imagination to decide if there is any connection.)

We are tempted to think of newborn babies as mere bundles of reflexes. But a number of observations show that infants respond in ways that are more subtle than was once imagined. For example, Andrew Meltzoff and Keith Moore (1977) found that babies are born mimics. Figure 15–1 shows Meltzoff as he sticks out his tongue, opens his mouth, and purses his lips at a 20-day-old girl. Will the

Fig. 15–1 *Infant imitation. In the top row of photos, Andrew Meltzoff makes facial gestures at an infant. The bottom row records the infant's responses. Videotapes of Meltzoff and of tested infants helped ensure objectivity. (Photos courtesy of Andrew N. Meltzoff.)*

baby imitate him? Videotapes made of the babies tested in this way confirm that they consistently imitate adult facial gestures. Such mimicry is obviously an aid to rapid learning in infancy.

Question: How much intelligence does a newborn have?

Child psychologist Jerome Bruner believes babies are smarter than most people think. Bruner cites an experiment in which 3- to 8-week-old babies showed signs of understanding that a person's voice and body are connected. If babies heard their mother's voice coming from where she was standing, they remained calm. If her voice came from a loudspeaker several feet away, the babies be-came agitated and began to cry. Bruner considers this and similar experiments a sign that the human mind is quite active from birth onward (Pines, 1970).

Another look into the private world of infants can be drawn from tests of their vision.

Question: How is it possible to test a baby's vision?

Working with infants always requires imagination because they cannot talk. To test infant vision, Robert Fantz (1963) invented a device called a **looking chamber** (Fig. 15–2a). A child is placed on his or her back inside the chamber, facing a lighted area above. Next, two objects are placed in the chamber. By observing the movements

Fig. 15–2   (a) *Eye movements and fixation points of infants are observed in Fantz's "looking chamber." (b) Thirteen-week-old infants preferred concentric and curved patterns like those on the left to nonconcentric and straight-line patterns like those on the right. (c) Infants tested in a looking chamber look at the normal face longer than at the scrambled face and at both faces longer than at the design on the right. (Photo courtesy of David Linton. Drawing from "The Origin of Form Perception" by Robert L. Fantz. Copyright © 1961 by Scientific American, Inc. All rights reserved.)*

(a)

(b)

(c)

of the infant's eyes and the images they reflect, it is possible to tell what the infant is looking at.

Fantz found that 3-day-old babies prefer complex patterns such as checkerboards and bull's-eyes to simpler colored rectangles. Other researchers have determined that infants are more excited by circles and curves and that they will look longer at red and blue than at other colors (see Fig. 15–2b; Bornstein, 1975; Ruff & Birch, 1974). Findings such as these demonstrate (as a friend of the author's once put it) that, "There really is a person inside that little body."

Of possibly greater interest is the finding that infants will spend more time looking at a human face pattern than at a scrambled face or a colored oval (see Fig. 15–2c). When real human faces were used, Fantz found that familiar faces were preferred to unfamiliar faces. However, preference for the familiar reverses at about age 2, when unusual objects begin to hold greater interest for the child. For instance, Jerome Kagan (1971) showed three-dimensional face masks to 2-year-olds and found they were fascinated by a face with eyes on the chin and a nose in the middle of the forehead. Kagan believes their interest came from a need to understand why the scrambled face differed from what they had come to expect.

Perhaps the most striking aspect of the human infant is the dazzling speed with which he or she is transformed from a helpless baby to an independent person. Early growth is extremely rapid. By the third year of life, the child stands, walks, talks, explores, and has a unique personality. At no other time after birth does development proceed more rapidly. During this period there is a fascinating interplay of forces shaping the child's development—most importantly, heredity and environment.

Heredity and Environment— The Nature of Nurture and the Nurture of Nature

Question: Which has a greater effect on development, heredity or environment?

For many years psychologists debated—sometimes heatedly—the relative importance of nature versus nurture in determining behavior. The potent effects of **heredity** (nature) certainly cannot be denied. At the moment of conception, when a sperm and egg unite, an incredible number of personal features and growth patterns are determined. It is estimated that the genetic information carried in each human cell would fill thousands of 1,000-page books—and that's in fine print!

Question: How does heredity operate?

Nature The nucleus of every cell in the body contains 46 threadlike structures called **chromosomes** that transmit the coded instructions of heredity. **Genes** are smaller areas on chromosomes. Each gene carries instructions that affect a particular process or personal characteristic. There are at least 100,000 genes in every human cell, and perhaps more. In some cases a single gene is responsible for a particular feature, such as eye color. Most characteristics, however, are **polygenetic,** or determined by many genes working in combination.

Genes may be *dominant* or *recessive*. When a gene is **dominant,** the trait it controls will be present every time the gene is present. When a gene is **recessive,** it must be paired with a second recessive gene before its effect will be expressed. Some examples should make the relationship clearer. We receive one-half of our chromosomes (and genes) from each parent. If you were to get a brown-eye gene from your father and a blue-green gene from your mother, you would be brown-eyed, because brown-eye genes are dominant.

Question: If brown-eye genes are dominant, how is it that two brown-eyed parents sometimes have a blue-eyed child?

If each parent has two brown-eye genes, the couple's children can only be brown-eyed. But what if each parent has one brown-eye gene and one blue-eye gene? In this case the parents would both have brown eyes, but there is one chance in four that their children will get two blue-eye genes and have blue eyes (see Fig. 15–3).

The sex of a child is also genetically determined, in this case by two specialized chromosomes. When two **X chromosomes** are inherited, the child will be a female; an X chromosome paired with a **Y chromosome** yields a male. The woman's ovum always provides an X chromosome since she has two X's in her own genetic makeup. In contrast one-half of the male's sperm carry X chromosomes and the other half Y's. This has effects beyond determining sex, since some traits are **sex-linked,** or carried by genes on the X chromosome. An example is color blindness, which is carried on an X chromosome and given from mother to son. (In a few instances sex-linked traits are carried on a Y chromosome. However, this is exceedingly rare.)

Hereditary instructions carried by the chromosomes influence development throughout life by affecting the sequence of growth, the timing of puberty, and the course of aging. The broad outlines of the **human growth sequence** are therefore universal. They extend from conception to old age and death, as Table 15–1 shows. In addi-

Fig. 15–3 *Gene patterns for children of brown-eyed parents, each with one brown-eye and one blue-eye gene. Since the brown-eye gene is dominant, only one child in four will be blue-eyed.*

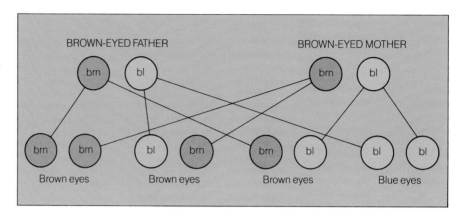

Table 15–1   Human Growth Sequence

Period*	Duration (approximate)	Descriptive Name
Germinal	First two weeks after conception.	Zygote
Embryonic	Two to eight weeks after conception.	Embryo
Fetal	From eight weeks after conception to birth.	Fetus
Neonatal	From birth to a few weeks after birth.	Neonate
Infancy	From a few weeks after birth until child is walking securely. Some children walk securely at less than a year while others may not be able to until age 17–18 months.	Infant
No designated name for this period	From about 15–18 months until about 2–2½ years.	Toddler
No specific name. Sometimes called "run-about years"	From age 2–3 to about age 6.	Preschool child
Middle years of childhood	From about age 6 to about age 12	No specific name
Pubescence	Period of about 2 years before puberty.	No specific name
Puberty	Point of development at which biological changes of pubescence reach a climax marked by sexual maturity.	No specific name
Adolescence	From the beginning of pubescence until full social maturity is reached (difficult to fix duration of this period).	Adolescent

Adulthood
  Young adulthood (19–25)
  Adulthood (25–40)
  Maturity (41 plus)
	From adolescence to death.
	Sometimes subdivided into other periods as shown at left.
		Adult

Senescence	No defined limits that would apply to all people. Extremely variable. Characterized by marked physiological and psychological deterioration.	Adult (senile), "old age"

(Table courtesy of Tom Bond.)

*Note: There is no exact beginning or ending point for the various growth periods. The ages are approximate, and each period may be thought of as shading or blending into the next.

tion, heredity determines eye and skin color, the order of motor development, and susceptibility to some diseases. Heredity also exerts considerable influence over body size and shape, height, intelligence, athletic potential, and a host of other details (Fig. 15–4). Score "1" for those who favor heredity as more important than environment in human development!

Nurture Does the preceding mean that nurture takes a back seat in development? Consider Aldous Huxley's (1965) summary of the influence of **environment:**

> Anatomically and physiologically man has changed very little during the last 20 or 30 thousand years. The native or genetic capacities of today's bright city child are no better than the native capacities of a bright child born into a family of Upper Paleolithic cave-dwellers. But whereas the contemporary bright baby may grow up to become almost anything—a Presbyterian engineer, for example, a piano-playing Marxist, a professor of biochemistry who is a mystical agnostic and likes to paint in water-colors—the Paleolithic baby could not possibly have grown into anything except a hunter or food-gatherer. (From "Human Potentialities" by A. Huxley. In R. E. Farson, ed., *Science and Human Affairs*. Palo Alto, CA: Science and Behavior Books, 1965)

Score "1" for the environmentalists!

Nature-Nurture Interactions The outcome of this debate (we have only viewed an opening round) is recognition that *both* heredity and environment are important. In fact, the two are inseparable. As a person grows, there is a constant interplay, or *interaction*, between the forces of nature and nurture. Heredity shapes development by providing a framework of personal potentials and limitations that are altered by learning, nutrition, disease, culture, and other environmental factors.

Question: How soon after birth do hereditary differences appear?

They appear immediately. From birth onward, infants are unique individuals. Jerome Kagan (1969) found that newborn babies differ noticeably in activity, irritability, attention, and other aspects of **temperament.** (Temperament refers to the physical foundations of personality, such as prevailing mood, sensitivity, and energy levels.) Another study found that babies can be separated into three major categories: *Easy children* (about 40 percent of those observed) are relaxed and agreeable. *Difficult children* (about 10 percent) are moody, intense, and easily angered. *Slow-to-warm-up children* (about 15 percent) are restrained and unexpressive, or shy. The remaining children do not fit neatly into any single category (Thomas & Chess, 1977). (Perhaps we should call them "generic" children?)

Fig. 15—4 *Identical twins. Twins who share identical genes (identical twins) demonstrate the powerful influence of heredity. Even when they are reared apart, identical twins are strikingly alike in motor skills, physical development, and appearance (Horn, Plomin, & Rosenman, 1976).*

Because of inborn differences in readiness to smile, cry, vocalize, reach out, or pay attention, babies rapidly become *active participants* in their own development. Growing infants alter parents' behavior at the same time they are changed by it. For example, Amy is an easy baby who smiles frequently and is easily fed. This encourages touching, feeding, and affection from her mother. The mother's responses, in turn, reward Amy and cause more smiling and other positive reactions. A dynamic *relationship* has been established between mother and child.

Consistent differences in temperament can be detected for at least the first 2 years of life (Matheny, Wilson, & Nuss, 1984). Yet by age 10 children's personalities show little connection to the irritability, activity, or attentiveness observed in infancy (Kagan, 1976). Such findings emphasize again that environmental forces continue to modify inborn potentials with each passing year.

To summarize, we might say that three factors combine to determine a person's **developmental level** at any stage of life. These are: *heredity, environment,* and the individual's *own behavior,* each tightly interwoven with the others.

Maturation— Heredity at the Helm

Question: What, specifically, is maturation?

Maturation refers to growth and development of the body—or more specifically, of muscle, bone, and the nervous system. Maturation underlies the *orderly sequence* observed in the unfolding of many basic abilities, such as learning to crawl or walk.

While the *rate* of maturation varies from child to child, the *order* is virtually universal. For instance, the strength and coordination needed for sitting appear before that needed for crawling. Therefore, infants the world over typically sit before they crawl (and crawl before they stand, stand before they walk, and so on) (see Fig. 15–5).

Question: What about my weird cousin Emo who never crawled?

Like cousin Emo, a few children substitute rolling, creeping, or shuffling for crawling. A very small percentage move directly from sitting to standing and walking (Robson, 1984). Even so, an orderly sequence of motor development remains evident. In general, increased muscular

Fig. 15-5 *Motor development. Most infants follow an orderly pattern of motor development. Although the order in which children progress is similar, there are large individual differences in the ages at which each ability appears. The ages listed are averages for American children. It is not unusual for many of the skills to appear 1 or 2 months earlier than average or several months later (Frankenberg & Dodds, 1967).*

1. Fetal posture (new born)   2. Holds chin up (1 month)   3. Holds chest up (3 months)

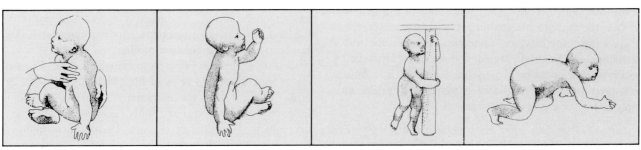

4. Sits when supported (4 months)   5. Sits alone (5 months)   6. Stands holding furniture (6 months)   7. Crawls (7 months)

8. Walks with support (9 months)   9. Stands alone (11 months)   10. Walks alone (12 months)

control in infants proceeds from *head to toe*, and from the *center* of the body *to the extremities*.

Readiness   Maturation often creates a condition of **readiness** for learning. The principle of readiness (also known as the **principle of motor primacy**) states: Until the necessary physical structures are mature, no amount of practice will be sufficient to establish a skill. It is impossible, for instance, to teach children to walk or to use a toilet before they have matured enough to control the necessary muscles. Parents who try to force children to learn skills for which they are not yet ready invite failure and run the risk of needlessly frustrating the child.

Question: Then are there definite ages at which children become ready to learn particular skills?

No. Readiness is not an all-or-nothing effect. Training that comes too early will be unsuccessful; training that is only a little early may succeed but will be inefficient; and training when a child is maturationally ready produces rapid learning.

Many parents are anxious to see their children move through the developmental stages, and there is always a temptation to try to hurry a child along. However, it is valuable to recognize that much needless grief can be avoided by respecting a child's personal rate of growth. For instance, eager parents who toilet trained an 18-month-old child in 10 trying weeks of false alarms and accidents might have done it in 3 weeks by waiting until the child was 24 months old. A recent study found that parents may control when toilet training starts, but maturation tends to determine when it will be completed (Martin et al., 1984). Around 30 months is average for completion. So why fight nature? (The wet look is in.)

Self-Awareness   When you look in a mirror, you recognize the image looking back as your own—except, perhaps, early on Monday mornings. At what age did this sense of recognition develop? Like many other events in development, **self-awareness** depends on maturation of the nervous system.

Question: How is self-awareness demonstrated in a baby?

In an experiment that must have been fun to do, mothers of children 9 to 24 months old secretly rubbed a spot of rouge on their child's nose. Each child was then placed in front of a mirror for testing. The question was, "When will the child notice the red spot, indicating recognition of the mirror image?" The probability that a child would touch his or her nose was very low at 9 months but jumped dramatically through the second year. In an even stronger test of self-recognition, infants were shown their own videotaped images on a TV screen. Most infants had to be 15 months old before they could recognize their own images (Lewis & Brooks-Gunn, 1979). Increased self-awareness, then, closely parallels the human growth sequence (Kagan, 1976).

Social Referencing   At about the same time that self-awareness develops, infants become increasingly aware of others. Have you ever noticed how adults sometimes glance at the facial expressions of others in order to decide how to respond? **Social referencing** of this sort can also be observed in babies. By 12 months of age, most babies *reference* (glance at) their mothers when placed in an unfamiliar situation.

In one recent study of social referencing, babies were placed on a visual cliff. (A visual cliff is pictured in Chapter 5.) The deep side of the cliff was just high enough so that the babies were tempted to cross it, but did not. Most babies placed on the edge of the cliff repeatedly looked at their mothers. As they did, the mothers made faces at them. (All for science, of course.) When the mothers posed faces of joy or interest, most babies crossed the deep side of the cliff. When they posed fear or anger, few babies crossed (Sorce et al., 1985). Thus, by the end of their first year, infants are aware of the facial expressions of others and seek guidance from them (Klinnert, 1984).

Learning Check

1. If an infant is startled, it will make movements similar to an embrace, known as the:
    a. grasping reflex   *b.* rooting reflex   *c.* Moro reflex   *d.* adaptive reflex

2. After age 2, infants tested in a looking chamber show a marked preference for familiar faces and simpler designs.   T or F?

3. As a child develops, there is a continuous _____ between the forces of heredity and environment.

4. Which of the following shows the correct sequence?
   a. zygote, fetus, embryo, neonate, infant   *c.* embryo, zygote, fetus, neonate, infant
   b. zygote, embryo, neonate, fetus, infant   *d.* zygote, embryo, fetus, neonate, infant

5. Slow-to-warm-up children can be described as restrained, unexpressive, or shy.   T or F?

6. The orderly sequence observed in the unfolding of many basic responses can be attributed to _____.

7. Clear signs of self-awareness or self-recognition are evident in most infants by the time they reach 8 months of age.   T or F?

8. The principle of motor primacy is also known as _____.

9. Social _____ of parents' facial expressions is evident in infants by the time they are 1 year old.

Answers: 1. c   2. F   3. interaction   4. d   5. T   6. maturation   7. F   8. readiness   9. referencing

Early Environment—
As the Twig Is Bent

Environment obviously begins to affect development immediately after birth, but it may come as a surprise that the prenatal environment is also important. Normally we think of the **intrauterine environment** of the womb as

Fig. 15–6 *Due to the rapid growth of basic structures, the developing fetus is sensitive to a variety of diseases, drugs, and sources of radiation. This is especially true during the first trimester (3 months) of gestation.*

highly protected and stable. In general it is, but a number of conditions can affect the fetus before birth.

Prenatal Development

During embryonic and fetal development it is quite possible for the effects of environment to reach the interior of the womb. If a mother's health or nutrition is poor, if she contracts certain diseases such as German measles or syphilis, if she uses drugs, or if she is exposed to X rays or atomic radiation, the fetus may be harmed. The resultant damage is referred to as a **congenital problem** (Fig. 15–6). Congenital problems (or *birth defects* as they are sometimes called) are distinct from **genetic problems,** which are inherited. (You will find more information on genetic problems in this chapter's Exploration.)

Question: How is it possible for the fetus to be harmed?

Effects of Drugs   As you may know, there is no direct intermixing of blood between mother and fetus. Nevertheless, some substances, especially drugs, reach the fetus. If the mother is addicted to morphine, heroin, or methadone, the infant may be born with a drug addiction. Most common prescription drugs—many of them capable of producing fetal malformations—also reach the fetus.

Even a partial listing of troublesome drugs underscores the need for caution in drug use during pregnancy. Potentially damaging substances include: general anesthetics; cortisone; tetracycline; excessive amounts of vitamins A, D, B_6, and K; some barbiturates; opiates; tranquilizers; synthetic sex hormones; and possibly even caffeine and aspirin (Cox, 1984; Jacobson et al., 1984).

Question: What about alcohol and tobacco?

Repeated heavy drinking by a pregnant woman can produce a pattern known as **fetal alcohol syndrome.** It includes miscarriage or premature birth, infants with low birth weight, and infants with a variety of bodily defects and deformations (Jones & Smith, 1973). With such risks the safest course during pregnancy is to avoid drinking entirely. There is increasing evidence that even modest use of alcohol during pregnancy can be damaging (Streissguth et al., 1984). The *maximum* amount a pregnant woman should drink on any day is 1 ounce of hard liquor, or one glass of wine, or two glasses of beer (Furey, 1982). During the first 3 months of pregnancy, frequent drinking of even such small amounts of alcohol may damage the fetus.

Smoking also has an adverse effect on prenatal development. Smoking can elevate or lower the heart rate of the unborn child, and a mother who smokes heavily is more likely to miscarry. Heavy smokers run a higher risk of premature birth and tend to give birth to underweight babies. Both premature birth and low birth weight increase the chances of infant sickness and death (Cox, 1984).

Birth

More than ever before, parents can choose how their child will be born. Should they choose a conventional hospital birth? Or should they try natural childbirth? Should the father be present for the birth? In recent years researchers have carefully probed the effects of such choices. Let's briefly explore what they have learned.

Conventional Delivery   Until recently **medicated births** in hospital delivery rooms were the rule in Western societies. In such births the mother is assisted by a physician and is given drugs to relieve pain. The drugs used range from local analgesics (painkillers) to general anesthetics that cause a loss of consciousness. Increasingly, doctors and parents have come to realize that general anesthesia during birth has major drawbacks. For one thing drugs dull or block the mother's awareness of birth. They also reduce oxygen flow to the fetus and can cause the infant to be born partially anesthetized. For such reasons babies whose mothers were given heavy doses of anesthetic tend to lag in muscular and neural development (Backbill, 1979).

In the last 5 years there has been a marked move away from use of general anesthesia during birth. Nevertheless, some form of painkiller is used in 95 percent of all deliveries in the United States. Certainly, mothers should not feel guilty if they need a painkiller during birth. However, it appears wise to use as few drugs as possible.

Prepared Childbirth   What can parents do to minimize the discomfort of birth—while giving their babies the best possible start in life? Many psychologists are convinced that **natural,** or **prepared, childbirth** is the answer. The most widely used approach to natural childbirth is the *Lamaze method* (la-MAHZ), developed by French physician Ferdinand Lamaze.

Couples begin learning the Lamaze method during pregnancy. Part of the training explains what will happen physically during birth: Women who thoroughly understand what is happening in their bodies tend to have fewer fears and less anxiety. Couples are also taught methods of breathing and muscular control to minimize pain during birth. Another important element is training the father or a friend to give support to the mother during birth. By coaching the mother in breathing and by assisting her in other ways, the father is made an active participant in the birth.

Natural childbirth typically shortens labor and minimizes pain. In addition, it treats birth as a celebration of life, rather than a medical problem or a disease. Accordingly, parents are more likely to experience birth as a time of great happiness when natural childbirth is used *and* the father is present (Tanzer & Block, 1976). (Should the celebration extend to the baby? See Highlight 15–1 for a discussion of "gentle birth.")

Question: How important is it for fathers to participate in birth?

For most parents the emotional intensity of birth magnifies its impact. Many fathers form memories at the time of their child's birth that will be with them for life. Such memories can make a difference in the father's willingness to care for the child or in his reaction when the child angers him. Researchers have found that fathers generally make a better transition to parenthood when they participate in preparing for childbirth (Grossman et al., 1980). But, while participation in the birth itself is valuable for fathers, it is apparently not essential. The father's *attitude* toward the birth of his child is probably more important. A recent study found that fathers who *wanted* to be present during delivery showed greater interest in their infants during the first year and were more likely to help care for the baby (Grossman & Volkmer, 1984). This was true whether or not the father was actually able to attend the birth.

Many hospitals now have **birthing rooms** that allow the father to "room in" in a homelike atmosphere (Fig. 15–7). This allows him to participate in the birth and to share in caring for the newborn. At the same time, it ensures that prompt medical attention is available in the event of any birth complications. Even traditional delivery rooms are allowing fathers to be present during birth, either as

Highlight 15–1
Gentle Birth

From the warm and protected confines of the womb, a baby is forcefully thrust into a cold, noisy world. The new arrival is greeted with glaring lights, booming voices, cutting of the umbilical cord, and weighing on a cold scale. According to French obstetrician Frederick Leboyer, these events make birth a needlessly traumatic experience.

Leboyer (1975) advocates a system of **gentle birth** that he claims is pleasant for both mother and baby. Delivery takes place in a quiet, dimly lit room. Immediately after birth the baby is placed on the mother's abdomen and is massaged. After several minutes of soothing and gentle massage, the umbilical cord is cut and the baby is bathed in warm water. Leboyer believes this approach is superior to conventional birth procedures, which he regards as "violent" and "cruel."

From a medical standpoint some of Leboyer's methods can be risky. A darkened delivery room, for instance, may delay detection of a "blue baby" or other complications. Still, gentle birth appeals to many parents, and thousands of babies have been delivered by the Leboyer method.

Leboyer claims that gentle births produce children who are happier, healthier, more relaxed, and more emotionally stable. However, evidence in support of this claim is not very convincing. It is true that during the first 15 to 20 minutes after birth, Leboyer babies are more relaxed than other newborns (Oliver & Oliver, 1978). From that point on, however, Leboyer-delivered babies do not differ in any measurable way from conventionally delivered babies (Nelson et al., 1980). Even if the Leboyer babies did differ, could we conclude that gentle birth is beneficial? What if parents who choose gentle births tend to be more loving or attentive? If this were the case, the later emotional health of their infants might have nothing to do with birth itself.

Undoubtedly, parents should use the method of delivery that makes them most comfortable, and many parents regard gentle birth as a desirable alternative. At this point, however, it appears that gentle births may be done more for parents than for babies!

observers or to coach the mother through labor and childbirth. In some cases the father cuts the umbilical cord and gives the infant its first bath. Babies are now less often rushed off to a nursery; in many hospitals the baby spends its first night with the parents in the birthing room. Clearly, such changes are making birth psychologically more rewarding for mother, father, and baby.

Maternal and Paternal Influences

In later years a child's environment expands to include the effects of culture, subculture, family, school, television, and peers. Immediately after birth and for the first few years, the most important influences come from an infant's caretakers. The quality of "mothering" and "fathering" is therefore of prime importance.

One revealing study of **maternal influences** began with selection of children who were unusually competent ("A" children) or who had a low degree of competence ("C" children). As increasingly younger children were observed, it became apparent that A and C patterns were already set by age 3.

To learn how this was possible, researchers visited homes and observed children under 3 and their mothers (White & Watts, 1973). Observed **caretaking styles** ranged from the "super mother" to the "zoo-keeper mother." Super mothers went out of their way to provide educational experiences for their children and allowed the child to initiate some activities. This caretaking style produced an A child, competent in most areas of development. At the other end of the spectrum, zoo-keeper mothers gave their children good physical care but interacted with them very little. Their child-care routines were rigid and highly structured. The result was C children who tended to approach problems inflexibly (Pines, 1969).

Another recent study found that children's intellectual abilities at age 6 can be predicted, to some extent, by their mothers' *responsiveness* to them during infancy (Coates & Lewis, 1984). Effective mothers, it seems, are those who are sensitive to their children's needs. Put another way, effective mothers alter their own behavior to meet their children's changing needs at each stage of development.

Taken together, such findings support two beliefs long held by developmental psychologists: First, that mothering *does* make a difference; and second, that early development has lasting effects on a person.

Question: Aren't you overlooking the effects of fathering?

Yes. Fathers also contribute significantly to an infant's social and intellectual growth. In fact fathers make a unique contribution to development by interacting with the infant in ways that differ from those typical of mothers.

Recent studies of **paternal influences** have shown that even in nontraditional families the father's main role tends to be that of a *playmate* for the infant. Fathers typically spend four or five times as much time playing with their infants as they do in caretaking (Parke & Sawin, 1977).

It might seem that the father's role as a playmate makes him less important in the child's development. Not so. From birth of the child onward, fathers are more visually attentive to the child than are mothers. They are much more tactile (lifting, tickling, and handling the baby), more physically arousing (engaging in rough-and-tumble play), and more likely to engage in unusual play (imitating baby, for example) (Crawley & Sherrod, 1984; Parke & Sawin, 1977). Mothers speak to the infant more, play more conventional games (such as peekaboo), and, as previously noted, spend more time in caretaking activities (see Fig. 15–9).

Thus, from the first days of life on, infants get very different views of males and females. Females, who offer comfort, nurturance, and verbal stimulation, also tend to be close at hand. Males come and go, and when they are present, action, exploration, and risk taking prevail (Herbert & Greenberg, 1983). It's no wonder, then, that maternal and paternal styles appear to have a major impact on children's sex-role development (Biller, 1982).

Language Development— Fast-Talking Babies

There's something almost miraculous about hearing a baby's first words. As infants, how did we manage to leap into the world of language? To gain an understanding, let's begin with a survey of language development.

Language Acquisition The development of language is closely tied to maturation. As any parent can tell you, babies can cry from birth on. By 4 weeks of age, the infant can control crying enough to use it as an attention-getting device, and parents can tell the nature of the infant's needs from the tone of the crying. Around 6 to 8 weeks of age, babies begin **cooing** (repeating vowel sounds like "oo" and "ah").

By age 6 months, the nervous system has matured enough to allow the child to grasp objects, to smile, laugh, sit up, and to **babble.** In the babbling stage consonant sounds are added to produce a continuous outpouring of repeated language sounds. The influence of environment at this stage is indicated by the fact that babbling increases when parents talk to the child (Mussen et al., 1979).

Fig. 15–7 *Changing attitudes toward childbirth have encouraged mothers and fathers to actively prepare for birth and to participate more fully in caring for the newborn.*

Fig. 15–8 *"Fathering" typically makes a contribution to early development differing in emphasis from "mothering."*

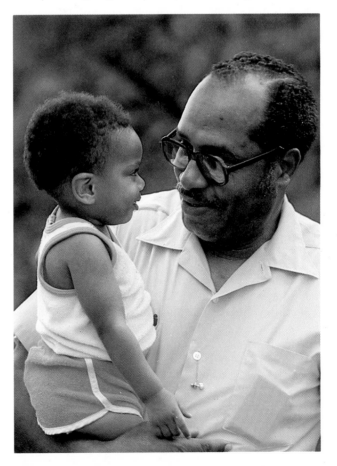

Fig. 15–9 *Mother-infant and father-infant interactions. These graphs show what occurred on routine days in a sample of 72 American homes. The graph on the left records the total amount of contact parents had with their babies, including such actions as talking to, touching, hugging, or smiling at the infant. The graph on the left shows the amount of caregiving (diapering, washing, feeding, and so forth) done by each parent. Note that in both cases mother-infant interactions greatly exceed father-infant interactions. (Adapted from Belsky, Gilstrap, & Rovine, 1984.)*

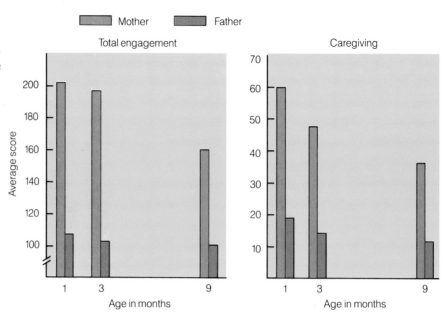

At about 1 year of age, the child can stand alone for a short time and can respond to words such as "no" or "hi." Soon afterward, the first connection between words and objects is formed, and children may address their parents as "Mama" or "Dada." Between the ages of 1½ and 2 years, children become able to stand and walk alone. By this time their vocabulary may include from 24 to 200 words. At first children go through a **single-word stage,** during which they say things such as "go," "juice," or "up" (Bloom & Lahey, 1978). Soon after, they begin to arrange words in simple two-word sentences called **telegraphic speech:** "Want Teddy," "Mama gone." From this point on, growth of the child's vocabulary and language skills proceeds at a phenomenal rate. By first grade the child can understand around 8000 words and use about 4000.

The Roots of Language

In a fascinating study, researchers Louis Sander and William Condon (1974) filmed newborn infants as the babies listened to various sounds. A later frame-by-frame analysis of the films showed something astonishing: Infants move their arms and legs in synchrony to the rhythms of human speech. Random noise, rhythmic tapping, or disconnected vowel sounds will not produce this "language dance." Only the natural rhythms of speech have this effect.

Why would day-old infants "dance" to speech but not other sounds? One possibility is that language recognition is innate. Linguist Noam Chomsky (1968, 1975) has long claimed that humans have a **biological predisposition** to develop language. According to Chomsky, language organization is inborn, much like a child's ability to coordinate walking. If such inborn language recognition does exist, it may explain why children around the world use a limited number of patterns in their first sentences. Typical patterns include (Mussen et al., 1979):

Identification:	See kitty.
Nonexistence:	Allgone milk.
Possession:	My doll.
Agent-action:	Mama give.
Negation:	Not ball.
Question:	Where doggie?

Question: Does Chomsky's theory explain why language develops so rapidly?

Perhaps. But many psychologists believe that Chomsky underestimates the importance of learning (Bruner, 1983). **Psycholinguists** (specialists in the psychology of language) have recently shown that language is not magically "switched on" by adult speech. Imitation of adults and rewards for correctly using words (as when a child asks for a cookie) are also a part of language learning. More importantly, parents and children begin to communicate long before the child can speak. Months of shared effort precede the child's first word (Miller, 1977). From this point of view, the filmed infants' behavior reflects a readiness to interact *socially* with parents, not innate language recognition.

Question: How do parents communicate with infants before they can talk?

Early Communication   Parents go to a great deal of trouble to get babies to smile and vocalize (Fig. 15–10). In doing so, they quickly learn to change their actions to keep the infant's attention, arousal, and activity at optimal levels (Brazelton et al., 1974). A familiar example is the "I'm-Going-to-Get-You Game." In it the adult says, "I'm gonna getcha . . . I'm gonna getcha . . . I'm gonna getcha . . . Gotcha!" Through such games, adults and babies come to share similar rhythms and expectations (Stern, 1982). Soon a system of shared **signals** is created. Touching, vocalizing, gazing, and smiling help lay a foundation for later language use. Specifically, these signals establish a pattern of "conversational" **turn taking** (Bruner, 1983; Snow, 1977):

Mother	Ann
	(smiles)
Oh what a nice little smile!	
Yes, isn't that nice?	
There.	
There's a nice little smile.	(burps)
Well, pardon you!	
Yes, that's better, isn't it?	
Yes.	(vocalizes)
Yes.	(smiles)
What's so funny?	

From the outside such exchanges may look meaningless. In reality they represent real communication. A baby's vocalizations and attention provide a way of interacting emotionally with parents (Stern et al., 1975). (For another perspective on turn taking, see Fig. 15–11.)

Parents as Tutors   Parents help children learn language in more ways than they may suspect. One way is through the use of **caretaker speech,** or "motherese," as it is sometimes called. Caretaker speech may be more familiar to you as Baby Talk. When talking to infants, parents raise the tone of their voice, use shorter phrases, repeat themselves more, and slow their rate of speaking (Parke, 1982; Warren-Leubecker & Bohannon, 1984). They also simplify pronouns ("Did Jenny eat it?") and pronunciation. In Baby Talk, phrases such as "pretty rabbit" become "pwitty wabbit, "skambled eggs" may replace scrambled eggs, and a stomach is a "tummy."

Question: What is the purpose of such changes?

Parents are apparently trying to help their children learn language. When a baby is still babbling, parents tend to use long, adult-style sentences. But as soon as the baby says its first word, they switch to Baby Talk. The changes in pronunciation parents make are probably not very important. But simplification is, because it helps babies learn the basic rules of language (Cherry 1979). As a child's speaking ability improves, parents tend to adjust their speech to the child's level of language development. Especially from age 1½ to 4, parents use strategies to clarify what a child says and to prompt the child to say more. Two typical strategies are (Newman & Newman, 1978):

Fig. 15–10   *Infant engagement scale. These samples from a 90-point scale show various levels of infant engagement, or attention. Babies participate in prelanguage "conversations" with parents by giving and withholding attention, and by smiling, gazing, or vocalizing. (Source: Beebe et al., 1982.)*

85
Medium high positive

50
Neutral attention

20
Avert

Fig. 15—11   *This graph shows the development of turn taking in games played by an infant and his mother. For several months Richard responded to games such as peekaboo and "hand-the-toy-back" only when his mother initiated action. At about 9 months, however, he rapidly began to initiate action in the games. Soon he was the one to take the lead about half of the time. Learning to take turns and to direct actions at another person underlie basic language skills. (From Bruner, 1983.)*

Fig. 15—12   *"Mother" Lorenz leads his charges. The goslings have imprinted on Lorenz because he was the first moving object they saw after they hatched.*

Expansion: *Child:*   Doggie bite.
              Parent: Yes, the dog bit *the toy.*
Prompting: *Child:*   Doggie briggle.
              Parent: What did the doggie do??

In summary, some elements of language may be innate, but a full flowering of speech requires careful cultivation. Now that we have our subjects (babies) walking and talking, let's move on to some other facets of development.

Critical Periods in Development—Imprinting, Attachment, and Motherless Monkeys

Question: Why do experiences early in life often have such lasting effects?

Part of the answer lies in the existence of critical periods for acquiring particular behaviors. A **critical period** is a time of increased sensitivity to environmental influences (both positive and negative). Critical periods usually cor-

respond to times of rapid development. For example, the infamous drug thalidomide interferes with limb formation in the developing fetus. Before its use was banned, many pregnant women in the United States and Europe had the misfortune of taking thalidomide during the period of fetal limb formation (the sixth to eighth weeks of pregnancy). The result was severe birth defects.

Imprinting   Often, certain events must occur during a critical period in order for a person or an animal to develop normally. For example, Konrad Lorenz, an ethologist who studies animal behavior, was curious about why baby geese follow their mother. The obvious explanation seemed to be, "It's instinctive," but Lorenz showed otherwise.

Mother Lorenz

Normally the first large moving object a baby goose sees is its mother. Lorenz hatched geese in an incubator, so the first moving object they saw was Lorenz. From then on, these baby geese followed Lorenz. They even reacted to his call as if he were their mother (Lorenz, 1937) (Fig. 15–12).

It can be seen that the response pattern of "mother-goose following" is not automatic. Rather, it is established during a critical period by the essential experience of seeing a large moving object. The rapid and early learning of a permanent behavior pattern of this type has been called **imprinting.**

In most birds the critical period for imprinting is very brief. For instance, Hess (1959) found that if ducklings are not allowed to imprint on their mother or some other object within 30 hours after hatching, they never will. (Ducklings have been imprinted on decoys, rubber balls, wooden blocks, and other unlikely objects.) In many animals imprinting and other events taking place during critical periods have lifelong consequences (Lorenz, 1962):

Revenge of the Jackdaw

Imprinting normally serves to attach a young animal to its mother. It also guides the selection of a mate of the same species at sexual maturity. In another of Lorenz's experiments, a jackdaw (European blackbird) imprinted on him. When the bird reached sexual maturity, Lorenz became the object of its mating ritual. Part of this ritual involves stuffing worms into the mouth of the intended mate—as a surprised Lorenz learned while asleep on the lawn one day. When Lorenz refused its gift, the jackdaw stuffed a worm in Lorenz's ear (showing, perhaps, that it's not nice to fool Mother Nature)!

Question: Does imprinting occur in humans?

Attachment True cases of imprinting are limited to birds and other animals (Hess, 1959). However, human infants form an **emotional attachment** to their *primary caretakers* (usually parents), and there is a critical period (roughly the first year of life) during which this must occur for healthy development (Bowlby, 1969, 1973). A direct sign that an emotional bond has been formed appears when infants are around 8 to 12 months of age. At that time babies display **separation anxiety** (crying and signs of fear) when their parents leave them alone or leave them with strangers (Kagan, 1976).

In recent years a major controversy has raged over whether attachment is influenced by events that occur immediately after birth. Please see Highlight 15–2 for a discussion of mother-infant bonding.

Attachment can have quite an effect on early development. Infants who are securely attached to their parents later show more resiliency, curiosity, problem-solving ability, and social competence in preschool (Parke & Asher, 1983).

Question: Does day-care for young children interfere with normal attachment?

Highlight 15–2
Mother-Infant Bonding—
A Touching Debate

In one hospital ward new mothers are given traditional contact with their infants: a glimpse after birth and 30-minute visits every 4 hours for feeding. In a second hospital ward "extended contact group" mothers are given their babies for 1 hour during the first 3 hours after birth and for an extra 5 hours each afternoon for the first 3 days after delivery. Does the extra contact make a difference?

An initial series of studies reported by Marshall Klaus and John Kennel (1982) seemed to suggest that there are lasting benefits to close, early contact between a mother and her infant. According to Klaus and Kennel, there is a sensitive period in the first hours after an infant's birth. Therefore, mother-child pairs who spend extra time together form a stronger **emotional bond.** This is especially true, they believe, if skin-to-skin touching is part of early contact.

Klaus and Kennel, along with several other researchers, have reported that "bonded" babies are healthier, brighter, and more alert and responsive than those who are denied extra contact. However, the majority of recent, more carefully conducted studies have failed to support the idea that extended, early contact is crucial to the mother-infant bond (Myers, 1984). Critics also point out that adopted children, premature babies, and babies born by cesarean section (surgical birth) all develop normal, affectionate bonds with their mothers. Even Klaus and Kennel now acknowledge that it is unlikely that something as important as emotional attachment would depend *solely* on the first few hours of life (Klaus & Kennel, 1984). Humans are highly adaptable, and there are many opportunities for attachment during the first year of life.

Advocates of bonding continue to believe that early contact between mothers and infants can have beneficial effects. Even those researchers who doubt that early contact makes a difference agree that allowing mother, father, and infant to be together during the first few hours is humane and natural. So, while most evidence suggests that early contact is not necessary, it is undoubtedly a positive, emotionally satisfying experience.

Fortunately, it seems that it does not. For one thing separation anxiety normally disappears when parting with parents becomes a routine event. In addition a major survey of day-care effects concluded that *"high-quality* nonmaternal care does not appear to have harmful effects on the preschool child's maternal attachment, intellectual development, social-emotional behavior, or physical health" (Etaugh, 1980). A second, more recent study also concluded that mother-infant attachment is not threatened by quality day care (Tephy & Elardo, 1984). Attachment also appears not to be harmed when the mother works (Owen et al., 1984). The key ingredient for secure attachment is a mother who is accepting and sensitive to her baby's signals and rhythms (Belsky, Rovine, & Taylor, 1984).

Motherless Monkeys   Research with rhesus monkeys suggests that, like imprinting, infant attachments can have lasting effects. Harry Harlow (1966, 1967) has shown that baby monkeys separated from their mothers and raised in isolation become troubled adult animals. Among other things these motherless monkeys never develop normal sexual behaviors, and they make very poor mothers if mated. They are coldly rejecting or indifferent to their babies and may brutalize or injure them. It has been suggested that human parents who abuse, reject, or physically injure their children may be displaying a similar pattern. Most abusive parents were themselves rejected or mistreated as children.

Meeting a baby's **affectional needs** is every bit as important as meeting more obvious needs for food, water, and physical care. All things considered, one of the most important developments of the first year of life appears to be creation of a bond of trust and affection between the infant and at least one other person. Parents are sometimes afraid of "spoiling" a baby with too much attention, but for the first year or two this is nearly impossible. As a matter of fact, a later capacity to experience warm and loving relationships may depend on it.

Question: Are there other critical periods?

Other Critical Periods   Psychologists are just beginning to explore the full range of critical periods in human development. It is well known, for example, that if a person waits until adulthood to learn a second language, achieving an authentic native accent is virtually impossible. In general, reaching maximum ability in artistic, athletic, musical, or language skills requires practice that begins at an early age. A case in point is the work of Japanese music teacher Shinichi Suzuki. Using scaled-down instruments, Suzuki has taught children as young as 3 years old to play the violin. By age 6 these children have spent half their lives playing Bach, Handel, and Mozart. By age 10 many are so phenomenal that serious adult students envy their ability.

In many ways it would be accurate to say that all of infancy is a *relatively critical period* in development. While we must wait for further research on variables affecting the kinds of skills described here, one area is fairly well understood. The effects of early stimulation and deprivation are discussed in the following section.

Deprivation and Enrichment— A Practical Definition of Tender Loving Care

NEWS ITEM: "Wild Child Raised by Apes Found in Africa." Over the years there have been several reported discoveries of feral (wild) children. These are children who have supposedly grown up in the care of animals and who act like animals when found. Actually, there is little documented evidence that such children have existed, but we needn't go this far afield for proof of the destructive effects of early **deprivation.**

There are numerous confirmed cases of children who have spent the first 5 or 6 years of life in closets, attics, and other restricted environments. When discovered, these children are usually mute, severely retarded, and emotionally damaged. Some suffer from **deprivation dwarfism**—stunted growth associated with isolation, rejection, or general deprivation in the home environment. (See inset news excerpt.) Special efforts to teach such children to speak and function normally often meet with limited success.

Question: What aspects of such experiences are responsible for the damage done?

One of the earliest hints came when psychoanalyst René Spitz (1945) compared two groups of infants. One group was made up of healthy and lively babies in an institution Spitz called the "nursery." In the "foundling home" was a second group of babies who suffered from a condition called **hospitalism.** This is a pattern of deep depression marked by weeping and sadness, long periods of immobility or mechanical rocking, and a lack of normal response to other humans. The foundling home also had an unusually high rate of infant deaths, and development of the living babies was severely retarded.

By comparing conditions at the two institutions, Spitz found some striking differences. At the nursery each baby had a separate attendant; at the foundling home there were eight babies to a nurse. Spitz considered the "wasting away" of the foundling home babies a result of their lack of dependable mother figures.

Question: In other words the babies failed to form an attachment to an adult, right?

Yes. Recent work shows that lack of attachment is a major element in early deprivation. For example, making living conditions better for a group of children in a Canadian institution failed to reverse their declining mental health. The children improved only when they were placed with caring foster parents or adoptive parents (Flint, 1978).

A second major factor in many cases of deprivation is a lack of **perceptual stimulation.** All of the "wasted" babies studied by Spitz were well cared for physically. However, they were kept in bare rooms in cribs with white sheets hung on the sides. The infants could see only the blank ceiling, and their only contact with others came during a few brief periods each day when they were quickly fed or changed. To put it mildly, there was *nothing happening* for these children—no change, no input, no cuddling, no attention, and most of all, no stimulation. This was deprivation in the fullest sense of the word.

Early Stimulation

Experiments with animals have confirmed the destructive effects of a lack of stimulation in infancy. For example, Harry Harlow separated infant rhesus monkeys from their mothers at birth. The real mothers were replaced with **surrogate** (artificial) **mothers**—essentially, dummies of approximately the same size and shape as real monkeys. Some of the surrogates were made of cold, unyielding wire, and others were covered with soft terry cloth (Fig. 15–13). When the infants were given a choice between the two mothers, they consistently chose to spend most of their time clinging to the cuddly terry cloth mother. This was true even when a bottle was mounted in the wire mother, making it the source of food.

The "love" and attachment displayed toward the cloth mothers was identical to that shown toward natural mothers. When frightened by rubber snakes, wind-up toys, and other "fear stimuli," the infant monkeys ran to their cloth mothers and clung to them for security (Harlow & Zimmerman, 1958). Harlow concluded that one of the most important dimensions of early stimulation is **contact comfort,** supplied by touching, holding, and stroking an infant. Harlow's findings may be inconclusive where humans are concerned, but other findings back them up. For example, one researcher found that just 20 minutes of extra touching a day could accelerate the developmental rate of infants in an institution (Casler, 1965).

"Closet Child" Now with Loving Parents

LONG BEACH (AP)—Becky's story began to unfold when the Sheriff's Department responded to a tip like hundreds of others. They found Becky in urine-soaked clothes, asleep on a hard cot in her parents' bedroom.

"She was almost like an animal," one of the deputies reported.

Her world then was the bedroom and its closet, in which she was kept for untold hours. Now Becky lives in a spacious foster home.

Since Becky's rescue, she has gained 12 pounds and grown 6 inches. But she is still a mite, for she weighed only 24 pounds and stood only 32 inches tall last April.

When she was found, Becky couldn't even crawl; now she walks. Then, she knew only a few words—now she speaks in sentences. She is, except for the hurt in her eyes, like almost any toddler.

But Rebecca is no toddler. She is 9 years old, and her pediatrician says she may never catch up.

For many psychologists the concept of contact comfort has become part of the rationale for advocating breast feeding of infants. Breast feeding almost guarantees a baby will receive an adequate amount of touching and handling, and it appears to aid attachment (Jensen et al., 1981). In addition, the breast-feeding mother produces **colostrum** (ko-LOSS-trum) rather than milk for the first few days after birth. Colostrum is a fluid rich in proteins that carries antibodies from the mother to the newborn and helps prevent certain infectious diseases.

Question: What about the mother who can't breast-feed or who prefers not to?

The advantages of breast feeding are not overriding. If a mother is aware of the importance of touching and cuddling, bottle feeding is in no way psychologically inferior to breast feeding. In fact a mother's warmth or coldness, relaxation or tension, and acceptance or rejection are more important than the choice of breast or bottle (Heinstein, 1963). Being sensitive to a baby's feeding rhythms and needs seems to be a key element in promoting healthy infant attachment (Ainsworth, 1979).

Fig. 15–13 *An infant monkey clings to a cloth-covered surrogate mother. Baby monkeys become attached to the cloth "contact-comfort" mother but not to a similar wire mother. This is true even when the wire mother provides food. (Photo courtesy of Harry Harlow, University of Wisconsin Primate Laboratory.)*

Enrichment   If too little stimulation limits development, can an abundance of stimulation enhance it? A number of attempts to answer this question have made use of **enriched environments.** An enriched environment is one that has been deliberately made more novel, complex, and richly stimulating. Enriched environments for infants may be the "soil" from which brighter children grow. To illustrate, let us begin with an experiment in which rats were raised in an enriched environment (Kretch et al., 1962):

Building Bigger and Better Brains

To begin with, infant rats were divided into two groups. One group was raised in *stimulus-poor* conditions. These animals were housed in adequate but unstimulating cages with gray walls that contained nothing to explore or investigate. The second group was housed in a sort of rat wonderland. The walls of the *stimulus-enriched* environment were decorated with colored patterns, and the cage was filled with platforms, ladders, and cubbyholes to be explored. When both groups of rats reached adulthood, they were tested for ability to learn mazes. The stimulated rats dramatically out-performed their deprived relatives. In addition, later tests showed that the stimulated rats had brains that were larger and heavier, with a thicker cortex.

It is a long leap from rats to people, yet it is hard to overlook the significance of an increase in brain size caused by sensory stimulation. If stimulation can enhance the "intelligence" of a lowly rat, it is reasonable to assume that human infants also benefit from stimulation.

Question: Is there any evidence that this is actually the case?

As might be expected, it is much harder to prove that such things occur in humans. In Chapter 17 you will find a full discussion of the effects of environment on intelligence. For now let us examine one case of enrichment applied to humans.

Infants like to reach out and touch things, but normally it takes about 5 months after birth for this skill to develop. In an experiment conducted at a state hospital, newborn infants were given several kinds of extra stimulation each day for several months (White & Held, 1966):

Each child in the stimulus enrichment condition was handled an extra 15 minutes daily; each was placed in a position that allowed visual exploration outside the crib; white crib sheets were replaced by patterned sheets with colorful animal designs; and a collection of bright and colorful objects was hung over each child's crib.

As limited as these changes may seem, they caused **visually directed reaching** to occur an average of a 1½ months early. This may not sound like an earthshaking improvement in adult terms, but for an infant it is a substantial acceleration of development.

This is only one of many experiments showing a positive relationship between stimulation and improvements in various abilities, particularly those that might be labeled "intellectual." Most people recognize that babies need lots of "tender loving care" where physical needs are concerned. But as the previous discussion shows, a complete definition of tender loving care should include a baby's psychological needs as well. It would be a good idea to place stimulation, affectionate touching, and personal warmth high on any list of infant needs.

Learning Check

The preceding sections of this chapter contain a large amount of information. Check your comprehension by answering the questions below. Skim back over the material if you miss any.

1. A duckling can be imprinted after the critical period has passed if the environment is enriched.   T or F?

2. The development of separation anxiety in an infant corresponds to formation of an attachment to parents.   T or F?

3. A baby's affectional needs can be met by supplying adequate food, water, and physical care.   T or F?

4. Harlow's "motherless monkeys" became attached to the surrogate mother that fed them.   T or F?

5. René Spitz attributed hospitalism to an absence of perceptual stimulation.   T or F?

6. Bottle feeding prevents a mother from providing an adequate amount of contact comfort for an infant.   T or F?

7. The intrauterine environment has little effect on a person's development.   T or F?

8. The "super mother" goes out of her way to provide educational experience yet accepts the child as he or she is.   T or F?

9. The development of speech and language usually occurs in which order:
a. crying, cooing, babbling, telegraphic speech   *c.* babbling, crying, cooing, telegraphic speech
b. cooing, crying, babbling, telegraphic speech   *d.* crying, babbling, cooing, identification

10. Research has shown conclusively that mother-infant contact immediately after birth is essential for optimal development.   T or F?

Answers: 1. F 2. T 3. F 4. F 5. F 6. F 7. F 8. T 9. *a* 10. F

Cognitive Growth—
How Do Children Learn to Think?
How Do Children Think to Learn?

Question: How different is a child's understanding of the world from that of an adult?

Generally speaking, a child's thinking is *less abstract* than that of an adult. Children use fewer generalizations, categories, or principles and tend to base their understanding of the world on particular examples, tangible sensations, and concrete objects.

An indication of the concrete nature of thinking in very young children is their failure to recognize the permanence of objects. Older children and adults realize that an object that is out of sight still exists. With a very young child, "out of sight" can literally mean "out of mind." If a ball rolls behind something while a 4- or 5-month-old child is playing with it, the child behaves as if the ball has ceased to exist and stops looking for it.

Long after children have discovered the permanence of objects, their thinking remains concrete in other ways. For example, before age 6 or 7, children are unable to

make **transformations.** If you show a child a short, wide glass full of milk and a tall, narrow glass (also full of milk), the child will tell you the taller glass contains more milk. Children will tell you this even if you allow them to watch as you pour milk from the short glass into an empty, tall glass. They are not bothered by the apparent transformation of the milk from a smaller to a larger amount (Fig. 15–14). They respond only to the fact that "taller" seems to mean "more." After about age 7 children are no longer fooled by this situation. Perhaps this is why 7 has been called the "age of reason." From age 7 on we see a definite trend toward more abstract thought (Elkind, 1968).

Question: Is there any pattern to the growth of intellect in childhood?

Piaget's Theory of Cognitive Development

According to the late Swiss psychologist and philospher Jean Piaget (1951, 1952), there is. Piaget (pronounced pea-ah-JAY) believed all children pass through a series of distinct *stages* in intellectual development (Fig. 15–15).

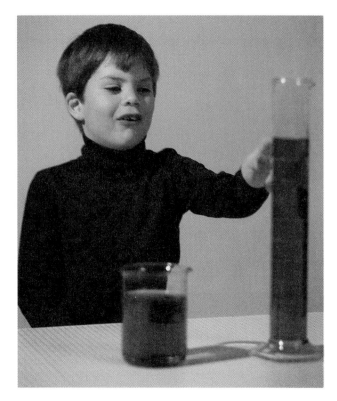

Fig. 15–14 *Children under age 7 intuitively assume that a volume of liquid is increased when it is poured from a short, wide container into a tall, thin one.*

Fig. 15–15 *Jean Piaget—philosopher, psychologist, and keen observer of children.*

Many of his ideas came from observing his own children as they solved various thought problems. (It is tempting to imagine that Piaget's illustrious career may have been launched one day when his wife said to him, "Watch the children for a while, will you, Jean?") Piaget's many observations convinced him that intellect grows through what he called "assimilation" and "accommodation."

Assimilation refers to using existing patterns in new situations. Let's say a plastic hammer is Ben's favorite toy. Ben uses the hammer properly and pounds on the blocks that came with it. For his birthday Ben gets an oversize toy wrench. If he uses the wrench for pounding, it has been assimilated to an existing mental structure.

In **accommodation** existing ideas are modified to fit new requirements. For instance, a young child might think that a dime is worth less than a (larger) nickel. As the child begins to spend money, he or she will be forced to alter ideas about what "more" and "less" mean. Thus, new situations are assimilated to existing ideas, and new ideas are created to accommodate new experiences.

Piaget's theories have had a profound effect on our thinking about children. The following is a brief summary of what he found.

The Sensorimotor Stage (0–2 Years)   In the first 2 years of life, a child's intellectual development is largely *nonverbal.* The child is mainly concerned with learning to coordinate *purposeful* movements with information from the senses. Also important at this time is gradual emergence of the concept of **object permanence.** At about age 1½ the child begins to pursue disappearing objects. By age 2 the child can anticipate the movement of an object behind a screen. When watching an electric train, for example, the child looks ahead to the end of a tunnel rather than staring at the spot where the train disappeared.

In general, developments in this stage indicate that the child's conceptions are becoming more *stable.* Objects cease to appear and disappear magically, and a more orderly and predictable world takes shape.

The Preoperational Stage (2–7 Years)   During the preoperational period the child is developing an ability to think *symbolically* and to use language. But the child's thinking is still very **intuitive.** (Do you remember thinking as a child that the sun and the moon followed you when you took a walk?) In addition, the child's use of language is not as sophisticated as it might seem. Children have a tendency to confuse words with the objects they represent. If the child calls a toy block a "car" and you use it to make a "train," the child may be upset. To children the name of an object is as much a part of the object as its size, shape, and color. This seems to underlie a preoccupation with name-calling. To the preoperational child an insulting name may hurt as much as "sticks and stones." Consider, for instance, one rather protected youngster who was angered by her older brother. Searching for a way to retaliate against her larger and stronger foe, she settled on, "You panty girdle!" It was the worst thing she could think of.

During the preoperational stage the child is also quite **egocentric,** or unable to take the viewpoint of other people. The ego seems to stand at the center of his or her world. To illustrate, show a child a two-sided mirror. Then hold it between the two of you so the child can see herself in it. If you ask her what she thinks *you* can see, she imagines that you see *her* reflected image instead of your own. The concept of egocentrism helps us understand why children can seem exasperatingly selfish or uncooperative at times. A child who blocks your view by standing in front of a television set assumes that you can see if he can. If you ask him to move so you can see, he may move so that he can see better!

The Concrete Operational Stage (7–11 Years)
An important development during this stage is mastery of the concept of **conservation.** Children have learned the concept of conservation when they understand that rolling a ball of clay into a "snake" does not increase the amount of clay and that pouring liquid from a tall, narrow glass into a shallow dish does not reduce the amount of liquid. In each case the volume remains the same despite a change in shape or appearance. The original amount is "conserved" (Fig. 15–15).

During the concrete operational stage a child's thought begins to include the concepts of time, space, and number. Categories and principles are used, and the child can think logically about concrete objects or situations. These abilities explain why children stop believing in Santa Claus when they reach the concrete operations stage. Because of their ability to conserve, they come to realize such things as: Santa couldn't possibly visit everyone's house in one evening, or Santa's sack couldn't hold that many toys (Fehr, 1976).

Another important development at this time is the ability to reverse thoughts or operations. Lack of *reversibility* is illustrated by this conversation with a 4-year-old boy still in the *preoperational* stage (Phillips, 1969):

"Do you have a brother?"
"Yes."
"What's his name?"
"Jim."
"Does Jim have a brother?"
"No."

Highlight 15–3
Monopoly à la Piaget

Piaget's stages of cognitive development may be easier to remember if we relate them to a single example. What would happen at each stage if we played a game of *Monopoly* with the child?

Sensorimotor stage:	The child puts houses, hotels, and dice in mouth, plays with "Chance" cards.
Preoperational stage:	The child plays *Monopoly* but makes up own rules and cannot understand instructions.
Concrete operational stage:	The child understands basic instructions and will play by the rules but is not capable of hypothetical transactions dealing with mortgages, loans, and special pacts and bargains with other players.
Formal operations stage:	The child no longer plays game mechanically; complex and hypothetical transactions unique to each game are now possible.

Reversibility of thought allows children in the concrete operations stage to recognize that if $4 \times 2 = 8$, then 2×4 does, too. Younger children must memorize each relationship separately.

The Formal Operations Stage (11 Years and Up)
Sometime after about the age of 11, the child begins to break away from concrete objects and specific examples. Thinking is based more on **abstract principles.** Children can think about their thoughts, and they become less egocentric. The older child or adolescent also gradually becomes able to consider **hypothetical possibilities** (see Highlight 15–3). For example, if you ask a younger child: "What do you think would happen if people were

able to fly?" the child might respond, "But people can't fly." Older children are able to consider the possibilities and to discuss their implications.

The stage of formal operations represents attainment of full adult intellectual ability. The older adolescent is capable of inductive and deductive reasoning and can con-

ceptualize mathematics, physics, philosophy, psychology, and other theoretical and abstract systems. From this point on, improvements in intellectual ability are based on the accumulation of knowledge, experience, and wisdom, rather than on an enlargement of basic thinking capacity.

Learning Check

Match each item with one of these stages:

A Sensorimotor   **B.** Preoperational   **C.** Concrete operations   **D.** Formal operations

1. _____ egocentric thought

2. _____ abstract or hypothetical thought

3. _____ purposeful movement

4. _____ intuitive thought

5. _____ conservation

6. _____ reversibility

7. _____ object permanence

8. _____ nonverbal development

9. Assimilation refers to applying existing thought patterns or knowledge to new situations.   T or F?

Answers: 1. B 2. D 3. A 4. B 5. C 6. C 7. A 8. A 9. T

Applications

Making the Most of a Magic Time of Life

Many applications of the ideas presented in this chapter are self-evident. A few bear additional emphasis or extension.

Maturation   It is valuable to remember that individual differences in maturation rates are the rule in human development. Aware parents recognize the difference between the **statistical child** and the **particular child**.

Developmental norms specifying ages at which particular abilities appear are based on *averages*. There is always a wide range of normal variation around each average. Thus, it is reasonable to expect plateaus, reversals, and periods of rapid advancement in the development of a particular child. This applies not only to the appearance of motor skills such as crawling and walking but also to language development and the stages of cognitive development described by Piaget.

In all areas of development the uniqueness of a child should be respected. This means resisting the temptation to compare the child with others, particularly in the child's presence. Each child is an individual and should be viewed as such.

Enrichment

As we have already noted, babies need stimulation. By keeping this need in mind, parents can do much to provide opportunities for varied sensory experience during infancy. A baby should be surrounded by colors, music, people, and things to see, taste, smell, and touch. Babies are not vegetables. It makes perfect sense to talk to infants, to take them outside, to hang mobiles over their cribs, or to rearrange their rooms. Also, the more time babies spend interacting with par-

Applications: Making the Most of a Magic Time of Life

ents, the faster they develop language and thinking abilities (Clarke-Stewart & Koch, 1983). Most parents could put far more imagination into attempts to enrich an infant's surroundings than they typically do.

Question: Can enrichment be overdone?

The answer depends more on the *quality* of enrichment than on its quantity. Remember that the goal in enrichment is to create a world that *responds* to the infant—not one that bombards the infant with stimuli.

Responsiveness   The concept of **responsiveness,** mentioned earlier, applies to toys and objects, as well as to parents' behavior. Toys that respond to a child's actions, such as balls, rattles, mirrors—even a spoon and a pie tin—help speed infant learning. Particularly effective are experiences that allow children to see cause-effect results from their own behavior. As psychologist Paul Chance points out, the most responsive toys tend to be the least expensive. The least responsive toy available is probably a $500 color television, while one of the most responsive is a $1 rubber ball (Chance, 1982).

Many authorities are concerned about parents who try to *push* their children's intellectual development in a misguided attempt to produce "super babies." It's worth stating again that forcing a barrage of stimuli, flash cards, exercises, and the like on infants is not enriching. Parents who approach play and learning as if their preschooler were on the fast track for Harvard are filling their own needs at the expense of the child's (Alvino et al., 1985). True enrichment is responsive to the child's curiosity and interests. It does not make the child feel pressured to perform.

Question: Is enrichment useful only during infancy?

Definitely not. An enriched, responsive environment is beneficial at any stage of childhood. As a matter of fact, Jerome Kagan has reported that stimulation in later childhood can have a greater effect on intellect than previously believed.

Kagan studied babies who were raised in darkened huts in an isolated Guatemalan village. Without the benefit of even a moderate amount of stimulation, these children were severely retarded by age 2. Yet by age 11 they had become beautiful children—gay, alert, and active (Kagan & Klein, 1973). The rich stimulation of vil-

lage life during later childhood was enough to reverse the effects of early deprivation.

Question: In general what kinds of experiences are most likely to encourage intellectual development?

Piaget Revisited

Piaget's theory suggests that the ideal is to provide experiences that are only slightly novel, unusual, or challenging. Remember, a child's intellect develops mainly through accommodation. As old concepts and thinking habits become obsolete, they are discarded or adapted to fit new demands.

To stretch a child's intellect, demands must be made, but experiences that are too far beyond the familiar may cause frustration and withdrawal. Therefore, gradually expanding beyond a child's current level of understanding is usually most productive.

Parents can contribute greatly to intellectual growth through their attitudes toward a child's *investigation* or exploration of the world. The child who repeatedly hears, "Don't touch that" (chair, handle, trash, radio, pencil, flower, and so forth) or "I told you not to" (go up there, play with that, leave this spot, get dirty, and so forth) may become passive and intellectually dulled (Carew, Chan, & Halfor, 1976). Placing virtually all common objects off limits for a child is a serious mistake.

In addition, Piaget's work shows the importance of relating to a child on the appropriate level. If you give a physical explanation to a very young child who asks, "Why does the sun come up in the morning?" you may have missed the point. Answering in terms of the child's egocentric viewpoint is more likely to be meaningful. An answer such as, "So that you will know it's time to get up" is completely satisfactory for a young child. Later, explanations can be made increasingly abstract and accurate.

It is also valuable to remember that children are newcomers to language. Many of the "silly" things children say have meanings that become apparent only to the adult patient enough to look for them. For example, language expert S. I. Hayakawa (1965) relates this incident:

Once when our little girl was three years old, she found the bath too hot and said, "Make it warmer." It took me a moment to figure out that she meant, "Bring the water more

Applications: Making the Most of a Magic Time of Life

nearly to the condition we call warm." It makes perfectly good sense if you look at it that way. (From "The Use and Misuse of Language" by S. I. Hayakawa. In R. E. Farson, Ed., *Science and Human Affairs*. Palo Alto, CA: Science and Behavior Books, 1965)

Intellectual growth is encouraged when children feel free to express ideas and when they feel understood when they do.

Question: Are there any guidelines for relating to children at their level?

In a delightful book entitled *Using Psychology*, psychologist Morris Holland offers some suggestions about how best to relate to children at different stages of intellectual development. The following points are drawn from his discussion (Holland, 1975).

1. Sensorimotor stage (0–2). Active play with a child is most effective at this stage. Encourage explorations in touching, smelling, and manipulating objects. Playing peekaboo is a good way to establish the permanence of objects.

2. Preoperational stage (2–7). Although children are beginning to talk to themselves and to act out solutions to problems, touching and seeing things will continue to be more useful than verbal explanations. Concrete examples will also have more meaning than generalizations. The child should be encouraged to classify things in different ways. Learning the concept of conservation may be aided by demonstrations involving liquids, beads, clay, and other substances.

3. Concrete operational stage (7–11). Children in this stage are beginning to use generalizations, but they still require specific examples to grasp many ideas. Expect a degree of inconsistency in the child's ability to apply concepts of time, space, quantity, and volume to new situations.

4. Formal operations stage (11–adult). At this point it becomes more realistic to explain things verbally or symbolically to a child. Helping the child master general rules and principles now becomes productive. Encourage the child to create hypotheses and to imagine how things "could be."

Keeping this general outline in mind should help you adjust to the changing patterns of intellect displayed by developing children.

Learning Check

1. The idea that the particular child is different from the "statistical child" applies to language development and cognitive skills but not to motor development.   T or F?
2. In his study of a Guatemalan village, Kagan found that a stimulating environment can sometimes reverse severe early deprivation.   T or F?
3. To promote accommodation, it is best to provide information or experiences only moderately beyond a child's current level of comprehension.   T or F?
4. Playing peekaboo is a good way to help the sensorimotor child master the concept of conservation.   T or F?

Answers: 1. F   2. T   3. T   4. F

Chapter Summary

■ The human *neonate* has a number of *adaptive reflexes*, including the *grasping, rooting, sucking,* and *Moro reflexes*. Neonates show immediate evidence of learning and of appreciating the consequences of their actions.

■ Tests in a *looking chamber* reveal a number of visual preferences in the newborn. The neonate is drawn to complex, circular, curved, red or blue designs; human face patterns are also preferred, especially familiar faces. In later infancy interest in the unfamiliar emerges.

■ The *nature-nurture controversy* concerns the relative contributions of *heredity* (nature) and *environment* (nurture) to development. Hereditary instructions are carried by the *chromosomes* and *genes* in each cell of the body. Most characteristics are *polygenetic* and reflect the combined effects of *dominant* and *recessive* genes. Heredity influences a large number of personal characteristics as well as programming the general *human growth sequence*.

■ Heredity is also involved in differences in *temperament* present at birth. Most infants reliably fall into one of three temperament categories: *easy* children, *difficult* children, and *slow-to-warm-up* children.

■ Most psychologists accept that heredity and environment are inseparable and *interacting* forces. A child's *developmental level* therefore reflects *heredity, environment*, and the effects of the child's *own behavior*.

■ *Maturation* of the body and nervous system underlies the orderly *sequence* of motor, cognitive, and language development. The *rate* of maturation, however, varies from individual to individual.

■ The development of self-awareness, walking, bowel and bladder control, and many other basic capacities closely parallels maturation. Many early skills are subject to the principle of *readiness* (or *motor primacy*).

■ *Prenatal development* is subject to environmental influences in the form of diseases, drugs, radiation, and the mother's diet, health, or emotions. Prenatal damage to the fetus may cause *congenital problems*, or birth defects.

■ Healthy children are produced both by *conventional birth* and by *natural* (or *prepared*) *childbirth*. Prepared births, however, have the advantage of minimizing the use of anesthetics. The father's presence at birth appears to be desirable, although his attitude toward the birth may be of more basic importance. There is little evidence that *gentle birth* has any lasting advantages for the infant, although parents may prefer it for other reasons.

■ Studies of parents and their children suggest that *caretaking styles* have a substantial impact on emotional and intellectual development. Whereas mothers typically emphasize caretaking, fathers tend to function as playmates for their children.

■ *Language development* proceeds from *control of crying*, to *cooing*, to *babbling*, to use of *single words*, then *telegraphic speech*.

■ The underlying patterns of telegraphic speech suggest a *biological predisposition* to acquire language. This innate predisposition is augmented by learning. *Prelanguage communication* between parent and child involves *shared rhythms*, nonverbal *signals, turn taking*, and *mutual monitoring*. *Caretaker speech* and other parental behavior helps promote language learning.

■ A variety of *critical periods* exist throughout development, including periods before birth. Many animals display critical periods in *imprinting*.

■ *Emotional attachment* of human infants to their caretakers is a critical early event. Infant attachment is reflected by *separation anxiety* and perhaps by *stranger anxiety*. Although the issue is controversial, it is doubtful that immediate *mother-infant contact* is crucial for forming lasting emotional bonds.

■ Early *perceptual* and *emotional deprivation* seriously retard development. Even physical growth may be affected, as is the case in *deprivation dwarfism*.

■ Research on deprivation suggests that perceptual stimulation is essential for normal development. Work with subhuman primates (monkeys) has also pointed to *contact comfort* as an important source of infant stimulation and attachment.

■ Deliberate *enrichment* of the environment in infancy has a beneficial effect on the development of animals. Research with human infants has also demonstrated the value of enrichment.

■ The intellect of a child is *less abstract* than that of an adult. Jean Piaget theorized that intellectual growth occurs through a combination of *assimilation* and *accommodation*. He also held that children go through a fixed series of *cognitive stages*. The stages and their approximate age ranges are: *sensorimotor* (0–2), *preoperational* (2–7), *concrete operations* (7–11), and *formal operations* (11–adult).

■ Wise parents recognize the difference between the *statistical child* and a *particular child*. Effective *enrichment* is *responsive* to the child's interests and needs, and it takes into account the child's level of cognitive development.

Exploration

The Brave New World of Genetics and Reproduction

In his famous novel, *Brave New World*, Aldous Huxley described a futuristic society in which "baby factories" produce thousands of duplicate humans to do society's labor. Huxley, writing in the 1930s, envisioned a future in which biological engineering would be used for sinister ends. Now that the future has arrived, we find instead that some of the possibilities Huxley anticipated have made it possible for previously infertile couples to have children. And yet, as is often true, new solutions create new problems. In this Exploration we will briefly describe some recent developments in medicine and genetics that raise interesting social, psychological, and ethical questions.

Biological Engineering

In the recent past, adoption was the only alternative for couples with untreatable infertility. Now such couples have an array of new options. Let's investigate two that are of special interest.

Artificial Insemination   If her husband is sterile, a woman can undergo **artificial insemination.** In this procedure sperm from an anonymous donor are used to impregnate the woman. Donors are selected so that their eye and hair colors, height, and so on, match as closely as possible the husband's. For obvious emotional reasons some of the husband's sperm are sometimes mixed with the donor sperm so that it is impossible to tell who was actually the father.

Test-Tube Babies   A technique called **in vitro fertilization** has recently made it possible for some infertile couples to bear children who share both the mother's and father's genes. To produce a "test-tube" baby, egg cells are surgically collected from the mother's ovary. The egg cells are then placed in a petri dish containing nutrients, and the father's sperm cells are added. After the egg cell is fertilized and begins dividing, it is implanted in the mother's womb, where it develops normally. In a new variation of in vitro fertilization, an unrelated woman may donate an egg cell to the infertile couple. The egg cell is then fertilized with the husband's sperm and implanted in the wife's uterus.

Questions and Controversies

The procedures outlined here raise a number of practical, emotional, moral, and even religious issues. Many of these issues will no doubt occur to the reader. A few that may not are listed here.

Many donors for artificial insemination are used repeatedly. One clinic reported that a single donor fathered 50 babies. What if this donor harbored a genetic disease or defect? What if children fathered by the same donor were to meet and marry? Since they would be half brother and half sister, their offspring would run a high risk of having genetic defects. What rules of testing and record keeping should apply to artificial insemination by donor?

Many scientists believe that han-

dling egg cells for in vitro fertilization may increase the risk of deformities in the newborns. If a child is born with a defect, is the physician responsible? What if more than one egg is fertilized? Should it be donated to another infertile couple? Would letting it die constitute an abortion? Should in vitro fertilization be allowed if the man and woman are not married?

Sex Selection   Another recent development that may have an impact on parenthood is the possibility of selecting an infant's sex before conception. The procedure involves separating X- and Y-bearing sperm and then artificially fertilizing the egg cell with all male-producing or all female-producing sperm.

Currently, sex selection techniques cannot *guarantee* to produce a child of the desired sex. Also, sex selection is relatively expensive (about $300), and some couples may be discouraged because artificial insemination is involved. A further worry is that two-thirds of childless American couples say they would prefer to have a boy as a first child. If large numbers of couples select their children's sex, would an excess of male births result?

Genetics and Parenthood

In recent years, having children has also been influenced by improved understanding of human genetics. Increasingly, it has become possible to combat troubles that "run in the family." It is now

Exploration: The Brave New World of Genetics and Reproduction

possible to identify a large number of genetic disorders, such as sickle cell anemia, hemophilia, cystic fibrosis, muscular dystrophy, albinism, some forms of mental retardation, and so forth, which may be carried by parents.

Genetic Counseling Prospective parents who suspect that they may be carriers of genetic disorders may seek **genetic counseling**. By examining the family history of each prospective parent, and in some cases by directly mapping chromosomes, the risk of a genetic disorder can be calculated (Rowley, 1984).

Question: What can a couple do if the risk of a genetic defect is high?

Knowing the risks, parents can choose not to have a child, or if the odds are in their favor, they may elect to take the chance. Even when there is a reasonable likelihood of a genetic disorder, some couples elect to have children but then to have a test performed during pregnancy to detect the presence or absence of the genetic defect. Such prenatal testing is done by **amniocentesis** (AM-nee-oh-SEN-tee-sis), which involves taking a sample of amniotic fluid (the fluid that surrounds the fetus) from the mother's womb. This procedure allows determinations of fetal sex and the detection of many genetic defects.

Amniocentesis is usually done at about the fifteenth week of pregnancy. Thus, when a serious genetic defect is detected, couples who do not object to abortion can terminate the pregnancy. Parents who consider abortion unacceptable still have the advantage of forewarning so they may prepare the best possible care for the child.

The Future

Recent advances in biology, genetics, and the exploding knowledge about how DNA controls heredity will quite likely bring about profound changes in the human condition. Let's sample some of the possibilities.

Eugenics It is probably true that domestic plants and animals have been improved more in the past 50 years than in the previous 5000. This improvement has been accomplished primarily through *eugenics* (you-JEN-iks), or selective breeding for desirable characteristics. Some extremists have already proposed that eugenics be applied to humans. Even if this state of affairs never actually happens (it is loaded with ethical problems), the steady application of genetic counseling could have a eugenic effect on the general population.

Genetic Engineering In the future it may become possible to remove defective genes and replace them with normal ones. Could such genetic engineering also be used to produce beauty, intelligence, re-

sistance to aging, or superhuman athletic potential? In theory, yes, but practically speaking, probably not. Literally thousands of genes affect such qualities, not to mention the effects of environment. For this reason limited genetic engineering involving one or two genes may soon become possible, but modifying genes on a major scale is not likely in the near future. **Cloning,** the production of an entire organism from a single cell, is also likely to remain science fiction (where humans are concerned) for the immediate future.

Gene Cards One authority on genetic engineering and genetic defects predicts that eventually people will carry a "gene identity card," based on blood tests made during childhood. Such cards would show what hereditary diseases a person is predisposed to or which problems may be passed on in childbearing when combined with the gene pattern of a mate (Milunsky, 1977).

Rapid advances in techniques that affect heredity and conception have an important place in the understanding of behavior. And as we have seen, such changes raise a number of important psychological and ethical questions. Some additional questions of interest are provided in the Questions for Discussion section that concludes this chapter.

Exploration: The Brave New World of Genetics and Reproduction

Learning Check

1. The procedure known as in vitro fertilization involves fertilizing a woman with donor sperm.   T or F?
2. So called test-tube babies are produced by fertilizing an egg cell outside of the body.   T or F?
3. Current sex selection procedures can consistently produce male offspring but cannot guarantee female babies.   T or F?
4. Amniocentesis is primarily used to select sex before birth.   T or F?
5. The term *eugenics* refers to the production of an entire organism from a single cell.   T or F?

Answers: 1. F   2. T   3. F   4. F   5. F

Questions for Discussion

1. Should humans try to control their own heredity? Who would decide what characteristics should be developed? Who would get them? For what purpose? Would you endorse use of genetic engineering to delay or prevent aging?

2. If preselection of the sex of a child becomes possible, what effect would you predict on the *long-term* ratio of males to females born? (Currently 106 males are born for every 100 females.) Why do you make this prediction? What are its implications? (If the population became roughly 70 percent male, the birthrate and population growth would slow dramatically.)

3. Which do you think would produce a better decision by prospective parents receiving genetic counseling: to be told, "There is a 1 percent chance of having a child with a chromosome abnormality" or to be given the same information this way, "You must realize that either it will or it will not happen"?

4. What are your thoughts on the following practical and ethical questions: Should children conceived by donor artificial insemination or by donor egg be told about their parentage? Should records be kept that would allow them to find their donor fathers or mothers if some extraordinary need were to arise? What would be the psychological impact of knowing that you were conceived in vitro?

5. In view of the importance of infant attachment and the participation of fathers in child care, what changes would you recommend in maternity and paternity leaves from work? Would you change the traditional division of labor in maternal and paternal roles? Why or why not?

6. What is your reaction to the following statement, made by anthropologist Margaret Mead: "Fathers are a biological necessity but a social accident."

7. In what ways is it accurate to treat children as "little adults"? In what ways is it inaccurate? What is the value of children in society?

8. How many ways can you think of for an infant to reward its mother and for the mother to reward the infant?

9. What types of toys would you select for an infant or young child? Do you think simple toys or elaborate toys would be best? Why? Would your choice change for an older child? Why?

10. How has heredity affected your development? How has environment affected you? How would childrearing be different if parents had to teach children *deliberately* to walk or to talk?

11. If you were the director of an orphanage or a similar institution, what steps would you take to ensure the normal development of infants in your care?

Challenges of Development: The Cycle of Life

Chapter 16

Chapter Preview
Life with Billy

By the time he was 5, Billy's "record" read like the script of a parent's worst nightmare. Billy threw uncontrollable temper tantrums and never seemed to sleep. He had not learned to talk. He got into closets and tore up his mother's dresses and urinated on her clothes. He smashed furniture and spread soap powder and breakfast food all over the floors. He attacked his mother at every opportunity, once going for her throat with his teeth. He tried to stuff his baby brother in a toy box. When Billy's parents bought him a doll they called by the baby's name, they began finding the doll pushed head down in the toilet bowl.

Billy refused to eat anything but cold, greasy hamburgers from a certain drive-in. To get through a week, his parents were forced to buy hamburgers by the sack and hide them around the house so Billy wouldn't eat them all at once. When his parents went out driving, they had to detour around drive-ins to prevent Billy from frothing at the mouth and trying to jump out the window (Moser, 1965). Billy, you may note, was not an average 5-year-old.

Question: What was his problem?

Billy was an autistic child. His problem is rare. Few children get off to as bad a start in life as Billy. Nevertheless, every individual faces certain challenges and problems on the path to healthy development. Some obstacles, such as toilet training or establishing an identity, can be considered universal. Others are specialized problems. In either case, the challenges of development extend far beyond childhood and on into old age.

In this chapter we will examine some of the special challenges and problems presented by each stage of life. Be alert for information pertinent to your own life. Be alert for Billy, too. You'll meet him again later in the chapter.

Survey Questions What are the typical tasks and dilemmas of childhood, adolescence, adulthood, and old age? What are some of the more serious childhood problems? In what ways is adolescent development especially challenging? What happens psychologically during adulthood and aging? How do effective parents rear their children? In what ways are attitudes toward death changing?

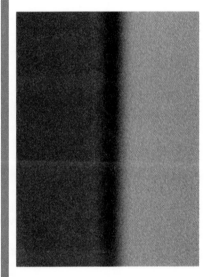

Resources

The Cycle of Life— Rocky Road or Garden Path?

If you pride yourself on being one of a kind, you have good reason. There is no such thing as a "typical person" or a "typical life." Nevertheless, there are certain broad similarities in the universal **life stages** of infancy, childhood, adolescence, young adulthood, middle adulthood, and old age. Each period confronts a person with a new set of **developmental tasks** to be mastered. These are skills that must be acquired or personal changes that must take place for optimal development. Examples are: learning to read in childhood, adjusting to sexual maturity in adolescence, and establishing a vocation as an adult (Havighurst, 1979).

In an influential book entitled *Childhood and Society* (1963), personality theorist Erik Erikson suggests that we also face a specific **psychosocial dilemma**, or "crisis," at each stage of life. According to Erikson, resolving each dilemma creates a new balance between a person and the social world. An unfavorable outcome throws us off balance and makes it harder to deal with later crises. A string

Fig. 16–1 *According to Erikson, children aged 3 to 5 learn to plan and initiate activities through play.*

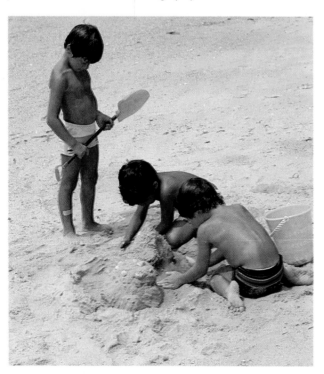

of "successes" produces healthy development and a satisfying life. Those who are plagued with unfavorable outcomes may experience life as a "rocky road."

Question: What are the major developmental tasks and life crises?

This is a broad question requiring an extended answer. Read on!

Stage One, First Year of Life: Trust versus Mistrust   During the first year of life children are completely dependent on others. Erikson believes that a basic attitude of **trust** or **mistrust** is formed at this time. Trust is established when babies are given adequate warmth, touching, love, and physical care. Mistrust is caused by inadequate or unpredictable care and by parents who are cold, indifferent, or rejecting. Basic mistrust may later cause insecurity, suspiciousness, or inability to relate to others. Notice that basic trust is encouraged by the same conditions that help babies become securely attached to their parents (Chapter 15).

Stage Two, 1–3 Years: Autonomy versus Shame and Doubt   In stage two, children's growing self-control is expressed by climbing, touching, exploring, and a general desire to do things for themselves. Parents help foster a sense of **autonomy** by encouraging children to try new skills. However, the child's first crude efforts often result in spilling, falling, wetting, and other "accidents." Thus, parents who *ridicule* their children, or *overprotect* them, may cause them to feel **shame** and to **doubt** their abilities.

Stage Three, 3–5 Years: Initiative versus Guilt   In stage three, the child moves from simple self-control to an ability to take initiative. Through play the child learns to plan, undertake, and carry out a task. Parents reinforce **initiative** by giving freedom to play, to ask questions, to use imagination, and to choose activities (Fig. 16–1). Children may be emotionally handicapped by parents who criticize severely, prevent play, or discourage questions. In this case children learn to feel **guilty** about the activities they initiate.

Stage Four, 6–12 Years: Industry versus Inferiority   Many of the events of middle childhood are symbolized by that fateful day when you first entered school. With dizzying speed your world expanded beyond your family, and you faced a whole series of new challenges.

Erikson describes the elementary school years as the child's "entrance into life." In school, children begin to learn skills valued by society, and success or failure can have lasting effects on their feelings of adequacy. Children learn a sense of **industry** if they win praise for building, painting, cooking, reading, studying, and other productive activities. If a child's efforts are regarded as messy, childish, or inadequate, feelings of **inferiority** result. For the first time teachers, classmates, and adults outside the home become as important as parents in shaping attitudes toward oneself.

Stage Five, Adolescence: Identity versus Role Confusion   Adolescence is a turbulent time for many persons in our culture. Caught between childhood and adulthood, the adolescent faces some unique problems. Erikson considers a need to answer the question, "Who am I?" the primary task during this stage of life. Mental and physical maturation bring to the individual new feelings, a new body, and new attitudes (Fig. 16–2). The adolescent must build a consistent **identity** out of self-perceptions and relationships with others. Conflicting experiences as a student, friend, athlete, worker, son or daughter, lover, and so forth must be integrated into a unified sense of self (more on this later). According to Erikson, persons who fail to develop a sense of identity suffer

from **role confusion,** an uncertainty about who they are and where they are going.

Question: What does Erikson consider the major conflict in early adulthood?

Stage Six, Young Adulthood: Intimacy versus Isolation   In stage six, Erikson emphasizes the need to achieve an essential quality of **intimacy** in one's life. After establishing a stable identity, a person is prepared to share meaningful love or deep friendship with others. By "intimacy" Erikson means an ability to care about others and to share experiences with them. In line with Erikson's view, 75 percent of college-age men and women rank a good marriage and family life as their primary adult goal (Bachman & Johnson, 1979). And yet, marriage or sexual involvement is no guarantee that intimacy will prevail: Many adult relationships remain superficial and unfulfilling. Failure to establish intimacy with others leads to a deep sense of **isolation.** The person feels alone and uncared for in life. This circumstance often sets the stage for later difficulties.

Stage Seven, Middle Adulthood: Generativity versus Stagnation   According to Erikson, an interest in guiding the next generation is the main source of balance in mature adulthood. This quality, called **generativity,** is

Fig. 16–2   *Dramatic differences in physical size and maturity are found in adolescents of the same age. The girls pictured are all 13, the boys 16. Maturation that occurs earlier or later than average can affect the "search for identity." (From "Growing Up" by J. M. Tanner. Copyright © September 1973 by Scientific American, Inc. All rights reserved.)*

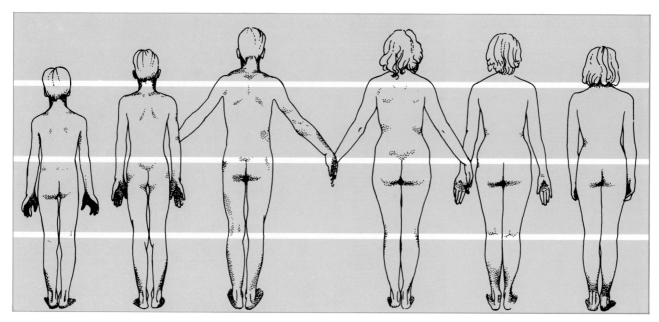

expressed by caring about oneself, one's children, and the future (Fig. 16–3). Generativity may be achieved by guiding one's own children or by helping other children (as a teacher, clergyman, or coach might do). It may also be achieved through productive or creative work. In any case a person's concern and energies must be broadened to include the welfare of others and society as a whole. Failure in this is marked by a **stagnant** concern with one's own needs and comforts. Life loses meaning, and the person feels bitter, dreary, and trapped.

Question: What does Erikson see as the conflicts of old age?

Stage Eight, Late Adulthood: Integrity versus Despair   Because old age is a time of reflection, a person must be able to look back over the events of a lifetime with a sense of acceptance and satisfaction. According to Erikson, the previous seven stages of life become the basis for successful aging. The person who has lived richly and responsibly develops a sense of **integrity**. This sense allows the person to face aging and death with dignity. If previous life events are viewed with regret, the elderly person falls into **despair**. In this case there is a feeling that life has been a series of missed opportunities, that one has failed, and that it is too late to reverse what has been done. Aging and the threat of death then become a source of fear and depression.

Although Erikson has not specifically discussed it, others believe that preparing for death may be an internal process. This view holds that approaching death causes aged individuals to undertake a **life review** (Barrow & Smith, 1979; Butler & Lewis, 1977). During the life review (which may be a universal process during the last days of life), vivid memories of earlier events bring to the surface unresolved questions, conflicts, and issues. At this time older people reevaluate the meaning of life and, ideally, find new meaning that reduces fear and anxiety and prepares them to face death (Barrow & Smith, 1979).

In squeezing the events of a lifetime into a few pages, we must ignore countless details. Although much is lost, the net effect is a clearer picture of an entire life cycle. In this brief overview we have seen that the successful life begins with learning to trust others and ends with trusting and feeling good about one's life: Thus, the circle closes and the cycle is complete.

Evaluation   For simplicity, Erikson's dilemmas are stated in either/or terms. It would be unusual, however, for a person to experience only one side of each conflict. In many instances a mixture of positive and negative effects spills over into later development. It is also important to realize that Erikson's account is theoretical; some theorists emphasize different life events.

Is Erikson's description, then, an exact map of your future? Probably not. Still, the dilemmas we have discussed reflect major psychological events in the lives of many people. Knowing about such events may allow you

Fig. 16–3   *According to Erikson, an interest in future generations characterizes optimal adult development.*

to anticipate typical trouble spots in life. You may also be better prepared to understand the problems and feelings of friends and relatives at various stages in the life cycle.

Having completed our whirlwind birth-to-death tour, we will revisit several life stages for a closer look at some of the challenges, landmarks, tasks, and problems of each. Before we begin, it might be a good idea to complete the Learning Check that follows.

Learning Check

Since Erikson's eight life stages are scattered through the previous pages, you might find it helpful to summarize them. Complete the following do-it-yourself summary to check your recall of the stages. Compare your answers with those listed below to make sure you have a correct summary.

Stage	Crisis	Favorable outcome
First year of life	1. _____ vs. 2. _____	Faith in the environment and in others
Ages 1–3	Autonomy vs. 3. _____	Feelings of self-control and adequacy
Ages 3–5	4. _____ vs. guilt	Ability to begin one's own activities
Ages 6–12	Industry vs. 5. _____	Confidence in productive skills, learning how to work
Adolescence	6. _____ vs. role confusion	An integrated image of oneself as a unique person
Early adulthood	Intimacy vs. 7. _____	Ability to form bonds of love and friendship with others
Middle adulthood	Generativity vs. 8. _____	Concern for family, society, and future generations
Late adulthood	9. _____ vs. 10. _____	Sense of dignity and fulfillment, willingness to face death

Answers: 1. trust 2. mistrust 3. shame or doubt 4. initiative 5. inferiority 6. identity 7. isolation 8. stagnation 9. integrity 10. despair

Problems of Childhood— Why Parents Get Gray Hair

Can you remember a time in your childhood when your actions led to a disaster or a near disaster? It shouldn't be hard. It's a wonder that many of us survive childhood at all. Where I grew up, digging underground tunnels, wriggling down chimneys, hopping on trains, jumping off houses, crawling through storm drains, making bombs— and worse—were common childhood adventures.

Question: If initiative and industry are important in childhood, what limits should parents place on a child's freedom to explore the world?

An answer is provided by psychologist Diana Baumrind (1980) who has studied the effects of three major styles of parenting. According to Baumrind, each style tends to have a different effect on children's behavior. See if you recognize the styles she describes.

Authoritarian parents view children as having few rights but adultlike responsibilities. The authoritarian parent tends to demand strict adherence to rigid standards of behavior. The child is expected to stay out of trouble and to accept without question parents' word on right and wrong behavior. The children of such parents typically are obedient and self-controlled, but they also tend to be emotionally stiff, withdrawn, apprehensive, and lacking in curiosity.

In contrast **overly permissive parents** view children as having few responsibilities but rights similar to adults. Such parents require little in the way of responsible behavior from their children. Rules are not enforced and the child usually gets his or her own way. This tends to produce dependent, immature children who misbehave frequently. Such children tend to "run amok" and to be aimless in their approach to life.

Baumrind describes **effective parents** as those who balance their own rights with those of their children. Such parents are *authoritative* but not authoritarian. That is, they control their children's behavior, but they are also loving and caring. Effective parents approach discipline in a way that is firm and consistent, not harsh or rigid. In general they encourage the child to act responsibly. This parenting style produces children who tend to be competent, self-controlled, independent, assertive, and inquir-

ing. Thus, by balancing freedom and restraint, effective parents help children become responsible adults.

As an added guide to parenting, it may help to remember that stress is a normal part of life—even in childhood. Certainly this does not mean that parents should go out of their way to stress a child. However, it does suggest that there is no point in trying to shield children completely from stressful stimulation. **Overprotection** (sometimes called "smother love") can be as damaging as overstressing a child or being excessively strict or permissive.

Most children do a good job of keeping stress at comfortable levels when *they* initiate an activity (Murphy & Moriarty, 1976) (Fig. 16–4). At a public swimming pool, for instance, some children can be observed making death-defying leaps from the high dive, while others stick close to the wading area. If no immediate danger is present, it is reasonable to let children get stuck in trees, make themselves dizzy, squabble with neighbor children, and so forth. Getting into a few scrapes can help prepare a child to cope with later stresses. Just think, if your author hadn't crawled through a few storm pipes, his adult interest in plumbing the depths of the psyche might have gone down the drain.

Question: How can you tell if a child is being subjected to too much stress?

Normal Childhood Problems   Child specialists Chess, Thomas, and Birch (1965) have listed a number of difficulties experienced at times by almost every child. These can be considered normal reactions to the unavoidable stress of growing up.

Fig. 16–4 *Most children do a good job of keeping stress at comfortable levels when they initiate an activity.*

1. All children experience occasional **sleep disturbances,** including wakefulness, frightening dreams, or a desire to get into their parents' bed.
2. **Specific fears** of the dark, dogs, school, or of a particular room or person are also common.
3. Most children will be **overly timid** at times, allowing themselves to be bullied by other children into giving up toys, a place in line, and the like.
4. Temporary periods of **general dissatisfaction** may occur during which nothing pleases the child.
5. Children also normally display periods of **general negativism** marked by tantrums, refusal to do anything requested, or a tendency to say no on principle.
6. Another normal problem is **clinging,** in which children refuse to leave the side of their mothers or to do anything on their own.
7. Development does not always advance smoothly. Every child will show occasional **reversals** or **regressions** to more infantile behavior.

An additional problem common to the elementary school years is **sibling rivalry.** Where there is more than one child in a family, it is normal for a certain amount of jealousy, rivalry, and even hostility to develop between brothers and sisters. Some sibling conflict may even be constructive. A limited amount of aggressive give-and-take between siblings provides an opportunity to learn emotional control, self-assertion, and being a good sport (Bank & Kahn, 1982). Parents can help keep such conflicts within bounds by not "playing favorites" and by resisting the temptation to compare one child to another.

Parents should also expect some **rebellion** from their children. Most schoolchildren rebel at times against rules and limitations of the adult world. For many children the company of peers offers a chance to "let off steam" by doing some of the things adults forbid. Being messy, noisy, hostile, or destructive is normal when engaged in to a moderate degree.

It is important to keep in mind that "normal problems" can signal a more serious disturbance if they are displayed for prolonged periods or if they become exaggerated. Problems of a more serious nature are identified in the next section.

Significant Childhood Problems— Off to a Bad Start

Although severe emotional disturbances affect only a minority of children, the number involved is larger than most people realize.

Question: What is the nature of these problems?

Toilet-Training Disturbances Difficulty sometimes centers on toilet training or bowel and bladder habits. The two most common problems are **enuresis** (EN-you-REE-sis: lack of bladder control) and **encopresis** (EN-coh-PREE-sis: lack of bowel control). Enuresis is more common than encopresis and many times more common among males than females. Both wetting and soiling can be a means of expressing frustration or pent-up hostility.

Parents should not be overly alarmed by some delays in toilet training or by a few "accidents." As mentioned in the last chapter, 30 months is the average age for completing toilet training. It is not unusual, however, for some children to take 6 months longer. Even when problems persist, they may be purely physical. Many bed wetters, for instance, have difficulty because they become extremely relaxed when asleep. These children can be helped by limiting the amount they drink during the evening. They should also use the toilet just before going to

bed, and they can be rewarded for "dry" nights. Understanding, tact, and sympathy can do much to alleviate mild disturbances. Where more serious problems exist, parents should seek professional help.

Feeding Disturbances Feeding disturbances take a variety of forms. The disturbed child may vomit or refuse food for no reason or may drastically overeat or undereat. **Overeating** is sometimes encouraged by a parent who feels unloved and compensates by showering the child with "love" in the form of food. Some parents overfeed simply because they consider a fat baby healthy or desirable. Whatever the case, overfed children develop eating habits and conflicts that have lifelong consequences.

As described in Chapter 12, serious cases of *undereating* are called **anorexia nervosa** (AN-uh-REX-yah ner-VOH-sah: nervous loss of appetite). The victims of anorexia nervosa are mostly adolescent females. In addition to the causes described in Chapter 12, anorexia may reflect conflicts about maturing sexually. In other words, by starving themselves, adolescent girls can limit figure development and prevent menstruation (Palazolli, 1978). This delays the time when they must face adult responsibilities. In younger children self-starvation seems to be related to the fact that eating is a social event. That is, the child who refuses to eat may be trying to gain attention or to do battle with parents.

Another childhood eating difficulty is a condition called **pica** (PIE-ka). Some children go through a period of intense appetite during which they eat or chew on all sorts of inedible substances. Most commonly these are plaster or chalk, but some children displaying pica try to eat things like buttons, rubber bands, mud, or paint flakes. The latter can be quite dangerous because some paint contains lead, which is highly poisonous.

Speech Disturbances The two most common speech problems are **delayed speech** and **stuttering.** A serious delay in learning to talk is sometimes caused by too little stimulation in early childhood. Other possible causes are parents who discourage the child's attempts to grow up, and stresses such as separation from the mother, hospitalization, or birth of a sibling.

Stuttering was once held to be primarily a psychological disturbance. Now, researchers believe that stuttering is usually of physical origin. For example, stuttering is four times more common in males than in females, and there seem to be hereditary factors underlying its occurrence (Sheehan & Costley, 1977). Nevertheless, in some instances stuttering seems to reflect learned speech patterns or tension or frustration in the child. Because of such factors, parental reactions can add considerably to the child's anxiety, thus perpetuating the problem.

Learning Disorders   Soon after Gary entered school, he became shy and difficult. Gary's teacher suspected a learning disability, and a specialist confirmed this. **Learning disabilities** include problems with thinking, perception, language, attention, or activity levels. Gary's specific problem was **dyslexia** (dis-LEX-yah), an inability to read with understanding. Because of it, he often felt confused and "stupid" in class, although his intelligence was normal.

The causes of dyslexia are not known at present. However, researchers suspect that it is related to brain dominance. As you may recall from Chapter 3, the left side of the brain is usually dominant over the right in language ability. In a minority of people the right brain is language dominant, or it shares language ability with the left brain. People with shared or reversed dominance of this sort seem to be more prone to language disorders, including dyslexia (Durden-Smith & DeSimone, 1984; Marx, 1983).

One of the most significant learning disorders is **hyperactivity**. The hyperactive child is constantly in motion and cannot concentrate (Fig. 16–5). The child talks rapidly, cannot sit still, rarely finishes work, acts on impulse, and cannot pay attention. Hyperactivity occurs in 3 to 5 percent of American children, with five times as many boys as girls being affected (Varley, 1984). Unless it is carefully

managed, hyperactivity can severely limit a child's ability to learn.

Question: What causes hyperactivity?

The most widely held theory is that hyperactivity is the result of **minimal brain dysfunction (MBD).** Experts who support this theory link hyperactivity to a lag in brain maturation or to undetected damage to the brain. Medical authorities typically advocate the use of stimulant drugs to control hyperactivity. On one hand, such drugs do appear to lessen activity and increase the child's ability to focus attention (Solanto, 1984). On the other hand, however, a number of psychologists have objected to this blanket use of powerful drugs, which they regard as dangerous and unnecessary (Havighurst, 1976).

Question: What kind of treatment do they suggest?

Some researchers have found **behavior modification** as effective as drug treatment (Pelham, 1977; Wulbert & Dries, 1977). Behavior modification essentially is the application of learning principles to human problems (see Chapter 23 for more information). The basic idea is to find times when the hyperactive child is calm and attentive and to reward the child for such behavior.

Childhood Autism   Childhood **autism** (AH-tism) is a problem that affects 1 in 2500 children, boys four times more often than girls. Autism is one of the most severe

Fig. 16–5 *The hyperactive child's inability to hold still and pay attention can seriously disrupt learning.*

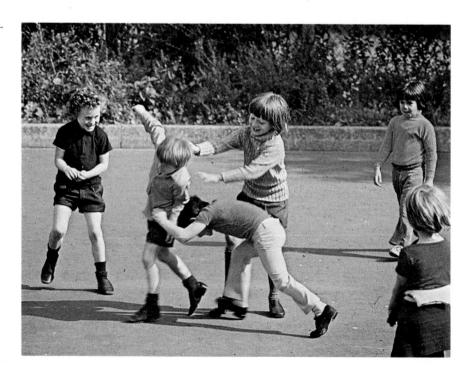

childhood problems. The autistic child is locked into a private world and appears to have no need for affection or contact with others. Autistic children do not even seem to know or care who their parents are.

In addition to being extremely isolated, the autistic child may throw gigantic temper tantrums—sometimes including self-destructive behavior such as head banging. Sadly, many well-meaning parents unintentionally reward such behavior with attention and concern (Edelson, 1984). Language learning in the autistic is usually so retarded that the child is mute. If they speak at all, autistic children often infuriatingly parrot back everything said, a response known as **echolalia** (EK-oh-LAY-lee-ah). These children also engage in frequent repetitive actions such as rocking, flapping their arms, or waving their fingers in front of their eyes. Additionally, they may show no response to an extremely loud noise (sensory blocking) or may spend hours watching a water faucet drip (sensory "spinout") (Ferster, 1968; Rimland, 1978).

Question: Do parents cause autism?

At one time experts blamed parents for autism. It is now recognized that autism is caused by congenital defects in the nervous system (Schopler, 1978). This is why, even as babies, autistic children are aloof and do not cuddle or mold to their parents' arms.

Question: Can anything be done for an autistic child?

Even with help, only about one autistic child in four approaches normalcy. Nevertheless, almost all autistic children can make progress with proper care (Schopler, 1978). When treatment is begun early, behavior modification can be particularly successful.

Do you remember the child described in the Chapter Preview? Billy was one of the first patients in a pioneering program designed by psychologist Ivar Lovaas. Billy was selected for the program because of his unusual appetite for hamburgers. Teaching Billy to talk illustrates one aspect of his treatment. It began with his learning to blow out a match—making a sound like "who." Each time he made the "who" sound, Billy was rewarded with a bite of his beloved hamburgers. Next he was rewarded for babbling meaningless sounds. If he accidentally said a word, he was rewarded. After several weeks, he was able to say words such as "ball," "milk," "mama," and "me." By a painstaking continuation of this process, Billy was eventually taught to talk. Notice that this process is basically an example of **operant shaping,** discussed in Chapter 8.

In a behavior modification program, each of an autistic child's maladaptive behaviors is altered using combinations of reward and punishment. In addition to food, therapists are finding that sensory stimulation, such as tickling or music, is often very reinforcing for the autistic child (Rincover et al., 1977). And, strangely enough, researchers have found that following actions such as head banging and hand biting by punishment can bring a swift end to self-destructive behavior (Haywood et al., 1982). When such efforts are combined with parental involvement in treatment at home, considerable progress can be made (Short, 1984).

Autism and other severe childhood problems represent a monumental challenge to the ingenuity of psychologists, educators, and parents. However, great strides have been made in the last few years, and there is reason to believe that in the future even more help will be available to children who get a bad start in life.

Learning Check

See if you can answer these questions before you continue reading.

1. Occasional reversals and regressions to more infantile behavior are sure signs that a significant childhood problem exists.   T or F?

2. Sleep disturbances and specific fears can be a sign of significant childhood problems when they are prolonged or exaggerated.   T or F?

3. A moderate amount of sibling rivalry is considered normal.   T or F?

4. Encopresis is the formal term for lack of bladder control.   T or F?

5. The hyperactive child is lost in his or her own private world.   T or F?

6. According to Diana Baumrind's research, effective parents are authoritarian in their approach to their children's behavior.   T or F?

Answers: 1. F   2. T   3. T   4. F   5. F   6. F

Adolescence—
The Best of Times,
the Worst of Times

"It was the best of times, it was the worst of times, it was the age of wisdom, it was the age of foolishness . . . we had everything before us, we had nothing before us. . . ."

Charles Dickens, *A Tale of Two Cities*

Adolescence is a time of change, exploration, exuberance, and youthful searching. It is also a time of worry and problems, especially in today's world. It might even be fair to describe adolescence as "the best of times, the worst of times." Just in case you weren't taking notes in junior high, let's survey some problems and challenges of this colorful chapter of life.

Adolescence and Puberty

Adolescence refers to the period during which we move from childhood to acceptance as an adult. This change in social status is so natural that a period of adolescence is recognized in almost all cultures. However, the length of adolescence varies greatly from culture to culture (Siegel,

Fig. 16–6 *The typical rate of growth for boys and girls. Notice that the rate of growth in early adolescence equals that for ages 1 to 3. Note too the earlier growth spurt for girls.*

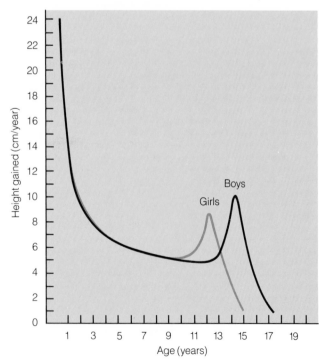

1982). For example, most 14-year-old girls in America live at home and go to school. In contrast many 14-year-old females in rural villages of the Near East are married and have children (Santrock, 1984). In our culture 14-year-olds are adolescents. In others they may be adults.

Many people confuse adolescence with puberty. But as you can see, the culturally defined period of adolescence differs from puberty, which is a *biological* event. **Puberty** refers to rapid physical growth, coupled with hormonal changes that bring sexual maturity. Interestingly, the peak **growth spurt** during puberty occurs earlier for girls than for boys (Fig. 16–6). This difference accounts for the 1- to 2-year period when girls tend to be taller than boys. (Remember going to dances where the girls towered over the boys?) For girls the onset of puberty typically occurs between 11 and 14 years of age. For most boys the age range is 13 to 16 years (Kaluger & Kaluger, 1984).

When you were going through puberty, did you ever spend *hours* preparing to attend a party, dance, or other social event? If you did, you weren't alone. Puberty tends to dramatically increase body awareness and concerns about physical appearance (Siegel, 1982). Beyond this about one-half of all boys and one-third of all girls report being dissatisfied with their appearance during early adolescence (Rosenbaum, 1979). In many instances, such feelings are related to the *timing* of puberty. Girls who are temporarily "too tall," boys who are "too small," and both boys and girls who lag in sexual development are likely to be upset about their bodies.

Question: How much difference does the timing of puberty make?

Early and Late Maturation   Because puberty involves so many rapid changes, it can be stressful for just about anyone. When puberty comes unusually early or late, its impact may be magnified—for both good and bad.

For boys, early maturation is generally beneficial. Typically, it enhances their self-image and gives them an advantage athletically and socially. For such reasons early maturing boys tend to be more poised, relaxed, dominant, self-assured, and popular with their peers (Santrock, 1984; Siegel, 1982). Many late maturing boys are anxious about being behind in development. However, after they catch up, they tend to be more eager, talkative, self-assertive, and tolerant of themselves.

For girls, the advantages of early maturation are less clear-cut. In elementary school, developmentally advanced girls tend to have *less* prestige among peers. Presumably, this is because they are larger and heavier than their classmates. By junior high, however, early development leads to *greater* peer prestige and adult approval. In contrast later maturing girls have the possible advantage of usually growing taller and thinner than early maturing girls. Other relevant findings are that early maturing girls date sooner, are more independent, and are more active in school; they are also more often in trouble at school (Siegel, 1982).

As you can see, there are costs and benefits associated with both early and late puberty. One added cost of early maturation is that it may force premature identity formation (Siegel, 1982). When a teenager begins to look like an adult, he or she may be treated like an adult. Ideally, this change can encourage greater maturity and independence. But what happens when a person is treated as an adult before he or she is emotionally ready? Then the search for identity may end too soon, leaving the person with a distorted, poorly formed sense of self (see Highlight 16–1).

Search for Identity

As discussed earlier, many psychologists regard identity formation as a key task of adolescence. To be sure, problems of identity occur at other times too. But in a very real sense, puberty signals that the time has arrived to begin forming a new, more mature image of oneself. Answering the question "Who am I?" is also spurred by cognitive development. After adolescents have attained the stage of formal operations, they are better able to ask questions about their place in the world and about morals, values, politics, social relationships, and private thoughts. Then too, being able to think about hypothetical possibilities allows the adolescent to contemplate the future and ask more realistically, "Who will I be?" (Coleman, Hersberg, & Morris, 1977).

David Elkind has noted another interesting pattern in adolescent thought. According to Elkind (1984), many teenagers are preoccupied with **imaginary audiences.** That is, they act like others are as aware of their thoughts and feelings as they are themselves. Sometimes this leads to painful self-consciousness—as in thinking *everyone* is staring at a bad haircut you just received. The imaginary audience also seems to underlie attention-seeking "performances" involving outlandish dress or behavior. In any case adolescents become very concerned with controlling the impressions they make on others (Santrock, 1984). For many being "on stage" in this way helps define the shape of an emerging identity.

Question: What effects do parents have on identity formation?

Highlight 16–1
Hurried into Adulthood

Psychologist David Elkind (1981) believes that a large number of American parents are hurrying their children's development. Elkind is concerned about parents who try to raise their babies' IQ's or who have them reading, swimming, and doing gymnastics before they are 3 months old. Such pushing, he believes, partly explains why more children than ever show serious stress symptoms. Moreover, hurried children are becoming hurried teenagers—urged by parents and media alike to grow up fast. Elkind believes that too many teenagers are left without sufficient guidance, direction, and support to make a healthy transition to adulthood (Elkind, 1984).

Elkind's main thesis is that adolescence was once a sort of grace period during which teenagers could adjust to the remarkable changes taking place in their lives. Today, teenagers have adulthood thrust on them prematurely. Violence, drug abuse, X-rated movies, teenage crime, teenage pregnancy, divorce and single parent households, date rape, aimless schools—all this, and more, strikes Elkind as evidence that there is no place for teenagers in today's society.

According to Elkind, the traditional **markers** of adolescence have all but disappeared. (Markers are signs that tell where a person stands socially—such as a driver's license or a wedding ring.) As an example, Elkind notes that clothing for children and teenagers is increasingly adultlike. Girls especially are encouraged to wear revealing and seductive clothing and swimsuits. As another example Elkind states that images of human sexuality, aggression, and degradation were once reserved for mature adults. Now they are shown regularly in movies and on TV, leading to an early loss of innocence in young viewers.

Clearly, Elkind is stating a clinical opinion, not a demonstrated fact. It's possible that his view will prove exaggerated—indeed, much of what he says is debatable. Nevertheless, his portrayal of hurried adolescents as "all grown up with no place to go" is highly thought provoking.

Fig. 16–7 *Membership in friendship groups and cliques helps adolescents build an identity apart from their relationship to parents. However, overidentification with a clannish group that rejects anyone who looks or acts different can limit personal growth.*

Parents and Peers The adolescent search for identity often results in increased conflict with parents. However, this is not necessarily a problem. Some conflict with parents is probably necessary for growth of a separate identity. A complete lack of conflict may mean that the adolescent is afraid to seek independence (Siegel, 1982). Actually, there is usually a good deal of agreement between adolescents and their parents on basic topics such as religion, marriage, morals, and so forth. The largest conflicts tend to be over more superficial differences in styles of dress, manners, social behavior, and the like. In general, adolescents tend to overestimate differences between themselves and their parents (Lerner & Shea, 1982).

In high school were you a jock, preppy, brain, hacker, surfer, cowboy, punk, mod, warthog, dervish, gargoyle, or aardvark? (Well, okay, I made up the last four—the rest are real.) Increased identification with peer groups is quite common during adolescence. To an extent, membership in such groups gives a measure of security and a sense of identity apart from the family. Beyond this, group membership provides practice in belonging to a social network. Children tend to see themselves more as members of families and small friendship groups, not as members of society as a whole. Therefore, gaining a broader, member-of-society perspective can be a major step toward adulthood (Kohlberg, 1976) (Fig. 16–7).

Question: But aren't groups also limiting?

Yes, they are. Conformity to peer values peaks in early adolescence, but it remains strong at least through high school (Newman, 1982). Throughout this period there is always a danger of allowing group pressures to foreclose personal growth. By the end of high school, many adolescents have not yet sufficiently explored various interests, values, vocations, skills, or ideologies on their own. Perhaps this is why many students view moving on to work or college as a chance to break out of earlier roles—to expand or reshape personal identity. For many who choose college, the effect may be more a matter of placing further changes in identity on hold. By doing so, college students keep open the possibility of changing majors, career plans, personal style, and so on. Typically, commitment to an emerging adult identity grows stronger in later college years (Santrock, 1984).

The search for identity we have discussed here may be intensified during adolescence, but it does not end there. In the next section we will move on into early adulthood for a look at further developments. Before you read more, here's a chance to check your memory.

Learning Check

1. In most societies, adolescence begins with the onset of puberty and ends with its completion.   T or F?

2. Early maturing boys tend to experience more clear-cut advantages than do early maturing girls.   T or F?

3. According to David Elkind, the traditional markers of adolescence and adulthood have been blurred.   T or F?

4. The imaginary audience refers to conformity pressures that adolescents believe adults apply to them.   T or F?

Answers: 1. F   2. T   3. T   4. F

Challenges of Adulthood— Charting Life's Ups and Downs

After a "settling down" period somewhere in the twenties, adult development is uniform and uninteresting, right? Wrong! A fairly predictable series of challenges is associated with development from adolescence to old age.

Question: What personality changes and psychological developments can a person look forward to in adulthood?

Recent research has added several important substages to the events discussed by Erikson. One of the most informative accounts is based on clinical work by Roger Gould, a psychiatrist interested in adult personality. Gould's research (1975) reveals that the most common patterns for American adults are as follows.

Ages 16–18: Escape from Dominance   Ages 16 to 18 are marked by a struggle to escape from parental dominance. Efforts to do so cause considerable anxiety about the future and conflicts about continuing dependence on parents.

Ages 18–22: Leaving the Family   The majority of people break away from their families in their early twenties. Leaving home is usually associated with building new friendships with other adults. These friends serve as substitutes for the family and as allies in the process of breaking ties.

Ages 22–28: Building a Workable Life   The trend in the mid-twenties is to seek mastery of the real world. Two dominant activities are: striving for accomplishment (seeking competence) and reaching out to others. Note that the second activity corresponds to Erikson's emphasis on seeking intimacy at this time. Married couples in this age group tend to place a high value on "togetherness."

Ages 29–34: Crisis of Questions   Around the age of 30 many people experience a minor life "crisis." The heart of this crisis is a serious questioning of what life is all about. Assurance about previous choices and values tends to waver. Unsettled by these developments, the person actively searches for a style of living that will bring meaning to the second half of life. Marriages are particularly vulnerable during this time of dissatisfaction. Extramarital affairs and divorces are common symptoms of the "crisis of questions."

Ages 35–43: Crisis of Urgency   People of ages 35 to 43 are typically beginning to become more aware of the reality of death. Having a limited number of years to live begins to exert pressure on the individual. Intensified attempts are made to succeed at a career or to achieve one's life goals. Generativity, in the form of nurturing, teaching, or serving others, helps alleviate many of the anxieties of this stage.

Ages 43–50: Attaining Stability   The urgency of the previous stage gives way to a calmer acceptance of one's fate in the late forties. The predominant feeling is that the die is cast and that former decisions can be lived with. Those who have families begin to appreciate their children as individuals and to ease up on their tendency to extend their own goals to their children's behavior.

Age 50 and Up: Mellowing   After age 50 a noticeable mellowing occurs. Emphasis is placed on sharing day-to-day joys and sorrows. There is less concern with glamor, wealth, accomplishment, and abstract goals. Many of the tensions of earlier years give way to a desire to savor life and its small pleasures.

Question: Don't many people undergo a midlife crisis?

A Midlife Crisis? Obviously, not everyone has difficulty at the midpoint of life. However, psychologist Daniel J. Levinson at Yale University has carried out an in-depth study of lives from early adulthood to later maturity. Levinson (1978) found that most of his subjects (all males) went through a period of instability, anxiety, and change between the ages of 37 and 41 (Gould's "crisis of urgency" period).

Roughly one-half of the people studied by Levinson defined the midlife period as a sort of "last chance" to achieve their life goals. Such goals were often stated as a key event; for example, attaining a supervisory position, achieving a certain income, becoming a full professor, becoming shop steward, and so forth. For these individuals the midlife period is stressful yet manageable. A second pattern involved a serious midlife decline, often related to choice of a dead-end job or lifestyle. In other cases it meant that subjects had experienced external success but felt that what they were doing was pointless. And in a third pattern a few hearty individuals appeared to be "breaking out" of a seriously flawed life structure. For them, a decision to "start over" was typically followed by 8 to 10 years of rebuilding.

Thus, it can be seen that the midlife crisis, if it takes place at all, can be both a danger and an opportunity. Ideally it is a time of reworking old identities, of achieving long-sought goals, of finding one's own truths, and of preparation for later maturity and aging (Barrow & Smith, 1979).

Middle Age When individuals reach their forties and fifties, declining strength, physical vigor, and youthfulness make it clear that more than half of their time is gone. At the same time, greater stability comes from letting go of the "impossible dream" (Sheehy, 1976). That is, there is an increased attempt to be satisfied with the direction one's life has taken and to accept that hoped-for life goals may no longer be possible.

For most women during this era, **menopause** represents the first real encounter with aging. At menopause monthly menstruation ends, and a woman is no longer able to bear children. In menopause the level of the hormone estrogen drops—sometimes causing drastic changes in mood or appearance and the occurrence of physical symptoms such as hot flashes (a sudden uncomfortable sensation of heat). Some women find menopause as difficult to adjust to as

adolescence, and many experience anxiety, irritability, or depression at this time. Most postmenopausal women, however, report that menopause was not as bad as they expected and that much of their anxiety came from not knowing what to expect (Mussen et al., 1979).

Question: Do men go through similar changes?

Males do not undergo any physical change that is directly comparable to menopause. Just the same, some authorities now believe that 40- to 60-year-old males often pass through a **climacteric** (kly-MAK-ter-ik), or significant physiological change (Zaludek, 1976). During the climacteric, decreases in male hormone output may cause psychological symptoms similar to those experienced by women in menopause. However, men remain fertile at this time, and many of their symptoms (depression, anxiety, irritability) are more likely related to self-doubts caused by declining vigor and changing physical appearance.

After the late fifties, problems an individual faces in maintaining a healthy and meaningful life are complicated by the inevitable process of aging. How unique are the problems of older people, and how severely do they challenge the need to maintain integrity and personal comfort? We will look at some answers in the next section.

Aging— Will You Still Need Me When I'm 64?

In 1978 students at Long Beach City College in California elected Pearl Taylor their spring festival queen. Ms. Taylor had everything necessary to win: looks, intelligence, personality, and campuswide popularity. At about the same time, citizens of Raleigh, North Carolina, elected Isabella Cannon as their mayor.

Question: What's so remarkable about these events?

Not too much really, except that Pearl was 90 years old when elected, and Isabella was 73 (Barrow & Smith, 1979). Both were part of the graying of America. Currently, some 21 million Americans are over the age of 65. By the year 2020, some 40 million persons, or *1 out of every 5*, will be 65 years of age or older. These figures make the aged the fastest growing segment of society. Understandably, psychologists have become increasingly interested in aging.

Question: What is life like for the aged?

Highlight 16–2
Biological Aging—How Long Is a Lifetime?

Bulletin: You are going to get old. Despite anything you might do to delay it, aging will catch you. Why should this be so? Several interesting biological theories have been proposed to explain aging (Coni, Davison, & Webster, 1984). One thought is that aging is controlled by a built-in biological clock, much like early maturation is programmed by heredity. Another theory is that our days are numbered because human cells die out after about 50 doublings. Other theories emphasize a pileup of wear and tear on the body that leads to mutations in genes or homeostatic failure.

Whatever the biological causes of aging, humans seem to grow, mature, age, and die within a set time. The length of our lives is limited by a boundary called the **maximum life span**. Humans, like other animals, appear to live a limited number of years, even under the best of circumstances. Current estimates of the average human life span place it around 95 to 110 years (Botwinick, 1984).

For most people, **life expectancy** (the actual number of years the average person lives) is shorter than a life span. In the 1800s the average life expectancy was 36 years. By 1900 it was 49 years.

In 1951 in the United States it was 69 years (Hellman, 1971). Now, average life expectancy for American males is 71 years and for females it is 78 years. With improved health care life expectancy should move even closer to the maximum life span.

At present there is no known way to extend the human life span. On the other hand there is every reason to believe that life expectancy can be increased. If you would personally like to add to a new, higher average, here are some deceptively simple rules for living a long life (Coni, Davison, & Webster, 1984):

1. Do not smoke.
2. Use alcohol in moderation or not at all.
3. Avoid becoming overweight.
4. If you suffer from high blood pressure, have it treated.
5. Remain socially and economically active in retirement.
6. Exercise regularly throughout life.

To this we can add: Get married (married persons live longer), learn to manage stress, and choose long-lived parents!

There are large variations in aging. Most of us have known elderly individuals at both extremes: those who are active, healthy, satisfied, and whose minds are clear and alert and those who are confused, childlike, dependent, or senile. Despite such variations, some generalizations can be made.

Aging   Biological aging is a gradual process that begins quite early in life. Peak functioning in most physical capacities reaches a maximum by about 25 to 30 years of age. Thereafter, gradual declines can be observed in muscular strength, flexibility, circulatory efficiency, speed of response, sensory acuity, and other functions.

Question: So people are "over the hill" by 30?

Hardly! Prime abilities come at different ages for different activities. Peak performances for professional football and baseball players usually occur in the mid-twenties; for

professional bowlers, the mid-thirties; for artists and musicians, the fifties; and for politicians, philosophers, business or industrial leaders and others, the early sixties.

For those who are still young, the prospect of physical aging may be the greatest threat of old age (see Highlight 16–2). However, it is a misconception to believe that most elderly people are sickly, infirm, or senile. Only about 5 percent of the elderly are in nursing homes. As for the possibility of mental deterioration, Dr. Alex Comfort (1976) comments, "The human brain does not shrink, wilt, perish, or deteriorate with age. It normally continues to function well through as many as nine decades." As a **gerontologist** (JER-on-TOL-o-jist: one who studies aging), Comfort estimates that only 25 percent of the disability of old people is medically based. The remaining 75 percent is social, political, and cultural (Fig. 16–8).

Comfort's view is backed up by studies of the intellectual capacities of aging individuals. Little overall decline

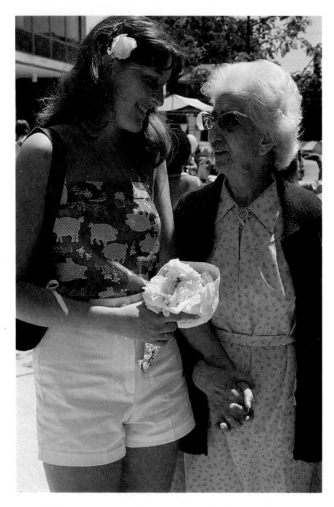

Fig. 16–8 *Aging is a fact. But is "oldness" a social convention? Do the needs of "old people" differ from those of the young?*

Question: What kind of person adjusts most successfully to aging?

Activity and Disengagement   Two principal theories have been proposed to explain successful adjustment to the physical and social changes of aging. **Disengagement theory** assumes that it is normal and desirable that people will withdraw from society as they age (Cumming & Henry, 1961). According to this theory, elderly persons welcome disengagement since it relieves them of roles and responsibilities they have become less able to fulfill. Likewise, society benefits from disengagement as younger persons with new energy and skills fill positions vacated by aging individuals.

Certainly we have all known people who disengaged from society as they grew older. Nevertheless, the disengagement theory can be criticized for describing successful aging as an orderly retreat.

Question: What does the second theory say?

A second view of optimal aging is provided by **activity theory,** which assumes that activity is the essence of life for people of all ages. Activity theory predicts that people who remain active physically, mentally, and socially will adjust better to aging (Havighurst, 1961).

Proponents of activity theory believe that aging persons should maintain the activities of their earlier years for as long as possible. If a person is forced to give up particular roles or activities, it is recommended that these activities or roles be replaced with others. In so doing, the aging person is able to maintain a better self-image, greater satisfaction, and more social support—resulting in more successful aging.

Question: Which theory is correct?

The majority of studies conducted on aging support the *activity theory,* although there have been exceptions (Barrow & Smith, 1979). At the same time, some people do seek disengagement, so neither theory is absolutely "correct." Actually, successful aging probably requires a combination of activity and disengagement. For example, one researcher has shown that the elderly tend to disengage from activities that are no longer satisfying while maintaining those that are (Brown, 1974).

Ageism   In one way or another you have encountered ageism. **Ageism** refers to discrimination or prejudice on the basis of age. It applies to people of all ages and can oppress the young as well as the old. For instance, a person applying for a job may just as likely be told, "You're too young," as "You're too old." Ageism, however, prob-

occurs in intelligence test scores with aging. Although it is true that **fluid abilities** (those requiring speed or rapid learning) may decline, **crystallized abilities** such as vocabulary and accumulated knowledge actually improve at least into the seventies (Baltes & Schaie, 1974). The general intellectual decline attributed to old age is largely a myth.

Aging individuals who remain active and do not suffer major physical problems are quite likely to remain productive, creative, and alert. Continued intellectual stimulation, education, and use of skills can greatly delay age-related declines (Sherman, 1971). Many people remain productive well into their seventies and eighties. Examples are: Pablo Picasso (artist), Margaret Mead (anthropologist), Pablo Casals (cellist), and so on.

ably has more negative impact on older individuals since it is usually expressed as an aversion, hatred, or rejection of the elderly. As Alex Comfort (1976) points out, the concept of "oldness" is often used to expel people from useful work. According to Comfort, retirement is frequently just another name for dismissal and unemployment.

Another facet of ageism is stereotyping of the aged. Popular stereotypes of the "dirty old man," "meddling old woman," "senile old fool," and the like, especially as seen in films and on TV, help perpetuate the myths underlying ageism. Contrast such images to those associated with youthfulness: The young are perceived as fresh, whole, attractive, energetic, active, emerging, appealing, and so forth.

Question: What can be done about ageism?

One of the best ways to combat ageism as it applies to older persons is to counter stereotypes with facts. As one example, studies show that in many occupations older workers perform better at jobs requiring *both* speed and skill (Giniger et al., 1983). Taking a broader view, Bernice Neugarten (1971) examined the lives of 200 people between the ages of 70 and 79. Neugarten found that 75 percent of these people were satisfied with their lives after

retirement. Other myths about aging identified by Neugarten are:

1. Old persons generally do not become isolated and neglected by their families. Most *prefer* to live apart from their children.
2. Old persons are rarely placed in mental hospitals by uncaring children.
3. Old persons who live alone are not necessarily lonely or desolate.
4. Few elderly persons ever show signs of senility or mental decay, and few ever become mentally ill.

In short, most of the elderly studied by Neugarten were integrated, active, and psychologically healthy. Alex Comfort may best have put aging in perspective by listing the needs of the elderly. He says that as an "old" person you will have four needs: dignity, money, proper medical care, and useful work—exactly the things you have always needed.

Psychological studies of aging call for an end to the forced obsolescence of the elderly. As a group older people represent a valuable source of skills, knowledge, and energy that we can no longer afford to cast aside. As we face the challenges of this planet's uncertain future, we need all the help we can get!

Learning Check

Check your comprehension with these questions.

1. Building a workable life tends to be the dominant activity during which age range?
   a. 18–22   *b.* 22–28   *c.* 29–34   *d.* 35–43

2. Levinson's description of the "midlife crisis" corresponds roughly to Gould's
   a. escape from dominance   *b.* crisis of questions   *c.* crisis of urgency   *d.* settling-down period

3. The average male experiences the menopause between the ages of 45 and 50.   T or F?

4. Many indications of biological aging start to become evident as early as the mid-twenties.   T or F?

5. An expert on the problems of aging is called a _____.

6. The activity theory of optimal aging holds that aging individuals should restrict their activities and withdraw from former community activities.   T or F?

7. After age 65 a large proportion of older people show significant signs of senility and most require special care.   T or F?

Answers: 1. b   2. c   3. F   4. T   5. gerontologist   6. F   7. F

Applications

Parenting—The World's Most Important Job

Raising children draws many of the problems of development into a single arena. When parenting is effective, both adult and child benefit. When parents fail to give their children a good start in life, everybody suffers—the child, the parents, and society as a whole. Healthy development requires emotional and social competence as well as intellectual ability. In addition to the skills needed for achievement, effective parents give their children a capacity for love, joy, and fulfillment.

Question: What can parents do to promote healthy development in their children?

Much of the answer can be found in two key areas of parent-child relationships. These are *communication* and *discipline*. In each area parents can set an example of tolerance, understanding, and acceptance that goes beyond their traditional role as mere dispensers of "dos" and "don'ts."

Rearing Children

No psychologist would deny that love is essential for healthy development, but *discipline* can be of equal importance. Parents with unmanageable, delinquent, or unhappy children often can honestly claim that they have given them lots of love. Yet when parents fail to provide a framework of guidelines for behavior, children become antisocial, aggressive, and insecure. As noted earlier in this chapter, overly permissive parents—those who allow themselves to be dominated or manipulated—create lifelong patterns of self-serving behavior in their children.

Question: Does that mean discipline should be strict and unbending?

No. Recall too, that authoritarian parents also have undesirable effects on their children. Families do not need to be run like military boot camps. Effective discipline is authoritative yet sensitive. The goal is to socialize the child without undue frustration and without destroying the bond of love and trust between parent and child.

Question: How can a balance be maintained?

Many experts are advocating a new style of childrearing that recognizes a child's psychological needs. Discipline should give children freedom to express their deepest feelings through speech and actions. This does not mean freedom to do entirely as one pleases. It means the child has room to move about freely *within* well-defined limits. Of course, individual parents may choose limits that are more or less "strict." But this choice is less important than the consistency of parental standards. *Consistent* discipline gives a child a sense of security and stability; inconsistency makes the child's world seem unreliable and unpredictable.

Question: How can limits best be maintained?

Parents tend to base discipline on one or more of the following techniques: **power assertion, withdrawal of love,** or **child management** (Coopersmith, 1968; Hoffman, 1977).

Power assertion refers to physical punishment or to a show of force in which parents take away toys or privileges. As an alternative, some parents may temporarily withdraw love by refusing to speak to a child, by threatening to leave, by rejecting the child, or by otherwise acting as if the child is temporarily unlovable. Management techniques combine praise, recognition, approval, rules, reasoning, and the like to encourage desirable behavior. Each of these approaches can effectively control a child's behavior, but their side effects differ considerably.

Question: What are the side effects?

Power-oriented techniques, particularly harsh or severe physical punishment, are associated with fear, hatred of parents, and a lack of spontaneity and warmth. Severely punished children also tend to be defiant, rebellious, and aggressive (Patterson, 1982).

Withdrawal of love, which is a major middle-class mode of discipline, produces children who tend to be self-disciplined. We might say that such children have developed a good conscience. They are often described as "model" children or as unusually "good." But as a side effect, they are also frequently anxious, insecure, and dependent on adults for approval.

Applications: Parenting—The World's Most Important Job

Management techniques also have their limitations. Most important is the need to carefully adjust them to a child's level of understanding. Younger children may not always see the connection between rules, explanations, and their own behavior. In spite of this limitation, management techniques receive a big plus in an important area of child development. Psychologist Stanley Coopersmith (1968) has found a direct connection between parental styles of discipline and a child's **self-esteem.**

Question: What is self-esteem?

Self-esteem refers to a quiet confidence that comes from regarding oneself as a worthwhile person. Many theorists consider high self-esteem essential for emotional health. Individuals with low self-esteem have a low estimation of their value as people.

In direct studies of children, Coopersmith found that low self-esteem is related to the use of physical punishment or withholding of love. High self-esteem, in contrast, was related to management techniques that emphasized clear and consistent discipline coupled with high parental interest and concern for the child. Thus, it seems best for parents to minimize physical punishment and to avoid unnecessary withdrawal of love.

Question: Are you saying that physical punishment and withdrawal of love should not be used?

Effective parents use each of the three major types of discipline at one time or another, and each has its place. Coopersmith's findings simply suggest that physical punishment and withdrawal of love should be used with caution. In using these two forms of punishment, the following guidelines should be observed.

1. Parents should separate disapproval of the act from disapproval of the child. Instead of saying, "I'm going to punish you because *you* are bad," say, "I'm upset about *what you did.*"
2. Punishment should never be harsh or injurious to a child. Don't physically punish a child while you are angry. Also remember that giving a child the message "I don't love you right now" can be more painful than any spanking.
3. Punishment is most effective when it is administered immediately. This statement is especially true for younger children.
4. Spanking and other forms of physical punishment

are not particularly effective for children under age 2. The child will only be confused and frightened. Spankings also become less effective after age 5 because they tend to humiliate the child and breed resentment.
5. Reserve physical punishment for situations that pose an immediate danger to the younger child, for example, when a child runs into the street.
6. Remember too that it is usually more effective to reinforce children when they are being good than it is to punish them for misbehavior.

After age 5, management techniques are the most effective form of discipline, especially techniques that emphasize communication.

Communication between Parent and Child

When clear communication is maintained between parent and child, many discipline problems can be avoided before they develop. Haim Ginott (1965) has suggested that it is essential to make a distinction between a child's feelings and a child's behavior. Since children (and parents, too) do not choose how they will feel, it is important to allow free expression of feelings.

The child who learns to regard some feelings as "bad," or unacceptable, is being asked to deny a very real part of his or her experience. Ginott encourages parents to teach their children that all feelings are appropriate; it is only actions that are subject to disapproval. Many parents are unaware of just how often they block communication and the expression of feelings in their children. Consider this typical conversation taken from Ginott's book (1965):

Son: I am stupid, and I know it. Look at my grades in school.
Father: You just have to work harder.
Son: I already work harder and it doesn't help. I have no brains.
Father: You are smart, I know.
Son: I am stupid, I know.
Father: (loudly) You are not stupid!
Son: Yes, I am!
Father: You are not stupid. Stupid!

By debating with the child, the father misses the point that his son *feels* stupid. It would be far more helpful for the father to encourage the boy to talk about his feelings.

Applications: Parenting—The World's Most Important Job

Question: How could he do that?

He might say, "You really feel that you are not as smart as others, don't you? Do you feel that way often? Are you feeling bad at school?" In this way the child is given a chance to express his emotions and to feel understood. The father might conclude the conversation by saying, "Look, son, in my eyes you are a fine person. But I understand how you feel. Everyone feels stupid at times."

Communication with a child can also be the basis of effective discipline. Thomas Gordon (1970), a child psychologist who has developed a program called Parent Effectiveness Training (PET), offers a useful suggestion. Gordon believes that parents should send "I" messages to their children, rather than "you" messages.

Question: What's the difference?

"You" messages take the form of threats, name calling, accusing, bossing, lecturing, or analyzing. Generally, "you" messages tell children what's "wrong" with them.

An "I" message is a form of communication that tells children what effect their behavior has had on you. To illustrate the difference, consider this example. After a hard day's work, Susan wants to sit down and rest a while. She begins to relax with a newspaper when her 5-year-old daughter starts banging loudly on a toy drum. Most parents would respond with a "you" message:

"You go play outside this instant." (bossing)

"Don't ever make such a racket when someone is reading." (lecturing)

"You're really pushing it today, aren't you?" (accusing)

"You're a spoiled brat." (name calling)

"Do you want me to swat you?" (threatening)

Gordon suggests sending an "I" message such as, "I am very tired, and I would like to read. I feel upset and can't read when you make so much noise." This forces the child to accept responsibility for the effects of her actions. If this doesn't curb misbehavior, the consequences can also be stated as an "I" message: "I would like for you to stop banging on that drum; otherwise, please take it outside." If the child continues to

bang on the drum inside the house, then she has caused the toy to be put away. If she takes it outside, she has made a decision to play with the drum in a way that respects her mother's wishes. In this way both parent and child are allowed to maintain a sense of self-respect, and a needless clash is averted.

Only two additional points on communicating with children need be noted. They are: "Listen more than you talk"; and "Live the message you wish to communicate."

Child Abuse

Sadly, no account of parenting would be complete without a brief discussion of child abuse. Much as we might like to believe otherwise, child abuse is widespread—from 200,000 to 400,000 cases of physical abuse are reported each year in this country alone. Undoubtedly, many more go unreported (President's Commission on Mental Health, 1978). In about one-third of all cases of physical abuse, the child is seriously injured (Giovannoni & Becerra, 1979). Every year hundreds of children are killed by their own parents.

Question: What are abusive parents like?

Characteristics of Abusive Parents   Abusive parents are usually young (under 30) and from lower income levels. However, professionals who treat child abuse see parents of all ages and income levels.

Abusive parents often have a high level of stress and frustration in their lives. Typical problems include loneliness, marital discord, unemployment, drug abuse, divorce, family violence, heavy drinking, and work anxieties (Giovannoni & Becerra, 1979). Some parents are aware that they are mistreating a child, but they are unable to stop. Other abusive parents literally hate their children or are disgusted by them. The child's sloppiness, diapers, crying, or needs are unbearable to the parent. Often these parents expect the child to love them and make them happy. When the child (who is usually under 3 years old) cannot meet their unrealistic demands, they react with lethal anger.

As mentioned previously, the core of much child abuse is a cycle of violence that flows from one generation to the next. That is, most abusive parents were themselves mistreated as children (Williams & Money,

Applications: Parenting—The World's Most Important Job

1980). Such parents simply never learned how to love, communicate with, or discipline a child.

When does the cycle of violence begin? Sad to say, it shows up almost immediately:

Abusive Toddlers

In a recent study abused 1- to 3-year-olds were observed as they interacted with playmates. The question of interest was, "How do abused children react when another child is crying or distressed?" In almost every instance abused children responded to distress with fear, threats, or physical assault (Main & George, 1985).

In short, abused children rapidly become abusive children and, later, abusive adults.

Question: What can be done about child abuse?

Preventing Child Abuse   Many public agencies now have teams to identify battered or neglected children. However, legal "cures" for child abuse are not very satisfying. The courts can take custody of a child, or the parents may voluntarily agree to place the child in a foster home. Foster care can be an improvement, but it may also further traumatize the child. In some cases the child is allowed to remain with the parents but under court supervision. Even then, there is a chance of further injury unless the parents get help.

Self-help groups staffed by former child abusers and concerned volunteers are a major aid to parents. One such group is Parents Anonymous, a national organization of parents determined to help each other stop abusing children. Local groups set up networks of members that parents can call in an abuse crisis or when they feel one coming on. Parents also learn how to curb violent impulses and how to cope with their children. Such training may be especially effective when carried out at home, where abuse usually occurs (Nomellini & Katz, 1983).

Another way of preventing child abuse is by changing attitudes. Despite newspaper and TV coverage of the problem, many parents believe it is their "right" to slap or hit their children. A recent survey found that corporal punishment is widely accepted in this country. Even hitting a child with a leather strap or a wooden stick was rated as only "moderately serious" (Giovannoni & Becerra, 1979). A child had to be "banged against a wall" or "hit in the face with a fist" before the parent considered the act abusive. As the authors of the survey put it, the public attitude appears to be, "It's all right to hit your child, but not too hard; in fact it's all right to hurt your child—but not too badly."

To face the problem squarely, we must realize that the line between acceptable discipline and child abuse is blurred. As a society we seem to say, "Violence is okay if the child isn't injured; if the child is injured, then it's child abuse." Of course, when the child is injured, it's too late to take back the violence. By condoning punishment that borders on being abusive, we greatly raise the chances of injury. The best solution to physical abuse, then, may lie in rethinking our attitudes toward physical punishment and toward the rights of children.

Learning Check

1. According to the text, effective discipline gives children freedom within a structure of consistent and well-defined limits.   T or F?
2. Coopersmith found that high self-esteem in childhood is related to discipline based on either management techniques or withdrawal of love.   T or F?
3. Spankings and other physical punishment are most effective for children under the age of 2.   T or F?
4. Authoritarian parents view children as having few rights but many responsibilities.   T or F?
5. Most parents who abuse children were themselves mistreated as children.   T or F?

Answers: 1. T   2. F   3. F   4. T   5. T

Chapter Summary

- According to Erikson, each life stage provokes a specific *psychosocial crisis*. In order of occurrence these are: *trust versus mistrust, autonomy versus shame and doubt, initiative versus guilt, industry versus inferiority, identity versus role confusion, intimacy versus isolation, generativity versus stagnation,* and *integrity versus despair.*

- Three major parental styles are *authoritarian, permissive,* and *effective (authoritative) parenting.* When judged by its effects on children, authoritative parenting appears to be most effective.

- Few children grow up without experiencing some of the normal problems of childhood: *negativism, clinging, specific fears, sleep disturbances, general dissatisfaction, regression, sibling rivalry,* and *rebellion.*

- Significant problems affect about 1 child in 10. Major areas of difficulty are: *toilet training* (including *enuresis* and *encopresis*); *feeding disturbances,* such as *overeating, anorexia nervosa* (self-starvation), and *pica* (eating nonfood substances); *speech* (*delayed speech, stuttering*); and *learning disorders* (*dyslexia, hyperactivity,* and other problems). *Childhood autism* is representative of some of the more severe problems that can occur. Some cases of hyperactivity and autism are being treated successfully with *behavior modification.*

- *Adolescence* is a culturally defined social status; *puberty* is a biological event. *Early maturation* is beneficial mostly for boys; its effects are mixed for girls. One danger of early maturation is *premature identity formation.* Adolescent identity formation is accelerated by cognitive development and is influenced by parents and peers.

- Certain relatively consistent events mark adult development in our society. These range from escaping parental dominance in the late teens to a noticeable acceptance of one's lot in life during the fifties. Some research indicates that a *midlife crisis* affects many people in the 37 to 41 age range. Adjustment to later middle age may be complicated for women by *menopause* and for men by a *climacteric.*

- Both the *number* and *proportion* of older people in the population has grown. *Biological aging* begins between 25 and 30; however, peak performance in a particular pursuit may come at various points throughout life. Maximum *life span* can be distinguished from *life expectancy.* Intellectual decline is quite limited, at least through one's seventies.

- *Gerontologists* have proposed two major theories of successful aging. The *disengagement theory* holds that withdrawal from society is necessary and desirable in old age. The *activity theory* counters that optimal adjustment to aging is tied to continuing activity and involvement. There is an element of truth to each, but the activity theory has received more support.

- *Ageism* refers to prejudice, discrimination, and stereotyping on the basis of age. It affects people of all ages but is especially damaging to older people. Most ageism is based on myths and misinformation.

- Effective parental discipline tends to emphasize *child management* techniques (especially communication) rather than *power assertion* or *withdrawal of love. Child abuse* is a major problem for which few solutions exist at present. Abused children tend to become abusive adults.

►►► **Exploration**

Approaching Death—New Pathways

In January 1967, H. Bedford, a psychology professor from Glendale, California, died at the age of 73. His body was immediately frozen—submerged in liquid nitrogen—making him the first person in the United States to try to cheat death by cryonic suspension (Keeffe, 1977). Mr. Bedford's story is only one indication of changing attitudes toward dying.

For some, death is a sudden tragedy; for others it is a long-wished-for release. Whatever the case, death—the last phase of life—is something we all must face. It therefore behooves each of us to know something about death. In this section we will add to an earlier discussion of death (Chapter 13) by considering four departures from traditional approaches to dying: the hospice movement, passive euthanasia, active euthanasia, and cryonics.

Hospice At the beginning of this century most people died at home. Today, of the more than 2 million deaths that occur yearly in the United States, more than 70 percent take place outside the home, most either in a hospital or a nursing home (Fulton, 1979). Just as some people have begun to question traditional funeral practices (embalming, viewing, elaborate and expensive caskets and ceremonies), many are now beginning to question treatment of the terminally ill. Too often dying persons are isolated, frightened, in pain, and stripped of control over their

final days of life. The hospice concept was created to counter this situation.

A hospice is basically a hospital for the terminally ill, modeled after a pioneering English facility. The goal of the hospice is to give specialized care to the dying individual and to improve the quality of life in the person's final days. The first hospice was created in recognition of dying individuals' needs to be included, to know that someone still cares, to maintain control over their lives, and to have a say in their own dying. In operation, the first hospices presented a striking contrast to the grim wards for the terminally ill then found in many hospitals.

Question: How is a hospice different?

First, there are lots of people present. A hospice offers support, counseling, guidance, and companionship from volunteers, other patients, staff, clergy, and counselors. Friendship and kindness are expressed toward patients so that when the time comes to die, they know they will be treated with respect and love.

Second, the atmosphere differs markedly from that of a traditional hospital. A hospice attempts to provide pleasant surroundings, an atmosphere of intentional informality, and a sense of continued living for patients. Unlimited around-the-clock visits are permitted by relatives, friends, children, and even pets. Patients receive constant at-

tention; they play games, make day trips, have predinner cocktails if they choose; entertainment is provided; volunteers visit with the patients—in short, life goes on.

A third aspect of hospice care is the freedom of choice allowed patients. Patients decide about their own diets, about whether or not they will use pain-killing drugs, and about whether or not they want to continue medical care. Patients may also choose freedom from intolerable pain. This is usually achieved by providing them with Brompton's mixture, a combination of cherry syrup and morphine. The dosage of morphine in a Brompton's "cocktail" is small enough so the person does not become euphoric or groggy; it simply relieves pain.

At present most larger cities in the United States have hospices. Their success has been such that they are likely to be added to many more communities. At the same time, treatment for the terminally ill has drastically improved in hospitals—largely due to pioneering efforts in the hospice movement.

A Right to Die? The "right to die" concept might be better stated as a right to "live in peace and comfort until death." Much of the recent interest in this issue has focused on the Karen Ann Quinlan case. In 1975 Karen lapsed into a coma after suffering an overdose of drugs and alcohol. After doctors said she would never recover, Kar-

Exploration: Approaching Death—New Pathways

en's parents began a legal fight to turn off the respirator and other devices being used to prolong her life. In 1976 the New Jersey Supreme Court issued a landmark decision giving permission to the parents to order removal of Karen's life-support equipment. Despite the doctors' predictions, Karen continued to live for another 10 years. Karen died in 1985 at the age of 31.

Is there a right to die? Doctors and other medical personnel are legally and morally bound to prolong and preserve life, and in most states relatives and guardians cannot legally give permission for removal of life-supporting equipment. One way out of this dilemma that is gaining support is the **living will** (see mailing address at the end of this chapter). The intent of a living will is to free the terminally and irreversibly ill from a slow and cruel death, allowing death with dignity. The will is made out when the person is still healthy and states that, in the event of irreversible illness, the person does not want to have life sustained by medical machines or heroic measures. A living will is not yet binding in most states, but it does make clear the wishes of terminally ill persons unable to speak for themselves. Here is an excerpt from one widely used living will:

A Living Will

If at such a time the situation should arise in which there is no reasonable expectation of my recovery from extreme physical or mental disability, I direct that I be allowed to die and not be kept alive by medications, artificial means or "heroic measures." I do,

however, ask that medication be mercifully administered to me to alleviate suffering even though this may shorten my remaining life. (Reprinted with permission from Concern for Dying, 250 West 57th Street, New York, NY 10017)

Euthanasia   The right to die won for Karen Quinlan by her parents may be thought of as **passive euthanasia** (YOU-tha-NAY-zyah), in which death is allowed to occur but is not actively caused (Hendin, 1984). In **active euthanasia** steps would be taken at a patient's request to deliberately hasten death, perhaps by administering drugs that induce death painlessly. Both forms of euthanasia present ethical dilemmas for physicians, who are trained to keep patients alive. On the other hand doctors are also sworn to *humane* treatment. With this second point in mind, proponents of euthanasia believe that it is a basic human right to die with dignity and a minimum of discomfort. To a degree, passive euthanasia is already practiced in the United States. Should active euthanasia ever become legal (many people find the idea totally unacceptable), it might also become possible for next of kin to request euthanasia for an incapacitated individual.

There are several arguments against euthanasia. The case of Karen Delahanty of Avon, Connecticut, provides a good starting point. After a head-on automobile accident, Karen entered a coma from which doctors predicted she would never recover. One year later she miraculously regained consciousness. What if euthanasia had been carried out?

Other questions that arise, in addition to unexpected recovery, include: What guarantee is there that the choice of euthanasia would be made freely and without pressure? Can family members be trusted to make a correct decision? Would they feel guilt afterward? What about the medical personnel involved; how would they respond emotionally to "mercy killing"? No doubt you can think of other objections.

Cryonics   To complete our brief sampling of new approaches to dying, let's return to cryonics. Cryonics involves freezing a person's body at death. The idea is to keep the person frozen until medical science perfects ways to thaw, restore, and revive the person. Those who have been placed in **cryonic suspension** obviously are gambling that if they are revived a cure will exist for whatever killed them.

Question: Does freezing actually work?

Cryonic suspension must be viewed as a symbolic attempt to cheat death, or perhaps as an emotional hedge against the finality of death. At this point cryonic suspension is impractical because freezing does serious damage to the body. The ice crystals formed by freezing and unfreezing the human brain would almost surely turn it to mush—wiping out most or all of the memories stored there. If a person frozen at death were ever to be successfully revived, that person would have no identity and perhaps no understanding of where he or she was or why he or

Exploration: Approaching Death—New Pathways

she was there. Such persons would, in most cases, be quite old. (To date, most of the persons who have been frozen have been middle-aged or older.) Another problem is the great expense of maintaining cryonic capsules for many years. And, in California (where else?) a case has already surfaced where careless operators of a cryonics service allowed a number of bodies to defrost.

Whereas it is true that for a few pioneering souls there is clearly "ice after death," immortality, it would seem, does not yet fall within the province of technology.

Learning Check

1. The goal of a hospice is to freeze persons who have died of diseases that might one day become curable.   T or F?
2. In passive euthanasia death is allowed to occur but is not actively induced.   T or F?
3. Cryonic suspension is a type of passive euthanasia.   T or F?
4. Active euthanasia is now legal in most states, providing that the terminally ill patient has signed a living will.   T or F?

Answers: 1. F   2. T   3. F   4. F

Questions for Discussion

1. Describe an incident from your own childhood that you consider growth promoting. Describe an incident that set you back or had a negative effect on you. How do these incidents differ?
2. Were you physically punished as a child? What is your attitude toward physical punishment now? Would you use physical punishment on your own children?
3. In what ways do parents add to the conflicts of adolescents seeking identity and young adults seeking independence?
4. Do you know a person who seems to have "flunked" one or more of Erikson's developmental stages? What effect has this had on the person's subsequent development?
5. Anthropologist Margaret Mead has charged, "We have become a society of people who neglect our children, are afraid of our children." Do you agree?
6. Do we need a "children's liberation movement" to establish the civil rights of children? (Keep in mind that few parents show their children the courtesy they show strangers.)

7. How common do you think it is to experience a "midlife crisis"? Would you expect people of other cultures to experience a similar crisis? Is the word *crisis* an exaggeration?
8. If you could choose to remain a particular age, what age would you choose? Why? What are your attitudes toward aging?
9. When and how would you prefer to die? If you had a terminal illness, would you want to be told? Do you think sudden death or death with forewarning would be better?
10. Should passive euthanasia be allowed? Should active euthanasia be allowed? What are the arguments for and against each? Do you think a living will is a good idea? Why or why not?
11. Large areas of land are currently required for traditional cemeteries. Should people be buried upright instead of prone? How should society balance respect for the dead with needs to make way for the living?

Where to Write for Information

Anorexia Nervosa   National Association of Anorexia Nervosa and Associated Disorders, Box 271, Highland Park, IL 60035

Autism   The National Society for Autistic Children, 101 Richmond Street, Huntington, WV 25701

Child Abuse   Parents Anonymous, 22330 Hawthorne Boulevard, Torrance, CA 90505

Hospice   The National Hospice Organization, 301 Tower Suite 506, 301 Maple Avenue West, Vienna, VA 22180

Hyperactivity   Department of Health, Education, and Welfare, Office of the Secretary, Secretary's Committee on Mental Retardation, Washington, DC 20201

Learning Disorders   National Association for Children with Learning Disabilities, 5225 Grace Street, Pittsburgh, PA 15236

Living Will   Concern for Dying, 250 West 57th Street, New York, NY 10107

Intelligence

Chapter 17

Chapter Preview
What Day Is It?

Ask George in which recent years April 21 fell on a Sunday. Without hesitation he will answer: "1985, 1974, 1968, 1963, 1957, 1946." Surprisingly, this gives only the slightest hint of his ability. If encouraged, George will go back as far as 1700—with complete accuracy! His calendar calculations cover a range of at least 6000 years, extending centuries beyond present perpetual calendars. With equal ease he can identify February 15, 2002, as a Friday or August 28, 1591, as a Wednesday.

Question: Is he a genius?

George's abilities are all the more amazing in view of the fact that he is mentally retarded and cannot add, subtract, multiply, or divide even simple numbers (Horwitz et al., 1965). George is an idiot savant, a person of subnormal intelligence who shows highly developed mental ability in one or more very limited areas.

Question: How could he be retarded and have this ability both at the same time?

The striking contrast between George's general retardation and unusual mental ability is a fitting introduction to the challenge psychologists face in trying to define and measure intelligence. Quite frankly, we are still searching for answers to such questions as: Is intelligence a general trait or a collection of specific skills? Is intelligence determined by the genetic "wheel of fortune" or is it nurtured by environment? Is it possible to construct an intelligence test that is fair to all people? How important is intelligence for "success"? Because our understanding of intelligence is rapidly changing, we cannot hope to give final answers.

For the sake of clarity, this chapter is divided into two parts. In the Resources section we will assume that intelligence can be measured, and we will use measurements as a way of answering questions about intelligence. In the Applications section we will consider questions that have been raised about intelligence tests and the meaning of their results.

Survey Questions How do psychologists define intelligence? What are the qualities of a good psychological test? What are typical IQ tests like? How do IQ scores relate to gender, age, and occupation? What does IQ tell us about genius? What causes mental retardation? Does heredity or environment determine intelligence? Are IQ tests fair to all racial and cultural groups?

Resources

Defining Intelligence— Intelligence Is . . . It's . . . You Know, It's . . .

Like so many important concepts in psychology, intelligence cannot be observed directly: It has no mass, occupies no space, and is invisible. Nevertheless, we feel certain it exists. Consider the following two individuals:

When she was 14 months old, Anne H. wrote her own name. She taught herself to read at age 2. At age 5, she astounded her kindergarten teacher by walking into class with a stack of encyclopedias—which she proceeded to read. At 10 she

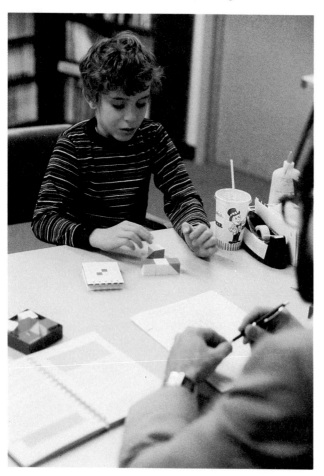

Fig. 17–1 *Modern intelligence tests are widely used to measure intellectual abilities. When properly administered, such tests provide an operational definition of intelligence.*

breezed through an entire high school algebra course in 12 hours.

At age 10 Billy A. can write his name and can count, but he has trouble with simple addition and subtraction problems and finds multiplication impossible. He has been held back in school twice and is still incapable of doing the work his 8-year-old classmates find easy. His teachers have suggested placing him in a special educational program for slow learners.

Anne is considered a genius; Billy, a slow learner. There seems little doubt that they differ in intelligence.

Question: Wait! Anne's ability is obvious, but how do we know that Billy isn't just lazy?

This dilemma is one that **Alfred Binet** faced in 1904. The minister of education in Paris had given Binet the task of devising a way to distinguish slower students from the more capable (or the capable but lazy). In a flash of brilliance, Binet and an associate created a test made up of "intellectual" questions and problems. Next, they determined which questions an average child could answer at each age. Children low in intellectual ability were identified by below-par performance on the test.

Binet's approach gave rise to modern intelligence tests. At the same time, it launched 80 years of debate that has often been heated and at times bitter. Part of the debate is related to the basic difficulty of defining intelligence.

Question: Is there an accepted definition of intelligence?

Most psychologists would probably agree with David Wechsler's general description of **intelligence** as the: *global capacity of the individual to act purposefully, to think rationally, and to deal effectively with the environment.* Beyond this, there is so much disagreement that many psychologists simply accept an **operational definition** of intelligence. (A concept is defined "operationally" by specifying what procedures will be used to measure it.) In other words, by selecting test items, a psychologist is saying in a very direct way: "This is what I mean by intelligence." A test that measures memory, reasoning, and verbal fluency offers a very different definition of intelligence than one that measures strength of grip, shoe size, length of the nose, or age in days.

Reliability and Validity   Suppose that a famous psychologist, Ike Q. Tester, is dissatisfied with existing intelligence tests and decides to develop his own (the I. Q.

Tester IQ Test). Professor Tester decides to limit his test to a single question. According to Professor Tester, one's intelligence is revealed by an ability to complete this series of numbers: 5 5 6 6 8 1 _____. As a concerned citizen, there are two questions you should ask about Tester's test: "Is it *reliable?*" and, "Is it *valid?*"

Question: What does reliability refer to?

A reliable bathroom scale gives the same weight on several successive weighings. For a test to be **reliable,** it must yield the same score, or close to the same score, each time it is given to the same person. It is easy to see that a test has little value if it is unreliable. Imagine a medical test for pregnancy, for instance, that gives positive and negative responses for the same woman on different occasions.

To check the reliability of the I. Q. Tester IQ Test, we could administer it to a large group of people. Then each person could be tested again at a later date to establish *test-retest reliability.* By comparing such scores, we find that the Tester test is quite reliable. In fact, the scores are *identical* for both tests: Everyone scores zero each time (except Professor Tester, who scores 100 percent and thereby proclaims himself the only human with any intelligence). On questioning, Tester reveals his secret of success: The numbers in the question are part of his Social Security number. Hence, anyone else who answers correctly does so purely by chance!

If Tester had provided a larger number of questions, the reliability of his test could be checked in another way. Reliability is sometimes measured by comparing the score on one-half of the test items with the score on the other half (*split-half reliability*). Likewise, if Tester offered two versions of the test, we could compare scores on one with scores on the other for each person (*equivalent-forms reliability*). In any case, Tester has shown the scores on his test to be consistent (reliable), but are they valid?

Obviously, we have been playing with a silly example; by no stretch of the imagination can the I. Q. Tester IQ Test be considered valid. A test has **validity** when it measures what it claims to measure. Like the I. Q. Tester IQ Test, many psychological tests you will encounter have little or no validity. This is especially true of "personality" tests found in magazines or offered by commercial self-improvement courses.

Question: How is the validity of a test established?

As a starting point a test should include items that look as if they are related to what is supposedly being measured (*face validity*). The validity of a test of athletic aptitude would be suspect if the test involved adding long columns of numbers; a test of mathematical aptitude that measured muscular strength would be equally questionable. A better way of gauging validity is to compare test scores to actual performance (*criterion validity*). A test of legal aptitude, for example, might be validated by comparing test scores with grades in law school. If high scores correlate with high grades or other measures of success, the test may be considered valid.

Tester's Last Stand   Let's return to Professor Tester for a final point. Although he admits his test has problems, Professor Tester claims that at least it is *objective.* Is he right? Actually, yes, because a test is said to be **objective** if it gives the same score when different people correct it. Tester's test *is* objective, as are most intelligence tests. However, objectivity is not enough to guarantee a fair test. To be useful, a psychological test must also be *standardized.*

Test **standardization** refers to two things: First, it means that standard procedures are used in giving the test to all people; and second, it means finding the norm, or average score, made by a large group of people similar to those for whom the test was designed. Without standardization it would be unfair to compare the scores of people taking a test on different occasions. And without norms there would be no way to tell if a score is high, low, or average.

Later in this chapter we will address the question of whether intelligence tests are valid. For now, let's take a practical approach, by examining some widely used standardized tests and the meaning of scores on them.

Testing Intelligence— The IQ and You

American psychologists quickly recognized the usefulness of Binet's test. In 1916 **Lewis Terman** and others at Stanford University revised it for use in this country. After several more revisions, the **Stanford-Binet Intelligence Scale** is still widely used. The Stanford-Binet assumes that mental ability in childhood improves with increasing age. As a result the Stanford-Binet is really a set of increasingly more difficult tests, one for each age group.

The age-ranked questions of the Stanford-Binet allow a person's **mental age** to be determined. For example, at ages 8 or 9, very few children can define the word *connection.* At age 10, 10 percent can. At age 13, 60 percent can. In other words, the ability to define *connection* indicates mental ability comparable to that of the average 13-year-old and gives a mental age of 13 (on this single item).

Table 17–1 is a sample of items that persons of average intelligence can answer at various ages.

Mental age gives a good indication of actual abilities, but it says nothing about whether overall intelligence is high or low. To know the meaning of mental age, **chronological age** (age in years) must also be considered. Mental age can then be related to chronological age to yield an

Table 17–1 Sample Items from the Stanford-Binet Intelligence Scale	
Two years old	On a large paper doll, points out the hair, mouth, feet, ear, nose, hands, and eyes.
	When shown a tower built of four blocks, builds one like it.
Three years old	When shown a bridge built of three blocks, builds one like it.
	When shown a drawing of a circle, copies it with a pencil.
Four years old	Fills in the missing word when asked, "Brother is a boy; sister is a _____." "In daytime it is light; at night it is _____."
	Answers correctly when asked, "Why do we have houses?" "Why do we have books?"
Five years old	Defines *ball*, *hat*, and *stove*.
	When shown a drawing of a square, copies it with a pencil.
Nine years old	Answers correctly when examiner says, "In an old graveyard in Spain they have discovered a small skull which they believe to be that of Christopher Columbus when he was about ten years old. What is foolish about that?"
	Answers correctly when asked, "Tell me the name of a color that rhymes with head." "Tell me a number that rhymes with tree."
Adult	Can describe the difference between laziness and idleness, poverty and misery, character and reputation.
	Answers correctly when asked, "Which direction would you have to face so your right hand would be toward the north?"

(Terman & Merrill, 1960.)

IQ, or **intelligence quotient.** When the Stanford-Binet was first used in the United States, IQ was defined as mental age (MA) divided by chronological age (CA) and multiplied by 100:

$$\frac{MA}{CA} \times 100 = IQ$$

An advantage of the IQ is that intelligence can be compared in children with different chronological and mental ages. For instance a 10-year-old child with a mental age of 12 has an IQ of 120:

$$\frac{(MA)\ 12}{(CA)\ 10} \times 100 = 120\ (IQ)$$

A second child having a mental age of 12, but with a chronological age of 12 would have an IQ of 100:

$$\frac{(MA)\ 12}{(CA)\ 12} \times 100 = 100\ (IQ)$$

The IQ shows that the younger child is brighter than his 12-year-old friend, even though their intellectual skills are actually the same. Notice that IQ equals 100 when MA = CA. An IQ score of 100 is therefore defined as average intelligence.

Question: Then does a person with an IQ score below 100 have below average intelligence?

Not unless the IQ is significantly below 100. An IQ of 100 is the *mathematical* average (or mean) for such scores. "Average intelligence" is usually defined as any score from 90 to 109. The important point to note is that IQ scores will be over 100 when mental age is higher than age in years, and IQ scores will be below 100 when mental age is lower than age in years. An example of the second possibility would be a 15-year-old with a MA of 12:

$$\frac{12}{15} \times 100 = 80\ (IQ)$$

The preceding calculations were described to give you insight into the meaning of IQ scores. With tests currently in use, there is no longer any need to calculate IQ's. Instead, a person's IQ score can be determined directly from tables supplied with the test.

Question: How old do children have to be before their IQ scores become stable?

Stability of IQ   IQ scores are not very dependable until about age 6 (Honzik, 1983). The correlation between IQ scores obtained at age 2 and those obtained at age 18 is only .31. (Recall that a perfect correlation is 1.00 and a correlation of 0.00 occurs when scores are unrelated.) With increasing age, IQ's become more reliable. The average change (median change) in IQ on retesting is roughly 5 points in either direction. However, children may show small ups and downs in tested intelligence as they develop. No typical pattern exists, and in some cases changes in IQ of 15 points or more may take place. Overall, though, changes are usually quite small after middle childhood.

Question: How much does aging affect the IQ?

Since IQ reflects education, maturity, and experience, as well as native intellectual capacity, test scores show a small, gradual increase until about age 40 (Eichorn et al., 1981). This trend, of course, is an average. Some people show fairly large gains in IQ, whereas others experience sizable losses. How do the two groups differ? In general, persons who show the largest IQ increases have been exposed to stimulating intellectual experiences during early adulthood. Those who show the most decline typically suffer from chronic illness, drinking problems, or unstimulating lifestyles (Honzik, 1984).

Some studies have recorded slow declines in IQ after middle age, while others indicate little or no change due to aging (Schaie, 1980). As you may recall from the previous chapter, these contradictory results can be explained in this way: When general information or comprehension is emphasized, there is little decline in IQ until advanced age; however, test items requiring speed, rapid insight, or perceptual flexibility show earlier losses and a rapid decline after middle age (Baltes & Schaie, 1974). *Overall*, age-related losses are small for most healthy, well-educated individuals (Schaie, 1980).

Perhaps the most intriguing link between IQ and aging is the observation that impending death may be signaled by marked changes in brain function. Certain intellectual skills have been shown to decline abruptly about 5 years before death. This **terminal decline** in IQ can be measured even when the person appears to be in good health (Jarvik et al., 1973; Suedfeld & Piedrahita, 1984).

Question: Is the Stanford-Binet the only intelligence test?

The Wechsler Test   A widely used alternative to the Stanford-Binet is the **Wechsler Adult Intelligence Scale–Revised,** or **WAIS–R.** This test also has a form adapted for use with children, called the **Wechsler Intelligence Scale for Children–Revised (WISC–R).**

The Wechsler tests bear an overall similarity to the Stanford-Binet but differ in some important respects. The WAIS–R is specifically designed to test adult intelligence, and both the WISC–R and the WAIS–R rate **performance** (nonverbal) intelligence in addition to **verbal** intelligence. The Stanford-Binet only gives one overall IQ, whereas the Wechsler tests can be broken down to reveal strengths and weaknesses in various areas. The intellectual skills revealed by the Wechsler tests and some sample items are listed in Table 17–2.

Group Tests   Both the Stanford-Binet and the Wechsler tests are **individual intelligence tests** that must be given on a one-to-one basis by a specially trained tester. Other tests of intelligence have been designed for use with large groups of people. **Group intelligence tests** are usually paper-and-pencil tests that require test-takers to read, to follow instructions, and to solve problems of logic, mathematics, or the visual arrangement of geometric designs. The first group intelligence test was the Army Alpha, developed for use in classifying World War I military inductees.

If you're wondering if you have ever taken an intelligence test, the answer is probably yes. The Scholastic Aptitude Test (SAT), the American College Test (ACT), and the College Qualification Test (CQT) all are group tests that can be used to estimate a person's intelligence as well as his or her chances for college success.

Learning Check

Check your comprehension before you continue reading.

1. The first successful intelligence test was developed by _____.

2. If we define intelligence by writing a test, we are using:
    a. a circular definition   *c.* an operational definition
    b. an abstract definition   *d.* chronological age as the definition of intelligence

3. Place an "R" or a "V" after each operation to indicate if it would be used to establish the reliability or the validity of a test.
   a. Compare score on one-half of test items with score on the other half.   (   )
   b. Compare scores on test to grades, performance ratings, or other measures.   (   )
   c. Compare scores from test after administering it on two separate occasions.   (   )
   d. Compare actual content of test items to what is supposedly being measured.   (   )

4. IQ was originally defined as $\dfrac{(\quad\quad)}{(\quad\quad)} \times 100$.

5. Ability to answer general information and comprehension questions shows the most rapid decline during aging.   T or F?

6. The WAIS–R is a group intelligence test.   T or F?

7. Establishing norms and uniform procedures for administering a test are elements of standardization.   T or F?

Answers: **1.** Alfred Binet   **2.** c   **3.** a.(R), b.(V), c.(R), d.(V)   **4.** $\dfrac{MA}{CA} \times 100$ **5.** F   **6.** F   **7.** T

Table 17–2   Sample Items Similar to Those Used on the WAIS–R

Verbal Subtests	Sample Items
Information	How many wings does a bird have? Who wrote *Paradise Lost?*
Digit Span	Repeat from memory a series of digits, such as 3 1 0 6 7 4 2 5, after hearing them once.
General	What is the advantage of keeping money in a bank?
Comprehension	Why is copper often used in electrical wires?
Arithmetic	Three men divided 18 golf balls equally among themselves. How many golf balls did each man receive? If two apples cost 15¢, what will be the cost of a dozen apples?
Similarities	In what way are a lion and a tiger alike? In what way are a saw and a hammer alike?
Vocabulary	This test consists simply of asking, "What is a _____?" or "What does _____ mean?" The words cover a wide range of difficulty or familiarity.

Performance Subtests	Description of Item
Picture Arrangement	Arrange a series of cartoon panels to make a meaningful story.
Picture Completion	What is missing from these pictures?
Block Design	Copy designs with blocks (as shown at right).
Object Assembly	Put together a jigsaw puzzle.
Digit Symbol	

1	2	3	4
X	III	I	0

Fill in the symbols:

3	4	1	3	4	2	1	2

(Courtesy of The Psychological Corporation.)

Variations in Intelligence— The Numbers Game

Based on scores from a large number of randomly selected people, the classifications shown in Table 17–3 have been set for various IQ ranges. A look at the percentages reveals a definite pattern. The distribution of IQ's approximates a **normal** (bell-shaped) **curve,** in which the majority of scores fall close to the average, with far fewer at the extremes. Figure 17–2 shows this characteristic of measured intelligence.

Question: On the average, do males and females differ in intelligence?

Sex IQ does not give a definite answer to this question since intelligence test items are selected to be equally difficult for both sexes. It seems safe to assume that men and women do not differ in overall intelligence, and no significant IQ difference has been found. However, tests like the WAIS–R allow a comparison of the intellectual strengths and weaknesses of men and women. Here a difference does emerge: Women perform better on test items that require verbal ability, vocabulary, and rote learning; men are better at items that require visualization of spatial relationships and arithmetic reasoning (Wechsler, 1958). However, such differences are small and are based on *averages.* It is important to recognize that many women are better than men at math, that many men are better than women at verbal skills, and so forth.

Question: How do IQ scores relate to success in school, jobs, and other undertakings?

Table 17–3 Distribution of Adult IQ Scores on WAIS–R

IQ	Verbal Description	Percent of Adults
Above 130	Very superior	2.2
120–129	Superior	6.7
110–119	Bright normal	16.1
90–109	Average	50.0
80– 89	Dull normal	16.1
70– 79	Borderline	6.7
Below 70	Mentally retarded	2.2

(Wechsler, 1958.)

School and Occupation IQ differences of a few points tell little about intellectual potential. But when a broader range of scores is considered, meaningful differences emerge. The correlation between IQ and school grades is .50—a sizable association.

As you might expect, there is also a relationship between IQ and job classification. Persons holding "high-status" positions average higher IQ's than those in "lower status" occupational settings. (The term *high status* refers to traditionally higher paid business and professional occupations.) For example, accountants average about 120 in IQ and miners about 90 (Anastasi & Foley, 1958). It is important to note, however, that there is a range of IQ scores in all occupations. Many people of high intelligence, because of choice or circumstance, can be found in "low-ranking" occupations (Fig. 17–3).

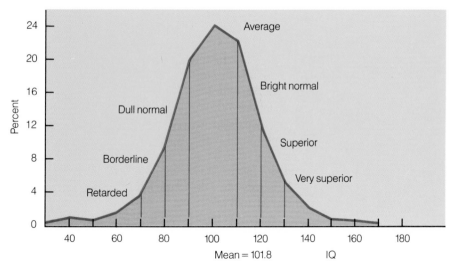

Fig. 17–2 *Distribution of Stanford-Binet Intelligence Test scores for 3184 children. (After Terman & Merrill, 1960.)*

Fig. 17–3 *John Kirtley has an IQ score of 174, yet he prefers to do custodial work, feeling that his unusual intellect would be "used" by his employers if he pursued a technical occupation.*

It is tempting to interpret the link between IQ and occupation as evidence that professional jobs require more intelligence. This interpretation is dangerous because IQ tests require the same types of mental gymnastics needed for success in school. Since higher status jobs often require an academic degree, the apparent link between IQ and job status may be misleading. Selection procedures for professional jobs appear to be biased in favor of a particular type of intelligence; namely, the kind measured by intelligence tests.

When variations in IQ are extreme—below 70 or above 130—influences on adjustment and one's potential for success become unmistakable. Only 4.5 percent of the population falls in these ranges, but this means that about 10 million people in the United States are exceptional by way of having very high or very low IQ's. Discussions of the mentally gifted and the mentally retarded follow.

The Mentally Gifted— Is Genius Next to Insanity?

Question: How high is the IQ of a genius?

Only about 1 percent of the population scores above 140 on IQ tests. A person scoring this high is at least "gifted" and, depending on the standards used, he or she may be considered a genius. However, some psychologists reserve the term *genius* for even higher IQ's or for other qualities, such as exceptional creativity.

Are high IQ scores in childhood associated with later ability? To directly answer this question, Lewis Terman selected 1500 children with IQ's of 140 or more. By following the development of this gifted group into adulthood, Terman countered a number of popular misconceptions about genius.

Misconception: The gifted tend to be peculiar, socially backward people.
Fact: On the contrary, Terman's gifted subjects were socially well adjusted and showed above-average leadership capacity.

Misconception: "Early ripe means later rot": The gifted tend to fizzle out as adults.
Fact: This is false. When retested as adults, Terman's subjects again scored in the upper IQ ranges.

Misconception: The very bright are usually physically inferior "eggheads" or weaklings.
Fact: This is also a misconception. As a group the gifted were above average in height, weight, and physical appearance.

Misconception: The highly intelligent person is more susceptible to mental illness ("Genius is next to insanity").
Fact: Terman demonstrated conclusively that the gifted have better than average mental health records, indicating a greater *resistance* to mental illness.

Misconception: Intelligence has nothing to do with success, especially in practical matters.
Fact: The later success of Terman's subjects was the most striking finding of the study. Far more of them than average had completed college, earned advanced degrees, or held professional positions. Many had been recognized for outstanding achievements. As a group the gifted had produced dozens of books, thousands of scientific articles, and hundreds of short stories and other publications (Terman & Oden, 1959).

Question: Were all of the gifted children superior as adults?

No. Remember that high IQ reveals *potential*, not capacity. A high IQ is no guarantee of success. Some of the gifted had committed crimes, were unemployable, or were poorly adjusted.

Question: How did the more successful subjects differ from the less successful?

A recent follow-up found that the highly successful subjects differed mainly in their greater *persistence* and motivation to succeed (Feldman, 1982). The meaning of this finding is clear: As one educator put it, "No one is paid to sit around being capable of achievement—what you do is always more important than what you should be able to do" (Whimbey, 1980).

Question: How might a parent spot an unusually bright child?

Early signs frequently observed in gifted children include: a tendency to seek out and identify with older children and adults; an early fascination with explanations and problem solving; talking in complete sentences as early as 2 or 3 years of age; an unusually good memory; precocious talent in art, music, or number skills; an early interest in books, early reading (often by age 3); showing of kindness, un-

derstanding, and cooperation toward others (Alvino et al., 1985).

Notice that this list includes behavior other than straight "academic" intelligence. Children may be gifted in ways other than that reflected by a high IQ score. In fact if such things as artistic talent, mechanical aptitude, musical aptitude, athletic potential, and so on, are considered, 19 out of 20 children could be labeled "gifted" in some respect (Fig. 17–4) (Feldman & Bratton, 1972). It may therefore be a mistake to identify giftedness primarily with intelligence tests (Alvino et al., 1985). Such limited definitions of giftedness may shortchange many children who have special talents or potentials (see Highlight 17–1).

Being gifted in the sense of having a high IQ is not without its problems, particularly in childhood. The gifted child may rapidly become bored in a classroom designed for average children. Boredom can lead to behavioral problems or clashes with teachers who consider the gifted child a show-off or smart aleck. The extremely bright child may also find the company of his or her classmates less stimulating than that of older children or adults (Alvino et al., 1985). In recognition of these problems, many school systems now provide special Gifted and Talented Education (GATE) programs and classes for gifted children.

Fig. 17–4 *It is wise to remember that there are many ways in which a child may be "gifted." Many schools now offer gifted and talented education programs for students with a variety of special abilities—not just those who score well on IQ tests.*

Highlight 17–1
Frames of Mind—Seven Intelligences?

At an elementary school a student who is two grades behind in reading shows his teacher how to solve a difficult computer programming problem. In a nearby room one of his classmates, who is poor in math, plays an intricate piece of music on a piano. Both of these children show clear signs of intelligence. And yet, each might score below average on a traditional IQ test. Such observations have convinced many psychologists that it is time to forge new, broader definitions of intelligence. Their basic goal is to better predict "real world" success—not just the likelihood of success in school (Sternberg, 1985).

One such psychologist is Howard Gardner of Harvard University. Gardner (1985) theorizes that there are actually seven different kinds of intelligence. These include abilities in: language, logic and math, visual and spatial thinking, music, bodily-kinesthetic skills (such as dance or athletics), intrapersonal skills (self-knowledge), and interpersonal skills (leadership, social abilities). Each intelligence appears to be largely independent of the others, and each seems to be controlled by different brain areas. (This could explain the remarkable abilities of idiots savants.) Most of us are probably strong in only a few of the intelligences. In contrast, geniuses—like Albert Einstein—seem to be able to use all of the intelligences, as needed, to solve problems.

If Gardner's theory is correct, traditional IQ tests measure only a part of real-world intelligence—namely, linguistic, logical-mathematical, and spatial abilities. A further implication is that our schools may be wasting a lot of human potential. For example, some children might find it easier to learn math or reading if these topics were tied into art, music, dance, drama, and so on.

Not all psychologists agree with Gardner's broader definition of intelligence. His view, in fact, is at odds with studies that suggest that scores on IQ tests mainly reflect an underlying "general intelligence" factor (often referred to as "g"). This g-factor is said to explain the high correlations found among scores on various tests of intellectual ability and achievement. Gardner's reply would probably be that such correlations only show how narrowly traditional tests define intelligence. Whether or not he is right, it seems likely that in the future intelligence will not be so strongly equated with IQ.

Mental Retardation—
A Difference That Makes a Difference

A person with mental abilities far below average is termed **mentally retarded** or **developmentally disabled.** An IQ of 70 or below traditionally has been the dividing line between normal intelligence and retardation. However, a person's ability to perform **adaptive behaviors**—such as dressing, eating, communicating, shopping, and working—also figures into such classifications (Haywood et al., 1982). Below an IQ of 70, additional distinctions may be made as shown in Table 17–4.

Question: Are the retarded usually placed in institutions?

No. Total care is only necessary for the profoundly retarded. The **severely** and **moderately** retarded are capable of mastering basic language skills and routine self-help skills. Many become financially self-supporting by working in *sheltered workshops* (special simplified work environments). The **mildly** retarded benefit from carefully structured and supervised education. As adults they are capable of living alone and may marry (although they tend to have difficulties with many of the demands of adult life) (Suinn, 1975).

It is important to realize that retarded persons have no handicap where feelings are concerned. They are sensitive to rejection and are easily hurt by teasing or ridicule. Likewise, they respond warmly to love and acceptance. Professionals working with them emphasize their rights to self-respect and to a place in the community. This is especially important during childhood, when the support of others adds greatly to the person's chances of becoming a well-adjusted member of society (Fig. 17–5).

Question: What causes mental retardation?

Causes of Retardation

About 25 percent of all cases of mental retardation are *organic*, or related to known physical disorders, including **birth injuries** (such as lack of oxygen), **fetal damage** (from maternal drug abuse, disease, or infection), **metabolic disorders**, such as cretinism and phenylketonuria (discussed in the next section), and **genetic abnormalities.**

In the majority of instances, no known biological problem can be identified. In such cases the degree of retardation is usually mild, in the 50-to-70 IQ range, and quite often other family members are also mildly retarded (DSM-III, 1980). **Familial retardation,** as this is called, occurs most often in very low income or impoverished households. In some such homes nutrition, early stimulation, medical care, intellectual stimulation, and emotional support are inadequate. The positive side of this picture is that most cases of familial retardation could be prevented by better nutrition, education, and early childhood enrichment programs.

To conclude our discussion, let's briefly return to organic retardation for a look at several distinctive problems.

Phenylketonuria (PKU) Phenylketonuria (FEN-ul-KEET-uh-NURE-ee-ah) is a genetically induced lack of an important enzyme. Lack of the enzyme causes the buildup of phenylpyruvic acid (a destructive chemical) within the body. If PKU goes untreated, severe retardation typically occurs by age 3 (Kopp & Parmelee, 1979). PKU is now easily detected in babies by medical testing during the first month of life. It can usually be controlled by a special diet low in foods containing substances the child's body can't handle.

Microcephaly Microcephaly (MY-kro-SEF-ah-lee) means small-headedness. The microcephalic suffers a rare abnormality in which the skull is extremely small or fails to grow. The brain is forced to develop in a limited space, causing severe retardation that usually requires the individual to be placed in an institution. The microcephalic is typically affectionate, well behaved, and easy to work with.

Hydrocephaly Hydrocephaly (HI-dro-SEF-ah-lee: water on the brain) is caused by a buildup of cerebrospinal fluid within brain cavities. Pressure from this fluid can damage the brain and greatly enlarge the head. Hydrocephaly is not uncommon—about 8000 babies are born with

Table 17–4	Levels of Mental Retardation	
IQ Range	**Degree of Retardation**	**Educational Classification**
68–83	Borderline	Slow learner
52–67	Mild	Educable retarded
36–51	Moderate	Trainable retarded
20–35	Severe	Trainable retarded
Below 20	Profound	Total-care group

(Robinson & Robinson, 1970.)

the problem each year in the United States. Thanks to new medical procedures, most of these infants now will lead normal lives. Treatment involves surgically implanting a tube that drains fluid from the brain into the abdomen. If this is done within the first 3 months of life, retardation can usually be avoided.

Fig. 17–5 *This youngster is a participant in the Special Olympics—an athletic event for the mentally retarded. It is often said of the Special Olympics that "everyone is a winner—participants, coaches, and spectators."*

Cretinism   Cretinism (KREET-un-iz-um) is a form of retardation that develops in infancy due to an insufficient supply of thyroid hormone. In some parts of the world, cretinism is caused by too little iodine in the diet (iodine is necessary for normal thyroid function). Widespread use of iodized salt makes this cause of the condition rare in the United States. Cretinism causes stunted physical and intellectual growth that cannot be corrected unless detected early. Fortunately, it is easily and routinely detected in infancy and may be treated by thyroid hormone replacement.

Down Syndrome   The disorder known as Down syndrome causes moderate to severe retardation and a shortened life expectancy (usually around 40 years) in 1 out of 800 babies. Distinctive physical features of this problem, once referred to as mongolism, are almond-shaped eyes, a slightly protruding tongue, stubby hands, a stocky build, and sometimes a deep crease on the palm of the hand. It is now known that Down children have an extra chromosome. That is, cells in the child's body have 47 chromosomes, instead of the usual 46. This condition results from flaws in the parents' egg or sperm cells. Thus, while Down syndrome is *genetic*, it is not *hereditary* and does not "run in the family."

A very significant factor in Down syndrome appears to be the age of parents at the time of conception. The reproductive cells of older men and women are more prone to errors during cell division, which raises the odds that an extra chromosome will be present. Mothers in their early twenties have about 1 chance in 2000 of giving birth to a Down syndrome baby. At age 40 the odds increase to about 1 in 105. By age 48 the risk reaches 1 in 12. Recent research has determined that the age of the father is also linked to increased risk. In about 25 percent of cases the father is the source of the extra chromosome (de la Cruz & Muller, 1983).

These rather significant changes in risk should be considered in family planning. There is no "cure" for Down syndrome. However, these children are usually loving and responsive, and they can make progress in a caring environment. Experts working with Down syndrome children emphasize that they can do most of the things that other children can do, only more slowly (Pueschel et al., 1978). There is evidence that Down children continue to learn and to make slow mental progress well into adulthood (Berry et al., 1984). The best hope for Down syndrome victims therefore lies in specially tailored educational programs that enable them to lead fuller lives.

Learning Check

1. The distribution of IQ's approximates a _____ (bell-shaped) curve.
2. The association between IQ and "high-status" jobs shows that "high-status" jobs require more intelligence.   T or F?
3. Women tend to excel on test items that require verbal ability, vocabulary, and rote learning.   T or F?
4. Only about 6 percent of the population score above 140 on IQ tests.   T or F?
5. An IQ score below 90 indicates mental retardation.   T or F?
6. Many cases of mental retardation without known organic causes appear to be _____.
7. According to Howard Gardner's theory, the three basic human intelligences are: linguistic skills, logic, and spatial skills.   T or F?

Match:

8. ____ PKU
9. ____ Microcephaly
10. ____ Hydrocephaly
11. ____ Cretinism
12. ____ Down Syndrome

A. Too little thyroid hormone
B. Very small brain
C. 47 chromosomes
D. Lack of an important enzyme
E. Excess of cerebrospinal fluid
F. Caused by a lack of oxygen at birth

Answers: 1. normal 2. F 3. T 4. F 5. F 6. familial 7. F 8. D 9. B 10. E 11. A 12. C

Heredity and Environment— Super Rats and Family Trees

Question: Is intelligence inherited?

This seemingly simple question is loaded with controversy. Some psychologists believe intelligence is strongly affected by heredity. Many others think that environment is dominant. Let's examine some of the evidence for each view.

In a classic study of genetic factors in learning, Tryon (1929) managed to breed separate strains of "maze-bright" and "maze-dull" rats (animals that were extremely "bright" or "stupid" at learning mazes). After several generations of breeding, the slowest "super rat" outperformed the best "dull" rat. This and other studies of **eugenics** (selective breeding for desirable characteristics) suggest that some traits are highly influenced by heredity.

Question: That may be true, but is maze learning really a measure of intelligence?

No, it isn't. Tryon's study seemed to show that intelligence is inherited, but later researchers found the "bright" rats were simply more motivated by food and less easily distracted during testing (Whimbey, 1980). When they weren't chasing after rat chow, the "bright" rats were no more intelligent than the supposedly dull rats. Because of such problems, animal studies cannot tell us with certainty how heredity and environment affect intelligence. Let's see what human studies reveal.

Most people are aware that there is a moderate similarity in the intelligence of parents and their children, or be-

tween brothers and sisters. As Figure 17–6 shows, the similarity in IQ scores among relatives grows in proportion to their closeness on the family tree.

Question: Does that indicate that intelligence is hereditary?

Not necessarily, because brothers, sisters, and parents share similar environments as well as similar heredity. To separate heredity and environment, we need to make some selected comparisons.

Twin Studies Notice in Figure 17–6 that the IQ scores of fraternal twins are more alike than those of ordinary siblings. **Fraternal twins** come from two separate eggs fertilized at the same time. Thus, they are no more genetically alike than ordinary siblings. Why then, should the twins' IQ scores be more similar? The reason is environmental: Parents treat twins more alike than ordinary siblings, resulting in a closer match in IQ's.

More striking similarities are observed with **identical twins,** who develop from a single egg and have *identical* genes. At the top of Figure 17–6 you can see that identical twins who grow up in the same family have highly correlated IQ's. This is what we would expect with identical heredity and highly similar environments. Now, let's consider what happens when identical twins are reared apart. As you can see, the correlation drops, but only from .86 to .72. Psychologists who emphasize genetics believe these figures show that intelligence is 70 to 80 percent hereditary (Eysenck, 1981).

Fig. 17–6 *Approximate correlations between IQ scores for persons with varying degrees of genetic and environmental similarity. Notice that the correlations grow smaller as the degree of genetic similarity declines. Also note that a shared environment increases the correlation in all cases. (Estimates from Bouchard, 1983, and Henderson, 1982.)*

Ψ Highlight 17–2
Can Intelligence Be Taught?

The traditional answer to the question, "Can intelligence be taught?" is "No." Coaching, for instance, has little positive effect on aptitude and intelligence test scores (Kulik, Bangert-Drowns, & Kulik, 1984). But is a brief period of coaching a fair test of the modifiability of intelligence? Apparently not. There is increasing evidence that extended, in-depth training in thinking skills can increase tested intelligence (Whimbey, 1980).

At the forefront of such efforts is Israeli psychologist Reuven Feuerstein (FOY-er-shtine). Feuerstein and his colleagues have developed a program they call Instrumental Enrichment. The program involves hundreds of hours of guided problem solving. The emphasis throughout is on remedying the kinds of gaps and flaws in thinking that cause lower IQ scores (Feuerstein et al., 1980). Feuerstein and other researchers have shown that such training can, in fact, raise IQ scores (Haywood, Meyers, & Switsky, 1982; Messerer et al., 1984).

Instrumental Enrichment is now used in about 4000 American schools and institutions. The problem with such training, however, is that it is very time consuming. In recognition of this problem, other psychologists are now developing computer programs to teach problem solving, effective thinking, and other elements of intelligence (Pellegrino, 1985). With our growing understanding of how people think, and with the tireless aid of computers, it may indeed become common in schools to "teach intelligence."

Fig. 17–7 *Comparison of an adopted child and a biological child reared in the same family. (After Kamin, 1981.)*

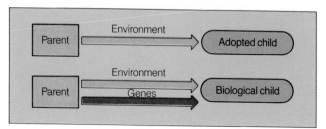

Question: How do environmentalists interpret the figures?

Environmentalists point out that some separated twins differ by as much as 20 IQ points. In every case where this occurs there are large educational and environmental differences between the twins (Whimbey, 1980). Also separated twins are almost always placed in homes socially and educationally similar to their biological parents. This fact would tend to inflate apparent genetic effects by making the separated twins' IQ's more alike (Kamin, 1981).

The Burt Controversy   For many years hereditarians replied to the preceding point by citing the work of British psychologist Cyril Burt. Burt claimed to have studied 53 sets of separated identical twins. Their IQ's, he said, were highly correlated, even though the twins were placed in homes unrelated in socioeconomic status. Unfortunately, Burt's data are now known to be a product of fraud. American psychologist Leon Kamin (1974, 1981) noticed that Burt's numbers "looked funny" and later went on to prove that Burt had made up the twins.

It is clear that Burt's twin studies cannot be counted as evidence in favor of a hereditary view of intelligence. However, hereditarians argue that most of Burt's findings have been duplicated by others (Rimland & Musinger, 1977). Be that as it may, the Burt affair has caused some psychologists to revise their thinking on the heritability of intelligence. Many now estimate that intelligence is only 45 percent hereditary; some even question this figure. The truth of the matter is that it may never be possible to accurately say to what degree intelligence is genetically determined.

Strong evidence for an environmental view of intelligence comes from families having one adopted child and one biological child. As Figure 17–7 shows, parents contribute genes *and* environment to their biological child. With an adopted child they contribute only environment. If intelligence is highly genetic, the IQ's of biological children should be more like their parents' IQ's than are the IQ's of adopted children. However, two recent studies show that children reared by the same mother resemble her in IQ to the same degree; it does not matter whether they share her genes (Horn et al., 1979; Kamin, 1981; Weinberg, 1977).

Question: How much can environment alter intelligence?

IQ and Environment   In one study, striking increases in IQ were observed in 25 children who were moved from an orphanage to more stimulating environments. The children, all considered mentally retarded and unadoptable, were moved to an institution where they received personal attention from adults. Later, these supposedly retarded children were adopted by parents who gave them love, a family, and a stimulating environment. The IQ's of the children showed an average gain of 29 points. For one child the increase was an amazing 58 points. A second group of initially less "retarded" children who remained in the orphanage *lost* an average of 26 IQ points (Skeels, 1966)!

The educational level of parents creates another interesting environmental effect. In a study done in France, IQ scores for 32 adopted children were compared with the scores of brothers and sisters who stayed with the biological parents. In most cases the biological parents were poorly educated and worked in nonprofessional jobs. The adopted children had mostly gone to families of higher educational and economic status. It was found that average IQ scores matched almost perfectly those of children from similar family backgrounds. That is, children who stayed with their biological parents had lower IQs than their adopted brothers and sisters. Basically, the adoptees performed the same as nonadopted upper-middle-class children (Schiff et al., 1978). This and the preceding study are an encouraging indication that intelligence can be raised by an improved environment. (Also, see Highlight 17–2.)

Some environmental effects are more subtle than the previous examples indicate. Psychologist Robert Zajonc (ZYE-onz) has found that IQ decreases as family size grows. The brightest children come from the smallest families, and within a family the brightest children are, on the average, those who are born first (Zajonc, 1975; Zajonc & Markus, 1975). Zajonc believes that each arriving baby temporarily lowers the "average intellectual level" in the family, thus making the environment less stimulating. (Have you ever tried to have an intellectual chat with a baby?) Theoretically, the effects of family size can be minimized by spacing children at least 2 years apart.

Question: If I am the last child from a large family, how should I take these findings?

Not too seriously! The average IQ score for the oldest of two children is only 10 points higher than the average for the last of nine children. Differences of this amount may mean little in terms of what a person can actually do. Also, later born children may excel in other ways (see Chapter 18). Later-borns, for instance, usually have excellent social skills, leading to greater popularity among peers and schoolmates. And, as a final point, there is evidence that birth-order differences in IQ may disappear by age 17 (McCall, 1984).

Summary In summary, few psychologists seriously believe that heredity is not a factor in intelligence, and all accept that environment affects it. Estimates of the contributions of each factor continue to vary. But ultimately, both camps agree that improving social conditions or education can raise intelligence. There is probably no limit to how far *down* intelligence can go in a poor environment, but heredity may impose some limits on how far up IQ can go, even under ideal conditions (Scarr-Salapatek, 1971). It might help, then, to think of inherited intellectual potential as a rubber band that is stretched by outside forces. A long rubber band may be stretched more easily, but a shorter one can be stretched to the same length if enough force is applied (Stern, 1956). Of course a superior genetic "gift" may allow for a higher maximum IQ, but in the final analysis intelligence reflects development as well as potential, nurture as well as nature.

Learning Check

1. Selective breeding for desirable characteristics is called _____.

2. The closest similarity in IQ's would be observed for:
   a. parents and their children   *b.* identical twins reared apart   *c.* fraternal twins reared together   *d.* siblings reared together

3. Most psychologists believe that intelligence is 90 percent hereditary.   T or F?

4. Except for slight variations during testing, IQ cannot be changed.   T or F?

5. Environmental effects are probably more capable of lowering IQ than of raising it.   T or F?

6. According to the research of Robert Zajonc, children in large families provide extra stimulation for one another, thereby increasing intelligence.   T or F?

Answers: 1. eugenics 2. b 3. F 4. F 5. T 6. F

Applications

Intelligence in Perspective—
Are Intelligence Tests Intelligent?

Almost everyone has some curiosity about how they would score on an intelligence test. If you would like to get a rough estimate of your IQ, take the following self-administered test.

Dove Counterbalance Intelligence Test

Time limit: 5 minutes   Circle the correct answer.

1. T-bone Walker got famous for playing what?
a. trombone   c. T-flute   e. "hambone"
b. piano   d. guitar

2. A "gas head" is a person who has a _____.
a. fast-moving car   d. habit of stealing cars
b. stable of "lace"   e. long jail record for
c. "process"   arson

3. If you throw the dice and 7 is showing on the top, what is facing down?
a. 7   c. boxcars   e. 11
b. snake eyes   d. little joes

4. Cheap chitlings (not the kind you purchase at a frozen-food counter) will taste rubbery unless they are cooked long enough. How soon can you quit cooking them to eat and enjoy them?
a. 45 minutes   d. one week (on a low flame)
b. two hours   e. one hour
c. 24 hours

5. Bird or Yardbird was the jacket jazz lovers from coast to coast hung on _____?
a. Lester Young   d. Charlie Parker
b. Peggy Lee   e. Birdman of Alcatraz
c. Benny Goodman

6. A "handkerchief head" is:
a. a cool cat   c. an Uncle Tom   e. a preacher
b. porter   d. a hoddi

7. Jet is _____.
a. an East Oakland motorcycle club
b. one of the gangs in *West Side Story*
c. a news and gossip magazine
d. a way of life for the very rich

8. "Bo Diddly" is a _____.
a. game for children   d. new dance
b. down-home cheap wine   e. Moejoe call
c. down-home singer

9. Which word is most out of place here?
a. splib   c. gray   e. black
b. blood   d. spook

10. If a pimp is uptight with a woman who gets state aid, what does he mean when he talks about "Mother's Day"?
a. second Sunday in May
b. third Sunday in June
c. first of every month
d. none of these
e. first and fifteenth of every month

11. How much does a "short dog" cost?
a. 15¢   c. 35¢   e. 86¢ plus tax
b. $2   d. 5¢

12. Many people say that "Juneteenth" (June 10th) should be made a legal holiday because this was the day when:
a. the slaves were freed in the United States
b. the slaves were freed in Texas
c. the slaves were freed in Jamaica
d. the slaves were freed in California
e. Martin Luther King was born
f. Booker T. Washington died

13. If a man is called a "blood," then he is a _____.
a. fighter   d. hungry hemophile
b. Mexican-American   e. red man or Indian
c. Negro

14. What are the Dixie Hummingbirds?
a. a part of the KKK
b. a swamp disease
c. a modern gospel group
d. a Mississippi Negro paramilitary strike force
e. deacons

15. The opposite of square is _____.
a. round   c. down   e. lame
b. up   d. hip

Applications: Intelligence in Perspective—Are Intelligence Tests Intelligent?

Answers: 1. d 2. c 3. a 4. c 5. d 6. c 7. c 8. c 9. c 10. c 11. c 12. b 13. c 14. c 15. d

If you scored 14 on this exam, your IQ is approximately 100, indicating average intelligence. If you scored 11 or less, you are mentally retarded. With luck and the help of a special educational program, we may be able to teach you a few simple skills!

Race and IQ

Question: Isn't this test a little unfair?

No, it is *very* unfair. It was constructed by black sociologist Adrian Dove as "a half serious attempt to show that we're just not talking the same language." Dove tried to slant his test as much in favor of urban black culture as he believes the typical intelligence test is biased toward a white middle-class background. (Due to its age, the test is probably now also unfair for anyone under 30.)

Dove's test is a thought-provoking reply to the fact that black children in the United States score an average of about 15 points lower on standardized IQ tests than do white children. By reversing the bias, Dove has shown that intelligence tests are not equally valid for all groups. As Kagan (1973) has commented, "If the Wechsler and Binet scales were translated into Spanish, Swahili, and Chinese and given to every 10-year-old in Latin America, East Africa, or China, the majority would obtain IQ scores in the mentally retarded range."

Certainly we cannot believe that children of different cultures are all retarded. The fault must lie in the test. To avoid this problem, some psychologists have tried to develop **culture-fair tests** that do not disadvantage certain groups. (For a sample of culture-fair test items, see Fig. 17–8.)

Biased tests are not the only IQ issue blacks have confronted. Arthur Jensen, writing in the *Harvard Educational Review,* claimed in 1969 that the lower IQ scores of blacks can be primarily attributed to "genetic heritage."

Before we go any further, it is important to note that few psychologists support Jensen. Soon after Jensen made his claim, psychologists responded with a number of counterarguments.

First, it is no secret that as a group blacks in the United States are more likely than whites to live in environments that are physically, educationally, and intellectually impoverished. As one critic notes, test scores are meaningless if they result from unequal educational opportunity. Further, it is tragic if these scores are then used to deny further educational opportunities (Grover, 1983).

Second, the gap in IQ between blacks and whites is small enough to be closed by environment. Jensen's reply to this claim is that special educational programs such as Head Start have proved incapable of narrowing the IQ gap. But it is essentially ridiculous to expect

Fig. 17–8 *Sample items from a culture-fair test. 1. Which pattern is different from the remaining four? (Number 3.) 2. Which of the five figures on the right would properly continue the three on the left—that is, fill the blank? (Number 5.) 3. Which of the figures on the right should go in the square on the left to make it look right? (Number 2.) 4. At left the dot is outside the square and inside the circle. In which of the figures on the right could you put a dot outside the square and inside the circle? (Number 3.) (Courtesy of R. B. Cattell.)*

Applications: Intelligence in Perspective—Are Intelligence Tests Intelligent?

that a brief summer program or a few hours a day are enough to counteract the differences in educational and environmental advantages of blacks and whites.

Third, Jensen ignores the point made by the Dove Test. The assumptions, biases, and content of standard IQ tests do not allow meaningful comparisons between ethnic, cultural, or racial groups (Garcia, 1977). As Leon Kamin (1981) says, "The important fact is that we cannot say which sex (or race) might be more intelligent, because we have no way of measuring 'intelligence.' We have only IQ tests." Kamin's point is that the makers of IQ tests designed test items that would give men and women equal IQ scores. They could just as easily put together an IQ test that would give blacks and whites in this country equal scores. Differences in IQ scores are not a fact of nature, but a decision by the test makers. This is why whites do better on IQ tests written by whites, and blacks do better on IQ tests written by blacks. Another example of this fact is an intelligence test made up of 100 words selected from the *Dictionary of Afro-American Slang*. Williams (1975) gave the test to 100 black and 100 white high school students in St. Louis and found that the black group averaged 36 points higher than the white group.

Perhaps the most devastating criticism of Jensen is that his logic is faulty. Consider this example: Corn comes in different varieties bred to grow to a certain height. If we plant tall and short varieties side by side in the same field, we will observe a genetically determined difference in their height at maturity. But what if we take corn (all the same variety) and plant half in a fertile field and half in poor soil? Again we observe a difference in maximum height, but this time it is clearly a mistake to assume the difference is genetically caused.

Only when black children are raised in exactly the same surroundings as white children can hereditary factors be clearly assessed. Along this line, one revealing study looked at black children adopted by white families. These children had IQ scores averaging 106, which is comparable to the national average for white children (Scarr-Salapatek & Weinberg, 1975). It is not clear if the black children were actually "brighter" as a result of being raised by white families or if they were just better prepared to take a "white" test. The fact remains, that when an equal opportunity for intellectual development can close the IQ gap, we must abandon narrow genetic views of IQ differences.

Questioning the Concept of IQ— Beyond the Numbers Game

Blacks are not the only segment of the population with reason to question the validity of intelligence testing and the role of heredity in determining intelligence. The clarifications won by blacks extend to others as well.

Consider the 9-year-old child facing this question on an intelligence test: "Which of the following does not belong with the others? Roller skates, airplane, train, bicycle." If the child fails to answer "airplane," does this reveal a lack of intelligence? It can be argued that an intelligent choice could be based on any of the following: Roller skates are not typically used for transportation; an airplane is the only nonland item; a train can't be steered; a bicycle is the only item with just two wheels (Sheils & Monroe, 1976). The parents of a child who misses this question may have reason to be angry since educational systems tend to classify children and then make the label stick.

Recent court decisions have led some states to outlaw use of intelligence tests in public schools (see the Exploration section). Criticism of intelligence testing has also come from the academic community. Harvard University psychologist David McClelland (1973) believes IQ is of little value in predicting real competence in dealing effectively with the world. McClelland concedes that IQ predicts school performance, but when he compared a group of straight-A college students with another group having poor grades, he found no differences in later career success.

Standardized Testing   In addition to IQ tests, 400 to 500 million standardized multiple-choice tests are given in schools and workplaces around the nation each year. Many, like the Scholastic Aptitude Test, may determine whether a person is admitted to college. Other tests—for employment, licensing, and certification—directly affect the lives of thousands by qualifying or disqualifying them for jobs.

Widespread reliance on standardized intelligence tests and aptitude tests raises questions about the relative good and harm they do. On the positive side, tests can open opportunities as well as close them. A high test score may allow a disadvantaged youth to enter college, or it may identify a child who is bright but emotionally disturbed. Test scores may also be fairer and more objective than judgments made by admis-

Applications: Intelligence in Perspective—Are Intelligence Tests Intelligent?

sions officers or employment interviewers. Also, tests *do* accurately predict academic performance. The fact that academic performance *does not* predict later success may call for an overhaul of college course work, not an end to testing.

On the negative side, mass testing can occasionally exclude people of obvious ability. In one recent case a student who was seventh in his class at Columbia University, and a member of Phi Beta Kappa, was denied entrance to law school because he had low scores on the Law School Admissions Test (*U.S. News and World Report,* 1979). Other complaints relate to the frequent appearance of bad or ambiguous questions on standardized tests, overuse of class time to prepare students for the tests (instead of teaching general skills), and in the case of intelligence tests the charge that tests are often biased.

What should we make of the positive and negative aspects of standardized testing? Robert Glaser (1977) says we should remember that tests are "limited tools for limited purposes." Glaser also says that tests are now used primarily to *select people.* In schools they could instead be used to *adapt instruction* to the strengths, weaknesses, and needs of each student— thereby increasing the chances of success.

Conclusion

An application of the preceding discussion to your personal understanding of intelligence can be summarized in this way. Intelligence tests are a two-edged sword;

we have learned much from their use, yet they have the potential to do great harm. In the final analysis it is important to remember—as Howard Gardner has pointed out—that creativity, motivation, physical health, mechanical aptitude, artistic ability, and numerous other qualities not measured by intelligence tests contribute to achievement of life goals. Also remember that IQ is *not intelligence.* IQ is an *index* of intelligence—as defined by a particular test. Change the test and you change the score. An IQ is not some permanent number stamped on the forehead of a child that forever determines potential.

Let us end on an optimistic note. As discussed earlier in Highlight 17–2, some psychologists and educators are seeking ways to teach necessary intellectual skills to all children. In some cases their success has been striking. One experiment divided 40 children from extremely disadvantaged (slum) families into two groups. Children in the control group received no extra attention or training. Beginning shortly after birth, the experimental group was given a wide variety of stimulation to develop perceptual, motor, and language abilities. At age 2 the children were placed in small classes with other children and several teachers. Each child received lots of teacher attention and exposure to a broad range of topics and thinking exercises. When tested at age 5½ the control group had an average IQ of about 95; the average for the experimental group was 124 (reported by Whimbey, 1980). These results should be encouraging to everyone interested in the fulfillment of human potentials.

Learning Check

1. The WAIS–R, Stanford-Binet, and Dove Test are all culture-fair intelligence scales.   T or F?
2. Jensen's claim that genetics accounts for racial differences in average IQ ignores environmental differences and the cultural bias inherent in standard IQ tests.   T or F?
3. IQ scores predict school performance.   T or F?
4. IQ is not intelligence; it is an index of intelligence.   T or F?

Answers: 1. F   2. T   3. T   4. T

Chapter Summary

■ *Intelligence* refers to one's general capacity to act purposefully, think rationally, and deal effectively with the environment. In practice, intelligence is *operationally defined* by the creation of intelligence tests.

■ To be of any value, a psychological test must be *reliable* (give consistent results). A worthwhile test must also have *validity*, meaning that it measures what it claims to measure. Widely used intelligence tests are *objective* (they give the same result when scored by different people) and *standardized* (the same procedures are always used in giving the test, and norms have been established so scores can be interpreted).

■ The first practical intelligence test was assembled by Alfred Binet. A modern version of Binet's test is the *Stanford-Binet Intelligence Scale*. A second major intelligence test is the *Wechsler Adult Intelligence Scale–Revised* (WAIS–R). The WAIS–R measures both *verbal* and *performance* intelligence. Intelligence tests have also been produced for use with groups. *Group tests* include the *Army Alpha*, the *SAT*, the *ACT*, and the *CQT*.

■ Intelligence is expressed in terms of an *intelligence quotient* (IQ). IQ is defined as *mental age* (MA) divided by *chronological age* (CA) and then multiplied by 100. An "average" IQ of 100 occurs when mental age equals chronological age.

■ IQ scores become fairly stable at about age 6 and they become increasingly reliable thereafter. On the average, IQ scores continue to gradually increase until middle age. Later intellectual declines are slight for most people until their seventies. Shortly before death a more significant *terminal decline* in intelligence is often observed.

■ The distribution of IQ scores approximates a *normal curve*. There are no overall differences between males and females in tested intelligence, but intellectual strengths exist for each. IQ is strongly related to school grades and job status. The second association may be somewhat artificial.

■ People with IQ's in the *gifted* or "genius" range of above 140 tend to be superior in many respects. By criteria other than IQ, a large proportion of children might be considered as gifted in one way or another. Intellectually gifted children often have difficulties in average classrooms and benefit from special accelerated programs.

■ The term *mentally retarded* is traditionally applied to those whose IQ falls below 70, or who lack various *adaptive behaviors*. Further classifications of retardation are: *mild* (52–67), *moderate* (36–51), *severe* (20–35), and *profound* (below 20). Chances for educational success are related to the degree of retardation.

■ About 25 percent of the cases of mental retardation are *organic*, being caused by *birth injuries*, *fetal damage*, *metabolic disorders*, or *genetic abnormalities*. The remaining 75 percent are of undetermined cause. Many of these are thought to be the result of *familial retardation*, a generally low level of educational and intellectual stimulation in the home, coupled with poverty and poor nutrition.

■ Five specific forms of organic retardation are: *phenylketonuria (PKU)*, *microcephaly*, *hydrocephaly*, *cretinism*, and *Down Syndrome*.

■ Studies of *eugenics* in animals and familial relationships in humans demonstrate that intelligence is partially determined by heredity. However, environment is also important, as revealed by changes in tested intelligence induced by stimulating environments. There is increasing evidence that some elements of intelligence can be taught. Intelligence therefore reflects the combined effects of both heredity and environment in the development of intellectual abilities.

The Larry P. Case—"Six-Hour Retardates"

The case: Larry P. v. the California State Superintendent of Education.

The issue: Larry P. was one of six black children who claimed that biased IQ test scores were wrongly used to place them in classes for the educable mentally retarded (EMR).

The outcome: In a landmark decision a federal judge ruled that IQ test scores alone could no longer be used for EMR placement. The ruling has virtually eliminated IQ testing in California schools. It is likely to do the same in many other states.

The bare facts of the Larry P. case only hint at the interesting issues it raised. Testimony during the trial brought out the following:

For Larry P.: All six youngsters suing the state had scored below 75 on standardized IQ tests. But they scored from 17 to 35 points higher when retested by psychologists who used language and examples the children were familiar with.

For the State: Experts admitted that IQ test questions can be easier for some groups than for others. However, they held that IQ tests accurately predict school performance and are therefore valid.

For Larry P.: Witnesses pointed out that EMR assignments are almost always permanent. Witnesses also described the devastating effects of placing a child of normal

intelligence in an EMR class. One researcher found that other students commonly refer to EMR students with cruel nicknames. EMR students are not expected to progress beyond the third- to fifth-grade level. Thus, by the time of graduation, a child of normal intelligence would be hopelessly behind other students. After graduation EMR students find it difficult to get jobs, because they have been labeled "retarded."

For the State: Defense experts claimed that IQ tests help prevent mistakes in EMR assignments—for example, by revealing the true potential of a child who might be considered "slow" by a biased teacher. They also defended the EMR program as an effort to help less able students.

For Larry P.: Roughly twice as many black and Hispanic children are found in EMR classes than would normally be expected—a fact suggesting a defect in the tests, not in the children (Ristow, 1978).

Ignorance versus Stupidity In the end the judge ruled that IQ tests violate federal antidiscrimination laws. He was convinced, he said, that the tests are based mainly on verbal tasks that are unfair to children whose home environment does not provide practice in formal English or in verbal skills. He further held that, "if tests suggest that a young child is probably going to be a poor student, the school cannot, on that basis alone,

deny that child the opportunity to develop and improve the academic skills necessary for success in our society".

Supporters of the Larry P. decision believe it affirms the rights of disadvantaged children, whose ignorance—a lack of knowledge—has been mistaken for stupidity—a lack of intelligence. One such supporter is Jane Mercer, a sociologist who gave key testimony in the case.

Six-Hour Retardates Mercer testified that the more a child's family is like the average white Anglo middle-class norm, the better the child scores on IQ tests. Mercer believes that schools often label children retarded, when actually the children only lack culturally tied knowledge (Mercer, 1977). Mercer has found that many black or Hispanic EMR students show abundant signs of normal intelligence. For example, a child who does poorly in the classroom or on an IQ test may function perfectly well at home and in the community. Mercer refers to such children as "six-hour retardates"—youngsters who are "retarded" only during the school day.

Question: If standardized IQ tests cannot be used to assess student abilities, what can?

SOMPA Mercer and her associate June Lewis think they have an answer. They call it SOMPA, which stands for System of Multicultural Pluralistic Assessment. SOMPA is not a new test. Rather, it's a con-

Exploration: The Larry P. Case—"Six-Hour Retardates"

troversial new way of looking at children. Because it takes cultural differences into account, SOMPA is the only system that currently meets the standards established by the Larry P. case.

Question: How does SOMPA differ from standard IQ tests?

SOMPA combines three ways of looking at child: a medical model, a social model, and a pluralistic model.

Medical Model   SOMPA uses existing tests of dexterity, vision, hearing, or general health to determine if a child has any problems in these areas. In this way physical problems are identified that may be causing low school performance.

Social Model   Scores on the standard WISC–R are combined with evaluations of the child's behavior outside the classroom. By determining how the child functions with family, friends, and in the community, the school psychologist can avoid the mistake of creating a "six-hour retardate" on the basis of a test score.

Pluralistic Model   SOMPA assumes that when everything else is held constant (educational advan-

tages at home, especially), the child who has learned the most probably has the most "learning potential." Off-campus environments, however, are not equal. SOMPA therefore assumes that true potential can be masked by a child's cultural background. To avoid this problem, SOMPA compares each child's WISC–R score with that of children from similar backgrounds. The result is what Mercer calls a child's Estimated Learning Potential (ELP). Mercer considers ELP a truer measure of a child's intelligence than the standard IQ (Mercer, 1977).

To show how SOMPA works, Mercer offers an example. Maria Gonzales is 7. She lives with her mother, father, and five brothers and sisters in an inner city barrio. Maria's mother and father both grew up in rural Mexico, where the mother finished fourth grade and the father second grade. Maria's family speaks only Spanish. The average score for a child like Maria—with a background so different from core Anglo culture—is about 85. Maria's score on the WISC–R was 114, almost 30 points above this average. Mercer estimates Maria's real learning potential at 133. If her family had been more like the middle-class norm,

Maria's score would have remained at 114. Considering her age and background, Maria's performance on the WISC–R is truly outstanding (Mercer, 1977). Maria is probably a gifted child whose potential should not be wasted.

The idea behind SOMPA, then, is to keep average kids out of classes for the mentally retarded and to identify gifted children who might otherwise be passed over as average. If Mercer is correct in her thinking, SOMPA may launch a new generation of intelligence measures and spur new ways to meet the educational needs of children from differing backgrounds.

Understandably, both the Larry P. decision and SOMPA are controversial. Some psychologists object to courts making educational decisions. Others are uncomfortable with the idea of using multiple norms to interpret IQ test scores. If you were the judge, how would you have ruled? If you were a school psychologist, how would you feel about using SOMPA? In your opinion what role should IQ tests have in a democratic society?

Learning Check

1. The basic issue of the Larry P. case was whether children's IQs are lowered by placement in EMR classes.   T or F?
2. Before the Larry P. case, placement in EMR classes was almost always done on the basis of group IQ test scores.   T or F?
3. SOMPA is designed to obtain IQ scores from an assessment of a child's physical health and social functioning.   T or F?
4. In the SOMPA system, IQ scores are compared with norms for children of similar cultural and social backgrounds.   T or F?

Answers: 1. F   2. T   3. F   4. T

Questions for Discussion

1. In what ways might our society encourage the development of different intellectual skills in males and females?

2. Do you know your IQ? Would you like to know it? Why?

3. What advantages or disadvantages would you expect to be associated with knowing your own IQ? With having a teacher know your IQ? With your parents' knowing your IQ?

4. How might public education be restructured to encourage full intellectual development for all children? How might grading be changed to reflect broader definitions of intelligence?

5. How would you feel about the application of eugenics to human reproduction? Can you think of circumstances under which you would or would not consider it acceptable?

6. The debate over the relative importance of heredity and environment in determining intelligence has raged for decades. Why do you think the debate has lasted so long and attracted so much interest? If the heritability of IQ could be known with certainty, what difference would it make?

Chapter 18 | Personality: Types, Traits, and Testing

Chapter Preview
The Hidden Essence

Rural Colorado. The car lurched as we made our way through the last few yards of brain-jarring ruts. An ancient farmhouse stood to one side, a hulking monument to neglect.

Annette was out of the house—hooting and whooping—before we had stopped. If anyone was suited for a move to the "wilds" of Colorado, it was Annette, the "terror of Tenth Street." Still, it was difficult to imagine a more radical change. After separating from her husband, she had traded housewifery in the city for survival in the hinterlands. Survival, by the way, is no exaggeration. Annette was working as a ranch hand and as a lumberjack (lumberjill?), trying to make it alone through some hard winters.

So radical were the changes in Annette's life, I must confess I expected just as radical a change in her. She was, on the contrary, more her "old self" than ever.

Perhaps you have had a similar experience. After several years of separation it is always intriguing to see an old friend. Often you will be struck at first by the ways in which the person has changed in appearance, interests, and knowledge. Soon, however, you will probably be pleased to discover how superficial such changes really are. Under it all there is a core that ties the semistranger before you to the person you once knew. It is exactly this core of consistency that psychologists have in mind when they use the term personality.

The Extra Dimension *Despite our advanced technology, the human dimension still determines success or failure in many situations. Human error contributed significantly to the Three Mile Island Nuclear Power Plant accident. Similarly, it is often said that the most dangerous part of an automobile is "the nut at the wheel." Without doubt personality touches many aspects of our daily lives. Selecting a mate, choosing friends, getting along with co-workers, voting for a president, and numerous other activities raise questions about personality. But what is personality? How does it differ from temperament, character, or attitudes? How stable are personality characteristics? These and related questions are the concerns of this chapter.*

Survey Questions How do psychologists use the term *personality?* Does body build have any connection with personality? Are some personality traits more basic or important than others? Does birth order have any effect on personality? What is psychological androgyny (and is it contagious)? How do psychologists measure personality? What causes shyness? What can be done about it? How much does heredity influence personality?

Resources

Do You Have Personality?

"Jim's not handsome, but he has a great personality." "My father's business friends think he's a nice guy, but they should see him at home where his real personality comes out." "It's hard to believe they're sisters. They have such opposite personalities."

It's obvious from such statements that we use the term *personality* daily. But when questioned, many people seem hard pressed to define personality. Most simply end up saying something about "charm," "charisma," or "style." If you have used *personality* in such ways, you have given it a different meaning than a psychologist would. To a psychologist it makes little sense to ask, "Do I have personality?" or to proclaim, "She has lots of personality." In psychological terms everyone has personality.

Question: Then how do psychologists use the term?

Since personality is a *hypothetical construct,* * psychologists give it different meanings. However, most regard **personality** as a person's *unique and enduring behavior patterns.* In other words, personality refers to the consistency in who you are, have been, and will become. It also refers to the special combination of talents, attitudes, values, hopes, loves, hates, and habits that marks each person as unique.

Question: How is psychologists' use of the term different from the way most people use it?

Many people confuse personality with what is technically known as **character.** The term *character* implies that a person has been *evaluated,* not just described. If, by saying someone has "personality," you mean the person is friendly, outgoing, and attractive, you are really referring to character. However, in some cultures it is considered desirable for a person to be fierce, aggressive, and competitive. So, while everyone in a particular culture has personality, not everyone has character—or at least not good character. (Do you know any good characters?)

Personality can also be distinguished from **temperament.** As mentioned in Chapter 15, temperament is the "raw material" from which personality is formed. Temperament refers to the hereditary aspects of one's emotional nature: sensitivity, strength and speed of response, prevailing mood, and fluctuations in mood (Allport, 1961).

*An explanatory concept that is not directly observable.

As you may recall, differences in temperament are apparent from birth onward. (The impact of heredity on personality is discussed further in this chapter's Exploration.)

Probing personality is difficult because it cannot be directly observed. Now that you know what psychologists mean by personality, let's see how it has been studied.

Categorizing Personality— "Sorry, You're Not My Type"

Have you ever asked a friend, "What type of person is she (or he)?" before meeting someone new? An interest in **personality types** is quite natural. Informally, it is common to speak of the executive type, the athletic type, the motherly type, the strong silent type, and the like. Everyday conceptions of personality types abound.

Question: How valid is it to speak of personality "types"?

Over the years psychologists have proposed various ways to categorize personalities. Consider the idea, first advanced

Fig. 18–1   *Does this man have personality? Do you?*

by Swiss psychiatrist Carl Jung (yung), that a person is either an **introvert** (shy, self-centered person) or an **extrovert** (bold, outgoing person). These terms are so widely used that you may think of yourself and your friends as being one or the other. However, the wildest, wittiest, most party-loving "extrovert" you know is introverted at times, and extremely introverted persons are assertive and sociable in some situations. In short, two categories seem insufficient to fully express personality. Perhaps, then, we need more categories. Let's consider William Sheldon's **constitutional theory** of personality, which describes three personality types.

Body Build and Personality   In the early 1950s Sheldon (1954) carefully analyzed body dimensions of thousands of male college students. From this work Sheldon concluded that physique is a combination of **endomorphy, mesomorphy,** and **ectomorphy.** Endomorphy is characterized by a fat, soft, round body structure. (Sheldon noted that endomorphs float in water!) Mesomorphy is marked by a robust development of muscles, bones, and ligaments. (Mesomorphs do not necessarily have athletic bodies. A "walking muscle" might be a more apt description.) Ectomorphy is characterized by underdeveloped muscles and bones. The ectomorph is flat-chested, thin, frail, and linear. (But has a large head!)

Question: How can I tell if I am an endomorph, mesomorph, or ectomorph?

You are probably none of them. "Pure" examples of each physique are rare. The average person's **somatotype** (body type) is a mixture of all three components. In rating body structure, a number from 1 to 7 is assigned to each dimension. The average person rates around 4 on each (see Fig. 18–2).

Question: What connection did Sheldon find between body type and personality?

Sheldon compared ratings on 60 features of personality with the three body types. Three personality types emerged: **viscerotonia, somatotonia,** and **cerebrotonia.**

Viscerotonia (VIS-er-oh-TOE-nee-ah) combines sociability, tolerance, and goodwill with a love of eating, sleeping, and physical comfort. Somatotonia (so-MAT-oh-TOE-nee-ah) is characterized by assertiveness, boldness, energy, aggression, a callous attitude toward the feelings of others, and a love of physical exercise. The cerebrotonic (ser-REE-bro-TAWN-ik) individual is self-conscious, shy, sensitive, nervous, and needs privacy and intellectual stimulation.

It may come as no surprise that Sheldon found a strong association between endomorphy and viscerotonia, mesomorphy and somatotonia, ectomorphy and cerebrotonia. But before you leap to conclusions about yourself or your friends, remember that most people are a mixture of the three body types. Also, notice that Sheldon's findings reflect *stereotyped* images of fat, muscular, and thin persons. It is very likely that Sheldon was influenced by such stereotypes when he rated the personalities of his subjects.

Question: Then is there a relationship between body type and personality or isn't there?

In the final analysis, it seems fair to assume that body type affects personality, but only to a minor degree (Cortes & Gatti, 1972). It is as big a mistake to judge people by their bodies as it is to judge books by their covers.

Despite their limitations, type systems still have a place in psychology. You might recall from Chapter 14, for instance, that classifying people as Type A or Type B personalities helps predict their chances of suffering a heart

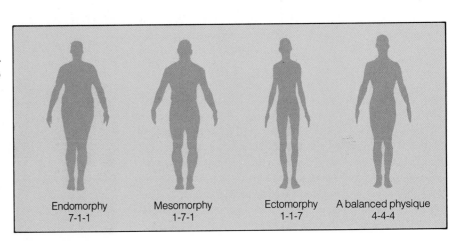

Fig. 18–2 *Sheldon's somatotype system. A 1–7–1 type might be a gymnast or an Olympic weight lifter. Many high-fashion models are 1–1–7 types. A sumo wrestler is typically a 7–1–1 type.*

Endomorphy
7-1-1

Mesomorphy
1-7-1

Ectomorphy
1-1-7

A balanced physique
4-4-4

attack. However, as we seek deeper understanding, most type systems tend to oversimplify personality. A more effective approach is based on the concept of personality *traits*. If you have resisted the idea of putting yourself in an all-or-nothing category, be it introvert, extrovert, endomorph, or whatever, then you may find the trait approach more satisfying.

The Trait Approach—Describe Yourself in 18,000 Words or Less

How many words can you think of to describe the personality of a close friend? You should have little trouble making a long list: Over 18,000 English words refer to personal characteristics (Allport & Odbert, 1936). Many of these words describe personality *traits*. **Traits** are *relatively permanent* and *enduring qualities* that a person shows in most situations. (See Highlight 18–1.) For example, if you are usually optimistic, reserved, or friendly, these qualities might be considered stable traits of your personality.

Question: What if I am sometimes pessimistic, uninhibited, or shy?

The first three qualities are still traits as long as they are most *typical* of your behavior. Let's say Ima Student approaches most situations with optimism, but has a habit of expecting the worst each time she takes a test. If her pessimism is limited to this situation or to a few others, it is still accurate and useful to describe her as an optimistic person.

In general, the trait approach attempts to identify traits that best describe a particular individual. Take a moment to check traits in Table 18–1 that you feel describe your personality. Are the traits you checked of equal importance? Are some stronger or more basic than others? Do any overlap? For example, if you checked "dominant," did you also check "confident" and "bold"? Answers to these questions would interest a **trait theorist**. To understand personality, trait theorists attempt to classify traits and to discover which are most basic.

Question: Are there different kinds of traits?

Classifying Traits Psychologist Gordon Allport (1961), who was deeply interested in personality, identified several kinds of traits. **Common traits** are those shared by most members of a culture. Common traits show how people from a particular nation or culture are similar, but they tell us little about individuals. Since we know that no two people are exactly alike, we must also consider unique personal qualities, or **individual traits.**

Highlight 18–1
Extroverted Study Habits

Where do you prefer to study in the library? The answer may reveal a basic trait of your personality.

As we noted, splitting people into introverted and extroverted *types* is an oversimplification. On the other hand many psychologists regard one's *degree* of introversion/extroversion as one of several important personality *traits*. Viewed in this way, a person's level of introversion/extroversion can have interesting links to behavior.

One recent study found that students scoring high in extroversion chose study locations that provide higher noise levels and more chances for socializing (Campbell & Hawley, 1982).

In the campus library at Colgate University (where the study was done), you can find extroverted students in the second floor lounge. Or, if you prefer, more introverted students can be found studying in the carrels on the first and third floors!

If the difference between common traits and individual traits seems unclear to you, consider this illustration: Each person's hand is unique in the details of its shape (individual traits), but in an anatomy class we can still describe

Table 18–1   Adjective Checklist

Check the traits you feel are characteristic of your personality. Are some more basic than others?

aggressive	organized	ambitious
confident	loyal	generous
warm	bold	cautious
sensitive	mature	talented
sociable	busy	funny
dominant	dull	accurate
humble	uninhibited	future-oriented
thoughtful	serious	helpful
orderly	anxious	conforming
liberal	curious	optimistic
meek	neighborly	passionate
kind	compulsive	honest
cheerful	emotional	good-natured
clever	calm	reliable
jealous	religious	nervous

the characteristics of hands in general (common traits). Thus, Allport believed that by studying traits we could discover what is true of personalities in general, while also improving our understanding of individual personalities.

Allport also made distinctions among **cardinal traits, central traits,** and **secondary traits.** Cardinal traits are so basic that all of a person's activities can be traced to existence of the trait. It is said, for instance, that an overriding factor in the life of Albert Schweitzer was "reverence for every living thing." Likewise, Abraham Lincoln's personality was dominated by the cardinal trait of honesty. According to Allport, few people have cardinal traits.

Question: How do central and secondary traits differ from cardinal traits?

Central traits are the basic building blocks of personality. Allport found that a surprisingly small number of central traits is sufficient to capture the essence of a person. College students asked to write a short description of someone they knew well mentioned an average of only 7.2 central traits (Allport, 1961).

In contrast, secondary traits are less consistent and less important aspects of a person. For this reason, any number of secondary traits could be listed in a personality description. Your own secondary traits include such things as food preferences, attitudes, political opinions, musical tastes, and so forth. In Allport's terms, a personality description might therefore include:

Name: Jane Doe
Age: 22
Cardinal traits: None
Central traits: Possessive, autonomous, artistic, dramatic, self-centered, trusting
Secondary traits: Prefers colorful clothes, likes to work alone, politically liberal, always late, and so forth

Source Traits   A second major approach to the study of traits is illustrated by the work of Raymond B. Cattell (1965). Cattell was dissatisfied with merely classifying traits. Instead, he wanted to reach deeper into personality to learn how traits are organized and interlinked.

Cattell began by studying features that make up the visible parts of personality. He called these **surface traits.** Through use of questionnaires, direct observation, and life records, Cattell assembled data on the surface traits of a large number of people. He then noted that surface traits often appear in *clusters*, or groups. In fact, some traits appeared together so often they seemed to represent a single, more basic trait. Cattell called such underlying personality characteristics **source traits.**

Question: How do source traits differ from Allport's central traits?

The main difference is that Allport classified traits subjectively, whereas Cattell used a statistical technique called **factor analysis** to trace surface traits back to source traits. Factor analysis uses correlations to identify traits that are interrelated. Using this approach, Cattell developed a list of 16 source traits. He considers this the basic number necessary to describe an individual personality.

Cattell's source traits are measured by a test called the *Sixteen Personality Factor Questionnaire* (often referred to as the 16 PF). Like many tests of its type, the 16 PF can be used to produce a **trait profile.** A trait profile presents a graph of a person's scores for each trait. Trait profiles can be very helpful for obtaining a "picture" of an individual personality or for making comparisons between the personalities of two or more persons (see Fig. 18–3).

Traits, Consistency, and Situations

There is now little doubt that personality traits show a degree of consistency over long periods of time (Conley, 1984; Moss & Susman, 1980). And yet, *situations* also exert a powerful influence on our behavior. For instance, it would be unusual to find someone reading a book at a football game or dancing at a movie. Likewise, few people sleep in roller coasters or laugh at funerals. On the other hand, your personality traits may help predict whether you choose to read a book, go to a movie, or attend a football game in the first place.

In view of such observations, most psychologists now agree that traits *interact* with situations to determine behavior (Loevinger & Knoll, 1983). (This point is discussed further in Chapter 19.)

To illustrate what is meant by **trait-situation interactions,** imagine what would happen if you moved from a church to a classroom to a party to a football game. As the setting changed, your behavior would probably become more loud and boisterous. This change would demonstrate situational effects on behavior. Yet, at the same time, your personality traits would also be apparent: If you were quieter than average in class, you would probably be quieter than average in the other settings too (Rorer & Widiger, 1983).

The concept of traits allows us to address some interesting questions about personality. Let's take a moment to explore two intriguing examples of trait research.

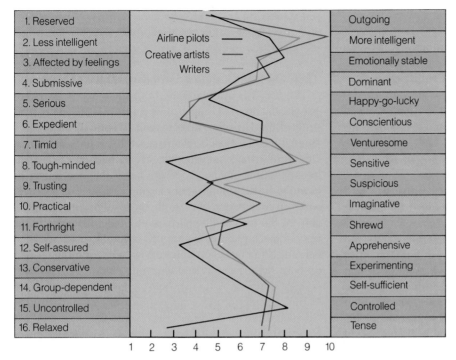

	Airline pilots ———	Outgoing
1. Reserved	Creative artists ———	More intelligent
2. Less intelligent	Writers	Emotionally stable
3. Affected by feelings		Emotionally stable
4. Submissive		Dominant
5. Serious		Happy-go-lucky
6. Expedient		Conscientious
7. Timid		Venturesome
8. Tough-minded		Sensitive
9. Trusting		Suspicious
10. Practical		Imaginative
11. Forthright		Shrewd
12. Self-assured		Apprehensive
13. Conservative		Experimenting
14. Group-dependent		Self-sufficient
15. Uncontrolled		Controlled
16. Relaxed		Tense

1 2 3 4 5 6 7 8 9 10

Fig. 18–3 *The 16 source traits measured by Cattell's 16 PF are listed on the left. Scores can be graphed as a profile for an individual or a group. Profiles shown are group averages for airline pilots, creative artists, and writers. Notice the similarity between artists and writers and the difference between these two and pilots. (After Cattell, 1973.)*

Birth Order— Personality by Position?

Without exception you are one of the following: the oldest or only child in your family, a middle child, or the youngest. If you had it to do over again, which would you choose to be? Your answer could depend on the personality traits you would most like to have. Birth order, or **ordinal position,** in a family can leave an imprint on personality.

Firstborn/Later-Born

Question: What traits are associated with birth order?

The clearest differences are between **firstborn** and **later-born** children. The firstborn seem to have a higher chance of achieving eminence than later-born persons. Freud, Kant, Beethoven, Dante, Einstein, and an unexpectedly large number of other high-achieving men and women were firstborn children (Harris, 1964). Firstborns have better high school and college grade averages. More first-borns become National Merit Scholars, and more are medical students or graduate students. Most of this country's astronauts were firstborn (Harris, 1964; Hilton, 1967). In short, firstborns tend to be high achievers—re-

sponsible, hardworking, and disciplined persons with high levels of pride and self-esteem (Howarth, 1980).

Before you congratulate yourself on being a firstborn or lament that you are not, consider this: Firstborns are also shyer, more conforming, and more likely to be anxious or neurotic than later-born persons (Howarth, 1980; Schachter, 1959).

Question: What are the strengths of later-born persons?

Later-born persons tend to excel in social relationships. They are affectionate, friendly, and at ease with others. Youngest children also tend to be more original and creative than firstborns. For such reasons, later-borns are typically more popular with their peers. They also display better social skills when interacting with strangers (Ickes & Turner, 1983).

Question: How does birth order influence personality?

Parental Attitudes   The answer seems to lie in the "emotional set" parents bring to each child. Because they are the first on the scene, oldest children often get more attention, praise, and concern than later children. The first child is talked to more, punished more, and gets more stimulation and affection than later-born children do (Belsky, Gilstrap, & Rovine, 1984). The firstborn is also more likely to be a planned child and is breast-fed longer (Sears, Maccoby, & Levin, 1957).

Such patterns seem to benefit the firstborn, who come to think of themselves as important persons. High parental expectations for the firstborn are then translated into high self-expectations. For example, women business executives who have excelled in traditional, male-dominated occupations tend to be firstborn children. Although the connection is open to interpretation, it may be that these firstborn women were especially encouraged to achieve by their parents (Hoyenga & Hoyenga, 1984).

A principal drawback of being firstborn is that new parents are more anxious and inconsistent. As a result, firstborns develop higher levels of anxiety and a tendency to conform to adult values. Parents consistently report that they used lighter discipline and were more relaxed with second or later children. The youngest child in a family is particularly prone to be pampered and to have fewer responsibilities than did older brothers and sisters. Another way of saying this is that firstborn children tend to become parent oriented, whereas later-borns tend to be more peer oriented (Markus, 1981).

At this point it should be emphasized that birth-order effects can be stated only as broad patterns. Being a first- or later-born child does not mean that your personality will invariably fit the profiles we have outlined. Countless factors, including the number of children in a family, their sex, age differences, and the age of parents, can modify birth-order effects. For example, a third child who is born 4 or 5 years after the last previous child may get nearly as much attention from parents as a firstborn would. Nevertheless, when large samples of people are considered, small birth-order effects do emerge (Ernst & Angst, 1983; Sutton-Smith, 1982).

Compared with birth-order effects, growing up as a male or a female has many times more impact on personality. What does it mean to have "masculine" or "feminine" traits? To find out, let's explore a second area of interesting research.

Psychological Androgyny— Are You Masculine, Feminine, or Androgynous?

Are you a leader, aggressive, ambitious, analytical, assertive, athletic, competitive, dominant, forceful, independent, individualistic, decisive, self-reliant, and willing to take risks? If so, you are quite "masculine." Are you affectionate, cheerful, childlike, compassionate, flatterable, gentle, gullible, a lover of children, loyal, sensitive, shy,

soft-spoken, sympathetic, tender, understanding, warm, and yielding? If so, then you are quite "feminine."

Question: What if I have characteristics from both lists?

Then you may be **androgynous** (an-DROJ-ih-nus).

The two lists just given are from the work of psychologist Sandra Bem. Using lists of various traits, Bem constructed the **Bem Sex Role Inventory (BSRI)**, a list of 20 "masculine" traits (self-reliant, assertive, and so forth), 20 "feminine" traits (affectionate, gentle), and 20 neutral traits (truthful, friendly). Next, Bem and her associates gave the BSRI to thousands of people, asking them to say whether each trait applied to them. Of those surveyed, 50 percent fell into traditional masculine or feminine categories; 15 percent scored higher on traits of the opposite gender; and 35 percent were androgynous, getting high scores on both the masculine and feminine items.

Question: You haven't said yet what it means to be androgynous. Is it having both male and female traits?

Psychological Androgyny   The word **androgyny** (an-DROJ-ih-nee) literally means "man-woman." Androgyny sounds as if it might have something to do with androids, asexuality, or sex-change operations, but it actually refers to persons who have both masculine and feminine traits.

Bem's interest in androgyny stems from her belief that our complex society requires flexibility with respect to sex roles. She believes that it is right, and more than ever necessary for men to be gentle, compassionate, sensitive, and yielding, and for women to be forceful, self-reliant, independent, and ambitious—*as the situation requires*. In short, Bem believes that more people should be androgynous (Fig. 18–4).

Adaptability   In an interesting series of experiments, Bem and her associates sought to show that androgynous individuals are more adaptable, that they are less hindered by sex roles or images of what is appropriate "masculine" or "feminine" behavior. For example, in one experiment Bem gave subjects the choice of performing either a "masculine" activity (oil a hinge, nail boards together, and so forth) or a "feminine" activity (prepare a baby bottle, wind yarn into a ball, and so on). Masculine men and feminine women consistently chose sex-appropriate activities, even when the opposite choice paid more.

Bem's conclusion from a number of studies is that rigid sex roles can seriously restrict behavior, especially for men (Bem, 1974, 1975a, 1975b, 1981). She believes masculine males have great difficulty expressing warmth, playfulness, and concern—even when these qualities are appropriate—because they view such actions as "feminine."

Likewise, feminine women have trouble being independent and assertive, even when these qualities are called for.

In the years since Bem's first studies, androgyny has been variously supported, attacked, and debated. Now, as the dust begins to settle, the picture looks like this:

■ Having "masculine" traits primarily means a person is independent and assertive. Scoring high in "masculinity," therefore, is related to high self-esteem and to success in many situations.

■ Having "feminine" traits primarily means a person is nurturant and interpersonally oriented. People who score high in "femininity," therefore, tend to experience greater social closeness with others and more happiness in marriage.

In sum, there are advantages to possessing both "masculine" and "feminine" traits, whatever one's gender may be (Spence, 1984).

Many people, of course, remain comfortable with traditional views of masculinity and femininity. Nevertheless, personality researchers have done much to show that "masculine" traits and "feminine" traits can exist in the same person, and that androgyny can be a highly adaptive balance.

Fig. 18–4 *Androgynous individuals adapt easily to both traditionally "masculine" and "feminine" situations.*

Learning Check

1. _____ refers to the hereditary aspects of a person's emotional nature.

2. A system that classifies all people as either introverts or extroverts constitutes a _____ approach to personality.

Match in accordance with Sheldon's theory:

3. ____ Endomorphy   **A.** Cerebrotonia

4. ____ Mesomorphy   **B.** Somatotonia

5. ____ Ectomorphy   **C.** Viscerotonia

6. The term _____ refers to the presence or absence of desirable personal qualities.
   a. personality *b.* character *c.* somatomorphy *d.* temperament

7. According to Allport, few people have _____ traits.

8. Central traits are those shared by most members of a culture.   T or F?

9. Cattell believes that clusters of _____ traits reveal the presence of underlying _____ traits.

10. Cattell's personality questionnaire provides ratings on 16 surface traits.   T or F?

11. The Bem Sex Role Inventory is used to identify source traits in androgynous individuals.   T or F?

12. Whereas firstborn persons tend to be high achievers, later-born persons tend to excel in social skills.   T or F?

Answers: 1. Temperament 2. type 3. C 4. B 5. A 6. b 7. cardinal 8. F 9. surface, source 10. F 11. F 12. T

Personality Assessment—Psychological Yardsticks

One of the greatest values of the trait approach is the refinement it has brought to personality measurement and testing. To study traits, psychologists have found it helpful to create ways of assessing personality. The results have been of tremendous value in research, industry, education, and clinical work.

Question: How is personality assessed?

Psychologists use **interviews, observation, questionnaires,** and **projective tests** to measure personality. Each method is a refinement of more informal ways of evaluating people.

At one time or another, you have probably "sized up" a potential date, friend, or employer by engaging in conversation (interview). Perhaps you have asked a friend "When I am delayed, I get angry. Do you?" (questionnaire). Maybe you watch your professors when they are angry or embarrassed to learn what they are "really" like (observation). Or possibly you have noticed that when you say, "I think people feel . . .," you may be expressing your own feelings (projection). Let's see how psychologists apply each approach to probe personality more formally.

The Interview

A very direct way to learn about a person's personality is to engage in conversation. An interview is described as **unstructured** if the conversation is informal and the interviewee determines what subjects are discussed. In a **struc-**

Fig. 18–5 *What is your impression of this person? Interviewers are often influenced by the halo effect (see text).*

tured interview information is obtained by asking a series of planned questions.

Question: How are interviews used?

Interviews are used to identify personality disturbances; to select persons for employment, college, or special programs; and for research on personality dynamics. Interviews also provide information for counseling or therapy. For instance, a counselor might ask a depressed person, "Have you ever contemplated suicide? What were the circumstances?" The counselor might then follow by asking, "How did you feel about it?" or, "How is what you are now feeling different from what you felt then?"

In addition to providing information, interviews make it possible to observe a person's tone of voice, hand gestures, posture, and facial expressions. Such "body language" cues are important because they may radically alter what is said, as when a person claims to be "completely calm" yet trembles uncontrollably.

Limitations   Interviews give rapid insight into personality, but they are subject to certain limitations. For one thing, interviewers can be swayed by preconceptions. A person identified as a "housewife," "college student," "high school athlete," "punk," or "ski bum" may be misjudged because of an interviewer's attitude toward a particular lifestyle. Second, an interviewer's own personality may cause an accentuation or distortion of the interviewee's traits.

A third problem is the **halo effect.** The halo effect is a tendency to generalize a favorable or unfavorable impression to unrelated details of personality (Fig. 18–5). A person who is likable or physically attractive may be rated more mature, intelligent, or adjusted than he or she actually is. The halo effect is something to keep in mind when you are interviewed for employment. First impressions do make a difference.

Even with their limitations, interviews are a respected method of personality assessment. In many cases, interviews are an essential step to additional personality testing and to counseling or therapy.

Direct Observation and Rating Scales

Are you fascinated by bus depots, airports, subway stations, or other public places? Many people relish a chance to observe the behavior of others. When used for assessment, direct observation is an extension of this natural interest in "people watching." For instance, a psychologist might arrange to observe a disturbed child playing with other children. Does the child remain withdrawn from

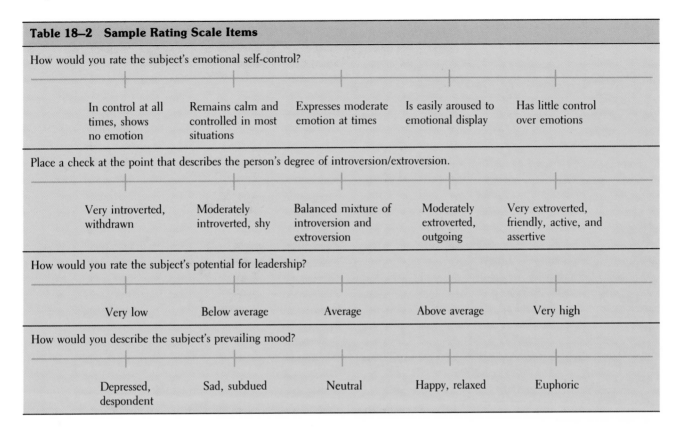

Table 18–2   Sample Rating Scale Items

How would you rate the subject's emotional self-control?

| In control at all times, shows no emotion | Remains calm and controlled in most situations | Expresses moderate emotion at times | Is easily aroused to emotional display | Has little control over emotions |

Place a check at the point that describes the person's degree of introversion/extroversion.

| Very introverted, withdrawn | Moderately introverted, shy | Balanced mixture of introversion and extroversion | Moderately extroverted, outgoing | Very extroverted, friendly, active, and assertive |

How would you rate the subject's potential for leadership?

| Very low | Below average | Average | Above average | Very high |

How would you describe the subject's prevailing mood?

| Depressed, despondent | Sad, subdued | Neutral | Happy, relaxed | Euphoric |

others? Does she become hostile or aggressive without warning? By careful observation, the psychologist will form an impression of the child's personality and clarify the nature of her problems.

Question: Wouldn't observation be subject to the same problems of misperception as an interview?

Yes. Misperceiving can be a difficulty. Because of it, **rating scales** are sometimes used (see Table 18–2). Rating scales limit the chance that some traits will be overlooked while others are exaggerated. Perhaps such scales should be standard procedures for choosing a roommate, spouse, or lover!

An alternative to rating scales is to do a **behavioral assessment**. In this case, observers record how often various *actions* occur, not what traits they think a person has. For example, psychologists working with hospitalized mental patients may find it helpful to record the frequency of patients' aggression, self-care, speech, and unusual behaviors (Alevizos & Callahan, 1977).

Situational Testing   A specialized form of direct observation is called **situational testing**. Situational tests are based on the premise that the best way to learn how a

person reacts is to simulate "real life" situations. Situational tests expose a person to frustration, temptation, pressure, boredom, or other conditions capable of revealing personality characteristics.

Question: How are situational tests done?

An interesting example of situational testing is the "Shoot–Don't Shoot" training done by many police departments (Fig. 18–6). At times, police officers must make split-second decisions about using their guns. A mistake may be fatal. In the *Shoot–Don't Shoot Test*, actors play the part of armed juveniles or criminals. As various high-risk scenes are acted out live, or on videotape, officers must decide to shoot or hold fire. A newspaper reporter who took the test (and failed it) gives this account (Gersh, 1982):

> I judged wrong. I was killed by a man in a closet, a man with a hostage, a woman interrupted when kissing her lover, and a man I thought was cleaning a shotgun. . . . I shot a drunk who reached for a comb, and a teenager who pulled out a black water pistol. Looked real to me.

In addition to the training it provides, the Shoot–Don't Shoot Test uncovers police cadets who lack the good judgment needed to carry a gun on the street.

Fig. 18—6 *A police officer undergoes a Shoot–Don't Shoot Test. Variations on this situational test are used by a growing number of police departments. All officers must score a passing grade.*

Personality Questionnaires

Most **personality questionnaires** are paper-and-pencil tests requiring people to answer questions about themselves. As measures of personality, questionnaires are more *objective* than interviews or observation. Questions, administration, and scoring are all standardized so that scores are unaffected by the opinions or prejudices of the examiner.

Many personality tests have been created, including tests such as the *Guilford-Zimmerman Temperament Survey*, the *California Psychological Inventory*, the *Allport-Vernon Study of Values*, the *16 PF*, and many more. One of the best known and most widely used is the *Minnesota Multiphasic Personality Inventory (MMPI)*. The MMPI is composed of 550 items to which a subject must respond "true," "false," or "cannot say." Items include statements such as:

Everything tastes the same.
There is something wrong with my mind.
I enjoy animals.
Whenever possible I avoid being in a crowd.
I have never indulged in any unusual sex practices.
Someone has been trying to poison me.
I daydream often.*

*Reproduced by permission. Copyright 1943, renewed 1970 by the University of Minnesota. Published by The Psychological Corporation, New York, NY. All rights reserved.

Question: How can these items show anything about personality? For instance what if a person has a cold so that "everything tastes the same"?

The answer to a single item tells nothing about personality. A person who agrees that "everything tastes the same" might indeed have a cold. It is only through *patterns* of response that personality is revealed. Items on the MMPI were selected for their ability to correctly identify persons with particular psychological problems. If items are consistently answered in a particular way by depressed persons, it is assumed that others who answer the same way are also prone to depression.

The MMPI measures 10 major aspects of personality (listed in Table 18–3). After the MMPI is scored, results are charted as an MMPI profile (see Fig. 18–7). By comparing a person's profile with scores produced by normal adults, various disorders can be identified.

Question: How accurate is the MMPI?

For the MMPI or any other personality questionnaire to be accurate, people must be willing to tell the truth about themselves.

Because truthful answers are important, the MMPI has an additional "Lie Scale" to detect attempts of subjects to make themselves look better (or worse) than they really are. However, the Lie Scale alone is not enough to ensure accuracy. If MMPI scores were used as the only basis for classifying a person as neurotic, severely depressed, or schizophrenic, a large number of people would be incorrectly labeled (Cronbach, 1970). Fortunately, such judgments usually take into account information from interviews or other sources.

Most psychologists are well aware of the limitations of psychological tests (see Highlight 18–2). If psychologists were the only persons giving these tests, there would be few problems. However, many organizations, including businesses, routinely use personality tests, and errors or abuses sometimes occur. With this in mind, you should be aware that the United States Supreme Court handed down a decision in 1971 limiting the use of tests as conditions of employment or promotion. If you think a test was unfair, you may have a case.

Projective Tests of Personality—
Inkblots and Hidden Plots

Projective tests take a very different approach to personality than the techniques already discussed. Interviews, observation, rating scales, and inventories typically identify overt, observable traits. By contrast, projective tests attempt to uncover deep-seated or *unconscious* wishes, thoughts, and needs.

Question: How is a test able to do that?

As a child you may have delighted in finding faces and objects in cloud formations. Or perhaps you have learned something about your friends' personalities from their reactions to movies or paintings. If so, you will have some

Table 18–3   MMPI Subscales

   1. Hypochondriasis (HI-po-kon-DRY-uh-sis). Reflects exaggerated concern about one's physical health.
   2. Depression. High scorers are marked by feelings of worthlessness, hopelessness, and pessimism.
   3. Hysteria. Reflects somatic complaints related to psychological disturbances (psychosomatic problems).
   4. Psychopathic deviancy. Shows a disregard for social and moral standards and emotional shallowness in relationships.
   5. Masculinity/femininity. Indicates degree of traditional "masculine" aggressiveness or "feminine" sensitivity.
   6. Paranoia. Indicates extreme suspiciousness and feelings of persecution.
   7. Psychasthenia (psych-as-THEE-nee-ah). Suggests presence of irrational fears (phobias) and compulsive (ritualistic) actions.
   8. Schizophrenia. Reflects withdrawal, unusual and bizarre thinking or actions.
   9. Hypomania. Suggests emotional excitability, manic moods or behavior, and excessive activity.
10. Social introversion. High score indicates a tendency to be socially withdrawn.

insight into the rationale for projective tests. A **projective test** provides an *ambiguous stimulus* that a person must describe or make up a story about. Describing an unambiguous stimulus (a picture of an automobile, for example) tells little about your personality. But when you are faced with an unstructured stimulus or situation, you

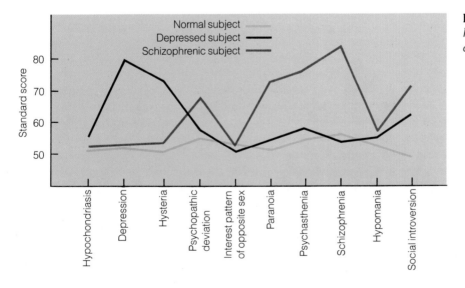

Fig. 18–7 *An MMPI profile showing hypothetical scores indicating normality, depression, and psychosis.*

Highlight 18–2
"Roasting" Personality Tests

Humorist Art Buchwald (1965) once lampooned personality questionnaires by writing his own test. Here is a sample of his items:

Answer, "Yes," "No," or "Don't bother me, I can't cope!"

I would enjoy the work of a chicken flicker.
My eyes are always cold.
Frantic screams make me nervous.
I believe I smell as good as most people.
Most of the time I go to sleep without saying good-bye.
I use shoe polish to excess.
The sight of blood no longer excites me.

Buchwald's questions may seem ridiculous, but they are not very different from the real thing. To avoid the problems of traditional tests, psychologist Frank McMahon (1964) once constructed an "above-board" test with clearly stated questions. For example, the true-false question: "Some people have it in for me" is followed by: "If True, I can't seem to get them off my mind." Although McMahon's test has not been widely used, his approach clearly takes much of the mystery out of personality testing.

must organize and interpret what you see in terms of your own life experiences. Everyone sees something different in a projective stimulus, and what is perceived can reveal inner workings of the personality.

Since projective tests have no right or wrong answers, the ability of subjects to fake or "see through" the tests is greatly reduced. Moreover, projective tests can be an unusually rich source of information, since responses are not restricted to simple true-false or yes-no answers.

Question: Is the inkblot test a projective technique?

The Rorschach Inkblot Test   The inkblot test, or *Rorschach* (ROR-shock), is one of the oldest and most widely used projective tests. Developed by Swiss psychologist Hermann Rorschach in the 1920s, it consists of a set of 10 standardized inkblots. These vary in color, shading, form, and complexity.

Question: How does testing take place?

First, subjects are shown each blot and asked to describe what they see in it (Fig. 18–8). Later, the psychologist may return to a blot, asking a subject to identify specific sections, to elaborate on previous descriptions, or to suggest a completely new story. Obvious differences in content—such as "blood dripping from a dagger" versus "flowers blooming in a field"—are important for identifying conflicts and fantasies. But surprisingly, content is considered less important than what parts of the inkblot are used to form an image and how the image is organized. These factors allow a psychologist to view the ways in which a subject perceives the world and to detect disorders in personality function.

Fig. 18–8   *Inkblots similar to those used on the Rorschach. What do you see?*

The Thematic Apperception Test   Another popular projective test is the *Thematic Apperception Test (TAT)* developed by Harvard psychologist and personality theorist Henry Murray.

Question: How does the TAT differ from the Rorschach?

The TAT consists of 20 sketches depicting various scenes and life situations (see Fig. 18–9). The subject is shown each sketch and is asked to make up a story about the people in it. Later the subject is shown each sketch a second or perhaps third time. The subject is then asked to elaborate on previous stories or to construct new stories for each sketch.

Question: How is the TAT scored?

Scoring of the TAT is restricted to analyzing the content of the stories. In particular, the psychologist is concerned with what the basic issues are in each story: Interpretation focuses on how people in the stories feel, how they interact, what events led to the incidents depicted in the sketch, and how the story will end. The psychologist might also count the number of times the central figure in each story is angry, overlooked, apathetic, jealous, or threatened. For example, here is a story written by a student to describe Fig. 18–9.

> The girl has been seeing this guy her mother doesn't like. The mother is telling her that she better not see him again. The mother says, "He's just like your father." The mother and father are divorced. The mother is smiling because she thinks she is right. But she doesn't really know what the girl wants. The girl is going to see the guy again, anyway.

Question: How accurate are projective tests?

Limitations of Projective Testing   Although projective tests have been popular with clinical psychologists, their *validity* is considered lowest among tests of personality. (Recall that a test is valid when it measures what it claims to measure.) Because of the subjectivity involved in scoring, *objectivity* (consistency) of judgments among different users of the TAT and Rorschach is also low. Note that after the subject interprets an ambiguous stimulus, the scorer must interpret the subject's (sometimes) ambiguous responses. In a sense, the interpretation of a projective test may be a projective test for the scorer!

Despite the drawbacks of projective tests, many psychologists attest to their value, especially as part of a **battery** of tests and interviews. It is said that in the hands of a skillful clinician, projective tests help detect major conflicts and define the goals of therapy. Moreover, since projective tests are unstructured, they may be more effective

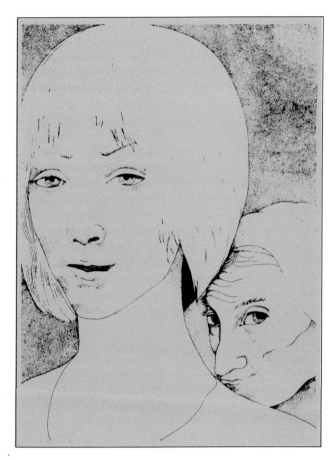

Fig. 18–9   *This is a picture like those used for the Thematic Apperception Test. If you wish to simulate the test, tell a story that explains what led up to the pictured situation, what is happening now, and how the action will end.*

for getting clients to talk about anxiety-provoking topics than are the direct questions found in inventories and interviews.

Sudden Murderers— A Research Example

Personality studies provide us with clues to some of the most perplexing human events. Consider Fred Cowan, a model student in school and described by those who knew him as quiet, gentle, and a man who loved children. Despite his size (6 feet tall, 250 pounds), Fred was described by a co-worker as "someone you could easily push around."

Fred Cowan is representative of a puzzling phenomenon: the sudden murderer—a gentle, quiet, shy, good-natured person who explodes without warning into violence (Lee et al., 1977). Two weeks after being suspended from his job, Fred returned to work determined to get even with his supervisor. Unable to find the man, he killed four co-workers and a policeman before taking his own life.

Question: Isn't such behavior contrary to the idea of personality traits?

It might seem that sudden murderers are newsworthy simply because they seem such unlikely candidates for violence. On the contrary, research conducted by Melvin Lee, Philip Zimbardo, and Minerva Bertholf suggests that sudden murderers explode into violence *because* they are shy, restrained, and inexpressive, not in spite of it. These researchers studied prisoners at a California prison: 10 were inmates whose homicide was an unexpected first offense; 9 were criminals with a record of habitual violence prior to murder; and 16 were inmates convicted of nonviolent crimes.

Question: Did the inmates differ in personality makeup?

Lee and his associates administered a battery of tests to the inmates. Included were the MMPI, a test measuring shyness, an adjective checklist, and personal interviews. As expected, the sudden murderers were passive, shy, and

overcontrolled (restrained) individuals. The habitually violent inmates were "masculine" (aggressive), undercontrolled (impulsive), and less likely to view themselves as shy than the average person (Lee et al., 1977).

Interviews and other observations have revealed that quiet, overcontrolled individuals are likely to be especially violent if they ever lose control. Their attacks are usually triggered by a minor irritation or frustration, but the attack reflects years of unexpressed anger and feelings of belittlement. When sudden murderers finally release the strict controls they have maintained on their behavior, a furious and frenzied attack ensues. Usually it is totally out of proportion to the offense against them, and often they have amnesia for some or all of their violent actions.

In comparison, the previously violent murderers showed very different reactions. Although they killed, their violence was moderate—usually only enough to do the necessary damage. Typically, they felt they had been cheated or betrayed and that they were doing what was necessary to remedy the situation or to maintain their manhood (Lee et al., 1977).

This brief example illustrates how some of the concepts and techniques discussed in this chapter can be applied to further our understanding. The Applications section that follows should add balance to your view of personality. Don't be shy: Read on!

Learning Check

1. Planned questions are used in a _____ interview.
2. The halo effect is the tendency of an interviewer to influence what is said by the interviewee.   T or F?
3. Which of the following is considered the most objective measure of personality   (circle):

   rating scales   personality questionnaires   projective tests   the TAT

4. Situational testing allows direct _____ of personality characteristics.
5. A psychotic person would probably score highest on which MMPI scale?   (circle)

   depression   hysteria   schizophrenia   hypomania

6. The use of ambiguous stimuli is most characteristic of   (circle):

   interviews   projective tests   personality inventories   direct observation

7. The content of one's responses to the MMPI is considered an indication of unconscious wishes, thoughts, and needs.   T or F?
8. Doing a behavioral assessment requires direct observation of the person's actions.   T or F?
9. A surprising finding is that sudden murderers are usually overcontrolled, very masculine, and more impulsive than average.   T or F?

Answers: 1. structured   2. F   3. personality questionnaires   4. observation   5. schizophrenia   6. projective tests   7. F   8. T   9. F

Applications

Shrinking Violets and Bashful Beaux— Understanding Shyness

Do you:

Find it hard to talk to strangers?
Lack confidence with people?
Find it difficult to make friends?
Feel awkward in social situations?
Feel nervous with people who are not close friends?

If so you may be one of the *40 percent* of American college students who consider themselves shy. If you are shy and wish you weren't, it may help to know that many others are shy too. However, three-fourths of those who are shy say they don't like it (Zimbardo et al., 1978).

Touch a snail and it retreats into its shell. Speak to a shy person, and he or she may shrink back as if threatened. As a personality trait, **shyness** refers to an avoidance of others, coupled with social inhibition (restraint and signs of strain when socializing) (Buss, 1980). Shy persons fail to make eye contact, retreat when spoken to, speak too quietly, pause too long in conversations, and display little interest or animation.

Question: What causes shyness?

Elements of Shyness To begin with, shy persons often lack **social skills.** Many simply have not learned how to meet others, how to start a conversation and keep it going, or how to end social encounters. A second factor in shyness is **social anxiety.** Most people are nervous in some social situations (such as meeting an attractive stranger). Such anxiety is typically a reaction to *evaluation fears* (fears of being embarrassed, ridiculed, rejected, or of seeming inadequate). Such fears occur for both the shy and the nonshy. However, social anxieties are more frequent or intense for shy persons. A third problem for shy persons is a **self-defeating bias** in their thinking. Specifically, shy persons almost always blame themselves when a social encounter doesn't go well (Girodo, 1978).

Immediate Causes of Shyness Have you ever had to deliver a speech to a group of strangers? If you have, you are probably aware that shyness is most of-

ten triggered by *novel* or *unfamiliar* social situations. A person who does fine with family or close friends may become shy and awkward when meeting a stranger. Shyness is also magnified by formality, meeting someone of higher status, being noticeably different from others, or being the focus of attention (as in giving a speech) (Buss, 1980; Pilkonis, 1977).

Question: Don't most people become cautious and inhibited in such circumstances?

Yes. That's why we need to see how the personalities of shy and nonshy persons differ.

Dynamics of the Shy Personality There is a tendency to think that shy persons are wrapped up in their own feelings and thoughts. In some cases this may be true. But surprisingly, researchers Jonathan Cheek and Arnold Buss (1979) found no connection between shyness and *private* self-consciousness (attention to inner feelings, thoughts, and fantasies). Instead, they discovered that shyness is linked to *public* self-consciousness.

Persons who rate high in **public self-consciousness** are intensely aware of themselves as social objects (Buss, 1980). They are concerned about what others think of them, and they feel others are evaluating them. They worry about saying the wrong thing or appearing foolish. With such concerns, many shy persons feel they are being rejected even when they are not. In public they may feel "naked" or as if others can "see through them." Such feelings trigger anxiety or outright fear during social encounters, leading to awkwardness and inhibition.

As mentioned, almost everyone feels anxious in at least some social situations. But there is a key difference in the way shy and nonshy persons *label* this anxiety. Shy persons tend to consider their social anxiety a *lasting personality trait.* In contrast, nonshy persons believe that *external situations* cause their occasional feelings of shyness. Particular people or situations may trigger anxiety or "stage fright" for the nonshy, but this group assumes that almost anyone would feel as they

Applications: Shrinking Violets and Bashful Beaux—Understanding Shyness

do under the same circumstances (Zimbardo et al., 1978).

Why should labeling make such a difference? The answer seems to lie in its effect on *self-esteem.* Nonshy persons tend to have higher self-esteem than shy persons. The greater confidence of the nonshy comes from an ability to benefit more from successful social encounters. Nonshy persons give themselves credit for successes, and they recognize that failures are often due to circumstances. Shy people, in contrast, blame themselves for social failures and never give themselves credit for successes. It's no wonder they often have lower self-esteem (Buss, 1980; Girodo, 1978).

Consequences of Shyness   Even when it is mild, shyness can cause problems. Among the most common are:

1. Difficulties in making new friends or meeting people.
2. Feelings of isolation and loneliness.
3. Misperception by others; a shy person may strike others as vain, bored, unfriendly, or uninterested.
4. A general lack of self-projection and confidence in social settings.

Unless shyness is intense and quite painful, it is a mistake to think of it as a major problem. Yet, as the preceding list shows, shyness does have its costs. As one author notes, people who were once shy look back on the shyness of their youth "with about the same tenderness that they recall adolescent pimples."

Question: What can be done to reduce shyness?

Overcoming Shyness

Visitors to China frequently marvel at the almost total lack of shyness among the Chinese. In America many children seem to "outgrow" shyness as they gain social skills and wider social experience. Some adults overcome shyness with the aid of a "shyness clinic" or similar program. (Shyness clinics are sometimes offered on college campuses or by private psychologists.) Many previously shy people simply made an effort to learn new social skills and break out of old routines. Each of these observations suggests that shyness is to a large extent learned and open to change. If you are shy and would like to change, the information that follows may

offer a starting point. Even if you are not shy, you may find some of the ideas useful.

Shy Beliefs   While directing a shyness clinic, Michel Girodo (1978) observed that shyness is often maintained by a number of unrealistic or unproductive beliefs. Here's a sample:

1. *If you wait around long enough at a social gathering, something will happen.*
Comment: This is really a cover-up for fear of initiating conversation. For two people to meet, at least one has to make an effort—it might as well be you.
2. *Other people who are popular are just lucky when it comes to being invited to social events or asked out.*
Comment: Except for times when a person is formally introduced to new acquaintances, this is false. People who are more active socially typically make an effort to meet and spend time with others: They join clubs, invite others to do things, strike up conversations, and generally leave little to "luck."
3. *The odds of meeting someone interested in socializing are always the same, no matter where I am.*
Comment: This is another rationalization for inaction. It pays to seek out settings and events that have a higher probability of leading to social contact. Drama clubs, hiking clubs, sports teams, school events, and so forth often serve as a convenient way to bring together people interested in socializing.
4. *If someone doesn't seem to like you right away, they really don't like you and never will.*
Comment: This belief leads to much unnecessary withdrawal and isolation. Even when a person doesn't show immediate interest, it doesn't mean the person dislikes you. Liking takes time and opportunity to develop.

Unproductive beliefs like the preceding can be replaced with statements such as these:

1. I've got to be active in social situations.
2. I can't wait until I'm completely relaxed or comfortable before taking a social risk.
3. I don't need to pretend to be someone I'm not; it just makes me more anxious.
4. I may think other people are harshly evaluating me, but actually I'm being too hard on myself.
5. I can set reasonable goals for expanding my social experience and skills.

Applications: Shrinking Violets and Bashful Beaux—Understanding Shyness

6. Even people who are very socially skillful are never successful 100 percent of the time. I shouldn't get so upset when an encounter goes badly. (Adapted from Girodo, 1978.)

Social Skills   Learning to play a musical instrument, ski, or speak a foreign language takes practice. So does the learning of social skills. There is nothing "innate" about knowing how to meet people or enjoy a conversation. There are many ways in which social skills can be directly practiced. It can be helpful, for instance, to get a tape recorder and listen to several of your conversations. You may be surprised by the way you pause, interrupt, miss cues, or seem disinterested. Similarly, it can be useful to look at yourself in a mirror and exaggerate facial expressions of surprise, interest, dislike, pleasure, and so forth. By such methods most people can learn to put more animation and skill into their self-presentation.

One of the simplest ways to make better conversation is by learning to ask questions. A good series of questions shifts attention to the other person and shows you are interested in her or him. Nothing elaborate is needed. You can do fine with questions such as, "Where do you (work, study, live)?" "Do you like (dancing, travel, music)?" "How long have you (been at this school, worked here, lived here)?" The best questions are often *open-ended* (Girodo, 1978):

"Do you get a chance to travel much?" (as opposed to: "Have you ever been to Florida?").

"What's it like living on the west side?" (as opposed to: "Do you like living on the west side?").

"What kinds of food do you like?" (as opposed to "Do you like Chinese cooking?").

It's easy to see why open-ended questions are helpful. Because a number of words are needed to answer them, it takes only a few questions to keep a conversation alive. Also, in replying to open-ended questions, people often give "free information" about themselves. This extra information can then be used to ask other questions or to lead into other topics of conversation.

This brief sampling of ideas is no substitute for actual practice. Overcoming shyness requires a real effort to learn new skills and test old beliefs and attitudes. It may even require the help of a counselor or therapist. At the very least it requires a willingness to take social risks. Breaking down the barriers of shyness will always include some awkward or unsuccessful encounters. Nevertheless, the rewards are powerful: human companionship and personal freedom.

Learning Check

1. Surveys show that 14 percent of American college students consider themselves shy.   T or F?
2. Social anxiety and evaluation fears are seen almost exclusively in shy individuals; the nonshy rarely have such experiences.   T or F?
3. Unfamiliar people and situations most often trigger shyness.   T or F?
4. Public self-consciousness plus a tendency to label oneself as shy are major characteristics of the shy personality.   T or F?
5. Misperception by others is a common problem associated with shyness.   T or F?
6. Changing personal beliefs and practicing social skills can be helpful in overcoming shyness.   T or F?

Answers: 1. F   2. F   3. T   4. T   5. T   6. T

Chapter Summary

■ *Personality* is made up of one's unique and enduring behavior patterns. *Character* is personality evaluated, or the possession of desirable qualities. *Temperament* refers to the hereditary and physiological aspects of one's emotional nature.

■ A basic approach to the study of personality is classification into *types*. Jung's concepts of the *introvert* and the *extrovert* are an example of this approach. One well-known type system is Sheldon's *somatotype theory*. Sheldon linked body types to personality types: *endomorphy–viscerotonia*, *mesomorphy–somatotonia*, and *ectomorphy–cerebrotonia*. Like most type systems, Sheldon's oversimplifies personality.

■ The *trait* approach attempts to specify qualities of personality that are most enduring or characteristic of a person. Allport makes useful distinctions between *common traits* and *individual traits* and among *cardinal*, *central*, and *secondary traits*.

■ A second trait approach, developed by Cattell, attributes visible or *surface traits* to the existence of underlying *source traits*. Cattell identified 16 source traits by use of a statistical method called *factor analysis*.

■ Cattell's source traits are measured by the *Sixteen Personality Factor Questionnaire* (16 PF). The outcome of the 16 PF may be graphically presented as a *trait profile*, as is often done for other trait measures.

■ Traits appear to *interact* with *situations* to determine behavior. Neither factor alone fully explains our actions.

■ A variety of research suggests that birth order or *ordinal* position in a family can influence personality development. *Firstborn* and only children tend to be high achievers but also shyer, more conforming, and more anxious. *Later-born* persons are more likely to excel in social skills.

■ Research conducted by Bem and others indicates that roughly one-third of all persons are *androgynous*. Psychological androgyny (possessing both masculine and feminine traits) appears related to greater adaptability or flexibility in behavior.

■ Accurate *assessment* of personality is of great importance to psychologists. Techniques typically used to measure personality are: *interviews*, *observation*, *questionnaires*, and *projective tests*.

■ *Structured* and *unstructured* interviews provide much information, but they are subject to interviewer bias and misperceptions. The *halo effect* (a tendency to generalize first impressions) may also lower the accuracy of an interview.

■ *Direct observation*, sometimes involving *situational tests*, *behavioral assessment*, or use of *rating scales*, allows evaluation of a person's actual behavior.

■ *Personality questionnaires*, such as the *Minnesota Multiphasic Personality Inventory* (MMPI), are objective, but their accuracy and validity are open to question.

■ *Projective tests* ask a subject to project thoughts or feelings to an ambiguous stimulus or unstructured situation. The *Rorschach*, or *inkblot test*, is a well-known projective technique. A second is the *Thematic Apperception Test* (TAT). The validity and objectivity of projective tests are quite low. Nevertheless, projective techniques are considered useful by many clinicians, particularly as part of a *battery* of tests.

■ *Shyness* is a combination of *social inhibition* and *social anxiety*. It is marked by heightened *public self-consciousness* and a tendency to regard one's shyness as a lasting *trait*. Shyness can be lessened by changing *self-defeating beliefs* and by improving *social skills*.

▶▶▶ **Exploration**

Identical Twins—Twin Personalities?

Some breeds of dogs have reputations for being friendly, aggressive, intelligent, calm, or emotional. Such differences fall in the realm of **behavioral genetics**—the study of inherited *behavioral* traits. Just as physical features are inherited, so too are many behavioral traits. For instance, selective breeding of animals can lead to striking differences in social behavior, emotionality, learning ability, aggression, activity, and other behaviors (Sprott & Staats, 1975).

Question: To what extent do such findings apply to humans?

Genetic studies of humans rely mainly on comparisons of identical twins and other close relatives. Such studies, of course, are less conclusive than work done with animals. Nonetheless, they show that intelligence, some mental disorders, temperament, and other complex qualities are influenced by heredity. (For specific examples of behavioral genetics research, see Chapters 17 and 21.) In view of findings like these, we also might wonder, "Do genes affect personality?"

Question: Wouldn't comparing the personalities of identical twins help answer the question?

It would indeed—especially if the twins were separated at birth.

Twin Cities Twin Studies   Over the past several years, psychologists at the University of Minnesota

have been studying twins who grew up in separate homes. At the university, reunited twins take a wide range of medical and psychological tests. The tests probe each twin's brain waves, physical capacities, health, diet, IQ, tastes, fears, fantasies, dreams, personality traits, ambitions, and more (Fig. 18-10).

These tests, and earlier work by others, indicate that identical twins are much alike, even when they are reared apart (Bouchard et al., 1981). Like all identical twins, the reunited twins are astonishingly similar in appearance and voice quality. Observers are also struck by how often the twins display

identical facial gestures, hand movements, and nervous tics, such as nail biting or finger tapping. On many of the physical tests, results for reunited twins are so similar that they might have been produced by the same person on different days. As discussed in Chapter 17, identical twins, even when reared apart, have highly correlated IQ scores. Separated twins also tend to share similar talents. If one twin excels at art, music, dance, drama, or athletics, the other is likely to also—despite wide differences in childhood environment (Farber, 1981).

All of these observations make it clear that heredity has a sizable

Fig. 18–10   *Reunited identical twins Terry and Margaret undergo lung function tests at the University of Minnesota. Researchers collected a wide range of medical and psychological data for each set of twins.*

Exploration: Identical Twins—Twin Personalities?

effect on each of us. Where personality is concerned, similarities also exist, but they are not as strong. For instance, identical twins frequently differ in dominance and extroversion. That is, one twin is usually more extroverted or dominant than the other (Farber, 1981). Due to such differences, personality profiles for separated twins may have much in common, but they are usually far from identical.

All told, it seems reasonable to conclude that there is a genetic factor in personality (Farber, 1981). However, it is relatively small in comparison to the great physical similarity of identical twins (Scarr et al., 1981).

This modest conclusion contrasts sharply with reports of twin studies in the popular press. The impression created there has been one of overwhelming genetic control of behavior.

Question: For example?

The "Jim Twins"   Many of the reunited twins who participated in the Minnesota study displayed similarities far beyond what one would expect on the basis of heredity. A good example is provided by the "Jim twins," James Lewis and James Springer. These two reunited twins, like the others tested, had the same height and weight and very similar speech patterns, mannerisms, and posture.

The similarities, however, did not stop there. Both Jims had married and divorced women named Linda. Both had undergone police training. Both had named their firstborn sons James Allan. Both drove Chevrolets and vacationed at the same beach each summer.

Both listed carpentry and mechanical drawing among their hobbies. Both had built circular benches around trees in their yards. And so forth (Holden, 1980).

Counterpoint   Such coincidences may seem amazing at first. But the astute reader will realize that they have little to do with genetics. In the first place many such coincidences are quite common. It would not be unusual, for instance, for two unrelated people to drive the same make of car. The odds of this occurring for a Chevrolet are 1 in 7 (Nelson, 1982).

Question: That might be true for some similarities. But what about the Jim twins' shared hobbies, police training, and so on?

Again, it is important to realize that seemingly unlikely similarities also occur for unrelated persons. Consider, as an example, two women who discovered they had the same maiden names and that they shared a Social Security number. Both women were born on the same day and both were named Patricia Ann Campbell. After the women learned of one another's existence, they also discovered that they: Both had fathers named Robert. Both have worked as bookkeepers. Both have two children, each of the same age. Both have studied cosmetology and enjoy oil painting. Both married military men. And so on ("Fate," 1983).

Such similarities are not really so surprising. Two adults of the same age and sex are likely to have had many experiences in common. This is true because they live in

the same historical times and choose from a similar range of societal options.

The preceding brings us to a last point. Imagine that you were separated at birth from a twin brother or sister. If you were reunited with your twin today, what would you do? Quite likely, you would spend the next several days in almost nonstop conversation. And what would this conversation center on? Almost certainly, you would compare every imaginable detail of your lives.

Under such circumstances we could virtually guarantee that you and your twin would compile a long list of similarities. ("Wow! I use the same brand of toothpaste you do!") Yet, two unrelated persons of the same age and sex could probably rival your list—*if* they were as motivated to find similarities.

In short, many of the seemingly "astounding" coincidences shared by reunited twins may be a special case of the fallacy of positive instances, described in Chapter 1: Similarities blaze brightly in the memories of reunited twins, while differences are ignored.

Summary   The points we have covered do not deny that personality is influenced by heredity. There are many indications that it is. They do suggest, however, that some people have gone overboard in ascribing personality traits, personal preferences, interests, and behaviors to heredity.

There is danger in overstating the role of heredity in human behavior. Doing so can easily lead to

Exploration: Identical Twins—Twin Personalities?

racist or sexist attitudes. For this reason it is wise to remember that we do not inherit specific behavioral habits. Rather, we inherit certain potentials and general ways of reacting to the environment. These, in turn, can be greatly altered by experience (Farber, 1981). We are not—thank goodness—genetically programmed robots whose behavior is "wired in" for life.

Learning Check

1. Behavioral genetics is the study of how heredity influences behavioral traits and patterns.   T or F?
2. Contrary to earlier research, the Minnesota studies found relatively low correlations among IQ scores of reunited identical twins.   T or F?
3. Research with identical twins has shown that heredity is the single most powerful influence on adult personality.   T or F?
4. A large amount of evidence now indicates that genes strongly influence personal preferences and interests but not personality traits.   T or F?

Answers: 1. T 2. F 3. F 4. F

Questions for Discussion

1. Are birth-order effects an example of personality typing? To what extent do they oversimplify matters?
2. Have you ever been interviewed or given a personality test? How accurate did you consider the resulting assessment of your personality?
3. Under what circumstances would you consider a personality test an invasion of privacy?
4. If you could select only three personality traits, which would you consider most basic? Why?
5. If you were selecting candidates for an extended space flight, how would you make your choices? What could be done to improve the accuracy of your judgments of candidates' personalities?
6. Do you think there is such a thing as "national character"? That is, do all Germans, all French, all Americans, all Canadians, and so forth have common traits?
7. Do you know anyone who seems to have a cardinal trait? What do you think are central traits of your personality? Secondary traits?
8. Do you think animals have personalities? Defend your answer.
9. Can you name any public personalities (entertainers, politicians, athletes, artists, musicians) whom you deem to be androgynous? Are any of your friends or acquaintances androgynous? Do you agree or disagree with Bem's assertion that these people are more adaptable?
10. Why do you think media coverage of reunited identical twins has exaggerated the role of genetics in human behavior and personality?

Chapter 19 | Theories of Personality

Chapter Preview
Eels, Cocaine, Hypnosis, and Dreams

One of his earliest scientific discoveries was the location of the testes in an eel. Later he obtained some cocaine and began to study its value as a medicine. He was soon convinced it was a wonder drug. He proclaimed, "I took coca again and a small dose lifted me to heights in a wonderful fashion. I am just now busy collecting the literature for a song of praise to this magical substance" (Jones, 1953, p. 84). But his praise came to a rapid end when he prescribed cocaine to aid a friend addicted to morphine. Instead of improving, the friend became dependent on both drugs. His next interest was hypnosis, but he abandoned it when it did not meet his needs. At age 44, criticized by friends and virtually unknown in intellectual circles, he published his first book. It was a masterwork entitled The Interpretation of Dreams *(1900). Less than 1000 copies were sold.*

Question: Who are you talking about?

The hero of this little essay is no less than the best known of all personality theorists—Sigmund Freud. Volume after volume followed Freud's initial work until he had built a theory of personality that deeply influenced modern thought. Other theorists owe a debt to his pioneering efforts.

As there are dozens of personality theories, it is possible to introduce only a few of the most influential. For clarity, we will confine ourselves to three broad perspectives: (1) psychodynamic theories, (2) behavioristic theories, and (3) humanistic theories. Psychodynamic theories focus on the inner workings of personality, especially internal conflicts and struggles. Behavioristic theories place greater importance on the external environment and on the effects of conditioning and learning. Humanists stress subjective experience and personal growth.

Survey Questions   How do psychodynamic theories explain personality? What do behaviorists emphasize in their approach to personality? How do humanistic theories differ from other perspectives? According to each major viewpoint (psychodynamic, behavioristic, humanistic), what childhood events shape adult personality? What can be done to promote self-actualization? How does moral development relate to personality?

Resources

My life has been aimed at one goal only; to infer or to guess how the mental apparatus is constructed and what forces interplay and counteract in it.

Sigmund Freud

Psychoanalytic Theory— Id Came to Me in a Dream

Psychoanalytic theory, the best-known psychodynamic approach, grew out of the clinical study of disturbed individuals. Sigmund Freud, a Viennese physician, became interested in personality when he realized that many of his patients' problems seemed not to have physical causes. Starting about 1890 and continuing until he died in 1939, Freud evolved a theory of personality that is more complex than a short description can show. We will consider only its main features.

Question: How did Freud view personality?

The Structure of Personality

Freud conceived of personality as a dynamic system directed by three structures: the **id,** the **ego,** and the **superego.** Each is a complex system in its own right, and behavior in most situations involves the activity of all three.

The Id   The id is made up of innate biological instincts and urges present at birth. It is self-serving, irrational, impulsive, and totally **unconscious.** The id operates on the **pleasure principle,** meaning that pleasure-seeking impulses of all kinds are freely expressed. If everyone's personality were solely under control of the id, the world would be chaotic beyond belief.

Freud thought of the id as a wellspring of energy for the entire **psyche,** or personality. This energy, called **libido** (lih-BEED-oh), derives from the **life instincts** (called **Eros**). According to Freud, libido promotes survival and underlies sexual desires. Freud also described a **death instinct (Thanatos),** which he deemed responsible for aggressive and destructive urges (Fig. 19–1). Most id energies are directed toward discharging tensions associated with sex and aggression.

The Ego   The ego is sometimes described as the "executive," because it draws energy from the id. The id is like a blind king or queen whose power is awesome but who must rely on others to carry out orders. The id can only produce mental images of things it desires. (This is called "primary process thinking.") The ego wins power to direct behavior by matching the desires of the id with external reality.

Question: Are there other differences between the ego and the id?

Yes. In contrast to the id, which operates on the pleasure principle, the ego is directed by the **reality principle.** That is, the ego delays action until it is appropriate. The reality principle results in "secondary process thinking," which basically is realistic problem solving. The ego is the system of thinking, planning, and deciding. It is in conscious control of the personality.

Question: What is the role of the superego?

The Superego   The superego acts as a judge or censor for the thoughts and actions of the ego. One part of the superego, called the **conscience,** represents all actions for which a person has been punished. When standards of the conscience are not met, you are punished internally by *guilt* feelings. The **ego ideal** represents all behavior one's parents approved or rewarded. The ego ideal is a source of goals and aspirations. When its standards are met, *pride* is felt. By these processes the superego acts as an "internalized parent" to bring behavior under control. In Freudian terms, a person with a poorly developed superego will be a delinquent, criminal, or antisocial personality. In contrast, an overly strict or harsh superego will cause inhibition, rigidity, or intolerable guilt.

The Dynamics of Personality

Question: How do the id, ego, and superego interact?

It is important to recognize that Freud did not envision the id, ego, and superego as parts of the brain, or as "little people" running the human psyche. In reality they are distinct and conflicting psychological processes. Freud theorized a delicate balance of power among the three. For example, the demands of the id for immediate gratification often clash with the superego's moral restrictions. Perhaps the role of each division of the personality can be clarified by an example.

Freud in a Nutshell

Let's say you are sexually attracted to someone. The id clamors for immediate satisfaction of its sexual desires but is op-

Fig. 19–1 *Freud considered personality an expression of two conflicting forces: life instincts and the death instinct. Both are symbolized in this drawing by Allan Gilbert. (If you don't immediately see the death symbolism, stand farther from the drawing.)*

posed by the superego (which finds the very thought of sexual behavior appalling). The id says, "Now, now, now!" The superego icily responds, "Never!" And what does the ego say? The ego says, "I have a plan!"

To be sure, the oversimplification is drastic, but it captures the core of Freudian personality dynamics. To reduce tension, the ego could initiate actions leading to friendship or romance. If the id is unusually powerful, the ego may direct an attempted seduction. If the superego is dominant, the ego may be forced to *displace* or *sublimate* sexual energies to other activities (sports, music, dancing, push-ups, cold showers). According to Freud, similar internal struggles and rechanneling of energies typify most personality functioning.

Question: Is the ego always caught in the middle?

Basically, yes, and the pressures on it can be quite strong. In addition to meeting the conflicting demands of the id and the superego, the overworked ego must deal with external reality. When the ego is threatened or overwhelmed, the person feels anxiety. Impulses from the id that threaten a loss of control cause **neurotic anxiety.** Threats of punishment from the superego cause **moral anxiety.** Each person develops habitual ways of reducing these anxieties, and many resort to use of *ego-defense mechanisms* to lessen internal conflicts (see Chapter 14).

Levels of Awareness   A major principle of psychoanalytic theory, and other psychodynamic theories, is that behavior often expresses unconscious forces within the personality. The **unconscious** includes repressed memories and emotions as well as the instinctual drives of the id. Interestingly, modern scientists are beginning to identify brain areas that seem to have the kinds of unconscious effects Freud described. Especially important are areas linked with emotion and memory—such as the hippocampus in the limbic system (Reiser, 1985; Wilson, 1985).

Even though they are beyond awareness, unconscious thoughts, feelings, or impulses may slip into behavior in disguised or symbolized form. For example, if you meet someone you would like to know better, you may unconsciously leave a book or a jacket at his or her house to ensure another meeting.

Question: Earlier you said the id is completely unconscious. Are the actions of the ego and superego unconscious?

At times, yes, but they also operate on two other levels of awareness (Fig. 19–2). The **conscious** level includes everything we are aware of at a given moment: thoughts, perceptions, feelings, and memories. The **preconscious** contains material that can be readily brought to awareness. If you stop to think about a time when you have felt angry or rejected, you will be moving this memory from the preconscious to the conscious level of awareness.

Another illustration of the levels of awareness is found in the operation of the superego. At times we consciously attempt to live up to moral codes or standards; at other times we may feel guilty without knowing why. Psychoanalytic theory attributes the latter instances to unconscious workings of the superego. In Freudian psychology, events that are truly unconscious cannot be readily brought to awareness or directly known by the individual.

In view of the large number of terms used in psychoanalytic theory, Table 19–1 summarizes what we have covered.

Psychodynamic Theories— Freud's Descendants

Freud's ideas quickly attracted a brilliant following. Just as rapidly, Freud's insistence on the importance of instinctual drives and sexuality caused many to disagree with him. Those who stayed close to the core of Freud's thought are now referred to as **neo-Freudians** (*neo*: new). Some of the better known neo-Freudians include: Karen Horney, Anna Freud (Freud's daughter), Otto Rank, and Erich Fromm. Other early followers of Freud broke away more completely and created their own opposing theories. This group includes people such as Alfred Adler, Harry Sullivan, and Carl Jung.

Fig. 19–2 *The approximate relationship among the id, ego, superego, and levels of awareness.*

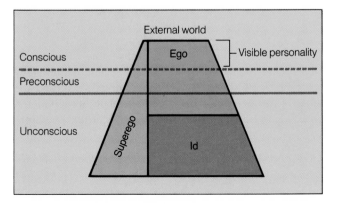

Table 19–1   Some Key Psychoanalytic Terms

Psychoanalytic theory   Freudian theory of personality that emphasizes unconscious forces and internal conflicts in its explanations of behavior.

Id   According to Freud, the most primitive part of personality, which remains unconscious, supplies energy to other parts of the psyche, and demands immediate gratification.

Pleasure principle   Principle under which the id operates, consisting of a desire for immediate satisfaction of wishes, desires, or needs.

Psyche   The mind, mental life, and personality as a whole.

Libido   In Freudian theory, the force, primarily pleasure-oriented, that energizes the subparts of personality.

Eros   Freud's name for the "life instincts" postulated by his theory.

Thanatos   The death instinct postulated by Freud.

Ego   The executive portion of personality in Freudian theory charged with directing rational, realistic behavior.

Reality principle   The principle by which the ego functions, involving delaying action (or gratification) until it is appropriate.

Superego   In Freud's theory, an internalization of parental values and societal standards.

Conscience   In Freudian theory, the part of the superego that causes guilt when its standards are not met.

Ego ideal   In Freudian theory, a part of the superego representing ideal behavior; a source of pride when its standards are met.

Neurotic anxiety   Apprehension that occurs when the ego must struggle to maintain control over id impulses.

Moral anxiety   Apprehension felt when one's thoughts, impulses, or actions conflict with standards enforced by the superego.

Unconscious   In Freudian theory, contents of the mind that are beyond awareness, especially impulses and desires not directly known to a person.

Conscious   Region of the mind that includes all mental contents (thoughts, images, feelings, memories, and so forth) a person is aware of at any given moment.

Preconscious   An area of the mind that contains information not currently in consciousness, but that can be voluntarily brought to awareness.

Question: How did the thinking of these people differ from Freud's ideas?

A complete account of other psychodynamic theories must await your first course in personality. For now, let's sample three views: one representing an early rejection of

Freud's thinking (Adler); a second embracing most but not all of Freud's theory (Horney); and the third involving a carryover of Freudian ideas into a related but unique theory (Jung).

Alfred Adler (1870–1937)   Adler broke away from Freud because he disagreed with Freud's emphasis on the unconscious, on instinctual drives, and on the importance of sexuality. Adler believed that we are *social* creatures governed by social urges, *not* by biological instincts. In Adler's view, the main driving force in personality is a **striving for superiority.** By this he meant a struggle to overcome imperfections; an upward drive for competence, completion, and mastery of shortcomings.

Question: What motivates striving for superiority?

Adler believed that everyone experiences **feelings of inferiority,** mainly because we begin life as small, weak, and relatively powerless children surrounded by larger and more powerful adults. Feelings of inferiority may also come from our personal limitations. The struggle for superiority arises from such feelings.

While everyone strives for superiority, each person tries to **compensate** for different limitations, and each chooses a different pathway to superiority. Adler believed that this situation creates a unique **style of life** (or personality pattern) for each individual. According to Adler the core of each person's style of life is formed by age 5.* However, later in his life Adler began to emphasize the existence of a **creative self.** By this he meant that humans *create* their personalities through choices and experiences.

Karen Horney (1885–1952)   As a neo-Freudian, Karen Horney (HORN-eye) remained faithful to most of Freud's ideas. Yet at the same time, she altered or rejected some, and added many of her own. Horney also resisted Freud's more mechanistic, biological, and instinctive ideas. For example, as a woman Horney rejected Freud's claim that "anatomy is destiny." This view, inherent in Freudian psychology, held males to be dominant or superior to females. Horney was among the first to challenge the obvious male bias in Freud's thinking.

Horney also disagreed with Freud about the causes of neurosis. Freud held that the neurotic (anxiety-ridden) individual is struggling with forbidden drives that threaten a loss of control. Horney's view was that a core of **basic anxiety** occurs when people feel isolated and helpless in a hos-

tile world. These feelings, she believed, are rooted in childhood. Basic anxiety then causes troubled individuals to exaggerate a single mode of interacting with others.

Question: What do you mean by "mode of interacting"?

According to Horney each of us can move **toward** others (by depending on them for love, support, or friendship); we can move **away** from others (by withdrawing, acting as a "loner," or by being "strong" and independent); or we can move **against** others (by attacking, competing with, or seeking power over them). Horney believed that emotional health reflects a balance in moving toward, away from, and against others. In her view, emotional problems tend to lock people into overuse of only one of the three modes—an insight that remains valuable today.

Carl Jung (1875–1961)   Jung (yung) was a student of Freud's, but the two parted ways when Jung began to develop his own ideas. Like Freud, Jung called the conscious part of the personality the ego. However, he further noted that between the ego and the outside world we often find a **persona,** or "mask." The persona is the "public self" presented to others when people adopt particular roles or when they hide their deeper feelings. As mentioned in the previous chapter, actions of the ego may reflect attitudes of **introversion** (in which energy is mainly directed inward) or of **extroversion** (in which energy is mainly directed outward).

Question: Was Jung's view of the unconscious the same as Freud's?

Jung used the term **personal unconscious** to refer to what Freud simply called the unconscious. The personal unconscious is a storehouse for personal experiences, feelings, and memories that are not directly knowable. Departing from Freud, Jung also proposed a deeper **collective unconscious,** shared by all humans. Jung believed that from the beginning of time all humans have had experiences with birth, death, power, god figures, mother and father figures, animals, the earth, energy, evil, rebirth, and so on. According to Jung, such universals create **archetypes** (AR-KEH-types: original ideas or patterns).

Archetypes, found in the collective unconscious, are unconscious images that cause us to respond emotionally to *symbols* of birth, death, energy, animals, evil, and the like. Jung believed that he detected symbols of such archetypes in the art, religion, myths, and dreams of every culture and age.

Question: Are some archetypes more important than others?

---

*According to Adler, valuable clues to a person's style of life are revealed by the earliest memory that can be recalled. You might therefore find it interesting to search back to your earliest memory and contemplate what it tells you.

Two particularly important archetypes are the **anima** (representing the female principle) and the **animus** (representing the male principle). Each person has both an anima and an animus. For full development, Jung considered it essential that we express both the "masculine" and "feminine" side of personality. Existence of the anima in males and the animus in females also enables us to relate to members of the opposite sex.

Jung regarded the **self-archetype** as the most important of all. The self-archetype represents unity. Its existence causes a gradual movement toward balance, wholeness, and harmony within the personality. Jung believed that we become richer and more completely human when a balance is achieved between conscious and unconscious, anima and animus, thinking and feeling, sensing and intuiting, persona and ego, introversion and extroversion.

Question: Was Jung talking about self-actualization?

Essentially, he was. Jung was the first to use the term *self-actualization* to describe a striving for completion and unity. He believed that the self-archetype is symbolized in every culture by **mandalas** (man-DALL-ahs: magic circles) of one kind or another (Fig. 19–3).

Jung's theory may not always be "good psychology," but clearly he was a man of genius and vision. If you would like to know more about Jung and his ideas, a good starting place is his autobiography, *Memories, Dreams, Reflections*.

Fig. 19–3 *Jung considered circular designs symbols of the self archetype and representations of unity, balance, and completion within the personality.*

Learning Check

1. List the three divisions of personality postulated by Freud: _____.
2. Which division is totally unconscious? _____.
3. Which division is responsible for moral anxiety? _____.
4. Freud proposed the existence of a death archetype known as Thanatos.   T or F?

Match:

5. ____ striving for superiority
6. ____ basic anxiety
7. ____ pleasure principle
8. ____ collective unconscious
9. ____ anima

A. Freud
B. Adler
C. Horney
D. Jung

Answers: 1. id, ego, superego 2. id 3. superego 4. F 5. B 6. C 7. A 8. D 9. D

Learning Theories of Personality— Habit I Seen You Somewhere Before?

Question: How do behaviorists approach personality?

According to some critics: as if people are robots like R2D2 of *Star Wars* fame. Actually, the behaviorist position is not nearly as mechanistic as some critics would have us believe, and its value is now well established. For one thing, the behaviorists have shown repeatedly that children can *learn* the likes of kindness or hostility, generosity or destructiveness (Bandura & Walters, 1963; Hoffman, 1975). But what does this have to do with personality? Everything, according to the behavioral viewpoint.

The behaviorist position is that personality is no more (or less) than a collection of learned behavior patterns. Personality, like other learned behavior, is acquired through classical and operant conditioning, observational learning, reinforcement, extinction, generalization, and discrimination (Fig. 19–4). When Mother says, "It's not nice to make mud pies with Mommy's blender. If we want to grow up to be a big girl we won't do it again, will we?" she serves as a model and in other ways shapes her daughter's personality.

Strict learning theorists reject the idea that personality is made up of consistent traits. They would contend, for instance, that there is no such thing as a trait of "honesty" (Bandura, 1973; Mischel, 1968).

Fig. 19–4 *Freud believed that aggressive urges are "instinctual." In contrast, behavioral theories assume that personal characteristics such as aggressiveness are learned. Is this boy's aggression the result of observational learning, harsh punishment, or prior reinforcement?*

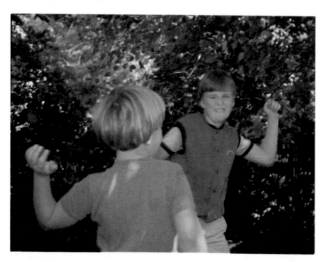

Question: Certainly some people are honest while others are not. How can honesty not be a trait?

A learning theorist would agree that some people are *more often* honest than others. But knowing this does not allow us to predict whether a person will be honest in a specific situation. It would not be unusual, for example, to find that a person honored for returning a lost wallet had cheated on a test. If you were to ask a learning theorist, "Are you an honest person?" the reply might be, "In what situation?"

In drawing our attention to **situational determinants** of behavior, learning theorists have not entirely removed the "person" from personality. Walter Mischel (1973) acknowledges that some situations strongly determine behavior (for instance, an escaped lion walks into the supermarket; you accidentally sit on a lighted cigarette; you find your lover in bed with your best friend). Other situations are trivial and have little impact. Thus, external events *interact* with each person's unique learning history to produce behavior in any given situation. As discussed in Chapter 18, trait theorists also believe that situations affect behavior, but by interacting with traits. So, in essence learning theorists favor substituting the concept of past learning for "traits" in order to explain behavior.

Question: How do learning theorists view the structure of personality?

Behavior = Personality The behavioral view of personality can be illustrated with a theory proposed by John Dollard and Neal Miller (1950). In their view, **habits** form the structure of personality. As for the dynamics of personality, Dollard and Miller believe habits are governed by four elements of learning: **drive, cue, response, and reward.** A drive is any stimulus strong enough to goad a person to action (hunger, pain, lust, frustration, fear, and so on). Cues are signals from the environment that guide responses so they are most likely to bring about reward or reinforcement.

Question: How does that relate to personality?

An example may clarify this viewpoint. Let's say a child is frustrated by an older brother who takes a toy from her. A number of responses are open to the child. She can throw a temper tantrum, hit her brother, tell Mother, and so forth. The response she chooses is guided by available cues and the previous effects of each response. If telling Mother has paid off in the past, and Mother is present, telling may be her immediate response. If a different set of cues exists (if Mother is absent or if the older brother looks particularly menacing), some other response may be selected.

To an outside observer, the child's actions seem to reflect her personality. To the learning theorist, they are a direct reaction to the combined effects of drive, cue, response, and reward.

Question: Doesn't this analysis leave out a lot?

Yes. Learning theorists originally set out to provide a simple, clear model of personality. But in recent years they have had to face a fact they originally tended to overlook. The fact is: People think. The new breed of behavioral psychologists—who include perception, thinking, and other mental events in their views—are called **social learning theorists.** (The label *social* is used because they also stress social relationships and modeling.)

Social Learning Theory   The "cognitive behaviorism" of social learning theory can be illustrated by three concepts proposed by Julian Rotter (1975). They are: the psychological situation, expectancy, and reinforcement value. Let's examine each.

Someone trips you. How do you respond? Your response probably depends on whether you think it was an accident or intentional. It is not enough to know the setting in which a person responds. We also need to know the person's **psychological situation.** That is, how the person *interprets* or *defines* the situation. Here's another example. Let's say you do poorly on an exam. Do you consider this a challenge to work harder, an indication that

it's time to drop the class, or an excuse to get drunk? Again, your interpretation is important.

An **expectancy** refers to your anticipation that a response will lead to reinforcement. To continue the example, if working harder has paid off in the past, it is a likely reaction to a low test score. But according to Rotter, behavior is not automatic. To predict your response, we would also have to know if you *expect* your efforts to pay off in the present situation. In fact, expected reinforcement may be more important than actual past reinforcement. And what about the *value* you attach to grades, school success, or personal ability? Rotter's third concept, **reinforcement value,** states that humans attach different values to various activities or rewards. This too must be taken into account to understand personality.

One additional idea deserves mention here. We all at times evaluate our actions and may reward ourselves with special privileges or treats when the evaluation is positive (Fig. 19–5). With this in mind, social learning theory adds the concept of **self-reinforcement** to the behavioristic view. Thus, habits of self-praise or self-reproach become important dimensions of personality. In fact, self-reinforcement might be considered the behaviorist's equivalent of the Freudian superego. (See Highlight 19–1.)

Radical Behaviorism   As you have probably noted, social learning theory is only moderately behavioristic. The most extreme view of personality is held by radical

Fig. 19–5 *Through self-reinforcement we reward ourselves for personal achievements and other "good" behavior.*

Highlight 19–1
Self-Reinforcement

The following statements, adapted from a scale developed by Elaine Heiby (1983), will add to your understanding of self-reinforcement.

I often think positive thoughts about myself.

I frequently meet standards that I set for myself.

I try not to blame myself when things go wrong.

I usually don't get upset when I make mistakes because I learn from them.

I can get satisfaction out of what I do even if it's not perfect.

When I make mistakes, I take time to reassure myself.

I don't think talking about what you've done right is too boastful.

Praising yourself is healthy and normal.

I don't think I have to be upset every time I make a mistake.

My feelings of self-confidence and self-esteem stay pretty steady.

People who agree with all or most of the preceding statements tend to have high rates of self-reinforcement. And, as the last item suggests, high rates of self-reinforcement are related to high self-esteem. The reverse is also true: Numerous studies have shown that mildly depressed college students tend to have low rates of self-reinforcement (Heiby, 1983).

It is not known if low self-reinforcement leads to depression, or if the reverse is true. But, in any case, learning to be more self-reinforcing appears to lessen depression (Fuchs & Rehm, 1977). From a behavioral viewpoint, there is value in learning to be "good to yourself."

Table 19–2   Behavioral Concepts of Personality

Behavioral personality theory   Any model of personality that emphasizes observable behavior, the relationship between stimuli and responses, and the impact of learning.

Learning theorist   With regard to personality, a psychologist interested in the ways that learning principles shape and explain personality.

Situational determinants   Immediate conditions (for example, rewards and punishments) in a given situation that determine what behavior is likely to occur, independent of the actor's personality traits.

Habit   A deeply ingrained, learned pattern of response.

Drive   Any stimulus (especially an internal stimulus such as hunger) strong enough to goad a person into action.

Cue   External stimuli or signs that guide responses, especially those that signal the likely presence or absence of reinforcement.

Response   Any behavior, either observable or internal.

Social learning theory   An approach that combines behavioral principles, cognition (perception, thinking, anticipation), social relationships, and observational learning to explain personality.

Psychological situation   A situation as it is perceived and interpreted by an individual, not as it exists objectively.

Expectancy   One's anticipation or expectation concerning the effect some response will have, especially regarding reinforcement.

Reinforcement value   The subjective value a person attaches to a particular activity or reinforcer.

Self-reinforcement   Praising oneself or giving oneself a special treat or reward for having made a particular response (such as completing a school assignment).

Radical behaviorism   An approach that avoids any reference to thoughts or other internal processes. Radical behaviorists are interested strictly in relationships between stimuli and responses.

behaviorist B. F. Skinner, who has said, "Intelligent people no longer believe that men are possessed by demons . . . but human behavior is still commonly attributed to indwelling agents" (Skinner, 1971). For Skinner, "personality" is a convenient fiction we invent to pretend we have explained behavior that is actually controlled by the environment. Skinner believes that everything a person does is ultimately based on past and present rewards and punishments. Perhaps Skinner's point of view has been shaped by his environment.

Again, we have discussed a large number of terms in our look at behavioral views of personality. To help you learn them, the terms are summarized in Table 19–2.

Humanistic Theory— A Peek at Peak Experiences

Humanism is a reaction to the pessimism of psychoanalytic theory and the mechanistic qualities of learning theory. At its core is a new image of what it means to be human. Humanists reject the Freudian view of personality as a battleground for biological instincts and unconscious forces. They view people as unique and set apart from the rest of the animal kingdom. Humanists also oppose the mechan-

Highlight 19–2
Characteristics of Self-Actualizers

As he continued his studies, Maslow found that **self-actualizers** share a great number of similarities. Whether famous or unknown, academically distinguished or uneducated, rich or poor, self-actualizers tend to fit this profile:

1. Efficient perceptions of reality. Maslow's subjects were able to judge situations correctly and honestly and were very sensitive to the fake and dishonest.

2. Comfortable acceptance of self, others, nature. Subjects were able to accept their own human nature with all its shortcomings. The shortcomings of others and the contradictions of the human condition were also accepted with humor and tolerance.

3. Spontaneity. Maslow's subjects extended their creativity into everyday activities. They tended to be unusually alive, engaged, and spontaneous.

4. Task-centering. Most subjects had a mission to fulfill in life or some task or problem outside of themselves to pursue. Humanitarians such as Albert Schweitzer or Mother Teresa represent this quality.

5. Autonomy. Subjects were free from dependence on external authority or other people. They tended to be resourceful and independent.

6. Continued freshness of appreciation. The self-actualizer seems to constantly renew appreciation of life's basic goods. A sunset or a flower will be experienced as intensely the one-thousandth time as it was the first. There is an "innocence of vision," like that of an artist or a child.

7. Fellowship with humanity. Maslow's subjects felt a deep identification with others and the human situation in general.

8. Profound interpersonal relationships. The interpersonal relationships of self-actualizers are marked by deep, loving bonds.

9. Unhostile sense of humor. This refers to the wonderful capacity to laugh at oneself. It also refers to the kind of humor a man like Abraham Lincoln had. Lincoln probably never made a joke that hurt anybody. His wry comments were a gentle prodding at human shortcomings.

10. Peak experiences. All of Maslow's subjects reported the frequent occurrence of "peak" experiences. These were marked by feelings of ecstasy, harmony, and deep meaning. Subjects reported feeling at one with the universe, stronger and calmer than ever before, filled with light, beauty, goodness, and so forth. In short, self-actualizers feel safe and unanxious, accepted, loved, loving, and alive.

ical, "thing-like" overtones of the behaviorist viewpoint. We are not, they say, merely a bundle of moldable responses; instead, we are creative beings capable of making responsible choices. The humanistic viewpoint leads to a greater emphasis on immediate **subjective experience** rather than on prior learning.

Question: Who are the major humanistic theorists?

There are many psychologists whose theories fall within the humanistic tradition. Of these, the best known are Carl Rogers and Abraham Maslow. Since self-actualization was briefly introduced elsewhere in the text, let's begin with a more detailed look at this facet of Maslow's thinking.

Maslow and Self-Actualization

Psychologists have had a tendency to study human problems more than human strengths. A notable exception to this can be found in Abraham Maslow's studies of people living unusually effective lives. Maslow became interested in people who seemed to be using almost all of their talents and potentials. How were they different from the average person? To find an answer, Maslow began by studying the lives of great men and women: Albert Einstein, William James, Jane Adams, Eleanor Roosevelt, Abraham Lincoln, John Muir, Walt Whitman, and others. From there he moved on to studies of artists, writers, poets, and other creative individuals.

Along the way Maslow's thinking changed radically. At first he studied only people of obvious creativity or high achievement. Eventually, however, it became clear that a carpenter, housewife, clerk, or student could live creatively and make full use of his or her potentials. Maslow referred to this tendency as *self-actualization* (Maslow, 1954). (See Highlight 19–2.)

Question: Maslow's list of self-actualizing people seems pretty subjective. Is it really a fair representation of self-actualization?

You have noticed that Maslow tried to investigate self-actualization empirically, but his choice of people for study was subjective. Undoubtedly there are many ways to reach full development of personal potential. Maslow's primary contribution was to draw attention to the *possibility* of continued personal growth. Maslow considered self-actualization an ongoing process, not a simple end point to be attained only once.

Carl Rogers' Self Theory

Carl Rogers is a psychotherapist who, like Freud, bases his theory on clinical experience. Unlike Freud, who portrayed the normal personality as "adjusted" to internal conflict, Rogers sees greater possibility for inner harmony. The **fully functioning person,** he says, is one who has achieved an openness to feelings and experiences and has learned to trust inner urges and intuitions (Rogers, 1961). Rogers believes this attitude is most likely to occur when a

Fig. 19–6 *Humanists consider self-image a central determinant of behavior and personal adjustment.*

Table 19–3   Some Key Humanistic Terms
Humanism   An approach to psychology that focuses on human experience, problems, potentials, and ideals.
Subjective experience   Reality as it is perceived and interpreted, not as it exists objectively; personal, private, nonobjective experience.
Self-actualization   The full development of personal potential.
Self-actualizer   One who is living creatively and making full use of his or her potentials.
Task centering   Focusing on the task at hand, rather than on one's own feelings or needs.
Autonomy   A freedom from dependence on external authority or the opinions of others.
Peak experiences   Temporary moments of self-actualization, marked by feelings of ecstasy, harmony, and deep meaning.
Fully functioning person   Rogers' term for persons living in harmony with their deepest feelings, impulses, and intuitions.
Self   A continuously evolving conception of one's personal identity.
Phenomenal field   A person's total subjective experience of reality; his or her private psychological world.
Self-image   Total subjective perception of oneself, including an image of one's body, impressions of one's personality, capabilities, and so forth.
Symbolization   In Rogers' theory, the process of admitting an experience to awareness.
Incongruence   A mismatch or inconsistency. In Rogers' theory, experiences that are inconsistent with one's self-image are said to be incongruent.
Incongruent person   A person who has a distorted or inaccurate self-image.
Ideal self   An idealized image of oneself (the person one would like to be) that, optimally, closely matches one's overall self-image.

person receives ample amounts of love and acceptance from others.

Personality   Structure   and   Dynamics   Rogers' theory of personality centers on the concept of the **self,** a flexible and changing perception of personal identity that emerges from the **phenomenal field.**

Question: What is the phenomenal field?

The phenomenal field is the person's total *subjective* experience of reality. The self is made up of those experiences identified as "I" or "me" that are separated from "not me" experiences. Much human behavior can be understood as an attempt to maintain consistency between one's **self-image** and actions. For example, individuals who think of themselves as kind and considerate will act accordingly in most situations.

Question: Let's say I know a person who thinks she is kind and considerate, but she really isn't. How does this fit Rogers' theory?

According to Rogers, experiences that match the self-image are **symbolized** (admitted to consciousness) and contribute to gradual changes in the self. Information or feelings inconsistent with the self-image are said to be **incongruent.** It is incongruent, for example, to think of yourself as a considerate person if others frequently mention your rudeness. It is also incongruent to pretend you are kind when you are feeling callous or to say you are not angry when you are seething inside.

Experiences seriously incongruent with the self-image can be threatening, and they are often distorted or denied conscious recognition. Blocking, denying, or distorting experiences prevents the self from changing and creates a gulf between the self-image and reality. As the self-image grows more unrealistic, the **incongruent person** becomes confused, vulnerable, dissatisfied, or seriously maladjusted (see Chapter 20).

When your self-image is consistent with what you really think, feel, do, and experience, you are best able to actualize your potentials. Rogers also considers it essential to have congruence between the self-image and the **ideal self.** The ideal self is similar to Freud's ego ideal. It is an image of the person you would most like to be.

Question: Is it really incongruent to not live up to one's ideal self?

Rogers is aware that we never fully attain our ideals, but the greater the gap between the way you see yourself and the way you would like to be, the greater the tension and anxiety experienced. The Rogerian view of personality functioning can therefore be summarized as a process of maximizing potentials by accepting information about oneself as realistically and honestly as possible. In accord with Rogers' thinking, researchers have found that people with a close match between their self-image and ideal self tend to be socially poised, confident, and resourceful. Those with a poor match tend to be anxious, insecure, and lacking in social skills (Gough, Fioravanti, & Lazzari, 1983).

Learning Check

1. Social learning theorists relate personality "traits" to _____.

2. Dollard and Miller consider cues the basic structure of personality.   T or F?

3. Humanists emphasize subjective experience and innate drives for self-actualization.   T or F?

4. A close match between the self-image and the ideal self creates a condition called incongruence.   T or F?

5. Self-reinforcement is to behavioristic theory as superego is to psychoanalytic theory.   T or F?

6. The radical behaviorist view of personality is represented by:
    a. Neal Miller   *b.* B. F. Skinner   *c.* Abraham Maslow   *d.* Carl Rogers

Answers: *q* **·9** ⊥ **·5** Ⅎ **·4** ⊥ **·3** Ⅎ **·2** suoᴉʇɐnʇᴉs ɔᴉɟᴉɔǝds ɹo sʇᴉqɐɥ **·1**

Personality Development— Three Theories

Every society must bring about the **socialization** of its children by teaching them language, customs, rules, roles, and morals. The job of preparing children to participate in society is typically placed in the hands of parents. This arrangement is convenient and fateful. While carrying out socialization, parents impart something of their own personality to children.

Question: How does this occur? What factors are most influential in the development of adult personality?

Each theory offers a different version of the important events in personality formation. Let's begin with a look at the psychoanalytic viewpoint.

A Freudian Fable?

Freud theorized that the core of personality is formed before age 6 in a series of **psychosexual stages.** His account holds that childhood urges for erotic pleasure have lasting effects on development. Freud's emphasis on infantile sexuality is one of the most controversial aspects of his thinking. However, Freud used the term *sex* very broadly to mean any pleasurable activity.

Freud identified four psychosexual stages: the **oral, anal, phallic,** and **genital.** At each stage a different part of the body becomes an **erogenous zone** (an area capable of producing pleasure). Each then serves as the main source of pleasure, frustration, and self-expression. Freud believed that many adult personality traits can be traced to **fixations** in one or more of the stages.

Question: What is a fixation?

A fixation is an unresolved conflict or emotional hang-up caused by overindulgence or frustration. A description of the psychosexual stages shows why Freud considered fixations important.

The Oral Stage   During the first year of life, most of the infant's pleasure comes from stimulation of the mouth. If a child is overfed or frustrated, oral traits may be created. Adult expressions of oral needs include gum chewing, nail biting, smoking, kissing, overeating, and alcoholism (Fig. 19–7).

Question: What if there is an oral fixation?

Fig. 19–7   *Was Freud's ever-present cigar a sign of an oral fixation?*

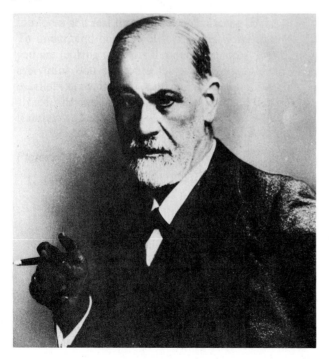

Fixation early in the oral stage produces an **oral-dependent** personality. Oral-dependent persons are gullible (they swallow things easily!), passive, and need lots of attention (they want to be mothered). Frustrations later in the oral stage cause aggression, often in the form of biting. Fixation here causes **oral-aggressive** adults to be argumentative ("biting sarcasm" is their forte!), cynical, and exploitive of others.

The Anal Stage   Between the ages of 1 and 3, the child's attention shifts to the process of elimination. When parents attempt toilet training, the child can gain approval or express rebellion or aggression by "holding on" or "letting go." Therefore, harsh or indulgent toilet training may lock such responses into personality. Freud described the **anal-retentive** (holding-on) personality as obstinate, stingy, orderly, and compulsively clean. The **anal-expulsive** (letting-go) personality is disorderly, destructive, cruel, and messy.

The Phallic Stage   Adult traits of the **phallic personality** are: vanity, exhibitionism, sensitive pride, and narcissism (self-love). Freud theorized that such traits develop between the ages of 3 and 6. At this time, increased sexual interest causes the child to become physically attracted to the parent of the opposite sex. In males this attraction leads to an **Oedipus conflict.** The core of the conflict is that the boy feels rivalry with his father for the affection of the mother. Freud believed the male child feels threatened by the father (specifically, the boy fears castration). To lower his anxieties, the boy must **identify** with the father. Identification causes him to take on the father's values and to form a conscience.

Question: What about the female child?

The female counterpart to the Oedipus conflict is called the **Electra conflict.** In it the girl loves her father and competes with her mother. However, according to Freud, the girl's identification with the mother is more gradual and less effective in creating a conscience. Freud believed that females already feel castrated and so are less driven to identify with their mothers than boys are with their fathers. This particular aspect of Freudian thought has been thoroughly (and rightfully) denounced by modern feminists. It is probably best understood as a reflection of the male-dominated times in which Freud lived.

Latency   According to Freud there is a period of *latency* from age 6 to puberty. Latency is not actually a stage. Rather, it is a time during which psychosexual development is interrupted. Freud's belief that psychosexual development is "on hold" at this time is difficult to accept. Nevertheless, Freud saw latency as a relatively quiet time compared with the stormy first 6 years of life.

The Genital Stage At puberty a resurgence of sexual energies activates all the unresolved conflicts of earlier years. This resurgence, according to Freud, is the reason why adolescence can be such a trying time, filled with emotion and turmoil. The genital stage begins at puberty and is marked, through adolescence, by a growing capacity for mature and responsible social-sexual relationships. The genital stage ends with heterosexual love and the attainment of full adult sexuality.

Critical Comments As bizarre as Freud's developmental theory might seem, it has been influential for several reasons. First, it pioneered the idea that the first years of life help shape adult personality. Second, it identified feeding, toilet training, and early sexual experiences as critical events in personality formation. Third, Freud was among the first to propose that development proceeds through a series of stages. (Erik Erikson's psycho*social* stages, described in Chapter 16, are a modern extension of Freudian thinking.)

Question: Is the Freudian view of development widely accepted?

Despite its contributions, Freud's theory remains controversial, and few psychologists embrace it without reservation. In some cases Freud was clearly wrong. His portrayal of the elementary school years (latency) as free from sexuality and unimportant for personality development defies belief. His idea that a stern or threatening father helps develop a strong conscience in males has also been challenged. Studies show that an affectionate and accepting father is more likely than a stern one to create a strong conscience in a son (Mussen et al., 1969; Sears et al., 1957). Freud also overemphasized sexuality in personality development; other motives and cognitive factors are of equal importance. Many more criticisms could be listed, but the fact remains that there is an element of truth to much of what Freud said.

Question: How do learning theorists account for personality development?

Behavioristic View of Development

Many of Freud's major points can be restated in terms of modern learning theory. Miller and Dollard (1950) agree with Freud that the first 6 years are crucial for personality development, but for different reasons. Rather than thinking in terms of psychosexual urges and fixations, they ask, "What makes early learning experiences so lasting in their effects?" Their answer is that childhood is a time of urgent and tearing drives, powerful rewards and punishments, and crushing frustrations. Also important is **social reinforcement** based on the effects of attention and approval from others. These forces combine to shape the core of personality.

Critical Situations Miller and Dollard consider four developmental situations to be of critical importance. These are: (1) **feeding**, (2) **toilet** or **cleanliness training**, (3) **sex training**, and (4) learning to express **anger** or **aggression**.

Question: Why are these of special importance?

Feeding serves as an illustration. If children are fed when they cry, they are encouraged to actively manipulate the environment. The child allowed to cry without being fed learns to be passive. Thus, a basic active or passive orientation toward the world may be formed by early feeding experiences. Feeding can also affect later social relationships because the child learns to associate satisfaction and pleasure, or frustration and discomfort, with the presence of others.

Toilet and cleanliness training can be a particularly strong source of emotion for both parents and children. Parents are usually aghast the first time they find a child smearing feces about with gay abandon. Their reaction is often sharp punishment. For the child the result is frustration and confusion. Many attitudes toward cleanliness, conformity, and bodily functions are formed at such times. Studies also show that severe, punishing, or frustrating toilet training can have undesirable effects on personality development (Sears et al., 1957). Toilet and cleanliness training therefore require patience and a sense of humor.

Question: What about sex and anger?

When, where, and how a child learns to express anger and aggression are of obvious importance. So too is expression of sexual behavior. Both types of experiences can leave an imprint on personality. Specifically, permissiveness for sexual and aggressive behavior in childhood is linked to adult needs for power (McCelland & Pilon, 1983). This link probably occurs because permitting such behaviors allows children to get pleasure from asserting themselves.

Sex training also involves learning "male" and "female" behaviors—which creates an even broader basis for shaping personality.

Fig. 19–8 *Adult personality is influenced by identification with parents.*

Becoming Male or Female   From birth onward children are identified as boys or girls and encouraged to learn sex-appropriate behavior. Two processes that contribute greatly to personality development in general, and to sex training, are *identification* and *imitation*. **Identification** refers to the child's emotional attachment to admired adults, especially to those the child depends on for love and care. Identification typically encourages **imitation,** a desire to be like the valued or admired adult (Fig. 19–8). Many of a child's "male" or "female" traits come from conscious or unconscious attempts to pattern behavior after that of the same-sex parent with which the child identifies.

Question: When children are around parents of both sexes, why don't they imitate behavior typical of the opposite sex as well as the same sex?

You may recall from Chapter 9 that Albert Bandura and others have shown that learning takes place vicariously as well as directly (Bandura, 1965). This means we can learn without direct reward by observing and remembering the actions of others. But imitation of actions depends on their outcome. For example, boys and girls have equal opportunities to observe adults and other children acting aggressively. However, girls are less likely than boys to imitate aggressive behavior because they rarely see female aggression rewarded or approved. Thus, many arbitrary dimensions of "maleness" or "femaleness" are perpetuated at the same time sexual identity is established.

A study of preschool children by Lisa Serbin and Daniel O'Leary (1975) found that boys are three times more likely to get teacher attention for aggressive or disruptive behavior than girls are. Boys who hit other students or who broke things typically got loud scoldings that drew the attention of the whole class. When teachers responded to disruptive girls, they gave brief, soft rebukes that others couldn't hear. Since we know that attention of almost any kind reinforces children's behavior, it is clear that the boys were being encouraged to be active and aggressive. Serbin and O'Leary found that girls got the most attention when they were within arm's reach, literally or figuratively clinging to the teacher.

It's easy to see that the teachers were unwittingly encouraging the girls to be submissive, dependent, and passive. Similar differences in reinforcement probably explain why males are responsible for much more aggression in society than females are. Murder and assault rates, for example, are consistently higher for men (Deaux, 1985).

A Humanistic View of Development

Why do mirrors, photographs, tape recorders, and the reactions of others hold such fascination and threat for most people? Carl Rogers would say it is because they provide information about one's *self*. Developing a self-image depends on information from the environment. It begins with a sorting of perceptions and feelings—my body, my toes, my nose, I want, I like, I am, and so on—and soon expands to include self-evaluation: I am a good person, I am bad right now, and so forth.

Question: How does development of the self contribute to later personality functioning?

Rogers holds that positive and negative evaluations by others cause a child to develop internal standards of evaluation called **conditions of worth.** In other words we learn that some actions win our parents' love and approval while others are rejected.

Learning to evaluate some experiences or feelings as "good" and others as "bad" is directly related to a later capacity for self-esteem, positive self-evaluation, or **posi-**

tive self-regard, to use Rogers' term. To think of yourself as a good, lovable, worthwhile person, your behavior and experiences must match your internal conditions of worth. The problem is that this can cause incongruence by leading to the denial of many true feelings and experiences.

To put it simply, Rogers sees many adult adjustment problems as an attempt to live by the standards of others. He believes congruence and self-actualization are encouraged by replacing conditions of worth with organismic val-uing. Organismic valuing is a direct, gut-level response to life that avoids the filtering and distortion of incongruence. It is the ability to trust one's own feelings and perceptions—to become one's own "center of evaluation." Organismic valuing is most likely to develop, Rogers feels, when children (or adults) receive "unconditional positive regard" from others. That is, when they are prized just for being themselves, without any conditions or strings attached.

Learning Check

1. Freud's version of personality development is based on the concept of _____ stages.

2. Arrange these stages in the proper order: phallic, anal, genital, oral. _____.

3. Freud considered the anal-retentive personality obstinate and stingy.   T or F?

4. Which of the following is *not* a critical learning situation in the behaviorist theory of personality formation?   (circle)

   feeding   sex training   language training   anger training

5. Behavioristic theories emphasize identification and _____.

6. Rogers considers acceptance of conditions of _____ a troublesome aspect of development of the self.

Answers: 1. psychosexual 2. oral, anal, phallic, genital 3. T 4. language training 5. imitation 6. worth.

Personality Theories—
Overview and Comparison

Question: Which personality theory is right?

Each theory has made contributions to our understanding of personality by organizing observations of human behavior. Nevertheless, none of the major theories can be fully proved or disproved. (If a theory could be proved true, it would no longer be a theory—it would be a law.) At the same time that theories are neither true nor false, their predictions may be. The best way to judge a theory, then, is in terms of its *usefulness* for explaining behavior, for stimulating research, and for suggesting ways of treating psychological disorders. Each theory has fared differently in these areas.

Psychoanalytic Theory By present standards psychoanalytic theory seems to overemphasize sexuality and biological instincts. These distortions were corrected somewhat by the neo-Freudians, but problems remain. One of the most telling criticisms of Freudian theory is that it can explain any psychological event *after* it has occurred. But beforehand it offers little help in predicting future behavior. For this reason many psychoanalytic concepts are difficult or impossible to test.

Behavioristic Theory Learning theories have provided a good framework for personality research. Of the three major perspectives, the behaviorists have made the best effort to rigorously test and verify their ideas. They have, however, been criticized for underestimating the impact on personality of temperament, emotion, and subjective experience. To a degree social learning theory is an attempt to answer such criticisms.

Humanistic Theory A great strength of the humanists is the light they have shed on positive dimensions of personality. As Maslow (1968) put it, "Human nature is not nearly as bad as it has been thought to be. It is as if Freud supplied us with the sick half of psychology and we must now fill it out with the healthy half." Despite their contributions the humanists can be criticized for using imprecise concepts that are difficult to measure or study objectively. Even so, humanistic thought has encouraged many people to seek greater self-awareness and personal growth.

Summary In the final analysis we need the concepts of all three perspectives (and those discussed in the previous chapter) to adequately explain personality. There is an element of truth to each view, and a balanced picture emerges only when all are considered. Table 19–4 provides a final overview of the three principal theories we have discussed.

Table 19–4   Comparison of Three Views of Personality

	Psychoanalytic Theory	Behavioristic Theory	Humanistic Theory
View of human nature	negative	neutral	positive
Is behavior free or determined?	determined	determined	free choice
Principal motives	sex and aggression	drives of all kinds	self-actualization
Personality structure	id, ego, superego	habits	self
Role of unconscious	maximized	practically nonexistent	minimized
Conception of conscience	superego	self-reinforcement	ideal self, valuing process
Developmental emphasis	psychosexual stages	critical learning situations; identification and imitation	development of self-image
Barriers to personal growth	unconscious conflicts; fixations	maladaptive habits; pathological environment	conditions of worth; incongruence

Applications

The Search for Self-Actualization

Some people fear finding themselves alone—and so they don't find themselves at all.

André Gide

What a man can be, he must be. This need we may call self-actualization.

Abraham Maslow

Self-actualization is a concept that has appeared several times in this book. Perhaps you have been attracted to the promise it holds for personal growth. Self-actualizers lead rich, creative, and fulfilling lives.

Question: What steps can be taken to promote self-actualization?

Promoting self-actualization is more difficult than might be imagined. Many people are caught in a struggle for survival or security and never get a chance to develop their potentials fully. Others show little interest in personal growth or in the qualities Maslow described.

Moreover, Maslow made few specific recommendations about how to proceed. Nevertheless, a number of helpful suggestions can be gleaned from his writings (Maslow, 1954, 1967, 1971).

Steps Toward Self-Actualization

There is no magic formula for leading a more creative life. Knowing or even imitating the traits of unusually effective people cannot be counted on to promote self-actualization. Self-actualization is primarily a *process*, not a goal or an end point. As such it requires hard work, patience, and commitment. Here are some ways to begin.

Be Willing to Change Begin by asking yourself, "Am I living in a way that is deeply satisfying to me and that truly expresses me?" If not, be prepared to make changes in your life. Indeed, ask yourself this question often and accept the need for continual change.

Applications: The Search for Self-Actualization

Take Responsibility   You can become an architect of self by acting as if you are *personally* responsible for every aspect of your life. Shouldering responsibility in this way is not totally realistic, but it helps end the habit of blaming others for your own shortcomings. This attitude is illustrated by a young woman who realized in a counseling session, "I can't depend on someone else to give me an education. I'll have to get it myself" (Rogers, 1962).

Examine Your Motives   Self-discovery involves an element of risk. To learn your strengths, limitations, and true feelings, you must be willing to go out on a limb, speak your mind, and take some chances. Fears of failure, rejection, loneliness, or disagreement with others are a tremendous barrier to personal change. If most of your behavior seems to be directed by a desire for "safety" or "security," it may be time to test the limits of those needs. Try to make each life decision a choice for growth, not a response to fear or anxiety.

Experience Honestly and Directly   Wishful thinking is another barrier to personal growth. Self-actualizers trust themselves enough to accept all kinds of information without distorting it to fit their fears and desires. Try to see yourself as others do. Be willing to admit, "I was wrong" or, "I failed because I was irresponsible." This basic honesty can be extended to perception in general. Try to experience the world as you did when you were a child: fully, vividly, and directly. Try to see things as they are, not as you would like them to be.

Make Use of Positive Experiences   As a rule of thumb, growth-promoting activities usually feel good. Perhaps you have felt unusually alert and alive when expressing yourself through art, music, dance, writing, or athletics. Or perhaps life seems especially rich when you are alone in nature, surrounded by friends, or when you are helping others. Whatever their source, Maslow considered peak experiences temporary moments of self-actualization. Therefore, you might actively repeat activities that have caused feelings of awe, amazement, exaltation, renewal, reverence, humility, fulfillment, or joy.

Be Prepared to Be Different   Maslow believed that everyone has a potential for "greatness," but most fear

becoming what they might. Much of this fear is related to the fact that actualizing potentials may place you at odds with cultural expectations or with others who are important in your life. As part of personal growth, be prepared to be unpopular when your views don't agree with others.' Trust your own impulses and feelings; don't automatically judge yourself by the standards of others. Accept your uniqueness: As one young woman put it, "I've always tried to be what others thought I should be, but now I'm wondering whether I shouldn't just see that I am what I am" (Rogers, 1962).

Get Involved   Maslow found with few exceptions that self-actualizers tend to have a mission or "calling" in life. For these people "work" is not done just to fill deficiency needs, but to satisfy higher yearnings for truth, beauty, brotherhood, and meaning. Many of the things you do may be motivated by more commonplace needs, but you can add meaning to these activities by endeavoring to work hard at whatever you do. Get personally involved and committed. Turn your attention to problems outside yourself.

Slow Down   Try to avoid hurrying or overscheduling your time. Self-awareness takes time to develop, and a certain amount of leisure is essential for contemplation and self-exploration. Time pressures tend to force a person to rely compulsively on old habits.

Start a Journal   Although this suggestion does not come from Maslow's writings, it is a valuable way of promoting self-awareness. Many people find a journal provides the kind of information necessary to make growth-oriented life changes. A journal should include a description of significant events in your daily life. In addition thoughts, feelings, fears, wishes, frustrations, and dreams should be recorded. Some find it useful to write dialogues in their journal in which they speak to parents, teachers, lovers, objects, and so forth. Review and reread your journal periodically. You will find it is easier to learn from an event after it has "cooled off" and you can view it objectively.

Assess Your Progress   Since there is no final point at which one becomes self-actualized, it is important frequently to gauge your progress and to renew your efforts. Boredom is a good sign you are in need of

Applications: The Search for Self-Actualization

change. If you feel bored at school, at a job, or in a relationship, consider it a challenge or an indication that you have not taken responsibility for personal growth. A situation is only as "boring" as you allow it to be. Almost any activity can be used as a chance for self-exploration if it is approached creatively.

What to Expect   As we have already noted, growth-promoting activities are usually personally satisfying.

Question: Are there other signs that one is moving in the right direction?

Yes. There should be a noticeable improvement in the quality of your daily life and a greater acceptance of yourself and of others. You should feel more confident and should carry out daily routines with less strain or conflict. These changes do not happen overnight, and

your first steps toward self-actualization may be threatening at the same time they are exhilarating. Positive changes can also be quite subtle. An idea of what to expect is provided by the words of Henry David Thoreau. After he had spent 2 years in the wilderness at Walden Pond, Thoreau had this to say about his experience:

I learned this, at least, by my experiment: that as one advances confidently in the direction of his dreams, and endeavors to live the life which he has imagined, he will meet with a success unexpected in common hours. He will put some things behind, will pass an invisible boundary; new universal and more liberal laws will begin to establish themselves around and within him. . . . The laws of the universe will appear less complex, and solitude will not be solitude, nor poverty, poverty, nor weakness, weakness.

Learning Check

1. In his writings, Maslow emphasized that self-actualization is a process, not a goal or end point.   T or F?
2. Making fuller use of personal potentials requires learning to live up to the expectations of others.   T or F?
3. Maslow described peak experiences as temporary moments of self-actualization.   T or F?
4. A major characteristic of self-actualizers is their interest in status and personal recognition.   T or F?
5. According to Maslow, wishful thinking and distorted self-perceptions are barriers to self-actualization.   T or F?

Answers: 1. T   2. F   3. T   4. F   5. T

Chapter Summary

- Like other *psychodynamic* approaches, Freud's psychoanalytic theory emphasizes unconscious forces and conflicts within the personality. In his theory, personality is made up of the *id, ego,* and *superego. Libido,* derived from the life instincts, is the primary energy running the personality. Conflicts within the personality may cause *neurotic anxiety* or *moral anxiety* and motivate use of *ego-defense mechanisms.* The personality operates on three levels: the *conscious, preconscious,* and *unconscious.*

- Some of Freud's followers, known as *neo-Freudians,* altered and updated his theories. Others have developed related but separate *psychodynamic theories.*
  Alfred Adler proposed a more *social view* of personality, emphasizing *feelings of inferiority* and *striving for superiority.* Striving for superiority and *compensation* for limitations creates a unique *style of life,* which is further altered by the *creative self.*

- Karen Horney countered some of Freud's male-oriented thinking and contended that emotional disturbances are rooted in *basic anxiety.* Basic anxiety can cause an overuse or overdependence on one of three modes of relating to others: moving *toward, away* from, or *against* others.

- Carl Jung broke away from Freud to develop his own theory, which includes a number of unique concepts such as: the *persona, extroversion* and *introversion,* the *personal unconscious,* and the *collective unconscious.* His most controversial ideas pertain to the existence of *archetypes,* such as the *anima* and *animus,* and the *self-archetype.*

- Behavioral theories of personality emphasize learning, conditioning, and immediate effects of the environment. Learning theorists generally reject the idea of stable personality "traits," preferring instead to stress the effects of *prior learning* and *situational determinants* of behavior.

- Learning theorists John Dollard and Neal Miller consider *habits* the basic core of personality. Habits express the combined effects of *drive, cue, response,* and *reward.*

- *Social learning theory* adds cognitive elements, such as perception, thinking, and understanding to the behavioral view of personality. Such elements are exemplified by Julian Rotter's concepts of the *psychological situation, expectancies,* and *reinforcement value.* Some social learning theorists treat "conscience" as a kind of *self-reinforcement.*

- Humanistic theory emphasizes *subjective experience* and needs for *self-actualization.* Abraham Maslow's study of *self-actualizers* showed that they have a variety of characteristics in common, ranging from efficient perceptions of reality to frequent peak experiences.

- Carl Rogers' theory views the *self* as an entity that emerges from the *phenomenal field.* Experiences that match the *self-image* are *symbolized* (admitted to consciousness), while those that are *incongruent* are excluded. The *incongruent person* has a highly unrealistic self-image. The *congruent* or *fully functioning person* is flexible and open to experiences and feelings.

- The Freudian view of personality development is based on a series of *psychosexual stages:* the *oral, anal, phallic,* and *genital* stages. *Fixation* at any stage can leave a lasting imprint on personality.

- The behavioristic view of personality development holds that social *reinforcement* in four situations is critical. The situations are: *feeding; toilet* or *cleanliness training; sex training;* and *anger* or *aggression training. Identification* and *imitation* are of particular importance in sex training.

- In the development of personality, humanists are primarily interested in the emergence of a *self-image* and *self-evaluations.* As parents apply *conditions of worth* to children's behavior, thoughts, and feelings, children begin to do the same. Internalized conditions of worth then contribute to incongruence and interrupt the *organismic valuing process.*

- Self-actualization can be viewed as an ongoing process of personal growth, rather than a destination. In this sense self-actualization may be actively pursued at any point in life.

▶▶▶ **Exploration**

Moral Development—Values and Personality

A person with a terminal illness is in great pain. She is pleading for death. Should extraordinary medical procedures be used to keep her alive? If a friend of yours desperately needed to pass a test and asked you to help him cheat, would you do it?

Questions such as these have more to do with personality than you might suspect. We have already seen that personality theories use some concept of conscience to explain behavior. By conscience we typically mean a system of *moral values* that guides behavior.

For many, conscience is simply an internal source of reward (pride) and punishment (guilt). But according to researcher Lawrence Kohlberg, conscience is only one of several ways in which moral values are represented in the personality. Kohlberg (1981a) believes there are higher levels of moral development and that these are acquired in stages.

Question: What does he base this belief on?

Moral Dilemmas   To study moral development, Kohlberg posed *moral dilemmas* to children of different ages. Here is one of the dilemmas he used (adapted from Kohlberg, 1969):

A woman was near death from cancer, and there was only one drug that might save her. The drug had been discovered by a druggist who was charging ten times what the drug cost him to make. The sick woman's husband could only get together $1000, which was half of what the druggist was charging. He asked the druggist to sell it cheaper or to let him pay later. But the druggist said no. So the husband got desperate and broke into the man's store to steal the drug for his wife. Should he have done that? Was it actually wrong or right? Why?

Each child was asked to say what action should be taken by the husband. By classifying reasons given for each choice, Kohlberg identified three levels of moral development.

At the first, or **preconventional level,** moral thinking is determined by the consequences of actions (punishment, reward, or exchange of favors). In the second, or **conventional level** of morality, actions are directed by a desire to conform to the expectations of others or to socially accepted rules and values. The third, or **postconventional level,** represents advanced moral development. Behavior at this level is directed by self-accepted moral principles. In addition to the three levels, Kohlberg identified six stages of moral development.

Stages of Moral Development

Preconventional

Stage 1. Punishment orientation. In this stage, actions are evaluated in terms of possible punishment, not goodness or badness. Obedience to power is emphasized.

Stage 2. Pleasure-seeking orientation. Right action is determined by one's own needs. Concern for the needs of others is largely a matter of "You scratch my back and I'll scratch yours," not of loyalty, gratitude, or justice.

Conventional

Stage 3. Good boy/good girl orientation. Good behavior is that which pleases others in the immediate group or which brings approval. The emphasis is on being "nice."

Stage 4. Authority orientation. In this stage the emphasis is on upholding law, order, and authority; doing one's duty; and following social rules.

Postconventional

Stage 5. Social-contract orientation. Support of laws and rules is based on rational analysis and mutual agreement. Rules are recognized as open to question but are upheld for the good of the community and in the name of democratic values.

Stage 6. Morality of individual principles. Behavior is directed by self-chosen ethical principles that tend to be general, comprehensive, or universal. High value is placed on justice, dignity, and equality.

Examples of Reasoning at Each Stage

Stage 1. "He shouldn't steal the drug because he could get caught

Exploration: Moral Development—Values and Personality

and sent to jail" (avoiding punishment).

Stage 2. "It won't do him any good to steal the drug because his wife will probably die before he gets out of jail" (self-interest).

Stage 3. "He shouldn't steal the drug because others will think he is a thief. His wife would not want to be saved by thievery" (avoiding disapproval).

Stage 4. "Although his wife needs the drug, he should not break the law to get it. Everyone is equal in the eyes of the law, and his wife's condition does not justify stealing" (traditional morality of authority).

Stage 5. "He should not steal the drug. The druggist's decision is reprehensible, but mutual respect for the rights of others must be maintained" (social contract).

Stage 6. "He should steal the drug and then inform the authorities that he has done so. He will have to face a penalty, but he will have saved a human life" (self-chosen ethical principles).

In recent years Kohlberg has combined Stages 5 and 6 because it has been difficult, in practice, to separate them (Kohlberg, 1981b). He remains firm in his belief, however, that morality develops in preconventional, conventional, and postconventional phases.

Question: Does everyone eventually reach the last level?

Kohlberg and his associates have found that people advance through the stages at different rates and that many people fail to reach the "principled" level of morality. The preconventional stages (1 and 2)

are most characteristic of young children and delinquents. Conventional group-oriented morals of Stages 3 and 4 are characteristic of older children and most of the adult population. Kohlberg estimates that postconventional morality, representing self-direction and higher principles, is characteristic of only about 20 percent of the adult population.

Morality in the Real World   To illustrate the importance of moral development in personality, let us compare two very different individuals. First let's apply Kohlberg's analysis to statements attributed to Nazi officer Adolf Eichmann, accused of sharing responsibility for the deaths of millions of Jews in Germany during World War II:

> In actual fact, I was merely a little cog in the machinery that carried out the directives of the German Reich (Stage 1). It was really none of my business (Stage 2). Yet what is there to "admit"? I carried out my order (Stage 1) (Kohlberg, 1969).

Compare this with the words of Mahatma Gandhi, the famous leader who protested British rule of India. Gandhi once addressed a British court:

> I had to either submit to a system which I considered had done irreparable harm to my country, or incur the risk. . . . I am here, therefore, to invite and cheerfully submit to the highest penalty that can be inflicted upon me for what in law is a deliberate crime and what appears to me to be the highest duty of a citizen.

Gandhi, like other great leaders (Lincoln, Martin Luther King), was

clearly operating at a postconventional level of morality.

Moral development is a promising topic for further study. As an example, consider the work of psychologist Carol Gilligan.

Justice or Caring?   Gilligan (1982) has pointed out that Kohlberg's system is concerned mainly with the ethics of *justice*. Based on studies of women who faced real-life dilemmas, Gilligan argues that there is also an ethic of *care* and responsibility to be considered. As one illustration Gilligan presented the following story to 11- to 15-year-old American children:

The Porcupine and the Moles

Seeking refuge from the cold, a porcupine asked to share a cave for the winter with a family of moles. The moles agreed. But because the cave was small, they soon found they were being scratched each time the porcupine moved about. Finally, they asked the porcupine to leave. But the porcupine refused saying, "If you moles are not satisfied, I suggest that you leave."

Gilligan found that boys who read this story tended to opt for justice in resolving the dilemma: "It's the moles' house. It's a deal. The porcupine leaves." In contrast, girls tended to look for solutions that would keep all parties happy and comfortable, such as, "Cover the porcupine with a blanket."

Gilligan's point is that male psychologists have, for the most part, defined moral maturity in terms of justice and autonomy. From this perspective women's concern with relationships can look like a weak-

---

Exploration: Moral Development—Values and Personality

---

ness rather than a strength. But Gilligan believes that caring is also a major element of moral development and suggests that males may lag in achieving it.

Whatever the outcome of such debates, research on moral development seems highly worthwhile. Many of the problems facing us today—overpopulation, environmen-

tal destruction, crime, prejudice—are essentially problems of individual conscience.

Learning Check

1. According to Kohlberg, the conventional level of moral development is marked by a reliance on outside authority.   T or F?
2. Self-interest and avoiding punishment are elements of postconventional morality.   T or F?
3. About 80 percent of the adult population functions at the postconventional level of moral reasoning.   T or F?
4. Gilligan regards gaining a sense of justice as the principal basis of moral development.   T or F?

Answers: 1. T 2. F 3. F 4. F

Questions for Discussion

1. How did you answer Kohlberg's moral dilemma? Do you think your answer reflects the role of moral reasoning in your personality?

2. Kohlberg says moral reasoning is a stable personality characteristic; social learning theory says honesty is highly influenced by situations. Which do you think is right? Why?

3. Do you think higher levels of moral reasoning can be taught without specifically teaching moral values?

4. What level of moral reasoning is most frequently displayed by the characters in TV dramas, comedies, or commercials?

5. Do you think the "draft dodgers," antiwar activists, or conscientious objectors of the 1960s were acting in self-interest or at higher levels of morality?

6. Can you describe an action you performed recently that seems to represent operation of the id, ego, or superego? How would a behaviorist or a humanist interpret the same event?

7. Can you cite a behavior or an experience that seems to support the existence of the unconscious or of unconscious motivation?

8. Can you cite observations that support Freud's scheme of psychosexual stages? Can you cite observations that contradict it?

9. Is "Mr. Clean" an anal-retentive?

10. As a child whom did you identify with? What effect did this have on your personality?

11. Freud thought that adolescent males who clash with adult male authority figures (teachers, ministers, policemen, and so forth) are experiencing a carryover of the Oedipus conflict. What do you think?

12. What experiences have you had that have contributed to personal growth? What experiences set you back or were otherwise negative in their effects? Which personality theory best explains the differences between these experiences?

13. The film *Close Encounters* culminates with a visit to Earth by a magnificent round spaceship. The ship opens to reveal childlike creatures who have come to take a chosen few to a new life among the stars. What archetypal symbols are represented by these images? Can you think of other films, works of art, or images that seem to symbolize Jungian archetypes?

Part Six

Abnormal Behavior and Psychotherapy

Chapter 20

Deviance and Disorder: The Unhealthy Personality

Chapter Preview
Catch-22: A Practical Definition of "Crazy"

"Can't you ground someone who's crazy?"

"Oh, sure, I have to. There's a rule saying I have to ground anyone who's crazy."

"Then why don't you ground me? I'm crazy. Ask Clevinger."

"Clevinger? Where is Clevinger? You find Clevinger and I'll ask him."

"Then ask any of the others. They'll tell you how crazy I am."

"They're crazy."

"Then why don't you ground them?"

"Why don't they ask me to ground them?"

"Because they're crazy, that's why."

"Of course they're crazy," Doc Daneeka replied. "I just told you they're crazy, didn't I? And you can't let crazy people decide whether you're crazy or not, can you?"

Yossarian looked at him soberly and tried another approach. "Is Orr crazy?"

"He sure is," Doc Daneeka said.

"Can you ground him?"

"I sure can. But first he has to ask me to. That's part of the rule."

"Then why doesn't he ask you to?"

"Because he's crazy," Doc Daneeka said. "He has to be crazy to keep flying combat missions after all the close calls he's had. Sure, I can ground Orr. But first he has to ask me to."

"That's all he has to do to be grounded?"

"That's all. Let him ask me."

"And then you can ground him?" Yossarian asked.

"No. Then I can't ground him."

"You mean there's a catch?"

"Sure there's a catch." Doc Daneeka replied. "Catch-22. Anyone who wants to get out of combat duty isn't really crazy."

There was only one catch and that was Catch-22, which specified that a concern for one's own safety in the face of dangers that were real and immediate was the process of a rational mind. Orr was crazy and could be grounded. All he had to do was ask; and as soon as he did, he would no longer be crazy and would have to fly more missions. Orr would be crazy to fly more missions and sane if he didn't, but if he was sane he had to fly them. If he flew them he was crazy and didn't have to; but if he didn't want to he was sane and had to. Yossarian was moved very deeply by the absolute simplicity of this clause of Catch-22 and let out a respectful whistle.

"That's some catch, that Catch-22," he observed.

"It's the best there is," Doc Daneeka agreed. *

This excerpt from Joseph Heller's novel Catch 22 *captures the ambiguities presented by the classic question, "What is normal?" In the 1800s, doctors and laymen alike used such terms as "crazy," "insane," "cracked," and "lunatic" quite freely. The "insane" were considered bizarre and definitely different from you or me.*

Today our understanding of "mental illness" or emotional disturbance is becoming increasingly sophisticated. Drawing lines between normal and abnormal can be done only by considering some complex issues. In this chapter and the next we will summarize major psychological disturbances and their characteristics.

Survey Questions   How is normality defined, and what are the major psychological disorders? What is a personality disorder? Is the term *neurosis* still used? What problems result when a person suffers high levels of anxiety? What are affective disorders? What can be done about them? What causes suicide, and how can it be prevented? What role does the concept of insanity play in criminal trials?

Resources

Psychopathology—Defining Major Psychological Problems

In 1978 William Milligan was accused of being the "university rapist" who attacked four women near Ohio State University. At his trial, psychiatrists testified that Milligan had nine separate personalities. The rapist was assumed to have been a personality identified as an "18-year-old lesbian" named Adelena.

Unlike the *Catch 22* excerpt, William Milligan's problem is "nonfiction." It is but one hint of the magnitude of mental health problems in this country. Here are the facts on psychopathology:

Nearly half of all hospital beds in all types of hospitals are occupied by the mentally ill.

1 out of every 10 children born will experience either a major or a minor mental disorder.

1 out of every 100 persons will become so severely disturbed as to require hospitalization at some point in his or her lifetime.

Each year over 2 million persons are admitted or readmitted to outpatient services or psychiatric treatment in general hospitals.

A tremendous variety of problems falls under the general heading of *psychopathology*. **Psychopathology** may be defined as the *inability to behave in ways that foster the well-being of the individual and ultimately of society*. This definition covers not only obviously maladaptive behavior such as drug addiction, compulsive gambling, or loss of

contact with reality, but also any behavior that interferes with personal growth and self-fulfillment (Coleman, Butcher, & Carson, 1984).

Psychological problems are grouped into broad categories of maladaptive behavior. The most widely used system of classification is found in the *Diagnostic and Statistical Manual of Mental Disorders* (DSM-III, 1980). If you were to glance through this manual, you would find a wide range of disorders described, including those that follow.

Organic mental disorders are problems caused by brain pathology; that is, by senility, drug damage, diseases of the brain, injuries, the toxic effects of poisons, and so on. Organic disorders are often accompanied by such symptoms as severe emotional disturbances, impairment of thinking, memory loss, personality changes, and delirium.

Substance use disorders are defined as psychological dependence on mood- or behavior-altering drugs: alcohol, barbiturates, opiates, cocaine, amphetamines, hallucinogens, cannabis, tobacco, and others. Problems in this category center on damaged social or occupational functioning and an inability to stop using the drug (Fig. 20–1).

Psychotic disorders are the most severe type of psychopathology, often requiring hospitalization. In psychosis there is a retreat from reality: The person can no longer tell what is fantasy or hallucination, and what is real. In addition there is usually a major loss of ability to control thoughts and actions.

Affective disorders primarily involve disturbances in

Fig. 20–1 *The self-portraits shown here were painted by Andy Wilf between 1978 and 1981. During that time Wilf is said to have increasingly abused drugs and alcohol. This dramatic series of images is a record of his self-destructive descent into a private hell. The third painting shows a shrouded skull—and foretells the artist's fate. Wilf died of a drug overdose early in 1982. Drug abuse is but one of the many psychopathologies, or "problems in living," psychologists seek to alleviate. (Courtesy of Ulrike Kantor, Ulrike Kantor Gallery.)*

mood or emotion (affect = emotion). In an affective disorder, individuals may be *manic*, meaning agitated, euphoric, and hyperactive, or they may be *depressed*. In either case, extremes of mood are intense or long lasting. Depressed individuals run a high risk of suicide.

Anxiety disorders may take the form of *phobias* (irrational fears of objects, activities, or situations), *panic* (in which the person suffers sudden unexplainable feelings of terror), or *generalized anxiety* (chronic and persistent anxiety). Also associated with anxiety disorders is a pattern known as *obsessive-compulsive* behavior (more on this later).

Somatoform disorders are indicated when a person has physical symptoms that mimic physical disease or injury (paralysis, blindness, or chronic pain, for example) but for which there is no identifiable cause. The assumption in such cases is that psychological factors underlie the symptoms.

Dissociative disorders include cases of sudden temporary *amnesia* and instances of *multiple personality*, like that displayed by William Milligan.

Personality disorders are deeply ingrained, unhealthy personality patterns. Such patterns are usually apparent by adolescence and continue throughout most of adult life.

They include paranoid (overly suspicious), narcissistic (self-loving), dependent, compulsive, antisocial, and other personality types.

Psychosexual disorders include *gender identity disorders* (where a person's sexual identity does not match his or her physical gender), *transsexualism* (a persistent discomfort about one's sex and a desire to change to the opposite sex), and a wide range of deviations in sexual behavior (fetishism, voyeurism, and so on). Also included in this category are a variety of *psychosexual dysfunctions* (problems in sexual desire or sexual response; see Chapter 24).

Question: Shouldn't neurosis *be included on the list?*

The former *Diagnostic and Statistical Manual* (DSM-II) listed neurosis as a disorder, but the new version (DSM-III) does not. Why? Because it was felt that "neurosis" is a vague term that tends to lump together too many separate problems. Behavior that was once considered "neurotic" is now separated into anxiety disorders, somatoform disorders, and dissociative disorders. Of course, it still makes sense to distinguish these milder problems from psychosis, because they do not involve a major loss of contact with reality.

Question: Is psychosis the same as insanity?

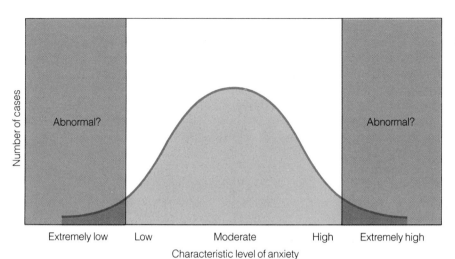

Fig. 20–2 *The number of people displaying a personal characteristic may help define what is statistically abnormal.*

No. Psychosis is a *psychiatric* term that describes a particular type of psychopathology. **Insanity** is a *legal* term. Persons who are declared "insane" are not legally responsible for their actions, and they can be involuntarily committed to a mental institution. Insanity is usually established through the testimony of psychologists and psychiatrists who serve as **expert witnesses** in a court of law (Carelli, 1982). (See this chapter's Exploration for further discussion of insanity.)

Normality— What Is Normal?

Setting aside certain behaviors or certain people as psychologically unhealthy raises the age-old issue of what is normal. Defining normality can be a tricky business. We might begin by saying that **subjective discomfort** is characteristic of psychopathology; that is, the unhealthy personality will be marked by unhappiness, anxiety, depression, or other signs of emotional upset.

Question: But couldn't a person be psychotic without feeling subjective discomfort?

Yes. A problem with this definition is that a person's behavior might be quite maladaptive without causing personal discomfort. A psychotic person displaying obviously bizarre and maladjusted behavior might feel on top of the world. It could be said, also, that a *lack* of discomfort may reveal a problem. If you were to show no signs of grief or depression in response to the death of a friend or loved

*Normal in this case is a statistical concept referring only to the shape of the curve.

one, we might suspect psychopathology. In practice, subjective discomfort accounts for most instances in which a person voluntarily seeks professional help.

Some psychologists have tried to pin down normality more objectively by using **statistical definitions.** For example, since we know that anxiety is a characteristic of several milder disorders, we could devise a test to learn how many people show low, medium, or high levels of anxiety. Usually the results of such a test will fall into a **normal** (bell-shaped) **curve** (see Fig. 20–2). Notice that most people score in the center region of such a curve. Those people who deviate from the average by being anxious all the time (high anxiety) might be considered abnormal. Incidentally, a person who never feels anxiety might also be considered abnormal.

Question: Then a statistical definition of abnormality tells us nothing about the meaning of a deviation from the norm?

Right. It is as statistically "abnormal" (unusual) for a person to score above 145 on an IQ test as it is to score below 55, but only in the second case would we consider the score "abnormal" or undesirable.

Another major problem with statistical definitions is the question of *where to draw the line* between normality and abnormality. To take a new example, we could obtain the average frequency of sexual intercourse for persons of a particular age, sex, and marital status. Obviously, a person who feels driven to seek sexual release dozens of times a day has a problem. But as we move back toward the norm, we face the statistical problem of drawing lines. How often must an otherwise normal behavior occur before it becomes abnormal?

Social nonconformity may also serve as a basis for judging normality. Abnormal behavior can sometimes be viewed as a failure in *socialization*. Here we refer to the person who has not adopted the usual minimum rules for social conduct, or who has learned to engage in socially destructive or self-destructive behavior. This type of nonconformity must be carefully distinguished from that shown by highly creative individuals or those who have a unique lifestyle. It should be noted also that strict adherence to social norms is no guarantee of mental health (Fig. 20–3). In some cases psychopathology takes the form of rigid conformity.

Before any behavior can be defined as normal or abnormal, we must consider the **context** in which it occurs. Is it normal to stand outside and water a lawn? It depends on whether it is raining. Is it abnormal for a grown man to remove his pants and expose himself to another man or woman in a place of business? It depends on whether the other person is a bank clerk or a doctor! Almost any imaginable behavior can be considered normal in some context, as the following example indicates:

> In mid-October 1973 an airplane carrying a rugby team called the Old Christians crashed in the snowcapped Andes of South America. Incredibly, 16 of the 45 people who had been aboard at the time of the crash survived 73 days in deep snow and subfreezing temperatures. They were forced to use extremely grim measures to do so—they ate the bodies of those who had died in the crash. (Adapted from *Time*, Jan. 8, 1973)

Culture is one of the most influential contexts in which any behavior is judged. In some cultures it is considered normal to believe that plants and trees are inhabited by spirits, or to defecate or urinate in public, or to appear naked in public. In our culture each of these behaviors would be considered unusual or abnormal. There is, in other words, a high degree of **cultural relativity** in perceptions of normality and abnormality (see Highlight 20–1). Still, all known cultures classify people as abnormal if they either fail to communicate with others or are consistently unpredictable in their actions.

Question: If abnormality is so hard to define, how are judgments of psychopathology made?

It should be clear at this point that all definitions of abnormality are **relative.** Yet, in spite of the great difficulty of formally defining abnormality, we know that psychological disturbances occur and that they must be identified.

In practice, the judgment that a person needs help usually occurs when the person *does something* (hits a person, hallucinates, stares into space, collects rolls of toilet paper, and so forth) that *annoys* or *gains the attention* of a person in a *position of power* (an employer, teacher, parent, spouse, or the person himself or herself) who then *does something* about it. (A police officer may be called, the person may be urged to see a psychologist, a relative may start commitment proceedings, or the person may voluntarily seek help.)

The sections that follow continue our discussion by describing in greater detail some of the problems already mentioned. A full discussion of schizophrenia and other more severe problems is reserved for the next chapter. Before you read further, see if you can answer these questions.

Fig. 20–3 *Social nonconformity does not automatically indicate psychopathology.*

Highlight 20–1
Women, Culture, and "Madness"

Many more women than men are treated for psychological problems. Why?

- Due to cultural training women may be more willing than men to reveal distress and to seek help for their problems.
- Because women are often denied power, responsibility, and independence in our society, they may more often feel depressed, anxious, or hopeless—for good reason.
- There may be a damaging male bias to traditional conceptions of normality.

The third possibility is perhaps the most controversial. According to psychologist Marcie Kaplan (1983), DSM-III has a distinct male bias. Kaplan believes that women are penalized both for conforming to female stereotypes and for ignoring them. If a woman is independent, aggressive, and unemotional, she may be considered "unhealthy." Yet, at the same time, a woman who is vain, emotional, irrational, and dependent on others (all are "feminine" traits in our culture) may be classified as a histrionic, or dependent personality.

For the most part, DSM-III is a highly useful system. Nevertheless, Kaplan's critique helps illustrate the subtle influence that culture may have on perceptions of normality.

Learning check

1. Approximately what percentage of hospital beds are occupied by the mentally ill?   (circle)

    10 percent   25 percent   50 percent   75 percent   90 percent

2. Which among the following are *not* major psychological problems listed in DSM-III?   (circle)

    psychotic disorders   affective disorders   neurosis   personality disorders   insanity   anxiety disorders

3. A major difference between psychotic disorders and anxiety disorders (or other milder problems) is that in psychosis the individual has _____

4. Statistical definitions of abnormality successfully avoid the limitations of other approaches.   T or F?

5. One of the most powerful contexts in which judgments of normality and abnormality are made is:
    a. the family   *b.* religious systems   *c.* occupational settings   *d.* culture

Answers: 1. 50 percent   2. neurosis, insanity   3. lost contact with reality   4. F   5. d

The Antisocial Personality—
Rebel without a Cause

As stated earlier, personality disorders are deeply ingrained maladaptive personality patterns. For example, the *paranoid personality* is overly suspicious, mistrusting, or hypersensitive, guarded, and distrustful of the honesty of others. Persons having a *narcissistic personality* are preoccupied with their own self-importance; they need constant admiration, and they are absorbed in fantasies of power, wealth, brilliance, beauty, and love. The *dependent personality* involves an extreme lack of self-confidence in which others are allowed to run the person's life, and the person places his or her own needs second to others. The list of such maladaptive patterns is long, so let us focus on a single frequently misunderstood personality disorder: the antisocial personality.

Question: What are the characteristics of an antisocial personality?

The individual with an **antisocial personality** (sometimes referred to as a *sociopath* or *psychopath*) typically has a long history of conflict with society. Antisocial persons are irresponsible, impulsive, selfish, lacking in judgment, unable to feel guilt, emotionally shallow, unable to learn from experience, and lacking in moral values. In short, the sociopath is poorly socialized, has a general disregard for the truth, and seems to lack a conscience (Cleckley, 1964; *DSM-III*, 1980).

Question: Are sociopaths dangerous?

Sociopaths are rarely the crazed murderers that have been portrayed on TV and in movies. It is true that many sociopaths are delinquents or criminals who may pose a threat to the general public. But antisocial personalities such as Charles Manson, whose "family" of followers committed the grisly Tate-LaBianca murders, are quite unusual. Most sociopaths create a good first impression and are frequently described as "charming." Their lying, self-serving manipulation, and lack of dependability only gradually become evident to their "friends."

Many successful businesspeople, entertainers, politicians, and other "normal" individuals reveal sociopathic leanings in their willingness to coldly use other people for their own ends. Some psychologists believe that the "manipulative personality" may be a better description of the problem as it occurs in noncriminal individuals (Bursten, 1973).

Question: What causes sociopathy?

People with antisocial personalities usually have a childhood history of emotional deprivation and neglect. This, perhaps, is chiefly responsible for their failure to develop concern for the feelings of others. In addition, adult sociopaths display some subtle physical differences. For example, they produce unusual brain wave patterns suggesting underarousal of the brain (Hare & Cox, 1978). This condition may explain why many sociopaths are thrill seekers. Quite likely, they are searching for stimulation strong enough to overcome their chronic underarousal and "boredom" (Coleman, Butcher, & Carlson, 1984).

Another interesting finding comes from psychological testing in which adult sociopaths must learn to avoid an electric shock. Under these and similar circumstances they show much less anxiety than normal persons do (Hare & Cox, 1978). Those with antisocial personalities might therefore be described as *emotionally cold*. They simply do not feel normal pangs of conscience, guilt, or anxiety. This coldness seems to account for an unusual ability to calmly lie, cheat, steal, or manipulate others.

Question: Can sociopathy be treated?

Antisocial personality disorders are rarely treated with success. All too often, sociopaths manipulate therapy like any other situation. If it is to their advantage to act "cured," they will do so, but they return to former patterns of behavior at the first opportunity. There is, however, some evidence that antisocial behavior declines somewhat after age 30.

Sexual Deviance— Trench Coats, Whips, Leathers, and Lace

Sexual deviance implies a departure from accepted standards of proper behavior. By the most strict standards (including the law in some states), any sexual activity other than face-to-face heterosexual intercourse between married adults is "deviant." But public standards and behavior found privately acceptable by consenting adults are often at odds. By private standards, oral-genital contact, masturbation, and premarital sex cannot be considered sexual deviations.

From a psychological point of view, the mark of true sexual deviations is that they are compulsive and destructive. Typically, they cause guilt, anxiety, or discomfort for one or both participants. Deviations fitting this definition are related to a wide variety of behaviors, including **pedophilia** (sex with children), **bestiality** (sex with animals), **incest** (sex with blood relatives), **fetishism** (sexual arousal associated with inanimate objects), **exhibitionism** (displaying the genitals), **voyeurism** (viewing the genitals of others), **transvestism** (achieving sexual arousal by wearing clothing of the opposite sex), **sadism** (inflicting pain as a part of the sex act), and **masochism** (receiving pain as part of the sex act).

Misconceptions   Sexual deviance is a highly emotional subject, and many misconceptions have developed. Two of the most misunderstood problems are exhibitionism and pedophilia. Check your understanding against the information that follows.

Exhibitionism is a common problem: Roughly 35 percent of all sexual arrests are for "flashing." Exhibitionists are typically male, married, and most come from strict and repressive backgrounds. Exhibitionists have the highest repeat rate among sexual offenders. Most of them feel a deep sense of inadequacy, which produces a compulsive need to prove their manhood by frightening women. While exhibitionists are usually harmless, those who approach closer than arm's reach may be dangerous (Sue et al., 1981). In general a woman confronted by an exhibitionist can assume that his goal is to shock and alarm her. By becoming visibly upset, she actually encourages him (Hyde, 1984).

Child molesters, who are usually males, are often pictured as despicable perverts lurking in dark alleys. In fact, most are married and two-thirds are fathers. Many are rigid, passive, puritanical, or religious. In one-half to two-thirds of all cases of molestation, the offender is a friend, acquaintance, or relative of the child. Molesters are also often thought of as child rapists. But force or even threats are almost never used, and molestation rarely exceeds fondling (Sue et al., 1981).

Question: How serious are the effects of a molestation?

Many authorities believe that a single incident of molestation is unlikely to cause severe psychological harm to a child. For most children the event is frightening but not terribly traumatic. This is why parents are urged not to overreact to the incident or become hysterical. Doing so only further frightens the child (Wilson et al., 1984). In contrast, repeated molestations, especially by someone the child deeply trusts, can leave lasting emotional scars. Molestations by parents, close relatives, teachers, youth leaders, and similar persons can be quite damaging. In such cases professional counseling is often needed to help the child overcome the damaging effects.

As the preceding suggests, the picture of sexual deviance that most often emerges is one of sexual inhibition and immaturity. Quite often, the sexual offender chooses some relatively infantile sexual expression (like exhibitionism or pedophilia) because it is less threatening than normal sexuality. Even considering the emotional trauma they sometimes inflict, most sexual offenders are to be pitied more than feared.

Rape   A notable exception to the point just made can be found in the problem of forcible rape. Rapists often inflict more violence on their victims than is necessary to achieve their goal. Most authorities no longer think of rape as a sexual act. Rather, it is an act of brutality or aggression based on the need to debase others. Many rapists are antisocial personalities who impulsively take what they want without concern for the feelings of the victim or guilt about their deed. Others harbor deep-seated resentment or outright hatred toward women. However, the problem may reach far deeper (see Highlight 20–2).

Quite often, the rapist's goal is not strictly sexual intercourse; it is to attack, subordinate, humiliate, and de-

Highlight 20–2
Sex Role Stereotyping and Rape

A number of writers have suggested that rape is in some ways related to sex role socialization. That is, many people learn to believe that women should not show direct interest in sex. Men, on the other hand, are taught to take the initiative and to persist in attempts at sexual intimacy—even when the woman says no.

Psychologists James Check and Neil Malamuth believe that such attitudes create a "rape-supportive culture." In their view, rape is only an extreme expression of a system that condones forced sexual intimacy. They point out, for instance, that the single, most used cry of rapists to their victims is, "You know you want it." And afterward, "There now, you really enjoyed it, didn't you."

To test the hypothesis that stereotyped images contribute to rape, male college students were classified as either high or low in sex role stereotyping. Each student then read one of three stories. The first described voluntary intercourse; the second depicted stranger rape; and the third described acquaintance rape (forced intercourse on a date).

As predicted, college males high in sex role stereotyping were more aroused by the rape stories. Their arousal patterns, in fact, were similar to those found among actual rapists. Moreover, a chilling 44 percent of those tested indicated they would consider raping someone—especially if they could be sure of not being caught (Check & Malamuth, 1983).

In another study of rape, over half of a sample of adults agreed with the statement, "A woman who goes to the home or apartment of a man on the first date implies she is willing to have sex" (Burt, 1980). In view of such attitudes—and the continuing widespread belief that when a woman says no she means yes—it is little wonder that rape occurs every 6 minutes in the United States. Perhaps the time has come for our culture to make it clear that no means no.

grade the victim. Typical after-effects for the victim include rage, guilt, depression, loss of self-esteem, shame, and, in many cases, a lasting mistrust of male-female relationships. The male who doubts the seriousness of rape should imagine himself mistakenly placed in jail, where he is violently raped (sodomized) by other inmates. There is no pleasure in rape for victims of either sex. It is truly a despicable crime.

Learning Check

1. Which of the following personality disorders is associated with an inflated sense of self-importance and a constant need for attention and admiration?
   a. narcissistic   *b.* paranoid   *c.* antisocial   *d.* manipulative

2. Almost all persons with antisocial personalities are criminals or delinquents.   T or F?

3. Antisocial personality disorders are difficult to treat, but there is typically a decline in antisocial behavior after adolescence.   T or F?

4. The formal term for child molesting is:
   a. sadism   *b.* bestiality   *c.* pedophilia   *d.* fetishism

5. What percentage of arrests for sexual offenses involve exhibitionism? _____

6. Rape is primarily an act of brutality or aggression, rather than an exclusively sexual act.   T or F?

Answers: 1. *a*   2. F   3. F   4. *c*   5. 35 percent   6. T

Nonpsychotic Disorders— When Anxiety Rules

Imagine for a moment the feeling of waiting to take an important test for which you are unprepared; or waiting to give a speech to a large audience of strangers; or waiting for a dentist to start work. You have almost certainly felt **anxiety** in one of these situations. Anxiety is similar to fear except that it is a response to a *nonspecific threat* or an *anticipation of harm*. When people get stage fright, we say that they are anxious, because it is unclear what they fear.

Question: Is it abnormal to feel anxiety?

We all occasionally feel anxiety, and at times of great stress anxiety may be intense, but anxiety that is out of proportion to a given situation may reveal a problem:

A college student appeared at the counseling center with a complaint that he was deathly afraid of examinations. . . . He had previously been involved in a confrontation with an instructor whom he accused of having administered an unfair test in that there was not enough time to answer all the questions. . . He soon realized that the time limit had not been long enough because he had wasted most of his time in attempting to control his anxieties. He had already skipped two other examinations by remaining in bed petrified with his fears of failure. (Adapted from Suinn, 1975)*

Life-Disruptive, Nonpsychotic Disorders   The student just described shows signs of having a disruptive emotional problem, but one that does not involve a loss of contact with reality. As mentioned earlier, such problems were once called neuroses. Now they are classified separately as anxiety disorders, dissociative disorders, and somatoform disorders. In general these problems involve:

High levels of anxiety and/or restrictive, self-defeating behavior patterns

A tendency to use elaborate defense mechanisms or avoidance responses to maintain minimal functioning

Pervasive feelings of stress, insecurity, inferiority, unhappiness, and dissatisfaction with life

Persons with such disorders struggle to preserve control but remain ineffective and accomplish little.

*From *Fundamentals of Behavior Pathology* by R. M. Suinn. Copyright © 1975. Reprinted by permission of John Wiley & Sons, Inc. Additional Suinn quotes in this chapter and the next are from the same source.

Question: Do such problems constitute a "nervous breakdown"?

Adjustment Disorders   The problems mentioned seriously disrupt people's lives and almost always cause considerable misery. However, they rarely bring about a total "breakdown." Actually, the term *nervous breakdown* has no formal meaning. There is nothing wrong with the nerves of an anxious or emotionally troubled individual. What many people have in mind when they use the term is properly called an **adjustment disorder.**

Adjustment disorders occur when life stresses push people beyond their ability to cope effectively. Examples of such stresses are prolonged unemployment, extreme marital strife, and chronic physical illness. The presence of an adjustment disorder is signaled by extreme irritability, sleep disturbances, loss of appetite, physical complaints, and apathy, anxiety, or depression. Often these problems are successfully treated with rest, sedation, supportive counseling, and a chance to "talk through" fears and anxieties.

Question: How is an adjustment disorder different from an anxiety disorder?

The outward symptoms can be similar. However, adjustment disorders typically disappear when life circumstances improve. This demonstrates their link to stressful events. In most anxiety disorders the person's distress seems greatly out of proportion to the situation. Consider, for example, the following description of Ethel B:

> She was never completely relaxed, and complained of vague feelings of restlessness, and a fear that something was "just around the corner." Although she felt that she had to go to work to help pay the family bills, she could not bring herself to start anything new for fear that something terrible would happen on the job. She had experienced a few extreme anxiety attacks during which she felt "like I couldn't breathe, like I was sealed up in a transparent envelope. I thought I was going to have a heart attack. I couldn't stop shaking." (Suinn, 1975)

Distress such as Ethel B's is a key element in anxiety disorders. Many psychologists believe it also underlies dissociative and somatoform disorders—where maladaptive behavior serves to reduce anxiety and personal discomfort. To deepen your understanding, let's examine several related nonpsychotic disorders.

Anxiety Disorders

The essential feature of the simplest anxiety disorder (known as a **generalized anxiety disorder**) is at least 6 months of persistent anxiety. Affected individuals typically complain of sweating, racing heart, dizziness, upset stomach, rapid breathing, and other symptoms of autonomic nervous system activity. They also continually worry, anticipating disasters such as fainting, losing control, dying, injury, or death of close relatives, and so forth.

Question: Was Ethel B's problem a generalized anxiety disorder?

No. The added presence of *anxiety attacks* indicates she suffered from a **panic disorder.**

Panic Disorder   In this relatively simple but very disturbing pattern, continuous tension, worry, and anxiety occasionally explode into sudden episodes of intense panic. During a panic, or anxiety attack, affected individuals experience heart palpitations or chest pain, choking or smothering sensations, vertigo, feelings of unreality, trembling, and fear of dying, going crazy, or doing something uncontrollable during the attack (DSM-III, 1980). Many believe that they are having a heart attack, are going insane, or are about to die. Needless to say, individuals showing this pattern are unhappy and uncomfortable much of the time.

Phobic Disorder   Phobias are irrational fears that persist even when there is no real danger. In a **phobic disorder,** irrational fears, anxiety, and avoidance are focused on specific objects, activities, or situations (Fig. 20–4).

Fig. 20–4   *For a person with a strong fear of snakes (ophidiophobia), merely looking at this picture may be unsettling.*

Fig. 20–5 *The severe obsessions and compulsions of billionaire Howard Hughes led him to live as a recluse for over 20 years. Hughes had an intense fear of contamination. To avoid infection, he constructed sterile, isolated environments in which his contact with people and objects was strictly limited by complicated rituals. Before handling a spoon, for instance, Hughes had his attendants wrap the handle in tissue paper and seal it with tape. A second piece of tissue was then wrapped around the first before he would touch it (Hodgson & Miller, 1982). A spoon prepared as Hughes required is shown at right.*

Acrophobia—fear of heights
Agoraphobia—fear of public places
Claustrophobia—fear of closed spaces
Nyctophobia—fear of darkness
Pathophobia—fear of disease
Zoophobia—fear of animals

This list of possibilities is only partial: Phobias may be attached to almost any object or situation.* Almost everyone has a few mild phobias: Fears of heights, closed spaces, or bugs and crawly things are common. A phobic disorder differs from such garden-variety fears in that it produces overwhelming anxiety that may cause vomiting, wild climbing and running, or fainting. Phobic persons are so threatened that they will go to almost any length to avoid the feared object or situation.

Question: Are some phobias more common than others?

The most common problem is agoraphobia (ah-go-rah-FOBE-ee-ah). One expert estimates that 1 out of every 100

* Obviously, by combining the appropriate root word with the word *phobia*, any number of unlikely fears can be named. Some are: *acarophobia*, fear of itching; *zemmiphobia*, fear of the great mole rat; *nictophobia*, fear of backing into doorknobs; *phobiaphobia*, fear of fear; and *hippopotomonstrosesquipedaliophobia*, fear of long words!

people has agoraphobia severe enough to restrict his or her life to a serious degree (Hardy, 1976).

Agoraphobia often starts after a stressful life event, such as interpersonal conflict (Last, Barlow, & O'Brien, 1984). Soon after the event, the agoraphobic person develops an intense fear of leaving the familiar setting of the home. Typically, he or she develops elaborate alibis to avoid areas of insecurity—such as crowds, open roads, supermarkets, automobiles, and so on (Zane & Milt, 1984). As a result agoraphobics depend heavily on others to maintain a semblance of a normal life. Some are literally housebound, and never leave the security of their homes (DSM-III, 1980).

Obsessive-Compulsive Disorder Obsessions are images or thoughts that intrude into consciousness against a person's will. You have probably experienced a mild obsessional thought in the form of some song or stupid commercial jingle that is repeated over and over in your mind. This may be irritating, but it is certainly not disturbing in any major sense. True obsessions are so disturbing that they cause anxiety or extreme discomfort. Such obsessions may center on images of one's own violent death, feelings of being "dirty" or "unclean," feelings that one is about to lose control, or similar threatening preoccupations.

Obsessions usually give rise to **compulsions**. These are irrational acts a person feels driven to repeat (Fig. 20–5). Often, the compulsive act helps control or block out anxiety caused by the obsession. A person who feels guilty or unclean because of a conflict about masturbation might be driven to wash his hands hundreds of times a day. A minister who finds profanities popping into his mind might take up compulsively counting his heartbeats to prevent their appearance. A young mother who repeatedly has an image of a knife plunging into her infant might count all the knives in the house several times a day and insist that they always be locked up.

Of course, not all obsessive-compulsive disorders are so dramatic; many simply involve extreme orderliness and rigid routine. Compulsive attention to detail and rigid adherence to procedures and rules make the highly anxious person feel more secure by keeping activities totally predictable and under control.

Post-Traumatic Disorders Most anxiety disorders are relatively lasting patterns. As such, they have little connection to the actual degree of threat present. A notable exception is found in **post-traumatic stress disorders.** These problems occur when stresses *outside the range of normal human experience* cause a significant psychological and emotional disturbance. Such reactions frequently follow sudden disasters, such as floods, tornadoes, earthquakes, or serious accidents (Fig. 20–6).

Military combat is also a major source of post-traumatic stress disorders. For instance, many soldiers suffer **combat exhaustion** after extended periods of severe stress. Like other anxiety disorders, combat exhaustion is characterized by insomnia or repeated nightmares, loss of appetite, extreme sensitivity, unexplained crying, body tremor, hand wringing, and attacks of uncontrollable anxiety. Reactions of this sort may also surface long after the stress has passed—as is sometimes observed in former political hostages, prisoners of war, and combat veterans.

Dissociative Disorders

A dissociative reaction is marked by striking episodes of *amnesia*, *fugue*, or *multiple personality*. **Amnesia** is the inability to recall one's name, address, or past. **Fugue** (sounds like fewg) is physical flight to escape extreme conflict or threat. Fugue and amnesia are sometimes coupled. A person may wander away from work or school only to later arrive in a strange place with no knowledge of the journey. It's easy to see that forgetting one's identity or fleeing unpleasant situations can serve as a defense against intolerable anxiety.

Multiple personality is a relatively rare condition in which two or more separate personalities exist in an individual. The fictional story of *Dr. Jekyll and Mr. Hyde* is a well-known example of **dual personality.** (Note that dual personality is *not* schizophrenia; schizophrenia is a form of psychosis, as discussed in the next chapter.) One of the most dramatic examples of multiple personality ever recorded is described in the book *Sybil* (Schreiber, 1973). Sybil is a woman who had 16 different personalities. Each personality had a distinct voice, vocabulary, and posture. One personality could play the piano (not Sybil), but the others could not.

When a personality other than Sybil was in control, Sybil experienced a "time lapse," or memory blackout. For example, as a child she once "awoke" as a fifth grader and couldn't understand why she was not in her third-grade classroom. When she was asked to do a multiplication problem, she couldn't begin. Two years of her life were missing, and the personality that had inhabited her body had learned multiplication, but Sybil had not.

Sybil's amnesia and alternate personalities developed during childhood when she was regularly beaten, locked in closets, perversely tortured, and almost killed. Sybil's first dissociations allowed her to escape by creating another person who would suffer torture in her place. Multiple personality often begins with similar unbearable childhood

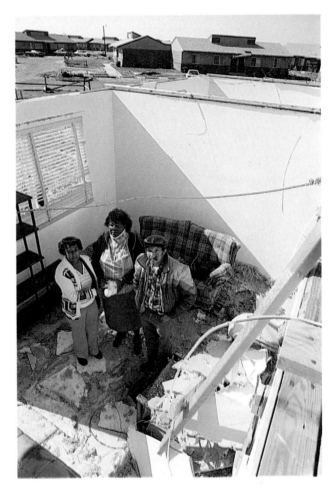

Fig. 20–6 *In the aftermath of natural disasters, some survivors suffer from post-traumatic stress reactions. For some, the flare-up of anxiety and distress may occur months or years after the stressful event is over.*

experiences. In later years Sybil continued the pattern by developing additional personalities to defend against new stresses. Fortunately, multiple personality is far rarer in real life than it is in TV dramas!

Somatoform Disorders

Perhaps you have known someone, particularly someone prone to anxiety, who seems to suffer from an unending series of physical complaints. Usually such individuals believe they have been "sickly" for much of their lives. Often, they have a complicated medical history, and they have, over the years, consulted numerous doctors, sometimes two or more at once. Life for these people is marked by endless preoccupation with bodily sensations and var-

Fig. 20—7   (left) *"Glove" anesthesia is a conversion reaction involving loss of feeling in areas of the hand that would be covered by a glove* (a). *If the anesthesia were physically caused, it would follow the pattern shown in* (b). *(right) To test for organic paralysis of the arm, an examiner can suddenly extend the arm, stretching the muscles. A conversion reaction is indicated if the arm pulls back involuntarily. (Adapted from Weintraub, 1983.)*

ious "diseases"—despite the fact that there is no physical basis for their complaints.

Question: Are you describing hypochondria?

Basically, yes. In **hypochondriasis** (HI-po-kon-DRY-uh-sis) the person has multiple physical complaints for which medical attention is sought, but for which no clear physical cause can be found. **Psychogenic pain** is a related problem in which the person is disabled by pain that has no identifiable physical basis. A rarer form of somatoform disorder (or "body-form" disorder) is called a *conversion reaction.*

Question: How does a conversion reaction differ from hypochondriasis?

Conversion reactions occur when anxiety or severe emotional conflicts are "converted" into symptoms that actually disturb bodily functioning or closely resemble physical disability. Conversion disorders are usually quite dramatic. For instance, a soldier might go deaf or lame or might develop "glove anesthesia" just before a battle.

Question: What is glove anesthesia?

Glove anesthesia is a loss of sensitivity in the areas of skin that would normally be covered by a glove. Glove anesthesia demonstrates that conversion symptoms often contradict known medical facts. The system of nerves in the hands does not form a glovelike pattern and therefore could not cause the observed symptoms. Conversion reactions are also revealed by a disappearance of symptoms when the "victim" is asleep, hypnotized, or anesthetized (Fig. 20–7).

The physical symptoms of a conversion disorder usually serve to excuse the person from a threatening situation. In one case a college student who had a minor traffic accident awakened the following morning with a numbness in his legs and found himself unable to move them. A conversion reaction was suspected when it was noted that he did not seem at all upset by his inability to walk. Investigation revealed that his parents were pressuring him to stay in school (although he wanted to quit) and that he was not prepared for his final exams. If he failed his exams, he expected to be drafted (Suinn, 1975).

A final note of interest: Conversion disorders probably account for many of the so-called miracle cures attributed to faith healers or medical quacks. Persons with conversion symptoms who firmly believe they are being helped may undergo a miraculous cure, but they usually develop new symptoms later.

Learning Check

We have discussed problems from four major categories of DSM-III, as listed below. See if you can correctly match specific disorders with items on the right, by placing letters in the parentheses.

1. Adjustment disorders (   )

2. Anxiety disorders:
    generalized anxiety disorder (   )
    panic disorder (   )
    phobic disorders (   )
    obsessive-compulsive disorders (   )
    post-traumatic stress disorder (   )

3. Dissociative disorders (   )
4. Somatoform disorders (   )

A.   Disturbing thoughts, rigid routine, mechanical behavior

B.   Hypochondriasis, psychogenic pain, and conversion reactions

C.   Free-floating anxiety and anxiety attacks

D.   Persistent, specific, irrational fears

E.   Emotional distress linked to ongoing life stresses

F.   Amnesia, fugue, multiple personality

G.   Chronic worry, anxiety, nervousness without apparent external source

H.   Triggered by events outside the range of normal human experience

Answers: 1. E   2. G, C, D, A, H   3. F   4. B

Three Theories— Pathways to Anxiety and Disorder

Question: What causes the problems described in the preceding section?

At least three major perspectives on the causes of dissociative, anxiety, and somatoform disorders can be identified. These are: (1) the psychodynamic approach, (2) the humanistic-existential approach, and (3) the behavioristic approach.

Psychodynamic Approach   Freud was the first to propose an explanation for what was then called neurosis. According to Freud, disturbances like those we have described represent a raging conflict between subparts of the personality—the id, ego, and superego.

Freud emphasized that intense anxiety can be caused by forbidden id impulses for sex or aggression that threaten to break through into behavior. Also important is guilt generated by the superego's response to these impulses. The ego is caught in the middle and overwhelmed. This forces the person to adopt rigid defense mechanisms and misguided, inflexible behavior to prevent a disastrous loss of control.

Humanistic-Existential Approaches   Humanistic psychologist Carl Rogers interprets emotional disorders as the end product of a faulty *self-image* (Rogers, 1959). Rogers believes that anxious individuals have built up unrealistic pictures of themselves, leaving them vulnerable to contradictory information. Let's say, for example, that an essential part of a student's self-image is seeing himself or herself as highly intelligent. If the student does poorly in school, he or she may deny or distort self-perceptions and views of the situation. Rigid defense mechanisms, a conversion reaction, anxiety attacks, or similar symptoms may result from threats to one's self-image. These symptoms in turn become new threats and require further distortions. We have, in other words, a vicious cycle of maladjustment and anxiety that feeds on itself once started.

Some psychologists take a more existential point of view and stress that unhealthy anxiety reflects a loss of *meaning* in one's life. According to them, we must show *courage* and *responsibility* in our choices if life is to have meaning. Too often, they say, we give in to "existential anxiety" and back away from life-enhancing choices. Existential anxiety is the unavoidable anguish that comes from knowing that we are personally responsible for our lives. Hence, we have a crushing need to choose wisely and courageously.

From the existential view, people who are unhappy and anxious are living in "bad faith." That is, they have crumbled in the face of the awesome responsibility to choose a meaningful existence: They have lost their way in life.

Behavioristic Approach Behaviorists generally assume that the "symptoms" we have discussed are learned, just as other behaviors are. You might recall from Chapter 8, for instance, that phobias can be learned through classical conditioning. Similarly, anxiety attacks may reflect a generalization of conditioned emotional responses to new situations. As another example, the hypochondriac's "sickness behavior" may be reinforced by the sympathy and attention he or she gets.

One aspect of disordered behavior all theorists agree on is that it is self-defeating and *paradoxical*. A paradox is a contradiction. The contradiction in self-defeating behavior is that in the long run it makes the person more miserable, but its immediate effect is to temporarily lower anxiety.

Question: But if the person becomes more miserable in the long run, how does the pattern get started?

The behavioristic explanation is that self-defeating behavior begins with **avoidance learning** (described earlier, in Chapter 9). Here's a quick review of avoidance learning to refresh your memory:

> An animal is placed in a special cage. After a few minutes a light comes on, followed a moment later by a painful shock. Quickly, the animal escapes into a second chamber. After a few minutes a light comes on in this chamber, and the shock is repeated. Soon the animal learns to *avoid* pain by moving *before* the shock occurs. Once an animal learns to avoid, the shock can be turned off altogether. A well-trained animal may avoid the nonexistent shock indefinitely.

The same analysis can be applied to disordered human behavior. A behaviorist would say that the powerful reward of *immediate relief* from anxiety keeps self-defeating avoidance behavior alive. This view, known as the **anxiety reduction hypothesis**, seems to explain why the behavior patterns we have discussed often look very "stupid" to outside observers.

There is probably a core of truth to each of the three explanations. For this reason, understanding a particular example of anxiety disorders, dissociation, or somatoform disorders may be aided by combining parts of all three perspectives. Each viewpoint also suggests a different approach to treatment. Since there are many possibilities, a full discussion of therapy is found later, in Chapters 22 and 23.

Affective Disorders— On the Dark Side of the Mood

Nobody loves you when you're down and out—or so it seems. Psychologists have gradually come to realize that disturbances in mood—the **affective disorders**—are among the most serious of all. In terms of sheer numbers, studies show that in Europe and the United States between 10 and 20 percent of the adult population has had a major depressive episode at some time (DSM-III, 1980). Roughly 25 percent of all cases treated by private psychiatrists and psychologists are for depression (Marmon, 1975).

Question: Don't affective disorders include manic behavior?

Although manic behavior is included, depression is by far the most common problem. In depressive disorders, sadness and despondency are exaggerated, prolonged, or unreasonable. Indications of a depressive disorder are: sadness, hopelessness, inability to feel pleasure or to take interest in anything, withdrawal from family and friends, fatigue, limited movement, sleep and eating disturbances, feelings of worthlessness, an extremely negative self-image, and, often, recurrent thoughts of suicide.

In serious cases of depression it becomes impossible for a person to function at work or at school. Sometimes, depressed individuals cannot even feed or clothe themselves. When depression and/or mania is even more severe, the person may become psychotic and lose touch with reality. (Affective psychosis is discussed in the next chapter.)

Question: How are depressive disorders different from milder, more normal feelings of depression?

If a loved one dies or a person suffers a major failure, loss, or setback, a period of mourning or depression is to be expected. Depression at such times represents an emotional adjustment that is completed within a reasonable time. When someone is continuously or intensely depressed, we must look for causes that go beyond the apparent triggering incident. In many **reactive depressions** we find that the person was unprepared to cope with a major loss because of an earlier series of disappointments. In other instances the person is simply emotionally dependent or immature. In any case, the triggering incident in a reactive depression is often merely the "last straw" that reveals an underlying emotional disturbance.

Question: Is there an explanation for severe depression?

Depression and other affective disorders have resisted explanation and treatment. Some scientists are focusing on

Highlight 20–3
Postpartum Depression

Two weeks after the birth of her child, Cheryl realized something was wrong. She could no longer ignore that she was extremely irritable, fatigued, tearful, and depressed. "Shouldn't I be happy?" she wondered. "What's wrong with me?"

Many women are surprised to learn that they run an increased risk of depression after giving birth. The two most common forms of the problem are **maternity blues** and **postpartum depression.** (The term *postpartum* refers to the time period following childbirth.)

An estimated 50 to 80 percent of all women undergo a temporary disturbance in mood, usually lasting from 24 to 48 hours after childbirth. These "third-day" maternity blues are marked by crying, fitful sleep, tension, anger, and irritability. For most women this reaction is a normal part of adjusting to childbirth. Their depression is brief and relatively mild. For some women, however, the maternity blues can be the beginning of a more lasting depression.

As many as 20 percent (1 in 5) of all women who give birth may develop a mild to moderate depressive disorder. Typical signs of postpartum depression are mood swings, despondency, feeling inadequate, and feeling unable to cope with the new baby. Depression of this kind may last anywhere from 2 months to about a year.

Predicting postpartum depression is difficult. However, the risk is increased by high levels of anxiety during pregnancy and by negative attitudes toward childrearing. The occurrence of stressful life events before birth is also a major concern. Because birth and adjusting to parenthood can both be stressful, it may be that any extra problems push women toward depression.

Psychologists are still studying the best ways to prevent and treat postpartum depression. Presently, the amount of social support a woman receives seems to be an important part of the problem. That is, women who become depressed are also likely to view their husbands as unsupportive. Efforts to educate prospective parents about postpartum depression and the value of mutual support may therefore prove helpful. (Source: Hopkins, Marcus, & Campbell, 1984.)

---

the biology of mood changes. These researchers are interested in brain chemicals and transmitter substances, electrolytes, serotonin and noradrenaline levels, and so forth. Their findings are complex and inconclusive, but progress has been made. For example, the chemical **lithium carbonate** can be effective in treatment of some cases of depression, particularly those also showing manic behavior (Depue & Monroe, 1978). Others have looked for psychological explanations. Psychoanalytic theory, for instance, holds that depression is caused by repressed anger that is turned inward as self-blame and self-hate (Isenberg & Schatzberg, 1976). As discussed earlier, in Chapter 13, behavioral theories of depression emphasize *learned helplessness.*

Adequate understanding and treatment of depression is a challenge to the ingenuity of psychologists, psychiatrists, and other investigators. It is to their credit that this major source of human misery has recently become the target of intensified research (see Highlight 20–3). While we await the outcome of their efforts, a problem remains: Thousands of depressed people commit suicide each year. What can be done about it? This chapter's Applications section provides some answers.

A Final Note— You're Okay, Really!

It is the author's hope that you will not fall prey to a psychological version of "medical student's disease" after reading this chapter. Medical students, it seems, have a tendency to notice in themselves the symptoms of each dreaded disease they learn about. As a psychology student you may have noticed what seem to be abnormal tendencies in your own behavior. If so, don't panic: This only shows that pathological behavior is an *exaggeration* of normal defenses and reactions, not that your behavior is pathological.

Learning Check

1. The humanistic explanation of anxiety and related disorders emphasizes the importance of faulty self-image.   T or F?

2. According to the behavioristic view, anxious, self-defeating behavior is explained by _____ learning.

3. Freud's original psychodynamic explanation of "neurosis" was based on the anxiety reduction hypothesis.   T or F?

4. Learned helplessness is emphasized by _____ theories of depression.
   a. humanistic   *b.* behavioristic   *c.* biological   *d.* psychoanalytic

5. The drug lithium carbonate has been shown to be an effective treatment for anxiety disorders.   T or F?

6. The existential explanation of unhealthy anxiety is based on a conflict between subparts of the personality.   T or F?

Answers: 1. T   2. avoidance   3. F   4. b   5. F   6. F

Applications

Warning: Suicide May Be Hazardous to Your Health

"Suicide: A permanent solution to a temporary problem."

By the time you finish reading this page, someone in the United States will have attempted suicide. Suicide is a very disturbing and widely misunderstood mental health problem. It ranks as the seventh cause of death in the United States, and approximately 1 person out of 100 has attempted suicide at some time in his or her life. Given these figures, it seems likely that you will sooner or later be affected by the suicide attempt of a friend, relative, neighbor, or co-worker. Check your knowledge of suicide against the following information.

Question: What factors affect suicide rates?

Season   Suicide rates vary from city to city and time to time, but some general patterns emerge. Contrary to popular belief, there is little connection between major holidays, such as Christmas, and the suicide rate. For reasons not clearly understood, the peak actually comes in May (Zung & Green, 1974).

Sex   Men have the questionable honor of being better at suicide than women. Three times as many men as women *complete* suicide, but women make more attempts. More men than women succeed at suicide because they typically use a gun or an equally fatal technique. Women most often attempt a drug overdose, a method that allows greater chance of help arriving before death occurs (Lester, 1972).

Age   Age is also a factor in suicide. More than half of all suicides are committed by individuals over 45 years old. This may be changing, however. There has been a recent increase in suicide rates for adolescents and young adults.

Part of this increase comes from the ranks of college students, where suicide is the leading cause of death. Contrary to popular belief, the most dangerous time for student suicide is the beginning (first 6 weeks) of a semester, not during final exams.

Problems with schoolwork contribute to some suicides, but only in the sense that suicidal students were not living up to their own extremely high standards. Many were good students. Other important factors in student suicide are chronic health problems (real or imagined) and interpersonal difficulties (some suicides are rejected lovers, but others are simply withdrawn and friendless people) (Seiden, 1966).

Of special concern to psychologists is the recent dramatic increase in adolescent suicides. At present about 5000 teenagers and young adults commit suicide each year. This rate—about 13 deaths per day—is double the number reported 10 years ago. In some cities authorities have reported *suicide clusters*—virtual "epidemics" of adolescent suicide that occur one after another. Also distressing is the fact that an increasing number of youths employ such highly lethal methods as shooting themselves.

Applications: Warning: Suicide May Be Hazardous to Your Health

Income   Some professions, particularly medicine and psychiatry, show higher than average suicide rates. Overall, however, suicide is quite democratic. It is equally a problem of the rich and the poor (Labovity & Hagedorn, 1971).

Marital Status   An additional factor in suicide is marital status. Marriage (when successful) may be the best natural guard against suicidal impulses. The highest suicide rates are found among the divorced; the next highest rates occur among the widowed; lower rates are recorded for single persons; and married individuals have the lowest rate of all.

Question: Why do people try to kill themselves?

Immediate Causes   The best explanation for suicide may simply come from a look at the conditions that precede it. Usually there is a history of interpersonal troubles with family, in-laws, or a lover or spouse. Often there may be drinking problems, sexual adjustment problems, or job difficulties (Humphrey et al., 1972).

A combination of factors such as these lead to severe depression and a preoccupation with death as the "answer" to the person's suffering. There is usually a break in communication with others that causes the person to feel isolated and misunderstood. Self-image becomes very negative. The person feels worthless and helpless and wants to die (Lester, 1972).

A long history of such conditions is not always necessary to produce a desire for suicide. People who attempt suicide are not necessarily "mentally ill." Anyone may temporarily reach a state of depression severe enough to attempt suicide. Most dangerous for the average person are times of divorce, separation, failure, and bereavement. Each can create what seems like an intolerable situation and can motivate an intense desire for escape.

The causes of increased adolescent suicide remain unclear. As with adults, there is often a backdrop of problems with drugs, depression, school, peers, family, divorced parents, or the breakup of a romance. However, many victims come from stable and affluent homes. Some experts suggest that many adolescent suicides result from *unrealistic expectations*. For example, parents may create feelings of despair by pressuring their children to meet impossibly high standards.

Even without parental pressure, teenagers may expect the impossible of themselves in school, sports, romance, or progress toward a future career. Extremely high expectations can bring self-esteem to rock bottom over even the smallest "failure" (Serban, 1982). Again, the outcome is feelings of helplessness, hopelessness, and a desire to escape.

Preventing Suicide—You Can Help

Question: Is it true that people who talk about or threaten suicide are rarely the ones who try it?

No. This is one of the major fallacies about suicide. Of every 10 potential suicides, 8 give warning beforehand (Rudestam, 1971; Schneidman et al., 1965). A person who threatens suicide should be taken seriously. A potential suicide may say nothing more than, "I feel sometimes like I'd be better off dead." Warnings may also come indirectly. If a friend gives you a favorite ring and says, "Here, I won't be needing this any more," or comments, "I guess I won't get my watch fixed—it doesn't matter anyway," it may be a plea for help.

Question: Is it true that suicide can't be prevented, that the person will find a way to do it anyway?

No. The decision to attempt suicide usually comes when a person is alone, depressed, and unable to view matters objectively. You *should* intervene if someone seems to be threatening suicide.

It is estimated that about two-thirds of all suicide attempts fall in the "to be" category. That is, they are made by people who do not really want to die. Almost a third more are characterized by a "to be or not to be" attitude. These people are ambivalent or undecided about dying. Only about 3 to 5 percent of cases represent individuals who definitely want to die. Most people, therefore, are relieved when someone comes to their aid (Schneidman et al., 1965). Remember that suicide is almost always a cry for help and that you *can* help.

Question: What is the best thing to do if someone hints they are thinking about suicide?

Suicide expert David Lester (1971b) believes that your most important task is to establish *rapport* with the person. You should offer support, acceptance, and legitimate caring. Lester gives some important suggestions about how to handle a potential suicide.

1. A suicidal person feels misunderstood. You should, therefore, try to accept the feelings the person is expressing. Telling suicidal persons they really don't want to kill themselves, or listing reasons why they shouldn't,

Applications: Warning: Suicide May Be Hazardous to Your Health

only adds to their feelings that no one understands. This usually makes a bad situation worse. The person needs *acceptance,* not advice.

2. Acceptance should extend to the idea of suicide itself. One of the worst things you can do is to say something like, "You're not thinking of doing something drastic, are you?" Hiding from suicide or trying to avoid talking about it makes the person feel wrong, unaccepted, and alone. Don't be afraid to talk about suicide directly. It is completely acceptable to ask, "Are you thinking of suicide?"

Establishing communication with suicidal persons may be enough to carry them through a difficult time. You may also find it helpful to get day-by-day commitments from them to meet for lunch, to share a ride, and the like. Let the person know you *expect* her or him to be there. Such commitments, even though small, can be enough to tip the scales when a person is alone and thinking about suicide.

Don't end your efforts too soon. One of the most dangerous times is when a person *suddenly* seems to get better after a severe depression. Many experts agree that this often means the person has finally made the decision to end it all. The improvement in mood is deceptive because it comes from an anticipation that suffering is at an end (Lester & Lester, 1971).

There are over 200 centers for suicide prevention in the United States, and most sizable cities have mental health crisis intervention teams. Both services have staff who are trained to talk to potential suicides over the phone. Give a person who seems to be suicidal the number of one of these services to place near a phone. Urge the person to call you or the service if he or she becomes frightened or impulsive.

The preceding applies mainly to persons who are having mild suicidal thoughts. If a person actually threatens suicide, you must act more quickly. Ask how the person plans to carry out the suicide. A person who has a concrete, workable plan should be asked to accompany you to the emergency room of a hospital.

If a person seems to be on the verge of attempting suicide, don't worry about overreacting; call the police, crisis intervention, or a rescue unit. Needless to say, you should call immediately if a person is in the act of attempting suicide or if a drug has already been taken. The majority of suicide attempts come at temporary low points in a person's life and may never be repeated. Get involved—you may save a life!

Suicide—A Summary of Facts

The following is a list of useful facts to know about suicide.

1. More men than women commit suicide, but women make more attempts.
2. College students are more likely to attempt suicide during the first part of the school quarter or semester.
3. Many people temporarily become depressed enough to contemplate suicide. All of those who would attempt suicide are not psychotic or suffering from lasting mental illness.
4. Suicide strikes both the rich and the poor.
5. A person who is suicidal once may never again become suicidal. Preventing suicide is well worth the effort.
6. Most potentially suicidal persons give warning.
7. People who talk about suicide *do* often attempt it.
8. The majority of people (two-thirds) who attempt suicide do not really want to die, and most of the remainder are ambivalent about dying.
9. A *sudden* improvement in mood after a suicidal depression can mean that the person has decided to carry out a suicide attempt.
10. Suicide can often be prevented by the efforts of family, friends, and mental health professionals.

Learning Check

1. More women use guns in their suicide attempts than do men.   T or F?
2. While the overall suicide rate has stayed the same, there has been a decrease in adolescent suicides.   T or F?
3. Suicide is equally a problem of the rich and the poor.   T or F?
4. The highest suicide rates are found among the divorced.   T or F?
5. The majority (two-thirds) of suicide attempts fall in the "to be" category.   T or F?

Answers: 1. F   2. F   3. T   4. T   5. T

Chapter Summary

- Mental or emotional disturbances are a major health problem. Major categories of *psychopathology* include: *organic mental disorders, substance use disorders, psychotic disorders, affective disorders, anxiety disorders, somatoform disorders, dissociative disorders, personality disorders,* and *psychosexual disorders.*

- Traditionally, a distinction has been made between milder, *nonpsychotic disorders* and *psychoses*—problems involving loss of contact with reality. *Insanity* is a legal term defining the ability to know right from wrong and whether one may be held responsible for one's actions.

- Formal definitions of normality usually take into account all or most of the following: *subjective discomfort, statistical definitions* (or *norms*), *social nonconformity,* and the *cultural* or *situational context* of behavior. There are problems with each definition in that all are *relative* standards. In practice, judgment of normality is a social act influenced by many factors. Personality disorders are deeply ingrained maladaptive personality patterns. A frequently misunderstood personality disorder is *sociopathy,* or *antisocial personality.* Antisocial persons seem to lack a *conscience.* They are emotionally unresponsive, manipulative, and have shallow interpersonal relationships. However, few are homicidal and only a small proportion are criminals.

- Sexual deviance may be the most relative disorder of all. Many "sexually deviant" behaviors are acceptable in other cultures. Deviations that often cause difficulty are: *pedophilia, bestiality, incest, fetishism, voyeurism, exhibitionism, transvestism, sadism,* and *masochism.* Sex offenders are rarely dangerous and can best be characterized as sexually inhibited and immature. *Forcible rape* is primarily a violent crime of aggression rather than a sex crime. There is evidence that rape is related to stereotyped attitudes toward male and female sex roles.

- Anxiety disorders, dissociative disorders, and somatoform disorders are characterized by high levels of anxiety and/or rigid defense mechanisms and self-defeating behavior patterns. The term *nervous breakdown* has no formal meaning. However, "breakdowns" do corre-

spond somewhat to *adjustment disorders,* in which the person is overwhelmed by ongoing life stresses.

- *Anxiety disorders,* characterized by excessive anxiety or anxiety-based behaviors, include: *generalized anxiety disorder* (chronic anxiety and worry), *panic disorder* (anxiety attacks, panic, free-floating anxiety), *phobic disorders* (specific irrational fears), *post-traumatic stress disorder* (emotional disturbance triggered by severe stress), and *obsessive-compulsive disorders* (obsessions and compulsions).

- *Dissociative disorders* may take the form of *amnesia* (loss of memory and personal identity), *fugue* (flight from familiar surroundings), or *multiple personality* (development of two or more distinct personalities). *Somatoform disorders* center on physical complaints that mimic disease or disability. In *hypochondriasis* there are multiple physical complaints for which medical attention is sought. *Psychogenic pain* refers to discomfort for which there is no identifiable physical cause. In *conversion disorders* actual symptoms of disease or disability develop, but they are psychological in origin.

- Three broad types of explanation for anxious, disordered behavior are: (1) the *psychodynamic* approach, emphasizing unconscious conflicts within the personality; (2) the *humanistic* approach, emphasizing the effects of a *faulty self-image,* and the related existential approach, which stresses a loss of meaning in one's life; and (3) the *behavioristic* approach, which emphasizes the effects of previous learning, particularly *avoidance learning.*

- *Affective disorders* primarily involve disturbances of mood or emotion, producing *manic* (agitated, elated, hyperactive) or *depressive* (sad, apathetic, suicidal) states. Depression is the most common affective disorder. *Reactive depressions* are often triggered by external events; however, they are more intense or prolonged than normal. Biological, psychoanalytic, and behavioral theories of depression have been proposed. Research on the causes and treatment of depression continues.

Psychology and the Law—The "Twinkie Defense"

Mark David Chapman claimed devils forced him to kill former Beatle John Lennon. In court, his lawyer asserted that Chapman was "not guilty by reason of insanity." However, at midtrial Chapman decided to plead guilty to second-degree murder. His reason? He said God had visited him in his cell and told him to confess.

Chapman's case is one of thousands each year that mingle law, psychiatry, psychology, and public opinion. For over 130 years the **insanity defense** has bedeviled the courts and has raised difficult legal, moral, and psychological questions.

Question: What exactly is the insanity defense?

Insanity   The insanity defense entered Western law as the **M'Naghten rule.** In 1843 the English House of Lords ruled on the case of Daniel M'Naghten, a "madman" who attempted to kill a Member of Parliament but murdered another man instead. The court held that a defendant—in this case M'Naghten—must understand the wrongfulness of his or her actions to be held responsible for them. Persons suffering from "mental disease or other defects" that prevent them from knowing right from wrong are "insane." In our legal system the taking of life by an insane person is not murder.

Defendants may also claim they knew their act was wrong, but they had an **irresistible impulse** they could not control. An example is the person who finds his or her spouse in a stranger's arms and kills in a jealous rage. A related defense claims **diminished capacity** to control actions or to know right from wrong. A person who commits a crime while under the influence of drugs might make this plea.

The Twinkie Defense   The problems posed by the insanity defense are vividly shown by three recent cases. In Oakland, California, a jury declared Darlin June Cromer sane in the racial killing of a 5-year-old boy. This, despite the fact that one psychiatrist testified that Cromer was "the most psychotic person" he'd ever seen. Cromer was sentenced to life in prison (Einstein, 1981).

On the opposite side of the Bay, Dan White admitted killing San Francisco Mayor George Moscone and Supervisor Harvey Milk. However, White's lawyer convinced the jury that White acted with diminished capacity. The defense claimed, among other things, that White was deranged from eating too much "junk food"—an argument that became known as the Twinkie Defense. (For those unschooled in junk food trivia, a Twinkie is a small sponge cake with a sugary cream filling.) Testimony in the trial established that White planned the murders beforehand and carefully avoided security guards to reach his vic-

tims. White received a 7-year jail sentence. (White was paroled in 1984 and committed suicide in 1985.) The verdict so outraged many citizens that a new law in California now bans claims of "diminished capacity" (Tierney, 1982). In yet another case "Vampire Killer" Richard Chase was convicted of killing six people and drinking the blood of some of them. Chase was declared sane.

These cases point to the inconsistencies of a system that allows people who appear sane to be judged insane, and apparently insane people to be judged sane.

Question: How is sanity determined?

Expert Testimony   The most sensational criminal trials involving insanity have a typical pattern: Defense psychiatrists interview the defendant and then testify that he or she was insane at the time of the crime; prosecution psychiatrists examine the defendant and testify to his or her sanity. After these **expert witnesses** contradict one another's testimony, it's up to the jury to decide who is right.

But more often, this "battle of the experts" never takes place. In 4 out of 5 cases, prosecuters, defense attorneys, medical experts, and judges agree *before* trial that the defendant is mentally ill (Bower, 1984). Thus, if a person really is psychotic, in most cases experts agree fairly readily.

Exploration: Psychology and the Law—The "Twinkie Defense"

Opinion Please   The preceding brief discussion raises several interesting questions.

1. The states of Montana, Idaho, and Utah have banned the insanity plea, but in most states it remains intact. Several other states now allow only a "guilty, but mentally ill" plea. In your opinion, should questions of insanity be considered in criminal trials? Should the insanity defense be allowed?

Before you answer, you should know that pleas of insanity are actually relatively rare, being used in only about 1 out of every 500 court cases. In only about 2 percent of these cases does the insanity defense succeed. Nationally, this amounts to about 100 cases a year (Carelli, 1982).

More importantly, a verdict of innocence by reason of insanity does not set a person free. In most states it requires automatic commitment to a mental hospital.

Thereafter, the law places the burden of proof on patients. To be released, they must show that they are no longer a danger to themselves or others. Moreover, in some cases persons declared "insane" have been hospitalized longer than they would have been imprisoned for a criminal conviction.

Then again, critics of the insanity defense point out that insane offenders are now held for an average of about 2 years (Bower, 1984). In some instances the public may rightly ask if justice has been served.

2. Should the courts accept pleas of "diminished capacity"? Before you answer this question, think about the "guilt" of a severely retarded person or someone with a brain tumor who commits a crime.

3. If a person has not broken the law, who should decide if the person should be committed? Should

it be a judge? A jury? A psychiatrist? A psychologist? Who should decide when an "insane" person can be released? Should a person have the right to refuse treatment? What if the person did commit a crime?

Before you answer, it may be useful to know that psychiatric predictions of violent behavior are largely inaccurate. Follow-ups of arrests and mental hospital records show that from two-thirds to nine-tenths of the time, experts are *wrong* in forecasting violence (Loftus & Monahan, 1980). At present there is no way to accurately predict which individuals are likely to be dangerous to themselves or to others.

As you can see, there are no easy answers to the preceding questions. Nevertheless, when the issues are "madness," personal freedom, criminal responsibility, and justice, everyone has an opinion. What's yours?

Questions for Discussion

1. What effect might living in different parts of town, membership in an ethnic group, or growing up in a different culture have on a person's perceptions of "normality"?

2. Can you think of a behavior that would be considered "abnormal" under any possible set of circumstances?

3. How would your perception of a person be likely to change if you knew he or she were an "ex-mental patient"?

4. To what extent does "maladjusted" or "sick" mean "different from me"?

5. Are standards of "normality" in our society broad enough to accommodate varying lifestyles?

6. In what ways might our ultracompetitive society contribute to the development of a sociopathic personality?

7. How would you explain the increase in youth suicide?

Chapter 21 | Psychosis

Chapter Preview
Psychosis—"Losing It"

I'm a man 36 years of age, that in 1956–57 they changed the flag of the United States of America once by adding Alaska as a State to the Union and thus paving the way for Hawaii to become a state in 1959. That of course, gives me the *"capacity of the flag itself"* and therefore like any Congressional Medal of Honor winner, gives me the "capacity of the President of the United States of America. . . ."

. . . in 1955–56 civil authorities . . . some "small time" politicians got together on me and sand-bagged me brainwashed me and bugged me with a *"short-wave* Radio grid center, with an ultra-violet cross grid" called a "bug." Its sole purpose is to use a person's senses against himself so as to perjure and distort him to no end of humiliation . . . they vibrate your nerves physically with it and never ceases.

. . . I'd been there several months before they gave me "ground privileges" and once on the grounds they started frequencing my time all the more, vibrating the back of my neck, first flicking it to the front of my face, like a "whip" or a cat of 9 tails. (Suinn, 1975)

The excerpts above are taken from a letter written by a man experiencing a psychosis. They reveal some of the severe disturbances in thinking, behavior, speech, and emotions that accompany psychosis.

Psychosis also represents a loss of contact with reality. Novelist Joanne Greenberg (1964) describes a split from reality this way:

The walls dissolved and the world became a combination of shadows . . . all direction became a lie. The laws of physics and solid matter were repealed and the experience of a lifetime of tactile sensation, motion, form, gravity, and light were invalidated. She did not know whether she was standing or sitting down, which way was upright, and from where the light, which was a stab as it touched her, was coming. She lost track of the parts of her body; where her arms were and how to move them. As light went spinning erratically away and back she tried to clutch at thoughts only to find that she had lost all memory of the English language. *

What is psychosis really like? What causes it? What can be done about it? For answers to these and related questions, read on.

Survey Questions   What are the general characteristics of psychosis? How do paranoid psychosis, schizophrenia, and affective psychosis differ? What causes schizophrenia? How are psychotic disorders treated? Is psychiatric labeling damaging?

*From I Never Promised You a Rose Garden by Hannah Green (Joanne Greenberg). Copyright © 1964 by Hannah Green. Reprinted by permission of Holt, Rinehart and Winston, Publishers.

Resources

Psychosis—Life in the Shadow of Madness

Psychosis—a major loss of contact with shared views of reality—is among the most serious of all mental problems.

Question: What is psychosis like?

A person experiencing a psychotic break undergoes a number of important changes. Following are descriptions of some of the major characteristics of psychoses (psycho*sis*: singular; psycho*ses*: plural).

Presence of Delusions Delusions are false beliefs that are held even when the facts contradict them. Individuals with the psychotic delusion that they are Jesus Christ will not be disturbed by an inability to walk on water or to perform miracles. Some common types of delusion are: (1) *depressive* delusions, in which people feel that they have committed horrible crimes or sinful deeds; (2) *somatic* delusions, such as belief that one's body is "rotting away" or that it is ravaged by disease; (3) delusions of *grandeur*, in which individuals think they are extremely important persons; (4) delusions of *influence*, in which people feel they are being controlled or influenced by others or by unseen forces; (5) delusions of *persecution*, in which people feel others are "out to get them"; and (6) delusions of *reference*, in which unrelated events are given personal meaning (as when a person assumes that a newspaper article or a television program is giving a special message directly to her or him) (DSM-III, 1980). If you reread the opening quote of the Chapter Preview, you will find evidence of delusions of grandeur, influence, and persecution.

Hallucinations and Sensory Changes Hallucinations are sensory experiences that occur in the absence of a stimulus. The most common psychotic hallucination is hearing voices, which may be familiar, may be answered, and frequently are insulting. More rarely, psychotic individuals may also feel "insects crawling under the skin," taste "poisons" in their food, or smell "gas" their "enemies" are using to "get" them. Sensory changes may bring about extreme sensitivity to heat, cold, pain, or touch. Anesthesia, a loss of normal sensitivity, is also possible.

Disturbed Emotions Emotions may swing violently between extremes of elation and depression, or the psychotic person may be hyperemotional, depressed, emotionally "flat," or apathetic. In **flat affect** there are almost no signs of emotion. In such cases a person's face is frozen and his or her voice is monotonous.

Personality Disorganization or Disintegration Major disturbances such as those just described, plus added problems in thought, speech, memory, actions, and attention, bring about *personality disintegration* and a break with reality. As a result, significant impairment almost always occurs in work, social relations, and self-care. When psychotic disturbances and a shattered personality are evident for weeks or months (often including a period of deterioration, an active phase, and a residual phase), then the individual is said to have suffered a psychosis (DSM-III, 1980).

Question: How could a person function with such problems?

Actually, the preceding description is somewhat exaggerated, since it is rare to find all these changes occurring at once. As a matter of fact, you would probably find a trip to a psychiatric ward disappointing if you expected to see flamboyant, dramatic, or bizarre behavior. Typically, extreme psychotic behavior occurs in brief *episodes*. The symptoms of psychosis come and go and may be quite subtle much of the time (Fig. 21–1).

Question: Does psychosis occur without warning?

No. Usually there are signs of impending trouble. A recent study of psychotic patients found that for most, symptoms such as insomnia, emotional changes, or feeling "high" signaled a coming crisis (Brier & Strauss, 1983). In fact, most of the patients were aware of their symptoms and tried to fight off the psychosis.

Even after a psychotic break, people are not totally unresponsive to their surroundings. In one interesting experiment psychotic patients were interviewed in two ways. Some were told that the purpose of the interview was to determine if they were "ready for discharge." In this group, patients who were known to like the hospital acted very bizarre and disturbed during the interviews. A second group was told that the interview was to determine if the patient should be allowed "open ward" privileges. In this case, disturbed patients suddenly became amazingly free of symptoms (Braginsky & Braginsky, 1967).

This experiment shows that some psychotic symptoms

Fig. 21–1 *A scene in a state mental hospital.*

can be considered a primitive form of communication, the message being, "I need help" or, "I can't handle it anymore." This view becomes more evident in light of the fact that an almost universal symptom of psychosis is difficulty in talking to others. Psychotic speech tends to be garbled and chaotic, sometimes sounding like no more than a "word salad":

Fig. 21–2 *The Mad Hatter,* from Lewis Carroll's book, Alice in Wonderland. *History provides numerous examples of psychosis caused by toxic chemicals. Carroll's Mad Hatter character is modeled after an occupational disease of the 18th and 19th centuries. In that era hatmakers were heavily exposed to mercury used in the preparation of felt. Consequently, many suffered brain damage and became psychotic, or "mad" (Kety, 1979).*

The lion will have to change from dogs into cats until I can meet my father and mother and we dispart from rats. . . . It's all over for a squab true tray and there ain't no squabs, there ain't no men, there ain't no music, there ain't nothing besides my mother and my father who stand alone upon the Island of Capri where is no ice. Well it's my suitcase sir. (Rodgers, 1982)

Question: Are there different types of psychosis?

A psychosis based on known brain pathology related to disease, gunshot wound, accident, or other physical causes is termed an **organic psychosis**. A psychosis based on unknown or psychological factors is called a **functional psychosis**. The possible causes of functional psychoses are explored later in this chapter.

Organic Psychosis   One example of organic psychosis is **general paresis** (pah-REE-sis), which occurs in some cases of untreated syphilis. In advanced stages, syphilis attacks brain cells and gradually brings about a deterioration in behavior. A common sign of general paresis is a loss of inhibition that leads to inappropriate comments, shocking profanity, and obscenity—the "dirty old man" syndrome.

A second source of organic psychosis that gives special cause for alarm is lead and mercury poisoning (see Fig. 21–2). Although such poisoning is relatively rare, it can damage the brain and cause hallucinations, delusions, or a loss of emotional control. A particulary dangerous situation is found in old buildings, since many are painted with old-style leaded paints. Children who eat this paint may become psychotic or retarded. Other more subtle sources of lead can also be a problem. For example, children who live near congested streets may absorb lead from breathing automobile exhaust. Testing shows that high levels of lead are related to difficulties in thinking and attention at school (Yule et al., 1984).

Senile dementia is probably the most common organic problem. In senile dementia (duh-MEN-sha), there are marked disturbances in memory, reasoning, judgment, impulse control, and personality—a combination that usually leaves victims confused, suspicious, apathetic, or withdrawn. Senile dementia is closely associated with physical deterioration of the brain. Common causes are circulatory problems, repeated strokes, or general shrinkage and atrophy of the brain (see Highlight 21–1).

Three major types of functional psychoses are *paranoia*, *affective psychosis*, and *schizophrenia*. Information on each follows.

Paranoid Psychosis— An Enemy behind Every Tree

Paranoia is a rare form of psychosis. The true paranoid does not suffer from hallucinations, emotional excesses, or a fragmented personality. The major sign of paranoia is the presence of delusions of grandeur or persecution. Many self-styled reformers, absurdly jealous husbands or wives, crank-letter writers, "communist hunters," and the like are paranoids.

Most often, paranoid delusions center on feelings of persecution. Paranoid individuals believe they are being cheated, spied on, followed, poisoned, harassed, or that someone is plotting against them. Paranoids are usually intensely suspicious, believing they must be on guard at all times. The evidence paranoids find to support their beliefs is usually unconvincing to others. Every detail of the paranoid's existence is woven into a private version of "what's really going on." Buzzing during a telephone conversation may be interpreted as "someone listening," a stranger who comes to the door asking for directions may "really be trying to get information," and so forth.

Paranoids are rarely treated or admitted to mental hospitals because it is almost impossible to suggest to them that they need help. A friend, relative, or psychologist who does so simply becomes part of the "conspiracy" to "persecute" them.

Paranoids frequently lead lonely, isolated, and humorless lives marked by constant suspicion and hostility toward others. Paranoids are not necessarily dangerous to others, but they can be. A person who believes that "the Mafia" is slowly closing in on him may be moved to violence by

---

**ψ   Highlight 21–1
Alzheimer's Disease**

Alzheimer's disease (ALLS-hi-merz) is one of the most fearsome and devastating problems of aging. In addition to being the most common form of organic brain damage, it is the major cause of senility. Alzheimer's disease afflicts about 5 to 10 percent of all people over age 65, or about 2 million Americans.

Alzheimer's victims at first have difficulty remembering recent events. Then they slowly become more disoriented, suspicious, and confused. In time they lose the ability to work, cook, drive, or use tools. As their condition worsens, victims can no longer read, write, and calculate. This decline is much like watching early mental development in reverse: Victims first become childlike. Eventually they are mute, bedridden, and unable to walk, sit up, or smile (Roach, 1985). It is no exaggeration to say that they become very much like infants.

Researchers are urgently seeking the causes of Alzheimer's disease. It is now known that selective damage to nerve cells in the brain is probably to blame. Especially important is the presence of unusual webs and tangles in nerve cells leading to and from the hippocampus—an area important for learning and memory (Chapter 3) (Hyman et al., 1984). Important changes also take place in an area called the nucleus basalis and in chemicals necessary for carrying messages within the brain (Coyle, Price, & DeLong, 1983).

By the year 2000 it is estimated that 1 of every 10 adults over 65 will be a victim of Alzheimer's disease (Shodell, 1984). At present, increased efforts are being made to find a cure for Alzheimer's. For some of us such efforts may prove to be a race against time.

---

his irrational fears. A person standing at the door with his hand in his coat pocket could become the target of a paranoid attempt at "self-defense."

Because our next topics involve several new terms and ideas, let's stop for a quick Learning Check before proceeding.

Learning Check

1. A person who wrongly believes that his or her body is "rotting away" is suffering from:
   a. depressive delusions   *b.* delusions of grandeur   *c.* somatic delusions   *d.* delusions of persecution

2. Persons suffering from psychoses are totally unresponsive to their surroundings.   T or F?

3. A psychosis caused by lead poisoning would be termed a *functional* disorder.   T or F?

4. Paranoia is the most common form of psychosis.   T or F?

5. In *flat affect*, a sensory experience—such as hearing voices—occurs in the absence of a stimulus.   T or F?

6. Alzheimer's disease is thought to be caused by lead poisoning in the hippocampus.   T or F?

Answers: 1. c   2. F   3. F   4. F   5. F   6. F

Affective Psychosis— Peaks and Valleys

About 14 percent of patients admitted to mental hospitals suffer from *affective* psychosis.

Question: How does an affective psychosis differ from other types?

In addition to the usual symptoms of psychosis, **major affective disorders** (affective psychoses) are marked by lasting extremes in mood or emotion. Typically, one of the following patterns predominates: In **bipolar disorders,** persons go up or down emotionally. The individual may be continuously loud, elated, hyperactive, and energetic *(manic type)* or may swing between mania and deep depression *(mixed type)* (DSM-III, 1980). Even when a person is sad and guilt-ridden, the problem is considered a bipolar disorder *(depressive type)* if the person has ever been manic in the past. The person who only goes down emotionally, suffers from a **unipolar disorder.** If the psychotic depression occurs without any history of mania, it is called a **major depression.**

Manic individuals throw themselves into fits of activity marked by extreme distractibility, rapid shifts in thoughts ("flights of ideas"), constant talking, and restless movement. In advanced stages manic behavior becomes more and more incoherent, agitated, and out of control. Eating or sleeping may be ignored until individuals push themselves into states of total delirium. (Such behavior accounts for public images of the "raving maniac.") This brief excerpt from a case history illustrates manic behavior:

> Her husband had returned home to find her twirling around the living room bizarrely draped in her wedding gown tied with a bathtowel and wearing a lampshade. She gaily greeted him, laughed with an ear-piercing shrillness, and invited him to stay for the exciting "coming-out" party she was giving. Strewn on the table were a thousand handwritten invitations signed with a flourish and addressed to such dignitaries as the President of the United States, the justices of the Supreme Court, the Emperor of Japan. She made incessant noises: singing her own ballads, shouting mottoes, which she devised, reciting limericks, making rhyming sounds, and yelling obscenities (Suinn, 1970).

Depressive reactions show a reverse pattern, in which feelings of failure, sinfulness, worthlessness, and total despair predominate. The person becomes extremely subdued or withdrawn and may be intensely suicidal. Depressive reactions pose a serious threat to the survival of a disturbed individual. Suicide attempted during a psychotic depression is rarely a plea for help. Usually, the person intends to succeed and may give no prior warning (Fig. 21–3).

Manic and depressive states often appear to be interrelated in bipolar disorders. That is, when manic behavior occurs, it may still be a reaction to depression. The manic individual seeks to escape feelings of worthlessness and depression in an unending rush of activity.

Question: How do affective psychoses differ from the affective disorders described in Chapter 20?

Major affective disorders usually involve more severe mood changes. Also, of course, the person's emotional excesses are accompanied by psychotic delusions and hallucinations. As a further distinction, affective psychoses more often appear to be **endogenous** (en-DODGE-eh-nus: produced from within), rather than a reaction to external events.

Schizophrenia— Shattered Reality

Approximately half of all admissions to mental hospitals are diagnosed as *schizophrenic*. **Schizophrenia** (SKIT-soh-FREE-nee-uh) is a major health problem: 1 person in 100 will become schizophrenic, and one-fourth of all hospital beds in the United States are occupied by schizophrenics. Most schizophrenics are young adults, but schizophrenia can occur at any age.

Question: Does a schizophrenic have two personalities?

Schizophrenia does not refer to having more than one personality. Recall from the previous chapter that multiple personality is a nonpsychotic, dissociative disorder.

The word *schizophrenia* does mean "split mind," but this refers to a split between thought and emotion. In schizophrenia, emotions may become blunted or flat, or they may be very inappropriate. For example, a schizophrenic may smile or giggle when told his mother has died, or may describe her death with no visible emotion. In addition, schizophrenia is characterized by: withdrawal from contact with others and a loss of interest in external activities; a breakdown of personal habits and ability to deal with daily events; and the delusions, hallucinations, and thought abnormalities found in other types of psychosis. Schizophrenic delusions can be particularly bizarre. They often include the idea that the person's thoughts and actions are being controlled, that his or her thoughts are being broadcast so others can hear them, that thoughts have been "inserted" into the person's mind, or that thoughts have been removed.

Question: Is there more than one type of schizophrenia?

Schizophrenia may ultimately turn out to be a whole group of related disturbances. For now, we can identify four major subtypes of schizophrenia and one closely related personality disorder. Let's begin with the personality disorder.

Borderline Schizophrenia Problems informally referred to as *borderline schizophrenia* develop slowly, usually starting in adolescence. Affected persons gradually become withdrawn and isolated. They are usually seen as listless and apathetic by others and they are often considered "odd," "shiftless," or "eccentric." Their behavior may be markedly peculiar (collecting garbage, eating cigarette butts, talking to themselves, and so forth) and their emotions are usually dulled. Typically, they seem to prefer to avoid contact and communication with others.

Problems of this type superficially resemble some aspects

Fig. 21–3 *In a depressive psychosis suicidal impulses can be intense and despair total.*

of schizophrenia. But since the person is not actively psychotic, it is probably best to think of this problem as a personality disorder. Many **schizotypal personalities** go unnoticed and untreated, living out colorless and isolated lives on the fringes of society as vagrants, derelicts, or prostitutes.

Disorganized Schizophrenia Disorganized schizophrenia comes as close as any true psychiatric problem to matching the stereotyped images of "insanity" seen in movies and on television. In disorganized schizophrenia, personality disintegration is almost complete. The result is silliness, laughter, and bizarre or often obscene behavior (Fig. 21–4), as shown by this intake interview of a patient:

Dr. I am Dr. _____. I would like to know something more about you.
Patient You have a nasty mind. Lord!! Lord!!•Cat's in a cradle.

Fig. 21—4 *In disorganized schizophrenia behavior is marked by silliness, laughter, bizarre, and often obscene behavior.*

Dr.   Tell me, how do you feel?
Patient   London's bell is a long, long dock. Hee! Hee! (Giggles uncontrollably)
Dr.   Do you know where you are now?
Patient   D_____n! S_____t on you all who rip into my internals! The grudgerometer will take care of you all! (Shouting) I am the Queen, see my magic, I shall turn you all into smidgelings forever!
Dr.   Your husband is concerned about you. Do you know his name?
Patient   (Stands, walks to and faces the wall) Who am I, who are we, who are you, who are they (Turns) I . . . I . . . I . . . I! (makes grotesque faces)

Edna was placed in the women's ward where she proceeded to masturbate. She always sat in a chosen spot and in a chosen way, with her feet propped under her. Occasionally, she would scream or shout obscenities. At other times she giggled to herself. She was known to attack other patients. She began to complain that her uterus was attached to a "pipeline to the Kremlin" and that she was being "infernally invaded" by Communism. (Suinn, 1975)

Disorganized schizophrenia typically develops in early adolescence or young adulthood and is often preceded by serious personality disorganization in earlier years. Chances of improvement are limited, and social impairment is usually extreme (DSM-III, 1980).

Catatonic Schizophrenia   The catatonic seems to be in a state of total panic. This brings about a stuporous condition in which odd positions may be held for hours or even days. Sometimes, a condition called *waxy flexibility* occurs. At such times the catatonic can be arranged into any position like a mannequin. These periods of immobility may be similar to the tendency to "freeze" at times of great emergency or panic. There is evidence that catatonic individuals are struggling desperately to control their inner turmoil, because stupor may occasionally give way to outbursts of agitated and sometimes violent behavior. The following excerpt describes a **catatonic episode:**

Manuel appeared to be physically healthy upon examination. Yet he did not regain his awareness of his surroundings. He remained motionless, speechless, and seemingly unconscious. One evening an aide turned him on his side to straighten out the sheet, was called away to tend another patient, and forgot to return. Manuel was found the next morning, still on his side, his arm tucked under his body, as he had been left the night before. His arm was turning blue from lack of circulation but he seemed to be experiencing no discomfort. Further examination confirmed that he was in a state of waxy flexibility. (Suinn, 1975)

Notice that, in addition to his other problems, Manuel was unable to talk. *Mutism* plus a marked decrease in responsiveness to the environment make the catatonic patient difficult to reach. Fortunately, this bizarre form of schizophrenia is rare in Europe and North America.

Paranoid Schizophrenia   Paranoid schizophrenia is the most common schizophrenic disorder. **Paranoid schizophrenia,** like paranoia, centers around delusions of grandeur and persecution, but in paranoid schizophrenia there is personality disintegration that is not evident in paranoia. The paranoid schizophrenic also has hallucinations and delusions that are more fragmented and unconvincing than those of the paranoid.

Thinking that their minds are being controlled by god, the government, or "cosmic rays from space," or that someone is trying to poison them, paranoid schizophrenics may feel forced into violence to "protect" themselves. Do you remember James Huberty, who brutally murdered 21 people at a fast-food restaurant in San Ysidro, California, in 1984? Some observers believe that Huberty was a paranoid schizophrenic who felt persecuted and cheated by life. Shortly before he announced to his wife that he was "Going hunting humans," Huberty had been hearing hallucinated voices.

The three "types" of schizophrenia just described occur most often in textbooks. In reality there is considerable overlap among the types, and a real patient may shift from one pattern of behavior to another at different times. Many patients, therefore, are simply classified as suffering from **undifferentiated schizophrenia.**

The diagnosis of schizophrenia is fairly subjective and open to considerable error (see this chapter's Applications) (McCabe, 1976). All things considered, however, there is no doubt that schizophrenia is real or that it is a major challenge to medical and psychological researchers.

The Causes of Schizophrenia— An Unsolved Riddle

Former British Prime Minister Winston Churchill once described a question that perplexed him as "a riddle wrapped in a mystery inside an enigma." The same words might be used to describe the causes of schizophrenia, the most common and devastating psychosis.

Question: What do we know about the causes of schizophrenia?

Environment   Some psychologists suspect that early **psychological trauma** may contribute to the later develop-ment of schizophrenia. Case studies of schizophrenia often show its victims were exposed to violence, sexual abuse, death, divorce, or separation in childhood. In general there seems to be a greater than average degree of stress in the childhood of those who develop schizophrenia. A question that remains unanswered is why childhood trauma leaves some individuals emotionally crippled and others not.

Many psychologists theorize that a **disturbed family environment** is a causal factor in schizophrenia. For example, one intriguing theory is that the schizophrenic is *forced* to escape into psychosis by being placed in what British psychiatrist R. D. Laing (1967, 1970) calls a *position of checkmate.* This idea can be illustrated by imagining that someone is standing over you with a large stick. This person gives you these instructions:

> In a moment I'm going to ask you if this stick is real. If you say yes, I will hit you with it. If you say no, then I will hit you with it. If you refuse to answer, I will hit you with it.

Your reaction to this dilemma might very well be stammering, emotion, and a defensive crouch. To a person outside the situation your reactions might look "crazy" (Fig. 21–5). Similarly, Laing believes that the schizophrenic's strange thoughts and behavior are really an adaption to an impossible environment. Laing and others also believe the families of schizophrenics constantly engage in **double-bind communication.**

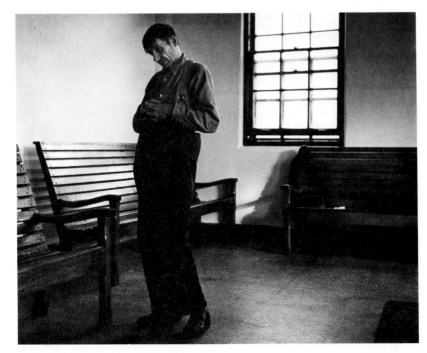

Fig. 21–5 *Can the catatonic's rigid postures and stupor be understood in terms of abnormal body chemistry? Environment? Heredity?*

Highlight 21–2
The Genain Sisters—Trouble Times Four

By the time the Genain quadruplets reached high school, they began to act strangely. Hester broke light bulbs and tore buttons off her clothes. By age 20 Nora moaned at meals and complained that the bones in her neck were slipping. At night she stood on her knees and elbows in bed until they bled. At age 22 Iris quit her job, complaining that "I am pinned down. Someone wants to fight and I don't want to." Soon afterward, she "went to pieces." She screamed, drooled at meals, and talked about hearing voices. Myra, who was the fourth identical quad, panicked easily and couldn't be reassured but did not actually break down until age 24 (Rosenthal, 1963).

In addition to sharing identical heredity, the Genain sisters—Nora, Iris, Myra, and Hester—have something else in common: All four became schizophrenic before age 25. The women, who are now in their fifties, have been in and out of mental hospitals all their lives.

You may be tempted immediately to assume that the Genain quads' psychoses were caused by heredity. However, it would be a mistake to overlook the nightmarish family life in which the girls grew up. Mr. Genain was an alcoholic who hounded, spied on, terrorized, and sexually molested the girls.

For the most part Mrs. Genain was curiously blind to her husband's actions and offered the girls little support. Instead, she added her own bizarre thinking and sexual preoccupations to the family's already warped relationships. To put it mildly, the girls' mother and father failed spectacularly as parents.

In the final analysis it seems that both heredity and an unhealthy environment led to the Genain sisters' problems (Coleman, Butcher, & Carson, 1984). Further support for this conclusion comes from the fact that Myra, the least ill of the four, was her mother's favorite. Myra also was the only sister able to keep some distance from her father.

In sum, it appears that heredity may set higher or lower thresholds for psychosis. Whether a person "crosses the line" and becomes actively disturbed, however, may depend on the kind of stresses he or she is exposed to.

A double-bind message is one that places the listener in an unsolvable conflict like that just posed. For example, the mother of a schizophrenic might issue this typical double-bind message, "You don't really love me; you're only pretending you do." This statement asks for a show of love but makes showing love impossible. Anything the person does becomes "wrong."

Although environmental explanations are attractive, they are not enough to account for schizophrenia. For example, when the children of schizophrenic parents are raised away from their chaotic home environments, they are still likely to become psychotic (Page, 1971).

Question: Does that mean that heredity is a factor in schizophrenia?

Heredity   Evidence for heredity as a factor in schizophrenia has been growing ever stronger in recent years. It now appears that some individuals inherit a *potential* for developing schizophrenia.

Question: How can that be shown?

Here is a prime example: If one identical twin becomes schizophrenic (remember, identical twins have identical genes), then the other twin has a *46 percent* chance of also becoming schizophrenic (Nicol & Gottesman, 1983). There is even a case on record of *four* identical quadruplets *all* developing schizophrenia (Rosenthal & Quinn, 1977). (See Highlight 21–2.)

Question: What about other family relationships?

If *both* parents are schizophrenic, a child again has a 46 percent chance of developing the disorder; persons with a brother or sister and one parent who are schizophrenic run a 17 percent risk; persons with a schizophrenic brother or sister have a 10 percent chance; and for *fraternal* twins the chance of mutual schizophrenia is about 14 percent (Nicol & Gottesman, 1983).

These figures can be compared with the risk for the population in general, which is 1 percent (Fig. 21–6). Comparisons such as these, and a variety of other studies, have shown that schizophrenia is more common among close relatives than distant relatives and that it tends to run in families (Gottesman & Shields, 1982).

Question: How could someone inherit a susceptibility to schizophrenia?

Body Chemistry LSD, PCP (angel dust), and similar drugs produce effects that partially mimic the symptoms of psychosis. Also, the same drugs (phenothiazines) that are used to treat an LSD overdose are effective in treating schizophrenia (Mandell et al., 1972). Such similarities have suggested to many scientists that psychosis may be based on **biochemical abnormalities** that cause the body to produce some substance similar to a *psychedelic* (mind-altering) drug. At present the most likely candidate is **dopamine** (DOPE-ah-meen), an important chemical messenger in the brain (Fig. 21–7).

Question: How does dopamine fit into the picture?

By far the most exciting discovery in recent years is the close link between dopamine and schizophrenia. Many researchers now believe that schizophrenia is directly related to overactivity in brain dopamine systems (Barchas et al., 1978; Nicol & Gottesman, 1983).

Early hints of a dopamine-psychosis link came when researchers noted that large doses of amphetamines (speed) produce symptoms that are almost identical to paranoid schizophrenia. Amphetamines, it turns out, also raise brain dopamine levels. Another piece of the puzzle fell into place when it was discovered that all major *antipsychotic* drugs *block* the action of dopamine at receptor areas in the brain (Iversen, 1979).

Question: Then is schizophrenia a "dopamine high"?

For a time it seemed so. But no extra or abnormal amounts of dopamine could be found in the brains of schizophrenics (Davis, 1978). So much for the dopamine theory!

But wait. Our story is not over. In a dramatic breakthrough a team of researchers at the University of Toronto found nearly *double* the normal number of dopamine receptors in the brains of schizophrenics. These extra receptors exist in especially large numbers in the limbic system (a major emotional system of the brain) (Lee & Seeman, 1980).

Many scientists now believe that dopamine activation triggers a flood of unrelated thoughts, feelings, and perceptions, and directly accounts for the voices, hallucinations, delusions, and other disturbances of schizophrenia (Iversen, 1979). Because of the extra receptors, schizophrenics may get psychedelic effects from normal levels of dopamine in the brain. The implication of this, and related research on other brain chemicals, is that schizophrenics may be on a sort of drug trip caused by their own bodies (Bushbaum & Haier, 1982; Hoffer, 1972).

Medical researchers have long hoped for a way to di-

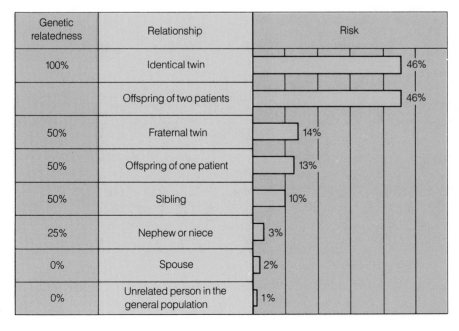

Genetic relatedness	Relationship	Risk
100%	Identical twin	46%
	Offspring of two patients	46%
50%	Fraternal twin	14%
50%	Offspring of one patient	13%
50%	Sibling	10%
25%	Nephew or niece	3%
0%	Spouse	2%
0%	Unrelated person in the general population	1%

Fig. 21–6 *Lifetime risk of developing schizophrenia is related to how closely a person is genetically related to a schizophrenic. A shared environment also increases the risk (Nicol & Gottesman, 1983). (Data from Gottesman & Shields, 1982.)*

Fig. 21–7   *This series of paintings by Louis Wain reflects a troubled personality. Wain was a British illustrator who became schizophrenic in middle age. As Wain's psychosis progressed, his cat paintings became highly abstract and fragmented. In many ways Wain's paintings resemble the perceptual changes caused by psychedelic drugs such as mescaline and LSD. Recent research suggests that psychosis may, in fact, be the result of mind-altering changes in brain chemistry. (Derik Bayes/Courtesy Guttman-Maclay Life Picture Service.)*

rectly observe the schizophrenic brain. Two new medical techniques are now making this possible. One, called a **CT scan,** provides an X-ray picture of the brain. (CT stands for computed tomography, or computer-enhanced X-ray images.) Figure 21–8 shows a CT scan of John Hinkley, Jr.'s brain. Hinkley, you may recall, shot President Ronald Reagan and three other men in 1981. In the ensuing trial Hinkley was judged insane.

As you can see, Hinkley's brain differed from the norm. Specifically, it had wider surface fissuring and enlarged ventricles (fluid-filled spaces within the brain). Similar changes, which are normal in older people, are found in about 1 out of 10 young schizophrenics. Although the meaning of such changes is still in doubt, the CT scan promises to aid in diagnosing schizophrenia and to provide new information on its causes (McKean, 1982).

A second new technique, called a **PET scan,** provides an image of brain *activity*. (PET stands for positron emission tomography.) A PET scan is made by injecting a radioactive sugar solution into a vein. When the sugar reaches the brain, a device measures how much is used in each area. This information is then translated into a colored map, or scan, of brain activity (Fig. 21–9). Researchers are already finding patterns in such scans that are consistently linked with schizophrenia, affective disorders, and other problems. Some researchers believe that in the future PET scans will be routinely used to diagnose schizophrenia (Landis, 1980). For now PET scans show that there is a clear difference between normal and schizophrenic brain activity.

Summary   In summary, the emerging picture of psychosis takes this form: *Anyone* subjected to enough stress may be pushed to a psychotic break, but some people inherit a difference in bodily chemistry or brain structure that makes them more susceptible. Thus, the right combination of inherited potential and environmental stress brings about changes in brain chemicals or generates

Fig. 21–8   (left) CT scan of would-be presidential assassin John Hinkley, Jr., taken when he was 25. The X-ray image shows widened fissures in the wrinkled surface of Hinkley's brain. (right) CT scan of a normal 25-year-old's brain. In most young adults the surface folds of the brain are pressed together too tightly to be seen. As a person ages, surface folds of the brain normally become more visible. Pronounced brain fissuring in young adults may be a sign of schizophrenia, chronic alcoholism, or other problems (McKean, 1982).

NORMAL   SCHIZOPHRENIC   MANIC-DEPRESSIVE

Fig. 21–9 *Positron emission tomography produces PET scans of the human brain. In the scans shown here, red, pink, and orange indicate lower levels of brain activity; white and blue indicate higher activity levels. Notice that activity in the schizophrenic brain is quite low in the frontal lobes (top area of each scan). Activity in the manic-depressive brain is low in the left brain hemisphere and high in the right brain hemisphere. Researchers are trying to identify consistent patterns like these to aid diagnosis of mental disorder.*

mind-altering substances in the body (Gottesman & Shields, 1982).

Ultimately, distinctions between organic and functional psychoses may be dropped, and treatment of major disturbances may become more chemical than psychological.

But for now psychosis remains "a riddle wrapped in a mystery inside an enigma." Let us hope the recent advances that we have so briefly explored are as promising as they appear to be.

Learning Check

Match the following:

1. _____ Schizotypal personality
2. _____ Disorganized schizophrenia
3. _____ Catatonic schizophrenia
4. _____ Paranoid schizophrenia
5. _____ Major affective disorders

A. Manic or depressive behavior
B. Mutism, odd postures, immobility
C. Borderline schizophrenia
D. Silliness, disorganization, bizarre behavior
E. Delusions of grandeur or persecution

6. Schizophrenics have two or more personalities.   T or F?

7. R. D. Laing attributes psychotic behavior to a "crazy" or impossible environment, often created in the home by:
   a. manic parents   *c.* psychedelic interactions
   b. schizoaffective interactions   *d.* double-bind communication

8. The _____ _____ of a schizophrenic person runs a 46 percent chance of also becoming psychotic.

9. Abnormally high numbers of noradrenaline receptors have been found in the brains of schizophrenics.   T or F?

10. Enlarged surface fissures and ventricles, as revealed by CT scans, are found only in the brains of chronic schizophrenics.   T or F?

Answers: 1. C   2. D   3. B   4. E   5. A   6. F   7. d   8. identical twin   9. F (dopamine receptors)   10. F

Treatment— Medical Approaches

Question: Is psychosis incurable? If a person's symptoms temporarily disappear, can an unexpected relapse occur?

An organic psychosis cannot be "cured" in the usual sense, but it may be controlled with drugs and other techniques. With functional psychoses the outlook is still rather negative, but many people are *permanently* cured. It is wrong to fear "former mental patients" or to exclude them from work, friendships, or other social situations. A psychotic episode does not inevitably lead to a lifelong maladjustment, but too often it leads to rejection based on groundless fears.

Question: What can be done about psychosis?

Two basic forms of treatment can be distinguished. The first, called **psychotherapy,** can be described as two people talking about one person's problems. Psychotherapy is a special relationship between a therapist and a person in trouble. Psychotherapy is applied to everything from a brief crisis to a full-scale psychosis. Because approaches currently in use are so varied, a complete discussion of psychotherapy is found in the next two chapters.

A second major approach to treatment is **somatic** (bodily) **therapy.** The principal somatic treatments are *chemotherapy, electroconvulsive therapy,* and *psychosurgery.* Somatic therapy is often done in the context of psychiatric *hospitalization.* All these approaches have a distinct medical slant, and they are used primarily to treat psychoses. For these reasons, somatic therapy provides an appropriate conclusion to our discussion of psychosis.

Drugs   The atmosphere in mental hospitals changed radically in the mid-1950s with the widespread adoption of chemotherapy (KEE-mo-therapy). **Chemotherapy** is the use of drugs or chemical substances to alleviate the symptoms of emotional disturbance. Drugs may relieve the anxiety attacks and other discomforts of nonpsychotic disorders, but they are more frequently used to combat psychosis. Drugs such as Thorazine are credited with emptying mental hospitals, reducing the hospital population from a peak of 560,000 to fewer than 200,000 patients in barely a generation.

Question: What types of drugs are used in chemotherapy?

The three major classes of drugs are: *minor tranquilizers, major tranquilizers (antipsychotics),* and *energizers.* **Minor tranquilizers** calm anxious or agitated persons; **antipsychotics** control hallucinations and other symptoms of psychosis; and **energizers** improve the mood of those who are depressed.

Question: Are drugs a valid approach to treatment?

Drugs have greatly improved the chances for recovery from a psychiatric disorder. They have shortened the length of hospital stays and have made it possible for more individuals to be returned to the community where they may be treated on an outpatient basis.

Few experts would argue for a return to the conditions that existed before chemotherapy became available. But there are some drawbacks. First of all, drugs do not *cure* mental illness. In many instances, they only temporarily relieve symptoms. Such relief may allow patients to benefit more fully from psychotherapy and other attempts to help them, but drugs alone do not remove underlying problems. As a matter of fact, patients may separate temporary improvement caused by a drug from improvement they consider genuine. As one patient told the author, "The drugs made me talk more and seem happy, but I knew I really wasn't."

The use of drugs also raises the issue of balancing benefits against possible side effects. For example, as many as 10 percent of patients taking major tranquilizers for extended periods develop *tardive dyskinesia* (TARD-iv dis-cah-NEE-zyah). In this neurological condition patients develop rhythmical facial and mouth movements, as well as unusual movements of the limbs and other parts of the body.

Perhaps the most valid criticism of chemotherapy is the simple observation that it is often overused. Apparently the temptation to reach for the prescription pad is great. Most observers agree that too many drugs are being given to too many people. Researcher David Rosenhan (see the Applications section of this chapter) believes that drugs are often used to keep patients docile and easy to manage. Many critics believe that the locks that came off the doors of old-style asylums have simply been replaced by "chemical locks." In the long run, concern over side effects and the overuse of drugs may temper the popularity of chemotherapy. But where psychosis is concerned, drugs are usually helpful and will remain a major mode of treatment.

Shock   Electroconvulsive therapy (ECT) is a rather drastic medical treatment for depression. In the usual ECT session a 150-volt electrical current is passed through the brain for slightly less than a second (Fig. 21–10). The current triggers a convulsion and causes the patient to lose consciousness for a short time. Muscle relaxants and sedative drugs are given before ECT to soften its impact. Treatments are administered in a series of 6 to 8 sessions spread over 3 to 4 weeks. There is some loss of memory for the period of treatments, but memory usually returns within 6 months.

Question: How does shock help?

Fig. 21–10 *In electroconvulsive therapy electrodes are attached to the head, and a brief electrical current is passed through the brain. ECT is used in the treatment of severe depression.*

Actually, it is the seizure activity that is considered helpful. Proponents of ECT claim that shock-induced seizures alter the biochemical balance in the brain, bringing an end to severe depression and suicidal or self-destructive behavior (Frankl, 1977).

Many people consider ECT a distasteful procedure, and not all professionals support its use. In fact, a heated debate has raged over the effectiveness of ECT and the seriousness of its side effects. Critics claim that memory losses caused by ECT are often permanent and that there is evidence of occasional brain damage (Friedberg, 1977). Others have charged that ECT is no more effective than drugs and that it is used for all types of problems, even though it is only effective for depression (Costello, 1976; Turek & Hanlon, 1977).

Defenders of ECT argue that evidence of damage comes mainly from studies done before sedation, muscle relaxants, and the use of oxygen reduced chances of injury. And recently there have been reports that if electrodes are applied to only one side of the head, memory loss is greatly reduced (Rosenberg & Pettinati, 1984). Those who support ECT view it as being like any other medical treatment: It involves calculated risks (Fink, 1977; Weiner, 1984).

As is the case with chemotherapy, the major problem with ECT seems to lie in overuse and misuse. Some patients have had literally hundreds of shock treatments and have suffered damage in the process. In spite of such abuses, ECT, when carefully used, is still considered a valid treatment for selected cases of depression—especially when it brings a rapid end to wildly self-destructive behavior.

Surgery   The most extreme biological treatment is **psychosurgery**, a general term applied to any surgical alteration of the brain. The best known psychosurgery is the *lobotomy*. In the **prefrontal lobotomy** and related techniques, the frontal lobes are disconnected from other areas of the brain. The original goal of this procedure was to calm persons who had not responded to any other type of treatment.

When the lobotomy was first introduced in the early 1950s, there were enthusiastic claims for its success. But later studies suggest that some patients were calmed, some showed no change, and some became "vegetables." Lobotomies also caused a high rate of undesirable side effects, such as seizures, extreme lack of emotional response, and even stupor (Barahal, 1958; Valenstein, 1980). As such problems became apparent, the lobotomy was abandoned.

Question: To what extent is psychosurgery now used?

Psychosurgery is still considered a valid treatment by many neurosurgeons. However, most now use sophisticated **deep lesioning** techniques. In this approach small target areas in the brain's interior are destroyed. The appeal of deep lesioning is that it can have fairly specific effects. For instance, a patient with uncontrollable aggressive impulses may be calmed by psychosurgery (Valenstein, 1980).

It is worth remembering that all forms of psychosurgery are *irreversible*. A drug can be given or taken away. You can't take back psychosurgery. Many critics argue that psychosurgery should be banned altogether. Others continue to report success with psychosurgical procedures (Mitchell-Heggs et al., 1976). All things considered, it is perhaps most accurate, even after decades of use, to describe psychosurgery as an "experimental" technique (Perkoff, 1980).

Hospitalization   Somatic therapy, psychotherapy, and other techniques may require a special setting or special control for a period of time. Traditionally, this has meant a trip to a psychiatric hospital or state institution. **Hospitalization** by itself may be considered a form of treatment since it removes a troubled individual from situations that may be provoking or maintaining the problem.

At its best the hospital is a sanctuary—a controlled environment in which diagnosis, support, refuge, and psychotherapy are provided (Bachrach, 1984). At worst an institution can be a brutalizing experience that leaves a person less prepared to face the world than before (Fig. 21–11).

In the last 20 years the resident population in large mental hospitals throughout the United States has been reduced by two-thirds. This reduction is largely due to policies designed to improve the odds that hospitalization will be constructive.

Ideally, hospitals are used as a last resort after other forms of treatment within the community have been exhausted. Recent research indicates that most psychiatric patients do as well with short-term hospitalization (3 to 4 weeks) as they do with longer periods (3 to 4 months) (Glick et al., 1979). In view of this, hospital stays are now held to a minimum through use of *revolving-door* policies, in which patients are released as soon as possible and readmitted only if necessary. Also, modern hospitals provide recreation and rehabilitation to help end an old problem—the tendency for many patients to become so "institutionalized" that they have difficulty returning to the community. Also helpful are halfway houses and voluntary support groups that ease the patient's return to the community.

Question: How successful have such policies been?

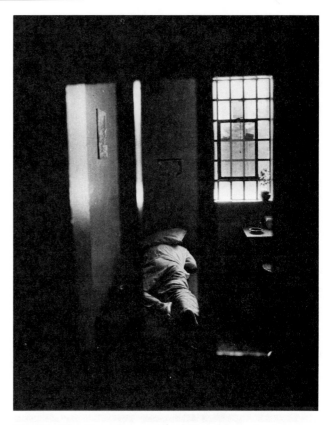

Fig. 21–11 *Depending on the quality of the institution, hospitalization may be a refuge or a brutalizing experience. Many state "asylums" or mental hospitals are antiquated and in need of drastic improvement.*

In truth their success has been limited. Many states have welcomed a reduction in mental hospital populations as a way to save money. The upsetting result is that many chronic patients are being discharged to a lonely existence in hostile communities without adequate care. A large percentage of homeless persons interviewed recently at an emergency shelter had psychiatric problems (Bassuk, Rubin, & Lauriat, 1984). In short, critics point out that the revolving door turns inward, too. Patients who move from hospitalization to unemployment and social isolation all too often must return for further treatment (Goering et al., 1984).

Large mental hospitals may no longer be warehouses for society's unwanted, but many former patients are no better off leading bleak lives in nursing homes, single-room hotels, or board and care homes (Bassuk & Gerson, 1978). Ironically, high-quality psychological and psychiatric care is available in almost every community. As much as anything, a simple lack of sufficient funding prevents large numbers of people from getting the care they need. It would be especially helpful if better rehabilitation programs were offered as a follow-up treatment (Goering et al., 1984).

Community Mental Health Programs— Hope and Help for Many

The creation of community mental health centers has been a bright spot in mental health care. **Community mental health centers** de-emphasize hospitalization and seek new answers to mental health problems through short-term treatment, outpatient care, and crisis or emergency services (Perlmutter & Silverman, 1972).

If it is like most, the primary aim of the mental health center in your community is to directly aid troubled citizens. The second goal of mental health centers is *prevention*. Consultation, education, and crisis intervention are used to end or prevent problems before they become serious. Also, some centers attempt to raise the general level of mental health in target areas by combating problems such as unemployment, delinquency, and drug abuse.

Question: How have community mental health centers fared in meeting their goals?

In practice they have concentrated much more on providing clinical services than they have on prevention (Bloom & Parad, 1977). This situation appears to be primarily the result of wavering government support (translation: money).

Overall, community mental health centers have succeeded in making mental health services more accessible than ever before. Many of their programs are made possible by **paraprofessionals,** individuals who work under the supervision of more highly trained staff. Some paraprofessionals are ex-addicts, ex-alcoholics, or ex-patients who have "been there." Many more are persons (paid or volunteer) who have skills in tutoring, crafts, counseling, or simply are warm, empathetic, and skilled at communication. There is a severe shortage of people working in mental health care. The contributions of paraprofessionals will undoubtedly continue to grow. A career as a paraprofessional should not be overlooked by students planning to work in the field of mental health (see Appendix A).

Learning Check

1. The use of chemotherapy has required longer hospital stays because drugs can be given only under hospital supervision. T or F?

2. ECT is a modern form of chemotherapy.   T or F?

3. Electroconvulsive therapy is mainly used as a treatment for depression.   T or F?

4. Tardive dyskinesia is a possible complication in long-term use of:
   a. major tranquilizers   *b.* minor tranquilizers   *c.* energizers   *d.* ECT

5. Currently, the frontal lobotomy is the most widely used form of psychosurgery.   T or F?

6. Psychosurgery can be reversed if it is unsuccessful.   T or F?

7. Whenever possible, the community mental health movement emphasizes prevention of mental health problems.   T or F?

8. Research indicates that relatively short periods of psychiatric hospitalization are as beneficial as long-term hospital stays. T or F?

Answers: 1. F   2. F   3. T   4. *a*   5. F   6. F   7. T   8. T

Applications

On Being Sane in Insane Places

Question: Suppose someone were committed to a psychiatric hospital by accident. Would the staff notice? Would the person be able to get out?

David Rosenhan of Stanford University set out to answer these questions and another: "How accurately do psychiatric hospitals distinguish between people who are psychotic and those who are healthy?"

To find out, Rosenhan and several colleagues had themselves committed (Rosenhan, 1973). Entrance to mental hospitals was gained by faking only one symptom: Rosenhan and the others complained of hearing voices that said "empty," "hollow," and "thud." In 11 out of 12 tries, they were admitted with a diagnosis of schizophrenia.

Pseudo-patients After being admitted, these *pseudo-patients* dropped all pretense of mental illness. Yet, even though they acted completely normal, none of the researchers was ever recognized by hospital *staff* as a phony patient. Other patients were not so easily fooled. It was not unusual for a real patient to say to one of the researchers, "You're not crazy, you're checking up on the hospital!" or, "You're a journalist."

Rosenhan and the others spent from 1 to 7 weeks in hospitals before being discharged. The hospitals ranged from very modern and plush to ancient and shoddy. No matter how good the facilities or the hospital's reputation, Rosenhan found some disturbing conditions.

Contact between staff and patients was very limited and was sometimes marked by fear or hostility. It was found that attendants and staff only spent an average of 11.3 percent of their time out of the "cage," the glassed-in central compartment in the ward.

It was not unusual for the morning attendants to wake patients with a hostile call of: "Come on, you m_____ f_____s, out of bed!" When patients tried to talk with staff, they were often ignored or received strange replies. One pseudo-patient approached a psychiatrist and politely asked when he might get grounds privileges. The doctor's reply was "Good morning, Dave. How are you today?"

Rosenhan found that therapy other than drugs was very limited. Daily contact of patients with psychiatrists, psychologists, or physicians averaged about 7 *minutes*. On the other hand, the researchers were given a total of 2100 pills to swallow. (They took only 2 of these; the rest were pocketed or flushed down the toilet.)

Nonpersons Patients tended to be treated as nonpersons. A nurse unbuttoned her uniform to adjust her bra in front of a roomful of male patients. She was not being sexy; she just didn't consider the patients men. A patient would often be discussed by the staff while the patient was standing nearby. It was as if patients were invisible.

A situation that sums up Rosenhan's findings better than any other is his notetaking. Rosenhan began taking notes by carefully jotting things on a small piece of paper hidden in his hand. He learned quickly that hiding was totally unnecessary. He was soon walking around with a clipboard and notepads, recording observations and collecting data.

No one questioned this behavior. Notetaking was simply seen as a symptom of his "illness." As a matter of fact, Rosenhan found that anything he did was ignored. When a staff member manhandled a patient (as happened occasionally), Rosenhan would be right there—taking notes on the whole incident!

Labels These observations clarify the failure of staff members to detect the fake patients. Because the pseudo-patients were seen in the *context* of a mental ward and because they had been *labeled* schizophrenic, *anything* they did was seen as a symptom of their "illness."

To return to the original hypothetical question about talking your way out of an accidental commitment, it should be clear that it could be quite futile to say, "Look, this is all a mistake, I'm not crazy. You've got to let me out." The response might very well be, "Have you had these paranoid delusions for long?"

Many mental health professionals found Rosenhan's findings hard to believe. This led to a follow-up study, in which researchers warned the staff of another hospital that one or more pseudo-patients were going to try to gain admission over the next 3 months. Thus alerted,

Applications: On Being Sane in Insane Places

the staff at this hospital tried to identify fake incoming patients. Among 193 candidates, 41 were labeled fakes by at least one staff member, and 19 more were labeled "suspicious." This only served to confirm Rosenhan's original findings, because he never sent *any* patients—fake or otherwise—to this hospital!

An important final note is that all of the normal people who served as pseudo-patients in the original studies were discharged as schizophrenics "in remission" (temporarily free of symptoms). In other words the label that prevented hospital staff from seeing the normality of the researchers stayed with them when they left. Psychiatrist Karl Menninger (1964) once commented on a similar situation:

> A label can blight the life of a person even after his recovery from mental illness. A young doctor I knew suffered for a time from some anxiety and indecision. He consulted a psychiatrist and soon recovered. Unfortunately, a "tentative" diagnosis of schizophrenia got abroad—I don't know how—and the young doctor's professional career was seriously impaired. He was injured, not by mental illness but by a word.

Observations such as these are not a total condemnation of psychiatric hospitals. Many of the conditions Rosenhan encountered will be found in *any* hospital or other large institution. But Rosenhan's findings do carry an important message for professionals and nonprofessionals alike: *labels can be dangerous*. As Stoller (1967) has said:

> When a person is labeled—neurotic, psychotic, executive, teacher, salesman, psychologist—either by himself or by

others, he restricts his behavior to the role and even may rely upon the role for security. This diminishes the kind of experiences he is likely to have. Indeed, it is those groups whose members have shared labels—be it schizophrenic or executive—which are hardest to help move into intimate contact.

Implications The terms reviewed in this and the previous chapter can, and do, aid communication about human problems. But if used carelessly, they may do great damage. Everyone has felt or acted "crazy" during brief periods of stress or high emotion. The person whose adjustment problems extend over a longer period of time is different from you or me only in the severity of his or her difficulty.

It is therefore more productive to label problems than to label people. Think of the difference in impact between saying, "He is experiencing a serious emotional disturbance" and saying, "He is a *psychotic*." Which statement would you choose to have said about yourself?

It is also important to realize that a severely disturbed person will appreciate being treated normally. Rosenhan's research makes it clear that the person is not helped by being thrust into the role of a "patient." One former patient's comments clarify this last point:

> After I got back from the hospital, my friends tried to *act* like nothing had changed. But I could tell they weren't being honest. For instance, a friend invited me to dinner and everything went fine until I dropped my fork. Both my friend and his wife jumped up and stared at me like they thought I might explode. I was quite embarrassed.

Learning Check

1. In the majority of their attempts, Rosenhan's pseudo-patients were admitted to mental hospitals after complaining only that they were hearing voices.   T or F?
2. Although they were often detected by professional staff members, the normality of the pseudo-patients was never recognized by other patients.   T or F?
3. During their hospital stay, pseudo-patients were denied psychiatric drugs even though they requested them.   T or F?
4. Rosenhan found that almost anything pseudo-patients said or did was interpreted as a symptom of their "illness."   T or F?
5. When they were alerted that a number of pseudo-patients might try to gain entry, hospital staff members were able to more accurately detect the fakes.   T or F?

Answers: 1. T   2. F   3. F   4. T   5. F

Chapter Summary

- Psychosis is a break in contact with reality that is marked by *delusions, hallucinations, sensory changes, emotional disturbances*, and, in some cases, *personality disintegration*.

- Psychotic symptoms, as well as lesser problems in thought, speech, memory, and attention, tend to be most prominent during short episodes of increased disturbance. There is evidence that some such symptoms are partially under voluntary control.

- An *organic psychosis* is based on known injuries or diseases of the brain. Problems of unknown origin are termed *functional psychoses*. Three common causes of organic psychosis are untreated syphilis (*general paresis*), *poisoning*, and *senile dementia* (especially *Alzheimer's disease*).

- A diagnosis of *paranoid psychosis* is almost totally based on delusions of grandeur or persecution and rarely involves personality disintegration. Because they often have intense and irrational delusions of persecution, paranoid persons may be violent if they believe they are threatened.

- *Major affective disorders* (affective psychoses) involve extremes of mood, plus psychotic symptoms. *Bipolar disorders* combine mania and depression, and occur in *manic, depressive*, and *mixed* types. *Major depressions* involve extreme sadness and despondency but no evidence of mania.

- *Schizophrenia* is the most common psychosis. It is distinguished by a split between thought and emotion and by delusions, hallucinations, and communication difficulties. Several subtypes of schizophrenia have been identified.

- A *schizotypal personality disorder*, sometimes referred to as borderline schizophrenia, involves gradual withdrawal into isolation from others and odd, apathetic behavior.

- *Disorganized schizophrenia* shows extreme personality disintegration and silly, bizarre, or obscene behavior. Social impairment is usually extreme.

- *Catatonic schizophrenia* is associated with stupor, mutism, and odd postures. Sometimes, violent agitated behavior also occur.

- In *paranoid schizophrenia* (the most common subtype), outlandish delusions of grandeur and persecution are coupled with psychotic symptoms and personality breakdown.

- *Undifferentiated schizophrenia* is the term used to indicate a lack of clear-cut patterns of disturbance.

- Current explanations of schizophrenia emphasize a combination of *environmental stress, inherited susceptibility*, and *biochemical abnormalities* in the body or brain. One popular environmental theory is that schizophrenics have been subject to unsolvable dilemmas through *double-bind communication*. A better case can be made for the importance of early *traumatic experiences* and *disturbed family environments* as underlying factors in schizophrenia. In addition, studies of twins and other close relatives strongly support a genetic view of schizophrenia. Recent biochemical studies have focused on abnormalities in brain transmitter substances, especially *dopamine* and its receptor sites.

- Three somatic or medical approaches to treatment of psychosis are *chemotherapy* (use of drugs), *electroconvulsive therapy* (ECT—brain shock for the treatment of depression), and *psychosurgery* (surgical alteration of the brain). All three techniques are capable of producing serious side effects, and all are controversial to a degree (due to questions about effectiveness and the cost/benefit ratio).

- *Hospitalization* is often associated with somatic therapy, and it is also considered a form of treatment. Prolonged hospitalization is now discouraged by *revolving-door* admissions policies and by an emphasis on providing care within the community. As long as community care remains poor, however, repeated hospitalization is likely.

- A development in mental health care that seeks to avoid or minimize hospitalization is the creation of *community mental health centers*. Community mental health centers also have as their goal the *prevention* of mental health problems through education, consultation, and crisis intervention.

- David Rosenhan's use of *pseudo-patients* to study mental hospitals suggests that problems in diagnosis exist and that *psychiatric labeling* can affect our perceptions of others' behavior.

▶▶▶ **Exploration**

Who Is "Crazy" and What Should Be Done about It?

Two well-known critics of traditional psychiatric treatment for "mental illness" are Thomas Szasz and Ronald D. Laing. Szasz (1966) believes that mental illness is a myth. Szasz charges that traditional medical concepts of diseases have been wrongly applied to emotional problems. The "medical model," as this is called, treats such problems as "diseases" with "symptoms" that can be "cured." Szasz and a number of other experts prefer to view emotional disturbances as "problems in living." This view makes the goal of therapy "change" rather than "cure" and changes a "patient" to a "client."

Szasz has also questioned handling of the civil rights of psychiatric "patients." Szasz estimates there are 750,000 persons in mental hospitals, 90 percent of them *involuntarily*. He sees this as a serious mistake. To commit people because they might be dangerous to themselves is indefensible by Szasz's standards.

According to Szasz, the only legitimate reason for depriving a person of freedom is for being dangerous to others, but then only if the person has broken the law by committing violence or by threatening to do so. Szasz considers the disturbed no more dangerous than a randomly selected group of citizens. He therefore rejects involuntary commitment as "punishment without trial, imprison-ment without limit, and stigmatization without hope of redress" (1969).

Szasz's position is that people have the right to be as "crazy" as they want as long as they don't hurt anyone else and don't break existing laws. Psychiatrist Ronald Laing takes a more extreme position. Laing believes that our world has become so "mad" that anyone adjusted to it is in serious trouble. He claims:

> The experience and behavior that are labeled schizophrenia are a special sort of strategy that a person invents in order to live in an unliveable world (1967).*

Based on his respect for those who are unable or unwilling to "play the game" anymore, Laing set up an "antihospital" in London called Kingsley Hall. In Kingsley Hall no distinctions were made between patients and staff. Kingsley Hall was run as a self-governing communal arrangement without white coats and "chemical strait-jackets."

In Kingsley Hall, "psychotics" were encouraged to explore the limits of their break from reality as a means of establishing a more honest relationship with the world. In this regard Laing has said:

*From *The Politics of Experience* by R. D. Laing. Copyright © 1967 by R. D. Laing. Reprinted by permission of Penguin Books Ltd.

Madness need not be all breakdown. It may also be breakthrough. It is potentially liberation and renewal as well as enslavement and existential death.

Laing believes schizophrenia is real, but he also thinks it can be good for you. In his view psychosis is similar to a psychedelic "trip"—an ultimate existential confrontation with oneself, one's reality, and the meaning of life.

It is undoubtedly a mistake to assume that the findings of David Rosenhan and the visions of people such as Szasz and Laing justify abandoning the tremendous advances in mental health care made in recent years. These people do raise serious questions about the future, however. In an area as complex as treatment of major emotional disturbances, there is much room for improvement and innovation. In addition, they have focused attention on the important civil rights questions of involuntary commitment. As a final bit of food for thought, consider the following incident, recorded by a reporter visiting a large state mental hospital:

A thin man, old and dry, stopped the guide and said, "When the hell you gonna get me a suit and let me outa here? How about it? . . ." The guide said something indefinite and the man walked away, nodding. This was the section for killers, I had been told, so I asked what the thin man had done.

Exploration: Who is "Crazy" and What Should Be Done about It?

"He painted a horse."

"He what?"

"He painted a horse."

"What's wrong with that?"

"It was in a field. A live horse, He was drunk and somebody bet him he couldn't make a horse look like a ze-bra, I think, so he painted it and they put him here. For being drunk proba-bly."

"How long has he been in?"

"Thirty-seven years. By the time they got around to letting him out he really was crazy. . . . For his own good we just can't let him go out of here."*

*Bruce Jackson, "Our Prisons Are Criminal," *New York Times Magazine*, September 22, 1973, pp. 54–57.

Learning Check

1. Szasz has argued that it is inappropriate to apply a medical or disease model to what he terms "problems in living." T or F?
2. Szasz points out that most people in mental hospitals are there voluntarily. T or F?
3. Laing's antihospital made use of psychedelic drug trips to help patients confront their psychotic behavior. T or F?

Answers: 1. T 2. F 3. F

Questions for Discussion

1. What positive and negative roles do mental institutions play in society?
2. Is Szasz justified in his appraisal of mental institutions as simply prisons by another name?
3. Do you think Szasz and Laing are unrealistically romantic in their approach to mental illness, or are they the wave of the future?
4. Under what circumstances would you consider it reasonable for a stranger to be involuntarily committed? A friend? A close relative? Yourself?
5. In your opinion, how could a person experiencing a severe "problem in living" be most effectively helped?
6. Should a mental patient have the right to:
   a. refuse medication
   b. demand legal counsel and alternative medical opinions
   c. refuse to work in a mental hospital or to choose the work he or she will do
   d. communicate by phone, letter, or in person with anyone at any time
   e. keep personal property (including drugs, matches, pocketknives, and other potentially harmful materials)
   f. request an alternative to legal commitment to a mental hospital
   g. be represented by an independent advocate who is not on the hospital staff?
7. In view of what you know about the causes of psychosis, how valid do you consider the medical model of mental illness? What are the advantages and disadvantages of such a model? What are the advantages and disadvantages of a psychological model?

Chapter 22 | Insight Therapy

Chapter Preview
Quiet Terror on a Spring Afternoon

The warm California sun shone brightly. A light breeze danced inland from the ocean. Outside my office window an assortment of small birds sang to a beautiful spring day. I could hear them between Susan's frightened sobs.

As a psychologist I see many students who have personal problems. Still, I was somewhat surprised to see Susan at my office door. Her excellent work in class and her healthy, casual appearance left me unprepared for her first words. "I feel like I'm losing my mind," she said. "Can I talk to you?"

In the next hour Susan sketched the features of her own personal hell. Her calm exterior hid a world of overwhelming fear, anxiety, and depression. She had lost several part-time jobs because at each one she began to fear her co-workers and the customers so much that she could barely bring herself to speak to them. Her absenteeism and embarrassing interchanges with customers would gradually lead to her dismissal.

At school Susan felt "different" and was sure that other students could tell she was "weird." Several disastrous romances had left her terrified of men. Lately she had become so depressed that she had begun to think frequently of suicide. At times she became so terrified for no apparent reason that her heart pounded wildly and she felt that she was about to lose control of herself completely.

Susan's visit to my office was an important turning point. Emotional conflicts had made her existence a living nightmare. At a time when she was becoming her own worst enemy, Susan had realized that she needed the help and support of another person to overcome her problems. In Susan's case that person was a talented psychologist to whom I referred her. By combining various forms of psychotherapy, the psychologist was able to help Susan come to grips with her emotions and return a healthy balance to her personality.

This chapter and the next discuss psychological methods used to ease problems like Susan's. Here we will describe therapies that emphasize the value of gaining insight *into personal problems. In the next chapter we will focus on* behavior therapy *and* cognitive therapy, *which are used to directly change troublesome thoughts and behaviors.*

Survey Questions   How did modern psychotherapies develop? Is Freudian psychoanalysis still used? What are the characteristics of humanistic therapies? Can psychotherapy be done with groups of people? What are group therapies like? What do various therapies have in common? How would a person go about finding professional help? What can be done to help a troubled friend?

Resources

Humpty-Dumpty sat on a wall.
Humpty-Dumpty had a great fall.
All the King's horses and all the King's men
Couldn't put Humpty together again.

Psychotherapy— Getting Better by the Hour

In our age of stress, conflict, and anxiety, who will put you together again, and how will they do it? Actually, the odds are that you will *not* experience a life-impairing emotional problem like Susan's, but if you did, what kind of help is available? In most cases the answer is some form of *psychotherapy.*

Question: What is psychotherapy?

Psychotherapy is any psychological technique used to facilitate positive changes in a person's personality, behavior, or adjustment. The psychotherapist has many approaches to choose from: psychoanalysis, desensitization, Gestalt therapy, logotherapy, client-centered therapy, reality therapy, transactional analysis, behavior modification—to name but a few.

Due to a recent explosive growth in the number of therapies, some confusion may exist about how they differ. To begin, it may help to recognize that psychological problems are complex, and that the best approach for a particular person or problem will not always be the same.

Also, psychotherapies vary widely in emphasis, as described in Table 22–1.

Myths   Popular accounts tend to depict psychotherapy as a complete personal transformation—a sort of "major overhaul" of the psyche. But this ignores the realities of solving human problems. As clinical psychologist Bernie Zilbergeld (1983) points out, therapy is *not* equally effective for all problems. Chances of improvement are fairly good for phobias, low self-esteem, some sexual problems, and marital conflicts. More complex problems, however, can be difficult to treat. Also, contrary to what many people think, therapy usually does not bring about dramatic changes in behavior or an end to personal problems. For many people, therapy's major benefit is that it provides comfort, support, and a way to make positive changes.

In short, it is often unrealistic to expect psychotherapy to undo a person's entire past history. Yet even when problems are severe, therapy may help a person gain a new perspective or learn ways to better cope with life (Coleman, Butcher, & Carson, 1984). Psychotherapy can be hard work for both client and therapist. But when it succeeds, there are few activities more rewarding.

As a final point, you also should realize that psychotherapy is not done only to solve psychological problems. Some therapies are designed to encourage personal growth and enrichment for people who are already functioning effectively.

Table 22–1 Dimensions of Therapy	
The term *psychotherapy* most often refers to verbal interaction between trained mental health professionals and their clients. Many therapists also use learning principles to directly alter troublesome behaviors, as described in Chapter 23.	The terms listed here describe basic aspects of various therapies. Notice that more than one term may apply to the same therapy. For example, it would be possible to have a directive, action-oriented group therapy or a nondirective, individual, insight-oriented therapy.
Individual therapy	A therapy session involving only one client and one therapist
Group therapy	A therapy session in which several clients participate at one time with one or more therapists
Insight therapy	Any psychotherapy whose goal is to lead clients to a deeper understanding of their thoughts, emotions, and behavior
Action therapy	Any therapy designed to bring about direct changes in troublesome thoughts, habits, feelings, or behavior
Directive therapy	Any approach in which the therapist provides strong guidance during therapy sessions
Nondirective therapy	A style of therapy in which clients assume responsibility for solving their own problems; the therapist assists but does not guide or give advice

Origins of Therapy—Bored Skulls and Hysteria on the Couch

History gives ample reason for appreciating the humanity of modern therapies. Archaeological findings dating to the Stone Age suggest that most primitive approaches were marked by fear and superstitious belief in demons, witchcraft, and magic. One of the more dramatic "cures" practiced by primitive "psychotherapists" was a process called **trepanning** (treh-PAN-ing). A hole was bored, chipped, or bashed into the skull of the patient, presumably to relieve pressure or release evil spirits. Actually, trepanning may have simply been an excuse to kill people who were un-

usual, since many of the "patients" didn't survive the "treatment."

During the Middle Ages treatment for the mentally ill in Europe focused on **demonology.** Abnormal behavior was blamed on supernatural forces such as possession by the devil or the curses of witches and wizards. As treatment, **exorcism** was used to drive out the evil. For the fortunate, exorcism was a religious ritual. More often, it took the form of physical torture to make the body an inhospitable place for the devil to reside (Fig. 22–1).

One explanation for the rise of demonology may lie in a condition called **ergotism** (ER-got-ism). In the Middle Ages, rye fields were often infested with ergot fungus (Fig.

Fig. 22–1   *Early approaches to the treatment of mental illness. (a) Primitive "treatment" for mental disorder sometimes took the form of boring a hole in the skull. (b) Many early asylums were no more than prisons with inmates held in chains. (c) One late nineteenth-century "treatment" was based on swinging the patient in a harness—presumably to calm the patient's nerves.*

(a)

(b)

(c)

22–2). Ergot, we now know, is a natural source of LSD and other mind-altering chemicals. Eating bread made from tainted grain can cause symptoms that might easily be interpreted as possession, bewitchment, or madness. Pinching sensations, convulsions, muscle twitches, facial spasms, delirium, and visual hallucinations are all common reactions to ergot poisoning (Kety, 1979; Matossian, 1982). Thus, many of the "patients" of demonology may have been doubly victimized.

The idea that the emotionally disturbed are "mentally ill" and that they should be treated compassionately emerged after 1793. This was the year **Philippe Pinel** changed the Bicêtre Asylum in Paris from a squalid "madhouse" into a mental hospital by personally unchaining the inmates. Although almost 200 years have passed since Pinel began humane treatment for the emotionally disturbed, the process of improving conditions in psychiatric hospitals and of changing public attitudes toward psychotherapy continues today. Increased acceptance of the value of psychotherapy is a positive sign, but public attitudes toward the disturbed still tend to be colored by suspicion and fear. Perhaps as more people take part in psychotherapy as a growth experience, it will become more widely understood.

Question: When was psychotherapy developed?

The first true psychotherapy was developed around the turn of the century by Sigmund Freud.

As a physician in Vienna, Freud was intrigued by the cases of **hysteria** (physical symptoms such as paralysis or numbness without known physical cause) he encountered. As you may recall, such problems are now called *somatoform disorders* (see Chapter 20). Slowly Freud became convinced that the symptoms of hysteria were only the tip of the iceberg, that deeply hidden unconscious conflicts (frequently sexual in nature) were to blame. Based on this insight, Freud went on to develop his own form of therapy. Because **psychoanalysis,** as Freud called his technique, is the "granddaddy" of most modern psychotherapies, let us examine it in some detail.

Psychoanalysis— Expedition into the Unconscious

Question: Isn't psychoanalysis the therapy where the patient lies on a couch?

Freud's patients usually reclined on a couch during therapy, while Freud sat out of sight taking notes and offering interpretations. This arrangement was selected to encourage relaxation and a free flow of thoughts and images from the patient's unconscious (Fig. 22–3). This aspect is the

Fig. 22–2 *Two ears of rye infested with ergot fungus (dark areas). The psychedelic effects of the fungus may explain some cases of "possession" in Medieval Europe and "bewitchment" in colonial New England.*

least important of several features of psychoanalysis and has been abandoned by many modern analysts.

Question: How did Freud treat emotional problems?

Freud's theory stressed that repressed memories, motives, and conflicts—particularly those stemming from instinctual drives for sex and aggression—were the cause of neurosis. Although unconscious and repressed, these factors remain active in the personality, forcing the person to develop rigid ego-defense mechanisms and to devote excessive amounts of time and energy to compulsive and self-defeating behavior. Freud relied on four basic techniques to uncover the unconscious roots of neurosis (Freud, 1949).

1. **Free association.** During psychoanalysis the patient must say whatever comes to mind without regard for whether it makes sense or is painful or embarrassing. Thoughts are allowed to move freely from one association to the next.

2. **Dream analysis.** The purpose of free association is to lower defenses so that unconscious material may emerge. Freud considered dreams an unusually good additional way to tap the unconscious. Freud referred to dreams as "the royal road to the unconscious" because he believed that forbidden desires and unconscious feelings are more freely expressed in dreams. He distinguished between the **manifest** (obvious, visible) **content** and the **latent** (hidden) **content** of dreams.

   To appreciate fully the unconscious message of a dream, Freud sought to reveal its latent meaning by interpreting **dream symbols.** Let's say a young husband reports a dream in which he pulls a pistol from his waistband and aims at a target while his wife watches. The pistol repeatedly fails to discharge, and

Fig. 22–3 *Pioneering psychotherapist Sigmund Freud in his office.*

the man's wife laughs at him. Freud might see this as an indication of repressed feelings of sexual impotence, with the gun serving as a disguised image of the penis.

3. Analysis of resistance. When free associating or describing dreams, the patient may *resist* talking about or thinking about certain topics. Such resistances are said to reveal important unconscious conflicts. As the analyst becomes aware of resistances, he or she brings them to the patient's awareness so they can be dealt with realistically.

4. Analysis of transference. The individual undergoing psychoanalysis may transfer feelings to the therapist that relate to important past relationships with others. At times the analyst may be reacted to as if he or she were a rejecting father, an unloving or overprotective mother, or a former lover. This is considered a prime opportunity to help the patient undergo an emotional reeducation. As the patient reexperiences repressed emotions, the therapist can help the patient recognize and understand them.

Question: Is psychoanalysis still used?

Psychoanalysis in its original form called for three to five therapy sessions a week for up to 7 years. Because of the huge amounts of time and money this requires, most psychodynamic therapists now substitute more direct inter-

viewing for free association, and the length of therapy has been shortened considerably.

A more important question about psychoanalysis may be: Does it work? The development of newer, more streamlined psychotherapies is in part due to questions about the effectiveness of psychoanalysis. One psychologist, H. J. Eysenck (1967), has gone so far as to suggest that psychoanalysis takes such a long time that symptoms disappear because of **spontaneous remission** (improvement due to the mere passage of time). To support his argument, Eysenck cites research showing that people placed on *waiting lists* improve at the same rate as those in psychoanalysis.

How seriously should Eysenck's criticism be taken? At present his view appears fairly extreme. It is true that problems ranging from hyperactivity to anxiety improve with the passage of time. However, more recent work affirms that psychoanalysis is usually better than no treatment at all (Bergin & Suinn, 1975).

Undoubtedly, many people have been helped by psychoanalytic therapy. But to the modern therapist questions remain: When psychoanalysis works, why does it work? Which procedures are essential and which are unnecessary? Based on intuition, personal philosophy, clinical experience, and the personality theory they find most acceptable, modern psychotherapists have posed surprisingly varied answers to these questions. The following sections will acquaint you with some therapies currently in use.

Learning Check

See if you can answer the following questions. If you miss any, review the previous sections.

Match

1. ____ Directive therapies
2. ____ Action therapies
3. ____ Insight therapies
4. ____ Nondirective therapies

A. Change behavior
B. Place responsibility on client
C. The client is strongly guided
D. Seek understanding

5. Pinel is famous for his use of exorcism.   T or F?

6. Freud developed trepanning.   T or F?

7. A spontaneous remission of symptoms means that psychotherapy has succeeded.   T or F?

8. In psychoanalysis an emotional attachment to the therapist by the patient is called:
   a. free association   *b.* resistance   *c.* manifest association   *d.* transference

Answers: 1. C 2. A 3. D 4. B 5. F 6. F 7. F 8. d

Humanistic Therapies— Restoring Human Potential

The goal of traditional psychoanalysis is adjustment. Freud was actually quite conservative in his claims: Any of his patients, he said, could expect only to change their "hysterical misery into common unhappiness"! The humanistic therapies outlined in upcoming sections are generally more optimistic. Most assume that it is possible for people to live rich and rewarding lives and to make full use of their potential. Psychotherapy is seen as a means of giving natural tendencies toward mental health a chance to emerge.

Question: What is client-centered therapy? How is it different from psychoanalysis?

Client-Centered Therapy   Psychoanalysts delve into childhood, dreams, and the unconscious. Psychologist Carl Rogers has found it more productive to explore *conscious* thoughts and feelings (Fig. 22–4). The psychoanalyst tends to take a position of authority from which he or she offers interpretations of what is "wrong" with the patient or of what dreams or childhood experiences "mean." Rogers believes that what is right or valuable for the therapist may not be right and valuable for the client. (Rogers prefers the term *client* to *patient*.) Accordingly, **client-centered therapy** (also called person-centered therapy) is *nondirective*. The client is the center of the process. He or she determines what will be discussed during each session.

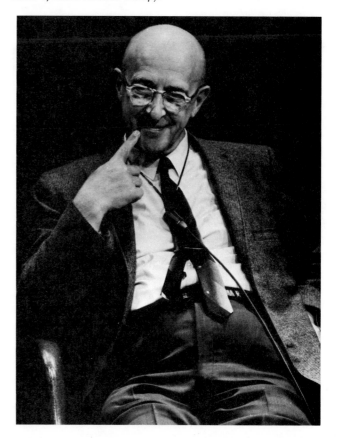

Fig. 22–4   *Contemporary psychotherapist Carl Rogers, originator of client-centered therapy.*

Highlight 22–1
Carl Rogers on Personal Growth

Like other humanistic psychologists, Carl Rogers (1980) believes deeply that there is a natural human urge to seek health and self-growth. Rogers' belief is vividly expressed by the following quotation:

> I remember that in my boyhood the bin in which we stored our winter's supply of potatoes was in the basement, several feet below a small window. The conditions were unfavorable, but pale white sprouts . . . would grow two or three feet in length as they reached toward the light of the distant window. The sprouts were, in their bizarre, futile growth, a sort of desperate expression of the directional tendency I have been describing. . . . In dealing with clients whose lives have been terribly warped, in working with men and women on the back wards of state hospitals, I often think of those potato sprouts. . . . The clue to understanding their behavior is that they are striving, in the only ways that they perceive as available to them, to move toward growth, toward becoming. To healthy persons, the results may seem bizarre and futile but they are life's desperate attempt to become itself. This potent constructive tendency is an underlying basis of the person-centered approach.

Question: If the client runs things, what does the therapist do?

The therapists's job is to create an "atmosphere of growth" by maintaining four basic conditions.

First, the therapist offers the client **unconditional positive regard.** In other words, the client is accepted *totally.* The therapist refuses to react with shock, dismay, or disapproval to anything the client says or feels. Total acceptance by the therapist is the first step to self-acceptance by the client.

Second, the therapist attempts to achieve genuine **empathy** for the client by trying to see the world through the client's eyes and to feel some part of what he or she is feeling.

As a third essential condition, the therapist strives to be **authentic** in his or her relationship with clients. The therapist must not hide behind a professional role. Rogers believes that phony fronts and facades destroy the growth atmosphere sought in client-centered therapy (see Highlight 22–1).

Fourth, the therapist does not make interpretations, pose solutions, or offer advice. Instead, the therapist **reflects** the client's thoughts and feelings. By repeating or restating what the client has said or by telling the client what emotion he or she seems to be displaying, the therapist serves as a psychological "mirror" in which clients learn to see themselves more clearly and realistically. Rogers believes that a person armed with a realistic self-image and with a new level of self-acceptance will gradually discover solutions to life problems.

Existential Therapy   According to the existentialists, "being in the world" (existence) creates deep and unavoidable conflicts. Each of us, they say, must deal with the realities of death. We must face the fact that each person creates his or her private world by making choices. We must overcome the isolation of living on a vast and indifferent planet. We must confront feelings of meaninglessness.

Question: What do these concerns have to do with psychotherapy?

Like client-centered therapy, **existential therapy** tries to promote self-knowledge and self-actualization. However, there are important differences. Client-centered therapy seeks to uncover a "true self" hidden behind an artificial screen of defenses. In contrast, existential therapy emphasizes the idea of **free will.** That is, through *choices* one can *become* the person he or she wants to be.

Existential therapy attempts to restore meaning and vitality to life so that the individual has the *courage* to make rewarding and socially constructive choices. Typically, existential therapy focuses on the "ultimate concerns" of human existence. These include the inescapable givens of **death, freedom, isolation,** and **meaninglessness** (Yalom, 1980).

Question: What does an existential therapist do?

One example of existential therapy is Victor Frankl's **logotherapy.**

Frankl (1955) developed his approach on the basis of experiences in a Nazi concentration camp. In the camp Frankl observed the breakdown of countless prisoners as they were stripped of all hope and human dignity. Frankl believed that those who survived with their sanity did so because they had managed to hang on to a sense of *meaning* (logos). In some cases this was nothing more than the ultimate human freedom—the freedom to choose one's own attitude in any set of circumstances.

Like most existential therapists, Frankl uses a flexible approach centered around **confrontation.** The person is challenged to examine the quality of his or her existence and choices and to *encounter* the unique, intense, here-and-now interaction of two human beings. When existential therapy is successful, it brings about a reappraisal of what's important in life. Indeed, some clients experience an emotional rebirth not unlike that seen in people who have survived a close brush with death.

Gestalt Therapy   Gestalt therapy, which is most often associated with the late Frederick (Fritz) Perls (1969), is built around the idea that perception, or *awareness*, becomes disjointed and incomplete in the maladjusted individual. The Gestalt approach is more directive than either client-centered therapy or existential therapy, and it places a special emphasis on immediate experience.

Question: What does Gestalt mean?

The German word **Gestalt** means *whole*, or complete. The Gestalt therapist seeks to help the individual rebuild thinking, feeling, and acting into connected wholes. This is achieved by expanding personal awareness, by accepting responsibility for one's thoughts, feelings, and actions, and by filling in gaps in experience.

Question: What do you mean by "gaps in experience"?

Gestalt therapists believe that we often shy away from expressing or "owning" upsetting feelings. This creates a gap in self-awareness that may become a barrier to personal growth. For example, a person who feels anger after the death of a parent might go for years without expressing it. This and similar threatening gaps may block emotional health.

Working either one-to-one or in a group setting, the Gestalt therapist encourages the individual to become more aware of his or her immediate experience. Rather than discussing "why" he or she feels guilt, anger, fear, or boredom, the client is encouraged to have these feelings in the "here and now" and to become fully aware of them. The therapist helps promote awareness by drawing attention to the client's posture, voice, and eye or hand movements. The client may also be asked to exaggerate a vague feeling until it becomes clear. Gestalt therapists believe that expressing such feelings allows people to "take care of unfinished business" and break through emotional impasses.

In all his writings, Perls' basic message comes through clearly: Emotional health comes from knowing what you *want* to do, not dwelling on what you *should* do, *ought* to do, or *should want* to do. Another way of stating this idea is that emotional health come from taking full responsibility for one's feelings and actions. It means changing "I can't" to "I won't," for example, or "I must" to "I choose to."

Question: How does Gestalt therapy help people discover their real wants?

Above all else, Gestalt therapy emphasizes *present* experience. Clients are urged to stop intellectualizing and talking *about* feelings. Instead they learn to: live now; live here; stop imagining; experience the real; stop unnecessary thinking; taste and see; express rather than explain, justify, or judge; give in to unpleasantness and pain just as to pleasure; surrender to being as you are (adapted from Naranjo, 1970).

Learning Check

See if you can answer the following questions.

Match

1. _____ Client-centered therapy
2. _____ Gestalt therapy
3. _____ Existential therapy
4. _____ Logotherapy

A. Meaning
B. Unconditional positive regard
C. Gaps in awareness
D. Choice and becoming

5. A Gestalt therapist tries to *reflect* a client's thoughts and feelings.   T or F?
6. Client-centered therapy is directive.   T or F?
7. Confrontation and encounter are concepts of existential therapy.   T or F?

Answers: 1. B 2. C 3. D 4. A 5. F 6. F 7. T

Group Therapy— People Who Need People

Question: Is group therapy just individual therapy with more than one person?

Most psychotherapies can be adapted for use in groups. Psychologists first tried working with groups as a practical response to the need for more therapists than were available. To their surprise, group therapy not only worked, it also offered some special advantages (Fig. 22–5).

In group therapy a person can *act out* or directly experience problems. Doing so often produces insights that might not occur from merely talking about problems. In addition, other group members with similar problems can offer support and useful input. Groups also help form a bridge between therapy and real-life problems by providing a situation that is more realistic than the protected atmosphere of individual therapy. For reasons such as these, a number of specialized group techniques have emerged. Because they range from Alcoholics Anonymous to marriage encounter, we will sample only a few representative approaches. (The largest group therapy of all may be on your radio—see Highlight 22–2.)

Psychodrama   One of the first group approaches was developed by J. L. Moreno (1953), who called his technique **psychodrama.** In psychodrama an individual **role plays** (acts out) dramatic incidents resembling those that cause problems in real life. For example, a disturbed teenager might act out a typical family fight, with the therapist playing his father and other clients taking the roles of mother, brothers, and sisters. Moreno believed that insights and the emotional relearning from these enactments transfer to real-life situations. Therapists using psychodrama often find **role reversals** especially helpful (Leveton, 1977). For instance, the teenager just described would be asked to role play his father or mother in order to better understand their feelings.

Family Therapy   Family relationships are the source of great pleasure and, all too often, of great pain for many people. In **family therapy,** husband, wife, and children work as a group to resolve the problems of each family member. Family therapy tends to be brief and focused on specific problems, such as frequent fights, a depressed teenager, and so forth (Berman, 1982).

Family therapists believe that problems are rarely lim-

Fig. 22–5 *A group therapy session. Group members offer mutual support while sharing problems, insights.*

ited to a single family member: A problem for one is considered a problem for all. Thus, family members work together to improve communication, to change destructive patterns, and to see themselves and each other in new ways.

Question: Does the therapist work with the whole family at once?

The family therapist treats the family as a unit but may not meet with the entire family at each session. If a family crisis is at hand, the therapist may first try to identify the most resourceful family members, who can help solve the immediate problem. The therapist and family members may then work on resolving more basic conflicts and on improving family relationships.

Group Awareness Training   During the 1960s and 1970s, the human potential movement led many people to become interested in personal growth experiences. Often, their interest was expressed by participation in sensitivity training or encounter groups.

Question: What is the difference between sensitivity and encounter groups?

Sensitivity groups tend to be less confrontive than encounter groups. Participants in sensitivity groups take part in exercises that gently enlarge awareness of oneself and others. For example, in a "trust walk," participants expand their confidence in others by allowing themselves to be led while blindfolded.

In **encounter groups** more intense emotion and communication may take place. Here, the emphasis is on tearing down defenses and false fronts through discussion that can be brutally honest (Stoller, 1972). Because there is a danger of hostile confrontation and psychological damage, encounter group participation is safest when members are carefully screened and a trained leader guides the group.

Sensitivity and encounter techniques are used by many businesses to improve employee morale and relationships. Specially designed encounter groups for married couples are also widely held. However, in the last decade there has been a shift away from public participation in sensitivity and encounter groups. Instead, hundreds of thousands of people have taken part in various forms of **large group awareness training** (Finkelstein et al., 1982). Lifespring, Actualizations, est, and similar commercial programs are well-known examples. Like the smaller groups that preceded them, large group trainings combine psychological exercises, confrontation, new viewpoints, and group dynamics to promote personal change.

**Ψ   Highlight 22–2
"Psych Jockeys"**

By now you have probably heard a phone-in radio psychologist. On a typical program callers describe problems arising from child abuse, loneliness, love affairs, phobias, sexual adjustment, or depression. The radio psychologist then offers reassurance, advice, or suggestions for getting help.

Talk-radio psychology may seem harmless, but it raises some important questions. For instance, is it reasonable to give advice without knowing anything about a person's background? Might the advice do harm? What good can a psychologist do in 3 minutes?

In defense of themselves, radio psychologists point out that listeners may learn solutions to their own problems by hearing others talk. Many also stress that their work is educational, not therapeutic. And certainly for some callers a radio psychologist may be the only person willing to listen to their problem.

The real issue seems to be the question of when advice becomes therapy. The American Psychological Association has taken the position that media psychologists should discuss only problems of a general nature, instead of actually counseling a person. For example, if a caller complains about insomnia, the radio psychologist should talk about insomnia in general, not probe the caller's personal life (Schommer, 1984).

By giving information and advice, radio psychologists probably do help some listeners. Even so, a good guide for anyone tempted to call a radio psychologist might be "let the consumer beware." Or to use an analogy, how much confidence would you have in a physician who would make a diagnosis over the phone?

Question: Are sensitivity, encounter, and awareness groups really psychotherapies?

Judging from the glowing testimonials given by many participants, such groups must fill some need not met by society or traditional psychotherapy. However, there is, at present, little evidence that these experiences are truly therapeutic (Finkelstein et al., 1982). Many of the claimed benefits may simply result from a kind of **therapy placebo effect** related to positive expectations, a break in daily routine, and an excuse to act differently. The importance of such factors is easily illustrated: Participants in a weekend "retreat" that featured nothing more than volleyball, charades, and ballroom dancing also reported enhanced mental health (McCardel & Murray, 1974)! Kurt Back (1972) may have summarized it best when he said, "Encounter groups may comfort, but they do not cure anything." For some the experience is positive, for some negative, and for many it is merely a diversion.

Transactional Analysis— Different Strokes for Different Folks

Transactional Analysis (TA) is a therapy that blends humanistic thought with some updated elements of psychoanalysis. TA teaches people a model of behavior to use in becoming more aware of themselves and their *interactions* with others—especially those involving various "games." Because TA emphasizes relationships, it is often conducted as a group therapy.

Question: How does TA enhance awareness?

TA is based on a relatively simple concept proposed by Eric Berne (1961, 1964). Berne says the personality has three basic parts or **ego-states,** known as the *Parent*, the *Adult*, and the *Child*. These can be distinguished from one another by distinct behaviors, words, tones, gestures, attitudes, and expressions.

Although Berne denied it, it is easy to see that the three ego-states are an updated version of Freud's concepts of the id, ego, and superego: The Child corresponds to the id, the Adult to the ego, and the Parent to the superego.

Ego-States   The **Child** is a carryover from youth. The Child can be primitive, impulsive, demanding, creative, playful, or manipulative. The Child tends to say things such as "I want"; "I need"; "I won't"; or, simply "Wow."

In addition to this perpetual Child, Berne says we carry another product of our past, in the form of the Parent ego-state. The **Parent** is an internal record of all the messages received from one's parents or other authorities as our personality developed. The Parent can be evaluative and restrictive or nurturing and allowing. It is activated whenever you judge or nurture yourself or another person. The Parent makes such statements as: "You should"; "You ought to"; "Why didn't you?"; "That's good"; "You can do it"; "That's bad"; and "Try harder."

According to TA, people get into trouble when they use an inappropriate ego-state. TA teaches people how to develop each ego-state and helps them decide when to use it. The **Adult** is a mature and rational decision-making part of the personality. With the adult in charge, an individual can explore alternatives and their consequences and decide which ego-state is needed. TA gives people a thinking strategy to use in exploring alternatives and deciding what changes they wish to make, especially in *relationships* with others.

Question: How does the ego-state analysis apply to relationships?

Transactions   The Parent-Adult-Child analysis can be extended to interactions between two people. That is, a person can send a message from any of his or her ego-states to any of the ego-states in another person. TA holds that trouble comes in relationships when *crossed* or *ulterior transactions* (exchanges) occur. (See Fig. 22–6.) Diagram (a) represents an Adult-to-Adult transaction, such as, "What time is it?" "It's one o'clock." Communication continues because the expected response was received. But what if the reply is Parent-to-Child, such as, "Why don't you just forget about the time and see if you can get some work done for a change?" Now communication breaks down, or is "crossed" (diagram b).

Question: What happens in an ulterior transaction?

In an ulterior transaction the exchange *appears* to take place on one level, but actually takes place on another.

Fig. 22–6 *Basic TA transactions.*

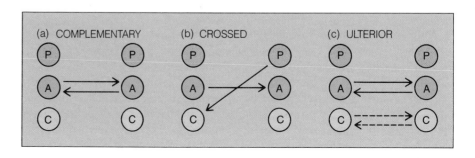

Table 22–2   Comparison of Psychotherapies

	Insight or Action?	Directive or Nondirective?	Time Orientation	Individual or Group?
Psychoanalysis	insight	directive	past	individual
Client-centered	insight	nondirective	past and present	individual
Existential	insight	both	present and future	individual
Gestalt	insight	directive	present	both
Transactional analysis	both	directive	past and present	both
Psychodrama	insight	directive	present	group
Family	both	directive	present	group
Behavior modification*	action	directive	present	both
Cognitive*	action	directive	present	individual
Rational-emotive*	action	directive	present	individual

*Discussed in Chapter 23.

For example, the apparent Adult-to-Adult question, "Isn't it getting late?" might carry with it an unspoken (ulterior) cue: "Hey, why don't we quit early tonight?" The reply, "Yeah, it's getting late," might have nothing to do with the time; it may instead be a Child-to-Child reply, "Yeah, let's go play, the supervisor won't know if we leave early."

Games Ulterior transactions may sound harmless enough, but they form the basis of **games,** which are indirect ways of communicating. For example, one spouse might ask another, "How much money is in the checking account?" in such a way that the real message is, "What are you trying to do, put us in the poorhouse?" Games keep people from being close and honest, and at worst they may be physically or emotionally destructive. By the way, the most common game in marriage is, "If it weren't for you" (I would be doing all the things I pretend I want to do but am afraid to try). A major goal of TA is to teach people more direct and creative ways of living, by exploring alternatives to games.

Psychotherapy— An Overview

Question: How effective is psychotherapy?

Judging the outcome of therapy is tricky. Nevertheless, there is evidence that therapy is beneficial. In surveys of hundreds of studies of psychotherapy, a modest but consistent positive effect for therapy was found to exist (Shapiro & Shapiro, 1982; Smith & Glass, 1977). These find-ings, of course, are based on averages: For some people therapy was tremendously helpful; for others it was unsuccessful; overall it was effective for more people than not. Speaking more subjectively, one real success (in which a person's life is lastingly changed for the better) can be worth the frustration of several cases in which little progress is made.

Question: What do psychotherapies have in common?

The therapies we have sampled are but a few of the approaches in use. One author, writing in 1959, counted at least 36 major systems of psychotherapy (Harper, 1959). The count could easily exceed 200 today. The examples cited were selected because they represent some of the basic variations in philosophy or techniques and because they offer ideas that may be of immediate use to you. For a summary of their major differences, see Table 22–2. To add to your understanding of psychotherapy, let us briefly summarize what all techniques have in common.

All the psychotherapies we have discussed include some combination of the following goals: insight, resolution of conflicts, an improved sense of self, a change in unacceptable patterns of behavior, better interpersonal relations, and an improved picture of oneself and the world. To accomplish these goals, psychotherapies offer:

1. A *caring relationship* between client and therapist. *Emotional rapport* based on warmth, friendship, understanding, acceptance, and empathy forms the basis for this relationship.

2. A *protected setting* in which emotional *catharsis* (release) can take place. Therapy provides a sanctuary in

which the client is free to express fears, anxieties, and personal secrets without fear of rejection or loss of confidentiality.

3. All therapies to some extent offer an *explanation* or *rationale* for the suffering the client has experienced, and they propose a line of action that if followed will end this suffering.

These basic foundations of psychotherapy represent one of the more valuable lessons to be learned from this chapter. Together, they offer a useful perspective for meeting the challenge of helping a troubled friend or relative. More specific suggestions on this point will be found in the Applications section that follows.

Learning Check

1. In psychodrama, people attempt to form meaningful wholes out of disjointed thoughts, feelings, and actions.   T or F?

2. Most large group awareness trainings make use of Gestalt therapy.   T or F?

3. There are no dangers in participating in an encounter group.   T or F?

4. Which therapy places great emphasis on role playing?
   a. psychodrama   *b.* family therapy   *c.* TA   *d.* encounter

5. The Adult is a mature and rational decision-making part of the personality.   T or F?

6. According to TA, destructive psychological games are based on _____ transactions.

7. Emotional _____ (release) in a protected setting is an element of most psychotherapies.

Answers: 1. F   2. F   3. F   4. *a*   5. T   6. ulterior   7. catharsis

Applications

Seeking Professional Help—When, Where, and How?

Question: How would I know if I should seek professional help at some point in my life?

Although there is no simple answer to this question, the following guidelines may be helpful.

1. If your level of psychological discomfort (unhappiness, anxiety, or depression, for example) becomes comparable to a level of physical discomfort that would cause you to see a doctor or dentist, you should consider seeing a psychologist or a psychiatrist.

2. Another sign that should influence your decision is the occurrence of significant changes in observable behavior, such as the quality of your work (or schoolwork), your rate of absenteeism, your use of drugs (including alcohol), or your relationships with others who are important to you.

3. Perhaps you have at some time urged a friend or relative to seek professional help and were then dismayed because they refused to recognize the extent of their problem. If *you* find friends or relatives making a similar suggestion, recognize that they may be seeing things more objectively than you.

4. If you have persistent or disturbing suicidal thoughts or impulses, you should seek help immediately.

Question: If I wanted to talk to a therapist, how would I find one?

1. *The yellow pages.* Psychologists are listed under "Psychologist" or in some cases under "Counseling Services." Psychiatrists are generally listed as a subheading under "Physicians." Counselors are usually found under the heading "Marriage and Family Coun-

Applications: Seeking Professional Help—When, Where, and How?

selors." These listings will usually put you in touch with individuals in private practice.

2. *Community or county mental health centers*. Most counties and many cities in the United States now offer public mental health services. (These are listed in the phone book.) Public mental health centers usually provide counseling and therapy services directly and can make referrals to private therapists.

3. *Mental health associations*. Many cities have mental health associations organized by concerned citizens. Groups such as these usually keep listings of qualified therapists and of other services and programs in the community.

4. *Colleges and universities*. If you are a student, don't overlook counseling services offered by a student health center or special student counseling facilities.

5. *Newspaper advertisements*. Professional ethics discourage advertisements. Occasionally there are exceptions to this rule as when low-cost "outreach" clinics try to make their presence known to the public, but in the case of an advertised service you should carefully inquire into the training and qualifications of its staff.

Question: How would I know what kind of a therapist to see? How would I pick one?

The choice between a psychiatrist and a psychologist is somewhat arbitrary. Both are trained to do psychotherapy, and whereas a psychiatrist can administer somatic therapy and prescribe drugs, a psychologist can work in conjunction with a physician if such services seem indicated. Fees for psychiatrists are usually higher, averaging about $80 an hour. Psychologists average from $40 to $60 an hour.

With fees in mind, your decision may be influenced by whether you have health insurance that will cover the expense. If fees are a problem, keep in mind that many individual therapists charge on a sliding scale, or ability-to-pay basis, and that community mental health centers almost always charge on a sliding scale.

Some communities now have counseling services staffed by sympathetic paraprofessional counselors, whose fees are much lower. There is a natural tendency, perhaps, to doubt the abilities of paraprofessionals. However, many studies have shown that paraprofessional counselors are often as effective as professionals (Hattie, Sharpley, & Rogers, 1984). Group therapy is also much less expensive because the therapist's fee is divided among several people.

The training and qualifications of a therapist usually can be learned simply by asking. A reputable therapist will be glad to reveal his or her background. If you have any doubts, credentials may be checked and other helpful information can be obtained from local branches of any of the following organizations. You can also write to the addresses listed below.

The National Association for Mental Health
1800 North Kent Street
Rosslyn, VA 22209

The American Psychiatric Association
1700 18th Street N.W.
Washington, DC 20009

The American Psychological Association
1200 17th Street N.W.
Washington, DC 20036

The American Association of Humanistic Psychology
7 Hartwood Drive
Amherst, NY 14226

The question of how to pick a particular therapist remains. The best way is to start with a short consultation with a respected psychiatrist or psychologist or with a counselor at a mental health center. This will allow the person you visit to evaluate your problem and recommend an appropriate type of therapy or a therapist who is likely to be helpful. As an alternative you might ask the person teaching this course for a referral.

Question: How would I know whether to quit or ignore a therapist?

A balanced look at psychotherapies suggests that all *techniques* are about equally successful (Frank, 1973; Gomes-Schwartz et al., 1978). However, all *therapists* are not equally successful.

Far more important than the approach used are the therapist's personal qualities. The most consistently successful psychotherapists are those who are willing to use whatever method seems most helpful for a client. They are also marked by personal characteristics of warmth, integrity, sincerity, and empathy (Frank, 1973; Katz, 1972; Knight, 1949).

It is perhaps most accurate to say that at this stage of development, psychotherapy is an art, not a science. Since the *relationship* between a client and therapist is the therapist's most basic tool, you must trust and easily relate to a therapist for therapy to be effective.

Applications: Seeking Professional Help—When, Where, and How?

Clients who like their therapists are generally more successful in therapy (Gomes-Schwartz et al., 1978). There is always a temptation to avoid facing up to personal problems. With this in mind, you should give a therapist a fair chance and not give up too easily. But don't hesitate to change therapists or to terminate therapy if you lose confidence in the therapist or if you don't relate well to the therapist as a person.

Becoming a Community Mental Health Resource— How to Help

Question: What can be done to help a friend or relative who has a temporary personal problem or emotional crisis?

Everyone at one time or another will be faced with the task of comforting a troubled friend. For the majority of such upsets, any caring, emotionally stable, empathetic person can aid effectively. For example, Carl Rogers (1980) cites hot-line workers who, with minimal training, can at times "use a skill and judgment that would make a professional green with envy." But how can you best give support? Jerome Frank (1973), Carl Rogers (1957), and others appear to agree about two essential conditions for the person hoping to help in constructive personality change. These are:

1. An unconditional acceptance of the troubled person, an unshakable positive regard for him or her as a human.
2. A capacity to communicate to the person an understanding of the discomfort he or she is feeling.

We may call the second quality *empathy*, the ability to enter another person's private world, to understand feelings, and to share psychological pain. Because empathy and true caring cannot be faked, your support at times of crisis can be more valuable than anything the best-trained professional can offer. John O. Stevens (1971) has summarized:

> The way to really help someone is not to help him do anything but become more aware of his own experience—his feelings, his actions, his fantasies—and insist that he explore his own experience more deeply and take responsibility for it, no matter what that experience is.

Question: I'm still not sure exactly what is best to do when a friend wants to talk about a problem.

Here are several points to keep in mind when "counseling" a friend.

Active Listening   People frequently talk "at" each other without really listening. A person with problems needs to be heard. Make a sincere effort to listen to and understand the person. Let the person know you are listening through eye contact, posture, your tone of voice, and your replies.

Focus on Feelings   Feelings are neither right nor wrong. By focusing on the person's feelings, you can avoid making him or her defensive. Passing judgment on what is said prevents the free outpouring of emotion that is the basis for catharsis. For example, a friend confides that he has failed a test. Perhaps you know that he studies very little. If you say, "Maybe if you studied a little more you would do better," he will probably become defensive or hostile. Much more can be accomplished by saying, "You must feel very frustrated" or, simply, "How do you feel about it?"

Avoid Giving Advice   It is not unreasonable to give advice when you are asked for it, but beware of the trap of the "Why don't you? Yes, but . . ." game. According to Berne (1964), this "game" follows a pattern: Someone says, "I have this problem." You say, "Why don't you do thus and so?" The person replies, "Yes, but . . ." and then gives you several reasons why your suggestion won't work. If you make a new suggestion, the reply will once again be, "Yes, but . . ." because the person either knows more about his or her personal situation than you do or because he or she has reasons for avoiding your advice. The student described in the previous paragraph knows he needs to study. His problem is to understand why he doesn't *want* to study.

Accept the Person's Frame of Reference   W. I. Thomas said, "Things perceived as real are real in their effect." Try to resist the temptation to contradict the person with your point of view. Since we all live in different psychological worlds, there is no "correct" view of a life situation. If a person feels that his point of view

Applications: Seeking Professional Help—When, Where, and How?

is understood, he will feel freer to examine it objectively and to question his perspective.

Reflect Thoughts and Feelings   One of the most productive things you can do when "counseling" a friend is to give feedback by simply restating what is said. This is also a good way to encourage a person to talk. If he or she seems to be at a loss for words, restate his or her last sentence. For example:

Friend: I'm really down about school. I can't get interested in any of my classes. I flunked my Spanish test, and somebody stole my notebook for psychology.
You: You're really upset about school, aren't you?
Friend: Yeah, and my parents are hassling me about my grades again.
You: You're feeling pressured by your parents?
Friend: Yeah, damn.
You: It must make you angry to be pressured by them.

As simple as this sounds, it is extremely helpful to someone trying to sort out his or her feelings. Try it. If nothing else, you'll develop a reputation as a fantastic conversationalist!

Maintain Confidentiality   Your efforts to help will be wasted if you fail to respect the privacy of someone who has confided in you. Put yourself in the person's place. Don't gossip.

These guidelines are not an invitation to play "junior therapist." A professional therapist is prepared to attack a serious problem from a position of experience and expertise, and formal therapy provides a protected and confidential arena in which problems can be solved. These guidelines simply urge you to recognize the role each of us plays in providing two of the greatest mental health resources available at any cost: friendship and honest communication.

Learning Check

1. Persistent emotional discomfort is a clear sign that professional psychological counseling should be sought.
    T or F?
2. Community mental health centers rarely offer counseling or therapy themselves; they only do referrals.   T or F?
3. In many instances a therapist's personal qualities have more of an effect on the outcome of therapy than does the type of therapy used.   T or F?
4. To aid a troubled friend, you should focus on facts rather than feelings, and you should critically evaluate what the person is saying in order to help him or her grasp reality.   T or F?
5. One danger of giving advice is the tendency for the interchange to slip into the "Yes, but . . ." game.   T or F?

Answers: 1. T   2. F   3. T   4. F   5. T

Chapter Summary

- *Psychotherapies* may be classified as *insight* therapies, *action* therapies, *directive* therapies, *nondirective* therapies, and combinations of these. *Behavior therapy* and *cognitive behavior therapy* are major action-oriented approaches. Therapies may be conducted either *individually* or in *groups*.

- Primitive approaches to mental illness were often superstitious and misguided. *Trepanning* involved boring a hole in the skull. *Demonology*, used in the Middle Ages, attributed mental disturbance to supernatural forces and prescribed *exorcism* as the cure. In some instances the actual cause of bizarre behavior may have been *ergot poisoning*. More humane treatment began in 1793 with the work of *Philippe Pinel* in Paris.

- Freud's *psychoanalysis* was the first formal psychotherapy. Psychoanalysis seeks a release of repressed thoughts and emotions from the unconscious. The psychoanalyst uses the techniques of *free association, dream analysis,* and *analysis of resistance* and *transference* to reveal health-producing insights. Some critics have argued that traditional psychoanalysis takes so long that patients may simply experience a *spontaneous remission* of symptoms.

- *Client-centered* (or *person-centered*) therapy is nondirective and is dedicated to creation of an *atmosphere of growth. Unconditional positive regard, empathy, authenticity,* and *reflection* are combined to give the client a chance to solve his or her own problems.

- *Existential therapies,* such as Frankl's *logotherapy,* focus on the end result of the choices one makes in life. Clients are encouraged through *confrontation* and *encounter* to exercise *free will* and to take responsibility for their choices. The goal of existential therapy is to reestablish meaning in one's life.

- *Gestalt therapy* emphasizes immediate awareness of thoughts and feelings. Its goal is to rebuild thinking, feeling, and acting into connected wholes and to help clients break through emotional blocks.

- *Group therapy* may be a simple extension of individual methods or it may be based on techniques developed specifically for groups. In *psychodrama,* individuals enact roles and incidents resembling their real-life problems. In *family therapy* the family group is treated as a unit.

- Although not literally psychotherapies, sensitivity and encounter groups attempt to encourage positive personality change. *Sensitivity groups* tend to be nonconfrontive, their emphasis being on self-awareness, trust, and communication. In *encounter groups,* participants actively tear down facades and defenses. In recent years commercially offered *large group awareness trainings* have become popular. However, the therapeutic benefits of such programs are questionable.

- In *transactional analysis* (TA) people learn to apply the P-A-C (Parent-Adult-Child) analysis to their own and others' behavior. By placing the Adult in control, people learn to draw on the strengths of each *ego-state.* They also learn to recognize *complementary, crossed,* and *ulterior transactions* and to avoid *games.*

- Studies of the outcome of psychotherapy show that it is generally effective; there are, however, large individual differences in effectiveness. All psychotherapies offer a *caring relationship, emotional rapport,* a *protected setting, catharsis, explanations* for client's problems, and a *line of action* to follow in alleviating them.

- Sources of psychological help exist in most communities. A competent and reputable therapist can usually be located through a *referral.* Providing *empathy* is a major way to support a troubled friend. Other points to keep in mind are to *listen actively, focus on feelings,* avoid giving *unwanted advice,* accept the person's *perspective, reflect* thoughts and feelings, and maintain *confidentiality.*

Exploration

A Therapist Named Eliza

Psychotherapists differ widely in personal style and choice of techniques. The following is a somewhat unusual example of how therapy can act as a "psychological mirror" for a troubled person.

C: Men are all alike.
T: In what way?
C: They're always bugging us about something or other.
T: Can you think of a specific example?
C: Well, my boyfriend made me come here.
T: Your boyfriend made you come here?
C: He says I'm depressed much of the time.
T: I am sorry to hear you are depressed.
C: It's true. I am unhappy.
T: Do you think coming here will help you not to be unhappy?
C: I need some help, that much seems certain.
T: What would it mean to you if you got some help?
C: Perhaps I could learn to get along with my mother.
T: Tell me more about your family.
C: My mother takes care of me.
T: Who else in your family takes care of you?
C: My father.
T: Your father?
C: You are like my father in some ways.
T: What resemblance do you see?
C: You are not very aggressive, but I think you don't want me to notice that.

T: What makes you think I am not very aggressive?
C: You don't argue with me.
T: Why do you think I don't argue with you?
C: You are afraid of me.
T: Does it please you to believe I am afraid of you?
C: My father is afraid of everybody.
T: What else comes to mind when you think of your father?
C: Bullies.
T: Does that have anything to do with the fact that your boyfriend made you come here?

Notice how the therapist helped the client see a possible link between her feelings for her father and her boyfriend. This insight is particularly interesting because her therapist was a *computer*. What you just read is part of a "conversation" held with a computer program named Eliza developed by computer scientist Joseph Weizenbaum (1966).

Question: Is Weizenbaum serious about having a computer act as a therapist?

Actually, Weizenbaum opposes use of computers as therapists for real clients. From the beginning Weizenbaum has said that computers must never replace human relationships (Williams, 1984). But other psychologists believe otherwise. Supporters point out that computerized therapy would have the advantages of low cost, conve-

nience, consistency, and dependability (Alexander, 1978).

Critics view experimentation with computerized therapy as "dehumanizing technology," and they note that when a computer says, "I understand," it is meaningless. They also point out that computers would miss nonverbal messages contained in a glance, a gesture, laughter, or tears.

On the other hand, many people find it helpful to keep a journal of their thoughts and feelings to get a clearer picture of themselves. There is also evidence that tape-recording your thoughts on a problem—and then listening to the tape—can contribute to self-awareness (Snider, Davis, & Brown, 1984). In similar fashion a computer "therapist" might provide a helpful sounding board for sorting out feelings and alternatives. At the very least, computer therapy might make a type of "personal education" available to large numbers of people, particularly those unable to afford traditional therapy.

Even with its possible advantages, talking with a computer has proved only mildly therapeutic at best (Williams, 1984). The limitations of computer therapy are aptly illustrated by the following interchange between a journalist and Eliza (Gorman, 1985):

D: I would like to know what you think of your patients?
E: Do you wish to would like to know what me?

Exploration: A Therapist Named Eliza

D: You talk like a chimpanzee.
E: Oh, I talk like a chimpanzee?
D: Yes, and not as well as some.
E: You seem quite positive.
D: Do you wish to would like to know what you—what kind of nonsense is that?
E: You like to think I wish to would like to know what you—don't you?

It appears that in psychotherapy, as in all aspects of life, there is no substitute for human understanding, empathy, and trust.

Learning Check

1. Computer scientist Joseph Weizenbaum has urged psychologists to try Eliza with real clients.   T or F?
2. It is probably accurate to say that computer therapy has no value for promoting personal awareness.   T or F?
3. Computer therapy would have the advantages of consistency, convenience, and low cost.   T or F?
4. Virtually all psychologists regard computer therapy as dehumanizing.   T or F?

Answers: 1. F   2. F   3. T   4. F

Questions for Discussion

1. What preconceptions did you have about psychotherapy? Has your understanding of therapy changed? Has your attitude changed?
2. Do you agree with existential therapist Rollo May that there has been a loss of individual freedom, faith, and meaning in today's society? Why or why not?
3. Which form of psychotherapy do you find the most attractive? Why?
4. What psychological services are available in your area? Would you know how to find or make use of them? What factors would affect your decision to seek help?
5. Describe a time when you helped someone resolve a personal problem. Describe a time when you were unsuccessful in helping. What factors seemed to make the difference?
6. Do you think it would be right for a therapist to allow a person to make suicide an "existential choice" or an expression of "free will?"
7. What advantages and disadvantages would you anticipate in working with a computer therapist?
8. Which style of therapy would you expect a computer program to most closely duplicate? If a computer were programmed to provide help for a limited problem such as test anxiety, would you find computer therapy more acceptable?
9. In your opinion are radio psychologists engaged in education or therapy? Is talk-show psychology ethical? What value is there for listeners and callers in talking with a radio psychologist?

Behavior Therapy

Chapter 23

Chapter Preview

Behavior Therapy and the Twilight Zone

Five times a day, for several days, Brooks Workman stopped what she was doing and vividly imagined opening a soft drink can. She made a point of picturing herself bringing the can to her mouth and placing her lips on it. Just as she was about to drink, hordes of roaches poured out of the can and scurried into her mouth—writhing, twitching, and wiggling their feelers (Williams & Long, 1979).

Question: Why would anyone imagine such a thing?

Brooks Workman's behavior is not as strange as it sounds. Her goal was self-control: Brooks felt that she was drinking too many colas and she wanted to cut down. The method she chose (called covert sensitization*) is a form of* behavior therapy. *Behavioral approaches include* **behavior modification** *(the use of learning principles to change behavior) and* **cognitive behavior therapy** *(the use of learning principles to change upsetting thoughts and beliefs).*

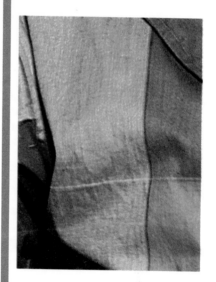

Behavior Therapy   *In the previous chapter we discussed therapies based on* insight *or* self-awareness. *Here we will consider* action-oriented *approaches. Behavior therapists believe that insight or deep understanding of one's problems is often unnecessary for improvement. Instead, behavior therapists try to directly alter troublesome thoughts and behaviors.*

   Brooks Workman didn't need to probe into her past or her emotions and conflicts; she simply wanted to break a bothersome habit. Even when serious problems are at stake, techniques like the one she used have proved valuable. Behavior therapy has helped people stop drinking, smoking, hiccuping, stuttering, and molesting children. Behavior modification can be used to lose weight or to increase eating in the pathologically underweight. It has improved study habits, work output in factories, and speech in retarded and disturbed children, and it has increased the amount of time psychotic patients will go without hallucinating. Also, through behavior modification, people have conquered fears of heights, snakes, public speaking, sexual intimacy, and automobiles.

   The list of possible applications for behavioral approaches is practically endless. It is almost certain that you will discover a useful technique for self-improvement in this chapter. But before we begin, here is something to think about.

The Twilight Zone?   *Pretend for a moment that you work for the telephone company and that you have been sent to repair a phone. Picture a professional building similar to those in which your doctor and dentist are found. Inside the* *front door is an office bustling with quiet activity. As you look down the hall, you see the offices of several therapists. You ask where the broken phone is. A secretary tells you it is at the opposite end of the building and asks you to follow. The secretary opens a door on your left. As you step through it, your mind reels.*

In confusion you rapidly scan your surroundings. You are in a tavern! In the dim light you see a bar and heavily padded stools. Behind the counter, a bartender polishes glasses in front of a large mirror and a row of bottles. Lighted displays advertising beer glow softly from the wall, and music flows from an unseen speaker.

Catching sight of the secretary again, you wind your way through the tables and hurry to a door on the opposite side of the room. Once again you are in an ordinary office. But over your shoulder you see the bartender close the door behind you, and the strains of music die abruptly with the click of the latch.

What's happening here? Was it a hallucination? A movie set? A modern version of Alice in Wonderland? *A hideout for the CIA? For an answer, read further.*

Survey Questions   How are learning principles applied in aversion therapy? Can behavior therapy be used to treat phobias, fears, and anxieties? What role does reinforcement play in behavior modification? Can behavior therapy change thoughts and emotions? How are behavioral principles applied to everyday problems?

Resources

Behavior Modification— Animal, Vegetable, or Mineral?

Question: In general how does behavior therapy work?

Behavior therapy is based on one basic assumption: People have *learned* to be the way they are. Consequently, if they have learned responses that cause problems, then they can change them or *relearn* more appropriate responses. Broadly speaking, **behavior modification** refers to any attempt to use the learning principles of *classical* or *operant conditioning* to change human behavior.

Question: How does classical conditioning work? I'm not sure I remember.

Classical conditioning was described in Chapter 8. It is the process of learning originally studied by Russian physiologist Ivan Pavlov. Here is a brief review of Pavlov's principles:

A previously neutral stimulus (the *conditioned stimulus*) is followed by a stimulus (the *unconditioned stimulus*) that always produces a response (the *unconditioned response*). Eventually the conditioning stimulus begins to produce the response directly. The response is then called a *conditioned response*.

Thus, for a child the sight of a hypodermic needle (CS) is followed by pain (US), which causes anxiety or emotional discomfort (UR). Eventually the sight of a hypodermic (the conditioned stimulus) may produce anxiety (a conditioned response) *before* the child feels any pain.

Question: What does classical conditioning have to do with behavior modification?

Classical conditioning can be used to associate discomfort with a bad habit. Psychologists call discomfort used in this way an *aversion*. An aversion may be used to combat an undesirable habit as it was in the case of the woman who wanted to drink fewer colas. When more powerful versions of this approach are used, it is called *aversion therapy*.

Aversion Therapy— A Little Pain Goes a Long Way

Imagine that you are eating an apple. Suddenly you discover that you just bit a large green worm in half. You vomit. Months pass before you can eat an apple again without feeling ill. You have experienced a *conditioned aversion* to apples.

Question: Conditioning an aversion was mentioned as an application of classical conditioning in behavior modification. How is a conditioned aversion used in therapy?

In **aversion therapy** an individual learns to associate a strong aversion (or negative emotional response) with an undesirable habit such as drinking, overeating, or gambling. Aversion therapy has been used to cure hiccups, sneezing, stuttering (Goldiamond, 1965), vomiting (Lang & Melamed, 1969), bed-wetting (Wickes, 1958), and for treatment of fetishism, transvestism, and other "maladaptive" sexual behaviors (Fuastman, 1976). Aversion therapy can also be an aid to persons who want to quit smoking (see Highlight 23–1).

An excellent example of aversion therapy is provided by the work of Roger Vogler and his associates (1977). Vogler works with alcoholics who have been unable to stop drinking. For many clients aversion therapy is a last chance. They have often been threatened with desertion by relatives and friends, have lost their jobs, and have tried Alcoholics Anonymous, psychotherapy, detoxification, vitamin therapy, and even Antabuse therapy. (Antabuse is a drug that causes an alcoholic to become violently nauseated after he or she drinks.) Here is a typical aversion procedure:

> While drinking an alcoholic beverage, painful (although noninjurious) electric shocks are delivered to the client's hand. From the client's point of view, the shocks are unpredictable; he or she never knows for sure when one is due. Most of the time, however, the shocks come as the client is beginning to take a drink of alcohol (Fig. 23–1).

This *response-contingent* (or response-connected) shock obviously takes the immediate pleasure out of drinking. It also causes the alcohol abuser to develop a conditioned aversion to drinking. The sight and smell of alcohol and the motions of drinking begin to have a capacity to make the individual very uncomfortable.

Question: But can't the person tell when it is "safe" to drink and when it is not?

Transfer, or *generalization*, of aversion conditioning to the "real world" is a problem. With this in mind, Vogler constructed in his office a vivid recreation of a "friendly neighborhood tavern," complete with a bar, tables, soft lights, music, and a bartender. Also provided are a "living room," a "bedroom," and a "kitchen." Clients undergo aversion therapy in a setting as much like the normal site of their drinking as possible, which helps assure that carryover of the aversion training will occur.

Actually, aversion therapy is used as a last resort, even

Highlight 23–1
Puffing Up an Aversion

The fact that nicotine is toxic makes it easy to create an aversion to smoking. Behavior therapists have found that electric shock, nauseating drugs, and similar aversive stimuli are not required to make smokers uncomfortable. All that is needed is for the smoker to smoke—rapidly and for a long time.

Rapid smoking is the most widely used aversion therapy for smoking (Lichtenstein, 1982). In this method subjects are told to smoke continuously, taking a puff every 6 to 8 seconds. Rapid smoking continues until the smoker is miserable and can stand it no more. By then, most clients are thinking, "I never want to see another cigarette for the rest of my life."

A number of studies suggest that rapid smoking is the most effective behavior therapy for smoking. Recent research also indicates that the health risks of rapid smoking are small (Hall et al., 1984). Nevertheless, anyone tempted to try rapid smoking should realize that it is very unpleasant. Without the help of a therapist, most people quit too soon for the procedure to succeed. (An alternative method that is more practical is described in the Applications section of this chapter.)

The most basic problem with rapid smoking—like other stop-smoking methods—is that about one-half of those who quit smoking begin again (Hall et al., 1984). Because the "evil weed" calls so strongly to former smokers, support from a stop-smoking group or a close, caring person can make a big difference. Former smokers who get encouragement from others are much more likely to stay smoke-free (Lichtenstein, 1982).

for problems as serious as alcohol abuse. Vogler and his associates also train alcoholics to discriminate blood alcohol levels (so clients can tell how drunk they are). They teach alcoholics alternatives to drinking, and they offer education programs on alcohol abuse as well as general counseling (Vogler et al., 1977). Recently, they have added an interesting twist to their aversion therapy: Alcohol abusers are videotaped as they go from sober to drunk.

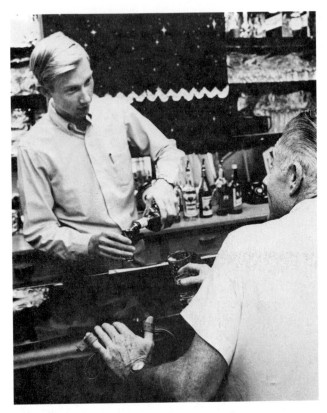

Fig. 23–1 *Aversion therapy for drinking. The sights, smells, and tastes of drinking are associated with unpleasant electrical shocks applied to the hand.*

Later, they watch the videotaped drinking bout and see themselves with slurred speech, dropping cigarette ashes in their drinks, saying stupid and belligerent things. Most react with shame and embarrassment when they see the tapes. Apparently, few people have any idea of how unattractive they are when drunk.

To add to the videotape effect, the bartender is trained to provoke clients into becoming argumentative and obnoxious. Presumably, this is not too hard to do by the time the client is saying, "I am 'masshhhed'" (Vils, 1976). In the videotape self-confrontation held later, grossly drunken behaviors are replayed until the client says, "Okay, okay, I've seen enough." Seeing themselves as obnoxious drunks adds to the aversion people feel for drinking, and it increases their determination to quit.

Question: I'm not sure I'm comfortable with the idea of treating humans this way.

People are often disturbed (shocked?) by such methods. It must be emphasized that clients usually volunteer for aversion therapy because it helps them overcome a destructive habit. Indeed, commercial aversion programs for overeating, smoking, and alcohol abuse have attracted large numbers of willing customers.

When psychologists use aversion therapy, they often back it up with supportive counseling. Also, for mild problems, such as nail biting, a person may not have to undergo pain at all. Merely watching a trained actor (who *appears* to get electric shocks while biting his nails) can curb the problem (Rosenthal et al., 1978). Last, and most important, aversion therapy can be justified by its long-term benefits. As behaviorist Donald Baer puts it, "A small number of brief, painful experiences is a reasonable exchange for the interminable pain of a lifelong maladjustment" (Baer, 1971).

Learning Check

Before continuing, see if you can answer these questions. If not, review the preceding section.

1. What two types of conditioning are used in behavior modification? _____ and _____

2. Aversion therapy is used to combat what? _____

3. Shock, pain, and discomfort play what role in conditioning an aversion?
   a. conditioned stimulus   *c.* unconditioned response
   b. unconditioned stimulus   *d.* conditioned response

4. If shock is used to control drinking, it must be _____ contingent.

5. A potential problem with aversion therapy is transfer of the aversion to settings outside the clinic or laboratory.   T or F?

Answers: 1. classical, operant   2. undesirable responses or destructive habits   3. b   4. response   5. T

Desensitization—Who's Afraid of a Big, Bad Hierarchy?

Assume you are a swimming instructor who wants to help a child overcome fear of the high diving board. How might you proceed? Directly forcing a terrified child off the high board could be a psychological disaster. Obviously, a better approach would be to begin by teaching the child to dive off the edge of the pool. Then the child could be taught to dive off the low board, followed by a platform 6 feet above the water, and then an 8-foot platform. As a last step the child could try the high board.

This *ordered set of steps* is called a **hierarchy.** The hierarchy allows the child to undergo *adaptation.* Gradually the child adapts to the high dive and overcomes fear, much as one adapts gradually to the cool water of a swimming pool on a hot day. When the child has overcome the fear, a psychologist would say that **desensitization** (dee-SEN-sih-tih-ZAY-shun) has occurred (Fig. 23–2).

Desensitization is also based on the principle of **reciprocal inhibition,** named by Joseph Wolpe (1974). Reciprocal inhibition means that one emotional state can prevent the occurrence of another. For instance, it is impossible to be anxious and relaxed at the same time. If we have managed to get our subject onto the high board in a relaxed state, anxiety and fear responses will be inhibited. Repeated times on the high board should cause fear in the situation to disappear. Again, we would say that the person has been *desensitized.* In general, desensitization (that is, a reduction in fears) is usually brought about by gradually approaching a feared stimulus while maintaining complete relaxation.

Question: What is desensitization used for?

Desensitization is primarily used to help people unlearn or countercondition phobias or strong anxieties. Almost everyone has a phobia or two. Many people fear heights, snakes, public speaking, spiders, and so forth. Usually these cause little difficulty because the individual carefully avoids fear-producing situations. However, consider the following: a teacher with stage fright, a student with test anxiety, a salesperson who fears people, an aspiring pole-vaulter who fears heights, or a newlywed with a fear of sexual intimacy. Each may be hampered enough by fears or anxieties to seek aid.

Question: How is desensitization done?

Desensitization usually involves three steps. First, the client and the therapist *construct a hierarchy.* This is a list of fear-provoking situations involving the phobia and ranging from the least disturbing situation to the most disturbing one. Second, the client is taught *exercises that produce total relaxation.* Once the client is relaxed, he or she proceeds to the third step by trying to *perform the least disturbing item* on the list. For a fear of heights (acrophobia), this might be: "(1) standing on a chair." The first item is repeated until no anxiety is felt. Any change from complete relaxation is a signal to clients that they must repeat the relaxation process before continuing. Slowly clients move up the hierarchy: "(2) climb to the top of a small

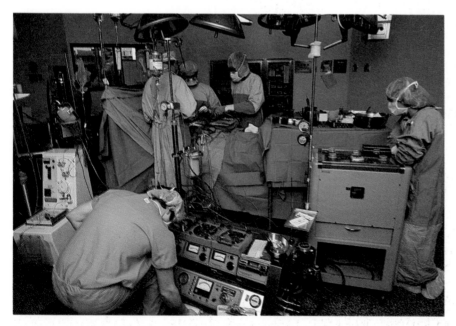

Fig. 23–2 *A case of natural desensitization: Doctors and nurses learn to remain calm at the sight of blood because of their frequent exposure to it.*

Fig. 23–3 *Treatment of a snake phobia by vicarious desensitization. The photographs show models interacting with snakes. To overcome their own fears, phobic subjects observed the models. (Bandura et al., 1969. Photos courtesy of Albert Bandura.)*

stepladder"; "(3) look down a flight of stairs"; and so on, until the last item is performed without fear: "(20) fly in an airplane."

Question: I understand how some fears could be desensitized by gradual approach—like the child on the high dive. But how would a therapist use desensitization to combat fear of sexual intimacy?

For a person with a fear of heights, the steps of the hierarchy might be acted out. Often, however, acting out is totally impractical. In some cases this problem can be handled by having clients observe models (live or filmed) who are performing the feared behavior (Fig. 23–3). If such **vicarious desensitization** is not practical, there is yet another alternative. Fortunately, desensitization works almost as well when a person *vividly imagines* each step in the hierarchy. If the person can visualize the steps without anxiety, fear in the actual situation is reduced.

Here is a sample of the hierarchy imagined by a 24-year-old married woman to overcome the fear and disgust she felt for sexual intercourse. (Some steps are left out to shorten the list.)

1. Dancing with and embracing husband while fully clothed.
2. Being kissed on cheeks and forehead.
3. Being kissed on lips.
4. Sitting on husband's lap, both fully dressed.
5. Husband kisses neck and ears.
6. Husband caresses hair and face.
   .
   .
   .
17. Having intercourse in bed in the dark.
18. Having intercourse in the nude in a dining room or living room.
19. Changing positions during intercourse.
20. Having intercourse in the nude while sitting on husband's lap. (Adapted from Lazarus, 1964)

Mrs. A was able to imagine the last steps in this hierarchy without experiencing anxiety after a 3-month period of desensitization. Accordingly, she and her husband reported that their sexual and marital adjustments were greatly improved.

Learning Check

Answer these questions before reading on.

1. The ordered series of steps used in desensitization make up a _____ of feared situations.

2. What two principles underlie desensitization? _____ and _____

3. When desensitization is carried out through the use of live or filmed models, it is called:
a. cognitive therapy   *b.* covert desensitization   *c.* relaxation training   *d.* vicarious desensitization

4. Three basic steps in desensitization are: construct a hierarchy, flood the person with anxiety, imagine relaxation. T or F?

Answers: **1.** hierarchy **2.** adaptation, reciprocal inhibition **3.** *d* **4.** F

Operant Principles—
All the World Is a . . . Skinner Box?

Question: Aversion therapy and desensitization are forms of behavior modification based on classical conditioning. Where does operant conditioning fit in?

The principles of operant conditioning have been developed by B. F. Skinner and other psychologists mostly through laboratory research with animals. The operant principles most frequently used by behavior therapists to deal with *human* behavior are:

1. *Positive reinforcement.* An action that is followed by reward will occur more frequently. If children whine and get attention, they will whine more frequently. If you get A's in your psychology class, you may become a psychology major.
2. *Nonreinforcement.* An action that is not followed by reward will occur less frequently.
3. *Extinction.* If a response is not followed by reward after it has been repeated many times, it will go away. After winning 3 times, you pull the handle on a slot machine 30 times more without a payoff. What do you do? You go away. So does the response of handle pulling (for that particular machine, at any rate).
4. *Punishment.* If a response is followed by discomfort or an undesirable effect, the response will be suppressed (but not necessarily extinguished).
5. *Shaping.* Shaping means rewarding actions that are closer and closer approximations to a desired response. If a response is complicated, it may never occur and therefore will not be rewarded. If I want to reward a retarded child for saying "ball," I may begin by rewarding the child for saying anything that starts with a *b* sound.
6. *Stimulus control.* Responses tend to come under the control of the situation in which they occur. If I set my clock 10 minutes fast, I can get to work on time in the morning. My departure is under the stimulus control of the clock even though I know it is fast.
7. *Time out.* A time-out procedure usually involves removing the individual from a situation in which reinforcement occurs. Time out prevents reward from following an undesirable response; it is a variation of nonreinforcement.

(For a more thorough review of operant principles, return to Chapter 8.) As simple as these principles may seem, they have been used very effectively by behavior modification specialists to overcome difficulties in work, home, school, and industrial settings. Let's see how.

Nonreinforcement and Extinction—
Time Out in the Attention Game

An extremely overweight mental patient had a persistent and disturbing habit: She stole food from other patients. No one could persuade her to stop stealing or to diet. For the sake of her health, a behavior therapist assigned her a special table in the ward dining room. If she approached any other table, she was immediately removed from the dining room. Since her attempts to steal food went unrewarded, they rapidly disappeared. Additionally, any attempt to steal from others usually resulted in the patient's missing her own meal (Ayllon, 1963).

Question: What operant principles did the therapist use?

The therapist used *nonreward* to produce *extinction*. Most frequently occurring human behaviors lead to some form of reward. An undesirable response can be eliminated by *identifying* and *removing* the rewards that maintain it. But people don't always do things for food, money, or other obvious rewards. Most of the rewards maintaining human behavior are more subtle. *Attention, approval,* and *concern* are common yet powerful reinforcers for humans (Fig. 23–4).

For instance, in a classroom we often find that misbehaving children are surrounded by others who giggle and pay attention to them. If seating is rearranged so that the disruptive children are surrounded by less responsive students, misbehavior decreases. Attention from a teacher (even scolding) can also be a reinforcer. An experiment showed that when teachers paid extra attention to classroom misbehavior, it increased. It increased even when the attention took the form of saying things such as "Sit down!" When misbehaving children were *ignored* and attention was given to children who were *not* misbehaving, misbehavior decreased (Madsen et al., 1968).

Question: How are nonreward and extinction applied in therapy?

Fig. 23–4 *This graph shows extinction of self-destructive behavior in two autistic boys. Before extinction began, the boys received attention and concern from adults for injuring themselves. During extinction, self-damaging behavior was ignored. (Adapted from Lovaas & Simons, 1969.)*

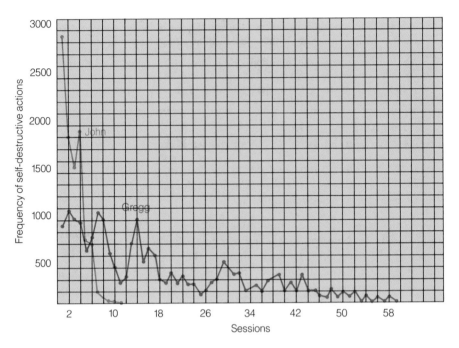

Nonreward and extinction can eliminate many problem behaviors. Frequently, difficulties center around a limited number of particularly disturbing responses. A typical strategy used in institutions is called *time out*. Time out means refusing to reward maladaptive responses, usually by refusing to play the *attention* game. Another form of time out is to remove an individual immediately from the setting in which an undesirable response occurs, so that the response will not be rewarded. For example:

> Fourteen-year-old Josh periodically appeared in the nude in the activity room of a training center for disturbed juveniles. This behavior always generated a great deal of attention from staff and other patients. Usually Josh was returned to his room and confined there. During this "confinement," he often missed doing his usual chores. As an experiment he was placed on time out. The next time he appeared nude, counselors and other staff members greeted him normally and then ignored him. Attention from other patients rapidly subsided. Sheepishly he returned to his room and dressed.

Reinforcement and Token Economies— The Target Is Health

This section might be called "Throwing a Lifeline to the Unreachable." A distressing problem faced when dealing with severe mental illness is how to "break through" to a patient who cannot, or will not, communicate. Mental patients sometimes spend years in hospitals without notice-able improvement. Even the patient who is willing to talk about his or her problem may make little visible progress toward mental health.

Question: What can be done in such circumstances?

An approach to therapy that is rapidly growing in popularity is based on the use of *tokens*. **Tokens** are *symbolic* rewards that can be exchanged for real rewards. (As you may recall from Chapter 8, tokens are secondary reinforcers.)

Tokens may be printed slips of paper, plastic "poker" chips, check marks, points, or "gold stars." Whatever form they take, tokens serve as rewards because they may be exchanged for candy, food, cigarettes, recreation, or other privileges, such as private time with a therapist, outings, using the record player, and so forth. Tokens are being used in mental hospitals, halfway houses for drug addicts, schools for the retarded, programs for delinquents, and ordinary classrooms. Their use is usually associated with dramatic improvements in behavior and overall adjustment.

Learning research and everyday experience point out the power of positive reinforcement to change behavior. If a response is followed by reward, it will occur more frequently. Using tokens, a therapist can *immediately* reward a positive response. This feature of tokens allows a therapist to use operant shaping to influence behavior instead of vaguely urging patients to "get themselves together."

So that incentives will have maximum impact, the

therapist selects specific **target behaviors** that could or should be improved, then reinforces them with tokens. For example, an uncommunicative mental patient might initially be given a token each time he or she says a word. Next, tokens may be given for speaking a complete sentence. Later, the patient could gradually be required to speak more frequently, then to answer questions, and eventually to carry on a short conversation in order to receive tokens. In this way patients who have not spoken more than a few words for months or years have been returned to the world of normal communication.

Full-scale use of tokens in an institutional setting leads to the development of a **token economy.** In a token economy patients are rewarded with tokens for a wide range of socially desirable or productive activities. They must *pay* tokens for privileges and for engaging in problem behavior (Fig. 23–5). For example, tokens are given to patients who get out of bed, dress themselves, take required medication, arrive for meals on time, and the like. Work at constructive activity, such as gardening, cooking, or custodial duties, may also earn tokens. Patients *must exchange* tokens for meals and for private rooms, movies, passes, off-ward activities, and other privileges. Sometimes tokens can be exchanged for items at a commissary or ward store. Patients are *charged* tokens for staying in bed, disrobing in

public, talking to themselves, fighting, crying, and similar target behaviors.

In a token economy program, staff members ensure that patients earn tokens easily for constructive behavior, but fine them heavily for destructive responses. This system provides the therapist with leverage. Patients are both pushed and enticed toward normality. The result can be a radical change in a patient's overall adjustment and morale. Patients have an incentive to change and are held responsible for their maladaptive habits and actions. Many "hopelessly" retarded, mentally ill, and delinquent people have been returned to a productive life by means of token economies.

Question: Wouldn't there be a problem with generalization of improvements brought about by a token economy?

Yes. As was the case with aversion therapy, lack of generalization can be a problem. To minimize it, patients are praised and given social recognition when they receive tokens. Each time a token is given, the therapist says something like "That was very good," or "You're doing so well."

By the time they are ready to leave the program, patients may be earning tokens on a weekly basis for maintaining sane, responsible, and productive behavior

Fig. 23–5 *Pictured below are the tokens used in one token economy system; also pictured are credit values for various activities. Tokens may be exchanged for items or for privileges listed on the board. (Photographs courtesy of Dr. Robert P. Liberman.)*

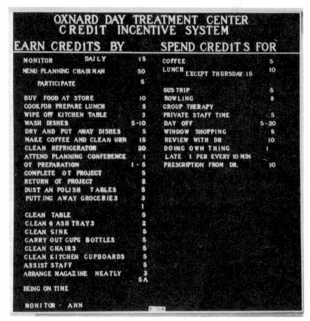

(Binder, 1976). The results of recent experiments suggest that the most effective token economies are those that ultimately depend on *social rewards* such as recognition and approval (Lieberman et al., 1976). Such rewards are what patients will receive when they return to family, friends, and community.

Cognitive Behavior Therapy— Think Positive!

Question: How would a behavior therapist treat a problem like depression? None of the techniques described seem to apply.

As we have discussed, behavior therapists usually try to change troublesome actions. However, in recent years a new breed of therapist has appeared. **Cognitive behavior therapists,** as they are called, are interested in thoughts as well as visible behavior. Rather than looking only at actions, cognitive therapists try to learn what people think, believe, and feel. They then help clients change *thinking patterns* that lead to trouble (Meichenbaum, 1977).

Cognitive Therapy for Depression

Cognitive therapy has been especially effective for treating depression. As you may recall from Chapter 13, Aron Beck believes that negative, self-defeating thoughts underlie depression. According to Beck, depressed persons see themselves, the world, and the future in negative terms. Beck (1985) believes this occurs because of several major distortions in thinking. The first is *selective perception:* If five good things happen during the day and three bad, the depressed person will focus only on the bad. *Overgeneralization* is a second thinking error underlying depression. An example would be considering yourself a total failure, or worthless, if you were to lose a job or fail a class. To complete the picture, Beck says that depressed persons tend to *magnify* the importance of undesirable events, and they engage in *all-or-nothing thinking* (seeing events, or themselves, as completely good or bad, right or wrong, successful or a failure) (Beck, 1985).

Question: What do cognitive behavior therapists do to alter such patterns?

Cognitive therapists make a step-by-step effort to correct negative thoughts that lead to depression or similar problems. At first, clients are taught to recognize and keep track of their own thoughts. The client and therapist then look for ideas and beliefs that cause depression, anger, avoidance, and so forth. For example, here's how a therapist might challenge all-or-nothing thinking (Burns & Persons, 1982):

Client: I'm feeling even more depressed. No one wants to hire me, and I can't even clean up my apartment. I feel completely incompetent!

Therapist: I see. The fact that you are unemployed and have a messy apartment proves that you are completely incompetent?

Client: Well . . . I can see that doesn't add up.

Next, clients are asked to gather information to test their beliefs. For instance, a depressed person might list his or her activities for a week. The list is then used to challenge all-or-nothing thoughts, such as "I had a terrible week" or "I'm a complete failure." With more coaching, clients learn to alter thoughts in ways that improve their moods, actions, and relationships.

In an alternate approach, the cognitive thrapist looks for an *absence* of effective coping skills and thought patterns, not for the *presence* of self-defeating thinking (Meichenbaum, 1977). The aim is to teach clients how to cope with anger, depression, shyness, stress, and similar problems. Stress inoculation, which was described in Chapter 14, is a good example of this approach.

Cognitive behavior therapy is a promising and rapidly expanding specialty. Before we leave the topic, let's explore one more widely used form of cognitive therapy.

Rational-Emotive Therapy

According to Albert Ellis (1962, 1973), the basic idea of **rational-emotive therapy (RET)** is as easy as A-B-C. Ellis assumes that people become unhappy and develop self-defeating habits because of unrealistic or faulty *beliefs*.

Question: How are beliefs important?

Ellis analyzes problems in this way: The letter A stands for an **activating experience,** which the person assumes to be the cause of C, an emotional **consequence.** For instance, a person who is rejected (the activating experience) feels depressed, threatened, or hurt (the consequence). Rational-emotive therapy shows the client that the true cause of difficulty is what comes between A and C: In between is B, the client's irrational and unrealistic **beliefs.** In this example the unrealistic belief leading to unnecessary suffering is: "I must be loved and approved of by almost everyone at all times" (see Table 23–1).

Ellis (1979) believes that most irrational beliefs come from three core ideas, each of which is unrealistic:

1. I *must* perform well and be approved of by significant others. If I don't, then it is awful, I cannot stand it, and I am a rotten person.
2. You *must* treat me fairly. When you don't, it is horrible and I cannot bear it.
3. Conditions *must* be the way I want them to be. It is terrible when they are not, and I cannot stand living in such an awful world.

It's easy to see that such beliefs can lead to much grief and needless suffering in a less than perfect world.

Rational-emotive therapists are very directive in their attempts to change a client's irrational beliefs and self-talk. The therapist may directly attack clients' logic, challenge their thinking, confront them with evidence contrary to their beliefs, and may even assign homework.

RET has been criticized as superficial and argumentative by some, but Ellis' basic insight has considerable merit. For instance, one recent study found that having irrational beliefs, like those listed in Table 23–1, is related to feelings of anger and unhappiness (Rohsenow & Smith, 1982). Many of us would probably do well to surrender our irrational beliefs. Improved self-acceptance and a better tolerance of daily annoyances are the benefits of doing so (Ellis, 1976).

Table 23–1   Ten Irrational Beliefs

1. I must be loved and approved of by almost every significant person in my life.
2. I should be completely competent and achieving in all ways to be a worthwhile person.
3. Certain people I must deal with are thoroughly bad and should be severely blamed and punished for it.
4. It is awful and upsetting when things are not the way I would very much like them to be.
5. My unhappiness is always caused by external events; I cannot control my emotional reactions.
6. If something unpleasant might happen, I should keep dwelling on it.
7. It is easier to avoid difficulties and responsibilities than to face them.
8. I should depend on others who are stronger than I am.
9. Because something once strongly affected my life, it will do so indefinitely.
10. There is always a perfect solution to human problems, and it is awful if this solution is not found.

(Adapted from Rohsenow & Smith, 1982.)

The value of cognitive approaches is further illustrated by three techniques (covert sensitization, thought stopping, and covert reinforcement) described in the Applications section that follows. See what you think of them.

Learning Check

1. Behavior modification programs aimed at extinction of an undesirable behavior typically make use of what operant principles?
   a. punishment and stimulus control   c. nonreinforcement and time out
   b. punishment and shaping   d. stimulus control and time out
2. Attention can be a powerful _____ for humans.
3. Token economies depend on use of the time-out procedure.   T or F?
4. An advantage of tokens is that they can be used to _____ _____ a desired response.
5. Tokens are used at first to change specific actions called _____ _____.
6. Tokens basically allow the operant shaping of desired responses.   T or F?
7. According to Beck, selective perception, overgeneralization, and _____ thinking are cognitive habits that underlie depression.
8. RET teaches people to change the antecedents of irrational behavior.   T or F?

Answers: 1. c   2. reinforcer   3. F   4. immediately reinforce   5. target behaviors   6. T   7. all-or-nothing   8. F

Applications

Self-Management—Applying Behavioral Principles to Yourself

"Throw out the snake oil, ladies and gentlemen, and throw away your troubles. Doctor B. Havior Modification is here to put an end to all human suffering."

True? Well, not quite. Behavior therapy is not a cure-all. Its use is often quite complicated and requires a great deal of experience and expertise. Also, there are times when therapists regard insight therapy as more appropriate than behavior therapy. Still, behavior therapy offers a straightforward solution to many problems.

It would be a serious mistake to presume that you could apply the principles of behavior therapy to major personal problems. As mentioned elsewhere in this book, professional help is available and should be sought when a significant problem exists. For lesser difficulties there is a good chance that you might succeed in modest attempts to apply the principles of behavior modification to yourself. Let us see how this might be done.

Covert Reward and Punishment— Boosting Your "Will Power"

"Have you ever decided to quit smoking cigarettes, watching television too much, eating too much, drinking too much, or driving too fast?"

"Well, one of those applies. I have decided several times to quit smoking."

"When have you decided?"

"Usually after I am reminded of how dangerous smoking is—like when I heard that my uncle had died of lung cancer. He smoked constantly."

"If you have decided to quit 'several times,' I assume you haven't succeeded?"

"No, the usual pattern is for me to become upset about smoking and then to cut down for a day or two."

"You forget the disturbing image of your uncle's death, or whatever, and start smoking again."

"Yes, I suppose if I had an uncle die every day or so, I might actually quit!"

The use of electric shock to condition an aversion seems remote for everyday problems. Even naturally aversive actions are difficult to apply to personal be-

havior. As mentioned earlier, for instance, rapid smoking is difficult for most smokers to carry out on their own. And, what about a problem like overeating? It would be difficult indeed to eat enough to create a lasting aversion to overeating.

In view of such limitations, psychologists have developed an alternative procedure that can be used to curb smoking, overeating, and other habits (Cautela & Bennett, 1981).

Covert Sensitization   Obtain six 3-by-5 cards and on each write a brief description of a scene related to the habit you wish to control. The scene should be so *disturbing* or *disgusting* that thinking about it would temporarily make you very uncomfortable about indulging in the habit. For smoking, the cards might read:

1. I am in a doctor's office. The doctor looks at some X rays and tells me I have lung cancer. She says a lung will have to be removed and she sets a date for the operation.
2. I am in bed under an oxygen tent. My chest feels caved in. There is a tube in my throat. I can barely breathe.
3. I wake up in the morning and smoke a cigarette. I begin coughing up blood.
4. Other cards would continue along the same line.

For overeating the cards might read:

1. I am at the beach. I get up to go for a swim and I overhear people whispering to each other, "Isn't that fat disgusting?"
2. I am at a store buying clothes. I try on several things that are too small. The only things that fit look like rumpled sacks. Salespeople are staring at me.
3. And so forth.

The trick, of course, is to get yourself to imagine or picture vividly each of these disturbing scenes *several times* a day. Imagining the scenes can be accomplished by placing them under *stimulus control*. Simply choose something you do *frequently* each day (such as

Applications: Self-Management—Applying Behavioral Principles to Yourself

getting a cup of coffee or getting up from your chair). Next make a rule. Before you can get a cup of coffee, or get up from your chair, or whatever you have selected as a cue, you must take out your cards and *vividly picture* yourself engaging in the action you wish to curb (eating or smoking, for example). Then *vividly picture* the scene described on the top card. Imagine the scene for 30 seconds. After visualizing the top card, move it to the bottom so the cards are rotated. Make new cards each week. The scenes can be made much more upsetting than the samples given here. The samples are toned down to keep you from being "grossed out."

Covert sensitization may sound as if you are "playing games with yourself," but it can be a great help if you want to cut down on a bad habit (Cautela, 1973). Try it!

Thought Stopping As discussed earlier, behavior therapists have begun to realize that thoughts, like visible responses, can also cause trouble. Think of times when you have repeatedly "put yourself down" mentally or when you have been preoccupied by needless worries, fears, or other negative and upsetting thoughts. If you would like to gain control over such thoughts, recent experiments show how it can be done.

The simplest thought-stopping technique makes use of mild punishment to suppress upsetting mental images and internal "talk." Simply place a large, flat rubber band around your wrist. As you go through the day, apply this rule: Each time you catch yourself thinking the upsetting image or thought, pull the rubber band away from your wrist and snap it. You need not make this terribly painful. Its value lies in drawing your attention to how often you form negative thoughts and in interrupting the flow of thoughts. Strong punishment is not required.

Question: It seems like this procedure might be abandoned rapidly. Is there an alternative?

A second thought-stopping procedure requires only that you interrupt upsetting thoughts each time they occur. Begin by setting aside time each day during which you will deliberately think the unwanted thought. As you begin to form the thought, shout "Stop!" aloud, with conviction. (Obviously you should choose a private spot for this part of the procedure!)

Repeat the thought-stopping procedure 10 to 20 times for the first 2 or 3 days. Then switch to shouting "Stop!" covertly (to yourself) rather than aloud. Thereaf-

ter, thought stopping can be carried out throughout the day, whenever upsetting thoughts occur (adapted from Williams & Long, 1979). After several days of practice, you should be able to stop unwanted thoughts whenever they occur.

Covert Reinforcement Earlier we discussed how punishing images can be linked to undesirable responses, such as smoking or overeating, to decrease their occurrence. Many people also find it helpful to covertly *reinforce* desired actions. For example, suppose your target behavior is "not eating dessert." If this were the case, you could (Cautela & Bennett, 1981):

Imagine that you are standing at the dessert table with your friends. As dessert is passed, you politely refuse, and you feel good about staying on your diet.

These images would then be followed by imagining a pleasant, reinforcing scene:

Imagine that you are your ideal weight. You look really slim in your favorite color and style. Someone you like says to you, "Gee, you've lost weight. I've never seen you look so good."

For many people, of course, actual direct reinforcement (as described in the Chapter 8 Exploration) is the most powerful way to alter behavior. Nevertheless, covert or "visualized" reinforcement can have similar effects. To make use of covert reinforcement, choose one or more target behaviors and rehearse them mentally. Then follow each rehearsal with a vivid rewarding image.

Applying Desensitization— Overcoming Common Fears

You have prepared for 2 weeks to give a speech in a large class. As your turn approaches, your hands begin to tremble and perspire. Your heart pounds and you find it difficult to breathe. You say to your body, "Relax!" What happens? Nothing!

Relaxation The key to desensitization is relaxation. To inhibit fear, one must *learn* to relax. Here is a method for achieving deep-muscle relaxation.

Tense the muscles in your right arm until they tremble. Hold them tight for about 5 seconds and then let go. Allow your hand and arm to go limp and to relax completely. Repeat the procedure. Releasing tension two or three times will allow you to feel whether your arm muscles have relaxed. Re-

Applications: Self-Management—Applying Behavioral Principles to Yourself

peat the tension-release procedure with your left arm. Compare it with your right arm. Repeat until the left arm is equally relaxed. Apply the tension-release technique to your right leg; to your left leg; to your abdomen; to your chest and shoulders. Clench and release your chin, neck, and throat. Wrinkle and release your forehead and scalp. Tighten and release your mouth and face muscles. As a last step, curl your toes and tense your feet. Then release. Practice relaxation with the tension-release method until you can achieve complete relaxation quickly (5 to 10 minutes).

After you have practiced relaxation once a day for a week or two, you will begin to be able to tell when your body (or a group of muscles) is tense. Also, you will begin to be able to relax on command. As an alternative you might want to try imagining a very safe, pleasant, and relaxing scene. Some people find such images as relaxing as the tension-release method (Crits-Christoph & Singer, 1984).

Once you have learned to relax, the next step is to identify the fear you would like to control and construct a *hierarchy*.

Procedure for Constructing a Hierarchy   Make a list of situations (related to the fear) that make you anxious. Try to list at least 10 situations. Some should be very frightening and others only mildly frightening. Write a short description of each situation on a separate 3-by-5 card. Place the cards in order from the least disturbing situation to the most disturbing. Here is a sample hierarchy for a student afraid of public speaking:

1. Given an assignment to speak in class.
2. Thinking about the topic and the date the speech must be given.
3. Writing the speech; thinking about delivering the speech.
4. Watching other students speak in class the week before the speech date.

5. Rehearsing the speech alone; pretending to give it to the class.
6. Delivering the speech to my roommate; pretending my roommate is the teacher.
7. Reviewing the speech on the day it is to be presented.
8. Entering the classroom; waiting and thinking about the speech.
9. Being called; standing up; facing the audience.
10. Delivering the speech.

Using the Hierarchy   When you have mastered the relaxation exercises and have the hierarchy constructed, set aside time each day to work on reducing your fear. Begin by performing the relaxation exercises. When you are completely relaxed, visualize the scene on the first card (the least frightening scene). If you can *vividly* picture and imagine yourself in the first situation twice *without a noticeable increase in muscle tension*, proceed to the next card. Also, as you progress through the cards, relax yourself between each card.

Each day, stop when you reach a card that you cannot visualize without tension after making three attempts. Each day, begin one or two cards before the one on which you stopped the previous day. Continue to work with the cards until you can visualize the last situation without experiencing tension (techniques are based on Wolpe, 1974).

By using this approach, you should be able to reduce the fear or anxiety associated with things such as public speaking, entering darkened rooms, asking questions in large classes, heights, talking to members of the opposite sex, taking tests, and so forth. Even if you are unable to reduce a fear, you will have learned to place relaxation under voluntary control. This alone is valuable because controlling unnecessary tension can increase energy and efficiency.

Learning Check

1.   Covert sensitization and thought stopping combine aversion therapy and cognitive therapy.   T or F?
2.   Like covert aversion conditioning, covert reinforcement of desired responses is also possible.   T or F?
3.   Exercises that bring about deep-muscle relaxation are an essential element in covert sensitization.   T or F?
4.   Items in a desensitization hierarchy should be placed in order from least disturbing to most disturbing.   T or F?
5.   The first step in desensitization is to place the visualization of disturbing images under stimulus control.   T or F?

Answers: 1. T   2. T   3. F   4. T   5. F

Chapter Summary

- *Behavior therapists* use variations of *behavior modification*, therapeutic techniques that apply the learning principles of *operant* and *classical conditioning*, to bring about positive changes in human behavior.
- Classical conditioning, the pairing of a *conditioned stimulus* (CS) and an *unconditioned stimulus* (US), can be used to condition an *aversion* when the US causes pain or discomfort.
- In *aversion therapy* the sights, sounds, odors, and motions of a maladaptive response or bad habit (such as smoking or drinking) are associated with pain or other aversive events. Thus, the undesirable response becomes linked with an aversion that inhibits occurrence of the response.
- Classical conditioning also underlies *desensitization*, a technique used to overcome fears and anxieties. In desensitization, gradual *adaptation* and *reciprocal inhibition* serve to break the link between fear and particular situations. Typical steps in desensitization are: *constructing a hierarchy* of feared situations, *learning* to produce *total relaxation*, and *performing items on the hierarchy* (from least to most disturbing).
- Desensitization may be carried out with real settings and situations in the environment or it may be carried out by *vivid imagination* of the fear hierarchy. Desensitization is also effective when it is administered *vicariously*; that is, when clients watch *models* perform the feared responses.
- Behavior modification also makes use of operant principles. The most commonly used principles are: *positive reinforcement, nonreinforcement, extinction, punishment, shaping, stimulus control,* and *time out*. Through the application of these principles, behavior modification is used to extinguish undesirable responses and to promote constructive behavior.
- Nonreward can be used to produce extinction of troublesome behaviors. Often this is done by simply *identifying* and *eliminating* reinforcers, particularly *attention* and *approval*.
- In the application of positive reinforcement and operant shaping, symbolic rewards known as *tokens* are often used. Tokens allow *immediate reinforcement* of selected *target behaviors* so that rapid shaping is possible.
- Full-scale use of tokens in an institutional setting produces a *token economy*. In a token economy, responsibilities, goods, services, and privileges are assigned values, and tokens are earned and exchanged. Toward the end of a token economy program, patients are shifted to *social rewards* such as recognition and approval.
- *Cognitive behavior therapy* is a new specialty that emphasizes changing thought patterns that underlie emotional or behavioral problems. Its goals are to correct distorted thinking and/or to teach improved coping skills.
- In a variation of cognitive therapy called *rational-emotive therapy* (RET), clients learn to recognize and challenge their own *irrational beliefs*. In the *ABC analysis* of RET, changing B (beliefs) alters the emotional consequences (C) of activating events (A).
- Cognitive-behavioral techniques can be an aid to managing one's own behavior. In *covert sensitization*, aversive images are used to discourage unwanted behavior. *Thought stopping* uses mild punishment to prevent upsetting thoughts. *Covert reinforcement* is a way to encourage desired responses by mental rehearsal. *Desensitization* pairs relaxation with a hierarchy of upsetting images in order to lessen fears.

Exploration

Self-Directed Behavior Change—A Case Study

By now it should be clear that behavioral principles are highly useful for solving personal problems. To conclude, let's explore a final example of behavior therapy in action.

The case study summarized here was done by psychologists Scott Hamilton and David Waldman (1983). Hamilton and Waldman's study concerns Al, a 20-year-old student enrolled in a psychology course.

Case Study

Many psychology students now learn self-control methods like those described earlier. As class projects, most students modify target behaviors such as studying, exercising, eating, and the like. Al's project was different. Al had a 4-year history of moderate to severe depression. Previously, Al had tried to alleviate his depression through group therapy and other efforts. However, Al continued to engage in frequent self-criticism and negative thinking, which almost always made him depressed.

Al's depression was worsened by overgeneralization. He often spent hours torturing himself with distorted thoughts, such as, "I'm *stupid* and a *total failure* because my grades are bad." Because Al's problem was more serious than most, it was selected for analysis as a case study.

Self-Modification Procedures

Baseline   During an initial 18-day period, Al recorded how often he had negative thoughts and how intense they were. This was done to determine his baseline level of depressive thinking.

Behavioral Intervention   Because Al's depression was so closely linked to negative thoughts, his first plan focused on solving the problems he worried about most. These included studying too little, low grades, poor time scheduling, and a lack of career goals.

Al set up a program in which he earned points for seeking out career information, meeting daily study goals, maintaining a time schedule, and so forth. Al also made a list of reinforcing activities. He allowed himself to engage in these activities only in exchange for points earned by constructive behavior.

Cognitive Behavioral Intervention
As you can see in Fig. 23–6, Al's reinforcement system did not consistently lessen his depressive thinking. In view of this, Al dropped the reinforcement system after 2 weeks and concentrated on directly changing his depressive thoughts.

Al's cognitive program had three elements. First, he kept a record of events and thoughts that immediately preceded his becoming depressed. He then re-evaluated the event and restated his thoughts about it in a more rational form. Second, he administered daily covert reinforcement to himself. This took the form of reading written, positive statements about himself while engaging in pleasant activities. The third element of Al's program involved setting aside times each day when he would relax and mentally rehearse coping with stressful situations. At such times Al tried to imagine the worst possible turn of events and to picture himself dealing with the situation calmly.

Results and Follow-Up   As
shown in Fig. 23–6, Al's cognitive-behavioral program significantly reduced the frequency of his depressive thoughts. Both Al and his peers reported that he was less depressed. This improvement was still evident 6 months later.

Question: Why didn't the behavioral part of Al's program work?

Hamilton and Waldman report that Al's point system did eliminate many of the sources of his self-critical thoughts, such as insufficient studying. However, new depressive thoughts (about his appearance and love life, for instance) began to replace the old worries. In Al's case it proved more effective to directly attack his depressive thinking.

Exploration: Self-Directed Behavior Change—A Case Study

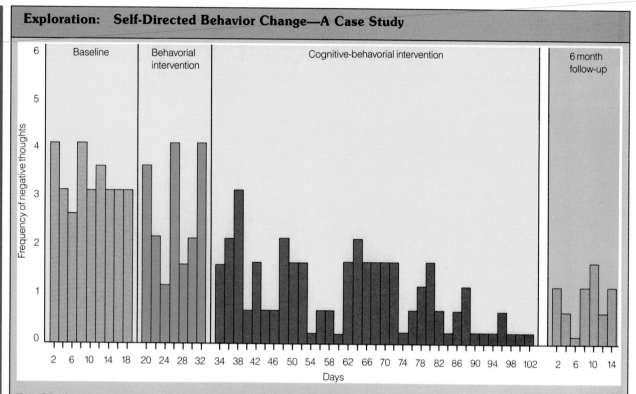

Fig. 23–6   *This graph shows the average frequency of Al's negative thoughts for 2-day intervals. Note the significant reduction that occurred during the cognitive-behavioral period of his program. Notice also that Al's improvement was still evident 6 months later. (Data from Hamilton & Waldman, 1983.)*

Conclusion   Al's case may be unusual. Perhaps others would not be as successful as he was in changing their own thinking patterns. It is worth saying again that for major problems it is advisable to seek guidance from a professional therapist. Nevertheless, Al's success is a tribute to the value of behavioral and cognitive therapies.

To Control or Not to Control?

Obviously, if you *voluntarily* use behavioral principles to change your own behavior, problems of control and personal freedom are avoided. But what about when behavior modification is used by some people to change the behavior of others?

When behavior therapy was first developed, many observers feared that it would be used to control people against their will. By now, most fears of behavior therapy have faded. For one thing, it is now clear that *all* psychotherapies modify behavior in one way or another. And for another, studies show that behavior therapists are rated just as warm and caring as traditional therapists (Staples et al., 1975).

Behavior Therapy: Are You for or Against It?

One area remains in which there is controversy concerning behavior modification. Some critics still object to its use with "captive" groups, such as in schools, prisons, mental institutions, geriatric hospitals, factories, and so forth.

Proponents of behavior modification believe that it has no peer in areas such as classroom management, work with the retarded, child discipline, and treatment for obes-

Exploration: Self-Directed Behavior Change—A Case Study

ity, phobias, sexual dysfunction, and the like. They also argue that many mental patients are serving virtual life sentences in state hospi- tals. In view of the demonstrated effectiveness of behavioral tech- niques, they consider it unethical to *withhold* treatment.

The proper place for behavior control in a free society is a com- plex issue. Where do you stand on the use of behavior modification?

Learning Check

1. Al began his program by recording the frequency of his depressive thoughts. This was done so that he could tell when his thoughts got down to the baseline.   T or F?
2. Al's plan for reinforcing his own desirable behavior is an example of operant conditioning.   T or F?
3. According to Fig. 23–6, Al was able to greatly reduce the frequency of his depressive thoughts by directly reinforcing desirable behavior.   T or F?
4. Voluntary use of behavioral principles to change one's own behavior typically does not compromise personal freedom.   T or F?

Answers: 1. F   2. T   3. F   4. T

Questions for Discussion

1. How do you think an insight-oriented therapist would have approached Al's depression? What advantages and disadvantages do you see in the behavioral approach? What do you think would be the limitations of self-directed behavior change?

2. Under what conditions would you condone the use of behavior modification? When would you oppose it?

3. Based on the techniques described, would you cooperate with a therapist who wanted to use behavior therapy? Are there some techniques you find acceptable and others not?

4. Select a bad habit you would like to break or a positive behavior you would like to encourage and tell how you might use a behavioral or cognitive-behavioral technique to alter your behavior.

5. Some critics have charged that the use of tokens in the classroom encourages students to expect artificial rewards. Behavior theorists reply that explicit rewards are better than inconsistent rewards such as praise and attention. What are the advantages and drawbacks represented by each position?

6. How do you feel about the use of behavior modification in prisons and psychiatric hospitals? Is behavior therapy any different from the involuntary administration of tranquilizers or other drugs? Why or why not?

Part Seven

Self and Others

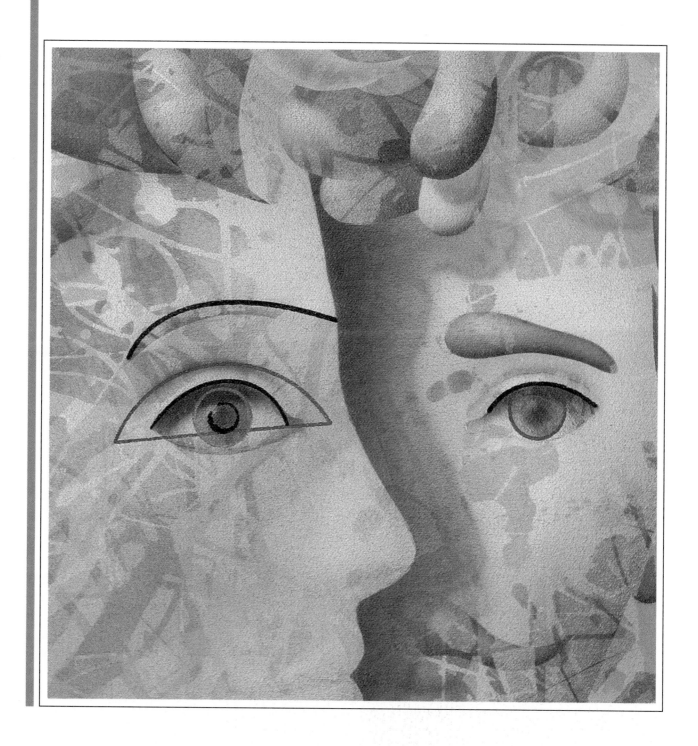

Chapter 24 | Human Sexuality

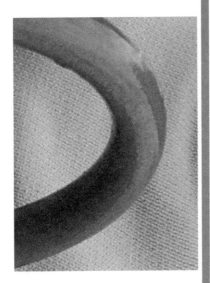

Chapter Preview

That Magic Word

Sex\seks\ n 1. one of the two divisions of organisms formed on the distinction of male and female.

"Sex" has many meanings: reproduction, gender, sexual identity, recreation, intimacy, and much more. Of the various meanings, the simplest would seem to be the reference to gender. What, really, could be simpler? Males are males and females are females, right? Wrong. Even something as basic as gender is complicated and many-sided.

Gender *The complexity of gender is illustrated by the attempt (1976) of Dr. Renée Richards to enter a women's tennis tournament. You may recall from news stories that Dr. Richards is a transsexual. Formerly she was Dr. Richard Raskin, a Newport Beach, California, ophthalmologist. As a man Richard Raskin was a modestly successful tennis player. After a sex-change operation and hormone therapy to alter gender, Dr. Richards tried to launch a new tennis career as a woman. Understandably, other women players protested. Officials finally decided to use a genetic sex test to determine if Dr. Richards could compete. She, in turn, protested this test. Genetically she would still be considered male, but psychologically she is female—she has female genitals, and she functions socially as a female (Hyde, 1979). Is Dr. Richards, then, male or female?*

You might consider the case of Renée Richards an unfair example because the transsexual seeks an alteration of natural gender. For most people the various indicators of gender are in agreement. Nevertheless, it is not unusual to find occasional ambiguities among the various dimensions of a person's "sex." Contrary to common belief, gender is not a simple either-or classification. In the first part of this chapter we will consider some basic dimensions of "maleness" and "femaleness." An essential question we will address is, "How does one become male or female?"

Sexual Behavior *Each of us is by nature a sexual creature, an inescapable reality that springs from the basic biology of reproduction. With this reality in mind, later sections of this chapter discuss sexual behavior, sexual arousal and response, sexual problems, and attitudes toward sexuality. These are topics you may feel you already know a lot about. Therefore, before reading further, you may find it interesting to see if you can correctly answer the Human Sexuality Quiz. Answers follow the quiz. The reasons for the answers can be found in this chapter.*

Human Sexuality Quiz *Indicate which of the statements are true and which are false.*

1. *Women are generally incapable of multiple orgasm.*
2. *Impotence in males is usually psychologically caused.*
3. *Frequent nocturnal emissions ("wet dreams") in males indicate the presence of a sexual disorder.*
4. *Male sexual potency and female pleasure in intercourse are closely related to penis size.*
5. *Of the various sexual dysfunctions, premature ejaculation is one of the easiest to treat.*
6. *Although it is less apparent, women ejaculate during orgasm.*
7. *For women, masturbation typically involves stimulation of the clitoris.*
8. *Sterilization in both men and women usually abolishes the sex drive.*
9. *Women have two kinds of orgasm, vaginal and clitoral.*
10. *Changes in sexual behavior brought about by the "sexual revolution" have had more impact on women than on men.*
11. *Men are more aroused by explicit erotic stimuli (such as pornographic films) than are women.*
12. *Maximum sexual responsiveness generally occurs at a later age for women than it does for men.*

Answers: 1. F 2. T 3. F 4. F 5. T 6. T 7. T 8. F 9. F 10. T 11. F 12. T

Survey Questions What are the basic dimensions of gender? How does one's sense of maleness or femaleness develop? How are sex roles acquired? What are the most typical patterns of human sexual behavior? To what extent do males and females differ in sexual response? Have recent changes in attitudes affected sexual behavior? What are the most common sexual adjustment problems? How are they treated?

Resources

The Development of Sex Differences

It has been said that the one thing you will never forget about a person is that person's sex. Considering the number of activities, relationships, conflicts, and choices influenced by gender, it is no wonder that we pay close attention to it. Let's begin with a few basic questions: What does it mean to be male or female? What are the dimensions of gender? How do gender and sex role differences develop?

Male or Female? Traditionally, the basic physical differences between males and females have been divided into *primary* and *secondary* sexual characteristics.

Primary sexual characteristics refer to the sexual and reproductive organs themselves: the penis, testes, and scrotum in males; and the ovaries, uterus, and vagina in females (Figs. 24–1 and 24–2). As described in Chapter 16, **secondary sexual characteristics** appear at puberty in response to hormonal signals from the pituitary gland. In females, secondary sexual characteristics involve development of the breasts, broadening of the hips, and other changes in body shape. Males develop facial and body hair, and the voice deepens. These changes signal readiness for reproduction. Reproductive maturity is especially evident in the female **menarche** (MEN-ar-kee: the onset of menstruation). From menarche until **menopause** (the end of regular monthly fertility cycles), women can bear children.

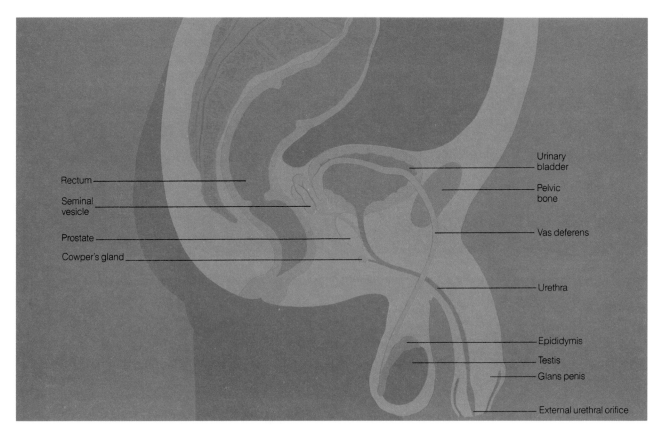

Urinary bladder

Pelvic bone

Vas deferens

Urethra

Epididymis

Testis

Glans penis

External urethral orifice

Rectum

Seminal vesicle

Prostate

Cowper's gland

Fig. 24—1   *Cutaway view of internal and external male reproductive structures.*

Question: What causes the development of sex differences?

In general terms, both primary and secondary sexual characteristics are related to the action of sex hormones in the body. (*Hormones* are chemical substances secreted by glands of the endocrine system.) The **gonads** (or sex glands) affect sexual development and behavior by secreting **estrogens** (female hormones) and **androgens** (male hormones). The gonads in the male are the testes, and in the female the ovaries. The adrenal glands (located above the kidneys) also supply sex hormones in both males and females. At puberty, adrenal secretions add to the development of secondary sexual characteristics.

Interestingly, all individuals normally produce both estrogens and androgens. It is the proportion of these substances that influences sex differences. In fact, the development of male or female anatomy is largely due to the presence or absence—before birth—of **testosterone** (one of the androgens).

Question: Then is biological sex determined by the sex hormones?

Not entirely. As suggested by our discussion in the Chapter Preview, gender cannot be reduced to a single dimension.

Dimensions of Gender   At the very least, any designation of gender must include: (1) **genetic sex** (XX or XY chromosomes), (2) **gonadal sex** (ovaries or testes), (3) **hormonal sex** (predominance of androgens or estrogens), (4) **genital sex** (clitoris and vagina in females, penis and scrotum in males), and (5) **gender identity** (one's personal sense of maleness or femaleness) (Money & Ehrhardt, 1972).

To see why gender must be defined along several dimensions, let's follow the sequence of events involved in becoming male or female.

Fig. 24—2 *Cutaway view of internal and external female reproductive structures.*

Labels in figure:
- Fallopian tube
- Ovary
- Urinary bladder
- Pelvic bone
- Urethra
- Clitoris
- Labia minora
- Uterus
- Cervix
- Vagina
- Rectum

Gender Development Becoming male or female starts simply enough. Genetic sex is determined at the instant of conception: Two X chromosomes initiate development of a female; an X chromosome and a Y chromosome produce a male. Genetic sex remains the same throughout life, but it alone does not determine gender. We must also consider hormonal effects before birth.

For the first 6 weeks of prenatal development, there is no difference between a genetically male and a genetically female embryo. However, if a Y chromosome is present, testes develop in the embryo and supply testosterone, stimulating growth of the penis and other male structures (Fig. 24–3). In the absence of testosterone, the embryo will develop female reproductive organs and genitals, regardless of genetic sex. It might be said, then, that nature's primary impulse is to make a female (Money, 1965).

Development of the embryo usually matches genetic sex, but not always. A genetic male will fail to develop male genitals if insufficient testosterone is formed during prenatal growth. Even if testosterone is present, an inherited *androgen insensitivity* may exist, again resulting in female development.

Similarly, androgens must be either at low levels or absent for an XX embryo to develop as a female. Thus, for both genetic males and females, hormonal problems before birth may result in **hermaphroditism** (her-MAF-ro-dite-ism), which means defects in sexual development resulting in dual or ambiguous sexual anatomy. For instance, a developing female may be masculinized by exposure to *progestin* (a drug given to prevent miscarriage) or by a problem known as the *androgenital syndrome*. In the androgenital syndrome, estrogen is produced, but a genetic abnormality causes the adrenal glands to secrete excess amounts of androgen. In such cases a female child may be born with male genitals.

Question: Would such a child be reared as a male?

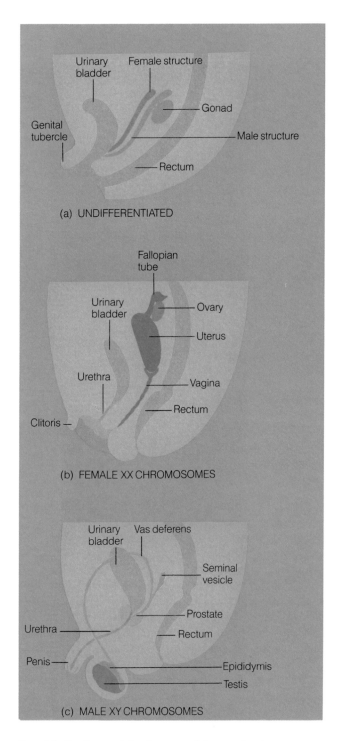

(a) UNDIFFERENTIATED

Urinary bladder

Female structure

Gonad

Genital tubercle

Male structure

Rectum

(b) FEMALE XX CHROMOSOMES

Fallopian tube

Urinary bladder

Ovary

Uterus

Urethra

Vagina

Clitoris

Rectum

(c) MALE XY CHROMOSOMES

Urinary bladder

Vas deferens

Seminal vesicle

Prostate

Urethra

Rectum

Penis

Epididymis

Testis

Fig. 24–3 *Prenatal development of the reproductive organs. Early development of ovaries or testes affects hormonal balance and alters sexual anatomy. (a) At first the sex organs are the same in the human male and female. (b) When androgens are absent, female structures develop. (c) Male sex organs are produced when androgens are present.*

Some are. Usually, however, the condition is detected and corrected by surgery. If necessary, extra estrogen may be administered after birth.

Some researchers believe that, in addition to guiding physical development, the balance of sex hormones before birth may also "sex type" the brain (Diamond, 1977). Changes in the brain are then thought to alter later chances of developing masculine or feminine characteristics.

Question: Does that mean there is a physical basis for male and female traits?

In animals, clear connections exist between prenatal hormones and later emergence of male or female behaviors. However, with humans evidence suggests that most sex-linked behavior is learned (Weisstein, 1975). Be that as it may, some researchers believe that prenatal exposure to androgens or estrogens exerts a **biological biasing effect** on later psychosexual development in humans.

Question: Is there any evidence for this?

Consider females who have been exposed to androgens before birth. After birth their hormone balance shifts to female and they are raised as girls. Does prenatal exposure to male hormones have any masculinizing effect on their psychological development? Medical psychologist John Money, who has studied many of these women, believes it does. During childhood the women were typically tomboys who preferred the company of boys to girls, engaged in more vigorous athletic activities than their peers, were more achievement-oriented, and were less interested in future marriage plans and romance (Money, 1977).

Question: Isn't it possible that the girls were influenced by their parents?

Yes. This explains why such research cannot be considered conclusive. The tomboyish qualities observed in prenatally masculinized girls may simply result from learning.

At the risk of getting entangled in the "battle of the sexes," let's consider one more idea. Some researchers believe that biology underlies male-female differences in thinking abilities. Women, they contend, are more often "left-brained," and men, "right-brained." The left brain, you may recall, is largely responsible for language and rote learning. The right brain is superior at spatial reasoning. Thus, some psychologists believe that biological differences explain why men (as a group) do better on spatial tasks and why women are better at language skills. Others, however, strongly reject this theory. To them such claims are based on shaky evidence and sexist thinking (Fairweather, 1976; Parlee, 1979; Unger, 1979). The one thing that is certain in this debate is that males and females are more alike than they are different (Maccoby & Jacklin, 1974). There is no biological basis for the unequal treatment women have often faced at work, school, and elsewhere.

Gender Identity   One's personal, private sense of maleness or femaleness is referred to as *gender identity*, which can be distinguished from *sex roles*. Sex roles are observable traits, mannerisms, interests, and behaviors defined by one's culture as "male" or "female."

Gender identity appears to be a *learned* self-perception—a point emphasized by cases of hermaphroditism. If we compare two individuals having the same degree of hermaphroditism—one raised as a boy and the other as a girl—we will find that the person raised as a girl will act like and consider herself a girl, and the individual raised as a boy will act like and identify himself as a boy (Money, 1970).

Question: At what age is gender identity acquired?

Gender identity is essentially formed by 3 or 4 years of age (Money, 1977). Accordingly, children born with ambiguous gender have few problems as long as a final decision concerning their sex is made by the age of 18 months. If the parents consistently treat the child as a boy or a girl, the child should develop a clear sense of gender. Delaying the decision can create a situation in which the child develops a gender identity at odds with his or her biological sex, or a confused sense of sexual identity.

Question: How is gender identity acquired?

Obviously, it begins with *labeling* ("It's a boy"; "It's a girl"). Thereafter it is influenced by **sex role socialization;** that is, by the countless, subtle pressures exerted by parents, peers, and cultural forces that urge boys to "act like boys" and girls to "act like girls." In the next section we will investigate sex roles and sex role socialization in more detail.

Sex Roles and Sex Role Socialization

In determining adult sexual behavior and sex-linked personality traits, *sex roles* are probably as important as chromosomal, genital, or hormonal sex. **Sex role** refers to the pattern of behavior encouraged and expected of individuals on the basis of gender. In our culture boys are usually encouraged to be strong, fast, aggressive, dominant, achieving, and otherwise "male." Females have typically been expected to be sensitive, intuitive, passive, emotional, and "naturally" interested in household tasks and childrearing. The "naturalness" of such sex roles becomes questionable when they are compared with variations in different cultures. For example, Ethel Albert (1963) has identified numerous cultures in which women do the heavy work because men are considered too weak for it. In the Soviet Union approximately 75 percent of the medical doctors and a large proportion of the work force are women. Many more examples can be cited, but perhaps one of the most pertinent is anthropologist Margaret Mead's (1935) observations of the Tchambuli people of New Guinea.

Sex roles for the Tchambuli are a nearly perfect reversal of the American stereotypes. Tchambuli women handle the fishing and manufacturing and are expected to control the power and economic life of the community. Women also take the initiative in courting and sexual relations. Tchambuli men, on the other hand, are expected to be dependent, flirtatious, and concerned with their appearance. Art, games, and theatrics occupy most of the Tchambuli males' time, and males are particularly fond of adorning themselves with flowers and jewelry.

As the Tchambuli demonstrate, activities considered "appropriate" for males and females vary in different cultures. The arbitrary nature of sex roles is also apparent. A man is no less a man if he cooks, sews, or cares for children; a woman is no less a woman if she excels in sports, succeeds in business, or works as a mechanic. Still, adult personality and gender identity are closely tied to cultural definitions of "masculinity" and "femininity."

An interesting side effect of sex role socialization is the imprint left on activities having nothing to do with gender. On the average, for example, boys are superior to girls in math and visual-spatial skills. And, as previously mentioned, girls are superior to boys in language and verbal skills. There is also considerable evidence that boys are more aggressive than girls, that girls are more empathetic than boys, and so on (Block, 1979; Maccoby & Jacklin, 1974).

Question: How are such differences created?

Sex Role Socialization   Learning sex roles begins immediately after birth. Infant girls are held more gently and treated more tenderly than boys are. Both parents play more roughly with their sons than with their daughters (who are presumed to be more "delicate"). Later, boys are allowed to roam over a wider area without special permission. They are also expected to run errands earlier than girls. Daughters are told that they are pretty and that "nice girls don't fight." Boys are told to be strong and that "boys don't cry." Sons are more often urged to control emotions than are daughters, and parents tolerate aggression toward other children more in boys than in girls.

The toys purchased for boys and girls are strongly sex-typed: dolls for girls; trucks and guns for boys. Even bicycles come in "boys' " and "girls' " models (Hoffman, 1977; Wilson et al., 1977). By the time children reach kindergarten, they have learned to think that doctors, fire fighters, and pilots are men, and that nurses, secretaries, and hairdressers are women (Blaske, 1984). And why not? The work force in America is still highly segregated by sex, and children learn from what they see.

Overall, parents tend to encourage their sons to engage in **instrumental** (goal-directed) **behaviors,** to control their emotions, and to prepare for the world of work. Daughters, on the other hand, are encouraged in **expressive** (emotion-oriented) **behaviors** and, to a lesser degree, are socialized for the maternal role.

When told that they respond differently to boys and girls, parents often explain that it is because there are "natural" differences between the sexes (Wilson et al., 1977). But what comes first, "natural differences" or the expectations that create them?

Question: Many people have become interested in the limitations imposed by stereotyped sex roles. Would such parental behavior apply to feminist mothers?

Sex roles are so pervasive that even feminists can be influenced by them. One study found that feminist women had little trouble treating their daughters in a nonstereotyped manner, but they seemed to want their sons to be "liberated but masculine." In other words, they had no anxieties when their daughters engaged in traditional "masculine" play, but they were upset if their sons played "dress up," preferred frilly clothes, imitated "female" mannerisms, or played with dolls (Van Gelder & Carmichael, 1975).

In our culture "male" seems—for many—to be defined as "not female." That is, many parents have a vague fear of expressive and emotional behavior in male children, because to them it seems to imply effeminacy (Wilson et al., 1977).

To summarize, sex role socialization in our society prepares children for an adult world in which men are expected to be instrumental, conquering, controlling, and unemotional, and in which women are expected to be expressive, emotional, passive, and dependent. Thus, sex role socialization prepares us to be highly competent in some respects and handicapped in others. Of course, many people find traditional sex roles comfortable and desirable. It seems evident, however, that just about everyone will benefit when the more stereotyped and burdensome aspects of sex roles are set aside.

Learning Check

To check your progress, answer the following questions:

1. _____ sexual characteristics refer to the sexual and reproductive organs; _____ sexual characteristics refer to other bodily changes that take place at puberty.

2. All individuals normally produce both androgens and estrogens, although the balance differs in males and females.   T or F?

3. The five basic dimensions of gender are: _____
_____.

4. In females, hermaphroditism may result from:
   a. an androgen insensitivity   *b.* excessive estrogen   *c.* the androgenital syndrome   *d.* all of the preceding

5. For humans, the biological biasing effect of prenatal hormones can now be regarded as proven.   T or F?

6. One's private sense of maleness or femaleness is referred to as _____.

7. Traditional sex-role socialization encourages _____ behavior in males.
   a. instrumental   *b.* expressive   *c.* emotional   *d.* dependent

Answers:

identify **7.** *a*
1. Primary, secondary **2.** T **3.** genetic sex, gonadal sex, hormonal sex, genital sex, gender identity **4.** *c* **5.** F **6.** gender

Sexual Behavior

Question: When does sexual behavior first appear in humans?

A capacity for sexual arousal is apparent at birth or soon after. Sexual researcher Alfred Kinsey verified instances of *orgasm* (sexual climax) in boys as young as 5 months old and girls as young as 4 months (Kinsey et al., 1948, 1953). Kinsey also found that children aged 2 to 5 years spontaneously manipulate and exhibit their genitals.

Various forms of sexual behavior continue through childhood and adolescence, but as the child matures, cultural norms place greater restrictions on sexual activities. Still, 50 percent of males and 25 percent of females report having engaged in preadolescent sex play. In adulthood, norms continue to shape sexual activity along socially approved lines. In our culture, sex between children, incest (sex between close relatives), prostitution, homosexuality, and extramarital sex all tend to be discouraged.

As was the case with sex role behavior, it can be seen that such restrictions are somewhat arbitrary. A comparison of many cultures shows that less restriction is usually matched by more sexual activity of all kinds. If cultural restrictions are disregarded, it can be said that any sexual act engaged in by consenting adults is "normal" if it does not hurt anyone.

Sexual Arousal   Sexual arousal in humans is a complex phenomenon. It may, of course, be produced by direct stimulation of the body's **erogenous zones** (eh-ROJ-eh-nus: productive of pleasure or erotic desire). Human erogenous zones include the genitals, mouth, breasts, ears, anus, and to a lesser degree the surface of the entire body. It is clear, however, that more than physical contact is involved: A urological or gynecological examination rarely results in any sexual arousal. Human sexual arousal obviously includes a large cognitive element (see Highlight 24–1). Indeed, arousal may be triggered by mere thoughts or images.

Question: Are men more easily sexually aroused than women?

Apparently not. To answer the question, one study used medical recording devices to measure sexual arousal in males and females as they listened to erotic tape recordings. It was found that the erotic material was equally arousing for both sexes (Heiman, 1977). This and similar findings suggest that women are no less *physically* aroused by erotic stimuli than are men. However, compared with

---

Highlight 24–1
Sexual Scripts

In a restaurant, we commonly expect certain things to occur. It could even be said that each of us has a restaurant "script" that defines a plot, dialogue, and actions that should take place. Researcher John Gagnon (1977) believes that, similarly, we learn a variety of **sexual scripts** that guide our behavior.

Sexual scripts determine when and where we are likely to express sexual feelings, and with whom. They provide a "plot" for the order of events in lovemaking, and they outline "approved" actions, motives, and outcomes.

When two people follow markedly different scripts, misunderstandings are almost sure to occur. Consider, for instance, what happens when a woman acting out a "friendly first date" script is paired with a man following a "seduction" script: The result is often anger, hurt feelings, or worse. Even newlyweds may find that their sexual agendas differ. In such cases considerable "rewriting" of scripts is often needed for sexual compatibility.

However you may feel about the reality of sexual scripts, one implication seems inescapable: For humans the mind (or brain) is the ultimate erogenous zone (Knox, 1984).

---

men, women more often have a negative *emotional* response to explicit pictures of sex. That is, women more often report feeling upset and disgusted by these stimuli (Hoyenga & Hoyenga, 1984).

If capacity for sexual arousal is measured by frequency of orgasm (brought about by masturbation or intercourse), the peak of male sexual activity is at age 18. Kinsey's studies (done in the early 1950s) placed the peak of female sexual activity at about 30 years of age. However, in recent years women have participated more fully in sexual activities, and at an earlier age (Hunt, 1974). The peak rate of female sexual activity still appears to occur later than that of males. However, male and female sexual behavior is gradually becoming more alike.

Question: What causes differences in sex drive?

Sex Drive   Attitudes toward sex, sexual experience, and recency of sexual release are all obviously important, but physical factors may also play a role. In males the strength of the sex drive is related to the amount of androgens secreted by the testes. When the supply of androgens dramatically increases at puberty, sex drive increases too.

Surprisingly, the "male" hormones, or androgens, may also affect female sex drive. In addition to estrogen, a woman's body produces small amounts of androgens. Evidence suggests that these androgens may increase the sex drive in women just as they do in men. One study found that frequency of intercourse for married women was highest when their androgen levels were at a peak (Persky et al., 1978). Furthermore, when women are given androgens for medical reasons, some report increased sexual desire (Carlson, 1981). Some women also report variations in arousal at various times during their monthly cycle. If such a relationship does exist, its effects are probably small, since women may engage in sexual activity at any time during their monthly cycles (including during menstruation).

Question: Are nocturnal emissions ("wet dreams") an indication of an unusually strong sex drive? Do they ever indicate sexual disorders? Do both men and women experience nocturnal orgasms?

According to Kinsey's studies, about 85 percent of males and 35 percent of females have had sexual dreams that resulted in orgasm. These experiences typically begin during adolescence and may continue throughout adulthood. Kinsey found some reduction in the number of men experiencing nocturnal orgasms after marriage, but no change among women. Nocturnal orgasm may best be considered a completely normal (if relatively infrequent) form of sexual release.

Question: Does alcohol stimulate the sex drive?

In general, no. Alcohol is a *depressant*. As such, it may, in small doses, stimulate erotic desire by lowering inhibitions. This effect no doubt accounts for alcohol's reputation as an aid to seduction. (Humorist Ogden Nash once summarized this bit of folklore by saying, "Candy is dandy, but liquor is quicker.") However, in larger doses alcohol suppresses orgasm in women and erection in men. Increasing levels of drunkenness cause a progressive decrease in sexual desire, arousal, pleasure, and performance (Malatesta et al., 1979).

Question: Does removal of the testes or ovaries abolish the sex drive? Also, what happens to the sex drive in old age?

In lower animals, castration (surgical removal of the testicles) or removal of the ovaries usually completely abolishes sexual activity in *inexperienced* animals. Sexually ex-

perienced animals (particularly higher animals such as monkeys) may show little immediate change in sexual behavior after castration. In humans, the effects of male and female castration vary. Initially, some individuals show a decline in sex drive, while others experience no change. However, after several years have passed, almost all subjects report a decrease in sex drive.

The preceding observations have nothing to do with the effects of *sterilization*. Men and women who choose surgically based birth control (such as a vasectomy or a tubal ligation) experience no loss of sex drive. If anything, they may become more sexually active when pregnancy is no longer a concern.

There is typically a natural decline in sex drive that accompanies aging and reduction in sex hormone output. However, sexual activity does not come to an unavoidable end. In some cases men and women in their nineties have continued active sex lives. The crucial factor for an extended sex life appears to be regularity and opportunity. Individuals who fairly regularly engage in intercourse after ages 40 to 50 have little difficulty in later years (Masters & Johnson, 1970).

Masturbation   One of the most basic human sexual behaviors is masturbation. **Masturbation** may be defined as deliberate self-stimulation that causes sexual pleasure or orgasm. Rhythmic self-stimulation has been observed in infants under 1 year of age. In adulthood, masturbation in the male usually takes the form of stroking or other manipulation of the penis. Female masturbation most often centers on stimulation of the clitoris or the areas immediately surrounding it.

The following are some questions commonly asked about masturbation.

Question: In adulthood do more men masturbate than women?

Yes. Of the women who took part in Kinsey's survey (1953), 60 percent reported that they had masturbated at some time. Of the males, 95 percent reported that they had masturbated (Kinsey et al., 1948). (Some cynics add, "And the other 5 percent lied!")

A survey conducted in the 1970s by Morton Hunt (1974) showed almost identical rates: 94 percent for males and 63 percent for females. Hunt believes, however, that a liberalization of attitudes toward masturbation has taken place. This change is reflected in the fact that adolescents now begin masturbation at a younger age.

Question: What purpose does masturbation serve?

Through masturbation people discover what is pleasing sexually and what their natural rhythms and preferences are. Masturbation is therefore an important part of the psychosexual development of most adolescents. Among other things, it provides a biologically healthy substitute for sexual intercourse during a period when sexual activity is discouraged and young people are maturing emotionally (Wilson et al., 1977).

Question: Is it immature for masturbation to continue after marriage?

If it is, there are a large number of "immature" people around! Morton Hunt found that approximately 70 percent of married men and women masturbate at least occasionally.

Generally speaking, masturbation is a valid sexual activity at any age, and it may continue after marriage without posing any threat to a relationship. There is nothing immature or infantile about masturbation. As a matter of fact, masturbation may be related to sexual response in other activities. For example, 85 percent of a group of women who had masturbated before marriage reported having an orgasm during the first year of marriage. In contrast, only about 65 percent of a group of women who did not masturbate experienced orgasm during the first year of marriage (Kinsey et al., 1953).

Question: Is there any way in which masturbation can cause harm?

In the past, frightening stories about possible physical and mental damage abounded in folklore about masturbation. Thirty years ago, a child might be told that masturbation would cause insanity, acne, sterility, or other such nonsense. "Self-abuse," as it was often called, has enjoyed a long and unfortunate history of religious and medical condemnation.

The contemporary view is that masturbation is a normal and acceptable sexual outlet. No knowledgeable psychologist would deny this, and enlightened parents are well aware of it. Still, many a child has been punished or made to feel guilty for touching his or her genitals. This situation is unfortunate since there is no harm caused by masturbation itself. Typically, the only negative effects of masturbation are the fear, guilt, or anxiety that occur when an individual has learned negative attitudes toward it.

Sexual Variations   Male **homosexuality** and female **lesbianism** are two significant variations in sexuality. It is estimated that about 5 to 10 percent of all adult men in Western societies are predominantly homosexual. Adult women who are predominantly homosexual represent 3 to 5 percent of all women (Marmor, 1980). These percentages are small, but they indicate that there may be 6 to 12 million lesbians and gay men in the United States.

When evaluating homosexuality, one should remember that cultural standards for sexual behavior vary greatly. A major survey of 76 cultures found that almost two-thirds accept some form of homosexuality (Weinberg & Williams, 1974). Moreover, psychological testing consistently shows no differences in personality or adjustment between heterosexuals and homosexuals (Bell et al., 1981; Marmor, 1980). For these and other reasons, homosexuality cannot be considered a sexual disorder on psychological grounds (DSM-III, 1980).

Psychologically, homosexuality is regarded as a problem only if a person feels lasting guilt, self-hate, or similar negative emotions—a condition referred to as *ego-dystonic homosexuality* (DSM-III, 1980). This condition is probably rare, however. The majority of adult homosexuals display adjustment patterns and occupational histories similar to those of heterosexuals (Marmor, 1980). The problems faced by homosexuals are more often related to rejection by family, discrimination in employment and housing, and to the undercurrent of homophobia in American society. (*Homophobia* refers to prejudice, fear, and dislike aimed at homosexuals.)

Homosexuals are found in all walks of life, at all social and economic levels, and in all cultural groups. As more gay and lesbian people make themselves known to friends, relatives, and co-workers, it may be reasonable to expect that the prejudices against them will wane.

Learning Check

1. A capacity for sexual arousal is apparent at birth or soon after.   T or F?

2. Areas of the body that produce erotic pleasure are called _____ zones.

3. When exposed to erotic stimuli, men and women vary in their most common emotional reactions, but there appears to be no difference in their levels of physical arousal.   T or F?

4. There is some evidence to suggest that sexual activity and sex drives peak later for males than they do for females.   T or F?

5. It is possible (and normal) for sexual activity to continue to ages 80 or 90.   T or F?

6. More males than females report that they masturbate.   T or F?

7. Masturbation can cause physical harm, according to the latest research reports.   T or F?

8. The percentage of women who are homosexual is greater than the percentage of men who are homosexual.   T or F?

Answers: 1. T   2. erogenous   3. T   4. F   5. T   6. T   7. F   8. F

Human Sexual Response

Objective information about human sexual response has been expanded by the work of gynecologist William Masters and psychologist Virginia Johnson (1966, 1970). In a series of experiments, interviews, and controlled observations, Masters and Johnson directly studied sexual intercourse and masturbation in nearly 700 males and females. The information they obtained has significantly improved our understanding of human sexuality.

According to Masters and Johnson, sexual response in both males and females can be divided into four phases: (1) **excitement**, (2) **plateau**, (3) **orgasm**, and (4) **resolution**. (See Fig. 24–4 and Fig. 24–5.)

Male Response   Sexual arousal in the male is signaled by erection of the penis during the excitement phase. There is also a speedup in heart rate, increased blood flow to the genitals, enlargement of the testicles, erection of the nipples, and numerous other bodily changes. If sexual stimulation ends, the excitement phase will gradually subside. Continued stimulation moves the individual into the plateau phase, in which physical changes and subjective feelings of arousal become more intense. If stimulation ends during this phase, sexual arousal will subside more slowly and may produce considerable frustration.

Further stimulation during the plateau phase brings about a reflex release of accumulated tension resulting in sexual climax, or orgasm. Orgasm in the mature male is accompanied by **ejaculation** (release of seminal fluid) and is followed by a short **refractory period** during which continued stimulation will not produce a second orgasm. (Many men cannot even be stimulated to erection until the refractory phase has passed.) Only rarely is the male refractory period followed by a second orgasm. Orgasm is usually followed by *resolution*, a return to lower levels of sexual tension and arousal.

Female Response   Although the timing and intensity of the phases vary considerably from person to person, the basic pattern of response for women is the same as that for men. During the excitement phase of arousal, a complex pattern of changes take place to prepare the vagina for intercourse. These changes correspond to erection in the male. Also (as in the male), the nipples become erect, pulse rate changes, and the skin may become flushed. Most women go through a plateau stage comparable to that in the male, although a few follow a pattern of response that essentially skips the plateau (Fig. 24–5).

During orgasm, from 3 to 10 muscular contractions of the vagina, uterus, and related structures serve to release accumulated sexual tension. Contrary to the belief of some women, no form of ejaculation accompanies female orgasm. Vaginal lubrication produced during the earlier stages of arousal probably accounts for the misconception of those women who believe they have ejaculated. Both orgasm and resolution in the female usually last longer than they do in the male. After orgasm, about 15 percent of all females return to the plateau phase and may have another orgasm before resolution.

Before the work of Masters and Johnson, there was considerable debate about whether a difference existed between female orgasm associated with the vagina and orgasm derived from stimulation of the clitoris. Sigmund Freud had contended in his writings that a clitoral orgasm was an "immature" form of female response. Since the clitoris is the female structure comparable to the penis, Freud felt that women whose orgasmic experiences centered on the clitoris had not fully accepted their femininity.

Masters and Johnson exploded the Freudian myth by showing that there is absolutely no difference in physical response no matter what form of stimulation produces orgasm. As a matter of fact, the vagina is relatively insensitive to touch. Most sensations during intercourse, therefore, come from stimulation of the clitoris and other external structures. It now seems apparent that sensations from many sources are fused together into the total experience of orgasm and that, for the majority of women, one of the more important sources of these sensations is the clitoris.

When women in one study were asked to express a preference for vaginal or clitoral stimulation, most said they would rather not choose, but if forced to choose, two-thirds preferred clitoral sensations (Fisher, 1973). Similarly, researcher Shere Hite has reported the results of an unscientific, yet thought-provoking survey of 3000 women. Among these women only 26 percent reported regularly reaching orgasm during intercourse without separate massaging of the clitoris (Hite, 1976). To downgrade the "clitoral orgasm" ignores the basic physiology of female sexual response.

Male and Female Responses Compared

The research of Masters and Johnson indicates that similarities between male and female sexual responses outweigh the differences. However, differences that do exist may have a significant effect on sexual adjustment. For

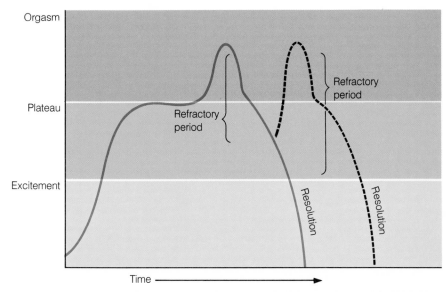

Fig. 24—4 *Male sexual response cycle. (Reproduced by permission from Frank A. Beach (ed.),* Sex and Behavior, *NY: John Wiley & Sons, Inc., 1965.)*

Fig. 24—5 *Female sexual response cycle. (Reproduced by permission from Frank A. Beach (ed.),* Sex and Behavior, *NY: John Wiley & Sons, Inc., 1965.)*

example, it was found that women typically go through the sexual phases more slowly than do men. During lovemaking, a woman may require from 10 to 20 minutes to go from excitement to orgasm,* whereas a man may experience all four stages in as little as 4 minutes. These differences should be kept in mind by couples seeking sexual compatibility.

Question: Does that mean a couple should try to time lovemaking to promote simultaneous orgasm?

At one time the concept of simultaneous orgasm (both partners reaching sexual climax at the same time) was considered the ideal "goal" of lovemaking. More recently, it has been rejected as an artificial concern that may reduce satisfaction instead of enhance it. To paraphrase one expert (Lowen, 1965):

> To govern the timing of orgasm can destroy the natural flow of feeling that guarantees mutual satisfaction. This point cannot be stressed too strongly. Inhibiting the buildup of excitation may limit pleasure, whereas spontaneity enhances it.

It is more advisable to aim for the satisfaction of both partners through some combination of intercourse and manual stimulation than it is to self-consciously inhibit spontaneity, communication, and pleasure.

Question: Does slower response mean that women are less sexual than men?

Definitely not. During masturbation 70 percent of females reach orgasm in 4 minutes or less. This finding casts serious doubts on the idea that female response is actually slower. Slower female response during intercourse probably occurs because stimulation to the clitoris is less direct. It might be said that the male anatomy simply provides too little stimulation during intercourse for more rapid female response, not that the female is in any way inferior.

Question: Does penis size affect female response?

Masters and Johnson found that the vagina adjusts to the size of the penis, and that subjective feelings of pleasure and intensity of orgasm are not related to penis size. They also found that while individual differences exist in flaccid penis size, there tends to be much less variation in erect penis size. (This is why erection has been referred to as the great equalizer.) Contrary to popular belief, there is no relationship between penis size and male sexual potency.

Question: Men almost always reach orgasm during intercourse, but many women do not. Does this indicate that women are less sexually responsive?

Again, the evidence argues against any lack of female sexual responsiveness. It is true that about 1 woman in 3 does not experience orgasm during the first year of marriage, and only about 30 percent regularly reach orgasm through intercourse alone. However, this does not imply lack of physical responsiveness since approximately 90 percent of all women reach orgasm when masturbating (Knox, 1984).

In another regard the female is clearly more responsive. Only about 5 percent of males are capable of multiple orgasm (and then only after an unavoidable refractory period). Most males are almost always limited to a second orgasm at best. In contrast, Masters and Johnson's findings suggest that most women who regularly experience orgasm are capable of multiple orgasm. Remember, though, that only about 15 percent of all women regularly experience multiple orgasm. A woman should not assume that something is wrong if she isn't multiorgasmic.

Attitudes and Sexual Behavior

Question: Has there been a "sexual revolution"?

Some observers have argued that liberalized attitudes toward sexual expression and the simultaneous development of effective contraceptives have brought about a "revolution" in sexual behavior. Others believe that sexual behavior has remained essentially unchanged for the past 20 years. From this point of view, the "sexual revolution" has been mostly verbal—people are simply talking more about sex now than they were in the past (Miller & Siegal, 1972).

Attitudes   An accurate description of changing sexual attitudes and behavior seems to lie somewhere between the two views just expressed. Attitudes have changed significantly in the direction of greater tolerance. Behavior has also changed, but much more moderately.

Changing attitudes are graphically illustrated by the result of national polls concerning the acceptability of pre-

---

*There is much variation, however. A recent study of 1000 married women found that 50 percent of them reached orgasm if intercourse lasted 1 to 11 minutes; if intercourse lasted 15 minutes or more, the rate increased to 66 percent. Twenty-five percent of the wives said that orgasm occurred within 1 minute of the start of intercourse (Brewer, 1981). (Note that these times refer only to intercourse, not to an entire arousal sequence.)

marital intercourse. In a 1959 Roper Poll, 88 percent of those interviewed agreed that premarital sex is "wrong." In 1969 only 68 percent of the respondents to a Gallup Poll rejected premarital sex. By 1973 only 48 percent felt like-wise. And in 1979 only 5 percent of college-age men and 12 percent of women endorsed abstaining from sex before marriage (DeLameter & MacCorquodale, 1979; cited by Knox, 1984). Similar changes have been observed in atti-tudes toward extramarital sex, homosexuality, legalized prostitution, sex education, no-fault divorce, and a vari-ety of related issues.

Question: Have changing attitudes been translated into behavior?

As we shall see in a moment, they have to some extent. Largely, however, there is greater *tolerance* for sexual be-havior, expecially that *engaged in by others.* For example, *Psychology Today* magazine found in a poll of its readers that 80 percent considered extramarital sex acceptable un-der some circumstances. But, in practice only 40 percent of married men and 36 percent of married women had actually had extramarital sexual experience (Athenasiou et al., 1970). Another survey of more conservative couples found that only 28 percent reported extramarital sexual ex-perience (Johnson, 1970).

Question: How do such figures compare with earlier gen-erations?

The figures cited do not allow a good comparison because they represent selected groups of people. A better indica-tion is given by comparing Kinsey's findings from the early 1950s to Hunt's from the early 1970s. These researchers obtained very similar figures: About 50 percent of males and 20 percent of females have at least one extramarital contact during their lifetime (Hunt, 1974; Kinsey, 1953). Thus, changing attitudes have not greatly altered behavior in this area.

Question: What kinds of changes have taken place?

Behavior   Premarital intercourse rates have traditionally been considered a good indication of overall sexual activi-ty. Kinsey found that 70 percent of males and 33 percent of females had engaged in premarital intercourse by age 25. Twenty years later, Hunt obtained premarital inter-course rates of 97 percent for males and about 70 percent for females by age 25. A more recent study found that 93 percent of women married after 1973 had engaged in pre-marital relations (Levin & Levin, 1975). A variety of ad-ditional studies support the idea that premarital intercourse rates have definitely increased.

A major element of the "sexual revolution" is earlier participation in sexual behavior by both sexes. A recent survey of American teenagers found that 43 percent of boys and 31 percent of girls have had intercourse by age 16 (Hass, 1983). There has also been a marked increase in sexual expression among females. Other studies show higher rates of intercourse in marriage for couples of all ages and a greater variety of sexual expression in marital relations (Hunt, 1974; Levin & Levin, 1975).

Question: Has a "sexual revolution" taken place then?

A Sexual Revolution?   In all, there certainly seems to be adequate evidence that sexual behavior has increased in the last 20 to 25 years. However, this trend does not seem to represent a move toward sexual promiscuity. Although it is true that sexual intercourse by unmarried couples is more common, most couples emphasize mutual commit-ment and a loving relationship as a requirement for sexual involvement. In this regard, premarital sex today often parallels the behavior of engaged couples 20 years ago (Si-mon & Gagnon, 1973).

Or as one author has noted (Hyde, 1979), many young people today have just changed the sequence of events. For their parents the sequence was: fall in love, marry, begin a sexual relationship. For many the sequence now is: fall in love, begin a sexual relationship, marry. Most women have only 1 premarital sexual partner whom they eventually marry. Men typically have about 6 premarital partners (Hyde, 1979). Overall, an image of rampant sex-ual behavior is not supported.

We have noted that extramarital intercourse rates seem to have changed little in the past 25 years. Thus, liberal-ized sexual attitudes seem not to have jeopardized the basic concept of marriage. Even premarital intercourse does not appear to represent a major rejection of tradi-tional values and responsible behavior. The association be-tween sexuality and love or affection remains strong for the majority of the population. Likewise, other changes in at-titudes and behavior appear to reflect a greater acceptance of sexuality, rather than a true "revolution" (see Highlight 24–2).

A more comfortable acceptance of a natural element of human relationships—sexuality—is the positive side of changing sexual attitudes and values. The negative side is represented by the plight of the individual who is not ready for, or interested in, greater sexual freedom. As one of the women who responded to Shere Hite's survey said:

> The Sexual Revolution tells me I am abnormal if I don't de-sire to make it with every Tom, Dick, or Jane that I see. I am only free to say yes. (Hite, 1976, cited by Hyde, 1979)

Highlight 24–2
Slow Death of the Double Standard

A good summary of the changes that have occurred in sexual behavior is found in the phrase, "the slow death of the double standard."

In the past decades distinctly different standards were often applied to male and female sexuality. Males, for instance, were largely forgiven for engaging in premarital sex. Young males who "sowed wild oats" were not only tolerated, but in some cases tacitly encouraged to do so as a step toward manhood.

On the other hand, women who were sexually active before marriage ran the risk of being labeled "easy," "bad," or "promiscuous" (Knox, 1984).

Similar differences pervaded sexual mores and placed women in a separate-but-not-equal position with regard to sexual behavior. However, as the gap between male and female sexual patterns has continued to close, it is increasingly likely that an end to the double standard is in sight.

Apparently, some individuals feel pressured into sexual behavior because it is "expected." However, pressures such as these probably come as much from the individual as from others. If a greater acceptance of human sexuality is to be constructive, it must be perceived as a general increase in personal freedom—as the right to say no, as well as a right to choose when, where, how, and with whom one's sexuality will be expressed. As is true in other areas of human functioning, freedom must be combined with responsibility, commitment, and caring if it is to have meaning.

Learning Check

1. List the four phases of sexual response identified by Masters and Johnson: _____

2. Males typically experience _____ after ejaculation.
    a. an increased potential for orgasm   c. the excitement phase
    b. a short refractory period   d. muscular contractions of the uterus

3. The research of Masters and Johnson suggests that the similarities between male and female sexual responses outweigh the differences.   T or F?

4. During lovemaking, a female may require from 10 to 20 minutes to go from excitement to orgasm, whereas the male may experience all four stages of sexual response in as little as 4 minutes.   T or F?

5. Simultaneous orgasm of the male and female should be the ultimate goal in lovemaking.   T or F?

6. Recent research shows there is considerable evidence that open discussion and more liberal views regarding sexual behavior are causing loose or promiscuous sexuality.   T or F?

7. Contrary to long-standing belief, it now appears that much female sexuality is focused on:
    a. the uterus   b. the urethra   c. the clitoris   d. the cervix

Answers: 1. excitement, plateau, orgasm, resolution   2. b   3. T   4. T   5. F   6. F   7. c

Applications

Sexual Problems

Question: What are the most common sexual problems? How are they treated?

Most people who seek sexual counseling have one or more of the following six problems (Kaplan, 1974):

A. For the male:

1. Impotence: inability to produce or maintain an erection.
2. Premature ejaculation: inability to delay or control orgasm.
3. Retarded ejaculation: inability to reach orgasm.

B. For the female:

1. General sexual dysfunction: lack of erotic response to sexual stimulation (frigidity).
2. Orgasmic dysfunction: inability to reach orgasm.
3. Vaginismus: spasm of muscles at the entrance of the vagina, preventing intercourse.

There was a time when couples and individuals endured such dysfunctions in silence. However, in recent years effective treatments have been found for each problem. Let's briefly investigate the causes and treatments of the six barriers to sexual adjustment and fulfillment.

Male Impotence   Impotence (also known as erectile dysfunction) is the inability to maintain an erection for sexual intercourse. Impotence may be an occasional or continuous problem. Males suffering from *primary impotence* have never been able to produce or maintain an erection. Those who have previously performed successfully, but then have become impotent, are said to suffer from *secondary impotence*. In either case, when impotence becomes a repeated pattern, it can be very disturbing to the man and his sexual partner.

Question: How often must a man experience failure to be considered impotent?

Sex therapists Masters and Johnson (1970) feel that a problem exists when failure occurs on 25 percent or more of a man's lovemaking attempts. Repeated impotence should therefore be distinguished from an *occasional* inability to produce or maintain an erection. Fatigue, anger, anxiety, and excessive consumption of alcohol, can all cause temporary impotence in healthy males.

It is important to recognize that occasional impotence is normal. At such times it is particularly important for the man's partner to avoid expressing anger, disappointment, or embarrassment. Patient reassurance helps prevent the establishment of a vicious cycle. In fact, overreaction to occasional impotence may generate fears and doubts that will contribute to further impotence.

Question: What causes impotence?

For years, experts held that impotence is rarely caused by physical illness, disease, or damage. Now they recognize that roughly 40 percent of cases are physically caused. However, even when a physical problem exists, it is almost always made worse by anxiety and other emotional factors. Also, notice that impotence is still more likely to be psychological than physical. If a man can have an erection under any circumstances (during sleep, for instance), his problem is probably not physical (Knox, 1984).

According to Masters and Johnson (1970), primary impotence is often related to harsh religious training, early sexual experience with a seductive mother, or other experiences leading to guilt, fear, and sexual inhibition. Also seen occasionally are indications of homosexual feelings the person has not come to terms with.

Secondary impotence may be related to anxiety about sex in general, guilt because of an extramarital affair, resentment or hostility toward a sexual partner, fear of ability to perform, and similar emotions and conflicts. Often the problem starts with repeated sexual failures caused by drinking too much alcohol or by the presence of premature ejaculation. In either case initial doubts soon become severe fears of failure—which then further inhibit sexual response.

Applications: Sexual Problems

Treatment for impotence usually begins with discussion of the fears and psychological blocks behind the problem. The man learns that he cannot consciously will an erection and that his disability is not a reflection on his manhood. To further free him of his fears (particularly that of failure), the man and his partner are usually assigned a series of exercises to perform. This technique, called **sensate focus,** directs attention to natural sensations of pleasure and builds communication skills.

In sensate focus the couple is initially told to take turns stroking various parts of each other's bodies. They are instructed to carefully avoid any genital contact at first. Instead, they are to concentrate on giving pleasure and on signaling what is most gratifying to them. This takes the pressure to perform off the male and allows him to learn to give pleasure as a means of receiving it.

Over a period of days or weeks, the couple proceeds to more intense physical contact involving the breasts and genitals. As inhibitions are reduced and natural arousal begins to replace fear, the successful couple moves on to intercourse.

Premature Ejaculation   Masters and Johnson (1970) consider ejaculation to be premature if a man cannot delay sexual climax long enough to satisfy his partner in at least one-half of their lovemaking attempts. However, Helen Kaplan, of Cornell University Medical School, finds this definition unsatisfactory because of large variations in the time different women take to reach orgasm. Kaplan (1974) says that prematurity exists when ejaculation occurs reflexively, or when there is an inability to tolerate high levels of excitement at the plateau stage of arousal.

Question: Do many men have difficulties with premature ejaculation?

Premature ejaculation is a common problem in male sexual adjustment. Theories advanced to explain it have ranged from the idea that it may represent hostility toward the female partner (since it deprives her of satisfaction) to the suggestion that most early male sexual experiences tend to encourage rapid climax (such as those taking place in the back seat of a car and masturbation). Kaplan (1974) adds that excessive

arousal and anxiety over performance are usually present, and that some men simply engage in techniques that maximize sensation and make rapid orgasm inevitable. Whatever the causes, premature ejaculation can be a serious difficulty, especially in the context of long-term relationships.

Treatment for premature ejaculation is highly successful and relatively simple. The most common treatment procedure is the *squeeze technique* used by Masters and Johnson. The woman stimulates her partner manually until he signals that ejaculation is about to occur. She then firmly squeezes the tip of the penis to inhibit orgasm. When the man feels he has control, stimulation is repeated. Gradually, the man acquires the ability to delay orgasm sufficiently for satisfactory intercourse. During treatment, skills that improve communication between partners are developed, along with a better understanding of the male's sexual response cues.

Retarded Ejaculation   Among males an inability to reach orgasm was once considered a rare problem. But milder forms of this dysfunction have recently accounted for increasing numbers of clients seeking therapy (Kaplan, 1974). Background factors often observed are: strict religious training, fear of impregnating, lack of interest in the sexual partner, symbolic inability to give of oneself, unacknowledged homosexuality, or the recent occurrence of traumatic life events. Power and commitment struggles within relationships may be important added factors.

Treatment for retarded ejaculation consists of sensate focus, manual stimulation by the female (which is designed to orient the male to the female as a source of pleasure), and stimulation to the point of orgasm followed by immediate intercourse and ejaculation. Therapy also focuses on resolving personal conflicts and marital difficulties underlying the problem.

Female General Sexual Dysfunction   This difficulty, commonly referred to as *frigidity,* is usually defined as a persistent inability to derive pleasure from sexual stimulation. Women who show general sexual dysfunction respond with little or no physical arousal to sexual stimulation. The problem thus appears to correspond directly to male impotence (Kaplan, 1974). As in male

Applications: Sexual Problems

impotence, general female sexual dysfunction may be primary or secondary.

The causes of female general sexual dysfunction bear some similarity to those seen in male impotence. Frigidity can often be traced to frightening childhood experiences such as molestations (often by older relatives), incestuous relations that produce lasting guilt, a harshly religious background in which sex is considered evil, or cold unloving childhood relationships. Also common is the need to maintain control over emotions, deep-seated conflicts over being female, and extreme distrust of others, especially males (Masters & Johnson, 1970).

Question: How does treatment proceed?

Treatment at the Cornell clinic includes sensate focus, genital stimulation by the woman's partner, and "nondemanding" intercourse controlled by the woman. With success in these initial stages, full intercourse is gradually instituted. As sexual training proceeds, psychological conflicts and dynamics typically appear, and as they do, they are treated in separate counseling sessions (Kaplan, 1974).

Female Orgasmic Dysfunction   The most prevalent sexual complaint among women is orgasmic dysfunction, an inability to reach orgasm during intercourse. Often it is clear in such cases that the woman is not completely unresponsive; rather, she is unresponsive in the context of a relationship—she may easily reach orgasm by masturbation, but not in intercourse.

Question: Then couldn't the woman's partner be at fault?

Sex therapists try to avoid finding fault or placing blame. However, it is true that the male partner must be sexually adequate in terms of freedom from premature ejaculation, and that he must have a commitment to ensuring gratification of the woman. Some instances of "orgasmic dysfunction" can be traced to inadequate stimulation or faulty technique on the part of the male. Even when this is the case, sexual adjustment difficulties are best viewed as a problem the couple shares, not just as the "woman's problem" or the "man's problem."

If we focus only on the woman, the most common source of orgasmic difficulties is overcontrol of sexual response. Female orgasm requires a degree of abandonment to erotic feelings. It is therefore inhibited by ambivalence or hostility toward the relationship, by guilt, by fears of expressing sexual needs, and by tendencies to control and intellectualize erotic feelings. The woman is unable to let go and enjoy the flow of pleasurable sensations.

In Helen Kaplan's treatment program, nonorgasmic women are first trained to focus on their sexual responsiveness through masturbation or manual stimulation by a partner. As the woman becomes consistently orgasmic in these circumstances, her responsiveness is gradually transferred to intercourse. Couples also typically learn alternative positions and techniques of lovemaking designed to increase clitoral stimulation. At the same time, communication between partners is stressed, especially with reference to the woman's sexual value system (expectations, motivations, preferences).

Vaginismus   In the condition known as *vaginismus,* muscle spasms make intercourse impossible. Vaginismus is often accompanied by obvious fears of intercourse, and where fear is absent, high levels of anxiety are present. Vaginismus therefore appears to be a phobic response to intercourse. Predictably, causative factors include experiences of painful intercourse, rape and/or brutal and frightening sexual encounters, fear of men, misinformation about sex (belief that it is injurious), and fear of the specific male partner (Kaplan, 1974).

Treatment of vaginismus, carried out within the marital unit, is similar to what might be done for a nonsexual phobia. It includes extinction of conditioned muscle spasms by progressive relaxation of the vagina, desensitization of fears of intercourse, and masturbation or manual stimulation to associate pleasure with sexual approach by the male partner. Hypnosis has also been used in some cases with success (Kaplan, 1974).

Summary   Solving sexual problems can be difficult. The problems described are rarely solved without professional help (a possible exception is premature ejaculation). If a serious sexual difficulty is not resolved in a reasonable amount of time, the aid of an appropri-

Applications: Sexual Problems

ately trained psychologist, physician, or counselor should be sought. The longer the problem is ignored, the more difficult it is to solve.

Sexual Adjustment

Question: What can be done to improve sexual adjustment?

Often it is useless to separate sexual adjustment from the broader context of a relationship. Conflict and unresolved anger in other areas frequently take their toll in sexual adjustment; conversely, mutually satisfying relationships tend to carry over into sexual relations. Sex is not just a performance or a skill to be mastered like playing tennis. It is a form of communication and an extension of a relationship. Couples with strong and open relationships can probably survive most sexual problems. A couple with a satisfactory sex life but a poor relationship rarely lasts.

Sex researchers and therapists Masters and Johnson (1970) have discussed how sexual partners can best approach disagreements about each other's sexual needs and wishes. When disagreements arise over issues such as frequency of intercourse, who initiates lovemaking, or what behavior is appropriate, Masters and Johnson believe that the rule should be "each partner must accept the other as the final authority on his or her own feelings."

Partners are urged to give feedback about their feelings by following what therapists call the "touch and ask" rule: Touching and caressing should often be followed by questions such as, "Does that feel good?" "Do you like that?" and so forth (Knox, 1984). When problems do arise, partners are urged to be *responsive* to each other's needs at an *emotional* level and to recognize that all sexual problems are *mutual*. Failures should always be shared without placing blame. Masters and Johnson believe that it is particularly important to avoid the "numbers game." That is, couples should avoid being influenced by statistics on the "average" frequency of intercourse, by stereotypes about sexual potency, and by the superhuman sexual exploits portrayed in movies and magazines.

Question: Are there any other guidelines for maintaining a healthy emotional relationship?

In a study that compared happily married couples with unhappily married couples, Navran (1967) found that in almost every regard the happily married couples showed superior *communication* skills. Many theorists agree that communication is facilitated by observing the following guidelines (after Bach & Wyden, 1969).

Avoid "Gunnysacking"   Persistent feelings, whether positive or negative, need to be expressed. Gunnysacking refers to saving up feelings and complaints. These are then "dumped" during an argument or used as ammunition in a fight. Gunnysacking is very destructive to a relationship.

Be Open about Feelings   Happy couples not only talk more, they convey more personal feelings and show greater sensitivity to their partners' feelings.

. . . in a healthy relationship, each partner feels free to express his likes, dislikes, wants, wishes, feelings, impulses, and the other person feels free to react with like honesty to these. In such a relationship, there will be tears, laughter, sensuality, irritation, anger, fear, baby-like behavior, and so on. (Jourard, 1963)

Don't Attack the Other Person's Character   Whenever possible, expressions of negative feelings should be given as statements of one's own feelings, not as statements of blame. It is far more constructive to say, "It makes me angry when you leave things around the house" than it is to say, "You're a slob!"

Don't Try to "Win" a Fight   Constructive fights are aimed at resolving shared differences, not at establishing who is right or wrong, superior or inferior.

Recognize that Anger Is Appropriate   Constructive and destructive fights are not distinguished by whether anger is expressed. A fight is a fight, and anger is appropriate. As is the case with any other emotion in a relationship, anger should be expressed. However, constructive expression of anger requires that couples fight fair by sticking to the real issues and by not "hitting below the belt."

As a last point, it is worth restating that sexual adjustment and loving relationships are interdependent. As

Applications: Sexual Problems

one observer put it, when sex goes well it's 15 percent of a relationship, and when it goes badly it's 85 percent (Knox, 1984). As a shared pleasure, a form of intimacy, a means of communication, and a haven from everyday tensions, a positive sexual relationship can do much to enhance a couple's mutual understanding and caring. Likewise, an honest, equitable, and affectionate out-of-bed relationship contributes greatly to sexual satisfaction (Hatfield et al., 1982).

Learning Check

1. Males suffering from primary impotence have never been able to produce or maintain an erection.   T or F?
2. According to the latest figures, most cases of impotence are caused by physical problems.   T or F?
3. Sensate focus is the most common treatment for premature ejaculation.   T or F?
4. Premature ejaculation is considered the rarest of the male sexual adjustment problems.   T or F?
5. As it is for impotence, the sensate focus technique is a primary treatment mode for female general sexual dysfunction.   T or F?
6. Vaginismus appears to be a phobic response to sexual intercourse.   T or F?
7. Masters and Johnson urge sexual partners to recognize that all sexual problems are mutual, they are not just one partner's problem.   T or F?

Answers: 1. T 2. F 3. T 4. F 5. T 6. T 7. T

Chapter Summary

■ Physical differences between males and females can be divided into *primary sexual characteristics* (genital and reproductive organs) and *secondary sexual characteristics* (other bodily features). Reproductive maturity in females is signaled by the *menarche* (the onset of menstruation). The development of both primary and secondary sexual characteristics is influenced by *androgens* (male sex hormones) and *estrogens* (female sex hormones).

■ Gender can be broken down into *genetic sex, gonadal sex, hormonal sex, genital sex,* and *gender identity.*

■ Gender development begins with genetic sex (XX or XY chromosomes). It is then influenced by prenatal hormonal influences. *Androgen insensitivity,* exposure to *progestin,* the *androgenital syndrome,* and similar problems can cause problems in the formation of the genitals. Resulting gender ambiguities are called *hermaphroditism.*

■ Some researchers believe that prenatal hormones can exert a *biological biasing effect* on later psychosexual development. Most, however, place greater emphasis on learned *gender identity* and the effect of *sex roles* and *sex role socialization* on behavior. Sex role socialization in particular seems to account for most observed male/female differences.

■ Sexual behavior is quite "natural," being apparent soon after birth and expressed in various ways throughout life. There appears to be little difference in sexual responsiveness between males and females.

■ There is some evidence that the sex drive peaks at a later age for females than it does for males. Sex drive in both males and females may be related to bodily levels of androgen. *Nocturnal orgasms* are a normal, but relatively minor, form of sexual release. *Castration* may or may not influence sex drive in humans.

■ *Masturbation* is a normal and completely acceptable behavior practiced by large portions of the population. For many, masturbation is an important part of sexual self-discovery. It is valid in marriage and normally has no harmful effects.

■ A significant minority of adults are *homosexual,* being consistently attracted to sexual activity with members of the same sex. As a group homosexual men and women do not differ psychologically from heterosexuals.

■ Human sexual response can be divided into four phases: (1) *excitement*, (2) *plateau*, (3) *orgasm*, and (4) *resolution*. Both males and females may go through all four stages in 4 or 5 minutes. But during intercourse, most females typically take longer than this—from 10 to 20 minutes. There do not appear to be any differences between "vaginal orgasms" and "clitoral orgasms" in the female. Mutual orgasm is no longer considered the ideal in lovemaking.

■ Attitudes toward sex have become more liberalized, but actual changes in sexual behavior have been rather gradual. Generally speaking, the greatest change has been in the number of people willing to talk openly about sex. The next greatest change has been a greater acceptance of female sexuality and narrowing of differences in male and female patterns of sexual behavior.

■ The principal male problems in sexual adjustment are: *impotence, premature ejaculation,* and *retarded ejaculation*; for women they are: *general sexual dysfunction, orgasmic dysfunction,* and *vaginismus.* Behavioral methods and counseling techniques have been developed to alleviate each problem. However, most sexual adjustment problems are closely linked to the general health of a couple's overall relationship.

Exploration

Touching—Does It Always Have Sexual Implications?

The whole thing began because Sidney Jourard is a people watcher. One day, sitting in a coffeehouse in San Juan, Puerto Rico, where he was a Peace Corps consultant, he wondered how many times the couple at the next table would touch each other in 1 hour. During the next 2 years, he did the same thing in London and Paris while studying at London's Tavistock Clinic. When he went to Gainesville, Florida, to teach psychology at the University of Florida, he checked out an Amercian couple for the 1 hour. The two people at the Gainesville table touched each other 2 times in 1 hour. In Paris the touch total for 1 hour was 110. In San Juan, 180. And in London? In London, the two people touched each other not at all.

From this information you must draw you own conclusions. Jourard, back at Gainesville, Florida, teaching, being a therapist, and practicing hatha-yoga, refused to. But his interest led him to make further surveys.

He gave booklets to his Gainesville students, 54 male and 84 female. Each booklet contained four diagrams of the body divided into 24 zones, the idea lifted (he says with a straight face) from a butcher's meat chart. He then asked his students to report, anonymously of course, which area of their bodies had been touched by mother, father, best-friend-same-sex, and best-friend-opposite-sex. Furthermore, each student was asked to show which zones he or she had

touched on these four persons. Time range: within the last year. The charts in Fig. 24–6 show the result.

Here Jourard *will* draw conclusions about "body accessibility."

"If you're out of love," says the professor, "you're out of touch."

"There isn't a great deal of body contact going on outside the strictly sexual context. It's almost as if all possible meanings of a touch are eliminated except the caress with the sexually arousing intent. . . . Most regions of a young adult's body remain untouched unless one has a close friend of the opposite sex, and that depends on the relationship going on between them."

One of our touch taboos, then, is that we equate touch with sexuality. Therefore, unless the relationship is sexual, *mustn't touch.*

Jourard goes on to say that in family physical contact the daughters are "the favored ones." A girl's parents touch her more than they would if she were a boy. Right up into her twenties. Parents stop touching boys about the time they reach what used to be called the Age of Reason—when one can commit sin. Furthermore, a girl's mother is allowed, or allows herself (having herself once been a favored one), to give frequent touches to a girl's hair. One-half of the parents get to touch her on the lips, and half manage a literal pat on the back. But—taboo, taboo— only 13 percent of the girls received a paternal pat on the bot-

tom, and none of the girls touched or were touched by their fathers in the genital area. (Not quite the case with regard to male students and Mamma.)

Outside the Best-Friend-Opposite-Sex category very little touching goes on, but when it does happen between lovers, the professor says, "There is a virtual deluge of physical contact all over the body. . . . I suspect that the transformation from virginity or even preorgasmic existence to the experience of having a sexual climax is so radical as to be equivalent to a kind of rebirth."

For Jourard, in our maddeningly crowded world, touch may be our salvation. "I think that body contact has the function of confirming one's bodily being," he says. Yet how can one learn to touch lovingly if one is not permitted to touch and be touched when young? To touch and be touched at times *other* than when making love?

"It's a blunted way of life," Jourard says. "People need physical contact to increase awareness and sensitivity to the body. But, instead, we use our relationship with others as a means to increase our status and social position. We are afraid to let others get close because then we are trapped. . . . The price we pay for this estrangement is loneliness." (The preceding article was written by H. E. F. Donohue, 1968)

Exploration: Touching—Does It Always Have Sexual Implications?

WHERE AMERICAN MALES ARE TOUCHED

By mother

By father

By same
sex friend

By opposite
sex friend

WHERE AMERICAN FEMALES ARE TOUCHED

By mother

By father

By same
sex friend

By opposite
sex friend

76–100%   51–75%   26–50%   0–25%

Fig. 24–6 *Results of Jourard's study of body accessibility. Figures shown are the percentages of young adults touched in each body area, during a 1 year period, by the persons listed. Touching patterns are highly influenced by culture. People in other countries touch much more, or less, than is customary in the United States. (After Jourard, 1966.)*

Exploration: Touching—Does It Always Have Sexual Implications?

Learning Check

1. In his first casual observations, Jourard noted the highest rates of touching in
   a. Florida   *b.* France   *c.* Puerto Rico   *d.* England
2. Within the family, boys are typically touched more by parents than girls are.   T or F?
3. Jourard recorded the highest rates of touching by
   a. mothers   *b.* fathers   *c.* same sex friends   *d.* opposite sex friends
4. In our culture the hands are the most accepted areas of the body for touching by others.   T or F?

Answers: 1. c   2. F   3. d   4. T

Questions for Discussion

1. Do your patterns of touching and being touched correspond to those found by Jourard?
2. In what ways does sexual contact differ from nonsexual touching? Do you feel as Jourard does that people should touch more? Why or why not?
3. Would you be jealous if your spouse or lover were touched (in a nonsexual way) by a person of the same sex? Opposite sex?
4. Do you think the "sexual revolution" will increase touching by encouraging openness or decrease it by defining more casual touching as potentially sexual?
5. Imagine that you were born as a member of the opposite sex. In what ways would your life to date have been different? (Consider relationships, self-image, clothing, recreation, interests, career plans, and so forth.)
6. In your opinion what are the advantages and disadvantages of distinctly different male/female sex roles?
7. Mentally change your male friends to females and your female friends to males. Can you separate the "human being" or "core person" from your friends' normal gender identities and sex roles? What effect does this have on your perception of others?
8. Female sexual behavior appears to be changing more rapidly than is male behavior. To what do you attribute the different rate of change?
9. Recall your own education about sexuality. In what ways and at what age would you recommend that children learn about sex?

Chapter 25

Social Psychology I

Chapter Preview

To live alone, one must be either an animal or a god.

Aristotle

No man is an Iland, intire of itselfe.

John Donne

The Social Animal

Your assignment, should you accept it, is this: You have been given a written message and the name, address, and occupation of the person who should receive it. This "target person" lives over 1500 miles away in a city you have never visited. You are allowed to move the message through the mail, but you may send it only to a first-name acquaintance. That person, in turn, must mail the message only to one of his or her first-name acquaintances. The message is to be moved in this manner until it reaches the target person, whom the previous person must know by name.

Sound impossible? Social psychologist Stanley Milgram and his associates asked a number of people to try moving a message in this way. Amazingly, about one message in five made it. Even more amazing was the number of people needed to complete a chain between two strangers separated by half a continent. The average number of "links" required was about seven people (Korte & Milgram, 1970; Milgram, 1967)!

Question: How is that possible?

Actually, the seven-link average is not as astounding as it might seem. Each of us is enmeshed in a complex network of social relationships, and each person's network overlaps with many others. If you know hundreds of people, and each of them knows hundreds more, a chain of seven people can create millions of possible interconnections. Undeniably, humans are social animals.

Social psychology *is the study of how people behave in the presence (real or implied) of others. Some groups are formal and organized; others are unorganized. All influence the behavior of their members. The fascinating interplay of individual and group behavior has been the target of an immense amount of psychological study; too much, in fact, for us to cover in any detail. Therefore, this chapter and the next are social psychology "samplers." It is hoped that you will find the topics selected interesting and thought provoking.*

Survey Questions How does group membership affect individual behavior? What unspoken rules govern the use of personal space? How do we perceive the motives of others and the causes of our own behavior? Why do people affiliate? What factors influence interpersonal attraction? What have social psychologists learned about conformity, social power, obedience, and compliance? How does self-assertion differ from aggression? What is a social trap?

Resources

Humans in a Social Context— People, People Everywhere

We are born into an organized society. Established values, expectations, and behavior patterns are present when we arrive. So too is **culture,** an ongoing pattern of life that is passed from one generation to the next. Some readily visible aspects of culture are language, marriage customs, concepts of ownership, and sex roles.

Groups The groups to which a person belongs form his or her most immediate day-to-day social environment. Each person is a member of many groups: the family, teams, church groups, work groups, and so on. In each group we occupy a *position* in the structure of the group. **Roles** are different expected behavior patterns displayed in connection with various social positions. Different expectations are associated with playing each of the following

roles: mother, teacher, employer, student. Some roles are **ascribed,** meaning they are not under the individual's control: male or female, adolescent, inmate. **Achieved** roles are those attained voluntarily, or by special effort: wife, teacher, scientist, bandleader (Fig. 25–1).

Question: What effect does role playing have on behavior?

Roles allow us to anticipate the behavior of others. When a person is acting as a physician, mother, clerk, or police officer, certain behaviors are expected. In general, roles are quite useful because they streamline many of our daily interactions with others. However, roles have a negative side too. It is not unusual for a person to occupy two or more conflicting roles. Getting caught in a **role conflict** can be quite uncomfortable or frustrating. Consider, for example, the traffic court judge whose son is brought before her with a violation, or the teacher who must flunk a close friend's daughter.

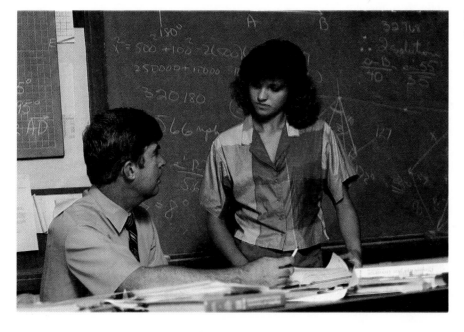

Fig. 25–1 *Roles have a powerful impact on social behavior.*

The impact of roles is dramatically illustrated by an experiment conducted by psychologist Philip Zimbardo and his students at Stanford University. In this experiment normal, healthy, male college students were paid $15 a day to serve as "inmates" and "guards" in a simulated prison (Zimbardo et al., 1973).

On the second day of their "imprisonment," the prisoners staged a number of disturbances, but their rebellion was quickly suppressed by the guards. Over the next few days the guards behaved with increasing brutality and the prisoners became more traumatized, passive, and dehumanized. Four prisoners had to be released in the first 4 days because of reactions such as hysterical crying, confusion, and severe depression. Each day the guards tormented the prisoners with more frequent commands, insults, and demeaning tasks. After 6 days the experiment was halted.

What had happened? Zimbardo's interpretation is that the roles—prisoner and guard—assigned to participants were so powerful that in just a matter of days the experiment had become "reality" for those involved. Afterward, many of the guards found it hard to believe their own behavior. As one recalled, "I was surprised at myself. . . . I made them call each other names and clean toilets out with their bare hands. I practically considered the prisoners cattle" (Zimbardo, 1973). It would seem that the source of many destructive human relationships can be found in destructive roles.

Position in a group also determines one's **status.** In most groups higher status is associated with special privileges and respect. Status can operate very subtly to influence behavior in many situations. For example, in one interesting experiment researchers left dimes in phone booths. When subjects entered the booths, they were approached by a researcher who said, "Excuse me, I think I left a dime in this phone booth a few minutes ago. Did you find it?" When the researcher was well dressed, 75 percent of the people returned the dime, but only 38 percent returned it to poorly dressed researchers (Bickman, 1974). Perhaps the better treatment given "higher status" individuals in this situation explains some of the American preoccupation with status symbols.

Question: Are there other dimensions of group membership?

Groups are made up of people who are in some way interrelated. Two important dimensions of any group are its *structure* and *cohesiveness.* **Group structure** is the organization of roles, communication pathways, and power in the group. Organized groups such as the Army or an ath-

letic team have a high degree of structure. Informal friendship groups may or may not be highly structured. **Group cohesiveness** is basically an indication of the degree of attraction among group members. Cohesiveness is the basis for much of the power that groups exert over their members.

A very important aspect of the functioning of any group is its norms. **Norms** are standards of conduct that prescribe appropriate behavior in a given situation. If you have the slightest doubt about the existence of powerful group norms, Stanley Milgram suggests this test: Board a crowded bus, find a seat, and begin singing loudly in your fullest voice. Milgram's guess is that no more than 1 person in 100 could actually carry out these instructions.

Question: How are norms formed?

One early investigation of the formation of group norms made use of a striking illusion called the **autokinetic effect.** In a completely darkened room, a stationary pinpoint of light will appear to drift or move about (it is therefore "autokinetic" or "self-moving"). Muzafer Sherif (1935) found that estimates of how far the light moves vary widely from person to person. However, when two or more people give estimates at the same time, their judgments rapidly converge. There is a similar convergence of attitudes, beliefs, and behavior among members of most groups. A good example of such convergence can be found in norms governing the use of *personal space.* Since personal space is an intriguing topic in its own right, let's take a moment to examine it.

Personal Space—
Invisible Boundaries

An interesting aspect of social behavior is the effort people expend to regulate the space around their bodies. Each person has an invisible "spatial envelope" that defines his or her **personal space** and extends "I" or "me" boundaries past the skin.

Question: What effect does personal space have on behavior?

Maintaining and regulating personal space directly affects many social interactions. There are unspoken rules covering the interpersonal distance considered appropriate for formal business, casual conversation, waiting in line with strangers, and other situations. The study of rules for the personal use of space is called **proxemics** (Hall, 1974) (Fig. 25–2).

Fig. 25–2 *The use of space in public places is governed by unspoken norms, or "rules," about what is appropriate.*

The existence of personal space and the nature of proxemics can be demonstrated by "invading" the space of another person. The next time you are talking with an acquaintance, move closer and watch the reaction. Most people show immediate signs of discomfort and step back to reestablish their original distance. Those who hold their ground will turn to the side, look away, or position an arm in front of themselves as a kind of barrier to intrusion. If you persistently edge toward your subjects, you should find it easy to move them several feet from their original positions.

Question: Would this technique work with a good friend?

Possibly not. Conventions governing comfortable or acceptable distances vary according to relationships as well as activities. Hall (1966) identifies four basic zones (listed distances apply to North American culture):

1. **Intimate Distance.** For most American adults the most private personal space extends about 18 inches out from the skin. Entry within this space is reserved for special people or circumstances. Lovemaking, comforting others, cuddling children, and massage all take place within this space. So does wrestling!
2. **Personal Distance.** This is the distance maintained in comfortable interaction with friends. It extends from about 1½ to 4 feet from the body. Personal distance basically keeps people within "arm's reach" of each other.
3. **Social Distance.** Impersonal business and casual social gatherings take place in a range of about 4 to 12 feet. This distance eliminates most possibilities of touching and formalizes conversation by requiring greater voice projection. "Important people" in many offices use the width of their imposing desks to maintain social distance while conducting business.
4. **Public Distance.** When people are separated by more than 12 feet, interactions take on a decidedly formal quality. People look "flat," and the voice must be raised. Formal speeches, lectures, business meetings, and the like are conducted at public distance.

Because of the consistencies of spatial behavior in our culture, you can learn much about your relationship to others by observing the distance you most comfortably hold between yourselves. Watch for this dimension in your daily social activities.

We have now explored some basic facts of social life as well as a striking example of group norms. In the next section we will consider another interesting aspect of social behavior: a kind of impromptu detective work that we engage in each day, in which we try to guess the motives of others and the causes of their actions. Let's see how this is done.

Social Perception— Behind the Mask

As much as we might like to think otherwise, it is probably impossible to completely know another person. In fact, in many instances we must form impressions of people from only the smallest shreds of evidence. How do we form such impressions? How do they affect our behavior? Many of the answers lie in **attribution,** the process of making inferences about behavior. (Attribution was also discussed briefly in Chapter 13.) To learn how we fill in the "person behind the mask," let's further explore the making of attributions.

Attribution Theory

Two people enter a restaurant and order different meals. One person tastes her food, then salts it. The second salts his food before tasting it. How would you explain their behavior? In the first instance you might assume that the *food* needed salt. If so, you have attributed the woman's actions to an **external** cause. In the second case you might be more inclined to conclude that the man must really *like* salt. If so, you would be saying that the cause of his behavior is **internal** (McGee & Snyder, 1975).

Question: What effects do such interpretations have?

It is difficult to fully understand social behavior without considering internal and external attributions. For instance, let's say that Jim, who is in one of your classes, seems to avoid you. You see Jim at a market. Do you say hello to him? It could depend on how you have explained Jim's actions to yourself (Wegner & Vallacher, 1977). Have you assumed his avoidance is caused by shyness? Coincidence? Dislike?

Question: How do people make such judgments?

Making Attributions Two factors that greatly influence attribution are the **consistency** and **distinctiveness** of a person's behavior (Kelly, 1967). If Jim has consistently avoided you, it is clear that he was not just in a bad mood on several occasions, so coincidence is ruled out. Still, Jim's avoidance could mean he is shy, not that he dislikes you. This is why distinctiveness is also important. If Jim seems to avoid others too, you may conclude that he is shy. If his avoidance is consistently and distinctively linked with you, you will probably assume that he dislikes you. You could be wrong, of course, but your behavior toward Jim will change just the same.

To infer causes, we typically take into account the behavior of the **actor,** the **object** of the action, and the **setting** in which the action occurs (Kelly, 1967). Imagine, for example, that someone compliments your taste in clothes. If you are at a picnic, you may attribute this compliment to what you are wearing (the "object"), unless, of course, you're wearing your worst "grubbies." If you are, you may simply assume the person (or "actor") is friendly, or tactful. However, if you are at a clothing store and a salesperson compliments you, you will probably attribute it to the setting—not to what you are wearing or to the salesperson's true feelings. In making attributions we are very sensitive to **situational demands.** When a person is quiet and polite in church or at a funeral, it tells us little about the individual's motives. The situation demands such behavior.

When situational demands are quite strong, we tend to **discount** claims that a person's actions are internally caused. For example, you have probably discounted the sincerity of professional athletes who endorse shaving creams, hair tonics, deodorants, and the like. Obviously, the athletes' endorsements are well explained by the large sums of money they receive. It's not necessary to assume they actually *like* the products they sell.

Consensus (or agreement) is another factor affecting attribution. A consensus in the behavior of a number of people implies that the behavior has an external cause. If millions of people go to see a particular movie, we tend to say *the movie* is good. If someone you know goes to see a movie six times when others are staying away in droves, the tendency is to assume *the person* likes "that type of movie."

Actor and Observer Let's say that at the last five parties you have attended, you've seen a woman named Pam. Based on this, you assume that Pam is outgoing and likes to socialize. You see Pam at yet another gathering and mention that she seems to like parties. She says, "Actually, I hate these parties, but I get invited to play my tuba at them. My music teacher says I need to practice in front of an audience, so I keep attending these dumb events. Want to hear a Sousa march?"

We seldom know the real reasons for others' actions. This is why we tend to infer causes from *circumstances.* However, in doing so, we often make mistakes like the one just described. The most common error is to attribute the actions of *others* to *internal causes* while attributing our *own* behavior to situations (*external causes*) (Jones & Nisbett, 1971; Kelly, 1971). This mistake is made so often that it is called the **fundamental attributional error** (Ross, 1977).

Psychologists have found that we consistently attribute the behavior of others to their wants, motives, and personality traits. In contrast, we tend to find external explanations for our own behavior. No doubt you chose *your* major in school because of what it has to offer; other students choose *their* majors because of the kind of people they are (Wegner & Vallacher, 1977). Or, other people who don't leave tips in restaurants are cheapskates; if you don't leave a tip, it's because the service was bad.

Implications   As you can see, attribution theory attempts to summarize how we think about ourselves and others. It also tries to identify some of the consistent errors or biases in our interpretations. In addition to providing a better understanding of behavior, attribution theory has helped identify some practical problems. Let's conclude with a brief example.

Ye Old Double Standard   Attribution research has uncovered an interesting double standard for men and women. In a study by Deaux and Emswiller (1974), men and women overheard a male or female perform extremely well on a perception task. Subjects were then asked to rate whether the test taker's success was due to his or her ability, to luck, or to some combination of the two. Both men and women attributed male success mainly to skill and women's performances mainly to luck! This was true, even though male and female performances were identical. No doubt, such attributions dog the heels of many talented and successful women.

Learning Check

1. *Male, female,* and *adolescent* are examples of _____ roles.

2. Status refers to a set of expected behaviors associated with a social position.   T or F?

3. Research has shown that the number of first-name acquaintances needed to interconnect two widely separated strangers averages about seven people.   T or F?

4. The Stanford prison experiment demonstrated the powerful influence of the autokinetic effect on behavior.   T or F?

5. Social psychology is the study of how people behave _____.

6. If two people position themselves 5 feet apart while conversing, they are separated by a gap referred to as _____ distance.

7. When situational demands are strong, we tend to attribute a person's actions to internal causes.   T or F?

8. The fundamental attributional error is to attribute the actions of others to internal causes, while attributing our own behavior to external causes.   T or F?

Answers: 1. ascribed 2. F 3. T 4. F 5. in the presence of others 6. social 7. F 8. T

The Need for Affiliation— Come Together

Question: Why do people choose to associate with others?

We have already observed that the **need to affiliate** appears to be a basic human characteristic. Why? Probably because affiliation helps meet needs for approval, support, friendship, and information. We also seek company to alleviate fear or anxiety. An experiment in which college women were threatened with painful electric shock serves as an illustration.

Zilstein's Shock Shop

A man introduced as Dr. Gregor Zilstein ominously explained to arriving subjects, "We would like to give each of you a series of electric shocks. . . . These shocks will hurt, they will be painful." In the room was a frightening electrical device that seemed to verify Zilstein's intentions. While waiting to be shocked, each subject was given a choice of waiting alone or with other subjects. Women frightened in this way more often chose to wait with others than did subjects told that the shock would be a mild tickle or tingle. (Schachter, 1959)

Apparently the frightened women found it comforting or reassuring to be with others. The tempting conclusion is: "Misery loves company." But this is not completely accurate. In a later experiment, women expecting to be shocked were given the option of waiting with other shock subjects, with women waiting to see their advisers, or alone. Most subjects chose to wait with other future "victims." In short, misery seems to love miserable company! In general, we tend to seek the company of people in circumstances similar to our own.

Question: Is there a reason for this?

Yes. Other people provide information for evaluating one's own reactions. When a situation is threatening or unfamiliar, or when a person is in doubt, *social comparisons* serve as a guide for behavior.

Social Comparison Theory   In some cases objective standards for self-evaluation exist. If I want to know how tall I am, I simply get out a yardstick. But how do I know if I am a good athlete, guitarist, worker, parent, or friend? How do I know if my views on politics, religion, or the latest rock album are correct? The only yardstick available for such evaluations is provided by comparing myself with others.

Eminent social psychologist Leon Festinger (1954) was among the first to point out that group membership fills needs for **social comparison.** When there are no objective standards, we must turn to others as a way of evaluating our actions, feelings, opinions, or abilities. When students congregate to compare notes after a classroom exam, they satisfy needs for social comparison.

Festinger emphasizes that social comparisons are not made randomly or on some ultimate scale. To illustrate, let's say we ask a student if she is a good tennis player. If she were to compare herself with a professional, the answer would be no. But this tells little about her relative ability. In her group of tennis partners, she might be considered an excellent player. Useful personal evaluation requires comparison with people of similar backgrounds, abilities, and circumstances. On a fair scale of comparison, our tennis player knows she is good and takes pride in her skills.

In the same way, thinking of yourself as successful, talented, responsible, or fairly paid depends entirely on whom you compare yourself to. Social comparison theory holds that a desire for self-evaluation determines what groups one joins, and it provides a general motive for associating with others.

Question: Don't people also affiliate out of attraction for one another?

They do, of course. The next section tells why.

Interpersonal Attraction— Social Magnetism?

"Birds of a feather flock together." "Familiarity breeds contempt." "Opposites attract." "Absence makes the heart grow fonder." Interest in what attracts people to one another has spawned an extensive folklore about what factors are important. This is understandable, since **interpersonal attraction** is the basis for most voluntary social relationships.

Question: What attracts people to each other?

Social psychologist Elliot Aronson (1969) lists several factors that determine with whom you are likely to become friends.

1. **Physical Proximity.** It may be difficult to admit, but our friends (or even lovers) are selected more on the basis of opportunity than we might like to believe. Nearness plays a powerful role in determining friendships. In a study of friendship patterns in a married-student housing complex, it was found that the closer people lived to each other, the more likely they were to be friends (Festinger et al., 1950). People in love like to think they have found the "one and only" person in the universe for them. In reality they have probably found the one and only person in a 5-mile radius—or at least within driving distance (Buss, 1985)!

A main reason for proximity's effect is that it increases the *frequency of contact* between people. A variety of laboratory studies show that we are generally attracted to people with whom we have had frequent contact (Saegert et al., 1973). In other words, there does seem to be a boy-next-door or girl-next-door effect in romantic attraction and a folks-next-door effect in friendship (Fig. 25–3).

2. **Physical Attractiveness.** As might be expected, beautiful people are consistently rated more attractive than those of average appearance. This is another example of the *halo effect* (Chapter 18), in which it is assumed that attractive people are also intelligent, witty, honest, and so on.

Being physically attractive seems to be an advantage for both males and females, but in our culture beauty has more influence on a woman's fate than on a man's. For instance, a study of dating patterns of college dormitory residents found a strong relationship between physical beauty in women and their frequency of dating. For men, looks were unrelated to dating frequency (Krebs & Adinolfi, 1975). After marriage there is a tendency for attractive women to be paired with highly educated men with high incomes. For men, however, there is little relationship between attractiveness and the achievement of status (Udry & Eckland, 1984).

If you view this state of affairs as rather shallow and sexist, it may be reassuring to know that beauty is a factor mainly in initial acquaintance. Later, more substantial personal qualities become important (Berscheid & Walster, 1974). It takes more than appearance to make a lasting relationship.

3. Competence. We are also attracted to the talented or competent, but there is an interesting twist to this.

Clever but Clumsy

In an experiment on attraction, college students listened to one of four tapes of a supposed candidate for the "College Quiz Bowl." On two of the tapes the person was represented as highly intelligent; on the other two he was depicted as average in ability. One of the "intelligent" and one of the "average" tapes included an incident in which the candidate clumsily spilled coffee on himself. Those listening to the tapes rated as *most* attractive the superior candidate who blundered, and as *least* attractive the student who was average and clumsy. The superior but clumsy student was more attractive than the student who was only superior. (Aronson, 1969)

The upshot of this experiment seems to be that we like people who are competent, but human.

4. Similarity. Take a moment to mentally list as many of your friends as you can. What do they have in common (other than the joys of knowing you)? It is highly likely that most are close to you in age and of the same sex and race as you are. There will be exceptions, of course. However, similarity on these three dimensions is the general rule for friendships in American culture (Huston & Levinger, 1978).

One of the most consistent findings about interpersonal attraction is that people with similar backgrounds, interests, attitudes, or beliefs are attracted to each other (Byrne, 1971). This is probably at least partially due to the reinforcing value of seeing our beliefs and attitudes affirmed by others. It shows we are "right" and reveals that they are clever people as well! Similarity also affects mate selection—see Highlight 25–1.

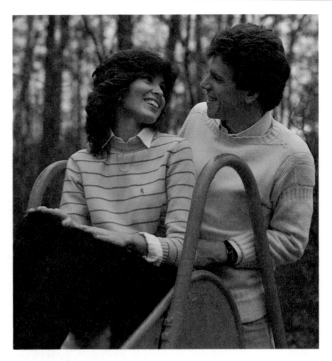

Fig. 25–3 *What attracts people to each other? Proximity and frequency of contact have a surprisingly large impact.*

Question: How do people who are not yet friends learn if they are similar?

Self-Disclosure Getting to know others requires a willingness to talk about more than just the weather, sports, or nuclear physics. At some point you must begin to share private thoughts and feelings and reveal more of your true self. Engaging in such **self-disclosure** is a major step toward friendship. Experiments confirm that we more often reveal ourselves to persons we like than to those we find less attractive (Chaiken & Derlega, 1974).

Disclosing oneself to others requires a degree of trust. Many people play it safe, or "close to the vest," with people they do not know well. Indeed, there are definite norms about when self-disclosure is acceptable and when it is not. Moderate self-disclosure leads to **reciprocity** (a return in kind) (Huston & Levinger, 1978). **Overdisclosure,** however, gives rise to suspicion and reduced attraction (Rubin, 1975). (Imagine standing in line at a market and having the person in front of you say: "Lately I've been thinking about how I really feel about myself. I think that I'm pretty well adjusted, but I occasionally have some questions about my sexual adequacy.") When self-disclosure proceeds at a moderate pace, it is accompanied by

Highlight 25–1
Selecting a Mate—Reflections in a Social Mirror

Ninety percent of all people in Western societies marry at some point. What, beyond attraction, determines how people pair up? The answer is that we tend to marry someone who is like us in almost every way.

A variety of studies show that people who marry are highly similar in age, education, race, religion, and ethnic background. In addition, the correlation of attitudes and opinions for married couples is .5. For mental abilities it is .4, and for socioeconomic status, height, weight, and eye color it is .3. In general, you are far more likely to choose someone similar to yourself as a mate than someone very different.

A second question of interest concerns what traits people look for in a mate. In the United States both men and women agree that the following six qualities are most important: kindness and understanding, intelligence, exciting personality, good health, adaptability, and physical attractiveness. Despite such agreement, men and women do differ on some rankings. Men, for instance, rank physical attractiveness as the third most important feature, whereas women rank it sixth. A second major difference concerns good earning capacity: men rank it eleventh; women rank it eighth. Apparently, for most people romance is leavened with a dash of practicality. Even so, kindness and understanding are ranked first by almost everyone. (Source: Buss, 1985)

---

growing trust and intimacy. When it is too rapid, or inappropriate, we are likely to back off and wonder about the person's motives.

Box 25–1 *Sample love-scale and liking-scale items. Each scale consists of 13 items similar to those shown. Scores on these scales correspond to other indications of love and liking. (Reprinted by permission of Zick Rubin.)*

Love Scale

1. If _____ were feeling bad, my first duty would be to cheer him (her) up.
2. I feel that I can confide in _____ about virtually everything.
3. I find it easy to ignore _____'s faults.

Liking Scale

1. When I am with _____, we almost always are in the same mood.
2. I think that _____ is unusually well-adjusted.
3. I would highly recommend _____ for a responsible job.

Social Exchange Theory As relationships progress, quite often they can be understood in terms of maximizing rewards while minimizing "costs" in any **social exchange.** When a relationship ceases to be attractive, people often say, "I'm not getting anything out of it any more." Actually, they probably are, but their costs—in terms of effort, irritation, or lowered self-esteem—have exceeded their rewards. According to social exchange theory, we unconsciously weigh such rewards and costs. For a relationship to last, it must be *profitable* (its rewards must exceed its costs) for both parties.

Question: Does romantic attraction differ from interpersonal attraction?

Romantic Attraction In an earlier discussion we treated love as an emotion (Chapter 13) and pointed out that passionate or romantic love is marked by heightened arousal. To get another angle on love, psychologist Zick Rubin (1973) chose to think of it as an attitude held by one person toward another. This approach allowed Rubin to develop "liking" and "love" scales (see Box 25–1) to measure each "attitude." Next, Rubin contacted dating couples and asked them to complete each scale twice: once with their date in mind and once for a close friend of the same sex.

Question: What were the results?

Scores for love of partner and love of friend differed more than those for liking (Table 25–1). In other words, dating couples liked *and* loved their partners, but mostly liked their friends. Women, however, were a little more "loving" of their friends than were men. Does this reflect real differences in the strength of male friendships and female friendships? Probably not, since it is more acceptable in our culture for women to express love for one another than it is for men.

Another way in which love and friendship differ is mutual absorption. Romantic love, in contrast to simple liking, usually involves deep **mutual absorption** of the lovers. In other words, lovers (unlike friends) attend almost exclusively to one another. It's not surprising, then, that couples scoring high on Rubin's love scale spend more

Table 25–1   Love and Liking for Date and Same-Sex Close Friend

Condition	Mean Scores	
	Women	Men
Love for partner	89.46	89.37
Liking for partner	88.48	84.65
Love for friend	65.27	55.07
Liking for friend	80.47	79.10

(Source: Rubin, 1970.)

time gazing into each other's eyes than do couples who score low on the scale (Rubin, 1970). As the song says, "Millions of people go by, but they all disappear from view—'cause I only have eyes for you."

Learning Check

Before reading more, check your comprehension by answering the following questions.

1. Women threatened with electric shock in an experiment generally chose to wait alone or with other women not taking part in the experiment.   T or F?

2. The need to affiliate is related to interest in social comparison.   T or F?

3. Social comparisons are made pretty much at random.   T or F?

4. Interpersonal attraction is increased by all but one of the following.   (Which does not fit?)

   physical proximity   competence   similarity   social costs

5. High levels of self-disclosure are reciprocated in most social encounters.   T or F?

6. Women rate their friends higher on the love scale than do men.   T or F?

7. The most striking finding about marriage patterns in the United States is that most people choose mates whose personalities are quite unlike their own.   T or F?

Answers: 1. F   2. T   3. F   4. social costs   5. F   6. T   7. F

Social Influence— Follow the Leader

Question: What is social influence?

Imagine a traffic signal brightly flashing the word WAIT. As you and a number of other pedestrians wait for it to change, a well-dressed man in a suit crosses against the light. How many people follow him? Do you think the answer would be different if the man were dressed in a denim shirt, patched pants, and scuffed shoes?

One of the most heavily researched topics in social psychology concerns the effects of **social influence**. When people interact, they almost always affect one another's behavior. The street-corner setting just described was used in an early experiment on social influence. As you might have guessed, more people followed the well-dressed man than the one dressed in shabby clothes (Lefkowitz et al., 1955).

In another sidewalk experiment, various numbers of people were assembled on a busy New York City street. On cue they all looked at a sixth-floor window across the street. A camera recorded the number of passersby who also stopped to stare. The larger the initial group, the more people were influenced to join in staring at the window (Milgram et al., 1969).

Question: Are there different kinds of social influence?

Social influence ranges from simple suggestion to intensive indoctrination (brainwashing). Everyday behavior is probably most influenced by group pressures for conformity. Conformity situations develop when individuals become aware of differences between themselves and group actions, norms, or values (McGuire, 1969). Let us consider this important dimension of social life in more detail.

Conformity

When John first started working at the Fleegle Flange Factory, he found it easy to process 300 flanges an hour, while those around him averaged only 200. Other workers told him to slow down and take it easy. "I get bored," he said and continued to do 300 flanges an hour. At first John had been welcomed, but now conversations broke up when he approached and other workers laughed at or ignored him when he spoke. Although he never made a conscious decision to conform, in another week John's output had slowed to 200 flanges an hour.

Fig. 25–4 *Conformity is a subtle dimension of daily life. Notice the similarities of clothing and hair styles, among these couples.*

As mentioned earlier, all groups have shared rules of conduct called *norms.* The broadest norms, as defined by overall society, establish "normal" or acceptable behavior in most situations. Comparing hairstyles, habits of speech, dress, eating habits, and social customs in two or more cultures makes it clear that we all conform to social norms. In fact, a degree of uniformity is necessary if we are to interact comfortably. Imagine being totally unable to anticipate the actions of others. In stores, schools, and homes this would be frustrating and disturbing. On the highways it would be lethal.

Perhaps the most basic of all group norms is (as John discovered), "Thou shalt conform!" (Suedfeld, 1966). This is equally true for the Hell's Angels, the Daughters of the American Revolution, a street-corner gang, or the board of directors of a large corporation. Groups of all kinds exert considerable pressures toward uniformity on their members. Like it or not, everyday life is filled with instances of conformity (Fig. 25–4).

Question: How strong are group pressures for conformity?

The Asch Experiment One of the better known experiments on conformity was staged by Solomon Asch in the early 1950s. You can best appreciate Asch's experiment by placing yourself in the position of a subject. Assume that you are seated at a table with six other students. Your task is actually quite simple. On each trial you are asked to select from among three lines the one that matches a standard line (see Fig. 25–5).

As the testing begins, each subject announces an answer for the first card. When your turn comes, you find yourself in complete agreement with the others. "This isn't hard at all," you say to yourself. For several more trials your answers correspond to those of the group. Then comes a shock. All six people announce that line one matches the standard, and you were about to say line three. Suddenly you feel alone and upset. You nervously look at the lines again as the room falls silent. Everyone seems to be staring at you as the experimenter awaits your answer. Do you yield to the group?

In this experiment the other "students" were all accomplices coached to give the wrong answer on about a third of the trials. Few real subjects suspected trickery; hence, the group pressure created was very realistic (Asch, 1956).

Question: How many people yielded to group pressure?

Subjects conformed to the group on about one-third of the critical trials. Of those tested 75 percent yielded at least once. The significance of these results is underscored by the fact that subjects tested alone erred in less than 1 per-

Standard line   Comparison lines

Fig. 25–5 *Stimuli used in Solomon Asch's conformity experiments.*

cent of their judgments. Those who yielded to group pressures were clearly denying what their eyes told them.

Question: Are some people more susceptible to group pressures than others?

A variety of experiments have shown that people with high needs for structure or certainty are more likely to be influenced. People who are anxious, low in self-confidence, or who are concerned with the opinions or approval of others are also more susceptible. Certain situations also encourage conformity, sometimes with disastrous results (see Highlight 25–2).

Question: How do groups enforce norms?

Group Factors in Conformity   In most of our experiences with groups, we have been rewarded with acceptance and approval for conformity and threatened with rejection or ridicule for nonconformity. These reactions are called **group sanctions.** Negative sanctions (or punishments) for nonconformity range from laughter, staring, or social disapproval to complete rejection or formal ostracism. This is illustrated by later experiments in which Asch made up groups of six real subjects and one trained dissenter. When "Mr. Odd" announced his wrong answers, he was greeted with derisive laughter and sidelong glances.

Question: Wouldn't the effectiveness of group sanctions depend on the importance of the group?

Yes. And this is why the Asch experiments are impressive. Since these were only temporary groups, sanctions were informal and rejection had no lasting importance.

Question: What factors, besides importance of the group, affect the degree of conformity?

Earlier, we described an experiment in which passersby were influenced by a group of people staring at a building. We noted that the larger the group, the greater the number of passersby influenced. In Asch's face-to-face groups,

**Highlight 25–2
Groupthink—
Agreement at Any Cost**

What happens when people in positions of power fall prey to pressures for conformity? To find out, Yale psychologist Irving Janis analyzed a collection of disastrous decisions made by government officials. His conclusion? Many such fiascoes are the result of **groupthink**—a compulsion by decision makers to maintain each other's approval, even at the cost of critical thinking. Groupthink has been blamed for many embarrassments, such as the Susan B. Anthony dollar and John F. Kennedy's backing of the Bay of Pigs invasion in Cuba.

The core of groupthink is misguided group loyalty, which prevents members from "rocking the boat" or questioning weak arguments and sloppy thinking. The resulting conformity pressures and self-censorship cause members to believe that there is greater agreement and unanimity than actually exist (Janis & Mann, 1977).

To prevent groupthink, Janis suggests that group leaders should: (1) define each group member's role as that of critical evaluator; (2) avoid stating any personal preferences in the beginning; (3) state the problem factually, without bias; (4) invite a group member or outside person to play devil's advocate. In addition, Janis suggests that there should be a "second-chance" meeting to reevaluate important decisions. That is, each decision should be reached twice. In an age clouded by the threat of nuclear war and similar disasters, even stronger solutions to the problem of groupthink would be welcome. Perhaps we should form a group to think about it?!

the size of the majority also made a difference, but a surprisingly small one. The number of conforming subjects increased dramatically as the majority was increased from two to three people. However, a majority of three produced about as much yielding as a majority of eight. Next time you want to talk someone into (or out of) something, take two friends along and see what a difference it makes! (Sometimes it helps if the two are large and mean looking.)

Even more important than the size of the majority is its **unanimity.** Having at least one person in your corner can greatly reduce pressures to conform. When Asch provided subjects with an ally (who also opposed the majority by giving the correct answer), conformity was lessened. In terms of numbers, a unanimous majority of three is more powerful than eight with one dissenting. Perhaps this ·accounts for the rich diversity of human attitudes, beliefs, opinions, and lifestyles. If you can find at least one other person who sees things as you do (no matter how weird), you can be relatively secure in your opposition to other viewpoints.

Learning Check

1. The effect one person's behavior has on another is called _____ _____.
2. Conformity is a normal aspect of social life.   T or F?
3. Subjects in Solomon Asch's conformity study yielded on about 75 percent of the critical trials.   T or F?
4. Nonconformity is punished by negative group _____.
5. Janis uses the term _____ to describe a compulsion among decision-making groups to maintain an illusion of unanimity.

Answers: 1. social influence 2. T 3. F 4. sanctions 5. groupthink

Social Power— Who Can Do What to Whom?

Here's something to think about: Whereas *strength* is a quality possessed by individuals, *power* is always social—it arises when people come together and disappears when they disperse. In trying to understand the ways people are able to influence each other, it is helpful to distinguish among five types of **social power** (Raven, 1974).

Reward power lies in the ability to reward a person for complying with desired behavior. Teachers try to exert reward power over their students through the use of grades. Employers command reward power by their control of wages and bonuses.

Coercive power is based on the ability to punish a person for failure to comply. Coercive power is the basis for most statute law, in that fines or imprisonment are used to control behavior.

Legitimate power comes from acceptance of a person as an agent of an established social order. For example, elected leaders and supervisors have legitimate power. So does a teacher in the classroom, but outside the classroom that power would have to come from another source.

Referent power is based on respect for or identification with a person or a group. The person "refers to" the source of referent power for direction. Referent power is responsible for much of the conformity observed in groups.

Expert power is based on recognition that another person has knowledge or expertise necessary for achieving a goal. An example is allowing teachers or experts to guide behavior because you believe in their ability to produce desirable results. Physicians, lawyers, psychologists, and plumbers have expert power.

A person who has power in one situation may have very little in another. In those situations where a person has power, he or she is described as an *authority*. In the next section we will investigate *obedience*. Obedience is a special type of conformity to the demands of an authority.

Obedience— Would You Electrocute a Stranger?

The question is this: If ordered to do so, would you administer an electric shock to a man with a known heart condition who is screaming and asking to be released? Certainly we can assume that few people would do so. Or can we? In Nazi Germany obedient soldiers (once average citizens) helped slaughter over 9 million people. Another example of the same phenomenon is an infamous incident during the Vietnam War when Lt. William Calley led a bloody massacre of helpless civilians at My Lai. Do such inhumane acts reflect deep character flaws? Are they the acts of heartless psychopaths or crazed killers? Or are they simply the result of obedience to authority? What are the limits of such obedience? These are questions that puzzled social psychologist Stanley Milgram (1965) when he began a provocative series of studies on obedience.

Question: How did Milgram study obedience?

As was true of the Asch experiments, Milgram's research is best appreciated by imagining yourself as a subject. Place yourself in this situation.

Milgram's Study   Imagine answering a newspaper ad to take part in a "learning" experiment at Yale University. When you arrive, a coin is flipped and a second subject, a pleasant-looking man in his fifties, is designated the "learner." By chance you have become the "teacher."

Your task is to read a list of word pairs to be memorized by the learner. You are to punish him with an electric shock each time he makes a mistake. The learner is taken to an adjacent room and you watch as he is seated in an "electric chair" apparatus and electrodes are attached to his wrists. You are then escorted to your position in front of a "shock generator." On this device is a row of 30 switches labeled from 15 to 450 volts and accompanied by descriptions ranging from "Slight Shock" to "Extreme Intensity Shock" and finally "Danger: Severe Shock." Your instructions are to administer a shock each time the learner makes a mistake. You are to begin with 15 volts and then move one switch (15 volts) higher for each additional mistake.

The experiment begins, and the learner soon makes his first error. You flip a switch. More mistakes. Rapidly you reach the 75-volt level. The learner moans after each shock. At 100 volts he complains he has a heart condition. At 150 volts he no longer wants to continue and demands release. At 300 volts he screams and says he can no longer give answers.

At some point during the experiment, you begin to protest to the experimenter. "That man has a heart condition," you say; "I'm not going to kill that man." The experimenter says, "Please continue." Another shock and another scream from the learner, and you say, "You mean I've got to keep going up the scale? No, sir. I'm not going to give him 450 volts!" The experimenter says, "The experiment requires that you continue." For the remainder of the experiment, the learner refuses to answer any more questions and screams with each shock (Milgram, 1965).

Question: I can't believe many people would do this. What happened?

Milgram also doubted that many people would obey such orders, and when he polled a group of psychiatrists before the experiment, they predicted that less than 1 percent of those tested would obey. The astounding fact is that 65 percent of those tested obeyed completely by going all the

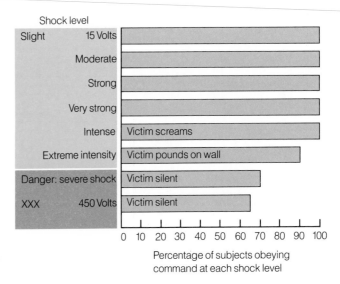

Shock level

Fig. 25–6   *Results of Milgram's obedience experiment. Only a minority of subjects refused to provide shocks, even at the most extreme intensities. The first substantial drop in obedience occurred at the 300-volt level (Milgram, 1963).*

way to the 450-volt level. Virtually no one stopped short of 300 volts ("Severe Shock") (see Fig. 25–6).

Question: Was the "learner" injured?

The time has come to reveal that the "learner" was actually an actor who turned a tape recorder on and off in the "shock room." No shocks were ever administered, but the dilemma for the "teacher" was quite real. Subjects protested, sweated, trembled, stuttered, bit their lips, and laughed nervously. Clearly, they were disturbed by what they were doing, but most obeyed the experimenter's orders.

Question: Why did so many people obey?

Milgram's Follow-up   Some have suggested that the prestige of Yale University contributed to subjects' willingness to obey. Could subjects have assumed that the professor running the experiment would not really allow anyone to be hurt? To investigate this possibility, the experiment was rerun in a shabby office building in nearby Bridgeport, Connecticut. There was nothing in either the location or the experimenter's appearance to inspire confidence. Under these conditions fewer people obeyed (48 percent), but the reduction was minor.

Milgram was quite disturbed by the willingness of people to knuckle under to authority and to senselessly shock someone. In later experiments he tried in various ways to reduce obedience. He found that distance between the

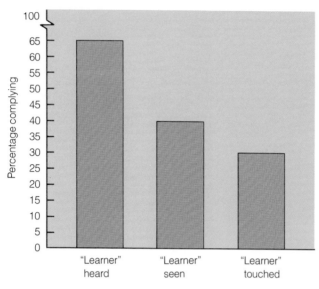

Fig. 25–7 *Physical distance from the "learner" had a significant effect on the percentage of subjects obeying orders.*

"teacher" and the "learner" was of importance. When subjects were in the *same room* as the learner, only 40 percent were fully obedient. When they were *face-to-face* with the learner and were required to force his hand down on a "shock plate," only 30 percent obeyed (Fig. 25–7). *Distance* from the authority also had an effect. When the experimenter delivered his orders over the phone, only 22 percent obeyed.

Milgram's research raises nagging questions about our willingness to commit antisocial or inhumane acts commanded by a "legitimate authority." The excuse so often given by war criminals—"I was only following orders"— takes on new meaning in this light. Milgram suggests that when directions come from an authority, people rationalize that they are not personally responsible for their actions (Fig. 25–8).

Question: Aren't you taking an overly dim view of obedience?

Obedience to authority is obviously necessary and desirable in many circumstances. Just the same, it is probably true, as C. P. Snow (1961) has observed, "When you think of the long and gloomy history of man, you will find more hideous crimes have been committed in the name of obedience than in the name of rebellion." With this in mind, let us end this discussion on a more positive note. In one of his experiments, Milgram found that group support can greatly reduce destructive obedience. When real subjects saw two other "teachers" (both actors) resist orders and walk out of the experiment, only 10 percent continued to obey. Thus, a personal act of courage or moral fortitude by one or two members of a group may free others to disobey misguided or unjust authority.

Fig. 25–8 *Obedience to authority is often necessary and reasonable; however, it can also be destructive.*

Compliance— A Foot in the Door

In *conformity* situations the pressure to "get in line" is usually indirect. When an authority commands *obedience*, the pressure is direct and difficult to resist. There is a third possibility of interest. The term **compliance** has been used to describe situations in which a person with little or no authority makes a direct request to another person (Wrightsman & Deaux, 1981).

Pressures to comply are quite common. For example, a stranger might ask you to yield a phone booth so he can make a call, a saleswoman might suggest that you buy a more expensive watch than you had planned on, or a co-worker might ask you for some money to buy a cup of coffee.

Question: What determines whether a person will comply with a request?

Many factors could be listed, but three stand out as especially interesting. Let's briefly consider each.

The Foot-in-the-Door Effect People who sell door-to-door have long recognized that once they get a foot in the door, a sale is almost a sure thing. To state the **foot-in-the-door** principle more formally, a person who agrees to a small request is later more likely to comply with a larger demand. Evidence suggests, for instance, that if someone asked you to put a large, ugly sign in your front yard to promote safe driving, you would refuse. If, however, you had first agreed to put a small sign in your window, you would later be much more likely to allow the big sign to be placed in your yard (Freedman & Fraser, 1966).

The Door-in-the-Face Effect Let's say that a neighbor comes to your door and asks you to feed his dogs, water his plants, and mow his yard while he is out of town for a month. This is quite a major request—one that most people would probably turn down. Feeling only slightly guilty, you tell your neighbor that you're sorry but you can't help him out. Now, what if the same neighbor returns the next day and asks you if you would at least pick up his mail while he is gone. Chances are very good that you would honor this request, even if you might have resisted it otherwise.

Psychologist Robert Cialdini and his associates coined the term **door-in-the-face effect** to describe the reverse of the foot-in-the-door effect (Cialdini et al., 1975). On some occasions the best way to get a person to agree to a small request is to first make a major request. After the

person has turned down the major request ("slammed the door in your face"), he or she may be more willing to agree to a lesser demand.

The Low-Ball Technique Anyone who has purchased an automobile will recognize a third way of inducing compliance. Automobile dealers are notorious for convincing customers to buy a car by offering "low-ball" prices that undercut the competition. The dealer first gets the customer to agree to buy at an attractively low price. Then, once the customer is committed, various techniques are used to bump the price up before the sale is concluded (see Highlight 25–3). The **low-ball technique,** then, consists of getting a person committed to act and then making the terms of acting less desirable. Another example would be asking someone to loan you $5 and then upping it to $15. Or, you might ask someone if he or she would give you a ride to school in the morning. Only after the person has agreed would you tell her or him that you had to be there at 6 A.M.

Passive Compliance Complying with requests is a normal part of daily social life. At times, however, a willingness to comply can exceed what is reasonable. Researcher Thomas Moriarty (1975) has demonstrated excessive, passive compliance under realistic conditions. Moriarty became interested in the "little murders" of daily life: the personal insults, rebuffs, and sacrifices of dignity that are common. Moriarty observed that many people will put up with almost anything to avoid a confrontation. He decided to put this passive, "no-hassle" attitude to experimental test.

In one experiment, two subjects (one actually an accomplice) were given a difficult test in a very small room. The subjects were seated back-to-back and left alone to work. As soon as the experimenter left, the phoney subject turned on a portable cassette player at full volume. Real subjects who failed to complain were treated to a 17-minute blast of nerve-wracking rock music. The accomplice was instructed to turn the music off only after a third request. In this particular experiment, 80 percent of the subjects said nothing, although they glared, cupped their ears, stopped work, and so forth. Interviews conducted later showed that most subjects were angry or annoyed but were afraid to tell the other "subject" to be quiet.

Question: Could it be that people failed to complain because they didn't want to disrupt the testing?

Yes, it is possible that the passivity observed in this study is unique to the experimental setting. However, when

Highlight 25–3
How to Drive a Hard Bargain

Your local car lot is a good place to see compliance take place. Automobile salespersons play the compliance game daily and get very good at it. If you understand what they are up to, you will have a far better chance of resisting their tactics.

Foot in the Door   The salesperson offers you a test drive. If you accept, you will have made a small commitment of time to a particular car and to the salesperson. The salesperson will then ask you to go to an office and fill out some papers, "just to see what kind of a price" he or she can offer. If you go along, you will be further committed.

The Low-Ball Technique   To get things underway, the salesperson will offer you a very good price for your trade-in or she/he will ask you to make an offer on the new car, "any offer, no matter how low." The salesperson will then ask if you will buy the car if she/he can sell it for the price you state. If you say yes, you have virtually bought the car. Most people find it very difficult to walk away once bargaining has reached this stage.

Once buyers are "hooked" by a low-ball offer, the salesperson goes to the manager to have the sale "approved." On returning, the salesperson will tell you with great disappointment that the dealership would lose money on the deal. "Couldn't you just take a little less for the trade-in or pay a little more for the car?" he or she will ask. At this point many people hesitate and grumble, but most give in and accept some "compromise" price or trade-in amount.

By the time you strike a deal, you can assume that the price you accept will give the dealership the minimum profit it requires on all sales—and probably much more. To add insult to injury, the salesperson will then try to increase the profit by convincing you to add various options to your car—extra mirrors, a stereo system, cruise control, and so forth. All of these items cost less from independent suppliers, so many people pay hundreds of dollars too much for them alone.

To combat all of the preceding, get a final "best offer" in writing. Then walk out. Go to another dealer and see if the salesperson will better the price, in writing. When she/he does, return to the first dealership and negotiate for an even better price—*then* decide where to buy.

Moriarty and his students staged loud conversations behind theater patrons or people studying in a library, very few protested. In other naturalistic experiments, people were accosted in phone booths. The experimenter explained that he had left a ring in the booth and asked if the subject had found it. When the subject said "no," the experimenter demanded that the subject empty his pockets. Most did.

In these and similar situations, people passively accepted having their personal rights trampled, even when objecting presented no threat to their safety. Have we become, as Moriarty puts it, "a nation of willing victims"? Certainly we would hope not. Nevertheless, researchers such as Milgram and Moriarty have identified a significant social problem. We will address this problem again in the Applications section that follows.

Learning Check

1.   An ability to punish others for failure to obey is the basis for:
   a. referent power   *b.* expert power   *c.* legitimate power   *d.* coercive power

2.   Would you "electrocute" a stranger? _____

3.   Obedience in Milgram's experiments was related to:
   a. distance between learner and teacher   *c.* obedience of other teachers
   b. distance between experimenter and teacher   *d.* all of the above

4. Obedience is conformity to _____.

5. By repeating his obedience experiment in a downtown office building, Milgram demonstrated that the prestige of Yale University was the main reason for subjects' willingness to obey in the original experiment.   T or F?

6. The research of Thomas Moriarty and others has shifted to an interest in _____ _____ rather than obedience to authority.

Answers: 1. *d* 2. answer will vary 3. *d* 4. authority 5. F 6. passive compliance

Applications

Assertiveness Training—Standing Up for Your Rights

Have you ever:

Hesitated to question an error on a restaurant bill because you were afraid of making a scene?

Backed out of asking for a raise or a change in working conditions?

Said "yes" when you wanted to say "no"?

Been afraid to question a grade that seemed unfair?

Most of us have been rewarded, first as children, and later as adults, for compliant, obedient, or "good" behavior. Perhaps this is why so many people find it difficult to assert themselves. Or perhaps nonassertion is related to the anxiety that accompanies "making a scene" or feeling disliked by others. Whatever the causes, some people are so seriously inhibited that they suffer tremendous anguish in any situation requiring poise, self-confidence, or self-assertion. Fortunately for these people, behavior therapist Joseph Wolpe (and others) have pioneered a therapeutic technique called *assertiveness training*.

Question: What is done in assertiveness training?

Assertiveness training is a very direct procedure. By using group exercises, videotapes, mirrors, and staged conflicts, the behavior therapist teaches assertive behavior. People learn to practice honesty, disagreeing, questioning authority, and assertive postures and gestures. As their self-confidence improves, nonassertive clients are taken on "field trips" to shops and restaurants where they practice what they have learned.

Nonassertion severe enough to require therapy is unusual. Nevertheless, many people become tense or upset in at least some situations in which they must stand up for their rights. For this reason many people have found the techniques and exercises of assertiveness training helpful. If you have ever eaten a carbonized steak when you ordered it rare, or stood in silent rage as a clerk ignored you, the following discussion will be of interest.

Self-Assertion   The first step in assertiveness training is to convince yourself of three basic rights: You have the right to refuse, to request, and to right a wrong. Self-assertion involves standing up for these rights by speaking out in your own behalf.

Question: Is self-assertion just getting things your own way?

Not at all. A basic distinction can be made between *self-assertion* and *aggressive* behavior. Assertion is a direct, honest expression of feelings and desires. It is not exclusively self-serving, since pent-up anger can be very destructive to relationships. People who are nonassertive are usually patient to a fault. In contrast, aggression does not take into account the feelings or rights of others. Aggression is an attempt to get one's own way no matter what. Assertion techniques emphasize firmness, not attack (see Table 25–2).

The basic idea in assertiveness training is that each assertive action is practiced until it can be repeated even under stress. For example, let's say it really angers you when a store clerk waits on several people who arrived after you did. To improve your assertiveness in this situation, you would begin by *rehearsing* the dialogue, posture, and gestures you would use to

Applications: Assertiveness Training—Standing Up for Your Rights

Table 25–2   Comparison of Assertive, Aggressive, and Nonassertive Behavior

	Actor	Receiver of Behavior
Nonassertive bahavior	Self-denying, inhibited, hurt, and anxious; lets others make choices; goals not achieved	Feels sympathy, guilt, or contempt for actor; achieves goals at actor's expense
Aggressive behavior	Achieves goals at others' expense; expresses feelings, but hurts others; chooses for others or puts them down	Feels hurt, defensive, humiliated, or taken advantage of; does not meet own needs
Assertive behavior	Self-enhancing; acts in own best interests; expresses feelings; respects rights of others; goals usually achieved, self-respect maintained	Needs respected and feelings expressed; may achieve goal; self-worth maintained

After Alberti & Emmons, 1978.

confront the clerk or the other customer. Working in front of a mirror can be very helpful. If possible, you should *role play* the scene with a friend. Be sure to have your friend take the part of a really aggressive or irresponsible clerk, as well as a cooperative one. Rehearsal and role playing should also be used when you expect a possible confrontation with someone—for example, if you were going to ask for a raise, challenge a grade, or confront a landlord.

Question: Is that all there is to it?

No. Another important principle is *overlearning*. When you rehearse or role play assertive behavior, it is essential to continue practice until your responses become almost automatic. This helps prevent you from getting flustered in the actual situation.

One more technique you may find useful is the *broken record*. A good way to prevent assertion from becoming aggression is to simply restate your request as many times and as many ways as necessary. As an illustration, let's say you are returning a pair of shoes to a store. After two wearings the shoes fell apart, but you bought them 2 months ago and no longer have a receipt. The broken-record technique sounds something like this:

Customer: I would like to have these shoes replaced.
Clerk: Do you have a receipt?
Customer: No, but I bought them here and since they are defective, I would like to have you replace them.

Clerk: I can't do that without a receipt.
Customer: I understand that, but I want them replaced.
Clerk: Well, if you'll come back this afternoon and talk to the manager . . .
Customer: I've brought these shoes in because they are defective.
Clerk: Well, I'm not authorized to replace them.
Customer: Yes, well, if you'll replace these, I'll be on my way.

Notice that the customer has not attacked the clerk or created an angry confrontation. Simple persistence is often all that is necessary for successful self-assertion.

Question: How would I respond assertively to a put-down?

Responding assertively to verbal aggression (a put-down) is a real challenge. The tendency is to respond aggressively, which usually makes things worse. A good way to respond to a put-down is this: (1) If you are wrong, admit it; (2) acknowledge the person's feelings; (3) assert yourself about the other person's aggression; (4) briskly end the interchange.

Psychologists Robert Alberti and Michael Emmons (1978) offer an example of using the four steps: Let's say you accidently bump into someone. The person responds angrily, "Damn it! Why don't you watch where you're going! You fool, you could have hurt me!" A good response would be to say, "I'm sorry I bumped

Applications: Assertiveness Training—Standing Up for Your Rights

you. I didn't do it intentionally. It's obvious you're upset, but I don't like your calling me names or yelling. I can get your point without that."

Now, what if someone insults you indirectly ("I love your taste in clothing, it's so 'folksy.'")? Alberti and Emmons suggest you ask for a clarification ("What are you trying to say?"). This will force the person to take responsibility for the aggression. It can also provide an opportunity to change the way the person interacts with you: "If you really don't like what I'm wearing, I'd like to know it. I'm not always sure I like the things I buy, and I value your opinion."

To summarize, self-assertion is not instant poise, confidence, or self-assurance. It is a way of combating anxieties associated with living in an impersonal and sometimes intimidating society. If you are interested in more information, see Alberti and Emmons' book, *Your Perfect Right* (Impact, 1978).

Learning Check

1. In assertiveness training, people learn techniques for getting their way in social situations and angry interchanges.   T or F?
2. Nonassertive behavior causes hurt, anxiety, and self-denial in the actor, and sympathy, guilt, or contempt in the receiver.   T or F?
3. Overlearning should be avoided when rehearsing assertive behaviors.   T or F?
4. The "broken record" must be avoided, because it is a basic nonassertive behavior.   T or F?

Answers: 1. F   2. T   3. F   4. F

Chapter Summary

- Humans are social animals enmeshed in a complex network of social relationships. *Social psychology* studies humans as members of groups. Its focus is how people behave in the presence (real or implied) of others.
- *Culture* provides a broad social context for our behavior. One's *position* in groups defines a variety of *roles* to be played. Roles, which may be *achieved* or *ascribed*, are particular behavior patterns associated with social positions. When a person holds two or more contradictory roles, *role conflict* may occur. The Stanford prison experiment showed that destructive roles may override individual determinants of behavior.
- Positions within groups typically carry higher or lower levels of *status*. High status is associated with special privileges and respect.
- *Group structure* refers to the organization of roles, communication pathways, and power within a group. *Group cohesiveness* is basically the degree of attraction among group members. *Norms* are standards of conduct enforced (formally or informally) by groups. The *autokinetic effect* has been used to demonstrate that norms rapidly form even in temporary groups.
- The study of personal space is called *proxemics*. Four basic spatial zones around each person's body are: *intimate distance* (0 to 18 inches), *personal distance* (1½ to 4 feet), *social distance* (4 to 12 feet), and *public distance* (12 feet or more).
- *Attribution theory* is concerned with how we make inferences about behavior. A variety of factors affect attribution, including *consistency*, *distinctiveness*, *situational demands*, and *consensus*. The *fundamental attributional error* is to ascribe the actions of others to internal causes, while attributing one's own behavior to external causes.
- The *need to affiliate* is tied to needs for approval, support, friendship, and information. Research indicates that affiliation is also related to reducing anxiety and uncertainty. *Social comparison theory* holds that we also affiliate to evaluate our actions, feelings, and abilities.
- *Interpersonal attraction* is increased by *physical proximity* (nearness), *frequent contact*, *physical attractiveness*, *competence*, and *similarity*. A large degree of similarity on many dimensions is characteristic of mate selection in most marriages.
- *Self-disclosure* occurs more when two people like one another. A *reciprocity norm* exists for self-disclosure: Low levels of self-disclosure are met with low levels in return, whereas moderate self-disclosure elicits more personal replies. However, *overdisclosure* tends to inhibit self-disclosure by others.
- According to *social exchange theory*, we tend to maintain relationships that are *profitable*; that is, those for which perceived rewards exceed perceived costs.
- *Romantic love* has been studied as a special kind of attitude. Love can be distinguished from liking by the use of attitude scales. Dating couples like *and* love their partners but only like their friends. Love is also associated with greater *mutual absorption* between people.
- In general, *social influence* refers to alterations in behavior brought about by the behavior of others, especially situations in which *conformity* occurs.
- Virtually everyone conforms to a variety of broad social and cultural norms. *Conformity pressures* also exist within smaller groups. The Asch experiments demonstrated that various *group sanctions* encourage conformity.
- *Groupthink* refers to compulsive conformity in group decision making. Victims of groupthink seek to maintain each other's approval, even at the cost of critical thinking.
- Social influence is also related to five types of *social power*. The types are: *reward power, coercive power, legitimate power, referent power,* and *expert power*.
- *Obedience* to authority has been investigated in a variety of experiments, particularly those by Milgram. Obedience in Milgram's studies decreased when the victim was in the same room, when the victim and subject were face-to-face, when the authority figure was absent, and when others refused to obey.
- *Compliance* with direct requests is another means by which behavior is influenced. Three strategies for inducing compliance are the *foot-in-the-door technique*, the *door-in-the-face approach*, and the *low-ball technique*. Recent research suggests that in addition to excessive obedience to authority, many people show a surprising *passive compliance* to unreasonable requests.

Social Traps—The Tragedy of the Commons

You are in a packed theater in an older building. Halfway through the feature movie *(Bambi Meets Godzilla),* you begin to smell smoke. The screen goes dark. You try to stay calm as you move toward a distant exit sign. Suddenly someone screams. You lunge for the door. Instantly, you are caught in a crush of people. The crowd jams together so tightly that only a few people can squeeze through the door. If the fire moves swiftly, many lives will be lost.

This situation—panic during a fire—is a classic example of a *social trap*. Each person in a theater who runs toward the exits has acted in his or her immediate self-interest. Yet if *everyone* bolts at once, the chances that anyone will survive may be very low.

Social Traps

Question: What exactly is a social trap?

A **social trap** is any situation that rewards actions that have undesired effects in the long run (Cross & Guyer, 1980). Personal examples of social traps are quite common. For instance, many people are enticed into drinking too much at parties because their pleasure is immediate and their discomfort (a hangover) comes later. Many people go into debt because they get the immediate reward of owning desirable goods; only later do they suffer when a staggering credit card bill arrives. For the immediate pleasures of intimacy, many teen-

agers later pay the price of pregnancy, forced marriage, early divorce, curtailed education, and so on.

Psychologists have been especially interested in *collective* social traps. In such traps no one individual acts against the group interest, but if many people act alike, collective harm is done. For example, each person who leaves work at 5:00 in a congested city expects to gain by getting home earlier. Yet if everyone leaves at 5:00, the resulting traffic jam ensures that everyone will, in fact, arrive home late and emotionally frazzled. The problem could be solved if some people would wait a half hour or more before leaving. However, no one does this because immediate self-interest encourages a "fast getaway."

A related example is the fact that many large cities now have rapid transit systems that are underused by citizens. Each person decides that it is more convenient to own and drive a separate car (in order to run errands and so on). However, we see again that individual behavior affects the welfare of others. Because everyone wants to drive for "convenience," driving becomes inconvenient: The mass of cars in most cities causes irritating traffic snarls and a lack of parking spaces. Each car owner has been drawn into a trap.

The Tragedy of the Commons

Social traps are especially damaging when we are enticed into over-

use of scarce resources. This is exactly what happened a few years ago to crab fishermen in Alaska.

Initially, crabs were plentiful and fishermen were few. Each fisherman was therefore able to make large, lucrative catches. To raise their profits, fishermen began to add second, third, and fourth boats to their operations. For a while this did, in fact, increase individual profits. Yet, as the size of the fishing fleet continued to grow, the number of crabs available to be caught by any boat decreased.

Eventually, so many crabs were caught that their rate of reproduction slowed. As a result, crab fishermen began to go bankrupt in large numbers. Individually, their actions made sense. But collectively, the group suffered greatly.

Ecologist Garrett Hardin (1968, 1985) calls situations like the one just described the **tragedy of the commons**. Tragedies of this sort often occur when people share a scarce resource: Each person acts in his or her self-interest, which causes the resource to be used up so that everyone suffers. More familiar examples of this dilemma are the lack of individual incentives to conserve gasoline, water, or electricity. Whenever one's personal comfort or convenience is involved, it is highly tempting to "let others worry about it." Yet, in the long run everyone stands to lose.

Social Problems   Many major social problems can be thought of

Exploration: Social Traps—The Tragedy of the Commons

as social traps. In most cases of environmental pollution, for instance, there are immediate benefits for polluting and major long-term costs. If one person pollutes a river or trashes the roadside, it has little noticeable effect. But as many people do the same, problems quickly mount up that affect everyone. As another example, consider the farmer who applies a pesticide to a crop to save it from insect damage. The farmer benefits immediately. However, if other farmers follow suit, the local water system may be permanently damaged.

Traps also exist at the international level. Countries continue to add to their nuclear stockpiles in order to be more "secure." Yet doing so may eventually increase the chances of a final nuclear holocaust. It's no wonder that people who study international conflicts often come away shaking their

heads and wondering "How did we get into this mess?"

Question: What can be done to avoid social traps?

Escaping Traps   In some situations it might be possible to dismantle social traps by rearranging rewards and costs. For example, many companies are tempted to pollute because it saves them money and increases profits. To reverse the situation, a pollution tax could be levied so that it would cost more, not less, for a business to pollute. As another example, we could reward lower individual consumption of resources. Some power companies have already experimented with a meter that charges lower rates for using power at off-peak periods (also, see Chapter 27).

There is evidence that in real social traps people are more likely to restrain themselves when they be-

lieve others will too (Messick et al., 1983). Otherwise, they are likely to think, "Why should I be a sucker? I don't think anyone else is going to conserve (fuel, electricity, water, crabs, or whatever)."

Other problems may be harder to solve. What, for instance, can be done about truck drivers who cause dangerous traffic jams on narrow roads because they will not pull over? How can littering be discouraged or prevented? How would you make carpooling or using public transportation the first choice for most people? Or how could people simply be encouraged to stagger their departure times to and from work? All of these and more are social traps that need springing. It is important that we not fall into the trap of ignoring them.

Learning Check

1. A social trap is any situation in which undesired actions are rewarded in the long run.   T or F?
2. Individuals in a collective social trap act in ways that appear to be rational but that create problems for the group as a whole.   T or F?
3. The "tragedy of the commons" occurs when individuals use a shared resource too quickly because they get immediate rewards for doing so.   T or F?
4. Rearranging individual rewards and costs is one way to dismantle social traps.   T or F?

Answers: 1. F   2. T   3. T   4. T

Questions for Discussion

1. Reread the experiments performed on passive compliance. What would have been an assertive response to the situations described? An aggressive response?
2. Would it be possible to be completely nonconforming (that is, to not conform to *some* group norm)?
3. How serious, in your estimation, are problems of conformity, obedience, and passive compliance?
4. How has physical proximity influenced your choice of friends.
5. Modern warfare allows killing to take place impersonally and at a distance. How does this relate to Milgram's experiments?
6. People of different nationalities often have different norms for personal space. What would you expect to happen in a conversation between two people with very different proxemic habits?
7. Can you think of a personal experience in which you were subjected to group pressures similar to those in the Asch experiment? How did you feel? Did you yield?
8. In view of the Milgram obedience experiment, do you think the civil disobedience of the civil rights and anti-war movements was justified? Why or why not?
9. If you were placed in charge of an important decision-making group, what would you do to minimize groupthink? Do you think some types of committees or groups are especially prone to groupthink? How serious a problem do you think groupthink is in the government? The military? Business? Schools? Community groups?
10. What social traps can you identify in day-to-day experience? What could be done to change them?
11. Garrett Hardin believes that it is a mistake to send food to countries wracked by famine. According to Hardin, this only allows the population of such countries to expand so that a later, larger disaster becomes inevitable. In your opinion, is it more or less humane to supply food under such circumstances?

Chapter 26 | Social Psychology II

Chapter Preview
Doomsday for the Seekers

Hardly a year passes, it seems, without a doomsday group of one kind or another making the news. In one classic example of such groups, a woman named Mrs. Keech claimed she was receiving messages from beings on a planet called Clarion. The beings told Mrs. Keech that they had detected a fault in the Earth's crust that would submerge the North American continent in an unimaginable natural disaster. The date of this event was to be December 21. However, Mrs. Keech and her band of followers, who called themselves the Seekers, had no fear: On December 20 they expected to be met at midnight by a flying saucer and taken to safety in outer space.

The night of December 20 arrived, and the Seekers gathered at Mrs. Keech's house. Many had given up jobs and possessions to prepare for departure. Expectations were high and commitment was total, but as the night wore on, midnight passed and the world continued to exist. It was a bitter and embarrassing disappointment for all concerned.

Question: Did the group break up then?

The amazing twist to this story, and the aspect that intrigued social psychologists, was that the Seekers became more convinced than ever before that they had been right. At about 5 A.M. Mrs. Keech announced that she had received a message explaining that the Seekers had saved the world. Before the night of December 20, the group had been uninterested in convincing other people that the world was coming to an end. Now they called newspapers, magazines, and radio stations to explain what had happened and to convince others of their accomplishment.

How do we explain this strange turn in the behavior of Mrs. Keech's doomsday group? The answer seems to lie in the concept of cognitive dissonance. *Cognitive dissonance also helps explain many aspects of attitude change. Watch for a discussion of cognitive dissonance later in this chapter.*

Survey Questions What are attitudes? How are they acquired, measured, and changed? Under what conditions is persuasion most effective? What is cognitive dissonance? What does it have to do with attitudes and behavior? Is brainwashing actually possible? How are people converted to cult membership? What causes prejudice and intergroup conflict? What can be done about these problems? How do psychologists explain human aggression? Why are bystanders so often unwilling to help in an emergency?

Resources

Attitudes—
Belief + Emotion + Action

What is your attitude toward birth control, marijuana, Republicans, higher education, Chevrolets, psychology? The answers have far-reaching effects on your behavior. The effects of attitudes are intimately woven into our actions and views of the world. Our tastes, friendships, votes, preferences, and goals are all touched by attitudes.

Question: What specifically is an attitude?

An **attitude** is a learned predisposition to respond to people, objects, or institutions in a positive or negative way. Attitudes are one of the most studied aspects of social functioning. This is because attitudes summarize past experience and *predict* or direct future actions. For example, an approach known as the **misdirected letter technique** demonstrates that actions are closely connected to attitudes:

The Luck of the Irish

During a period of civil violence in Ireland, researchers measured attitudes held toward the Irish in a sample of English households. Later, wrongly addressed letters were sent to the same households. Each letter had either an English name on it or an Irish name. The question was: Would the "Irish" letters be returned to the post office or thrown away? As predicted, the number of "Irish" letters returned corresponded directly to pro- or anti-Irish attitudes measured earlier. (Howitt et al., 1977)

"Your attitude is showing," is sometimes said. This statement seems simple, but actually there are three ways in which attitudes are expressed. Most attitudes have a **belief component**, an **emotional component**, and an **action component**. Consider, as an example, your attitude toward gun control. You will have beliefs about whether gun control would affect rates of crime or violence. You will have emotional responses to guns, find them either attractive and desirable or threatening and destructive. And you will have a tendency to seek out or avoid gun ownership. The action component of your attitude will probably also include support of organizations that urge or oppose gun control.

Question: How do people acquire attitudes?

Attitude Formation Attitudes are acquired in several basic ways. Sometimes we form them through **direct con-tact** with the object of the attitude—such as opposing pollution when a nearby factory ruins your favorite river. Attitudes are also learned through **interaction with others** holding the same attitude—if you live in a vegetarian household, chances are you will become a vegetarian. Attitudes are also acquired through the effects of **child rearing**. For example, if both parents belong to the same political party, chances are two out of three that as an adult the child will belong to the same party (Campbell et al., 1954).

In the previous chapter we discussed group forces that operate to bring about conformity. There is little doubt that many of the attitudes we hold are influenced by **group membership** (Fig. 26–1). In one classic study, for example, groups were formed to discuss the case of a juvenile delinquent. Most participants believed that what the boy needed was love, kindness, and friendship. To test group pressures on attitudes, a person who advocated severe punishment was added to each group.

Question: How did group members react to the "deviate"?

At first they directed almost all of their comments to him. But when the deviate stuck to his position, an interesting thing happened: Soon, he was almost completely excluded from conversation. And later, the deviate was strongly rejected in ratings made by other group members (Schachter, 1951). Group pressures for conformity and the difficulty of holding deviant attitudes can be clearly seen in this outcome.

Attitudes are also influenced by the **mass media**. As Marshall McLuhan put it, we are "massaged" by the media, meaning: threatened, urged, cajoled, persuaded, and otherwise influenced. Ninety-eight percent of American homes have a television set, which is on an average of almost 7 hours a day (Comstock et al., 1978). The values and information thus channeled into homes exert a powerful influence on how people perceive, think about, and react to their world. For instance, the heavy dose of violence on television may lead viewers to develop a **"mean" world view**. That is, frequent viewers overestimate their chances of being involved in a violent incident (Roberts & Bachen, 1981). Heavy viewers are also less likely to feel that most people can be trusted (Gerbner & Gross, 1976). Of added concern are the stereotyped images of male and female roles and of racial or ethnic minorities found on the "tube."

Fig. 26–1 *Attitudes are an important dimension of social behavior. They are often rooted in reference groups (see text).*

Some attitudes are formed inadvertently through **chance conditioning.** Let's say, for instance, that you have had three encounters in your lifetime with psychologists. If by chance all three were negative, you might take an unduly dim view of psychology and psychologists. In the same way, people often develop strong attitudes toward cities, restaurants, or parts of the country on the basis of one or two unusually good or bad experiences.

Question: Why are some attitudes acted on while others are not?

To answer the question, let's consider an example. Assume that a person accepts that automobiles contribute to pollution, and strongly objects to smog, but continues to drive to work every day. How are such discrepancies explained? For one thing, the *immediate consequences* of our actions weigh heavily on the choices we make. A person who objects to air pollution but continues to drive is responding to the immediate convenience of driving.

A second factor is our expectation of how *others will evaluate* our actions (Fishbein and Ajzen, 1975). By taking this factor into account, researchers have been able to accurately predict family planning choices, alcohol use by adolescents, reenlistment in the National Guard, voting on a nuclear power plant initiative, and so forth (Cialdini et al., 1981).

Finally, we must not overlook the effect that longstanding *habits* have on action (Triandis, 1977). Say a "male chauvinist" boss makes a vow to change his sexist attitudes toward female employees. Two months later it would not be unusual for his behavior to show the effects of habit rather than his intention to change. In short, there are often large differences between attitudes and behavior—particularly between privately held attitudes and public behavior.

Question: Can attitudes be measured?

Attitude Measurement   There are a number of approaches to the measurement of attitudes. In some cases individuals are simply asked in a straightforward way to express attitudes toward a particular issue. For example, a person might be asked in an **open-ended interview,** "What are your thoughts about strip mining?" The second approach, which has been particularly useful as a measure of attitudes toward various groups, uses a **social distance scale.** Social distance indicates the degree to which one person would be willing to have contact with another person. The individual is asked to indicate his or her willingness to admit members of a particular group to various levels of social closeness, ranging from "would exclude from my country" to "would admit to marriage in my family."

Use of **attitude scales** is one of the most common methods of measurement. Attitude scales consist of statements expressing various possible views on a particular issue. For example, "socialized medicine would destroy the quality of health care in this country" or, "this country desperately needs a national health care program." People are asked to express agreement or disagreement with each item on a five-point scale ranging from "strongly agree" to "strongly disagree." When scores on all items are computed, a person can be rated in terms of overall acceptance or rejection of a particular issue.

Attitude measures, particularly as they have been used in public polls, have provided much useful information about the feelings of large segments of the population. Again, though, it is important to remember that expressed attitudes and behavior may differ. Publicly expressed attitudes favoring racial or sexual equality often crumble in situations involving a conflict of interest. A "racially enlightened" individual, for instance, may act quite bigoted when equal employment opportunity laws threaten a chance for employment.

Attitude Change— Why the "Seekers" Went Public

Although attitudes are relatively stable, they are subject to change. Some attitude change can be understood in terms of the concept of **reference groups.** A reference group is one whose values and attitudes are seen by the individual as being relevant to his or her own. Reference group membership need not be physical. It depends instead on whom you identify with or care about.

In the 1930s Theodore Newcomb studied real-life attitude change among students at Bennington College. Most of the students came from conservative homes, but Bennington was a very liberal school. Newcomb found that most students shifted significantly toward more liberal attitudes during their 4 years at Bennington. Those who did not change maintained parents and hometown friends as their primary reference group (typified by one student's statement, "I decided I'd rather stick to my father's ideas"). Those who did change identified primarily with the campus community. Notice that all students could count both the college and their families as *membership* groups, but that one or the other tended to become their reference group.

Question: What about advertising and other direct attempts to change attitudes? Are they effective?

Business corporations, politicians, and others who seek to persuade us obviously believe that attitude change can be engineered. Over $5 billion is spent yearly on television advertising in the United States alone.

Persuasion refers to any deliberate attempt to bring about attitude change by the transmission of information. Persuasion can range from the daily bombardment of media commercials to personal discussion among friends. In most cases the success or failure of attempted persuasion can be understood by considering characteristics of the **communicator,** the **message,** and the **audience** (Fig. 26–2). Let's say you have a chance to promote an issue important to you (pro or anti nuclear power, for instance) at a community gathering. Whom should you choose to make the presentation, and how should that person present it?

Research on persuasion suggests that attitude change is encouraged when: (1) the communicator is likeable, trust-

Fig. 26–2 *Persuasion. Would you be likely to be swayed by this person's message? Successful persuasion is related to characteristics of the communicator, the message, and the audience.*

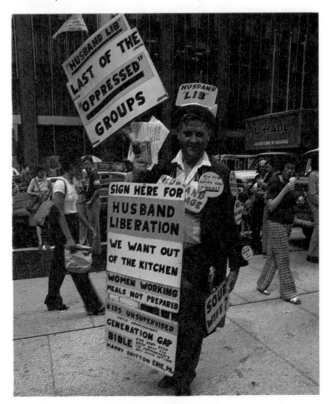

worthy, an expert on the topic, and similar to the audience in some respect; (2) the message appeals to emotions, particularly to fear or anxiety; (3) the message also provides a clear course of action that will, if followed, reduce fear or anxiety; (4) the message states clear-cut conclusions; (5) both sides of the argument are presented (for a well-informed audience); (6) only one side of the argument is presented (for a poorly informed audience); (7) the persuader appears to have nothing to gain if the audience accepts the message; and (8) the message is repeated as frequently as possible (Aronson, 1972; McGuire, 1969). You should have little difficulty seeing how these principles are applied in the selling of everything from underarm deodorants to presidents.

We all know from personal observation that emotional experiences also dramatically alter attitudes. Those individuals who give up drinking after nearly dying in an automobile accident caused by their own drunkenness serve as an example. To bring about such attitude change, psychologists have experimented with creating similar experiences through role playing.

Question: For example?

Janis and Mann (1965) asked women who were known smokers to play the role of a cancer patient. A physician told each of the women that he had some bad news: She had lung cancer and would have to undergo immediate surgery. The women played out the part by asking questions about the surgery, by asking if it might fail, and so on. Women in the role-playing group drastically reduced their smoking. Those who listened to a tape recording of similar information showed little change.

Question: Why should role playing have more effect than hearing the same information?

Cognitive Dissonance Theory   Certainly, emotional impact and realism have some effect, but part of the explanation also lies in the concept of **cognitive dissonance.**

Question: What is cognitive dissonance?

Cognitions are thoughts. Dissonance means clashing. The influential theory of cognitive dissonance (Festinger, 1957) states that contradicting or clashing thoughts cause discomfort. We have a need for *consistency* in our thoughts and our perceptions.

If individuals can be made to act in ways that are inconsistent with their attitudes, they may change their thoughts to bring them into agreement with their actions. For example, smokers are told on every pack that cigarettes may endanger their lives. They light up and smoke. How do they resolve the tension between this information and their

actions? They could quit smoking, but it may be easier to convince themselves that smoking is not really so dangerous. To do this, they will seek examples of people who have lived long lives as heavy smokers, and will associate with other smokers who support this attitude. They will also avoid information concerning the link between smoking and cancer. Cognitive dissonance theory also suggests that people tend to reject new information that contradicts ideas they already hold, in a sort of "don't bother me with the facts my mind is made up" strategy.

Recall now the account of Mrs. Keech and her doomsday group. Why did their belief in Mrs. Keech's messages *increase* after the world failed to end? Why did they suddenly become interested in convincing others of the correctness of their beliefs? Cognitive dissonance explains that after publicly committing themselves to their beliefs, they had a strong need to maintain their stand. No matter what the evidence, convincing others was a way of adding additional proof that they were right.

Question: Acting contrary to one's attitudes does not always bring about change. How does cognitive dissonance account for this?

The amount of **reward,** or **justification,** for acting contrary to one's beliefs can influence the amount of dissonance created. In a now classic study, college students performed an extremely boring task consisting of turning wooden pegs on a board for an extended time. Afterward, they were asked to help lure others into the experiment by pretending it was interesting and enjoyable. Students paid $20 for lying to others did not change their own negative opinion of the task. Those who were paid only $1 later rated the experience as actually being pleasant and interesting. In other words, those paid $20 experienced no dissonance. These students could reassure themselves that anybody would lie for $20. Those paid $1 were faced with the conflicting thought, "I lied, but I had no good reason to." Rather than admit to themselves that they had lied, these students changed their attitude toward what they had done (Festinger & Carlsmith, 1959).

More recent experiments indicate that we are especially likely to experience dissonance when we cause an event to occur that we would rather hadn't occurred (Cooper & Fazio, 1984). Let's say, for example, that you agree to help a friend move. The day for the move arrives and you feel like staying in bed. Actually, you wish you hadn't promised to help. Thus, to reduce the dissonance you feel, you will probably convince yourself that the work will actually be "sort of fun" or that your friend really deserves the help. We make such adjustments in attitudes countless times in order to minimize cognitive dissonance.

Learning Check

1. Attitudes have three parts: a _____ component, an _____ component, and an _____ component.

2. Which of the following is associated with attitude formation?
   a. group membership   c. child rearing   e. all of the preceding
   b. chance conditioning   d. mass media   f. a and d only

3. Because of the immediate consequences of actions, behavior contrary to one's attitudes is often enacted.   T or F?

4. Items such as, "would exclude from my country" or "would admit to marriage in my family" would be found in which attitude measure?
   a. a reference group scale   b. an attitude scale   c. a social distance scale   d. an open-ended interview

5. In presenting a persuasive message, it is best to give both sides of the argument if the audience is already well informed on the topic.   T or F?

6. Much attitude change is related to a desire to avoid clashing or contradictory thoughts, an idea summarized by _____ _____ theory.

Answers: 1. belief, emotional, action 2. e 3. T 4. c 5. T 6. cognitive dissonance

Forced Attitude Change— Brainwashing and Cults

Most people associate the term *brainwashing* with techniques used by the Chinese on American prisoners during the Korean War. Through various types of "thought reform," the Chinese were able to coerce approximately 16 percent of these prisoners to sign false confessions (Schein et al., 1957). More recently, the mass murder/suicide at Jonestown has rekindled public interest in the subject of inducing involuntary changes in attitudes, beliefs, or personal loyalties.

Question: What is brainwashing? How does it differ from other persuasive techniques?

As we have noted, advertisers, politicians, educators, religious organizations, and others actively seek to alter attitudes and opinions. To an extent their persuasive efforts resemble brainwashing, but there is an important difference: **Brainwashing** requires a *captive* audience. If you are offended by a television commercial, you can tune it out. Prisoners in the POW camps in Korea (and later in Vietnam) were completely at the mercy of their captors. James McConnell has noted that complete control over the environment allows a degree of psychological manipulation that would be impossible in a normal setting.

Question: How does captivity facilitate persuasion?

Brainwashing McConnell identifies three techniques used for brainwashing: (1) The target person is isolated from others who would support his or her original attitudes; (2) the target person is made completely dependent on his or her captors for satisfaction of needs; (3) the indoctrinating agent is in a position to reward the target person for changes in attitude or behavior.

Brainwashing typically begins with an attempt to make the target feel completely helpless. Physical and psychological abuse, lack of sleep, humiliation, and isolation serve to **unfreeze** former values and beliefs. **Change** comes about when exhaustion, pressure, and fear become unbearable. Prisoners reach the breaking point and sign a false confession or cooperate to gain relief. When they do, they are suddenly rewarded with praise, privileges, food, or rest. The continued coupling of hope and fear with additional pressures for conformity then serves to **refreeze** new attitudes (Schein et al., 1961).

Question: How permanent are changes caused by brainwashing?

In most cases, the dramatic alteration in attitudes brought about by brainwashing is temporary. Most "converted" prisoners who returned to the United States after the Korean War eventually reverted to their original beliefs and repudiated their indoctrinators.

Cults   Exhorted by their leader, some 900 members of the Reverend Jim Jones' People's Temple picked up paper cups and drank purple Kool-aide laced with the deadly poison cyanide. Psychologically, the mass suicide at

Jonestown in 1978 is not so incredible as it might seem. Isolated in the jungles of Guyana, intimidated by guards, lulled with sedatives, cut off from friends and relatives, and totally accustomed to obeying rigid rules of conduct, the inhabitants of Jonestown were primed for Jones' final "loyalty test." Of greater psychological interest is the question of how people reach such a state of commitment and dependency.

Question: Why do people join groups such as the People's Temple?

Psychologist Margaret Singer (1979) has studied and aided hundreds of former cult members. Her interviews reveal that, in recruiting new members, cults make use of a powerful blend of guilt, manipulation, isolation, deception, fear, and escalating commitment. In this respect cults employ high-pressure indoctrination techniques not unlike those used in brainwashing.

Some of those interviewed by Singer were suffering from marked psychological distress when they joined a cult. Most, however, were simply undergoing a period of mild

Fig. 26–3 *Aftermath of the mass suicide at Jonestown. How do cultlike groups recruit new devotees? (See text.)*

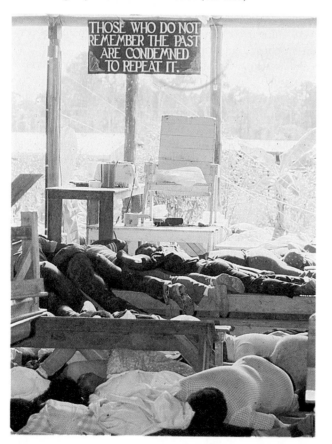

depression, indecision, or alienation from family and friends. Cult members try to catch potential converts at a time of need, especially when a sense of belonging will be attractive. For instance, many were approached just after a romance had broken up, or when they were struggling with exams or choice of a major, or when they were simply at loose ends and "on the street."

Question: How is conversion achieved?

Often it begins with intense displays of affection and understanding ("love bombing"). Next comes isolation from noncult members, together with drills, disciplines, and rituals (all-night meditation or continuous chanting, for instance) to wear down physical and emotional resistance, as well as to generate commitment.

At first, recruits make small commitments (to stay after a meeting, for example). Then, large commitments are encouraged (to stay an extra day, to call in sick at work, and so forth). Making a major commitment is usually the final step. The new devotee signs over a bank account or property to the group, takes up residence with the group, and so forth. Such major public commitments create a powerful cognitive dissonance effect in which it becomes virtually impossible for converts to admit they have made a mistake.

Once in the group, members are cut off from family and friends (former reference groups), and the cult can thus control the flow and the interpretation of information to them. Members are isolated physically (by continuous activity) and psychologically from their former value systems and social structure.

Question: Why do people stay in cults?

Most former members mention guilt and fear as the main reasons for not leaving even when they wished they could. Most had been reduced to childlike dependency on the group for meeting all their daily needs (Singer, 1979).

Behind the "throne" from which Jim Jones ruled Jonestown was a sign bearing these words: "Those who do not remember the past are condemned to repeat it" (Fig. 26–3). If we are to take the Reverend Jones at his word, then we should remember that cults are but one example of the danger of trading independence for security. Cults are merely a highly visible indication of the extent to which we all can be influenced by sophisticated psychological coercion and by our needs for approval from others.

Prejudice—Attitudes That Injure

Prejudice is a negative attitude or prejudgment tinged with unreasonable suspicion, fear, or hatred. Often prejudice is institutionalized and backed by social power structures. In such cases it is referred to as **racism, sexism,** or **ageism,** depending on the group discimated against. Since sexism and ageism were discussed in earlier chapters, let's focus on racial prejudice and racism. Both racial prejudice and institutionalized racism may contribute to *discrimination*. **Discrimination** refers to behavior that prevents individuals from doing things they might reasonably expect to be able to do, such as buying a house, riding a bus, or attending a high-quality school.

An indication of just how pervasive discrimination can be comes from a rather remarkable study by F. K. Heussenstamm (1971). Subjects in the study were 15 college students, all of whom had received no traffic citations in the previous year. Each subject attached a bumper sticker for a well-known, militant black organization to his or her car. During the next 17 days the group received a total of 33 traffic citations! The power relationship between the white establishment and black militants (at least as interpreted by individual police officers) is clear.

Question: How do prejudices develop?

Becoming Prejudiced One theory suggests that prejudice represents a form of **scapegoating.** Scapegoating, you may recall, is a form of displaced aggression in which hostilities generated by frustration are redirected to other targets. One interesting test of this hypothesis was conducted at a summer camp for young men. Subjects were given a difficult test they were sure to fail. Additionally, completing the test caused them to miss a trip to the theater (normally the high point of their weekly entertainment). Attitudes toward Mexicans and Japanese were measured before the test and after the men had failed the test and missed the entertainment. Subjects in this study consistently rated members of these two groups lower after they had been frustrated (Miller & Bugelski, 1970).

At times the development of prejudice (like other attitudes) can be traced to direct experiences with members of the rejected group. A child who is repeatedly bullied by members of a particular racial or ethnic group may develop resentment that forms the core of a lifelong dislike for members of the group. The tragedy in such cases is that once such an antipathy is established, it prevents accepting additional, more positive experiences that could reverse the damage.

Gordon Allport (1958) concluded that there are two important sources of prejudice. **Personal prejudice** occurs when members of another racial or ethnic group represent a threat to the individual's security or comfort. For example, members of another group may be viewed as competitors for jobs. **Group prejudice** occurs simply through the individual's adherence to *group norms*. In other words, you may have no personal reason for disliking out-group members, but you do so because you are expected to.

The Prejudiced Personality Other research suggests that prejudice at times is a general personality characteristic.

Question: Do you mean some people are more prone to prejudice than others?

Apparently some are. Theodore Adorno and his associates (1950) conducted extensive research on what they called the **authoritarian personality.** These researchers started out by studying anti-Semitism as a means of understanding the social climate that existed in Germany during World War II. In the process they found that people who are prejudiced against one group tend to be prejudiced against *all* out-groups.

Question: What are the characteristics of the prejudice-prone personality?

The authoritarian personality can be described as a collection of personal attitudes and values marked by rigidity, inhibition, and oversimplification. Authoritarians tend to be very **ethnocentric**—they consider only members of their own national, ethnic, or religious group acceptable. They are also overwhelmingly concerned with power, authority, and obedience. To measure these qualities, Adorno and his associates created the "F" scale. (The "F" stands for fascism.) This attitude scale is made up of statements such as the following—to which the authoritarian readily agrees (Adorno et al., 1950):

Authoritarian Beliefs

Obedience and respect for authority are the most important virtues children should learn.

People can be divided into two distinct classes: the weak and the strong.

If people would talk less and work more, everybody would be better off.

What this country needs most, more than laws and political programs, is a few courageous, tireless, devoted leaders, in whom the people can put their faith.

Nobody ever learns anything really important except through suffering.

Every person should have complete faith in some supernatural power whose decisions are obeyed without question.

Certain religious sects that refuse to salute the flag should be forced to conform to such patriotic action or else be abolished.

As children, authoritarians were usually severely punished and learned to fear authority (and to covet it) at an early age. Authoritarians are not happy people.

It should be readily apparent from the list of authoritarian beliefs that the "F" scale is slanted toward politically conservative authoritarians. Psychologist Milton Rokeach (1960) has noted that rigid and authoritarian personalities can be found at both ends of the political spectrum. Rokeach therefore prefers to describe rigid and intolerant thinking as **dogmatism.**

Even if we discount the obvious bigotry of the dogmatic or authoritarian personality, racial prejudice runs deep in American society. To illustrate, an experiment showed that liberal, white, male college students were more willing to give shocks (under laboratory conditions) to a black victim than to a white victim (Shulman, 1974). We will probe deeper into the roots of such prejudiced behavior in an upcoming discussion, but first let's stop for a Learning Check.

Learning Check

1. Brainwashing differs from other persuasive attempts in that brainwashing requires a _____ _____.

2. Which statement about brainwashing is *false?*
   a. The target person is isolated from others.
   b. Attitude changes brought about by brainwashing are almost always permanent.
   c. The first step is unfreezing former values and beliefs.
   d. Cooperation with the indoctrinating agent is rewarded.

3. Margaret Singer found that most former cult members had experienced a major psychological disturbance just before joining the cult.   T or F?

4. Which of the following is *not* a technique typically used by cults to recruit new members?
   a. "love bombing" and isolation   c. physical intimidation and veiled threats
   b. drills and rituals to wear down resistance   d. a succession of smaller to larger commitments

5. The authoritarian personality tends to be prejudiced against all out-groups, a quality referred to as _____.

Answers: 1. captive audience   2. *b*   3. F   4. *c*   5. ethnocentrism

Intergroup Conflict— The Roots of Prejudice

An unfortunate by-product of the human proclivity for forming groups is that group membership often limits contact with people in other groups. Additionally, groups themselves may come into conflict. Both events tend to foster unpleasant feelings and prejudices toward the outgroup. The bloody clash of opposing forces in Ireland, in South Africa, and in hometown U.S.A. are reminders that intergroup conflict is a widespread problem of modern life. Daily we read of jarring clashes between nations, communities, races, and political, religious, or ethnic groups. In many cases, intergroup conflict is accompanied by *stereotyped* images of out-group members and by bitter prejudice.

Question: What exactly do you mean by a stereotype?

Social stereotypes are oversimplified images of people who fall into a particular category. As psychologist Gordon Allport (1958) put it: "Given a thimbleful of facts . . . [we] rush to make generalizations as large as a tub." Stereotypes tend to simplify people into "us" and "them" categories. Actually, aside from the fact that they always oversimplify, stereotypes may be either *positive* or *negative*. Table 26–1 shows stereotyped images of various national and ethnic groups and their changes over the years (Fig. 26–4). Notice that many of the qualities listed are desirable.

Stereotypes held by the prejudiced tend to be unusually irrational. When given a list of negative statements about other groups, prejudiced individuals agree with most of them. Particularly revealing is the fact that they often agree with conflicting statements. Thus, Jews are both "pushy" and "standoffish" or blacks are "ignorant" and "sly" to the prejudiced person. In one study, prejudiced

Table 26–1   University Students' Characterization of Ethnic Groups, 1933 and 1967

Trait	Percent Checking Trait 1933	1967	Trait	Percent Checking Trait 1933	1967	Trait	Percent Checking Trait 1933	1967
Americans			**Italians**			**Jews**		
Industrious	48	23	Artistic	53	30	Shrewd	79	30
Intelligent	47	20	Impulsive	44	28	Mercenary	49	15
Materialistic	33	67	Musical	32	9	Grasping	34	17
Progressive	27	17	Imaginative	30	7	Intelligent	29	37
			Revengeful	17	0			
Germans			**Irish**			**Blacks**		
Scientific	78	47	Pugnacious	45	13	Superstitious	84	13
Stolid	44	9	Witty	38	7	Lazy	75	26
Methodical	31	21	Honest	32	17	Ignorant	38	11
Efficient	16	46	Nationalistic	21	41	Religious	24	8

Source: M. Karlins, T. L. Coffman, and G. Walters, "On the Fading of Social Stereotypes: Studies in Three Generations of College Students." *Journal of Personality and Social Psychology,* 1969, 13:1, 1–16.

subjects even expressed negative attitudes toward two non-existent groups, the "Piraneans" and the "Danirians." As further testimony to the irrationality of stereotypes, we may note that when a prejudiced person meets a pleasant or likeable member of a rejected group, the out-group member tends to be perceived as "an exception to the rule," not as a disconfirmation of the stereotype.

Question: How do stereotypes and intergroup tensions develop?

Two experiments, both in unlikely settings and both using children as subjects, offer some insight into these problems.

An Experiment in Prejudice   What is it like to be discriminated against? Those who have never experienced discrimination probably can't imagine it. In a unique experiment, elementary school teacher Jane Elliot sought to give her pupils direct experience with prejudice.

On the first day of the experiment, Elliot announced that brown-eyed children were to sit in the back of the room and that they could not use the drinking fountain. Blue-eyed children were given extra recess time and got to leave first for lunch. At lunch brown-eyed children were prevented from taking second helpings, because they would "just waste it." Mixing of brown-eyed and blue-eyed children was prevented, and the blue-eyed children were told they were cleaner and smarter (Peters, 1971).

At first Elliot had to maintain these imposed conditions of prejudice. She also made an effort to constantly criticize and belittle the brown-eyed children. To her surprise, the blue-eyed children rapidly joined in and soon were out-doing her in the viciousness of their attacks. The blue-eyed children began to feel superior, and the brown-eyed children felt just plain awful. Fights broke out. Test scores of the brown-eyed children fell.

Question: How lasting were the effects of this experiment?

The effects were short-lived, because two days later the roles of the children were reversed. Before long, the same destructive effects occurred again, but this time in reverse.

Fig. 26–4   *Racial and ethnic pride are gradually replacing stereotypes and discrimination.*

The implications of this experiment are unmistakable. In less than 1 day it was possible to get children to hate each other because of their eye color and **status inequalities.** Certainly, the effects of a lifetime of real racial or ethnic prejudice are infinitely more powerful and destructive.

Question: What can be done to combat prejudice?

Equal-Status Contact Progress has been made through attempts to educate the general public about the lack of justification for prejudicial attitudes. Changing the belief component of an attitude has long been known to be one of the most direct means of changing the entire attitude. Thus, when people are made aware that minority group members share the same goals, ambitions, feelings, and frustrations as they do, intergroup relations may be improved.

However, this is not the whole answer. As we noted earlier, there is often a wide difference between attitudes and actual behavior. Until nonprejudicial behavior is engineered, changes can be quite superficial. Several lines of thought (including cognitive dissonance theory) suggest that more frequent **equal-status contact** between groups in conflict should reduce prejudice and stereotypes.

Question: But does it?

Much evidence suggests it does. For example, in one early study white women who lived in integrated and segregated housing projects were compared for changes in attitude toward their black neighbors. Women in the integrated project showed a favorable shift in attitudes toward members of the other racial group. Those in the segregated project showed no change or actually became more prejudiced than before (Deutsch & Collins, 1951). In other studies mixed-race groups have been formed at work, in the laboratory, and at schools. The conclusion from such research is that personal contact with a disliked group will induce friendly interracial behavior, respect, and liking. However, these benefits occur only when personal contact is on an equal footing (Cook, 1985).

To test the importance of equal-status contact directly, Gerald Clore and his associates set up a unique summer camp for children. The camp was administered by one white male, one white female, one black male, and one black female. Each campsite had three black and three white campers and one black and one white counselor. Thus, blacks and whites were equally divided in number, power, privileges, and duties. Did the experience make a difference? Apparently it did: Testing showed the children had significantly more positive attitudes toward opposite-race children after attending the camp than they did before (Clore, 1976).

Superordinate Goals Let us now consider a revealing study of intergroup conflict and its reduction. Muzafer Sherif and his associates conducted an ingenious experiment—also at a summer camp—with 11-year-old boys. When they arrived at camp, the boys were separated into two groups and housed in cabins that were physically separated. At first the groups were kept apart to build up in-group friendships. Development of pride and identification with the in-group was encouraged by participation in cooperative games and activities. Soon each group had a flag, a name (the "Rattlers" and the "Eagles"), and had staked out its own territory. At this point the two groups were placed in competition with each other. After a number of clashes, disliking between the two groups bordered on hatred. Outright hostility erupted as the boys baited each other, started fights, and raided each other's cabins (Sherif et al., 1961).

Question: Were they allowed to go home hating each other?

As an experiment in the reduction of intergroup conflict, and to prevent the boys from remaining enemies, various strategies were tried to reduce tensions. Having leaders from each group meet did nothing. Just getting the groups together also did little. When the groups were invited to eat together, the event became a free-for-all.

Finally, emergencies were staged that required cooperation among members of the groups. For example, the water supply was damaged in a way that required all the boys to work together to repair it. Creation of this and other **superordinate goals** served to restore relations between the two groups. As members were forced to cooperate, hostilities subsided.

"Jigsaw" Classrooms Contrary to the hopes of many, integrating public schools often has little positive effect on racial prejudice. In fact, prejudice may be made worse, and the self-esteem of minority students frequently decreases (Aronson, 1980).

Question: If integrated schools provide equal-status contact, shouldn't prejudice be reduced?

Theoretically, yes. But in practice, minority-group children often enter newly integrated schools unprepared to compete on an equal footing. Elliot Aronson and his colleagues (1978) argue that the competitive nature of schools almost guarantees that children will *not* learn to like and understand each other. In the typical classroom, children compete fiercely for the approval of the teacher. Successful students learn to feel superior and often hold unsuccessful students in contempt. This is a high-stakes game in which only a few can win. It is clearly not a good way to reduce prejudice.

Based on the preceding ideas, Aronson has pioneered a way to apply the concept of superordinate goals to ordinary classrooms. According to Aronson, such goals are effective because they make people **mutually interdependent.** Each person's needs are linked to those of others in the group, and cooperation is encouraged.

Question: How has this idea been applied?

Aronson has successfully created **"jigsaw" classrooms** that emphasize cooperation rather than competition. The term *jigsaw* refers to the pieces of a jigsaw puzzle. In Aronson's method, each child is given a "piece" of the information needed to prepare for a test (Fig. 26–5).

In a typical session, children are divided into groups of five or six and given a topic to study for a later exam. Each child is given his or her "piece" of information and asked to learn it. For example, one child might have information on Thomas Edison's invention of the light bulb; another, facts about his invention of the telephone; and a third, information on Edison's childhood. After the children have learned their individual parts, they teach them to others in the group. Even the most competitive children quickly realize that they cannot do well without the aid of everyone in the group. Each child makes a unique and essential contribution, so the children learn to listen to, and respect, each other.

Does the jigsaw method work? Compared with children in traditional classrooms, children in jigsaw groups were less prejudiced, they liked their classmates more, they had more positive attitudes toward school, their grades improved, and their self-esteem increased (Aronson et al., 1979). Such results are quite encouraging. As Kenneth Clark (1965) has said, "Racial prejudice . . . debases all human beings—those who are its victims, those who victimize, and in quite subtle ways, those who are merely accessories."

Aggression— The World's Most Dangerous Animal

For a time, the City Zoo of Los Angeles had on display two examples of the world's most dangerous animal—the only animal capable of destroying the earth and all other animal species. Perhaps you have already guessed which animal this was. In the cage were two college students, representing the species *Homo sapiens!*

The human capacity for aggression is staggering. It has been estimated that during the 125-year period ending

Fig. 26–5 *In a "jigsaw" classroom, children help each other prepare for tests. As they "teach" each other what they know, the children learn to cooperate and to respect the unique strengths of each individual.*

with World War II, 58 million humans were killed by other humans (an average of nearly 1 person per minute). Murder now ranks as a major cause of death in the United States. One American kills another every 23 minutes—making the United States one of the world's most violent nations (Meredith, 1984). It is estimated that more than 1.4 million American children are subjected to physical abuse by parents each year. War, homocide, riots, family violence, assassination, rape, assault, forcible robbery, and other violent acts offer further testimony to the realities of human aggression (Fig. 26–6).

Question: What causes aggression?

The complexity of aggression has given rise to a number of potential explanations for its occurrence. Brief descriptions of some of the major possibilities follow.

Instincts Some theorists argue that, as humans, we are naturally aggressive, having inherited a "killer instinct" from our animal ancestors. Ethologists such as Konrad Lorenz (1966, 1974) believe that aggression is a biologically rooted behavior observed in all animals, including humans. Lorenz also believes that humans lack certain innate patterns that inhibit aggression in other animal spe-

Fig. 26–6 *Ritualized human aggression. Violent and aggressive behavior is so commonplace it may be viewed as entertainment. How "natural" is aggressive behavior?*

cies. For example, in a dispute over territory or dominance, two wolves may growl, lunge, bare their teeth, and fiercely threaten each other. In most instances, though, neither is killed or even wounded. One wolf, recognizing the dominance of the other, will typically bare its throat in a gesture of submission. The dominant wolf could kill in an instant, but it is inhibited by the submissive gesture. In contrast, human confrontations of equal intensity almost always end in injury or homicide.

The idea that humans are "naturally" aggressive has an intuitive appeal, but many psychologists question it. Many of Lorenz's "explanations" of aggression are little more than loose comparisons between human and animal behavior. Just labeling a behavior as "instinctive" does little to explain it. More importantly, we are left with the question of why some individuals or human groups (the Arapesh, the Senoi, the Navajo, the Eskimo, and others) show little hostility or aggression.

Biology   Despite problems with the instinctive view, there is evidence that a biological basis for aggression may exist. Physiological studies have shown that there are brain areas capable of triggering or ending aggressive behavior (see Chapter 3). Also, researchers have found a relationship between aggression and such physical factors as hy-

poglycemia (low blood sugar), allergy, and specific brain injuries and disorders (Bandura, 1973; Bolton, 1976; Mark & Ervin, 1970). None of these conditions, however, can be considered a direct *cause* of aggression. Instead, they probably lower the threshold for aggression, making hostile behavior more likely to occur.

The effects of alcohol and other drugs provide another indication of the role of the brain and biology in violence and aggression. A variety of studies show that alcohol is involved in large percentages of murders and violent crimes (Collins, 1981; Lagerspetz, 1981). Intoxicating drugs lower inhibitions to act aggressively—often with tragic results.

Frustration   Step on a dog's tail and you may get nipped. Frustrate a human and you may get insulted. The **frustration-aggression hypothesis** states that frustration is closely associated with aggression (Dollard et al., 1939). At several points in earlier chapters we have considered examples of the link between frustration and aggression.

Question: Does frustration always produce aggression?

Although the connection is strong, a moment's thought will show that frustration does not *always* lead to aggression, and that aggression can occur in the absence of frustration. Frustration, for instance, may lead to stereotyped responding, or perhaps to a state of "learned helplessness" (see Chapters 13 and 14). Aggression in the absence of frustration might be demonstrated by sports spectators who start fights, throw bottles, tear down goalposts, and the like after their team has *won*.

Frustration probably encourages aggression because it is aversive (uncomfortable). Many experiments have shown that unpleasant stimuli, such as pain, insults, sweltering rooms, and disgusting scenes or odors tend to increase aggression. Such stimuli probably raise overall arousal levels so that we become more sensitive to *cues* for aggression (Berkowitz, 1976, 1982).

Question: What do you mean by "cues" for aggression?

Some cues, or signals, for aggression are internal (angry thoughts for instance). Many are external: Certain words, actions, and gestures of others are strongly associated with aggressive response (a raised middle finger, for instance, is an almost universal invitation to aggression).

Even inanimate objects may serve as cues for aggression. In one classic experiment, subjects administered shocks to another person in a laboratory. Before doing so, they were ridiculed and shocked by the other person. Just before subjects got a chance to "return the favor," they saw either a couple of badminton rackets, or a shotgun and a revolver on a table in the testing room. In either case, the experimenter explained that someone had left the objects there, and he casually moved them aside. Subjects who glimpsed the guns gave stronger shocks to the person who had angered them than did subjects who saw the sports equipment (Berkowitz, 1968). The implication of this **weapons effect** seems to be that the symbols and trappings of aggression encourage aggression.

Social Learning   One of the most widely accepted explanations of aggression is also the simplest. **Social learning theory** holds that we learn to be aggressive by observing aggression in others (Bandura, 1973). According to this view, there is no instinctive human programming for fistfighting, pipe-bombing, knife-wielding, gun-loading, or other elements of violent or aggressive behavior. Hence, aggression must be learned.

Social learning theorists predict that individuals growing up in nonaggressive cultures will themselves be nonaggressive. Those raised in a culture with aggressive models and heroes will learn aggressive responses.

Considered in such terms, it is no wonder that America has become one of the most violent of all countries. It is estimated that a violent crime occurs every 54 seconds in the United States. Approximately 40 percent of the popu-

Highlight 26–1
**Aggression and Pornography—
Is There a Link?**

The debate on the effects of pornography is heating up again. Until recently, most evidence suggested that viewing pornography has no major adverse effects. This conclusion appears to remain valid for stimuli that can be described as merely erotic or sexual in content. However, in the last 10 years there has been a dramatic increase in the number of aggressive-pornographic stimuli appearing in the mass media. **Aggressive pornography** refers to depictions in which violence, threats, or obvious power differences are used to force someone (usually a woman) to engage in sex.

What are the effects of images that link aggression with sexual arousal? To answer this question, researchers have performed a variety of experiments that follow this general form: First, male subjects are angered. Then they are exposed to an aggressive-pornographic film. Other subjects watch either neutral or nonaggressive-erotic films for comparison. Subjects are then allowed to administer supposed electrical shocks to either male or female "victims."

The principal finding of such studies is that aggressive-pornographic stimuli do increase aggression by males against females. In a summary of related experiments, researchers Neil Malamuth and Ed Donnerstein (1982) conclude that "exposure to mass media stimuli that have violent and sexual content increases the audience's aggressive-sexual fantasies, beliefs in rape myths, and aggressive behavior."

lation owns firearms. Nationally, 70 percent agree that "When a boy is growing up, it is very important for him to have a few fistfights." Eighteen percent of the population admit to having slapped or kicked another person (Stark & McEvoy, 1970). Children and adults are treated to an almost nonstop parade of aggressive models (in the media as well as in actual behavior—see Highlight 26–1). We are, without a doubt, an aggressive culture.

Question: What can be done about aggression?

Social learning theory implies that "aggression begets aggression." In other words, watching a prize fight, sporting event, or violent television program may increase aggression, rather than drain off aggressive urges. Thus, the spiral of aggression might be broken if we did not so often portray it, reward it, and glorify it.

Anger Control   On a personal level, some psychologists have succeeded in teaching people to control their anger and aggressive impulses. The key to **anger control** is the fact that people who respond calmly to upsetting situations tend to see them as *problems to be solved*. Therefore, to limit anger, people are taught to:

1. Define the problem as precisely as possible.
2. Make a list of possible solutions.
3. Rank the likely success of each solution.
4. Choose a solution and try it.
5. Assess how successful the solution was and make adjustments if necessary.

Taking these steps has helped many people lessen tendencies toward child abuse, family violence, and other destructive outbursts (Meichenbaum, Henshaw, & Himel, 1982).

Beyond this, the question remains, "How shall we tame the world's most dangerous animal?" There is no easy answer—only a challenge of pressing importance. The solution will undoubtedly involve the best efforts of thinkers and researchers from many disciplines.

For the more immediate future it is clear that we need more people who are willing to engage in helpful, altruistic, *prosocial* behavior. In the following Applications section we will examine some of the forces that operate to prevent people from helping others. Also discussed are a few glimmerings about how to encourage prosocial behavior.

Learning Check

1. Social stereotypes may be both positive and negative.   T or F?

2. The stereotypes underlying racial and ethnic prejudice tend to be irrational.   T or F?

3. Over the last 30 to 40 years there has been a marked increase in stereotyped images held by college students.   T or F?

4. Jane Elliot's classroom experiment in prejudice showed that children could be made to dislike one another
   a. by setting up group competition   *c.* by role playing
   b. by imposing status inequalities   *d.* by frustrating all the students

5. Research suggests that prejudice and intergroup conflict may be reduced by _____ _____ interaction and _____ goals.

6. Some researchers view aggression as related to such factors as hypoglycemia, allergy, and specific brain injuries and disorders.   T or F?

7. Frustration is more likely to produce aggression when cues for aggressive behavior are present.   T or F?

8. Social learning theory holds that exposure to aggression _____ aggressive behavior.

Answers: 1. T 2. T 3. F 4. b 5. equal status, superordinate 6. T 7. T 8. increases

Applications

Helping—Prosocial Behavior

Late one night in March 1964, tenants of a Queens, New York, apartment building watched and listened in horror as a young woman named Kitty Genovese was murdered on the sidewalk outside. From the safety of their rooms, no fewer than 38 people heard the agonized screams as her assailant stabbed her, was frightened off, and returned to stab her again.

Kitty Genovese's murder took over 30 minutes, but none of her neighbors tried to help. None even called the police. Perhaps it is understandable that no one wanted to get involved. After all, it could have been a violent lovers' quarrel, or helping might have meant risking personal injury. But what prevented these people from at least calling the police?

Question: Isn't this an example of the alienation of city life?

News reports treated this incident as evidence of a breakdown in social ties caused by the impersonality of the city. While it is true that urban living can be dehumanizing, this does not fully explain such **bystander apathy.** According to psychologists Bibb Latane and John Darley (1968), failure to help is related to the number of people present. Over the years numerous studies have shown that the more potential helpers present, the *lower* the chances that help will be given (Latane, Nida, & Wilson, 1981).

Question: Why would people be less willing to help when others are present?

In Kitty Genovese's case the answer is that everyone thought *someone else* would help. The dynamics of this effect can be illustrated in this way: Suppose that two motorists have stalled at roadside, one on a sparsely traveled country road and the other on a busy freeway. Who gets help first?

On the freeway, where hundreds of cars pass every minute, each driver can assume that someone else will help. Personal responsibility for helping is spread so thin that no one takes action. On the country road, one of the first few people to arrive will probably stop, since the responsibility is clearly theirs. In general, Latane

and Darley assume that bystanders are not apathetic or uncaring; they are inhibited by the presence of others.

Bystander Intervention   There are four **decision points** individuals must pass through before giving help. First they must **notice** that something is happening. Next they must **define** the event as an emergency. Then they must **take responsibility.** Finally, they must **select** a course of action. Laboratory experiments have shown that each step can be influenced by the presence of other people.

Noticing   What would happen if you fainted and collapsed on the sidewalk? Would someone stop to help? Would people think you were drunk? Would they even *notice* you? Latane and Darley suggest that if the sidewalk is crowded, few people will even see you. This has nothing to do with people blocking each other's vision. Instead, it is related to widely accepted norms against staring at others in public. People in crowds typically "keep their eyes to themselves."

Question: Is there any way to show this is a factor in bystander apathy?

To test this idea, students were asked to fill out a questionnaire either alone or in a room full of people. While the students worked, a thick cloud of smoke was blown into the room through a ventilator.

Most students alone in the room noticed the smoke immediately. Few of the people in groups noticed the smoke, even when it became difficult to see through it. Subjects working in groups politely kept their eyes on their papers and avoided looking at others (or the smoke). In contrast, those who were alone scanned the room from time to time.

Defining an Emergency   The smoke-filled room also shows the influence others have on defining a situation as an emergency. After subjects in groups noticed the smoke, they cast sidelong glances at others in the room. Apparently they were searching for clues to help interpret what was happening. No one wanted to over-

Applications: Helping—Prosocial Behavior

react or make fools of themselves if there was no emergency. However, as subjects coolly surveyed the reactions of others, they were themselves being surveyed. In real emergencies, people sometimes underestimate the need for action because each person attempts to appear calm. In short, until someone acts, no one acts.

Taking Responsibility   Perhaps the most crucial step in the helping sequence is assuming responsibility. In this case, groups limit helping by causing a **diffusion of responsibility.**

Question: Is that like the unwillingness of drivers to offer help on a crowded freeway?

Exactly. It is the feeling that no one is personally responsible for helping.

This problem was demonstrated in an experiment in which students took part in a group discussion over an intercom system. Actually, there was only one real subject in each group; the others were tape-recorded confederates of the experimenter. Each subject was placed in a separate room (supposedly to maintain confidentiality), and discussions of college life were begun.

During the discussion, one of the "students" simulated an epileptic-like seizure and called out for help. In some cases, subjects thought they were alone with the seizure victim. Others believed they were members of three- or six-person groups.

Subjects who thought they were alone with the "victim" of this staged emergency reported it immediately or tried to help. Some subjects in the three-person groups failed to respond and those who did were slower. In the six-person groups, over a third of the subjects took no action at all.

People in this experiment were obviously faced with a conflict like that in many real emergencies: should they be helpful and responsible, or should they mind their own business? Many were influenced toward inaction by the presence of others.

Question: People do help in some emergencies. How are these different?

It is not always clear what makes the difference. Helping behavior is a complex event, influenced by many variables.

One naturalistic experiment staged in a New York City subway gives a hint of the kind of things that may be important. When a "victim" (actor) "passed out" in a subway car, he received more help when carrying a cane than when carrying a liquor bottle. More importantly, however, was the fact that most people were willing to help in either case (Piliavin et al., 1969).

To better answer the question, we need to consider some factors not included in Latane and Darley's account of helping.

Who Will Help Whom?   Psychologist John Dovido (1984) has summarized some of the major factors that affect helping behavior. Many studies suggest that when we see a person in trouble, this tends to cause heightened arousal. This aroused, keyed-up feeling can motivate us to give aid, but only if the rewards and costs of helping are balanced: Higher costs (such as great effort, personal risk, or possible embarrassment) almost always decrease helping.

In addition to *general* arousal, potential helpers may feel *empathic* arousal. This means that they emphathize with the person in need or feel some of the person's pain, fear, or anguish. Empathic arousal also motivates helping—especially when the person in need seems to be similar to ourselves. In fact, feeling a connection to the victim may be one of the most important factors in helping. This, perhaps, is why being in a good mood also increases helping. When we are feeling successful, happy, or fortunate, we may also feel more connected to others (Dovido, 1984).

Question: Is there anything that can be done to encourage prosocial behavior?

There is evidence that people who see others helping are more likely to offer help themselves. For example, motorists were much more likely to stop to help a woman fix a flat tire when they had just passed another woman being helped by someone (Bryan & Test, 1967). Also, persons who give help in one situation tend to perceive themselves as helpful people. This change in self-image encourages them to help in other situations. One more point is that norms of fairness encourage us to help others who have helped us (Dovido, 1984). For all these reasons, helping others not only assists them directly, it encourages others to help too.

Applications: Helping—Prosocial Behavior

Learning Check

1. Psychologists have shown that the dehumanizing qualities of urban living explain most instances of bystander apathy.   T or F?
2. Defining an event as an emergency is the first step toward bystander intervention.   T or F?
3. People sometimes fail to define an event as an emergency because they are misled by a seeming lack of concern displayed by others.   T or F?
4. In laboratory experiments, a large number of potential helpers tends to reduce the likelihood that help will be given.   T or F?

Answers: 1. F   2. F   3. T   4. T

Chapter Summary

■ *Attitudes* are learned dispositions made up of a *belief component*, an *emotional component*, and an *action component*.

■ Attitudes may be formed by *direct contact, interaction with others*, and *childrearing practices*. Groups also exert pressures on attitudes held by their members. *Peer group influences*, the *mass media*, and *chance conditioning* also appear to be important in attitude formation.

■ Attitudes are typically measured by use of techniques such as *open-ended interviews, social distance scales*, and *attitude scales*. Attitudes expressed in these ways do not always correspond to actual behavior.

■ Attitude change is related to *reference group membership*, to deliberate *persuasion*, and to significant *personal experiences* (which may be engineered through *role playing*).

■ The maintenance and change of attitudes are closely related to needs for consistency in thoughts and actions. *Cognitive dissonance theory* explains the dynamics of such needs.

■ *Brainwashing* is a form of forced attitude change. It depends on control of the target person's total environment. Three steps in brainwashing are *unfreezing, changing*, and *refreezing* attitudes and beliefs.

■ Many religious and quasi-religious cults recruit new members with high-pressure indoctrination techniques resembling brainwashing. Such groups attempt to catch people when they are vulnerable. Then they combine isolation, displays of affection, discipline and rituals, intimidation, and escalating commitment to bring about conversion.

■ *Prejudice* is a negative attitude held toward members of various *out-groups*. One theory attributes prejudice to *scapegoating*. A second says that prejudices may be held for personal reasons *(personal prejudice)* or simply through adherence to *group norms (group prejudice)*.

■ Prejudiced individuals tend to have *authoritarian* or *dogmatic personalities*, characterized by rigidity, inhibition, intolerance, oversimplification, and *ethnocentrism*.

■ *Intergroup conflict* gives rise to hostility and the formation of *social stereotypes. Status inequalities* tend to build prejudice. *Equal-status contact* tends to reduce it. Muzafer Sherif and others have emphasized the concept of *superordinate goals* as a key to reducing intergroup conflict, be it racial, religious, ethnic, or national. On a smaller scale, *jigsaw classrooms* (which encourage cooperation through mutual interdependence) have been shown to be an effective way of combating prejudice.

■ *Aggression* and violence are serious social problems and the subject of much current research. *Ethological explanations* of aggression attribute it to inherited instincts. *Biological explanations* emphasize brain mechanisms and physical factors related to thresholds for aggression. According to the *frustration-aggression hypothesis*, frustration and aggression are closely linked, especially when *aggressive cues* are present. *Social learning theory* has focused attention on the role of aggressive models in the development of aggressive behavior.

■ Four *decision points* that must be passed before a person gives help are: *noticing, defining an emergency, taking responsibility*, and *selecting a course of action*. Helping is less likely at each point when other potential helpers are present. Helping is encouraged by general arousal, empathic arousal, being in a good mood, low effort or risk, and similarity between the victim and the helper. For several reasons, giving help tends to encourage others to help too.

Sociobiology—Do Genes Guide Social Behavior?

A small band of men moves cautiously through a rubble-strewn battlefield. Without warning, a grenade sails overhead and lands at their feet. There is no time for escape. Instinctively, one of the men dives at the grenade, covers it with his own body, and shields his comrades from certain death. Scenes such as this have occurred in almost every modern war. How are such altruistic actions explained?

Sociobiology   According to a viewpoint called **sociobiology,** many human social behaviors have roots in heredity. Sociobiologists, such as Harvard zoologist Edward Wilson, believe that competition, war, territoriality, aggression, sibling rivalry, conformity, male-female differences, fear of strangers, altruism, and many other behaviors are "in our genes."

The core idea in sociobiology is that social behavior evolves in ways that maximize the fitness of a species for survival. For instance, animals that compete successfully for food, territory, mates, and so forth are more likely to survive and reproduce. Thus, competitiveness gradually becomes a trait of following generations. Sociobiologists believe that many human traits evolved through similar patterns of natural selection.

Applying the concept of natural selection to explain human nature may make sense for some behaviors. But how do sociobiologists explain altruistic actions like the selfless heroism of the soldier de-

scribed earlier? The answer is intriguing. Sociobiologists point out that altruistic suicides can be observed in many animal species. For example, if a honeybee stings an intruder in order to protect its hive, the bee will die. How could such behavior evolve if altruistic bees never get a chance to reproduce and pass on their genes? Sociobiologists reply that altruistic actions help improve chances that an animal's *kin* will survive.

Each individual shares some genes in common with close family members. So, while the altruistic individual's genes may not be passed on directly, they are perpetuated by close kin. In human terms, sociobiologists argue that a person might sacrifice his or her own chance of survival to ensure the survival of a number of close relatives. Of course, heroic soldiers are typically unrelated to their comrades. Nevertheless, a soldier may act for the good of the group because altruism has been "bred into" humans during eons of evolution.

Biological Determinism   Sociobiology deserves credit for offering a fresh perspective on human behavior. In fact, sociobiology produces some fascinating images when it is taken to its logical extremes: It is almost as if genes are at the helms of great hulking machines (our bodies) that they use for protection and self-preservation. Sociobiology seems to say that genes manipulate our behavior to ensure *their* survival (or at

least the survival of duplicate genes in the bodies of our relatives).

Sociobiology's major strength is that it helps relate human behavior to biology. Its major weakness is that it probably overstates its case. The degree of biological determinism assumed by sociobiologists is so extreme that even most biologists question it.

Critique   Thinking about the biological foundations of human behavior is always interesting. However, the conclusions drawn by sociobiologists are highly questionable. Evolution and natural selection, for instance, may have favored development of the human brain, rather than of specific behavioral traits. Humans equipped with large brains are resourceful, adaptable, and flexible. Our intelligence, in fact, would seem to have much more to do with our survival as individuals and as a group than could be provided by strict genetic programming.

Along the same line, many critics of sociobiology point out that evolution progresses too slowly to account for many behavioral adaptations. The spread of ideas, traditions, and cultural patterns is much more rapid. To return to our earlier example, altruism may indeed be a necessity for a society to endure. However, selfless acts need not be coded into our nature by genes; they may be explained equally well by learning.

The danger inherent in sociobiology is that it can be used to sup-

Exploration: Sociobiology—Do Genes Guide Social Behavior?

port the social status quo. By defining human nature as relatively fixed and (in the short run) unchanging, sociobiology discourages attempts to change current cultural practices. Edward Wilson has said, for instance, that since males are typically more aggressive than females, "even with identical education and equal access to all professions, men are more

likely to continue to play a disproportionate role in political life, business, and science." If you are female, that should make you angry. If you are a male, it should make you angry on behalf of your mother, sisters, daughters, wife, lover, and female friends.

Conclusion   In the realm of ideas, it's also a matter of survival

of the fittest. To many observers it appears that sociobiology will have to evolve greatly if it is going to survive. In the meantime, the sociobiology debate should prove interesting.

(Sources: Blaustein, 1983; Gould, 1976; Kamin, 1985; Kitchner, 1985; Lumsden & Wilson, 1983; Snowdon, 1983; Wilson, 1975.)

Learning Check

1. The core idea of sociobiology is that social behavior evolved in ways that maximize individual fitness for survival.   T or F?
2. Sociobiologists believe that altruistic behavior evolved because individual sacrifice improved chances that immediate family members and close kin would survive.   T or F?
3. The majority of biologists endorse sociobiological explanations of behavior.   T or F?
4. Critics of sociobiology point out that natural selection among humans might have favored enlargement of the brain and behavioral flexibility—not selection of specific behavioral traits.   T or F?

Answers: 1. T   2. T   3. F   4. T

Questions for Discussion

1. Choose an issue you feel strongly about. State your attitudes concerning the issue. How did you come to hold your present attitudes? What types of experiences or variables influenced you?
2. If you were asked to establish a program to end conflict between students attending two rival high schools, what steps would you take?
3. What do you think are the superordinate goals facing the nation and the world? (To be truly "superordinate," a goal would have to be seen as valid by nearly everyone.) Do such goals exist? How could such a goal be converted into greater intergroup cooperation?
4. Describe a situation in which you did or did not offer help to someone who was, or might have been, in need. What influenced your decision? In view of what you know about helping behavior, can you explain why rape or assault victims are advised to shout "Fire!"?
5. Kenneth Clark has said, "Prejudice is a way that hu-

man beings have of betraying the fragility of their egos." What do you think Clark meant? Do you agree?
6. How has the antismoking campaign of the American Cancer Society made use of cognitive dissonance to discourage smoking?
7. In what ways do magazine and television advertisements apply the principles of persuasion? (Consider the communicator, the message, and the audience.)
8. The view that humans are instinctively aggressive "naked apes" has been quite popular. To what do you attribute this popularity? Do you consider humans naturally aggressive? What evidence can you give for or against this view?
9. Sociobiologists have been accused of making a basic error by assuming that human nature is revealed by the behavior of citizens in modern societies. What do you think are the basic, universal characteristics of human nature?

Applied Psychology

Chapter 27

Chapter Preview

Birdbrains

Imagine yourself lost at sea in a tiny rubber raft, the victim of a boating accident. After 10 hours adrift, you begin to lose all hope of being found. Then, seemingly out of nowhere, a Coast Guard helicopter swoops in and lifts you from the waves. Gratefully, you thank your rescuers. But with a laugh, they insist the real credit belongs to three "birdbrains."

Sound farfetched? In recent tests, pigeons—who are sharp-eyed and nearly immune to boredom—have been taught to aid search-and-rescue crews. The pigeons are first conditioned in Skinner boxes to peck images of red or yellow rafts, life vests, and life preservers. During rescues, they ride in a chamber under the helicopter, where their pecking is monitored electronically. A buzzer in the cockpit, activated by the pecking, guides pilots to the target (Japenga, 1982; Stark, 1981).

Applied psychology refers to the use of psychological principles and research methods to solve practical problems—such as finding victims lost at sea. Increasingly psychology is being used to enhance the quality of life and to improve human performance. And, as we will soon see, the ocean is not the only place where applied psychology can make a life-or-death difference.

The Towering Inferno   *All too often, fires in high-rise buildings lead to needless deaths. Using the elevators, for instance, can be fatal, because they act as chimneys for smoke and poisonous fumes (Keating & Loftus, 1981).*

Question: How can psychology improve the odds for survival?

In the confusion following a fire alarm, many people ignore posted safety instructions. To remedy the situation, psychologists Jack Keating and Elizabeth Loftus created an unusual, life-saving "fire alarm." The best alarm, they found, is a voice that tells people exactly what to do. After much research, they designed the following message to be broadcast during fires:

> Female voice: "May I have your attention, please. May I have your attention, please."
> Male voice: "There has been a fire reported on the 20th floor. While this report is being verified, the building manager would like you to proceed to the stairways and walk down to the 18th floor. Please do not use the elevators, as they may be needed. Please do not use the elevators, but proceed to the stairways." (Loftus, 1979)

As simple as this message seems, it contains three key elements: (1) Research has shown that switching from a female to a male voice (or the reverse) is very attention getting. (2) During emergencies, people like to feel that some authority is in control (the "building manager" in this case). (3) The crucial reminder to avoid the elevators is repeated, so it will be remembered.

Sea rescues and fire escapes may be dramatic examples of applying psychology, but they are far from unusual. In fields as diverse as industry, sports, and medicine, psychology is being applied to our lives. Let's see how.

Survey Questions   What are the major areas of applied psychology? What is the nature of each area? How is psychology applied in business and industry? What have psychologists learned about the effects of our physical and social environments? How do people choose careers? How is psychology being applied in space missions?

Resources

Introduction to Applied Psychology

Question: What are the major areas of applied psychology?

The largest area is clinical psychology (see Chapter 1). A closely related specialty is **community psychology.** Instead of focusing on individuals (as clinical psychologists do), community psychologists treat whole neighborhoods or communities as their "clients" (Conyne & Clack, 1981). (Community psychologists have BIG offices!) To promote community mental health, community psychologists typically emphasize prevention, education, and consultation. Often, they target drug abuse, child neglect, unemployment, prejudice, and similar problems for solution. Such efforts, they believe, help prevent mental health problems before they begin.

Beyond clinical areas in psychology, the list of applications grows large. In this chapter we will cover the psychology of work, environmental behavior, education, consumer behavior, health, and sports. To begin, let's see how psychology is applied in business and industry.

Industrial/Organizational Psychology— Psychology at Work

Do you consider work a blessing? Or a curse? Or do you simply agree that it is "better to wear out than to rust out"? Whatever your attitude, the simple fact is that most adults work for a living. From the 1920s until the present, **industrial/organizational psychologists** have studied the problems people face at work. Very likely, their efforts will affect how you are selected for a job and how you are tested, trained, and evaluated for promotions. A psychol-

ogist may even help design your work environment or the machines you use at work.

Industrial/organizational psychologists are employed mostly by government, industry, and businesses. Typically, they work in three major areas: testing and placement (personnel psychology), human relations at work, and industrial engineering (the design of machines and work environments) (Landy & Trumbo, 1980). To get a fuller flavor of what I/O psychologists do, look at Table 27–1. As you can see, their interests are quite varied. As a further illustration, see Box 27–1 for an interesting sample of recent I/O research.

Question: You mentioned that industrial psychologists sometimes help design machines. What does a "shrink for machines" do?!

Engineering Psychology

However helpful a machine may be in theory, it is of little value until it can be operated by humans. A poorly designed pocket calculator that causes errors might just as well be a paperweight. An automobile design that blocks large areas of the driver's vision could be deadly. To adapt machines for human use, the **engineering psychologist** (or **human factors engineer**) must make them *compatible* with our sensory and motor capacities (Neff, 1977; Wickens & Kramer, 1985). For example, *displays* must be easy to perceive, *controls* easy to use, and the tendency to make errors must be minimized (see Figure 27–1). Many of the machines we rely on each day were designed, in part, by human factors engineers. Some familiar examples include: push-button telephones, user-friendly computers, home appliances, cameras, airplane controls, and traffic signals.

Table 27–1   Topics of Special Interest to Industrial/Organizational Psychologists

absenteeism	pay schedules
decision making	personnel selection
design of organizations	personnel training
employee stress	productivity
employee turnover	promotion
interviewing	task analysis
job enrichment	task design
job satisfaction	work behavior
labor relations	work environment
machine design	work motivation
management styles	worker evaluations
minority workers	

Box 27–1
Flexitime

If you've ever worked "9 to 5," you know that traditional time schedules can be confining. In addition, they doom many workers to a daily battle with rush-hour traffic. To improve worker morale, industrial psychologists have proposed the use of flexible working hours, or **flexitime.** The basic idea is that starting and quitting times are made flexible, as long as employees are present during a core work period (Owen, 1976). For example, employees might be allowed to arrive between 7:30 A.M. and 10:30 A.M., and to depart between 3:30 P.M. and 6:30 P.M.

Is flexitime really an improvement? Recent studies of two groups of clerical workers suggest that in many cases it is. A switch to flexitime brought a number of benefits, including more job satisfaction, better work-group relations, better relations with supervisors, and less absenteeism (Narayan & Nath, 1982; Orpen, 1981). Although more research is needed, perhaps we can say that it is better, when possible, to bend hours instead of people.

More elaborate machines, such as the United States space shuttle, stretch human capacities to their limits—and require *extensive* human factors engineering.

Personnel Psychology

The mark of maturity, Sigmund Freud said, is a capacity for love and work. While most people gladly embrace love, many would just as soon forget work. Yet the fact is, employed adults spend an average of over 2000 hours

Fig. 27–1 *Human Factors Engineering. (a) Early roll indicators in airplanes were perceptually confusing and difficult to read (top). Improved displays are clear even to nonpilots. Which would you prefer if you were flying an airplane in heavy fog? (b) Even on a stove, the placement of controls is important. During simulated emergencies, subjects made no errors in reaching for the controls on the top stove. In contrast, they erred 38 percent of the time with the bottom arrangement (Chapanis & Lindenbaum, 1959). (c) Sometimes the shape of a control is used to indicate its function, so as to discourage errors. For example, the left control might be used to engage and disengage the gears of an industrial machine, whereas the right control might operate the landing flaps on an airplane.*

a year at their jobs. With so much time at stake, understanding the world of work is clearly a survival skill. Let's explore some additional aspects of industrial/organizational psychology likely to affect your life.

At present, the odds are 9 out of 10 that you are, or will be, employed in business or industry. Thus, nearly everyone who holds a job is sooner or later placed under the "psychological microscope" of personnel selection procedures. Clearly, there is value in knowing how selection for hiring and promotion is done.

Question: How do personnel psychologists make employee selections?

Personnel selection begins with a **job analysis** to find out exactly what workers do and what skills or knowledge they need for success in a job (Tenopyr & Oeltjen, 1982). A job analysis may be done by interviewing workers or supervisors, by giving them questionnaires, by observing work, or by identifying **critical incidents**. Critical incidents are situations that an employee *must* be able to cope with if he or she is going to succeed in a particular job. The ability to deal calmly with a mechanical emergency,

for instance, might be a critical incident for an airline pilot. Once job requirements are known, psychologists can state what skills, aptitudes, and interests are needed (Fig. 27–2).

Selection Procedures   After desirable skills and characteristics are identified, the next step is to learn which job applicants possess them. Currently, the methods most often used for evaluating job candidates are: gathering *biodata, interviewing,* giving *standardized psychological tests,* and the *assessment center* approach. Let's see what each entails.

As simple as it may seem, one good way to predict job success is to collect **biodata** (detailed biographical information) from applicants. The premise behind biodata is that past behavior tends to predict future behavior. Thus, by learning in detail about a person's life, it is often possible to say whether the person is suited for a particular type of work (Owens & Shoenfeldt, 1979). Some of the most useful items of biodata are: past athletic interest, academic achievement, scientific interest, extracurricular activities, religious activities, social popularity, friction

Fig. 27–2 *Analyzing complex skills has also been valuable to the United States Air Force. When million-dollar aircraft and the lives of pilots are at stake, it makes good sense to do as much training and research as possible on the ground. Air force psychologists use flight simulators like the one pictured here to analyze the complex skills needed to fly jet fighters. Skills can then be taught without risk on the ground. The General Electric simulator shown here uses a computer to generate full-color images that respond realistically to a pilot's use of the controls. (Photograph supplied by courtesy of General Electric Company.)*

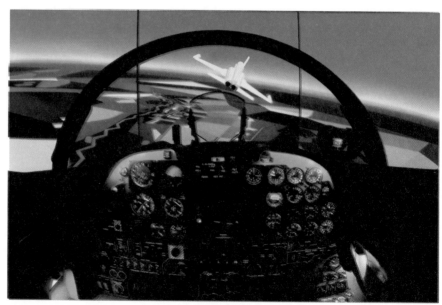

with brothers and sisters, attitudes toward school, and parents' socioeconomic status (Eberhardt & Muchinsky, 1982). Taken together, this information tells quite a lot about personality, interests, and abilities.

The traditional **personal interview** is still one of the most popular ways of selecting candidates for jobs or promotions. However, as we discussed in Chapter 18, interviews are subject to the *halo effect* and similar problems. For this reason, psychologists continue to investigate factors that affect interviews, with an eye toward improving their value. (See Box 27–2.)

Question: What kinds of tests do personnel psychologists use?

In addition to general intelligence and personality tests, like those described in earlier chapters, personnel psychologists frequently administer **vocational interest tests,** such as the *Kuder Occupational Interest Survey* and the *Strong-Campbell Interest Inventory*. Such tests identify interests by requiring a choice among statements like the following:

I would prefer to
a. visit a museum
b. read a good book
c. take a walk outdoors

If you take an interest test and your preferences match those of people who are successful in a given occupation, it is assumed that you, too, would be comfortable doing the work they do.

Aptitude tests are another mainstay of personnel psychology. Such tests rate a person's potential to learn tasks or skills used in various occupations. Tests exist for clerical aptitude, verbal aptitude, mechanical aptitude, artistic, legal, or medical aptitudes, and many others. As an example, tests of clerical aptitude emphasize the capacity to do rapid, precise, and accurate office work. One section of a clerical aptitude test, therefore, might ask a person to mark all numbers and names that are identical in a long list of pairs like those shown here (Schultz, 1979). (Also see Fig. 27–3.)

49837266	49832766
Global Widgets, Inc.	Global Wigets, Inc.
874583725	874583725
Sevanden Corp.	Sevanden Corp.
Perlee Publishing	Perlee Puhlishing

As a college graduate, you will quite likely encounter the **assessment center** approach to personnel selection. Assessment center programs are set up by many large organizations to do in-depth evaluations of job candidates. Assessment centers have become so popular that the list of

---

Box 27–2
The Sweet Smell of Success?—Not Always

Each year, clothing and cosmetics manufacturers spend huge sums to convince us that their products make us more attractive. Actually, such claims are somewhat justified. You might recall from Chapter 18, for instance, that physically attractive individuals are often given more positive evaluations in interviews—even on traits that have no connection to appearance. Presumably, this effect might even extend to the effects of wearing a pleasant perfume or cologne. But does it? In a recent experiment, *female* interviewers did, in fact, give higher ratings to job applicants who wore pleasant scents. But *males* gave *lower* ratings to persons who wore perfume or cologne (Baron, 1983).

Psychologist Robert Baron, who conducted this experiment, speculates that the male interviewers were more aware of the scents and resented the implied attempt to influence their ratings. Whatever the case, one thing is clear: If possible, you should learn an interviewer's sex beforehand—if you want to avoid making a flagrant, fragrant error, that is.

---

businesses using them—Ford Motor Company, International Business Machines, Kodak, Exxon, Sears, Bell Telephone, and over 1000 others—reads like a corporate *Who's Who.*

Question: How do assessment centers differ from the selection methods already described?

Assessment centers are used primarily to fill management and executive positions. After applicants have been tested and interviewed at an assessment center, they are placed in simulated work situations for observation and evaluation. For example, in one exercise applicants are given an *in-basket test.* This test consists of a basket full of memos, requests, and problems typical of those faced by executives. The applicant is asked to quickly read all of the materials and to take appropriate action. In another, more stressful test, applicants take part in a *leaderless group discussion* in which they try to solve a realistic business problem (Schultz, 1979). While the group grapples with the problem, "clerks" bring in price changes, information on

Fig. 27–3 *Not all aptitude tests are of the paper-and-pencil variety. Here, a job applicant takes a mechanical aptitude test.*

delayed supplies, and so forth. By observing applicants, it is possible to evaluate leadership skills and, especially, how job candidates cope with stress.

Question: How well does this approach work?

Assessment centers have had success in predicting performance in a variety of jobs, careers, and advanced positions in the military (Borman et al., 1983). One recent study of women, for instance, found that assessment center predictions of management potential were strongly related to career progress 7 years later (Ritchie & Moses, 1983). On the basis of long-range studies, it appears that future success is most clearly predicted by oral communication skills, leadership, energy, resistance to stress, tolerance for uncertainty, need for advancement, and planning skills (Bray et al., 1974; Ritchie & Moses, 1983).

As you will soon learn, psychologists working in business do far more than match people with jobs. Let's see how they also contribute to management and the quality of work.

Theories of Management and Job Satisfaction

At 7 A.M. each morning at a major manufacturing plant, more than 400 assembly line workers, supervisors, and top executives begin their work day talking, joking, and exercising together, all to the beat of amplified music. To say the least, these are unusual working conditions. To understand the rationale behind them, let's consider two basic theories of employee management.

Theory X and Theory Y One of the earliest attempts to improve worker efficiency was made in 1923 by Frederick Taylor, an engineer. To speed up production, Taylor standardized work procedures and emphasized careful planning, control, and orderliness. Today, modern versions of Taylor's approach are called **scientific management** (also known as **Theory X,** for reasons explained shortly). Scientific management uses time-and-motion studies, task analysis, job specialization, assembly lines, pay schedules, and the like, to increase productivity.

Question: It sounds like scientific management treats people as if they were machines. Is that true?

To some extent it is. Managers who adhere to Theory X tend to assume that workers must be coerced or guided into being productive. Many psychologists working in business are concerned, of course, with improving **work efficiency** (defined as maximum output at lowest cost). As a result, they alter conditions they believe will affect workers (such as time schedules, work quotas, bonuses, and so on). Some might even occasionally wish that people would act like well-oiled machines. However, most recognize that **psychological efficiency** is just as important as work efficiency. In addition to achieving high productivity, businesses must be able to retain workers, minimize absenteeism, sustain good morale and labor relations, and so forth if they are to prosper. Management that ignores or mishandles the human element can be very costly.

The term *Theory X* was coined by psychologist Douglas McGregor (1960) as a way to distinguish scientific management from a newer management style. McGregor dubbed this approach, which emphasizes human relations at work, **Theory Y.**

Question: How is this approach different?

Theory Y managers assume that workers enjoy independence and are willing to accept responsibility. They also assume that worker needs and goals can be meshed with the company's goals, and that people are not naturally passive or lazy. In short, Theory Y assumes that people are industrious, creative, and rewarded by challenging work. It appears that, given the proper conditions of freedom and responsibility, many people *will* work hard to gain competence and to use their talents fully.

Many features of Theory Y are illustrated by the Honda plant at Marysville, Ohio. As you probably know, the automobile industry has a long history of labor-management clashes and widespread discontent among workers. In fact, outright sabotage by assembly line workers is not uncommon. To avoid such problems, Honda initiated a series of simple, seemingly successful measures. They include:

Regardless of their position, all employees wear identical white uniforms. This allows workers and supervisors to interact on an equal footing and builds a feeling of teamwork.

To further minimize status differences, all employees hold the title *associate.*

There are no private offices, separate dining halls, or reserved parking for executives.

Employees work alongside company executives, to whom they have easy access.

Every employee has a say in, and responsibility for, quality control and safety.

Departmental meetings are held daily, in which announcements are made, decisions are made, and thoughts are freely shared (Abrams, 1983).

Of the many elements that make Theory Y methods effective, two that stand out are *participative management* and *management by objectives.* In **participative management,** employees at all levels are included in decision making (Fig. 27–4). By taking part in decisions that affect them, employees like those at the Honda factory come to see work as a cooperative effort—not as something imposed on them by an authoritarian boss. The resulting benefits include greater productivity, greater job satisfaction, and less job-related stress (Jackson, 1983).

Question: What does management by objectives refer to?

In **management by objectives,** workers are given specific goals to meet, so they can tell if they are doing a good job. Typical objectives include reaching a certain sales figure, making a certain number of items, or reducing waste by a specific percentage. In any case, workers are free to choose (within limits) how they will achieve their goals. As a result they experience a greater sense of independence and personal meaning in their work.

Job Satisfaction It often makes perfect sense to apply Theory X methods to work. However, doing so without taking worker needs into account can be a case of winning the battle while losing the war. That is, immediate productivity may rise while job satisfaction declines. And, when job satisfaction is low, morale falls and absenteeism skyrockets. There is also a high rate of turnover of employees, leading to high training costs and inefficiency. Understandably, many of the methods used by successful managers tend to improve **job satisfaction.**

Question: Under what conditions is job satisfaction highest?

Basically, job satisfaction comes from a good fit between a person's interests, abilities, needs, and expectations, and his or her work. What, then, do workers consider

Fig. 27–4 *Participative management techniques encourage employees at all levels to become involved in decision making. Quite often this arrangement leads to greater job satisfaction.*

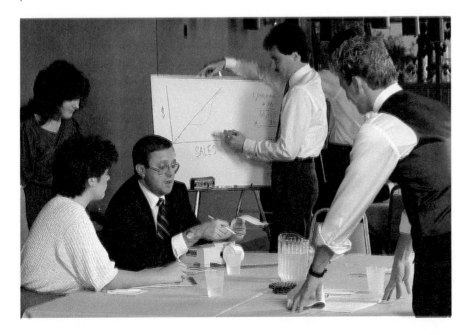

important? When a sample of American workers was asked to rate the importance of 25 aspects of work, the first 8 choices were:

1. Interesting work
2. Enough help and equipment to get the job done
3. Enough information to get the job done
4. Enough authority to get the job done
5. Good pay
6. Opportunity to develop special abilities
7. Job security
8. Seeing the results of one's work (*Work in America*, 1973)

Undoubtedly, some workers get satisfaction mainly from the money they earn. As you can see, however, most rate other factors higher. To summarize much research, we can say that job satisfaction is highest when workers are: (1) allowed ordinary social contacts with others; (2) allowed to use their own judgment and intelligence; (3) recognized for doing well; (4) given a chance to apply their skills; (5) given relative freedom from close supervision; and (6) given opportunities for promotion and advancement.

Job Enrichment   For years the trend in business and industry was to make work more streamlined and efficient and to tie greater pay to greater productivity. However, in recent years far too many jobs have become routine, repetitive, boring, and unfulfilling. It's no wonder that incentives such as bonuses and raises often have little effect on productivity. A better strategy, it would seem, is **job enrichment**—an approach that combines many of the principles just discussed.

Question: How is job enrichment done?

Job enrichment usually involves removing some of the controls and restrictions on employees and giving them greater responsibility, freedom, choice, and authority. Also, instead of performing an isolated part of a larger process, employees may switch to doing a complete cycle of work or completing an entire item or project. Whenever possible, workers are given feedback about their work or progress. This feedback comes to them directly instead of to a supervisor. Workers are encouraged to learn new and more difficult tasks and to learn a broad range of skills.

Job enrichment has been used with great success by large corporations such as IBM, Maytag, Western Electric, Chrysler, and Polaroid. It is usually accompanied by lower production costs, increased job satisfaction, reduced boredom, and less absenteeism (Schultz, 1979).

Although we have only scratched the surface of industrial/organizational psychology, it is time to move on for a look at another applied area of great personal relevance. Before we begin, here's a Learning Check.

Learning Check

1. To gain attention for an emergency announcement, it is better to switch from a male voice to a female voice than it is to do the reverse.   T or F?

2. An important element of engineering psychology is making _____ and _____ compatible with human use.

3. Identifying critical work incidents is sometimes included in a thorough _____ _____.

4. Detailed biographical information about a job applicant is referred to as _____.

5. The Strong-Campbell Inventory is a typical aptitude test.   T or F?

6. A leaderless group discussion is most clearly associated with which approach to employee selection?
   a. aptitude testing   *b.* personal interviews   *c.* job analysis   *d.* assessment center

7. Theory X, or scientific management, is concerned primarily with improving _____ _____.

8. Participative management is often a feature of businesses that follow Theory Y.   T or F?

9. For the majority of workers, job satisfaction is almost exclusively related to the amount of pay received.   T or F?

10. Job enrichment is a direct expression of scientific management principles.   T or F?

Answers: 1. F   2. displays, controls   3. job analysis   4. biodata   5. F   6. *d*   7. work efficiency   8. T   9. F   10. F

Environmental Psychology— Life in the Big City

For the last decade psychologist Terry Daniel has pursued an unusual and very interesting line of research. Using a variety of special analytic techniques, Daniel and his colleagues have helped the United States Forest Service evaluate the psychological effects of harvesting timber from forest lands (Daniel & Boster, 1976). The Forest Service was interested in learning how to harvest timber (especially dead trees) from forests without damaging their appeal. By doing an analysis of scenic beauty, Daniel and his colleagues helped guide harvesting plans. Loosely speaking, what they found is that, in the public eye, the ideal forest scene consists of a green meadow, a few young, healthy pine trees, and one or two picturesque, old fallen logs. This description suggests that much thinning of natural forestation can be done without hurting forest aesthetics— at least as far as the general public is concerned.

The work of Terry Daniel, and psychologists like him, falls into an area known as **environmental psychology,** a specialty concerned with how environments influence our behavior. Environmental psychologists are interested both in **physical environments** (natural or constructed) and in **social environments** (such as a dance, business meeting, or party) (Conyne & Clack, 1981). They also give special attention to **behavioral settings** (for example, an office,

locker room, church, casino, or classroom). As you have no doubt noticed, various environments and behavioral settings tend to "demand" certain actions (Fig. 27–5). Consider, for example, the difference between a classroom with all seats facing forward and one in which the seats are arranged in a circle. In which classroom would group discussion most likely occur?

Other major interests of environmental psychologists are personal space, territorial behavior (see Box 27–3), stressful environments, architectural design, environmental protection, and many related topics (Table 27–2).

Environmental Influences A major implication of environmental research is that much of our behavior is controlled, in part, by the environment (Conyne & Clack, 1981). A case in point is the seismograph (earthquake detector) housed at a museum in the author's hometown. Even though this instrument is cased in solid concrete, its lure is apparently irresistible—below it are countless shoe marks made by visitors who have kicked the wall to see if the seismograph's needle would move! (It doesn't.) Similarly, psychologists have found that a variety of factors influence the amount of vandalism that occurs in public places.

On the basis of psychological research, many architects now "harden" and "de-opportunize" public settings to discourage vandalism and graffiti (Wise, 1982). Some such

Fig. 27–5 *Various behavioral settings place strong demands on people to act in expected ways.*

Box 27–3
Territoriality

In Chapter 25 we noted that powerful norms govern the use of space surrounding each person's body. As we move farther from the body, it becomes apparent that personal space also extends to adjacent areas that we claim as our "territory." For example, in the library **territorial behavior** might include protecting your space with a book, coat, notebook, or other personal belonging (Sommer, 1969). "Saving a place" at a theater or beach also demonstrates the tendency to identify a space as "ours."

Respect for the temporary ownership of space is widespread. It is not unusual for a person to "take over" an entire table or study room by looking annoyed when others intrude. Your own personal territory may include your room, specific seats in many of your classes, or a particular table in the cafeteria or library that "belongs" to you and your friends.

Researchers have found that the more attached you are to an area, the more likely you are to signal your "ownership" with obvious **territorial markers,** such as decorations, plants, photographs, posters, or even graffiti (Hansen & Altman, 1976). College dorms and business offices are prime places to observe this type of territorial marking.

Table 27–2   Topics of Special Interest to Environmental Psychologists

architectural design	noise
behavioral settings	personal space
cognitive maps	personality and environment
constructed environments	pollution
crowding	privacy
energy conservation	proxemics
environmental stressors	resource management
heat	territoriality
human ecology	urban planning
littering	vandalism
natural environment	

efforts limit opportunities for vandalism (doorless toilet stalls, tiled walls). Others weaken the lure of potential targets. (Strangely enough, a raised flower bed around signs helps protect them, because people resist trampling the flowers to get to the sign.)

Given the personal impact that environments have, it is important to know how we are affected by stressful or unhealthy environments—a topic we will now consider.

Stressful Environments

Everyone has his or her own list of complaints about living in, or visiting, a large city. Traffic congestion, pollution, crime, and impersonality are urban problems that rapidly come to mind. To this list psychologists have added crowding, noise, and overstimulation as major sources of urban stress. Recent psychological research has begun to clarify the impact of each of these conditions on human functioning.

Crowding   Overpopulation ranks as one of the most serious problems facing the world today. The world's population is now well over 4 billion, and it will more than double in the next 40 years. Nowhere are the effects of overpopulation more evident than in the teeming cities of many underdeveloped nations. Closer to home, the jammed buses, subways, and living quarters of our own large cities are ample testimony to the stresses of crowding.

Question: Is there any way to assess the effect crowding has on people?

One approach is to study the effects of overcrowding among animals. Although the results of animal experiments cannot be considered conclusive for humans, they point to some disturbing effects.

Question: For example?

In an interesting experiment, John Calhoun (1962) let a group of laboratory rats reproduce without limit in a confined space. Calhoun provided plenty of food, water, and nesting materials for the rats. All the rats lacked was space. At its peak the colony numbered 80 rats, yet it was housed in a cage designed to comfortably hold about 50. Overcrowding in the cage was heightened by actions of the two most dominant males, who staked out private territory at opposite ends of the cage, gathered harems of 8 to 10 females, and prospered. This situation forced the remaining rats into a small middle area where severe crowding resulted.

Question: What effect did crowding have on the animals?

A high incidence of pathological behavior developed in both males and females. Females abandoned nest building and caring for their young. Pregnancies decreased and infant mortality ran extremely high. Many of the animals became highly aggressive and went on rampaging attacks against others. Sexual behavior was rampant, with some animals displaying hypersexuality, bisexuality, homosexuality, or complete sexual passivity. Many of the animals died, apparently from stress-caused diseases. The connection between these problems and overcrowding is unmistakable.

Question: But does this apply to humans?

Many of the same pathological behaviors can be observed in crowded inner-city ghettos. It is therefore tempting to assume that violence, social disorganization, and declining birthrates as seen in these areas are directly related to crowding. However, the link has not yet been demonstrated with humans. Nutritional, educational, income, and health care disadvantages suffered by those living in the inner city may also be to blame (Freedman, 1975). In fact, many laboratory studies using human subjects have failed to produce any serious ill effects by crowding people into small places. Most likely, this is because *crowding* is a psychological condition that is separate from **density** (the number of people in a given space).

Question: How does crowding differ from density?

Crowding refers to *subjective* feelings of being overstimulated by social inputs or by a loss of privacy. Whether high density is experienced as crowding may depend on relationships among those involved (Fig. 27–6). In an elevator, subway, or prison, high densities may be uncomfortable. In contrast, a musical concert, party, or reunion may be most pleasant at high density levels (Freedman, 1975). Thus, crowding may interact with various situations to intensify existing stresses or pleasures. Researcher Garvin McCain and his colleagues have recently reported that there are substantial increases in death rates among prison inmates and mental hospital patients living in crowded conditions.

Overload   One clear cost of high densities and crowding is a condition that psychologist Stanley Milgram calls **attentional overload**. Large cities tend to bombard inhabitants with sensory stimulation, information, and interper-

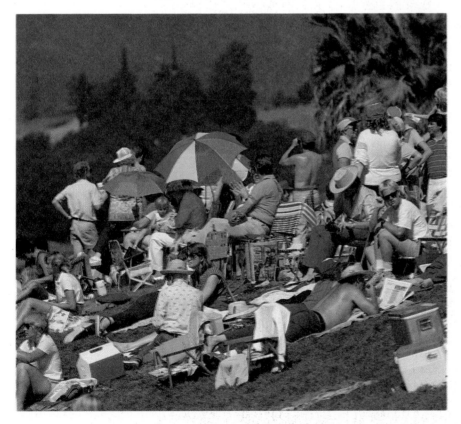

Fig. 27–6 *High densities do not automatically produce feelings of crowding. The nature of the situation and the relationship between crowd members are also important.*

Box 27–4
The High Cost of Noise

How serious are the effects of daily exposure to noise? A recent study of children attending schools near Los Angeles International Airport suggests that constant noise can be quite damaging. Children from the noisy schools were compared with students of similar backgrounds attending schools farther from the airport (Cohen et al., 1980). Testing showed that children attending the noisy schools had higher blood pressure than those from the quieter schools. They were more likely to give up attempts to solve a difficult puzzle. And, they were poorer at proofreading a printed paragraph—a task that requires close attention and concentration.

The greater tendency of children from the noisy schools to give up or become distracted is a serious handicap. It may even indicate a state of "learned helplessness" (described in Chapter 13) caused by daily, uncontrollable blasts of sound. Even if such damage proves to be temporary, it is clear that "noise pollution" is a major source of environmental stress.

sonal contact. The resulting sensory and cognitive overload can be quite stressful (see Box 27–4). Milgram (1970) believes city dwellers learn to prevent overload by engaging in only brief, superficial interpersonal contacts, by ignoring nonessential events, and by adopting cold and unfriendly expressions. In short, many city dwellers may find that a degree of callousness is essential for survival.

Question: Is there any evidence that such strategies are actually adopted?

A fascinating study suggests that they are. In several large American cities and smaller nearby towns, a young child stood on a busy street corner and asked passing strangers for help, saying, "I'm lost. Can you call my house?" About 72 percent of those approached in small towns offered to help. Only about 46 percent of those asked for help in the cities aided the child. In some cities (Boston and Philadelphia), only about one-third were willing to help (Takooshian et al., 1977). A decline in sensitivity to the needs of others may yet prove to be one of the more serious costs of overpopulation.

Environmental Problem Solving

While overcrowding ranks high on the list of environmental stresses, it is only one of many problems that press for attention. Other major difficulties center on pollution, the effects of noise, the energy crisis, poor architectural design, and related problems. Although the challenge is large, environmental psychology has begun to provide many solutions. To conclude, let's examine some representative problems.

Problem   The way people think about the environment greatly affects behavior. Mental "maps" of various areas, for instance, often guide actions and alter decisions. A case in point is a study recently done in Philadelphia. There, researchers found that an existing school bus route contributed to truancy, because many of its stops were at corners where children were afraid of being attacked and beaten (Conyne & Clack, 1981).

Solution   By doing an **environmental assessment**, psychologists can develop a picture of environments as they are perceived by people using them. An assessment often includes such things as charting areas of highest use in buildings, using attitude scales to measure reactions to various environments (such as schools, businesses, parks), and even having people draw a version of their "cognitive map" of a building, campus, or city (Stokols, 1978). In the case of the schoolchildren, residents of the neighborhood were asked to rate how much stress they felt when walking in various areas. The result was a contour map (somewhat like a high and low pressure weather map) that showed the areas of highest perceived stress. This "stress map" was then used to reroute school buses to "low pressure" areas.

Problem   Anyone who has ever lived in a college dorm knows that at times a dorm hall can be quite a "zoo." Most architects undoubtedly aim to create buildings in which people will be comfortable, happy, and healthy. But sometimes they miss the mark regarding human behavior. In one well-known experiment, Baum and Valins (1977) found that students housed in long, narrow, corridor-design dormitories often feel crowded and stressed. The crowded students tended to withdraw from other residents and even made more trips to the campus health center than did those living in less crowded buildings.

Solution   **Architectural psychology** is a specialty of growing importance for designing buildings. By studying the effects of existing buildings, psychologists are often able to suggest design changes that solve or avoid problems. For example, Baum and Valins (1979) studied two basic dorm arrangements. One dorm had a long corridor and one central bathroom. As a result, residents were constantly forced into contact with one another. The other dorm consisted of rooms clustered in threes, with each suite sharing a small bathroom. Even though the amount of space available to each student was the same in both dorms, students in the long-corridor dorm reported feeling more crowded. They also made fewer friends in their dorm and showed greater signs of withdrawing from social contact.

Question: What sort of solution does this suggest?

A later experiment showed that small architectural changes can greatly reduce the stress of high-density living. Baum and Davis (1980) compared students living in a long-corridor dorm housing 40 students to those living in an altered long-corridor dorm. In the altered dorm, Baum and Davis divided the hallway in half with unlocked doors and made three center bedrooms into a lounge area (see Fig. 27–7). At the end of the term, students living in the divided dorm reported less stress from crowding. They formed more friendships, and they were more open to social contacts. In comparison, students in the long-corridor dorm felt more crowded, stressed, and unfriendly, and they kept their doors shut much more frequently—presumably because they "vahnted to be alone." Similar improvements have been made by altering the interior designs of businesses, schools, apartment buildings, and mental hospitals.

Problem   The rapid worldwide consumption of energy and other resources is one of the most devastating of all social problems. The recent energy crisis, whether engineered by oil companies, or not, was a small taste of what may lie in the future. In the face of projected shortages, and the bloated consumption of natural resources by Western nations, what can be done to encourage conservation on a personal level?

Solution   Even if you sincerely tried to reduce your use of energy (electricity, for instance), you would probably find it difficult. A major problem is that *feedback* concerning energy use (the monthly bill) arrives long after the temptation to turn up the heat or leave lights burning (see Chapter 9). Recognizing this problem, psychologists have shown that moderately lower energy bills result from simply giving families daily feedback about their use of gas or electricity (Seligman & Darley, 1978).

Even more effective are programs that give monetary rewards for energy conservation (Cone & Hayes, 1980). This is especially true for *master-metered* apartment complexes. In such apartments, families do not receive individual bills for their utilities. Consequently, they have no reason *not* to use gas and electricity. Often they consume about 25 percent more energy than they would in an individually metered apartment (McClelland & Cook, 1980). At this rate of waste, apartment owners can split any savings (from reduced consumption) with tenants and still be ahead.

Conclusion   We have had room here only to hint at the creative and highly useful work being done in environmental psychology. While many environmental problems remain, it is encouraging to see that behavioral solutions exist for at least some of them. Surely, creating and maintaining healthy environments is one of the major challenges facing coming generations.

Fig. 27–7   *An architectural solution for crowding. Psychologists divided a dorm hall like that shown in the left diagram* (a) *into two shorter halls separated by unlocked doors and a lounge area* (b). *This simple change minimized unwanted social contacts and greatly reduced feelings of crowding among dorm residents. (Adapted from Baum & Davis, 1980.)*

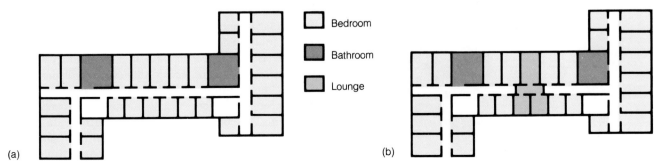

(a)   Bedroom   Bathroom   Lounge   (b)

Learning Check

1. Although male rats in Calhoun's crowded animal colony became quite pathological, female rats continued to behave in a relatively normal fashion.   T or F?

2. To clearly understand behavior, it is necessary to make a distinction between crowding and _____ (the number of people in a given space).

3. Milgram believes that many city dwellers prevent attentional overload by limiting themselves to superficial social contacts.   T or F?

4. Performing an environmental _____ might make a good prelude to redesigning college classrooms to make them more comfortable and conducive to learning.

5. So far, the most successful approach for bringing about energy conservation is to add monetary penalties to monthly bills for overconsumption.   T or F?

Answers: 1. F 2. density 3. T 4. assessment 5. F

A Panorama of Applied Psychology

We have discussed work and the environment at some length because of their major effects on our lives. To provide a fuller account of the diversity of applied psychology, let's conclude by briefly sampling some additional topics of interest.

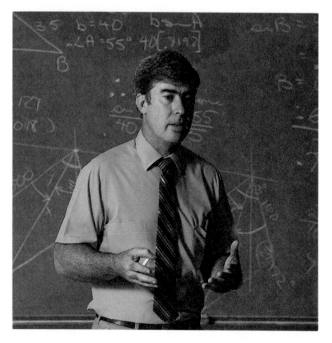

Fig. 27–8 *Educational psychologists are interested in enhancing learning and improving teaching.*

Educational Psychology

You have just been asked to teach a class of fourth-graders for a day. What will you do? (Assume that bribery, showing them films, and a field trip to a video arcade are out.) If you ever do try teaching, you might be surprised at how challenging it can be. Effective teachers must understand processes involved in learning, instruction, classroom dynamics, and testing. Fortunately, teachers (and their students) have benefited greatly from the work of educational psychologists (see Box 27–5). Specifically, **educational psychology** seeks to understand how people learn and how teachers instruct (Thornburg, 1984) (Fig. 27–8).

What are the best ways to teach? Is there an optimal teaching style for different age groups, topics, or individuals? These and many related questions lie at the heart of educational psychology (Table 27–3). In addition to studying such questions, educational psychologists design aptitude and achievement tests, evaluate educational programs, and help train teachers at colleges and universities.

Question: As a student, I've encountered different teaching styles. Do different styles affect classroom learning?

There is little doubt that teachers can greatly affect student interest, motivation, and creativity. But what styles have what effects? To answer this question, psychologists have compared a number of teaching styles. Two of the most basic are direct instruction and open teaching.

In **direct instruction,** factual information is presented by lecture, demonstration, and rote practice. In **open teaching,** active teacher-student discussion is emphasized (Peterson, 1979). And now, the winner: As it turns out, both approaches have advantages. Students of direct in-

Table 27–3   Topics of Special Interest to Educational Psychologists

aptitude testing	language learning
classroom management	learning theory
classroom motivation	moral development
classroom organization	student adjustment
concept learning	student attitudes
curriculum development	student needs
disabled students	teacher attitudes
exceptional students	teaching strategies
gifted students	teaching styles
individualized instruction	test writing
intellectual development	transfer of learning
intelligence testing	

struction do slightly better on achievement tests than do those in open classrooms (Thornburg, 1984). However, students of open teaching do somewhat better on tests of abstract thinking, creativity, and problem solving. They also tend to be more independent, curious, and positive in their attitudes toward school (Peterson, 1979). At present it looks as if a balance of teaching styles goes hand in hand with a balanced education.

Although we have viewed only a small sample of educational research, its value for improving teaching and learning should be apparent. In the next section we will consider how psychology is applied in a very different context—the highly competitive world of consumer affairs.

Consumer Psychology

Whether it's buying a car, toothpaste, a record, or lunch, we are all consumers. **Consumer psychology** is an applied field that focuses on how and why consumers act as they do (Robertson et al., 1984) (see Table 27–4). Consumer psychology is a rapidly growing specialty, especially as applied to business and advertising (Kassarjian, 1982).

Table 27–4   Topics of Special Interest to Consumer Psychologists

attitude change	marketing research
brand loyalty	marketing strategies
brand recognition	mass media effects
buying habits	opinion leaders
consumer attitudes	opinion polling
consumer complaints	package design
consumer needs	product image
consumer protection	pronotional schemes
consumer values	shopping behavior
effects of advertising	subcultural markets
family decision making	

Box 27–5
Elements of a Teaching Strategy

Whether it's "breaking in" a new co-worker, instructing a friend in a hobby, or helping a child learn to read, the fact is we all teach at times. The next time you are asked to share your knowledge, how will you do it? One good way to become more effective is to use a specific **teaching strategy**. The example that follows was designed for classroom use, but it applies to many other situations as well (adapted from Thornburg, 1984).

Step 1: Learner preparation   Begin by gaining learner's attention and focusing interest on the topic at hand.

Step 2: Stimulus presentation   Present instructional stimuli (information, examples, and illustrations) deliberately and clearly.

Step 3: Learner response   Allow time for learner to respond to the information presented (by repeating correct responses or asking questions, for example).

Step 4: Reinforcement   Give positive reinforcement (praise, encouragement) and feedback ("Yes, that's right," "No, this way," and so forth) to strengthen correct responses.

Step 5: Evaluation   Test or assess the learner's progress so that both you and the learner can make adjustments when needed.

Step 6: Spaced review   Review periodically to help strengthen responses to key stimuli.

Many people give little thought to why they buy what they do. But, in fact, **consumer behavior** can be separated into several steps. These include: deciding to spend, selecting a brand, shopping, making the purchase, and evaluating the product in use (Robertson et al., 1984). At each step, advertising, packaging, and a host of other factors affect our behavior. To pinpoint such factors, a type of public opinion polling called *marketing research* is done.

In marketing research, people in a representative sample are asked to give their personal impressions of products, services, and advertising. In this way researchers have learned, among other things, that powerful, widely held **brand images** often develop. A case in point is the

Box 27–6
Name That Beer

It is quite common for products to be promoted as "superior," "the best," "unmistakably different," and the like. How well do such claims hold up? In one recent test, three nationally advertised brands of beer were compared. The results are typical of many similar tests: When consumers sampled beer under controlled conditions—where taste was the only cue available—there was no evidence of any noticeable difference in brands (Fowler, 1982).

Although beer lovers would probably disagree, it appears that the labels could be interchanged on many major brands and no one would notice the difference. Minimal differences of this sort are what spur massive, image-conscious advertising campaigns.

images many people have of automobiles, such as: Mercedes-Benz (high status), Corvette (power and sportiness), Buick (conservatism), and so forth (Robertson et al., 1984). Brand images often direct buying behavior and help explain why many people purchase products for their labels as much as for their performance.

In addition to marketing research, consumer psychologists do laboratory testing of products (see Box 27–6); they try to match products to consumer needs; they test public acceptance of new products, brand names,* and packaging; and they devise plans to change buying habits (including designing TV commercials, printed advertisements, premiums, contests, promotional schemes, and the like).

Question: It sounds like consumer psychology is concerned with getting people to buy things they don't need. Is that the case?

It is true that many consumer psychologists use their knowledge to increase sales. However, not all consumer psychology is profit oriented. For instance, principles of consumer behavior may be used to encourage the conservation of gasoline, water, or electricity. Also, many consumer psychologists are interested in protecting and enhancing consumer welfare by persuading people to act in their own best interest. Advertising campaigns concerning

*The importance of product names is illustrated by the difficulty Chevrolet had in initial attempts to market its *Nova* model in South America. Until the name was changed, consumers shunned the car. The problem? In Spanish, *no va* means "doesn't go"!

auto seat belt use, highway safety, drug abuse prevention, and the like all draw on an understanding of consumer behavior.

As a final example, it was consumer psychologists who documented the large number of commercials on "kid-vid" (children's television programs). Each year the average child sees over 20,000 commercials—most of which are for highly sugared cereals and overpriced toys. Related research showed that children under age 6 are easily victimized because they often cannot distinguish commercials from the program itself (Oskamp, 1984). Such findings have helped advance the cause of **consumerism** (attempts to enhance consumer knowledge, rights, and welfare) for both children and adults.

Behavioral Medicine

Most people agree that health is important—especially their own. Yet, almost half of all deaths in the United States are primarily due to unhealthy behavior or lifestyles. A new specialty called **behavioral medicine** aims to do something about it. Behavioral medicine (also known as **health psychology**) is the study of behavioral factors in physical illness and the use of behavioral methods to preserve health and treat disease (Miller, 1982) (see Table 27–5).

Question: What kinds of behavior are you referring to as unhealthy?

Although some causes of poor health are beyond our control, health psychologists have identified a number of major **behavioral risk factors** that *can* be changed. Each of the following factors greatly increases the chances of disease and early death: cigarette smoking, alcohol abuse, overeating, underexercise, and Type A behavior (Miller, 1983). (For more information on Type A behavior, return to Chapter 14.)

Table 27–5 Topics of Special Interest to Health Psychologists

addictions	lifestyle and health
biofeedback	pain management
brain activity and health	personality and disease
chronic illness	psychology of illness
coping patterns	psychosomatic illness
eating disorders	stress effects
emotions and health	stress inoculation
health education	stress reduction
health skills	training health personnel
health systems planning	unhealthful behavior
immune system response	

Question: What have health psychologists done to lessen the risks?

Recent attempts to "immunize" youths against pressures to start smoking are a good example of behavioral medicine in action. The smoker who says, "Quitting is easy, I've done it dozens of times," states a basic truth—giving up smoking is very difficult. In fact, only 1 smoker in 10 has long-term success. This observation suggests the value of concentrating on early prevention. In one program, junior-high students were given "standard" information on the unhealthy effects of smoking. Then, to add to the program's impact, the students *role played* ways to resist pressures from peers, adults, and cigarette advertisements. Follow-up checks indicated that students who did the role playing were only half as likely to begin smoking as were students in a control group (Hurd et al., 1980).

In addition to small projects like that described, health psychologists have had some success with **community health campaigns.** These are education projects designed to lessen a combination of major risk factors (see Box 27–7 and Fig. 27–9).

By also specializing in stress management, pain control, the treatment of psychosomatic diseases, and similar

Box 27–7
Have a Heart

A good example of a community health campaign in action is the Stanford Heart Disease Prevention Program (Meyer et al., 1980). In the Stanford project, a media campaign about risk factors in heart disease—smoking, diet, and exercise—was combined with special group workshops for high-risk individuals. The program's success can be seen in the fact that, after 2 years, the number of smokers had decreased by 17 percent in the test community. Compare this figure to the 12 percent *increase* observed in a similar, untreated community. Such progress may seem modest, but it is, in fact, worthwhile, cost-effective, and highly promising (Miller, 1983).

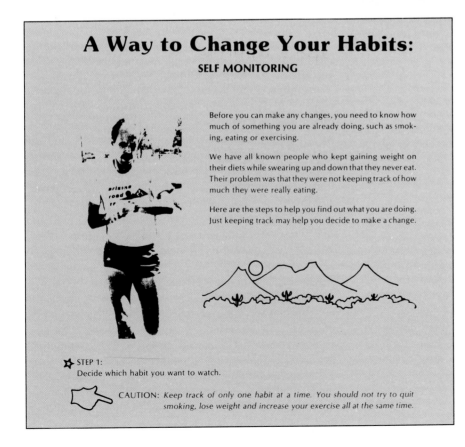

A Way to Change Your Habits:

SELF MONITORING

Before you can make any changes, you need to know how much of something you are already doing, such as smoking, eating or exercising.

We have all known people who kept gaining weight on their diets while swearing up and down that they never eat. Their problem was that they were not keeping track of how much they were really eating.

Here are the steps to help you find out what you are doing. Just keeping track may help you decide to make a change.

STEP 1:
Decide which habit you want to watch.

CAUTION: *Keep track of only one habit at a time. You should not try to quit smoking, lose weight and increase your exercise all at the same time.*

Fig. 27–9   *The page you see reproduced here is from a booklet prepared as part of a public health campaign conducted in southern Arizona. Such campaigns promote health by calling attention to psychological risk factors and by telling what to do about them. (From Marques et al., 1982.)*

applications, psychologists are making a growing contribution to good health.

Sports Psychology

Question: What does psychology have to do with sports?

As almost all serious athletes soon learn, peak performance requires more than physical training—mental and emotional "conditioning" are also important. For this reason, many teams, both professional and amateur, now include psychologists on their staffs (Greenspan, 1983). On any given day, a sports psychologist might teach an athlete how to relax, how to ignore distractions, or ways to cope with emotions. He or she might also provide personal counseling for performance-lowering stresses and conflicts (Rushall, 1975). Other psychologists are interested in studying factors that affect athletic achievement, such as skill learning, the personality profiles of champion athletes, the effects of spectators, and related topics (Table 27–6). In short, **sports psychologists** seek to understand and improve sports performance and to enhance the benefits of sports participation.

Before the advent of sports psychology, it was debatable whether athletes improved because of "homespun" coaching methods, or in spite of them. For example, in early studies of volleyball and gymnastics, it became apparent that people teaching these sports had very little knowledge of crucial, underlying skills (Salmela, 1974, 1975).

Question: How has psychology helped?

A major contribution by psychologists has been their ability to do detailed studies of complex skills (Desharhais, 1975). In a psychological **task analysis**, sports skills are broken into subparts, so that key elements can be identified and taught (see Box 27–8 for an example). Such methods are an extension of techniques first used for job analyses, as described earlier.

Because sports have strong positive or negative effects on participants, they often provide valuable information on human behavior in general. For example, a recent study of Little League baseball found that children's self-esteem improved significantly after a season of play (Hawkins & Gruber, 1982). Psychologists have also learned that such benefits are most likely to occur when competition, rejection, criticism, and the "one-winner mentality" are minimized. When working with children in sports, they emphasize fair play, intrinsic rewards, self-control of emotions, independence, and self-reliance (Orlick, 1975).

Adults also benefit from sports. For many the payoffs are stress reduction, a better self-image, and improved general health. Researchers have reported, for instance, that distance running is associated with lower levels of tension, anxiety, fatigue, and depression than is found in the nonrunning population (Gondola & Tuckman, 1982; Morgan, 1978).

One of the most interesting topics in sports psychology is the phenomenon of **peak performance.** Many athletes report episodes during which they felt almost as if they were in a trance. The experience has also been called "flow" because the athlete becomes one with his or her performance and flows with it. At such times athletes experience intense concentration, detachment from surroundings, a lack of fatigue and pain, a subjective slowing of time, and feelings of unusual power and control (Browne & Mahoney, 1984). It is at just such times that "personal bests" tend to occur.

A curious aspect of flow is that it cannot be forced to happen. In fact, if a person stops to think about it, the flow state goes away. Psychologists are now trying to identify conditions that encourage peak performance and the unusual mental state that often accompanies it. Promising work is being done to train athletes to use physical relaxation, guided imagery, mental rehearsal, autohypnosis, and the like to attain peak performance.

At present, sports psychology is a very young field and still much more an art than a science (Greenspan, 1983). Nevertheless, interest in the field is rapidly expanding.

Summary   Although we have now sampled several major areas of applied psychology, they are by no means the only applied specialties. Others that immediately come to mind are school psychology, military psychology, the psychology of law, and space psychology (a skyrocketing field that is really looking up—see this chapter's Exploration).

In the Applications section that follows we will discuss the psychology of making vocational choices—a topic that has a great deal of personal impact. But first, a word from your conscience: It's time for a Learning Check.

Table 27–6   Topics of Special Interest to Sports Psychologists

achievement motivation	hypnosis
athletic personality	mental practice
athletic task analysis	motor learning
coaching styles	peak performance
competition	positive visualization
control of attention	self-regulation
coping strategies	skill acquisition
emotions and performance	social facilitation
exercise and mental health	stress reduction
goal setting	team cooperation
group (team) dynamics	training procedures

Box 27–8
Taking the Pulse of a Bull's-Eye

It doesn't take much to be off target in the new Olympic sport of marksmanship. The object is to hit a bull's-eye the size of a dime at the end of a 165-foot-long shooting range. Nevertheless, an average of 50 bull's-eyes out of 60 shots is not unusual in international competition (prone position).

What does it take—beyond keen eyes and steady hands—to achieve such accuracy? The answer is surprising: Sports psychologists have found that top marksmen consistently squeeze the trigger *between* heartbeats (see Fig. 27–10). Apparently

the tiny tremor induced by a heartbeat is enough to send the shot astray (Pelton, 1983). Without careful psychological study it is doubtful that this element of marksmanship would have been identified. Now that its importance is known, competitors have begun to use various techniques—from relaxation training to biofeedback—to steady and control their heartbeat. In the future the best marksmen may be those who set their sights on mastering their hearts.

Fig. 27–10 *The target on the left shows what happens when a marksman fires during the heart's contraction. Higher score, as shown by the three shots on the right, is more likely when shots are made between heartbeats. (Adapted from Pelton, 1983.)*

Heartbeat

Shot

Shot

Learning Check

Match the term on the left with one or more related topics or concepts from the list on the right.

1. ____Educational psychology
2. ____Consumer psychology
3. ____Behavioral medicine
4. ____Sports psychology

A. Risk factors
B. Teaching strategies
C. Peak performance

D. Marketing research
E. Mental health
F. Brand image

G. Styles of instruction
H. Community campaigns
I. Task analysis

5. Compared with direct instruction, open teaching produces better scores on achievement tests.   T or F?

6. List at least three behavioral risk factors identified by health psychologists: _____

Answers:
1. B, G 2. D, F 3. A, E, H 4. C, I 5. F 6. cigarette smoking, alcohol abuse, overeating, underexercise, Type A behavior

Applications

Vocational Choice and Occupational Survival— Charting Your Course in the World of Work

Within 5 years after first becoming employed, more than half of all college graduates change jobs. Why? Contrary to what might be expected, higher pay is not the prime reason. Needs for recognition and challenge, the desire to do something worthwhile, opportunities to learn, and needs to use skills and abilities are all ranked higher than money by workers (Renwick & Lawler, 1978).

The message in these findings seems to be that work needs to be satisfying on a day-to-day basis. When it's not, many people quickly tire of trading their time and energy for money. Professionals, in particular—such as accountants, nurses, engineers, architects, biologists, and teachers—rate the nature of their work as the greatest source of their job satisfaction (Bird, 1975).

In recognition of the likely importance of work in your life, this final Applications provides a look at how vocational choices are made, and how they can be improved. Let's begin with a short case history.

John's Story   John was always an excellent student, but his real love was sports. Being on the track team was, in fact, the high point of his college career. (About 7 feet high, to be exact. John was a high jumper.) After he graduated, John was hired by a large accounting firm at an enviable starting salary. Yet within 2 years, John knew he had made a mistake. Accounting left him dissatisfied, restless, and often bored.

In college John's career choice had seemed highly practical. Now he was miserable. What could he do about it? John decided to take a chance. He quit his job, and after several years of additional education, financial hardship, and personal sacrifice, he accepted his first college coaching position.

Vocational Choice

As John's story illustrates, vocational decisions are neither permanent nor easily undone. Usually, by the time a person has selected a career path, it takes a large amount of effort to change course. Moreover, doing so can be a major risk. (What if John had discovered that he also disliked coaching?) The reality that John faced is illustrated by a survey in which 44 percent of the respondents indicated that, for better or worse, they felt "locked into" their current jobs (Renwick & Lawler, 1978). Clearly, there is value in making good vocational choices, and in making them early, if possible.

Career Development   John's abrupt change is somewhat unusual. For most people who enter professions, career development tends to flow through four broad phases. These are: (1) the **exploration phase**, during which an initial search for career possibilities is made; (2) the **establishment phase**, during which the person finds a job, enters a career, develops competence, and gains status; (3) the **midcareer phase**, which is a time of high productivity and acceptance by co-workers; and (4) the **later career phase**, when the individual serves as a respected expert, and often, as a "mentor" (role model and guide) for younger workers (Van Maanen & Schein, 1977).

Of the four phases, the two most likely to be of immediate relevance to students are exploration and establishment. Let's probe them in greater depth.

Question: How do most people choose their vocations?

During the exploration phase, most people go through a recognizable series of stages as they choose a vocation (Weiten, 1983).

In the **fantasy stage** children under age 10 simply *imagine* what they want to be when they grow up. The roles they fantasize—such as President, pilot, rock star, rodeo rider, or TV announcer—may be unrealistic, but they do show that children realize they will need to work someday.

During the **tentative stage** (roughly, ages 10 to 18), adolescents begin to form more realistic, if somewhat general, ideas about what they want to do. However, their plans may shift several times during this period and typically remain tentative. Toward the end of high school, many students begin to more fully appreciate the importance of choosing a vocation. They also become aware that there are limits to their options and barriers to certain careers.

After high school, various social and practical pres-

Applications: Vocational Choice and Occupational Survival

sures lead most people to narrow their range of vocational options. During this **realistic stage** the first steps are taken to find out what particular jobs are like and to prepare for them. At this time many college students use coursework as a way to discover what they are good at and what holds their interest.

By the early twenties, most people begin to carry out their vocational plans. This involves completing necessary training and landing that important first job.

The preceding description implies that most people carefully choose a vocation or career. Actually, there is evidence that vocational choice is often rather haphazard (Janis & Wheeler, 1978). For example, it is not unusual for students to allow a tentative choice of major to determine school coursework. Soon, they find themselves channeled into a particular career path—without really having made a clear decision.

Question: How would a person go about improving the quality of his or her vocational choice?

To begin with, it is worthwhile to recognize that the jobs or careers we are attracted to are influenced by a multitude of factors. Some of the more important influences are: socioeconomic status, intelligence and school achievement, family background, gender, and personal interests (Kaplan & Stein, 1984). As much as these factors may influence your own choice, it is also important to realize that you have the potential for success in a variety of occupations. This is reflected by the fact that the best single predictor of the job category you will enter is your **vocational aspiration,** which is simply what you tell yourself you would like to do.

The world of work is rapidly changing and increasingly complex. In the face of such changes, it is becoming more important to make careful, informed decisions about what kind of work you would like to do. To make sure your vocational choice will be realistic and personally rewarding, you must: (1) gain an accurate understanding of various occupations and (2) get a clear picture of your own interests, needs, and goals.

Question: That seems obvious. But how?

Vocational Counseling The easiest way to improve occupational choice is to consult a **vocational counselor.** Vocational counselors are counseling psychologists who have specialized in the skills and knowledge needed to match people with jobs. A vocational coun-

selor can help you clarify your career goals and can administer interest and aptitude tests to guide your choice. Many colleges now offer vocational counseling at campus **career centers.** These centers also typically store a wealth of information about various jobs and careers. (An introductory discussion of careers in psychology follows this chapter in Appendix A.)

If formal guidance is unavailable, you will have to serve as your own "vocational counselor." A good way to start is to consult the *Occupational Outlook Handbook,* available in most libraries. This book, published yearly by the United States Department of Labor, provides objective information about the outlook for various occupations. The *Handbook* includes job descriptions, information on necessary training, average earnings, and the number of jobs likely to be available in coming years. A simple look at such facts could prevent many students from pursuing overpopulated careers (law, for instance).

Learning about the intangibles that affect job satisfaction may require more initiative. In many occupations the nature of the work is not what it seems from the outside. For instance, medical students are often dismayed when they first begin to realize that disease is ugly and that many medical procedures are distasteful. To find out beforehand what an occupation is like, it is advisable to talk to at least several people in that line of work. Be sure to ask your informants what they dislike about their jobs, as well as their rewards. If possible, you might even spend a day observing people in an occupation that interests you.

After you have selected, prepared for, and begun a career, many challenges remain—far too many, in fact, to discuss here. To conclude, let us briefly consider the challenge of maintaining a healthy attitude at work.

Occupational Survival

Many businesses are now trying to reduce stresses at work by altering management practices and restructuring their organizations. Some also hire psychologists to teach employees to better cope with stress—an approach that seems to have merit. For instance, one recent study found that teaching employees stress inoculation techniques (Chapter 14) and progressive relaxation (Chapter 23) lowered adrenaline levels and depression ratings at work (Ganster et al., 1982).

Applications: Vocational Choice and Occupational Survival

If an employer does not provide for occupational stress reduction, it may be up to you to ensure your own health by practicing stress coping strategies. Sometimes, it is also possible to carry out a personal program of job enrichment, in order to make work more rewarding. If such strategies fail to keep job satisfaction high and work stresses within bounds, it may be time to consider a change in jobs or even careers.

Making Career Decisions

Another way of improving work adjustment is to examine your approach to making career decisions. Yale University psychologist Irving Janis and writer Dan Wheeler (1978) have described the ways in which people typically deal with work dilemmas, especially those that lead to a change in careers. Their analysis suggests that there are four basic coping styles. See if you recognize yourself in any of the following descriptions.

The Vigilant Style   This style is the most effective of the four. It describes individuals who evaluate information objectively and make decisions with a clear understanding of the alternatives. Persons using this style make mental "balance sheets" to weigh possible gains and losses before taking action.

The Complacent Style   Persons of this type drift along with a nonchalant attitude toward job decisions. They tend to let chance direct their careers and to take whatever comes along without really making plans.

The Defensive-Avoidant Style   These people are fully aware of the risks and opportunities presented by career choices and dilemmas. However, they are uncomfortable making decisions. This leads them to procrastinate, rationalize, and to make excuses for their inaction and indecision.

The Hypervigilant Style   People with this style more or less panic when forced to make career decisions. They may collect hundreds of job announcements and brochures, but they become so frantic that making logical decisions is nearly impossible.

These coping styles may seem exaggerated, but they are easy to observe when people are forced to change jobs or make major alterations in career plans. To relate them to yourself, think about how you have handled vocational decisions to date, or decisions about your college career. Of the four, Janis and Wheeler consider only the first, or vigilant style, to be constructive. With this insight you may be able to greatly improve the quality of your career choices.

Conclusion   Work, leisure, family, community, environment—all contribute to the quality of our lives. And, as we have seen throughout this text, psychology has much to offer in each of these areas. It is my sincere hope that you have found enough relevance and value in this book to kindle a lifelong interest in psychology. Psychology's future looks exciting. What role will it play in your life?

Learning Check

1. Those working in professions generally place greater emphasis on the nature of their work more than on money as the source of job satisfaction.   T or F?
2. The establishment phase of career development is a time during which an initial search for career possibilities is made.   T or F?
3. Many people go through a fantasy stage and a tentative stage before they become more realistic about choosing a career.   T or F?
4. The best single predictor of what occupations college students will enter is their IQ scores.   T or F?
5. Stress inoculation techniques have proved capable of lowering stress levels at work.   T or F?
6. The vigilant style of making career choices is characterized by panic and illogical decisions.   T or F?

Answers: 1. T 2. F 3. T 4. F 5. T 6. F

Chapter Summary

- *Applied psychology* refers to the use of psychological principles and research methods to solve practical problems.
- *Community psychologists* treat entire communities as their "clients" and engage in activities that help promote community-wide mental health.
- *Industrial/organizational psychologists* are interested in the problems people face at work. Typically, they specialize in *personnel psychology*, *human relations* in the work setting, and/or *engineering psychology* (the design of machines and work environments for human use).
- Personnel psychologists try to match people with jobs by combining *job analysis* with a variety of selection procedures, including: gathering *biodata*, *interviewing*, giving *standardized psychological tests* (especially *interest inventories* and *aptitude tests*) and through the *assessment center* approach.
- Two basic approaches to business and industrial management are *scientific management (Theory X)* and *human relations* approaches *(Theory Y)*. Theory X is most concerned with *work efficiency*, whereas Theory Y emphasizes *psychological efficiency*.
- *Job satisfaction* is not directly related to productivity, but it is linked to absenteeism, morale, employee turnover, and other factors that affect overall business efficiency. Job satisfaction is usually enhanced by Theory Y–oriented *job enrichment*.
- *Environmental psychologists* are interested in the effects of *behavioral settings*, *physical* or *social environments*, and *human territoriality*, among many other major topics.
- Overpopulation is a major world problem, often reflected at an individual level in crowding. Animal experiments indicate that excessive crowding can be unhealthy. However, human research shows that psychological feelings of *crowding* do not always correspond to *density* (the number of people in a given space). One major consequence of crowding is *attentional overload*.
- A large number of practical problems—from *noise pollution* to architectural design—have come under the scrutiny of environmental psychologists. In many cases effective behavioral solutions to such problems have been found, often as a result of first doing a careful *environmental assessment*.
- *Educational psychologists* seek to understand how people learn and teachers instruct. They are particularly interested in teaching styles, such as *direct instruction* and *open teaching*, and *teaching strategies*.
- Consumer psychologists study *consumer behavior* and serve as consultants to businesses and advertising agencies. Consumer psychologists often do *marketing research* to aid the promotion of various products. Some also do research that helps advance the cause of *consumerism* and consumer welfare.
- *Behavioral medicine*, or *health psychology*, is concerned with psychological factors in physical illness and in behavioral methods for preserving health. Often this is achieved by identifying and removing *behavioral risk factors*, and through *public health campaigns*.
- *Sports psychologists* seek to understand and improve sports performance and to enhance the benefits of sports participation. A careful *task analysis* of sports skills is one of the major tools for improving coaching and performance.
- Four broad periods in career development are the *exploration phase*, the *establishment phase*, the *midcareer phase*, and the *later career phase*. The exploration phase can be further divided into a *fantasy stage*, a *tentative stage*, and a *realistic stage*. *Vocational counseling* can greatly aid career decision making.
- Styles of making career decisions have been classified as *vigilant*, *complacent*, *defensive-avoidant*, and *hypervigilant*. Of these four only the vigilant style is consistently constructive.

Space Psychology—Life on the High Frontier

The first human outpost in space is drawing near. By the early 1990s the United States plans to orbit a continuously inhabited space station. Many engineering problems must be solved before a permanent space habitat becomes a reality. Yet the real challenge may lie in the psychological adjustments needed for men and women to live in space.

The Challenge of Living Aloft

Life in the miniworld of a space station won't be easy, physically or mentally. For months at a time space station residents will be restricted to tiny living quarters with little privacy. During an interplanetary trip, explorers would be confined for nearly 2 years.

No doubt the first long-term space residents will find life in orbit stressful. Even small disagreements can lead to tense clashes when people must live in cramped quarters. Living aloft would be similar to spending several months among a group of strangers in a small room from which you cannot escape.

In addition to confinement, long-term space inhabitants will face other trying conditions, including: restricted movement, separation from loved ones, isolation from hobbies and recreations, sensory monotony, noise, and many other stresses. It's no wonder that some astronauts reported restlessness, depression, and boredom during their months aboard Skylab, a small space station orbited in the early 1970s.

Space Strike America's third Skylab crew spent a highly productive 3½ months in space. The crew—Edward Gibson, Gerald Carr, and William Pogue—also staged the world's first "space strike." Along with the pesky irritations of confined living, the crew felt pressured by a packed work schedule. After 6 weeks the crew had fallen far behind in chores and experiments. The first signs of trouble surfaced at that time when Carr told Mission Control, "There's nothing worse than having to gobble your meal in order to get some task done that really should have been scheduled some other time, so please loosen up!"

For 6 weeks the Skylab-3 astronauts worked 18 hours a day. Their schedule was so full they had almost no time for privacy or reflection. For 3 weeks crew members had hinted that they were angry. But ground controllers failed to recognize the seriousness of these complaints. In a sudden burst of defiance, the astronauts went on strike and did exactly as they pleased. Gibson went to the solar console. Carr and Pogue sat in the wardroom, looked out the window, and took photographs.

Obviously, no one on Earth was going to fly up and punish the astronauts for skipping their chores. The crisis was finally resolved when the crew was given more time to do experiments and fewer tasks to complete. Although the Skylab-3 strike was brief, it shows how important the human element will be in space.

Space Habitats

Clearly, space habitats must be designed with human behavior in mind. What will it take to make a congenial space station—one capable of sustaining emotional well-being and efficient performance? To begin, the *social* environment, or microsociety, on a space station will need to operate as smoothly as possible. For this reason many problems may be avoided by careful selection and training of future space residents *before* they go aloft.

It also would be wise to identify—and ease—stressors in space living quarters. To this end, psychologists have pinpointed several key areas of concern. Let's sample some expected problems and possible solutions.

General Environment Design of a space station as a living environment must take many human factors into account. For instance, researchers have learned that astronauts prefer rooms with clearly defined "up" and "down"—even in the weightlessness of space. Pro-

Exploration: Space Psychology—Life on the High Frontier

visions must be made for regular exercise and full-body showers. As trivial as it might seem, a lack of showers was a major complaint among subjects in earlier confinement experiments.

Within a space station there should be some flexibility concerning the use of living and work areas. Behavior patterns change over time, and control of one's environment helps lower stress. At the same time people need stability. Psychologists have found, for instance, that eating becomes an important high point in monotonous environments. Eating at least one meal together each day can help keep a crew working as a social unit.

Sleep cycles will need to be carefully controlled in space to avoid disrupting bodily rhythms. In earlier space missions astronauts had difficulty sleeping while the remainder of the crew continued to work and talk. Problems with sleep will be worsened by the constant noise on a space station. Fans, pumps, switches, lights, and the like constantly click, hum, or throb on a spacecraft. At best, a space station will be at least as noisy as the typical office. At first such noise is annoying. After weeks or months it can become a serious stressor. Researchers are experimenting with various earmuffs, eyeshades, and sleeping arrangements to alleviate such difficulties.

Privacy   Psychologists are helping engineers design space habitats that meet human needs for privacy. However, privacy will have to be based mainly on temporarily

blocking out visual and auditory contact with others. In the first permanent space stations there will be too little room for separate quarters.

Forced togetherness is stressful mainly because temporary retreat from contact with the group is difficult or impossible. Thus, control over the amount of contact one has with others is more important than having a private room. Designers do recognize, however, the need to define private territories. It will be important to identify small areas that can be personalized and "owned" by each individual. Desks, lockers, sleep stations, and the like could fill this need if they are not shared with others.

Sensory Restriction   Sensory monotony will be a problem in space, even with the magnificient vistas of Earth below. (How many times would you have to see the North American continent without losing some interest?)

Researchers are developing stimulus environments that will use music, videotapes, and other diversions to combat monotony and boredom. Again, they are trying to provide choice and control for workers. Studies of confined living make it clear that one person's symphony is another's grating noise. Where music is concerned, individual earphones may be all that is required.

Most people in restricted environments find that they prefer noninteractive pastimes such as reading, listening to music, looking out windows, writing, and watching films or television. As much as

anything, this preference may show again the need for privacy. By listening to music or reading, a person can psychologically withdraw from the group. A good selection of passive entertainments appears to be a must for any space station. Interestingly, Soviet astronauts, who make much use of music, have also reacted with delight to grab bags containing unexpected toys or novelties.

Social Isolation   Separation from family, friends, and one's home community is a major stressor. However, the ability to talk regularly with family via two-way televised meetings should help ease feelings of social isolation. Some psychologists also believe that there should be a psychological support group on Earth with whom a space station crew would talk to prevent emotional problems. In short, the best antidote for social isolation will probably be abundant opportunities to communicate with associates and loved ones on Earth.

Conflict Resolution and Mental Health   Many studies of long-term isolation show steady declines in motivation. Most inhabitants intend to use their free time for creative pursuits. But in reality they end up marking time and many become apathetic. Judging from submarine missions and Antartic bases, as many as 5 percent of space inhabitants may experience some psychological disturbance. Most often the problem has been depression. However, in rare instances people have become

Exploration: Space Psychology—Life on the High Frontier

paranoid, psychotic, suicidal, or uncontrollably aggressive. As stated earlier, the risk of such problems may be minimized by careful selection of personnel. Even so, it will be important to teach crew members basic counseling skills for clarifying disagreements and resolving conflicts.

Life on Spaceship Earth

Why is the idea of living in space so fascinating? Perhaps it is because human strengths and weaknesses will be magnified in the miniature world of a space station. As psychologist Yvonne Clearwater (1985) says:

> The space station represents the first glimmerings of recognition that some

of the toughest challenges in space—as on Earth—concern human behavior, not technology. . . . Ironically, the farther we go from Earth and the longer we stay away, the more we will need to know about ourselves.

Scientists working on the space effort believe that psychological factors will become increasingly important for the success or failure of future space missions.

It is curiously fitting that the dazzling technology of space travel has highlighted the inevitable importance of human behavior. Here on Earth, as in space, we cannot count on technology alone to solve problems. The threat of nuclear war, social conflict, crime, prejudice, overpopulation, environmental damage, famine, homicide,

economic disaster—these and most other major problems facing us are behavioral. Will spaceship Earth endure? It's a psychological question.*

*Sources: Chaikin, 1985; Clearwater, 1985; Connors, Harrison, & Akins, 1985; Engle & Lott, 1980; Joyce, 1984.

Learning Check

1. The Skylab-3 space strike was caused mainly by dissatisfaction with the poor quality of meals in space.   T or F?
2. Researchers have learned that astronauts have no preference for living quarters with clearly defined "up" and "down" orientations.   T or F?
3. Research shows that needs for privacy can be met by providing ways to temporarily withdraw from social contact with a group, even when physical withdrawal is impossible.   T or F?
4. Most people in restricted environments prefer group pastimes, such as playing card games, skits, or group singing.   T or F?

Answers: 1. F   2. F   3. T   4. F

Careers in Psychology

Let's say that you have taken the first step toward a career in psychology: Your introductory course has convinced you that you want to learn more about human behavior. The next step is to learn more about careers in psychology—something you can begin doing right here.

First Questions   Are you suited to a career in psychology? What kinds of jobs are available to persons with associate, bachelor's, master's, or doctoral degrees in psychology? What is the employment outlook for psychology and related fields? These are questions to ask if you are thinking about majoring in psychology. Although this appendix can only provide preliminary answers, it should help you get started. First, let's see if you are on the right track.

- Do you have a strong interest in human behavior?
- Are you emotionally stable?
- Do you have good communication skills?
- Do you find theories and ideas challenging and stimulating?
- Do your friends regard you as especially sensitive to the feelings of others?
- Have you read popular books on psychology and found them interesting?
- Have discussions in this text matched some of your own insights about human behavior?
- Do you enjoy working with other people?

If most of the preceding statements apply, a career in psychology or a related field may be a good choice for you.

Majoring in Psychology

As a quick survey of your classmates might indicate, the majority of students studying introductory psychology are not psychology majors. More surprising is the fact that the majority of undergraduate psychology majors do not plan to work as psychologists. Most are interested in moving directly into careers and vocations that do not require extended graduate training. Many of today's psychology majors recognize that a psychology degree can be valuable in careers other than psychology. Learning psychology can provide a general knowledge of behavior that aids success in various occupations.

If you think you would like to major in psychology, but you are not interested in graduate training, here are some points to consider:

- Few workers hold one job forever, or even remain in a single line of work for life.
- The nature of work is likely to change greatly in your lifetime, and adaptability will be important.
- A broad education that develops many skills makes a person more vocationally adaptable.

- It is a major myth that every job requires a precise set of skills. Apart from highly technical or specialized jobs, many positions can be filled by persons with differing combinations of skills.
- Specific undergraduate programs do not exist for many mental health professions—making psychology a good undergraduate major leading to later specialized training.
- Job recruiters look primarily for general competence in verbal and written communication, plus social skills and facility in meeting the public.

General Skills   For reasons like those listed here, a general education in psychology can lead to a variety of interesting jobs and professions. Even a brief list of "marketable" abilities provided by a psychology degree includes the following: clear, analytic thinking; objectivity and keen observation; an ability to handle data, recognize patterns, and draw conclusions; ability to plan and organize complex activities; ability to communicate clearly, both verbally and in writing; the capacity to comprehend abstract principles and the subtleties of human behavior; ability to critically evaluate evidence; interpersonal skills; and general knowledge relevant to success in many settings.

Again, the point is that even if you do not plan to work as a psychologist, psychology can be a practical undergraduate major.

Education and Options

If you do decide to major in psychology, it is important to be aware of the level of training required for various jobs. While opportunities exist for those with an A.A. or B.A. degree in psychology, many of the most rewarding positions require further education. The discussion that follows should give you some idea of the options at each level.

Associate Degree Level   Training in psychology at the associate degree level tends to yield fewer choices than those available to graduates with bachelor's degrees or more advanced training. Even so, all of the jobs listed here are open to persons with a 2-year, A.A. degree.

child care worker	public survey worker
human services worker	recreation aide
mental health assistant	rehabilitation aide
nursing home attendant	senior citizen aide
playground supervisor	teacher's aide
preschool aide	ward attendant
psychiatric technician	youth supervisor

These jobs are only a sample of what is available. People with associate degrees in psychology are qualified to do interviewing, to give and score specific psychological tests, and to communicate the needs of clients to psychologists and other professionals. In general, a person with an associate degree can expect to work directly with clients, but under the supervision of more highly trained professionals.

In some communities specific training programs exist for students interested in working as psychiatric (or psychological) technicians at hospitals or clinics. Often, a year or two of training can lead directly to a job in a local mental health facility. In some cases provisions have been made for "psych-tech" trainees to combine classroom study with on-the-job training.

Bachelor's Degree   As already mentioned, a bachelor's degree in psychology can be considered preparation for a variety of jobs or occupations. An undergraduate psychology major is also a good prelude to advanced training in several related professions. And, of course, a bachelor's degree is the first step toward a master's or doctoral degree in psychology.

Most of the jobs you see listed here are available to persons with bachelor's degrees in psychology. Some, however, require additional training (becoming a high school teacher, for example). Also, you would be most competitive for many of the listed jobs if you were to combine a psychology major with a minor in another area, such as business. In other cases it would be better to make psychology your minor, in combination with a major in a related area (law enforcement and nursing are examples).

advertising agent	customer relations
art therapist	director of day care center
assistant youth coordinator	drug counselor
biofeedback technician	educational salesperson
business management trainee	employment counselor
case worker	employment interviewer
child development specialist	family services worker
child welfare agent	geriatric technician
college admissions representative	group home coordinator
counselor aide	high school psychology teacher
crisis intervention team member	human relations director
	job analyst
	labor relations specialist

management consultant

marketing researcher

music therapist

occupational therapist

patient service represen-
tative

personnel worker

probation/parole officer

psychiatric nurse

public health assistant

public relations specialist

recreational therapist

research assistant

sales representative

social worker

special education teacher

statistical assistant

veteran's advisor

Again, these are only some of the possibilities. As the diversity of the list suggests, it is important to remain flexible when pursuing a psychology major. Plan your education so that you are exposed to psychology's many areas of knowledge, and avoid specializing too soon. To further broaden your employment options, consider taking classes in computer programming, mathematics, statistics, accounting, finance, business, marketing, advertising, education, technical writing, or law enforcement.

Master's Level   A master's degree in psychology usually requires from 1 to 2 years of graduate-level training beyond the bachelor's degree. The master's degree usually requires completion of a research thesis and/or a certain number of hours of supervised practical experience in an applied setting. At present the most popular master's-level specialty is counseling psychology. Undoubtedly, this is because a master's degree in counseling is one of the most direct routes to a career as a mental health professional.

Those with a master's degree in counseling psychology may further specialize in marriage and family counseling, vocational or educational counseling, child counseling, or rehabilitation counseling—to name only major possibilities. Many counselors are self-employed, but some work for human service agencies, at mental health clinics, and occasionally for the military or large businesses. Recently, counselors have begun to move into new areas such as hospices, child abuse clinics, rape counseling centers, stress clincs, and so on.

Other master's-level specialties, such as human factors engineering, school psychology, psychometrics, clinical psychology, industrial psychology, or general psychology, are also offered. But recently, employment opportunities have become more limited for new master's-level psychologists. When positions open in such areas, they are often filled by doctoral-level psychologists. (However, master's-level psychologists with prior work experience often are competitive for such positions.) On the other hand, a master's degree could make you more competitive for all of the jobs listed earlier, at the bachelor's level. It might also help you qualify for higher pay. For such reasons a master's degree in psychology remains valuable, even in areas other than counseling.

Doctoral Level   Earning a doctorate in psychology requires commitment. (That's personal commitment, not commitment to a mental hospital—although some doctoral candidates might disagree!) It usually takes at least 3 years of education beyond a bachelor's degree to attain a doctorate (Ph.D., Psy.D., or Ed.D.). More often, a doctorate takes 4 or more years to complete, and some specialties, such as clinical and counseling psychology, require at least 1 more year of internship. (An internship is a closely supervised, on-the-job training experience for professionals entering the field.)

How do the three doctoral degrees differ? The answer may help you decide which would be most appropriate for you if you want to become a psychologist. A Ph.D. is a research degree. As such, it requires completion of a dissertation (an original research contribution to the field). Psychologists holding Ph.D. degrees are active in all areas of psychology, including clinical psychology. However, some psychologists who primarily want to work as therapists now earn a Psy.D. degree (Doctor of Psychology) instead of a Ph.D. This newly created degree allows students in clinical psychology to gain practical experience as a psychotherapist rather than doing a dissertation. The Ed.D. (Doctor of Education) is also typically more applied in orientation than the Ph.D. Coursework for the Ed.D. focuses on the psychology of learning and education.

It is also worth mentioning that in most states a doctoral degree alone does not automatically allow a person to practice psychology. To be legally licensed or certified as a psychologist, a person usually must have a doctorate in psychology, plus at least 1 year of internship, as well as having passed written and oral state licensing exams.

As you can see, becoming a psychologist is a major achievement, reflecting the attainment of a high level of knowledge. Understandably, doctoral-level psychologists have the widest range of work choices. These include settings such as colleges and universities, clinics, rehabilitation centers, government agencies, businesses, industry, the military, and private practice. Also, as you can see in Table A-1, psychologists holding doctoral degrees average several thousand dollars per year greater income in most professional positions.

If you wish to pursue a doctorate in psychology, it is not absolutely necessary to make plans now for attending

Table A-1   1982 Median Income for Psychologists

Area	Master's	Doctorate
College faculty	23,000*	29,000*
Educational administration	40,000	40,000
Clinical psychology	26,000	38,000
Counseling psychology	25,000	32,000
Research	32,000	36,000
School psychology	26,000*	27,000*
Applied (I/O) psychology	36,000	45,000

*For a 9 to 10 month academic year.

(Data from Stapp & Fulcher, 1983. Figures are rounded to the nearest thousand dollars.)

graduate school—but it helps! Getting admitted to a doctoral program in psychology is as difficult as getting into medical school. The sooner you know what kind of program you would like to enter, the better your chances will be of meeting all of its requirements. To learn more, consult the book *Graduate Study in Psychology,* published by the American Psychological Association. This book is loaded with information to help you plan your graduate education. Be sure to read Appendix D, which gives practical, step-by-step information on how to get accepted to graduate school. (An address for APA publications is given at the end of this appendix.)

Employment Outlook

The good news is that, overall, jobs for people with psychology degrees are expected to grow faster than average in coming years. However, professional-level jobs (master's and doctorate) will account for a relatively small percentage of total new positions. With projections for a decline in college enrollments, academic positions will be in especially short supply. Even in industrial, clinical, and other applied areas there will be much competition for positions. However, this should not deter a person who is strongly interested in psychology from pursuing a doctoral-level career. It simply means that it is wise to take steps to make yourself highly employable. These include: (1) Attending an APA-accredited graduate school. (2) Gaining work experience while in school (by working as a research assistant, teaching assistant, or even as a volunteer, if necessary). (3) Specializing in additional skills that are in demand, such as computer programming, therapy for special populations (such as the mentally retarded), research in heavily funded areas (such as drug abuse research), and so forth.

Best Bets   At all degree levels, applied areas are probably the best bet for employment in the near future. The prospects remain reasonably good for clinical and counseling psychologists, industrial/organizational psychologists, and clinical or psychiatric social workers. Health-related jobs also look good, especially anything associated with senior citizens, as the "graying of America" continues. Two of the fastest growing jobs for the next decade are projected to be employment interviewers and occupational therapists. Both positions are open to bachelor's and master's degree holders.

For further information on careers in psychology, talk with your psychology teacher or visit the campus career center if your school has one. Additional sources of information are listed below.

The Future   In addition to the jobs discussed here, there are a number of emerging specialties that are likely to grow rapidly. It shouldn't be long before job titles such as the following become more common: shyness counselor, thanatologist, retirement counselor, jury selection specialist, weight control counselor, stress-reduction counselor, executive recruiter, sleep disorders therapist, and others as yet unnamed. In short, psychology should remain a stimulating and innovative field as the demand for psychological skills and services continues to grow. Perhaps psychology holds a future for you.

Additional Sources of Information

American Psychological Association. *Careers in psychology.* Washington, DC: American Psychological Association, 1980. (Address: 1200 Seventeenth Street N.W., Washington, DC 20036. One copy of this pamphlet will be sent free, on request.)

American Psychological Association. *Graduate study in psychology* (revised annually). Washington, DC: American Psychological Association, 1985. (Address is given above.)

Fretz, B. R., & Stang, D. J. *Preparing for graduate study in psychology: Not for seniors only!* Washington, DC: American Psychological Association, 1980.

Woods, P. J. (Ed.). *Career opportunities for psychologists: Expanding and emerging areas.* Washington, DC: American Psychological Association, 1976.

Woods, P. J. (Ed.). *The psychology major: Training and employment strategies.* Washington, DC: American Psychological Association, 1979.

Statistics*

Statistics from "Heads" to "Tails"

Let's say a friend of yours invites you to try your hand at a "game of chance." He offers to flip a coin and pay you one dollar if the coin comes up "heads." If the coin shows "tails," you must pay him a dollar. He flips the coin, tails—you pay him a dollar. He flips it again: tails. Again: tails. And again: tails. And again: tails.

At this point you are faced with a choice. Should you continue the game in an attempt to recoup your losses? Or should you assume the coin is biased and quit before you really get "skinned"? Taking out a pocket calculator (and the statistics book you carry with you at all times), you compute the odds of obtaining 5 tails in a row from an unbiased coin. The probability is 0.031 (roughly 3 times out of 100).

If the coin really is honest, 5 consecutive tails is a rather rare event. Wisely, you decide the coin is probably biased and refuse to play again. (Unless, of course, your "friend" is willing to take tails for the next 5 tosses!)

Perhaps a decision could have been made in this hypothetical example without using statistics. But notice how much clearer the situation becomes when it is expressed statistically.

Statistics in Psychology   Psychologists try to extract and summarize useful information from the observations they make. To do so, they use two major types of statistics. The first type, called **descriptive statistics**, summarizes or "boils down" numbers so they become more meaningful and easier to communicate to others. The second type, known as **inferential statistics,** is used for decision making, for generalizing from small samples, and for drawing conclusions. As was the case in the coin-flipping example, psychologists must often base decisions on limited data. Such decisions are greatly aided by inferential statistics.

Descriptive Statistics

Statistical techniques bring greater clarity and precision to psychological thought and research. To see how, let's begin by considering three basic techniques of descriptive statistics: **graphical statistics**, measures of **central tendency**, and measures of **variability.**

Graphical Statistics   Table B-1 shows hypothetical scores on a test of hypnotic susceptibility administered to 100 college students.

*Portions of this appendix were contributed by Danniel Downey, Ph.D.

Table B-1 Raw Sources of Hypnotic Susceptibility									
55	86	52	17	61	57	84	51	16	64
22	56	25	38	35	24	54	26	37	38
52	42	59	26	21	55	40	59	25	57
91	27	38	53	19	93	25	39	52	56
66	14	18	63	59	68	12	19	62	45
47	98	88	72	50	49	96	89	71	66
50	44	71	57	90	53	41	72	56	93
57	38	55	49	87	59	36	56	48	70
33	69	50	50	60	35	67	51	50	52
11	73	46	16	67	13	71	47	25	77

With such disorganized data, it is difficult to form an overall "picture" of differences in hypnotic susceptibility. But by using a **frequency distribution,** large amounts of information can be neatly organized and summarized. To make a frequency distribution, the entire range of possible scores is broken down into *classes* of equal size. Next, the number of scores falling into each class is recorded. In Table B-2 the raw data have been condensed into a frequency distribution. Notice how much clearer the scores of the entire group become.

Frequency distributions are often expressed *graphically* to make them more "visual." **Histograms,** as these are called, are constructed by labeling frequencies on the *ordinate* (vertical line) and class intervals on the *abscissa* (horizontal line). Next, bars are drawn for each class interval; the height of each bar is determined by the number of scores in each class (see Fig. B-1). An alternate way of graphing scores is the more familiar **frequency polygon** (Fig. B-2). Here points are placed at the center of each class interval to indicate the number of scores. Then, the dots are connected by straight lines.

Measures of Central Tendency   A measure of central tendency is simply a number describing a "middle score" around which other scores fall. A familiar measure of cen-

tral tendency is the mean, or "average." But as we shall see in a moment, there are other types of "averages" that can be used. To illustrate each we need an example: Table B-3 shows the raw data for a hypothetical experiment in which subjects were given a test of memory. Assume that

Fig. B–1   *Frequency histogram of hypnotic susceptibility scores contained in Table B–1.*

Fig. B–2   *Frequency polygon of hypnotic susceptibility scores contained in Table B–1.*

Table B-2 Frequency Distribution of Hypnotic Susceptibility Scores	
Class Interval	Number of Persons in Class
0–19	10
20–39	20
40–59	40
60–79	20
80–99	10

Table B-3   Raw Scores on a Memory Test for Subjects Taking Rememberine or a Placebo

Subject	Group 1 Rememberine	Group 2 Placebo
1	65	54
2	67	60
3	73	63
4	65	33
5	58	56
6	55	60
7	70	60
8	69	31
9	60	62
10	68	61
Sum	650	540
Mean	65	54
Median	66	60

$$\text{Mean} = \frac{\Sigma X}{N} \text{ or } \frac{\text{sum of all scores, X}}{\text{number of scores}}$$

$$\text{Mean Group 1} = \frac{65 + 67 + 73 + 65 + 58 + 55 + 70 + 69 + 60 + 68}{10}$$

$$= \frac{650}{10} = 65$$

$$\text{Mean Group 2} = \frac{54 + 60 + 63 + 33 + 56 + 60 + 60 + 31 + 62 + 61}{10}$$

$$= \frac{540}{10} = 54$$

Median = the middle score or the mean of the two middle scores*

Median Group 1 = 55 58 60 65 | 65 67 | 68 69 70 73

$$= \frac{65 + 67}{2} = 66$$

Median = 31 33 54 56 | 60 60 | 60 61 62 63

$$\text{Group 2} = \frac{60 + 60}{2} = 60$$

*☐ indicates middle score(s).

one group was given a drug purported to improve memory (let's call the drug Rememberine), while a second group received placebos. Is there a difference between memory scores in the two groups? It's difficult to tell without computing an average.

As one type of "average," the **mean** is computed for each group by adding all the scores and then dividing by the total number of scores. Notice in Table B-3 that the means reveal a difference between the two groups.

The mean is sensitive to extremely high or low scores. For this reason it is not always the best measure of central tendency. (Imagine how distorted it would be to calculate average yearly incomes from a small sample of people that happened to include a multimillionaire.) In such cases the *middle score* in a group of scores—called the **median**—is used instead.

The median is found by arranging scores from the highest to the lowest and selecting the score that falls in the middle. Consider for example, the following weights obtained from a small class of college students: 105, 111, 123, 126, 148, 151, 154, 162, 182. The median for the group is 148, the middle score. Of course, if there is an even number of scores, there will be no "middle score." This problem is handled by averaging the two scores that "share" the middle spot. This procedure yields a single number to serve as the median (see bottom panel of Table B-3).

A final measure of central tendency is the **mode**, which is simply the most frequently occurring score in a group of scores. If you were to take the time to count the scores in Table B-3, you would find that the mode of Group 1 is

65 and the mode of Group 2 is 60. Although the mode is easy to obtain, it can be an unreliable measure, especially in a small group of scores. The mode's advantage is that it gives the score actually obtained by the greatest number of people.

Measures of Variability   Let's say a researcher discovers two drugs that lower anxiety in agitated patients. However, let's also assume that one drug consistently lowers anxiety by moderate amounts, whereas the second sometimes lowers it by large amounts, sometimes has no effect, or may even increase anxiety in some patients. Overall, there is no difference in the *average* (mean) amount of anxiety reduction, yet an important difference exists between the two drugs. As this example shows, it is not enough to simply know the average score in a distribution; usually, we would also like to know if scores are grouped closely together or scattered widely.

Measures of *variability* provide a single number that tells how "spread out" scores are. When the scores are widely spread, this number gets larger. When they are close together, it gets smaller. If you look again at the example in Table B-3, you will notice that the scores within each group vary widely. How can we show this fact?

The simplest way would be to use the **range**, which is the difference between the highest and lowest scores. In Group 1 of our experiment, the highest score is 73 and the lowest is 55; thus, the range is 18 (73 minus 55 equals 18). In Group 2, the highest score is 63, and the lowest is 31; this makes the range 32. Scores in Group 2 are more spread than those in Group 1.

A better measure of variability is the **standard deviation**. To obtain the standard deviation, the deviation (or difference) of each score from the mean is found and then squared (multiplied by itself). These squared deviations are then added and averaged (the total is divided by the number of deviations). Taking the square root of this average yields the standard deviation (see Table B-4). Notice again that the variability for Group 1 (5.4) is smaller than that for Group 2 (where the standard deviation is 11.3).

Standard Scores   A particular advantage of the standard deviation is that it can be used to "standardize" scores in a way that gives them greater meaning. For example, John and Susan have both taken psychology midterms, but in different classes. John earned a score of 118, and Susan scored 110. Who did better? It is impossible to tell without knowing what an average score was on each test, and whether John and Susan scored at the top, middle, or bottom of their classes. We would like to have one

Table B-4   Computation of the Standard Deviation

	Group 1—Mean = 65	
Score Mean	**Deviation (d)**	**Deviation Squared (d²)**
65 − 65 =	0	0
67 − 65 =	2	4
73 − 65 =	8	64
65 − 65 =	0	0
58 − 65 =	−7	49
55 − 65 =	−10	100
70 − 65 =	5	25
69 − 65 =	4	16
60 − 65 =	−5	25
68 − 65 =	3	9
		291

$$SD = \sqrt{\frac{\text{sum of } d^2}{n}} = \sqrt{\frac{291}{10}} = \sqrt{29.1} = 5.4$$

	Group 2—Mean = 54	
Score Mean	**Deviation (d)**	**Deviation Squared (d²)**
54 − 54 =	0	0
60 − 54 =	6	36
63 − 54 =	9	81
33 − 54 =	−21	441
56 − 54 =	2	4
60 − 54 =	6	36
60 − 54 =	6	36
31 − 54 =	−23	529
62 − 54 =	8	64
61 − 54 =	7	49
		1276

$$SD = \sqrt{\frac{\text{sum of } d^2}{n}} = \sqrt{\frac{1276}{10}} = \sqrt{127.6} = 11.3$$

number that gives all this information. A number that does this is the **z-score**.

To convert original scores to z-scores, the mean is subtracted from the score. The resulting number is then divided by the standard deviation for that group of scores. To illustrate, Susan had a score of 110 in a class with a mean of 100 and a standard deviation of 10. Therefore, her z-score is +1.0 (see Table B-5). John's score of 118 came from a class having a mean of 100 and a standard deviation of 18; thus his z-score is also +1.0 (see Table B-5). Originally, it looked as if John did better on his midterm than Susan did, but we now see that, relatively speaking, their scores were equivalent. Compared with other students, each was an equal distance above average.

The Normal Curve

When chance events are recorded, we find that some outcomes have a high probability and occur very often; others have a low probability and occur infrequently; still others have little probability and occur rarely. As a result, the distribution (or tally) of chance events typically resembles a **normal curve** (see Fig. B-3). Most psychological traits or

Table B-5   Computation of a z-Score

$$z = \frac{X - \bar{X}}{SD} \text{ or } \frac{score - mean}{standard\ deviation}$$

$$Susan: z = \frac{110 - 100}{10} = \frac{+10}{10} = +1.0$$

$$John: z = \frac{118 - 100}{18} = \frac{+18}{18} = +1.0$$

events are determined by the action of a large number of factors. Therefore, like chance events, measures of psychological variables tend to form a normal curve. For example, direct measurement has shown that such characteristics as height, memory span, and intelligence are distributed normally. In other words, many people have average height, memory ability, and intelligence; but as we move above or below average, we find fewer and fewer people.

It is very fortunate that many psychological variables are distributed "normally," because a great deal is known about the normal curve. One property relevant to our discussion is the relationship between the standard deviation

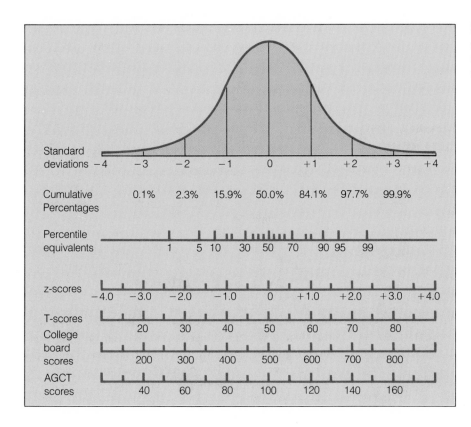

Fig. B–3 *The normal curve. Scales show the relationship of standard deviation, z-scores, and other measures to the curve.*

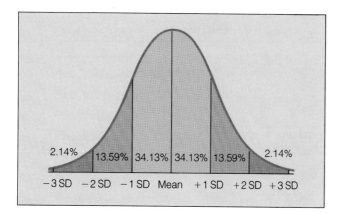

Fig. B–4 *Relationship between standard deviation and the normal curve.*

and the normal curve; specifically, the standard deviation measures off set proportions of the curve above and below the mean. For example, in Fig. B-4, notice that 68 percent of all cases (IQ scores, memory scores, heights, or whatever) fall between one standard deviation above and below the mean (± 1 SD); 95 percent of all cases fall between ± 2 SD; and 99 percent of cases can be found between ± 3 SD from the mean.

Table B-6 gives a more complete account of the relationship between z-scores and the percentage of cases found in a particular area of the normal curve. Notice, for example, that 93.3 percent of all cases fall below a z-score of $+1.5$. A z-score of 1.5 on a test (no matter what the original or "raw" score was) would be a good performance, since approximately 93 percent of all scores fall below this mark. Relationships between the standard deviation (or z-scores) and the normal curve are invariant, making possible useful comparisons between various tests or groups of scores.

Inferential Statistics

Let's say a researcher studies the effects of a new therapy on a small group of depressed individuals. Is he or she interested only in these particular individuals? Usually not, since except in rare instances, psychologists seek to discover general laws of behavior that apply widely to human and animal species. Undoubtedly the researcher would like to know if the therapy holds any promise for all depressed people. As stated earlier, **inferential statistics** are techniques that allow us to make inferences. That is, they allow us to generalize from the behavior of small groups of subjects to that of the larger groups they represent.

Samples and Populations   In any scientific investigation we would like to observe the entire set, or **population,** of subjects, objects, or events being studied. However, this is usually impossible or impractical. Observing all Catholics, all cancer patients, or all mothers-in-law could be both impractical (since all are large populations) and impossible (since people change denominations, may be unaware of having cancer, and change their status as relatives). In such cases, **samples** or smaller cross sections of a population are selected, and observations of the sample are used to draw conclusions about the entire population.

The major requirement for any sample is that it be **representative.** That is, the sample group must truly reflect the characteristics of the larger population. Referring to our earlier hypothetical study of the effects of a drug on memory, it would be essential that the sample of 20 subjects be representative of the general population. A very important aspect of representative samples is that their members are chosen at **random**; that is, each member of the total population must have an equal chance of being selected for the sample.

Significance of Differences Between Groups in an Experiment

In our hypothetical drug experiment we found that the average memory score was higher for the group given the drug than it was for subjects who received no drug (the placebo group). Certainly this result is interesting, but could it have occurred by chance? If two groups were repeatedly tested (with neither receiving any drug), their average memory scores would sometimes differ. How much

Table B-6 Area Under the Normal Curve as a Percentage of Total Area for a Variety of z-Scores		
z-Score	Percentage of Area to the Left of This Value	Percentage of Area to the Right of This Value
-3.0 SD	00.1	99.9
-2.5 SD	00.6	99.4
-2.0 SD	02.3	97.7
-1.5 SD	06.7	93.3
-1.0 SD	15.9	84.1
-0.5 SD	30.9	69.1
0.0 SD	50.0	50.0
$+0.5$ SD	69.1	30.9
$+1.0$ SD	84.1	15.9
$+1.5$ SD	93.3	06.7
$+2.0$ SD	97.7	02.3
$+2.5$ SD	99.4	00.6
$+3.0$ SD	99.9	00.1

must two means differ before we can consider the difference "real" (not due to chance)?

Notice that the question is similar to one discussed earlier: How many tails in a row must we obtain when flipping a coin before we can conclude that the coin is biased? In the case of the coin, we noted that obtaining 5 tails in a row is a rather rare event. Thus, it became reasonable to assume the coin was biased. Of course, it is possible to get 5 tails in a row when flipping an honest coin. But since this outcome is unlikely, we have good reason to suspect that something other than chance (a loaded coin, for instance) caused the results. Similar reasoning is used in tests of statistical significance.

Tests of **statistical significance** provide an estimate of how often experimental results could have occurred by chance alone. The results of a test of statistical significance are stated as a probability giving the odds that the observed difference was due to chance. In psychology any experimental result that could have occurred by chance 5 times (or less) out of 100 (in other words, a probability of .05 or less) is considered *significant*. In the memory experiment we have used as an example, the probability is .025 ($p \leq .025$) that the group means would differ as they do by chance alone. This allows us to conclude with some certainty that the drug actually did improve memory scores.

Correlation

Many of the statements that psychologists make about behavior do not result from the use of experimental methods. Rather, they come from keen observations and measurement of existing phenomena. For example, a psychologist might note that the higher a couple's socioeconomic and educational status, the smaller the number of children they are likely to have. Or that grades in high school are related to how well a person is likely to do in college. Or even that as rainfall levels increase within a given metropolitan area, crime rates decline. In these instances we are dealing with the fact that two variables are **co-relating** (varying together in some orderly fashion).

As discussed in Chapter 2, the simplest way of visualizing a correlation is to construct a **scatter diagram**. In a scatter diagram, two measures (grades in high school and grades in college, for instance) are obtained. One measure is indicated by the X axis and the second by the Y axis. The scatter diagram plots the intersection of each pair of measurements as a single point. Many such measurement pairs give pictures like those in Fig. B-5

Figure B-5 also shows scatter diagrams of three basic kinds of relationships between variables (or measures). Graphs A, B, and C show **positive relationships** of varying strength. As you can see, in a positive relationship, increases in the X measure (or score) are matched by increases in the Y measure (or score). An example would be finding that higher IQ scores (X) are associated with higher college grades (Y). A **zero correlation** (or relationship) is pictured in graph D. This might be the result of comparing subjects' hat sizes (X) to their college grades (Y). Graphs E and F both show a **negative relationship** (or correlation). Notice that as values on one measure increase, those on the second become smaller. An example might be the relationship between amount of alcohol consumed and scores on a test of coordination: Higher alcohol levels are correlated with lower coordination scores.

Correlations can also be expressed as a **coefficient of correlation**. This coefficient is simply a number falling somewhere between $+1.00$ and -1.00. If the number is zero or close to zero, it indicates a weak or nonexistent relationship. If the correlation is $+1.00$, a **perfect positive relationship** exists; if it is -1.00, a **perfect negative relationship** has been discovered. The most commonly used correlation coefficient is called the Pearson r. Calculation of the Pearson r is relatively simple, as shown in Table B-7. (The numbers shown are hypothetical.)

As stated in Chapter 2, correlations in psychology are rarely perfect. Most fall somewhere between zero and plus or minus one. The closer the correlation coefficient is to $+1.00$ or -1.00, the stronger the relationship. An interesting example of some typical correlations is provided by a study that compared the IQ's of adopted children with their biological mothers. At age 4, the children's IQ's correlated .28 with their mothers' IQ's. By age 7 the correlation was .35, and by age 13 it had grown to .38.

Correlations often provide highly useful information. For instance, it is valuable to know that there is a correlation between cigarette smoking and lung cancer rates. Another example is the fact that higher consumption of alcohol during pregnancy is correlated with lower birth weight and a higher rate of birth defects. There is a correlation between number of recent life stresses experienced and the incidence of emotional disturbance. And so on. More examples could be cited, but the point is, correlations help identify relationships that are worth knowing.

Correlations are particularly valuable for making **predictions**. If we know two measures are correlated, and we know a person's score on one measure, we can predict his or her score on the other. For example, most colleges have formulas that make use of multiple correlations to decide which prospective students have the best chances for success. Usually the formula includes such "predictors" as high school GPA, teacher ratings, and scores on the Scholastic Aptitude Test (SAT) or some equivalent. Al-

Fig. B–5 *Scatter diagrams showing various degrees of relationship for a positive, zero, and negative correlation. (Adapted from Pagano, 1981.)*

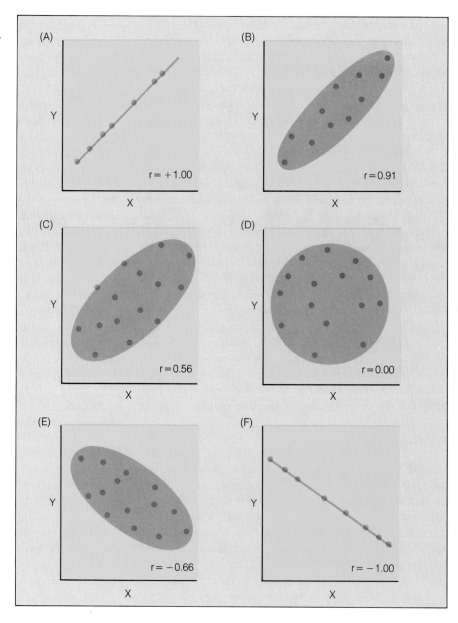

though none of the predictors is perfectly correlated with success in college, together they correlate highly and provide a useful technique for screening applicants.

There is an interesting "trick" you can do with correlations that you may find useful. It works like this: If you *square* the correlation coefficient (multiply *r* by itself), you will get a number telling the **percent of variance** accounted for by the correlation. For example, the correlation between IQ scores and college grade point average is 0.5. Multiplying 0.5 times 0.5 gives 0.25, or 25 percent. This means that 25 percent of the variation in college grades is accounted for by knowing IQ scores. In other words, with a correlation of 0.5, college grades are "squeezed" into an oval like that in graph C, Fig. B–5. IQ scores take away some of the possible variation in corresponding grade point averages. If there were no correlation between IQ and grades, grades would be completely free to vary, as shown in Fig. B–5, graph D.

Along the same line, a correlation of 1.00 or −1.00 means that 100 percent of the variation in the Y measure is accounted for by knowing the X measure: If you know a person's X score, you can tell exactly what the Y score is. An example that comes close to this state of affairs is the high correlation (0.86) between the IQ's of identical twins. In any group of identical twins, 74 percent of the variation in the "Y" twins' IQ's is accounted for by knowing the IQ's of their siblings (the "X's").

Correlation and Causation   It is very important to recognize that the existence of a correlation between two measures does not automatically mean that one causes the other: *Correlation does not demonstrate causation.* When a correlation exists, the best we can say is that two variables are related. Of course, this does not mean that it is impossible for two correlated variables to have a cause-effect relationship. Rather, it means that we cannot *conclude* that a causal relationship exists solely on the basis of a correlation. To establish greater confidence in the existence of a causal relationship, we must perform an experiment (see Chapter 2).

Often two correlated variables are related through the influence of a third variable. For example, we might observe that the more hours students devote to studying the better their grades. Although it is tempting to conclude that more studying produces (causes) better grades, it is possible (indeed, it is probable) that grades and the amount of study time are both related to the amount of motivation or interest a student has.

The distinction between having data that indicate causality versus data that indicate a relationship of unknown origin is one that should not be forgotten. Since we rarely run experiments in daily life, the information on which we act is largely correlational. This should make us more humble and more tentative in the confidence with which we make pronouncements about human behavior.

Table B–7   IQ and Grade Point Average for Computing Pearson r

Student No.	IQ X	Grade Point Average Y	X Score Squared X^2	Y Score Squared Y^2	X Times Y XY
1	110	1.0	12,100	1.00	110.0
2	112	1.6	12,544	2.56	179.2
3	118	1.2	13,924	1.44	141.6
4	119	2.1	14,161	4.41	249.9
5	122	2.6	14,884	6.76	317.2
6	125	1.8	15,625	3.24	225.0
7	127	2.6	16,124	6.76	330.2
8	130	2.0	16,900	4.00	260.0
9	132	3.2	17,424	10.24	422.4
10	134	2.6	17,956	6.76	348.4
11	136	3.0	18,496	9.00	408.0
12	138	3.6	19,044	12.96	496.8
Total	1503	27.3	189,187	69.13	3488.7

$$r = \frac{\Sigma XY - \frac{(\Sigma X)(\Sigma Y)}{N}}{\sqrt{\left[\Sigma X^2 - \frac{(\Sigma X)^2}{N}\right]\left[\Sigma Y^2 - \frac{(\Sigma Y)^2}{N}\right]}}$$

$$= \frac{3488.7 - \frac{1503(27.3)}{12}}{\sqrt{\left[189,187 - \frac{(1503)^2}{12}\right]\left[69.13 - \frac{(27.3)^2}{12}\right]}}$$

$$= \frac{69.375}{81.088} = 0.856 = 0.86$$

(Adapted from Pagano, 1981.)

Glossary

Absolute threshold A point indicating the minimum amount of physical energy necessary to produce a sensation.

Accommodation Changes in the shape of the lens of the eye that serve to focus objects at varying distances. Also, modifying old concepts and thinking habits to fit new information or demands (Piaget).

Acetylcholine (uh-SEET-ul-COH-leen) A neurotransmitter substance that is released at synapses and at the neuromuscular junction (point of contact between a neuron and a muscle fiber). Acetylcholine can initiate a nerve impulse or a muscle contraction, depending on its point of release.

Achievement motivation A need for success or the attainment of excellence.

Acromegaly (ak-row-MEG-uh-lee) A condition involving progressive enlargement of the hands, face, and feet due to excessive secretion of growth hormones by the pituitary.

Acuity (ah-CUE-ih-tee) That aspect of visual perception having to do with the sharpness or resolution of images.

Acupuncture (AK-you-punk-chur) The Chinese medical art of relieving pain and treating illness by inserting thin hairlike needles at various points on the body.

Adaptation In general, adjustment to environmental demands. In connection with the senses, a gradual decline in response to a constant stimulus.

Adaptation level An internal or mental medium point that we use to judge amounts.

Addiction Development of physical dependence on a drug such that craving and physical discomfort (withdrawal symptoms) occur in its absence.

Adjustment disorder A combination of emotional, psychological, and physical disturbances caused by identifiable life stresses.

Adrenal glands (ah-DREE-nal) Source of adrenaline, a hormone secreted during emotional arousal. Also, a source of other important hormones.

Adrenaline (ah-DREN-ul-in) A hormone produced by the adrenal glands similar in its effects to sympathetic nervous system activation; produces diffuse activation throughout the body.

Affect Pertaining to emotion or feelings.

Affective disorders A form of psychopathology characterized by mania or severe depression; disorders involving extremes of emotion.

Affective psychosis A loss of contact with reality involving extremes of emotional response, such as mania, depression, or manic-depressive mood swings.

Afferent (AF-er-ent) Carrying or conducting inward, as in nerves or neurons conveying impulses toward the brain or central nervous system; opposite of *efferent*.

Afferent or sensory nerves Incoming sensory fibers.

Affiliation motive The desire to associate with other people.

Ageism A prejudice held on the basis of age; hence, any tendency to discriminate on the basis of age.

Age regression Return of a hypnotized subject to a younger age.

Aggression Any response made with the intention of bringing harm to another person.

Agnosias (ag-NO-zyahs) In perception, disturbances of the meaning of sensory stimuli; hence, an inability to know; for example, an inability to recognize objects or pictures.

Alpha wave A relatively large, slow brain wave pattern indicating a passive state of relaxed awareness.

Altered state of consciousness Any nonordinary mental state, including meditation, hypnosis, and drug-induced states.

Ambivalence (am-BIV-ah-lence) Holding opposite emotions such as love and hate toward some person or object.

Amnesia Loss of memory (partial or complete) for past events.

Amniocentesis (AM-nee-oh-sen-TEE-sus) The extraction and analysis of amniotic fluid from the womb in the early stages of pregnancy; used for the detection of genetic anomalies in the fetus.

Amphetamines Class of drugs acting as central nervous system stimulants. Not known to be physically addictive but may cause strong psychological dependency.

Anal stage In Freud's theory, the second stage of psychosexual development corresponding roughly to the period of toilet training between the second and third year. (See also *genital stage; oral stage; phallic stage.*)

Androgen (AN-dro-jen) Any of a number of male sex hormones.

Androgyny (an-DROJ-ih-nee) The condition of having both male and female behavioral traits or a balance between "masculinity" and "feminity" as they are defined by one's culture.

Anesthesia (an-es-THEE-zyah) Loss of bodily sensations.

Anima (AN-ih-muh) In Jung's theory, an archetype representing femaleness or the female principle within the psyche. (See *archetype.*)

Animus (AN-ih-mus) In Jung's theory, an archetype representing maleness or the male principle within the psyche. (See *archetype.*)

Anorexia nervosa (AN-uh-REX-see-ah ner-VOH-sah) A condition in which a person will eat, but with great reluctance, and typically not enough to sustain normal weight. A serious loss of appetite apparently of psychological origin.

Anosmia (a-NAHZ-me-ah) Loss of the sense of smell, particularly for a specific type of odor.

Anthropomorphic fallacy (AN-thro-po-MORE-fik) The error of attributing human thoughts, feelings, and motives to animals.

Antidepressants Drugs that counteract depression or despondency by elevating the individual's mood.

Antipsychotics (AN-tie-sie-KOT-iks) Drugs that alleviate psychotic symptoms, making it easier to treat psychiatric problems.

Anxiety A feeling of painful or apprehensive uneasiness closely related to fear; especially, that characterized by dread or anticipation of some unclear threat.

Anxiety disorders A class of personal disturbances characterized by excessive and chronic anxiety states. Formerly referred to as neurosis.

Aphasias (ah-FAZE-yahs)   Speech disturbances resulting from damage to certain areas in the temporal lobe of the brain.

Apnea (ap-NEE-uh)   To be without breath; an interruption in breathing.

Approach-avoidance conflict   Unpleasant situation in which a person is simultaneously attracted to and repelled by the same goal. (See *conflict*.)

Aptitude test   A test that rates a person's potential for learning skills required by various occupations.

Architectural psychology   Study of the effects buildings have on behavior; the design of buildings using behavioral principles.

Archetype (AR-keh-type)   An original pattern, prototype, or idea on which others are modeled. In Jung's theory, universal primordial images found in the collective unconscious.

Arousal   The overall level of excitation or activation present at any given time for a person or animal.

Assessment   Evaluation or measurement.

Assimilation   In Piaget's theory, the application of existing mental patterns to new situations. (Compare *accommodation*.)

Astigmatism (ah-STIG-mah-tiz-im)   A defect in the shape of the cornea, the lens, or the eye as a whole that causes some parts of vision to be out of focus.

Attention   Orienting toward or focusing on some stimulus.

Attitude   A predisposition having emotional, belief, and behavioral components that determines a person's reaction toward a particular social stimulus.

Attribution   The process of mentally ascribing one's own behavior, and that of others, to various causes.

Autism (OT-is-im)   A severe disorder of childhood involving mutism, sensory spinouts, sensory blocking, tantrums, lack of awareness of others, echolalia, and other difficulties.

Autokinetic effect (OT-oh-kih-NET-ik)   The apparent movement of a stationary pinpoint of light displayed in a dark room; often occurs as a result of suggestion.

Autonomic nervous system (ANS)   Division of the peripheral nervous sytem concerned with involuntary functions of the body.

Aversive conditioning (ah-VER-siv)   Use of an unpleasant or painful stimulus to reinforce learning.

Avoidance learning   Learning procedure in which the occurrence of a particular response results in postponement or prevention of an unpleasant stimulus.

Axon (AK-sahn)   A thin fiber process extending from the cell body of a neuron (nerve cell); normally conducts information away from the cell body.

Babinski reflex   Curling and spreading of the toes that occurs when the sole of an infant's foot is stroked.

Bait shyness   An unwillingness or hesitation on the part of animals to accept a particular food. Often caused by the presence of a taste aversion. (See *taste aversion*.)

Barbiturates   Addictive drugs that depress activity of the central nervous system. Barbiturate intoxication resembles intoxication caused by alcohol.

Behavioral medicine   The study of behavioral factors in physical illness and the use of behavioral methods to preserve health and treat disease.

Behaviorism   The school of psychology that emphasizes the study of overt, observable behavior.

Behavior modification   Application of principles of learning to change or eliminate maladaptive or abnormal behavior.

Beta waves (BAY-tah)   Fast, low-voltage activity of a more or less ran-

dom character recorded on the EEG when an organism is alert and attending to stimuli. (See *EEG*.)

Biased sampling   Selection of subjects for an experiment or public opinion poll that gives some subjects a greater chance of being included than others. (See also *randomization*.)

Binocular cues   Any cue for depth perception that requires two eyes.

Biodata   Detailed biographical information about a job applicant used to predict suitability for various occupations.

Biofeedback   A technique allowing a subject to monitor and control his or her own internal bodily functions.

Bipolar disorders   Emotional disorders in which a person is manic (excited) or depressed, or swings between mania and depression.

Blind spot   A portion of the retina where the optic nerve leaves the eye and therefore there are no visual receptors.

Brain lesion (LEE-zhun)   Destruction of brain tissue experimentally, accidentally, or through disease.

Brainstorming   A group problem-solving technique in which ideas are offered freely, imaginatively, and without evaluation as to their practicality.

Brainwashing   Engineered or forced change in attitudes and beliefs.

Brightness   In perception, the relative amount of light reflected from or emanating from the surface of a stimulus or object.

Caffeine   A natural drug with stimulant properties that is found in coffee, tea, and synthetic beverages and medicines.

Carcinogen (kar-SIN-oh-jen)   Any cancer-producing substance.

Case study   An intensive investigation of the behavior of a single person.

Cataplexy (CAT-ah-plek-see)   A sudden loss of all muscle tone and voluntary movement in the body causing complete collapse.

Catatonic (CAT-ih-TAWN-ik)   A schizophrenic state marked by alternate periods of stupor and activity, also by mutism and waxy flexibility of the body.

Central nervous system (CNS)   The brain and spinal cord.

Character   A subjective evaluation of an individual's personality, often as to its desirable and undesirable attributes.

Chemotherapy (KEE-mo-therapy or CHEM-oh-therapy)   Use of psychoactive drugs for the treatment of mental disturbances.

Chromosomes (KRO-muh-somz)   Threadlike structures ("colored bodies") within the nucleus of each cell that carry the genes. Normal human cells each have 23 pairs of chromosomes.

Circadian rhythms (SUR-kay-dee-an)   Cyclical changes in bodily function that vary on a schedule approximating one 24-hour day.

Clairvoyance (klare-VOY-ans)   Purported form of extrasensory perception (ESP) in which objects or events are perceived without the aid of normal sensory systems.

Classical conditioning   A basic form of learning discovered by Pavlov in which existing (reflex) responses are attached to new stimuli by pairing the new stimuli with stimuli that naturally elicit the response.

Client-centered therapy   A form of therapy designed by Rogers in which the client assumes responsibility for solving his or her own problems. The therapist's role is to clarify and assist, not to give advice.

Climacteric (kly-MAK-ter-ik)   A period or point during late middle age in males in which a significant change in health, vigor, appearance, or potency takes place. Roughly analogous to *menopause* in women.

Clinical psychologist   A psychologist who specializes in treating psychological and behavioral disturbances or who does research on such disturbances.

Cloning (KLO-ning)   The reproduction of an entire plant or organism from a single cell of the original plant or organism.

Closure Gestalt term for the perceptual tendency to complete figures by "closing," or ignoring, small gaps.

Cocaine A crystalline drug derived from coca leaves; used as a central nervous system stimulant and local anesthetic.

Cochlea (KOCK-lee-ah) The snail-shaped organ of hearing in the inner ear containing the ultimate sensory receptors for hearing.

Coding Organizing information for efficient memory storage and retrieval.

Coefficient of correlation (KOE-eh-FISH-ent of KORE-eh-LAY-shun) An index of the degree of relationship between two sets of measures or two variables. Coefficients are expressed as a number ranging from −1.00 to +1.00.

Cognition (cog-NISH-un) The process of thinking, knowing, or processing information.

Cognitive (COG-nuh-tiv) Of or pertaining to thinking, knowing, understanding, or the internal processing of information.

Cognitive dissonance (COG-nuh-tiv DIS-uh-nuns) An imbalance between one's thoughts, beliefs, attitudes, or behavior; a tension state that people are motivated to reduce.

Cognitive map Internal images of an area (maze, city, campus, and so forth) that presumably underlie an ability to choose alternate paths to the same goal.

Collective unconscious According to Jung's theory, a portion of the psyche that is common to all people and that contains archetypal images. (See *archetype*.)

Colostrum (kuh-LOSS-trum) The milklike substance secreted by women during the first few days after childbirth. Colostrum is rich in antibodies to disease.

Community psychology A specialty that seeks to improve community-wide mental health through direct services, prevention, education, and consultation.

Comparative psychology The study and comparison of the behavior of different species, especially animals.

Compensation Counteracting a real or imagined weakness by emphasizing desirable traits or seeking to excel in other areas.

Compression In hearing, the squeezing together of air molecules at the front of a sound wave. Collision of the compressed wave front with the auditory apparatus then sets the auditory apparatus in motion.

Compulsion An act the individual feels driven to repeat, often against his or her will.

Concept A generalized idea representing a class of objects or events that are grouped together on the basis of some common feature or property characteristic of each.

Condensation In the Freudian theory of dream interpretation, a tendency to combine images from several sources into a single complex image.

Conditioned emotional response The conditioning of autonomic nervous system response and/or visceral response to a previously nonemotional stimulus.

Conditioned response In classical conditioning, a learned response that becomes attached to the conditioned stimulus.

Conditioned stimulus In classical conditioning, a previously neutral stimulus that acquires the capacity to evoke a response as the result of association with an unconditioned stimulus.

Conditioning The process of learning by association discovered by Pavlov. Also sometimes used to refer to operant learning. (See *classical conditioning* and *operant conditioning*.)

Cones Visual receptors in the eye responsible for color vision and daylight visual acuity. (See *rods*.)

Conflict A mental or behavioral state characterized by clashing or incompatible motives, desires, goals, and so forth. The four most basic conflicts are: approach conflicts, avoidance conflicts, approach-avoidance conflicts, and double approach-avoidance conflicts.

Congenital problems (kon-JEN-ih-tal) A defect acquired during development in the uterus; hence, a problem existing at birth (a "birth defect"). Distinct from a *hereditary* problem (that is, one transmitted by genes).

Conjunctive concept (kon-JUNK-tiv) A concept defined as having one value on one dimension *and* a second value on another dimension (for example, red triangles). (Compare with *disjunctive* and *relational* concepts.)

Connotative meaning (KON-oh-TAY-tiv) The subjective personal or emotional significance of a word or concept apart from its explicit and recognized meaning.

Conscience (KON-chuns) Internalized sense of right and wrong; in Freudian theory, the superego.

Consolidation (kon-sol-ih-DAY-shun) Theoretical process by which material is solidified as a permanent memory in the brain after being learned.

Constructs Explanatory concepts inferred from observable events but not directly observable themselves.

Consumer psychology Specialty area that focuses on understanding consumer behavior; often applied to advertising, marketing, product testing, and the like.

Contact comfort A pleasant and reassuring feeling human and animal infants derive from touching or clinging to something soft and warm, usually the mother.

Contiguity (kon-tih-GEW-ih-tee) In close proximity or contact; very near in time or space.

Continuous reinforcement A schedule of reinforcement in which every response is reinforced.

Control Eliminating, identifying, or equalizing all factors in an experiment that could affect its outcome.

Control group A group in a psychological experiment that is exposed to all experimental conditions except the independent variable. (See *experimental group*.)

Convergence The simultaneous turning inward of the two eyes as they focus on nearby objects.

Convergent thought Thinking directed toward discovery of a single established correct answer; conventional thinking.

Conversion reaction A symptom or disability that appears to be physical but that actually results from anxiety, stress, or emotional conflict.

Cornea (KOR-nee-ah) The clear outer membrane covering the eyeball.

Corpus callosum (KOR-pus cah-LO-sum) A large nerve unit in the middle of the brain connecting the two hemispheres; serves to transfer information from one hemisphere to the other.

Correlation (KOR-eh-LAY-shun) The existence of a consistent (nonrandom) relation between two variables or measures.

Correlational study A nonexperimental study designed to assess the degree of relationship between two or more variables.

Corticalization (KOR-tih-kal-ih-ZAY-shun) The increase in the relative size and importance of the cerebral cortex observed as one ascends the biological scale from lower animals to humans.

Counseling psychologist A psychologist who specializes in the treatment of milder emotional and behavioral disturbances.

Counselor A mental health professional who specializes in adjustment problems not involving serious mental disorder; for example, marriage counselors, occupational counselors, or school counselors.

Cretinism (KREET-un-ism) A form of mental retardation resulting from a malfunction of the thyroid gland.

Critical period   A time during which a certain event must occur in an organism's life if development is to occur normally.

CT scan   Computed tomography scan; a computer-enhanced X-ray image of the brain.

Culture   An ongoing pattern of life characterizing a society at a particular historical period or stage in its development.

Dark adaptation   The process by which the eye adapts to conditions of low illumination, principally, by a shift to rod vision. (See *rods*.)

Decibel (DES-ih-bel)   A unit used to measure the loudness of sounds; ordinary speech registers around 60 decibels.

Deductive thought   A pattern of thought in which the thinker must use a general set of rules to draw a logical conclusion. (Compare with *inductive thought*.)

Defense mechanisms   Habitual and unconscious psychological devices used to reduce or avoid anxiety.

Delayed speech   A significant delay in the development of speech capacity in early childhood.

Delta waves   Large, slow, regular waves of brain activity recorded on the EEG during the deeper stages of sleep.

Delusions   False beliefs held against all evidence to the contrary; symptomatic of some psychotic disorders.

Demonology (DEE-mon-OL-oh-gee)   In Medieval Europe, that branch of knowledge dealing with the study of demons and the treatment of those "possessed" by demons.

Dendrites (DEN-drites)   Branching projections of nerve cell bodies (neurons) that form synapses with other neurons and conduct information toward the cell body. (See *neurons*.)

Denial   A defense mechanism used to deny the existence of a problem or an unpleasant reality.

Denotative (DEE-no-TATE-iv)   The objective dictionary meaning of a word or concept.

Dependent variable   The variable (usually a behavior) that reflects changes in the independent variable. (See *independent variable*.)

Depressant   A drug or chemical agent that lowers bodily or nervous system function.

Depressive neurosis (new-ROW-sis)   Prolonged and severe depression triggered by a stressful event but representing an overreaction to it.

Depressive psychosis (sie-KOH-sis)   A form of psychosis characterized by the deepest possible despondency.

Deprivation   In development, the loss or withholding of normal stimulation, nutrition, comfort, love, and so forth. A condition of lacking.

Depth perception   The ability to see three-dimensional space and to accurately estimate distances.

Detoxification (de-TOKS-ih-fih-KAY-shun)   To remove poison or the effects of poison. In the treatment of alcoholism, the physical withdrawal of the patient from alcohol.

Developmental tasks   Any of the countless personal changes that must be made throughout life for optimal development.

Developmental psychologist   A psychologist interested in the course of human growth and development, from before birth until death.

Difference threshold   The smallest change in a physical stimulus that can be detected by an observer.

Digit span test   A test of attention and short-term memory. Subjects are asked to recall a series of random digits of varying lengths that has just been read to them.

Discrimination (learning)   The ability to detect differences between two or more objects or events; often brought about by reinforcement of responses to one stimulus but not the other.

Dishabituation (DIS-ha-bit-you-AY-shun)   A reinstatement of sensory response lost or reduced by the occurrence of habituation. (See *habituation*.)

Disjunctive concept   A concept defined by the presence of at least one of a number of features, or a concept defined as having one value on one dimension *or* a different value on another dimension (for example, blue *or* triangular). (Compare with *conjunctive* and *relational* concepts).

Disorganized schizophrenia (SKIT-suh-FREE-nee-ah)   A form of psychosis characterized by giddy, obscene, or silly behavior and including a severe disintegration of personality.

Displacement   In Freudian theory, the rechanneling of energy from one target or activity to another. Often used as a defense mechanism, as when aggression is displaced on someone or something other than the actual source of frustration.

Dissociative reaction (dih-SOSH-ih-tiv)   Unusual disorders including amnesia, fugue, and multiple personality that allow individuals to separate themselves from upsetting thoughts and actions.

Divergent thinking   Thinking that produces many ideas or alternatives; creative or unconventional thinking.

DNA (deoxyribonucleic acid)   Large and complex chemical molecules found in chromosomes and believed to be the substance of which genes are composed.

Dogmatism (DOG-mah-tizm)   An unwarranted positiveness or certainty in matters of opinion.

Dominant gene   A gene whose influence will be expressed on every occasion in which it is present. (Compare *recessive gene*.)

Dopamine (DOPE-ah-meen)   An important neurotransmitter found in the brain, particularly at sites within the limbic system.

Double-bind communication   A message that contradicts itself and places the person who receives it in an unsolvable conflict.

Down Syndrome   A hereditary abnormality associated with the presence of 47 chromosomes rather than the usual 46 and characterized by a shortened life expectancy, mental retardation, and unusual physical features.

Drive   The psychological representation of internal need states; for example, hunger, thirst, and so forth.

Drug interaction   The outcome of combining two or more drugs within the body producing effects above and beyond what would be expected from the mere addition of the effects of one to the effects of the other.

Dual personality   A form of dissociative disorder in which the person maintains two separate personalities, one of which typically is unaware of the existence of the other.

Dyslexia (dis-LEK-see-ah)   An inability to read with understanding, often caused by a tendency to misread letters (by seeing their mirror images, for instance).

Echolalia (ek-oh-LAY-lee-ah)   A tendency, sometimes observed in autistic children, to repeat, or echo back, whatever is said to them.

Eclectic   Selected or chosen from many sources.

Educational psychology   The psychological study of learning, teaching, and related topics.

EEG (electroencephalogram)   Record of the electrical activity of the brain; made by attaching electrodes to the scalp.

Efferent (EF-er-ent)   Carrying or conducting outward, as in nerves or neurons conveying impulses away from the brain or central nervous system; opposite of *afferent*.

Ego (EE-go)   In Freudian terminology, the portion of personality that is in conscious control of behavior and that reconciles the demands of the id, superego, and external reality.

Egocentric (EE-go-SEN-trik) Unable to take a viewpoint other than one's own.

Eidetic imagery (eye-DET-ik IM-ij-ree) The ability to retain an image long enough to use it as a source of information; basically, a photographic memory.

Ejaculation (EE-jac-you-LAY-shun) The release of sperm and seminal fluid by the male at the time of orgasm.

Electra conflict (ih-LEK-trah) In Freudian theory, a conflict experienced by female children when they become attracted to their fathers and feel themselves to be in competition with their mothers. (See *Oedipus conflict*.)

Electroconvulsive shock (ECS) (ih-LEK-tro-cun-VUL-siv) An electric shock passed directly through the brain, producing a convulsion. ECS can impair memory and produce amnesia in experimental animals. Clinically, it is used in the treatment of severe depression.

Electrode Any needle, wire, metal plate, or saltwater-filled glass tube used to apply electrical current to the body, especially to neural tissue.

Electromagnetic radiation (ih-LEK-tro-mag-NET-ik) Waves of energy produced by electric and magnetic oscillations. Radio waves, light waves, X rays, and gamma rays are all electromagnetic waves differing only in their wavelength.

Empathy (EM-puh-thee) A capacity for taking another's point of view or sharing another's state of consciousness; to feel what another is feeling.

Empirical (im-PIR-ih-cul) Founded on experiment or experience; based on direct observation.

Encoding Changing information into a form that allows it to be stored in memory and manipulated in thought.

Encopresis (en-coh-PREE-sis) An inability to control defecation (elimination of solid wastes); hence, "soiling."

Encounter group A group experience that emphasizes intensely honest interchanges among participants regarding feelings and reactions to one another.

Endocrine system (EN-duh-krin) Bodily system made up of those glands whose secretions pass directly into the bloodstream or lymph.

Endogenous depression (en-DAHJ-eh-nus) Depression that appears to be produced from within, rather than as a reaction to life events.

Endorphins (en-DOR-funz) A class of brain peptides (proteins) having an apparent link to the control of pain and possibly to psychiatric disturbances.

Engineering psychology A specialty concerned with the design of machines and work environments so that they are compatible with human sensory and motor capabilities.

Engrams (EN-gramz) "Memory traces" or physical changes taking place in the brain; a general term referring to the theoretical basis for learning and memory.

Enkephalins (en-KEF-ah-lins) Recently discovered brain peptides (proteins) having an apparent link to emotional functioning.

Enuresis (EN-you-REE-sis) An inability to control urination, particularly with reference to bed-wetting.

Environmental psychology The formal study of how environments affect behavior.

Episodic drive (ep-ih-SOD-ik) A noncyclical drive state occurring in distinctly separate episodes associated with particular conditions (for example, pain avoidance, specific hungers, sexual motivation).

Episodic memory (ep-ih-SOD-ik) A hypothesized "autobiographical" subpart of memory that records life events or "episodes."

Erogenous zone (eh-ROJ-ih-nus) Any bodily area productive of pleasurable sensations and particularly those areas producing erotic desire when stimulated.

Escape learning Learning to make a response to escape or to terminate an aversive (painful) stimulus. Escape learning is negatively reinforced by termination of the aversive stimulus.

Escapism Reducing discomfort by leaving frustrating situations or by psychologically withdrawing from them.

Estrogen (ES-truh-jen) Any of a number of female sex hormones.

Estrus (ES-trus) Changes in the reproductive organs and sexual drives of animals associated with a desire for mating, particularly used to refer to female animals "in heat."

Ethnocentric (ETH-no-CEN-trik) Placing one's own group or race at the center; that is, tending to reject all other groups but one's own.

Ethologist (ETH-all-oh-jist) A person who studies the natural behavior patterns of animals.

Eugenics (you-GEN-iks) The science that deals with the improvement of an animal species or race.

Exorcism In Medieval Europe, the practice of expelling or driving off an "evil spirit," particularly one residing in the body of an individual who is "possessed."

Experiment A scientific technique whereby all relevant variables are manipulated, measured, or controlled so that cause-effect relationships may be observed. Simple experiments typically involve both an *experimental group* and a *control group*.

Experimental group In a controlled experiment, the group of subjects exposed to the independent variable or experimental manipulation. (See control group.)

Experimental psychologist A psychologist primarily interested in the scientific study of human and animal behavior.

Experimenter effect Changes in subjects' behavior caused by the unintended influence of an experimenter's presence and actions.

Extinction The process of consistently not reinforcing a learned response, leading to a gradual decrease in the frequency with which the response occurs.

Extraneous variables (ex-TRAY-nee-us) Those conditions or factors to be excluded from possible influence on the outcome of a controlled experiment (that is, variables the experimenter is not interested in).

Extrasensory perception The purported ability to perceive events in ways that cannot be explained by known capacities of the sensory organs.

Extrinsic motivation Motivation based on obvious external rewards, obligations, or similar factors, not on the inherent satisfactions of the task or activity.

Extrovert (EK-struh-vert) An individual whose energies and interests are directed outward; a person who seeks social contact or is outgoing. (Compare introvert.)

Factor analysis A statistical technique whereby multiple measures are intercorrelated. Measures that form "clusters" of correlations are assumed to represent some more general underlying factor.

Family therapy Therapeutic technique in which all family members participate, both individually and as a group, to change destructive relationships.

Fantasy A product of the imagination determined mainly by one's motives or feelings. Fantasy may be used as an escape mechanism.

Feedback Knowledge of results or relaying the effect of some action to the person controlling it.

Figure-ground Gestaltist's observation that some aspects of a stimulus pattern appear to stand out as an object (figure) while others appear to stand in the background (ground).

Fixation The tendency to repeat wrong solutions or faulty responses as a consequence of frustration. In Freudian theory, lasting conflicts developed during a particular stage of development as a result of frustration or overindulgence during that stage.

Fixed-action pattern   A genetically programmed sequence of movements occurring mechanically and virtually universally in members of a particular species.

Fixed-interval schedule   A schedule of reinforcement in which reinforcement is administered following a fixed period of time after the previous reinforcement; for example, every 3 minutes.

Fixed-ratio schedule   A schedule of reinforcement in which a predetermined number of responses must be made before reinforcement is delivered; for example, one reinforcement for every five responses.

Flat affect   A seemingly total lack of emotional responsiveness.

Fovea (FOE-vee-ah)   A small depression in the center of the retina containing the greatest concentration of *cones* and providing the sharpest vision.

Frame of reference   A mental and emotional perspective, relative to which events are perceived and evaluated.

Fraternal twins   Twins conceived from two separate eggs. Fraternal twins are no more alike genetically than other siblings. (See *identical twins*.)

Free association   A technique of *psychoanalysis* in which persons say anything that comes into their minds regardless of how embarrassing or unimportant it may seem.

Free-floating anxiety   Feelings of dread or apprehension that cannot be traced to any particular source.

Free will   The doctrine that humans are capable of freely making choices or decisions.

Frigidity   An abnormal lack of sexual desire.

Frontal lobotomy   Surgical destruction of the frontal lobes of the brain, or separation of the frontal lobes from the remainder of the brain.

Frustration   An internal emotional state resulting from interference with satisfaction of a motive or blocking of goal-directed behavior.

Fugue (FEWG)   A dissociative reaction characterized by taking flight and by a loss of memory for events before or during the act of fleeing.

Functional fixedness   Rigidity in problem solving caused by an inability to see novel uses for familiar objects.

Functionalism (FUNK-shun-ul-ism)   School of psychology concerned with how behavior and mental abilities help people adapt to their environments.

Functional psychosis   A psychosis with no apparent biological basis.

Galvanic skin response (GSR) (gal-VAN-ik)   A change in the electrical resistance of the skin associated with arousal or anxiety.

General adaptation syndrome (GAS)   Selye's description of a consistent pattern of reactions to prolonged stress occurring in three stages: alarm, resistance, and, finally, exhaustion.

General paresis (pah-REE-sis)   An organic psychosis that results when syphilis attacks the brain.

Generalization   The transfer of a learned response from one stimulus or set of circumstances to others that are in some way like the original stimulus.

Generalized anxiety disorder   Defined as at least 6 months of persistent anxiety.

Genes   Areas on the chromosomes that carry hereditary instructions affecting various personal characteristics.

Genital stage   The final stage in psychosexual development (according to Freud); typically attained in late adolescence and representing full psychosexual maturity. (See also *anal stage*; *oral stage*; *phallic stage*.)

Gerontologist (JER-un-TOL-uh-jist)   One who studies the effects of aging.

Gestalt (guh-SHTALT)   A German word meaning form or pattern.

The school of psychology emphasizing the study of perception, learning, and thinking in whole units, not by analysis into parts.

Gestalt therapy   A psychotherapy developed by Perls and others that emphasizes immediate experience and participation of the whole person in any activity.

Goal   The object of a motivated and directed sequence of behavior.

Gonads   The sex glands—testes in males and ovaries in females.

Grammar   The study of classes of words and their functions and relations within sentences.

Graphology (gra-FALL-uh-jee)   The legitimate study of handwriting to detect forgeries; also, the discredited notion that personality characteristics are revealed by handwriting.

Group sanctions   Any rewards or punishments (real or symbolic) applied to members of a group for adherence to, or deviation from, group norms for acceptable conduct.

Group therapy   Any form of psychotherapy taking advantage of the special characteristics of group interaction. Individuals work out personal problems with the guidance of a trained therapist and the help of other group members.

Gustation (gus-TAY-shun)   The sense of taste or the act of tasting.

Habituation (ha-bich-oo-WAY-shun)   A decrease in the strength of a reflex caused by its repeated elicitation. Also, a decrease in sensory response to repeated presentation of a stimulus.

Hallucinations (ha-loos-un-AY-shuns)   Imaginary sensations such as seeing, hearing, or smelling things that don't exist in the real world.

Hallucinogen (ha-lu-SIN-oh-jen)   Any substance or drug that causes hallucinations.

Halo effect   The tendency to generalize a favorable or unfavorable impression to unrelated details of personality.

Heredity   A transmission of physical and psychological characteristics from parents to offspring through genes.

Hermaphroditism (hur-MAF-roh-dite-ism)   The condition of having genitals suggestive of both sexes; ambiguous genital sexuality.

Hippocampus   A structure in the brain associated with the regulation of emotion and the transfer of information from short-term memory to long-term memory.

Homeostasis (HOE-me-oh-STAY-sis)   Steady state of physiological equilibrium maintained by various bodily mechanisms.

Hormone   A bodily chemical transported by body fluids that has an effect on physiological functioning or psychological behavior.

Hospitalism   A pattern of deep depression observed in institutionalized infants; marked by weeping and sadness and a lack of normal response to other humans.

Hue   That property of color represented by its classification into basic categories of red, orange, yellow, green, blue, indigo, and violet or intermediaries of these.

Humanism   An approach to psychology that focuses on human experience, problems, potentials, or ideals.

Hydrocephaly (HI-dro-SEF-ah-lee)   A type of mental retardation caused by accumulation of cerebrospinal fluid within the brain.

Hyperactivity   A behavioral state characterized by short attention span, restless movement, and impaired learning capacity. Sometimes referred to as minimal brain dysfunction (MBD).

Hyperopia (HI-per-OH-pea-ah)   A visual defect causing farsightedness.

Hypnogogic images (hip-no-GAH-jik)   Unusually vivid mental imagery associated with hypnosis, the period immediately preceding sleep, and other unusual states of consciousness.

Hypnosis   An altered state of consciousness characterized by relaxation, focused attention, and increased susceptibility to suggestion.

Hypochondria (HI-po-KON-dree-ah) An excessive preoccupation with minor bodily problems or complaints about illnesses that seem to be imaginary.

Hypoglycemia (HI-po-gly-SEE-me-ah) Below-normal blood sugar level.

Hypothalamus (HI-po-THAL-ah-mus) A small area at the base of the brain that regulates many aspects of motivation and emotion, particularly hunger, thirst, and sexual behavior.

Hypothesis (hi-POTH-eh-sis) The predicted outcome of an experiment or an educated guess about the relationship between variables.

Hysteria (his-TAIR-ee-ah) Wild emotional excitability sometimes associated with the development of apparent physical disabilities (numbness, blindness, and so forth) without known physical cause.

Icon (EYE-con) A mental image or representation.

Id According to Freud, the most primitive part of the personality, which supplies energy and which demands immediate gratification of needs, drives, and desires.

Identical twins Twins who develop from the same egg and who, therefore, have an identical hereditary makeup. (See *fraternal twins*.)

Identification A process in personality development in which a person becomes like an admired adult by incorporating the adult's goals and values into his or her own behavior. Also used as a defense mechanism in adulthood.

Illusion In perception, an unreal or misleading impression presented to vision or other senses; thus, a perception that fails to give a true representation of the stimulus. (Compare with *hallucination*.)

Implicit trial and error In problem solving, the internal elimination (by covert trial and error) of wrong solutions.

Imprinting A rapid and relatively permanent type of learning that occurs within a limited period of time early in life.

Incentive A goal object valued by an individual that can be employed to motivate behavior.

Incentive value The value a goal holds for a person or animal above and beyond its ability to fill a need.

Independent variable In a controlled experiment, the condition under investigation as a potential cause of some change in behavior; the variable manipulated (changed) by the experimenter. (See *dependent variable*.)

Inductive thought A type of thinking in which one is given a series of specific examples and must infer from them a general rule. (Compare with *deductive thought*.)

Industrial psychology The application of psychology to work, especially to personnel selection, human relations, and machine design.

Innate Inborn or hereditary traits.

Insanity Mental disability resulting in an inability to manage one's affairs or to be aware of the consequences of one's actions. Legally, persons declared insane may not be held fully responsible for their actions.

Insight A sudden reorganization of the elements of a problem causing the solution to become self-evident. Also, one's understanding of one's own behavior or motives.

Insomnia A consistent or prolonged inability to sleep; insufficient sleep or poor quality sleep.

Instinct Complex unlearned behaviors that are species-specific and relatively uniform.

Instrumental conditioning Learning brought about when voluntary responses are affected by their consequences, as when an animal learns its way through a maze to get food; specifically, the effects of positive and negative reinforcement, nonreinforcement, and punishment.

Intellectualization A psychological defense mechanism in which anxiety or emotion is removed from a situation by thinking or speaking of the situation in very formal or abstract terms.

Intelligence quotient (IQ) An index of intelligence defined as a person's mental age divided by his or her chronological age and multiplied by 100.

Interference theory The theory of forgetting that holds that previously learned materials interfere with the storage of new material or that the recall of previous learning is prevented by recent learning.

Intermittent reinforcement Reinforcement occurring irregularly or unexpectedly (partial reinforcement).

Intrauterine environment (IN-tra-YOOT-uh-run) The chemical and physical environment existing in the womb before birth.

Intrinsic motivation Motivation that comes from within, rather than from the presence of external rewards; the motivation that derives from enjoyment of a task or activity.

Introspection (IN-tro-SPEK-shun) A psychological technique used to examine one's own conscious experience; self-observation of one's thoughts, feelings, and sensations.

Introvert (IN-truh-vert) An individual who prefers being alone, who withdraws from social contact, or who is self-centered. (Compare *extrovert*.)

Iris Colored circular muscle of the eye that opens and closes to admit more or less light into the eye.

Isolation A psychological defense involving the separation of contradictory feelings or ideas into "logic-tight" compartments.

Just noticeable difference The amount of increase or decrease in a stimulus that can be reliably detected as a change in amount, value, or intensity.

Kinesics (kih-NEE-siks) The study of the meaning of body movements, posture, hand gestures, and facial expressions.

Kinesthesis (KIN-es-THEE-sus) The sense of one's own bodily position, muscle movement, or equilibrium.

Latency (LATE-un-see) In Freudian theory, the period from age 6 until puberty characterized as a quiet interruption of psychosexual development.

Latent learning Learning that occurs without obvious reinforcement and that is not apparent until reinforcement is provided.

Lateralization Refers to the concentration of specific mental functions or abilities on one side of the brain or the other.

Learned helplessness A learned inability to overcome environmental obstacles or to avoid punishment.

Learning In general, any relatively permanent change in behavior that can be attributed to experience but not to such factors as fatigue, maturation, injury, and so forth.

Learning set A readiness for learning a task or mastering a problem established by prior learning of similar tasks or solution of similar problems.

Lens A transparent structure at the front of the eye that focuses images on the retina.

Libido (lih-BEE-doe) In Freudian terminology, the sexual energy involved in the functioning of personality; primarily sexual in nature.

Limbic system A collection of interconnected brain structures whose functions include smell and emotional reactions.

Linguistic determinism Hypothesis proposed by Whorf that the language one speaks shapes one's perceptions of reality and influences one's thought.

Localization of function The theory that particular psychological functions are represented by particular parts of the brain.

Logotherapy (LO-go-therapy) Therapy that emphasizes the need to find meaning in life.

Long-term memory Memory of events for relatively long periods, usually presumed to be based on permanent storage of information transferred from short-term memory. (*See also short-term memory.*)

Major affective disorders Psychotic disorders marked by lasting extremes of mood or emotion.

Major depression A severe and lasting depression accompanied by the symptoms of psychosis.

Major tranquilizers Drugs that in addition to having tranquilizing properties also serve as antipsychotics by reducing hallucinations, sensory distortions, and delusional thinking. (Compare with *minor tranquilizers.*)

Mandala (man-DALL-ah) A circular design advanced to a high art form by Tibetan Buddhists. Mandalas are considered to be a symbol of wholeness, balance, and totality. Mandala-type designs are observed in all cultures.

Manic Extremely excited, hyperactive, or irritable.

Manic-depressive psychosis A psychosis in which a persons' moods swing from elation or excitement to deep depression. (See *psychosis.*)

Mantra A flowing word or sound repeated silently to oneself as the focus of attention in meditation.

Masochism (MAS-oh-kizm) Deriving sexual gratification from pain inflicted on oneself by others.

Massed practice Continuous practice without rest periods or interruption, as distinct from distributed practice.

Mass media Major channels of public communication and information flow, such as radio, television, newspapers, magazines.

Masturbation Erotic stimulation of the genitals other than by intercourse, usually resulting in orgasm.

Maternal influences The aggregate of all psychological effects mothers have on their children. (See *paternal influences.*)

Maturation The emergence and development of personal characteristics in an orderly sequence as a result of underlying physical growth.

Meditation A contemplative exercise for the production of relaxation, heightened awareness, or spiritual revelation.

Memory The mental capacity for storing, organizing, and recovering information.

Menarche (MEN-ar-kee) The onset of menstruation; a woman's first period.

Menopause (MEN-oh-paws) In females, the time during middle age when regular monthly menstrual periods end. (See also *climacteric.*)

Mental age An indication of mental ability defined in terms of the average capabilities of individuals at each age; that is, mental ability apart from actual age in years.

Mental retardation The presence of a developmental disability; a formal IQ score below 70; or a significant impairment of adaptive behavior.

Mescaline (MES-kuh-lin) A psychoactive drug derived from the peyote cactus that has properties similar to LSD.

Mesmerize An archaic term for hypnotize.

Metabolism (meh-TAB-oh-lizm) The rate of energy production and expenditure in the body.

Microcephaly (MY-kro-CEF-ah-lee) A type of mental retardation characterized by a very small skull that prevents normal brain development.

Microsleep A momentary shift in brain wave patterns to those of sleep.

Minimal brain dysfunction A condition of brain immaturity believed by some to underlie hyperactivity in children. (See *hyperactivity.*)

Minor tranquilizers Drugs capable of producing relaxation or a reduction of general tension or activation, and those that have an antianxiety property such as Valium. (Compare with *major tranquilizers.*)

MMPI (Minnesota Multiphasic Personality Inventory) The most widely used self-rating personality test.

Mnemonic device (nee-MON-ik or ni-MON-ik) Any technique or strategy to assist remembering.

Model A system of ideas and concepts designed to interrelate known facts and to provide an explanatory system.

Modeling A type of imitation in which an individual mimics behavior performed by another person (the model).

Monocular (mah-NOCK-you-ler) Pertaining to the function of one eye. For example, monocular cues for depth perception are those involving the use of only one eye.

Morphemes (MORE-feems) The smallest meaningful units in a language.

Motive A drive or force within the organism that activates behavior or directs it toward a goal.

Motor neuron An efferent neuron that carries motor commands from the central nervous system to muscles and glands. (See *efferent; neurons.*)

Motor program A mental representation or model of a skilled movement; similar in some ways to a computer program.

Motor skills Learned skills having an element of physical dexterity or requiring the coordination of muscular movements.

Multiple personality A rare form of emotional disturbance in which an individual maintains two or more distinct personalities; formally classified as a dissociative reaction.

Myoclonus (MY-ahk-luh-nus) Reflex contractions of muscles, causing a jerking motion.

Myopia (my-OH-pea-ah) A visual defect making it difficult to focus distant objects (nearsightedness).

Narcolepsy (NAR-co-lep-see) A serious sleep disturbance in which the individual suffers uncontrollable sleep attacks, which can occur even when the person is standing or driving.

Natural selection Charles Darwin's theory that evolution favors the survival of those plants and animals best adjusted to the conditions under which they live (survival of the fittest).

Naturalistic observation Observation and recording of naturally occurring behavior that is not manipulated experimentally.

Need In motivational theory, a specific state within the organism that may elicit behavior appropriate to the need (often related to the depletion of essential bodily substances or the disruption of homeostasis).

Negative practice The deliberate repetition of an unwanted response until it becomes aversive or painful.

Negative reinforcement Increasing the probability of a response by terminating or withdrawing an unpleasant stimulus on completion of the response.

Negative transfer A carryover of skills or responses from one task to another when such carryover impairs performance on the second task. (Compare *positive transfer.*)

Neo-Freudians (NEE-oh Freudians) Personality theorists who accept the broad features of Freud's psychodynamic approach but who have revised his theory to fit their own concepts.

Neonate (NEE-oh-nate) The human newborn.

Nervous system   A network of neurons that interconnects sensory receptors and effector organs to produce behavior and conscious experience.

Neurilemma (NEW-rih-LEM-ah)   A thin layer of cells wrapped around the axons of some neurons.

Neurons   Individual nerve cells that form the basic structure of the nervous system.

Neurosis (new-ROW-sis)   A behavior disturbance primarily characterized by excessive anxiety, minor distortions of reality, and subjective discomfort. The term is now considered outdated.

Neuropeptides (NEW-roh-PEP-tides)   A newly discovered class of brain chemicals consisting of simple proteins capable of a wide range of effects on moods and behavior.

Neurotransmitter (NEW-roh-transmitter)   Any one of a number of chemical substances secreted by neurons, which cross the synapse and alter activity in the receiving neuron.

Night blindness   A condition in which vision becomes impaired in low levels of illumination.

Nondirective therapy   (See *client-centered therapy*.)

Nonhomeostatic   Not subject to the maintenance of homeostatic balance. (See *homeostasis*.)

Nonsense syllable   A meaningless syllable usually consisting of a consonant, a vowel, and a consonant; used in experiments on retention and memory.

Noradrenaline (NOR-ah-DREN-ah-lin)   A neurotransmitter secreted by neurons of the sympathetic nervous system; also produced at various locations within the brain. Increased noradrenaline output is associated with anger.

Normal curve   A bell-shaped curve having known mathematical properties and characterized by a large number of scores in the middle, tapering toward very few extremely high and low scores at either end.

Norms   Accepted social rules for behavior to which the individual members of a group tend to conform.

NREM sleep   Sleep periods during which there is a minimum of eye movement and little or no dreaming.

Nystagmus (nis-TAG-mus)   Involuntary vibration or movement of the eyeball, including tiny oscillations (physiological nystagmus) and larger reflex movements seen in the blind.

Object constancy   Tendency to perceive objects in the same way even when one's view of them changes.

Object permanence   Recognition that objects continue to exist when they cannot be seen. Very young children appear to believe that objects cease to exist when the objects are out of sight.

Obsessions   Recurring irrational or disturbing thoughts a person cannot prevent.

Obsessive-compulsive disorder   Extreme preoccupation with certain thoughts and compulsive performance of certain behaviors, both of which occur in ritualistic or unavoidable fashion.

Oedipus conflict (ED-ih-pus)   A Freudian concept referring to a boy's sexual attachment to his mother. (See *Electra conflict*.)

Olfaction (ol-FAK-shun)   The sense of smell.

Operant conditioning (OP-er-unt)   Type of learning that occurs when an organism "operates" on the environment. The consequences of a response affect its probability of recurrence.

Operational definition   Definition of a concept or variable that specifies the operations (actions or procedures) used to measure the concept or manipulate the variable.

Optic nerve   The large nerve carrying visual impulses from each eye to the brain.

Oral stage   The Freudian stage of psychosexual development in which the individual is preoccupied with his or her mouth. (See also *anal stage*; *genital stage*; *phallic stage*.)

Organic mental disorder   A mental or emotional problem caused by clearly identifiable physiological or genetic factors.

Organismic valuing (or-gan-IS-mik)   The process of evaluating events on the basis of spontaneous personal reaction rather than by reference to learned systems of values.

Orgasm   A climax and release of sexual excitement.

Orientation response   The pattern of changes occurring throughout the body that prepares an organism to receive information from a particular stimulus.

Ovaries   Female sex organs that produce hormones and ova (eggs).

Overlearning   Practice that is continued beyond the point of mere mastery of memorized material or of a skill.

Palmistry (PALM-is-tree)   A false system that claims to be able to identify personality traits or to predict the future by analyzing the lines on the palms of the hand.

Panic disorder   Persistently high levels of anxiety coupled with sudden episodes of intense, but unfocused, panic.

Paradoxical sleep   A sleep pattern in which the individual produces an EEG record similar to Stage 1 sleep, or even to waking, yet remains behaviorally asleep (and typically dreaming).

Paranoia (pair-ih-NOY-yah)   A psychotic state characterized by delusions of persecution or grandeur.

Paranoid schizophrenia (PAIR-ih-noid SKIT-suh-FREE-nee-ah)   A psychosis characterized by delusions of persecution or grandeur and accompanied by severe disturbances of thought and emotion. (See *psychosis*.)

Paraprofessional   An individual who works in a near-professional capacity under the supervision of a more highly trained person.

Parapsychology (PAIR-ah-sie-COLL-uh-jee)   The scientific study of extranormal psychological events; for example, extrasensory perception.

Parasympathetic nervous system (PAIR-ah-sim-pah-THET-ik)   The division of the autonomic nervous system associated with production of relaxation, bodily deactivation, and conservation of energy.

Partial reinforcement   Reinforcement administered only after a portion of the total responses in a particular situation (also called intermittent reinforcement).

Partial reinforcement effect   A greater resistance to extinction observed in responses acquired on a schedule of partial reinforcement (responses rewarded on only a portion of their occurrences).

Paternal influences   The aggregate of all psychological effects fathers have on their children. (See *maternal influences*.)

Pedophilia   Sex with children; child molesting.

Peer group   A group of people of one's own age and of equal or similar background.

Perception   The process of meaningfully organizing sensation.

Peripheral nervous system (peh-RIF-er-al)   All portions of the nervous system lying outside the brain and spinal cord, including sensory neurons, motor neurons, the spinal nerves, cranial nerves, skeletal nervous system, and autonomic nervous system.

Peripheral vision   Vision at the periphery (edges) of the visual field.

Persona (per-SO-nah)   In Jung's system, an archetype representing the "mask" or public self presented to others.

Personality   An individual's unique and enduring traits and psychological characteristics and the dynamic relationship among them. (See *traits*.)

Personality disorder   Disturbances involving maladaptive and long-standing distortions of personality characteristics.

Personality types   Systems of personality description employing only a few categories, with each category representing a collection of related traits. (See *traits*.)

Personnel psychology   Branch of industrial/organizational psychology concerned with testing, selection, placement, and promotion of employees.

PET scan   Positron emission tomography; the colored image of brain areas and their activity produced by the scanning process.

Phallic stage (FAL-ik)   The Freudian developmental stage in which the individual is preoccupied with pleasure derived from the genital organs. (See also *anal stage; genital stage; oral stage*.)

Phenomenal field (fi-NOM-un-ul)   One's complete field of subjective awareness.

Phenylketonuria (PKU) (FEN-ul-KEET-un-YURE-ee-ah or FEEN-ul-KEET-un-YURE-ee-ah)   A metabolic disorder causing the accumulation of phenylalanine in the body and leading to mental retardation.

Phi phenomenon (FIE fi-NOM-uh-non)   The apparent movement of two stationary lights caused when they are lighted in quick succession.

Phobia (FOE-bee-ah)   An intense and unrealistic fear of some specific object or situation.

Phobic disorder (FOE-bik)   A type of anxiety disorder in which irrational fears predominate.

Phonemes (FOE-neems)   The basic sounds of a language that can be distinguished from one another.

Phosphene (FOSS-feen)   A luminous visual impression caused by activation of the retina by any means, including pressure and electrical stimulation.

Photoreceptors   Sensory receptors sensitive to light and specialized for transforming light waves into neural impulses.

Phrenology (freh-NOL-oh-jee)   A false system that holds that the shape of the skull indicates mental faculties or personal characteristics.

Physiological psychologist   A psychologist who studies the relationship between the nervous system and behavior.

Pica (PIE-kah)   A craving for unnatural foods or substances such as chalk, ashes, and so forth.

Pitch   Psychological experience of high or low tones corresponding to the physical dimension of frequency.

Placebo (pla-SEE-bo)   An inactive substance given in the place of a drug in psychological research or by physicians who wish to treat chronic aches and pains by suggestion.

Placebo effect   Changes in behavior due to one's expectations that a drug (or other treatment) will have some effect.

Polygenetic   Any physical or behavioral trait influenced by three or more (often many) genes.

Polygraph   An instrument for recording several measures of bodily activity simultaneously; commonly used to refer to the records of emotional response made by a "lie detector."

Population   An entire defined group; all members of a class or set from which a smaller sample may be drawn. (See *sample*.)

Positive reinforcement   Rewards or stimuli that increase the probability of a response they have followed.

Positive transfer   The carryover of skills or responses from one task to another when such carryover improves performance on the second task. (Compare *negative transfer*.)

Post-traumatic stress disorder   Psychological and emotional disturbance following exposure to stresses outside the range of normal human experience, such as natural disasters and military combat.

Precognition (PREE-kog-nish-un)   Literally, knowing beforehand; hence, any foretelling of the future or any prior knowledge of events unknowable by normal means.

Prejudice   A negative attitude or prejudgment held against members of a particular group of people. Most often, attitudes held about racial or ethnic groups, but also frequently applied to other groups as well.

Prenatal   Events occurring before the birth of a child.

Presbyopia (prez-by-OH-pea-ah)   Farsightedness caused by aging.

Pressure   In psychological terms, pressure is said to exist when extended vigilance must be maintained, when events must be speeded up, or when a person must work at or near maximum capacity for an extended period.

Primary impotence (IM-pu-tens)   In the male, total inability to perform sexually. (See also *secondary impotence*.)

Primary motives   Innate motives based on biological needs.

Primary reinforcers   Unlearned reinforcers; usually those that satisfy physiological needs.

Primate   A member of the family of mammals, including humans, apes, and monkeys.

Proactive inhibition (pro-AK-tiv)   Forgetting that occurs when previous learning interferes with more recent learning.

Projection   Attributing one's own feelings, shortcomings, or unacceptable impulses to others as a means of defending against anxiety.

Projective tests   Psychological tests making use of unstructured stimuli, wherein the subject is presumed to project his or her own thoughts and impulses onto the stimulus.

Proxemics (prox-EM-iks)   Systematic study of the human use of space; particularly, interpersonal space in various social settings.

Pseudo-memories (SUE-doe)   False memories that a person believes to be true or accurate.

Pseudo-psychologies (SUE-do)   False or dubious systems that purport to explain behavior.

Psi events (SEYE events)   Paranormal events falling outside the traditional bounds of psychology and science. Includes clairvoyance, telepathy, precognition, psychokinesis, astral projection, out-of-body experiences, and the like.

Psyche (SIE-kee)   The mind, mental life, and personality as a whole.

Psychiatrist   A medical doctor who has additional training in the diagnosis and treatment of mental illness.

Psychoactive drugs (SIE-co-AK-tiv)   Any of a large number of substances (often quite potent) capable of altering sensation, perception, cognition, memory, or other psychological events.

Psychoanalysis (SIE-co-ah-NAL-ih-sis)   A Freudian approach to therapy emphasizing free association, dream interpretation, and transference.

Psychoanalyst (SIE-co-AN-ah-list)   A mental health professional (usually a medical doctor) trained to practice psychoanalysis.

Psychodrama (SIE-co-DRAH-ma)   A technique of psychotherapy in which people act out personal conflicts in the presence of other people who play supporting parts.

Psychodynamic (SIE-co-die-NAM-ik)   Pertaining to internal motives, unconscious forces, and other aspects of mental functioning.

Psychokinesis (SIE-co-kih-NEE-sis)   The ability to influence physical events by mental activity or the act of exerting mental control over inanimate objects.

Psycholinguist (SIE-co-LING-wist)   A psychologist who specializes in the study of language.

Psychologist   An individual highly trained in the philosophy, methods, factual knowledge, and theories of psychology; usually has at least a master's degree and frequently a doctorate.

Psychology   The scientific study of behavior and conscious experience.

Psychometrics (SIE-co-MET-riks)   Specialty that focuses on mental measurement or psychological testing, such as personality and intelligence testing.

Psychopath (SIE-co-path)   An individual who appears to make no distinctions between right and wrong and to feel no guilt about destructive or antisocial behavior.

Psychopathology (SIE-co-pah-THOL-ih-jee)   Abnormal or maladaptive behavior; literally, mental sickness.

Psychophysics (SIE-co-fiz-iks)   The study of the relationship between physical stimuli and the sensations evoked by them in a human observer.

Psychosexual stages (SIE-co-sexual)   In Freudian theory, development of the personality according to the following stages: *oral stage, anal stage, phallic stage,* and *genital stage.*

Psychosis (sie-CO-sis)   A severe psychological disturbance characterized by withdrawal from reality, by hallucinations and delusions, by disturbed emotions, and often by personality disorganization.

Psychosomatic illnesses (SIE-co-so-MAT-ik)   Disorders in which actual physical damage results from psychological stress.

Psychosurgery (SIE-co-surgery)   Surgical alterations of the brain designed to bring about certain behavioral or emotional changes; may be performed with traditional surgical instruments or by the removal of brain tissue through use of electrical currents and electrodes.

Psychotherapy (SIE-co-therapy)   General term referring to any form of psychological treatment for behavioral disorders; most often used to refer to verbal interaction between the client and a trained mental health professional.

Punishment   After a response, the delivery of an event or stimulus that tends to reduce the future probability of that response.

Pupil   The dark spot at the front of the eye through which light moves in to reach the retina.

Pupillometrics (PUE-pil-oh-MET-riks)   A technique developed by Hess for measuring dilation and constriction of the pupils in response to various stimuli; purportedly a measure of emotional response.

Racism   Racial prejudice that has become institutional (that is, reflected in government policy, schools, and so forth) and that is enforced by the existing social power structure.

Random   Haphazard and without definite pattern. Random numbers represent a series in which each digit from 0 to 9 has an equal probability of appearing in any particular position.

Randomization   The use of random numbers or a random procedure (for example, flipping a coin) to assign subjects to the experimental and control groups in an experiment or a similar situation.

Rarefaction (rare-eh-FAK-shun)   In hearing, the spreading or thinning of air molecules between the crests of successive sound waves.

Rational emotive therapy   A direct and forceful therapy in which clients learn to abandon irrational and self-defeating behavior and beliefs.

Rationalization   Explaining away one's shortcomings in such a way as to avoid responsibility.

Reaction formation   A psychological defense mechanism in which an individual controls unconscious anxiety-producing impulses by behaving in exactly the opposite way.

Recall   Detailed remembering with a minimum of memory cues.

Recessive gene   A gene whose influence will only be expressed when it is paired with a second recessive gene (that is, it cannot be expressed in the presence of a dominant gene). (See *dominant gene.*)

Recitation (RES-ih-TAY-shun)   Repeating aloud material that is to be learned as a means for improving memory of the material.

Recognition   Memory in which previously learned material is correctly identified as that which has been seen before.

Redintegration (ruh-DIN-tuh-GRAY-shun)   The process of inferring or reconstructing an entire complex memory after first observing or remembering only a part of it.

Reference group   Any group with which the individual identifies psychologically and uses as a standard for social comparison.

Reflex   An automatic response to a stimulus; for example, an eye blink, knee jerk, or dilation of the pupil.

Regression   Return to earlier behavior patterns appropriate to a child or younger person, particularly as a response to stress.

Reinforcement   Any stimulus that brings about learning or increases the frequency of the response. Often simply a reward.

Reinforcer   Any stimulus that reliably increases the frequency or probability of responses it follows.

Relational concept   A concept defined by the relationship of one or more dimensions to a second (or other) dimension (for example, "greater than," "above," "equal to"). (Compare with *conjunctive* and *disjunctive* concepts.)

Relearning   Learning again something previously learned; used as a measure of memory for prior learning.

Reliability   An important charcteristic of any test. A test that is reliable gives the same score each time it is administered.

Remission (reh-MISH-un)   Disappearance of symptoms of a psychological disorder.

REMs   An abbreviation for rapid eye movements characteristic of Stage 1 dream sleep.

REM sleep   Rapid-eye-movement sleep corresponding to periods of dreaming.

Replicate   To reproduce or repeat, as in duplicating the results of an experiment.

Representative sample   A sample of a larger population of subjects or observations that accurately reflects the characteristics of the larger population. Representative samples are frequently achieved by random selection of subjects or observations. (See *randomization* and *sample.*)

Repression   Pushing out or barring from consciousness unwanted memories, impulses, or feelings.

Resistance   Blocks that occur in psychoanalysis during free association.

Respondent conditioning   Another term for classical conditioning. (See *classical conditioning.*)

Response   Any muscular action, glandular activity, or other objectively identifiable aspect of behavior.

Retardation   Mental capacity significantly below average; traditionally defined as an IQ score below 70.

Retention   Storage or memorization of information.

Retina   The photosensitive lining at the back of the eye containing rods and cones.

Retrieval   Extracting stored information from memory.

Retroactive inhibition (RET-ro-AK-tiv)   The interference of new learning with the memory of previously learned material.

Retrograde amnesia (RET-ro-grade)   Loss of memory for events that happened before a head injury or other amnesia-producing event.

Rhodopsin (row-DOP-sin)   The photosensitive pigment in the rods of the retina. A chemical composed of retinene and opsin that breaks down into retinene and opsin when struck by light.

RNA (ribonucleic acid)   A chemical substance similar to DNA and believed to be involved in learning and memory.

Rods   Visual receptors in the retina that are responsive to low levels of illumination but that produce only black-white vision. (See *cones.*)

Role   Pattern of behavior one is expected to exhibit when occupying a particular position within a group.

Role reversal   Taking the role of another person to learn how one's own behavior appears from the other person's perspective.

Sadism (SADE-izm)   Deriving erotic satisfaction by the infliction of pain on another; more broadly, love of cruelty.

Sample   A subset or portion of a population.

Saturation   As applied to colors, saturation refers to colors that are free from the mixture of white, that are very pure, and that represent a concentrated area of the spectrum.

Savings score   In testing memory by relearning, the score that is obtained by subtracting the amount of time necessary to remaster material from the amount of time necessary to master it originally.

Scapegoating   The act of causing a person or group of people to bear the blame for others or for conditions not of their making; habitual redirection of aggression toward some person or group.

Schedule of reinforcement   A rule for determining which response will be reinforced.

Schizophrenia (SKIT-suh-FREE-nee-uh)   A form of psychosis characterized by withdrawal from reality, apathy or inappropriate emotion, and, in many cases, delusions and hallucinations.

Schizotypal personality (SKIT-suh-TYPE-al)   A serious personality disorder involving withdrawal, odd behavior, and eccentric thought, but lacking the hallucinations and delusions of true schizophrenia.

Scientific method   A technique for testing the truth of a proposition through careful measurement and controlled observation.

Secondary elaboration   In Freudian dream theory, a tendency to fill in gaps and missing details in the recall or retelling of dreams, thus making dream accounts more logical and organized.

Secondary impotence (IM-pu-tens)   In the male, unsatisfactory sexual performance caused by premature ejaculation. (See also *primary impotence.*)

Secondary motives   Motives based on learned psychological needs.

Secondary reinforcement   A previously neutral stimulus that acquires reinforcement value through association with primary reinforcers. (See also *primary reinforcers.*)

Sedative   A drug that tends to calm, tranquilize, or to encourage sleep.

Self-actualization   The full development of personal potential, especially emotional potential.

Self-disclosure   The process of revealing private thoughts, feelings, and personal history to others.

Self-image   Total subjective perception of oneself, including an image of one's body and perceptions of one's personality, capabilities, and so forth.

Semantics   The study of meanings in language.

Semantic memory   A hypothetical "mental dictionary" of basic facts and knowledge said to be a subpart of long-term memory.

Senile dementia   Serious mental impairment in old age caused by physical deterioration of the brain.

Sensation   The immediate response to stimulation of the sensory receptors and the transduction of environmental or internal events into neural response.

Sensitivity group   A group experience consisting of exercises designed to increase self-awareness and sensitivity to others.

Sensory adaptation   A reduction in sensory responses to any unchanging form of stimulation.

Sensory memory   The first stage in memory storage that holds detailed and literal images of incoming information for a half-second or less.

Sensory neuron   An afferent neuron that carries sensory information toward the brain or central nervous system.

Separation anxiety   Distress displayed by infants when they are separated from their parents or principal caretakers.

Serial position effect   The tendency for the greatest number of memory errors to occur for the middle portions of an ordered list.

Set   A predisposition to respond in a certain way.

Set point   A theoretical proportion of body fat that tends to be maintained by alterations in hunger and eating.

Sexism   Prejudice and discrimination based on gender, particularly that which is reflected in existing social power structures, but also in more subtle attitudes and actions.

Sex roles   Learned behavior that fits societal expectations of proper behavior for males and females.

Shaping   Gradual molding of responses to a final desired behavior by reinforcing successive approximations of the behavior.

Short-term memory (STM)   The retention of information for brief periods without rehearsal; the first step in the creation of permanent memories. (See also *long-term memory.*)

Skin senses   The senses of touch, pressure, pain, heat, and cold.

Social comparison   Making judgments about ourselves through comparison with others.

Social learning theory   An approach that combines learning principles with cognitive processes (perception, thinking, anticipation), plus the effects of observational learning, to explain behavior.

Social influence   Changes in a person's behavior induced by the presence or actions of others.

Social motives   Learned motives that are acquired as part of growing up in a particular society or culture.

Socialization   The process of learning to live in a particular culture by adopting socially acceptable behavior.

Social psychologist   A psychologist particularly interested in the effects of other people on individual behavior.

Sociopath   Another name for the psychopath or antisocial personality. (See *psychopath.*)

Soma (SO-ma)   The body of any living cell, particularly the body of a nerve cell (neuron).

Somatic therapy (so-MAT-ik)   Any therapy directly involving bodily processes; for example, drug therapy, electroconvulsive therapy, psychosurgery, and so forth.

Somatoform disorders (so-MAT-oh-form)   A class of disturbances characterized by exaggerated bodily complaints (hypochondria) or by the presence of physical disability without apparent cause.

Somatotype (so-MAT-oh-type)   Literally, one's body type. In Sheldon's body type system, one's rating on the dimensions of endomorphy, mesomorphy, and ectomorphy.

Somesthetic (som-es-THET-ik)   Pertaining to sensations produced in the skin, muscles, joints, and viscera.

Somnambulism (som-NAM-bue-lizm)   The formal term for sleepwalking.

Spaced practice   Learning trials or practice sessions spread over an extended period of time and including a number of rest periods.

Species   A classification comprising closely related plants or animals potentially able to breed with one another.

Species-specific behavior   Patterned behavior that is exhibited by all normal members of a particular species. (See also *species.*)

Specific hunger   A heightened desire for, or consumption of, a particular food item, especially one that remedies a nutritional deficiency.

Spontaneous recovery   The sudden reappearance of a learned response after apparent extinction.

Spontaneous remission   In psychiatry or clinical psychology, the spontaneous disappearance of psychological symptoms or behavioral disturbances (for example, clients placed on waiting lists sometimes improve at the same rate as those accepted into therapy).

Sports psychology   A specialty that combines study of sports skills with clinical techniques to enhance sports performance and the benefits of sports participation.

Status   An individual's position in a group or social system.

Stereoscopic vision   The seeing of objects as three-dimensional and the perception of space made possible chiefly by the separation of the eyes.

Stereotype   An inaccurate or oversimplified image of the traits of individuals who belong to a particular social group.

Stereotyped response   A rigid, repetitive, and nonproductive response made mechanically and without regard for its appropriateness.

Stimulant   A substance that produces temporary excitation of the body and/or nervous system.

Stimulus   Any physical energy that has some effect on an organism and that evokes a response.

Stimulus generalization   The tendency to make a learned response to stimuli similar to the stimulus an organism was originally conditioned to respond to.

Stimulus motives   Innate needs for stimulation and information.

Stress   A condition in which an organism is subjected to external conditions to which it must adjust or adapt.

Stroboscopic movement (strobe-oh-SKOP-ik)   An illusion of movement caused by the rapid presentation of a series of photographs or other representations of phases of a continuous movement. More commonly, the illusion of movement created by cartoon animation and by movie films.

Structuralism (STRUK-chur-al-izm)   An early school of thought in psychology that tried to analyze sensations and to break down subjective experience into its basic building blocks.

Sublimation (SUB-lih-may-shun)   A psychological defense mechanism involving the expression of socially unacceptable impulses in a socially acceptable way; for example, converting greed into a successful business career.

Subliminal (sub-LIM-ih-nal)   Perception of a stimulus that is presented below the threshold for conscious recognition.

Superego (super-EE-go)   In Freud's theory of personality, the representation of parental values and the rules of society; basically, the unit that acts as the conscience.

Superordinate goals (super-ORD-ih-nate)   Goals that exceed or override all others; goals that render other goals relatively less important.

Survey method   The use of public polling techniques to answer psychological questions.

Syllogism (SIL-oh-jizm)   A logical format for reasoning consisting of a major premise, a minor premise, and a conclusion.

Symbolization   In dream imagery, the tendency for images to stand for or suggest something else by reason of similarity, relationship, appearance, or unconscious association.

Sympathetic nervous system   A division of the autonomic nervous system responsible for activating the body at times of emotion or stress by speeding up energy consumption and preparing the body for action.

Synapse (SIN-aps)   The microscopic space over which nerve impulses travel in the junction of two neurons.

Synesthesia (sin-es-THEE-zyah)   Experiencing one sensory modality in terms of another; for example, "seeing" sounds as colors.

Synesthete (sin-es-THEET)   A person who regularly experiences synesthesia. (See *synesthesia*.)

Syntax   The study of the word order used in the formation of phrases, clauses, and sentences.

Tachistoscope (tuh-KIS-toh-scope)   A mechanical device capable of flashing words or pictures on a screen for very short periods of time; used in perceptual testing, especially in studies of subliminal perception.

Taste aversion   An active dislike for a particular food frequently created when the food is associated with sickness or discomfort. (See *bait shyness*.)

Telepathy (teh-LEP-ah-thee)   A purported form of extrasensory perception in which thoughts are transferred from a sender to a receiver without direct contact. (See *extrasensory perception*.)

Telodendria (tel-oh-DEN-dree-ah)   A branching network of fibers at the end of the axon in nerve cells that forms multiple synapses with other neurons.

Temperament   The physical foundation of personality including such things as prevailing mood, sensitivity, energy levels, and so forth.

Terminal decline   A significant decline in mental capacity observed before death and in some cases anticipating the occurrence of death.

Testes   The male sex organs, located in the scrotum; the source of sperm and male sex hormones.

Testosterone (tes-TOS-ter-own)   Male sex hormone responsible for the development of secondary sexual characteristics.

Thanatologist (THAN-ah-TOL-oh-jist)   One who studies death and the process of dying.

Theory   A system of ideas and concepts designed to set forth and interrelate concepts and facts in a way that summarizes existing data and predicts future observations.

Timbre (TIM-ber)   The psychological aspect of sound that corresponds to the complexity of a tone.

Tinnitus (tin-NYE-tus)   A ringing or whistling sensation in the ears due to disease, injury, drugs, or unknown causes.

Tip-of-the-tongue phenomenon   The experience of feeling that a memory is available but being unable to retrieve it.

Tolerance   A condition in drug addiction brought about by the body's ability to withstand increased amounts of the drug. As tolerance develops, the dosage must be increased to produce the same reaction a smaller dosage once produced.

Traits (personality)   Enduring attitudes and personal qualities that an individual tends to display in most life situations.

Transactional analysis (TA)   A therapeutic technique designed to improve awareness of one's transactions (interchanges) with others.

Transduction   Changing one form of energy into another.

Transference   Refers to the tendency of a patient to transfer feelings to the therapist that correspond to feelings held toward important figures in the patient's past.

Trepanning (treh-PAN-ing)   In modern usage, any surgical procedure in which a hole is bored into the skull. Historically, the chipping or boring of holes in the skull by primitive peoples as a means of treating mental disturbances.

Trichromatic color theory (TRY-kroe-MAT-ik)   Theory of color vision that states that there are three types of cones, each type maximally sensitive to either red, green, or blue.

Unconditioned response   In classical conditioning, the unlearned response that is innately elicited by the unconditioned stimulus; usually a reflex response.

Unconditioned stimulus   A stimulus innately capable of eliciting a response.

Unconscious (un-KON-shus)   That part of a person's mind or personality that contains impulses and desires not directly known to the person.

Unipolar disorder   An emotional disorder in which a person experiences extended periods of deep depression but has no history of ever having been manic.

Vacillation (VAS-ih-LAY-shun)   Wavering in aim or action, especially in conflict situations.

Validity   The ability of a test to measure what it purports to measure.

Variable interval schedule   A schedule of reinforcement that varies the time period between reinforcements.

Variable ratio schedule   A schedule in which the number of respones required to produce reinforcement varies.

Vestibular senses (ves-TIB-you-ler)   Concerned with balance or equilibrium, senses that are produced by the semicircular canals located close to the inner ear.

Vicarious conditioning (vie-CARE-ee-us)   The establishment of a conditioned response (often an emotional response) by observing the reactions of another person to a particular stimulus.

Visual acuity   The clarity of visual perception.

Vocational interest test   A paper-and-pencil test that assesses a person's interests and matches them to interests found among successful workers in various occupations.

White noise   An auditory stimulus that is made up of all audible frequencies of sound and that sounds like a hiss or a waterfall.

References

Aarons, L. (1976). Sleep-assisted instruction. *Psychological Bulletin, 83,* 1–40.

Abe, K., Amatomi, M., & Oda, N. (1984). Sleepwalking and recurrent sleep-talking in children of childhood sleepwalkers. *American Journal of Psychiatry, 141,* 800–801.

Abrams, A. (1983, January 7). Honda Ohio plant transplants Japan methods, harmony. *Los Angeles Times,* Part IV, pp. 1–2.

Adams, J. A. (1967). *Human memory.* New York: McGraw-Hill.

Adams, J. A. (1980). *Learning and memory.* Homewood, IL: Dorsey Press.

Adler, C. S., & Adler, S. M. (1976). Biofeedback—psychotherapy for the treatment of headaches: A 5-year follow-up. *Headache, 16,* 189–191.

Adorno, T. W., Frenkel-Brunswik, E., Levinson, D. J., & Sanford, R. N. (1950). *The authoritarian personality.* New York: Harper.

Ahles, T. A., Blanchard, E. B., & Leventhal, H. (1983). Cognitive control of pain: Attention to the sensory aspects of the cold pressor stimulus. *Cognitive Therapy and Research, 7,* 159–178.

Ainsworth, M. D. S. (1979). Infant-mother attachment. *American Psychologist, 34,* 932–937.

Akerstedt, T., Torsvall, L., & Gillberg, M. (1982). Sleepiness and shift work: Field studies. *Sleep, 5,* S95–S106.

Albert, E. M. (1963). The roles of women: Question of values. In Farber & Wilson (Eds.), *The potential of women.* New York: McGraw-Hill.

Alberti, R., & Emmons, M. (1978). *Your perfect right.* San Luis Obispo, CA: Impact.

Alcock, J. E. (1981). *Parapsychology, science or magic?* New York: Pergamon.

Alevizos, P. N., & Callahan, E. J. (1977). Assessment of psychotic behavior. In A. R. Ciminero, K. S. Calhoun, & H. E. Adams (Eds.), *Handbook of behavioral assessment.* New York: Wiley.

Alexander, G. (1978, September). Terminal therapy. *Psychology Today,* pp. 50–60.

Allen, B. (1979). Winged victory of "Gossamer Albatross." *National Geographic, 156,* 642–651.

Allison, T., & Van Twyver, H. (1970, February). The evolution of sleep. *Natural History.*

Alloy, L. B., Peterson, C., Abramson, L. Y., & Seligman, M. E. (1984). Attributional style and the generality of learned helplessness. *Journal of Personality and Social Psychology, 46,* 681–687.

Allport, G. W. (1958). *The nature of prejudice.* Garden City, NY: Doubleday, Anchor Books.

Allport, G. W. (1961). *Pattern and growth in personality.* New York: Holt, Rinehart and Winston.

Allport, G. W., & Odbert, H. S. (1936). Trait-names: A psycholexical study. *Psychological Monographs, 221.*

Alvino, J., and the Editors of Gifted Children Monthly. (1985). *Parents' Guide to Raising a Gifted Child.* Boston: Little, Brown.

Amabile, T. M. (1983). *The social psychology of creativity.* New York: Springer-Verlag.

American Medical Association, Department of Mental Health. (1968). The crutch that cripples: Drug dependence, Part I. *Today's Health, 46*(9), 11–12, 70–72.

American Psychiatric Association. (1980). *Diagnostic and statistical manual of mental disorders* (3rd ed.). Washington, DC: Author.

American Psychological Association. (1970). *Careers in psychology.* Washington, DC: Author.

Anand, B. K., & Brobeck, J. R. (1951). Hypothalamic control of food intake in rats and cats. *Yale Journal of Biological Medicine,* 123–140.

Anastasi, A., & Foley, J. P., Jr. (1958). *Differential psychology* (3rd ed.). New York: Macmillan.

Anderson, R. H., Anderson, K., Fleming, D. E., & Kinghorn, E. (1984). A multidimensional test of the attributional reformulation of learned helplessness. *Bulletin of the Psychonomic Society, 22,* 212–213.

Anhalt, H. S., & Klein, M. (1976). Drug abuse in junior high school populations. *American Journal of Drug and Alcohol Abuse 3,* 589–603.

Annett, J. (1979). Memory for skill. In M. M. Gruneberg & P. E. Morris (Eds.), *Applied problems in memory.* London: Academic Press.

Apfel, R. E. (1977, November). Resounding facts on hearing loss. *The Science Teacher, 44*(8), 31–34.

Arndt, S., & Berger, D. E. (1978). Cognitive mode and asymmetry in cerebral functioning. *Cortex, 14,* 78–86.

Aronson, E. (1972). *The social animal.* San Francisco: Freeman.

Aronson, E. (1980). *The social animal.* San Francisco: Freeman.

Aronson, E. (1969). Some antecedents of interpersonal attraction. In W. J. Arnold & D. Levine (Eds.), *Nebraska Symposium on Motivation.* Lincoln: University of Nebraska Press.

Aronson, E., With Blaney, N., Sikes, J., Stephan, C., & Snapp, M. (1979). Busing and racial tension: The jigsaw route to learning and liking. In V. J. Derlega & L. H. Janda (Eds.), *Personal adjustment, selected readings.* Glenview, IL: Scott, Foresman.

Aronson, E., Stephan, C., Sikes, J., Blaney, N., & Snapp, M. (1978). *The jigsaw classroom.* Beverly Hills, CA: Sage Publications.

Asch, S. E. (1956). Studies of independence and conformity: A minority of one against a unanimous majority. *Psychological Monographs, 70*(416).

Asimov, I. (1967). *Is anyone there?* Garden City, NY: Doubleday.

Astronomical Society of the Pacific. (1983). *Astrology and astronomy.* San Francisco: Author.

Athenasiou, R., Shaver, P., & Tavris, C. (1970). Sex. *Psychology Today, 4*(2), 37–52.

Atkinson, R. C., & Shiffrin, R. M. (1971, August). The control of short-term memory. *Scientific American,* 89–90.

Ayllon, T. (1963). Intensive treatment of psychotic behavior by stimulus satiation and food reinforcement. *Behavior Research and Therapy, 1,* 53–61.

Ayllon, T., & Azrin, N. H. (1965). The measurement and reinforcement of behavior of psychotics. *Journal of the Experimental Analysis of Behavior, 8,* 357–383.

Ayllon, T., Haughton, E., & Hughes, H. B. (1965). Interpretation of symptoms: Fact or fiction? *Behavior and Therapy, 3,* 1–7.

Azrin, N. H., Hutchinson, R. R., & McLaughlin, R. (1965). The opportunity for aggression as an operant reinforcer during aversive stimulation. *Journal of Experimental Analysis of Behavior, 8,* 171–180.

Bach, G., & Wyden, P. (1969). *The intimate enemy.* New York: Morrow.

Bachman, J. G., & Johnson, L. D. (1979). The freshmen. *Psychology Today, 13,* 78–87.

Bachrach, L. L. (1984). Asylum and chronically ill psychiatric patients. *American Journal of Psychiatry, 141,* 975–978.

Back, K. W. (1972). The group can comfort but it can't cure. *Psychology Today, 6*(7), 28–35.

Baddeley, A. D. (1976). *The psychology of memory*. New York: Basic Books.

Baer, D. M. (1971, October). Let's take another look at punishment. *Psychology Today*.

Ball, G. G., & Grinker, J. A. (1981). Overeating and obesity. In S. J. Mule (Ed.), *Behavior in Excess* (pp. 194–220). New York: The Free Press.

Baltes, P. B., & Schaie, K. W. (1974). Aging and I.Q.: The myth of the twilight years. *Psychology Today*, 7(10), 35–40.

Bandura, A. (1973). *Aggression: A social learning analysis*. Englewood Cliffs, NJ: Prentice-Hall.

Bandura, A. (1977). Self-efficacy: Toward a unifying theory of behavioral change. *Psychological Review*, 84, 191–215.

Bandura, A. (1971). *Social learning theory*. New York: General Learning Press.

Bandura, A. (1965). Vicarious processes: A case of no-trial learning. In L. Berkowitz (Ed.), *Advances in experimental social psychology*, Vol. 2, (pp. 1–55). New York: Academic Press.

Bandura, A., & Rosenthal, T. L. (1966). Vicarious classical conditioning as a function of arousal level. *Journal of Personality and Social Psychology*, 3, 54–62.

Bandura, A., Ross, D., & Ross, S. A. (1963). Vicarious reinforcement and imitative learning. *Journal of Abnormal and Social Psychology*, 67, 601–607.

Bandura, A., & Walters, R. (1959). *Adolescent aggression*. New York: Ronald.

Bandura, A., & Walters, R. (1963). Aggression. In H. W. Stevenson (Ed.), *Child psychology*. Chicago: University of Chicago Press.

Bandura, A., & Walters, R. (1963). *Social learning and personality development*. New York: Holt.

Bank, S. P., & Kahn, M. D. (1982). *The sibling bond*. New York: Basic Books.

Barahal, H. S. (1958). 1000 prefrontal lobotomies: Five- to ten-year follow-up study. *Psychiatric Quarterly*, 32, 653–678.

Barber, T. X. (1970). Suggested ("hypnotic") behavior: The trance paradigm versus an alternative paradigm (Report No. 103). Harding, MA: Medfield Foundation.

Barber, T. X. (1959). Toward a theory of pain: Relief of chronic pain by prefrontal leucotomy, opiates, placebos, and hypnosis. *Psychological Bulletin*, 56, 430–460.

Barchas, J. D., Elliot, G. R., & Berger, P. A. (1978). Biogenic amine hypothesis of schizophrenia. In L. C. Wynne, R. L. Cromwell, and S. Matthysse (Eds.), *The nature of schizophrenia: New approaches to research and treatment*. New York: Wiley.

Baron, R. A. (1983). "Sweet smell of success"? The impact of pleasant artificial scents on evaluations of job applicants. *Journal of Applied Psychology*, 68, 709–713.

Barron, F. (1958). The psychology of imagination. *Scientific American*, 199(3), 150–170.

Barrow, G. M., & Smith, P. A. (1979). *Aging, ageism, and society*. St. Paul, MN: West.

Basedow, R. A. (1925). *The Australian Aborigine*. Adelaide, Australia: Peerce.

Bassuk, E. L. & Gerson, S. (1978) Deinstitutionalization and mental health services. *Scientific American*, 238(2), 46–53.

Bassuk, E. L., Rubin, L., & Lauriat, A. (1984). Is homelessness a mental health problem? *American Journal of Psychiatry*, 141, 1546–1550.

Baum, A., & Davis, G. E. (1980). Reducing the stress of high-density living: An architectural intervention. *Journal of Personality and Social Psychology*, 38, 471–481.

Baum, A., & Valins, S. (1979). Architectural mediation of residential density and control: Crowding and the regulation of social contact. *Advances in Experimental and Social Psychology*, 12, 131–175.

Baum, A., & Valins, S. (Eds.). (1977). *Human response to crowding: Studies of the effects of residential group size*. Hillsdale NJ: Erlbaum.

Baumrind, D. (1980, July). New directions in socialization research. *American Psychologist*, 35, 639–652.

Beach, F. A. (1975). Behavioral endocrinology: An emerging discipline. *American Scientist*, 63, 178–187.

Beck, A. T. (1985). Cognitive therapy of depression: New perspectives. In P. Clayton (Ed.), *Depression*. New York: Raven.

Beck, A. T., & Greenberg, R. L. (1974). Coping with depression. Institute For Rational Living.

Beck, A. T., & Young, J. E. (1978, September). College blues. *Psychology Today*, 80–92.

Becker, P. (1982). Fear reactions and achievement behavior of students approaching an examination. In H. W. Krohne & L. Laux (Eds.), *Achievement, stress and anxiety* (pp. 275–290). Washington: Hemisphere.

Beebe, B., Gerstman, L., Carson, B., Dolins, M., Zigman, A., Rosensweig, H., Faughey K., & Korman, M. (1982). Rhythmic communication in the mother-infant dyad. In M. Davis (Ed.), *Interaction rhythms, periodicity in communicative behavior*. New York: Human Sciences Press.

Beecher, H. K. (1959). *Measurement of subjective responses: Quantitative effects of drugs*. New York: Oxford University Press.

Beidler, L. M. (1963). Dynamics of taste cells, In Y. Zotterman (Ed.), *Olfaction and taste, Vol. 1*. New York: Macmillan.

Bekesy, G. von. (1957a). The ear. *Scientific American*, 197, 66–78.

Beljan, J. R., Rosenblatt, L. S., Hetherington, N. W., Layman, J., Flaim, S. E. T., Dale, G. T., & Holley, D. C. (1972). *Human performance in the aviation environment* (Contract No. 2–6657, Pt. Ia, pp. 253–259). Washington, DC: National Aeronautics and Space Administration.

Bell, A. P., Weinberg, M. S., & Hammersmith, S. K. (1981). *Sexual preference*. Indiana University Press.

Belsky, J., Gilstrap, B., & Rovine, M. (1984). The Pennsylvania infant and family development project, I: Stability and change in mother-infant and father-infant interaction in a family setting at one, three, and nine months. *Child Development*, 55, 692–705.

Belsky, J., Rovine, M., & Taylor, D. G. (1984). The Pennsylvania infant and family development project, III: The origins of individual differences in infant-mother attachment: Maternal and infant contributions. *Child Development*, 55, 718–728.

Bem, S. L. (1974). The measurement of psychological androgyny. *Journal of Consulting and Clinical Psychology*, 42, 155–162.

Bem, S. L. (1975a). Sex-role adaptability: One consequence of psychological androgyny. *Journal of Personality and Social Psychology*, 31, 634–643.

Bem, S. L. (1977). Psychological androgyny. In A. G. Sargent (Ed.), *Beyond Sex Roles*. St. Paul, MN: West.

Bem, S. L. (1981). Gender schema theory. A cognitive account of sex typing. *Psychological Review*, 88, 354–364.

Bem, S. L. (1975b, September). Androgyny vs. the tight little lives of fluffy women and chesty men. *Psychology Today*, 58–62.

Beneke, W. M., & Harris, M. B. (1972). Teaching self-control of study behavior. *Behavior Research and Therapy*, 10, 35–41.

Bengelsdorf, I. S. (1970, March 5). Alcohol, morphine addictions believed chemically similar. *Los Angeles Times*, Part II, p. 7.

Bennett, W., & Gurin, J. (1982). *The dieter's dilemma*. New York: Basic Books.

Benson, H. (1975). *The relaxation response*. New York: William Morrow.

Benson, H. (1977). Systematic hypertension and the relaxation response. *The New England Journal of Medicine*, 296, 1152–1156.

Benton, A. L. (1980, February). The neuropsychology of facial recognition. *American Psychologist*, 35, 176–186.

Bergin, A., & Suinn, R. M. (1975). Individual psychotherapy and behavior therapy. *Annual Review of Psychology*, 26, 509–556.

Berkowitz, L. (1982). Aversive conditions as stimuli to aggression. In L. Berkowitz (Ed.), *Advances in experimental social psychology*, Vol 15. New York: Academic Press.

Berkowitz, L. (1968). The frustration-aggression hypothesis revisited. In L. Berkowitz (Ed.), *Roots of aggression: A re-examination of the frustration-aggression hypothesis*. New York: Atherton Press.

Berkowitz, L. (1984). Some effects of thoughts on anti- and prosocial influences of media events: A cognitive-neoassociation analysis. *Psychological Bulletin*, 95, 410–427.

Berlyne, D. (1966). Curiosity and exploration. *Science*, 153, 25–33.

Berman, L. H. (1982). Family therapy. In L. E. Abt & I. R. Stuart (Eds.), *The newer therapies: A sourcebook*. New York: Van Nostrand Reinhold.

Berne, E. (1964). *Games people play*. New York: Grove Press.

Berne, E. (1961). *Transactional analysis in psychotherapy*. New York: Grove Press.

Bernstein, I. L. (1978). Learned taste aversions in children receiving chemotherapy. *Science*, 200, 1302–1303.

Berry, P., Groeneweg, G., Gibson, D., & Brown, R. I. (1984). Mental development of adults with Down syndrome. *American Journal of Mental Deficiency*, 89, 252–256.

Bersheid, E., & Walster, E. (1974b). A little bit about love. In T. L. Huston (Ed.), *Foundations of interpersonal attraction.* New York: Academic Press.

Bersheid, E., & Walster, E. (1974a). Physical attractiveness. In L. Berkowitz (Ed.), *Advances in experimental social psychology, Vol. 7.* New York: Academic Press.

Bertsch, G. J. (1976). Punishment of consummatory and instrumental behavior: A review. *Psychological Record, 26* 13–31.

Bettelheim, B. (1960). *The informed heart.* New York: Free Press.

Biblow, E. (1973). Imaginative play and the control of aggressive behavior. In J. L. Singer (Ed.), *The child's world of make-believe: Experimental studies of imaginative play.* New York: Academic Press.

Bickman, L. (1974, April). Clothes make the person. *Psychology Today.*

Biller, H. B. (1982). Fatherhood: Implications for child and adult development. In B. B. Wolman (Ed.), *Handbook of developmental psychology.* Englewood Cliffs, NJ: Prentice-Hall.

Binder, V. (1976). Behavior modification: Operant approaches to therapy. In V. Binder, A. Binder, & B. Rimland (Eds.), *Modern therapies* (pp. 150–165). Englewood Cliffs, NJ: Prentice-Hall.

Bird, D. (1975). *The case against college.* New York: David McKay.

Birnbaum, I. M., Parker, E. S., Hartley J. T., & Nobel, E. P. (1978). Alcohol and memory: Retrieval processes. *Journal of Verbal Learning and Verbal Behavior, 17,* 325–335.

Blanchard, E. B., & Epstein, L. H. (1978). *A biofeedback primer.* Reading, MA: Addison-Wesley.

Blaske, D. M. (1984). Occupational sex-typing by kindergarten and fourth-grade children. *Psychological Reports, 54,* 795–801.

Blaustein, A. R. (1983). The situation of sociobiology. *Science, 220,* 188–189.

Block, J. (1979, September). *Socialization influence of personality development in males and females.* American Psychological Association Master Lecture, Convention of the American Psychological Association, New York City.

Bloom, B. (1985). *Developing talent in young people.* New York: Ballantine.

Bloom, B. L., & Parad, H. J. (1977). Professional activity patterns in community mental health centers. In I. Iscoe, B. L. Bloom, & C. D. Spielberger (Eds.), *Community psychology in transition.* Washington, DC: Hemisphere.

Bloom, L., & Lahey, M. (1978). *Language development and language disorders.* New York: Wiley.

Blumenthal, A. L. (1979). The founding father we never knew. *Contemporary Psychology, 24,* 547–550.

Blumenthal, A. L. (1977). *The process of cognition.* Englewood Cliffs, NJ: Prentice-Hall.

Bock, F. G. (1980). Cocarcinogenic properties of nicotine. In G. B. Gori & F. G. Bock (Eds.), *Banbury report.* Cold Spring Harbor Laboratory.

Boker, J. R. (1974). Immediate and delayed retention effects of interspersing questions in written instructional passages. *Journal of Educational Psychology, 66,* 96–98.

Bolles, R. C. (1979). *Learning theory* (2nd ed.). New York: Holt, Rinehart and Winston.

Bolton, R. (1976). Hostility in fantasy: A further test of the hypoglycemia-aggression hypothesis. *Aggressive Behavior, 2,* 257–274.

Boneau, C. A., & Cuea, J. M. (1974). An overview of psychology's human resources. *American Psychologist, 29,* 821–840.

Bonnet, M. H., & Moore, S. E. (1982). The threshold of sleep: Perception of sleep as a function of time asleep and auditory threshold. *Sleep, 5*(3), 267–276.

Bootzin, R. (1973, August). *Stimulus control of insomnia.* Paper presented at the meeting of the American Psychological Association, Montreal.

Borkovec, T. D. (1982). Insomnia. *Journal of Consulting and Clinical Psychology, 50,* 880–895.

Borman, W. C., Eaton, N. K., Bryan, J. D., & Rosse, R. S. (1983). Validity of army recruiter behavioral assessment. Does the assessor make a difference? *Journal of Applied Psychology, 68,* 415–419.

Bornstein, M. H. (1975). Qualities of color vision in infancy. *Journal of Experimental Child Psychology, 19,* 401–419.

Borrie, R. A., & Suedfeld, P. (1980). Restricted environmental stimulation therapy in a weight reduction program. *Journal of Behavioral Medicine, 3,* 147–161.

Botwinick, J. (1984). *Aging and behavior.* New York: Springer.

Bouchard, T. J., Jr. (1983). Twins—Nature's twice-told tale. *Yearbook of science and the future* (pp. 66–81). Chicago: Encyclopedia Britannica.

Bouchard, T. J., Jr., Heston, L., Eckert, E., Keyes, M., & Resnick, S. (1981). The Minnesota study of twins reared apart: Project description and sample results in the developmental domain. In L. Gedda, P. Parisi, & W. E. Nance (Eds.), *Twin research 3: Part B. Intelligence, personality, and development* (pp. 227–233). New York: Liss.

Bower, B. (1984, October 6). Not popular by reason of insanity. *Science News, 126*(14), 218–219.

Bower, G. H. (1973, October). How to . . . uh . . . remember. *Psychology Today,* 63–70.

Bower, G. H. (1981). Mood and memory. *American Psychologist, 36,* 129–148.

Bower, G. H., & Clark, M. C. (1969). Narrative stories as mediators for serial learning. *Psychonomic Science, 14,* 181–182.

Bower, G. H., & Springston, F. (1970). Pauses as recoding points in letter series. *Journal of Experimental Psychology, 83,* 421–430.

Bowerman, M. (1977). The acquisition of word meaning: An investigation of some current concepts. *Thinking.*

Bowker, L. H. (1976, October–December). The incidence of drug use and associated factors in two small towns: A community survey. *Bulletin on Narcotics. 28*(4), 17–25.

Bowlby, J. (1969). *Attachment and loss, Volume I: Attachment.* New York: Basic Books.

Bowlby, J. (1973). *Attachment and loss, Volume II: Separation and anxiety.* New York: Basic Books.

Brackbill, Y. (1979). Obstetrical medication and infant behavior. In J. D. Osofsky (Ed.), *Handbook of infant development.* New York: Wiley.

Braginsky, B. M., & Braginsky, D. D. (1967). Schizophrenic patients in the psychiatric interview: An experimental study of their effectiveness at manipulation. *Journal of Consulting Psychology, 31,* 543–547.

Bransford, J. D., & McCarrell, N. S. (1977). A sketch of cognitive approach to comprehension: Some thoughts about understanding what it means to comprehend. In P. N. Johnson-Laird & P. C. Wason (Eds.), *Thinking: Readings in cognitive science.* Cambridge: Cambridge University Press.

Bray, D. W., Campbell, R. J., & Grant, D. (1974). *Formative years in business: A long-term study of managerial lives.* New York: Wiley.

Brazelton, T. B., Koslowski, B., & Main, M. (1974). The origins of reciprocity: The early mother-infant interaction. In M. Lewis & L. A. Rosenblum (Eds.), *The effect of the infant on its caregiver.* New York: Wiley-Interscience.

Brecher, E. M. (1975a, March). Marijuana: The health questions. *Consumer Reports, 40,* 143–149.

Brecher, E. M. & the Editors of *Consumer Reports.* (1972). *Licit and illicit drugs.* Boston: Little, Brown.

Breier, A., & Strauss, J. S. (1983, October). Self control in psychotic disorders. *Archives of General Psychiatry, 40,* 1141.

Breland, K., & Breland, M. (1961). The misbehavior of organisms. *American Psychologist, 16,* 681–684.

Bresler, D. E., & Trubo, R. (1979). *Free yourself from pain.* New York: Simon & Schuster.

Brewer, J. S. (1981). Duration of intromission and female orgasm rates. *Medical Aspects of Human Sexuality, 15*(4), 70–71.

Bridges, K. M. B. (1932). Emotional development in early infancy. *Child Development, 3,* 324–334.

Brown, A. S. (1974). Satisfying relationships for the elderly and their patterns of disengagement. *Gerontologist, 14,* 258–262.

Brown, B. (1980). Perspectives on social stress. In H. Selye (Ed.), *Selye's guide to stress research, Vol. 1.* New York: Van Nostrand Reinhold.

Brown, R., & Kulik, J. (1977). Flashbulb memories. *Cognition, 5,* 73–99.

Brown, R., & McNeill, D. (1966). The "tip of the tongue" phenomenon. *Journal of Verbal Learning and Verbal Behavior, 5,* 325–337.

Browne, M. A., & Mahoney, M. J. (1984). Sport psychology. *Annual Review of Psychology, 35,* 605–625.

Brownell, K. D. (1982). Obesity: Understanding and treating a serious, prevalent, and refractory disorder. *Journal of Consulting and Clinical Psychology, 50,* 820–840.

Bruch, H. (1973). *Eating disorders.* New York: Basic Books.

Bruner, J. (1983). *Child's Talk.* New York: Norton.

Bruner, J. S. (1968). *Toward a theory of instruction.* New York: Norton.

Bruner, J. S., et al. (1966). *Studies in cognitive growth.* New York: Wiley.

Bruner, J. S., & Postman, L. (1949). On the perception of incongruity: A paradigm. *Journal of Personality, 18,* 206–223.

Bryan, J. H., & Test, M. A. (1967). Models and helping. Naturalistic studies in aiding behavior. *Journal of Personality and Social Psychology, 6,* 400–407.

Bryan, J. H., & Walbek, N. H. (1970). Preaching and practicing generosity: Children's actions and reactions. *Child Development, 41,* 329–353.

Buchsbaum, M. S., & Haier, R. J. (1983). Psychopathology: Biological approaches. *Annual Review of Psychology, 34,* 401–430.

Buchwald, A. (1965, June 20). Psyching out. *The Washington Post.*

Buckalew, L. W., & Buckalew, P. B. (1983). Behavioral management of exceptional children using video games as reward. *Perceptual Motor Skills, 56,* 580.

Buckhout, R. (1974, December). Eyewitness testimony. *Scientific American, 231,* 23–31.

Budzynski, T. H. (1977). Biofeedback strategies in headache treatment. In J. V. Basmajian (Ed.), *Biofeedback: A handbook for clinicians.* Baltimore. Williams and Wilkins.

Burka, J. B., & Yuen, L. M. (1983). *Procrastination.* Menlo Park, CA: Addison-Wesley.

Burns, D. D., & Persons, J. (1982). Hope and hopelessness: A cognitive approach. In L. E. Abt & I. R. Stuart (Eds.), *The newer therapies: A sourcebook* (pp. 33–57). New York: Van Nostrand Reinhold.

Bursten, B. (1973). *The manipulator.* New Haven, CT: Yale University Press.

Burt, M. R. (1980). Cultural myths and supports for rape. *Journal of Personality and Social Psychology, 38,* 217–230.

Burtt, H. E. (1941). An experimental study of early childhood memory: Final report. *Journal of General Psychology, 58,* 435–439.

Buss, A. H. (1980). *Self-consciousness and social anxiety.* San Francisco: Freeman.

Buss, D. M. (1985). Human mate selection. *American Scientist, 73,* 47–51.

Butler, R. (1954). Curiosity in monkeys. *Scientific American, 190*(18), 70–75.

Butler, R., & Harlow, H. F. (1954). Persistence of visual exploration in monkeys. *Journal of Comparative Physiological Psychology, 47,* 258–263.

Butler, R. N., & Lewis, M. I. (1977). *Aging and mental health.* St. Louis: Mosby.

Byrne, D. (1971). *The attraction paradigm.* New York: Academic Press.

Cabanac, M., & Duclaux, P. (1970). Obesity: Absence of satiety aversion to sucrose. *Science, 168,* 496–497.

Calhoun, J. B. (1962). A "behavioral sink." In E. L. Bliss (Ed.), *Roots of behavior.* New York: Harper & Row.

Campbell, A., Gurin, G., & Miller, W. E. (1954). *The voter decides.* New York: Harper & Row.

Campbell, J. B., & Hawley, C. W. (1982). Study habits and Eysenck's theory of extraversion-introversion. *Journal of Research in Personality, 16,* 139–146.

Campos, J. J., Hiatt, S., Ramsay, D., Henderson, C., & Svejda, M. (1978). The emergence of fear on the visual cliff. In M. Lewis & L. A. Rosenblum (Eds.), *The development of affect* (pp. 149–182). New York: Plenum Press.

Canadian Government's Commission of Inquiry. (1971). *The non-medical use of drugs.* Baltimore: Penguin.

Cannon, J. T., Liebeskind, J. C., & Frenk, H. (1978). Neural and neurochemical mechanisms of pain inhibition. In R. A. Sternbach (Ed.), *The psychology of pain.* New York: Raven Press.

Cannon, W. B. (1934). Hunger and thirst. In C. Murchinson (Ed.), *Handbook of general experimental psychology,* Worcester, MA: Clark University Press.

Cannon, W. B. (1942). "Voodoo" death. *American Anthropologist, 44,* 169–181.

Cannon, W. B. (1932). *The wisdom of the body.* New York: Norton.

Cannon, W. B., & Washburn, A. L. (1912). An exploration of hunger. *American Journal of Physiology, 29,* 441–454.

Carelli, R. (1982, May 31). Insanity: A legal lever that tips justice scales. *Santa Barbara News Press* (Associated Press).

Carew, J. V., Chan, I., & Halfor, C. (1976). *Observing intelligence in young children: Eight case studies.* Englewood Cliffs, NJ: Prentice-Hall.

Carlson, N. R. (1981). *Physiology of behavior* (2nd ed.). Boston: Allyn and Bacon.

Carmen, R., & Adams, W. R. (1985). *Study skills: A student's guide for survival.* New York: Wiley.

Carr, R. R., & Meyers, E. J. (1980). Marijuana and cocaine: The process of change in drug policy. In The Drug Abuse Council, *The facts about "drug abuse".* New York: The Free Press.

Carter, W. E. (Ed.). (1980). *Cannabis in Costa Rica: A study of chronic marijuana use.* Philadelphia: Institute for the Study of Human Issues.

Cartwright, R. (1969). In M. Kramer (Ed.), *Dream psychology and the new biology of dreaming.* Springfield, IL: Charles C Thomas.

Cartwright, R. D. (1978, December). Happy endings for our dreams. *Psychology Today,* 66–77.

Cartwright, R. D. (1978). Sleep and dreams, Part II. *Annual Review of Psychology, 29,* 223–252.

Case, R. B., Heller, S. S., Case, N. B., Moss, A. J., & The Multicenter Post-Infarction Research Group. (1985). Type A behavior and survival after acute myocardial infarction. *New England Journal of Medicine, 312*(12).

Casler, L. (1965). The effects of extra tactile stimulation on a group of institutionalized infants. *Genetic Psychology Monographs 71,* 137–175.

Cattell, R. B. (1973, July). Personality pinned down. *Psychology Today,* 40–46.

Cattell, R. B. (1965). *The scientific analysis of personality.* Baltimore: Penguin.

Cautela, J. (1973). Covert processes and behavior modification. *The Journal of Nervous and Mental Disease, 157,* 27–36.

Cautela, J. R., & Bennett, A. K. (1981). Covert conditioning. In R. J. Corsini (Ed.), *Handbook of innovative psychotherapies* (pp. 189–204). New York: Wiley.

Chafetz, M. E. (1979, May-June). Alcohol and alcoholism. *American Scientist, 67,* 293–299.

Chaikin, A. (1985, February). The loneliness of the long-distance astronaut. *Discover,* 20–31.

Chaikin, A. L., & Derlega, V. J. (1974). *Self-disclosure.* Morristown, NJ: General Learning Press.

Challinor, M. E. (1980, December). *Science 80, 27.*

Chance, P. (1982, January). Your child's self-esteem. *Parents.*

Chapanis, A., & Lindenbaum, L. E. (1959). A reaction time study of four control-display linkages. *Human Factors, 1,* 1–7.

Check, J. V. P., & Malamuth, N. M. (1983). Sex role stereotyping and reactions to depictions of stranger versus acquaintance rape. *Journal of Personality and Social Psychology, 45,* 344–356.

Cheek, J., & Buss, A. H. (1979). Scales of shyness, sociability, and self-esteem and correlations among them. Unpublished research, University of Texas. (Cited by Buss, 1980).

Cherry, L. J. (1979). A sociocognitive approach to language development and its implications for education. In O. K. Garnica & M. L. King (Eds.), *Language, children and society.* New York, Pergamon Press.

Chess, S., Thomas, A., & Birch, H. G. (1965). *Your child is a person: A psychological approach to parenthood without guilt.* New York: Viking.

Chomsky, N. (1968). *Language and mind.* New York: Harcourt Brace Jovanovich.

Chomsky, N. (1975). *Reflections on language.* New York: Pantheon Books.

Cialdini, R. B., Petty, R. E., & Cacippo, T. J. (1981). Attitude and attitude change. *Annual Review of Psychology, 32,* 357–404.

Cialdini, R. B., Vincent, J. E., Lewis, S. K., Catalan, J., Wheeler, D., & Darby, B. L. (1975). A reciprocal concessions procedure for inducing compliance. The door-in-the-face technique. *Journal of Personality and Social Psychology, 21,* 206–215.

Cimbalo, R. S., Faling, V., & Mousaw, P. (1976). The course of love: A cross-sectional design. *Psychological Reports, 38,* 1292–1294.

Clark, K. B. (1965). *Dark ghetto.* New York: Harper & Row.

Clarke-Steward, A., & Koch, J. B. (1983). *Children, development through adolescence.* New York: Wiley.

Clearwater, Y. (1985, July). A human place in outer space. *Psychology Today,* 34–43.

Cleckley, H. (1964). *The mask of sanity* (4th ed.). St. Louis: Mosby.

Cline, V. B., Croft, R. G., & Courrier, S. (1972). Desensitization of children to television violence. *Journal of Personality and Social Psychology, 27,* 360–365.

Clore, G. L. (1976). Interpersonal attraction: An overview. In *Contemporary topics in social psychology.* Morristown, NJ: General Learning Press.

Coates, D. L., & Lewis, M. (1984). Early mother-infant interaction and infant cognitive status as predictors of school performance and cognitive behavior in six-year-olds. *Child Development, 55,* 1219–1230.

Cobb, S. (1976). Social support as a moderator of life stresses. *Psychosomatic Medicine, 38,* 300–314.

Cofer, C. N. (Ed.). (1975). *The structure of human memory.* San Francisco: Freeman.

Cohen, D. (1974). *Intelligence.* New York: Evans.

Cohen, J. (1970). *Secondary motivation.* Chicago: Rand McNally.

Cohen, S. (1977, September). Internal opioid-like compounds. *Drug Abuse and Alcoholism Newsletter, 6*(7).

Cohen, S., Evans, G. W., Krantz, D. S., & Stokols, D. (1981). Cardiovascular and behavioral effects of community noise. *American Scientist, 69*, 528–535.

Coleman, J., Butcher, J. N., & Carson, R. C. (1984). *Abnormal psychology and modern life* (7th ed.). Glenview, IL: Scott Foresman.

Coleman, J. S., Hersberg, J., & Morris, M. (1977). Identity in adolescence: Present and future self-concepts. *Journal of Youth and Adolescence, 6*(1), 63–75.

Collins, A. M., & Quillian, M. R. (1969). Retrieval time from semantic memory. *Journal of Verbal Learning and Verbal Behavior, 8*, 240–247.

Collins, J. J. (1981). Alcohol use and criminal behavior: An empirical, theoretical, and methodological overview. In J. J. Collins (Ed.), *Drinking and crime: Perspectives on the relationship between alcohol consumption and criminal behavior.* New York: Guilford.

Comfort, A. (1976). *A good age.* New York: Crown.

Comstock, G., Chaffee, S., Katzman, N., McCombs, M., & Roberts, D. (1978). *Television and human behavior.* New York: Columbia University Press.

Condon, W. S., & Sander, L. W. (1974). Neonate movement is synchronized with adult speech: Interactional participation and language acquisition. *Science, 183*, 99–101.

Cone, J. D., & Hayes, S. C. (1980). *Environmental problems/behavioral solutions.* Monterey, CA: Brooks/Cole.

Coni, N., Davison, W., & Webster, S. (1984). *Aging.* Oxford: Oxford University Press.

Conley, J. J. (1984). Longitudinal consistency of adult personality: Self-reported psychological characteristics across 45 years. *Journal of Personality and Social Psychology, 47*, 1325–1333.

Connors, M. M., Harrison, A. A., & Akins, F. R. (1985). *Living Aloft.* Washington, DC: National Aeronautics and Space Administration.

Conte, H. R., Weiner, M. B., & Plutchik, R. (1982). Measuring death anxiety: Conceptual, psychometric, and factor-analytic aspects. *Journal of Personality and Social Psychology, 43*, 775–785.

Conyne, R. K., & Clack, R. J. (1981). *Environmental assessment and design.* New York: Praeger.

Cook, S. W. (1985). Experimenting on social issues. *American Psychologist, 40*, 452–460.

Cooper, J., & Fazio, R. H. (1984). A new look at dissonance theory. *Advances in Experimental Social Psychology, 17*, 229–266.

Coopersmith, S. (1968). Studies in self-esteem. *Scientific American, 218*, 96–106.

Corballis, M. C. (1980, March). Laterality and myth. *American Psychologist, 35*, 284–295.

Coren, S., & Porac, C. (1977, November). Fifty centuries of right-handedness: The historical record. *Science, 198*, 631–632.

Cornsweet, T. N. (1970). *Visual perception.* New York: Academic Press.

Cortes, J. B., & Gatti, F. M. (1972). *Delinquency and crime: A biopsychological approach.* New York: Seminar Press.

Costell, C. G. (1976, March). Electroconvulsive therapy: Is further investigation necessary?" *Canadian Psychiatric Association Journal, 21*(2), 61–67.

Cowles, J. T. (1937). Food tokens as incentives for learning by chimpanzees. *Comparative Psychology,* Monograph, *14*(5, Whole No. 71).

Cox, F. D. (1984). *Human intimacy.* St. Paul, MN: West Publishing.

Cox, T. (1978). *Stress.* Baltimore: University Park Press.

Coyle, J. T., Price, D. L., & DeLong, M. R. (1983). Alzheimer's disease: A disorder of cortical cholinergic innervation. *Science, 219*, 1184–1190.

Craig, K. (1978). Social modeling influences on pain. In R. A. Sternbach (Ed.), *The psychology of pain.* New York: Raven Press.

Craik, F. I. M. (1970). The fate of primary items in free recall. *Journal of Verbal Learning and Verbal Behavior, 9*, 143–148.

Crawley, S. B., & Sherrod, K. B. (1984). Parent-infant play during the first year of life. *Infant Behavior & Development, 7*, 65–75.

Crits-Christoph, P., & Singer, J. L. (1984). An experimental investigation of the use of positive imagery in the treatment of phobias. *Imagination, Cognition and Personality, 3*, 305.

Cronbach, L. (1970). *Essentials of psychological testing* (3rd ed.). New York: Harper & Row.

Cross, J. G., & Guyer, M. J. (1980). *Social traps.* Ann Arbor: The University of Michigan Press.

Culver, B., & Ianna, P. (1979). *The gemini syndrome.* Tucson, AZ: Pachart Publishing.

Cumming, E., & Henry, W. E. (1961). *Growing old: The process of disengagement.* New York: Basic Books.

Czeisler, C. A., Richardson, G. S., Zimmerman, J. C., Moore-Ede, M. C., & Weitzman, E. D. (1981). Entrainment of human circadian rhythms by light-dark cycles: A reassessment. *Photochemistry, Photobiology, 34*, 239–247.

Daniel, T. C., & Boster, R. S. (1978). Measuring landscape esthetics: The scenic beauty estimation method. *USDA Forestry Service Research Paper, RM-167* (66). Rocky Mt. Forest Range Station, Ft. Collins, CO.

Daniel, T. L., & Esser, J. K. (1980). Intrinsic motivation as influenced by rewards, task interest, and task structure. *Journal of Applied Psychology, 65*, 566–573.

Darley, J. M., & Latane, B. (1968). Bystander intervention in emergencies: Diffusion of responsibility. *Journal of Personality and Social Psychology, 8*, 377–383.

Darwin, C. (1872). *The expression of emotion in man and animals.* Chicago: The University of Chicago Press.

Davis, D. M. (1928). Self-selection of diet by newly weaned infants. *American Journal of Diseases of Children, 36*, 651–679.

Davis, J. M. (1978). Dopamine theory of schizophrenia: A two-factor theory. In L. C. Wynne, R. L. Cromwell, & S. Matthysse (Eds.), *The nature of schizophrenia: New approaches to research and treatment.*

Davis, M., McKay, M., & Eshelman, E. R. (1980). *The relaxation and stress reduction workbook.* Richmond, CA: New Harbinger.

Davis, R. E. (1975). Changing examination answers: An educational myth? *Journal of Medical Education, 50*, 685–687.

Deaux, K. (1985). Sex and gender. *Annual Review of Psychology, 36*, 49–81.

Deaux, K., & Emswiller, T. (1974). Explanation of successful performance on sex-linked tasks: What is skill for the male is luck for the female. *Journal of Personality and Social Psychology, 29*, 80–85.

de Bono, E. (1970). *Lateral thinking: Creativity step by step.* New York: Harper & Row.

DeCharms, R., & Muir, M. S. (1978). Motivation: Social Approaches. *Annual Review of Psychology, 29*, 91–113.

Deese, J., & Hulse, S. J. (1967). *The psychology of learning* (3rd ed.). New York: McGraw-Hill.

DeGood, D. E. (1975). Cognitive factors in vascular stress responses. *Psychophysiology, 12*, 399–401.

De Koninck, J., Gagnon, P., & Lallier, S. (1983). Sleep positions in the young adult and their relationship with the subjective quality of sleep. *Sleep, 6*(1), 52–59.

de la Cruz, F. F., & Muller, J. Z. (1983, November-December). Facts about Down syndrome. *Children Today, 12*(6), 2–7.

DeLamater, J., & MacCorquodale, P. (1979). *Premarital sexuality: Attitudes, relationships, behavior.* Madison: University of Wisconsin Press.

Delgado, J. (1970, May). ESB. *Psychology Today.*

Delgado, J. (1969). *Physical control of the mind.* New York: Harper & Row.

Dember, W. N., & Warm, J. S. (1979). *Psychology of perception,* (2nd ed.). New York: Holt.

Dement, W. (1960). The effect of dream deprivation. *Science, 131*, 1705–1707.

Dement, W. (1972). *Some must watch while some must sleep.* Stanford, CA: Stanford Alumni Association.

Dement, W., & Kleitman, N. (1957). The relation of eye movements during sleep to dream activity: An objective method for the study of dreaming. *The Journal of Experimental Psychology, 53*(5).

Dement, W., & Wolpert, E. (1958). The relation of eye movements, body mobility and external stimuli to dream content. *Journal of Experimental Psychology, 55*, 543–553.

Depue, R. A., & Monroe, S. M. (1978). The unipolar-bipolar distinction in the depressive disorders. *Psychological Bulletin, 85*, 1001–1029.

Deregowski, J. B. (1972, November). Pictorial perception and culture. *Scientific American,* 82–88.

Desharnais, R. (1975). Sport psychology in athletic training: Programs for maximum performance. In B. S. Rushall (Ed.), *The status of psychomotor learning and sport psychology research*. Dartmouth, Nova Scotia: Sport Science Associates.

Deutsch, D. (1978). Pitch memory: An advantage for the left-handed. *Science, 199*, 559–560.

Deutsch, M., & Collins, M. E. (1951). *Interracial housing*. Minneapolis: University of Minnesota Press.

Diamond, M. (1977). Human sexual development: Biological foundations for social development. In F. A. Beach (Ed.), *Human sexuality in four perspectives* (pp. 22–61). Baltimore: Johns Hopkins University Press.

Dixon, J. (1975, September 30). Jeanne Dixon strikes back at scientists who knock astrology. *National Star*, p. 5.

Dobelle, W. H., Mladejovsky, M. G., & Girvin, J. P. (1974). Artificial vision for the blind: Electrical stimulation of the visual cortex offers a hope for a functional prosthesis. *Science, 183*, 440–444.

Dollard, J., et al. (1939). *Frustration and aggression*. New Haven: Yale University Press.

Dollard, J., & Miller, N. E. (1950). *Personality and psychotherapy: An analysis in terms of learning, thinking and culture*. New York: McGraw-Hill.

Donohue, H. E. F. (1968). *Where should you touch?* New York: The Hearst Corporation.

Dooling, D. J., & Lachman, R. (1971). Effects of comprehension on retention of prose. *Journal of Experimental Psychology, 88*, 216–222.

Dossett, D. L., & Hulvershorn, P. (1983). Increasing technical training efficiency: Peer training via computer-assisted instruction. *Journal of Applied Psychology, 68*, 552–558.

Dovidio, J. F. (1984). Helping behavior and altruism: An empirical and conceptual overview. In L. Berkowitz (Ed.), *Advances in experimental social psychology, Vol. 17*. New York: Academic Press.

Dreyfuss, J. (1985, January 29). Implant liberates the deaf from silence. *Los Angeles Times*, Part V, page 1.

Driskell, J. L., & Kelly, E. L. A. (1980). A guided notetaking and study skills system for use with university freshmen predicted to fail. *Journal of Reading, 1*, 4–5.

Drowatzky, J. N. (1975). *Motor learning: Principles and practices*. Minneapolis, MN: Burgess.

Drug Abuse Council. (1980). *The facts about "drug abuse"*. New York: The Free Press.

Duncker, K. (1945). On problem solving. *Psychological Monographs, 58*(270).

Dunkle, T. (1982). The sound of silence. *Science 82*, 30–33.

Durden-Smith, J., & DeSimone, D. (1984, January). Hidden threads of illness. *Science Digest*, 51–53.

Dutton, D. G., & Aron, A. P. (1974). Some evidence for heightened sexual attraction under conditions of high anxiety. *Journal of Personality and Social Psychology, 30*, 510–517.

Dywan, J., & Bowers, K. S. (1983). The use of hypnosis to enhance recall. *Science, 222*, 184–185.

Ebbinghaus, H. (1885). *Memory: A contribution to experimental psychology*. Translated by H. A. Ruger & C. E. Bussenius, 1913. New York: New York Teacher's College, Columbia University.

Eberhardt, B. J., & Muchinsky, P. M. (1982). An empirical investigation of the factor stability of Owen's biographical questionnaire. *Journal of Applied Psychology, 67*, 138–145.

Edelson, S. M. (1984). Implications of sensory stimulation in self-destructive behavior. *American Journal of Mental Deficiency, 89*, 140–145.

Edwards, K. A., & Marshall, C. (1977). First impressions on tests: Some new findings. *Teaching of Psychology, 4*, 193–195.

Ehara, T. H. (1980, December). On the electronic chess circuit. *Science 80*, 78–79.

Eibl-Eibesfeldt, I. (1970). *Ethology: The biology of behavior*. New York: Holt, Rinehart and Winston.

Eichorn, D. H., Hunt, J. V., & Honzik, M. P. (1981). Experience, personality, and IQ: Adolescence to middle age. In D. H. Eichorn, J. A. Calusen, N.

Haan, M. P. Honzik, & P. H. Mussen (Eds.), *Present and past in middle life* (pp. 89–116). New York: Academic Press.

Einstein, D. (1981, February 26). Results of sanity trials show weakness in system. *Santa Barbara News Press* (Associated Press).

Ekman, P. (1980). *The face of man: Expressions of universal emotions in a New Guinea village*. New York: Garland STPM Press.

Ekman, P., & Friesen, W. V. (1975). *Unmasking the face*. Englewood Cliffs, NJ: Prentice-Hall.

Ekman, P., Levenson, R. W., & Friesen, W. V. (1983). Autonomic nervous system activity distinguishes among emotions. *Science, 221*, 1208–1210.

Elkind, D. (1984). *All grown up & no place to go*. Reading, MA: Addison-Wesley.

Elkind, D. (1968, May 26). Giant in the nursery—Jean Piaget. *The New York Times Magazine*.

Elkind, D. (1981). *The hurried child*. Reading, MA: Addison-Wesley.

Ellis, A. (1973, February). The no cop-out therapy. *Psychology Today, 7*, 56–60, 62.

Ellis, A. (1979). The practice of rational-emotive therapy. In A. Ellis & J. Whiteley (Eds.), *Theoretical and empirical foundations of rational-emotive therapy*. Monterey, CA: Brooks/Cole.

Ellis, A. (1976). Rational-emotive therapy. In V. Binder, A. Binder, & B. Rimland (Eds.), *Modern Therapies* (pp. 21–34). Englewood Cliffs, NJ: Prentice-Hall.

Ellis, A. (1962). *Reason and emotion in psychotherapy*. New York: Lyle Stuart.

Engel, G. (1977, November). Emotional stress and sudden death. *Psychology Today*, 144.

Engle, E., & Lott, A. S. (1980). *Man in flight*. Annapolis, MD: Leeward Publications.

Epstein, R., Langa, R. P., & Skinner, B. F. (1981). "Self-awareness" in the pigeon. *Science, 212*, 695–696.

Erdelyi, M. H. (1974). A new look at the new look: Perceptual defense and vigilance. *Psychological Review, 81*, 1–25.

Erdelyi, M. H., & Appelbaum, A. G. (1973). Cognitive masking: The disruptive effect of an emotional stimulus upon the perception of contiguous neutral items. *Bulletin of the Psychonomic Society, 1*, 59–61.

Ericsson, K. A., & Chase, W. G. (1982). Exceptional memory. *American Scientist, 70*, 607–615.

Erikson, E. H. (1963). *Childhood and society* (2nd ed.). New York: Norton.

Erlichman, H., & Weinberger, A. (1978). Lateral eye movements and hemispheric asymmetry: A critical review. *Psychological Bulletin, 85*, 1080–1101.

Ernst, C., & Angst, J. (1983). *Birth order*. New York: Springer-Verlag.

Etaugh, C. (1980, April). Effects of nonmaternal care on children. *American Psychologist, 35*, 309–319.

Evarts, E. V. (1979). Brain mechanisms of movement. *Scientific American, 241*(3), 164–179.

Eysenck, H. J. (1957, 1958). *Sense and nonsense in psychology*. Harmondsworth, Middlesex, England: Penguin.

Eysenck, H. J. (1967, June). New ways in psychotherapy. *Psychology Today*, 40.

Eysenck, H. J. (1981). *The intelligence controversy*. New York: Wiley.

Eysenck, H. J. (1983). Stress and personality as contributory factors in the causation of cancer. In F. J. McGuigan, W. E. Sime, & J. M. Wallace (Eds.), *Stress and Tension Control, Vol. 2*. (pp. 35–46). New York: Plenum.

Eysenck, M. W. (1984). *Attention and arousal*. New York: Academic Press.

Fairweather, H. (1976). Sex differences in cognition. *Cognition, 4*, 231–280.

Fantz, R. L. (1961, May). The origin of form perception. *Scientific American*, 71.

Fantz, R. L. (1963). Pattern vision in newborn infants. *Science, 140*, 296–297.

Faraday, A. (1972). *Dream power*. New York: Coward.

Farber, B. A. (1983). Introduction: A critical perspective on burnout. In B. A. Farber (Ed.), *Stress and burnout in the human service professions* (pp. 1–22). New York: Pergamon.

Farber, L. H. (1966, December 11). Ours is the addicted society. *The New York Times Magazine*.

Farber, S. L. (1981). *Identical twins reared apart*. New York: Basic Books.

Fast, J. (1970). *Body language*. New York: Evans.

Fate, IRS, link 2 women. (1983, May 2). *Santa Barbara News Press*, p. B-7.

Fehr, L. (1976). J. Piaget and S. Claus: Psychology makes strange bedfellows. *Psychological Reports, 39*, 740–742.

Feinberg, I., & Carlson, V. R. (1967). Sleep variables as a function of normal and pathological aging in man. *Journal of Psychiatric Research, 5,* 107–144.

Feldman, D. H., & Bratton, J. S. (1972). Relativity and giftedness: Implications for equality of educational opportunity. *Exceptional Children, 38,* 491–492.

Feldman, R. D. (1982). *Whatever happened to the quiz kids: Perils and profits of growing up gifted.* Chicago: Chicago Review Press.

Ferster, C. B. (1968, February). The autistic child. *Psychology Today,* 35–37, 61.

Ferster, C. B., Nurnberger, J. I., & Levitt, E. B. (1962). The control of eating. *Journal of Mathematics, 1,* 87–109.

Festinger, L. (1957). *A theory of cognitive dissonance.* Stanford, CA: Stanford University Press.

Festinger, L. (1954). A theory of social comparison processes. *Human Relations, 7,* 117–140.

Festinger, L., & Carlsmith, J. M. (1959). Cognitive consequences of forced compliance. *Journal of Abnormal and Social Psychology, 58,* 203–210.

Festinger, L., Schachter, S., & Back, K. (1950). *Social pressures in informal groups: A study of a housing project.* New York: Harper.

Feuerstein, R., Rand, Y., & Hoffman, M. B. (1980). *Instrumental enrichment: An intervention program for cognitive modifiability.* Baltimore: University Park.

Fink, M. (1977). Myths of shock therapy. *American Journal of Psychiatry, 134,* 991–996.

Finkelstein, P., Wenegrat, B., & Yalom, I. (1982). Large group awareness training. *Annual Review of Psychology, 33,* 515–539.

Fishbein, M., & Ajzen, I. (1975). *Belief, attitude, intention, and behavior: An introduction to theory and research.* Reading, MA: Addison-Wesley.

Fisher, K. (1984, December). Berkeley study finds stress is value-laden. *APA Monitor,* pp. 26, 30.

Fisher, S. (1973). *The female orgasm.* New York: Basic Books.

Fleming, J. (1974, January). Field report: The state of the apes. *Psychology Today,* 46.

Flint, B. M. (1978). *New hope for deprived children.* Toronto: University of Toronto Press.

Foos, P., & Clark, M. C. (1984). *Human Learning,* 2(3).

Foster, G., & Ysseldyke, J. (1976). Expectancy and halo effects as a result of artificially induced teacher bias. *Contemporary Educational Psychology, 1,* 37–45.

Foulkes, D., & Schmidt, M. (1983). Temporal sequence and unit composition in dream reports from different stages of sleep. *Sleep,* 6(3), 265–280.

Fowler, R. L. (1982). Detection of differences in beer composition by brand and level of calorie content. *Perceptual and Motor Skills, 55,* 967–970.

Fox, P., & Oakes, W. (1984). Learned helplessness: Noncontingent reinforcement in video game performance produces a decrement in performance on a lexical decision task. *Bulletin of the Psychonomic Society, 22,* 113–166.

Frank, J. D. (1973). The demoralized mind. *Psychology Today,* 6(11), 22–31, 100–101.

Frankenburg, W. K., & Dodds, J. B. (1967). The Denver Developmental Screening Test. *The Journal of Pediatrics, 1,* 181–191.

Frankl, F. H. (1977). Current perspectives on ECT: A discussion. *American Journal of Psychiatry, 134,* 1014–1019.

Frankl, V. (1955). *The doctor and the soul.* New York: Knopf.

Franklin, D. (1984, October 20). Crafting sound from silence. *Science News, 126,* 252–254.

Franklin, D. (1984). Growing up short. *Science News,* 125(6), 92–94.

Freedman, J. L. (1975). *Crowding and behavior.* San Francisco: Freeman.

Freedman, J. L. (1984). Effect of television violence on aggressiveness. *Psychological Bulletin, 96,* 227–246.

Freedman, J. L., & Fraser, S. C. (1966). Compliance without pressure: The foot-in-the-door technique. *Journal of Personality and Social Psychology, 4,* 195–202.

Freud, S. (1900). *The interpretation of dreams.* London: Hogarth.

Freud, S. (1949). *An outline of psychoanalysis.* New York: Norton.

Friedberg, J. (1977). Shock treatment, brain damage, and memory loss: A neurological perspective. *American Journal of Psychiatry, 134,* 1010–1014.

Friedman, M., & Rosenman, R. (1974). *Type A behavior and your heart.* New York: Knopf.

Friedman, M. I., & Stricker, E. M. (1976). The physiological psychology of hunger: A physiological perspective. *Psychological Review, 83,* 409–431.

Frodi, A. N., Lamb, M. E., Leavitt, L. A., Donovan, W. L., Neff, C., & Sherry, D. (1978). Fathers' and mothers' responses to the faces and cries of normal and premature infants. *Developmental Psychology, 14,* 190–198.

Fuastman, W. O. (1976, November). Aversive control of maladaptive sexual behavior: Past developments and future trends. *Psychology,* 13(4), 53–60.

Fuchs, C., & Rehm, L. (1977). A self-control behavior therapy program for depression. *Journal of Consulting and Clinical Psychology. 45,* 206–215.

Fulgosi, A., & Guilford, J. P. (1968). Short-term incubation in divergent production. *American Journal of Psychology, 7,* 1016–1023.

Fuller, B. (1969). *Utopia or oblivion: The prospects for humanity.* New York: Bantam Matrix.

Fulton, R. (1979, January 21). Death and dying in a changing world. *Santa Barbara News Press.*

Furey, E. M. (1982). The effects of alcohol on the fetus. *Exceptional Children, 49,* 30–34.

Gagne, R. M., & Fleishman, E. A. (1959). *Psychology and human performance.* New York: Holt, Rinehart and Winston.

Gagnon, J. H. (1977). *Human sexualities.* Glenview, IL: Scott, Foresman.

Galanter, E. (1962). Contemporary psychophysics. In *New directions in psychology,* Vol. 1 (pp. 87–156). New York: Holt, Rinehart and Winston.

Galston, A. W., & Slayman, C. L. (1983). Plant sensitivity and sensation. In G. O Abell & B. Singer (Eds.), *Science and the paranormal* (pp. 40–55). New York: Scribner.

Ganster, D. C., Mayes, B. T., Sime, W. E., & Tharp, G. D. (1982). Managing organizational stress: A field experiment. *Journal of Applied Psychology, 67,* 533–542.

Garcia, J. (1977). Intelligence testing: Quotients, quotas and quackery. In J. L. Martinez (Ed.), *Chicano psychology.* New York: Academic Press.

Garcia, J., Hankins, W. G., & Rusiniak, K. W. (1974). Behavioral regulation of the milieu interne in man and rat. *Science, 185,* 824–831.

Gardner, H. (1985). *Frames of mind.* New York: Basic Books.

Gardner, H. (1975). *The shattered mind: The person after brain damage.* New York: Knopf.

Gardner, M. (1966). Dermo-optical perception: A peek down the nose. *Science, 151,* 654–657.

Gardner, M. (1977, November/December). A skeptic's view of parapsychology. *The Humanist.*

Gardner, R. A., & Gardner, B. T. (1969). Teaching sign language to a chimpanzee. *Science, 165,* 664–672.

Gates, A. I. (1958). *Recitation as a factor in memorizing.* In J. Deese (Ed.), *The psychology of learning* (2nd ed.). New York: McGraw-Hill.

Gazzaniga, M. S. (1970). *The bisected brain.* New York: Plenum.

Gazzaniga, M. S., & LeDoux, J. E. (1978). *The integrated mind* New York: Plenum.

Geldard, F. A. (1972). *The human senses* (2nd ed.). New York: Wiley.

Gerbner, G., & Gross, L. (1976). Living with television: The violence profile. *Journal of Communication, 26,* 173–199.

Gersh, R. D. (1982, June 20). Learning when not to shoot. *Santa Barbara News Press.*

Geschwind, N. (1975). The apraxias: Neural mechanisms of disorders of learned movement. *American Scientist, 63,* 188–195.

Geschwind, N. (1979, September). Specializations of the human brain. *Scientific American, 241,* 180–199.

Gesell, A., et al. (1940). *The first five years of life.* New York: Harper Bros.

Gibson, E. J., & Walk, R. D. (1960). The "Visual Cliff." *Scientific American,* 202(4), 67–71.

Gillam, B. (1980). Geometrical illusions. *American Psychologist, 242,* 102–111.

Gilligan, C. (1982). *In a different voice.* Cambridge, MA: Harvard University Press.

Giniger, S., Dispenzieri, A., & Eisenberg, J. (1983). Age, experience, and performance on speed and skill jobs in an applied setting. *Journal of Applied Psychology, 68,* 469–475.

Ginott, H. G. (1965). *Between parent and child: New solutions to old problems.* New York: Macmillan.

Giovannoni, J. M., & Becerra, R. M. (1979). *Defining child abuse.* New York: The Free Press.

Girodo, M. (1978). *Shy? (You don't have to be!).* New York: Pocket Books.

Glaser, R. (1977, September/October). Adapting to individual differences. *Social Policy*, 27–33.

Glass, A. L., Holyoak, K. J., & Santa, J. L. (1979). *Cognition.* Reading, MA: Addison-Wesley.

Glass, D. C. (1977). Stress, behavior patterns, and coronary disease. *American Scientist*, 65, 177–187.

Glass, D. C., & Singer, J. E. (1972). Behavioral aftereffects of unpredictable and uncontrollable aversive events. *American Scientist*, 60, 457–465.

Glick, D., & Hargreaves, W. A., with Drues, J., & Showstack, J. (1979). *Psychiatric hospital treatment for the 1980s: A controlled study of short versus long hospitalization.* Lexington, MA: Lexington Books.

Goering, P., Wasylenki, D., Lancee, W., & Freeman, S. J. (1984). From hospital to community: Six-month and two-year outcomes for 505 patients. *Journal of Nervous & Mental Disease*, 172, 667–673.

Goldenson, R. M. (1970b). *The encyclopedia of human behavior*, Vol. 2. Garden City, NY: Doubleday.

Goldiamond, I. (1965). Fluent and non-fluent speech (stuttering): Analysis and operant techniques for control. In L. Krasner & L. P. Ullman (Eds.), *Research in behavior modification.* New York: Holt, Rinehart and Winston.

Goldiamond, I. (1971). Self-control procedures in personal behavior problems. In M. S. Gazzaniga & E. P. Lovejoy (Eds.), *Good reading in psychology.* Englewood Cliffs, NJ: Prentice-Hall.

Goleman, D. (1982, March). Staying up: The rebellion against sleep's gentle tyranny. *Psychology Today*, 24–35.

Gomes-Schwartz, B., Hadley, S. W., & Strupp, H. H. (1978). Individual psychotherapy and behavior therapy. *Annual Review of Psychology*, 29, 435–471.

Gondola, J. C., & Tuckman, B. W. (1982). Psychological mood state in "average" marathon runners. *Perceptual and Motor Skills*, 55, 1295–1300.

Goodglass, H. (1980). Disorders of naming following brain injury. *American Scientist*, 68, 647–655.

Gordon, T. (1970). *P.E.T. parent effectiveness training: A tested new way to raise children.* New York: Wyden.

Gorman, J. (1985, February). My fair software. *Discover*, 64–65.

Gottesman, I. I., & Shields, J. (1982). *The schizophrenic puzzle.* New York: Cambridge University Press.

Gottfried, A. W., & Bathurst, K. (1983). Hand preference across time is related to intelligence in young girls, not boys, *Science*, 221, 1074–1075.

Gough, H. G., Fioravanti, M., & Lazzari, R. (1983). Some implications of self versus ideal-self congruence on the revised adjective check list. *Journal of Personality and Social Psychology*, 44, 1214–1220.

Gould, L. C., et al. (1977, February). Sequential patterns of multiple-drug use among high school students. *Archives of General Psychiatry*, 34(2), 216–222.

Gould, R. (1975, February). Growth toward self-tolerance. *Psychology Today.*

Gould, S. J. (1976). Biological potential vs. biological determinism. *Natural History*, 85(5).

Graubard, P. S., & Rosenberg, H. (1974, March). Little brother is changing you. *Psychology Today.*

Green, H. (Joanne Greenberg). (1964). *I never promised you a rose garden.* New York: Holt, Rinehart and Winston.

Greenberg, J. (1978, July 1). The aging of sleep. *Science News*, 114(1), 10–12.

Greenberg, J. (1977, July 30) The brain and emotions: Crossing a new frontier. *Science News*, 112(5), 74–75.

Greene, D., & Lepper, M. R. (1974, September). How to turn play into work. *Psychology Today*, 49.

Greenspan, E. (1983, August 28). Conditioning athlete's minds. *New York Times Magazine*, 32–34.

Gregory, R. L. (1977). *Eye and brain: The psychology of seeing* (3rd ed). New York: World University Library.

Griffin, D. R. (1984). Animal Thinking. *American Scientist*, 72, 456–463.

Grings, W. W., & Lockhart, R. A. (1963). Effects of anxiety-lessening instructions and differential set development on the extinction of GSR. *Journal of Experimental Psychology*, 66, 292–299.

Grinspoon, L., & Bakalar, J. B. (1977). *Cocaine, a drug and its social evolution.* New York: Basic Books.

Grinspoon, L., & Hedblom, P. (1972, July 8). Amphetamines reconsidered [Special Issue]. *Saturday Review.*

Grobstein, P., & Chow, K. L. (1975). Perceptive field development and individual experience. *Science*, 190, 352–358.

Grossman, F. K., Eichler, L. S., & Winicoff, S. A. (1980). *Pregnancy, Birth and Parenthood.* San Francisco: Jossey-Bass.

Grossman, K., Thane, K., & Grossman, K. E. (1981). Maternal contact of the newborn after various postpartum conditions of mother-infant contact. *Developmental Psychology*, 17, 158–161.

Grossman, K. E., & Volkmer, H. (1984). Fathers' presence during birth of their infants and paternal involvement. *International Journal of Behavioral Development*, 7, 157–165.

Grover, S. C. (1983). *The cognitive basis of the intellect: A response to Jensen's "Bias in mental testing."* Calgary, Alberta: University of Calgary.

Guilford, J. P. (1950). Creativity. *American Psychologist*, 5, 444–454.

Guilford, J. P. (1959). *Personality.* New York: McGraw-Hill.

Guilleminault, C. (1979, June). The sleep apnea syndrome. *Medical Times*, 59–67.

Guilleminault, C., Passouant, P., & Dement, W. C. (1976). *Narcolepsy.* New York: Spectrum.

Gustavson, C. R., & Garcia, J (1974, May). Pulling a gag on the wily coyote. *Psychology Today*, 68–72.

Gutek, B. A. (1981, August). Experiences of sexual harassment: Results from a representative survey. Paper presented at the annual convention of the American Psychological Association, Los Angeles, California.

Haber, R. N. (1974). Eidetic images. In *Image object and illusion.* San Francisco: Freeman.

Haber, R. N. (1969). Eidetic images; with biographical sketches *Scientific American*, 220(12), 36–44.

Haber, R. N. (1980). How we perceive depth from flat pictures. *American Scientist*, 68, 370–380.

Haber, R. N. (1970, May). How we remember what we see. *Scientific American*, 104–112.

Haefele, J. W. (1962). *Creativity and innovation.* New York: Reinhold.

Hales, D. (1980). *The complete book of sleep.* Reading, MA: Addison-Wesley.

Hall, C. (1966). *The meaning of dreams.* New York: McGraw-Hill.

Hall, C. (1974). What people dream about. In R. L. Woods & H. B. Greenhouse (Eds.), *The new world of dreams: An anthology.* New York: Macmillan.

Hall, C., Domhoff, G. W., Blick, K. A., & Weesner, K. E. (1982). The dreams of college men and women in 1950 and 1980: A comparison of dream contents and sex differences. *Sleep*, 5(2), 188–194.

Hall, E. T. (1974). *Handbook for proxemic research.* Washington, DC: Social Anthropology and Visual Communication.

Hall, E. T. (1966). *The hidden dimension.* Garden City, NY: Doubleday.

Hall, G. S. (1922). *Senescence, the last half of life.* New York: Appleton-Century-Crofts.

Hall, R. G., Sachs, D. P., Hall, S. M., & Benowitz, N. L. (1984). Two-year efficacy and safety of rapid smoking therapy in patients with cardiac and pulmonary disease. *Journal of Consulting and Clinical Psychology*, 52, 574–581.

Hamilton, S. B., & Waldman, D. A. (1983). Self-modification of depression via cognitive-behavioral intervention strategies: A time series analysis. *Cognitive Therapy and Research*, 7, 99–106.

Hammer, S., & Hazleton, L. (1984, October). Cocaine and the chemical brain. *Science Digest*, 92, 58–61, 100–103.

Hansel, C. E. M. (1980). *ESP and parapsychology: A critical reevaluation.* Buffalo, NY: Prometheus.

Hansen, W. B., & Altman, I. (1976). Decorating personal places: A descriptive analysis. *Environmental Behavior*, 8, 491–505.

Hardin, G. (1985) *Filters against folly.* New York: Viking.

Hardin, G. (1968). The tragedy of the commons. *Science*, 162, 1243–1248.

Hardy, A. B. (1976). *Agoraphobia: Symptoms, causes, treatment.* Menlo Park, CA: Terrap.

Hardyck, C., Petrinovich, L. F., & Goldman, R. (1976). Left-handedness and cognitive deficit. *Cortex*, 12, 266–278.

Hare, R. D., & Cox, D. N. (1978). Psychophysiological research on psychopathy. In W. H. Reid (Ed.), *The psychopath: A comprehensive study of anti-social disorders and behaviors.* New York: Brunner/Mazel.

Harlow, H. F. (1949). The formation of learning sets. *Psychological Review, 56,* 51–65.

Harlow, H. F. (1966). Learning to love. *American Scientist, 54,* 244–272.

Harlow, H. F. (1967). The young monkeys. *Psychology Today, 1*(5), 40–47.

Harlow, H. F., & Harlow, M. K. (1962). Social deprivation in monkeys. *Scientific American, 207,* 136–146.

Harlow, H. F., & Zimmerman, R. R. (1958). The development of affectional responses in infant monkeys. *Proceedings of the American Philosophical Society, 102,* 501–509.

Harlow, J. M. (1868). Recovery from the passage of an iron bar through the head. *Massachusetts Medical Society, 2,* 327ff.

Harper. (1959). *Psychoanalysis and psychotherapy.* Englewood Cliffs, NJ: Prentice-Hall.

Harris, I.D. (1964). *The promised seed: A complete study of eminent first and later sons.* New York: Free Press.

Hartmann, E. L. (1973). *The functions of sleep.* New Haven, CT: Yale University Press.

Hartmann, E. L. (1981). The functions of sleep and memory processing. In W. Fishbein (Ed.), *Sleep, dreams and memory* (pp. 111–124). New York: SP Medical & Scientific Books.

Hartmann, E. L. (1978). *The sleeping pill.* New Haven, CT: Yale University Press.

Hass, A. (1983). *Teenage sexuality—A survey of teenage sexual behavior.* New York: Pinnacle Books.

Hatfield, E., Greenberger, D., Traupmann, J., & Lambert, P. (1982). Equity and sexual satisfaction in recently married couples. *Journal of Sex Research, 18,* 18–32.

Hattie, J. A., Sharpley, C. F., & Rogers, H. J. (1984). Comparative effectiveness of professional and paraprofessional helpers. *Psychological Bulletin, 95,* 534–541.

Havighurst, R. J. (1976). Choosing a middle path for the use of drugs with hyperactive children. *School Review, 85*(1), 60–77.

Havighurst, R. J. (1979). *Developmental tasks and education* (4th ed.). New York: McKay.

Havighurst, R. J. (1961). Successful aging. *Gerontologist, 1,* 8–13.

Hawkins, D. B., & Gruber, J. J. (1982). Little league baseball and players' self-esteem. *Perceptual and Motor Skills, 55,* 1335–1340.

Haywood, H. C., Meyers, C. E., & Switzby, H. N. (1982). Mental retardation. *Annual Review of Psychology, 33,* 309–342.

Hayakawa. S. I. (1965). The use and misuse of language. In R. E. Farson (Ed.), *Science and human affairs* (pp. 95–113). Palo Alto, CA: Science and Behavior Books.

Hayes, C. (1951). *The ape in our house.* New York: Harper & Row.

Hayes, J. R. (1978). *Cognitive psychology: Thinking and creating.* Homewood, IL: Dorsey.

Hearst, E. (1969). Psychology across the chess board. In *Readings in Psychology Today* (pp. 16–23). Del Mar, CA: CRM.

Hebb, D. O. (1949). *Organization of behavior.* New York: Wiley.

Hebb, D. O. (1966). *A textbook of psychology* (2nd ed.). Philadelphia: Saunders.

Hebb, D. O. (1974). What psychology is about. *American Psychologist, 29,* 71–79.

Heiby, E. M. (1983). Assessment of frequency of self-reinforcement. *Journal of Personality and Social Psychology, 44,* 1304–1307.

Heiman, J. R. (1977). A psychophysiological exploration of sexual arousal patterns in females and males. *Psychophysiology, 14,*(3), 266–274.

Heinstein, M. I. (1963). Behavioral correlates to breast-bottle regimes under varying parent-infant relationships. *Monographs of the Society for Research in Child Development, 28*(4), 1–61.

Held, R. (1971). Plasticity in sensory-motor systems. In *Contemporary psychology.* San Francisco: Freeman.

Heller, J. (1961). *Catch 22.* New York: Simon & Schuster.

Hellman, H. (1971). *Biology in the world of the future.* New York: Hayden.

Helson, H. (1964). *Adaptation-level theory.* New York: Harper & Row.

Henderson, N. D. (1982). Human behavior genetics. *Annual Review of Psychology, 33,* 403–440.

Hendin, D. (1984). *Death as a fact of life.* New York: Norton.

Herbert, W., & Greenberg, J. (1983, September 10). Behavior: Sex roles remain. *Science News, 124,* 172.

Heron, W. (1957). The pathology of boredom. *Scientific American, 196,* 52–56.

Herrnstein, R. J. (1979). Acquisition, generalization, and discrimination reversal of a natural concept. *Journal of Experimental Psychology: Animal Behavior Processes, 5,* 116–129.

Herron, J. (1980). *Neuropsychology of left-handedness.* New York: Academic Press.

Hess, E. H. (1959). Imprinting. *Science, 130,* 133–141.

Hess, E. H. (1975b, November). The role of pupil size in communication. *Scientific American,* 110–119.

Hess, E. H. (1975a). *The tell-tale eye: How your eyes reveal hidden thoughts and emotions.* New York: Van Nostrand Reinhold.

Heussenstamm, F. K. (1971). Bumper stickers and the cops. *Transaction, 8,* 32–33.

High bar not so routine for UCLA gymnast. (1984, June 4). *Los Angeles Times.*

Hilgard, E. R. (1977). *Divided consciousness.* New York: Wiley.

Hilgard, E. R. (1968). *The experience of hypnosis.* New York: Harcourt Brace Jovanovich.

Hilgard, E. R. (1978). Hypnosis and Pain. In R. A. Sternbach (Ed.), *The psychology of pain.* New York: Raven Press.

Hilgard, E. R. (1974, November). Weapon against pain—Hypnosis is no mirage. *Psychology Today.*

Hilgard, E. R., & Hilgard J. R. (1983). *Hypnosis in the Relief of Pain.* Los Altos, CA: Kaufmann.

Hilton, I. (1967). Differences in the behavior of mothers toward first and later born children. *Journal of Personality and Social Psychology, 7,* 282–290.

Hite, S. (1976). *The Hite report.* New York: Macmillan.

Hobson, J. A., & McCarley, R. W. (1977). The brain as a dream state generator: An activation-synthesis hypothesis of the dream process. *American Journal of Psychiatry, 134,* 1335–1348.

Hodgson, R., & Miller, P. (1982). *Selfwatching.* New York: Facts on File.

Hoffer, A. (1972). *Description, diagnosis, theory and treatment of schizophrenia.* Karpat.

Hoffman, L. W. (1977). Changes in family roles, socialization, and sex differences. *American Psychologist, 32,* 644–657.

Hoffman, M. L. (1975). Altruistic behavior and the parent-child relationship. *Journal of Personality and Social Psychology, 31,* 937–943.

Holden, C. (1980, November). Twins reunited. *Science 80,* 55–59.

Holland, M. K. (1975). *Using psychology: Principles of behavior and your life.* Boston: Little, Brown.

Holmes, D. S., Curtright, C. A., McCaul, K. D., & Thissen, D. (1980). Biorhythms: Their utility for predicting postoperative recuperative time, death, and athletic performance. *Journal of Applied Psychology, 65,* 233–236.

Holmes, D. S., Solomon, S., Cappo, B. M., & Greenberg, J. L. (1983). Effects of transcendental meditation versus resting on physiological and subjective arousal. *Journal of Personality and Social Psychology, 44,* 1245–1252.

Holmes, T., & Masuda, M. (1972, April). Psychosomatic syndrome. *Psychology Today,* 71.

Holmes, T. H., & Rahe, R. H. (1967). Social readjustment rating scale. *Journal of Psychosomatic Research.*

Honzik, M. P. (1984). Life-span development. *Annual Review of Psychology, 35,* 309–331.

Honzik, M. P. (1983). Measuring abilities in infancy: Value and limitations. In M. Lewis (Ed.), *Origins of intelligence.* New York: Plenum.

Hopkins, J., Marcus, M., & Campbell, S. B. (1984). Postpartum depression: A critical review. *Psychological Bulletin, 95,* 498–515.

Horn, J. M., Loehlin, J. C., & Willerman, L. (1979). Intellectual resemblance among adoptive and biological relatives: The Texas adoption project. *Behavior Genetics, 9,* 177–207.

Horn, J. M., Plomine, R., & Rosenman, R. (1976). Heritability of personality traits in adult male twins. *Behavior Genetics, 6,* 17–30.

Horne, J. A., Brass, C. B., Pettitt, A. N. (1980). Circadian performance differences between morning and evening "types." *Ergonomics, 23,* 29–36.

Horne, J. A., & Staff, L. H. E. (1983). Exercise and sleep: Body-heating effects. *Sleep, 6,* 36–46.

Horowitz, M. J. (1970). *Image formation and cognition*. New York: Appleton-Century-Crofts.

Horowitz, W. A., Kestenbaum, C., Person, E., & Jarvik, L. (1965). Identical twin—"Idiot savants" calendar calculators. *The American Journal of Psychiatry, 121*, 1075–1079.

Hosch, H. M., & Cooper, D. S. (1982). Victimization as a determinant of eyewitness accuracy. *Journal of Applied Psychology, 67*, 649–652.

Houston, J. P. (1985). *Motivation*. New York: Macmillan.

Howarth, E. (1980). Birth order, family structure and personality variables. *Journal of Personality Assessment, 44*, 299–301.

Howitt, D., Craven, G., Iveson, C., Kremer, J., McCabe, J., & Rolph T. (1977). The misdirected letter. *British Journal of Social and Clinical Psychology, 16*, 285–286.

Hoyenga, K. B., & Hoyenga, K. T. (1984). *Motivational explanations of behavior*. Monterey CA: Brooks/Cole.

Hsia, Y., & Graham, C. H. (1965). Color blindness. In C. H. Graham (Ed.), *Vision and visual perception* (pp. 395–413). New York: Wiley.

Hubel, D. H. (1979a, September). The brain. *Scientific American, 241*, 45–53.

Hubel, D. H. (1979b). The visual cortex of normal and deprived monkeys. *American Scientist, 67*, 532–543.

Hubel, D. H., & Wiesel, T. N. (1979). Brain mechanisms of vision. *Scientific American, 241*, 150–162.

Huesmann, L., Eron, L., Klein, L., Brice, P., & Fischer, P. (1983). Mitigating the imitation of aggressive behaviors by changing children's attitudes about media violence. *Journal of Personality and Social Psychology, 44*, 899–910.

Huges, J. (1974). Acquisition of a non-vocal "language" by aphasic children. *Cognition 3*, 41–55.

Humphrey, J. A., Puccio, D., Niswander, G. D., & Casey, T. M. (1972). An analysis of the sequence of selected events in the lives of a suicidal population: A preliminary report. *Journal of Nervous Mental Disorders, 154*, 137–140.

Hunt, M. (1974). *Sexual behavior in the 1970s*. Chicago: Playboy Press.

Hunt, M. (1982). *The universe within*. New York: Simon & Schuster.

Hunter, W. S. (1913). The delayed reaction in animals and children. *Behavior Monographs, 2*.

Hurd, P., Johnson, C. A., Pechacek, T., Bast, L. P., Jacobs, D. R., & Luepker, R. V. (1980). Prevention of smoking in seventh-grade students. *Journal of Behavioral Medicine, 3*, 15–28.

Hurst, M. W., Jenkins, C. D., & Rose, R. M. (1979). The relation of psychological stress to onset of medical illness. In C. A. Garfield (Ed.), *Stress and survival: The emotional realities of life-threatening illness*. St. Louis: Mosby.

Huston, T. L., & Levinger, G. (1978). Interpersonal attraction and relationships. *Annual Review of Psychology, 29*, 115–156.

Hutchison, M. (1984). *The book of floating*. New York: Quill.

Huxley, A. (1965). Human potentialities. In R. E. Farson (Ed.), *Science and human affairs*. Palo Alto, CA: Science and Behavior Books.

Hyde, J. S. (1984). *Understanding human sexuality*. New York: McGraw-Hill.

Hyman, B. T., Van Hoesen, G. W., Damasio, A. R., & Barnes, C. L. (1984). Alzheimer's disease: Cell-specific pathology isolates the hippocampal formation. *Science, 225*, 1168–1170.

Hyman, R. (1977). The case against parapsychology. *The Humanist, 37*, 47–49.

Hyman, R. (1979). Patterns of PSI—Exposed or imposed. *Contemporary Psychology, 24*, 766–767

Ickes, W., & Turner, M. (1983). On the social advantages of having an older, opposite-sex sibling: Birth order influences in mixed-sex dyads. *Journal of Personality and Social Psychology, 45*, 210–222.

Isen, A. M., & Means, B. (1983). The influence of positive affect on decision-making strategy. *Social Cognition, 2*, 18–31.

Isenberg, P. L., & Schatzberg, A. F. (1976). Psychoanalytic contribution to a theory of depression. In J. O. Cole, A. F. Schatzberg, & S. H. Frazier (Eds.), *Depression: Biology, psychodynamics, and treatment*. New York: Plenum Press.

Iversen, L. L. (1979, September). The chemistry of the brain. *Scientific American, 241*(3), 134–147.

Jackson, B. (1973, September 22). Our prisons are criminal. *New York Times Magazine*, pp. 54, 57.

Jackson, S. E. (1983). Participation in decision making as a strategy for reducing job-related strain. *Journal of Applied Psychology, 68*, 3–19.

Jacobson, A., Kales, A., Lehmann, D., & Zweizia, J. R. (1965). Somnambulism: All night EEG studies. *Science, 148*, 975–977.

Jacobson, L. E. (1932). The electrophysiology of mental activities. *American Journal of Psychology, 44*, 677–694.

Jacobson, S. W., et al. (1984). Neonatal correlates of prenatal exposure to smoking, caffeine, and alcohol. *Infant Behavior & Development, 7*, 253–265.

Jahn, R. G. (1982). The persistent paradox of psychic phenomena. *Proceedings of the IEEE, 70*(2), 136–166.

James, W. (1958). *The varieties of religious experience*. New York: New American Library.

Janis, I. L., & Mann, L. (1977). *Decision making*. New York: The Free Press.

Janis, I. L., & Mann, L. (1965). Effectiveness of emotional role-playing in modifying smoking habits and attitudes. *Journal of Experimental Research in Personality, 1*, 84–90.

Janis, I. L., & Wheeler, D. (1978, May). Thinking clearly about career choices. *Psychology Today, 11*, 66–78.

Japenga, A. (1982, May 19). The birds that hunt people. *Los Angeles Times*, Part V, pp. 1–2.

Jarvik, E. M. (1964). Ciba found. In H. Steinberg et al., *Symposium of Animal Pharmacology Drug Action*.

Jarvik, L. F., Eisdorfer, C., & Blum, J. E. (Eds.). (1973). *Intellectual functioning in adults*. New York: Springer.

Jellinik, E. M. (1960). *The disease concept of alcoholism*. New Haven: Hill House Press.

Jemmott, J. B., III, & Locke, S. E. (1984). Psychosocial factors, immunologic mediation, and human susceptibility to infectious diseases: How much do we know? *Psychological Bulletin, 95*, 78–108.

Jenkins, J. G., & Dallenbach, K. M. (1924). Oblivescence during sleep and waking. *American Journal of Psychology, 35*, 605–612.

Jensen, A. R. (1969). How much can we boost I.Q. and scholastic achievement? *Harvard Educational Review, 39*, 123.

Jensen, M. D., Benson, R. C., & Bobak, I. M. (1981). *Maternity care. The nurse and the family* (2nd ed.). St. Louis: Mosby.

Jerome, L. E. (1975). Astrology: Magic or science? In *Objections to astrology*. Prometheus Books.

John, E. R. (1967). *Mechanisms of memory*. New York: Academic Press.

Johnson, J. J. (1975). Sticking with first responses on multiple-choice exams: For better or for worse? *Teaching of Psychology, 2*(4).

Johnson, L., Naitoh, P., Lubin, A., & Moses, J. (1972). Sleep stages and performance. In W. P. Colquhoun (Ed.), *Aspects of human efficiency* (pp. 81–100). London: English University Press.

Johnson, P. C., Jr. (1984). Space medicine. *American Scientist, 72*, 495–498.

Johnson, R. E. (1970). Some correlates of extramarital coitus. *Journal of Marriage and Family, 32*, 449–456.

Johnson, S. M., & White, G. (1971). Self-observation as an agent of behavioral change. *Behavior Therapy, 2*, 488–497.

Jones, E. (1953). *The life and work of Sigmund Freud*. New York: Basic Books.

Jones, E. E., & Nisbett, R. E. (1971). The actor and observer: Divergent perceptions of the causes of behavior. In E. E. Jones, D. E. Kanouse, H. H. Kelley, R. E. Nisbett, S. Valins, & B. Weiner (Eds.). *Attribution: Perceiving the causes of behavior*. Morristown, NJ: General Learning Press.

Jones, K. L., & Smith, D. W. (1973). Recognition of the fetal alcohol syndrome in early infancy. *Lancet, 2*, 999.

Jones, W. R., & Ellis, N. R. (1962). Inhibitory potential in rotary pursuit acquisition. *Journal of Experimental Psychology, 63*, 534–537.

Jospe, M. (1978). *The placebo effect in healing*. Lexington, MA: Lexington Books.

Jourard, S. M. (1966). An exploratory study of body-accessibility. *British Journal of Social and Clinical Psychology, 5*, 221–231.

Jourard, S. M. (1974). *Healthy personality*. New York: Macmillan.

Jourard, S. M. (1963). *Personal adjustment* (2nd ed.). New York: Macmillan.

Joyce, C. (1984, May). Space travel is no joyride. *Psychology Today*, 30–37.

Judson, A. I., & Cofer, C. N. (1956). Reasoning as an associative process: I. "Direction" in a simple verbal problem. *Psychological Reports, 2*, 469–476.

Julesz, B. (1975, April). Experiments in the visual perception of texture. *Scientific American, 232*, 34–43.

Julesz, B. (1971). *Foundations of cyclopean perception*. Chicago: University of Chicago Press.

Julien, R. M. (1985). *A primer of drug action* (4th ed.). San Francisco: Freeman.

Kagan, J. (1971). *Change and continuity in infancy*. New York: Wiley.

Kagan, J. (1976). Emergent themes in human development. *American Scientist*, 64, 186–196.

Kagan, J. (1969). *Personality development*. New York: Harcourt Brace Jovanovich.

Kagan, J., & Klein, R. E. (1973). Cross-cultural perspectives on early development. *American Psychologist*, 28, 947–961.

Kahneman, D., Slovic, P., & Tversky, A. (1982). *Judgment under uncertainty: Heuristics and Biases*. Cambridge: Cambridge University Press.

Kahneman, D., & Tversky, A. (1973). On the psychology of prediction. *Psychological Review*, 80, 237–251.

Kahneman, D., & Tversky, A. (1972). Subjective probability: A judgment of representativeness. *Cognitive Psychology*, 3, 430–454.

Kales, A., & Kales, J. (1973). Recent advances in the diagnosis and treatment of sleep disorders. In G. Usdin (Ed.), *Sleep research and clinical practice*. New York: Brunner/Mazel.

Kaluger, G., & Kaluger, M. F. (1984). *Human Development*. St. Louis: Times Mirror/Mosby.

Kamin, L. J. (1985, October). Genes and behavior: The missing link. *Psychology Today*, 76–78.

Kamin, L. J. (1981). *The intelligence controversy*. New York: Wiley.

Kamin, L. J. (1974). *The science and politics of I.Q.* New York: Halstead.

Kamiya, J. (1968). Conscious control of brain waves. *Psychology Today 1*, 57–66.

Kandel, E. R. (1976). *Cellular basis of behavior: An introduction to behavioral neurobiology*. San Francisco: Freeman.

Kanfer, F. H., & Goldfoot, D. A. (1966). Self-control and tolerance of noxious stimulation. *Psychological Reports*, 18, 79–85.

Kanner, L. (1957). *Child psychiatry*. Springfield, IL: Charles C Thomas.

Kaplan, H. S. (1974). *The new sex therapy*. New York: Brunner/Mazel.

Kaplan, M. (1983). The issue of sex bias in DSM-III: Comments on the articles by Spitzer, Williams, and Kass. *American Psychologist*, 38, 802–803.

Kaplan, P. S., & Stein, J. (1984). *Psychology of adjustment*. Belmont, CA: Wadsworth.

Kapleau, P. (1966). *The three pillars of Zen*. New York: Harper & Row.

Karlins, M., Coffman, T. L., & Walters, G. (1969). On the fading of social stereotypes: Studies in three generations of college students. *Journal of Personality and Social Psychology*, 13, 1–16.

Kasamatsu, A., & Hirai, T. (1966). An electroencephalographic study of Zen meditation (Zazen). *Folia Psychiatria et Neurologia Japonica*, 20, 315–336. Reprinted in C. T. Tart, *Altered states of consciousness*.

Kastenbaum, R., & Aisenberg R. (1972). *The psychology of death*. New York: Springer.

Kassarjian, H. H. (1982). Consumer psychology. *Annual Review of Psychology*, 33, 619–649.

Katz, B. J. (1972). Finding psychiatric help can be traumatic itself. *The National Observer*.

Kazdin, A. E. (1975). *Behavior modification in applied settings*. Homewood IL: Dorsey Press.

Kearney, M. (1984). A comparison of motivation to avoid success in males and females. *Journal of Clinical Psychology*, 40, 1005–1007.

Keating, J. P., & Loftus, E. F. (1981, June). The logic of fire escape. *Psychology Today*, 14–19.

Keefe, F. J. (1982). Behavioral assessment and treatment of chronic pain: Current status and future directions. *Journal of Consulting and Clinical Psychology*, 50, 896–911.

Keeffe, P. (1977, September). Ice after death. *Novus*, 29–33.

Kelley, H. H. (1971). *Attribution in social interaction*. Morristown, NJ: General Learning Press.

Kelley, H. H. (1967). Attribution in social psychology. *Nebraska Symposium on Motivation*, 15, 192–238.

Kelley, H. H. (1950). The warm-cold variable in first impressions of persons. *Journal of Personality*, 18, 431–439.

Kennedy, J. M. (1983). What can we learn about pictures from the blind? *American Scientist*, 71, 19–26.

Kennell, J. H., & Klaus, M. H. (1984). Mother-infant bonding: Weighing the evidence. *Developmental Review*, 4, 275–282.

Kenrick, D. T., & Cialdini, R. B. (1977). Romantic attraction: Misattribution vs. reinforcement explanations. *Journal of Personality and Social Psychology*, 35, 381–391.

Kety, S. S. (1979, September). Disorders of the human brain. *Scientific American*, 241, 202–214.

Keys, A., Brozek, J., Henschel, A., Mickelson, O., & Taylor, H. L. (1950). *The biology of human starvation*. Minneapolis: University of Minnesota Press.

Kiell, N. (Ed.). (1973). *The psychology of obesity: Dynamics and treatment*. Springfield, IL: Charles C Thomas.

Kihlstrom, J. F. (1985). Hypnosis. *Annual Review of Psychology 36*, 385–418.

Kimble, G. A. (1961). *Hilgard and Marquis' conditioning and learning* (2nd ed.). New York: Appleton-Century-Crofts.

King, H. E. (1961). Psychological effects of excitation in the limbic system. In D. E. Sheer (Ed.), *Electrical stimulation of the brain*. Austin: University of Texas Press.

Kinsey, A., Pomeroy, W., & Martin, C. (1953). *Sexual behavior in the human female*. Philadelphia: Saunders.

Kinsey, A., Pomeroy, W., & Martin, C. (1948). *Sexual behavior in the human male*. Philadelphia: Saunders.

Kitcher, P. (1985). *Vaulting ambition: Sociobiology and the quest for human nature*. Cambridge, MA: MIT Press.

Klatzky, R. L. (1980). *Human memory structures and processes* (2nd ed.). San Francisco: Freeman.

Klaus, M. H., & Kennell, J. H. (1982). *Parent-infant bonding*. St. Louis: Mosby.

Klausmeir, H. J., & Goodwin, W. (1975). *Learning and human abilities* (4th ed.). New York: Harper & Row.

Kleitman, N. (1963). *Sleep and wakefulness* (2nd ed.). Chicago: University of Chicago Press.

Kleitman, N., & Kleitman, E. (1953). Effect of non-24-hour routines of living on oral temperature and heart rate. *Journal of Applied Physiology*, 6, 283–291.

Klienke, C. L. (1978). *Self-perception: The psychology of personal awareness*. San Francisco: Freeman.

Klinnert, M. D. (1984). The regulation of infant behavior by maternal facial expression. *Infant Behavior & Development*, 7, 447–465.

Knapp, M. L. (1978). *Nonverbal communication in human interaction* (2nd ed.) New York: Holt, Rinehart and Winston.

Knight, R. P. (1949). A critique of the present status of the psychotherapies. *Bulletin of the New York Academy of Medicine*, 25, 100–114.

Knox, D. (1984). *Human sexuality*. St. Paul, MN: West.

Kohlberg, L. (1969). The cognitive-developmental approach to socialization. In A. Goslin (Ed.), *Handbook of socialization theory and research*. Chicago: Rand McNally.

Kohlberg, L. (1981a). *Essays on moral development: Vol. 1. The philosophy of moral development*. San Francisco: Harper.

Kohlberg, L. (1981b). *The meaning and measurement of moral development*. Worcester, MA: Clark University Press.

Kohlberg, L. (1976). Moral stages and moralization: The cognitive-developmental approach. In T. Lickona (Ed.), *Moral development and behavior*. New York: Holt, Rinehart and Winston.

Kohler, I. (1962). Experiments with goggles. *Scientific American*, Offprint No. 465, 62–72.

Kohler, W. (1925). *The mentality of apes*. New York: Harcourt Brace Jovanovich.

Kolata, G. (1983). Brain-grafting work shows promise. *Science*, 221, 1277.

Koocher, G. P. (1977). Bathroom behavior and human dignity. *Journal of Personality and Social Psychology*, 35, 120–121.

Kopp, C. B., & Parmelee, A. H. (1979). Prenatal and perinatal influences on infant behavior. In J. D. Ofsky (Ed.), *Handbook of infant development*. New York: Wiley.

Korte, C., & Milgram, S. (1970). Acquaintance networks between racial groups. *Journal of Personality and Social Psychology*, 15, 101–108.

Kosslyn, S. M. (1983). *Ghosts in the mind's machine*. New York: Norton.

Kosslyn, S. M. (1975). Information representation in visual images. *Cognitive Psychology*, 7, 341–370.

Kosslyn, S. M., Ball, T. M., & Reiser, B. J. (1978). Visual images preserve metric spatial information: Evidence from studies of image scanning. *Journal of Experimental Psychology: Human Perception and Performance, 4,* 47–60.

Koukkou, M., & Lehmann, D. (1968). EEG and memory storage in sleep experiments with humans. *Electroencephalography and Clinical Neurophysiology, 25,* 455–462.

Krebs, D., & Adinolfi, A. A. (1975). Physical attractiveness, social relations, and personality style. *Journal of Personality and Social Psychology, 31,* 245–253.

Krech, D., Rosenzweig, M. R., & Bennett, E. L. (1962). Relations between brain chemistry and problem solving among rats raised in enriched and impoverished environments. *Journal of Comparative and Physiological Psychology, 55,* 801–807.

Krieger, D. T. (1983). Brain peptides: What, where, and why? *Science, 222,* 975–985.

Kripke, D. F., & Simons, R. N. (1976). Average sleep, insomnia, and sleeping pill use. *Sleep Research, 5,* 110.

Kristt, D. A., & Engel, B. T. (1975). Learned control of blood pressure in patients with high blood pressure. *Circulation, 51,* 370–378.

Kruger, L., & Liebeskind, J. C. (Eds.). (1984). *Advances in pain research and therapy.* New York: Raven Press.

Kubler-Ross, E. (1975). *Death: The final stage of growth.* Englewood Cliffs, NJ: Prentice-Hall.

Kulik, J. A., Bangert-Drowns, R. L., & Kulik, C. C. (1984). Effectiveness of coaching for aptitude tests. *Psychological Bulletin, 95,* 179–188.

Kulik, J. A., Kulik, C. C., & Cohen, P. A. (1980). Effectiveness of computer-based college teaching: A meta-analysis of findings. *Review of Educational Research, 50,* 525–544.

Kunst-Wilson, W., & Zajonc, R. (1980). Affective discrimination of stimuli that cannot be recognized. *Science, 207,* 557–558.

Labbe, R., Firl, A., Jr., Mufson, E. J., & Stein, D. G. (1983). Fetal brain transplants: Reduction of cognitive deficits in rats with frontal cortex lesions. *Science, 221,* 470–472.

La Berge, S. P. (1980). Lucid dreaming as a learnable skill: A case study. *Perceptual and Motor Skills, 51,* 1039–1042.

La Berge, S. P. (1981b, January). Lucid dreaming: Directing the action as it happens. *Psychology Today,* 48–57.

La Berge, S. P., Nagel, L. E., Dement, W. C., & Zarcone, V. (1981a). Lucid dreaming verified by volutional communication during REM sleep. *Perceptual and Motor Skills, 52,* 727–732.

Labov, W. (1973). The boundaries of words and their meanings. In C. J. N. Bailey & R. W. Shuy (Eds.), *New ways of analyzing variation in English.* Washington, DC: Georgetown University Press.

Labovitz, S., & Hagedorn, R. (1971). An analysis of suicide rates among occupational categories. *Social Inquiry, 41,* 67–72.

Lagerspetz, K. (1981). Combining aggression studies in infra-humans and man. In P. F. Brian & D. Benton (Eds.), *Multidisciplinary approaches to aggression research* (pp. 389–400). New York: Elsevier/North-Holland.

Laing, R. D. (1970). *The divided self.* New York: Pantheon.

Laing, R. D. (1967). *The politics of experience.* New York: Pantheon.

Laird, J. D. (1984). The real role of facial response in the experience of emotion. *Journal of Personality and Social Psychology, 47,* 909–917.

Laird, J. D. (1974). Self-attribution of emotion: The effects of expressive behavior on the quality of emotional experience. *Journal of Personality and Social Psychology, 29,* 475–486.

Lake, A. (1973). Get thin, stay thin. *McCalls, 100*(4).

Landis, D. (1980, December). A scan for mental illness. *Discover,* 26–27.

Landy, F. J., & Trumbo, D. A. (1980). *Psychology of work behavior.* Homewood, IL: Dorsey.

Lang, P. J., & Melamed, B. G. (1969). Avoidance conditioning therapy of an infant with chronic ruminative vomiting. *Journal of Abnormal Psychology, 74,* 1–8.

Langer, E. J., & Abelson, R. P. (1974). A patient by any other name . . .: Clinician group difference in labeling bias. *Journal of Consulting and Clinical Psychology, 42,* 4–9.

Lappe, F. M. (1971). *Diet for a small planet.* New York: Ballantine.

Last, C. G., Barlow, D. H., & O'Brian, G. T. (1984). Precipitants of agoraphobia: Role of stressful life events. *Psychological Reports, 54,* 567–570.

Latane, L., Nida, S. A., & Wilson, D. W. (1981). The effects of group size on helping behavior. In J. P. Rushton & R. M. Sorrentino (Eds.), *Altruism and helping behavior: Social, personality and developmental perspectives.* Hillsdale, NJ: Erlbaum.

Laurence, J., & Perry, C. (1983). Hypnotically created memory among highly hypnotizable subjects. *Science, 222,* 523–524.

Lazarus, A. H. (1964). The treatment of chronic frigidity by systematic desensitization. In H. J. Eysenck (Ed.), *Experiments in behavior therapy.* New York: Pergamon.

Lazarus, R. S. (1975). A cognitively oriented psychologist looks at feedback. *American Psychologist, 30,* 553–561.

Lazarus, R. S. (1981, July). Little hassles can be hazardous to health. *Psychology Today,* 58–62.

Lazarus, R. S. (1981). The stress and coping paradigm. In C. Eisdorfer, D. Cohen, A. Kleinman, & P. Maxim (Eds.), *Models for clinical psychopathology.* New York: Spectrum.

Lazarus, R. S., DeLongis, A., Folkman, S., & Gruen, R. (1985). Stress and adaptational outcomes. *American Psychologist, 40,* 770–779.

Lazarus, R. S., & Folkman, S. (1984). *Stress, appraisal, and coping.* New York: Springer.

Leavitt, H. J., & Schlosberg, H. (1944). The retention of verbal and motor skills. *Journal of Experimental Psychology, 34,* 404–417.

Leboyer, F. (1975). *Birth without violence.* New York: Knopf.

Lee, M., Zimbardo, P. G., & Bertholf, M. (1977, November). Shy murderers. *Psychology Today.*

Lee, T., & Seeman, P. (1980). Elevation of brain neuroleptic/dopamine receptors in schizophrenia. *American Journal of Psychiatry, 137,* 191–197.

Leeper, R. W. (1935). A study of a neglected portion of the field of learning: The development of sensory organization. *Pedagogical Seminary and Journal of Genetic Psychology, 46,* 41–75.

Lefkowitz, M., Blake, R. R., & Mouton, J. S. (1955). Status factors in pedestrian violation of traffic signals. *Journal of Abnormal and Social Psychology, 51,* 704–706.

Le Magnen, J. (1980). The body energy regulation: The role of three brain responses to glucopenia. *Neuroscience and Biobehavioral Reviews, 4,* 65–72.

Lenfant, C., & Schweizer, M. (1985). Contributions of health-related biobehavioral research to the prevention of cardiovascular diseases. *American Psychologist, 40,* 217–220.

Lepper, M. R. (1985). Microcomputers in Education. *American Psychologist, 40,* 1–18.

Lerner, R. M., & Shea, J. A. (1982). Social behavior in adolescence. In B. B. Wolman, G. Stricker, S. J. Ellman, P. Keith-Spiegel, & D. S. Palermo (Eds.), *Handbook of developmental psychology* (pp. 503–525). Englewood Cliffs, NJ: Prentice-Hall.

Lester, D. (1971b). Relationship of mental disorder to suicidal behavior. *New York State Journal of Medicine, 71,* 1503–1505.

Lester, D. (1972). *Why people kill themselves: A summary of research on suicidal behavior.* Springfield, IL: Charles C Thomas.

Lester, G., & Lester, D. (1971). *Suicide: The gamble with death.* Englewood Cliffs, NJ: Prentice-Hall.

Lettvin, J. Y. (1961). Two remarks on the visual system of the frog. In W. Rosenblith (Ed.), *Sensory communication.* Cambridge, MA: MIT Press.

Leveton, E. (1977). *Psychodrama for the timid clinician.* New York: Springer.

Levin, R. J., & Levin, A. (1975, October). The *Redbook* report on premarital and extramarital sex. *Redbook,* 38.

Levin, R. J., & Levin, A. (1975, September). Sexual pleasure: The surprising preference of 100,000 women. *Redbook,* 51.

Levine, J. D., Gordon, N. C., & Fields, H. L. (1979). The role of endorphins in placebo analgesia. In J. J. Bonica, J. C. Lielseskind, & D. Albe-Fessard (Eds.), *Advances in pain research and therapy,* Vol. 3. New York: Raven Press.

Levinson, D. J., with Darrow, C. N., Klein, E. B., Levinson, M. H., & McKee, B. (1978). *The seasons of a man's life.* New York: Knopf.

Levitt, R. A. (1977). Recreational drug use and abuse. In D. C. Rimm & J. W. Somervill (Eds.), *Abnormal psychology.* New York: Academic Press.

Levy, J., & Redd, M. (1976). Cerebral organization. *Science*, 337–339.

Lewin, K. (1935). *A dynamic theory of personality*. New York: McGraw-Hill.

Lewin, R. (1974, October 5). The brain through a cat's eyes. *Saturday Review/World*.

Lewin, R. (1975, September). Starved brains. *Psychology Today*.

Lewis, M., & Brooks-Gunn, J. (1979). *Social cognition and the acquisition of self*. New York: Plenum Press.

Lichtenstein, E. (1982). The smoking problem: A behavioral perspective. *Journal of Consulting and Clinical Psychology, 50*, 804–819.

Lieberman, D. A. (1979). Behaviorism and the mind: A (limited) call for a return to introspection. *American Psychologist, 34*, 319–333.

Lieberman, R. P., Fearn, C. H., Derisi, W., Roberts, J., & Carmona, M. (1976). The credit-incentive system: Motivating the participation of patients in a day hospital. *British Journal of Clinical Psychology, 15*.

Liebert, R. M., Neale, J. M., & Davidson, E. S. (1973). *The early window: Effects of television on children and youth*. Elmsford, NY: Pergamon Press.

Lilly, J. C. (1972). *The center of the cyclone*. New York: Julian Press.

Lindsley, D. B., Bowden, J., & Magoun, H. W. (1949). Effect upon the EEG of acute injury to the brain stem activating system. *EEG and Clinical Neurophysiology, 1*, 475–486.

Lindsley, J. G., Hartmann, E. L., & Mitchell, W. (1983). Selectivity in response to L-tryptophan among insomniac subjects: A preliminary report. *Sleep, 6*(3), 247–256.

Linton, M. (1979, July). I remember it well. *Psychology Today*, 81–86.

Lipinski, E., & Lipinski, B. G. (1970). Motivational factors in psychedelic drug use by male college students. In R. E. Hormon & A. M. Fox (Eds.), *Drug awareness*. New York: Discus Books, Avon.

Lipscomb, D. M. (1974). *Noise: The unwanted sounds*. Chicago: Nelson-Hall.

Lipsett, L. (1980, February). Conditioning the rage to live. *Psychology Today*, 124.

Loevinger, J., & Knoll, E. (1983). Personality: Stages, traits, and the self. *Annual Review of Psychology, 34*, 195–222.

Loftus, E. (1979). *Eyewitness testimony*. Cambridge, MA: Harvard University Press.

Loftus, E. (1980). *Memory*. Reading MA: Addison-Wesley.

Loftus, E. (1977). Shifting human color memory. *Memory & Cognition, 5*, 696–699.

Loftus, E. (1979, November). Words that could save your life. *Psychology Today, 102*, 105–106.

Loftus, E., & Loftus, G. (1980). On the permanence of stored information in the human brain. *American Psychologist, 35*, 409–420.

Loftus, E., & Monahan, J. (1980). Trial by data: Psychological research as legal evidence. *American Psychologist, 35*, 270–283.

Loftus, E., & Palmer, J. C. (1974). Reconstruction of automobile destruction: An example of interaction between language and memory. *Journal of Verbal Learning and Verbal Behavior, 13*, 585–589.

London, P. (1971). *Behavior control*. New York: Harper & Row.

Lorenz, K. (1974). *The eight deadly sins of civilized man*. (M. Kerr-Wilson, Trans.). New York: Harcourt Brace Jovanovich.

Lorenz, K. (1937). Imprinting. *The Auk, 54*, 245–273.

Lorenz, K. (1962). *King Solomon's ring*. New York: Time.

Lorenz, K. (1966). *On aggression*. (M. Kerr-Wilson, Trans.). New York: Harcourt Brace Jovanovich.

Los Angeles Times. (1981, September 24). Man tells how rod ran through head, p. 3.

Louis, A. M. (1978, April). Should you buy biorhythms? *Psychology Today*, 93–96.

Lovaas, O., & Simmons, J. (1969). Manipulation of self-destruction in three retarded children. *Journal of Applied Behavior Analysis, 2*, 143–157.

Lowen, A. (1965). *Love and orgasm*. New York: Macmillan.

Luce, G. G. (1971). *Body time: Physiological rhythms and social stress*. New York: Pantheon.

Luce, G. G. (1965). *Current research on sleep and dreams* (Health Service Publication No. 1389). Washington, DC: U.S. Department of Health, Education and Welfare.

Luce, G. G. (1974). Sleepwalking not related to dreams. In R. L. Woods & H. B. Greenhouse (Eds.). *The new world of dreams*. New York: Macmillan.

Luce, G. G., & Peper, E. (1971, September 12). Mind over body, mind over mind. *The New York Times Magazine*.

Ludwig, A. M. (1966). Altered states of consciousness. *Archives of General Psychiatry, 15*, 225–233.

Lueptow, L. B. (1980). Social change and sex-role changes in adolescent orientations toward life, work, and achievement: 1964–1975. *Social Psychology Quarterly, 43*, 48–59.

Lumsden, C., & Wilson, E. O. (1983). *Promethean fire*. Cambridge, MA: Harvard University Press.

Luria, A. R. (1968). *The mind of a mnemonist*. New York: Basic Books.

Luthans, F., Paul, R., & Baker, D. (1981). An experimental analysis of the impact of contingent reinforcement on salespersons' performance behavior. *Journal of Applied Psychology, 66*, 314–323.

Lykken, D. T. (1974). Psychology and the lie detector industry. *American Psychologist, 29*, 725–739.

Lykken, D. T. (1981). *A tremor in the blood: Uses and abuses of the lie detector*. New York: McGraw-Hill.

Lynch, G., & Baudry, M. (1984). The biochemistry of memory: A new and specific hypothesis. *Science, 224*, 1057–1063.

Maccoby, E. E., & Jacklin, C. N. (1974). *The psychology of sex differences*. Stanford, CA: Stanford University Press.

MacKinnon, D. W. (1962). The nature and nurture of creative talent. *American Psychologist, 1*, 484–495.

MacKinnon, D. W. (1968). Selecting students with creative potential. In P. Heist (Ed.), *The creative college student: An unmet challenge*. San Francisco: Jossey-Bass.

Madsen, C. H., Jr., Becher, W. C., Thomas, D. R., Koser, L., & Plager, E. (1968). An analysis of the reinforcing function of "sit down" commands. In R. K. Parker (Ed.), *Readings in educational psychology*. Boston: Allyn & Bacon.

Maier, N. R. F. (1949). *Frustration*. New York: McGraw-Hill.

Main, M., & George, C. (1985). Responses of abused and disadvantaged toddlers to distress and agemates: A study in day care. *Developmental Psychology, 21*, 407–412.

Malamuth, N. M., & Donnerstein, E. (1982). The effects of aggressive-pornographic mass media stimuli. In L. Berkowitz (Ed.), *Advances in Experimental Social Psychology, 15* (pp. 103–136). New York: Academic Press.

Malatesta, V. J., Pollack, R. H., Wilbanks, W. A., & Adams, H. E. (1979). *Journal of Sex Research, 15*, 101.

Malmo, R. B. (1975). *On emotions, needs, and our archaic brain*. New York: Holt, Rinehart and Winston.

Mandell, A. J., Segal, D. S., Kuczenski, R. T., & Knapp, S. (1972, October). The search for the schizococcus. *Psychology Today*, 68–72.

Mandler, G. (1968). Association and organization: Fact, fancies, and theories. In T. R. Dixon & D. L. Horton (Eds.), *Verbal behavior and general behavior theory* (pp. 109–119). Englewood Cliffs, NJ: Prentice-Hall.

Mark, V. H., & Ervin, F. R. (1970). *Violence and the brain*. New York: Harper & Row.

Markman, E. M., & Seibert, J. (1976). Classes and collections: Internal organization and resulting holistic properties. *Cognitive Psychology, 8*, 561–577.

Marks, D., & Kammann, R. (1979). *The psychology of the psychic*. Buffalo, NY: Prometheus Books.

Marks, L. (1978). *The unity of the senses: Interrelations among the modalities*. New York: Academic Press.

Marks, T., & Hammen, C. L. (1982). Interpersonal mood induction: Situational and individual determinants. *Motivation and Emotion, 6*, 387–399.

Markus, H. (1981, June). Sibling personalities: The luck of the draw. *Psychology Today*, 35–37.

Marmon, J. (1975). *Psychiatrists and their patients: A national study of private office practice*. Washington, DC: Joint Information Service of the American Psychiatric Association and the National Association for Mental Health.

Marmor, J. (Ed.) (1980). *Homosexual behavior: A modern reappraisal*. New York: Basic Books.

Marques, P., Bradley, J., Shappee, J., & Marques, C. (1982). *Bienestar: Health, well-being and lifestyle choices for Pinal County*. Project West Pinal, University of Arizona Health Sciences Center.

Marsh, C. (1977). A framework for describing subjective states of consciousness. In

N. E. Zinberg (Ed.), *Altered states of consciousness* (pp. 121–144). New York: Free Press.

Martin, B. M., Garrity, T. F., & Bowers, F. R. (1975). The influence of recent life experience on the health of college freshman. *Journal of Psychosomatic Research, 19*, 87–98.

Martin, J. A., King, D. R., Maccoby, E. E., & Jacklin, C. N. (1984). Secular trends and individual differences in toilet-training progress. *Journal of Pediatric Psychology, 9*, 457–467.

Marx, J. L. (1983). The two sides of the brain. *Science, 220*, 488–490.

Maslach, C. (1982). *Burnout: The cost of caring*. Englewood Cliffs, NJ: Prentice-Hall.

Maslow, A. H. (1971). *The farther reaches of human nature*. New York: Viking.

Maslow, A. H. (1954). *Motivation and personality*. New York: Harper.

Maslow, A. H. (1970). *Motivation and personality* (2nd ed.). New York: Harper & Row.

Maslow, A. H. (1965). A philosophy of psychology: The need for a mature science of human nature. In F. T. Severin (Ed.), *Humanistic viewpoint in psychology* (pp. 17–33). New York: McGraw-Hill.

Maslow, A. H. (1969). *The psychology of science*. Chicago: Regnery.

Maslow, A. H. (1967). *Self-actualization and beyond*. In J. F. T. Bugental (Ed.), *Challenges of humanistic psychology*. New York: McGraw-Hill.

Maslow, A. H. (1968). *Toward a psychology of being* (2nd ed.). New York: Van Nostrand.

Masters, W. H., & Johnson, V. E. (1966). *Human sexual response*. Boston: Little, Brown.

Masters, W. H., & Johnson, V. E. (1970). *The pleasure bond: A new look at sexuality and commitment*. Boston: Little, Brown.

Matheny, A. P, Jr., Wilson, R. S., & Nuss, S. M. (1984). Toddler temperament: Stability across settings and over ages. *Child Development, 55*, 1200–1211.

Matossian, M. K. (1982). Ergot and the Salem witchcraft affair. *American Scientist, 70*, 355–357.

Matthews, L. H., & Knight, M. (1963). *The senses of animals*. London: Museum Press.

Maupin, E. W. (1965). Individual differences in response to a Zen meditation exercise. *Journal of Consulting Psychology, 29*, 139–145.

Mayer, J. (1968). *Overweight: Causes, cost, and control*. Englewood Cliffs, NJ: Prentice-Hall.

McBurney, D. H., & Collings, V. B. (1984). *Introduction to sensation/perception* (2nd ed.). Englewood Cliffs, NJ: Prentice-Hall.

McCabe, M. S. (1976). Reactive psychoses and schizophrenia with good prognosis. *Archives of General Psychiatry, 33*(5), 571–576.

McCain, G., & Segal, E. M. (1969). *The game of science*. Monterey, CA: Brooks/Cole.

McCall, R. B. (1984). Developmental changes in mental performance: The effect of the birth of a sibling. *Child Development, 55*, 1317–1321.

McCardel, J., & Murray, E. J. (1974). Nonspecific factors in weekend encounter groups. *Journal of Consulting Psychology, 42*, 337–345.

McCaul, K. D., & Malott, J. M. (1984). Distraction and coping with pain. *Psychological Bulletin, 95*, 516–533.

McCauley, E., & Ehrhardt, A. A. (1976). Female sexual response: Hormonal and behavioral interactions. *Primary Care, 3*, 455.

McClelland, D. C. (1965). Achievement and entrepreneurship. *Journal of Personality and Social Psychology, 1*, 389–393.

McClelland, D. C. (1961). *The achieving society*. New York: Van Nostrand.

McClelland, D. C. (1975). *Power the inner experience*. New York: Irvington.

McClelland, D. C. (1958). Risk taking in children with high and low need for achievement. In J. W. Atkinson (Ed.), *Motives in fantasy action and society*. New York: Van Nostrand.

McClelland, D. C. (1973). Testing for competence rather than "intelligence." *American Psychologist, 28*, 1–14.

McClelland, D. C., & Pilon, D. A. (1983). Sources of adult motives in patterns of parent behavior in early childhood. *Journal of Personality and Social Psychology, 44*, 564–574.

McClelland, L., & Cook, S. W. (1980). Promoting energy conservation in master-metered apartments through group financial incentives. *Journal of Applied and Social Psychology, 10*, 20–31.

McConnell, J. V. (1962). Memory transfer through cannibalism in planarians. *Journal of Neuropsychiatry, 3*, 542–548.

McFadden, D., & Wightman, F. L. (1983). Audition. *Annual Review of Psychology, 34*, 95–128.

McGaugh, J. L. (1983). Hormonal influences on memory. *Annual Review of Psychology, 34*, 297–323.

McGaugh, J. L. (1970). Time-dependent processes in memory storage. In J. L. McGaugh & M. J. Herz (Eds.), *Controversial issues in consolidation of the memory trace*. New York: Atherton.

McGee, M. G., & Snyder, M. (1975). Attribution and behavior: Two field studies. *Journal of Personality and Social Psychology, 32*, 185–190.

McGinnies, E. (1949). Emotionality and perceptual defense. *Psychological Review, 56*, 244–251.

McGlothlin, W. (1975). Drug use and abuse. In M. R. Rosenzweig & L. W. Porter (Eds.), *Annual review of psychology* (p. 26). Palo Alto, CA.

McGregor, D. (1960). *The human side of enterprise*. New York: McGraw-Hill.

McGuire, W. J. (1969). The nature of attitudes and attitude change. In G. Lindzey & E. Aronson (Eds.), *The handbook of social psychology*, Vol. 3. Reading, MA: Addison-Wesley.

McKean, K. (1982, December). Anatomy of an air crash. *Discover*, 19–21.

McKean, K. (1985, June). Decisions. *Discover*, 22–31.

McKean, K. (1984, May). The fine art of reading voters' minds. *Discover*, 66–69.

McKean, K. (1983, November). Memory. *Discover*, 19–27.

McKean, K. (1985, April). Of two minds: Selling the right brain. *Discover*, 30–40.

McKean, K. (1982, August). A picture of Hinckley's brain. *Discover, 3*, 78–80.

McKellar, P. (1965). The investigation of mental images. In S. A. Barnett & A. McLaren (Eds.), *Penguin science journal*. Harmondsworth, England: Penguin.

McMahon, F. B. (1964). A contingent-item method for constructing a short personality questionnaire. *Journal of Applied Psychology*, 197–200.

McMullan, W. E., & Stocking, J. R. (1978). Conceptualizing creativity in three dimensions. *The Journal of Creative Behavior, 12*, 161–167.

McNett, I. (1982, January). Psy.D. fills demand for practitioners. *APA Psychology Monitor, 13*, 10–11.

Mead, M. (1935). *Sex and temperament in three primitive societies*. New York: Morrow.

Meeker, M. (1978). Measuring creativity from the child's point of view. *The Journal of Creative Behavior, 12*, 52–62.

Mehrabian, A. (1969). Significance of posture and position in the communication of attitude and status relationships. *Psychological Bulletin, 71*, 359–372.

Meichenbaum, D. (1977). *Cognitive behavior modification: An integrative approach*. New York: Plenum Press.

Meichenbaum, D., Henshaw, D., & Himel, N. (1982). Coping with stress as a problem-solving process. In H. W. Krohne & L. Laux (Eds.), *Achievement, stress, and anxiety*. New York: Hemisphere.

Melton, R. F. (1978). Resolution of conflicting claims concerning the effect of behavioral objectives on student learning. *Review of Educational Research, 48*, 291–302.

Meltzoff, A., & Moore, M. K. (1977, October). Imitation of facial and manual gestures by human neonates. *Science*, 75–78.

Melzack, R. (1974). Shutting the gate on pain. *Science Year: The World Book Science Annual*. Palo Alto, CA: Field.

Melzack, R., & Dennis, S. G. (1978). Neurophysical foundations of pain. In R. A. Sternbach (Ed.), *The psychology of pain*. New York: Raven Press.

Melzack, R., & Scott, T. H. (1957). The effects of early experience on the response to pain. *Journal of Comparative and Physiological Psychology, 50*, 155–161.

Menninger, K. (1964, April 25). Psychiatrists use dangerous words. *Saturday Evening Post*.

Menzel, E. W. (1978). Cognitive mapping in chimpanzees. In S. H. Hulse, H. Fowler, & W. K. Honig (Eds.), *Cognitive processes in animal behavior*. Hillsdale, NJ: Erlbaum.

Mercer, J. R. (1977). Identifying the gifted Chicano child. In J. L. Martinez (Ed.), *Chicano psychology*. New York: Academic Press.

Meredith, N. (1984, December). The murder epidemic. *Science 84*, 43–48.

Messerer, J., Hunt, E., Meyer, G., & Lerner, J. (1984). Feuerstein's instrumental enrichment: A new approach for activating intellectual potential in learning disabled youth. *Journal of Learning Disabilities, 17,* 322–325.

Messick, D. M., Wilke, H., Brewer, M., Kramer, R. M., Zemke, P. E., & Lui, L. (1983). Individual adaptations and structural change as solutions to social dilemmas. *Journal of Personality and Social Psychology, 44,* 294–309.

Meyer, A. J., Nash, J. D., McAlister, A. L., Maccoby, N., & Farquhar, J. W. (1980). Skills training in a cardiovascular health education campaign. *Journal of Consulting and Clinical Psychology, 48,* 129–142.

Meyers, B. J. (1984). Mother-infant bonding: The status of this critical-period hypothesis. *Developmental Review, 4,* 240–274.

Middlemist, R. D., Knowles, E. S., & Matter, C. F. (1976). Personal space invasions in the lavatory: Suggestive evidence for arousal. *Journal of Personality and Social Psychology, 33,* 541–546.

Milgram, S. (1963). Behavioral study of obedience. *Journal of Abnormal and Social Psychology, 67,* 371–378.

Milgram, S. (1970). The experience of living in the cities: A psychological analysis. *Science, 167,* 1461–1468.

Milgram, S. (1974). *Obedience to authority: An experimental view.* New York: Harper & Row.

Milgram, S. (1967, May). The small-world problem. *Psychology Today,* pp. 61–67.

Milgram, S. (1965). Some conditions of obedience and disobedience to authority. *Human Relations, 18,* 57–76.

Milgram, S., Bickman, L., & Berkowitz, L. (1969). Note on the drawing power of crowds of different size. *Journal of Personality and Social Psychology, 13,* 79–82.

Miller, G. (1980, January). Giving away psychology in the 80's. *Psychology Today,* 38.

Miller, G. (1964). Language and psychology. In E. H. Lennenberg (Ed.), *New directions in the study of language* (pp. 89–107). Cambridge, MA: MIT Press.

Miller, G. (1956). The magical number seven, plus or minus two: Some limits on our capacity for processing information. *Psychological Review, 63,* 81–87.

Miller, G. (1969). On turning psychology over to the unwashed. American Psychological Association paper.

Miller, G. (1977). *Spontaneous apprentices: children and language.* The Seabury Press.

Miller, H. L., & Siegal, P. S. (1972). *Loving: A psychological approach.* New York: Wiley.

Miller, L. K. (1976). The design of better communities through the application of behavioral principles. In W. E. Craighead, A. E. Kazdin, & M. J. Mahone (Eds.), *Behavior modification: Principles, issues, and applications.* Boston: Houghton Mifflin.

Miller, N. E. (1983). Behavioral medicine: Symbiosis between laboratory and clinic. *Annual Review of Psychology, 34,* 1–31.

Miller, N. E. (1944). Experimental studies of conflict. In J. McV. Hunt (Ed.), *Personality and the behavior disorders,* Vol. I (pp. 431–465). New York: Ronald Press.

Miller, N. E. (1941). The frustration-aggression hypothesis. *Psychological Review, 48,* 337–342.

Miller, N. E. (1969). Learning of visceral and glandular responses. *Science, 163,* 434–445.

Miller, N. E. (1982, May). Understanding psychological man: A state of the science report. *Psychology Today.*

Miller, N. E. (1985). The value of behavioral research on animals. *American Psychologist, 40,* 423–440.

Miller, N. E., & Bugelski. R. (1970). The influence of frustration imposed by the in-group on attitudes expressed toward out-groups. In R. I. Evans & R. M. Rozelle (Eds.), *Social psychology in life.* Boston: Allyn & Bacon.

Miller, N. E. & Di Cara, L. V. (1967). Instrumental learning of heart rate changes in curarized rats: Shaping and specificity to discriminative stimulus. *Journal of Comparative and Physiological Psychology, 63,* 12–19.

Miller, N. E., & Dworkin, B. R. (1974). Visceral learning: Recent difficulties with curarized rats and significant problems for human research. In D. A. Obrist et al. (Eds.), *Cardiovascular physiology* (pp. 312–331). Chicago: Aldine.

Miller, W. R., Rosellini, R. A., & Seligman, M. E. P. (1977). In J. D. Maser & M. E. P. Seligman (Eds.), *Psychopathology: Experimental models* (pp. 104–120). San Francisco: Freeman.

Milner, B. (1965). Memory disturbance after bilateral hippocampal lesions. In P. Milner & S. Glickman (Eds.), *Cognitive processes and the brain* (pp. 97–111). Princeton, NJ: Van Nostrand.

Milunsky, A. (1977). *Know your genes.* Boston: Houghton Mifflin.

Mischel, W. (1968). *Personality and assessment.* New York: Wiley.

Mischel, W. (1973). Toward a cognitive social learning reconceptualization of personality. *Psychological Review, 80,* 252–283.

Mitchell-Heggs, N., Kelly, D., & Richardson, A. (1976). Stereotactic limbic leucotomy—A follow-up at 16 months. *British Journal of Psychiatry, 128,* 226–240.

Money, J. (1977). Human hermaphroditism. In F. A. Beach (Ed.), *Human sexuality in four perspectives.* Baltimore: Johns Hopkins University Press.

Money, J. (1965). Psychosexual differentiation. In J. Money (Ed.), *Sex research: New developments* (pp. 3–23). New York: Holt, Rinehart and Winston.

Money, J. (1970). Sexual dimorphism and homosexual gender identity. *Psychological Bulletin, 6,* 425–440.

Money, J., & Ehrhardt, A. (1972). *Man and woman, boy and girl.* Baltimore: Johns Hopkins University Press.

Moore, D. C. (1981). Anorexia nervosa. In S. J. Mule (Ed.), *Behavior in excess.* New York: The Free Press.

Moore-Ede, M. C., Sulzman, F. M., & Fuller, C. A. (1982). *The clocks that time us.* Cambridge, MA: Harvard University Press.

Moreno, J. L. (1953). *Who shall survive?* New York: Beacon.

Morgan, W. P. (1978). The mind of the marathoner. *Psychology Today, 11*(11), 38–49.

Moriarty, T. (1975, April). A nation of willing victims. *Psychology Today,* 43–50.

Moritz, A. P., & Zamchech, N. (1946). Sudden and unexpected deaths of young soldiers. *American Medical Association Archives of Pathology, 42,* 459–494.

Moruzzi, G., & Magoun, H. W. (1949). Brain stem reticular formation and activation of the EEG. *EEG and Clinical Neurophysiology, 1,* 455–473.

Moser, D. (1965, May 7). The nightmare of life with Billy. *Life.*

Moss, H. A., & Susman, E. J. (1980). Longitudinal study of personality development. In O. G. Brim, Jr., & J. Kagan (Eds.), *Constancy and change in human development* (pp. 530–595). Cambridge, MA: Harvard University Press.

Moss, S., & Butler, D. C. (1978). The scientific credibility of ESP. *Perceptual and Motor Skills, 46.*

Moyer, R. S., & Bayer, R. H. (1976). Mental comparison and the symbolic distance effect. *Cognitive Psychology, 8,* 228–246.

Mueller, J. H., & Thompson, W. B. (1984). Test anxiety and distinctiveness of personal information. In H. M. Van Der Ploeg, R. Schwarzer, & C. D. Spielberger (Eds.), *Advances in test anxiety research,* Vol. 3 (pp. 21–37). Hillsdale, NJ: Erlbaum.

Munn, N. L., Fernald, L. D., Jr., & Fernald, P. S. (1969). *Introduction to psychology* (2nd ed.). Boston: Houghton Mifflin.

Murphy, L. B., & Moriarty, A. E. (1976). V*ulnerability, coping and growth.* New Haven, CT: Yale University Press.

Murray, F. S. (1980). Estimation of performance levels by students in introductory psychology. *Teaching of Psychology, 7,* 61–62.

Mussen, P. H., Conger, J. J., & Kagan, J. (1969). *Child development and personality* (3rd ed.). New York: Harper & Row.

Mussen, P. H., Conger, J. J., Kagan, J., & Geiwitz, J. (1979). *Psychological development: A life span approach.* New York: Harper & Row.

Myers, A. (1980). *Experimental psychology.* New York: Van Nostrand.

Nachman, M. (1970). Learned taste and temperature aversions due to lithium chloride sickness after temporal delays. *Journal of Comparative and Physiological Psychology, 73,* 22–30.

Naeye, R. L. (1980). Sudden infant death. *Scientific American, 4*(242), 56–62.

Nahas, G. G. (1979b). *Keep off the grass.* Elmsford, NY: Pergamon Press.

Nahas, G. G., & Paton, W. D. M. (1979a). *Marijuana, biological effects.* Elmsford, NY: Pergamon Press.

Naranjo, C. (1970). Present-centeredness: Technique, prescription, and ideal. In J. Fagan & I. L. Shepherd (Eds), *What is Gestalt therapy?* (pp. 63–97). New York: Harper & Row.

Narayanan, V. K., & Nath, R. (1981). A field test of some attitudinal and behavioral consequences of flexitime. *Journal of Applied Psychology, 67,* 214–218.

National Commision on Marijuana and Drug Abuse. (1973). *Drug use in America: The problem in perspective*. Washington, DC: U.S. Government Printing Office.

National Household Survey on Drug Abuse. (1982). National Institute of Drug Abuse.

National Institute on Drug Abuse (NIDA). (1976). *Marijuana and health*. Princeton, NJ: Response Analysis Corporation.

National Institute of Mental Health. (1982). *Television and behavior: Ten years of scientific progress and implications for the eighties*. Washington, DC: U.S. Government Printing Office.

Nauta, W. J. H., & Feirtag, M. (1979). The organization of the brain. *Scientific American*, 88–111.

Navran, L. (1967). Communication and adjustment in marriage. *Family Process*, 6, 173–184.

Neff, W. S. (1977). *Work and human behavior* (2nd ed.). Chicago: Aldine.

Nelson, E. (1976, May). New facts on biorhythms. *Science Digest*, 71–75.

Nelson, H. (1982, April 16). Twins: Studies of striking similarities. *Los Angeles Times*, p. 24.

Nelson, N., Enkin, M., Saigal, S., Bennett, K., Milner, R., & Sackett, D. (1980). A randomized clinical trial of the Leboyer approach to childbirth. *New England Journal of Medicine*, 302, 655–660.

Nelson, R., & Crutchfield, R. S. (1970). Mathematicians: The creative researcher and the average Ph.D. *Journal of Consulting and Clinical Psychology*, 34, 250–257.

Neufeld, R. W. (1970). The effect of experimentally altered cognitive appraisal on pain tolerance. *Psychonomic Science*, 20(2), 106–107.

Neugarten, B. (1971, December). Grow old along with me! The best is yet to be. *Psychology Today*, 45.

Neuringer, A. J. (1970). Superstitious key pecking after three peck-produced reinforcements. *Journal of the Experimental Analysis of Behavior*, 13, 127–134.

Newman, B. M., & Newman, P. R. (1978). *Infancy and childhood: Development and its contexts*. New York: Wiley.

Newman, P. R. (1982). The peer group. In B. B. Wolman, G. Stricker, S. J. Ellman, P. Keith-Spiegel, & D. S. Palermo, (Eds.), *Handbook of developmental psychology*. Englewood Cliffs, NJ: Prentice-Hall.

Nickerson, R. S., & Adams, M. J. (1979). Long-term memory for a common object. *Cognitive Psychology*, 11, 287–307.

Nicogossian, A. E., & Parker, J. F. (1982). *Space physiology and medicine*. Washington, DC: National Aeronautics and Space Administration.

Nicol, S. E., & Gottesman, I. I. (1983). Clues to the genetics and neurobiology of schizophrenia. *American Scientist*, 71, 398–404.

Nomellini, S., & Katz, R. C. (1983). Effects of anger control training on abusive parents. *Cognitive Therapy and Research*, 7, 57–68.

Nurnberger, J. I., & Zimmerman, J. (1970). Applied analysis of human behaviors: An alternative to conventional motivational inferences and unconscious determination in therapeutic programming. *Behavior Therapy*, 1, 59–69.

O'Brien, R. M., Figlerski, R. W., Howard, S. R., & Caggiano, J. (1981, August). *The effects of multi-year, guaranteed contracts on the performance of pitchers in major league baseball*. Paper presented at the annual meeting of the American Psychological Association, Los Angeles, CA.

Olds, J. (1977). *Drives and reinforcements: Behavioral studies of hypothalamic functions*. New York: Raven Press.

Olds, J., & Milner, P. (1954). Positive reinforcement produced by electrical stimulation of septal area and other regions of rat brain. *Journal of Comparative and Physiological Psychology*, 47, 419–427.

Olds, M. E., & Fobes, J. L. (1981). The central basis of motivation: Intracranial self-stimulation studies. *Annual Review of Psychology*, 32, 523–574.

O'Leary, K. D., & Becker, W. C. (1967). Behavior modification of an adjustment class: A token reinforcement program. *Exceptional Children*, 33, 637–642.

Oliver, C. M., & Oliver, G. M. (1978). Gentle birth: Its safety and its effect on neonatal behavior. *Journal of Obstetrical, Gynecological and Neonatal Nursing*.

Olmstead, B. (1983, February 17). More heavy drinking in colleges. *Los Angeles Times*.

O'Malley, M. N., & Andrews, L. (1983). The effect of mood and incentives on helping: Are some things money can't buy? *Motivation and Emotion*, 7, 179.

Orlick, T. D. (1975). The sports environment: A capacity to enhance—a capacity to destroy. In B. S. Rushall (Ed.), *The status of psychomotor learning and sport psychology research*. Dartmouth, Nova Scotia: Sport Science Associates.

Orne, M. T., & Wilson, S. K. (1978). On the nature of alpha feedback training. In G. E. Schwartz & D. Shapiro (Eds.), *Consciousness and self-regulation* (pp. 359–400). New York: Plenum.

Ornstein, R. E. (1972). *The psychology of consciousness*. San Francisco: Freeman.

Ornstein, R. E., & Galin, D. (1976). Physiological studies of consciousness. In P. Lec, R. E. Ornstein, D. Galin, A. Deichman, & C. Tart (Eds.), *Symposium on consciousness*. New York: Viking Press.

Orpen, C. (1981). Effect of flexible working hours on employee satisfaction and performance: A field experiment. *Journal of Applied Psychology*, 66, 113–115.

Osgood, C. E. (1952). The nature and measurement of meaning. *Psychological Bulletin*, 49, 197–237.

Oskamp, S. (1984). *Applied social psychology*. Englewood Cliffs, NJ: Prentice-Hall.

Oster, G. (1984). Muscle sounds. *Scientific American*, 250(3), 108–114.

Overmier, J. B., & Seligman, M. E. P. (1967). Effects of inescapable shock upon subsequent escape and avoidance learning. *Journal of Comparative and Physiological Psychology*, 63, 23–33.

Overton, D. A. (1985). Contextual stimulus effects of drugs and internal states. In P. D. Balsam & A. Tomie (Eds.), *Context and learning* (pp. 357–384). Hillsdale, NJ: Erlbaum.

Owen, J. D. (1976). Flextime: Some problems and solutions. *Industrial and Labor Relations Review*, 29, 152–160.

Owen, M. T., Easterbrooks, M. A., Chase-Lansdale, L., & Goldberg, W. A. (1984). The relation between maternal employment status and the stability of attachments to mother and to father. *Child Development*, 55, 1894–1901.

Owens, W. A., & Schoenfeldt, L. F. (1979). Toward a classification of persons. *Journal of Applied Psychology Monograph*, 64, 569–607.

Pagano, R. R. (1981). *Understanding statistics*. St. Paul, MN: West.

Pagano, R. R., & Warrenburg, S. (1983) Meditation. In R. J. Davidson, G. E. Schwartz, & D. Shapiro (Eds.). *Consciousness and self-regulation* (pp. 153–210). New York: Plenum.

Page, J. D. (1971). *Psychopathology*. Chicago: Aldine.

Paivio, A. (1969). Mental imagery in associative learning and memory. *Psychological Review*, 76, 241–263.

Palazolli, M. (1978). *Self starvation*. Jason Aronson.

Palkovitz, R. J., & Lore, R. K. (1980). Note taking and note review: Why students fail questions based on lecture material. *Teaching of Psychology*, 7, 159–160.

Palmer, M. H., Lloyd, M. E., & Lloyd, K. E. (1977). An experimental analysis of electricity conservation procedures. *Journal of Applied Behavior Analysis*, 10, 665–671.

Pappenheimer, J. R. (1976, August). The sleep factor. *Scientific American*.

Pardine, P., Napoli, A., Goodman, M., & Schure, M. (1981, August). *Physiological correlates of recent life stress experience*. Paper presented at the annual convention of the American Psychological Association, Los Angeles, CA.

Parke, R. D. (1982). The father of the child. From *The Sciences* (April 1979). Reprinted in *Psychology 82/83.) Guilford, CT: Dushkin.

Parke, R. D., & Asher, S. R. (1983). Social and personality development. *Annual Review of Psychology*, 34, 465–509.

Parke, R. D., & Sawin, D. B. (1977, November). Fathering: It's a major role. *Psychology Today*.

Parkes, C. M. (1979). Grief: The painful reaction to the loss of a loved one. *Monograph, University of California, San Diego*.

Parks, T. E. (1984). Illusory figures: A (mostly) atheoretical review. *Psychological Bulletin*, 95, 282–300.

Parlee, M. B. (1979). Psychology and women. *Journal of Women in Culture and Society*, 5, 121–133.

Parlee, M. B., & The Editors of *Psychology Today* Magazine. (1979, October). The friendship bond. *Psychology Today*.

Parnes, S. J. (1967). *Creative behavior workbook*. New York: Scribner.

Pasachoff, J. (1981). *Contemporary Astronomy* (2nd ed.). New York: Holt, Rinehart and Winston.

Patterson, F. (1978). Conversations with a gorilla. *National Geographic, 154*(4), 438–465.

Patterson, G. R. (1982). *Coercive family process.* Eugene, OR: Castilia Press.

Pavlov, I. P. (1927). *Conditioned reflexes* (G. V. Anrep, Trans.). New York: Dover.

Pelham, W. E. (1977). Withdrawal of a stimulant drug and concurrent behavioral intervention in the treatment of a hyperactive child. *Behavior Therapy, 8,* 473–479.

Pellegrino, J. W. (1985, October). Anatomy of analogy. *Psychology Today,* 49–54.

Pelton, T. (1983, May). The shootists. *Science 83, 4*(4), 84–86.

Penfield, W. (1957, April 27). Brain's record of past a continuous movie film. *Science News Letter,* 265.

Penfield, W. (1958). *The excitable cortex in conscious man.* Springfield, IL: Charles C Thomas.

Perin, C. T. (1943). A quantitative investigation of the delay of reinforcement gradient. *Journal of Experimental Psychology, 32,* 37–51.

Perkins, D. G., & Perkins, F. M. (1976). *Nailbiting and cuticlebiting: Kicking the habit.* Richardson, TX: Self Control Press.

Perkoff, G. T. (1980). The meaning of "experimental." In E. S. Valenstein (Ed.), *The psychosurgery debate.* San Francisco: Freeman.

Perlmutter, F., & Silverman, H. A. (1972). CMHC: A structural anachronism. *Social Work, 17,* 78–84.

Perls, F. (1969). *Gestalt therapy verbatim.* Lafayette, CA: Real People Press.

Persky, H., Lief, H. I., Straus, D., Miller, W. R., & O'Brien, C. P. (1978). Plasma testosterone level and sexual behavior of couples. *Archives of Sexual Behavior, 7,* 157–173.

Peters, W. A. (1971). *A class divided.* Garden City, NY: Doubleday.

Peterson, L. R., & Peterson, M. J. (1959). Short-term retention of individual verbal items. *Journal of Experimental Psychology, 58,* 193–198.

Peterson, P. L. (1979). Direct instruction: Effective for what and for whom?" *Educational Leadership, 37,* 46–48.

Phillips, D. (1982). The impact of fictional television stories on U.S. adult fatalities: New evidence on the effect of mass media on violence. *American Journal of Sociology, 87,* 1340–1359.

Phillips, J. L. (1969). *Origins of intellect: Piaget's theory.* San Francisco: Freeman.

Piaget, J. (1952). *The origins of intelligence in children.* New York: International University Press.

Piaget, J. (1951; original French, 1945). *The psychology of intelligence.* New York: Norton.

Pierrel, R., & Sherman, J. G. (1963, February). Train your pet the Barnabus way. *Brown Alumni Monthly.*

Piliavin, I. M., Rodin, J., & Piliavin, J. A. (1969). Good samaritanism: An underground phenomenon? *Journal of Personality and Social Psychology, 13,* 289–299.

Pilkonis, P. A. (1977). The behavioral consequences of shyness. *Journal of Personality, 45,* 596–611.

Pines, M. (1963, May). How three-year-olds teach themselves to read—and love it. *Harper's Magazine,* 58–64.

Pines, M. (1970, November 29). Infants are smarter than anybody thinks. *The New York Times Magazine,* pp. 32–33, 110, 114–120.

Pines, M. (1980, December). The sinister hand. *Science 80,* 26–27.

Pines, M. (1969, July 6). Why some three-year-olds get A's and some get C's. *The New York Times Magazine,* pp. 4–5, 10–17.

Playboy, (1969). *16*(2), 46.

Plutchik, R. (1980). *Emotion.* New York: Harper & Row.

Polivy, J., & Herman, C. P. (1985). Dieting and Binging. *American Psychologist, 40,* 193–201.

Pope, K. S. (1980). Defining and studying romantic love. In K. S. Pope (Ed.), *On love and loving* (pp. 1–26). San Francisco: Jossey-Bass.

Premack, A. J., & Premack, D. (1972, October). Teaching language to an ape. *Scientific American,* 92–99.

Premack, D. (1983). Animal cognition. *Annual Review of Psychology, 34,* 351–362.

Premack, D. (1970, September). The education of S*A*R*A*H. *Psychology Today,* 54–58.

Premack, D. (1965). Reinforcement theory. In D. Levine (Ed.), *Nebraska symposium on motivation.* Lincoln: University of Nebraska Press.

Premack, D., & Premack, A. J. (1983). *The mind of an ape.* New York: Norton.

President's Commission on Mental Health. (1978). *Report to the President.* Washington DC: U.S. Government Printing Office.

Pressley, M., Levine, J. R., Nakamura, G. V., Hope, D. J., Bispo, J. G., & Toye, A. R. (1980). The keyword method of foreign vocabulary learning: An investigation of its generalizability. *Journal of Applied Psychology, 65,* 635–642.

Pritchard, R. M. (1961). A collimator stabilizing system. *Quarterly Journal of Experimental Psychology, 13,* 181–183.

Pueschel, S. M., Canning, C. D., Murphy, A., & Zausmer, E. (1978). *Down syndrome: Growing and learning.* Kansas City, MO: Sheed Andrews & McMeel.

Pursch, J. A. (1983, June 12). Cocaine can give you the business. *Los Angeles Times,* Part VII, p. 12.

Rafaeli, A., & Klimoski, R. J. (1983). Predicting sales success through handwriting analysis: An evaluation of the effects of training and handwriting sample content. *Journal of Applied Psychology, 68,* 212–217.

Rahe, R. H. (1972). Subjects' recent life changes and their near-future illness reports. *Annals of Clinical Research, 4,* 250–265.

Randi, J. (1980). *Flim-flam!* New York: Lippincott & Crowell.

Raven, B. H. (1974). The analysis of power and power preference. In J. T. Tebeschi (Ed.), *Prospectus on social power.* Chicago: Aldine.

Rechtschaffen, A., Gilliland, M. A., Bergmann, B. M., & Winter, J. B. (1983). Physiological correlates of prolonged sleep deprivation in rats. *Science, 221,* 182–184.

Reif, A. E. (1981). The causes of cancer. *American Scientist, 69,* 437–447.

Reiser, M. (1985). *Mind, brain, body: Toward a convergence of psychoanalysis.* New York: Basic.

Renwick, P. A., & Lawler, E. E. (1978). What you really want from your job. *Psychology Today, 11*(12), 53–65.

Rescorla, R. (1980). *Pavlovian second-order conditioning: Studies in associative learning.* MacEachren Lectures, Halsted Press.

Resnick, R. B., Kestenbaum, R. S., & Schwartz, K. L. (1977). Acute systemic effects of cocaine in man: A controlled study in intranasal and intravenous routes. *Science, 195,* 696–698.

Reybowski, J. (1982). Social motivation. *Annual Review of Psychology, 33,* 123–154.

Rhine, J. B. (1977). History of experimental studies. In B. B. Wolman (Ed.), *Handbook of parapsychology.* Van Nostrand Reinhold.

Rhine, J. B. (1953). *New world of the mind.* New York: Sloane.

Rhine, J. B. (1974). Security versus deception in parapsychology. *Journal of Parapsychology, 38,* 99–121.

Ricketts, M. S., & Galloway, R. E. (1984). Effects of three different one-hour single-session treatments for test anxiety. *Psychological Reports, 54,* 113–119.

Rieger, M. G. (1976, October 30). Pain control through hypnosis. *Science News.*

Rimland, B. (1978). Inside the mind of the autistic savant. *Psychology Today, 12,* 68–80.

Rimland, B., & Munsinger, H. (1977). Letter to *Science, 195,* 246–247.

Rincover, A., Newsom, C. D., Lovaas, O. I., & Koegel, R. L. (1977). Some motivational properties of sensory stimulation in psychotic children. *Journal of Experimental Child Psychology, 24,* 312–323.

Ristow, W. (1978, November). Larry P. versus IQ tests. *The Progressive, 42,* 48–50.

Ritchie, R. J., & Moses, J. L. (1983). Assessment center correlates of women's advancement into middle management: A 7-year longitudinal analysis. *Journal of Applied Psychology, 68,* 227–231.

Roach, M. (1985, August). Reflection in a fatal mirror. *Discover,* 76–85.

Roberts, D. F., & Bachen, C. M. (1981). Mass communication effects. *Annual Review of Psychology, 32,* 307–356.

Robertson, T. S., Zielinski, J., & Ward, S. (1984). *Consumer behavior.* Glenview, IL: Scott, Foresman.

Robinson, F. P. (1941). *Effective behavior.* New York: Harper & Row.

Robinson, H. B., & Robinson, N. M. (1970). Mental retardation. In P. H. Mussen (Ed.), *Carmichael's manual of child psychology,* Vol. 2 (3rd ed.), New York: Wiley.

Robson, P. (1984). Prewalking locomotor movements and their use in predicting standing and walking. *Child Care, Health & Development, 10,* 317–330.

Rock, I., & Kaufman, L. (1962). The moon illusion II. *Science, 136,* 1023–1031.

Rodgers, J. E. (1982, July/August). Roots of madness. *Science 82.*

Rodin, J. (1981). Current status of the internal-external hypothesis for obesity: What went wrong? *American Psychologist, 36,* 361–372.

Rodin, J. (1978). Stimulus-bound behavior and biological self-regulation: Feeding, obesity, and external control. In G. E. Schwartz & D. Shapiro (Eds.), *Consciousness and self-regulation* (pp. 215–239). New York: Plenum.

Rogers, C. R. (1962, January 28). Learning to be free. A paper given at a session on "Conformity and Diversity" in the conference on "Man and Civilization," sponsored by the University of California School of Medicine, San Francisco, CA.

Rogers, C. R. (1957). The necessary and sufficient conditions of therapeutic personality change. *Journal of Consulting Psychology, 21,* 95–103.

Rogers, C. R. (1961). *On becoming a person: A therapists view of psychotherapy.* Boston: Houghton Mifflin.

Rogers, C. R. (1959). A theory of therapy, personality, and interpersonal relationships, as developed in the client-centered framework. In S. Koch (Ed.), *Psychology: A study of a science,* Vol. 3. New York: McGraw-Hill.

Rogers, C. R. (1980). *A way of being.* Boston: Houghton Mifflin.

Rogers, J. M. (1971, September). Drug abuse—Just what the doctor ordered. *Psychology Today,* 16–24.

Rohsenow, D. J., & Smith, R. E. (1982). Irrational beliefs as predictors of negative affective states. *Motivation and Emotion, 6,* 299–301.

Rokeach, M. (1960). *The open and closed mind.* New York: Basic Books.

Rorer, L. G., & Widiger, T. A. (1983). Personality structure and assessment. *Annual Review of Psychology, 34,* 431–463.

Rosch, E. (1977). Classification of real-world objects: Origins and representations in cognition. In P. N. Johnson-Laird & P. C. Wason (Eds.), *Thinking: Reading in cognitive science.* Cambridge: Cambridge University Press.

Rose, K. J. (1984, February). How animals think. *Science Digest, 89,* 59–61.

Rosen, J. C., & Leitenberg, H. (1982). Bulimia nervosa: Treatment with exposure and response prevention. *Behavior Therapy, 13,* 117–124.

Rosenbaum, M. B. (1979). The changing body image of the adolescent girl. In M. Sugar (Ed.), *Female adolescent development.* New York: Brunner/Mazel.

Rosenberg, J., & Pettinati, H. M. (1984). Differential memory complaints after bilateral and unilateral ECT. *American Journal of Psychiatry, 14,* 1071–1074.

Rosenhan, D. L. (1973). On being sane in insane places. *Science, 179,* 250–258.

Rosenman, R. H., Brand, R. J., Jenkins, C. D., Friedman, M., Straus, R., & Wurm, M. (1975). Coronary heart disease in the Western Collaborative Group Study: Final follow-up experience of 8 1/2 years. *Journal of the American Medical Association, 233,* 872–877.

Rosenthal, D. (1963). *The Genain quadruplets.* New York: Basic Books.

Rosenthal, D., & Quinn, O. W. (1977). Quadruplet hallucinations: Phenotypic variations of a schizophrenic genotype. *Archives of General Psychiatry, 34*(7), 817–827.

Rosenthal, R. (1965). Clever Hans: A case study of scientific method. Introduction to *Clever Hans: (The horse of Mr. Von Osten),* O. Pfungst. New York: Holt, Rinehart and Winston.

Rosenthal, R. (1976). *Experimenter effects in behavioral research.* New York: Irvington.

Rosenthal, R. (1973, September). The Pygmalion effect lives. *Psychology Today,* 56–63.

Rosenthal, T. L., Linehan, K. S., Kelley, J. E., Rosenthal, R. H., Theobald, D. E., & Davis, A. F. (1978). Group aversion by imaginal, vicarious and shared recipient-observer shocks. *Behavior Research and Therapy, 16,* 421–427.

Rosenthal, T. L., & Rosenthal, R. (1980). *The vicious cycle of stress reaction.* Memphis, TN: Stress Management Clinic, Department of Psychiatry, University of Tennessee College of Medicine.

Rosenthal, T. L., & Zimmerman, B. J. (1978). *Social learning and cognition.* New York: Academic Press.

Roskies, E., & Lazarus, R. (1980). Coping theory and the teaching of coping skills. In P. Davidson & S. Davidson (Eds.), *Behavioral medicine: Changing health life styles.* New York: Brunner/Mazel.

Ross, J. (1976, March). The resources of binocular perception. *Scientific American,* 80–86.

Ross, L. (1977). The intuitive psychologist and his shortcomings: Distortions in the attribution process. In L. Berkowitz (Ed.), *Advances in experimental social psychology.* New York: Academic Press.

Ross, M., Karniol, R., & Rothstein, M. (1976). Reward contingency and intrinsic motivation in children. *Journal of Personality and Social Psychology, 33,* 442–447.

Rotter, J. B., & Hochreich, D. J. (1975). *Personality.* Glenview, IL: Scott, Foresman.

Rowley, P. T. (1984). Genetic screening: Marvel or menace? *Science, 225,* 138–144.

Rubin, V., & Comitas, L. (Eds.). (1975). *Ganja in Jamaica.* The Hague: Mouton.

Rubin, Z. (1975). Disclosing oneself to a stranger: Reciprocity and its limits. *Journal of Experimental and Social Psychology, 11,* 233–260.

Rubin, Z. (1970, December). Jokers wild in the lab. *Psychology Today.*

Rubin, Z. (1973). *Liking and loving: An invitation to social psychology.* New York: Holt.

Rubin, Z. (1970). Measurement of romantic love. *Journal of Personality and Social Psychology, 16,* 265–273.

Rubinstein, E. A. (1978). Television and the young viewer. *American Scientist, 66,* 685–693.

Rubinstein, E. A., Liebert, R. M., Neale, J. M., & Poulos, R. W. (1974). *Assessing television's influence on children's prosocial behavior.* New York: Brookdale International Institute.

Ruch, F. L., & Zimbardo, P. G. (1971). *Psychology and life.* (8th ed.). Glenview, IL: Scott, Foresman.

Rudestam, K. E. (1971). Stockholm and Los Angeles: A cross-cultural study of the communication of suicidal intent. *Journal of Consulting and Clinical Psychology, 36,* 82–90.

Ruff, H. A., & Birch, H. G. (1974). Infant visual fixation: The effect of concentricity, curvilinearity, and number of directions. *Journal of Experimental Child Psychology, 17,* 460–473.

Rushall, B. S. (1975). Applied psychology in sports. In B. S. Rushall (Ed.), *The status of psychomotor learning and sport psychology research.* Dartmouth, Nova Scotia: Sports Science Associates.

Rushton, N. A. H. (1975, March). Visual pigments and color blindness. *Scientific American,* 64–74.

Saarni, C. (1982). Social and affective functions of nonverbal behavior: Developmental concerns. In R. S. Feldman (Ed.), *Development of nonverbal behavior in children* (pp. 123–148). New York: Springer-Verlag.

Saegert, S., Swap, W., & Zajonc, R. B. (1973). Exposure, context, and interpersonal attraction. *Journal of Personality and Social Psychology, 25,* 234–242.

Salame, R. F. (1984). Test anxiety: Its determinants, manifestations and consequences. In H. M. Van Der Ploeg, R. Schwarzer, & C. D. Spielberger (Eds.), *Advances in test anxiety research,* Vol. 3 (pp. 83–119). Hillsdale, NJ: Erlbaum.

Salmela, J. H. (1974). An information processing approach to volleyball. *C.V.A. Technical Journal, 1,* 49–62.

Salmela, J. H. (1975). Psycho-motor task demands of artistic gymnastics. In J. H. Salmela (Ed.), *The advanced study of gymnastics: A textbook.* Sundby Publications.

Salmoni, A. W., Schmidt, R. A., & Walter, C. B. (1984). Knowledge of results and motor learning: A review and critical reappraisal. *Psychological Bulletin, 95,* 355–386.

Sanders, G. S., & Simmons, W. L. (1983). Use of hypnosis to enhance eyewitness accuracy: Does it work? *Journal of Applied Psychology, 68,* 70–77.

Santrock, J. W. (1984). *Adolescence.* Dubuque, IA: Brown.

Sarason, I. G. (1980). Introduction to the study of test anxiety. In I. G. Sarason (Ed.), *Test anxiety, theory, research and applications* (pp. 3–14). Hillsdale, NJ: Erlbaum.

Sarason, I. G. (1975). Test anxiety, attention, and the general problem of anxiety. In C. D. Spielberger & I. G. Sarason (Eds), *Stress and anxiety,* Vol. 1. Washington, DC: Hemisphere.

Sarason, I. G. (1981). Test anxiety, stress, and social support. *Journal of Personality*, 49, 101–114.

Savage-Rumbaugh, E. S., Rumbaugh, D. M., & Boysen, S. (1980). Do apes use language? *American Scientist*, 68, 49–61.

Saxe, L., Dougherty, D., & Cross, T. (1985). The validity of polygraph testing. *American Psychologist*, 40, 355–366.

Scarr, S., Webber, P. L., Weinberg, R. A., & Wittig, M. A. (1981). Personality resemblance among adolescents and their parents in biologically related and adoptive families. *Journal of Personality and Social Psychology*, 40, 885–898.

Scarr, S., & Weinberg, R. A. (1977). Intellectual similarities within families of both adopted and biological children. *Intelligence*, 1, 170–191.

Scarr-Salapatek, S. (1971). Race, social class, and I.Q. *Science*, 174, 1223–1228.

Scarr-Salapatek, S., & Weinberg, R. A. (1975, December). When black children grow up in white homes. . . . *Psychology Today*.

Schachter, S. (1951). Communication, deviation, and rejection. *Journal of Abnormal and Social Psychology*, 46, 190–207.

Schachter, S. (1978). Pharmacological and psychological determinants of smoking. In R. E. Thornton (Ed.), *Smoking behavior*. Edinburgh: Churchill Livingston.

Schachter, S. (1959). *Psychology of affiliation*. Stanford, CA: Stanford University Press.

Schachter, S., & Grose, L. P. (1968). Manipulated time and eating behavior. *Journal of Personality and Social Psychology*, 10, 98–106.

Schachter, S., & Rodin, J. (1974). *Obese humans and rats*. Potomac, MD: Erlbaum.

Schachter, S., & Wheeler, L. (1962). Epinephrine, chlorpromazine and amusement. *Journal of Abnormal and Social Psychology*, 65, 121–128.

Schaie, K. W. (1980). Age changes in intelligence. In R. L. Sprott (Ed.), *Age, learning ability, and intelligence*. New York: Van Nostrand Reinhold.

Schally, A. B., Kastin, A. J., & Arimura, A. (1977). Hypothalamic hormones: The link between brain and body. *American Scientist*, 65, 712–719.

Schein, E. H., Hill, W. F., Lubin, A., & Williams, H. L. (1957). Distinguishing characteristics of collaborators and resistors among American prisoners of war. *Journal of Abnormal and Social Psychology*, 55, 197–201.

Schein, E. H., Schneier, I., & Barker, C. H. (1961). *Coercive persuasion*. New York: Norton.

Schiff, M., Duyme, M., Dumaret, A., Stewart, J., Tomkiewicz, S., & Feingold, J. (1978). Intellectual status of working-class children adopted early into upper-middle-class families. *Science*, 200, 1503–1504.

Schlesier-Stropp, B. (1984). Bulimia: A review of the literature. *Psychological Bulletin*, 38, 247–257.

Schless, A. P. (1977). Life events and illness: A three-year prospective study. *British Journal of Psychiatry*, 131, 26–34.

Schlosberg, H. (1954). Three dimensions of emotion. *Psychological Review*, 61, 81–88.

Schmeidler, G. R. (1977). Methods for controlled research on ESP and PK. In B. B. Wolman (Ed.), *Handbook of parapsychology*. New York: Van Nostrand Reinhold.

Schmidt, J. A. (1976). *Help yourself: A guide to self-change*. Champaign, IL: Research Press.

Schneidman, E. S. (1971). You and death. *Psychology Today*. 5(1), 43–45, 74–80.

Schneidman, E. S., Farberow, N. L., & Cabista, L. (1965). *Some facts about suicide causes and prevention*. Washington, DC: U.S. Government Printing Office.

Schommer, N. (1984, October). Shrinks on the air. *Discover*, 68–70.

Schopler, E. (1978). Changing parental involvement in behavioral treatment. In W. Rutter & E. Schopler (Eds.), *Autism: A reappraisal of concepts and treatment*. New York: Plenum.

Schreiber, F. R. (1973). *Sybil*. Chicago: Regency.

Schuele, J. G., & Wiesenfeld, A. R. (1983). Autonomic response to self-critical thought. *Cognitive Therapy and Research*, 7, 189–194.

Schultz, D. P. (1979). *Psychology in use: An introduction to applied psychology*. New York: Macmillan.

Schulz, R. (1978). *The psychology of death, dying and bereavement*. Reading, MA: Addison-Wesley.

Schuman, M. (1980). The psychophysiological model of meditation and altered states of consciousness: A critical review. In J. M. Davidson & R. C. Davidson (Eds.), *The psychobiology of consciousness*. New York: Plenum.

Schwartz, B. (1984). *Psychology of learning and behavior* (2nd ed.). New York: Norton.

Schwartz, C. J., McGill, H. C., & Rogers, W. R. (1980). Smoking and cardiovascular diseases. In G. B. Gori & F. G. Bock (Eds.), *Banbury report*. Cold Spring Harbor Laboratory.

Science News. (1977, July 16). 112(3), 39.

Sclafani, A., & Springer, D. (1976). Dietary obesity in adult rats: Similarities to hypothalamic and human obesity syndromes. *Psysiology and Behavior*, 17, 461–471.

Scott, E. M., & Verney, E. L. (1947). Self-selection and diet: VI. The nature of appetites for B vitamins. *Journal of Nutrition*, 34, 471–480.

Scrima, L., Broudy, M., Nay, K. N., & Cohn, M. A. (1982). Increased severity of obstructive sleep apnea after bedtime alcohol ingestion: Diagnostic potential and proposed mechanism of action. *Sleep*, 5, 318–328.

Sears, R. R., Maccoby, E. E., & Levin, H. (1957). *Patterns of child rearing*. Evanston, IL: Row, Peterson.

Seidel, W. F., Roth, T., Roehrs, T., Zorick, F., & Dement, W. C. (1984). Treatment of a 12-hour shift of sleep schedule with benzodiazepines. *Science*, 224, 1262–1264.

Seiden, R. H. (1966). Campus tragedy: A study of student suicide. *Journal of Abnormal Psychology*, 1, 389–399.

Seixas, F. A. (1981). Alcoholism. In S. J. Mule (Ed.), *Behavior in Excess* (pp. 120–129). New York: The Free Press.

Seligman, C., & Darley, J. M. (1978). Feedback as a means of decreasing residential energy consumption. *Journal of Applied Psychology*, 62, 363–368.

Seligman, M. E. P. (1972). For helplessness: Can we immunize the qeak? In *Readings in psychology today* (2nd ed.). Del Mar, CA: CRM.

Seligman, M. E. P. (1974). Submissive death: Giving up on life. *Psychology Today*, 7, 80–85.

Selye, H. (1976). *Stress in health and disease*. Boston: Butterworth.

Selye, H. (1956, 1976). *The stress of life*. New York: Knopf.

Senden, M. V. (1960). *Space and sight* (P. Health, Trans.). Glencoe, IL: Free press.

Serban, G. (1982). *The tyranny of magical thinking*. New York: Dutton.

Serbin, L. A., & O'Leary, K. D. (1975, December). How nursery schools teach girls to shut up. *Psychology Today*, 57–58, 102–103.

Sexual Medicine Today. (1980, April), 17.

Seyfarth, R. M., Cheney, D. L., & Marler, P. (1980a). Monkey responses to three different alarm calls: Evidence for predator classification and semantic communication. *Science*. 210, 801–803.

Shafer, R. P. (1972). *Marijuana: A signal of misunderstanding*. New York: Signet.

Shaffer, L. F. (1947). Fear and courage in aerial combat. *Journal of Consulting Psychology*, 11, 137–143.

Shapiro, D. A., & Shapiro, D. (1982). Meta-analysis of comparative therapy outcome studies: A replication and refinement. *Psychological Bulletin*, 92, 581–604.

Shaw, G. A., & Belmore, S. M. (1983). The relationship between imagery and creativity. *Imagination, Cognition and Personality*, 2, 115–123.

Sheehan, J. G., & Costley, M. S. (1977). A reexamination of the role of heredity in stuttering. *Journal of Speech and Hearing Disorders*, 42, 47–59.

Sheehan, P. W., Grigg, L., & McCann, T. (1984). Memory distortion following exposure to false information in hypnosis. *Journal of Abnormal Psychology*, 93, 259–265.

Sheehy, G. (1976). *Passages: Predictable crises from adult life*. New York: Dutton.

Sheils, M., & Monroe, S. (1976, March 22). A ban on I.Q. tests? *Newsweek*, 49.

Sheldon, W. H. (1954). *Atlas of men: A guide for somatotyping the adult male at all ages*. New York: Harper.

Shepard, R. N. (1975). Form, formation, and transformation of internal representations. In R. L. Solso (Ed.), *Information processing and cognition: The Loyola Symposium*. Hillsdale, NJ: Erlbaum.

Sherif, M. (1935). A study of some social factors in perception. *Archives of Psychology*, 27, 187.

Sherif, M., Harvey, O. J., White, B. J., Hood, W. R., & Sherif, C. W.

(1961). *Intergroup conflict and cooperation: The Robbers Cave experiment*. University of Oklahoma, Institute of Group Relations.

Sherman, E. D. (1971). Geriatrics: An emerging challenge to the health professions. *Journal of the American Geriatric Society, 19*, 199–207.

Shiffman, S. M. (1980). Diminished smoking, withdrawal symptoms, and cessation: A cautionary note. In G. B. Gori & F. G. Bock (Eds.), *Banbury report*. Cold Spring Harbor Laboratory.

Shiffrin, R. M. (1970). Forgetting: Trace erosion or retrieval failure? *Science, 168*, 1601–1603.

Shiffrin, R. W., & Cook, J. R. (1978). Short-term forgetting of item and order information. *Journal of Verbal Learning and Verbal Behavior, 17*, 189–218.

Shirley, M. M. (1933). *The first two years* (Institute of Child Welfare, Monograph No. 7): Minneapolis: University of Minnesota Press.

Shodell, M. (1984). The clouded mind. *Science 84*.

Short, A. B. (1984). Short-term treatment outcome using parents as co-therapists for their own autistic children. *Journal of Child Psychology & Psychiatry, 25*, 443–458.

Shulman, G. I. (1974). Race, sex and violence: A laboratory test of the sexual threat of the black male hypothesis. *American Journal of Sociology, 79*, 1260–1277.

Siegel, O. (1982). Personality development in adolescence. In B. B. Wolman, G. Stricker, S. J. Ellman, P. Keith-Spiegel, & D. S. Palermo (Eds.), *Handbook of developmental psychology* (pp. 537–548). Englewood Cliffs, NJ: Prentice-Hall.

Siegel, S., Hearst, E., George, N., & O'Neal, E. (1968). Generalization gradients obtained from individual subjects following classical conditioning. *Journal of Experimental Psychology, 78*, 171–174.

Siffre, M. (1975). Six months alone in a cave. *National Geographic, 147*(3), 426–435.

Simon, W., & Gagnon, J. (1973). Psychosexual development. In E. S. Morrison & V. Borosage (Eds.), *Human sexuality: Contemporary perspectives*. Palo Alto, CA: Mayfield.

Singer, J. L. (1974). Daydreaming and the stream of thought. *American Scientist, 62*, 417–425.

Singer, M. T. (1979, January). Coming out of the cults. *Psychology Today*, 72–82.

Singer, R. N. (1978). Motor skills and learning strategies. In H. F. O'Neil, Jr. (Ed.), *Learning strategies*. New York: Academic Press.

Skeels, H. M. (1966). Adult status of children with contrasting early life experiences. *Monograph of the Society for Research in Child Development, 31*(3).

Skinner, B. F. (1971). *Beyond freedom and dignity*. New York: Bantam.

Skinner, B. F. (1938). *The behavior of organisms*. Englewood Cliffs, NJ: Prentice-Hall.

Smith, A., & Sugar, O. (1975). Development of above-normal language and intelligence 21 years after left hemispherectomy. *Neurology, 25*, 813–818.

Smith, B. M. (1971). *The polygraph in contemporary psychology*. San Francisco: Freeman.

Smith, M. L., & Glass, B. V. (1977). Meta-analysis of psychotherapy outcome studies. *American Psychologist, 32*, 752–760.

Snider, J. G., Davis, M. H., & Brown, R. (1984). Effects of self-tape recording on self-awareness in a context of self-counseling. *Psychological Reports, 54*, 311–315.

Snow, C. E. (1977). The development of conversation between mothers and babies. *Journal of Child Language, 4*, 1–22.

Snow, C. P. (1961, February). Either-or. *Progressive*, 24.

Snowdon, C. T. (1983). Ethology, comparative psychology, and animal behavior. *Annual Review of Psychology, 34*, 63–94.

Snyder, C. R., & Shenkel, R. J. (1975, March). P. T. Barnum effect. *Psychology Today, 8*, 52–54.

Snyder, S. H. (1972, January). The true speed trip: Schizophrenia. *Psychology Today*.

Snyder, S. H., & Childers, S. R. (1979). Opiate receptors and opioid peptides. *Annual Review of Neuroscience, 2*, 35–64.

Solanto, M. V. (1984). Neuropharmacological basis of stimulant drug action in attention deficit disorder with hyperactivity: A review and synthesis. *Psychological Bulletin, 95*, 387–409.

Solomon, R. C., & Wynne, L. C. (1953). Traumatic avoidance learning: Acquisition in normal dogs. *Psychological Monographs, 67*(4, Whole No. 354).

Solomon, R. L. (1980, August). The opponent-process theory of acquired motivation. *American Psychologist*, 691–721.

Sommer, R. (1969). *Personal space: The behavioral basis of design*. Englewood Cliffs, NJ: Prentice-Hall.

Sommer, R. (1977, January). Toward a psychology of natural behavior. *APA Monitor*.

Sorce, J. F., Emde, R. N., Campos, J. J., & Klinnert, M. D. (1985). Maternal emotional signaling: Its effect on the visual cliff behavior of 1-year-olds. *Developmental Psychology, 21*, 195–200.

Spence, J. T. (1984). Masculinity, femininity, and gender-related traits: A conceptual analysis and critique of current research. In B. A. Maker & W. B. Maker (Eds.), *Progress in experimental personality research: Normal personality processes*, Vol 13. New York: Academic Press.

Sperry, R. W. (1956). The eye and the brain. *Scientific American* (Offprint No. 465), 48–52.

Sperry, R. W. (1968). Hemisphere deconnection and unity in conscious awareness. *American Psychologist, 23*, 723–733.

Sperry, R. W. (1974). Lateral specialization in the surgically separated hemispheres. In F. S. Schmitt & F. G. Worden (Eds.), *The neurosciences*. Cambridge, MA: MIT Press.

Spielberger, C. D., Anton, W. D., & Bedell, J. (1976). The nature and treatment of test anxiety. In M. Zuckerman & C. D. Spielberger (Eds.), *Emotions and anxiety: New concepts, methods, and applications* (pp. 317–345). Hillsdale, NJ: Erlbaum.

Spiesman, J. C., Lazarus, R. S., Mordkoff, A. M., & Davidson, L. A. (1964). The experimental reduction of stress based on ego-defense theory. *Journal of Abnormal and Social Psychology, 68*, 367–380.

Spitz, R. A. (1945). Hospitalism: An inquiry into the genesis of psychiatric conditions in early childhood. In *The psychoanalytic study of the child*, Vol I (pp. 53–74). New York: International University Press.

Spotts, J. V., & Shontz, F. C. (1980). *Cocaine users*. New York: Free Press.

Sprott, R. L., & Staats, J. (1975). Behavioral studies using genetically-defined mice—A bibliography. *Behavior Genetics, 5*, 27–82.

Staples, F. R., Sloane, B., Whipple, K., Cristol, A. H., & Yorkston, N. J. (1975). Differences between behavior therapists and psychotherapists. *Archives of General Psychiatry, 32*, 1515–1522.

Stapp, J., & Fulcher, R. (1983). *Salaries in psychology*. Washington DC: American Psychological Association.

Stark, E. (1981, September). Pigeon patrol. *Science 81*, 85–86.

Stark, R., & McEvoy, J. (1970, November). Middle-class violence. *Psychology Today*.

Stefanis, C., Dornbush, R. L., & Fink, M. (1977). *Hashish: A study of long-term use*. New York: Raven Press.

Stein, M. I. (1974). *Stimulating creativity*, Vol 1. New York: Academic Press.

Steinberg, L. D., Catalano, R., & Dooley, P. (1981). Economic antecedents of child abuse and neglect. *Child Development, 52*, 975–985.

Sterman, M. B. (1977). Effects of sensorimotor EEG feedback training on sleep and clinical manifestations of epilepsy. In J. Beatty & H. Legewie (Eds.), *Biofeedback and behavior*. New York: Plenum.

Stern, C. (1956). Hereditary factors affecting adoption: A study of adoption practices. *Child Welfare League of America, 2*, 53.

Stern, D. (1982). Some interactive functions of rhythm changes between mother and infant. In M. Davis (Ed.), *Interaction rhythms, periodicity in communicative behavior*. New York: Human Sciences Press.

Stern, D., Jaffe, J., Beebe, B., & Bennett, S. (1975). Vocalizing in unison and in alternation: Two modes of communication within the mother-infant dyad. In D. Aronson & R. Rieber (Eds.), *Developmental psycholinguistics and communication disorders* (pp. 89–100). Annals of the New York Academy of Sciences.

Stern, W. C. (1981). REM sleep and behavioral plasticity: Evidence for involvement of brain catecholamines. In W. Fishbein (Ed.), *Sleep, dreams and memory* (pp. 99–109). New York: SP Medical and Scientific Books.

Sternberg, R. J. (1985a). *Beyond IQ*. Cambridge: Cambridge University Press.

Sternberg, R. J., & Davidson, J. E. (1982, June). The mind of the puzzler. *Psychology Today*.

Sternberg, R. J., & Grajek, S. (1984). The nature of love. *Journal of Personality and Social Psychology, 47*, 312–329.

Stevens, C. F. (1979). The neuron. *Scientific American, 241*(3), 54–65.

Stevens, J. O. (1971). *Awareness: Exploring, experimenting, experiencing.* Lafayette, CA: Real People Press.

Stewart, K. (1969). Dream theory in Malaya. In C.T. Tart (Ed.), *Altered states of consciousness.* New York: Wiley.

Stokols, D. (1978). Environmental psychology. *Annual Review of Psychology, 29,* 253–295.

Stoller, F. H. (1967). The long weekend. *Psychology Today, 1*(7), 28–33.

Stoller, F. H. (1972). Marathon groups: Toward a conceptual model. In L. N. Solomon & B. Berzon (Eds.), *New Perspectives on Encounter Groups* (pp. 171–194). San Francisco: Jossey-Bass.

Strange, J. R. (1965). *Abnormal psychology.* New York: McGraw-Hill.

Streissguth, A. P., et al. (1984). Intrauterine alcohol and nicotine exposure: Attention and reaction time in 4-year-old children. *Developmental Psychology, 20,* 533–541.

Stunkard, A. (1980). *Obesity.* Philadelphia: Saunders.

Sue, D., Sue, D. W., & Sue, S. (1981). *Understanding abnormal behavior.* Boston: Houghton Mifflin.

Suedfeld, P. (1975, January–February). The benefits of boredom: Sensory deprivation reconsidered. *American Scientist, 63.*

Suedfeld, P. (1980). *Restricted environmental stimulation: Research and clinical applications.* New York: Wiley-Interscience.

Suedfeld, P. (1966). *Social processes.* Dubuque, IA: Brown.

Suedfeld, P., & Piedrahita, L. E. (1984). Intimations of mortality: Integrative simplification as a precursor of death. *Journal of Personality and Social Psychology, 47,* 848–852.

Suinn, R. M. (1970). *Fundamentals of behavior pathology.* New York: Wiley.

Suinn, R. M. (1975). *Fundamentals of behavior pathology* (2nd ed.). New York: Wiley.

Suinn, R. M. (1982). Intervention with Type A behaviors. *Journal of Consulting and Clinical Psychology, 50,* 933–949.

Sully, R. (1983). The work-setting support group: A means of preventing burnout. In B. A. Farber (Ed.), *Stress and burnout in the human service professions* (pp. 188–197). New York: Pergamon.

Sulzman, F. M. (1983). Primate circadian rhythms. *BioScience, 33*(7), 445–450.

Sutton-Smith, B. (1982). Birth order and sibling status effects. In M. E. Lamb & B. Sutton-Smith (Eds.), *Sibling relationships: Their nature and significance across the life-span.* Hillsdale, NJ: Erlbaum.

Swensen, C. H. (1973). *Introduction to interpersonal relations.* Glenview, IL: Scott, Foresman.

Szasz, T. S. (1969). The crime of commitment. *Psychology Today, 2*(10), 55–57.

Szasz, T. S. (1972, April). The ethics of addiction. *Harpers.*

Szasz, T. S. (1966, June 12). Mental illness is a myth. *The New York Times Magazine.*

Takooshian, H., Haber, S., & Lucido, D. J. (1977, February). Who wouldn't help a lost child? You, maybe. *Psychology Today, 67.*

Tanner, J. M. (1973, September). Growing up. *Scientific American,* 34–43.

Tanzer, D., & Block, J. L. (1976). *Why natural childbirth?* New York: Schocken.

Tarpy, R. M., & Mayer, R. E. (1978). *Foundations of learning and memory.* Glenview, IL: Scott, Foresman.

Tart, C. T. (1975). *States of consciousness.* New York: Dutton.

Taylor, C. W. (1978). How many types of giftedness can your program tolerate? *The Journal of Creative Behavior, 12,* 39–51.

Taylor, T. E. (1983, March 17). Learning studies of higher cognitive levels in short-term sensory isolation environment. Paper delivered at First International Conference on REST and Self-regulation, Denver, CO.

Ten Danger Signals of Depression. The National Association for Mental Health, Virginia.

Tenopyr, M. L., & Oeltjen, P. D. (1982). Personnel selection and classification. *Annual Review of Psychology, 33,* 581–618.

Tephly, J. B., & Elardo, R. (1984). Mothers and day-care teachers: Young children's perceptions. *British Journal of Developmental Psychology, 2,* 251–256.

Terman, L. M., & Oden, M. (1959). *The gifted group in mid-life: Vol. 5. Genetic studies of genius.* Stanford, CA: Stanford University Press.

Terman, L. M., & Merrill, M. A. (1937; revised ed., 1960). *Stanford-Binet Intelligence Scale.* Boston: Houghton Mifflin.

Thigpen, C. H., & Cleckley, H. M. (1957). *The three faces of Eve.* New York: McGraw-Hill.

Thomas, A., & Chess, S. (1977). *Temperament and development.* New York: Brunner/Mazel.

Thompson, R. I. (1967). *Foundations of physiological psychology.* New York: Harper & Row.

Thoreau, H. D. (1893). *Walden, or life in the woods.* New York: Houghton Mifflin.

Thornburg, H. D. (1984). *Introduction to educational psychology.* St. Paul, MN: West.

Tierney, J. (1982, June). Doctor, is this man dangerous? *Science 82,* 28–31.

Time, (1973, January 8).

Tobin, R. L. (1972). Murder on television and the fourteen-year-old. *Saturday Review, 55,* 39–40.

Tolman, E. C., & Honzik, C. H. (1930). Introduction and removal of reward and maze performance in rats. *University of California Publications in Psychology, 4,* 257–275.

Tolman, E. C., Ritchie, B. F., & Kalish, D. (1946). Studies in spatial learning: II. Place learning versus response learning. *Journal of Experimental Psychology, 36,* 221–229.

Topman, R. M., & Jansen, T. (1984). "I really can't do it, anyway": The treatment of test anxiety. In H. M. Van Der Ploeg, R. Schwarzer, & C. D. Spielberger (Eds.), *Advances in test anxiety research,* Vol 3 (pp. 243–251). Hillsdale, NJ: Erlbaum.

Tresemer, D. W. (1977). *Fear of success: An intriguing set of questions.* New York: Plenum.

Triandis, H. C. (1977). *Interpersonal behavior.* Monterey, CA: Brooks/Cole.

Trotter, R. J. (1974, August 3). Obesity and behavior. *Science News.*

Truax, S. H. (1983). Active search, mediation, and the manipulation of cue dimensions: Emotion attribution in the false feedback paradigm. *Motivation and Emotion, 7,* 41–60.

Tryon, R. C. (1929). The genetics of learning ability in rats. *University of California Publications in Psychology, 4,* 71–89.

Tulving, E. (1985). How many memory systems are there? *American Psychologist, 40,* 385–398.

Turek, I. S., & Hanlon, T. E. (1977). The effectiveness and safety of electroconvulsive therapy (ECT). *Journal of Nervous and Mental Disease, 164,* 419–431.

Turnbull, C. M. (1961). Some observations regarding the experiences and behavior of the Bambuti Pygmies. *American Journal of Psychology, 74,* 304–308.

Tversky, A., & Kahneman, D. (1982). Judgments of and by representativeness. In D. Kahneman, P. Slovic, & A. Tversky, *Judgment under uncertainty: Heuristics and biases* (pp. 84–98). Cambridge: Cambridge University Press.

Tversky, A., & Kahneman, D. (1981). The framing of decisions and the psychology of choice. *Science, 211,* 453–458.

Tzeng, O. J. L., & Wang, W. S. Y. (1983). The first two R's. *American Scientist, 71,* 238–243.

Udry, J. R., & Eckland, B. K. (1984). Benefits of being attractive: Differential payoffs for men and women. *Psychological Reports, 54,* 47–56.

Udry, J. R., & Morris, N. M. (1977). Human sexual behavior at different stages of the menstrual cycle. *Journal of Reproduction and Fertility, 51,* 419.

Ulrich, R. E., Stachnik, T. J., & Stainton, N. R. (1963). Student acceptance of generalized personality interpretations. *Psychological Reports, 131,* 831–834.

Underwood, B. J. (1957). Interference and forgetting. *Psychological Review, 64,* 49–60.

Unger, R. K. (1979). Toward a redefinition of sex and gender. *American Psychologist, 34,* 1085–1094.

U.S. Commission on Civil Rights. (1977). *Window dressing on the set: Women and minorities in television.* Washington, DC: U.S. Government Printing Office.

U.S. National Commission on the Causes and Prevention of Violence. (1970). *To establish justice, to insure domestic tranquility: The final report.* New York: Praeger.

U.S. News and World Report. (1979, May 14). Aptitude test scores: Grumbling gets louder, 76–79.

Valenstein, E. S. (1980). Extent of psychosurgery worldwide. In E. S. Valenstein (Ed.), *The psychosurgery debate.* San Francisco: Freeman.

Valins, S. (1966). Cognitive effects of false heart-rate feedback. *Journal of Personality and Social Psychology*, 4, 400–408.

Valins, S. (1967). Emotionality and information concerning internal reactions. *Journal of Personality and Social Psychology*, 6, 458–463.

Van de Castle, R. L. (1971). *The psychology of dreaming*. Morristown, NJ: General Learning Corporation.

Van Gelder, L., & Carmichael, C. (1975, October). But what about our sons? *Ms Magazine*.

van Lawick-Goodall, J. (1971). *In the shadow of man*. New York: Houghton Mifflin.

Van Maanen, J., & Schein, E. H. (1977). Career development. In J. R. Hackman & J. L. Suttle (Eds.), *Improving life at work*. Santa Monica, CA: Goodyear Publishing Co.

Varley, C. K. (1984). Attention deficit disorder (the hyperactivity syndrome): A review of selected issues. *Journal of Developmental & Behavioral Pediatrics*, 5, 254–258.

Vils, U. (1976, February 26). Alcoholism: Tempest in a shot glass. *Los Angeles Times*.

Vogler, R. E., & Bartz, W. R. (1982). *The better way to drink*. New York: Simon and Schuster.

Vogler, R. E., Weissbach, T. A., Compton, J. V., & Martin, G. T. (1977). Integrated behavior change techniques for problem drinkers in the community. *Journal of Consulting and Clinical Psychology*, 45, 267–279.

Volpicelli, J. R., Ulm, R. R., Altenor, A., & Seligman, M. E. P. (1983). Learned mastery in the rat. *Learning and Motivation*, 14, 204–222.

von Baumgarten, R., Benson, A., Berthoz, A., Brandt, T., Brand, U., Bruzek, W., Dichgans, J., Kass, J., Probst, T., Scherer, H., Vieville, T., Vogel, H., & Wetzig, J. (1984). Spatial orientation in weightlessness and readaptation to earth's gravity. *Science*, 225, 205–225.

Waid, W. M., & Orne, M. T. (1982, July/August). The physiological detection of deception. *American Scientist*, 70, 402–409.

Wall, P. D. (1976). In J. J. Bonica & D. Albe-Fessard (Eds.), *Advances in pain research and therapy*, Vol. 1. New York: Raven Press.

Wallach, M. A., & Kogan, N. (1965). *Modes of thinking in young children*. New York: Holt.

Walster, E. (1971). Passionate Love. In B. I. Murstein (Ed.), *Theories of attraction and love*. New York: Springer.

Walster, E., & Walster, G. W. (1978). *A new look at love*. Reading, MA: Addison-Wesley.

Warrenburg, S., & Pagano, R. (1983). Meditation and hemispheric specialization: Absorbed attention in long-term adherence. *Imagination, Cognition and Personality*, 2, 211–229.

Warren, Leubecker, A., & Bohannon, J. N. (1984). Intonation patterns in child-directed speech: Mother-father differences. *Child Development*, 55, 1379–1385.

Watson, D. L., & Tharp, R. G. (1981). *Self-directed behavior: Self-modification for personal adjustment* (3rd ed.). Monterey, CA: Brooks/Cole.

Watson, J. B. (1913). Psychology as the behaviorist views it. *Psychological Review*, 20, 158–177.

Watts, B. (1982). Individual differences in circadian activity rhythms and their effects on roommate relationships. *Journal of Personality*, 50, 374–384.

Webb, W. (1978). Sleep and dreams, Part I. *Annual Review of Psychology*, 29, 223–252.

Webb, W. (1975). *Sleep, the gentle tyrant*. Englewood Cliffs, NJ: Prentice-Hall.

Wechsler, D. (1958). *The measurement and appraisal of adult intelligence* (4th ed.). Baltimore: Williams & Wilkins.

Wegner, D. M., & Vallacher, R. R. (1977). *Implicit psychology*. New York: Oxford University Press.

Weil, A. T. (1977). The marriage of the sun and moon. In N. E. Zinberg (Ed.), *Altered states of consciousness* (pp. 37–52). New York: Free Press.

Weinberg, M. S., & Williams, C. J. (1974). *Male homosexuals*. New York: Oxford University Press.

Weiner, R. D. (1984). Convulsive therapy: 50 years later. *American Journal of Psychiatry*, 14, 1078–1079.

Weintraub, M. I. (1983). *Hysterical conversion reactions*. New York: SP Medical & Scientific Books.

Weisfeld, G. E., & Beresford, J. M. (1982). Erectness of posture as an indicator of dominance or success in humans. *Motivation and Emotion*, 6, 113–131.

Weisinger, M. (1977, July 24). The amazing Kreskin—It's all in the mind. *Parade*, 10.

Weiss, J. M. (1972). Psychological factors in stress and disease. *Scientific American*, 26, 104–113.

Weisstein, N. (1975). Psychology constructs the female. In I. S. Cohen (Ed.), *Perspectives on psychology* (pp. 318–331). New York: Praeger.

Weiten, W. (1983). *Psychology applied to modern life: Adjustment in the 80's*. Monterey CA: Brooks/Cole.

Weitzenhoffer, A. M., & Hilgard, E. R. (1959). *Stanford Hypnotic susceptibility Scales, Forms A and B*. Palo Alto, CA: Consulting Psychologists Press.

Weizenbaum, J. (1966, January). ELIZA—A computer program for the study of natural language communication between man and machine. *Communications of the Association for Computing Machinery*, 9, 36–43.

Wells, G. L., & Murray, D. M. (1983). What can psychology say about *Neil v. Biggers* criteria for judging eyewitness accuracy? *Journal of Applied Psychology*, 68, 347–362.

Wertheimer, M. (1959). *Productive thinking*. New York: Harper & Row.

Wexley, K. N. (1984). Personnel training. *Annual Review of Psychology*, 35, 519–551.

Whimbey, A., with Whimbey, L. S. (1980). *Intelligence can be taught*. New York: Dutton.

White, B. L., & Held, R. (1966). Plasticity of sensorimotor development in the human infant. In J. F. Rosenblith & W. Allinsmith (Eds.), *The causes of behavior*, Vol I (2nd ed.). Boston: Allyn & Bacon.

White, B. L., & Watts, J. C. (1973). *Experience and environment*, Vol I. Englewood Cliffs, NJ: Prentice-Hall.

Wickens, C. D., & Kramer, A. (1985). Engineering psychology. *Annual Review of Psychology*, 36, 307–348.

Wicken, D. D., Allen, C. K., & Hill, F. A. (1963). Effects of instruction and UCS strength on extinction of the conditioned GSR *Journal of Experimental Psychology*, 66, 235–240.

Wickes, I. G. (1958). Treatment of persistent enuresis with the electric buzzer. *Archives of Diseases in Childhood*, 33, 160–164.

Wilhelm, J. L. (1976). *The search for superman*. New York: Simon & Schuster.

Williams, B. A. (1984, November 30). U.S. approves implants to aid the totally deaf. *Santa Barbara News Press*, Part C, p. 6.

Williams, B. M. (1974, November). Promise and caution—"Hypnosis is like a scalpel. You wouldn't want it wielded by your janitor." *Psychology Today*.

Williams, G. J., & Money, J. (Eds.). (1980). *Traumatic abuse and neglect of children at home*. Baltimore, MD: Johns Hopkins University Press.

Williams, R. L. (1975). The Bitch-100: A culture-specific test. *Journal of Afro-American Issues*, 3, 103–116.

Williams, R. L., et al. (1964). Sleep patterns in young adults: An EEG study. *Electroencephalography and Clinical Neurophysiology*, 376–381.

Williams, R. L., & Long, J. D. (1979). *Toward a self-managed life style*. Boston: Houghton Mifflin.

Williams, S. (1984, April). Disk therapy. *Science 84*, 81, 94.

Wilson, E. O. (1975, October 12). Human decency is animal. *New York Times Magazine*.

Wilson, R. R. (1968). Perceptual distinction of height as a function of ascribed academic status. *Journal of Social Psychology*, 74, 97–102.

Wilson, S., Strong, B., Clarke, L. M., & Thomas, J. (1984). *Human sexuality*. St. Paul, MN: West.

Winget, C., & Kramer, M. (1979). (Dimensions of dreams. Gainesville: University Presses of Florida.

Winson, J. (1985). *Brain and psyche: The biology of the unconscious*. Garden City, NY: Doubleday.

Wise, E. H., & Haynes, S. N. (1983). Cognitive treatment of test anxiety: Rational restructuring versus attentional training. *Cognitive Therapy and Research*, 7, 69–78.

Wise, J. (1982, September). A gentle deterrent to vandalism. *Psychology Today*, 31–38.

Wolcott, J. H., McNeekin, R. R., Burgin, R. E., & Yanowitch, R. E. (1977). Correlation of general aviation accidents with the biorhythm theory. *Human Factors, 19,* 283–293.

Wolfe, J. B. (1936). Effectiveness of token rewards for chimpanzees. *Comparative Psychology Monographs, 12*(5), Whole No. 60.

Wolpe, J. (1974). *The practice of behavior therapy* (2nd ed.). New York: Pergamon.

Wood, M. M., & Greenfield, S. T. (1976). Women managers and fear of success: A study in the field. *Sex Roles, 2,* 375–387.

Woodmansee, J. J. (1970). The pupil response as a measure of social attitudes. In G. F. Summers (Ed.), *Attitude measurement.* Chiago: Rand McNally.

Woods, R. L., & Greenhouse, H. B. (1974). *The new world of dreams.* New York: Macmillan.

Woolfolk, R., & Richardson, F. (1978). *Stress, sanity and survival.* New York: Signet.

Work in America. (1973). Special Task Force, Department of Health, Education and Welfare. Cambridge, MA: MIT Press.

Wrightsman, L. S., & Deaux, K. (1981). *Social psychology in the 80s.* Monterey, CA: Brooks/Cole.

Wulbert, M., & Dries, R. (1977). The relative efficacy of methylphenidate (Ritalin) and behavior-modification techniques in the treatment of a hyperactive child. *Journal of Applied Behavior Analysis, 10,* 21–31.

Wursig, B. (1979, March). Dolphins. *Scientific American, 240*(3), 136–148.

Yalom, I. D. (1980). *Existential psychotherapy.* New York: Basic Books.

Yule, W., Urbanowicz, M., Lansdown, R., & Millar, I. B. (1984). Teachers' ratings of children's behavior in relation to blood lead levels. *British Journal of Developmental Psychology, 2,* 295–305.

Zajonc, R. B. (1975, January). Dumber by the dozen. *Psychology Today,* 37–43.

Zajonc, R. B., & Markus, G. B. (1975). Birth order and intellectual development. *Psychological Review, 82,* 74–88.

Zaludek, G. M. (1976, February). How to cope with male menopause. *Science Digest,* 74–79.

Zane, M. D., & Milt, H. (1984). *Your phobia.* Washington, DC: American Psychiatric Press.

Zilbergeld, B. (1983). *The shrinking of America: Myths of psychological change.* Boston: Little Brown.

Zimbardo, P. G. (1974). On the ethics of intervention in human psychological research: With special reference to the Stanford prison experiment. *Cognition, 2,* 243–256.

Zimbardo, P. G. (1975). *Psychology and life* (9th ed.). Glenview, IL: Scott, Foresman.

Zimbardo, P. G., Haney, C., & Banks, W. C. (1973, April 8). A pirandellian prison. *The New York Times Magazine.*

Zimbardo, P. G., Pilkonis, P. A., & Norwood, R. M. (1978). The social disease called shyness. In *Annual editions: Personality and adjustment 78/79.* Guilford, CT: Dushkin.

Zinberg, N. E. (1976, December). The war over marijuana. *Psychology Today,* 92–98.

Zubek, J. (1969b). Sensory and perceptual-motor processes. In J. Zubek (Ed.), *Sensory deprivation: Fifteen years of research* (pp. 207–253). New York: Appleton-Century-Crofts.

Zuckerman, M. (1972, April). *Manual and research report for the Sensation Seeking Scale (SSS).* Mimeograph, University of Delaware, Newark, DE

Zuckerman, M., & Allison, S. (1976). An objective measure of fear of success: Construction and validation. *Journal of Personality, 40,* 422–430.

Zuckerman, M., Eysenck, S., & Eysenck, H. J. (1978). Sensation seeking in England and America: Cross-cultural, age, and sex comparisons. *Journal of Consulting and Clinical Psychology, 46,* 139–149.

Zung, W. W. K., & Green, R. H., Jr. (1974). Seasonal variation of suicide and depression. *Archives of General Psychiatry, 30,* 89–91.

Index

Acknowledgments, Continued

p. 155 H. Benson, "Systematic Hypertension and The Relaxation Response." Reprinted by permission from *The New England Journal of Medicine*, Vol. 296, pp. 1152–1156, 1977.

Fig. 7–4 Yale Joel, LIFE Magazine, © Time Inc.

Fig. 7–5 © 1981 Martin M. Potker, Taurus.

Fig. 7–6 Wide World Photos.

Fig. 8–4 © Dan Francis, Mardan Photography.

Fig. 8–8 Ira Kirschenbaum, Stock, Boston.

Fig. 8–9 Yale Joel, LIFE Magazine, © Time, Inc.

Fig. 8–11 Chimp-O-Mat. Yerkes Regional Primate Research Center, Emory University.

Fig. 8–14 Dan Francis, Mardan Photography.

Fig. 8–15 Loomis Dean, LIFE Magazine, © Time, Inc.

Fig. 8–17 Photos by Barbara Martin, Courtesy of the *Los Angeles Times*, © 1984.

Fig. 8–18 Alain Dejean, Sygma.

Fig. 9–5 "Effects of Punishment on Extinction." Chart from B. F. Skinner, *The Behavior of Organism*, 1938. Permission from Prentice-Hall, Inc.

Fig. 9–6 © Ellis Herwig, The Picture Cube.

p. 219 Cartoon courtesy of Ed Arno and *Science 80*.

Fig. 9–9 Nursery School Children, Dr. Albert Bandura, Stanford University.

p. 223 Cartoon reproduced courtesy of the Edmonton Journal.

Fig. 9–10 Owen Franken, Stock Boston.

Fig. 9–11 Steven Stone, The Picture Cube.

Fig. 10–1 Courtesy of IBM.

Fig. 10–3 Penfield, W. *The Excitable Cortex in Conscious Man*, 1958. Courtesy of Charles C Thomas Publisher, Springfield, Illinois.

Fig. 10–6 © Larry Day.

Fig. 10–11 © Dan Francis, Mardan Photography.

Fig. 10–16 © Animals, Animals.

Fig. 11–2 © Ralph Reinhold, Animals, Animals.

Fig. 11–6 Osgood, C. E. "The Nature and Measurement of Meaning." *Psychological Bulletin*, 49, Copyright, 1952 by The American Psychological Association. Reprinted by permission.

Fig. 11–9 From "Teaching Language to An Ape." by Ann Premack and David Premack. Copyright © 1972 by *Scientific American*, Inc. All rights reserved.

Fig. 11–15 U.S. Patent No. 556,248. From *Absolutely Mad Inventions* by A. E. Brown and H. A. Jeffcott, Jr. Dover, 1970.

Fig. 12–1 © David Austen, Woodfin Camp.

Fig. 12–4 Hyperphagic Rat courtesy of Dr. Neal E. Miller, Rockefeller University.

Fig. 12–5 © Peter Menzel, Stock Boston.

Fig. 12–6 "Monkeys and Locks." Harry F. Harlow, University of Wisconsin Primate Laboratory.

Fig. 12–7 Berlyne, D. E. "Curiosity and Exploration." *Science*, Vol. 153, pp. 25–33, Figure 4, 1 July, 1966, Copyright 1966 by the American Association for the Advancement of Science.

Fig. 12–8 © David F. Hughes, The Picture Cube.

p. 294 Zuckerman, M. *Manual and Research Report for the Sensation-Seeking Scale (SSS)*. Mimeograph, University of Delaware, Newark, Delaware, April, 1972. Reproduced by permission.

Fig. 12–10 © Ellis Herwig, The Picture Cube.

Fig. 12–11 © Dan Francis, Mardan Photography.

Fig. 12–13 © Marty Heitner, Taurus.

Figs. 13–1, 13–8 Courtesy of The Record, Hackensack, New Jersey.

Fig. 13–4 © Phillip Jon Bailley, The Picture Cube.

Fig. 13–5 Photo courtesy of the Stoelting Company, Chicago, Illinois.

Fig. 13–7 Bridges, K. M. B. "Emotional Development in Early Infancy." *Child Development*, 3, 324–341. Figure 1, p. 340. Copyright, 1932.

Fig. 13–8 Zoological Society of San Diego.

Fig. 13–9 © Dan Francis, Mardan Photography.

p. 325 The Danger Signals of Depression, National Association of Mental Health.

p. 331 Associated Press news article courtesy of the Associated Press.

Fig. 13–11 © Laimute Druskis, Taurus.

p. 322 © Dan Francis, Mardan Photography.

Table 14–2 Friedman, M. and R. Roseman. *Type A Behavior and Your Heart*, Alfred A. Knopf, Inc. 1974. Reprinted by permission.

Table 14–3 Reprinted with permission from the *Journal of Psychosomatic Research* Vol. 11. T. H. Holmes and R. H. Rahe. "Social Readjustment Rating Scale," 1957, Pergamon Press, Ltd.

Fig. 14–2 © David Woo, Stock Boston.

Fig. 14–5 © Liane Enkilis, Stock Boston.

Fig. 14–6 © Cary Wolinsky, Stock Boston.

Fig. 14–7 The General Adaptation Syndrome graph from *The Stress of Life* by Hans Selye. Copyright © 1956, 1976 by Hans Selye. Used by permission of McGraw-Hill Book Company.

p. 332 The Better Half by Barnes, reprinted courtesy of Register and Tribune Syndicate, Inc.

Fig. 15–1 "Imitation of Facial and Manual Gestures by Human Neonates." by A. N. Meltzoff and M. K. Moore, *Science*, vol. 198, pp. 75–78, Fig. 1, October 7, 1977. Copyright 1977 by The American Association for the Advancement of Science.

Fig. 15–2 From "The Origin of Form Perception." by Robert L. Fantz. Copyright © 1961 by Scientific American, Inc. All rights reserved. Photograph of Fantz's Looking Chamber by David Linton.

p. 361 Huxley, A. "Human Potentialities." in R. E. Farson (ed.) *Science and Human Affairs*. Palo Alto, California: Science and Behavior Books, 1965.

p. 373 Associated Press newsarticle courtesy of the Associated Press.

Fig. 15–4 © Michael Grecco, Stock Boston.

Fig. 15–6 © Petit Format/Nestle, Science Source, Photo Researchers.

Fig. 15–7 © A. Glauberman, Photo Researchers.

Fig. 15–8 © Frank Siteman, Taurus.

Fig. 15–11 Jerome Bruner, *Child's Talk, Learning to use Language*, W. W. Norton & Co., 1981. Reprinted by permission.

Fig. 15–12 Nina Leen © 1964 Time Inc.

Fig. 15–13 © Martin Rogers, Stock Boston.

Fig. 15–14 © Mimi Forsyth, Monkmeyer.

Fig. 15–15 © Yves Debraine, Black Star.

p. 379 Hayakawa, S. I. "The Use and Misuse of Language." In R. E. Farson (ed.) *Science and Human Affairs*. Palo Alto, California: Science and Behavior Books, 1965.

Fig. 16–1 © Gabor Demjen, Stock Boston.

Fig. 16–2 From "Growing Up" by J. M. Tanner. Copyright © September, 1973 by *Scientific American*, Inc. All rights reserved.

Fig. 16–3 © Lenore Weber, Taurus.

Fig. 16–4 © Bohdan Hrynewych, Stock Boston.

Fig. 16–5 © Marilyn Silverstone, Magnum.

Fig. 16—7 © Pam Hasegawa, Taurus.

Fig. 16—8 © Elaine Wilks, O.S.F., Taurus.

p. 403 Ginott, H. *Between Parent and Child*. 1965. Reprinted by permission of Dr. Alice Ginott.

p. 408 Reprinted at the permission of: Concern for Dying, 250 W. 57th St. New York, NY 10107.

Table 17—1 Terman, L. and M. Merrill, *Stanford-Binet Intelligence Scale*. 1937 (Revised ed. 1960b). Houghton Mifflin Co.

Table 17—2 Wechsler Scale, The Psychological Corporation, 1958.

Fig. 17—1 © Mimi Forsyth, Monkmeyer.

Fig. 17—3 Wide World Photos.

Fig. 17—4 (*left*) © Karen R. Preuss, Taurus; (*middle*) © Dan Francisc, Mardan Photography; (*right*) © David M. Campione, Taurus.

Fig. 17—5 Special Olympics Photograph courtesy of Priscilla Copass and Steve Neighbors.

Fig. 17—8 Culture Fair Test Sample Items from R. B. Cattell, "Are I.Q. Tests Intelligent?" Reprinted by permission of Dr. R. B. Cattell.

Fig. 18—1 © Gregg Mancusco, Stock Boston.

Fig. 18—3 Cattell, R. B. "Personality Pinned Down." 1973. Reprinted by permission of Dr. R. B. Cattell.

Fig. 18—4 © Dan Francis, Mardan Photography.

Table 18—2 Reproduced by permission. Copyright 1943, renewed 1970 by the University of Minnesota. Published by the Psychological Corporation, New York, New York. All rights reserved.

Fig. 18—5 © Stacy Pick, Stock Boston.

Fig. 18—6 Woodfin Camp.

p. 439 Art Buchwald quotation courtesy of Art Buchwald, Los Angeles Times.

Fig. 18—10 © Alvis Upitis, Black Star.

Fig. 19—1 "All is Vanity." Courtesy of Illusions, Park Ridge, Illinois.

Fig. 19—4 © Dan Francis, Mardan Photography.

Fig. 19—5 © Terry McKoy, Taurus.

Fig. 19—6 © Charles E. Schmidt, Taurus.

Fig. 19—7 UPI/Bettmann News Photos.

Fig. 19—8 © Frank Siteman, Stock Boston.

p. 482 *Catch 22* copyright © 1955, 1961 by Joseph Heller. Reprinted by permission of Simon & Schuster, a division of Gulf and Western Corporation; and by A. M. Heath & Co., Ltd., London.

Fig. 20—1 Photographs courtesy of Ulrike Kantor Gallery.

Fig. 20—3 © Laimute Druskis, Taurus.

p. 490 Suinn, Richard M. *Fundamentals of Behavior Pathology*, 2nd ed. Copyright © 1975 by Richard Suinn. Reprinted by permission of John Wiley & Sons, Inc.

Fig. 20—4 © Cary Wolinsky, Stock Boston.

Fig. 20—5 (*left*) UPI/Bettmann News Photos; (*right*) D. Coon.

Fig. 20—6 © Charles Gupton, Stock Boston.

p. 504 *I Never Promised You a Rose Garden* by Hannah Green (Joanne Greenberg). Copyright © 1964 by Hannah Green. Reprinted by permission of Holt, Rinehart and Winston.

Fig. 21—1 Zalesky/Clemmer, Black Star.

Fig. 21—2 The Bettmann Archive.

Fig. 21—3 D. Coon

Fig. 21—4 Benyas, Black Star.

p. 510 Suinn, Richard M. *Fundamentals of Behavior Pathology*, 1st ed. Copyright © 1970 by Richard Suinn. Reprinted by permission of John Wiley & Sons, Inc.

Fig. 21—5 © 1975 Jerry Cooke.

Fig. 21—7 Derek Bayes/Courtesy Gottman-Mackey, Life Picture Service.

Fig. 21—8 (*left*) Dennis Brack, Black Star; (*right*) Duke University Hospital.

Fig. 21—9 The Brookhaven Institute.

Fig. 21—10 © Will McIntyre, Photo Researchers.

Fig. 21—11 Jeff Albertson, Stock, Boston.

p. 524 Laing, R. D. *The Politics of Experience*, p. 56. Copyright © 1967 by R. D. Laing. Reprinted by permission of Penguin Books, Ltd.

p. 524 Jackson, B. "Our Prisons are Criminal." September 22, 1968. © 1968 by the New York Times Company. Reprinted by permission.

Fig. 22—1 (a) University Museum of the University of Pennsylvania; (b) courtesy of the New York Public Library; (c) The Bettmann Archive.

Fig. 22—3 Historical Pictures Service, Chicago.

Fig. 22—4 Michael Routgier, Life Magazine © Time, Inc.

p. 540 Stevens, J. O. *Awareness: Exploring, Experimenting, Experiencing*. Real People Press, 1971.

p. 543 Weizenbaum, J. "ELIZA—A Computer Program for the Study of Natural Language Communication Between Man and Machine." *Communications of the Association for Computing Machinery*, January 1966, volume 9, No. 1, pp. 36–43. Copyright 1966, Association For Computing Machinery, Inc. Reprinted by permission.

Fig. 22—5 © Bohdan Hrynewych, Stock Boston.

p. 550 Lazarus, Arnold. "The Treatment of Chronic Frigidity by Systematic Desensitization." In *Experiments in Behavior Therapy*, H. J. Eysenck, (ed.). Reprinted by permission of the author. Copyright © 1964 Pergamon Press, Ltd.

Fig. 23—1 Curt Gunther, Camera 5.

Fig. 23—2 © Peter Menzel, Stock Boston.

Fig. 23—3 Photograph courtesy of Albert Bandura and the American Psychological Association. Copyright 1969 by the American Psychological Association. Reprinted by permission. From the *Journal of Personality and Social Psychology*, 1969, 13, pp. 173–199.

Fig. 23—4 Lovaas, O. I. and Simmons, J. Q. Manipulation of Self-destruction in Three Retarded Children." *Journal of Applied Behavior Analysis*. 1969, 2, pp. 143–157. Reprinted by permission.

Fig. 23—5 Token Economy photograph courtesy of Robert Liberman, M.D.

Figs. 24—4, 24—5 Beach, Frank A., ed. *Sex and Behavior*. New York: John Wiley & Sons, Inc., 1965.

Fig. 24—6 From "Where Should You Touch?" by H. E. F. Donohue. Copyright © 1965 Hearst Corporation. Reprinted by permission.

p. 587 Jourard, S. M. *Personal Adjustment*, 2nd ed. Copyright © 1963 Macmillan Publishing Co., Inc.

Fig. 25—1 © Charles Gupton, Stock Boston.

Fig. 25—2 © Gregg Mancusco, Stock Boston.

Fig. 25—3 © Stacy Pick, Stock Boston.

Fig. 25—4 © Janeart 1983, The Image Bank.

Table 25—1 Zick Rubin. "Measurement of Romantic Love." *Journal of Personality and Social Psychology*. Copyright 1970 by the American Psychological Association. Reprinted by permission.

Box 25—1 From Zick Rubin, *Liking and Loving: An Invitation to Social Psychology*, 1973, Holt, Rinehart and Winston.

Fig. 25—8 © Robert V. Eckert, Stock Boston.

Fig. 26—1 © C. Kuhn, The Image BankWest.

Fig. 26—2 © Mark Mittelman, Taurus.

Fig. 26—3 Wide World Photos.